New Era of Management

RICHARD L. DAFT

Vanderbilt University

DAFT

NINTH EDITION

SOUTH-WESTERN
CENGAGE Learning™

Australia • Brazil • Japan • Korea • Mexico • Singapore • Spain • United Kingdom • United States

SOUTH-WESTERN
CENGAGE Learning™

New Era of Management, Ninth Edition
Richard L. Daft, with the assistance of
Patricia G. Lane

Vice President of Editorial, Business: Jack
W. Calhoun

Editor-in-Chief: Melissa S. Acuña

Executive Editor: Joe Sabatino

Managing Developmental Editor: Emma
Newsom

Developmental Editor: Erin Berger

Editorial Assistant: Ruth Belanger

Executive Marketing Manager: Kimberly
Kanakes

Marketing Manager: Clint Kernen

Sr. Marketing Coordinator: Sarah Rose

Sr. Marketing Communications Manager:
Jim Overly

Sr. Content Project Manager: Martha Conway

Media Editor: Rob Ellington

Sr. Frontlist Buyer, Manufacturing: Doug Wilke

Production Service: Macmillan Publishing
Solutions

Sr. Art Director: Tippy McIntosh

Internal Designer: Joe Devine, Red Hangar
Design

Cover Image: Shutterstock

Photography Manager: Don Schlotman

Photo Researcher: Chris Caperton, O'Donnell
and Associates; Susan Van Etten

Text Permissions Manager: Margaret
Chamberlain-Gaston

Text Permissions Researcher: James Reidel

For product information and technology assistance, contact us at
Cengage Learning Customer & Sales Support, 1-800-354-9706
For permission to use material from this text or product,
submit all requests online at **www.cengage.com/permissions**
Further permissions questions can be emailed to
permissionrequest@cengage.com

Library of Congress Control Number: 2008943508

International Student Edition ISBN 13: 978-0-324-59819-3

International Student Edition ISBN 10: 0-324-59819-X

Cengage Learning International Offices
Asia
cengageasia.com
tel: (65) 6410 1200

Australia/New Zealand
cengage.com.au
tel: (61) 3 9685 4111

Brazil
cengage.com.br
tel: (011) 3665 9900

India
cengage.co.in
tel: (91) 11 30484837/38

Latin America
cengage.com.mx
tel: +52 (55) 1500 6000

UK/Europe/Middle East/Africa
cengage.co.uk
tel: (44) 207 067 2500

Represented in Canada by Nelson Education, Ltd.
nelson.com
tel: (416) 752 9100 / (800) 668 0671

For product information: **www.cengage.com/international**
Visit your local office: **www.cengage.com/global**
Visit our corporate website: **www.cengage.com**

Printed in Canada
1 2 3 4 5 6 7 13 12 11 10 09

New Era of Management

RICHARD L. DAFT

With deep appreciation to Dorothy,
the playwright and partner in my life,
and to my parents, who started my life
toward outcomes that I could not understand at the time.

About the Author

Richard L. Daft, PhD, is the Brownlee O. Currey, Jr., Professor of Management in the Owen Graduate School of Management at Vanderbilt University. Professor Daft specializes in the study of organization theory and leadership. Dr. Daft is a Fellow of the Academy of Management and has served on the editorial boards of *Academy of Management Journal*, *Administrative Science Quarterly*, and *Journal of Management Education*. He was the associate editor-in-chief of *Organization Science* and served for three years as associate editor of *Administrative Science Quarterly*.

Professor Daft has authored or co-authored 12 books, including *Organization Theory and Design* (South-Western, 2007), *The Leadership Experience* (South-Western, 2008), and *What to Study: Generating and Developing Research Questions* (Sage, 1982). He published *Fusion Leadership: Unlocking the Subtle Forces That Change People and Organizations* (Berrett-Koehler, 2000, with Robert Lengel). He has also authored dozens of scholarly articles, papers, and chapters. His work has been published in *Administrative Science Quarterly*, *Academy of Management Journal*, *Academy of Management Review*, *Strategic Management Journal*, *Journal of Management*, *Accounting Organizations and Society*, *Management Science*, *MIS Quarterly*, *California Management Review*, and *Organizational Behavior Teaching Review*. Professor Daft is currently working on a new book, *The Executive and the Elephant.* He also is an active teacher and consultant. He has taught management, leadership, organizational change, organizational theory, and organizational behavior.

Professor Daft served as associate dean, produced for-profit theatrical productions, and helped manage a start-up enterprise. He has been involved in management development and consulting for many companies and government organizations, including the American Banking Association, Bridgestone, Bell Canada, the National Transportation Research Board, Nortel, TVA, Pratt & Whitney, State Farm Insurance, Tenneco, the United States Air Force, the United States Army, J. C. Bradford & Co., Central Parking System, Entergy Sales and Service, Bristol-Myers Squibb, First American National Bank, and the Vanderbilt University Medical Center.

Preface

Managing for Innovation in a Changing World

In recent years, organizations have been buffeted by massive and far-reaching social, technological, and economic changes. Any manager who still believed in the myth of stability was rocked out of complacency when, one after another, large financial institutions in the United States began to fail. Business schools, as well as managers and businesses, were scrambling to keep up with the fast-changing story and evaluate its impact. This edition of *New Era of Management* addresses themes and issues that are directly relevant to the current, fast-shifting business environment. I revised *New Era of Management* with a goal of helping current and future managers find innovative solutions to the problems that plague today's organizations—whether they are everyday challenges or once-in-a-lifetime crises. The world in which most students will work as managers is undergoing a tremendous upheaval. Ethical turmoil, the need for crisis management skills, e-business, rapidly changing technologies, globalization, outsourcing, global virtual teams, knowledge management, global supply chains, the Wall Street meltdown, and other changes place demands on managers that go beyond the techniques and ideas traditionally taught in management courses. Managing today requires the full breadth of management skills and capabilities. This text provides comprehensive coverage of both traditional management skills and the new competencies needed in a turbulent environment characterized by economic turmoil, political confusion, and general uncertainty.

In the traditional world of work, management was to control and limit people, enforce rules and regulations, seek stability and efficiency, design a top-down hierarchy, and achieve bottom-line results. To spur innovation and achieve high performance, however, managers need different skills to engage workers' hearts and minds as well as take advantage of their physical labor. The new workplace asks that managers focus on leading change, harnessing people's creativity and enthusiasm, finding shared visions and values, and sharing information and power. Teamwork, collaboration, participation, and learning are guiding principles that help managers and employees maneuver the difficult terrain of today's turbulent business environment. Managers focus on developing, not controlling, people to adapt to new technologies and extraordinary environmental shifts, and thus achieve high performance and total corporate effectiveness.

My vision for the ninth edition of *New Era of Management* is to present the newest management ideas for turbulent times in a way that is interesting and valuable to students while retaining the best of traditional management thinking. To achieve this vision, I have included the most recent management concepts and research and have shown the contemporary application of management ideas in organizations. I have added a questionnaire at the beginning of each chapter that draws students personally into the topic and gives them some insight into their own management skills. A chapter feature for new managers, called the New Manager Self-Test, gives students a sense of what will be expected when they become managers. The combination of established scholarship, new ideas, and real-life applications gives students a taste of the energy, challenge, and adventure inherent in the dynamic field of management. The South-Western/Cengage Learning staff and I have worked together to provide a textbook better than any other at capturing the excitement of organizational management.

I revised *New Era of Management* to provide a book of utmost quality that will create in students both respect for the changing field of management and confidence that they can understand and master it. The textual portion of this book has been enhanced through the engaging, easy-to-understand writing style and the many in-text examples, boxed items, and short exercises that make the concepts come alive for students. The graphic component has been enhanced with several new exhibits and a new set of photo essays that illustrate specific management concepts. The well-chosen photographs provide vivid illustrations and intimate glimpses of management scenes, events, and people. The photos are combined with brief essays that explain how a specific management concept looks and feels. Both the textual and graphic portions of the textbook help students grasp the often abstract and distant world of management.

Focus on Innovation: New to the Ninth Edition

The ninth edition of *New Era of Management* is especially focused on the future of management education by identifying and describing emerging ideas and examples of innovative organizations and by providing enhanced learning opportunities for students.

Learning Opportunities

The ninth edition has taken a leap forward in pedagogical features to help students understand their own management capabilities and learn what it is like to manage in an organization today. New to this edition is an opening questionnaire that directly relates to the topic of the chapter and enables students to see how they respond to situations and challenges typically faced by real-life managers. New Manager Self-Tests in each chapter provide further opportunity for students to understand their management abilities. These short feedback questionnaires give students insight into how they would function in the real world of management. End-of-chapter questions have been carefully revised to encourage critical thinking and application of chapter concepts. End-of-chapter cases and ethical dilemmas help students sharpen their diagnostic skills for management problem solving.

Chapter Content

Within each chapter, many topics have been added or expanded to address the current issues managers face. At the same time, chapter text has been tightened and sharpened to provide greater focus on the key topics that count for management today. This tightening has resulted in a shortening of the text from 21 to 19 chapters. The essential elements about operations and technology have been combined into one chapter. An appendix on entrepreneurship and small business has been provided for students who want more information on managing in small businesses start-ups.

Chapter 1 includes a section on making the leap from being an individual contributor in the organization to becoming a new manager and getting work done primarily through others. The chapter introduces the skills and competencies needed to manage organizations effectively, including issues such as managing diversity, coping with globalization, and managing crises. In addition, the chapter discusses today's emphasis within organizations on innovation as a response to a rapidly changing environment.

Chapter 2 continues its solid coverage of the historical development of management and organizations. It also examines new management thinking for turbulent times. The chapter includes a new section on systemic thinking and an expanded discussion of post-World War II management techniques. The final part of the chapter looks at issues of managing the technology-driven workplace, including supply chain management, customer relationship management, and outsourcing.

Chapter 3 contains an updated look at current issues related to the environment and corporate culture, including a new section on issues related to the natural environment and managers' response to environmental advocates. The chapter also illustrates how managers shape a high–performance culture as an innovative response to a shifting environment.

Chapter 4 takes a look at the growing power of China and India in today's global business environment and what this means for managers around the world. The chapter discusses the need for *cultural intelligence,* and a new section looks at understanding communication differences as an important aspect of learning to manage internationally or work with people from different cultures. In addition, the complex issues surrounding globalization are discussed, including a consideration of the current globalization backlash. A new section on human resources points out the need for evaluating whether people are suitable for foreign assignments.

Chapter 5 makes the business case for incorporating ethical values in the organization. The chapter includes a new discussion of the *bottom-of-the-pyramid* business concept and how managers are successfully applying this new thinking. The chapter also has an expanded discussion of ethical challenges managers face today, including responses to recent financial scandals. It considers global ethical issues, as well, including a discussion of corruption rankings of various countries.

Chapter 6 provides a more focused discussion of the overall planning process and a new discussion of using strategy maps for aligning goals. This chapter also takes a close look at crisis planning and how to use scenarios. The chapter's final section on planning for high performance has been enhanced by a new discussion of intelligence teams and an expanded look at using performance dashboards to help managers plan in a fast-changing environment.

Chapter 7 continues its focus on the basics of formulating and implementing strategy. It includes a new section on diversification strategy, looking at how managers use unrelated diversification, related diversification, or vertical integration as strategic approaches in shifting environments. This chapter also looks at new trends in strategy, including the dynamic capabilities approach and partnership strategies.

Chapter 8 gives an overview of managerial decision making with an expanded discussion of how conflicting interests among managers can create uncertainty regarding decisions. A new section on why managers often make bad decisions looks at the biases that can cloud judgment. The chapter also includes a new section on innovative group decision making and the dangers of groupthink.

Chapter 9 discusses basic principles of organizing and describes both traditional and contemporary organizational structures in detail. The chapter includes a discussion of organic versus mechanistic structures and when each is more effective. Chapter 9 also provides a description of the virtual network organization form.

Chapter 10 includes a more focused discussion of the critical role of managing change and innovation today. The chapter includes a new discussion of the ambidextrous approach for both creating and using innovations and has expanded material on exploration and creativity, the importance of internal and external cooperation, and the growing trend toward open innovation.

Chapter 11 includes an expanded discussion of the strategic role of HRM in building human capital. The chapter has new sections on coaching and mentoring and the trend toward part-time and contingent employment. New ways of doing background checks on applicants, such as checking their pages on social networks, are discussed, and the chapter also looks at the changing social contract between employers and employees.

Chapter 12 has been revised and updated to reflect the most recent thinking on organizational diversity issues. The chapter looks at how diversity is changing the domestic and global workforce and includes a new section on the traditional versus inclusive models for managing diversity. This chapter also contains new coverage of the dividends of diversity; an expanded discussion of prejudice, discrimination, and stereotypes; and a new look at the difference between stereotyping and valuing cultural differences. The chapter includes a new five-step process for achieving cultural competence.

Chapter 13 provides an overview of financial and quality control, including Six Sigma, ISO certification, and a new application of the balanced scorecard, which views employee learning and growth as the foundation of high performance. The discussion of hierarchical versus decentralized control has been updated and expanded. The chapter also addresses current concerns about corporate governance and finding a proper balance of control and autonomy for employees.

Chapter 14 has been thoroughly revised to discuss recent trends in operations management, information technology, and e-business. The chapter begins by looking at the organization as a value chain and includes an expanded discussion of supply chain management and new technologies such a radio frequency identification (RFID). The discussion of information technology has been updated to include the trend toward user-generated content through wikis, blogs, and social networking. The chapter explores how these new technologies are being applied within organizations along with traditional information systems. The chapter also discusses e-commerce strategies, the use of business intelligence software, and knowledge management.

Chapter 15 continues its solid coverage of the basics of organizational behavior, including personality, values and attitudes, perception, emotional intelligence, learning and problem-solving styles, and stress management. Many exercises and questionnaires throughout this chapter enhance students' understanding of organizational behavior topics and their own personalities and attitudes.

Chapter 16 has been enriched with a discussion of followership. The chapter emphasizes that good leaders and good followers share common characteristics. Good leadership can make a difference, often through subtle, everyday actions. The discussion of power and influence has been expanded to include the sources of power that are available to followers as well as leaders. The discussions of charismatic, transformational, and interactive leadership have all been revised and refocused.

Chapter 17 covers the foundations of motivation and also incorporates recent thinking about motivational tools for today, including an expanded treatment of employee engagement. The chapter looks at new motivational ideas such as the importance of helping employees achieve work-life balance, incorporating fun and learning into the workplace, giving people a chance to fully participate, and helping people find meaning in their work.

Chapter 18 begins with a discussion of how managers facilitate strategic conversations by using communication to direct everyone's attention to the vision, values, and goals of the organization. The chapter explores the foundations of good communication and includes a new section on gender differences in communication, an enriched discussion of dialogue, and a refocused look at the importance of effective written communication in today's technologically connected workplace, including the use of new forms of manager communication such as blogs.

Chapter 19 includes a new section on the dilemma of teams, acknowledging that teams are sometimes ineffective and looking at the reasons for this, including such problems as free riders, lack of trust among team members, and so forth. The chapter then looks at how to make teams effective, including a significantly revised discussion of what makes an effective team leader. The chapter covers the types of teams and includes a new look at effectively using technology in virtual teams. The chapter also includes a section on managing conflict, including the use of negotiation.

In addition to the topics listed above, this text integrates coverage of the Internet and new technology into the various topics covered in each and every chapter.

Organization

The chapter sequence in *New Era of Management* is organized around the management functions of planning, organizing, leading, and controlling. These four functions effectively encompass both management research and characteristics of the manager's job.

Part One introduces the world of management, including the nature of management, issues related to today's chaotic environment, the learning organization, historical perspectives on management, and the technology-driven workplace.

Part Two examines the environments of management and organizations. This section includes material on the business environment and corporate culture, the global environment, ethics and social responsibility, and the natural environment.

Part Three presents three chapters on planning, including organizational goal setting and planning, strategy formulation and implementation, and the decision-making process.

Part Four focuses on organizing processes. These chapters describe dimensions of structural design, the design alternatives managers can use to achieve strategic objectives, structural designs for promoting innovation and change, the design and use of the human resource function, and the ways managing diverse employees are significant to the organizing function.

Part Five describes the controlling function of management, including basic principles of total quality management, the design of control systems, information technology, and techniques for control of operations management.

Part Six is devoted to leadership. The section begins with a chapter on organizational behavior, providing grounding in understanding people in organizations. This foundation paves the way for subsequent discussion of leadership, motivation of employees, communication, and team management.

Innovative Features

A major goal of this book is to offer better ways of using the textbook medium to convey management knowledge to the reader. To this end, the book includes several innovative features that draw students in and help them contemplate, absorb, and comprehend management concepts. South-Western has brought together a team of experts to create and coordinate color photographs, video cases, beautiful artwork, and supplemental materials for the best management textbook and package on the market.

Chapter Outline and Objectives. Each chapter begins with a clear statement of its learning objectives and an outline of its contents. These devices provide an overview of what is to come and can also be used by students to guide their study and test their understanding and retention of important points.

Opening Questionnaire. The text grabs student attention immediately by giving the student a chance to participate in the chapter content actively by completing a short questionnaire related to the topic.

Take a Moment. At strategic places through the chapter, students are invited to Take a Moment to apply a particular concept or think about how they would apply it as a practicing manager. This call to action further engages students in the chapter content. Some of the Take a Moment features also refer students to the associated New Manager Self-Test, or direct students from the chapter content to relevant end-of-chapter materials, such as an experiential exercise or an ethical dilemma.

New Manager Self-Test. A New Manager Self-Test in each chapter of the text provides opportunities for self-assessment as a way for students to experience management issues in a personal way. The change from individual performer to new manager is dramatic, and these self-tests provide insight into what to expect and how students might perform in the world of the new manager.

Concept Connection Photo Essays. A key feature of the book is the use of photographs accompanied by detailed photo essay captions that enhance learning. Each caption highlights and illustrates one or more specific concepts from the text to reinforce student understanding of the concepts. Although the photos are beautiful to look at, they also convey the vividness, immediacy, and concreteness of management events in today's business world.

Contemporary Examples. Every chapter of the text contains several written examples of management incidents. They are placed at strategic points in the chapter and are designed to illustrate the application of concepts to specific companies. These in-text examples—indicated by an icon in the margin—include well-known U.S. and international companies such as Toyota, Facebook, UPS, LG Electronics, Google, Unilever, Siemens, and eBay, as well as less-well-known companies and not-for-profit organizations such as Red 5 Studios, Strida, Genmab AS, ValueDance, and the U.S. Federal Bureau of Investigation (FBI). These examples put students in touch with the real world of organizations so that they can appreciate the value of management concepts.

Manager's Shoptalk Boxes. A Manager's Shoptalk box in each chapter addresses a specific topic straight from the field of management that is of special interest to students. These boxes may describe a contemporary topic or problem that is relevant to chapter content, or they may contain a diagnostic questionnaire or a special example of how managers handle a problem. The boxes heighten student interest in the subject matter and provide an auxiliary view of management issues not typically available in textbooks.

Video Cases. The six parts of the text conclude with video cases, one per chapter, that illustrate the concepts presented in that part. The 19 videos enhance class discussion, because students can see the direct application of the management theories they have learned. Each video case explores the issues covered in the video, allowing students to synthesize the material they've just viewed. The video cases culminate with several questions that can be used to launch classroom discussion or as homework. Suggested answers are provided in the Media Case Library.

Exhibits. Several exhibits have been added or revised in the ninth edition to enhance student understanding. Many aspects of management are research based, and some concepts tend to be abstract and theoretical. The many exhibits throughout this book enhance students' awareness and understanding of these concepts. These exhibits consolidate key points, indicate relationships among concepts, and visually illustrate concepts. They also make effective use of color to enhance their imagery and appeal.

Glossaries. Learning the management vocabulary is essential to understanding contemporary management. This process is facilitated in three ways. First, key concepts are boldfaced and completely defined where they first appear in the text. Second, brief definitions are set out in the margin for easy review and follow-up. Third, a glossary summarizing all key terms and definitions appears at the end of the book for handy reference.

A Manager's Essentials and Discussion Questions. Each chapter closes with a summary of the essential points that students should retain. The discussion questions are a complementary learning tool that will enable students to check their understanding of key issues, to think beyond basic concepts, and to determine areas that require further study. The summary and discussion questions help students discriminate between main and supporting points and provide mechanisms for self-teaching.

Management in Practice Exercises. End-of-chapter exercises called "Management in Practice: Experiential Exercise" and "Management in Practice: Ethical Dilemma" provide a self-test for students and an opportunity to experience management issues in a personal way. These exercises take the form of questionnaires, scenarios, and activities, and many also provide an opportunity for students to work in teams. The exercises are tied into the chapter through the Take a Moment feature that refers students to the end-of-chapter exercises at the appropriate point in the chapter content.

Case for Critical Analysis. Also appearing at the end of each chapter is a brief but substantive case that provides an opportunity for student analysis and class discussion. Some of these cases are about companies whose names students will recognize; others are based on real management events but the identities of companies and managers have been disguised. These cases allow students to sharpen their diagnostic skills for management problem solving.

Continuing Case. Located at the end of each part, the Continuing Case is a running discussion of management topics appropriate to that part as experienced by General Motors Company. Focusing on one company allows students to follow the managers' and the organization's long-term problems and solutions in a sustained manner.

Supplementary Materials

Instructor's Manual. Designed to provide support for instructors new to the course, as well as innovative materials for experienced professors, the Instructor's Manual includes Chapter Outlines, annotated learning objectives, Lecture Notes, and sample Lecture Outlines. Additionally, the Instructor's Manual includes answers and teaching notes to end-of-chapter materials, including the video cases and the continuing case. The files for the Instructor's Manual can be found at www.cengage .com/international.

Test Bank. Scrutinized for accuracy, the Test Bank includes more than 2,000 true/false, multiple-choice, short-answer, and essay questions. Page references are indicated for every question, as are designations of either factual or application so that instructors can provide a balanced set of questions for student exams. Each question is also tagged based on AACSB guidelines.

ExamView. Available on www.cengage.com/international, ExamView contains all of the questions in the printed Test Bank. This program is an easy-to-use test creation software compatible with Microsoft Windows. Instructors can add or edit questions, instructions, and answers, and select questions (randomly or numerically) by previewing them on the screen. Instructors can also create and administer quizzes online, whether over the Internet, a local area network (LAN), or a wide area network (WAN).

PowerPoint Lecture Presentation. Available on the Web site (www.cengage.com/ international), the PowerPoint Lecture Presentation enables instructors to customize their own multimedia classroom presentation. Containing an average of 27 slides per chapter, the package includes figures and tables from the text, as well as outside materials to supplement chapter concepts. Material is organized by chapter and can be modified or expanded for individual classroom use. PowerPoint slides are also easily printed to create customized Transparency Masters.

Study Guide. Packed with real-world examples and additional applications for helping students master management concepts, this learning supplement is an excellent resource. For each chapter of the text, the Study Guide includes a summary and completion exercise; a review with multiple-choice, true/false, and short-answer questions; a mini case with multiple-choice questions; management applications; and an experiential exercise that can be assigned as homework or used in class.

Video Package. The video package for *New Era of Management,* ninth edition, contains two options: On the Job videos and BizFlix videos. *On the Job* videos use real-world companies to illustrate management concepts as outlined in the text. Focusing on both small and large business, the videos give students an inside perspective on the situations and issues that corporations face. *BizFlix* are film clips taken from popular Hollywood movies such as *8 Mile, Backdraft,* and *The Bourne Identity,* and integrated into the ninth edition of Daft. Clips are supported by short cases and discussion questions at the end of each chapter.

Web Site (www.cengage.com/international). Discover a rich array of online teaching and learning management resources that you won't find anywhere else. Resources include interactive learning tools, links to critical management Web sites, and password-protected teaching resources available for download.

Acknowledgments

A gratifying experience for me was working with the team of dedicated professionals at South-Western who were committed to the vision of producing the best management text ever. I am grateful to Joe Sabatino, executive editor, whose enthusiasm, creative ideas, assistance, and vision kept this book's spirit alive. Emma Newsom, managing developmental editor, provided superb project coordination and offered excellent ideas and suggestions to help the team meet a demanding and sometimes arduous schedule. Kimberly Kanakes, executive marketing manager, and Clint Kernen, marketing manager, provided keen market knowledge and innovative ideas for instructional support. Martha Conway, senior content project manager, cheerfully and expertly guided me through the production process. Tippy McIntosh contributed her graphic arts skills to create a visually dynamic design. Ruth Belanger, editorial assistant, and Sarah Rose, marketing coordinator, skillfully pitched in to help keep the project on track. Joe Devine deserves a special thank you for his layout expertise and commitment to producing an attractive, high-quality textbook. Additionally, BJ Parker, Copyshop, USA, contributed the Continuing Case.

Here at Vanderbilt I want to extend special appreciation to my assistant, Barbara Haselton. Barbara provided excellent support and assistance on a variety of projects that gave me time to write. I also want to acknowledge an intellectual debt to my colleagues, Bruce Barry, Ray Friedman, Neta Moye, Rich Oliver, David Owens, Ranga Ramanujam, Bart Victor, and Tim Vogus. Thanks also to Deans Jim Bradford and Bill Christie who have supported my writing projects and maintained a positive scholarly atmosphere in the school. Another group of people who made a major contribution to this textbook are the management experts who provided advice, reviews, answers to questions, and suggestions for changes, insertions, and clarifications. I want to thank each of these colleagues for their valuable feedback and suggestions on the ninth edition:

David Alexander
*Christian Brothers
University*

Reginald L Audibert
*California State
University—Long Beach*

Burrell A. Brown
*California University of
Pennsylvania*

Paula Buchanan
*Jacksonville State
University*

Diane Caggiano
Fitchburg State College

Bruce Charnov
Hofstra University

Gloria Cockerell
Collin College

Jack Cox
Amberton University

Paul Ewell
Bridgewater College

Mary M. Fanning
*College of Notre Dame of
Maryland*

Merideth Ferguson
Baylor University

Karen Fritz
Bridgewater College

Yezdi H. Godiwalla
*University of Wisconsin—
Whitewater*

James Halloran
Wesleyan College

Stephen R. Hiatt
Catawba College

Betty Hoge
Bridgewater College

Jody Jones
*Oklahoma Christian
University*

Jerry Kinard
*Western Carolina
University*

Sal Kukalis
*California State
University—Long Beach*

Joyce LeMay
Bethel University

Wade McCutcheon
East Texas Baptist College

Tom Miller
Concordia University

W J Mitchell
Bladen Community College

John Okpara
Bloomsburg University

Lori A. Peterson
Augsburg College

Michael Provitera
Barry University

Abe Qastin
Lakeland College

Holly Caldwell Ratwani
Bridgewater College

Terry L. Riddle
Central Virginia Community College

Thomas Sy
California State University—Long Beach

Kevin A. Van Dewark
Humphreys College

Noemy Watchel
Kean University

Peter Wachtel
Kean University

I would also like to continue to acknowledge those reviewers who have contributed comments, suggestions and feedback on previous editions:

David C. Adams
Manhattanville College

Erin M. Alexander
University of Houston–Clear Lake

Hal Babson
Columbus State Community College

Reuel Barksdale
Columbus State Community College

Gloria Bemben
Finger Lakes Community College

Pat Bernson
County College of Morris

Art Bethke
Northeast Louisiana University

Thomas Butte
Humboldt State University

Peter Bycio
Xavier University, Ohio

Diane Caggiano
Fitchburg State College

Douglas E. Cathon
St. Augustine's College

Jim Ciminskie
Bay de Noc Community College

Dan Connaughton
University of Florida

Bruce Conwers
Kaskaskia College

Byron L. David
The City College of New York

Richard De Luca
William Paterson University

Robert DeDominic
Montana Tech

Linn Van Dyne
Michigan State University

John C. Edwards
East Carolina University

Mary Ann Edwards
College of Mount St. Joseph

Janice M. Feldbauer
Austin Community College

Daryl Fortin
Upper Iowa University

Michael P. Gagnon
New Hampshire Community Technical College

Richard H. Gayor
Antelope Valley College

Dan Geeding
Xavier University, Ohio

James Genseal
Joliet Junior College

Peter Gibson
Becker College

Carol R. Graham
Western Kentucky University

Gary Greene
Manatee Community College

Ken Harris
Indiana University Southeast

Paul Hayes
Coastal Carolina Community College

Dennis Heaton
Maharishi University of Management, Iowa

Jeffrey D. Hines
Davenport College

Bob Hoerber
Westminster College

James N. Holly
University of Wisconsin–Green Bay

Genelle Jacobson
Ridgewater College

C. Joy Jones
Ohio Valley College

Kathleen Jones
University of North Dakota

Sheryl Kae
Lynchburg College

Jordan J. Kaplan
Long Island University

J. Michael Keenan
Western Michigan University

Gloria Komer
Stark State College

Paula C. Kougl
Western Oregon University

Cynthia Krom
Mount St. Mary College

Mukta Kulkarni
University of Texas–San Antonio

William B. Lamb
Millsaps College

Robert E. Ledman
Morehouse College

George Lehma
Bluffton College

Cynthia Lengnick-Hall
University of Texas–San Antonio

Janet C. Luke
Georgia Baptist College of Nursing

Jenna Lundburg
Ithaca College

Walter J. MacMillan
Oral Roberts University

Myrna P. Mandell
California State University, Northridge

Daniel B. Marin
Louisiana State University

Michael Market
Jacksonville State University

James C. McElroy
Iowa State University

Dennis W. Meyers
Texas State Technical College

Alan N. Miller
University of Nevada–Las Vegas

Irene A. Miller
Southern Illinois University

James L. Moseley
Wayne State University

Micah Mukabi
Essex County College

David W. Murphy
Madisonville Community College

Nora Nurre
Upper Iowa University

Tomas J. Ogazon
St. Thomas University

Allen Oghenejbo
Mills College

Linda Overstreet
Hillsborough Community College

Ken Peterson
Metropolitan State University

Clifton D. Petty
Drury College

James I. Phillips
Northeastern State University

Linda Putchinski
University of Central Florida

Kenneth Radig
Medaille College

Gerald D. Ramsey
Indiana University Southeast

Barbara Redmond
Briar Cliff College

William Reisel
St. John's University–New York

Terry Riddle
Central Virginia Community College

Walter F. Rohrs
Wagner College

Meir Russ
University of Wisconsin–Green Bay

Marcy Satterwhite
Lake Land College

Don Schreiber
Baylor University

Kilmon Shin
Ferris State University

Daniel G. Spencer
University of Kansas

Gary Spokes
Pace University

M. Sprencz
David N. Meyers College

Shanths Srinivas
California State Polytechnic University, Pomona

Jeffrey Stauffer
Ventura College

William A. Stower
Seton Hall University

Mary Studer
Southwestern Michigan College

Bruce C. Walker
Northeast Louisiana University

Mark Weber
University of Minnesota

Emilia S. Westney
Texas Tech University

Stan Williamson
Northeast Louisiana University

Alla L. Wilson
University of Wisconsin–Green Bay

Ignatius Yacomb
Loma Linda University

Imad Jim Zbib
Ramapo College of New Jersey

Vic Zimmerman
Pima Community College

James Swenson
Moorhead State University, Minnesota

Irwin Talbot
St. Peter's College

Andrew Timothy
Lourdes College

Frank G. Titlow
St. Petersburg Junior College

John Todd
University of Arkansas

Philip Varca
University of Wyoming

Dennis L. Varin
Southern Oregon University

Gina Vega
Merrimack College

George S. Vozikis
University of Tulsa

Bruce C. Walker
Northeast Louisiana University

Mark Weber
University of Minnesota

Emilia S. Westney
Texas Tech University

Stan Williamson
Northeast Louisiana University

Alla L. Wilson
University of Wisconsin– Green Bay

Ignatius Yacomb
Loma Linda University

Imad Jim Zbib
Ramapo College of New Jersey

Vic Zimmerman
Pima Community College

I'd like to pay special tribute to my long-time editorial associate, Pat Lane. I can't imagine how I would ever complete such a comprehensive revision on my own. Pat provided truly outstanding help throughout every step of writing the ninth edition of *New Era of Management*. She skillfully drafted materials for a wide range of chapter topics, boxes, and cases; researched topics when new sources were lacking; and did an absolutely superb job with the copyedited manuscript and page proofs. Her commitment to this text enabled us to achieve our dream for its excellence. I also want to pay tribute to Mary Draper, who stepped in to help with the research and revision of this edition. Mary also did a superb job with the copyedited manuscript and page proofs. We could not have completed this revision without Mary's excellent assistance.

Finally, I want to acknowledge the love and contributions of my wife, Dorothy Marcic. Dorothy has been very supportive during this revision as we share our lives together. I also want to acknowledge the love and support from my five daughters— Danielle, Amy, Roxanne, Solange, and Elizabeth—who make my life special during our precious time together. Thanks also to B. J. and Kaitlyn and Kaci and Matthew for their warmth and smiles that brighten my life, especially during our days together skiing and on the beach.

Richard L. Daft
Nashville, Tennessee
December 2008

Brief Contents

Contents

Part 3

PLANNING

Part 4

ORGANIZING

Part 5

CONTROLLING

Part 6

LEADING

New Era of Management

RICHARD L. DAFT

Vanderbilt University

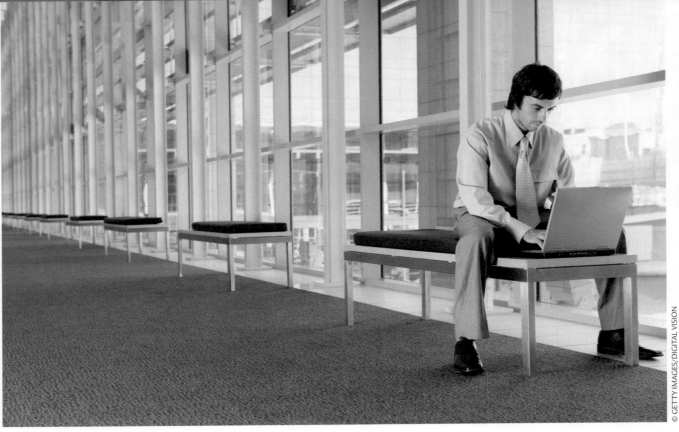

© GETTY IMAGES/DIGITAL VISION

Chapter Outline

Learning Outcomes

After studying this chapter, you should be able to:

1. Describe the four management functions and the type of management activity associated with each.

2. Explain the difference between efficiency and effectiveness and their importance for organizational performance.

3. Describe conceptual, human, and technical skills and their relevance for managers.

4. Describe management types and the horizontal and vertical differences between them.

5. Define ten roles that managers perform in organizations.

6. Appreciate the manager's role in small businesses and nonprofit organizations.

7. Understand the personal challenges involved in becoming a new manager.

8. Discuss characteristics of the new workplace and the new management competencies needed to deal with today's turbulent environment.

Innovative Management for Turbulent Times

1 Introduction
2 Environment
3 Planning
4 Organizing
5 Controlling
6 Leading

ARE YOU READY TO BE A MANAGER?[1]

Welcome to the world of management. Are you ready for it? This questionnaire will help you see whether your priorities align with the demands placed on today's managers. Rate each of the following items based on what you think is the appropriate emphasis for that task to your success as a new manager of a department. Your task is to rate the top four priority items as "High Priority" and the other four as "Low Prioity." You will have four of the items rated high and four rated low.

	High Priority	Low Priority
1. **Spend 50 percent or more of your time in the care and feeding of people.**	_____	_____
2. **Make sure people understand that you are in control of the department.**	_____	_____
3. **Use lunches to meet and network with peers in other departments.**	_____	_____
4. **Implement the changes you believe will improve department performance.**	_____	_____
5. **Spend as much time as possible talking with and listening to subordinates.**	_____	_____
6. **Make sure jobs get out on time.**	_____	_____
7. **Reach out to your boss to discuss his expectations for you and your department.**	_____	_____
8. **Make sure you set clear expectations and policies for your department.**	_____	_____

SCORING & INTERPRETATION: All eight items in the list may be important, but the odd-numbered items are considered more important than the even-numbered items for long-term success as a manager. If you checked three or four of the odd-numbered items, consider yourself ready for a management position. A successful new manager discovers that a lot of time has to be spent in the care and feeding of people, including direct reports and colleagues. People who fail in new management jobs often do so because they have poor working relationships or they misjudge management philosophy or cultural values. Developing good relationships in all directions is typically more important than holding on to old work skills or emphasizing control and task outcomes. Successful outcomes typically will occur when relationships are solid. After a year or so in a managerial role, successful people learn that more than half their time is spent networking and building relationships.

Many new managers expect to have power, to be in control, and to be personally responsible for departmental outcomes. A big surprise for many people when they first step into a management role is that they are much less in control of things than they expected. Managers are dependent on subordinates more than vice-versa because they are evaluated on the work of other people rather than on their own work. In a world of rapid change, unexpected events, and uncertainty, organizations need managers who can build networks and pull people together toward common goals.

The nature of management is to motivate and coordinate others to cope with diverse and far-reaching challenges. For example, Bruce Moeller, CEO of DriveCam, begins his work day by walking around visiting managers in operations, marketing, sales, engineering, finance, and so forth. Those managers, in turn, walk around talking with their direct reports, and on down the line. Moeller believes continual, free-flowing communication keeps everyone "on the same page" and helps employees meet goals at DriveCam, a company that sells and installs video recorders that monitor the behavior of commercial drivers.[2]

In the past, many managers did exercise tight control over employees. But the field of management is undergoing a revolution that asks managers to do more with less, to engage whole employees, to see change rather than stability as natural, and to inspire vision and cultural values that allow people to create a truly collaborative and productive workplace. In today's work environment, managers rely less on command and control and more on coordination and communication. This approach differs significantly from a traditional mind-set that emphasizes tight top-down control, employee separation and specialization, and management by impersonal measurement and analysis.

This textbook introduces and explains the process of management and the changing ways of thinking about the world that are critical for managers. By reviewing the actions of some successful and not-so-successful managers, you will learn the fundamentals of management. By the end of this chapter, you will already recognize some of the skills managers use to keep organizations on track, and you will begin to understand how managers can achieve astonishing results through people. By the end of this book, you will understand fundamental management skills for planning, organizing, leading, and controlling a department or entire organization.

WHY INNOVATION MATTERS

The theme of this text is innovation. To gain or keep a competitive edge, managers have renewed their emphasis on innovation, shifting away from a relentless focus on controlling costs toward investing in the future. In a survey of nearly 1,000 executives in North America, Europe, South America, and Asia, 86 percent agreed that "innovation is more important than cost reduction for long-term success."[3]

Why does innovation matter? Innovations in products, services, management systems, production processes, corporate values, and other aspects of the organization are what keeps companies growing, changing, and thriving. Without innovation, no company can survive over the long run. The growing clout and expertise of companies in developing countries, particularly China and India, have many Western managers worried. In a hypercompetitive global environment, companies must innovate more—and more quickly—than ever. Throughout this text, we will spotlight various companies that reflect this new innovation imperative. In addition, Chapter 10 discusses innovation and change in detail. First, let's begin our adventure into the world of management by learning some basics about what it means to be a manager.

THE DEFINITION OF MANAGEMENT

Every day, managers solve difficult problems, turn organizations around, and achieve astonishing performances. To be successful, every organization needs good managers.

What characteristic do all good managers have in common? They get things done through their organizations. Managers are the *executive function* of the organization, responsible for building and coordinating an entire system rather than performing specific tasks. That is, rather than doing all the work themselves, good managers create the systems and conditions that enable others to perform those tasks. As a boy, Wal-Mart founder Sam Walton made $4,000 a year at his paper route. How? Walton had a natural talent for management, and he created a system whereby he hired and coordinated others to help deliver papers rather than simply delivering what he could on his own.[4]

By creating the right systems and environment, managers ensure that the department or organization will survive and thrive beyond the tenure of any specific supervisor or manager. Consider that Jack Welch was CEO of General Electric through 20 amazingly successful years, but the leadership transition to Jeff Immelt in 2001 was as smooth as silk, and GE has stayed at or near the top of lists such as *Fortune* magazine's "Most Admired Companies," the *Financial Times* "most respected" survey, and *Barron's* most admired companies. People who have studied GE aren't surprised. The company has thrived for more than a century because managers created the right environment and systems. In the late 1800s, CEO Charles Coffin emphasized that GE's most important product was not lightbulbs or transformers, but *managerial talent*. Managers at GE spend a huge amount of time on human resources issues—recruiting, training, appraising, mentoring, and developing leadership talent for the future.[5]

Recognizing the role and importance of other people is a key aspect of good management. Early twentieth-century management scholar Mary Parker Follett defined management as "the art of getting things done through people."[6] More recently, noted management theorist Peter Drucker stated that the job of managers is to give direction to their organizations, provide leadership, and decide how to use organizational resources to accomplish goals.[7] Getting things done through people and other resources and providing leadership and direction are what managers do. These activities apply not only to top executives such as Eric Schmidt of Google or Indra Nooyi of PepsiCo, but also to the manager of a restaurant in your home town, the leader of an airport security team, a supervisor of an accounting department, or a director of sales and marketing. Thus, our definition of management is as follows:

Management is the attainment of organizational goals in an effective and efficient manner through planning, organizing, leading, and controlling organizational resources.

This definition holds two important ideas: (1) the four functions of planning, organizing, leading, and controlling, and (2) the attainment of organizational goals in an effective and efficient manner. Let's first take a look at the four primary management functions. Later in the chapter, we'll discuss organizational effectiveness and efficiency, as well as the multitude of skills managers use to successfully perform their jobs.

Concept Connection   A business may develop from a founder's talent, but **good management** and vision can take it to the next level. Tattoo artists Ami James (left) and Chris Núñez (right) started the business Miami Ink, which is the namesake of the TLC/Discovery reality television program in its fourth season in 2008. The partners pitched the concept for the show with a friend and turned their business into the most well-known tattoo design studio in the United States. Planning for life after reality TV, James and Núñez are creating another Miami tattoo studio, Love Hate Tattoo, because TLC/Discovery will own the rights to the name Miami Ink when the series ends.

As a new manager, remember that management means getting things done through other people. You can't do it all yourself. As a manager, your job is to create the environment and conditions that engage other people in goal accomplishment.

TakeaMoment

THE FOUR MANAGEMENT FUNCTIONS

Exhibit 1.1 illustrates the process of how managers use resources to attain organizational goals through the functions of planning, organizing, leading, and controlling. Although some management theorists identify additional management functions, such as staffing, communicating, or decision making, those additional functions will be discussed as subsets of the four primary functions in Exhibit 1.1. Chapters of this book are devoted to the multiple activities and skills associated with each function, as well as to the environment, global competitiveness, and ethics, which influence how managers perform these functions.

Planning

Planning means identifying goals for future organizational performance and deciding on the tasks and use of resources needed to attain them. In other words, managerial planning defines where the organization wants to be in the future and how

management The attainment of organizational goals in an effective and efficient manner through planning, organizing, leading, and controlling organizational resources.

planning The management function concerned with defining goals for future organizational performance and deciding on the tasks and resources needed to attain them.

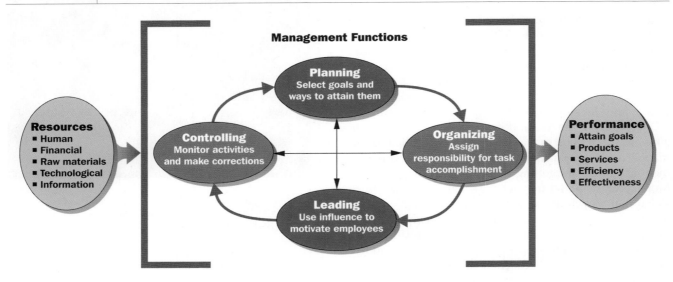

EXHIBIT | 1.1 The Process of Management

to get there. An example of good planning comes from Time Warner, Inc., where the marketing chiefs of the various divisions—HBO, Time Inc., Turner Broadcasting, Warner Bros., AOL, New Line Cinema, and Time Warner Cable—get together every three weeks to talk about future projects and how the divisions can work together to make them more successful. Thanks to careful planning, for example, almost every division is involved in promoting major films such as *The Golden Compass*, *Hairspray*, and *The Lord of the Rings* trilogy.[8]

organizing The management function concerned with assigning tasks, grouping tasks into departments, and allocating resources to departments.

leading The management function that involves the use of influence to motivate employees to achieve the organization's goals.

Organizing

Organizing typically follows planning and reflects how the organization tries to accomplish the plan. **Organizing** involves assigning tasks, grouping tasks into departments, delegating authority, and allocating resources across the organization. In recent years, companies as diverse as IBM, the Catholic Church, Motorola, and the Federal Bureau of Investigation have undergone structural reorganizations to accommodate their changing plans. At Avon Products, where sales have stalled and overhead costs have run amok, CEO Andrea Jung recently trimmed seven layers of management and reorganized the company into a structure where more decisions and functions are handled on a global basis to achieve greater efficiency of scale.[9]

Leading

Leading is the use of influence to motivate employees to achieve organizational goals. Leading means creating a shared culture and values, communicating goals to employees throughout the organization, and infusing employees with the desire to perform at a high level. Leading involves motivating entire departments and divisions as well as those individuals working immediately with the manager. In an era of uncertainty, global competition, and a growing diversity of the workforce, the ability to shape culture, communicate goals, and motivate employees is critical to business success.

Concept Connection As Chairman and CEO of Google, Eric Schmidt works with co-founders Sergey Brin and Larry Page to strike the right balance between innovation and discipline. These managers place a high priority on **leading** through shared values and goals to keep Google's employees motivated and energized. Yet from his experience of engineering a turnaround at struggling Novell, Schmidt knows the other **management functions** of planning, organizing, and controlling are just as important for success. In discussing his management role at Google, Schmidt says, "I keep things focused."

One doesn't have to be a well-known top manager to be an exceptional leader. Many managers working quietly in both large and small organizations around the world also provide strong leadership within departments, teams, nonprofit organizations, and small businesses. For example, Cara Kakuda is an area general manager in Hawaii for Nextel Partners, the rural-market division of Nextel Communications. Kakuda earned the job because of her ability to motivate and inspire employees. "People give her 150 percent," said a Nextel executive.[10]

Controlling

Controlling is the fourth function in the management process. **Controlling** means monitoring employees' activities, determining whether the organization is on target toward its goals, and making corrections as necessary. Managers must ensure that the organization is moving toward its goals. Trends toward empowerment and trust of employees have led many companies to place less emphasis on top-down control and more emphasis on training employees to monitor and correct themselves.

Information technology is helping managers provide needed organizational control without strict top-down constraints. Companies such as Cisco Systems and Oracle use the Internet and other information technology to coordinate and monitor virtually every aspect of operations, which enables managers to keep tabs on performance without maintaining daily authoritarian control over employees.[11]

ORGANIZATIONAL PERFORMANCE

The other part of our definition of management is the attainment of organizational goals in an efficient and effective manner. Management is so important because organizations are so important. In an industrialized society where complex technologies dominate, organizations bring together knowledge, people, and raw materials to perform tasks no individual could do alone. Without organizations, how could technology be provided that enables us to share information around the world in an instant; electricity be produced from huge dams and nuclear power plants; and thousands of videogames, compact discs, and DVDs be made available for our entertainment? Organizations pervade our society, and managers are responsible for seeing that resources are used wisely to attain organizational goals.

Our formal definition of an **organization** is a social entity that is goal directed and deliberately structured. *Social entity* means being made up of two or more people. *Goal directed* means designed to achieve some outcome, such as make a profit (Wal-Mart), win pay increases for members (AFL-CIO), meet spiritual needs (United Methodist Church), or provide social satisfaction (college sorority). *Deliberately structured* means that tasks are divided and responsibility for their performance is assigned to organization members. This definition applies to all organizations, including both profit and nonprofit. Small, offbeat, and nonprofit organizations are more numerous than large, visible corporations—and just as important to society.

Based on our definition of management, the manager's responsibility is to coordinate resources in an effective and efficient manner to accomplish the organization's goals. Organizational **effectiveness** is the degree to which the organization achieves a *stated goal*, or succeeds in accomplishing what it tries to do. Organizational effectiveness means providing a product or service that customers value. Organizational **efficiency** refers to the amount of resources used to achieve an organizational goal. It is based on how much raw materials, money, and people are necessary for producing a given volume of output. Efficiency can be calculated as the amount of resources used to produce a product or service. Efficiency and effectiveness can both be high in the same organization. Managers at retailer Target, for instance, continually look for ways to increase efficiency while also meeting the company's quality and customer satisfaction goals.

controlling The management function concerned with monitoring employees' activities, keeping the organization on track toward its goals, and making corrections as needed.

organization A social entity that is goal directed and deliberately structured.

effectiveness The degree to which the organization achieves a stated goal.

efficiency The use of minimal resources—raw materials, money, and people—to produce a desired volume of output.

Target

Innovative Way

Expect more, pay less. An astonishing 97 percent of Americans recognize Target's red-and-white bull's-eye brand, and almost as many are familiar with the slogan. "Sometimes we focus a little bit more on the 'pay less,' sometimes on the 'expect more,' but the guardrails are there," says Gregg Steinhafel, who took over as CEO of the trendy retailer in May 2008.

Target's slogan not only offers a promise to customers, it also reflects the company's emphasis on both effectiveness and efficiency. Target has an elite, secret team, called the "creative cabinet" that is made up of outsiders of various ages, interests, and nationalities who provide ideas and insights that keep the company on the cutting edge of consumer trends and give their input regarding managers' strategic initiatives. Innovation, design, and quality are key goals, and managers focus on providing a fun store experience and a unique, exciting product line. At the same time, they keep a close eye on costs and operating efficiencies to keep prices low. "I talk a lot about gross margin rate and the key drivers to improve our metrics and performance," Steinhafel says. In its SuperTarget centers, the retailer is able to consistently underprice supermarkets on groceries by about 10 percent to 15 percent and comes very close to Wal-Mart's rock-bottom prices.

As the economy slows, Target, like other retailers, has found the need to adjust worker hours and look for other efficiencies, which has drawn unfavorable attention from worker advocacy groups. Managers have to walk a fine line to continue to meet their goals for both efficiency and effectiveness.[12]

All managers have to pay attention to costs, but severe cost cutting to improve efficiency can sometimes hurt organizational effectiveness. The ultimate responsibility of managers is to achieve high **performance**, which is the attainment of organizational goals by using resources in an efficient *and* effective manner.

MANAGEMENT SKILLS

A manager's job is complex and multidimensional and, as we shall see throughout this book, requires a range of skills. Although some management theorists propose a long list of skills, the necessary skills for managing a department or an organization can be summarized in three categories: conceptual, human, and technical.[13] As illustrated in Exhibit 1.2, the application of these skills changes as managers move up in the organization. Although the degree of each skill necessary at different levels of an organization may vary, all managers must possess skills in each of these important areas to perform effectively.

Conceptual Skills

performance The organization's ability to attain its goals by using resources in an efficient and effective manner.

conceptual skill The cognitive ability to see the organization as a whole and the relationships among its parts.

Conceptual skill is the cognitive ability to see the organization as a whole system and the relationships among its parts. Conceptual skill involves the manager's thinking, information processing, and planning abilities. It involves knowing where one's department fits into the total organization and how the organization fits into the industry, the community, and the broader business and social environment. It means the ability to *think strategically*—to take the broad, long-term view—and to identify, evaluate, and solve complex problems.[14]

EXHIBIT | **1.2**   Relationship of Conceptual, Human, and Technical Skills to Management

Management Level
Top Managers

Middle Managers

First-Line Managers

Nonmanagers (Individual Contributors)

Conceptual skills are needed by all managers but are especially important for managers at the top. Many of the responsibilities of top managers, such as decision making, resource allocation, and innovation, require a broad view. Consider how recent strategic changes at General Electric reflect the conceptual skills of CEO Jeff Immelt. Immelt is remaking GE by thinking on a broad, long-term scale about the types of products and services people around the world are going to need in the future. He's pushing for growth by investing heavily in basic scientific and technological research, looking toward the needs of developing countries, and making structural and cultural changes that focus GE toward creating innovative products and services to meet shifting customer needs.[15]

Human Skills

Human skill is the manager's ability to work with and through other people and to work effectively as a group member. Human skill is demonstrated in the way a manager relates to other people, including the ability to motivate, facilitate, coordinate, lead, communicate, and resolve conflicts. A manager with human skills allows subordinates to express themselves without fear of ridicule, encourages participation, and shows appreciation for employees' efforts. Heather Coin, manager of the Sherman Oaks, California, branch of The Cheesecake Factory, demonstrates exceptional human skills. She considers motivating and praising her staff a top priority. "I really try to seek out moments because it's so hard to," she says. "You could definitely go for days without doing it. You have to consciously make that decision [to show appreciation]."[16]

Human skills are essential for managers who work with employees directly on a daily basis. Organizations frequently lose good people because of front-line bosses who fail to show respect and concern for employees.[17] However, human skills are becoming increasingly important for managers at all levels. In the past, many CEOs could get by without good people skills, but no longer. Today's employees, boards, customers, and communities are demanding that top executives demonstrate an ability to inspire respect, loyalty, and even affection rather than fear. "People are expecting more from the companies they're working for, more from the companies they're doing business with, and more from the companies they're buying from," says Raj Sisodia, a professor of marketing at Bentley College and co-author of a recent book called *Firms of Endearment*.[18]

Technical Skills

Technical skill is the understanding of and proficiency in the performance of specific tasks. Technical skill includes mastery of the methods, techniques, and equipment involved in specific functions such as engineering, manufacturing, or finance. Technical skill also includes specialized knowledge, analytical ability, and the competent use of tools and techniques to solve problems in that specific discipline. Technical skills are particularly important at lower organizational levels. Many managers get promoted to their first management jobs by having excellent technical skills. However, technical skills become less important than human and conceptual skills as managers move up the hierarchy. For example, in his seven years as a manufacturing engineer at Boeing, Bruce Moravec developed superb technical skills in his area of operation. But when he was asked to lead the team designing a new fuselage for the Boeing 757, Moravec found that he needed to rely heavily on human skills in order to gain the respect and confidence of people who worked in areas he knew little about.[19]

human skill The ability to work with and through other people and to work effectively as a group member.

technical skill The understanding of and proficiency in the performance of specific tasks.

Complete the experiential exercise on page 25 that pertains to management skills. Reflect on the strength of your preferences among the three skills and the implications for you as a manager.

TakeaMoment

When Skills Fail

Everyone has flaws and weaknesses, and these shortcomings become most apparent under conditions of rapid change and uncertainty.[20] Therefore, during turbulent times, managers really have to stay on their toes and apply all their skills and competencies in a way that benefits the organization and its stakeholders—employees, customers, investors, the community, and so forth. In recent years, numerous highly publicized examples showed us what happens when managers fail to effectively and ethically apply their skills to meet the demands of an uncertain, rapidly changing world. Companies such as Enron, Tyco, and WorldCom were flying high in the 1990s but came crashing down under the weight of financial scandals. Others, such as Rubbermaid and Kmart, are struggling because of years of management missteps.

Although corporate greed and deceit grab the headlines, many more companies falter or fail less spectacularly. Managers fail to listen to customers, misinterpret signals from the marketplace, or can't build a cohesive team and execute a strategic plan. Over the past several years, many CEOs, including Bob Nardelli at Home Depot, Carly Fiorina at Hewlett-Packard, and Michael Eisner at Disney have been ousted due to their failure to implement their strategic plans or keep stakeholders happy.

Recent examinations of struggling organizations and executives offer a glimpse into the mistakes managers often make in a turbulent environment.[21] One of the biggest blunders is managers' failure to comprehend and adapt to the rapid pace of change in the world around them. A related problem is top managers who create a climate of fear in the organization so that people are afraid to tell the truth and strive primarily to avoid the boss's wrath. Thus, bad news gets hidden and important signals from the marketplace are missed. People stop thinking creatively, avoid responsibility, and may even slide into unethical behavior if it keeps them on the boss's good side.[22]

Other critical management missteps include poor communication skills and failure to listen; poor interpersonal skills; treating employees as instruments to be used; a failure to clarify direction and performance expectations; suppressing dissenting viewpoints; and the inability to build a management team characterized by mutual trust and respect.[23] Bob Nardelli was forced out at Home Depot largely because he was unable to build trust and cohesiveness among his board and management team, and his brusque and unfeeling style alienated executives and rank and file workers alike. Using expletives for emphasis at one meeting soon after his arrival as CEO, Nardelli reportedly said, "You guys don't know how to run a . . . business." At the annual meeting where shareholder advocates were protesting Nardelli's extravagant pay package, the CEO limited shareholder questions to one minute, sealing his image as a callous executive unwilling to listen and compromise. He tried to redeem himself by going on a "listening tour," but the damage had been done.[24] Contrast Nardelli's approach with that of Jim McNerney, who spent his first six months as CEO of Boeing talking with employees around the company to understand Boeing's strengths and challenges and emphasizing the need for cooperation and teamwork.[25]

MANAGEMENT TYPES

Managers use conceptual, human, and technical skills to perform the four management functions of planning, organizing, leading, and controlling in all organizations—large and small, manufacturing and service, profit and nonprofit, traditional and Internet-based. But not all managers' jobs are the same. Managers are responsible for different departments, work at different levels in the hierarchy, and meet different requirements for achieving high performance. Twenty-five-year-old Daniel Wheeler is a first-line supervisor in his first management job at Del Monte Foods, where he is directly involved in promoting products, approving packaging sleeves, and organizing people to host sampling events.[26] Kevin Kurtz is a middle manager at Lucasfilm, where he works with employees to develop marketing campaigns for some of the entertainment company's hottest films.[27] And Domenic Antonellis is CEO of the New England Confectionary Co. (Necco), the company that makes those tiny pastel candy hearts stamped with phrases such as "Be Mine" and "Kiss Me."[28] All three are managers and must contribute to planning, organizing, leading, and controlling their organizations—but in different amounts and ways.

Vertical Differences

An important determinant of the manager's job is hierarchical level. Exhibit 1.3 illustrates the three levels in the hierarchy. A recent study of more than 1,400 managers examined how the manager's job differs across these three hierarchical levels and found that the primary focus changes at different levels.[29] For first-level managers, the main concern is facilitating individual employee performance. Middle managers, though, are concerned less with individual performance and more with linking groups of people, such as allocating resources, coordinating teams, or putting top management plans into action across the organization. For top-level managers, the primary focus is monitoring the external environment and determining the best strategy to be competitive.

Let's look in more detail at differences across hierarchical levels. **Top managers** are at the top of the hierarchy and are responsible for the entire organization. They have such titles as president, chairperson, executive director, chief executive officer (CEO), and executive vice president. Top managers are responsible for setting organizational goals, defining strategies for achieving them, monitoring and interpreting the external environment, and making decisions that affect the entire organization. They look to the long-term future and concern themselves with general environmental trends and the organization's overall success. Top managers are also responsible for communicating a shared vision for the organization, shaping corporate culture, and nurturing an entrepreneurial spirit that can help the company innovate and keep pace with rapid change.[30]

top manager A manager who is at the top of the organizational hierarchy and is responsible for the entire organization.

EXHIBIT | **1.3** Management Levels in the Organizational Hierarchy

© SUZANNE PLUNKETT/ASSOCIATED PRESS

Concept Connection Supported in part by USAID and published by The Killid Group, a media company headquartered in Kabul, *Mursal* is the first nationally distributed women's magazine in Afghanistan's history. Aimed at average women, most of whom are illiterate due to the lack of educational opportunities, the publication makes liberal use of photographs to cover a wide range of women's issues. It is the job of **middle managers,** such as the *Mursal* editors shown here talking with board member Palwasha Hassan, to help realize an organization's strategic goals, which are typically defined by top management.

middle manager A manager who works at the middle levels of the organization and is responsible for major departments.

project manager A manager responsible for a temporary work project that involves the participation of other people from various functions and levels of the organization.

first-line manager A manager who is at the first or second management level and is directly responsible for the production of goods and services.

functional manager A manager who is responsible for a department that performs a single functional task and has employees with similar training and skills.

Middle managers work at middle levels of the organization and are responsible for business units and major departments. Examples of middle managers are department head, division head, manager of quality control, and director of the research lab. Middle managers typically have two or more management levels beneath them. They are responsible for implementing the overall strategies and policies defined by top managers. Middle managers generally are concerned with the near future rather than with long-range planning.

The middle manager's job has changed dramatically over the past two decades. Many organizations improved efficiency by laying off middle managers and slashing middle management levels. Traditional pyramidal organization charts were flattened to allow information to flow quickly from top to bottom and decisions to be made with greater speed. Exhibit 1.3 illustrates the shrinking middle management.

Yet even as middle management levels have been reduced, the middle manager's job has taken on a new vitality. Rather than managing the flow of information up and down the hierarchy, middle managers create horizontal networks that can help the organization act quickly. Research shows that middle managers play a crucial role in driving innovation and enabling organizations to respond to rapid shifts in the environment.[31] As Ralph Stayer, CEO of Johnsonville Sausage said, "Leaders can design wonderful strategies, but the success of the organization resides in the execution of those strategies. The people in the middle are the ones who make it work."[32]

Middle managers' status has also escalated because of the growing use of teams and projects. Strong project managers are in hot demand. A **project manager** is responsible for a temporary work project that involves the participation of people from various functions and levels of the organization, and perhaps from outside the company as well. Many of today's middle managers work with a variety of projects and teams at the same time, some of which cross geographical and cultural as well as functional boundaries.

First-line managers are directly responsible for the production of goods and services. They are the first or second level of management and have such titles as supervisor, line manager, section chief, and office manager. They are responsible for groups of nonmanagement employees. Their primary concern is the application of rules and procedures to achieve efficient production, provide technical assistance, and motivate subordinates. The time horizon at this level is short, with the emphasis on accomplishing day-to-day goals. For example, Alistair Boot manages the menswear department for a John Lewis department store in Cheadle, England.[33] Boot's duties include monitoring and supervising shop floor employees to make sure sales procedures, safety rules, and customer service policies are followed. This type of managerial job might also involve motivating and guiding young, often inexperienced workers, providing assistance as needed, and ensuring adherence to company policies.

Horizontal Differences

The other major difference in management jobs occurs horizontally across the organization. **Functional managers** are responsible for departments that perform a single functional task and have employees with similar training and skills. Functional departments include advertising, sales, finance, human resources, manufacturing, and accounting. *Line managers* are responsible for the manufacturing and marketing departments that make or sell the product or service. *Staff managers* are in charge of departments such as finance and human resources that support line departments.

General managers are responsible for several departments that perform different functions. A general manager is responsible for a self-contained division, such as a Macy's department store or a General Motors assembly plant, and for all the functional departments within it. Project managers also have general management responsibility because they coordinate people across several departments to accomplish a specific project.

WHAT IS IT LIKE TO BE A MANAGER?

Unless someone has actually performed managerial work, it is hard to understand exactly what managers do on an hour-by-hour, day-to-day basis. The manager's job is so diverse that a number of studies have been undertaken in an attempt to describe exactly what happens. The question of what managers actually do to plan, organize, lead, and control was answered by Henry Mintzberg, who followed managers around and recorded all their activities.[34] He developed a description of managerial work that included three general characteristics and ten roles. These characteristics and roles, discussed in the following sections, have been supported in subsequent research.[35]

More recent research has looked at what managers *like* to do. The research found that both male and female managers across five different countries reported that they most enjoy activities such as leading others, networking, and leading innovation. Activities managers like least include controlling subordinates, handling paperwork, and managing time pressures.[36] Many new managers in particular find the intense time pressures of management, the load of administrative paperwork, and the challenge of directing others to be quite stressful as they adjust to their new roles and responsibilities. Indeed, the initial leap into management can be one of the scariest moments in a person's career.

© NEWSCOM

Concept Connection The father-son team of Don (left) and Donnie (right) Nelson have both held the position of **general manager** for the NBA Mavericks. In 1997, when Don Nelson took over as general manager and head coach of the Mavericks, the basketball team was in a freefall. Donnie joined his father the next year as assistant coach to help build the team. They were rewarded for their efforts in 2003 when the team broke through with a dynamic defense. Donnie moved into the general manager position in 2005 when his father stepped down and enjoyed overseeing the Mavericks play in the NBA finals in 2007 and 2008.

How will you make the transition to a new manager's position? Complete the New Manager Self-Test on page 14 to see how prepared you are to step into a management role.

TakeaMoment

Making the Leap: Becoming a New Manager

Many people who are promoted into a manager position have little idea what the job actually entails and receive little training about how to handle their new role. It's no wonder that, among managers, first-line supervisors tend to experience the most job burnout and attrition.[37]

Organizations often promote the star performers—those who demonstrate individual expertise in their area of responsibility and have an ability to work well with others—both to reward the individual and to build new talent into the managerial ranks. But making the shift from individual contributor to manager is often tricky. Dianne Baker, an expert nurse who was promoted to supervisor of an out-patient cardiac rehabilitation center, quickly found herself overwhelmed by the challenge of supervising former peers, keeping up with paperwork, and understanding financial and operational issues.[38] Baker's experience is duplicated every day as new managers struggle with the transition to their new jobs. Harvard professor Linda Hill

general manager A manager who is responsible for several departments that perform different functions.

New Manager Self-Test

Manager Achievement

Rate each item below based on your orientation toward personal achievement. Read each item and check either Mostly True or Mostly False as you feel right now.

	Mostly True	Mostly False
1. I enjoy the feeling I get from mastering a new skill.	_____	_____
2. Working alone is typically better than working in a group.	_____	_____
3. I like the feeling I get from winning.	_____	_____
4. I like to develop my skills to a high level.	_____	_____
5. I rarely depend on anyone else to get things done.	_____	_____
6. I am frequently the most valuable contributor to a team.	_____	_____
7. I like competitive situations.	_____	_____
8. To get ahead, it is important to be viewed as a winner.	_____	_____

SCORING AND INTERPRETATION: Give yourself one point for each Mostly True answer. In this case, a *low score* is better. A high score means a focus on personal achievement separate from others, which is ideal for a specialist or individual contributor. However, a manager is a generalist who gets things done through others. A desire to be a winner may put you in competition with your people rather than a focus on developing their skills. As a manager, you will not succeed as a lone achiever who does not facilitate and coordinate others. If you checked three or fewer as Mostly True, your basic orientation is good. If you scored six or higher, your focus is on being an individual winner. You will want to shift your perspective to become an excellent manager.

followed a group of 19 managers over the first year of their managerial careers and found that one key to success is to recognize that becoming a manager involves more than learning a new set of skills. Rather, becoming a manager means a profound transformation in the way people think of themselves, called *personal identity*, that includes letting go of deeply held attitudes and habits and learning new ways of thinking.[39] Exhibit 1.4 outlines the transformation from individual performer to manager.

Recall our earlier discussion of the role of manager as the executive function of the organization, the person who builds systems rather than doing specific tasks. The individual performer is a specialist and a "doer." His or her mind is conditioned to think in terms of performing specific tasks and activities as expertly as possible. The manager, on the other hand, has to be a generalist and learn to coordinate a broad range of activities. Whereas the individual performer strongly identifies with his or her specific tasks, the manager has to identify with the broader organization and industry.

In addition, the individual performer gets things done mostly through his or her own efforts, and develops the habit of relying on self rather than others. The manager, though, gets things done through other people. Indeed, one of the most common mistakes new managers make is wanting to do all the work themselves rather than

EXHIBIT | **1.4**

Making the Leap from
Individual Performer to
Manager

From Individual Identity	To Manager Identity
• Specialist, performs specific tasks	• Generalist, coordinates diverse tasks
• Gets things done through own efforts	• Gets things done through others
• An individual actor	• A network builder
• Works relatively independently	• Works in highly interdependent manner

SOURCE: Based on Exhibit 1.1, "Transformation of Identity," in Linda A. Hill, *Becoming a Manager: Mastery of a New Identity,* 2nd ed. (Boston, MA: Harvard Business School Press, 2003): 6.

delegating to others and developing others' abilities.[40] Lisa Drakeman made this mistake when she moved from teaching religion to being CEO of a biotechnology startup.

Innovative Way

Lisa Drakeman, Genmab AS

Lisa Drakeman was teaching religion at Princeton when her husband asked her to help out at Medarex, a new biotechnology company he founded to develop antibody-based medicines for cancer, inflammation, and infectious disease. Drakeman began performing various tasks part-time, but soon found herself heading up a spinoff company, Genmab AS of Denmark.

One of the toughest things Drakeman had to learn was to stop doing everything herself. In the beginning, she attended every meeting, interviewed every job candidate, and read every draft of clinical trial designs. She soon realized that she couldn't master every detail and that trying to do so would stall the company's growth. Although it was hard to step back, Drakeman eventually made the transition from doing individual tasks to performing the executive function. She established clear procedures and began delegating the details of products and clinical trials to others. Rather than interviewing job candidates herself, she set up human resources systems to enable others to interview, hire, and train employees. By developing from individual performer to manager, Drakeman helped Genmab grow from 25 employees to around 200 within a few years.[41]

Another problem for many new managers is that they expect to have greater freedom to do what they think is best for the organization. In reality, though, managers find themselves hemmed in by interdependencies. Being a successful manager means thinking in terms of building teams and networks, becoming a motivator and organizer within a highly interdependent system of people and work. Although the distinctions may sound simple in the abstract, they are anything but. In essence, becoming a manager means becoming a new person and viewing oneself in a completely new way.

Can you make a personal transformation from individual performer to manager, accomplishing work by engaging and coordinating other people? Look back at your results on the questionnaire at the beginning of this chapter to see how your priorities align with the demands placed on a manager.

TakeaMoment

Many new managers have to make the transformation in a "trial by fire," learning on the job as they go, but organizations are beginning to be more responsive to the need for new manager training. The cost to organizations of losing good employees who can't make the transition is greater than the cost of providing training to help new managers cope, learn, and grow. In addition, some of today's organizations are using great care in selecting people for managerial positions, including ensuring that each candidate understands what management involves and really wants to be a manager. A career as a manager can be highly rewarding, but it can also be stressful and frustrating. The Manager's Shoptalk further examines some of the challenges new managers face. After reading the Shoptalk, can you answer "Yes" to the question "Do I really want to be a manager?"

Manager's Shoptalk

Do You Really Want To Be A Manager?

Is management for you? Becoming a manager is considered by most people to be a positive, forward-looking career move and, indeed, life as a manager offers appealing aspects. However, it also holds many challenges, and not every person will be happy and fulfilled in a management position. Here are some of the issues would-be managers should consider before deciding they want to pursue a management career:

1. **The increased workload.** It isn't unusual for managers to work 70 to 80 hours per week, and some work even longer hours. A manager's job always starts before a shift and ends hours after the shift is over. When Ray Sarnacki was promoted to manager at an aerospace company, he found himself frustrated by the incessant travel, endless paperwork, and crowded meeting schedule. He eventually left the job and found happiness in a position earning about one-fifth of his peak managerial salary.

2. **The challenge of supervising former peers.** This issue can be one of the toughest for new managers. They frequently struggle to find the right approach, with some trying too hard to remain "one of the gang," and others asserting their authority too harshly. In almost all cases, the transition from a peer-to-peer relationship to a manager-to-subordinate one is challenging and stressful.

3. **The headache of responsibility for other people.** A lot of people get into management because they like the idea of having power, but the reality is that many managers feel overwhelmed by the responsibility of hiring, supervising, and disciplining others. New managers are often astonished at the amount of time it takes to handle "people problems." Kelly Cannell, who quit her job as a manager, puts it this way: "What's the big deal [about managing people]? The big deal is that people are human. . . . To be a good manager, you have to mentor them, listen to their problems, counsel them, and at the end of the day you still have your own work on your plate. . . . Don't take the responsibility lightly, because no matter what you think, managing people is not easy."

4. **Being caught in the middle.** Except for those in the top echelons, managers find themselves acting as a backstop, caught between upper management and the workforce. Even when managers disagree with the decisions of top executives, they are responsible for implementing them.

For some people, the frustrations of management aren't worth it. For others, management is a fulfilling and satisfying career choice and the emotional rewards can be great. One key to being happy as a manager may be carefully evaluating whether you can answer yes to the question, "Do I really want to be a manager?"

SOURCES: Erin White, "Learning to Be the Boss," *The Wall Street Journal*, November 21, 2005; Jared Sandberg, "Down Over Moving Up: Some New Bosses Find They Hate Their Jobs," *The Wall Street Journal*, July 27, 2005; Heath Row, "Is Management for Me? That Is the Question," *Fast Company* (February–March 1998): 50–52; Timothy D. Schellhardt, "Want to Be a Manager? Many People Say No, Calling Job Miserable," *The Wall Street Journal*, April 4, 1997; and Matt Murray, "Managing Your Career—The Midcareer Crisis: Am I in This Business to Become a Manager?" *The Wall Street Journal*, July 25, 2000.

Manager Activities

Most new managers are unprepared for the variety of activities managers routinely perform. One of the most interesting findings about managerial activities is how busy managers are and how hectic the average workday can be.

Adventures in Multitasking Managerial activity is characterized by variety, fragmentation, and brevity.[42] The widespread and voluminous nature of a manager's involvements leaves little time for quiet reflection. The average time spent on any one activity is less than nine minutes.

Managers shift gears quickly. Significant crises are interspersed with trivial events in no predictable sequence. Every manager's job, while in most cases not as potentially dangerous, is similar in its diversity and fragmentation to that of U.S. Marine Corps officers managing the reconstruction efforts in Iraq. Consider the diverse events in a typical day for Capt. Sean Miller in Fallujah, Iraq:[43]

- Begins the day meeting with tribal sheiks and local officials to decide which projects to finance.
- Drives to a command center to check the status of a job that a contractor has left unfinished.
- Walks to a nearby school to discuss awards for students who recite passages from the Koran.
- Is interrupted by a handful of people who have come with questions or demands: one asks about a relative he says had been detained several years ago; another pushes a contract for review into Miller's hands; a third is seeking work; and so on.
- Finally returns to the discussion of student awards.
- Agrees to a tour of the school, where a contractor explains his request for a $50,000 generator that Miller thinks can be obtained for $8,000.
- Checks the recently cleaned grounds at another school and finds that papers and other trash once again litter the area.
- Notices a man running a pipe from his roof and warns him against running his sewage to the school.
- Calms and directs his marines, who grow skittish as children, some in their upper teens, rush from the school building.
- Stops by a café to hear young men's complaints that they are asked to pay bribes to get a job on the police force.
- Near sunset, takes photos of a still-damaged cemetery door that contractors have been paid to repair.

Life on Speed Dial The manager performs a great deal of work at an unrelenting pace.[44] Managers' work is fast paced and requires great energy. The managers observed by Mintzberg processed 36 pieces of mail each day, attended eight meetings, and took a tour through the building or plant. As soon as a manager's daily calendar is set, unexpected disturbances erupt. New meetings are required. During time away from the office, executives catch up on work-related reading, paperwork, phone calls, and e-mail. Technology, such as e-mail, instant messaging, cell phones, and laptops, intensifies the pace. For example, Brett Yormark of the New Jersey Nets typically responds to about 60 messages before he even shaves and dresses for the day.[45]

The fast pace of a manager's job is illustrated by Heather Coin, the Cheesecake Factory manager we introduced earlier in the chapter. "I really try to keep the plates spinning," Coin says, comparing her management job to a circus act. "If I see a plate slowing down, I go and give it a spin and move on." She arrives at work about 9:30 a.m. and checks the financials for how the restaurant performed the day before. Next comes a staff meeting and various personnel duties. Before and after the lunch shift, she's pitching in with whatever needs to be done—making salads in the kitchen, expediting the food, bussing the tables, or talking with guests. After lunch, from 3:00 to 4:30 p.m., Heather takes care of administrative duties, paperwork, or meetings with upper management, media, or community organizations. At 4:30, she holds a shift-change meeting to ensure a smooth transition from the day crew to the night crew. Throughout the day, Heather also mentors staff members, which she considers the most rewarding part of her job. After the evening rush, she usually heads for home about 10 p.m., the end of another 12.5-hour day.[46]

Manager Roles

Mintzberg's observations and subsequent research indicate that diverse manager activities can be organized into 10 roles.[47] A **role** is a set of expectations for a manager's behavior. Exhibit 1.5 provides examples of each of the roles. These roles are divided into three conceptual categories: informational (managing by information); interpersonal (managing through people); and decisional (managing through action). Each role represents activities that managers undertake to ultimately accomplish the functions of planning, organizing, leading, and controlling. Although it is necessary to separate the components of the manager's job to understand the different roles and activities of a manager, it is important to remember that the real job of management cannot be practiced as a set of independent parts; all the roles interact in the real world of management. As Mintzberg says, "The manager who only communicates or only conceives never gets anything done, while the manager who only 'does' ends up doing it all alone."[48]

role A set of expectations for one's behavior.

Informational Roles Informational roles describe the activities used to maintain and develop an information network. General managers spend about 75 percent

EXHIBIT | 1.5

Ten Manager Roles

Category	Role	Activity
Informational	Monitor	Seek and receive information, scan periodicals and reports, maintain personal contacts.
	Disseminator	Forward information to other organization members; send memos and reports, make phone calls.
	Spokesperson	Transmit information to outsiders through speeches, reports, memos.
Interpersonal	Figurehead	Perform ceremonial and symbolic duties such as greeting visitors, signing legal documents.
	Leader	Direct and motivate subordinates; train, counsel, and communicate with subordinates.
	Liaison	Maintain information links both inside and outside organization; use e-mail, phone calls, meetings.
Decisional	Entrepreneur	Initiate improvement projects; identify new ideas, delegate idea responsibility to others.
	Disturbance handler	Take corrective action during disputes or crises; resolve conflicts among subordinates; adapt to environmental crises.
	Resource allocator	Decide who gets resources; schedule, budget, set priorities.
	Negotiator	Represent department during negotiation of union contracts, sales, purchases, budgets; represent departmental interests.

SOURCES: Adapted from Henry Mintzberg, *The Nature of Managerial Work* (New York: Harper & Row, 1973), pp. 92–93; and Henry Mintzberg, "Managerial Work: Analysis from Observation," *Management Science* 18 (1971): B97–B110.

of their time talking to other people. The *monitor* role involves seeking current information from many sources. The manager acquires information from others and scans written materials to stay well informed. The *disseminator* and *spokesperson* roles are just the opposite: The manager transmits current information to others, both inside and outside the organization, who can use it. One colorful example of the spokesperson role is Mick Jagger of the Rolling Stones. The rock band is run like a large, multinational organization with Jagger as the CEO. Jagger surrounds himself not only with talented artists, but also with sophisticated and experienced business executives. Yet it is Jagger who typically deals with the media and packages the band's image for a worldwide audience.[49]

COURTESY OF SBTV.COM

Concept Connection   Small business owners often assume multiple management roles. Here on the right Susan Solovic, founder and CEO of sbtv.com, functions as **spokesperson** in an interview with Tess Rafols of KTVK. She also is an **entrepreneur,** developing new ideas for the online television channel. Solovic fills the **monitor** role by keeping an eye on current trends that might be helpful to her evolving company as well as to the small businesses her channel serves.

Interpersonal Roles   Interpersonal roles pertain to relationships with others and are related to the human skills described earlier. The *figurehead* role involves handling ceremonial and symbolic activities for the department or organization. The manager represents the organization in his or her formal managerial capacity as the head of the unit. The presentation of employee awards by a division manager at Taco Bell is an example of the figurehead role. The *leader* role encompasses relationships with subordinates, including motivation, communication, and influence. The *liaison* role pertains to the development of information sources both inside and outside the organization. Stephen Baxter, managing director of Scotland's Glasgow Airport, illustrates the liaison role. Baxter led a rapid expansion of the airport by coordinating with executives at other organizations to find ways to woo new airlines to use Glasgow. He recently took on an extra role as president of the Glasgow chamber of commerce, enabling him to develop more sources of information and support.[50]

Decisional Roles   Decisional roles pertain to those events about which the manager must make a choice and take action. These roles often require conceptual as well as human skills. The *entrepreneur* role involves the initiation of change. Managers are constantly thinking about the future and how to get there.[51] Managers become aware of problems and search for innovations that will correct them. Susan Whiting, Chief of Research for Nielsen Media Research, scheduled dozens of individual and group meetings with clients to talk about how to adapt the Nielsen ratings for an era in which more and more shows are being viewed on computers, video iPods, and other digital devices.[52] The *disturbance handler* role involves resolving conflicts among subordinates or between the manager's department and other departments. The *resource allocator* role pertains to decisions about how to allocate people, time, equipment, money, and other resources to attain desired outcomes. The manager must decide which projects receive budget allocations, which of several customer complaints receive priority, and even how to spend his or her own time. The *negotiator* role involves formal negotiations and bargaining to attain outcomes for the manager's unit of responsibility. The manager meets and formally negotiates with others—a supplier about a late delivery, the controller about the need for additional budget resources, or the union about a worker grievance.

The relative emphasis a manager puts on these ten roles depends on a number of factors, such as the manager's position in the hierarchy, natural skills and abilities, type of organization, or departmental goals to be achieved. For example, Exhibit 1.6 illustrates the varying importance of the leader and liaison roles as reported in a survey of top-, middle-, and lower-level managers. Note that the importance of the leader role typically declines while the importance of the liaison role increases as a manager moves up the organizational hierarchy.

EXHIBIT | 1.6

Hierarchical Levels and
Importance of Leader and
Liaison Roles

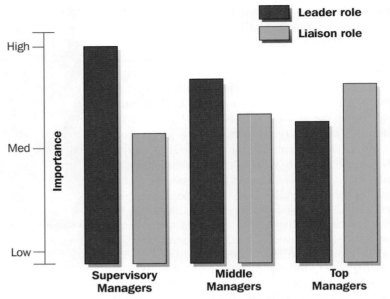

SOURCE: Based on information from A. I. Kraut, P. R. Pedigo, D. D. McKenna, and M. D. Dunnette, "The Role of the Manager: What's Really Important in Different Management Jobs," *Academy of Management Executive* 3 (1989), 286–293.

Other factors, such as changing environmental conditions, may also determine which roles are more important for a manager at any given time. A top manager may regularly put more emphasis on the roles of spokesperson, figurehead, and negotiator. However, the emergence of new competitors may require more attention to the monitor role, or a severe decline in employee morale and direction may mean that the CEO has to put more emphasis on the leader role. A marketing manager may focus on interpersonal roles because of the importance of personal contacts in the marketing process, whereas a financial manager may be more likely to emphasize decisional roles such as resource allocator and negotiator. Despite these differences, all managers carry out informational, interpersonal, and decisional roles to meet the needs of the organization. Managers stay alert to needs both within and outside the organization to determine what roles are most critical at various times.

MANAGING IN SMALL BUSINESSES AND NONPROFIT ORGANIZATIONS

Small businesses are growing in importance. Hundreds of small businesses are opened every month, but the environment for small business today is highly complicated. Small companies sometimes have difficulty developing the managerial dexterity needed to survive in a turbulent environment. One survey on trends and future developments in small business found that nearly half of respondents saw inadequate management skills as a threat to their companies, as compared to less than 25 percent of larger organizations.[53] Appendix A provides detailed information about managing in small businesses and entrepreneurial startups.

One interesting finding is that managers in small businesses tend to emphasize roles different from those of managers in large corporations. Managers in small companies often see their most important role as that of spokesperson because they must promote the small, growing company to the outside world. The entrepreneur role is also critical in small businesses because managers have to be innovative and help their organizations develop new ideas to remain competitive. Small-business managers tend to rate lower on the leader role and on information-processing roles, compared with their counterparts in large corporations.

Nonprofit organizations also represent a major application of management talent. Organizations such as the Salvation Army, Nature Conservancy, Greater Chicago Food Depository, Girl Scouts, and Cleveland Orchestra all require excellent management. The functions of planning, organizing, leading, and controlling apply to nonprofits just as they do to business organizations, and managers in nonprofit organizations use similar skills and perform similar activities. The primary difference is that managers in businesses direct their activities toward earning money for the company, whereas managers in nonprofits direct their efforts toward generating some kind of social impact. The unique characteristics and needs of nonprofit organizations created by this distinction present unique challenges for managers.[54]

Financial resources for nonprofit organizations typically come from government appropriations, grants, and donations rather than from the sale of products or services to customers. In businesses, managers focus on improving the organization's products and services to increase sales revenues. In nonprofits, however, services are typically provided to nonpaying clients, and a major problem for many organizations is securing a steady stream of funds to continue operating. Nonprofit managers, committed to serving clients with limited resources, must focus on keeping organizational costs as low as possible.[55] Donors generally want their money to go directly to helping clients rather than for overhead costs. If nonprofit managers can't demonstrate a highly efficient use of resources, they might have a hard time securing additional donations or government appropriations. Although the Sarbanes-Oxley Act (the 2002 corporate governance reform law) doesn't apply to nonprofits, for example, many are adopting its guidelines, striving for greater transparency and accountability to boost credibility with constituents and be more competitive when seeking funding.[56]

In addition, because nonprofit organizations do not have a conventional *bottom line*, managers often struggle with the question of what constitutes results and effectiveness. It is easy to measure dollars and cents, but the metrics of success in nonprofits are much more ambiguous. Managers have to measure intangibles such as "improve public health," "make a difference in the lives of the disenfranchised," or "increase appreciation for the arts." This intangible nature also makes it more difficult to gauge the performance of employees and managers. An added complication is that managers often depend on volunteers and donors who cannot be supervised and controlled in the same way a business manager deals with employees.

The roles defined by Mintzberg also apply to nonprofit managers, but these may differ somewhat. We might expect managers in nonprofit organizations to place more emphasis on the roles of spokesperson (to "sell" the organization to donors and the public), leader (to build a mission-driven community of employees and volunteers), and resource allocator (to distribute government resources or grant funds that are often assigned top-down).

Managers in all organizations—large corporations, small businesses, and nonprofit organizations—carefully integrate and adjust the management functions and roles to meet challenges within their own circumstances and keep their organizations healthy.

MANAGEMENT AND THE NEW WORKPLACE

Rapid environmental shifts, such as changes in technology, globalization, and shifting social values, are causing fundamental transformations that have a dramatic impact on the manager's job. These transformations are reflected in the transition to a new workplace, as illustrated in Exhibit 1.7.

New Workplace Characteristics

The primary characteristic of the new workplace is the *digitization* of business, which has radically altered the nature of work, employees, and the workplace itself.[57] The *old workplace* is characterized by routine, specialized tasks, and

EXHIBIT | 1.7

The Transition to a
New Workplace

	The New Workplace	The Old Workplace
Characteristics		
Technology	Digital	Mechanical
Work	Flexible, virtual	Structured, localized
Workforce	Empowered; diverse	Loyal employees; homogeneous
Management Competencies		
Leadership	Empowering	Autocratic
Doing Work	By teams	By individuals
Relationships	Collaboration	Conflict, competition

standardized control procedures. Employees typically perform their jobs in one specific company facility, such as an automobile factory located in Detroit or an insurance agency located in Des Moines. Individuals concentrate on doing their own specific tasks, and managers are cautious about sharing knowledge and information across boundaries. The organization is coordinated and controlled through the vertical hierarchy, with decision-making authority residing with upper-level managers.

In the *new workplace*, by contrast, work is free-flowing and *flexible.* Structures are flatter, and lower-level employees make decisions based on widespread information and guided by the organization's mission and values.[58] *Empowered employees* are expected to seize opportunities and solve problems as they emerge. Knowledge is widely shared, and people throughout the company keep in touch with a broad range of colleagues via advanced technology. The valued worker is one who learns quickly, shares knowledge, and is comfortable with risk, change, and ambiguity. People expect to work on a variety of projects and jobs throughout their careers rather than staying in one field or with one company.

The new workplace is organized around *networks* rather than rigid hierarchies, and work is often *virtual*, with managers having to supervise and coordinate people who never actually "come to work" in the traditional sense.[59] Flexible hours, telecommuting, and virtual teams are increasingly popular ways of working that require new skills from managers. Using virtual teams allows organizations to tap the best people for a particular job, no matter where they are located. Teams may include outside contractors, suppliers, customers, competitors, and interim managers. **Interim managers** are managers who are not affiliated with a specific organization but work on a project-by-project basis or provide expertise to organizations in a specific area.[60] This approach enables a company to benefit from specialist skills without making a long-term commitment, and it provides flexibility for managers who like the challenge, variety, and learning that comes from working in a wide range of organizations.

Technology also enables companies to shift significant chunks of what were once considered core functions to outsiders via *outsourcing, joint ventures,* and other complex *alliances.* U.S. companies have been sending manufacturing work to other countries for years to cut costs. Now, high-level knowledge work is also being outsourced to countries such as India, Malaysia, and South Africa.[61]

interim manager A manager who is not affiliated with a specific organization but works on a project-by-project basis or provides expertise to organizations in a specific area.

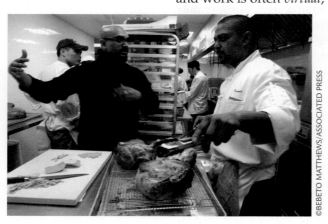

©BEBETO MATTHEWS/ASSOCIATED PRESS

Concept Connection   At New York City's Colors, a project of the Restaurant Opportunities Center, **collaboration** and **teamwork** are the keys to success. Many of the restaurant's employee-owners, immigrants hailing from about 22 different nations, worked in the World Trade Center's North Tower Windows on the World restaurant before its destruction on September 11, 2001. They share a strong commitment to a mission of honoring the 73 Windows employees who died and improving the restaurant industry working conditions. General manager Stefan Mailvaganam (left), shown with head chef Raymond Mohan (right), says the goal of Colors is to be "a restaurant with a conscience."

New Management Competencies

In the face of these transitions, managers must rethink their approach to organizing, directing, and motivating employees. Today's best managers give up their command-and-control mind-set to focus on coaching and providing guidance, creating organizations that are fast, flexible, innovative, and relationship-oriented.

Instead of "management-by-keeping-tabs," managers employ an *empowering leadership* style.[62] When people are working at scattered locations, managers can't continually monitor behavior. In addition, they are sometimes coordinating the work of people who aren't under their direct control, such as those in partner organizations. They have to set clear expectations, guide people toward goal accomplishment through vision, values, and regular communication, and develop a level of trust in employees' commitment to getting the job done.

Read the ethical dilemma on page 26 that pertains to managing in the new workplace. Think about what you would do and why to begin understanding how you will solve thorny management problems.

TakeaMoment

Success in the new workplace depends on the strength and quality of *collaborative relationships.* New ways of working emphasize collaboration across functions and hierarchical levels as well as with other companies. *Team-building skills* are crucial. Instead of managing a department of employees, many managers act as team leaders of ever-shifting, temporary projects. When a manager at IBM needs to staff a project, he or she gives a list of skills needed to the human resources department, which provides a pool of people who are qualified. The manager then puts together the best combination of people for the project, which often means pulling people from many different locations. IBM estimates that about 40 percent of its employees participate in virtual teams.[63]

The shift to a new way of managing isn't easy for traditional managers who are accustomed to being "in charge," making all the decisions, and knowing where their subordinates are and what they're doing at every moment. Even many new managers have a hard time with today's flexible work environment. Managers of departments participating in Best Buys' Results-Only Work Environment program, which allows employees to work anywhere, anytime as long as they complete assignments and meet goals, for example, find it difficult to keep themselves from checking to see who's logged onto the company network.[64]

Even more changes and challenges are on the horizon for organizations and managers. It's an exciting time to be entering the field of management. Throughout this book, you will learn much more about the new workplace, about the new and dynamic roles managers are playing in the twenty-first century, and about how you can be an effective manager in a complex, ever-changing world.

ch1   A MANAGER'S ESSENTIALS: WHAT HAVE WE LEARNED?

- This chapter introduced the topic of management and defined the types of roles and activities managers perform. Managers are responsible for attaining organizational goals in an efficient and effective manner through the four management functions of planning, organizing, leading, and controlling. Managers are the executive function of the organization. Rather than performing specific tasks, they are responsible for creating systems and conditions that enable others to achieve high performance.

- To perform the four functions, managers need three types of skills—conceptual, human, and technical. Conceptual skills are more important at top levels of the organization; human skills are important at all levels; and technical skills are most important for first-line managers.

- A manager's job varies depending on whether one is a top manager, middle manager, or first-line manager. A manager's job may also differ across the organization, to include project managers and interim managers as well as functional managers (including line managers and staff managers) and general managers.

- Becoming a manager requires a shift in thinking. New managers often struggle with the challenges of coordinating a broad range of people and activities, delegating to and developing others, and relating to former peers in a new way.

- Managers' activities are associated with ten roles: the informational roles of monitor, disseminator, and spokesperson; the interpersonal roles of figurehead, leader, and liaison; and the decisional roles of entrepreneur, disturbance handler, resource allocator, and negotiator.

- Rapid and dramatic change in recent years has caused significant shifts in the workplace and the manager's job. Rather than managing by command and control, managers of today and tomorrow use an empowering leadership style that focuses on vision, values, and communication. Team-building skills are crucial. Instead of just directing tasks, managers focus on building relationships, which may include customers, partners, and suppliers.

ch1   DISCUSSION QUESTIONS

1. How do you feel about having a manager's responsibility in today's world characterized by uncertainty, ambiguity, and sudden changes or threats from the environment? Describe some skills and qualities that are important to managers under these conditions.

2. Assume you are a project manager at a biotechnology company, working with managers from research, production, and marketing on a major product modification. You notice that every memo you receive from the marketing manager has been copied to senior management. At every company function, she spends time talking to the big shots. You are also aware that sometimes when you and the other project members are slaving away over the project, she is playing golf with senior managers. What is your evaluation of her behavior? As project manager, what do you do?

3. Jeff Immelt of GE said that the most valuable thing he learned in business school was that "there are 24 hours in a day, and you can use all of them." Do you agree or disagree? What are some of the advantages to this approach to being a manager? What are some of the drawbacks?

4. Why do some organizations seem to have a new CEO every year or two, whereas others have top leaders who stay with the company for many years (e.g., Jack Welch's 20 years as CEO at General Electric)? What factors about the manager or about the company might account for this difference?

5. What is the difference between efficiency and effectiveness? Which is more important for performance? Can managers improve both simultaneously?

6. You are a bright, hard-working entry-level manager who fully intends to rise up through the ranks. Your performance evaluation gives you high marks for your technical skills but low marks when it comes to people skills. Do you think people skills can be learned, or do you need to rethink your career path? If people skills can be learned, how would you go about it?

7. If managerial work is characterized by variety, fragmentation, and brevity, how do managers perform basic management functions such as planning, which would seem to require reflection and analysis?

8. A college professor told her students, "The purpose of a management course is to teach students about management, not to teach them to be managers." Do you agree or disagree with this statement? Discuss.

9. Discuss some of the ways organizations and jobs changed over the past 10 years. What changes do you anticipate over the next 10 years? How might these changes affect the manager's job and the skills a manager needs to be successful?

10. How might the teaching of a management course be designed to prepare future managers to deal with globalization and workforce diversity? What problems and opportunities do you think globalization and diversity present for managers?

ch1 MANAGEMENT IN PRACTICE: EXPERIENTIAL EXERCISE

Management Aptitude Questionnaire

Rate each of the following questions according to the following scale:

① I am never like this.
② I am rarely like this.
③ I am sometimes like this.
④ I am often like this.
⑤ I am always like this.

1. When I have a number of tasks or homework to do, I set priorities and organize the work around deadlines.
   1 2 3 4 5

2. Most people would describe me as a good listener.
   1 2 3 4 5

3. When I am deciding on a particular course of action for myself (such as hobbies to pursue, languages to study, which job to take, special projects to be involved in), I typically consider the long-term (three years or more) implications of what I would choose to do.
   1 2 3 4 5

4. I prefer technical or quantitative courses rather than those involving literature, psychology, or sociology.
   1 2 3 4 5

5. When I have a serious disagreement with someone, I hang in there and talk it out until it is completely resolved.
   1 2 3 4 5

6. When I have a project or assignment, I really get into the details rather than the "big picture" issues.
   1 2 3 4 5

7. I would rather sit in front of my computer than spend a lot of time with people.
   1 2 3 4 5

8. I try to include others in activities or discussions.
   1 2 3 4 5

9. When I take a course, I relate what I am learning to other courses I took or concepts I learned elsewhere.
   1 2 3 4 5

10. When somebody makes a mistake, I want to correct the person and let her or him know the proper answer or approach.
    1 2 3 4 5

11. I think it is better to be efficient with my time when talking with someone, rather than worry about the other person's needs, so that I can get on with my real work.
    1 2 3 4 5

12. I know my long-term vision of career, family, and other activities and have thought it over carefully.
    1 2 3 4 5

13. When solving problems, I would much rather analyze some data or statistics than meet with a group of people.
    1 2 3 4 5

14. When I am working on a group project and someone doesn't pull a fair share of the load, I am more likely to complain to my friends rather than confront the slacker.
    1 2 3 4 5

15. Talking about ideas or concepts can get me really enthused or excited.
    1 2 3 4 5

16. The type of management course for which this book is used is really a waste of time.
    1 2 3 4 5

17. I think it is better to be polite and not to hurt people's feelings.
    1 2 3 4 5

18. Data or things interest me more than people.
    1 2 3 4 5

Scoring and Interpretation

Subtract your scores for questions 6, 10, 14, and 17 from the number 6, and then add the total points for the following sections:

1, 3, 6, 9, 12, 15   Conceptual skills total score _____

2, 5, 8, 10, 14, 17   Human skills total score _____

4, 7, 11, 13, 16, 18   Technical skills total score _____

These skills are three abilities needed to be a good manager. Ideally, a manager should be strong (though not necessarily equal) in all three. Anyone noticeably weaker in any of the skills should take courses and read to build up that skill. For further background on the three skills, please refer to the explanation on pages 8–9.

NOTE: This exercise was contributed by Dorothy Marcic.

ch1 MANAGEMENT IN PRACTICE: ETHICAL DILEMMA

Can Management Afford to Look the Other Way?

Harry Rull had been with Shellington Pharmaceuticals for 30 years. After a tour of duty in the various plants and seven years overseas, Harry was back at headquarters, looking forward to his new role as vice president of U.S. marketing.

Two weeks into his new job, Harry received some unsettling news about one of the managers under his supervision. Over casual lunch conversation, the director of human resources mentioned that Harry should expect a phone call about Roger Jacobs, manager of new product development. Jacobs had a history of being "pretty horrible" to his subordinates, she said, and one disgruntled employee asked to speak to someone in senior management. After lunch, Harry did some follow-up work. Jacobs' performance reviews had been stellar, but his personnel file also contained a large number of notes documenting charges of Jacobs' mistreatment of subordinates. The complaints ranged from "inappropriate and derogatory remarks" to subsequently dropped charges of sexual harassment. What was more disturbing was that the amount as well as the severity of complaints had increased with each of Jacobs' ten years with Shellington.

When Harry questioned the company president about the issue, he was told, "Yeah, he's had some problems, but you can't just replace someone with an eye for new products. You're a bottom-line guy; you understand why we let these things slide." Not

sure how to handle the situation, Harry met briefly with Jacobs and reminded him to "keep the team's morale up." Just after the meeting, Sally Barton from HR called to let him know that the problem she'd mentioned over lunch had been worked out. However, she warned, another employee had now come forward demanding that her complaints be addressed by senior management.

What Would You Do?

1. Ignore the problem. Jacobs' contributions to new product development are too valuable to risk losing him, and the problems over the past ten years have always worked themselves out anyway. No sense starting something that could make you look bad.

2. Launch a full-scale investigation of employee complaints about Jacobs, and make Jacobs aware that the documented history over the past ten years has put him on thin ice.

3. Meet with Jacobs and the employee to try to resolve the current issue, then start working with Sally Barton and other senior managers to develop stronger policies regarding sexual harassment and treatment of employees, including clear-cut procedures for handling complaints.

SOURCE: Based on Doug Wallace, "A Talent for Mismanagement: What Would You Do?" *Business Ethics* 2 (November–December 1992): 3–4.

ch1 CASE FOR CRITICAL ANALYSIS

Elektra Products, Inc.

Barbara Russell, a manufacturing vice president, walked into the monthly companywide meeting with a light step and a hopefulness she hadn't felt in a long time. The company's new, dynamic CEO was going to announce a new era of employee involvement and empowerment at Elektra Products, an 80-year-old, publicly held company that had once been a leading manufacturer and retailer of electrical products and supplies. In recent years, the company experienced a host of problems: market share was declining in the face of increased foreign and domestic competition; new product ideas were few and far between; departments such as manufacturing and sales barely spoke to one another; morale was at an all-time low, and many employees were actively seeking other jobs. Everyone needed a dose of hope.

Martin Griffin, who had been hired to revive the failing company, briskly opened the meeting with a

challenge: "As we face increasing competition, we need new ideas, new energy, new spirit to make this company great. And the source for this change is you—each one of you." He then went on to explain that under the new empowerment campaign, employees would be getting more information about how the company was run and would be able to work with their fellow employees in new and creative ways. Martin proclaimed a new era of trust and cooperation at Elektra Products. Barbara felt the excitement stirring within her; but as she looked around the room, she saw many of the other employees, including her friend Simon, rolling their eyes. "Just another pile of corporate crap," Simon said later. "One minute they try downsizing, the next reengineering. Then they dabble in restructuring. Now Martin wants to push empowerment. Garbage like empowerment isn't a substitute for hard work and a little faith in the people who have been with this company for years. We made it great once, and we can do it again. Just get out of our way." Simon had been a manufacturing engineer with Elektra Products for more than 20 years. Barbara knew he was extremely loyal to the company, but he—and a lot of others like him—were going to be an obstacle to the empowerment efforts.

Top management assigned selected managers to several problem-solving teams to come up with ideas for implementing the empowerment campaign. Barbara loved her assignment as team leader of the manufacturing team, working on ideas to improve how retail stores got the merchandise they needed when they needed it. The team thrived, and trust blossomed among the members. They even spent nights and weekends working to complete their report. They were proud of their ideas, which they believed were innovative but easily achievable: permit a manager to follow a product from design through sales to customers; allow salespeople to refund up to $500 worth of merchandise on the spot; make information available to salespeople about future products; and swap sales and manufacturing personnel for short periods to let them get to know one another's jobs.

When the team presented its report to department heads, Martin Griffin was enthusiastic. But shortly into the meeting he had to excuse himself because of a late-breaking deal with a major hardware store chain. With Martin absent, the department heads rapidly formed a wall of resistance. The director of human resources complained that the ideas for personnel changes would destroy the carefully crafted job

categories that had just been completed. The finance department argued that allowing salespeople to make $500 refunds would create a gold mine for unethical customers and salespeople. The legal department warned that providing information to salespeople about future products would invite industrial spying.

The team members were stunned. As Barbara mulled over the latest turn of events, she considered her options: keep her mouth shut; take a chance and confront Martin about her sincerity in making empowerment work; push slowly for reform and work for gradual support from the other teams; or look for another job and leave a company she really cares about. Barbara realized she was looking at no easy choices and no easy answers.

Questions

1. How might top management have done a better job changing Elektra Products into a new kind of organization? What might they do now to get the empowerment process back on track?

2. Can you think of ways Barbara could have avoided the problems her team faced in the meeting with department heads?

3. If you were Barbara Russell, what would you do now? Why?

SOURCE: Based on Lawrence R. Rothstein, "The Empowerment Effort That Came Undone," *Harvard Business Review* (January–February 1995): 20–31.

---

ch1 ON THE JOB VIDEO CASE

Original Penguin Rides Out Turbulence

Penguins have always been cool. But golf shirts with a little flapping bird printed on them experienced a lull in coolness. In fact, their popularity remained frozen for two decades largely because they were worn by aging golfers. Now the penguins are back, flapping furiously—and, many would argue, coolly—not just on golf shirts but also on a wide array of men's and women's clothing and accessories, including shirts, shoes, hats, belts, neckties, handbags, and even bathing suits. These items represent the extreme makeover of a 50-year-old brand of clothing called Original Penguin. Now owned by Perry Ellis International, the Original Penguin brand of clothing is experiencing rejuvenation—thanks largely to Penguin's vice president, Chris Kolbe.

Chris Kolbe knows that thawing out an old brand is a daunting task under the best circumstances. But the fashion industry is particularly difficult—the pace is dizzying, and the turbulence is sometimes terrifying. Kolbe's activities as a manager are clearly characterized by variety, fragmentation, and brevity. For example, in a single day, Kolbe may be expecting several hundred samples from sources around the globe to arrive in time for a fashion show. He may have to decide whether to extend credit to a retailer or whether to drop one retailer in favor of another. He may have to review ad copy, return calls from fashion magazines, thumb through swatches of fabric, welcome sales reps arriving for a meeting, and fix his own computer. "We are always way behind and scrambling," he says with a chuckle. But Kolbe thrives on these activities because he is convinced that the time is right for his penguins to regain their place in the market among other legendary figures such as alligators and polo ponies—and he intends to make it happen.

Because the Penguin division is a tiny component of the much larger Perris Ellis company, Kolbe serves all the management functions of planning, organizing, leading, and controlling—often during the course of one work day. "I take personal responsibility and accountability for everything that has the Penguin brand on it," Kolbe notes.

Kolbe also fulfills all the roles of a top manager. He considers himself a hands-on manager, communicating constantly with his staff and keeping himself "involved in every detail so I don't lose sight" of things. He develops relationships with employees so that they can work well together. "My job is really the A to Z in assembling a team of people who can focus on certain pieces of that business and deliver on the strategic goals for the company," he explains. "I feel very fortunate to have such a good team." He makes decisions about where to take the brand. Right now, he has his sights set on a more upscale market. He envisions his customers as comfortable suburbanites who want high-quality, fashionable casual clothing. But he doesn't worry too much about direct competitors in the clothing industry. Instead, he focuses on how Original Penguin can compete for consumer dollars. "My role as vice president of Penguin really is . . . I'm acting president of a very small division—a startup company attached to a larger company," Kolbe observes. "So I really took on the A to Z of running a brand or running a company, from the . . . creative vision of the brand, to marketing the brand, to the business operations and sales of the brand."

As for that turbulence? Kolbe shrugs it off. "In every business there are roadblocks. So your ability to focus on the roadblock or work around the roadblock sometimes comes down to your ability to be successful." This is true even when the roadblock happens to be a shipment of women's flip-flops that hasn't arrived in time for the fashion show.

Questions

1. Describe the conceptual skills you think Chris Kolbe needs for his job as vice president of Original Penguin.

2. Suppose those flip-flops—or other components of the upcoming fashion show—don't arrive in time. Describe how Chris Kolbe might manage the situation.

3. What do you think is the most difficult part of Kolbe's job? Why?

SOURCES: Company Web site, *http://www.originalpenguin.com*, accessed July 30, 2004; "Pick up an Original Penguin," *Fashion UK*, July 8, 2004, *http://www.widemedia.com/fashionuk/news/2004*; Carl Swanson, "A Senior Moment," *The New York Times*, Spring 2004, p. 44; Stephanie Thomson, "Perry Ellis Banks on Brand Resurrections," *Advertising Age*, March 15, 2004, p. 14; Rima Sugi, "The Bird Is the Word," *New York Metro.com*, December 8, 2003, *http://www. newyorkmetro.com*.

---

ch1   BIZ FLIX VIDEO CASE

8 Mile

Jimmy "B-Rabbit" Smith, Jr. (Eminem) wants to be a successful rapper and to prove that a white man can create moving sounds. He works days at a plant run by the North Detroit Stamping Company and pursues his music at night, sometimes on the plant's grounds. The film's title refers to Detroit's northern city boundary which divides Detroit's white and African American populations. This film gives a gritty look at Detroit's hip-hop culture in 1995 and Jimmy's desire to be accepted by it. Eminem's original songs "Lose Yourself" and "8 Mile" received Golden Globe and Academy Award nominations.

This scene is an edited composite of two brief sequences involving the stamping plant. The first half of the scene appears early in the film as part of "The Franchise" sequence. The second half appears in the last 25 minutes of the film as part of the "Papa Doc Payback" sequence. In the first part of the scene, Jimmy's car won't start so he rides the city bus to work and arrives late. The second part occurs after he is beaten by Papa Doc (Anthony Mackie) and Papa Doc's gang. Jimmy's mother (Kim Basinger) returns to their trailer and tells him she won $3,200 at bingo. The film continues to its end with Jimmy's last battle (a rapper competition).

What to Watch for and Ask Yourself

1. What is your perception of the quality of Jimmy's job and his work environment?

2. What is the quality of Jimmy's relationship with Manny, his foreman (Paul Bates)? Does it change? If it does, why?

3. How would you react to this type of work experience?

ch1 ENDNOTES

1. This questionnaire is adapted from research findings reported in Linda A. Hill, *Becoming a Manager: How New Managers Master the Challenges of Leadership*, 2nd ed. (Boston, MA: Harvard Business School Press, 2003); and John J. Gabarro, *The Dynamics of Taking Charge* (Boston, MA: Harvard Business School Press, 1987).

2. Bruce Moeller, as told to Stephanie Clifford, "The Way I Work," *Inc. Magazine* (July 2007): 88–91.

3. Darrell Rigby and Barbara Bilodeau, "The Bain 2005 Management Tool Survey," *Strategy & Leadership* 33, no. 4 (2005): 4–12.

4. Todd G. Buchholz, "The Right Stuff to be CEO," *The Conference Review Board* (November–December 2007): 13.

5. Geoffrey Colvin, "What Makes GE Great?" *Fortune* (March 6, 2006): 90–96; and Betsy Morris, "The GE Mystique," *Fortune* (March 6, 2006): 98–104.

6. James A. F. Stoner and R. Edward Freeman, *Management*, 4th ed. (Englewood Cliffs, NJ: Prentice Hall, 1989).

7. Peter F. Drucker, *Management Tasks, Responsibilities, Practices* (New York: Harper & Row, 1974).

8. George Anders, "AOL's True Believers," *Fast Company* (July 2002): 96–104.

9. Nanette Byrnes, "Avon: More Than Cosmetic Changes," *BusinessWeek* (March 12, 2007): 62–63.

10. Jacy L. Youn, "True Calling," *Hawaii Business* (July 1, 2005): 13.

11. Eryn Brown, "Nine Ways to Win on the Web," *Fortune* (May 24, 1999): 112–125.

12. Jennifer Reingold, "Target's Inner Circle," *Fortune* (March 31, 2008): 74–86.

13. Robert L. Katz, "Skills of an Effective Administrator," *Harvard Business Review* 52 (September–October 1974): 90–102.

14. Troy V. Mumford, Michael A. Campion, and Frederick P. Morgeson, "The Leadership Skills Strataplex: Leadership Skills Requirements Across Organizational Levels," *The Leadership Quarterly* 18 (2007): 154–166.

15. Geoffrey Colvin, "The Bionic Manager," *Fortune* (September 19, 2005): 88–100.

16. Spielberg, "The Cheesecake Factory."

17. Sue Shellenbarger, "From Our Readers: The Bosses That Drove Me to Quit My Job," *The Wall Street Journal* (February 7, 2000): B1.

18. Quoted in Linda Tischler, "The CEO's New Clothes," *Fast Company* (September 2005): 27–28.

19. Eric Matson, "Congratulations, You're Promoted. (Now What?)," *Fast Company* (June–July 1997): 116–130.

20. Clinton O. Longenecker, Mitchell J. Neubert, and Laurence S. Fink, "Causes and Consequences of Managerial Failure in Rapidly Changing Organizations," *Business Horizons* 50 (2007): 145–155.

21. Based on Sydney Finkelstein, "7 Habits of Spectacularly Unsuccessful Executives," *Fast Company* (July 2003): 84–89; S. Finkelstein, *Why Smart Executives Fail* (New York: Portfolio, 2003); Charan and Useem, "Why Companies Fail"; and John W. Slocum Jr., Cass Ragan, and Albert Casey, "On Death and Dying: The Corporate Leadership Capacity of CEOs," *Organizational Dynamics* 30, no. 3 (Spring 2002): 269–281.

22. Patricia Wallington, "Toxic!" *CIO* (April 15, 2006): 34–36.

23. Based on Longenecker, et al., *Causes and Consequences of Managerial Failure in Rapidly Changing Organizations*; Finkelstein, "7 Habits of Spectacularly Unsuccessful Executives"; Charan and Useem, "Why Companies Fail"; and Slocum et al., "On Death and Dying."

24. Alan Murray, "Behind Nardelli's Abrupt Exit; Executive's Fatal Flaw: Failing to Understand New Demands on CEOs," *The Wall Street Journal*, January 4, 2007; Brian Grow, "Out at Home Depot," *BusinessWeek* (January 15, 2007): 56–62.

25. Diane Brady, "'Being Mean is So Last Millennium,'" *BusinessWeek* (January 15, 2007), sidebar in Murray, "Behind Nardelli's Abrupt Exit."

26. Eileen Sheridan, "Rise: Best Day, Worst Day," *The Guardian* (September 14, 2002): 3.

27. Heath Row, "Force Play" (Company of Friends column), *Fast Company* (March 2001): 46.

28. Charles Fishman, "Sweet Company," *Fast Company* (February 2001): 136–145.

29. A. I. Kraut, P. R. Pedigo, D. D. McKenna, and M. D. Dunnette, "The Role of the Manager: What's Really Important in Different Management Jobs," *Academy of Management Executive* 19, no. 4 (2005): 122–129.

30. Christopher A. Bartlett and Sumantra Ghoshal, "Changing the Role of Top Management: Beyond Systems to People," *Harvard Business Review* (May–June 1995): 132–142; and Sumantra Ghoshal and Christopher A. Bartlett, "Changing the Role of Top Management: Beyond Structure to Processes," *Harvard Business Review* (January–February 1995): 86–96.

31. Quy Nguyen Huy, "In Praise of Middle Managers," *Harvard Business Review* (September 2003): 72–79; Rosabeth Moss Kanter, *On the Frontiers of Management* (Boston: Harvard Business School Press, 2003).

32. Lisa Haneberg, "Reinventing Middle Management," *Leader to Leader* (Fall 2005): 13–18.

33. Miles Brignall, "Rise; Launch Pad: The Retailer; Alistair Boot, An Assistant Manager at the John Lewis Store in Cheadle, Talks to Miles Brignall," *The Guardian* (October 4, 2003): 3.

34. Henry Mintzberg, *The Nature of Managerial Work* (New York: Harper & Row, 1973); and Mintzberg, "Rounding Out the Manager's Job," *Sloan Management Review* (Fall 1994): 11–26.

35. Robert E. Kaplan, "Trade Routes: The Manager's Network of Relationships," *Organizational Dynamics* (Spring 1984): 37–52; Rosemary Stewart, "The Nature of Management: A Problem for Management Education," *Journal of Management*

Studies 21 (1984): 323–330; John P. Kotter, "What Effective General Managers Really Do," *Harvard Business Review* (November–December 1982): 156–167; and Morgan W. McCall, Jr., Ann M. Morrison, and Robert L. Hannan, "Studies of Managerial Work: Results and Methods," Technical Report No. 9, Center for Creative Leadership, Greensboro, NC, 1978.

36. Alison M. Konrad, Roger Kashlak, Izumi Yoshioka, Robert Waryszak, and Nina Toren, "What Do Managers *Like* to Do? A Five-Country Study," *Group and Organizational Management* 26, no. 4 (December 2001): 401–433.

37. For a review of the problems faced by first-time managers, see Linda A. Hill, "Becoming the Boss," *Harvard Business Review* (January 2007): 49–56; Loren B. Belker and Gary S. Topchik, *The First-Time Manager: A Practical Guide to the Management of People*, 5th ed. (New York: AMACOM, 2005); J. W. Lorsch and P. F. Mathias, "When Professionals Have to Manage," *Harvard Business Review* (July–August 1987): 78–83; R. A. Webber, *Becoming a Courageous Manager: Overcoming Career Problems of New Managers* (Englewood Cliffs, NJ: Prentice Hall, 1991); D. E. Dougherty, *From Technical Professional to Corporate Manager: A Guide to Career Transition* (New York: Wiley, 1984); J. Falvey, "The Making of a Manager," *Sales and Marketing Management* (March 1989): 42–83; M. K. Badawy, *Developing Managerial Skills in Engineers and Scientists: Succeeding as a Technical Manager* (New York: Van Nostrand Reinhold, 1982); and M. London, *Developing Managers: A Guide to Motivating and Preparing People for Successful Managerial Careers* (San Francisco: Jossey-Bass, 1985).

38. Erin White, "Learning to Be the Boss; Trial and Error Is the Norm as New Managers Figure Out How to Relate to Former Peers," *The Wall Street Journal*, November 21, 2005.

39. This discussion is based on Linda A. Hill, *Becoming a Manager: How New Managers Master the Challenges of Leadership*, 2nd ed. (Boston, MA: Harvard Business School Press, 2003), pp. 6–8; and L.A. Hill, "Becoming the Boss," *Harvard Business Review* (January 2007): 49–56.

40. See also "Boss's First Steps," sidebar in White, "Learning to Be the Boss"; and Belker and Topchik, *The First-Time Manager*.

41. Jeanne Whalen, "Chance Turns a Teacher into a CEO; Religion Lecturer Leaves Academic Path and Learns to Run a Biotech Start-Up," Theory & Practice column, *The Wall Street Journal*, October 17, 2005.

42. Henry Mintzberg, "Managerial Work: Analysis from Observation," *Management Science* 18 (1971): B97–B110.

43. Based on Damien Cave, "A Tall Order for a Marine: Feeding the Hand That Bit You," *The New York Times*, December 30, 2007.

44. Mintzberg, "Managerial Work."

45. Matthew Boyle and Jia Lynn Yang, "All in a Day's Work," *Fortune* (March 20, 2006): 97–104.

46. Spielberg, "The Cheesecake Factory."

47. Lance B. Kurke and Howard E. Aldrich, "Mintzberg Was Right!: A Replication and Extension of *The Nature of Managerial Work*," *Management Science* 29 (1983): 975–984; Cynthia M. Pavett and Alan W. Lau, "Managerial Work: The Influence of Hierarchical Level and Functional Specialty," *Academy of Management Journal* 26 (1983): 170–177; and Colin P. Hales, "What Do Managers Do? A Critical Review of the Evidence," *Journal of Management Studies* 23 (1986): 88–115.

48. Mintzberg, "Rounding out the Manager's Job."

49. Andy Serwer, "Inside the Rolling Stones Inc.," *Fortune* (September 30, 2002): 58–72.

50. Valerie Darroch, "High Flyer with Feet on Home Ground; Gorbals-Born Stephen Baxter Combines His Role as Glasgow Airport Boss with Heading the City's Chamber of Commerce," *Sunday Herald*, February 6, 2005.

51. Harry S. Jonas III, Ronald E. Fry, and Suresh Srivastva, "The Office of the CEO: Understanding the Executive Experience," *Academy of Management Executive* 4 (August 1990): 36–48.

52. Carol Hymowitz, "Smart Executives Shed Some Traditional Tasks to Focus on Key Areas," *The Wall Street Journal*, June 19, 2006.

53. Edward O. Welles, "There Are No Simple Businesses Anymore," *The State of Small Business* (1995): 66–79.

54. This section is based on Peter F. Drucker, *Managing the Non-Profit Organization: Principles and Practices* (New York: HarperBusiness, 1992); and Thomas Wolf, *Managing a Nonprofit Organization* (New York: Fireside/Simon & Schuster, 1990).

55. Christine W. Letts, William P. Ryan, and Allen Grossman, *High Performance Nonprofit Organizations* (New York: Wiley & Sons, 1999), pp. 30–35.

56. Carol Hymowitz, "In Sarbanes-Oxley Era, Running a Nonprofit Is Only Getting Harder," *The Wall Street Journal*, June 21, 2005; and Bill Birchard, "Nonprofits by the Numbers," *CFO* (June 2005): 50–55.

57. This section is based on "The New Organization: A Survey of the Company," *The Economist* (January 21, 2006); Harry G. Barkema, Joel A. C. Baum, and Elizabeth A. Mannix, "Management Challenges in a New Time," *Academy of Management Journal* 45, no. 5 (2002): 916–930; Michael Harvey and M. Ronald Buckley, "Assessing the 'Conventional Wisdoms' of Management for the 21st Century Organization," *Organizational Dynamics* 30, no. 4 (2002): 368–378; and Toby J. Tetenbaum, "Shifting Paradigms: From Newton to Chaos," *Organizational Dynamics* (Spring 1998): 21–32.

58. Caroline Ellis, "The Flattening Corporation," *MIT Sloan Management Review* (Summer 2003): 5.

59. Christopher Rhoads and Sara Silver, "Working at Home Gets Easier," *The Wall Street Journal*, December 29, 2005; Edwards, "Wherever You Go, You're on the Job"; and Kelley Holland, "When Work Time Isn't Face Time," *The New York Times*, December 3, 2006.

60. Kerr Inkson, Angela Heising, and Denise M. Rousseau, "The Interim

Manager: Prototype of the 21st Century Worker," *Human Relations* 54, no. 3 (2001): 259–284.

61. Keith H. Hammonds, "Smart, Determined, Ambitious, Cheap: The New Face of Global Competition," *Fast Company* (February 2003): 91–97.

62. Holland, "When Work Time Isn't Face Time."

63. Carla Johnson, "Managing Virtual Teams," *HR Magazine* (June 2002): 69–73; "The New Organisation," *The Economist* (January 21, 2006).

64. Holland, "When Work Time Isn't Face Time."

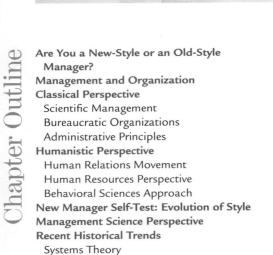

© GETTY IMAGES/DIGITAL VISION

Learning Outcomes

After studying this chapter, you should be able to:

1. Understand how historical forces influence the practice of management.

2. Identify and explain major developments in the history of management thought.

3. Describe the major components of the classical and humanistic management perspectives.

4. Discuss the management science perspective and its current use in organizations.

5. Explain the major concepts of systems theory, the contingency view, and total quality management.

6. Explain what a learning organization is and why this approach has become important in recent years.

7. Describe the management changes brought about by a technology-driven workplace, including the role of supply chain management, customer relationship management, and outsourcing.

The Evolution of Management Thinking

ARE YOU A NEW-STYLE OR AN OLD-STYLE MANAGER?[1]

The following are various behaviors that a manager may engage in when relating to subordinates. Read each statement carefully and rate each one Mostly True or Mostly False to reflect the extent to which you would use that behavior.

	Mostly True	Mostly False
1. Closely supervise my subordinates in order to get better work from them.	_____	_____
2. Set the goals and objectives for my subordinates and sell them on the merits of my plans.	_____	_____
3. Set up controls to ensure that my subordinates are getting the job done.	_____	_____
4. Make sure that my subordinates' work is planned out for them.	_____	_____
5. Check with my subordinates daily to see if they need any help.	_____	_____
6. Step in as soon as reports indicate that the job is slipping.	_____	_____
7. Push my people to meet schedules if necessary.	_____	_____
8. Have frequent meetings to learn from others what is going on.	_____	_____

SCORING AND INTERPRETATION: Add the total number of Mostly True answers and mark your score on the scale below. Theory X tends to be "old-style" management and Theory Y "new-style," because the styles are based on different assumptions about people. To learn more about these assumptions, you can refer to Exhibit 2.4 and review the assumptions related to Theory X and Theory Y. Strong Theory X assumptions are typically considered inappropriate for today's workplace. Where do you fit on the X–Y scale? Does your score reflect your perception of yourself as a current or future manager?

X-Y Scale

Theory X	10	5	0	Theory Y

The field of management is undergoing tremendous change. The questionnaire you just completed describes two differing philosophies about how people should be managed, and you will learn more about these ideas in this chapter. Both approaches still apply in today's organizations. However, many managers find themselves caught in a situation where the methods and patterns that kept the organization successful in the past no longer seem right to keep it thriving today and into the future.

Management philosophies and organizational forms change over time to meet new needs. The workplace of today is different from what it was 50 years ago—indeed, from what it was even 10 years ago. Yet some ideas and practices from the past are still highly relevant and applicable to management.

Many students wonder why history matters to managers. A historical perspective provides a broader way of thinking, a way of searching for patterns and determining whether they recur across time periods. For example, certain management practices that seem modern, such as open-book management or employee stock ownership, have actually been around for a long time. These techniques have repeatedly gained and lost popularity since the early twentieth century because of historical forces.[2] A study of the past contributes to understanding both the present and the future. It is a way of learning from others' mistakes so as not to repeat them; learning from others' successes so as to repeat them in the appropriate situation; and most of all, learning to understand why things happen to improve our organizations in the future.

This chapter provides an overview of the ideas, theories, and management philosophies that have contributed to making the workplace what it is today. We examine

1
Introduction

2
Environment

3
Planning

4
Organizing

5
Controlling

6
Leading

several management approaches that have been popular and successful throughout the twentieth century. The final section of the chapter looks at some recent trends and current approaches that build on this foundation of management understanding. This foundation illustrates that the value of studying management lies not in learning current facts and research but in developing a perspective that will facilitate the broad, long-term view needed for management success.

MANAGEMENT AND ORGANIZATION

Studying history doesn't mean merely arranging events in chronological order; it means developing an understanding of the impact of societal forces on organizations. Studying history is a way to achieve strategic thinking, see the big picture, and improve conceptual skills. Let's start by examining how social, political, and economic forces have influenced organizations and the practice of management.[3]

Social forces refer to those aspects of a culture that guide and influence relationships among people. What do people value? What do people need? What are the standards of behavior among people? These forces shape what is known as the *social contract*, which refers to the unwritten, common rules and perceptions about relationships among people and between employees and management.

A significant social force today is the changing attitudes, ideas, and values of Generation Y employees (sometimes called Nexters).[4] These young workers, the most educated generation in the history of the United States, grew up technologically adept and globally conscious. Unlike many workers of the past, they typically are not hesitant to question their superiors and challenge the status quo. They want a work environment that is challenging and supportive, with access to cutting-edge technology, opportunities to learn and further their careers and personal goals, and the power to make substantive decisions and changes in the workplace. In addition, Gen Y workers have prompted a growing focus on work/life balance, reflected in trends such as telecommuting, flextime, shared jobs, and organization-sponsored sabbaticals.

Political forces refer to the influence of political and legal institutions on people and organizations. Political forces include basic assumptions underlying the political system, such as the desirability of self-government, property rights, contract rights, the definition of justice, and the determination of innocence or guilt of a crime. The spread of capitalism throughout the world has dramatically altered the business landscape. The dominance of the free-market system and growing interdependencies among the world's countries require organizations to operate differently and managers to think in new ways. At the same time, strong anti-American sentiments in many parts of the world create challenges for U.S. companies and managers.

Economic forces pertain to the availability, production, and distribution of resources in a society. Governments, military agencies, churches, schools, and business organizations in every society require resources to achieve their goals, and economic forces influence the allocation of scarce resources. One trend is the growing economic power of less-developed countries. The rapid growth of China and India and their rise in the global marketplace dominated the 2007 World Bank-International Monetary Fund annual meetings, for example.[5] Another force is the shifting of the economy of the United States and other developed countries, with the sources of wealth, the fundamentals of distribution, and the nature of economic decision making undergoing significant changes. Today's economy is based as much on ideas, information, and knowledge as it is on material resources. Supply chains and distribution of resources have been revolutionized by digital technology. Surplus inventories, which once could trigger recessions, are declining or completely disappearing.[6]

social forces The aspects of a culture that guide and influence relationships among people—their values, needs, and standards of behavior.

political forces The influence of political and legal institutions on people and organizations.

economic forces Forces that affect the availability, production, and distribution of a society's resources among competing users.

TakeaMoment | As a new manager, do you appreciate a historical perspective to help you interpret current opportunities and problems? Social, economic, and political forces often repeat themselves, so your understanding will facilitate a broader view of how organizations adapt and succeed in today's environment.

Management practices and perspectives vary in response to these social, political, and economic forces in the larger society. During difficult times, managers look for ideas to help them cope with environmental turbulence and keep their organizations vital. The Manager's Shoptalk lists a wide variety of ideas and techniques used by today's managers. Management idea life cycles have been growing shorter as the pace of change has increased. A recent study by professors at the University of Louisiana at Lafayette found that, from the 1950s to the 1970s, it typically took more than a decade for interest in a popular management idea to peak. By the 1990s, the interval had shrunk to fewer than three years.[7]

Manager's Shoptalk

Contemporary Management Tools

Over the history of management, many fashions and fads have appeared. Critics argue that new techniques may not represent permanent solutions. Others feel that managers adopt new techniques for continuous improvement in a fast-changing world.

In 1993, Bain and Company started a large research project to interview and survey thousands of corporate executives about the 25 most popular management tools and techniques. The list for 2007 and their usage rates are below. How many tools do you know? For more information on specific tools, visit the Bain website: http://www.bain.com/management_tools/home.asp.

Fashion. Over the last decade, tools such as *activity-based management, one-to-one marketing, scenario planning,* and *virtual teams* have dropped out

of the top 25. *Business process reengineering* has been mercurial, with 69% usage in 1995, dropping to 38% in 2000, increasing again to 69% in 2007.

Global. North American executives are more likely to look outward, using *strategic alliances* and *collaborative innovation* more than companies in other parts of the world. European executives are big users of *customer segmentation*. Latin American executives use the fewest number of tools. Asia-Pacific executives report higher use of newer tools like *consumer ethnography* and *corporate blogs*.

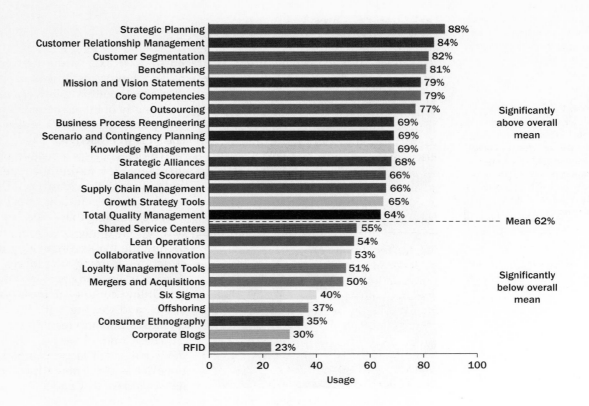

Tool	Usage
Strategic Planning	88%
Customer Relationship Management	84%
Customer Segmentation	82%
Benchmarking	81%
Mission and Vision Statements	79%
Core Competencies	79%
Outsourcing	77%
Business Process Reengineering	69%
Scenario and Contingency Planning	69%
Knowledge Management	69%
Strategic Alliances	68%
Balanced Scorecard	66%
Supply Chain Management	66%
Growth Strategy Tools	65%
Total Quality Management	64%
Shared Service Centers	55%
Lean Operations	54%
Collaborative Innovation	53%
Loyalty Management Tools	51%
Mergers and Acquisitions	50%
Six Sigma	40%
Offshoring	37%
Consumer Ethnography	35%
Corporate Blogs	30%
RFID	23%

Significantly above overall mean

Mean 62%

Significantly below overall mean

EXHIBIT 2.1 Management Perspectives over Time

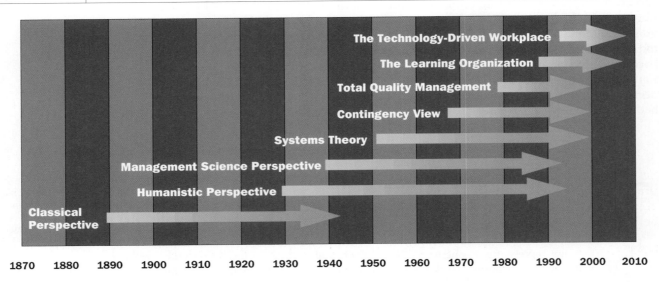

The Technology-Driven Workplace

The Learning Organization

Total Quality Management

Contingency View

Systems Theory

Management Science Perspective

Humanistic Perspective

Classical Perspective

1870   1880   1890   1900   1910   1920   1930   1940   1950   1960   1970   1980   1990   2000   2010

Recent challenges such as a tough economy and rocky stock market, environmental and organizational crises, lingering anxieties over war and terrorism, and the public suspicion and skepticism resulting from corporate scandals have left today's executives searching for any management tool—new or old—that can help them get the most out of limited resources. This search for guidance is reflected in a proliferation of books, scholarly articles, and conferences dedicated to examining management fashions and trends.[8] Exhibit 2.1 illustrates the evolution of significant management perspectives over time, each of which will be examined in the remainder of this chapter. The timeline reflects the dominant time period for each approach, but elements of each are still used in today's organizations.

classical perspective A management perspective that emerged during the nineteenth and early twentieth centuries that emphasized a rational, scientific approach to the study of management and sought to make organizations efficient operating machines.

CLASSICAL PERSPECTIVE

The practice of management can be traced to 3000 B.C., to the first government organizations developed by the Sumerians and Egyptians, but the formal study of management is relatively recent.[9] The early study of management as we know it today began with what is now called the **classical perspective**.

The classical perspective on management emerged during the nineteenth and early twentieth centuries. The factory system that began to appear in the 1800s posed challenges that earlier organizations had not encountered. Problems arose in tooling the plants, organizing managerial structure, training employees (many of them non-English-speaking immigrants), scheduling complex manufacturing operations, and dealing with increased labor dissatisfaction and resulting strikes.

These myriad new problems and the development of large, complex organizations demanded a new approach to coordination and control, and a "new sub-species

Concept Connection
Frederick Winslow Taylor (1856–1915). Taylor's theory that labor productivity could be improved by scientifically determined management practices earned him the status of "father of scientific management."

©THE GRANGER COLLECTION, NEW YORK

of economic man—the salaried manager"[10]—was born. Between 1880 and 1920, the number of professional managers in the United States grew from 161,000 to more than 1 million.[11] These professional managers began developing and testing solutions to the mounting challenges of organizing, coordinating, and controlling large numbers of people and increasing worker productivity. Thus began the evolution of modern management with the classical perspective.

This perspective contains three subfields, each with a slightly different emphasis: scientific management, bureaucratic organizations, and administrative principles.[12]

Scientific Management

Scientific management emphasizes scientifically determined jobs and management practices as the way improve efficiency and labor productivity. In the late 1800s, a young engineer, Frederick Winslow Taylor (1856–1915), proposed that workers "could be retooled like machines, their physical and mental gears recalibrated for better productivity."[13] Taylor insisted that improving productivity meant that management itself would have to change and, further, that the manner of change could be determined only by scientific study; hence, the label *scientific management* emerged. Taylor

> **scientific management** A subfield of the classical management perspective that emphasized scientifically determined changes in management practices as the solution to improving labor productivity.

suggested that decisions based on rules of thumb and tradition be replaced with precise procedures developed after careful study of individual situations.[14]

© UNDERWOOD & UNDERWOOD/CORBIS

Taylor's philosophy is encapsulated in his statement, "In the past the man has been first. In the future, the system must be first."[15] The scientific management approach is illustrated by the unloading of iron from rail cars and reloading finished steel for the Bethlehem Steel plant in 1898. Taylor calculated that with correct movements, tools, and sequencing, each man was capable of loading 47.5 tons per day instead of the typical 12.5 tons. He also worked out an incentive system that paid each man $1.85 a day for meeting the new standard, an increase from the previous rate of $1.15. Productivity at Bethlehem Steel shot up overnight.

Although known as the *father of scientific management*, Taylor was not alone in this area. Henry Gantt, an associate of Taylor's, developed the *Gantt chart*—a bar graph that measures planned and completed work along each stage of production by time elapsed. Two other important pioneers in this area were the husband-and-wife team of Frank B. and Lillian M. Gilbreth. Frank B. Gilbreth (1868–1924) pioneered *time and motion study* and arrived at many of his management techniques independently of Taylor. He stressed efficiency and was known for his quest for the one best way to do work. Although Gilbreth is known for his early work with bricklayers, his work had great impact on medical surgery by drastically reducing the time patients spent on the operating table. Surgeons were able to save countless lives through the application of time and motion study. Lillian M. Gilbreth (1878–1972) was more interested in the human aspect of work. When her husband died at the age of 56, she had 12 children ages 2 to 19. The undaunted "first lady of management" went right on with her work. She presented

Concept Connection
Lillian M. Gilbreth (1878–1972), Frank B. Gilbreth (1868–1924). This husband-and-wife team contributed to the principles of scientific management. His development of **time and motion studies** and her work in **industrial psychology** pioneered many of today's management and human resource techniques.

© THE GRANGER COLLECTION

Concept Connection Automaker Henry Ford made extensive use of Frederick Taylor's **scientific management** techniques, as illustrated by this assembly of an automobile at a Ford plant circa 1930. Ford replaced workers with machines for heavy lifting and moving autos from one worker to the next. This reduced worker hours and improved efficiency and productivity. Under this system, a Ford rolled off the assembly line every 10 seconds.

EXHIBIT | 2.2

Characteristics of Scientific
Management

General Approach
- Developed standard method for performing each job.
- Selected workers with appropriate abilities for each job.
- Trained workers in standard methods.
- Supported workers by planning their work and eliminating interruptions.
- Provided wage incentives to workers for increased output.

Contributions
- Demonstrated the importance of compensation for performance.
- Initiated the careful study of tasks and jobs.
- Demonstrated the importance of personnel selection and training.

Criticisms
- Did not appreciate the social context of work and higher needs of workers.
- Did not acknowledge variance among individuals.
- Tended to regard workers as uninformed and ignored their ideas and suggestions.

a paper in place of her late husband, continued their seminars and consulting, lectured, and eventually became a professor at Purdue University.[16] She pioneered in the field of industrial psychology and made substantial contributions to human resource management.

Exhibit 2.2 shows the basic ideas of scientific management. To use this approach, managers should develop standard methods for doing each job, select workers with the appropriate abilities, train workers in the standard methods, support workers and eliminate interruptions, and provide wage incentives.

The ideas of scientific management that began with Taylor dramatically increased productivity across all industries, and they are still important today. A recent *Harvard Business Review* article discussing innovations that shaped modern management puts scientific management at the top of its list of 12 influential innovations. Indeed, the ideas of creating a system for maximum efficiency and organizing work for maximum productivity are deeply embedded in our organizations.[17]

However, because scientific management ignored the social context and workers' needs, it led to increased conflict and sometimes violent clashes between managers and employees. Under this system, workers often felt exploited—a sharp contrast from the harmony and cooperation that Taylor and his followers had envisioned.

Bureaucratic Organizations

A systematic approach developed in Europe that looked at the organization as a whole is the **bureaucratic organizations** approach, a subfield within the classical perspective. Max Weber (1864–1920), a German theorist, introduced most of the concepts on bureaucratic organizations.[18]

During the late 1800s, many European organizations were managed on a personal, family-like basis. Employees were loyal to a single individual rather than to the organization or its mission. The dysfunctional consequence of this management practice was that resources were used to realize individual desires rather than organizational goals. Employees in effect owned the organization and used resources for their own gain rather than to serve customers. Weber envisioned organizations that would be managed on an impersonal, rational basis. This form of organization was called a *bureaucracy*. Exhibit 2.3 summarizes the six characteristics of bureaucracy as specified by Weber.

Weber believed that an organization based on rational authority would be more efficient and adaptable to change because continuity is related to formal structure and positions rather than to a particular person, who may leave or die. To Weber, rationality in organizations meant employee selection and advancement based

bureaucratic organizations
A subfield of the classical management perspective that emphasized management on an impersonal, rational basis through such elements as clearly defined authority and responsibility, formal record-keeping, and separation of management and ownership.

EXHIBIT | 2.3 Characteristics of Weberian Bureaucracy

SOURCE: Adapted from Max Weber, *The Theory of Social and Economic Organizations,* ed. and trans. A.M. Henderson and Talcott Parsons (New York: Free Press, 1947), pp. 328–337.

not on whom you know, but rather on competence and technical qualifications, which are assessed by examination or according to training and experience. The organization relies on rules and written records for continuity. In addition, rules and procedures are impersonal and applied uniformly to all employees. A clear division of labor arises from distinct definitions of authority and responsibility, legitimized as official duties. Positions are organized in a hierarchy, with each position under the authority of a higher one. The manager depends not on his or her personality for successfully giving orders but on the legal power invested in the managerial position.

Read the ethical dilemma on page 54 that pertains to problems of bureaucracy. What would it be like for you to be a manager in a bureaucratic organization? Would you thrive in that environment?

TakeaMoment

The term *bureaucracy* has taken on a negative meaning in today's organizations and is associated with endless rules and red tape. We have all been frustrated by waiting in long lines or following seemingly silly procedures. However, rules and other bureaucratic procedures provide a standard way of dealing with employees. Everyone gets equal treatment, and everyone knows what the rules are. This foundation enables many organizations to become extremely efficient. Consider United Parcel Service (UPS), sometimes called *Big Brown.*

**United Parcel
Service (UPS)**

Innovative Way

UPS specializes in the delivery of small packages, delivering more than 13 million every business day. In addition, UPS is gaining market share in air service, logistics, and global information services. Why has UPS been so successful? One important factor is the concept of bureaucracy. UPS is bound up in rules and regulations. It teaches drivers an astounding 340 steps for how to correctly deliver a package—such as how to load the truck, how to fasten their seat belts, how to walk, and how to carry their keys. Specific safety rules apply to drivers, loaders, clerks, and managers. Strict dress codes are enforced—clean uniforms (called *browns*), every day, black or brown polished shoes with nonslip soles, no beards, no hair below the collar, and so on. Supervisors conduct three-minute inspections of drivers each day. The company also has rules specifying cleanliness standards for buildings, trucks, and other properties. No eating or drinking is permitted at employee desks. Every manager is given bound copies of policy books and is expected to use them.

UPS has a well-defined division of labor. Each plant consists of specialized drivers, loaders, clerks, washers, sorters, and maintenance personnel. UPS thrives on written records, and it has been a leader in using new technology to enhance reliability and efficiency. Drivers use a computerized clipboard to track everything from miles per gallon to data on parcel delivery. All drivers have daily worksheets that specify performance goals and work output.

Technical qualification is the criterion for hiring and promotion. The UPS policy book says the leader is expected to have the knowledge and capacity to justify the position of leadership. Favoritism is forbidden. The bureaucratic model works just fine at UPS, "the tightest ship in the shipping business."[19]

Administrative Principles

Another major subfield within the classical perspective is known as the administrative principles approach. Whereas scientific management focused on the productivity of the individual worker, the **administrative principles** approach focused on the total organization. The contributors to this approach included Henri Fayol, Mary Parker Follett, and Chester I. Barnard.

Henri Fayol (1841–1925) was a French mining engineer who worked his way up to become head of a major mining group known as Comambault. Comambault survives today as part of Le Creusot-Loire, the largest mining and metallurgical group in central France. In his later years, Fayol wrote down his concepts on administration, based largely on his own management experiences.[20]

In his most significant work, *General and Industrial Management*, Fayol discussed 14 general principles of management, several of which are part of management philosophy today. For example:

- ■ *Unity of command.* Each subordinate receives orders from one—and only one—superior.

- ■ *Division of work.* Managerial work and technical work are amenable to specialization to produce more and better work with the same amount of effort.

- ■ *Unity of direction.* Similar activities in an organization should be grouped together under one manager.

- ■ *Scalar chain.* A chain of authority extends from the top to the bottom of the organization and should include every employee.

Fayol felt that these principles could be applied in any organizational setting. He also identified five basic functions or elements of management: *planning, organizing, commanding, coordinating,* and *controlling*. These functions underlie much of the general approach to today's management theory.

Mary Parker Follett (1868–1933) was trained in philosophy and political science at what today is Radcliffe College. She applied herself in many fields, including social psychology and management. She wrote of the importance of common superordinate goals for reducing conflict in organizations.[21] Her work was popular with business-people of her day but was often overlooked by management scholars.[22] Follett's ideas

administrative principles A subfield of the classical management perspective that focuses on the total organization rather than the individual worker, delineating the management functions of planning, organizing, commanding, coordinating, and controlling.

served as a contrast to scientific management and are reemerging as applicable for modern managers dealing with rapid changes in today's global environment. Her approach to leadership stressed the importance of people rather than engineering techniques. She offered the pithy admonition, "Don't hug your blueprints," and analyzed the dynamics of management-organization interactions. Follett addressed issues that are timely today, such as ethics, power, and how to lead in a way that encourages employees to give their best. The concepts of *empowerment*, facilitating rather than controlling employees, and allowing employees to act depending on the authority of the situation opened new areas for theoretical study by Chester Barnard and others.[23]

Chester I. Barnard (1886–1961) studied economics at Harvard but failed to receive a degree because he lacked a course in laboratory science. He went to work in the statistical department of AT&T and in 1927 became president of New Jersey Bell. One of Barnard's significant contributions was the concept of the informal organization. The *informal organization* occurs in all formal organizations and includes cliques and naturally occurring social groupings. Barnard argued that organizations are not machines and stressed that informal relationships are powerful forces that can help the organization if properly managed. Another significant contribution was the *acceptance theory of authority*, which states that people have free will and can choose whether to follow management orders. People typically follow orders because they perceive positive benefit to themselves, but they do have a choice. Managers should treat employees properly because their acceptance of authority may be critical to organization success in important situations.[24]

The overall classical perspective as an approach to management was very powerful and gave companies fundamental new skills for establishing high productivity and effective treatment of employees. Indeed, the United States surged ahead of the world in management techniques, and other countries, especially Japan, borrowed heavily from American ideas.

COURTESY, MARY PARKER FOLLETTE FOUNDATION AND READING UNIVERSITY, UK

Concept Connection

Mary Parker Follett (1868–1933). Follett was a major contributor to the **administrative principles** approach to management. Her emphasis on worker participation and shared goals among managers was embraced by many businesspeople of the day and has been recently "rediscovered" by corporate America.

FROM NATIONAL ARCHIVES

Concept Connection

This 1914 photograph shows the initiation of a new arrival at a Nebraska planting camp. This initiation was not part of the formal rules and illustrates the significance of the **informal organization** described by Barnard. Social values and behaviors were powerful forces that could help or hurt the planting organization depending on how they were managed.

HUMANISTIC PERSPECTIVE

Mary Parker Follett and Chester Barnard were early advocates of a more **humanistic perspective** on management that emphasized the importance of understanding human behaviors, needs, and attitudes in the workplace as well as social interactions and group processes.[25] We will discuss three subfields based on the humanistic perspective: the human relations movement, the human resources perspective, and the behavioral sciences approach.

humanistic perspective
A management perspective that emerged near the late nineteenth century and emphasized understanding human behavior, needs, and attitudes in the workplace.

Human Relations Movement

The **human relations movement** was based on the idea that truly effective control comes from within the individual worker rather than from strict, authoritarian control.[26] This school of thought recognized and directly responded to social pressures for enlightened treatment of employees. The early work on industrial psychology and personnel selection received little attention because of the prominence of scientific management. Then a series of studies at a Chicago electric company, which came to be known as the **Hawthorne studies**, changed all that.

Beginning about 1895, a struggle developed between manufacturers of gas and electric lighting fixtures for control of the residential and industrial market.[27] By 1909, electric lighting had begun to win, but the increasingly efficient electric fixtures used less total power. The electric companies began a campaign to convince industrial users that they needed more light to get more productivity. When advertising did not work, the industry began using experimental tests to demonstrate their argument. Managers were skeptical about the results, so the Committee on Industrial Lighting (CIL) was set up to run the tests. To further add to the tests' credibility, Thomas Edison was made honorary chairman of the CIL. In one test location—the Hawthorne plant of the Western Electric Company—some interesting events occurred.

The major part of this work involved four experimental and three control groups. In all, five different tests were conducted. These pointed to the importance of factors *other* than illumination in affecting productivity. To more carefully examine these factors, numerous other experiments were conducted.[28] The results of the most famous study, the first Relay Assembly Test Room (RATR) experiment, were extremely controversial. Under the guidance of two Harvard professors, Elton Mayo and Fritz Roethlisberger, the RATR studies lasted nearly six years (May 10, 1927 to May 4, 1933) and involved 24 separate experimental periods. So many factors were changed and so many unforeseen factors uncontrolled that scholars disagree on the factors that truly contributed to the general increase in performance over that time period. Most early interpretations, however, agreed on one thing: Money was not the cause of the increased output.[29] It was believed that the factor that best explained increased output was *human relations*. Employees performed better when managers treated them in a positive manner. Recent re-analyses of the experiments have revealed that a number of factors were different for the workers involved, and some suggest that money may well have been the single most important factor.[30] An interview with one of the original participants revealed that just getting into the experimental group had meant a huge increase in income.[31]

These new data clearly show that money mattered a great deal at Hawthorne. In addition, worker productivity increased partly as a result of the increased feelings of importance and group pride employees felt by virtue of being selected for this important project.[32] One unintended contribution of the experiments was a rethinking of field research practices. Researchers and scholars realized that the researcher can influence the outcome of an experiment by being too closely involved with research subjects. This phenomenon has come to be known as the *Hawthorne effect* in research methodology. Subjects behaved differently because of the active participation of researchers in the Hawthorne experiments.[33]

From a historical perspective, whether the studies were academically sound is of less importance than the fact that they stimulated an increased interest in looking at employees as more than extensions of production

human relations movement A movement in management thinking and practice that emphasizes satisfaction of employees' basic needs as the key to increased worker productivity.

Hawthorne studies A series of experiments on worker productivity begun in 1924 at the Hawthorne plant of Western Electric Company in Illinois; attributed employees' increased output to managers' better treatment of them during the study.

FROM WESTERN ELECTRIC PHOTOGRAPHIC SERVICES

Concept Connection   This is the Relay Room of the Western Electric Hawthorne, Illinois, plant in 1927. Six women worked in this relay assembly test room during the controversial experiments on employee productivity. Professors Mayo and Roethlisberger evaluated conditions such as rest breaks and workday length, physical health, amount of sleep, and diet. Experimental changes were fully discussed with the women and were abandoned if they disapproved. Gradually the researchers began to realize they had created a change in supervisory style and **human relations**, which they believed was the true cause of the increased productivity.

machinery. The interpretation that employees' output increased when managers treated them in a positive manner started a revolution in worker treatment for improving organizational productivity. Despite flawed methodology or inaccurate conclusions, the findings provided the impetus for the human relations movement. This approach shaped management theory and practice for well over a quarter-century, and the belief that human relations is the best approach for increasing productivity persists today.

Before reading on, take the New Manager Self-Test on page 44. This test will give you feedback about how your personal manager frame of reference relates to the human resources and other perspectives described in this chapter.

TakeaMoment

Human Resources Perspective

The human relations movement initially espoused a *dairy farm* view of management— contented cows give more milk, so satisfied workers will give more work. Gradually, views with deeper content began to emerge. The **human resources perspective** maintained an interest in worker participation and considerate leadership but shifted the emphasis to consider the daily tasks that people perform. The human resources perspective combines prescriptions for design of job tasks with theories of motivation.[34] In the human resources view, jobs should be designed so that tasks are not perceived as dehumanizing or demeaning but instead allow workers to use their full potential. Two of the best-known contributors to the human resources perspective were Abraham Maslow and Douglas McGregor.

Abraham Maslow (1908–1970), a practicing psychologist, observed that his patients' problems usually stemmed from an inability to satisfy their needs. Thus, he generalized his work and suggested a hierarchy of needs. Maslow's hierarchy started with physiological needs and progressed to safety, belongingness, esteem, and, finally, self-actualization needs. Chapter 17 discusses his ideas in more detail.

Douglas McGregor (1906–1964) had become frustrated with the early simplistic human relations notions while president of Antioch College in Ohio. He challenged both the classical perspective and the early human relations assumptions about human behavior. Based on his experiences as a manager and consultant, his training as a psychologist, and the work of Maslow, McGregor formulated his Theory X and Theory Y, which are explained in Exhibit 2.4.[35] McGregor believed

human resources perspective A management perspective that suggests jobs should be designed to meet higher-level needs by allowing workers to use their full potential.

EXHIBIT | 2.4

Theory X and Theory Y

Assumptions of Theory X
- The average human being has an inherent dislike of work and will avoid it if possible.
- Because of the human characteristic of dislike for work, most people must be coerced, controlled, directed, or threatened with punishment to get them to put forth adequate effort toward the achievement of organizational objectives.
- The average human being prefers to be directed, wishes to avoid responsibility, has relatively little ambition, and wants security above all.

Assumptions of Theory Y
- The expenditure of physical and mental effort in work is as natural as play or rest. The average human being does not inherently dislike work.
- External control and the threat of punishment are not the only means for bringing about effort toward organizational objectives. A person will exercise self-direction and self-control in the service of objectives to which he or she is committed.
- The average human being learns, under proper conditions, not only to accept but to seek responsibility.
- The capacity to exercise a relatively high degree of imagination, ingenuity, and creativity in the solution of organizational problems is widely, not narrowly, distributed in the population.
- Under the conditions of modern industrial life, the intellectual potentialities of the average human being are only partially utilized.

SOURCE: Douglas McGregor, *The Human Side of Enterprise* (New York: McGraw-Hill, 1960), pp. 33–48.

New Manager Self-Test

Evolution of Style

This questionnaire asks you to describe yourself. For each item, give the number "4" to the phrase that best describes you, "3" to the item that is next best, and on down to "1" for the item that is least like you.

1. My strongest skills are:
   _____ **a.** Analytical skills
   _____ **b.** Interpersonal skills
   _____ **c.** Political skills
   _____ **d.** Flair for drama

2. The best way to describe me is:
   _____ **a.** Technical expert
   _____ **b.** Good listener
   _____ **c.** Skilled negotiator
   _____ **d.** Inspirational leader

3. What has helped me the most to be successful is my ability to:
   _____ **a.** Make good decisions
   _____ **b.** Coach and develop people
   _____ **c.** Build strong alliances and a power base
   _____ **d.** Inspire and excite others

4. What people are most likely to notice about me is my:
   _____ **a.** Attention to detail
   _____ **b.** Concern for people
   _____ **c.** Ability to succeed in the face of conflict and opposition
   _____ **d.** Charisma

5. My most important leadership trait is:
   _____ **a.** Clear, logical thinking
   _____ **b.** Caring and support for others
   _____ **c.** Toughness and aggressiveness
   _____ **d.** Imagination and creativity

6. I am best described as:
   _____ **a.** An analyst
   _____ **b.** A humanist
   _____ **c.** A politician
   _____ **d.** A visionary

INTERPRETATION: New managers typically view their world through one or more mental frames of reference. (1) The *structural frame* of reference sees the organization as a machine that can be economically efficient and that provides a manager with formal authority to achieve goals. This manager frame became strong during the era of **scientific management** and **bureaucratic administration**. (2) The *human resource frame* sees the organization as people, with manager emphasis given to support, empowerment, and belonging. This manager frame gained importance with the rise of the **humanistic perspective**. (3) The *political frame* sees the organization as a competition for resources to achieve goals, with manager emphasis on negotiation and hallway coalition building. This frame reflects the need within **systems theory** to have all parts working together. (4) The *symbolic frame* of reference sees the organization as theater—a place to achieve dreams—with manager emphasis on symbols, vision, culture, and inspiration. This manager frame is important for **learning organizations**.

Which frame reflects your way of viewing the world? *The first two frames of reference—structural and human resource—are more important for new managers.* These two frames usually are mastered first. As new managers gain experience and move up the organization, they should acquire political skills and also learn to use symbols for communication. It is important for new managers not to be stuck for years in one way of viewing the organization because their progress may be limited. Many new managers evolve through and master each of the four frames as they become more skilled and experienced

SCORING: Higher score represents your way of viewing the organization and will influence your management style. Compute your scores as follows:

ST = 1a + 2a + 3a + 4a + 5a + 6a = _____

HR = 1b + 2b + 3b + 4b + 5b + 6b = _____

PL = 1c + 2c + 3c + 4c + 5c + 6c = _____

SY = 1d + 2d + 3d + 4d + 5d + 6d = _____

that the classical perspective was based on Theory X assumptions about workers. He also felt that a slightly modified version of Theory X fit early human relations ideas. In other words, human relations ideas did not go far enough. McGregor proposed Theory Y as a more realistic view of workers for guiding management thinking.

Look back at your scores on the questionnaire at the beginning of this chapter related to Theory X and Theory Y. How will your management assumptions about people fit into an organization today?

TakeaMoment

The point of Theory Y is that organizations can take advantage of the imagination and intellect of all their employees. Employees will exercise self-control and will contribute to organizational goals when given the opportunity. A few companies today still use Theory X management, but many are using Theory Y techniques. Consider how hearing-aid maker Oticon applies Theory Y assumptions to tap into employee creativity and mind power.

Oticon

Innovative Way

Oticon, a Danish company that made the world's first digital hearing aid, was once a typical hierarchical organization with a rather stodgy culture. That all changed in the early 1990s, when chief executive Lars Kolind turned everything on its head by throwing out the old structures and controls.

Kolind believed workers would be more creative, more productive, and more satisfied if they had fewer controls and limitations. Suddenly, employees were free to work on any project and join any team they chose. There was no hierarchy, no organization charts, no titles, and few rules. Permanent desks were done away with in favor of filing cabinets on wheels that people pushed from project to project. Kolind called it "the spaghetti organization" because the company held together without a fixed structure. Ideas began bubbling up and turning into hot new products, such as a hearing aid that required less adjustment. Productivity increased, and sales and profits soared.

Some of the old structures were reinstated as the company grew larger and after Kolind left the company. For example, everyone now reports to a direct supervisor, and people no longer have complete freedom to choose projects. New top leaders believe some structure is helpful as long as workers aren't constrained and burdened by tight controls. The Theory Y spirit survives at Oticon, helping to keep the company an innovation leader.[36]

Behavioral Sciences Approach

The **behavioral sciences approach** uses scientific methods and draws from sociology, psychology, anthropology, economics, and other disciplines to develop theories about human behavior and interaction in an organizational setting. This approach can be seen in practically every organization. When IBM conducts research to determine the best set of tests, interviews, and employee profiles to use when selecting new employees, it is using behavioral science techniques. When Best Buy electronics stores train new managers in the techniques of employee motivation, most of the theories and findings are rooted in behavioral science research.

One specific set of management techniques based in the behavioral sciences approach is *organization development* (OD). In the 1970s, organization development evolved as a separate field that applied the behavioral sciences to improve the organization's health and effectiveness through its ability to cope with change, improve internal relationships, and increase problem-solving capabilities.[37] The techniques and concepts of organization development have since been broadened and expanded to address the increasing complexity of organizations and the environment, and OD

behavioral sciences approach
A subfield of the humanistic management perspective that applies social science in an organizational context, drawing from economics, psychology, sociology, and other disciplines.

is still a vital approach for managers. OD will be discussed in detail in Chapter 10. Other concepts that grew out of the behavioral sciences approach include matrix organizations, self-managed teams, ideas about corporate culture, and management by wandering around. Indeed, the behavioral sciences approach has influenced the majority of tools, techniques, and approaches that managers have applied to organizations since the 1970s.

All the remaining chapters of this book contain research findings and management applications that can be attributed to the behavioral sciences approach.

MANAGEMENT SCIENCE PERSPECTIVE

World War II caused many management changes. The massive and complicated problems associated with modern global warfare presented managerial decision makers with the need for more sophisticated tools than ever before. The **management science perspective** emerged to address those problems. This view is distinguished for its application of mathematics, statistics, and other quantitative techniques to management decision making and problem solving. During World War II, groups of mathematicians, physicists, and other scientists were formed to solve military problems. Because those problems frequently involved moving massive amounts of materials and large numbers of people quickly and efficiently, the techniques had obvious applications to large-scale business firms.[38]

Management scholar Peter Drucker's 1946 book *Concept of the Corporation* sparked a dramatic increase in the academic study of business and management. Picking up on techniques developed for the military, scholars began cranking out numerous mathematical tools for corporate managers, such as the application of linear programming for optimizing operations, statistical process control for quality management, and the capital asset pricing model.[39]

These efforts were enhanced with the development and perfection of the computer. IBM introduced the first automatic, general purpose computer in 1944. It was essentially a calculator with 760,000 parts and 500 miles of wire that took 11 seconds to perform simple division.[40] Further developments over the 1950s and 1960s made this new tool increasingly useful as a data processor, reporting system, and data repository for managers.[41] Coupled with the growing body of statistical techniques, computers made it possible for managers to collect, store, and process large volumes of data for quantitative decision making.[42] Let's look at three subsets of the management science perspective.

Operations research grew directly out of the World War II military groups (called *operational research teams* in Great Britain and *operations research teams* in the United States).[43] It consists of mathematical model building and other applications of quantitative techniques to managerial problems.

Operations management refers to the field of management that specializes in the physical production of goods or services. Operations management specialists use quantitative techniques to solve manufacturing problems. Some commonly used methods are forecasting, inventory modeling, linear and nonlinear programming, queuing theory, scheduling, simulation, and break-even analysis.

Information technology (IT) is the most recent subfield of the management science perspective, which is often reflected in management information systems. These systems are designed to provide relevant information to managers in a timely and cost-efficient manner. More recently, information technology within organizations evolved to include intranets and extranets, as well as various software programs that help managers estimate costs, plan and track production, manage projects, allocate resources, or schedule employees. Most of today's organizations have departments of information technology specialists who use management science techniques to solve complex organizational problems.

management science perspective A management perspective that emerged after World War II and applied mathematics, statistics, and other quantitative techniques to managerial problems.

RECENT HISTORICAL TRENDS

The post–World War II period saw the rise of new concepts, along with a continued strong interest in the human aspect of managing, such as team and group dynamics and other concepts that relate to the humanistic perspective, as described earlier in the chapter. Among the approaches we've discussed, the humanistic perspective has remained most prevalent from the 1950s until today. Three new concepts that appeared were systems theory, the contingency view, and total quality management.

Systems Theory

A **system** is a set of interrelated parts that function as a whole to achieve a common purpose.[44] A system functions by acquiring inputs from the external environment, transforming them in some way, and discharging outputs back to the environment. Exhibit 2.5 shows the basic **systems theory** of organizations. It consists of five components: inputs, a transformation process, outputs, feedback, and the environment. *Inputs* are the material, human, financial, or information resources used to produce goods and services. The *transformation process* is management's use of production technology to change the inputs into outputs. *Outputs* include the organization's products and services. *Feedback* is knowledge of the results that influence the selection of inputs during the next cycle of the process. The *environment* surrounding the organization includes the social, political, and economic forces noted earlier in this chapter.

Some ideas in systems theory significantly affected management thinking. They include open and closed systems, synergy, and subsystem interdependencies.[45]

Open systems must interact with the environment to survive; **closed systems** need not. In the classical and management science perspectives, organizations were frequently thought of as closed systems. In the management science perspective, closed system assumptions—the absence of external disturbances—are sometimes used to simplify problems for quantitative analysis. In reality, however, all organizations are open systems, and the cost of ignoring the environment may be failure.

Synergy means that the whole is greater than the sum of its parts. When an organization is formed, something new comes into the world. Management, coordination, and production that did not exist before are now present. Organizational units working together can accomplish more than those same units working alone. The sales department depends on production, and vice versa.

system A set of interrelated parts that function as a whole to achieve a common purpose.

systems theory An extension of the humanistic perspective that describes organizations as open systems characterized by entropy, synergy, and subsystem interdependence.

open system A system that interacts with the external environment.

closed system A system that does not interact with the external environment.

synergy The concept that the whole is greater than the sum of its parts.

EXHIBIT | **2.5**

The Systems View of Organizations

Subsystems depend on one another as parts of a system. Changes in one part of the organization affect other parts. The organization must be managed as a coordinated whole. Managers who understand subsystem interdependence are reluctant to make changes that do not recognize subsystem impact on the organization as a whole. Consider Toyota's highly successful application of the "just-in-time" inventory control system, which aims to keep inventory at its lowest. Managers knew that the best way to make the system work was to let employees on the factory floor control the flow of materials. Thus, the change in production required that the company also make changes in culture and structure. Toyota decentralized decision making so that employees doing the work were empowered to make choices about how to accomplish it. Cultural values were shifted to encourage every employee to think creatively about improving his or her particular piece of the organization and to see problems as opportunities for learning and improving.[46]

As the example of Toyota shows, when managers learn to think systemically, they have a powerful tool for changing outcomes and improving performance. **Systemic thinking** means looking both at the distinct elements of a situation and at the interaction among those elements.[47] The fundamental assumption of systemic thinking is that everything in the world affects and is affected by the things around it. For example, all managers know that price, cost, volume, quality, and profit are all interrelated. Changing one will affect the others. However, most managers tend to think *analytically*, by breaking things down to their distinct elements. Systemic thinking takes a further step. To think systemically, managers look not only at the distinct parts of a system or situation but also at the interactions among those parts, which are continually changing and affecting each other differently. A systemic thinking process allows managers to get a handle on highly complex problems and situations in a way that analytical thinking cannot.

Contingency View

A second contemporary extension to management thinking is the **contingency view**. The classical perspective assumed a *universalist* view. Management concepts were thought to be universal; that is, whatever worked—leader style, bureaucratic structure—in one organization would work in another. In business education, however, an alternative view exists. In this *case* view, each situation is believed to be unique. Principles are not universal, and one learns about management by experiencing a large number of case problem situations. Managers face the task of determining what methods will work in every new situation.

To integrate these views the contingency view emerged, as illustrated in Exhibit 2.6.[48] Here neither of the other views is seen as entirely correct. Instead, certain contingencies, or variables, exist for helping management identify and understand situations. The contingency view tells us that what works in one setting might not work in another. Contingency means that one thing depends on other things and a manager's response to a situation depends on identifying key contingencies in an organizational situation.

subsystems Parts of a system that depend on one another for their functioning.

systemic thinking Seeing both the distinct elements of a situation and the complex and changing interaction among those elements.

contingency view An extension of the humanistic perspective in which the successful resolution of organizational problems is thought to depend on managers' identification of key variations in the situation at hand.

EXHIBIT | **2.6**   Contingency View of Management

As a new manager, learn to think systemically. Learn to see both the discrete elements of a situation as well as the ever-changing interactions among elements. Identify important contingencies that will help you understand a situation and find good solutions.

TakeaMoment

One important contingency, for example, is the industry in which the organization operates. The organizational structure that is effective for an Internet company such as Google would not be successful for a large auto manufacturer such as Ford. A management-by-objectives (MBO) system that works well in a manufacturing firm, in turn, might not be right for a school system. When managers learn to identify important patterns and characteristics of their organizations, they can then fit solutions to those characteristics.

total quality management (TQM) A concept that focuses on managing the total organization to deliver quality to customers. Four significant elements of TQM are employee involvement, focus on the customer, benchmarking, and continuous improvement.

Total Quality Management

The theme of quality is another concept that permeates current management thinking. The quality movement is strongly associated with Japanese companies, but these ideas emerged partly as a result of American influence after World War II. The ideas of W. Edwards Deming, known as the "father of the quality movement," were initially scoffed at in the United States, but the Japanese embraced his theories and modified them to help rebuild their industries into world powers.[49] Japanese companies achieved a significant departure from the American model by gradually shifting from an inspection-oriented approach to quality control toward an approach emphasizing employee involvement in the prevention of quality problems.[50]

During the 1980s and into the 1990s, **total quality management (TQM)**, which focuses on managing the total organization to deliver quality to customers, moved to the forefront in helping U.S. managers deal with global competition. The approach infuses quality values throughout every activity within a company, with front-line workers intimately involved in the process. Four significant elements of quality management are employee involvement, focus on the customer, benchmarking, and continuous improvement.

Employee involvement means that achieving quality requires companywide participation in quality control. All employees are *focused on the customer*; companies find out what customers want and try to meet their needs and expectations. *Benchmarking* refers to a process whereby companies find out how others do something better than they do and then try to imitate or improve on it. *Continuous improvement* is the implementation of small, incremental improvements in all areas of the organization on an ongoing basis. TQM is not a quick fix, but companies such as General Electric, Texas Instruments, Procter & Gamble, and DuPont achieved astonishing results in efficiency, quality, and customer satisfaction through total quality management.[51] TQM is still an important part of today's organizations, and managers consider benchmarking in particular a highly effective and satisfying management technique.[52]

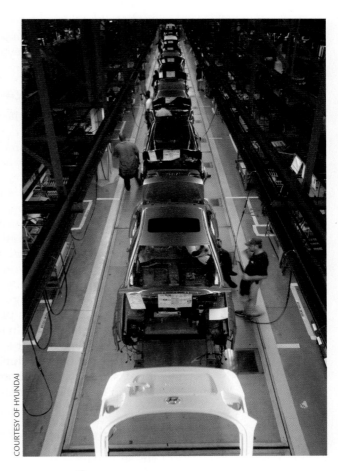

COURTESY OF HYUNDAI

Concept Connection The inclusion of Hyundai Motor Company's Elantra SE and Santa Fe in the 2008 top ten autos by *Consumer Reports* shows how commitment to **total quality management** can improve a company's products and market position. When Hyundai entered the U.S. market in 1999, its autos got low quality ratings from consumers. First, managers increased the quality team from 100 to 865 people and held quality seminars to train employees. They also **benchmarked** products, using vehicle lifts and high-intensity spotlights to compare against competing brands. Committing to **continuous improvement**, Hyundai delayed several new models to resolve problems. Within five years Hyundai earned quality ratings comparable to Honda and just behind Toyota.

Some of today's companies pursue highly ambitious quality goals to demonstrate their commitment to improving quality. For example, *Six Sigma*, popularized by Motorola and General Electric, specifies a goal of no more than 3.4 defects per million parts. However, the term also refers to a broad quality control approach that emphasizes a disciplined and relentless pursuit of higher quality and lower costs. TQM will be discussed in detail in Chapter 13.

INNOVATIVE MANAGEMENT THINKING FOR TURBULENT TIMES

All of the ideas and approaches discussed so far in this chapter go into the mix that makes up modern management. A recent book on management thinking indicates dozens of ideas and techniques in current use that can trace their roots to these historical perspectives.[53] In addition, innovative concepts continue to emerge to address management challenges in today's turbulent world. Organizations experiment with new ways of managing that more adequately respond to the demands of today's environment and customers. Two recent innovations in management include the shift to a learning organization and managing the technology-driven workplace.

The Learning Organization

One of the toughest challenges for managers today is to get people focused on adaptive change to meet the demands of an uncertain and rapidly changing environment. Few problems today come with ready-made solutions, and they require that people throughout the company think in new ways and learn new values and attitudes.[54] These needs demand a new approach to management and a new kind of organization.

Managers began thinking about the concept of the learning organization after the publication of Peter Senge's book, *The Fifth Discipline: The Art and Practice of Learning Organizations*.[55] Senge described the kind of changes managers needed to undergo to help their organizations adapt to an increasingly chaotic world. These ideas gradually evolved to describe characteristics of the organization itself. The **learning organization** can be defined as one in which everyone is engaged in identifying and solving problems, enabling the organization to continuously experiment, change, and improve, thus increasing its capacity to grow, learn, and achieve its purpose.

The essential idea is problem solving, in contrast to the traditional organization designed for efficiency. In the learning organization all employees look for problems, such as understanding special customer needs. Employees also solve problems, which means putting things together in unique ways to meet a customer's needs. Today's best managers know that sustained competitive advantage can come only by developing the learning capacity of everyone in the organization.

Managing the Technology-Driven Workplace

learning organization An organization in which everyone is engaged in identifying and solving problems, enabling the organization to continuously experiment, improve, and increase its capability.

supply chain management Managing the sequence of suppliers and purchasers, covering all stages of processing from obtaining raw materials to distributing finished goods to final customers.

The shift to the learning organization goes hand-in-hand with the current transition to a technology-driven workplace. Today, many employees perform much of their work on computers and may work in virtual teams, connected electronically to colleagues around the world. Even in factories that produce physical goods, machines have taken over much of the routine and uniform work, freeing workers to use more of their minds and abilities. Moreover, companies are using technology to keep in touch with customers and collaborate with other organizations on an unprecedented scale.

Supply Chain Management **Supply chain management** refers to managing the sequence of suppliers and purchasers, covering all stages of processing from obtaining raw materials to distributing finished goods to consumers.[56] Exhibit 2.7 illustrates

EXHIBIT 2.7 Supply Chain for a Retail Organization

Suppliers	Manufacturers	Distributors	Retailers

Flow of Products

SOURCE: Adapted from an exhibit from Global Supply Chain Games Project, Delft University and the University of Maryland, R. H. Smith School of Business, http://www.gscg.org:8080/opencms/export/sites/default/gscg/images/supplychain_simple.gif (accessed February 6, 2008).

a basic supply chain model. A supply chain is a network of multiple businesses and individuals that are connected through the flow of products or services.[57] Today, many organizations manage the supply chain with sophisticated electronic technology. In the retail industry, Wal-Mart used end-to-end digital supply chain technology as a competitive weapon to expand rapidly in the United States and is now trying to do the same around the world. In India, for example, Wal-Mart managers are investing in an efficient supply chain that will electronically link farmers and small manufacturers directly to the stores, maximizing value for both ends.[58] Supply chain management will be discussed in detail in Chapter 14.

customer relationship management (CRM)
Systems that help companies keep in close touch with customers, collect and manage customer data, and collaborate with customers to provide the most valuable products and services.

Take a Moment

As a new manager in today's workplace, be prepared to apply technology as a tool to build relationships with employees, customers, and other organizations and to help employees think and act creatively.

Customer Relationship Management One of today's most popular applications of technology is for customer relationship management. **Customer relationship management (CRM)** systems use the latest information technology to keep in close touch with customers and to collect and manage large amounts of customer data. These data can help employees and managers act on customer insights, make better decisions, and provide superior customer service. For example, when you check in at a Marriott hotel, it is likely that the desk clerk is well aware of your past requests for a king-size bed, non-smoking room, and access to the Internet in your room.[59]

There has been an explosion of interest in CRM in just a few short years. In the Manager's Shoptalk on page 35, CRM is the second most used management tool at 84 percent. Only 35 percent of companies reported using CRM in 2000. How things have changed! Meeting customer needs and desires is a primary goal for organizations, and using CRM to give customers what they really want provides a tremendous boost to customer service and satisfaction.

© BMW FINANCIAL SERVICES NA, LLC/PRNEWSFOTO (NEWSCOM)

Concept Connection The BMW subsidiary MINI offers customers a voice in everything from personalizing their credit cards to designing their cars. BMW Financial Services's MINI Platinum Visa cardholders can customize the MINI image that graces their card by accessing the Web page, shown here. There they can choose from four body styles, 36 different wheels, 21 body colors, and 24 roof options. Similar software allows individuals to customize their actual MINI vehicles. "No two MINIs are exactly alike," the MINI Web site proclaims. This type of collaborative customer experience is the next step in **customer relationship management (CRM)**, as companies court Internet-savvy Gen X and Gen Y consumers.

Outsourcing Information technology has also contributed to the rapid growth of **outsourcing**, which means contracting out selected functions or activities to other organizations that can do the work more cost efficiently. Today's companies are outsourcing like crazy to free up cash for investment in long-term research and innovation. Outsourcing, like supply chain management and CRM, requires that managers not only be technologically savvy but that they learn to manage a complex web of relationships. These relationships might reach far beyond the boundaries of the physical organization; they are built through flexible e-links between a company and its employees, suppliers, partners, and customers.[60]

outsourcing Contracting out selected functions or activities of an organization to other organizations that can do the work more cost efficiently.

ch2   A MANAGER'S ESSENTIALS: WHAT HAVE WE LEARNED?

- An understanding of the evolution of management helps current and future managers appreciate where we are now and continue to progress toward better management. Elements of various historical approaches go into the mix that makes up modern management.

- Three major perspectives on management evolved since the late 1800s: the classical perspective, the humanistic perspective, and the management science perspective. Each perspective encompasses several specialized subfields that provided important ideas still relevant in organizations today.

- Recent extensions of those perspectives include systems theory, the contingency view, and total quality management. Systemic thinking, which means looking not just at discrete parts of a situation but also at the continually changing interactions among the parts, is a powerful tool for managing in a complex environment.

- The most recent thinking about organizations was brought about by today's turbulent times and the shift to a new workplace described in Chapter 1. Many managers are redesigning their companies toward the learning organization, which fully engages all employees in identifying and solving problems.

- The shift to a learning organization goes hand-in-hand with the transition to a technology-driven workplace. Important new management approaches include supply chain management, customer relationship management, and outsourcing. These approaches require managers to think in new ways about the role of employees, customers, and partners. Today's best managers value employees for their ability to think, build relationships, and share knowledge, which is quite different from the scientific management perspective of a century ago.

ch2   DISCUSSION QUESTIONS

1. Why is it important to understand the different perspectives and approaches to management theory that have evolved throughout the history of organizations?

2. How do societal forces influence the practice and theory of management? Do you think new management techniques are a response to these forces?

3. Based on your experience at work or school, describe some ways in which the principles of scientific management and bureaucracy are still used in organizations. Do you believe these characteristics will ever cease to be a part of organizational life? Discuss.

4. A management professor once said that for successful management, studying the present was most important, studying the past was next, and studying the future was least important. Do you agree? Why?

5. Which of the three characteristics of learning organizations do you find most appealing? As a manager, which would be hardest for you to adopt? Why?

6. As organizations become more technology-driven, which do you think will become more important—the management of the human element of the organization or the management of technology? Discuss.

7. Why do you think Mary Parker Follet's ideas tended to be popular with business people of her day, but were ignored by management scholars? Why are her ideas appreciated more today?

8. Explain the basic idea underlying the contingency view. How would you go about identifying the key contingencies facing an organization?

9. Why can an event such as the Hawthorne studies be a major turning point in the history of management even if the idea is later shown to be in error? Discuss.

10. Identify the major components of systems theory. Is this perspective primarily internal or external to the organization? Explain.

11. Do you think management theory will ever be as precise as theories in the fields of finance, accounting, or experimental psychology? Why or why not?

12. To what degree do you think that effective control comes from within the individual worker, or do workers need rules, rewards, and punishments to perform effectively? Explain your reasoning.

ch2 MANAGEMENT IN PRACTICE: EXPERIENTIAL EXERCISE

Theory X and Theory Y Scale

The following are various types of behavior that a manager may engage in when relating to subordinates. Read each statement carefully and rate each one in terms of the extent to which you would use that behavior, according to the following scale.

① Make a great effort to do this

② Tend to do this

③ Tend to avoid doing this

④ Make a great effort to avoid this

1. Closely supervise my subordinates in order to get better work from them.

   1 2 3 4

2. Set the goals and objectives for my subordinates and sell them on the merits of my plans.

   1 2 3 4

3. Set up controls to assure that my subordinates are getting the job done.

   1 2 3 4

4. Encourage my subordinates to set their own goals and objectives.

   1 2 3 4

5. Make sure that my subordinates' work is planned out for them.

   1 2 3 4

6. Check with my subordinates daily to see if they need any help.

   1 2 3 4

7. Step in as soon as reports indicate that the job is slipping.

   1 2 3 4

8. Push my people to meet schedules if necessary.

   1 2 3 4

9. Have frequent meetings to keep in touch with what is going on.

   1 2 3 4

10. Allow subordinates to make important decisions.

    1 2 3 4

Scoring and Interpretation

Subtract each of your scores for Questions 4 and 10 from the number 5. Then, add the total points and mark your score on the scale below. Refer back to Exhibit 2.4 and review the assumptions related to Theory X and Theory Y. A person who fully subscribes to the assumptions of Theory X would have a score of 10, whereas a person who fully subscribes to the assumptions of Theory Y would have a score of 40. Strong Theory X assumptions are typically considered inappropriate for today's workplace. Where do you fit on the X–Y scale? Does your score reflect your perception of yourself as a current or future manager?

Theory X	10	20	30	40	Theory Y

SOURCE: J. William Pfeiffer and John E. Jones, eds., "Supervisory Attitudes: The X–Y Scale," *The 1972 Annual Handbook for Group Facilitators* (New York: John Wiley & Sons, 1972): 65–68. This material is used by permission of John Wiley & Sons, Inc. The X–Y scale was adapted from an instrument developed by Robert N. Ford of AT&T for in-house manager training.

ch2   MANAGEMENT IN PRACTICE: ETHICAL DILEMMA

The Supervisor

Karen Lowry, manager of a social service agency in a midsized city in Illinois, loved to see her employees learn and grow to their full potential. When a rare opening for a supervising clerk occurred, Karen quickly decided to give Charlotte Hines a shot at the job. Charlotte had been with the agency for 17 years and had shown herself to be a true leader. Charlotte worked hard at being a good supervisor, just as she had always worked hard at being a top-notch clerk. She paid attention to the human aspects of employee problems and introduced modern management techniques that strengthened the entire agency.

However, the Civil Service Board decided that a promotional exam should be given to find a permanent placement for the supervising clerk position. For the sake of fairness, the exam was an open competition—anyone, even a new employee, could sign up and take it. The board wanted the candidate with the highest score to get the job but allowed Karen, as manager of the agency, to have the final say-so.

Because she had accepted the provisional opening and proved herself on the job, Charlotte was upset that the entire clerical force was deemed qualified to take the test. When the results came back, she was devastated. Charlotte placed twelfth in the field of candidates while one of her newly hired clerks placed first. The Civil Service Board, impressed by the high score, is urging Karen to give the new clerk the permanent supervisory job. Karen wonders whether it is fair to base her decision only on the results of a written test.

What Would You Do?

1. Ignore the test. Charlotte has proved herself and deserves the job.

2. Give the job to the candidate with the highest score. You don't need to make enemies on the Civil Service Board, and, after all, it is an objective way to select a permanent placement.

3. Devise a more comprehensive set of selection criteria—including test results as well as supervisory experience, ability to motivate employees, and knowledge of agency procedures—that can be explained and justified to the board and to employees.

SOURCE: Based on Betty Harrigan, "Career Advice," *Working Woman* (July 1986): 22–24.

ch2   CASE FOR CRITICAL ANALYSIS

SIA Corporation

In the early years of the new century, it wasn't hard to see that SIA Corporation couldn't keep doing business the old-fashioned twentieth-century way. Chief knowledge officer Jerry Seibert fully realized he owed his new position in the newly created knowledge management department to this challenge.

Headquartered in the Midwest, SIA was an umbrella organization offering a wide range of insurance products to commercial customers of all sizes throughout the country and, increasingly, to multinational corporations throughout the world. Over the years it had diversified into various types of insurance by absorbing smaller companies until it now consisted of more than 30 separate business units. Each had its own hierarchy, characterized by strong top-down administration and the well-defined rules and procedures typical of the insurance industry; virtually every employee possessed specialized knowledge about a narrowly defined market niche.

Upper-level management had given the matter considerable attention and concluded that SIA's refined division of labor into technical specialists needed to give way to a collaborative learning organization, one where employee empowerment and open information made it possible for a single underwriter to be knowledgeable about a variety of products. Jerry's knowledge management department, housed within human resources, could make a contribution toward this goal.

Jerry devised an elegant solution, if he did say so himself. He oversaw the development of software that allowed any SIA employee to post a query, have that question directed only to those employees with relevant expertise, and then receive an answer, often in a matter of minutes and usually before the day was out. The only hitch was that hardly anyone was posting queries on the easy-to-use system.

Why? Rachel Greenwell, a veteran SIA underwriter, clued him in. Especially after weathering a turbulent period, one that had seen plenty of layoffs in the insurance industry, many employees viewed the restructuring as the first step in a process that would lead to pink slips landing on their desks. Some employees, in fact, saw their own highly specialized knowledge as a kind of job insurance policy. "I know that's not what your knowledge-sharing efforts are about and that their fears are unfounded," she reassured him. "But you've got about 9,999 other employees who are at least willing to entertain the possibility that sharing what they know isn't in their best interests."

Questions

1. What are some of the social, political, and economic forces that are influencing SIA's decision to become a learning organization?

2. If you were a specialist at SIA, how and why would you respond to the proposed changes? What steps would you suggest Jerry take to increase employee utilization of the knowledge-sharing system in particular? How can he encourage SIA employees to share information?

3. What general obstacles would you foresee in a company such as SIA trying to make the transition from a hierarchical, or bureaucratic, to a learning organization? What are some general measures managers can take to smooth the way?

SOURCES: Based on Megan Santosus, "Case Files: CNA Underwriting Knowledge," *CIO Magazine* (September 1, 2002): http://www.cio.com/archive/090102/underwriting.html; and Eric Lesser and Laurence Prusak, "Preserving Knowledge in an Uncertain World," *MIT Sloan Management Review* (Fall 2001): 101–102.

ch2   ON THE JOB VIDEO CASE

Original Penguin Becomes a Learning Organization

Taking charge of a company is both a challenge and a dream for any young manager. Chris Kolbe, vice president of Original Penguin, a division of Perry Ellis International, is no exception. Original Penguin is experiencing a total makeover, courtesy of Chris Kolbe and a small staff of designers, marketers, and finance managers. Once the domain of middle-aged golfers, the penguin logo now graces hats, neckties, shoes, and an entire line of fashionable women's clothing and accessories ranging from T-shirts and skirts to belts, shoes, handbags, and bathing suits. Original Penguin clothing now appears in such upscale department stores as Barney's and Saks—as well as its own retail store in midtown Manhattan. This hip new brand of clothing has come a long way from the golf courses of half a century ago.

Remaking a brand involves remaking an organization. In 1955, marketers for Munsingwear Penguin approached celebrities such as Bing Crosby and Bob Hope with the request to provide shirts for their golf tournaments. Then they contacted the Golf Association, asking for a list of its members—all men—to whom they sent sample golf shirts. The penguin logo quickly became associated with the men's pro golf tour. The company was run as a traditional organization, manufacturing a traditional product. But not any more.

Perry Ellis has made a strategy of acquiring languishing brands, such as Jantzen bathing suits and Penguin golf wear, and breathing new life into them. When Chris Kolbe was hired by the company to turn Original Penguin around, he was given a small New York office and two staffers. There was no way he could run the company as a traditional large corporation, nor did he want to. Original Penguin was about to become a learning organization, complete with teams, empowered employees, and a free flow of information.

Kolbe relies on collaboration and communication across departments—usually just across cubicles—among team members. He helps them set goals, makes sure they have the information they need, and then allows them to take responsibility for their own performance. "If you have a team, you have to give them ownership of what they do," Kolbe explains. He communicates regularly with the design team and marketing team but says that he prefers to limit the time everyone spends in meetings. "I'm a one-on-one guy. I try not to schedule a lot of meetings because meetings can be stifling."

Kolbe believes firmly in empowering employees with the freedom and resources to initiate their own ideas, make their own decisions, and perform their best. "Chris is easy to work with," says marketing manager Laura Bellafronto. "He makes you feel comfortable and secure . . . he makes you want to be here and be working with him." Kolbe is happy that he inspires that kind of loyalty. "I try to respect and treat everybody as I wish to be treated, but also I'm very comfortable with pushing people and asking a lot of them," he remarks.

The free flow of information between Kolbe and his staff is key to the rejuvenation of Original Penguin. Kolbe makes sure he communicates with every employee the goals and needs of the company. "He has a vision that he makes clear to everyone," says Laura Bellafronto.

Today, Original Penguin products sport an updated, more youthful look. "[They are] fashionably new, but not avant-garde," says Kolbe. If the clothes are vintage inspired, Penguin's new customers are too young to remember leisure suits or wall-to-wall shag carpeting. Kolbe's management style is as deceptively casual as the clothing itself—comfortable but made to last. "My authority [really derives] from what I do and how I communicate with people, my directness. I know when to have fun and I know when to be serious. I try to strike that balance."

Questions

1. As the organization has grown from just three employees, Chris Kolbe has had to delegate more decisions to others. How important is this transition to Original Penguin's success as a learning organization? Explain.

2. Do you think that Kolbe views knowledge among his employees as an important resource? Why or why not?

3. What steps might Original Penguin as a company take to ensure the satisfaction of its employees?

SOURCES: Company Web site, *http://www.originalpenguin.com*, accessed July 30, 2004; Carl Swanson, "A Senior Moment," in "Men's Fashions of the Times," *The New York Times*, spring 2004, p. 44; Mary Lisa Gavenas, "Brands on the Run," *DNR*, April 28, 2004, p. 17; Stephanie Thompson, "Perry Ellis Banks on Brand Resurrections," *Advertising Age*, March 15, 2004, p. 14.

---

ch2   BIZ FLIX VIDEO CASE

Backdraft

Two brothers follow in the footsteps of their late father, a legendary Chicago firefighter, and join the department. Stephen "Bull" McCaffrey (Kurt Russell) joins first and rises to the rank of lieutenant. Younger brother Brian (William Baldwin) joins later and becomes a member of Bull's Company 17. Sibling rivalry tarnishes their work relationships, but they continue to successfully fight Chicago fires. Add a plot element about a mysterious arsonist and you have the basis of an ordinary film. The film, however, rises above its otherwise formulaic plot thanks to great acting and amazing special effects. The intense, unprecedented special effects give the viewer an unparalleled experience of what it is like to fight a fire. Chicago firefighters applauded the realism of the fire scenes.[1]

This scene appears early in the film as part of "The First Day" sequence. Brian McCaffrey has graduated from the fire academy, and the fire department has assigned him to his brother's company. This scene shows him fighting his first real fire at a garment factory. The film continues with Company 17 fighting the fire and Brian receiving some harsh first-day lessons.

What to Watch for and Ask Yourself

1. What elements of the Chicago fire department culture does this scene show? Does the scene show any cultural artifacts or symbols? If it does, what are they?

2. Does the scene show any values that guide the firefighters' behavior?

3. What does Brian McCaffrey learn on his first day at work?

[1] J. Craddock, Ed. *VideoHound's Golden Movie Retriever*, (Farmington Hills, MI: The Gale Group, Inc.), 2000.

ch2 ENDNOTES

1. This questionnaire is from William Pfeiffer and John E. Jones, eds., "Supervisory Attitudes: The X–Y Scale," *The 1972 Annual Handbook for Group Facilitators* (New York: John Wiley & Sons, 1972), pp. 65–68. This material is used by permission of John Wiley & Sons, Inc. The X–Y scale was adapted from an instrument developed by Robert N. Ford of AT&T for in-house manager training.

2. Eric Abrahamson, "Management Fashion," *Academy of Management Review* 21, no. 1 (January 1996): 254–285. Also see "75 Years of Management Ideas and Practice," a supplement to the *Harvard Business Review* (September–October 1997), for a broad overview of historical trends in management thinking.

3. Daniel A. Wren, *The Evolution of Management Thought*, 4th ed. (New York: Wiley, 1994). Much of the discussion of historical forces comes from Arthur M. Schlesinger, *Political and Social History of the United States, 1829–1925* (New York: Macmillan, 1925); and Homer C. Hockett, *Political and Social History of the United States, 1492–1828* (New York: Macmillan, 1925).

4. Based on Stephanie Armour, "Generation Y: They've Arrived at Work with a New Attitude," *USA Today* (November 6, 2005): www.usatoday.com/money/workplace/2005-11-06-gen-y_x.htm; and Marnie E. Green, "Beware and Prepare: The Government Workforce of the Future," *Public Personnel Management* (Winter 2000): 435ff.

5. Aziz Hannifa, "India, China Growth Dominates World Bank Meet," *India Abroad* (New York edition), November 2, 2007.

6. Thomas Petzinger, Jr., "So Long Supply and Demand," *The Wall Street Journal*, January 1, 2000.

7. Study reported in Phred Dvorak, "Why Management Trends Quickly Fade Away (Theory and Practice column), *The Wall Street Journal*, June 26, 2006.

8. See Keith Leslie, Mark A. Loch, and William Schaninger, "Managing Your Organization by the Evidence,"

McKinsey Quarterly, Issue 3 (2006); Thomas H. Davenport, Laurence Prusak, and H. James Wilson, *What's the Big Idea? Creating and Capitalizing on the Best New Management Thinking* (Boston: Harvard Business School Press, 2003); Daniel James Rowley, "Resource Reviews," *Academy of Management Learning and Education* 2, no. 3 (2003): 313–321; Jane Whitney Gibson, Dana V. Tesone, and Charles W. Blackwell, "Management Fads: Here Yesterday, Gone Today?" *SAM Advanced Management Journal* (Autumn 2003): 12–17; David Collins, *Management Fads and Buzzwords: Critical-Practices Perspective*, (London, UK: Routledge, 2000); Timothy Clark, "Management Research on Fashion: A Review and Evaluation," *Human Relations* 54, no. 12 (2001): 1650–1661; Brad Jackson, *Management Gurus and Management Fashions* (London: Routledge, 2001); Patrick Thomas, *Fashions in Management Research: An Empirical Analysis* (Aldershot, UK: Ashgate, 1999).

9. Daniel A. Wren, "Management History: Issues and Ideas for Teaching and Research," *Journal of Management* 13 (1987): 339–350.

10. Business historian Alfred D. Chandler, Jr., quoted in Jerry Useem, "Entrepreneur of the Century," *Inc.* (20th Anniversary Issue, 1999): 159–174.

11. Useem, "Entrepreneur of the Century."

12. The following is based on Wren, *Evolution of Management Thought*, Chapters 4, 5; and Claude S. George, Jr., *The History of Management Thought* (Englewood Cliffs, NJ: Prentice-Hall, 1968), Chapter 4.

13. Cynthia Crossen, "Early Industry Expert Soon Realized a Staff Has Its Own Efficiency," *The Wall Street Journal*, November 6, 2006.

14. Alan Farnham, "The Man Who Changed Work Forever," *Fortune* (July 21, 1997): 114; Charles D. Wrege and Ann Marie Stoka, "Cooke Creates a Classic: The Story Behind F. W. Taylor's Principles of Scientific Management," *Academy of Management Review* (October 1978): 736–749; Robert Kanigel, *The*

One Best Way: Frederick Winslow Taylor and the Enigma of Efficiency (New York: Viking, 1997); and "The X and Y Factors: What Goes Around Comes Around," special section in "The New Organisation: A Survey of the Company," *The Economist* (January 21–27, 2006): 17–18.

15. Quoted in Ann Harrington, "The Big Ideas," *Fortune* (November 22, 1999): 152–154.

16. Wren, *Evolution of Management Thought*, 171; and George, *History of Management Thought*, 103–104.

17. Gary Hamel, "The Why, What, and How of Management Innovation," *Harvard Business Review* (February 2006): 72–84; Peter Coy, "Cog or Co-Worker?" *BusinessWeek* (August 20 & 27, 2007): 58–60.

18. Max Weber, *General Economic History*, trans. Frank H. Knight (London: Allen & Unwin, 1927); Max Weber, *The Protestant Ethic and the Spirit of Capitalism*, trans. Talcott Parsons (New York: Scribner, 1930); and Max Weber, *The Theory of Social and Economic Organizations*, ed. and trans. A. M. Henderson and Talcott Parsons (New York: Free Press, 1947).

19. Kelly Barron, "Logistics in Brown," *Forbes* (January 10, 2000): 78–83; Scott Kirsner, "Venture Vérité: United Parcel Service," *Wired* (September 1999): 83–96; "UPS," *The Atlanta Journal and Constitution*, April 26, 1992; and Kathy Goode, Betty Hahn, and Cindy Seibert, "United Parcel Service: The Brown Giant" (unpublished manuscript, Texas A&M University, 1981).

20. Henri Fayol, *Industrial and General Administration*, trans. J. A. Coubrough (Geneva: International Management Institute, 1930); Henri Fayol, *General and Industrial Management*, trans. Constance Storrs (London: Pitman and Sons, 1949); and W. J. Arnold et al., *BusinessWeek, Milestones in Management* (New York: McGraw-Hill, vol. I, 1965; vol. II, 1966).

21. Mary Parker Follett, *The New State: Group Organization: The Solution of Popular Government* (London: Longmans, Green, 1918); and Mary

Parker Follett, *Creative Experience* (London: Longmans, Green, 1924).

22. Henry C. Metcalf and Lyndall Urwick, eds., *Dynamic Administration: The Collected Papers of Mary Parker Follett* (New York: Harper & Row, 1940); Arnold, *Milestones in Management*.

23. Follett, *The New State*; Metcalf and Urwick, *Dynamic Administration* (London: Sir Isaac Pitman, 1941).

24. William B. Wolf, *How to Understand Management: An Introduction to Chester I. Barnard* (Los Angeles: Lucas Brothers, 1968); and David D. Van Fleet, "The Need-Hierarchy and Theories of Authority," *Human Relations* 9 (Spring 1982): 111–118.

25. Gregory M. Bounds, Gregory H. Dobbins, and Oscar S. Fowler, *Management: A Total Quality Perspective* (Cincinnati, OH: South-Western Publishing, 1995), pp. 52–53.

26. Curt Tausky, *Work Organizations: Major Theoretical Perspectives* (Itasca, IL: F. E. Peacock, 1978), p. 42.

27. Charles D. Wrege, "Solving Mayo's Mystery: The First Complete Account of the Origin of the Hawthorne Studies—The Forgotten Contributions of Charles E. Snow and Homer Hibarger," paper presented to the Management History Division of the Academy of Management (August 1976).

28. Ronald G. Greenwood, Alfred A. Bolton, and Regina A. Greenwood, "Hawthorne a Half Century Later: Relay Assembly Participants Remember," *Journal of Management* 9 (Fall/Winter 1983): 217–231.

29. F. J. Roethlisberger, W. J. Dickson, and H. A. Wright, *Management and the Worker* (Cambridge, MA: Harvard University Press, 1939).

30. H. M. Parson, "What Happened at Hawthorne?" *Science* 183 (1974): 922–932; John G. Adair, "The Hawthorne Effect: A Reconsideration of the Methodological Artifact," *Journal of Applied Psychology* 69, no. 2 (1984): 334–345; and Gordon Diaper, "The Hawthorne Effect: A Fresh Examination," *Educational Studies* 16, no. 3 (1990): 261–268.

31. R. G. Greenwood, A. A. Bolton, and R. A. Greenwood, "Hawthorne a Half Century Later," pp. 219–221.

32. F. J. Roethlisberger and W. J. Dickson, *Management and the Worker*.

33. Ramon J. Aldag and Timothy M. Stearns, *Management*, 2d ed. (Cincinnati, OH: South-Western Publishing, 1991), pp. 47–48.

34. Tausky, *Work Organizations: Major Theoretical Perspectives*, p. 55.

35. Douglas McGregor, *The Human Side of Enterprise* (New York: McGraw-Hill, 1960), pp. 16–18.

36. Jack Ewing, "No-Cubicle Culture," *BusinessWeek* (August 20 & 27, 2006): 60.

37. Wendell L. French and Cecil H. Bell Jr., "A History of Organizational Development," in Wendell L. French, Cecil H. Bell Jr., and Robert A. Zawacki, *Organization Development and Transformation: Managing Effective Change* (Burr Ridge, IL: Irwin McGraw-Hill, 2000), pp. 20–42.

38. Mansel G. Blackford and K. Austin Kerr, *Business Enterprise in American History* (Boston: Houghton Mifflin, 1986), Chapters 10, 11; and Alex Groner and the editors of *American Heritage* and *BusinessWeek*, *The American Heritage History of American Business and Industry* (New York: American Heritage Publishing, 1972), Chapter 9.

39. Geoffrey Colvin, "How Alfred P. Sloan, Michael Porter, and Peter Drucker Taught Us All the Art of Management," *Fortune* (March 21, 2005): 83–86.

40. "90 Years in Business," *The Conference Board Review* (September–October 2006): 30–39.

41. Wren, *The Evolution of Management Thought*.

42. Joyce Thompson Heames and Michael Harvey, "The Evolution of the Concept of the 'Executive' from the 20th Century Manager to the 21st Century Global Leader," *Journal of Leadership and Organizational Studies* 13, no. 2 (2006): 29–41.

43. Larry M. Austin and James R. Burns, *Management Science* (New York: Macmillan, 1985).

44. Ludwig von Bertalanffy, Carl G. Hempel, Robert E. Bass, and Hans Jonas, "General Systems Theory: A New Approach to Unity of Science," *Human Biology* 23 (December 1951): 302–361; and Kenneth E. Boulding, "General Systems Theory—The Skeleton of Science," *Management Science* 2 (April 1956): 197–208.

45. Fremont E. Kast and James E. Rosenzweig, "General Systems Theory: Applications for Organization and Management," *Academy of Management Journal* (December 1972): 447–465.

46. "Teaming with Bright Ideas," special section in "The New Organisation: A Survey of the Company," *The Economist* (January 21–27, 2006): 4–16.

47. The discussion of systemic thinking is based on Gary Bartlett, "Systemic Thinking: A Simple Technique for Gaining Systemic Focus," paper presented at the International Conference on Thinking (2001), http://www.probsolv.com (accessed February 5, 2008).

48. Fred Luthans, "The Contingency Theory of Management: A Path Out of the Jungle," *Business Horizons* 16 (June 1973): 62–72; and Fremont E. Kast and James E. Rosenzweig, *Contingency Views of Organization and Management* (Chicago: Science Research Associates, 1973).

49. Samuel Greengard, "25 Visionaries Who Shaped Today's Workplace," *Workforce* (January 1997): 50–59; and Harrington, "The Big Ideas."

50. Mauro F. Guillen, "The Age of Eclecticism: Current Organizational Trends and the Evolution of Managerial Models," *Sloan Management Review* (Fall 1994): 75–86.

51. Jeremy Main, "How to Steal the Best Ideas Around," *Fortune* (October 19, 1992): 102–106.

52. Darrell Rigby and Barbara Bilodeau, "Bain's Global 2007 Management Tools and Trends Survey," *Strategy & Leadership* 35, no. 5 (2007): 9–16.

53. Thomas H. Davenport and Laurence Prusak, with Jim Wilson, *What's the Big Idea? Creating and Capitalizing on the Best Management Thinking* (Boston, MA: Harvard Business School Press, 2003). Also see Theodore Kinni, "Have We Run Out of Big Ideas?" *Across the Board* (March–April 2003): 16–21, and Joyce Thompson Heames and Michael Harvey, "The Evolution of the Concept of the Executive from the 20th Century Manager to the 21st Century Global Leader," *Journal of Leadership and Organizational Studies* 13, no. 2 (2006): 29–41.

54. Ronald A. Heifetz and Donald L. Laurie, "The Leader as Teacher: Creating the Learning Organization," *Ivey Business Journal* (January–February 2003): 1–9.

55. Peter Senge, *The Fifth Discipline: The Art and Practice of Learning*

Organizations (New York: Doubleday/Currency, 1990).

56. Definition based on Steven A. Melnyk and David R. Denzler, *Operations Management: A Value Driven Approach* (Burr Ridge, IL: Richard D. Irwin, 1996): 613.

57. Global Supply Chain Games project, http://www.gscg.org (accessed July 16, 2008).

58. Eric Bellman and Cecilie Rohwedder, "Western Grocer Modernizes Passage to India's Markets," *The Wall Street Journal*, November 28, 2007.

59. "How Marriott Never Forgets a Guest," *BusinessWeek* (February 12, 2000): 74.

60. Andy Reinhardt, "From Gearhead to Grand High Pooh-Bah," *Business-Week* (August 28, 2000): 129–130.

1
Introduction

General Motors
Part One: Introduction to Management
General Motors Celebrates 100 Years of Change and Innovation

Of the many important dates in automotive history, September 16, 2008, marks both the end of an era and a bold new beginning. On that historic Tuesday, eager crowds packed the Renaissance Center in Detroit, Michigan, to celebrate a once-in-a-lifetime event: the 100-year anniversary of General Motors (GM).

Following months of centennial-themed pageantry and parades, the American automaker's towering headquarters had taken on a museumlike aura. On the ground floor sat immaculate showroom classics from the company's fabled past: an orange 1963 Corvette Sting Ray, a pistachio 1952 Saab, a shiny black 1955 Chevrolet Bel Air coupe, an apple-green 1973 Opel GT. Auto enthusiasts, reporters, and GM employees alike gazed nostalgically on the rows of vintage cars as the clock turned back to a glorious, bygone era in America's history.

Despite the irresistible charm projected by these solid-steel visitors from GM's legendary past, it was a concept vehicle from the company's future that had the crowd's engines revving on the main floor. For years, management at GM had talked of introducing alternative-energy models that excite consumers and protect the environment. Now, at this momentous celebration, the talk was over, and GM pulled back the curtain on what it says is the future of the auto industry: the Chevy Volt.

With its aerodynamic design and 40 miles of emissions-free driving on a single electric charge, GM's first-ever plug-in electric vehicle is a far cry from the gas-guzzling trucks and SUVs that delivered the company's greatest financial successes in recent decades. Indeed, the Volt represents a sea change for the world's largest auto manufacturer. Unlike hybrids that use electric power to improve the mileage of their gasoline engines, the Volt uses a gasoline generator to assist the range of its battery-powered electric drive unit. According to GM, driving the Volt will save owners $1,500 annually in energy costs. It's no wonder company officials cite the concept as proof of GM's intention to lead the reinvention of the automobile.

But the arrival of the Volt comes at a pivotal moment in GM's history. Ripple effects from an international mortgage crisis in 2008 triggered the industry's worst sales slump since 9/11. Soaring energy prices in the same period forced management to abandon Hummer and other super-sized models that once represented hope for a financial recovery. But the list goes on. GM also faces slumping shares, stupefying quarterly losses, ballooning debt, steep competition from Toyota, precarious dealings with labor unions, and almost insurmountable fuel-efficiency regulations from the federal government.

If history is any indication, GM will tackle these challenges head on, displaying the same innovative spirit that gave the business its first 100 years of manufacturing excellence. Since its founding in 1908, the automaker has repeatedly demonstrated its strong capacity for innovation and change. From speedometers (1901 Oldsmobile) and electric headlights (1909 Cadillac) to automatic transmissions (1940 Oldsmobile) and mass-produced V-8 engines (1914 Cadillac), GM teams have given the world hundreds of innovative firsts.

Whether it's big-idea concepts that reshape the future or smaller innovations that improve existing products, CEO Rick Wagoner and his management teams are developing the strategies that will guide the company successfully for the next 100 years. In his speech introducing the Volt's historic unveiling, Wagoner underscored the remarkable times in which we are living. "GM's centennial comes at an incredible time in our industry. The entire world is watching, hoping for a breakthrough in personal transportation that will address the very real energy and environmental challenges facing the globe."

The stakes have never been higher. If GM is to avoid becoming a museum of America's great automobile manufacturing past, management must deliver breakthrough ideas that once again stoke consumers' passions. With the Chevy Volt in production and a large cache of renowned brands including Cadillac, Chevrolet, Pontiac, and Saturn, there is every reason to believe GM will succeed.

Questions

1. Which management functions and skills enabled GM's leaders to create a bold vision for reinventing the automobile around green technology?

2. Identify social, political, and economic forces that affect the auto industry and the practice of management at GM.

3. Which historical management perspective fueled GM's transformation into a manufacturing powerhouse in the early twentieth century?

SOURCES: Robert Snell, "GM Unveils Its Chevy Volt at Centennial Celebration," *The Detroit News*, September 16, 2008, http://www .detnews.com (accessed October 8, 2008); Anita Lienert, "Aerodynamic Chevrolet Volt Electrifies GM's 100th-Anniversary Celebration," *Inside Line* (September 16, 2008), http://www.edmunds.com/insideline (accessed October 10, 2008); David Phillips, "Innovations Propel Success," *The Detroit News*, September 16, 2008, http://www.detnews.com (accessed October 7, 2008); "GM Starts Its Next 100 Years with New Approach," *The Bay City Times*, September 28, 2008, http://blog.mlive .com/bcopinion/2008/09/gm_starts_its_next_100_years_w.html (accessed October 11, 2008); David Kiley, "J.D. Power: Retail Sales To Be 2 Million Lower in 2008," *BusinessWeek Online*, October 8, 2008, http://www.businessweek.com/autos/autobeat/archives/2008/10/ jd_power_retail.html (accessed October 11, 2008).

© GETTY IMAGES/DIGITAL VISION

pt2   chapter3

Learning Outcomes

After studying this chapter, you should be able to:

1. Describe the general and task environments and the dimensions of each.

2. Explain the strategies managers use to help organizations adapt to an uncertain or turbulent environment.

3. Define corporate culture and give organizational examples.

4. Explain organizational symbols, stories, heroes, slogans, and ceremonies and their relationships to corporate culture.

5. Describe how corporate culture relates to the environment.

6. Define a cultural leader and explain the tools a cultural leader uses to create a high-performance culture.

1 Introduction

2 Environment

3 Planning

4 Organizing

5 Controlling

6 Leading

The Environment and Corporate Culture

ARE YOU FIT FOR MANAGERIAL UNCERTAINTY?[1]

Do you approach uncertainty with an open mind? Think back to how you thought or behaved during a time of uncertainty when you were in a formal or informal leadership position. Please answer whether each of the following items was Mostly True or Mostly False in that circumstance.

	Mostly True	Mostly False
1. Enjoyed hearing about new ideas even when working toward a deadline.		
2. Welcomed unusual viewpoints of others even if we were working under pressure.		
3. Made it a point to attend industry trade shows and company events.		
4. Specifically encouraged others to express opposing ideas and arguments.		
5. Asked "dumb" questions.		
6. Always offered comments on the meaning of data or issues.		
7. Expressed a controversial opinion to bosses and peers.		
8. Suggested ways of improving my and others' ways of doing things.		

SCORING AND INTERPRETATION: Give yourself one point for each item you marked as Mostly True. If you scored less than 5 you might want to start your career as a manager in a stable rather than unstable environment. A score of 5 or above suggests a higher level of mindfulness and a better fit for a new manager in an organization with an uncertain environment.

In an organization in a highly uncertain environment everything seems to be changing. In that case, an important quality for a new manager is "mindfulness," which includes the qualities of being open-minded and an independent thinker. In a stable environment, a manager with a closed mind may perform okay because much work can be done in the same old way. In an uncertain environment, even a new manager needs to facilitate new thinking, new ideas, and new ways of working. A high score on the preceding items suggests higher mindfulness and a better fit with an uncertain environment.

The environments in which businesses operate are increasingly dynamic, requiring managers to be ready to react and respond to even subtle environmental shifts. Mattel was shaken when it learned that a Chinese subcontractor used lead paint while manufacturing its toys. Because of the potential health hazard, Mattel recalled nearly 850,000 of its most popular toys—months before its holiday selling season. Not only did the recall frighten consumers, but it sparked a global debate about the safety of Chinese-made products. Mattel managers moved swiftly to reassure nervous parents of its high safety standards in its Chinese factories. In addition, CEO Robert Eckert explained the recall to consumers on the company's Web site and announced steps Mattel was taking to prevent further recalls.[2]

Mattel's prompt response, teamed with its long-standing history of successful manufacturing in China, led many independent analysts and watchdog groups to say that it may be the best role model for how to operate prudently in China. "Mattel realized very early that they were always going to be in the crosshairs of sensitivities about child labor and product safety, and they knew they had to play it straight. Mattel was in China before China was cool, and they learned to do business there in a good way," says M. Eric Johnson, a Dartmouth management professor.[3]

Environmental surprises, like the one Mattel faced in China, leave some managers unable to adapt their companies to new competition, shifting consumer interests, or new technologies. The study of management traditionally focused on factors within the organization—a closed-systems view—such as leading, motivating, and controlling employees. The classical, behavioral, and management science schools described in Chapter 2 looked at internal aspects of organizations over which managers have direct control. These views are accurate but incomplete. To be effective, managers must monitor and respond to the environment—an open-systems view. The events that have the greatest impact on an organization typically originate in the external environment. In addition, globalization and worldwide societal turbulence affect companies in new ways, making the international environment of growing concern to managers everywhere.

This chapter explores in detail components of the external environment and how they affect the organization. The chapter also examines a major part of the organization's internal environment—corporate culture. Corporate culture is shaped by the external environment and is an important part of the context within which managers do their jobs.

THE EXTERNAL ENVIRONMENT

The tremendous and far-reaching changes occurring in today's world can be understood by defining and examinng components of the external environment. The external **organizational environment** includes all elements existing outside the boundary of the organization that have the potential to affect the organization.[4] The environment includes competitors, resources, technology, and economic conditions that influence the organization. It does not include those events so far removed from the organization that their impact is not perceived.

The organization's external environment can be further conceptualized as having two layers: general and task environments, as illustrated in Exhibit 3.1.[5] The **general environment** is the outer layer that is widely dispersed and affects organizations

organizational environment
All elements existing outside the organization's boundaries that have the potential to affect the organization.

general environment The layer of the external environment that affects the organization indirectly.

EXHIBIT | **3.1**

Location of the Organization's General, Task, and Internal Environments

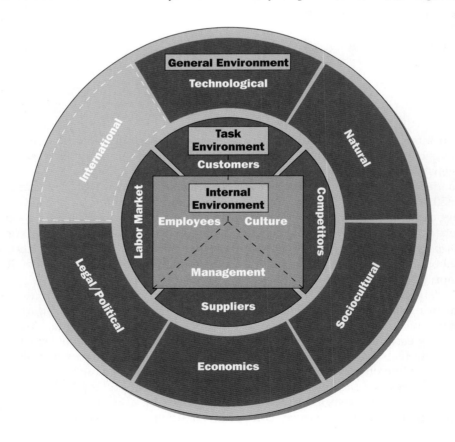

indirectly. It includes social, economic, legal/political, international, natural, and technological factors that influence all organizations about equally. Increases in the inflation rate or the percentage of dual-career couples in the workforce are part of the organization's general environment. These events do not directly change day-to-day operations, but they do affect all organizations eventually. The **task environment** is closer to the organization and includes the sectors that conduct day-to-day transactions with the organization and directly influence its basic operations and performance. It is generally considered to include competitors, suppliers, customers, and the labor market.

The organization also has an **internal environment**, which includes the elements within the organization's boundaries. The internal environment is composed of current employees, management, and especially corporate culture, which defines employee behavior in the internal environment and how well the organization will adapt to the external environment.

Exhibit 3.1 illustrates the relationship among the general, task, and internal environments. As an open system, the organization draws resources from the external environment and releases goods and services back to it. We will now discuss the two layers of the external environment in more detail. Then we will discuss corporate culture, the key element in the internal environment. Other aspects of the internal environment, such as structure and technology, will be covered in later chapters of this book.

task environment The layer of the external environment that directly influences the organization's operations and performance.

internal environment The environment that includes the elements within the organization's boundaries.

international dimension Portion of the external environment that represents events originating in foreign countries as well as opportunities for U.S. companies in other countries.

General Environment

The general environment represents the outer layer of the environment. These dimensions influence the organization over time but often are not involved in day-to-day transactions with it. The dimensions of the general environment include international, technological, sociocultural, economic, legal-political, and natural.

International The **international dimension** of the external environment represents events originating in foreign countries as well as opportunities for U.S. companies in other countries. Note in Exhibit 3.1 that the international dimension represents a context that influences all other aspects of the external environment. The international environment provides new competitors, customers, and suppliers and shapes social, technological, and economic trends as well.

Today, every company has to compete on a global basis. High-quality, low-priced automobiles from Japan and Korea have permanently changed the American automobile industry. In cell phones and handhelds, U.S.-based companies face stiff competition from Korea's Samsung, Finland's Nokia, and Taiwan's High Tech Computer Corporation (HTC). For many U.S. companies, such as Google, domestic markets have become saturated, and the only potential for growth lies overseas. Google's mission is to reach even the most far-flung corners of the globe by providing search results in more than 35 languages and a translation feature to users regardless of their native tongue.[6]

The most dramatic change in the international environment in recent years is the shift of economic power to China and India. Together, these countries have the population, brainpower, and dynamism to transform the

© BEN MARGOT/ASSOCIATED PRESS

Concept Connection "The big idea behind fair trade is that you can actually make globalization work for the poor," says Paul Rice, founder and CEO of TransFair USA. TransFair is the only U.S. organization authorized to grant the Fair Trade logo to products made from a growing list of crops, such as coffee, cocoa, and sugar, for which farmers in developing countries have been paid a fair price. The Oakland, California-based nonprofit is influencing the **international dimension** of today's business environment by helping increase the sales of fair trade products around the world. Rice says adhering to TransFair standards is just good business as the global environment grows increasingly important.

global economy of the twenty-first century. If things continue on the current track, some analysts predict that India will overtake Germany as the world's third-largest economy within three decades, and China will overtake the United States as number one by midcentury. In China, per capita income has tripled in a generation, and leaders are building the infrastructure for decades of expansion, as reflected in the country's hunger for raw materials. In 2005, China represented roughly 47 percent of the global cement consumption, 30 percent of coal, and 26 percent of crude steel. No one can predict the future, but it is clear that however things in India and China shake out, U.S. and other western firms have no choice but to pay attention.

The global environment represents a complex, ever-changing, and uneven playing field compared with the domestic environment. Managers who are used to thinking only about the domestic environment must learn new rules to remain competitive. When operating globally, managers have to consider legal, political, sociocultural, and economic factors not only in their home countries but in other countries as well. Global managers working in China, for example, recognize that their competitive success begins with their ability to build personal relationships and emotional bonds with their Chinese contacts. The Manager's Shoptalk offer tips for creating successful business relationships in China.

technological dimension
The dimension of the general environment that includes scientific and technological advancements in the industry and society at large.

sociocultural dimension
The dimension of the general environment representing the demographic characteristics, norms, customs, and values of the population within which the organization operates.

Technological The **technological dimension** includes scientific and technological advancements in a specific industry as well as in society at large. In recent years, this dimension created massive changes for organizations in all industries. Twenty years ago, many organizations didn't even use desktop computers. Today, computer networks, Internet access, handheld devices, videoconferencing capabilities, cell phones, and laptops are the minimum tools for doing business. A new generation of handhelds allows users to check their corporate e-mail, daily calendars, business contacts, and even customer orders from any location with a wireless network. Cell phones can now switch seamlessly between cellular networks and corporate WiFi connections. Some companies hand out wireless key fobs with continually updated security codes that enable employees to log onto their corporate networks and securely view data or write e-mails from any PC with a broadband connection.[7]

Other technological advances will affect organizations and managers. The decoding of the human genome could lead to revolutionary medical advances. Cloning technology and stem cell research are raising both scientific and ethical concerns. Because of microchip innovations, Motorola can now make the MotoFone F3 affordable to the world's poor, opening up vast economic opportunities for entrepreneurs in developing countries.[8] Nanotechnology, which refers to manipulating matter at its tiniest scale, is moving from the research lab to the marketplace. Some 1,200 nanotechnology start-ups have emerged around the world, and smart managers at established organizations such as 3M, Dow Chemical, Samsung, NASA, Intel, Johnson & Johnson, and IBM are investing research dollars in this technological breakthrough.[9]

© ELIPHOTO.COM/POWDERMONARCH LLC

Concept Connection Want to get the best out of Generation Y employees? Why not let your current Gen Y workers show you how? That's what Monarch Mountain, a ski and snowboard area near Salida, Colorado, does. As millions of Gen Y employees flood the job market, companies are finding ways to adapt to this shift in the **sociocultural dimension** of the environment. At Monarch, young employees, not managers, talk with prospective hires to answer questions and address their concerns from the perspective of the job seeker. Through the "First Responder" program, the employee provides a realistic picture of what it's like to work at Monarch and often becomes a mentor if the candidate is hired.

Sociocultural The **sociocultural dimension** of the general environment represents the demographic characteristics as well as the norms, customs, and values of the general population. Important sociocultural characteristics are geographical distribution and population density, age, and education levels. Today's demographic profiles are the foundation of tomorrow's workforce and consumers. Forecasters see increased globalization of both consumer markets

Manager's Shoptalk

Creating *Guanxi* in China

With its low labor costs and huge potential market, China is luring thousands of U.S. companies in search of growth opportunities. Yet University of New Haven's Usha C. V. Haley recently found that only one-third of multinationals doing business in China have actually turned a profit. One reason Western businesses fall short of expectations, experts agree, is that they fail to grasp the centuries-old concept of *guanxi* that lies at the heart of Chinese culture.

At its simplest level, guanxi is a supportive, mutually beneficial connection between two people. Eventually, those personal relationships are linked together into a network, and it is through these networks that business gets done. Anyone considering doing business in China should keep in mind the following basic rules:

- *Business is always personal*. It is impossible to translate "don't take it so personally—it's only business" into Chinese. Western managers tend to believe that if they conclude a successful transaction, a good business relationship will follow. The development of a personal relationship is an added bonus, but not really necessary when it comes to getting things done. In the Chinese business world, however, a personal relationship must be in place before managers even consider entering a business transaction. Western managers doing business in China should cultivate personal relationships—both during and outside of business hours. Accept any and all social invitations—for drinks, a meal, or even a potentially embarrassing visit to a karaoke bar.

- *Don't skip the small talk.* Getting right down to business and bypassing the small talk during a meeting might feel like an efficient use of time to an American manager. To the Chinese, however, this approach neglects the all-important work of forging an emotional bond. Be aware that the real purpose of your initial meetings with potential business partners is to begin building a relationship, so keep your patience if the deal you are planning to discuss never even comes up.

- *Remember that relationships are not short-term.* The work of establishing and nurturing guanxi relationships in China is never done. Western managers must put aside their usual focus on short-term results and recognize that it takes a long time for foreigners to be accepted into a guanxi network. Often, foreign companies must prove their trustworthiness and reliability over time. For example, firms that weathered the political instability that culminated in the 1989 student protests in Tiananmen Square found it much easier to do business afterwards.

- *Make contact frequently.* Some experts recommend hiring ethnic Chinese staff members and then letting them do the heavy lifting of relationship building. Others emphasize that Westerners themselves should put plenty of time and energy into forging links with Chinese contacts; those efforts will pay off because the contacts can smooth the way by tapping into their own guanxi networks. Whatever the strategy, contact should be frequent and personal. In addition, be sure to keep careful track of the contacts you make. In China, any and all relationships are bound to be important at some point in time.

SOURCES: Michelle Dammon Loyalka, "Doing Business in China," *BusinessWeek Online* (January 6, 2006), www.businessweek.com/smallbiz/; Los Angeles Chinese Learning Center, "Chinese Business Culture," http://chinese-school.netfirms.com/guanxi.html; and Beijing British Embassy, "Golden Hints for Doing Business in China," http://chinese-school.netfirms.com/goldenhints.html.

and the labor supply, with increasing diversity both within organizations and consumer markets.[10] Consider the following key demographic trends in the United States:

1. The United States is experiencing the largest influx of immigrants in more than a century. The Hispanic population is expected to grow to 102.6 million, an increase of 188 percent since 2000, and it will make up about a quarter of the U.S. population by 2050. In this same time period, non-Hispanic whites will make up only about 50 percent of the population, down from 74 percent in 1995 and 69 percent in 2004.[11]

2. Members of Generation Y are flooding the workplace. To replace the 64 million skilled workers who will start retiring by the end of this decade, companies will be poised to attract Gen Y workers if they offer competitive salaries, flat hierarchies, support networks, work-life balance, challenging work, and feedback on performance.[12]
3. The fastest-growing type of living arrangement is single-father households, which rose 62 percent in 10 years, even though two-parent and single-mother households are still much more numerous.[13]

Demographic trends affect organizations in other countries just as powerfully. Japan, Italy, and Germany are all faced with an aging workforce and customer base due to years of declining birth rates. In both Italy and Japan, the proportion of people over the age of 65 reached 20 percent in 2006.[14]

Economic The **economic dimension** represents the general economic health of the country or region in which the organization operates. Consumer purchasing power, the unemployment rate, and interest rates are part of an organization's economic environment. Because organizations today are operating in a global environment, the economic dimension has become exceedingly complex and creates enormous uncertainty for managers. The economies of countries are more closely tied together now. For example, the economic recession and the decline of consumer confidence in the United States in the early 2000s affected economies and organizations around the world. Similarly, economic problems in Asia and Europe had a tremendous impact on companies and the stock market in the United States.

One significant recent trend in the economic environment is the frequency of mergers and acquisitions. Citibank and Travelers merged to form Citigroup, IBM purchased Pricewaterhouse Coopers Consulting, and Cingular acquired AT&T Wireless. In the toy industry, the three largest toy makers—Hasbro, Mattel, and Tyco—gobbled up at least a dozen smaller competitors within a few years. At the same time, however, a tremendous vitality is evident in the small business sector of the economy. Entrepreneurial start-ups are a significant aspect of today's U.S. economy and will be discussed in Appendix A.

Legal-Political The **legal-political dimension** includes government regulations at the local, state, and federal levels, as well as political activities designed to influence company behavior. The U.S. political system encourages capitalism, and the government tries not to overregulate business. However, government laws do specify rules of the game. The federal government influences organizations through the Occupational Safety and Health Administration (OSHA), Environmental Protection Agency (EPA), fair trade practices, libel statutes allowing lawsuits against business, consumer protection legislation, product safety requirements, import and export restrictions, and information and labeling requirements. Many organizations also have to contend with government and legal issues in other countries. The European Union (EU) adopted environmental and consumer protection rules that are costing American companies hundreds of millions of dollars a year. Companies such as Hewlett-Packard, Ford Motor Company, and General Electric have to pick up the bill for recycling the products they sell in the EU, for example.[15]

Managers must also recognize a variety of **pressure groups** that work within the legal-political framework to influence companies to behave in socially responsible ways. Wake Up Wal-Mart, a union-backed campaign group, drums up public awareness of Wal-Mart's business practices to force the retailer to improve worker's wages and health care benefits. The group's campaign director hopes smaller companies will then follow suit.[16] Other activists have boldly petitioned Home Depot, which introduced the Eco Option brand for its environmentally friendly products, to stop advertising on Fox News, whose hosts and commentators dismiss global warming as ludicrous.[17]

economic dimension The dimension of the general environment representing the overall economic health of the country or region in which the organization operates.

legal-political dimension The dimension of the general environment that includes federal, state, and local government regulations and political activities designed to influence company behavior.

pressure group An interest group that works within the legal-political framework to influence companies to behave in socially responsible ways.

Natural In response to pressure from environmental advocates, organizations have become increasingly sensitive to the earth's diminishing natural resources and the environmental impact of their products. As a result, the natural dimension of the external environment is growing in importance. The **natural dimension** includes all elements that occur naturally on earth, including plants, animals, rocks, and natural resources such as air, water, and climate.

The natural dimension is different from other sectors of the general environment because it has no voice of its own. Influence on managers to meet needs in the natural environment may come from other sectors, such as government regulation, consumer concerns, bad press in the media, competitors' actions, or even employees.[18] For example, environmental groups advocate various action and policy goals that include reduction and clean up of man-made pollution, development of renewable energy resources, and sustainable use of scarce resources such as water, land, and air. More recently, there has been a strong concern about climate change such as global warming caused by greenhouse gases, most notably carbon dioxide.

Concern about the environment has prompted companies to take these actions:

- *Eliminating nonbiodegradable plastic bags from the environment.* Whole Foods will stop offering disposable, plastic grocery bags in all 270 stores, replacing them with recyclable bags. This change means roughly 100 million plastic bags will be kept out of the environment in the first eight months of the new program.[19]

- *Improving efficiency of plants and factories.* Nissan's Sunderland (UK) factory will use eight wind turbines to generate 6 percent of the plant's energy requirement, cutting carbon dioxide emissions by 4,000 tons per year. Toyota recycles 100,000 tons of wastewater a year in its reverse osmosis facility in its Burnaston (UK) plant.[20]

- *Investing in cleaner technologies.* GE, which once polluted the Hudson River with polychlorinated biphenyls (PCBs) as it manufactured transformers, now promises that it will invest $1.5 billion annually in researching cleaner forms of technology by 2010, up from $700 million in 2004.[21]

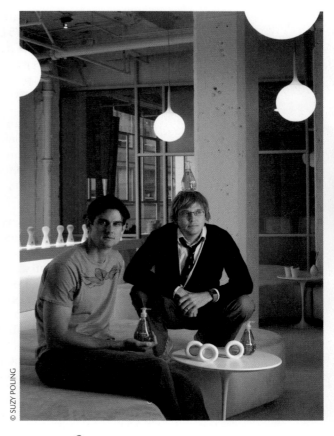

© SUZY POLING

Concept Connection High-school buddies Eric Ryan (left) and Adam Lowry (right) make environmentally friendly products look good. Their company, Method, produces nontoxic cleaning products with a concern for the **natural environment** and packages them in designer-looking bottles. Lowry, a chemical engineer, and Ryan, with an advertising background, founded Method in 2000 and sales grew to nearly $100 million in 2007.

Task Environment

As described earlier, the task environment includes those sectors that have a direct working relationship with the organization, among them customers, competitors, suppliers, and the labor market.

Customers Those people and organizations in the environment that acquire goods or services from the organization are **customers.** As recipients of the organization's output, customers are important because they determine the organization's success. Patients are the customers of hospitals, students the customers of schools, and travelers the customers of airlines. Many companies are searching for ways to reach the coveted teen and youth market by tying marketing messages into online social

natural dimension The dimension of the general environment that includes all elements that occur naturally on earth, including plants, animals, rocks, and natural resources such as air, water, and climate.

customers People and organizations in the environment that acquire goods or services from the organization.

networks such as MySpace.com and Facebook.com. With high school and college students representing a $375 billion consumer spending market, it's serious business for managers at companies such as Target, Apple, Coca-Cola, and Disney. Apple sponsors an Apple-lovers group on Facebook.com, giving away iPod Shuffles in weekly contests. Target has sponsored a group on MySpace.com that features a 15-year-old professional snowboarder wearing a Target logo on his helmet.[22]

Customers today have greater power because of the Internet, which presents threats as well as opportunities for managers. Today's customers can directly affect the organization's reputation and sales, for example, through gripe sites such as untied. com, where United Airlines employees and disgruntled fliers rail against the air carrier. "In this new information environment," says Kyle Shannon, CEO of e-commerce consultancy Agency.com, "you've got to assume everyone knows everything."[23]

Competitors   Specific competitive issues characterize each industry. Other organizations in the same industry or type of business that provide goods or services to the same set of customers are referred to as **competitors**. The recording industry differs from the steel industry and the pharmaceutical industry.

Competitive wars are being waged worldwide in all industries. Market leader MySpace keeps a close eye on Facebook's growing popularity. Both are battling it out for market leadership and advertising market share.[24] Netflix and Blockbuster use innovative pricing and distribution to win the loyalty of online movie customers. Internet jeweler Blue Nile clashes with Tiffany's, Zale's, and Kay's in a contest for leadership in the diamond ring market. Using its low overhead and strong purchasing power, Blue Nile sells diamond rings for 35 percent below most bricks-and-mortar stores.[25]

Suppliers   **Suppliers** provide the raw materials the organization uses to produce its output. A steel mill requires iron ore, machines, and financial resources. A small, private university may use hundreds of suppliers for paper, pencils, cafeteria food, computers, trucks, fuel, electricity, and textbooks. Companies from toolmakers to construction firms and auto manufacturers were hurt recently by an unanticipated jump in the price of steel from suppliers. Just as they were starting to see an upturn in their business, the cost of raw materials jumped 30 percent in a two-month period.[26] Consider also that China now produces more than 85 percent of the Vitamin C used by companies in the United States. An agreement among China's four largest producers led to an increase in the price of Vitamin C from $3 a kilogram to as high as $9 a kilogram.[27]

Many companies are using fewer suppliers and trying to build good relationships with them so that they will receive high-quality parts and materials at lower prices. The relationship between manufacturers and suppliers has traditionally been an adversarial one, but managers are finding that cooperation is the key to saving money, maintaining quality, and speeding products to market.

competitors Other organizations in the same industry or type of business that provide goods or services to the same set of customers.

suppliers People and organizations that provide the raw materials the organization uses to produce its output.

labor market The people available for hire by the organization.

TakeaMoment | As a new manager, you can get a leg up by paying attention to the external environment and international events. Stay in tune with what's going on in the general environment, including social, economic, technological, natural, and political trends. Pay particular attention to the task environment, including your customers, competitors, and suppliers. Be sure to connect the dots among the things you see.

Labor Market   The **labor market** represents people in the environment who can be hired to work for the organization. Every organization needs a supply of trained, qualified personnel. Unions, employee associations, and the availability of certain classes of employees can influence the organization's labor market. Labor market forces affecting organizations right now include: (1) the growing need for computer-literate knowledge workers; (2) the necessity for continuous investment in human resources through recruitment, education, and training to meet the competitive demands of the borderless world; and (3) the effects of international trading blocs, automation, outsourcing, and shifting facility locations on labor dislocations, creating unused labor pools in some areas and labor shortages in others.

Changes in these various sectors of the general and task environments can create tremendous challenges, especially for organizations operating in complex, rapidly changing industries. Nortel Networks, a Canadian company with multiple U.S. offices, is an example of an organization operating in a highly complex environment.

Nortel Networks

Innovative Way

Nortel Networks is a global company that connects people to the information they need through advanced communication technologies. With customers in more than 150 countries, Nortel designs and installs new networks and upgrades and supports and manages existing systems.[28] Nortel's complex external environment, illustrated in Exhibit 3.2, directly influences its operations and performance. The Canadian-based company began in 1895 as a manufacturer of telephones and has reinvented itself many times to keep up with changes in the environment. In the late 1990s, the company transformed itself into a major player in wireless technology and equipment for connecting businesses and individuals to the Internet. In 1997, the company was about to be run over by rivals such as Cisco Systems that were focused on Internet gear. Then-CEO John Roth knew he needed to do something bold to respond to changes in the technological environment. A name change to Nortel Networks symbolized and reinforced the company's new goal of providing unified network solutions to customers worldwide.

Today, Nortel's purpose is clear—to create a high-performance twenty-first-century communications company leveraging innovative technology that simplifies the complicated, hyperconnected world.[29] To achieve this goal, Nortel adapts and responds to the uncertainty of the external environment. One response to the competitive environment was to spend billions to acquire data and voice networking companies, including Bay Networks (which makes Internet and data equipment), Cambrian Systems (a hot maker of optical technology), Periphonics (maker of voice-response systems), and Clarify (customer relationship management software). These companies brought Nortel top-notch technology, helping the company snatch customers away from rivals Cisco and Lucent Technologies. In addition, even during rough economic times, Nortel kept spending nearly 20 percent of its revenues on research and development to keep pace with changing technology.

Internationally, Nortel has made impressive inroads in Taiwan, China, Brazil, Mexico, Colombia, Japan, and Sweden, among other countries. China's Ministry of Railways selected mobile communications railway technologies from Nortel to provide a secure, wireless network for trains traveling up to 350 km/hr.[30] It also won customers by recognizing the continuing need for traditional equipment and offering hybrid gear that combines old telephone technology with new Internet features, allowing companies to transition from the old to the new. Bold new technologies for Nortel include 4G broadband wireless, Carrier Ethernet, optical, next-generation services and applications, and secure networking.[31] Nortel is considered a leader in wireless gear and won contracts from Verizon Communications and Orange SA, a unit of France Telecom, to supply equipment that sends phone calls as packets of digital data like that used over the Internet. Nortel also capitalizes on strategic alliances by teaming with Microsoft, Dell, and IBM.[32]

Companies moving in a Net speed environment risk a hard landing, and when the demand for Internet equipment slumped in the early 2000s, Nortel's business was devastated. The company cut more than two-thirds of its workforce and closed dozens of plants and offices. An accounting scandal that led to fraud investigations and senior executive dismissals made things even worse. At one point, Nortel's stock was trading for less than a dollar. By early 2006, however, positive changes in the economic environment, along with a savvy new CEO, put Nortel back on an uphill swing. Bright spots for the company in 2007 included improved earnings, a boost in orders, and improved profitability. But Wall Street skeptics want to see more strong quarters before they are convinced of a turnaround.[33] As one analyst said, "It's a tough business," and Nortel's managers have to stay on their toes to help the organization cope in an ever-changing, difficult environment.[34]

2 Environment

EXHIBIT | **3.2**   The External Environment of Nortel

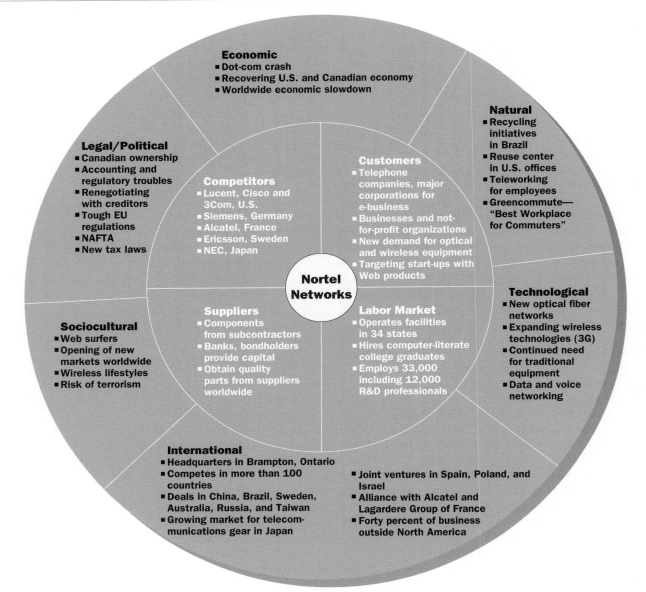

SOURCES: "Chinese Ministry of Railways Chooses Nortel Mobile Network," *M2Presswire*, Business and Company Resource Center database, (accessed January 29, 2008); Nortel Web site, http:www.nortel.com (accessed February 5, 2008); W. C. Symonds, J. B. Levine, N. Gross, and P. Coy, "High-Tech Star: Northern Telecom Is Challenging Even AT&T," *BusinessWeek* (July 27, 1992): 54–58; I. Austen, "Hooked on the Net," *Canadian Business* (June 26–July 10, 1998): 95–103; J. Weber with A. Reinhardt and P. Burrows, "Racing Ahead at Nortel," *BusinessWeek* (November 8, 1999): 93–99; "Nortel's Waffling Continues: First Job Cuts, Then Product Lines, and Now the CEO," *Telephony* (May 21, 2001): 12; and M. Heinzl, "Nortel's Profits of 499 Million Exceeds Forecast," *The Wall Street Journal*, January 30, 2004.

THE ORGANIZATION–ENVIRONMENT RELATIONSHIP

Why do organizations care so much about factors in the external environment? The reason is that the environment creates uncertainty for organization managers, and they must respond by designing the organization to adapt to the environment.

Environmental Uncertainty

Organizations must manage environmental uncertainty to be effective. *Uncertainty* means that managers do not have sufficient information about environmental factors

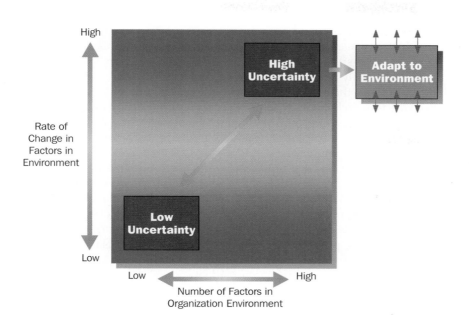

EXHIBIT | 3.3

The External Environment
and Uncertainty

2 Environment

to understand and predict environmental needs and changes.[35] As indicated in Exhibit 3.3, environmental characteristics that influence uncertainty are the number of factors that affect the organization and the extent to which those factors change. A large multinational like Nortel Networks has thousands of factors in the external environment creating uncertainty for managers. When external factors change rapidly, the organization experiences high uncertainty; examples are telecommunications and aerospace firms, computer and electronics companies, and e-commerce organizations that sell products and services over the Internet. Companies have to make an effort to adapt to the rapid changes in the environment. When an organization deals with only a few external factors and these factors are relatively stable, such as those affecting soft-drink bottlers or food processors, managers experience low uncertainty and can devote less attention to external issues.

boundary-spanning roles
Roles assumed by people and/or departments that link and coordinate the organization with key elements in the external environment.

Adapting to the Environment

If an organization faces increased uncertainty with respect to competition, customers, suppliers, or government regulations, managers can use several strategies to adapt to these changes, including boundary-spanning roles, interorganizational partnerships, and mergers or joint ventures.

Boundary-Spanning Roles Departments and **boundary-spanning roles** link and coordinate the organization with key elements in the external environment. Boundary spanners serve two purposes for the organization: They detect and process information about changes in the environment, and they represent the organization's interests to the environment.[36] Employees in engineering or research and development scan for new technological developments, innovations, and raw materials. People in departments such as marketing and purchasing span the boundary to work with customers and suppliers, both face-to-face and

© CAMPBELL'S SOUP COMPANY

Concept Connection A consumer focus group in Mexico evaluates Campbell's soups, reviewing qualities such as packaging, preparation, appearance, and taste. The passage of NAFTA broadened market opportunities in Mexico, where nearly 9 billion servings of soup are consumed each year. Marketing executives act as **boundary spanners** to test reactions and assess whether products meet local needs. Boundary spanning provided competitive intelligence that Mexican consumers like convenient dry-soup varieties as well as condensed and ready-to-serve soups.

through market research. Some organizations are staying in touch with customers through the Internet, such as by monitoring gripe sites, communicating with customers on company Web sites, and contracting with market-research firms that use the Web to monitor rapidly changing marketplace trends.[37] Another recent approach to boundary spanning is the use of *business intelligence*, which results from using sophisticated software to search through large amounts of internal and external data to spot patterns, trends, and relationships that might be significant. For example, Verizon uses business intelligence software to actively monitor customer interactions and fix problems almost immediately.[38]

Business intelligence is related to the growing area of boundary spanning known as *competitive intelligence (CI)*, which refers to activities to get as much information as possible about one's rivals. Competitive intelligence specialists use Web sites, commercial databases, financial reports, market activity, news clippings, trade publications, personal contacts, and numerous other sources to scan an organization's environment and spot potential threats or opportunities.[39] Visa has an employee who searches the Web for two hours each day for insights on MasterCard and other competitors. Harley-Davidson hires an outside research firm to search through massive amounts of data and reveal patterns that help decipher and predict competitors' actions.[40]

Boundary spanning is an increasingly important task in organizations because environmental shifts can happen so quickly in today's world. Managers need good information about their competitors, customers, and other elements of the environment to make good decisions. Thus, the most successful companies involve everyone in boundary-spanning activities.

TakeaMoment | **Read the ethical dilemma on pages 87–88 that pertains to competitive intelligence. Do you have the courage to risk your job by challenging the boss's inappropriate use of confidential information?**

Interorganizational Partnerships An increasingly popular strategy for adapting to the environment is to reduce boundaries and increase collaboration with other organizations. North American companies have typically worked alone, competing with one another, but an uncertain and interconnected global environment changed that tendency. Companies are joining together to become more effective and to share scarce resources. Disney has agreed to sell Rayovac brand batteries at all its theme and water parks in packaging that features popular Disney characters such as Mickey Mouse. This move will boost Rayovac battery sales and increase consumer exposure to the Disney brand.[41] Sony, Toshiba, and IBM are collaborating to produce a new, tiny computer chip. Supermarket chains Kroger, Albertsons, and Safeway banded together to negotiate with labor unions. Head-to-head competition among independent firms is giving way to networks of alliances that compete for business on a global basis. For example, the aerospace industry is controlled by two networks—those of Boeing and Airbus, each of which is made up of more than 100 partner organizations.[42]

Managers in partnering organizations are also shifting from an adversarial orientation to a partnership orientation. The new paradigm, shown in Exhibit 3.4, is based on trust and the ability of partners to work out equitable solutions to conflicts so that everyone profits from the relationship. Managers work to reduce costs and add value to both sides, rather than trying to get all the benefits for their own company. The new model is also characterized by a high level of information sharing, including e-business links for automatic ordering, payments, and other transactions. In addition, person-to-person interaction provides corrective feedback and solves problems. People from other companies may be onsite or participate in virtual teams to enable close coordination. Partners are frequently involved in one another's product design and production, and they are committed for the long term. It is not unusual for business partners to help one another, even outside of what is specified in the contract.[43]

EXHIBIT | 3.4

The Shift to a Partnership
Paradigm

From Adversarial Orientation ———————▶	To Partnership Orientation
• Suspicion, competition, arm's length	• Trust, value added to both sides
• Price, efficiency, own profits	• Equity, fair dealing, everyone profits
• Information and feedback limited	• E-business links to share information and conduct digital transactions
• Lawsuits to resolve conflict	• Close coordination; virtual teams and people onsite
• Minimal involvement and up-front investment	• Involvement in partner's product design and production
• Short-term contracts	• Long-term contracts
• Contracts limit the relationship	• Business assistance goes beyond the contract

Mergers and Joint Ventures A step beyond strategic partnerships is for companies to become involved in mergers or joint ventures to reduce environmental uncertainty. A frenzy of merger and acquisition activity both in the United States and internationally in recent years is an attempt by organizations to cope with the tremendous volatility of the environment.[44] A **merger** occurs when two or more organizations combine to become one. For example, Wells Fargo merged with Norwest Corporation to form the nation's fourth largest banking corporation.

A **joint venture** involves a strategic alliance or program by two or more organizations. A joint venture typically occurs when a project is too complex, expensive, or uncertain for one firm to handle alone. Oprah Winfrey's Harpo Inc. formed a joint venture with Hearst Magazines to launch *O, The Oprah Magazine*.[45] Despite her popularity and success with her television show, Winfrey recognized the complexity and uncertainty involved in starting a new magazine. The combined resources and management talents of the partners contributed to the most successful start-up ever in the magazine publishing industry.

Joint ventures are on the rise as companies strive to keep pace with rapid technological change and compete in the global economy. Chrysler and Nissan have created a product-sharing alliance that involves Nissan supplying Chrysler with a much-needed fuel-efficient car to be sold in South America. The Nissan–Chrysler arrangement could grow to include Chrysler providing pickup trucks to Nissan for sale in the United States. Interorganizational partnerships like this one occur frequently in the automobile industry.[46]

Many small businesses are also turning to joint ventures with large firms or with international partners. A larger partner can provide sales staff, distribution channels, financial resources, or a research staff. Small businesses seldom have the expertise to deal internationally, so a company such as Nypro, Inc., a plastic injection-molding manufacturer in Clinton, Massachusetts, joins with overseas experts who are familiar with the local rules. Nypro now does business in four countries.[47]

As a new manager, learning to span the boundary to other units that influence your success is important. As you progress to higher management positions, learn how to use interorganizational partnerships, and even mergers or joint ventures, to help your organization adapt and stay competitive in a shifting environment.

TakeaMoment

THE INTERNAL ENVIRONMENT: CORPORATE CULTURE

The internal environment within which managers work includes corporate culture, production technology, organization structure, and physical facilities. Of these, corporate culture surfaces as extremely important to competitive advantage. The

merger The combining of two or more organizations into one.

joint venture A strategic alliance or program by two or more organizations.

HONDA/ASSOCIATED PRESS

Concept Connection Equality stands at the heart of Japanese automaker Honda's **corporate culture**, and visible manifestations of the cultural values are everywhere. For example, at facilities such as this automobile manufacturing plant in Lincoln, Alabama, there are open offices, no assigned parking spaces, and the 4,500 employees, called *associates*, all eat in the same cafeteria and call each other by their first names. Everyone, from the president on down, comes to work, walks into the locker room, and changes into a gleaming white two-piece uniform emblazoned with the Honda insignia. It's no accident that it's hard to tell the managers from the front-line workers.

internal culture must fit the needs of the external environment and company strategy. When this fit occurs, highly committed employees create a high-performance organization that is tough to beat.[48]

Most people don't think about culture; it's just "how we do things around here" or "the way things are here." However, managers have to think about culture, because it typically plays a significant role in organizational success. The concept of culture has been of growing concern to managers since the 1980s as turbulence in the external environment has grown, often requiring new values and attitudes. Organizational culture has been defined and studied in many and varied ways. For the purposes of this chapter, we define **culture** as the set of key values, beliefs, understandings, and norms shared by members of an organization.[49] The concept of culture helps managers understand the hidden, complex aspects of organizational life. Culture is a pattern of shared values and assumptions about how things are done within the organization. This pattern is learned by members as they cope with external and internal problems and taught to new members as the correct way to perceive, think, and feel.

Culture can be analyzed at three levels, as illustrated in Exhibit 3.5, with each level becoming less obvious.[50] At the surface level are visible artifacts, which include such things as manner of dress, patterns of behavior, physical symbols, organizational ceremonies, and office layout. Visible artifacts are all the things one can see, hear, and observe by watching members of the organization. At a deeper level are the expressed values and beliefs, which are not observable but can be discerned from how people explain and justify what they do. Members of the organization hold these values at a conscious level. They can be interpreted from the stories, language, and symbols organization members use to represent them.

Some values become so deeply embedded in a culture that members are no longer consciously aware of them. These basic, underlying assumptions and beliefs are the essence of culture and subconsciously guide behavior and decisions. In some organizations, a basic assumption might be that people are essentially lazy and will shirk their duties whenever possible; thus, employees are closely supervised and given little freedom, and colleagues are frequently suspicious of one another. More

culture The set of key values, beliefs, understandings, and norms that members of an organization share.

EXHIBIT | 3.5

Levels of Corporate Culture

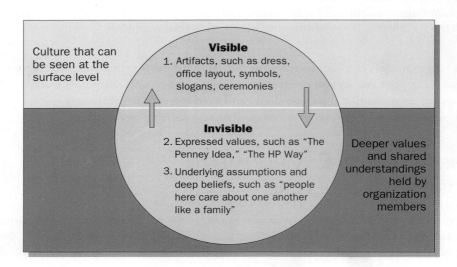

enlightened organizations operate on the basic assumption that people want to do a good job; in these organizations, employees are given more freedom and responsibility, and colleagues trust one another and work cooperatively.

The fundamental values that characterize an organization's culture can be understood through the visible manifestations of symbols, stories, heroes, slogans, and ceremonies.

Symbols

A **symbol** is an object, act, or event that conveys meaning to others. Symbols can be considered a rich, nonverbal language that vibrantly conveys the organization's important values concerning how people relate to one another and interact with the environment.[51] For example, managers at a New York-based start-up that provides Internet solutions to local television broadcasters wanted a way to symbolize the company's unofficial mantra of "drilling down to solve problems." They bought a dented old drill for $2 and dubbed it The Team Drill. Each month, the drill is presented to a different employee in recognition of exceptional work, and the employee personalizes the drill in some way before passing it on to the next winner.[52]

Stories

A **story** is a narrative based on true events and is repeated frequently and shared among organizational employees. Stories paint pictures that help symbolize the firm's vision and values and help employees personalize and absorb them.[53] A frequently told story at UPS concerns an employee who, without authorization, ordered an extra Boeing 737 to ensure timely delivery of a load of Christmas packages that had been left behind in the holiday rush. As the story goes, rather than punishing the worker, UPS rewarded his initiative. By telling this story, UPS workers communicate that the company stands behind its commitment to worker autonomy and customer service.[54] A story of Toyota's founder Kiichiro Toyoda, described below, illustrates his commitment to the "Toyota Way," a set of values that serve as the foundation of Toyota's success.

symbol An object, act, or event that conveys meaning to others.

story A narrative based on true events and repeated frequently and shared among organizational employees.

hero A figure who exemplifies the deeds, character, and attributes of a strong corporate culture.

Innovative Way | **Toyota**

Toyota Motor Corporation, an automotive powerhouse, is the most profitable automaker in the world. Known for award-winning reliability and quality, Toyota leads the industry in manufacturing and customer service. At a time when GM and Ford are closing plants, Toyota plans to open six more plants in the next few years. Toyota is also a leader and innovator in hybrid technology. Toyota offers six Toyota and Lexus hybrid vehicles in the United States, where it has sold more than 500,000 hybrids, surpassing the rest of the industry combined.[55]

What makes this company so successful? For Toyota, the answer is a strong corporate culture based on "The Toyota Way." A popular story of Toyota's founder Kiichiro Toyoda demonstrates his commitment to the culture during the early days of the company's history. Toyoda visited a plant and found a worker scratching his head and muttering about how his grinding machine would not run. Toyoda rolled up his sleeves and thrust his hands into the machine's oil pan. He came up with two handfuls of sludge and threw them to the floor. "How can you expect to do your job without getting your hands dirty," he exclaimed. This was the origin of one of the key elements of Toyota's culture: *genchi genbutsu*, meaning "go and see." To Toyota employees, this means go and seek out facts and information that help you make good decisions—even if it means rolling up your sleeves and getting dirty.[56]

Heroes

A **hero** is a figure who exemplifies the deeds, character, and attributes of a strong culture. Heroes are role models for employees to follow. Sometimes heroes are real, such as the female security supervisor who once challenged IBM's chairman because he wasn't carrying the appropriate clearance identification to enter a security area.[57] Heroes show how to do the right thing in the organization. Companies with strong cultures take advantage of achievements to define heroes who uphold key values.

At 3M Corporation, top managers keep alive the image of heroes who developed projects that were killed by top management. One hero was a vice president who was fired earlier in his career for persisting with a new product even after his boss had told him, "That's a stupid idea. Stop!" After the worker was fired, he would not leave. He stayed in an unused office, working without a salary on the new product idea. Eventually he was rehired, the idea succeeded, and he was promoted to vice president. The lesson of this hero as a major element in 3M's culture is to persist at what you believe in.[58]

Slogans

A **slogan** is a phrase or sentence that succinctly expresses a key corporate value. Many companies use a slogan or saying to convey special meaning to employees. The Ritz-Carlton adopted the slogan, "Ladies and gentlemen taking care of ladies and gentlemen" to demonstrate its cultural commitment to take care of both employees and customers. "We're in the service business, and service comes only from people. Our promise is to take care of them, and provide a happy place for them to work," said General Manager Mark DeCocinis, who manages the Portman Hotel in Shanghai, recipient of the "Best Employer in Asia" for three consecutive years.[59] Cultural values can also be discerned in written public statements, such as corporate mission statements or other formal statements that express the core values of the organization. The mission statement for Hallmark Cards, for example, emphasizes values of excellence, ethical and moral conduct in all relationships, business innovation, and corporate social responsibility.[60]

Ceremonies

A **ceremony** is a planned activity at a special event that is conducted for the benefit of an audience. Managers hold ceremonies to provide dramatic examples of company values. Ceremonies are special occasions that reinforce valued accomplishments, create a bond among people by allowing them to share an important event, and anoint and celebrate heroes.[61] In a ceremony to mark its 20th anniversary, Southwest Airlines rolled out a specialty plane it created called the "Lone Star One" that was designed like the Texas state flag to signify the company's start in Texas. Later, when the NBA chose Southwest Airlines as the league's official airline, Southwest launched another specialty plane, the "Slam Dunk One," designed in blue and orange with a large basketball painted toward the front of the plane. Today, ten specialty planes celebrate significant milestones in Southwest's history and demonstrate key cultural values.[62]

In summary, organizational culture represents the values, norms, understandings, and basic assumptions that employees share, and these values are signified by symbols, stories, heroes, slogans, and ceremonies. Managers help define important symbols, stories, and heroes to shape the culture.

ENVIRONMENT AND CULTURE

slogan A phrase or sentence that succinctly expresses a key corporate value.

ceremony A planned activity at a special event that is conducted for the benefit of an audience.

A big influence on internal corporate culture is the external environment. Cultures can vary widely across organizations; however, organizations within the same industry often reveal similar cultural characteristics because they are operating in similar environments.[63] The internal culture should embody what it takes to succeed in the environment. If the external environment requires extraordinary customer service, the culture should encourage good service; if it calls for careful technical decision making, cultural values should reinforce managerial decision making.

EXHIBIT | 3.6

Environmentally Adaptive versus Unadaptive Corporate Cultures

	Adaptive Corporate Cultures	Unadaptive Corporate Cultures
Visible Behavior	Managers pay close attention to all their constituencies, especially customers, and initiate change when needed to serve their legitimate interests, even if it entails taking some risks.	Managers tend to behave somewhat insularly, politically, and bureaucratically. As a result, they do not change their strategies quickly to adjust to or take advantage of changes in their business environments.
Expressed Values	Managers care deeply about customers, stockholders, and employees. They also strongly value people and processes that can create useful change (e.g., leadership initiatives up and down the management hierarchy).	Managers care mainly about themselves, their immediate work group, or some product (or technology) associated with that work group. They value the orderly and risk-reducing management process much more highly than leadership initiatives.

SOURCE: Adapted with the permission of The Free Press, a division of Simon & Schuster Adult Publishing Group, from CORPORATE CULTURE AND PERFORMANCE by John P. Kotter and James L. Heskett. Copyright © 1992 by Kotter Associates, Inc. and James L. Heskett. All rights reserved.

As a new manager, pay attention to culture. Recognize the ways in which cultural values can help or hurt your department's performance. Consciously shape adaptive values through the use of symbols, stories, heroes, ceremonies, and slogans.

TakeaMoment

Adaptive Cultures

Research at Harvard on 207 U.S. firms illustrated the critical relationship between corporate culture and the external environment. The study found that a strong corporate culture alone did not ensure business success unless the culture encouraged healthy adaptation to the external environment. As illustrated in Exhibit 3.6, adaptive corporate cultures have different values and behavior from unadaptive corporate cultures. In adaptive cultures, managers are concerned about customers and those internal people and processes that bring about useful change. In the unadaptive corporate cultures, managers are concerned about themselves, and their values tend to discourage risk taking and change. Thus, a strong culture alone is not enough, because an unhealthy culture may encourage the organization to march resolutely in the wrong direction. Healthy cultures help companies adapt to the environment.[64]

adaptability culture A culture characterized by values that support the company's ability to interpret and translate signals from the environment into new behavior responses.

Complete the experiential exercise on page 87 that pertains to adaptive cultures. How would you shape adaptive values in a company for which you worked?

TakeaMoment

Types of Cultures

In considering what cultural values are important for the organization, managers consider the external environment as well as the company's strategy and goals. Studies suggest that the right fit between culture, strategy, and the environment is associated with four categories or types of culture, as illustrated in Exhibit 3.7. These categories are based on two dimensions: (1) the extent to which the external environment requires flexibility or stability and (2) the extent to which a company's strategic focus is internal or external. The four categories associated with these differences are adaptability, achievement, involvement, and consistency.[65]

The **adaptability culture** emerges in an environment that requires fast response and high-risk decision making. Managers encourage values that support the company's ability to rapidly detect, interpret, and translate signals from the environment into new behavior responses.

© MISTY KEASLER

Concept Connection   John Zapp, general manager of a group of dealerships in Oklahoma City, realized his Buick-Pontiac-GMC and Dodge-Chrysler-Jeep outlets were losing sales to neighboring Toyota and Honda shops. To maximize sells on the current floor traffic, Zapp reconfigured his inventory to focus on selling pre-owned vehicles, which increased profit per auto. The key to keeping the pre-owned vehicles moving off the lot is the company's **achievement culture**. Zapp sets high goals and gives cash incentives to sales people who move the pre-owned inventory faster.

2 Environment

EXHIBIT | 3.7

Four Types of Corporate
Cultures

SOURCES: Based on D. R. Denison and A. K. Mishra, "Toward a Theory of Organizational Culture
and Effectiveness," *Organization Science*, 6,no. 2 (March–April 1995): 204–223; R. Hooijberg and
F. Petrock, "On Cultural Change: Using the Competing Values Framework to Help Leaders Execute
a Transformational Strategy," *Human Resource Management* 32, no.1 (1993): 29–50; and R. E. Quinn,
Beyond Rational Management: Mastering the Paradoxes and Competing Demands of High Performance (San
Francisco: Jossey-Bass, 1988).

Employees have autonomy to make decisions and act freely to meet new needs, and responsiveness to customers is highly valued. Managers also actively create change by encouraging and rewarding creativity, experimentation, and risk taking. Lush Cosmetics, a fast-growing maker of shampoos, lotions, and bath products made from fresh ingredients such as mangoes and avocados, provides a good example of an adaptability culture. A guiding motto at the company is "We reserve the right to make mistakes." Founder and CEO Mark Constantine is passionately devoted to change and encourages employees to break boundaries, experiment, and take risks. The company kills off one-third of its product line every year to offer new and offbeat products.[66] Other companies in the cosmetics industry, as well as those involved in electronics, e-commerce, and fashion, often use an adaptability culture because they must move quickly to respond to rapid changes in the environment.

The **achievement culture** is suited to organizations concerned with serving specific customers in the external environment but without the intense need for flexibility and rapid change. This results-oriented culture values competitiveness, aggressiveness, personal initiative, and willingness to work long and hard to achieve results. An emphasis on winning and achieving specific ambitious goals is the glue that holds the organization together.[67] Siebel Systems, which sells complex software systems, thrives on an achievement culture. Professionalism and aggressiveness are core values. Employees are forbidden to eat at their desks or to decorate with more than one or two personal photographs. People who succeed at Siebel are focused, competitive, and driven to win. Those who perform and meet stringent goals are handsomely rewarded; those who don't are fired.[68]

The **involvement culture** emphasizes an internal focus on the involvement and participation of employees to adapt rapidly to changing needs from the environment. This culture places high value on meeting the needs of employees, and the organization may be characterized by a caring, family-like atmosphere. Managers emphasize values such as cooperation, consideration of both employees and customers, and avoiding status differences. Consider the involvement culture at Valero, which is partly responsible for helping the company become the top oil refinery in the United States.

achievement culture A
results-oriented culture that values competitiveness, personal initiative, and achievement.

involvement culture A culture that places high value on meeting the needs of employees and values cooperation and equality.

Valero

When Hurricane Katrina hit New Orleans in late August 2005, companies throughout the region set their disaster plans into action. But few matched the heroic efforts put forth by employees at Valero's St. Charles oil refinery. Just eight days after the storm, the St. Charles facility was up and running, while a competitor's plant across the road was weeks away from getting back online. During the same time period, St. Charles's disaster crew managed to locate every one of the plant's 570 employees.

Part of the credit goes to Valero's family-like, let's-get-it-done-together culture, which has given Valero a distinctive edge during an era of cutthroat global competition in the oil industry. As CEO Bill Greehey transformed Valero, once primarily a natural-gas-pipeline company, into the nation's largest oil refinery business, he also instilled a culture where people care about one another and the company. Many of the refineries Valero bought were old and run-down. After buying a refinery, Greehey's first steps would be to assure people their jobs were secure, bring in new safety equipment, and promise employees that if they worked hard he would put them first, before shareholders and customers. Employees held up their end of the bargain, and so did Greehey.

Putting employees first has engendered amazing loyalty and dedication. When Greehey visited the St. Charles facility after Katrina, he was surprised to be greeted at a giant tent with a standing ovation. Even in the aftermath of a hurricane, employees had held to their tradition of throwing a plantwide barbecue lunch whenever Greehey visits a plant. "Right now morale is so high in this refinery you can't get at it with a space shuttle," an electrical superintendent at St. Charles said. "Valero has been giving away gas, chain saws, putting up trailers for the employees. They've kept every employee paid. Other refineries shut down and stopped paying. What else can you ask?"[69]

Some managers might think putting employees ahead of customers and shareholders is nice, but not very good for business. But at Valero, a strong involvement culture based on putting employees first has paid off in terms of high employee performance and rising market share, profits, and shareholder value.

The final category of culture, the **consistency culture**, uses an internal focus and a consistency orientation for a stable environment. Following the rules and being thrifty are valued, and the culture supports and rewards a methodical, rational, orderly way of doing things. In today's fast-changing world, few companies operate in a stable environment, and most managers are shifting toward cultures that are more flexible and in tune with changes in the environment. However, one thriving company, Pacific Edge Software, successfully implemented elements of a consistency culture, ensuring that all its projects are on time and on budget. The husband-and-wife team of Lisa Hjorten and Scott Fuller implanted a culture of order, discipline, and control from the moment they founded the company. The emphasis on order and focus means employees can generally go home by 6:00 P.M. rather than working all night to finish an important project. Hjorten insists that the company's culture isn't rigid or uptight, just *careful*. Although sometimes being careful means being slow, so far Pacific Edge has managed to keep pace with the demands of the external environment.[70]

Would you rather work in an organization with an adaptability, achievement, involvement, or consistency culture? Complete the New Manager Self-Test on page 82 to get an idea of what type of culture you would be most comfortable working in.

TakeaMoment

Each of these four categories of culture can be successful. In addition, organizations usually have values that fall into more than one category. The relative emphasis on various cultural values depends on the needs of the environment and the organization's focus. Managers are responsible for instilling the cultural values the organization needs to be successful in its environment.

consistency culture A culture that values and rewards a methodical, rational, orderly way of doing things.

New ManagerSelf-Test

Culture Preference

The fit between a new manager and organization culture can determine success and satisfaction. To understand your culture preference, <u>rank order</u> the items below from 1 to 8 based on the strength of your preference (1 = strongest preference).

1. The organization is very personal, much like an extended family.

2. The organization is dynamic and changing, where people take risks.

3. The organization is achievement oriented, with the focus on competition and getting jobs done.

4. The organization is stable and structured, with clarity and established procedures.

5. Management style is characterized by teamwork and participation.

6. Management style is characterized by innovation and risk-taking.

7. Management style is characterized by high performance demands and achievement.

8. Management style is characterized by security and predictability.

SCORING AND INTERPRETATION: Each question pertains to one of the four types of culture in Exhibit 3.7. To compute your preference for each type of culture, add together the scores for each set of two questions as follows:

Involvement culture—total for questions 1, 4:
_____

Adaptability culture—total for questions 2, 6:
_____

Achievement culture—total for questions 3, 7:
_____

Consistency culture—total for questions 4, 8:
_____

A lower score means a stronger culture preference. You will likely be more comfortable and more effective as a new manager in a corporate culture that is compatible with your personal preferences. A higher score means the culture would not fit your expectations, and you would have to change your style and preference to be comfortable. Review the text discussion of the four culture types. Do your cultural preference scores seem correct to you? Can you think of companies that fit your culture preferrence?

SOURCE: Adapted from Kim S. Cameron and Robert D. Quinn, *Diagnosing and Changing Organizational Culture* (Reading, MA: Addison-Wesley, 1999).

SHAPING CORPORATE CULTURE FOR INNOVATIVE RESPONSE

Research conducted by a Stanford University professor indicates that the one factor that increases a company's value the most is people and how they are treated.[71] In addition, surveys found that CEOs cite organizational culture as their most important mechanism for attracting, motivating, and retaining talented employees, a capability they consider the single best predictor of overall organizational excellence.[72] In a survey of Canadian senior executives, fully 82 percent believe a direct correlation exists between culture and financial performance.[73]

Corporate culture plays a key role in creating an organizational climate that enables learning and innovative responses to threats from the external environment, challenging new opportunities, or organizational crises. However, managers realize they can't focus all their effort on values; they also need a commitment to solid business performance.

Managing the High-Performance Culture

Companies that succeed in a turbulent world are those that pay careful attention to both cultural values *and* business performance. Cultural values can energize and motivate employees by appealing to higher ideals and unifying people around shared goals. In addition, values boost performance by shaping and guiding employee behavior, so that everyone's actions are aligned with strategic priorities.[74] Exhibit 3.8 illustrates four organizational outcomes based on the relative attention managers pay to cultural values and business performance.[75] A company in Quadrant A pays little attention to either values or business results and is unlikely to survive for long. Managers in Quadrant B organizations are highly focused on creating a strong cohesive culture, but they don't tie organizational values directly to goals and desired business results. When cultural values aren't connected to business performance, they aren't likely to benefit the organization during hard times. The corporate culture at Lego headquarters in Billund, Denmark, nearly doomed

© GETTY IMAGES

Concept Connection   The idea for this vertical fashion show at Rockefeller Center, where an acrobatic rappelling troupe walked down the side of a building, was born in Target's **high performance culture**. Target has quarterly Big Idea internal contests in which departments compete for additional budget allocations awarded for innovative ideas. The fun, creative competition encourages a sense of employee ownership and reinforces shared values. Tapping into employee talent helps Target meet its mission of providing customers with more for less.

the toymaker in the 1990s when sales plummeted as children turned away from traditional toys to video games. Imagination and creativity, not business performance, were what guided Lego. The attitude among employees was, "We're doing great stuff for kids—don't bother us with financial goals." New leader Jorgen Vig Knudstorp upended the corporate culture with a new employee motto: "I am here to make money for the company." The shift to bottom-line results appears to be making a difference, although Lego still has a long way to go.[76]

Quadrant C represents organizations that are focused primarily on bottom-line results and pay little attention to organizational values. This approach may

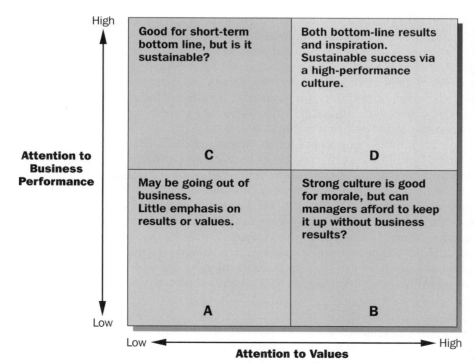

EXHIBIT | **3.8**

Combining Culture and Performance

SOURCE: Adapted from Jeff Rosenthal and Mary Ann Masarech, "High-Performance Cultures: How Values Can Drive Business Results," *Journal of Organizational Excellence* (Spring 2003): 3–18.

be profitable in the short run, but the success is difficult to sustain over the long term because the "glue" that holds the organization together—that is, shared cultural values—is missing. Think about the numerous get-rich-quick goals of dot-com entrepreneurs. Thousands of companies that sprang up in the late 1990s were aimed primarily at fast growth and quick profits, with little effort to build a solid organization based on long-term mission and values. When the crash came, these companies failed. Those that survived were typically companies with strong cultural values that helped them weather the storm. For example, both eBay and Amazon.com managers paid careful attention to organizational culture, as did smaller e-commerce companies like Canada's Mediagrif Interactive Technologies, an online B2B brokerage that allows businesses to meet online and trade their goods.[77]

Finally, companies in Quadrant D put high emphasis on both culture and solid business performance as drivers of organizational success. Managers in these organizations align values with the company's day-to-day operations—hiring practices, performance management, budgeting, criteria for promotions and rewards, and so forth. A 2004 study of corporate values by Booz Allen Hamilton and the Aspen Institute found that managers in companies that report superior financial results typically put a high emphasis on values and link them directly to the way they run the organization.[78] A good example is the fast-growing Umpqua Bank, which expanded from 11 branches and $140 million in assets in 1994 to 92 branches and $5 billion in assets nine years later. At Umpqua, every element of the culture focuses on serving customers, and every aspect of operations reflects the cultural values. Consider training programs. To avoid the "it's not my job" attitude that infects many banks, managers devised the "universal associate" program, which trains every bank staffer in every task, so that a teller can take a mortgage application and a loan officer can process your checking account deposit. Employees are empowered to make their own decisions about how to satisfy customers, and branches have free reign to devise unique ways to coddle the clientele in their particular location. Umpqua also carefully measures and rewards the cultural values it wants to maintain. The bank's executive vice president of cultural enhancement devised a software program that measures how cultural values are connected to performance, which the bank calls "return on quality" (ROQ). The ROQ scores for each branch and department are posted every month, and they serve as the basis for determining incentives and rewards.[79]

Quadrant D organizations represent the **high-performance culture**, a culture that (1) is based on a solid organizational mission or purpose, (2) embodies shared adaptive values that guide decisions and business practices, and (3) encourages individual employee ownership of both bottom-line results and the organization's cultural backbone.[80] This chapter's Unlocking Innovative Solutions Through People box describes the high-performance culture at Semco, where the company's unique cultural values have contributed to amazing business success.

One of the most important things managers do is create and influence organizational culture to meet strategic goals because culture has a significant impact on performance. In *Corporate Culture and Performance*, Kotter and Heskett provided evidence that companies that intentionally managed cultural values outperformed similar companies that did not. Recent research validated that some elements of corporate culture are positively correlated with higher financial performance.[81] A good example is Caterpillar Inc. Caterpillar developed a Cultural Assessment Process (CAP) to measure and manage how effectively the culture contributes to organizational effectiveness. The assessment gave top executives hard data documenting millions of dollars in savings attributed directly to cultural factors.[82]

high-performance culture
A culture based on a solid organizational mission or purpose that uses shared adaptive values to guide decisions and business practices and to encourage individual employee ownership of both bottom-line results and the organization's cultural backbone.

TakeaMoment | Even as a new manager you can manage for high performance by creating an adaptive culture and tying cultural values to the accomplishment of business results. Act as a cultural leader by communicating the desired values and outcomes and then modeling them in your daily behavior and decisions.

Cultural Leadership

A primary way in which managers shape cultural norms and values to build a high-performance culture is through *cultural leadership*. Managers must *overcommunicate* to ensure that employees understand the new culture values, and they signal these values in actions as well as words.

A **cultural leader** defines and uses signals and symbols to influence corporate culture. Cultural leaders influence culture in two key areas:

1. *The cultural leader articulates a vision for the organizational culture that employees can believe in.* The leader defines and communicates central values that employees believe in and will rally around. Values are tied to a clear and compelling mission, or core purpose.

2. *The cultural leader heeds the day-to-day activities that reinforce the cultural vision.* The leader makes sure that work procedures and reward systems match and reinforce the values. Actions speak louder than words, so cultural leaders "walk their talk."[83]

Managers widely communicate the cultural values through words and actions. Values statements that aren't reinforced by management behavior are meaningless or even harmful for employees and the organization. Whole Foods founder and CEO John Mackey wants his managers to place more value on creating "a better person, company, and world" than on pursuing personal financial gain. To demonstrate his personal commitment to this belief, he asked the board of directors to donate all his future stock options to the company's two foundations, the Animal Compassion Foundation and the Whole Planet Foundation.[84]

Cultural leaders also uphold their commitment to values during difficult times or crises, as illustrated by the example of Bill Greehey at Valero earlier in this chapter. On *Fortune* magazine's list of 100 Best Companies to Work For, Valero zoomed from Number 23 to Number 3 based on its treatment of employees following the devastating 2005 hurricanes. Despite the costs, Valero kept people on the payroll throughout the crisis, set up special booths to feed volunteers, and donated $1 million to the American Red Cross for hurricane relief efforts.[85] Upholding the cultural values helps organizations weather a crisis and come out stronger on the other side. Creating and maintaining a high-performance culture is not easy in today's turbulent environment and changing workplace, but through their words—and particularly their actions—cultural leaders let everyone in the organization know what really counts.

cultural leader A manager who uses signals and symbols to influence corporate culture.

| ch3 | A MANAGER'S ESSENTIALS: WHAT HAVE WE LEARNED? |

- The organizational environment includes all elements existing outside the organization's boundaries that have the potential to affect the organization. Events in the external environment are considered important influences on organizational behavior and performance. The external environment consists of two layers: the task environment and the general environment. The task environment includes customers, competitors, suppliers, and the labor market. The general environment includes technological, sociocultural, economic, legal-political, international, and natural dimensions. Management techniques for helping the organization adapt to the environment include boundary-spanning roles, interorganizational partnerships, and mergers and joint ventures.

- The organization also has an internal environment, which includes the elements within the organization's boundaries. A major internal element for helping organizations adapt to the environment is culture. Corporate culture is an important part of the internal organizational environment and includes the key values, beliefs, understandings, and norms that organization members share. Organizational activities that illustrate corporate culture include symbols, stories, heroes, slogans, and ceremonies. For the organization to be effective, corporate culture should be aligned with organizational strategy and the needs of the external environment.

■ Four types of culture are adaptability, achievement, involvement, and consistency. Strong cultures are effective when they enable an organization to meet strategic goals and adapt to changes in the external environment.

■ Culture is important because it can have a significant impact on organizational performance. Managers emphasize both values and business results to create a high-performance culture, enabling the organization to achieve solid business performance through the actions of motivated employees who are aligned with the mission and goals of the company.

■ Managers create and sustain adaptive high-performance cultures through cultural leadership. They define and articulate important values that are tied to a clear and compelling mission, and they widely communicate and uphold the values through their words and particularly their actions. Work procedures, budgeting, decision making, reward systems, and other day-to-day activities are aligned with the cultural values.

ch3   DISCUSSION QUESTIONS

1. What can you do now as a student—both inside and outside the classroom—to train yourself to be a more effective manager in an increasingly global business environment?

2. Would the task environment for a cellular phone company contain the same elements as that for a government welfare agency? Discuss.

3. What do you think are the most important forces in the external environment creating uncertainty for organizations today? Do the forces you identified typically arise in the task environment or the general environment?

4. Contemporary best-selling management books often argue that customers are the most important element in the external environment. Do you agree? In what company situations might this statement be untrue?

5. Why do you think many managers are surprised by environmental changes and unable to help their organizations adapt? Can a manager ever be prepared for an environmental change as dramatic as that experienced by airlines in the United States following the September 11, 2001, terrorist attacks in New York and Washington?

6. Why are interorganizational partnerships so important for today's companies? What elements in the current environment might contribute to either an increase or a decrease in interorganizational collaboration? Discuss.

7. Consider the chairs you have seen in an office. How does the assistant's chair, the manager's chair, and executive's chair differ? What do the differences mean?

8. Why are symbols important to a corporate culture? Do stories, heroes, slogans, and ceremonies have symbolic value? Discuss.

9. Both China and India are rising economic powers. How might your approach to doing business with Communist China be different from your approach to doing business with India, the world's most populous democracy? In which country would you expect to encounter the most rules? The most bureaucracy?

10. General Electric is famous for firing the lowest-performing 10 percent of its managers each year. With its strict no-layoff policy, Valero Energy believes people need to feel secure in their jobs to perform their best. Yet both are high-performing companies. How do you account for the success of such opposite philosophies?

ch3   MANAGEMENT IN PRACTICE: EXPERIENTIAL EXERCISE

Working in an Adaptive Culture

Think of a specific full-time job you have held. Please answer the following questions according to your perception of the *managers above you* in that job. Circle a number on the 1–5 scale based on the extent to which you agree with each statement about the managers above you: 5 Strongly agree; 4 Agree; 3 Neither agree nor disagree; 2 Disagree; 1 Strongly disagree.

1. Good ideas got serious consideration from management above me.

   1   2   3   4   5

2. Management above me was interested in ideas and suggestions from people at my level in the organization.

   1   2   3   4   5

3. When suggestions were made to management above me, they received fair evaluation.

   1   2   3   4   5

4. Management did not expect me to challenge or change the status quo.

   1   2   3   4   5

5. Management specifically encouraged me to bring about improvements in my workplace.

   1   2   3   4   5

6. Management above me took action on recommendations made from people at my level.

   1   2   3   4   5

7. Management rewarded me for correcting problems.

   1   2   3   4   5

8. Management clearly expected me to improve work unit procedures and practices.

   1   2   3   4   5

9. I felt free to make recommendations to management above me to change existing practices.

   1   2   3   4   5

10. Good ideas did not get communicated upward because management above me was not very approachable.

    1   2   3   4   5

Scoring and Interpretation

To compute your score: Subtract each of your scores for questions 4 and 10 from 6. Using your adjusted scores, add the numbers for all 10 questions to give you the total score. Divide that number by 10 to get your average score: _____.

An adaptive culture is shaped by the values and actions of top and middle managers. When managers actively encourage and welcome change initiatives from below, the organization will be infused with values for change. These 10 questions measure your management's openness to change. A typical average score for management openness to change is about 3. If your average score was 4 or higher, you worked in an organization that expressed strong cultural values of adaptation. If your average score was 2 or below, the culture was probably nonadaptive.

Thinking about your job, is the level of management openness to change correct for the organization? Why? Compare your scores to those of another student, and take turns describing what it was like working for the managers above your jobs. Do you sense a relationship between job satisfaction and your management's openness to change? What specific management characteristics and corporate values explain the openness scores in the two jobs?

SOURCES: S. J. Ashford, N. P. Rothbard, S. K. Piderit, and J. E. Dutton, "Out on a Limb: The Role of Context and Impression Management in Issue Selling," *Administrative Science Quarterly* 43 (1998): 23–57; and E. W. Morrison and C. C. Phelps, "Taking Charge at Work: Extrarole Efforts to Initiate Workplace Change," *Academy of Management Journal* 42 (1999): 403–419.

ch3   MANAGEMENT IN PRACTICE: ETHICAL DILEMMA

Competitive Intelligence Predicament

Miquel Vasquez was proud of his job as a new product manager for a biotechnology start-up, and he loved the high stakes and tough decisions that went along with the job. But as he sat in his den after a long

day, he was troubled, struggling over what had happened earlier that day and the information he now possessed.

Just before lunch, Miquel's boss had handed him a stack of private strategic documents from their closest competitor. It was a competitive intelligence gold mine—product plans, pricing strategies, partnership agreements, and other documents, most clearly marked "proprietary and confidential." When Miquel asked where the documents came from, his boss told him with a touch of pride that he had taken them right off the competing firm's server. "I got into a private section of their intranet and downloaded everything that looked interesting," he said. Later, realizing Miquel was suspicious, the boss would say only that he had obtained "electronic access" via a colleague and had not personally broken any passwords. Maybe not, Miquel thought to himself, but this situation wouldn't pass the *60 Minutes* test. If word of this acquisition of a competitor's confidential data ever got out to the press, the company's reputation would be ruined.

Miquel didn't feel good about using these materials. He spent the afternoon searching for answers to his dilemma, but found no clear company policies or regulations that offered any guidance. His sense of fair play told him that to use the information was unethical, if not downright illegal. What bothered him even more was the knowledge that this kind of thing might happen again. Using this confidential

information would certainly give him and his company a competitive advantage, but Miquel wasn't sure he wanted to work for a firm that would stoop to such tactics.

What Would You Do?

1. Go ahead and use the documents to the company's benefit, but make clear to your boss that you don't want him passing confidential information to you in the future. If he threatens to fire you, threaten to leak the news to the press.

2. Confront your boss privately and let him know you're uncomfortable with how the documents were obtained and what possession of them says about the company's culture. In addition to the question of the legality of using the information, point out that it is a public relations nightmare waiting to happen.

3. Talk to the company's legal counsel and contact the Society of Competitive Intelligence Professionals for guidance. Then, with their opinions and facts to back you up, go to your boss.

SOURCE: Adapted from Kent Weber, "Gold Mine or Fool's Gold?" *Business Ethics* (January–February 2001): 18.

---

ch3   CASE FOR CRITICAL ANALYSIS

Rio Grande Supply Company

Jasper Hennings, president of Rio Grande Supply Company, knew full well that a company's top executives were largely responsible for determining a firm's corporate culture. That's why he took such personal pride in the culture of his Texas-based wholesale plumbing supply company. It didn't just pay lip service to the values it espoused: integrity, honesty, and a respect for each individual employee. His management team set a good example by living those principles. At least that's what he'd believed until the other day.

The importance Jasper attached to respecting each individual was apparent in the company's Internet use policy. It was abundantly clear that employees weren't to use Rio Grande's computers for anything but business-related activities. However, Jasper himself had vetoed the inclusion of what was becoming a standard provision in such policies that management had the right to access and review anything employees created, stored, sent, or received on company equipment. He cut short any talk of installing software filters that would prevent abuse of the corporate computer system. Still, the company

reserved the right to take disciplinary action, including possible termination, and to press criminal charges if an employee was found to have violated the policy.

So how was he to square his cherished assumptions about his management team with what he'd just discovered? Henry Darger, his hard-working chief of operations and a member of his church, had summarily fired a female employee for having accessed another worker's e-mail surreptitiously. She hadn't taken her dismissal well. "Just ask Darger what he's up to when he shuts his office door," she snarled as she stormed out of Jasper's office. She made what Jasper hoped was an idle threat to hire a lawyer.

When Jasper asked Henry what the fired employee could possibly have meant, tears began to roll down the operations chief's face. He admitted that ever since a young nephew had committed suicide the year before and a business he'd helped his wife start had failed, he'd increasingly been seeking escape from his troubles by logging onto adult pornography sites. At first, he'd indulged at home, but of late he'd found himself spending hours at work visiting pornographic sites, the more explicit the better. Jasper was stunned. After a few speechless minutes, he told Henry to take the rest of the day off, go home, and think things over.

The president himself needed the afternoon to gather his wits. How should he handle this turn of events? On the one hand, Henry's immediate dismissal of the woman who'd tapped into another employee's e-mail when the operations chief was violating the Internet policy himself was hypocritical, to say the least. The person charged with enforcing that policy needed to be held to the highest standards. On the other hand, Jasper knew that Rio Grande employees routinely used computers at their desks to check personal e-mail, do banking transactions, check the weather, or make vacation arrangements. The company had turned a blind eye because it didn't seem worth the effort of enforcing the hard-and-fast policy for such minor infractions. Besides, Henry was a valued, if clearly troubled, employee. Replacing him would be costly and difficult. If Jasper decided to keep him on, the president clearly had no choice but to cross the line and get involved in Henry's private life, and he would be treating Darger differently from the treatment the female employee received.

When he met with Henry again first thing in the morning, he needed to have a plan of action.

Questions

1. What environmental factors have helped to create the situation Jasper Hennings faces? What factors does Jasper need to consider when deciding on his course of action?

2. Analyze Rio Grande's culture. In addition to the expressed cultural values and beliefs, what other subconscious values and beliefs do you detect? Are conflicting values present? When values are in conflict, how would you decide which ones take precedence?

3. Assume you are Jasper. What are the first two action steps you would take to handle the Henry Darger situation? How would your role as a cultural leader influence your decision? What message will your solution send to the other managers and rank-and-file employees?

SOURCES: Based on Willard P. Green, "Pornography at Work," *Business Ethics* (Summer 2003): 19; Patrick Marley, "Porn-Viewing Parole Agent Regains Job," *Milwaukee Journal Sentinel* (January 24, 2006): http://www.jsonline.com/story/idex.aspx?id=387492; "Sample Internet Policies for Businesses and Organizations," *Websense*, http://www.websense-sales.com/internet-access-policy.html; and Art Lambert, "Technology in the Workplace: A Recipe for Legal Trouble," *Workforce* (February 14, 2005): http://www.workforce.com/archive/article/23/95/08.php.

ch3 ON THE JOB VIDEO CASE

Lonely Planet Creates an Adventurous Culture

When you think of corporate culture, the image of suits and ties, pantyhose and pumps often springs to mind. But at Lonely Planet, the values, beliefs, understandings, and norms of the firm are expressed by staff members and managers who wear T-shirts, khakis, soft skirts, and sandals or clogs to work. Lonely Planet is a publishing company based in Australia with offices in several other countries—including the United States—that produces series of travel books, guides, and language phrasebooks for people who want adventure.

Founded in 1971 by Tony and Maureen Wheeler, who admit that they started the company as a way to fund their own travel dreams, Lonely Planet has grown to become a major force in the travel publishing industry. The company publishes books—like *South America on a Shoestring*—for travelers who want to visit off-beat places, often on a budget. To do so, Lonely Planet employs people who love to

travel and who love books. They are happy wending their way through a jungle path or along an ancient, cobblestone street as part of the job. They also delight in putting together the photos and text that will entice other travelers to explore. "I would say that the culture of Lonely Planet is sort of embodied in a sense of pioneering," observes Cindy Cohen of Lonely Planet's public relations department. "We like to give people a scoop on the 'inside' places to be." Lonely Planet describes trips for the curious, nonmainstream traveler.

Lonely Planet fosters an internal culture in which employees are free to be themselves—to exchange ideas and try new approaches to problems. The work space itself is informal and open, so that people can communicate easily with each other. Successes are celebrated by everyone with office parties, and employees are naturally friends who socialize together outside of work. In addition, although there is a Lonely Planet approach and format to the guides, the voices of individual travel writers are valued, which is unusual among travel publishers.

Lonely Planet's informal culture lends itself readily to adapting quickly to an ever-changing external environment. Not only do staff members have a broader view of the world because of their travel experience, but they are also sensitive to changes in the environment that signal changes Lonely Planet should make to capture new markets. For instance, Lonely Planet's books were originally geared toward Australian, European, and Asian markets, where travelers tend to take longer trips. Europeans often have a month to six weeks of vacation, so they take off on long jaunts. But Americans take shorter trips, for a variety of reasons. One is that they only get an average of two weeks' vacation from work per year. Another factor is the economy—only recently have American consumers begun to show confidence in the U.S. economy after the recession. A third factor is the practice of "cocooning," or staying close to home in the wake of the terrorist attacks of September 11, 2001, and the ensuing war on terrorism.

In addition, Americans still love to drive their cars—despite a recent spike in gasoline prices. Even if gasoline is more expensive than it used to be, it is still less expensive—at least for a family—to drive to a destination than to fly to it. So, Lonely Planet has refocused in the United States, developing a series of guidebooks to the National Parks, including the Grand Canyon, Yosemite, Yellowstone, and the Grand Tetons. In addition, the series includes popular parks in Canada that are accessible by car, such as Banff, Glacier, and Jasper. Then there are the *Road Trip Guides*—a series of guides to destinations around the United States that are off the beaten path but still accessible for weekend getaways. Travelers can drive the famous Route 66 or California Highway 1; they can cruise up the Hudson River Valley; or they can follow one of Lonely Planet's hottest new guides—*Blues and Barbecue*—through the South. In short, just about anywhere a traveler wants to go, Lonely Planet is ready to guide.

Questions

1. Describe the task environment for Lonely Planet.
2. Describe factors in the external environment that could create uncertainty for Lonely Planet.
3. Give an example of Lonely Planet's corporate culture at each of the three levels identified in Exhibit 3.5.

SOURCES: Company Web site, *http://www.lonelyplanet.com*, accessed August 5, 2004; "Lonely Planet Publications Company Profile," *Hoover's Online*, *http://biz.yahoo.com*, accessed July 30, 2004; Lonely Planet press packet.

ch3 BIZ FLIX VIDEO CASE

Mr. Baseball

The New York Yankees trade aging baseball player Jack Elliot (Tom Selleck) to the Chunichi Dragons, a Japanese team. This lighthearted comedy traces Elliot's bungling entry into Japanese culture where he almost loses everything including Hiroko Uchiyama (Aya Takanashi). As Elliot slowly begins to understand Japanese culture and Japanese baseball, he finally is accepted by his teammates. This film shows many examples of Japanese culture, especially their love for baseball.

Unknown to Hiroko's father, she and Jack develop an intimate relationship. Meanwhile, Jack does not know that Hiroko's father is "The Chief" (Ken Takakura), the manager of the Chunichi Dragons. This scene takes place after "The Chief" has removed Jack from a baseball game. The scene shows Jack dining with Hiroko and her grandmother (Mineko Yorozuya), grandfather (Jun Hamamura), and father.

What to Watch for and Ask Yourself

1. Does Jack Elliot behave as if he had had crosscultural training before arriving in Japan?
2. Is he culturally sensitive or insensitive?
3. What do you propose that Jack Elliot do for the rest of his time in Japan?

ch3 ENDNOTES

1. The self-test questions are based on ideas from R. L. Daft and R. M. Lengel, *Fusion Leadership* (San Francisco: Berrett Koehler, 2000): Chapter 4; B. Bass and B. Avolio, *Multifactor Leadership Questionnaire*, 2nd ed. (Menlo Park, CA: Mind Garden, Inc., 2004); and Karl E. Weick and Kathleen M. Sutcliffe, *Managing the Unexpected: Assuring High Performance in an Age of Complexity* (San Francisco: Jossey-Bass, 2001).

2. Christopher Palmeri, "What Went Wrong at Mattel" *BusinessWeek Online*, August 14, 2007, http://www.businessweek.com/bwdaily/dnflash/content/aug2007/db20070814_154726_page_2.htm (accessed February 5, 2008).

3. David Barboza and Louise Story, "Dancing Elmo Smackdown," *The New York Times Online*, July 26, 2007, http://www.nytimes.com/2007/07/26/business/26toy.html?_r=1&scp=1&sq=dancing+elmo+smackdown&st=nyt&oref=slogin (accessed February 5, 2008).

4. This section is based on Richard L. Daft, *Organization Theory and Design*, 8th ed. (Cincinnati, OH: South-Western, 2004), pp. 136–140.

5. L. J. Bourgeois, "Strategy and Environment: A Conceptual Integration," *Academy of Management Review* 5 (1980): 25–39.

6. Google Web site. Retrieved February 7, 2008, from http://www.google.com.

7. Cliff Edwards, "Wherever You Go, You're On the Job," *BusinessWeek* (June 20, 2005): 87–90.

8. "Tools for Better Living," *Fortune* (December 11, 2006): 135.

9. Stephen Baker and Adam Astor, "The Business of Nanotech," *BusinessWeek* (February 14, 2005): 64–71.

10. William B. Johnston, "Global Work Force 2000: The New World Labor Market," *Harvard Business Review* (March–April 1991): 115–127.

11. U.S. Census Bureau, "The Face of Our Population," *U.S. Census Bureau*, 2008, http://factfinder.census.gov/jsp/saff/SAFFInfo.jsp?_pageId=tp9_race_ethnicity (accessed January 28, 2008).

12. "You Raised Them, Now Manage Them," *Fortune* (May 28, 2007): 38–46.

13. U.S. Census, *www.census.gov/*.

14. Sebastian Moffett, "Senior Moment: Fast-Aging Japan Keeps Its Elders on the Job Longer," *The Wall Street Journal*, June 15, 2005.

15. Samuel Loewenberg, "Europe Gets Tougher on U.S. Companies," *The New York Times*, April 20, 2003.

16. Barney Gimbel, "Attack of the Wal-Martyrs," *Fortune* (December 11, 2006): 125.

17. Andrew Adam Newman, "Environmentalists Push, but Home Depot Refuses to Drop Ads on Fox News," *The New York Times*, July 30, 2007, http://www. http://www.nytimes.com/2007/07/30/business/media/30depot.html?scp=1&sq=Environmentalists+Push%2C+but+Home+Depot&st=nyt (accessed July 30, 2007).

18. Etzion, Dror. "Research on Organizations and the Natural Environment," *Journal of Management* 33 (August 2007): 637–654.

19. Bruce Horovitz, "Whole Foods Sacks Plastic Bags," *USA Today*, January 22, 2008.

20. Stuart Birch, "Now Companies Are Going Green Right from the Start," *The Times*, Green Motoring Focus Report 7, January 25, 2008.

21. Matthew L. Wald, "What's Kind to Nature Can be Kind to Profits," *The New York Times*, May 17, 2006, http://www.nytimes.com/2006/05/17/business/businessspecial2/17giant.html?scp=1&sq=What%27s+Kind+to+Nature+Can+Be+Kind+to+Profits&st=nyt (accessed January 30, 2008).

22. Jessi Hempel, "The MySpace Generation," *BusinessWeek* (December 12, 2005): 86–94.

23. John Simons, "Stop Moaning About Gripe Sites and Log On," *Fortune* (April 2, 2001): 181–182.

24. Jon Swartz, "MySpace Cranks Up Heat in Turf War with Facebook," *USA Today*, December 21, 2007, http://www.usatoday.com/tech/webguide/2007-12-20-myspace_n.htm (accessed December 21, 2007).

25. Gary Rivlin, "When Buying a Diamond Starts with a Mouse," *The New York Times*, January 7, 2007, http://www.nytimes.com/2007/01/07/business/yourmoney/07nile.html?_r=1&scp=1&sq=When+buying+a+diamond+starts+with+a+mouse&st=nyt&oref=slogin (accessed January 15, 2007).

26. Paul Glader, "Steel-Price Rise Crimps Profits, Adds Uncertainty," *The Wall Street Journal*, February 23, 2004.

27. John R. Wilke and Kathy Chen, "Planned Economy; As China's Trade Clout Grows, So Do Price-Fixing Accusations," *The Wall Street Journal*, February 10, 2006.

28. Nortel Web site, http:www.nortel.com (accessed February 2, 2008).

29. Ibid.

30. "China's Ministry of Railways Chooses Nortel Mobile Network to Enable High-Speed Railway to Run Smoother GSM-R Wireless Staff Communication and Signaling Optimize Train Performance," *M2 Presswire*, January, 29, 2008, Business and Company Resource Center database (accessed February 11, 2008).

31. Acquired from Nortel Networks *Corporate Backgrounder*, 1.

32. Ibid.

33. Roger O. Crockett, "Finally Good News From Nortel," *BusinessWeek* (November 6, 2007), http://www.businessweek.com/technology/content/nov2007/tc2007116_384831.htm?chan=search (accessed February 12, 2008).

34. Olga Kharif, "Nortel's New Lease on Life," *BusinessWeek Online*, January 26, 2006 (accessed February 3, 2008); Roger O. Crockett, "Nortel: Desperately Seeking Credibility," *BusinessWeek* (January 17, 2005): 60–61; Bernard Simon, "A Bright New Day for the Telecom Industry, If the Public Will Go Along," *The New York Times*, January 12, 2004; Mark Heinzl, "Nortel's Profit of $499 Million Exceeds Forecast," *The Wall Street Journal*, January 30, 2004; Joseph Weber with Andy Reinhardt and Peter Burrows, "Racing Ahead at Nortel," *BusinessWeek* (November 8, 1999): 93–99; Ian Austen, "Hooked on the Net," *Canadian Business*

2
Environment

(June 26–July 10, 1998): 95–103; "Nortel's Waffling Continues; First Job Cuts, Then Product Lines, and Now the CEO. What's Next?" *Telephony* (May 21, 2001): 12.

35. Robert B. Duncan, "Characteristics of Organizational Environment and Perceived Environmental Uncertainty," *Administrative Science Quarterly* 17 (1972): 313–327; and Daft, *Organization Theory and Design*.

36. David B. Jemison, "The Importance of Boundary Spanning Roles in Strategic Decision-Making," *Journal of Management Studies* 21 (1984): 131–152; and Marc J. Dollinger, "Environmental Boundary Spanning and Information Processing Effects on Organizational Performance," *Academy of Management Journal* 27 (1984): 351–368.

37. Sarah Moore, "On Your Markets," *Working Woman* (February 2001): 26; and John Simons, "Stop Moaning about Gripe Sites and Log On," *Fortune* (April 2, 2001): 181–182.

38. Tom Duffy, "Spying the Holy Grail," *Microsoft Executive Circle* (Winter 2004): 38–39.

39. Gary Abramson, "All Along the Watchtower," *CIO Enterprise* (July 15, 1999): 24–34.

40. Girard, "Snooping on a Shoestring," *Business 2.0* (May 2003): 64–66.

41. "Rayovac Batteries in a Partnership with a World of Disney Characters," *New York Times*, December 18, 2007, http://www.nytimes.com/2007/12/18/business/media/18adco.html?_r=1&scp=1&sq=rayovac+batteries&st=nyt&oref=slogin (accessed December 18, 2007).

42. Lynn A. Isabella, "Managing an Alliance Is Nothing Like Business as Usual," *Organizational Dynamics* 31, no. 1 (2002): 47–59; Cyrus F. Freidheim, Jr. *The Trillion-Dollar Enterprise: How the Alliance Revolution Will Transform Global Business* (New York: Perseus Books, 1998).

43. Stephan M. Wagner and Roman Boutellier, "Capabilities for Managing a Portfolio of Supplier Relationships," *Business Horizons* (November–December 2002): 79–88; Peter Smith Ring and Andrew H. Van de Ven, "Developmental Processes of Corporate Interorganizational Relationships," *Academy of Management Review* 19 (1994): 90–118; Myron Magnet, "The New Golden

Rule of Business," *Fortune* (February 21, 1994): 60–64; and Peter Grittner, "Four Elements of Successful Sourcing Strategies," *Management Review* (October 1996): 41–45.

44. Richard L. Daft, "After the Deal: The Art of Fusing Diverse Corporate Cultures into One," paper presented at the Conference on International Corporate Restructuring, Institute of Business Research and Education, Korea University, Seoul, Korea (June 16, 1998).

45. Patricia Sellers, "The Business of Being Oprah," *Fortune* (April 1, 2002): 50–64.

46. Micheline Maynard, "Chrysler and Nissan in Production Deal," *The New York Times*, January 11, 2008, http://www.nytimes.com/2008/01/12/business/12auto.html?scp=1&sq=Chrysler+and+Nissan&st=nyt (accessed January 30, 2008).

47. James E. Svatko, "Joint Ventures," *Small Business Reports* (December 1988): 65–70; and Joshua Hyatt, "The Partnership Route," *Inc.* (December 1988): 145–148.

48. Yoash Wiener, "Forms of Value Systems: A Focus on Organizational Effectiveness and Culture Change and Maintenance," *Academy of Management Review* 13 (1988): 534–545; V. Lynne Meek, "Organizational Culture: Origins and Weaknesses," *Organization Studies* 9 (1988): 453–473; John J. Sherwood, "Creating Work Cultures with Competitive Advantage," *Organizational Dynamics* (Winter 1988): 5–27; and Andrew D. Brown and Ken Starkey, "The Effect of Organizational Culture on Communication and Information," *Journal of Management Studies* 31, no. 6 (November 1994): 807–828.

49. Joanne Martin, *Organizational Culture: Mapping the Terrain* (Thousand Oaks, CA: Sage Publications, 2002); Ralph H. Kilmann, Mary J. Saxton, and Roy Serpa, "Issues in Understanding and Changing Culture," *California Management Review* 28 (Winter 1986): 87–94; and Linda Smircich, "Concepts of Culture and Organizational Analysis," *Administrative Science Quarterly* 28 (1983): 339–358.

50. Based on Edgar H. Schein, *Organizational Culture and Leadership*,

2nd ed. (San Francisco: Jossey-Bass, 1992): 3–27.

51. Michael G. Pratt and Anat Rafaeli, "Symbols as a Language of Organizational Relationships," *Research in Organizational Behavior* 23 (2001): 93–132.

52. Christine Canabou, "Here's the Drill," *Fast Company* (February 2001): 58.

53. Chip Jarnagin and John W. Slocum, Jr. "Creating Corporate Cultures through Mythopoetic Leadership," *Organizational Dynamics* 36, no. 3 (2007): 288–302.

54. Robert E. Quinn and Gretchen M. Spreitzer, "The Road to Empowerment: Seven Questions Every Leader Should Consider," *Organizational Dynamics* (Autumn 1997): 37–49.

55. Toyota Web site, http://www.toyota.com (accessed February 12, 2008).

56. Jarnagin and Slocum, "Creating Corporate Cultures through Mythopoetic Leadership."

57. Martin, *Organizational Culture*, pp. 71–72.

58. Terrence E. Deal and Allan A. Kennedy, *Corporate Cultures: The Rites and Rituals of Corporate Life* (Reading, MA: Addison-Wesley, 1982).

59. Arthur Yeung, "Setting People Up for Success: How the Portman Ritz-Carlton Hotel Gets the Best From Its People," *Human Resource Management* 45, no. 2 (Summer 2006): 267–275.

60. Patricia Jones and Larry Kahaner, *Say It and Live It: 50 Corporate Mission Statements That Hit the Mark* (New York: Currency Doubleday, 1995).

61. Harrison M. Trice and Janice M. Beyer, "Studying Organizational Cultures Through Rites and Ceremonials," *Academy of Management Review* 9 (1984): 653–669.

62. PRWeb, November 3, 2005, http://www.prweb.com/releases/2005/11/prweb306461.php (accessed February 7, 2008).

63. Jennifer A. Chatman and Karen A. Jehn, "Assessing the Relationship Between Industry Characteristics and Organizational Culture: How Different Can You Be?" *Academy of Management Journal* 37, no. 3 (1994): 522–553.

64. John P. Kotter and James L. Heskett, *Corporate Culture and Performance* (New York: The Free Press, 1992).

65. This discussion is based on Paul McDonald and Jeffrey Gandz, "Getting Value from Shared Values," *Organizational Dynamics* 21, no. 3 (Winter 1992): 64–76; Daniel R. Denison and Aneil K. Mishra, "Toward a Theory of Organizational Culture and Effectiveness," *Organization Science* 6, no. 2 (March–April 1995): 204–223; and Richard L. Daft, *The Leadership Experience*, 3rd ed. (Cincinnati, OH: South-Western, 2005), pp. 570–573.

66. Lucas Conley, "Rinse and Repeat," *Fast Company* (July 2005): 76–77.

67. Robert Hooijberg and Frank Petrock, "On Cultural Change: Using the Competing Values Framework to Help Leaders Execute a Transformational Strategy," *Human Resource Management* 32, no. 1 (1993): 29–50.

68. Patrick Lencioni, "Make Your Values Mean Something," *Harvard Business Review* (July 2002): 113–117, and Melanie Warner, "Confessions of a Control Freak," *Fortune* (September 4, 2000): 130–140.

69. Tim Young, "Rewarding Work," *HR Management,* Issue 172 (2005), http://www.hrmreport.com; and Janet Guyon, "The Soul of a Money-making Machine," *Fortune* (October 3, 2005): 113–120.

70. Rekha Balu, "Pacific Edge Projects Itself," *Fast Company* (October 2000): 371–381.

71. Jeffrey Pfeffer, *The Human Equation: Building Profits by Putting People First* (Boston: Harvard Business School Press, 1998).

72. Jeremy Kahn, "What Makes a Company Great?" *Fortune* (October 26, 1998): 218; James C. Collins and Jerry I. Porras, *Built to Last: Successful Habits of Visionary Companies* (New York: HarperCollins, 1994); and James C. Collins, "Change Is Good—But First Know What Should Never Change," *Fortune* (May 29, 1995): 141.

73. Andrew Wahl, "Culture Shock," *Canadian Business* (October 10–23, 2005): 115–116.

74. Jennifer A. Chatman and Sandra Eunyoung Cha, "Leading by Leveraging Culture," *California Management Review* 45, no. 4 (Summer 2003): 20–34.

75. This section is based on Jeff Rosenthal and Mary Ann Masarech, "High Peformance Cultures: How Values Can Drive Business Results," *Journal of Organizational Excellence* (Spring 2003): 3–18.

76. Nelson D. Schwartz, "One Brick at a Time," *Fortune* (June 12, 2006): 45–46.

77. Katherine Mieszkowski, "Community Standards," *Fast Company* (September 2000): 368; Rosabeth Moss Kanter, "A More Perfect Union," *Inc.* (February 2001): 92–98; Raizel Robin, "Net Gains" segment of "E-Biz That Works," *Canadian Business* (October 14–October 26, 2003): 107.

78. Reggie Van Lee, Lisa Fabish, and Nancy McGaw, "The Value of Corporate Values: A Booz Allen Hamilton/ Aspen Institute Survey," *Strategy + Business* 39 (Spring 2005): 52–65.

79. Lucas Conley, "Cultural Phenomenon," *Fast Company* (April 2005): 76–77.

80. Rosenthal and Masarech, "High-Performance Cultures."

81. John P. Kotter and James L. Heskett, *Corporate Culture and Performance* (New York: The Free Press, 1992); Eric Flamholtz and Rangapriya Kannan-Narasimhan, "Differential Impact of Cultural Elements on Financial Performance," *European Management Journal* 23, no. 1 (2005): 50–64. Also see J. M. Kouzes and B. Z. Posner, *The Leadership Challenge: How to Keep Getting Extraordinary Things Done in Organizations*, 3rd ed. (San Francisco: Jossey-Bass, 2002).

82. Micah R. Kee, "Corporate Culture Makes a Fiscal Difference," *Industrial Management* (November–December 2003): 16–20.

83. Rosenthal and Masarech, "High-Performance Cultures"; Lencioni, "Make Your Values Mean Something"; and Thomas J. Peters and Robert H. Waterman, Jr., *In Search of Excellence* (New York: Warner, 1988).

84. Jarnagin and Slocum, "Creating Corporate Cultures through Mythopoetic Leadership."

85. Guyon, "The Soul of a Moneymaking Machine"; and Geoff Colvin, "The 100 Best Companies to Work for in 2006," *Fortune* (January 23, 2006).

2 Environment

© GETTY IMAGES/DIGITAL VISION

Learning Outcomes

After studying this chapter, you should be able to:

1. Describe the emerging borderless world and some issues of particular concern for today's managers.

2. Describe market entry strategies that businesses use to develop foreign markets.

3. Define international management and explain how it differs from the management of domestic business operations.

4. Indicate how dissimilarities in the economic, sociocultural, and legal-political environments throughout the world can affect business operations.

5. Describe how regional trading alliances are reshaping the international business environment.

6. Describe the characteristics of a multinational corporation.

7. Explain cultural intelligence and why it is necessary for managers working in foreign countries.

Managing in a Global Environment

ARE YOU READY TO WORK INTERNATIONALLY?[1]

Are you ready to negotiate a sales contract with someone from another country? Companies large and small deal on a global basis. To what extent are you guilty of the behaviors below? Please answer each item as Mostly True or Mostly False for you.

Are You Typically:	Mostly True	Mostly False
1. **Impatient? Do you have a short attention span? Do you want to keep moving to the next topic?**	_____	_____
2. **A poor listener? Are you uncomfortable with silence? Does your mind think about what you want to say next?**	_____	_____
3. **Argumentative? Do you enjoy arguing for its own sake?**	_____	_____
4. **Unfamiliar with cultural specifics in other countries? Do you have limited experience in other countries?**	_____	_____
5. **Short-term oriented? Do you place more emphasis on the short-term than on the long-term in your thinking and planning?**	_____	_____
6. **"All business"? Do you think that it is a waste of time getting to know someone personally before discussing business?**	_____	_____
7. **Legalistic to win your point? Do you hold others to an agreement regardless of changing circumstances?**	_____	_____
8. **Thinking "win/lose" when negotiating? Do you usually try to win a negotiation at the other's expense?**	_____	_____

SCORING AND INTERPRETATION: American managers often display cross-cultural ignorance during business negotiations compared to counterparts in other countries. American habits can be disturbing, such as emphasizing areas of disagreement over agreement, spending little time understanding the views and interests of the other side, and adopting an adversarial attitude. Americans often like to leave a negotiation thinking they won, which can be embarrassing to the other side. For this quiz, a low score shows better international presence. If you answered "Mostly True" to three or fewer questions, then consider yourself ready to assist with an international negotiation. If you scored six or more "Mostly True" responses, it is time to learn more about other national cultures before participating in international business deals. Try to develop greater focus on other people's needs and an appreciation for different viewpoints. Be open to compromise and develop empathy for people who are different from you.

Do you think if you stay in your hometown as a manager you won't have to interact with people from other cultures? Think again. Many people who grew up in small towns with little diversity fail to appreciate the importance of cross-cultural skills. Yet in today's world, every manager needs to think globally. Rapid advances in technology and communications have made the international dimension an increasingly important part of the external environment discussed in Chapter 3. The future of our businesses and our societies is being shaped by global rather than local relationships.

A global mind-set and international experience are fast becoming prerequisites for managerial success. Many organizations based in the United States, including Wal-Mart, FedEx, Starbucks, and Nike, have learned that the greatest potential for growth lies overseas. In addition, the demand for raw materials such as steel, aluminum,

1 Introduction
2 Environment
3 Planning
4 Organizing
5 Controlling
6 Leading

cement, and copper has slowed in the United States but is booming in countries such as China, India, and Brazil.[2] For online companies, too, going global is a key to growth. The number of residential Internet subscribers in China is growing significantly faster than that of the United States. Western Europe and Japan together account for a huge share of the world's e-commerce revenue.[3]

The environment for today's organizations has become extremely competitive and highly complex. Less-developed countries are challenging mature countries in a number of industries. China is the world's largest maker of consumer electronics and is rapidly and expertly moving into biotechnology, computer manufacturing, and semiconductors. At least 19 advanced new semiconductor plants are in or nearing operation in China.[4] The pace of innovation in India is startling in industries as diverse as precision manufacturing, health care, and pharmaceuticals, and some observers see the beginnings of hypercompetitive multinationals in that country.[5]

This chapter introduces basic concepts about the global environment and international management. First, we consider the difficulty managers have operating in an increasingly borderless world. We then touch on various types of strategies and techniques for entering foreign markets and address the economic, legal-political, and sociocultural challenges companies encounter within the global business environment. The chapter also describes multinational corporations, looks at the impact of trade agreements, and considers the globalization backlash. The final section of the chapter talks about some of the challenges managers face when working cross-culturally.

A BORDERLESS WORLD

A manager's reality is that isolation from international forces is no longer possible. Consider that the FBI now ranks cyber crime as one of its top priorities because electronic boundaries between countries are virtually nonexistent. This openness has many positive aspects, but it also means hackers in one nation can steal secrets from companies in another or unleash viruses, worms, or other rogue programs to destroy the computer systems of corporations and governments around the world. The FBI has more than 150 agents in some 56 international offices, including Iraq and China, up from about a dozen offices in the early 1990s.[6]

Business has also become a unified, global field as trade barriers fall, communication becomes faster and cheaper, and consumer tastes in everything from clothing to cellular phones converge. Thomas Middelhoff of Germany's Bertelsmann AG, which purchased U.S. publisher Random House, put it this way: "There are no German and American companies. There are only successful and unsuccessful companies."[7] The difficulties and risks of a borderless world are matched by benefits and opportunities.

Today, even small companies can locate different parts of the organization wherever it makes the most business sense. Virtual connections enable close, rapid coordination among people working in different parts of the world, so it is no longer necessary to keep everything in one place. Organizations can go wherever they want to find the lowest costs or the best brainpower. Many companies outsource certain functions to contractors in other countries

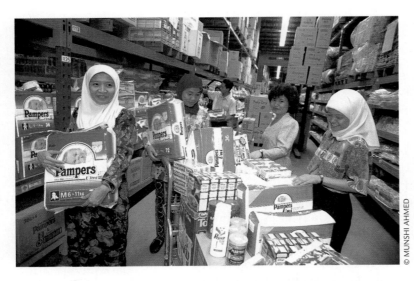

Concept Connection   Today's companies compete in a **borderless world**. Procter & Gamble sales in Southeast Asia make up a rapidly growing percentage of the company's worldwide sales. These shoppers are purchasing P&G's diaper products, Pampers, in Malaysia.

© MUNSHI AHMED

as easily as if the contractor were located right next door. For example, Excel Foundry and Machine in Pekin, Illinois, makes parts for machinery used in heavy-construction and mining operations. President Doug Parsons uses a strategy of outsourcing the easily duplicated parts to contractors in China so that Excel can focus more money and energy on making specialty products and innovating for the future.[8]

As a new manager, learn to "think globally." Take an interest in international people and issues. Don't hinder your own or your company's success by thinking only in terms of domestic issues, competitors, and markets. Expand your thinking by reading and networking broadly.

TakeaMoment

A borderless world means consumers can no longer tell from which country they're buying. U.S.-based Ford Motor Company owns Sweden's Volvo, while the iconic American beer Miller is owned by a South African company. Toyota is a Japanese corporation, but it has manufactured more than 10 million vehicles in North American factories. The technology behind Intel's Centrino wireless components was born in a lab in Haifa, Israel, and Chinese researchers designed the microprocessors that control the pitch of the blade on General Electric's giant wind turbines.[9]

For managers who think globally, the whole world is a source of ideas, resources, information, employees, and customers. Managers can move their companies into the international arena on a variety of levels. The process of globalization typically passes through four distinct stages, as illustrated in Exhibit 4.1.

1. In the *domestic stage*, market potential is limited to the home country, with all production and marketing facilities located at home. Managers may be aware of the global environment and may want to consider foreign involvement.

2. In the *international stage*, exports increase, and the company usually adopts a *multidomestic* approach, meaning that competition is handled for each country independently. Product design, marketing, and advertising are adapted to the specific needs of each country, requiring a high level of sensitivity to local values and interests. Typically, these companies use an international division to deal with the marketing of products in several countries individually.

3. In the *multinational stage*, the company has marketing and production facilities located in many countries, with more than one-third of its sales outside the home country. These companies adopt a *globalization* approach, meaning they focus on delivering a similar product to multiple countries. Product design, marketing, and advertising strategies are standardized throughout the world.

4. Finally, the *global* (or *stateless*) *stage* of corporate international development transcends any single home country. These corporations operate in true global fashion, making sales and acquiring resources in whatever country offers the best opportunities and lowest cost. At this stage, ownership, control, and top management tend to be dispersed among several nationalities.[10]

EXHIBIT | **4.1** Four Stages of Globalization

	1. Domestic	2. International	3. Multinational	4. Global
Strategic Orientation	Domestically oriented	Export-oriented, multidomestic	Multinational	Global
Stage of Development	Initial foreign involvement	Competitive positioning	Explosion of international operations	Global
Cultural Sensitivity	Of little importance	Very important	Somewhat important	Critically important
Manager Assumptions	"One best way"	"Many good ways"	"The least-cost way"	"Many good ways"

SOURCE: Based on Nancy J. Adler, *International Dimensions of Organizational Behavior*, 4th ed. (Cincinnati, OH: South-Western, 2002), pp. 8–9.

Today, the number of global or stateless corporations is increasing and the awareness of national borders decreasing, as reflected in the frequency of foreign participation at the top management level. Consider what's happening in the corner office of corporate America, where 14 of the *Fortune* 100 companies are now run by foreign-born CEOs. Citigroup tapped India-born Vikram S. Pandit as its CEO. Alcoa's top leader was born in Morocco, and Dow Chemical is headed by a native Australian.[11] The trend is seen in other countries as well. Wales-born Howard Stringer was named Sony's first non-Japanese CEO in 2004, and Nancy McKinstry is the first American to head Dutch publisher Wolters Kluwer.[12] Increasingly, managers at lower levels are also expected to know a second or third language and have international experience.

GETTING STARTED INTERNATIONALLY

Organizations have a couple of ways to become involved internationally. One is to seek cheaper sources of materials or labor offshore, which is called *offshoring* or *global outsourcing*. Another is to develop markets for finished products outside their home countries, which may include exporting, licensing, and direct investing. These **market entry strategies** represent alternative ways to sell products and services in foreign markets. Most firms begin with exporting and work up to direct investment. Exhibit 4.2 shows the strategies companies can use to enter foreign markets.

Exporting

market entry strategy An organizational strategy for entering a foreign market.

exporting An entry strategy in which the organization maintains its production facilities within its home country and transfers its products for sale in foreign countries.

With **exporting**, the corporation maintains its production facilities within the home nation and transfers its products for sale in foreign countries.[13] Exporting enables a company to market its products in other countries at modest resource cost and with limited risk. Exporting does entail numerous problems based on physical distances, government regulations, foreign currencies, and cultural differences, but it is less expensive than committing the firm's own capital to building plants in host countries. For example, a high-tech equipment supplier called Gerber Scientific Inc. prefers not to get involved directly in foreign country operations. Because machinery and machine tools are hot areas of export, executives are happy to ship overseas. Small to midsized U.S. companies are benefiting from increased exporting. Henry Estate, a winery in

EXHIBIT | 4.2   Strategies for Entering International Markets

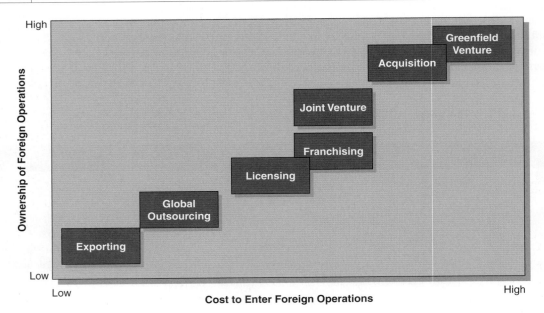

Umpqua, Oregon, exports quality wines to Canada, Japan, and the United Kingdom and has recently begun exporting to China to tap into the 1.3 billion potential wine drinkers in that country. Multiplex Co., a St. Louis manufacturer of beverage-dispensing equipment for fast-food service, exports about 40 percent of its products.[14]

A form of exporting to less-developed countries is called **countertrade,** which is the barter of products for products rather than the sale of products for currency. Many less-developed countries have products to exchange but have no foreign currency. An estimated 20 percent of world trade is countertrade.

Outsourcing

Global outsourcing, also called *offshoring,* means engaging in the international division of labor so that work activities can be done in countries with the cheapest sources of labor and supplies. Millions of low-level jobs such as textile manufacturing, call center operations, and credit card processing have been outsourced to low-wage countries in recent years. The Internet and plunging telecommunications costs are enabling companies to outsource more and higher-level work as well. Netgear, a Santa Clara, California-based company, makes networking equipment that is designed and marketed in the United States, engineered in Taiwan, and manufactured in China, helping the small company take advantage of the efficiencies it can gain in three different countries.[15]

The most recent trend is outsourcing core processes, which Joe McGrath, CEO of Unisys, refers to as the "natural next phase of the offshoring movement."[16] After the Sarbanes-Oxley Act went into effect, Unisys had a hard time finding enough internal auditors in the United States, so managers outsourced their core auditing practice to China. Large pharmaceutical companies farm out much of their early-stage chemistry research to cheaper labs in China and India.[17] Many organizations are even outsourcing aspects of innovation. One survey found that 65 percent of companies reported that part of their research and development takes place overseas. Both Microsoft and General Electric have research centers in China, and IBM has established an R&D center in India.[18]

Licensing

The next stage in pursuing international markets is licensing. With **licensing,** a corporation (the licensor) in one country makes certain resources available to companies in another country (the licensee). These resources include technology, managerial skills, and/or patent and trademark rights. They enable the licensee to produce and market a product similar to what the licensor has been producing. Heineken, which has been called the world's first truly global brand of beer, usually begins by exporting to help boost familiarity with its product; if the market looks enticing enough, Heineken then licenses its brands to a local brewer. Licensing offers a business firm relatively easy access to international markets at low cost, but it limits the company's participation in and control over the development of those markets.

One special form of licensing is **franchising,** which occurs when a franchisee buys a complete package of materials and services, including equipment, products, product ingredients, trademark and trade name rights, managerial advice, and a standardized operating system. Whereas with licensing, a licensee generally keeps its own company name, autonomy, and operating systems, a franchise takes the name and systems of the franchisor. The fast-food chains are some of the best-known franchisors. The story is often told of the Japanese child visiting Los Angeles who excitedly pointed out to his parents, "They have McDonald's in America."

© ROBERT HAGADONE

Concept Connection

Christopher Norman Chocolates found that perfection-obsessed Japanese customers appreciate the difference between their New York company's hand-painted chocolates and French and Belgium chocolates. Joe Guiliano (left) and John Down (right), partners in the high-end specialty chocolate company, first **exported** the chocolates through a Japanese distributor with experience in this niche market. Later they moved to a **licensing agreement,** with the distributor making the confections in a facility near Tokyo.

countertrade The barter of products for other products rather than their sale for currency.

global outsourcing Engaging in the international division of labor so as to obtain the cheapest sources of labor and supplies regardless of country; also called *offshoring.*

licensing An entry strategy in which an organization in one country makes certain resources available to companies in another to participate in the production and sale of its products abroad.

franchising A form of licensing in which an organization provides its foreign franchisees with a complete package of materials and services.

Direct Investing

A higher level of involvement in international trade is direct investment in facilities in a foreign country. **Direct investing** means that the company is involved in managing the productive assets, which distinguishes it from other entry strategies that permit less managerial control.

Currently, the most popular type of direct investment is to engage in strategic alliances and partnerships. In a **joint venture**, a company shares costs and risks with another firm, typically in the host country, to develop new products, build a manufacturing facility, or set up a sales and distribution network.[19] A partnership is often the fastest, cheapest, and least risky way to get into the global game. For example, Wal-Mart teamed up with local retailer Cifra SA in 1991 to get a foothold in Mexico. Despite early losses and difficulties, Wal-Mart is now the biggest private employer in Mexico and the largest single retailer in Latin America.[20] Auburn Farms, a Sacramento, California, manufacturer of all-natural snack foods, formed a joint venture with South Africa's Beacon Sweets & Chocolates.[21] Internet companies have also used joint ventures as a way to expand. AOL created a joint venture with Venezuela's Cisneros Group to smooth its entry into Latin America.[22] In addition to joint ventures, the complexity of today's global business environment is causing managers at many companies to develop alliance networks, which refer to collections of partnerships with various other firms, often across international boundaries.[23] These alliance networks help companies reduce costs, enhance their competitive position in the international environment, and increase knowledge on a global scale.

© ELIZABETH DALZIEL/ASSOCIATED PRESS

Concept Connection   Wal-Mart had $90.6 billion in international sales for the fiscal year ending January 2008 and operates more than 3,000 stores overseas, including this one which opened in Beijing in 2005. But the world's largest retailer isn't stopping there. Managers plan to increase the international division's share of total sales and earnings through a **direct investment** market entry strategy that includes **joint ventures**, **acquisitions**, and **greenfield ventures**. Wal-Mart is currently moving strongly into India, recently announcing a joint venture with Bharti Enterprises to establish Bharti Wal-Mart Private Limited, for wholesale cash-and-carry and back-end supply chain management operations in that country.

direct investing An entry strategy in which the organization is involved in managing its production facilities in a foreign country.

joint venture A variation of direct investment in which an organization shares costs and risks with another firm to build a manufacturing facility, develop new products, or set up a sales and distribution network.

wholly owned foreign affiliate A foreign subsidiary over which an organization has complete control.

greenfield venture The most risky type of direct investment, whereby a company builds a subsidiary from scratch in a foreign country.

The other choice is to have a **wholly owned foreign affiliate**, over which the company has complete control. Direct *acquisition* of an affiliate may provide cost savings over exporting by shortening distribution channels and reducing storage and transportation costs. Local managers also have heightened awareness of economic, cultural, and political conditions. Home Depot purchased the number two home-improvement retailer in Mexico, Home Mart, and turned it into today's leading chain with 50 stores. Philip Morris recently acquired Indonesia's third largest cigarette maker to tap into the lucrative Asian cigarette market.[24]

The most costly and risky direct investment is called a **greenfield venture**, which means a company builds a subsidiary from scratch in a foreign country. The advantage is that the subsidiary is exactly what the company wants and has the potential to be highly profitable. The disadvantage is that the company has to acquire all market knowledge, materials, people, and know-how in a different culture, and mistakes are possible. An example of a greenfield venture is the Nissan plant in Canton, Mississippi. The plant represents the first auto factory ever built in Mississippi, where the Japanese company had to rely on an untested and largely inexperienced workforce. The logistical and cultural hurdles were so enormous and the risks so high that one Nissan executive later said, "We did what nobody thought was possible." The U.S. auto parts maker Delphi is taking a similar leap by building a $40 million, 200,000-square-foot car electronics parts plant in Suzhou, China.[25]

China Inc.

Many companies today are going straight to China or India as a first step into international business. Business in both countries is booming, and U.S. and European companies are taking advantage of opportunities for all of the tactics we've discussed in this section: exporting, outsourcing, licensing, and direct investment. Foreign companies are investing more in business in China than they are spending anywhere else in the world.[26] In addition, multinationals based in the United States and Europe manufacture more and more products in China using design, software, and services from India. This trend prompted one business writer to coin the term *Chindia* to reflect the combined power of the two countries in the international dimension.[27]

Outsourcing is perhaps the most widespread approach to international involvement in China and India. China manufactures an ever-growing percentage of the industrial and consumer products sold in the United States—and in other countries as well. China produces more clothes, shoes, toys, television sets, DVD players, and cell phones than any other country. U.S. furniture and cabinetmakers have also shifted much of their production to that country in recent years, and manufacturers in China are moving into higher-ticket items such as automobiles, computers, and airplane parts.

China can manufacture almost any product at a much lower cost than Western manufacturers. Despite the advantages, however, companies are finding that operating smoothly in China isn't automatic. Mattel learned the hard way after having to recall millions of Chinese-made toys tainted with lead paint, as mentioned in Chapter 3, hurting the company financially and damaging its reputation. If a company like Mattel that has been operating in China since the late 1950s can run into trouble, think of the uncertainty newcomers must face.[28]

India, for its part, is a rising power in software design, services, and precision engineering. Nearly 50 percent of microchip engineering for Conexant Systems is done in India.[29] The California company makes the intricate brains behind Internet access for home computers and satellite-connection set-top boxes for televisions. Google sees India as the perfect place for finding the next set of ideas to keep the company on the cutting edge in global information services.

Google

Innovative Way

Google didn't go to India for cheap labor. It went there for technological talent. When the company wanted to open a new R&D center, it chose Bangalore, partly because many of the Indian engineers working at Google's California headquarters wanted to return home and participate in India's growth. Managers knew Google would have a hard time finding the technological brainpower the company needed in the United States alone. The company also has a larger facility in Hyderabad and two smaller offices in Mumbai and Delhi.

In addition to its hopes for India as a hotbed of innovation, Google also sees India as a vast potential market. The country's online advertising industry is miniscule today but projected to grow rapidly. Managers also believe that people in India are perfectly suited to help Google develop products for emerging markets where billions of people aren't yet on the Internet. "The fact that they come from this culture, the fact that they've seen the population of the world that's not on the Internet . . . puts them in a fairly unique position to transcend both worlds and be creative about emerging-world products," says Prasad Ram who heads the Bangalore research center.

For one thing, Indian engineers know that developing markets have different priorities. For most people in developed countries like the United States, Internet use is about lifestyle, but for those in developing nations such as India and China, it's about *livelihood*. They want to know how the Internet can help them generate income, improve their communities, and further their own and the country's economic development. That entrepreneurial spirit is a perfect fit for Google, where the guiding philosophy is to take risks and be aggressive in finding new applications to serve new markets.[30]

Google isn't the first U.S. company to see India as a major source of technological talent. Yahoo employs about 900 engineers at a research center in India, and IBM has become the country's largest foreign employer with more than 50,000 people employed there.

THE INTERNATIONAL BUSINESS ENVIRONMENT

International management is the management of business operations conducted in more than one country. The fundamental tasks of business management—including the financing, production, and distribution of products and services—do not change in any substantive way when a firm is transacting business across international borders. The basic management functions of planning, organizing, leading, and controlling are the same whether a company operates domestically or internationally. However, managers will experience greater difficulties and risks when performing these management functions on an international scale. Consider the following blunders:

- When U.S. chicken entrepreneur Frank Purdue translated a successful advertising slogan into Spanish, "It takes a tough man to make a tender chicken" came out as "It takes a virile man to make a chicken affectionate."[31]

- It took McDonald's more than a year to figure out that Hindus in India do not eat beef. The company's sales took off only after McDonald's started making burgers sold in India out of lamb.[32]

- In Africa, the labels on bottles show pictures of what is inside so illiterate shoppers can know what they're buying. When a baby-food company showed a picture of an infant on its label, the product didn't sell very well.[33]

- United Airlines discovered that even colors can doom a product. The airline handed out white carnations when it started flying from Hong Kong, only to discover that, to many Asians, such flowers represent death and bad luck.[34]

Some of these examples might seem humorous, but there's nothing funny about them to managers trying to operate in a highly competitive global environment. What should managers of emerging global companies look for to avoid obvious international mistakes? When they are comparing one country with another, the economic, legal-political, and sociocultural sectors present the greatest difficulties. Key factors to understand in the international environment are summarized in Exhibit 4.3.

international management
The management of business operations conducted in more than one country.

EXHIBIT | 4.3

Key Factors in the
International Environment

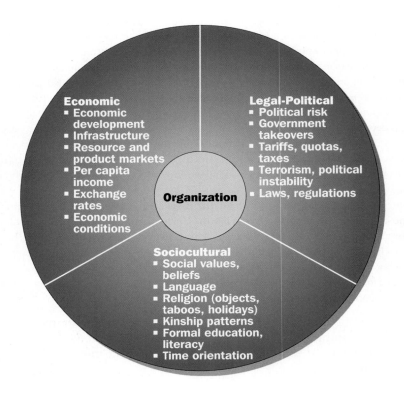

Economic
- Economic development
- Infrastructure
- Resource and product markets
- Per capita income
- Exchange rates
- Economic conditions

Legal-Political
- Political risk
- Government takeovers
- Tariffs, quotas, taxes
- Terrorism, political instability
- Laws, regulations

Organization

Sociocultural
- Social values, beliefs
- Language
- Religion (objects, taboos, holidays)
- Kinship patterns
- Formal education, literacy
- Time orientation

THE ECONOMIC ENVIRONMENT

The economic environment represents the economic conditions in the country where the international organization operates. This part of the environment includes such factors as economic development, resource and product markets, and exchange rates, each of which is discussed in the following sections. In addition, factors such as inflation, interest rates, and economic growth are also part of the international economic environment.

Economic Development

Economic development differs widely among the countries and regions of the world. Countries can be categorized as either *developing* or *developed*. Developing countries are referred to as *less-developed countries (LDCs)*. The criterion traditionally used to classify countries as developed or developing is *per capita income*, which is the income generated by the nation's production of goods and services divided by total population. The developing countries have low per capita incomes. LDCs generally are located in Asia, Africa, and South America. Developed countries are generally located in North America, Europe, and Japan. Most international business firms are headquartered in the wealthier, economically advanced countries, but smart managers are investing heavily in Asia, Eastern Europe, Latin America, and Africa.[35] These companies face risks and challenges today, but they stand to reap huge benefits in the future.

Each year, the World Economic Forum analyzes data to gauge how companies are doing in the economic development race and releases its Global Competitivenenss Report, which tallies 113 factors that contribute to an economy's competitiveness.[36] The report considers both hard data and perceptions of business leaders around the world and considers government policies, institutions, market size, the sophistication of finan-

cial markets, and other factors that drive productivity and thus enable sustained economic growth. Exhibit 4.4 shows the top ten countries in the overall ranking, along with several other countries for comparison. Note that highly developed countries rank higher in the competitiveness index. One important factor in gauging competitiveness is the country's **infrastructure**, that is, the physical facilities such as highways, airports, utilities, and telephone lines that support economic activities.

infrastructure A country's physical facilities that support economic activities.

Resource and Product Markets

When operating in another country, company managers must evaluate the market demand for their products. If market demand is high, managers may choose to export products to that country. To develop plants, however, resource markets for providing needed raw materials and labor must also be available. For example, the greatest challenge for McDonald's, which sells Big Macs on every continent except Antarctica, is to obtain supplies of everything from potatoes to hamburger

Concept Connection While working as a New York investment banker, Bangladesh native Iqbal Quadir realized that connectivity equals productivity. He also knew his impoverished homeland was one of the least connected places on earth. That prompted him to collaborate with countryman Muhammad Yunus, Grameen Bank founder and 2006 Nobel Peace Prize winner, to create Village Phone. Entrepreneurs, mostly women, use Grameen Bank microloans to purchase cell phones. "Telephone ladies," such as Monwara Begum pictured here, then earn the money to repay the debt by providing phone service to fellow villagers. Village Phone results in thousands of new small businesses, as well as an improved communication **infrastructure** that makes a wide range of **economic development** possible.

EXHIBIT | 4.4

World Economic Forum
Global Competitiveness
Index 2007–2008

Country	Overall Ranking
United States	1
Switzerland	2
Denmark	3
Sweden	4
Germany	5
Finland	6
Singapore	7
Japan	8
United Kingdom	9
Netherlands	10
South Korea	11
Chile	26
Kuwait	30
China	34
Lithuania	38
South Africa	44
India	48

SOURCE: The Global Competitiveness Report 2007–08, World Economic Forum, http://www.gcr.weforum.org (accessed April 30, 2008).

buns to plastic straws. At McDonald's in Cracow, the burgers come from a Polish plant, partly owned by Chicago-based OSI Industries; the onions come from Fresno, California; the buns come from a production and distribution center near Moscow; and the potatoes come from a plant in Aldrup, Germany.[37]

Exchange Rates

Exchange rate is the rate at which one country's currency is exchanged for another country's. Volatility in exchange rates is a major concern for companies doing business internationally.[38] Changes in the exchange rate can have major implications for the profitability of international operations that exchange millions of dollars into other currencies every day.[39] For example, assume that the U.S. dollar is exchanged for 0.8 euros. If the dollar increases in value to 0.9 euros, U.S. goods will be more expensive in France because it will take more euros to buy a dollar's worth of U.S. goods. It will be more difficult to export U.S. goods to France, and profits will be slim. If the dollar drops to a value of 0.7 euros, by contrast, U.S. goods will be cheaper in France and can be exported at a profit.

THE LEGAL-POLITICAL ENVIRONMENT

Businesses must deal with unfamiliar political systems when they go international, as well as with more government supervision and regulation. Government officials and the general public often view foreign companies as outsiders or even intruders and are suspicious of their impact on economic independence and political sovereignty.

political risk A company's risk of loss of assets, earning power, or managerial control due to politically based events or actions by host governments.

   Political risk is defined as the risk of loss of assets, earning power, or managerial control due to politically based events or actions by host governments.[40] One example is a new government effort in Russia to tighten financial monitoring. Critics charge that tax authorities demand confidential client information without a legal basis and vary their interpretation of Russian law as it pleases them. PricewaterhouseCoopers has had its Moscow offices raided and was ordered to pay $15 million in back taxes that the firm said it didn't owe.[41] Political risk also includes government takeovers of property and acts of violence directed against a firm's properties or employees. In Mexico, for example, business executives and their families are prime targets for gangs of kidnappers, many of which are reportedly led by state and local police. Estimates are that big companies in Mexico typically spend between 5 and 15 percent of their annual budgets on security,[42] and organizations in other countries face similar security issues.

Some companies buy political risk insurance, and risk management has emerged as a critical element of management strategy for multinational organizations.[43] To reduce uncertainty, companies sometimes rely on the *Index of Economic Freedom*, which ranks countries according to the impact political intervention has on business decisions, and the *Corruption Perception Index*, which assesses 91 countries according to the level of perceived corruption in government and public administration.[44]

Concept Connection Despite the **political risk**, **political instability**, and the local **laws and regulations** of countries such as Morocco, The Coca-Cola Company earns about 80 percent of its profits from markets outside North America. The soft-drink company suffered in global markets after complaints of tainted products from Belgium bottling plants. Managers are busily trying to rebuild relationships because of the importance of international sales.

Another frequently cited problem for international companies is **political instability**, which includes riots, revolutions, civil disorders, and frequent changes in government. In recent decades, civil wars and large-scale violence occurred in the Ukraine, Indonesia, Thailand, Sri Lanka (Ceylon), and Myanmar (Burma). China is highly vulnerable to periods of widespread public unrest due to the shifting political climate. The Middle East remains an area of extreme instability as the United States pursues a difficult and protracted reconstruction following the Iraqi war. U.S. firms or companies linked to the United States often are subject to major threats in countries characterized by political instability.

Differing laws and regulations also make doing business a true challenge for international firms. Host governments have myriad laws concerning libel statutes, consumer protection, information and labeling, employment and safety, and wages. International companies must learn these rules and regulations and abide by them. In addition, the Internet increases the impact of foreign laws on U.S. companies because it expands the potential for doing business on a global basis. First Net Card, started in 1999 to provide credit for online transactions to anyone in the world, found the complication of dealing with international credit and banking laws mind-boggling. After two years and a mountain of legal research, the company was licensed to provide credit only in the United States, Canada, and Britain.[45]

THE SOCIOCULTURAL ENVIRONMENT

A nation's culture includes the shared knowledge, beliefs, and values, as well as the common modes of behavior and ways of thinking among members of a society. Cultural factors can be more perplexing than political and economic factors when working or living in a foreign country.

Social Values

Many U.S. managers fail to realize that the values and behaviors that typically govern how business is done in the United States don't translate to the rest of the world.

political instability Events such as riots, revolutions, or government upheavals that affect the operations of an international company.

One way managers can get a handle on local cultures is to understand differences in social values.

Hofstede's Value Dimensions In research that included 116,000 IBM employees in 40 countries, Geert Hofstede identified four dimensions of national value systems that influence organizational and employee working relationships.[46] Examples of how countries rate on the four dimensions are shown in Exhibit 4.5.

power distance The degree to which people accept inequality in power among institutions, organizations, and people.

1. *Power distance.* High **power distance** means that people accept inequality in power among institutions, organizations, and people. Low power distance means that people expect equality in power. Countries that value high power distance are Malaysia, the Philippines, and Panama. Countries that value low power distance are Denmark, Austria, and Israel.

uncertainty avoidance A value characterized by people's intolerance for uncertainty and ambiguity and resulting support for beliefs that promise certainty and conformity.

2. *Uncertainty avoidance.* High **uncertainty avoidance** means that members of a society feel uncomfortable with uncertainty and ambiguity and thus support beliefs that promise certainty and conformity. Low uncertainty avoidance means that people have high tolerance for the unstructured, the unclear, and the unpredictable. High uncertainty avoidance countries include Greece, Portugal, and Uruguay. Countries with low uncertainty avoidance values are Singapore and Jamaica.

individualism A preference for a loosely knit social framework in which individuals are expected to take care of themselves.

collectivism A preference for a tightly knit social framework in which individuals look after one another and organizations protect their members' interests.

3. *Individualism and collectivism.* **Individualism** reflects a value for a loosely knit social framework in which individuals are expected to take care of themselves. **Collectivism** means a preference for a tightly knit social framework in which individuals look after one another and organizations protect their members' interests. Countries with individualist values include the United States, Canada, Great Britain, and Australia. Countries with collectivist values are Guatemala, Ecuador, and China.

masculinity A cultural preference for achievement, heroism, assertiveness, work centrality, and material success.

femininity A cultural preference for relationships, cooperation, group decision making, and quality of life.

4. *Masculinity/femininity.* **Masculinity** stands for preference for achievement, heroism, assertiveness, work centrality (with resultant high stress), and material success. **Femininity** reflects the values of relationships, cooperation, group decision making, and quality of life. Societies with strong masculine values are Japan, Austria, Mexico, and Germany. Countries with feminine values are Sweden, Norway, Denmark, and France. Both men and women subscribe to the dominant value in masculine and feminine cultures.

EXHIBIT 4.5

Rank Orderings of Ten Countries along Four Dimensions of National Value Systems

Country	Power Distance[a]	Uncertainty Avoidance[b]	Individualism[c]	Masculinity[d]
Australia	7	7	2	5
Costa Rica	8 (tie)	2 (tie)	10	9
France	3	2 (tie)	4	7
West Germany	8 (tie)	5	5	3
India	2	9	6	6
Japan	5	1	7	1
Mexico	1	4	8	2
Sweden	10	10	3	10
Thailand	4	6	9	8
United States	6	8	1	4

a_1 = highest power distance
10 = lowest power distance
b_1 = highest uncertainty avoidance
10 = lowest uncertainty avoidance
c_1 = highest individualism
10 = lowest individualism
d_1 = highest masculinity
10 = lowest masculinity

SOURCES: Dorothy Marcic, *Organizational Behavior and Cases*, 4th ed. (St. Paul, MN: West, 1995). Based on two books by Geert Hofstede: *Culture's Consequences* (London: Sage Publications, 1984) and *Cultures and Organizations: Software of the Mind* (New York: McGraw-Hill, 1991).

Hofstede and his colleagues later identified a fifth dimension, long-term orientation versus short-term orientation. The **long-term orientation**, found in China and other Asian countries, includes a greater concern for the future and highly values thrift and perseverance. A **short-term orientation**, found in Russia and West Africa, is more concerned with the past and the present and places a high value on tradition and meeting social obligations.[47] Researchers continue to explore and expand on Hofstede's findings. For example, in the last 25 years, more than 1,400 articles and numerous books were published on individualism and collectivism alone.[48]

Read the ethical dilemma on page 121 that pertains to social and cultural differences. | TakeaMoment

GLOBE Project Value Dimensions Recent research by the Global Leadership and Organizational Behavior Effectiveness (GLOBE) Project extends Hofstede's assessment and offers a broader understanding for today's managers. The GLOBE Project used data collected from 18,000 managers in 62 countries to identify nine dimensions that explain cultural differences, including those identified by Hofstede.[49]

1. *Assertiveness.* A high value on assertiveness means a society encourages toughness, assertiveness, and competitiveness. Low assertiveness means that people value tenderness and concern for others over being competitive.

2. *Future orientation.* Similar to Hofstede's time orientation, this dimension refers to the extent to which a society encourages and rewards planning for the future over short-term results and quick gratification.

3. *Uncertainty avoidance.* As with Hofstede's study, this dimension gauges the degree to which members of a society feel uncomfortable with uncertainty and ambiguity.

4. *Gender differentiation.* This dimension refers to the extent to which a society maximizes gender role differences. In countries with low gender differentiation, such as Denmark, women typically have a higher status and stronger role in decision making. Countries with high gender differentiation accord men higher social, political, and economic status.

5. *Power distance.* This dimension is the same as Hofstede's and refers to the degree to which people expect and accept equality or inequality in relationships and institutions.

6. *Societal collectivism.* This term defines the degree to which practices in institutions such as schools, businesses, and other social organizations encourage a tightly knit collectivist society in which people are an important part of a group or a highly individualistic society.

7. *Individual collectivism.* Rather than looking at how societal organizations favor individualism versus collectivism, this dimension looks at the degree to which individuals take pride in being members of a family, close circle of friends, team, or organization.

8. *Performance orientation.* A society with a high performance orientation places high emphasis on performance and rewards people for performance improvements and excellence. A low performance orientation means people pay less attention to performance and more attention to loyalty, belonging, and background.

9. *Humane orientation.* The final dimension refers to the degree to which a society encourages and rewards people for being fair, altruistic, generous, and caring. A country high on humane orientation places high value on helping others and being kind. A country low on this orientation expects people to take care of themselves. Self-enhancement and gratification are of high importance.

long-term orientation A greater concern for the future and high value on thrift and perseverance.

short-term orientation A concern with the past and present and a high value on meeting social obligations.

Manager'sShoptalk

How Well Do You Play The Culture Game?

How good are you at understanding cross-cultural differences in communication and etiquette? For fun, see how many of the following questions you can answer correctly. The answers appear at the end.

1. You want to do business with a Greek company, but the representative insists on examining every detail of your proposal for several hours. This time-consuming detail means that the Greek representative:
   a. Doesn't trust the accuracy of your proposal.
   b. Is being polite, and really doesn't want to go ahead with the deal.
   c. Is signaling you to consider a more reasonable offer, but doesn't want to ask directly.
   d. Is uncomfortable with detailed proposals and would prefer a simple handshake.
   e. Is showing good manners and respect to you and your proposal.

2. Male guests in many Latin American countries often give their visitors an *abrazzo* when greeting them. An *abrazzo* is:
   a. A light kiss on the nose
   b. A special gift, usually wine or food
   c. Clapping hands in the air as the visitor approaches
   d. A strong embrace, or kiss with hand on shoulder
   e. A firm two-handed handshake, lasting almost one minute

3. Japanese clients visit you at your office for a major meeting. Where should the top Japanese official be seated?
   a. Closest to the door
   b. As close to the middle of the room as possible
   c. Anywhere in the room; seating location isn't important to Japanese businesspeople
   d. Somewhere away from the door with a piece of artwork behind him or her
   e. Always beside rather than facing the host

4. One of the most universal gestures is:
   a. A pat on the back (congratulations)
   b. A smile (happiness or politeness)
   c. Scratching your chin (thinking)
   d. Closing your eyes (boredom)
   e. Arm up, shaking back and forth (waving)

5. While visiting a German client, you make a compliment about the client's beautiful pen set. What will probably happen?
   a. The client will insist very strongly that you take it.
   b. The client will tell you where to buy such a pen set at a good price.
   c. The client will accept the compliment and get on with business.
   d. The client will probably get upset that you aren't paying attention to the business at hand.
   e. The client will totally ignore the comment.

6. Managers from which country are least likely to tolerate someone being 5 minutes late for an appointment?
   a. United States
   b. Australia
   c. Brazil
   d. Sweden
   e. Saudi Arabia

7. In which of the following countries are office arrangements *not* usually an indicator of the person's status?
   a. United Kingdom
   b. Germany
   c. Saudi Arabia
   d. China
   e. United States

8. In many Asian cultures, a direct order such as "Get me the Amex report" is most likely to be given by:
   a. Senior management to most subordinates
   b. A junior employee to a peer
   c. Senior management only to very junior employees
   d. Junior employees to outsiders
   e. None of the above

9. In the United States, scratching one's head usually means that the person is confused or skeptical. In Russia, it means:
   a. "You're crazy!"
   b. "I am listening carefully."
   c. "I want to get to know you better."
   d. "I'm confused or skeptical."
   e. None of the above

10. A polite way to give your business card to a Japanese businessperson is:
    a. Casually, after several hours of getting to know the person
    b. When first meeting, presenting your card with both hands
    c. At the very end of the first meeting
    d. Casually during the meeting, with the information down to show humility
    e. Never; it is considered rude in Japan to give business cards

SOURCES: Steven L. McShane and Mary Ann Von Glinow, *Organizational Behavior: Emerging Realities for the Workplace Revolution*, 3rd ed. (New York: McGraw-Hill/Irwin, 2004); "Cross-Cultural Communication Game," developed by Steven L. McShane, based on material in R. Axtell, *Gestures: The Do's and Taboos of Body Language Around the World* (New York: Wiley, 1991); R. Mead, *Cross-Cultural Management Communication* (Chichester, UK: Wiley, 1990), chapter 7; and J. V. Thill and C. L. Bovée, *Excellence in Business Communication* (New York: McGraw-Hill, 1995), chapter 17.

Answers

1. e; 2. d; 3. d; 4. b; 5. c; 6. d; 7. c; 8. c; 9. d; 10. b

Exhibit 4.6 gives examples of how some countries rank on several of the GLOBE dimensions. These dimensions give managers an added tool for identifying and managing cultural differences. Although Hofstede's dimensions are still valid, the GLOBE research provides a more comprehensive view of cultural similarities and differences.

Social values greatly influence organizational functioning and management styles. Consider the difficulty that managers encountered when implementing self-directed work teams in Mexico. As shown in Exhibit 4.5, Mexico is characterized by very high power distance and a relatively low tolerance for uncertainty, characteristics that often conflict with the American concept of teamwork, which emphasizes shared power and authority, with team members working on a variety of problems without formal guidelines, rules, and structure. Many workers in Mexico, as well as in France and Mediterranean countries, expect organizations to be hierarchical. In Russia, people are good at working in groups and like competing as a team rather than on an individual basis. Organizations in Germany and other central European countries typically strive to be impersonal, well-oiled machines. Effective management styles differ in each country, depending on cultural characteristics.[50]

As a new manager, remember that understanding national culture is as important as paying attention to economic and political matters when working in or with a foreign country. Prepare yourself by studying how the foreign country's social and cultural values compare to your own country. Avoid an ethnocentric attitude and recognize how the ethnocentrism of others may affect your perspective or work attitudes.

TakeaMoment

Communication Differences

People from some cultures tend to pay more attention to the social context (social setting, nonverbal behavior, social status) of their verbal communication than Americans do. For example, American managers working in China have discovered that social context is considerably more important in that culture, and they need to learn to suppress their impatience and devote the time necessary to establish personal and social relationships.

Exhibit 4.7 indicates how the emphasis on social context varies among countries. In a **high-context culture**, people are sensitive to circumstances surrounding social exchanges. People use communication primarily to build personal

high-context culture A culture in which communication is used to enhance personal relationships.

Dimension	Low	Medium	High
Assertiveness	Sweden Switzerland Japan	Egypt Iceland France	Spain United States Germany (former East)
Future Orientation	Russia Italy Kuwait	Slovenia Australia India	Denmark Canada Singapore
Gender Differentiation	Sweden Denmark Poland	Italy Brazil Netherlands	South Korea Egypt China
Performance Orientation	Russia Greece Venezuela	Israel England Japan	United States Taiwan Hong Kong
Humane Orientation	Germany France Singapore	New Zealand Sweden United States	Indonesia Egypt Iceland

EXHIBIT | 4.6

Examples of Country Rankings on Selected GLOBE Value Dimensions

SOURCE: Mansour Javidan and Robert J. House, "Cultural Acumen for the Global Manager: Lessons from Project GLOBE," *Organizational Dynamics* 29, no. 4 (2001): 289–305.

EXHIBIT | 4.7

High-Context and
Low-Context Cultures

High
Context

Chinese
Korean
Japanese
Vietnamese
Arab
Greek
Spanish
Italian
English
North American
Scandinavian
Low   Swiss
Context   German

SOURCE: Edward T. Hall, *Beyond Culture* (Garden City, NY: Anchor Press/Doubleday, 1976); and J. Kennedy and A. Everest, "Put Diversity in Context," *Personnel Journal* (September 1991): 50–54.

social relationships; meaning is derived from context—setting, status, and non-verbal behavior—more than from explicit words; relationships and trust are more important than business; and the welfare and harmony of the group are valued. In a **low-context culture**, people use communication primarily to exchange facts and information; meaning is derived primarily from words; business transactions are more important than building relationships and trust; and individual welfare and achievement are more important than the group.[51]

To understand how differences in cultural context affect communications, consider the U.S. expression, "The squeaky wheel gets the oil." It means that the loudest person will get the most attention, and attention is assumed to be favorable. Equivalent sayings in China and Japan are "Quacking ducks get shot," and "The nail that sticks up gets hammered down," respectively. Standing out as an individual in these cultures clearly merits unfavorable attention.

High-context cultures include Asian and Arab countries. Low-context cultures tend to be American and Northern European. Even within North America, cultural subgroups vary in the extent to which context counts, explaining why differences among groups can hinder successful communication. White females, Native Americans, and African Americans all tend to prefer higher context communication than do white males. A high-context interaction requires more time because a relationship has to be developed, and trust and friendship must be established. Furthermore, most male managers and most people doing the hiring in organizations are from low-context cultures, which conflicts with people entering the organization from a background in a higher context culture.

TakeaMoment

Refer back to your score on the questionnaire at the beginning of this chapter, which will give you some insight into whether you lean toward low-context or high-context communications. A higher score indicates low-context behavior, which would clash when trying to do business in a high-context culture.

Other Cultural Characteristics

Other cultural characteristics that influence international organizations are language, religion, social organization, education, and attitudes. Some countries, such as India, are characterized by *linguistic pluralism*, meaning that several languages exist there. Other countries rely heavily on spoken versus written language. Religion includes sacred objects, philosophical attitudes toward life, taboos, and rituals. Social organization includes such matters as status systems, kinship and families, social institutions, and opportunities for social mobility. Education influences the literacy level, the availability of qualified employees, and the predominance of primary or secondary degrees.

low-context culture A culture in which communication is used to exchange facts and information.

Attitudes toward achievement, work, and people can all affect organizational productivity. For example, one study found that the prevalent American attitude that treats employees as a resource to be used (an *instrumental* attitude toward people) can be a strong impediment to business success in countries where people are valued as an end in themselves rather than as a means to an end (a *humanistic* attitude). U.S. companies sometimes use instrumental human resource policies that conflict with local humanistic values.[52]

Ethnocentrism, which refers to a natural tendency of people to regard their own culture as superior and to downgrade or dismiss other cultural values, can be found in all countries. Strong ethnocentric attitudes within a country make it difficult for foreign firms to operate there. American managers are regularly accused of an ethnocentric attitude that assumes the American way is the best way. Take the quiz in this chapter's Manager's Shoptalk box to see how much you know about cross-cultural communication and etiquette.

As business grows increasingly global, U.S. managers are learning that cultural differences cannot be ignored if international operations are to succeed. South Korean appliance maker LG Electronics rules in emerging markets because of managers' attention to cultural factors.

Innovative Way

LG Electronics

Two decades ago, managers at South Korea's LG Electronics decided to solve a longtime problem for homemakers: how to keep the kimchi from stinking up the fridge. Kimchi, made from fermented cabbage seasoned with garlic and chili, is served with most meals in Korea. Any leftovers in the refrigerator are inevitably going to taint other foods and leave a pungent odor that lingers for weeks. LG built a refrigerator with a special compartment to isolate the smelly kimchi, and it quickly became a must-have in Korean homes.

LG managers realized that their understanding of Korean culture led to an amazingly successful new product. So, they reasoned, why not apply that concept to designing products for other markets? LG doesn't just build a standard appliance and expect the whole world to love it. Instead, it taps into local idiosyncrasies in key markets by opening in-country research, manufacturing, and marketing facilities, enabling the company to "speak to consumers individually," as one manager put it. The approach led to products such as the kebab microwave in Iran, which includes a microwave-safe skewer rack and a preset for reheating shish kebabs, and the karaoke phone in Russia that can be programmed with the top 100 Russian songs, whose lyrics scroll across the screen when they're played. The phone was an instant hit in a country where people like to entertain at home during the long winters.

In India, LG has introduced a number of successful products, such as refrigerators with larger vegetable- and water-storage compartments, surge-resistant power supplies, and brightly colored finishes that reflect local preferences. Microwaves are designed with a dark interior to hide masala stains. After learning that many Indians use their televisions to listen to music, LG came out with a model featuring an ultra sound system. These efforts made LG the unprecedented leader in appliance sales in India, with market share in some categories nearly twice that of the competition.[53]

By making an effort to learn about local tastes and preferences, LG has become the appliance maker to beat in emerging global markets. Managers have now turned their attention to China, where LG is building extensive in-country facilities and learning all it can about local cultural preferences in the world's biggest consumer market.

INTERNATIONAL TRADE ALLIANCES

One of the most visible changes in the international business environment in recent years has been the development of regional trading alliances and international trade agreements. These developments are significantly shaping global trade.

ethnocentrism A cultural attitude marked by the tendency to regard one's own culture as superior to others.

GATT and the World Trade Organization

The General Agreement on Tariffs and Trade (GATT), signed by 23 nations in 1947, started as a set of rules to ensure nondiscrimination, clear procedures, the negotiation of disputes, and the participation of lesser-developed countries in international trade.[54] GATT sponsored eight rounds of international trade negotiations aimed at reducing trade restrictions. The 1986 to 1994 Uruguay Round (the first to be named for a developing country) involved 125 countries and cut more tariffs than ever before. In addition to lowering tariffs 30 percent from the previous level, it boldly moved the world closer to global free trade by calling for the establishment of the World Trade Organization (WTO).

The WTO represents the maturation of GATT into a permanent global institution that can monitor international trade and has legal authority to arbitrate disputes on some 400 trade issues. As of July 2007, 151 countries, including China, were members of the WTO. As a permanent membership organization, the WTO is bringing greater trade liberalization in goods, information, technological developments, and services; stronger enforcement of rules and regulations; and greater power to resolve disputes among trading partners.

European Union

An alliance begun in 1957 to improve economic and social conditions among its members, the European Economic Community has evolved into the 27-nation European Union (EU) illustrated in Exhibit 4.8. The biggest expansion came in 2004, when the EU welcomed ten new members from southern and eastern Europe.[55]

EXHIBIT | 4.8

The Nations of the
European Union

The goal of the EU is to create a powerful single market system for Europe's millions of consumers, allowing people, goods, and services to move freely. The increased competition and economies of scale within Europe enable companies to grow large and efficient, becoming more competitive in the United States and other world markets. Some observers fear that the EU will become a trade barrier, creating a *fortress Europe* that will be difficult to penetrate by companies in other nations.

Another aspect of significance to countries operating globally is the introduction of the euro. Fifteen member states of the EU have adopted the **euro**, a single European currency that replaced national currencies in Austria, Belgium, Cyprus, Finland, France, Germany, Greece, Ireland, Italy, Luxembourg, Malta, the Netherlands, Portugal, Slovenia, and Spain. Several other countries are using the euro under formal agreements, although they haven't yet met all the conditions to officially adopt the single currency.[56] The implications of a single European currency are enormous, within as well as outside Europe. Because it potentially replaces up to 27 European domestic currencies, the euro will affect legal contracts, financial management, sales and marketing tactics, manufacturing, distribution, payroll, pensions, training, taxes, and information management systems. Every corporation that does business in or with EU countries will feel the impact.[57]

North American Free Trade Agreement (NAFTA)

The North American Free Trade Agreement (NAFTA), which went into effect on January 1, 1994, merged the United States, Canada, and Mexico into the world's largest trading bloc with more than 421 million consumers. Intended to spur growth and investment, increase exports, and expand jobs in all three nations, NAFTA broke down tariffs and trade restrictions over a 15-year-period in a number of key areas. Thus, by 2008, virtually all U.S. industrial exports into Canada and Mexico were duty-free.

Over the first decade of NAFTA, U.S. trade with Mexico increased more than threefold, while trade with Canada also rose dramatically.[58] Significantly, NAFTA spurred the entry of small businesses into the global arena. Jeff Victor, general manager of Treatment Products, Ltd., which makes car cleaners and waxes, credits NAFTA for his surging export volume. Prior to the pact, Mexican tariffs as high as 20 percent made it impossible for the Chicago-based company to expand its presence south of the border.[59]

However, opinions over the benefits of NAFTA appear to be as divided as they were when talks began, with some people calling it a spectacular success and others referring to it as a dismal failure.[60] Although NAFTA has not lived up to its grand expectations, experts stress that it increased trade, investment, and income and continues to enable companies in all three countries to compete more effectively with rival Asian and European firms.[61]

THE GLOBALIZATION BACKLASH

As the world becomes increasingly interconnected, a backlash over globalization is occurring. In a *Fortune* magazine poll, 68 percent of Americans say other countries benefit the most from free trade. The sentiment is reflected in other countries such as Germany, France, even India. "For some reason, everyone thinks they are the loser," said former U.S. trade representative Mickey Kantor.[62]

In the United States, the primary concern is the loss of jobs as companies expand their offshoring activities by exporting more and more work overseas. Consider, for example, that Boeing uses aeronautical specialists in Russia to design luggage bins and wing parts for planes. They make about $650 a month, compared to a counterpart in the United States making $6,000.[63] The transfer of jobs such as making shoes, clothing, and toys began two decades ago. Today, services and knowledge work are rapidly moving to developing countries. An analyst at Forrester Research

euro A single European currency that replaced the currencies of 15 European nations.

© AFP/GETTY IMAGES

Concept Connection   Protesters shout slogans during a demonstration against the World Trade Organization outside a hotel in Jakarta, Indonesia, February 2007. Hundreds of activists held a demonstration to protest the visit of WTO director general Pascal Lamy and to urge the Indonesian government to not waiver on its stance favoring product exemptions. With increased globalization has come a **globalization backlash**, with most groups thinking other groups and countries benefit more from international trade.

multinational corporation (MNC) An organization that receives more than 25 percent of its total sales revenues from operations outside the parent company's home country; also called global corporation or *transnational corporation.*

Inc. predicts that at least 3.3 million mostly white-collar jobs and $136 billion in wages will shift from the United States to low-wage countries by 2015.[64] Many American shoppers say they'd be willing to pay higher prices to keep down foreign competition. Democratic presidential candidate Barack Obama tapped into strong sentiments when he declared, "People don't want a cheaper T-shirt if they're losing a job in the process."[65]

Business leaders, meanwhile, insist that economic benefits flow back to the U.S. economy in the form of lower prices, expanded markets, and increased profits that can fund innovation.[66] Some American companies are clearly benefiting from free trade. When Kalexsyn, a small chemistry research company in Kalamazoo, Michigan, couldn't get contracts with major U.S. pharmaceutical companies that were sending work to India and China, the owners found that European companies were eager to outsource chemical research to the United States.[67] U.S. exports grew 12 percent in 2006, based partly on the need for equipment and supplies for building infrastructure in place such as China, Brazil, and India.[68] United Technologies, which makes Pratt & Whitney engines, Sikorsky helicopters, and Otis elevators, has seen both its revenues and its stock price surge.[69] Yet the antiglobalization fervor is just getting hotter—and is not likely to dissipate anytime soon. In the end, it is not whether globalization is good or bad, but how business and government managers can work together to ensure that the advantages of a global world are fully and fairly shared.

MULTINATIONAL CORPORATIONS

The size and volume of international businesses are so large that they are hard to comprehend. For example, the value added (the sum of total wages, pretax profits, and depreciation and amortization) of ExxonMobil is comparable to the gross national product (GNP) of the Czech Republic. The value added of Wal-Mart is comparable to the size of Peru's GNP, and that of Toyota to the GNP of Kuwait.[70]

As discussed earlier in this chapter, a large volume of international business is being carried out in a seemingly borderless world by large international businesses that can be thought of as *global corporations, stateless corporations,* or *transnational corporations.* In the business world, these large international firms typically are called *multinational corporations (MNCs),* which have been the subject of enormous attention. MNCs can move a wealth of assets from country to country and influence national economies, politics, and cultures.

Although the term has no precise definition, a **multinational corporation (MNC)** typically receives more than 25 percent of its total sales revenues from operations outside the parent's home country. A recent report indicates that by

© NEWSCOM/GETTY IMAGES

Concept Connection   The Maharaja Mac and Vegetable Burger served at this McDonald's in New Delphi, India, represent how this **multinational corporation** changed its business model by decentralizing its operations. When McDonald's initiated international units, it copied what it did and sold in the United States. Today, though, the fast-food giant seeks local managers who understand the culture and laws of each country. McDonald's country managers have the freedom to use different furnishings and develop new products to suit local tastes.

2007 as much 42 percent of the global sales of U.S. manufacturing multinationals came from sales by their foreign affiliates.[71] MNCs also have the following distinctive managerial characteristics:

1. An MNC is managed as an integrated worldwide business system in which foreign affiliates act in close alliance and cooperation with one another. Capital, technology, and people are transferred among country affiliates. The MNC can acquire materials and manufacture parts wherever in the world it is most advantageous to do so.

2. An MNC is ultimately controlled by a single management authority that makes key strategic decisions relating to the parent and all affiliates. Although some headquarters are *binational*, such as the Royal Dutch/Shell Group, some centralization of management is required to maintain worldwide integration and profit maximization for the enterprise as a whole.

3. MNC top managers are presumed to exercise a global perspective. They regard the entire world as one market for strategic decisions, resource acquisition, and location of production, advertising, and marketing efficiency.

In a few cases, the MNC management philosophy may differ from that just described. For example, some researchers have distinguished among *ethnocentric companies*, which place emphasis on their home countries, *polycentric companies*, which are oriented toward the markets of individual foreign host countries, and *geocentric companies*, which are truly world oriented and favor no specific country.[72] The truly global companies that transcend national boundaries are growing in number. These companies no longer see themselves as American, Chinese, or German; they operate globally and serve a global market.

MANAGING IN A GLOBAL ENVIRONMENT

New managers who want their careers to move forward recognize the importance of global experience.[73] But working in a foreign country can present tremendous personal and organizational challenges. A clue to the complexity of working internationally comes from a study of the factors that contribute to global manager failures. Based on extensive interviews with global managers, researchers found that personal traits, the specific cultural context, or management mistakes made by the organization could all contribute to failure in an international assignment.[74]

Before reading the next section, find out your CQ (cultural intelligence) by answering the questions in the New Manager Self-Test on page 117. Your answers will indicate your level of cultural intelligence and help you relate to the concepts that follow. As a new manager, begin soon to develop cultural intelligence so you can work effectively with people from other countries.

TakeaMoment

Developing Cultural Intelligence

Managers will be most successful in foreign assignments if they are culturally flexible and able to adapt easily to new situations and ways of doing things. In other words, managers working internationally need cultural intelligence. **Cultural intelligence (CQ)** refers to a person's ability to use reasoning and observation skills to interpret unfamiliar gestures and situations and devise appropriate behavioral responses.[75]

It is important for a manager working in a foreign country to study the language and learn as much as possible about local norms, customs, beliefs, and taboos. However, that information alone cannot prepare the manager for every conceivable situation. Developing a high level of CQ enables a person to interpret unfamiliar situations and adapt quickly. Rather than a list of global "dos and don'ts," CQ is a practical learning approach that enables a person to ferret out clues to a culture's shared

cultural intelligence (CQ)
A person's ability to use reasoning and observation skills to interpret unfamiliar gestures and situations and devise appropriate behavioral responses.

understandings and respond to new situations in culturally appropriate ways. Consider what Pat McGovern does whenever he travels to a foreign country. McGovern is the founder and CEO of IDG, a technology publishing and research firm in Massachusetts that owns magazines such as *CIO* and *Computerworld*. IDG operates in 85 countries and gets 80 percent of profits from outside the United States. When McGovern goes to country for the first time, he spends the weekend just wandering around observing people. By watching how people in a foreign country behave, McGovern says he gets a sense of the culture—how fast people walk, how much they gesture, what they wear, how the treat one another.[76] McGovern believes you can be in sync anywhere if you pay attention.

Cultural intelligence includes three components that work together: cognitive, emotional, and physical.[77] The cognitive component involves a person's observational and learning skills and the ability to pick up on clues to understanding. The emotional aspect concerns one's self-confidence and self-motivation. A manager has to believe in his or her ability to understand and assimilate into a different culture. Difficulties and setbacks are triggers to work harder, not a cause to give up. Working in a foreign environment is stressful, and most managers in foreign assignments face a period of homesickness, loneliness, and culture shock from being suddenly immersed in a culture with completely different languages, foods, values, beliefs, and ways of doing things. **Culture shock** refers to the frustration and anxiety that result from constantly being subjected to strange and unfamiliar cues about what to do and how to do it. A person with high CQ is able to move quickly through this initial period of culture shock.

The third component of CQ, the physical, refers to a person's ability to shift his or her speech patterns, expressions, and body language to be in tune with people from a different culture. Most managers aren't equally strong in all three areas, but maximizing cultural intelligence requires that they draw upon all three facets. In a sense, CQ requires that the head, heart, and body work in concert.

High CQ also requires that a manager be open and receptive to new ideas and approaches. One study found that people who adapt to global management most easily are those who have grown up learning how to understand, empathize, and work with others who are different from themselves. For example, Singaporeans consistently hear English and Chinese spoken side by side. The Dutch have to learn English, German, and French, as well as Dutch, to interact and trade with their economically dominant neighbors. English Canadians must not only be well-versed in American culture and politics, but they also have to consider the views and ideas of French Canadians, who, in turn, must learn to think like North Americans, members of a global French community, Canadians, and Quebecois.[78] People in the United States who have grown up without this kind of language and cultural diversity typically have more difficulties with foreign assignments, but willing managers from any country can learn to open their minds and appreciate other viewpoints.

Managing Cross-Culturally

Which two of the following three items go together: a panda, a banana, and a monkey? If you said a monkey and a banana, you answered like a majority of Asians; if you said a panda and a monkey, you answered like a majority of people in Western Europe and the United States. Where Westerners see distinct categories (animals), Asians see relationships (monkeys eat bananas).[79] Although this test is not definitive, it serves to illustrate an important fact for managers. The cultural differences in how people think and see the world affect working relationships. To be effective on an international level, managers need to interpret the culture of the country and organization in which they are working and develop the sensitivity required to avoid making costly cultural blunders.[80]

In addition to developing cultural intelligence, managers can prepare for foreign assignments by understanding how the country differs in terms of the Hofstede and GLOBE social values discussed earlier in this chapter. These values greatly influence

culture shock Feelings of confusion, disorientation, and anxiety that result from being immersed in a foreign culture.

New ManagerSelf-Test

Are You Culturally Intelligent?

The job of a manager demands a lot, and before long your activities will include situations that will test your knowledge and capacity for dealing with people from other national cultures. Are you ready? To find out, think about your experiences in other countries or with people from other countries. To what extent does each of the following statements characterize your behavior? Please answer each of the following items as Mostly True or Mostly False for you.

	Mostly True	Mostly False
1. I plan how I'm going to relate to people from a different culture before I meet them.		
2. I understand the religious beliefs of other cultures.		
3. I understand the rules for nonverbal behavior in other cultures.		
4. I seek out opportunities to interact with people from different cultures.		
5. I can handle the stresses of living in a different culture with relative ease.		
6. I am confident that I can befriend locals in a culture that is unfamiliar to me.		
7. I change my speech style (e.g., accent, tone) when a cross-cultural interaction requires it.		
8. I alter my facial expressions and gestures as needed to facilitate a cross-culture interaction.		
9. I am quick to change the way I behave when a cross-culture encounter seems to require it.		

SCORING AND INTERPRETATION: Each question pertains to some aspect of cultural intelligence. Questions 1–3 pertain to the head (*cognitive CQ* subscale), questions 4–6 to the heart (*emotional CQ* subscale), and questions 7–9 to behavior (*physical CQ* subscale). If you have sufficient international experience and CQ to have answered "Mostly True" to two of three questions for each subscale or six of nine for all the questions, then consider yourself at a high level of CQ for a new manager. If you scored one or fewer "Mostly True" on each subscale or three or fewer for all nine questions, it is time to learn more about other national cultures. Hone your observational skills and learn to pick up on clues about how people from a different country respond to various situations.

SOURCES: Based on P. Christopher Earley and Elaine Mosakowski, "Cultural Intelligence," *Harvard Business Review* (October 2004): 139–146; and Soon Ang, Lynn Van Dyne, Christine Koh, K. Yee Ng, Klaus J. Templer, Cheryl Tay, and N. Anand Chandrasekar, "Cultural Intelligence: Its Measurement and Effects on Cultural Judgment and Decision Making, Cultural Adaptation and Task Performance," *Management and Organization Review* 3 (2007): 335–371.

2 Environment

how a manager should interact with subordinates and colleagues in the new assignment. For example, the United States scores extremely high on individualism, and a U.S. manager working in a country such as Japan, which scores high on collectivism, will have to modify his or her approach to leading and controlling to be successful. The following examples are broad generalizations, but they give some clues to how expatriate managers can be more successful. **Expatriates** are employees who live and work in a country other than their own.

Human Resources Not every manager will thrive in an international assignment, and careful screening, selection, and training of employees to serve overseas increase the potential for corporate global success. Human resource managers consider global skills in the selection process. In addition, expatriates receive cross-cultural training that develops language skills and provides cultural and historical orientation.[81] Equally important is honest self-analysis by overseas candidates and their families. Before seeking or accepting an assignment in another country, a candidate should ask himself or herself such questions as the following:

- Can you initiate social contacts in a foreign culture?
- Can you adjust well to different environments and changes in personal comfort or quality of living, such as the lack of television, limited hot water, varied cuisine, and national phone strikes?
- Can you manage your future reentry into the job market by networking and maintaining contacts in your home country?[82]

Employees working overseas must adjust to all of these conditions. In addition, managers going global often find that their management styles need adjustment to succeed in a country other than their native one.

TakeaMoment | Complete the experiential exercise on pages 120–121 that pertains to your global management potential. How well do your knowledge and preferences reflect a global perspective?

Leading In relationship-oriented societies that rank high on collectivism, such as those in Asia, the Arab world, and Latin America, leaders typically use a warm, personalized approach with employees. One of the greatest difficulties U.S. leaders encounter in doing business in China, for example, is failing to recognize that to the Chinese any relationship is a personal relationship.[83] Managers are expected to have periodic social visits with workers, inquiring about morale and health. Leaders should be especially careful about how and in what context they criticize others. To Asians, Africans, Arabs, and Latin Americans, the loss of self-respect brings dishonor to themselves and their families. The principle of *saving face* is highly important in some cultures.

Decision Making In the United States, mid-level managers may discuss a problem and give the boss a recommendation. On the other hand, managers in Iran, which reflects South Asian cultural values, expect the boss to make a decision and issue specific instructions.[84] In Mexico, employees often don't understand participatory decision making. Mexico ranks extremely high on power distance, and many workers expect managers to exercise their power in making decisions and issuing orders. American managers working in Mexico have been advised to rarely explain a decision, lest workers perceive this as a sign of weakness.[85] In contrast, managers in many Arab and African nations are expected to use consultative decision making in the extreme.

Motivating Motivation must fit the incentives within the culture. Recent data from Towers Perrin give some insight into what motivates people in different countries based on what potential employees say they want most from the company. In the United States,

Expatriates Employees who live and work in a country other than their own.

competitive base pay is considered most important, whereas prospective employees in Brazil look for career opportunities. In China, people want chances to learn, and employees in Spain put work-life balance at the top of their list.[86] Another study also found that intrinsic factors such as challenge, recognition, and the work itself are less effective in countries that value high power distance. It may be that workers in these cultures perceive manager recognition and support as manipulative and therefore demotivating.[87] A high value for collectivism in Japan means that employees are motivated in groups. An individual bonus for a high performer would be considered humiliating, but a reward for the team could be highly motivating. Managers in Latin America, Africa, and the Middle East can improve motivation by showing respect for employees as individuals with needs and interests outside of work.[88]

Controlling When things go wrong, managers in foreign countries often are unable to get rid of employees who do not work out. Consider the following research finding: When asked what to do about an employee whose work had been subpar for a year after 15 years of exemplary performance, 75 percent of Americans and Canadians said fire her; only 20 percent of Singaporeans and Koreans chose that solution.[89] In Europe, Mexico, and Indonesia, as well, to hire and fire based on performance seems unnaturally brutal. In addition, workers in some countries are protected by strong labor laws and union rules.

Managers also have to learn not to control the wrong things. A Sears manager in Hong Kong insisted that employees come to work on time instead of 15 minutes late. The employees did exactly as they were told, but they also left on time instead of working into the evening as they had previously. A lot of work was left unfinished. The manager eventually told the employees to go back to their old ways. His attempt at control had a negative effect.

---

ch4   A MANAGER'S ESSENTIALS: WHAT HAVE WE LEARNED?

- Successful companies are expanding their business overseas and successfully competing with foreign companies on their home turf. International markets provide many opportunities but are also fraught with difficulty.

- Major alternatives for entering foreign markets are outsourcing exporting, licensing, and direct investing through joint ventures or wholly owned subsidiaries.

- Business in the global arena involves special risks and difficulties because of complicated economic, legal-political, and sociocultural forces. Moreover, the global environment changes rapidly, as illustrated by the emergence of the World Trade Organization, the European Union, and the North American Free Trade Agreement.

- The expansion of free-trade policies has sparked a globalization backlash among people who are fearful of losing their jobs and economic security.

- Much of the growth in international business has been carried out by large businesses called multinational corporations (MNC). These large companies exist in an almost borderless world, encouraging the free flow of ideas, products, manufacturing, and marketing among countries to achieve the greatest efficiencies.

- Managers in MNCs as well as those in much smaller companies doing business internationally face many challenges and must develop a high level of cultural intelligence (CQ) to be successful. CQ, which involves a cognitive component (head), an emotional component (heart), and a physical component (body), helps managers interpret unfamiliar situations and devise culturally appropriate responses.

- Social and cultural values differ widely across cultures and influence appropriate patterns of leadership, decision making, motivation, and managerial control.

ch4 DISCUSSION QUESTIONS

1. What specifically would the experience of living and working in another country contribute to your skills and effectiveness as a manager in your own country?

2. What might be some long-term ramifications of the war in Iraq for U.S. managers and companies operating internationally?

3. What do you think is your strongest component of cultural intelligence? Your weakest? How would you go about shoring up your weaknesses?

4. What steps could a company take to avoid making product design and marketing mistakes when introducing new products into East Germany? How would you go about hiring a plant manager for a facility you are planning to build in East Germany?

5. Compare the advantages associated with the foreign-market entry strategies of exporting, licensing, and wholly owned subsidiaries. What information would you need to collect and what factors would you consider when selecting a strategy?

6. Should a multinational corporation operate as a tightly integrated, worldwide business system, or would it be more effective to let each national subsidiary operate autonomously?

7. What does it mean to say that the world is becoming *borderless*? That large companies are *stateless*?

8. Two U.S. companies are competing to take over a large factory in the Czech Republic. One delegation tours the facility and asks questions about how the plant might be run more efficiently. The other delegation focuses on ways to improve working conditions and produce a better product. Which delegation do you think is more likely to succeed with the plant? Why? What information would you want to collect to decide whether to acquire the plant for your company?

9. What is meant by the cultural values of individualism and power distance? How might these values affect organization design and management processes?

10. How do you think trade alliances such as NAFTA, the EU, and ASEAN might affect you as a future manager?

ch4 MANAGEMENT IN PRACTICE: EXPERIENTIAL EXERCISE

Rate Your Global Management Potential

A global environment requires that managers learn to deal effectively with people and ideas from a variety of cultures. How well-prepared are you to be a global manager? Read the following statements and circle the number on the response scale that most closely reflects how well the statement describes you.

Good Description 10 9 8 7 6 5 4 3 2 1 Poor Description

1. I reach out to people from different cultures.

   10 9 8 7 6 5 4 3 2 1

2. I frequently attend seminars and lectures about other cultures or international topics.

   10 9 8 7 6 5 4 3 2 1

3. I believe female expatriates can be equally as effective as male expatriates.

   10 9 8 7 6 5 4 3 2 1

4. I have a basic knowledge about several countries in addition to my native country.

   10 9 8 7 6 5 4 3 2 1

5. I have good listening and empathy skills.

   10 9 8 7 6 5 4 3 2 1

6. I have spent more than two weeks traveling or working in another country.

   10 9 8 7 6 5 4 3 2 1

7. I easily adapt to the different work ethics of students from other cultures when we are involved in a team project.

   10 9 8 7 6 5 4 3 2 1

8. I can speak a foreign language.

   10 9 8 7 6 5 4 3 2 1

9. I know which countries tend to cluster into similar sociocultural and economic groupings.

   10 9 8 7 6 5 4 3 2 1

10. I feel capable of assessing different cultures on the basis of power distance, uncertainty avoidance, individualism, and masculinity.

    10 9 8 7 6 5 4 3 2 1

Total Score: _____

Scoring and Interpretation

Add up the total points for the ten questions. If you scored 81–100 points, you have a great capacity for developing good global management skills. A score of 61–80 points indicates that you have potential but may lack skills in certain areas, such as language or foreign experience. A score of 60 or less means you need to do some serious work to improve your potential for global management. Regardless of your total score, go back over each item and make a plan of action to increase scores of less than five on any question.

SOURCE: Based in part on "How Well Do You Exhibit Good Inter-cultural Management Skills?" in John W. Newstrom and Keith Davis, *Organizational Behavior: Human Behavior at Work* (Boston, MA: McGraw-Hill Irwin, 2002), pp. 415–416.

ch4   MANAGEMENT IN PRACTICE: ETHICAL DILEMMA

2 Environment

AH Biotech

Dr. Abraham Hassan knew he couldn't put off the decision any longer. AH Biotech, the Bound Brook, New Jersey-based company started up by this psychiatrist-turned-entrepreneur, had developed a novel drug that seemed to promise long-term relief from panic attacks. If it gained FDA approval, it would be the company's first product. It was now time for large-scale clinical trials. But where should AH Biotech conduct those tests?

David Berger, who headed up research and development, was certain he already knew the answer to that question: Albania. "Look, doing these trials in Albania will be quicker, easier and a lot cheaper than doing them in the States," he pointed out. "What's not to like?"

Dr. Hassan had to concede Berger's arguments were sound. If they did trials in the United States, AH Biotech would spend considerable time and money advertising for patients and then finding physicians who'd be willing to serve as clinical trial investigators. Rounding up U.S. doctors prepared to take on that job was getting increasingly difficult. They just didn't want to take time out of their busy practices to do the testing, not to mention all the recordkeeping such a study entailed.

In Albania, it was an entirely different story. It was one of the poorest Eastern European countries, if not *the* poorest, with a just barely functioning health-care system. Albanian physicians and patients would practically arrive at AH Biotech's doorstep asking to take part. Physicians there could earn much better money as clinical investigators for a U.S. company than they could actually practicing medicine, and patients saw signing up as test subjects as their best chance for receiving any treatment at all, let alone cutting-edge Western medicine. All of these factors meant that the company could count on realizing at least a 25 percent savings, maybe more, by running the tests overseas.

What's not to like? As the Egyptian-born CEO of a start-up biotech company with investors and employees hoping for its first marketable drug, there was absolutely nothing not to like. It was when he thought like a U.S.-trained physician that he felt qualms. If he used U.S. test subjects, he knew they'd likely continue to receive the drug until it was approved. At that point, most would have insurance that covered most of the cost of their prescriptions. But he already knew it wasn't going to make any sense to market the drug in a poor country like Albania, so when the study was over, he'd have to cut off treatment. Sure, he conceded, panic attacks weren't usually fatal. But he knew how debilitating these sudden bouts of feeling completely terrified were—the pounding heart, chest pain, choking sensation, and nausea. The severity and unpredictability of these attacks often made a normal life all but impossible. How could he offer people dramatic relief and then snatch it away?

What Would You Do?

1. Do the clinical trials in Albania. You'll be able to bring the drug to market faster and cheaper, which will be good for AH Biotech's employees and investors and good for the millions of people who suffer from anxiety attacks.

2. Do the clinical trials in the United States. Even though it will certainly be more expensive and time-consuming, you'll feel as if you're living up to the part of the Hippocratic Oath that instructed you to "prescribe regimens for the good of my patients according to my ability and my judgment and never do harm to anyone."

3. Do the clinical trials in Albania, and if the drug is approved, use part of the profits to set up a compassionate use program in Albania, even though setting up a distribution system and training doctors to administer the drug, monitor patients for adverse effects, and track results will entail considerable expense.

SOURCES: Based on Gina Kolata, "Companies Facing Ethical Issue as Drugs Are Tested Overseas," *The New York Times*, March 5, 2004; and Julie Schmit, "Costs, Regulations Move More Drug Tests Outside USA," *USA Today*, June 16, 2005, http://www.usatoday.com/money/industries/health/drugs/2005-05-16-drug-trials-usat_x.htm.

ch4   CASE FOR CRITICAL ANALYSIS

Shui Fabrics

Ray Betzell, general manager for the past five years of a joint venture between Ohio-based Rocky River Industries and Shanghai Fabric Ltd., was feeling caught in the middle these days.

As he looked out over Shanghai's modern gleaming skyline from his corner office, Ray knew his Chinese deputy general manager, Chiu Wai, couldn't be more pleased with the way things were going. Ten years ago, Rocky River had launched Shui Fabrics, a 50-50 joint venture between the U.S. textile manufacturer and the Chinese company, to produce, dye, and coat fabric for sale to both Chinese and international sportswear manufacturers. After many obstacles, considerable red tape, and several money-losing years, the joint venture was fulfilling Chiu Wai's expectations—and those of the local government and party officials who were keeping careful tabs on the enterprise—much more quickly than he'd anticipated. By providing jobs to close to 3,000 people, Shui was making a real contribution to the local economy. Job creation was no small accomplishment in a country where outside experts estimated that the actual (as opposed to the official) unemployment rate routinely hovered at 20 percent.

From Chiu Wai's point of view, Shui was generating just the right level of profit—not too little and, just as importantly, not too much. With so many U.S.-Chinese joint ventures still operating in the red, Chiu Wai saw no reason Ray's American bosses shouldn't be more than satisfied with their 5 percent annual return on investment. But those earnings weren't going to land him in hot water with local authorities, many of whom still viewed profits made by Western companies on Chinese soil as just one more instance of exploitation in a long history of foreign attempts at domination.

If Chiu Wai had been eavesdropping on the conversation Ray had just had with Rocky River president Paul Danvers, the Chinese manager would have certainly been dismayed. Ray, who'd thoroughly enjoyed his time in China, was painfully aware of the quiet frustration in his boss's voice as it traveled over the phone lines from the other side of the world. To be sure, Paul conceded, Shui had cut Rocky River's labor costs, given the company access to the potentially huge Chinese market, and helped inoculate the firm against the uncertainty surrounding the periodic, often contentious U.S.–Chinese textile trade negotiations. Current U.S. tariffs and quotas could change at any time.

"But a 5 percent ROI is just pathetic," Paul complained. "And we've been stuck there for three years now. At this point, I'd expected to be looking at something more on the order of 20 percent." He pointed out that greater efficiency plus incorporating more sophisticated technology would allow Shui to reduce its workforce substantially and put it on the road to a more acceptable ROI. "I'm well aware of the fact that the Chinese work for a fraction of what we'd have to pay American workers, and I do appreciate the pressure the government is putting on you guys. But still, it doesn't make any sense for us to hire more workers than we would in a comparable U.S. plant."

After an uncomfortable silence, during which Ray tried and failed to picture broaching the subject of possible layoffs to his Chinese counterparts, he heard Paul ask the question he'd been dreading: "I'm beginning to think it's time to pull the plug on Shui. Is there any way you can see to turn this around, Ray, or should we start thinking about other options? Staying in China is a given, but there has to be a better way to do it."

Questions

1. How would you characterize the main economic, legal-political, and sociocultural differences influencing the relationship between the partners in Shui Fabrics? What GLOBE Project dimensions would help you understand the differences in Chinese and American perspectives illustrated in the case?

2. How would you define Shui's core problem? Are sociocultural differences the main underlying cause of this problem? Why or why not? How would you handle the conflict with your boss back in the United States?

3. If you were Ray Betzell, what other options to the 50-50 joint venture would you consider for manufacturing textiles in China? Make the argument that one of these options is more likely to meet Rocky River's expectations than the partnership already in place.

SOURCES: Based on Katherine Xin and Vladimir Pucik, "Trouble in Paradise," *Harvard Business Review* (August 2003): 27–35; Lillian McClanaghan and Rosalie Tung, "Summary of 'Negotiating and Building Effective Working Relationships with People in China,'" presentation by Sidney Rittenberg, Pacific Region Forum on Business and Management Communication, Simon Fraser University, Harbour Centre, Vancouver, B.C., March 21, 1991, http://www.cic.sfu.ca/forum/rittenbe.html; and Charles Wolfe Jr., "China's Rising Unemployment Challenge," Rand Corporation Web page, http://www.rand.org/commentary/070704AWSJ.html.

ch4 ON THE JOB VIDEO CASE

2
Environment

Lonely Planet Travels the World

For a company such as Lonely Planet, the idea of a borderless world is nothing new. Founded in Australia by Tony and Maureen Wheeler so that they could fund their own travel dreams, the travel publisher now has offices in Australia, the United States, the United Kingdom, and France, with a total of about 450 employees. Its writers, photographers, and marketers span the globe on a regular basis in search of the best destinations for their customers to explore. However, despite the fact that the idea of globalization is built into the firm's culture, its managers face international challenges every day.

Howard Ralley, director of global marketing and promotions, is now based in Australia, after having worked at the Lonely Planet office in the United Kingdom. He's a decisive manager who says what he means and means what he says. "You can get caught up in a lot of navel gazing, asking, 'What does *global* really mean?'" he quips. "Global doesn't really exist in a lot of senses. When you talk about global marketing, marketing is really all about talking with [a particular] customer, and that customer isn't global. [He or she] is concerned about the immediate environment." Thus, when Ralley and his staff get together to discuss a particular project, they consider the features of the destination, the characteristics of its culture, and the needs of the traveler as they relate to the location. The focus of a book on weekend escapes for the European traveler will be much different from the focus of a book on China.

Still, Ralley and his staff, along with the rest of the Lonely Planet employees around the world, strive to achieve consistency in the message they convey to consumers and other members of the travel industry. "There is a lot of 'globalness' that we achieve," says Ralley. "It's not about product . . . we're talking to an audience which shares many things, including a passion for travel. They believe that travel can change the world. So we work that message into individual markets." In addition, Lonely Planet employees around the world need to achieve consistency in the messages they convey to each other. The Internet has proved to be an excellent tool for handling both types of audiences. For instance, an image representing a specific book or series of books can be transmitted anywhere in the world, among Lonely Planet offices, to travel industry professionals, and to the home computers of consumers. This consistency in

messages helps reinforce the Lonely Planet brand worldwide.

Ralley emphasizes the importance of conveying a unique message about Lonely Planet to distinguish the publisher from its competitors. "If a brand tries to work in all kinds of markets and you try to dumb down to the lowest common denominator," he notes, then you get "blanding" instead of branding. "We all agree that travel is important," Ralley continues. "If we just did a message on that, it would make us no different from National Geographic, Fodor's, or Discovery—so that is blanding. You have to get brave in saying something new to the world. Branding is all about that distinction." Ralley doesn't mind that not every consumer likes Lonely Planet books. He feels that it is more important to speak with a decisive, distinctive voice.

To that end, Ralley is a decisive manager. "The world is not all happy," he said during one recent meeting when discussing with his staff the selection of representative photos for a pictorial book covering 230 countries. Ralley wanted to include a potentially controversial photo of an Ethiopian woman whose facial expression did not appear to be welcoming. His staff expressed concern that the photo would be interpreted as too political. But Ralley insisted that the photo was consistent with Lonely Planet's direct, frank approach to the world. "You face different challenges every day," he later explained when discussing his role as an international manager. "Everything you thought you knew . . . all your assumptions [about a certain culture or market] . . . you have to rethink that." And in the end, he makes the decisions. "At some point," Ralley says, "you have to call the shot."

Questions

1. Identify at least three ways that Lonely Planet can benefit from the use of technology around the world.

2. Why is a global presence particularly important for Lonely Planet?

3. Describe at least two personal challenges that Howard Ralley faces as a manager.

SOURCES: Company Web site, *http://www.lonelyplanet.com*, accessed August 5, 2004; "Lonely Planet Publications Company Profile," *Hoover's Online, http://biz.yahoo.com*, accessed July 30, 2004; Lonely Planet press packet.

ch4   BIZ FLIX VIDEO CASE

Emperor's Club

William Hundert (Kevin Kline), a professor at Saint Benedict's preparatory school, believes in teaching his students about living a principled life as well as teaching them his beloved classical literature. Hundert's principled ways are challenged, however, by a new student, Sedgewick Bell (Emile Hirsch). Bell's behavior during the 73rd annual Julius Caesar competition causes Hundert to suspect that Bell leads a less than principled life.

Years later Hundert is the honored guest of his former student Sedgewick Bell (Joel Gretsch) at Bell's estate. Depaak Mehta (Rahul Khanna), Bell, and Louis Masoudi (Patrick Dempsey) compete in a reenactment of the Julius Caesar competition. Bell wins the competition, but Hundert notices that Bell is wearing an ear-piece. Earlier in the film Hundert had suspected that the young Bell also wore an earpiece during the competition, but Headmaster Woodbridge (Edward Herrmann) had pressed him to ignore his suspicion.

This scene appears at the end of the film. It is an edited portion of the competition reenactment. Bell announced his candidacy for the U.S. Senate just before talking to Hundert in the bathroom. He carefully desribed his commitment to specific values that he would pursue if elected.

What to Watch for and Ask Yourself

1. Does William Hundert describe a specific type of life that one should lead? If so, what are its elements?

2. Does Sedgewick Bell lead that type of life? Is he committed to any specific ethical view or theory?

3. What consequences or effects do you predict for Sedgewick Bell because of the way he chooses to live his life?

ch4   ENDNOTES

1. Adapted from Cynthia Barnum and Natasha Wolniansky, "Why Americans Fail at Overseas Negotiations," *Management Review* (October 1989): 54–57.

2. Ted C. Fishman, "How China Will Change Your Business," *Inc. Magazine* (March 2005): 70–84; and Stephen Baker, "The Bridges Steel Is Building," *BusinessWeek* (June 2, 1997): 39.

3. Figures provided by CXO Media, reported in Steve Ulfelder, "All the Web's a Stage," *CIO* (October 1, 2000): 133–142; and Pete Engardio, "A New World Economy," *BusinessWeek* (August 22–29, 2005): 52–58.

4. Jason Dean, "Upgrade Plan: Long a Low-Tech Player, China Sets Its Sights on Chip Making," *The Wall Street Journal*, February 17, 2004.

5. Engardio, "A New World Economy."

6. Cassell Bryan-Low, "Criminal Network: To Catch Crooks in Cyberspace, FBI Goes Global," *The Wall Street Journal*, November 21, 2006.

7. Joseph B. White, "There Are No German or U.S. Companies, Only Successful Ones," *The Wall Street Journal*, May 7, 1998.

8. Ted C. Fishman, "Half a World Away, An Entrepreneur Grapples With (and Profits from) China's Boom," special section in "How China Will Change Your Business," *Inc* (March 2005): 70–84.

9. Adam Lashinsky, "Intel Outside," and Patricia Sellers, "Blowing in the Wind," special supplement,, "Fortune 500: The World of Ideas," *Fortune* (July 25, 2005): 127–138.

10. Nancy J. Adler, *International Dimensions of Organizational Behavior*, 4th ed. (Cincinnati, OH: South-Western, 2002), pp. 8–9; William Holstein, Stanley Reed, Jonathan Kapstein, Todd Vogel, and Joseph Weber, "The Stateless Corporation," *BusinessWeek* (May 14, 1990): 98–105; and Richard L. Daft, *Organization Theory and Design* (Cincinnati, OH: South-Western 2005).

11. Louise Story, "Seeking Leaders, U.S. Companies Think Globally," *The New York Times*, December 12, 2007.

12. Phred Dvorak and Merissa Marr, "In Surprise Move, Sony Plans to Hand Reins to a Foreigner," *The Wall Street Journal*, March 7, 2005; Carol Hymowitz, "More American Chiefs Are Taking Top Posts at Overseas Concerns," *The Wall Street Journal*, October 17, 2005; Justin Martin, "The Global CEO: Overseas Experience Is Becoming a Must on Top Executives' Resumes," *Chief Executive* (January–February 2004): 24.

13. Jean Kerr, "Export Strategies," *Small Business Reports* (May 1989): 20–25.

14. Allen P. Roberts Jr., "Localizing the Brand," *Inc.* (October 2005): 54–56; Robert S. Greenberger, "As U.S. Exports Rise, More Workers Benefit," *The Wall Street Journal*, September 10, 1997.

15. Fishman, "How China Will Change Your Business."

16. Jennifer Pellet, "The New Logic of Outsourcing: The Next Generation of Offshoring—Innovating and Engineering—Is at Hand (Roundtable)," *Chief Executive* (September 2007): 36–41.

17. Alison Stein Wellner, "Turning the Tables" *Inc.* (May 2006): 55–59.

18. Pellet, "The New Logic of Outsourcing."

19. Kathryn Rudie Harrigan, "Managing Joint Ventures," *Management Review* (February 1987): 24–41; and Therese R. Revesz and Mimi Cauley de Da La Sierra, "Competitive Alliances: Forging Ties Abroad," *Management Review* (March 1987): 57–59.

20. John Lyons, "Southern Hospitality: In Mexico, Wal-Mart Is Defying Its Critics," *The Wall Street Journal*, March 5, 2007.

21. Lora Kolodny, "Building a Global Alliance," *Inc.* (September 2005): 48; "Importing Can Help a Firm Expand and Diversify," *Nation's Business* (January 1995): 11.

22. Ian Katz and Elizabeth Malkin, "Battle for the Latin American Net," *BusinessWeek* (November 1, 1999): 194–200.

23. Anthony Goerzen, "Managing Alliance Networks: Emerging Practices of Multinational Corporations," *Academy of Management Executive* 19, no. 2 (2005): 94–107.

24. Lorrie Grant, "An 'Infinite' Opportunity for Growth: CEO Bob Nardelli Sees Expansion in Home Depot's Future," *USA Today*, July 28, 2005; Donald Greenlees, "Philip Morris to Buy Indonesian Cigarette Maker," *The New York Times*, March 14, 2005, www.nytimes.com.

25. G. Pascal Zachary, "Dream Factory," *Business 2.0* (June 2005): 96–102; Jothan Sapsford and James T. Areddy, "Why Delphi's Asia Operations Are Booming," *The Wall Street Journal*, October 17, 2005.

26. Fishman, "How China Will Change Your Business."

27. Engardio, "A New World Economy."

28. Louise Story, "After Stumbling, Mattel Cracks Down in China," *The New York Times*, August 29, 2007, http://www.nytimes.com/2007/08/29/business/worldbusiness/29mattel.html?ref=business... (accessed August 29, 2007).

29. James Flanigan, "Now, High-Tech Work Is Going Abroad," *The New York Times*, November 17, 2005.

30. Sheridan Prasso, "Google Goes to India," *Fortune* (October 29, 2007): 160–166.

31. Cited in Gary Ferraro, *Cultural Anthropology: An Applied Perspective*, 3rd ed. (Belmont, CA: West/Wadsworth, 1998), p. 68.

32. Jim Holt, "Gone Global?" *Management Review* (March 2000): 13.

33. Ibid.

34. "Slogans Often Lose Something in Translation," *The New Mexican*, July 3, 1994.

35. Louis S. Richman, "Global Growth Is on a Tear," in *International Business 97/98, Annual Editions*, ed. Fred Maidment (Guilford, CT: Dushkin Publishing Group, 1997), pp. 6–11.

36. "The Global Competitiveness Report 2007–2008," World Economic Forum, www.gcr.weforum.org, (accessed April 30, 2008).

37. Andrew E. Serwer, "McDonald's Conquers the World," *Fortune* (October 17, 1994): 103–116.

38. David W. Conklin, "Analyzing and Managing Country Risks," *Ivey Business Journal* (January–February 2002): 37–41.

39. Bruce Kogut, "Designing Global Strategies: Profiting from Operational Flexibility," *Sloan Management Review* 27 (Fall 1985): 27–38.

40. Ian Bremmer, "Managing Risk in an Unstable World," *Harvard Business Review* (June 2005): 51–60; and Mark Fitzpatrick, "The Definition and Assessment of Political Risk in International Business: A Review of the Literature," *Academy of Management Review* 8 (1983): 249–254.

41. Jason Bush, "Business in Russia Just Got Riskier," *BusinessWeek* (April 23, 2007): 43.

42. Kevin Sullivan, "Kidnapping Is Growth Industry in Mexico; Businessmen Targeted in Climate of Routine Ransoms, Police Corruption," *The Washington Post*, September 17, 2002.

43. Conklin, "Analyzing and Managing Country Risks"; Nicolas Checa, John Maguire, and Jonathan Barney, "The New World Disorder," *Harvard Business Review* (August 2003): 71–79; Jennifer Pellet, "Top 10 Enterprise Risks: What Potential Threats Keep CEOs Up at Night? (Roundtable),"

Chief Executive (October–November 2007): 48–53.

44. See Conklin, "Analyzing and Managing Country Risks."

45. Barbara Whitaker, "The Web Makes Going Global Easy, Until You Try to Do It," *The New York Times*, September 2000.

46. Geert Hofstede, "The Interaction between National and Organizational Value Systems," *Journal of Management Studies* 22 (1985): 347–357; and Geert Hofstede, "The Cultural Relativity of the Quality of Life Concept," *Academy of Management Review* 9 (1984): 389–398.

47. Geert Hofstede, "Cultural Constraints in Management Theory," *Academy of Management Executive* 7 (1993): 81–94; and G. Hofstede and M. H. Bond, "The Confucian Connection: From Cultural Roots to Economic Growth," *Organizational Dynamics* 16 (1988): 4–21.

48. For an overview of the research and publications related to Hofstede's dimensions, see "Retrospective: *Culture's Consequences*," a collection of articles focusing on Hofstede's work, in *The Academy of Management Executive* 18, no. 1 (February 2004): 72–93. See also Michele J. Gelfand, D. P. S. Bhawuk, Lisa H. Nishii, and David J. Bechtold, "Individualism and Collectivism," in *Culture, Leadership and Organizations: The Globe Study of 62 Societies*, ed. R. J. House, P. J. Hanges, M. Javidan, and P. Dorfman (Thousand Oaks, CA: Sage, 2004).

49. Robert J. House, Paul J. Hanges, Mansour Javidan, and Peter W. Dorfman, eds., *Culture, Leadership, and Organizations: The GLOBE Study of 62 Societies* (Thousand Oaks, CA: Sage Publications, 2004); M. Javidan and R. J. House, "Cultural Acumen for the Global Manager: Lessons from Project GLOBE," *Organizational Dynamics* 29, no. 4 (2001): 289–305; and R. J. House, M. Javidan, Paul Hanges, and Peter Dorfman, "Understanding Cultures and Implicit Leadership Theories Across the Globe: An Introduction to Project GLOBE," *Journal of World Business* 37 (2002): 3–10.

50. Chantell E. Nicholls, Henry W. Lane, and Mauricio Brehm Brechu, "Taking Self-Managed Teams to Mexico," *Academy of Management Executive*

13, no. 2 (1999): 15–27; Carl F. Fey and Daniel R. Denison, "Organizational Culture and Effectiveness: Can American Theory Be Applied in Russia?" *Organization Science* 14, no. 6 (November–December 2003): 686–706; Ellen F. Jackofsky, John W. Slocum, Jr., and Sara J. McQuaid, "Cultural Values and the CEO: Alluring Companions?" *Academy of Management Executive* 2 (1988): 39–49.

51. J. Kennedy and A. Everest, "Put Diversity in Context," *Personnel Journal* (September 1991): 50–54.

52. Terence Jackson, "The Management of People Across Cultures: Valuing People Differently," *Human Resource Management* 41, no. 4 (Winter 2002): 455–475.

53. Elizabeth Esfahani, "Thinking Locally, Succeeding Globally," *Business 2.0* (December 2005): 96–98.

54. This discussion is based on "For Richer, for Poorer," *The Economist* (December 1993): 66; Richard Harmsen, "The Uruguay Round: A Boon for the World Economy," *Finance & Development* (March 1995): 24–26; Salil S. Pitroda, "From GATT to WTO: The Institutionalization of World Trade," *Harvard International Review* (Spring 1995): 46–47, 66–67; and World Trade Organization, www.wto.org (accessed February 11, 2008).

55. "The History of the European Union," www.europa.eu.int/abc/history/index_en.htm (accessed February 11, 2008).

56. European Commission Economic and Financial Affairs Web site, http://ec.europa.eu/economy_finance/the_euro/index_en.htm?cs_mid=2946 (accessed August 8, 2008).

57. Lynda Radosevich, "New Money," *CIO Enterprise*, section 2 (April 15, 1998): 54–58.

58. Tapan Munroe, "NAFTA Still a Work in Progress," *Knight Ridder/Tribune News Service* (January 9, 2004), p. 1; and J. S. McClenahan, "NAFTA Works," *IW* (January 10, 2000): 5–6.

59. Amy Barrett, "It's a Small (Business) World," *BusinessWeek* (April 17, 1995): 96–101.

60. Eric Alterman, "A Spectacular Success?" *The Nation* (February 2, 2004): 10; Jeff Faux, "NAFTA at 10: Where Do We Go From Here?" *The Nation* (February 2, 2004): 11; Geri Smith and Cristina Lindblad, "Mexico: Was NAFTA Worth It? A Tale of What Free Trade Can and Cannot Do," *BusinessWeek* (December 22, 2003): 66; Jeffrey Sparshott, "NAFTA Gets Mixed Reviews," *The Washington Times*, December 18, 2003; and Munroe, "NAFTA Is Still Work in Progress."

61. Munroe, "NAFTA Is Still Work in Progress"; Jeffrey Sparshott, "NAFTA Gets Mixed Reviews," *The Washington Times*, December 18, 2003; Amy Borrus, "A Free-Trade Milestone, with Many More Miles to Go," *BusinessWeek* (August 24, 1992): 30–31.

62. Nina Easton, "Make the World Go Away," *Fortune* (February 4, 2008): 105–108.

63. Pete Engardio, Aaron Bernstein, and Manjeet Kripalani, "Is Your Job Next?" *BusinessWeek* (February 3, 2003): 50–60.

64. Jyoti Thottam, "Is Your Job Going Abroad?" *Time* (March 1, 2004): 26–36.

65. Easton, "Make the World Go Away."

66. Michael Schroeder and Timothy Aeppel, "Skilled Workers Sway Politicians with Fervor Against Free Trade," *The Wall Street Journal*, December 10, 2003.

67. Alison Stein Wellner, "Turning the Tables," *Inc. Magazine* (May 2006): 55–59.

68. Easton, "Make the World Go Away."

69. William J. Holstein, "Haves and Have-Nots of Globalization," *The New York Times*, July 8, 2007.

70. World Bank and *Fortune* magazine, as reported in Paul DeGrauwe, University of Leuven and Belgian Senate, and Filip Camerman, Belgian Senate, "How Big Are the Big Multinational Companies?" unpublished paper (2002).

71. Reported in Thomas J. Duesterberg, "Exporting Offers a Global Advantage," *Industry Week* (May 2007): 13.

72. Howard V. Perlmutter, "The Tortuous Evolution of the Multinational Corporation," *Columbia Journal of World Business* (January–February 1969): 9–18; and Youram Wind, Susan P. Douglas, and Howard V. Perlmutter, "Guidelines for Developing International Marketing Strategies," *Journal of Marketing* (April 1973): 14–23.

73. Christopher Bartlett, *Managing Across Borders*, 2nd ed. (Boston: Harvard Business School Press, 1998); and quote from Buss, "World Class."

74. Morgan W. McCall Jr. and George P. Hollenbeck, "Global Fatalities: When International Executives Derail," *Ivey Business Journal* (May–June 2002): 75–78.

75. The discussion of cultural intelligence is based on P. Christopher Earley and Elaine Mosakowski, "Cultural Intelligence," *Harvard Business Review* (October 2004): 139; Ilan Alon and James M. Higgins, "Global Leadership Success Through Emotional and Cultural Intelligence," *Business Horizons* 48 (2005): 501–512; P. C. Earley and Soon Ang, *Cultural Intelligence: Individual Actions Across Cultures* (Stanford, CA: Stanford Business Books); and David C. Thomas and Kerr Inkson, *Cultural Intelligence* (San Francisco: Berrett-Koehler, 2004).

76. Pat McGovern, "How to Be a Local, Anywhere," *Inc. Magazine* (April 2007): 113–114.

77. These components are from Earley and Mosakowski, "Cultural Intelligence."

78. Karl Moore, "Great Global Managers," *Across the Board* (May–June 2003): 40–43.

79. Richard E. Nisbett, *The Geography of Thought: How Asians and Westerners Think Differently . . . and Why* (New York: The Free Press, 2003), reported in Sharon Begley, "East vs. West: One Sees the Big Picture, The Other Is Focused," *The Wall Street Journal*, March 28, 2003.

80. Robert T. Moran and John R. Riesenberger, *The Global Challenge* (London: McGraw-Hill, 1994), pp. 251–262.

81. Joann S. Lublin, "Companies Use Cross-Cultural Training to Help Their Employees Adjust Abroad," *The Wall Street Journal*, August 4, 1992.

82. Gilbert Fuchsberg, "As Costs of Overseas Assignments Climb, Firms Select Expatriates More Carefully," *The Wall Street Journal*, January 9, 1992.

83. Valerie Frazee, "Keeping Up on Chinese Culture," *Global Workforce* (October 1996): 16–17; and Jack Scarborough, "Comparing Chinese and Western Cultural Roots: Why 'East Is East and . . . ,'" *Business*

Horizons (November–December 1998): 15–24.

84. Mansour Javidan and Ali Dastmal-chian, "Culture and Leadership in Iran: The Land of Individual Achievers, Strong Family Ties, and Powerful Elite," *Academy of Management Executive* 17, no. 4 (2003): 127–142.

85. Randall S. Schuler, Susan E. Jackson, Ellen Jackofsky, and John W. Slocum, Jr., "Managing Human Resources in Mexico: A Cultural Understanding," *Business Horizons* (May–June 1996): 55–61.

86. Towers Perrin data reported in "Workers Want . . ." sidebar in Peter Coy, "Cog or Co-Worker?" *BusinessWeek* (August 20 & 27, 2007): 58–60.

87. Xu Huang and Evert Van De Vliert, "Where Intrinsic Job Satisfaction Fails to Work: National Moderators of Intrinsic Motivation," *Journal of Organizational Behavior* 24 (2003): 159–179.

88. Shari Caudron, "Lessons from HR Overseas," *Personnel Journal* (February 1995): 88.

89. Reported in Begley, "East vs. West."

© CORBIS

Chapter Outline

Learning Outcomes

After studying this chapter, you should be able to:

1. Define ethics and explain how ethical behavior relates to behavior governed by law and free choice.

2. Explain the utilitarian, individualism, moral-rights, and justice approaches for evaluating ethical behavior.

3. Describe the factors that shape a manager's ethical decision making.

4. Identify important stakeholders for an organization and discuss how managers balance the interests of various stakeholders.

5. Explain the bottom-of-the-pyramid concept and some of the innovative strategies companies are using.

6. Explain the philosophy of sustainability and why organizations are embracing it.

7. Define corporate social responsibility and how to evaluate it along economic, legal, ethical, and discretionary criteria.

8. Discuss how ethical organizations are created through ethical leadership and organizational structures and systems.

Managing Ethics and Social Responsibility

1 Introduction

2 Environment

3 Planning

4 Organizing

5 Controlling

6 Leading

WILL YOU BE A COURAGEOUS MANAGER?

It probably won't happen right away, but soon enough in your duties as a new manager you will be confronted with a situation that will test the strength of your moral beliefs or your sense of justice. Are you ready? To find out, think about times when you were part of a student or work group. To what extent does each of the following statements characterize your behavior? Please answer each of the following items as Mostly True or Mostly False for you.

	Mostly True	Mostly False
1. I risked substantial personal loss to achieve the vision.	___	___
2. I took personal risks to defend my beliefs.	___	___
3. I would say no to inappropriate things even if I had a lot to lose.	___	___
4. My significant actions were linked to higher values.	___	___
5. I easily acted against the opinions and approval of others.	___	___
6. I quickly told people the truth as I saw it, even when it was negative.	___	___
7. I spoke out against group or organizational injustice.	___	___
8. I acted according to my conscience even if I would lose stature.	___	___

SCORING AND INTERPRETATION: Each of these questions pertains to some aspect of displaying courage in a group situation, which often reflects a person's level of moral development. Count the number of checks for Mostly True. If you scored five or more, congratulations! That behavior would enable you to become a courageous manager about moral issues. A score below four indicates that you may avoid difficult issues or have not been in situations that challenged your moral courage.

Study the specific questions for which you scored Mostly True and Mostly False to learn more about your specific strengths and weaknesses. Think about what influences your moral behavior and decisions, such as need for success or approval. Study the behavior of others you consider to be moral individuals. How might you increase your courage as a new manager?

What does courage have to do with a chapter on ethics? Unfortunately, many managers slide into unethical or illegal behavior simply because they don't have the courage to stand up and do the right thing. Remember WorldCom? The small long-distance company became a dazzling star during the late 1990s telecom boom. Just as quickly, it all came crashing down as one executive after another was hauled away on conspiracy and securities fraud charges. For controller David Myers, it was one small step that put him on a slippery slope. When CEO Bernard Ebbers and chief financial officer Scott Sullivan asked Myers to reclassify some expenses that would boost the company's earnings for the quarter, Myers admits that he "didn't think it was the right thing to do," but he didn't want to oppose his superiors. After that first mistake, Myers had to keep making—and asking his subordinates to make—increasingly irregular adjustments to try to get things back on track.[1]

WorldCom is one of many examples of widespread moral lapses and corporate financial scandals that have brought the topic of ethics to the forefront. The pervasiveness of ethical lapses in the early 2000s was astounding. Once-respected firms such as Enron, Arthur Andersen, Tyco, and HealthSouth became synonymous with greed, deceit, and financial chicanery. No wonder a public poll found that 79 percent of respondents in the United States believe questionable business practices are widespread. Fewer than one-third said they think most CEOs are honest.[2] The sentiment is echoed in other countries as well. Recent investigations of dozens of top executives in

Germany for tax evasion, bribery, and other forms of corruption have destroyed the high level of public trust business leaders there once enjoyed, with just 15 percent of respondents now saying business leaders are trustworthy.[3]

This chapter expands on the ideas about environment, corporate culture, and the international environment discussed in Chapters 3 and 4. We first focus on the topic of ethical values, which builds on the idea of corporate culture. We examine fundamental approaches that can help managers think through difficult ethical issues, and we look at factors that influence how managers make ethical choices. Understanding these ideas will help you build a solid foundation on which to base future decision making. We also examine organizational relationships to the external environment as reflected in corporate social responsibility. The final section of the chapter describes how managers build an ethical organization using codes of ethics and other organizational policies, structures, and systems.

WHAT IS MANAGERIAL ETHICS?

Ethics is difficult to define in a precise way. In a general sense, **ethics** is the code of moral principles and values that governs the behaviors of a person or group with respect to what is right or wrong. Ethics sets standards as to what is good or bad in conduct and decision making.[4] An ethical issue is present in a situation when the actions of a person or organization may harm or benefit others.[5] Yet ethical issues can sometimes be exceedingly complex. People in organizations may hold widely divergent views about the most ethically appropriate or inappropriate actions related to a situation.[6] Managers often face situations in which it is difficult to determine what is right. In addition, they might be torn between their misgivings and their sense of duty to their bosses and the organization. Sometimes, managers want to take a stand but don't have the backbone to go against others, bring unfavorable attention to themselves, or risk their jobs.

Ethics can be more clearly understood when compared with behaviors governed by law and by free choice. Exhibit 5.1 illustrates that human behavior falls into three categories. The first is codified law, in which values and standards are written into the legal system and enforceable in the courts. In this area, lawmakers set rules that people and corporations must follow in a certain way, such as obtaining licenses for cars or paying corporate taxes. The courts alleged that executives at companies such as WorldCom and Enron broke the law, for example, by manipulating financial results, such as using off-balance-sheet partnerships to improperly create income and hide debt.[7] The domain of free choice is at the opposite end of the scale and pertains to behavior about which the law has no say and for which an individual or organization enjoys complete freedom. A manager's choice of where to eat lunch or a music company's choice of the number of CDs to release is an example of free choice.

ethics The code of moral principles and values that governs the behaviors of a person or group with respect to what is right or wrong.

Between these domains lies the area of ethics. This domain has no specific laws, yet it does have standards of conduct based on shared principles and values about moral conduct that guide an individual or company. Executives at Enron, for example, did not break any specific laws by encouraging employees to buy more shares of stock even when they believed the company was in financial trouble and the price of

EXHIBIT | 5.1

Three Domains of Human Action

the shares was likely to decline. However, this behavior was a clear violation of the executives' ethical responsibilities to employees.[8] These managers were acting based on their own interests rather than their duties to employees and other stakeholders.

Many companies and individuals get into trouble with the simplified view that choices are governed by either law or free choice. This view leads people to mistakenly assume that if it's not illegal, it must be ethical, as if there were no third domain.[9] A better option is to recognize the domain of ethics and accept moral values as a powerful force for good that can regulate behaviors both inside and outside organizations.

ETHICAL DILEMMAS: WHAT WOULD YOU DO?

Ethics is always about making decisions, and some issues are difficult to resolve. Because ethical standards are not codified, disagreements and dilemmas about proper behavior often occur. An **ethical dilemma** arises in a situation concerning right or wrong when values are in conflict.[10] Right and wrong cannot be clearly identified.

The individual who must make an ethical choice in an organization is the *moral agent*.[11] Here are some dilemmas that a manager in an organization might face. Think about how you would handle them:

1. Your company requires a terrorist watch list screening for all new customers, which takes approximately 24 hours from the time an order is placed. You can close a lucrative deal with a potential long-term customer if you agree to ship the products overnight, even though that means the required watch list screening will have to be done after the fact.[12]

2. As a sales manager for a major pharmaceuticals company, you've been asked to promote a new drug that costs $2,500 per dose. You've read the reports saying the drug is only one percent more effective than an alternate drug that costs less than $625 per dose. The VP of sales wants you to aggressively promote the $2,500-per-dose drug. He reminds you that, if you don't, lives could be lost that might have been saved with that one percent increase in the drug's effectiveness.

3. Your company is hoping to build a new overseas manufacturing plant. You could save about $5 million by not installing standard pollution control equipment that is required in the United States. The plant will employ many local workers in a poor country where jobs are scarce. Your research shows that pollutants from the factory could potentially damage the local fishing industry. Yet building the factory with the pollution control equipment will likely make the plant too expensive to build.[13]

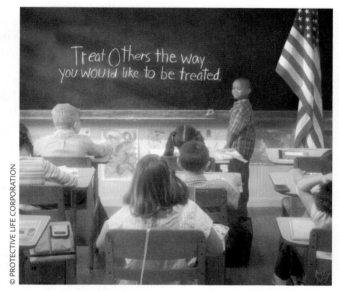

© PROTECTIVE LIFE CORPORATION

Concept Connection Protective Life Corporation shows its commitment to ethics through its corporate strategy: "Offer great products at highly competitive prices and provide the kind of attentive service we'd hope to get from others." Treating others the way you want to be treated is one approach to making ethically-responsible decisions and handling **ethical dilemmas**. However, insurance companies often have to rely on a **utilitarian approach** to ethical decision making that considers how to provide the greatest good to the greatest number of policyholders.

4. You have been collaborating with a fellow manager on an important project. One afternoon, you walk into his office a bit earlier than scheduled and see sexually explicit images on his computer monitor. The company has a zero-tolerance sexual harassment policy, as well as strict guidelines regarding personal use of the Internet. However, your colleague was in his own office and not bothering anyone else.[14]

These kinds of dilemmas and issues fall squarely in the domain of ethics. How would you handle each of the above situations? Now consider the following hypothetical dilemma, which scientists are using to study human morality.[15]

ethical dilemma A situation that arises when all alternative choices or behaviors are deemed undesirable because of potentially negative consequences, making it difficult to distinguish right from wrong.

■ A runaway trolley is heading down the tracks toward five unsuspecting people. You're standing near a switch that will divert the trolley onto a siding, but there is a single workman on the siding who cannot be warned in time to escape and will almost certainly be killed. Would you throw the switch?

■ Now, what if the workman is standing on a bridge over the tracks and you have to push him off the bridge to stop the trolley with his body in order to save the five unsuspecting people? (Assume his body is large enough to stop the trolley and yours is not.) Would you push the man, even though he will almost certainly be killed?

These dilemmas show how complex questions of ethics and morality can sometimes be. In *Time* magazine's readers' poll, 97 percent of respondents said they could throw the switch (which would almost certainly lead to the death of the workman), but only 42 percent said they could actually push the man to his death.[16]

CRITERIA FOR ETHICAL DECISION MAKING

Most ethical dilemmas involve a conflict between the needs of the part and the whole—the individual versus the organization or the organization versus society as a whole. For example, should a company perform surveillance on managers' nonworkplace conduct, which might benefit the organization as a whole but reduce the individual freedom of employees? Or should products that fail to meet tough Food and Drug Administration (FDA) standards be exported to other countries where government standards are lower, benefiting the company but potentially harming world citizens? Sometimes ethical decisions entail a conflict between two groups. For example, should the potential for local health problems resulting from a company's effluents take precedence over the jobs it creates as the town's leading employer?

Managers faced with these kinds of tough ethical choices often benefit from a normative strategy—one based on norms and values—to guide their decision making. Normative ethics uses several approaches to describe values for guiding ethical decision making. Four of these approaches that are relevant to managers are the utilitarian approach, individualism approach, moral-rights approach, and justice approach.[17]

Utilitarian Approach

The **utilitarian approach**, espoused by the nineteenth-century philosophers Jeremy Bentham and John Stuart Mill, holds that moral behavior produces the greatest good for the greatest number. Under this approach, a decision maker is expected to consider the effect of each decision alternative on all parties and select the one that optimizes the benefits for the greatest number of people. In the trolley dilemma above, for instance, the utilitarian approach would hold that it would be moral to push one person to his death in order to save five. In organizations, because actual computations can be complex, simplifying them is considered appropriate. For example, a simple economic frame of reference could be used by calculating dollar costs and dollar benefits. The utilitarian ethic is cited as the basis for the recent trend among companies to monitor employee use of the Internet and police personal habits such as alcohol and tobacco consumption, because such behavior affects the entire workplace.[18]

Individualism Approach

The **individualism approach** contends that acts are moral when they promote the individual's best long-term interests. Individual self-direction is paramount, and external forces that restrict self-direction should be severely limited[19] Individuals calculate the best long-term advantage to themselves as a measure of a decision's

utilitarian approach The ethical concept that moral behaviors produce the greatest good for the greatest number.

individualism approach The ethical concept that acts are moral when they promote the individual's best long-term interests.

goodness. The action that is intended to produce a greater ratio of good to bad for the individual compared with other alternatives is the right one to perform. In theory, with everyone pursuing self-direction, the greater good is ultimately served because people learn to accommodate each other in their own long-term interest. Individualism is believed to lead to honesty and integrity because that works best in the long run. Lying and cheating for immediate self-interest just causes business associates to lie and cheat in return. Thus, individualism ultimately leads to behavior toward others that fits standards of behavior people want toward themselves.[20]

One value of understanding this approach is to recognize short-term variations if they are proposed. People might argue for short-term self-interest based on individualism, but that misses the point. Because individualism is easily misinterpreted to support immediate self-gain, it is not popular in the highly organized and group-oriented society of today. This approach is closest to the domain of free choice described in Exhibit 5.1.

Moral-Rights Approach

The **moral-rights approach** asserts that human beings have fundamental rights and liberties that cannot be taken away by an individual's decision. Thus, an ethically correct decision is one that best maintains the rights of those affected by it.

Six moral rights should be considered during decision making:

1. *The right of free consent.* Individuals are to be treated only as they knowingly and freely consent to be treated.
2. *The right to privacy.* Individuals can choose to do as they please away from work and have control of information about their private life.
3. *The right of freedom of conscience.* Individuals may refrain from carrying out any order that violates their moral or religious norms.
4. *The right of free speech.* Individuals may criticize truthfully the ethics or legality of actions of others.
5. *The right to due process.* Individuals have a right to an impartial hearing and fair treatment.
6. *The right to life and safety.* Individuals have a right to live without endangerment or violation of their health and safety.

To make ethical decisions, managers need to avoid interfering with the fundamental rights of others. Performing experimental treatments on unconscious trauma patients, for example, might be construed to violate the right to free consent. A decision to monitor employees' nonwork activities violates the right to privacy. Sexual harassment is unethical because it violates the right to freedom of conscience. The right of free speech would support whistle-blowers who call attention to illegal or inappropriate actions within a company.

moral-rights approach The ethical concept that moral decisions are those that best maintain the rights of those people affected by them.

justice approach The ethical concept that moral decisions must be based on standards of equity, fairness, and impartiality.

distributive justice The concept that different treatment of people should not be based on arbitrary characteristics. In the case of substantive differences, people should be treated differently in proportion to the differences among them.

Go back to the section on ethical dilemmas on page 131 and select two. First apply the utilitarian approach to reach a decision in each situation, and then apply the moral-rights approach. Did you reach the same or different conclusions? As a new manager, do you think one approach is generally better for managers to use?

TakeaMoment

Justice Approach

The **justice approach** holds that moral decisions must be based on standards of equity, fairness, and impartiality. Three types of justice are of concern to managers. **Distributive justice** requires that different treatment of people not be based on arbitrary characteristics. Individuals who are similar in ways relevant to a decision should be treated similarly. Thus, men and women should not receive different salaries if they are performing the same job. However, people who differ in a substantive way, such as job skills or job responsibility, can be treated differently in proportion to the differences in skills or responsibility among them. This difference should have a clear relationship to organizational goals and tasks.

Procedural justice requires that rules be administered fairly. Rules should be clearly stated and consistently and impartially enforced.

Compensatory justice argues that individuals should be compensated for the cost of their injuries by the party responsible. Moreover, individuals should not be held responsible for matters over which they have no control.

The justice approach is closest to the thinking underlying the domain of law in Exhibit 5.1 because it assumes that justice is applied through rules and regulations. This theory does not require complex calculations such as those demanded by a utilitarian approach, nor does it justify self-interest as the individualism approach does. Managers are expected to define attributes on which different treatment of employees is acceptable. Questions such as how minority workers should be compensated for past discrimination are extremely difficult. However, this approach justifies the ethical behavior of efforts to correct past wrongs, play fair under the rules, and insist on job-relevant differences as the basis for different levels of pay or promotion opportunities. Most of the laws guiding human resource management (Chapter 11) are based on the justice approach.

Understanding these various approaches is only a first step. Managers still have to consider how to apply them. The approaches offer general principles that managers can recognize as useful in making ethical decisions.

procedural justice The concept that rules should be clearly stated and consistently and impartially enforced.

compensatory justice The concept that individuals should be compensated for the cost of their injuries by the party responsible and also that individuals should not be held responsible for matters over which they have no control.

MANAGER ETHICAL CHOICES

A number of factors influence a manager's ability to make ethical decisions. Individuals bring specific personality and behavioral traits to the job. Personal needs, family influence, and religious background all shape a manager's value system. Specific personality characteristics, such as ego strength, self-confidence, and a strong sense of independence, may enable managers to make ethical choices despite personal risks.

One important personal trait is the stage of moral development.[21] A simplified version of one model of personal moral development is shown in Exhibit 5.2.

EXHIBIT | 5.2   Three Levels of Personal Moral Development

Level 3: Postconventional

Follows self-chosen principles of justice and right. Aware that people hold different values and seeks creative solutions to ethical dilemmas. Balances concern for individual with concern for common good.

Level 2: Conventional

Lives up to expectations of others. Fulfills duties and obligations of social system. Upholds laws.

Level 1: Preconventional

Follows rules to avoid punishment. Acts in own interest. Obedience for its own sake.

Leadership Style: Autocratic/coercive   Guiding/encouraging, team oriented   Transforming, or servant leadership

Employee Behavior: Task accomplishment   Work group collaboration   Empowered employees, full participation

SOURCE: Based on L. Kohlberg, "Moral Stages and Moralization: The Cognitive-Developmental Approach," in *Moral Development and Behavior: Theory, Research, and Social Issues*, ed. T. Lickona (New York: Holt, Rinehart, and Winston, 1976), pp. 31–53; and Jill W. Graham, "Leadership, Moral Development and Citizenship Behavior," *Business Ethics Quarterly* 5, no. 1 (January 1995): 43–54.

At the *preconventional level*, individuals are concerned with external rewards and punishments and obey authority to avoid detrimental personal consequences. In an organizational context, this level may be associated with managers who use an autocratic or coercive leadership style, with employees oriented toward dependable accomplishment of specific tasks.

At level two, called the *conventional level*, people learn to conform to the expectations of good behavior as defined by colleagues, family, friends, and society. Meeting social and interpersonal obligations is important. Work group collaboration is the preferred manner for accomplishment of organizational goals, and managers use a leadership style that encourages interpersonal relationships and cooperation.

At the *postconventional*, or *principled* level, individuals are guided by an internal set of values based on universal principles of justice and right and will even disobey rules or laws that violate these principles. Internal values become more important than the expectations of significant others. This chapter's Manager's Shoptalk gives some tips for how postconventional managers can effectively challenge their superiors concerning questionable ethical matters. One example of the postconventional or principled approach comes from World War II. When the *USS Indianapolis* sank after being torpedoed, one Navy pilot disobeyed orders and risked his life to save men who were being picked off by sharks. The pilot was operating from the highest level of moral development in attempting the rescue despite a direct order from superiors. When managers operate from this highest level of development, they use transformative or servant leadership, focusing on the needs of followers and encouraging others to think for themselves and to engage in higher levels of moral reasoning. Employees are empowered and given opportunities for constructive participation in governance of the organization.

The great majority of managers operate at level two, meaning their ethical thought and behavior is greatly influenced by their superiors, colleagues, and other significant people in the organization or industry. A few have not advanced beyond level one. Only about 20 percent of American adults reach the level-three postconventional stage of moral development. People at level three are able to act in an independent, ethical manner regardless of expectations from others inside or outside the organization. Managers at level three of moral development will make ethical decisions whatever the organizational consequences for them.

© ROS WURZER/ASSOCIATED PRESS

Concept Connection Oprah Winfrey is an Emmy-winning television talk show host, heads multimedia empire Harpo Productions, and is personally worth an estimated $1.5 billion. Yet Winfrey is motivated not by a desire for influence, power, or money, but by her "calling," a mission to serve others by uplifting, enlightening, encouraging, and transforming how people see themselves. Winfrey demonstrates a **postconventional level of moral development**. Rather than listening to "the voice of the world," she says she listens to "the still small voice" inside that tells her what to do based on her deep moral values and standards of integrity. Winfrey evaluates every staff idea in terms of how it connects to service to others.

Review your responses to the questions at the beginning of this chapter, which will give you some insight into your own level of manager courage, which is related to moral development. As a new manager, strive for a high level of personal moral development. You can test yours by completing the New Manager Self-Test on page 137.

TakeaMoment

Manager's Shoptalk

How to Challenge the Boss on Ethical Issues

Many of today's top executives put a renewed emphasis on ethics in light of serious ethical lapses that tarnished the reputations and hurt the performance of previously respected and successful companies. Yet keeping an organization in ethical line is an ongoing challenge, and it requires that people at all levels be willing to stand up for what they think is right. Challenging the boss or other senior leaders on potentially unethical behaviors is particularly unnerving for most people. Here are some tips for talking to the boss about an ethically questionable decision or action. Following these guidelines can increase the odds that you'll be heard and your opinions will be seriously considered.

- *Do your research.* Marshall any facts and figures that support your position on the issue at hand, and develop an alternative policy or course of action that you can suggest at the appropriate time. Prepare succinct answers to any questions you anticipate being asked about your plan.

- *Begin the meeting by giving your boss the floor.* Make sure you really do understand what the decision or policy is and the reasons behind it. Ask open-ended questions, and listen actively, showing through both your responses and your body language that you're seriously listening and trying to understand the other person's position. In particular, seek out information about what the senior manager sees as the decision or policy's benefits as well as any potential downsides. It'll give you information you can use later to highlight how your plan can produce similar benefits while avoiding the potential disadvantages.

- *Pay attention to your word choice and demeanor.* No matter how strongly you feel about the matter, don't rant and rave about it. You're more likely to be heard if you remain calm, objective, and professional. Try to disagree without making it personal. Avoid phrases such as "you're wrong," "you can't," "you should,"

or "how could you?" to prevent triggering the other person's automatic defense mechanisms.

- *Take care how you suggest your alternative solution.* You can introduce your plan with phrases such as "here's another way to look at this" or "what would you think about . . . ?" Check for your superior's reactions both by explicitly asking for feedback and being sensitive to body language clues. Point out the potential negative consequences of implementing decisions that might be construed as unethical by customers, shareholders, suppliers, or the public.

- *Be patient.* Don't demand a resolution on the spot. During your conversation, you may realize that your plan needs some work, or your boss might just need time to digest the information and opinions you've presented. It's often a good idea to ask for a follow-up meeting.

If the decision or action being considered is clearly unethical or potentially illegal, and this meeting doesn't provide a quick resolution, you might need to take your concerns to higher levels, or even blow the whistle to someone outside the organization who can make sure the organization stays in line. However, most managers don't want to take actions that will harm the organization, its people, or the community. In many cases, questionable ethical issues can be resolved by open and honest communication. That, however, requires that people have the courage—and develop the skills—to confront their superiors in a calm and rational way.

SOURCE: Kevin Daley,"How to Disagree: Go Up Against Your Boss or a Senior Executive and Live to Tell the Tale," *T&D* (April 2004); Diane Moore,"How to Disagree with Your Boss—and Keep Your Job," *Toronto Star*, November 12, 2003; "How to Disagree with Your Boss," *WikiHow*, http://wiki.ehow .com/Disagree-With-Your-Boss; and"How to Confront Your Boss Constructively," *The Buzz* (October 23–29, 1996), www .hardatwork.com/Buzz/ten.html.

Globalization makes ethical issues even more complicated for today's managers.[22] For example, although tolerance for bribery is waning, bribes are still considered a normal part of doing business in many foreign countries. Transparency International, an international organization that monitors corruption, publishes an annual report ranking 30 leading exporting countries based on the propensity of

New Manager Self-Test

Self and Others

Leaders differ in how they view human nature and the tactics they use to get things done through others. Answer the questions below based on how you view yourself and others. Think carefully about each question and be honest about what you feel inside. Please answer whether each item below is Mostly True or Mostly False for you.

	Mostly True	Mostly False
1. I prefer not to depend on anyone else to get things done.	_____	_____
2. I appreciate that I am a special person.	_____	_____
3. I help orient new people even though it is not required.	_____	_____
4. I like to be the center of attention.	_____	_____
5. I am always ready to lend a helping hand to those around me.	_____	_____
6. I tend to see my co-workers as competitors.	_____	_____
7. I am quick to see and point out others' mistakes.	_____	_____
8. I frequently interrupt someone to make my point.	_____	_____
9. I often have to admit that people around me are not very competent.	_____	_____

SCORING AND INTERPRETATION: This scale is about orientation toward self versus others. A high score suggests you could be ego-centered, and may come across to others as something of a jerk. To compute your score, give yourself one point for each Mostly False answer to items 3 and 5, and one point for each Mostly True answer to items 1, 2, 4, 6, 7, 8, and 9. A score of 7 to 9 points suggests a self-oriented person who might take the *individualism approach* to the extreme or function at the *pre-conventional level 1* of moral development (Exhibit 5.2). A score from 4 to 6 points suggests a balance between self and others. A score from 0 to 3 points would indicate an "other" orientation associated with a *utilitarian* or *moral-rights approach* and *level 2 or level 3 moral development,* suggesting little likelihood of coming across as a jerk.

2 Environment

international businesses to offer bribes. Exhibit 5.3 shows results of the organization's most recent available report. Emerging export powers rank the worst, with India showing the greatest propensity for bribery and China, which has become the world's fourth largest exporter, almost as bad. However, multinational firms in the United States, Japan, France, and Spain also reveal a relatively high propensity to pay bribes overseas.[23]

These are difficult issues for managers to resolve. Companies that don't oil the wheels of contract negotiations in foreign countries can put themselves at a competitive disadvantage, yet managers walk a fine line when doing deals overseas. Although U.S. laws allow certain types of payments, tough federal antibribery laws are also in place. Many companies, including Monsanto, ScheringPlough, and IBM, have gotten into trouble with the U.S. Securities and Exchange Commission (SEC) for using incentives to facilitate foreign deals.

EXHIBIT | 5.3

The Transparency
International Bribe
Payers Index

A score of 10 represents zero propensity to pay bribes, while a score of
0 reflects very high levels of bribery.

Rank		Score	Rank		Score
1	Switzerland	7.81	16	Portugal	6.47
2	Sweden	7.62	17	Mexico	6.45
3	Australia	7.59	18	Hong Kong	6.01
4	Austria	7.50	18(tie)	Israel	6.01
5	Canada	7.46	20	Italy	5.94
6	United Kingdom	7.39	21	South Korea	5.83
7	Germany	7.34	22	Saudi Arabia	5.75
8	Netherlands	7.28	23	Brazil	5.65
9	Belgium	7.22	24	South Africa	5.61
9(tie)	United States	7.22	25	Malaysia	5.59
11	Japan	7.10	26	Taiwan	5.41
12	Singapore	6.78	27	Turkey	5.23
13	Spain	6.63	28	Russia	5.16
14	UAE	6.62	29	China	4.94
15	France	6.50	30	India	4.62

SOURCE: Transparency International, *www.transparency.org/policy_research/surveys_indices/bpi/bpi_2006*
(accessed February 18, 2008).

WHAT IS CORPORATE SOCIAL RESPONSIBILITY?

corporate social responsibility
The obligation of organization
management to make decisions
and take actions that will enhance
the welfare and interests of society as well as the organization.

Now let's turn to the issue of corporate social responsibility. In one sense, the concept
of social responsibility, like ethics, is easy to understand: It means distinguishing
right from wrong and doing right. It means being a good corporate citizen. The formal definition of **corporate social responsibility** (CSR) is management's obligation
to make choices and take actions that will contribute to the welfare and interests of
society as well as the organization.[24]

As straightforward as this definition seems, CSR can
be a difficult concept to grasp because different people
have different beliefs as to which actions improve society's welfare.[25] To make matters worse, social responsibility covers a range of issues, many of which are
ambiguous with respect to right or wrong. If a bank
deposits the money from a trust fund into a low-interest
account for 90 days, from which it makes a substantial
profit, is it being a responsible corporate citizen? How
about two companies engaging in intense competition?
Is it socially responsible for the stronger corporation to
drive the weaker one into bankruptcy or a forced merger?
Or consider companies such as Chiquita, Kmart, or Dana
Corporation, all of which declared bankruptcy—which is
perfectly legal—to avoid mounting financial obligations
to suppliers, labor unions, or competitors. These examples contain moral, legal, and economic considerations
that make socially responsible behavior hard to define.

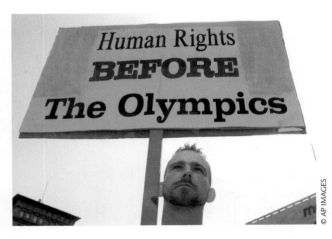

© AP IMAGES

Concept Connection   The International Olympic Committee
(IOC) must respond to numerous **stakeholders**, including the 205
National Olympic Committees that make up its membership, the
countries and cities at which various Olympic events will be held, the
business community that will cater to attendees, numerous sponsors,
media organizations, the participating athletes, and an international
public that has varying and conflicting interests. The symbolic running
of the torch for the 2008 Olympics was plagued by protests over China's
alleged human rights violations. In this photo, Ross Lahive protests
as the torch passes through San Francisco.

Organizational Stakeholders

One reason for the difficulty understanding and applying CSR is that managers must confront the question,
"Responsibility to whom?" Recall from Chapter 3 that
the organization's environment consists of several

sectors in both the task and general environment. From a social responsibility perspective, enlightened organizations view the internal and external environment as a variety of stakeholders.

A **stakeholder** is any group within or outside the organization that has a stake in the organization's performance. Each stakeholder has a different criterion of responsiveness because it has a different interest in the organization.[26] For example, Wal-Mart uses aggressive bargaining tactics with suppliers so that it is able to provide low prices for customers. Some stakeholders see this type of corporate behavior as responsible because it benefits customers and forces suppliers to be more efficient. Others, however, argue that the aggressive tactics are unethical and socially irresponsible because they force U.S. manufacturers to lay off workers, close factories, and outsource from low-wage countries. One supplier said clothing is being sold so cheaply at Wal-Mart that many U.S. companies could not compete even if they paid their employees nothing.[27]

The organization's performance affects stakeholders, but stakeholders can also have a tremendous effect on the organization's performance and success. Consider the case of Monsanto, a leading competitor in the life sciences industry.

Over the past decade or so, Monsanto has been transformed from a chemicals firm into a biotechnology company. The organization's vast array of stakeholders around the world includes customers, investors, suppliers, partners, health and agricultural organizations, regulatory agencies, research institutes, and governments.

Monsanto experienced some big problems in recent years because of its failure to satisfy various stakeholder groups. For example, the company's genetic seed business has been the target of controversy and protest. Small farmers were concerned about new dependencies that might arise for them with using the new seeds. European consumers rebelled against a perceived imposition of unlabeled, genetically modified food ingredients. Research institutes and other organizations took offense at what they perceived as Monsanto's arrogant approach to the new business. Activist groups accused the company of creating "Frankenstein foods." To make matters even worse, in seeking to sell genetically modified seeds in Indonesia, managers allegedly bribed government officials, which got Monsanto into hot water with the SEC.

In light of these stakeholder issues, CEO Hendrik Verfaillie offered an apology to some stakeholders at a *Farm Journal* Conference in Washington, D.C., saying that Monsanto "was so blinded by its enthusiasm for this great new technology that it missed the concerns the technology raised for many people." Verfaillie also announced a five-part pledge that aims to restore positive stakeholder relationships. Each of the five commitments requires an ongoing dialogue between Monsanto managers and various stakeholder constituencies. The company paid $1.5 million to settle the SEC charges and is voluntarily cooperating with regulatory investigators. Monsanto managers understand the importance of effectively managing critical stakeholder relationships.[28]

Monsanto

Innovative Way

Exhibit 5.4 illustrates important stakeholders for Monsanto. Most organizations are similarly influenced by a variety of stakeholder groups. Investors and shareholders, employees, customers, and suppliers are considered primary stakeholders, without whom the organization cannot survive. Investors, shareholders, and suppliers' interests are served by managerial efficiency—that is, use of resources to achieve profits. Employees expect work satisfaction, pay, and good supervision. Customers are concerned with decisions about the quality, safety, and availability of goods and services. When any primary stakeholder group becomes seriously dissatisfied, the organization's viability is threatened.[29]

Other important stakeholders are the government and the community, which have become increasingly important in recent years. Most corporations exist only under the proper charter and licenses and operate within the limits of safety laws, environmental protection requirements, antitrust regulations, antibribery legislation, and other laws and regulations in the government sector. The community includes local government, the natural and physical environments, and the quality of life

stakeholder Any group within or outside the organization that has a stake in the organization's performance.

2 Environment

EXHIBIT 5.4 Major Stakeholders Relevant to Monsanto Company

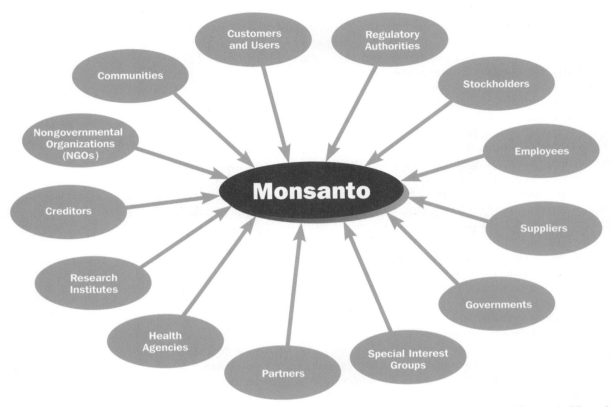

SOURCES: Based on information in D. Wheeler, B. Colbert, and R. E. Freeman, "Focusing on Value: Reconciling Corporate Social Responsibility, Sustainability, and a Stakeholder Approach in a Networked World," *Journal of General Management* 28, no. 3 (Spring 2003): 1–28; and J. E. Post, L. E. Preston, and S. Sachs, "Managing the Extended Enterprise: The New Stakeholder View," *California Management Review* 45, no. 1 (Fall 2002): 6–28.

provided for residents. Special interest groups, still another stakeholder, may include trade associations, political action committees, professional associations, and consumerists. Socially responsible organizations consider the effects of their actions on all stakeholder groups. Some large businesses with the resources needed to serve developing countries are extending their field of stakeholders by serving the *bottom of the pyramid*.

The Bottom of the Pyramid

The **bottom of the pyramid (BOP) concept**, sometimes called *base of the pyramid*, proposes that corporations can alleviate poverty and other social ills, as well as make significant profits, by selling to the world's poorest people. The term *bottom of the pyramid* refers to the more than four billion people who make up the lowest level of the world's economic "pyramid" as defined by per capita income. These people earn less than US $1,500 a year, with about one-fourth of them earning less than a dollar a day.[30] Traditionally, these people haven't been served by most large businesses because products and services are too expensive, inaccessible, and not suited to their needs. A number of leading companies are changing that by adopting BOP business models geared to serving the poorest of the world's consumers.

The BOP motive is two-fold. Of course, companies are in business with a goal to make money, and managers see a vast untapped market in emerging economies. However, another goal is to play a pivotal role in addressing global poverty and other problems such as environmental destruction, social decay, and political instability in

bottom of the pyramid concept The idea that large corporations can both alleviate social problems and make a profit by selling goods and services to the world's poorest people.

the developing world. Although the BOP concept has gained significant attention only recently, the basic idea is nothing new. Here's an example of a company that has been practicing bottom of the pyramid activities for more than a hundred years.

Unilever/Hindustan Lever

The World Health Organization estimates that diarrhea-related illnesses kill more than 1.8 million people a year. One way to prevent the spread of these diseases is better hand-washing, and marketing managers for Lifebuoy soap are trying to make sure people know that fact.

British soap maker Lever Brothers (now the global organization Unilever) introduced Lifebuoy to India more than a century ago, promoting it as the enemy of dirt and disease. The basic approach today is the same. Several years ago, the company's India subsidiary, Hindustan Lever Limited, introduced a campaign called *Swasthya Chetna* (Glowing Health), sending Lifebuoy teams into rural villages with a "glo-germ kit" to show people that even clean-looking hands can carry dangerous germs—and that soap-washed hands don't.

Sales of Lifebuoy have risen sharply since the campaign, aided by the introduction of a smaller-size bar that costs five rupees (about 12 cents). Just as importantly, says Hindustan Lever's chairman Harish Manwani, the campaign has reached around 80 million of the rural poor with education about how to prevent needless deaths.[31]

Marketing manager Punit Misra, who oversees the Lifebuoy brand, emphasizes that "profitable responsibility" is essential for companies to have a true impact on solving the world's problems. "If it's not really self-sustaining, somewhere along the line it will drop off," Misra says.[32] Other proponents of bottom-of-the pyramid thinking agree that BOP works because it ties social responsibility directly into the heart of the company. Businesses contribute to lasting change when the profit motive goes hand-in-hand with the desire to make a contribution to humankind.

THE ETHIC OF SUSTAINABILITY

Corporations involved in bottom-of-the-pyramid activities, as well as a number of other companies around the world, are also embracing a revolutionary idea called *sustainability* or *sustainable development*. **Sustainability** refers to economic development that generates wealth and meets the needs of the current generation while saving the environment so future generations can meet their needs as well.[33] With a philosophy of sustainability, managers weave environmental and social concerns into every strategic decision, revise policies and procedures to support sustainability efforts, and measure their progress toward sustainability goals. One of the most ardent, and perhaps unlikely, advocates of sustainability is a carpet manufacturer.

sustainability Economic development that generates wealth and meets the needs of the current population while preserving the environment for the needs of future generations.

Interface

For Ray Anderson, who founded the carpet tile company Interface, the approach to the environment used to be "to follow the law." Then he started reading about environmental issues and had an epiphany: "I was running a company that was plundering the earth," Anderson says.

How things have changed since then. Anderson challenged Interface to become a "restorative enterprise," an operation that does no harm to the biosphere and that takes nothing out of the earth than cannot be recycled or quickly regenerated.

Since 1994, Interface's use of fossil fuels is down 45 percent, with net greenhouse gas production down 60 percent. The company's global operations use only one-third the water they formerly used. Interface's contributions to garbage landfills have been cut by 80 percent. One key to the company's success, Anderson says, is a comprehensive approach that incorporates sustainability into every aspect of the business. Rather than going green by tacking on this or that environmental program, managers looked at and revised the whole system.[34]

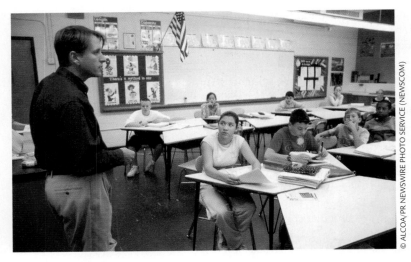

Concept Connection   Bob Smet, an Alcoa Power Generating Inc. (APGI) natural resources specialist, talks to Badin, North Carolina, elementary school students as part of parent company Alcoa Inc.'s "Taking Action" initiative. This annual employee volunteer program represents only one facet of the company's commitment to **sustainable development**. Alcoa's *2020 Strategic Framework for Sustainability* spells out goals for integrating **sustainability principles** into its ongoing operations and establishes specific benchmarks. The World Economic Forum named Alcoa one of the world's most sustainable corporations, and in recognition of its 80 percent reduction of greenhouse gas perfluorocarbon, *BusinessWeek* and The Climate Group cited the world's leading aluminum producer as a top "green" company of the decade.

Ray Anderson's mission is a lot easier than it used to be. Even companies that have typically paid little attention to the green movement are grappling with issues related to sustainability, partly because of the growing clout of environmentalists. Surveys show that American consumers find nonprofit green groups more credible than businesses, for example.[35] Another study found that MBA students would forgo an average of $13,700 in compensation to work for a company that had a good reputation for environmental sustainability.[36] Even Wal-Mart is paying attention. The company teamed up with Conservation International to help develop ways to cut energy consumption, switch to renewable power, and sell millions of energy-efficient fluorescent bulbs.[37] Sustainability argues that organizations can find innovative ways to create wealth at the same time they are preserving natural resources. General Mills used to pay to have oat hulls from its cereal production process hauled to the landfill. Now customers compete to buy the company's solid waste to be burned as fuel. GM earns more money from recycling than it once spent on disposal.[38]

EVALUATING CORPORATE SOCIAL RESPONSIBILITY

A model for evaluating corporate social performance is presented in Exhibit 5.5. The model indicates that total corporate social responsibility can be subdivided into four primary criteria: economic, legal, ethical, and discretionary responsibilities.[39] These four criteria fit together to form the whole of a company's social responsiveness.

EXHIBIT | **5.5**

Criteria of Corporate Social Performance

SOURCES: Based on Archie B. Carroll, "A Three-Dimensional Conceptual Model of Corporate Performance," *Academy of Management Review* 4 (1979): 499; A. B. Carroll, "The Pyramid of Corporate Social Responsibility: Toward the Moral Management of Corporate Stakeholders," *Business Horizons* 34 (July–August 1991): 42; and Mark S. Schwartz and Archie B. Carroll, "Corporate Social Responsibility: A Three-Domain Approach," *Business Ethics Quarterly* 13, no. 4 (2003): 503–530.

The first criterion of social responsibility is *economic responsibility*. The business institution is, above all, the basic economic unit of society. Its responsibility is to produce the goods and services that society wants and to maximize profits for its owners and shareholders. Economic responsibility, carried to the extreme, is called the *profit-maximizing view*, advocated by Nobel economist Milton Friedman. This view argues that the corporation should be operated on a profit-oriented basis, with its sole mission to increase its profits as long as it stays within the rules of the game.[40] The purely profit-maximizing view is no longer considered an adequate criterion of performance in Canada, the United States, and Europe. This approach means that economic gain is the only social responsibility and can lead companies into trouble.

Legal responsibility defines what society deems as important with respect to appropriate corporate behavior.[41] That is, businesses are expected to fulfill their economic goals within the framework of legal requirements imposed by local town councils, state legislators, and federal regulatory agencies. Examples of illegal acts by corporations include corporate fraud, intentionally selling defective goods, performing unnecessary repairs or procedures, deliberately misleading consumers, and billing clients for work not done. Organizations that knowingly break the law are poor performers in this category. For example, Dow Chemical was fined $2 million for violating an agreement to halt false safety claims about its pesticide products. Prudential Insurance also came under fire for misleading consumers about variable life insurance policies.[42]

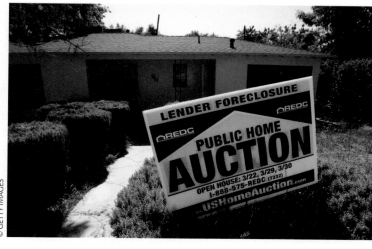

© GETTY IMAGES

Concept Connection   The fall of financial services icon Bear Sterns grabbed the headlines, but numerous mortgage companies were declaring bankruptcy at the same time. When looking for who failed to meet their **economic and ethical responsibilities** in the mortgage industry meltdown, there is plenty of blame to go around. Some mortgage brokers and companies had lenient lending policies and offered exotic mortgage types that borrowers did not fully understand. Some homebuyers and real estate investors over-extended in their purchasing. Some financial institutions bundled mortgages into investment securities. The resulting large number of foreclosed mortgages left empty houses, failed companies, and devastated families that will negatively impact some communities for years.

Ethical responsibility includes behaviors that are not necessarily codified into law and may not serve the corporation's direct economic interests. As described earlier in this chapter, to be *ethical*, organization decision makers should act with equity, fairness, and impartiality, respect the rights of individuals, and provide different treatment of individuals only when relevant to the organization's goals and tasks.[43] *Unethical* behavior occurs when decisions enable an individual or company to gain at the expense of other people or society as a whole. Consider what's happening in the student loan industry, which has come under close scrutiny after an investigation found that Student Loan Xpress paid financial aid directors at three universities a total of $160,000 in consulting fees, personal tuition reimbursement, and other payments as a gateway to being placed on the universities' preferred lenders lists. Investigators are seeking to determine whether lenders are being recommended to students because of the hidden payments officials are receiving rather than the fact that they offer the best lending terms to students.[44]

Read the ethical dilemma on page 150 that pertains to legal and ethical responsibilities. How important is it to you to protect the natural environment?

TakeaMoment

Discretionary responsibility is purely voluntary and is guided by a company's desire to make social contributions not mandated by economics, law, or ethics. Discretionary activities include generous philanthropic contributions that offer no payback to the company and are not expected. For example, General Mills spends more than five percent of pre-tax profits on social responsibility initiatives and charitable giving.[45] Another good illustration of discretionary behavior occurred when Emigrant Savings deposited $1,000 into the accounts of nearly 1,000 customers living in

discretionary responsibility
Organizational responsibility that is voluntary and guided by the organization's desire to make social contributions not mandated by economics, law, or ethics.

areas hit hardest by Hurricane Katrina.[46] Discretionary responsibility is the highest criterion of social responsibility because it goes beyond societal expectations to contribute to the community's welfare.

MANAGING COMPANY ETHICS AND SOCIAL RESPONSIBILITY

An expert on the topic of ethics said, "Management is responsible for creating and sustaining conditions in which people are likely to behave themselves."[47] Exhibit 5.6 illustrates ways in which managers create and support an ethical organization. One of the most important steps managers can take is to practice ethical leadership. *Ethical leadership* means that managers are honest and trustworthy, fair in their dealings with employees and customers, and behave ethically in both their personal and professional lives. Managers and first-line supervisors are important role models for ethical behavior, and they strongly influence the ethical climate in the organization by adhering to high ethical standards in their own behavior and decisions. Moreover, managers are proactive in influencing employees to embody and reflect ethical values.[48]

Managers can also implement organizational mechanisms to help employees and the company stay on an ethical footing. Some of the primary ones are codes of ethics, ethical structures, and measures to protect whistle-blowers.

Code of Ethics

A **code of ethics** is a formal statement of the company's values concerning ethics and social issues; it communicates to employees what the company stands for. Codes of ethics tend to exist in two types: principle-based statements and policy-based statements. *Principle-based statements* are designed to affect corporate culture; they define fundamental values and contain general language about company responsibilities, quality of products, and treatment of employees. General statements of principle are often called *corporate credos*. One good example is Johnson & Johnson's "The Credo."

code of ethics A formal statement of the organization's values regarding ethics and social issues.

TakeaMoment　｜　Do an Internet search for Johnson & Johnson's Credo, which is available in 36 languages. For more than 60 years, the Credo has guided Johnson & Johnson's managers in making decisions that honor the company's responsibilities to employees, customers, the community, and stockholders.

EXHIBIT ｜ 5.6

Building An Ethical Organization

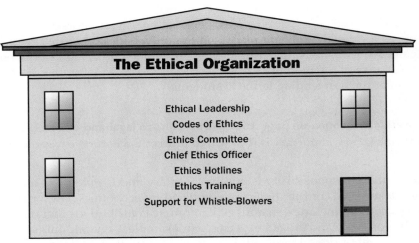

SOURCE: Adapted from Linda Klebe Treviño, Laura Pincus Hartman, and Michael Brown, "Moral Person and Moral Manager," *California Management Review* 42, no. 4 (Summer 2000): 128–142.

Policy-based statements generally outline the procedures to be used in specific ethical situations. These situations include marketing practices, conflicts of interest, observance of laws, proprietary information, political gifts, and equal opportunities. Examples of policy-based statements are Boeing's "Business Conduct Guidelines," Chemical Bank's "Code of Ethics," GTE's "Code of Business Ethics" and "Anti-Trust and Conflict of Interest Guidelines," and Norton's "Norton Policy on Business Ethics."[49]

Codes of ethics state the values or behaviors expected and those that will not be tolerated. A survey of *Fortune* 1,000 companies found that 98 percent address issues of ethics and business conduct in formal corporate documents, and 78 percent of those have separate codes of ethics that are widely distributed.[50] When top management supports and enforces these codes, including rewards for compliance and discipline for violation, ethics codes can boost a company's ethical climate.[51] The code of ethics for *The Milwaukee Journal Sentinel* gives employees some guidelines for dealing with ethical questions.

In recent years, charges of plagiarism and other ethical violations cast a spotlight on newspaper publishers and other media outlets. Executives at Journal Communications, the parent company of *The Milwaukee Journal Sentinel*, hope the company's clear and comprehensive code of ethics will reinforce the public's trust as well as prevent misconduct. This excerpt from the opening sections of the code outlines some broad provisions defining what the company stands for:

> Journal Communications and its subsidiaries operate in a complex and changing society. The actions of the company's employees, officers and directors clearly affect other members of that society. Therefore, every employee has an obligation to conduct the day-to-day business of the company in conformity with the highest ethical standards and in accordance with the various laws and regulations that govern modern business operations. . . .
>
> Journal Communications' ethical standards embrace not only the letter of the law, but also the spirit of the law. To that end, we must apply plain old-fashioned honesty and decency to every aspect of our job. We must never sacrifice ethics for expedience. Broadly put, we should treat others fairly and with respect.
>
> If faced with an ethical question, we should ask:

- Is this action legal?
- Does it comply with company policies and/or good business conduct?
- Is it something I would not want my supervisors, fellow employees, subordinates or family to know about?
- Is it something I would not want the general public to know about?

> We must not condone illegal or unethical behavior . . . by failing to report it, regardless of an employee's level of authority. . . . The company will protect us if we bring unethical activity to its attention.

> The *Journal*'s code of ethics also includes statements concerning respect for people, respect for the company, conflicts of interest, unfair competition, relationships with customers, suppliers, and news sources, confidential information, and accepting gifts and favors.[52]

Innovative Way

Milwaukee Journal Sentinel

By giving people some guidelines for confronting ethical questions and promising protection from recriminations for people who report wrongdoing, the *Journal*'s code of ethics gives all employees the responsibility and the right to maintain the organization's ethical climate.

Ethical Structures

Ethical structures represent the various systems, positions, and programs a company can undertake to implement ethical behavior. One of the newest positions in organizations is the *chief accounting officer*, a response to widespread financial wrongdoing in recent years. These high-level executives handle reporting and compliance, ensure due diligence, and work with outside auditors.[53] An **ethics committee** is a group of executives appointed to oversee company ethics. The committee provides rulings on questionable ethical issues and assumes responsibility for disciplining wrongdoers. Motorola's Ethics Compliance Committee, for instance, is charged with interpreting, clarifying, and communicating the company's code of ethics and with adjudicating suspected code violations.

ethics committee A group of executives assigned to oversee the organization's ethics by ruling on questionable issues and disciplining violators.

chief ethics officer A company executive who oversees ethics and legal compliance.

ethics training Training programs to help employees deal with ethical questions and values.

whistle-blowing The disclosure by an employee of illegal, immoral, or illegitimate practices by the organization.

Many companies set up ethics offices with full-time staff to ensure that ethical standards are an integral part of company operations. These offices are headed by a **chief ethics officer**, a company executive who oversees all aspects of ethics and legal compliance, including establishing and broadly communicating standards, ethics training, dealing with exceptions or problems, and advising senior managers in the ethical and compliance aspects of decisions.[54] The title of *chief ethics officer* was almost unheard of a decade ago, but highly publicized ethical and legal problems in recent years sparked a growing demand for these ethics specialists. The Ethics and Compliance Officers Association, a trade group, reports that membership soared 70 percent, to more than 1,260 companies, in the five years following the collapse of Enron due to financial wrongdoing.[55] Most ethics offices also work as counseling centers to help employees resolve difficult ethical issues. A toll-free confidential *ethics hotline* allows employees to report questionable behavior as well as seek guidance concerning ethical dilemmas.

TakeaMoment | Complete the experiential exercise on page 149 that pertains to ethical work environments. With what level of ethical climate are you most comfortable? As a manager, how might you improve the ethical climate of a department for which you are responsible?

Ethics training programs also help employees deal with ethical questions and translate the values stated in a code of ethics into everyday behavior.[56] Training programs are an important supplement to a written code of ethics. General Electric implemented a strong compliance and ethics training program for all 320,000 employees worldwide. Much of the training is conducted online, with employees able to test themselves on how they would handle thorny ethical issues. In addition, small group meetings give people a chance to ask questions and discuss ethical dilemmas or questionable actions. Every quarter, each of GE's business units reports to headquarters the percentage of division employees who completed training sessions and the percentage that have read and signed off on the company's ethics guide, "Spirit and Letter."[57] At McMurray Publishing Company in Phoenix, all employees attend a *weekly* meeting on workplace ethics, where they discuss how to handle ethical dilemmas and how to resolve conflicting values.[58]

© AP IMAGES

Concept Connection When American Airlines and Southwest Airlines were allowed to continue flying planes that Federal Aviation Administration inspectors thought needed repairs, some inspectors were allegedly threatened or punished to keep them quiet. The resulting **whistle-blower** complaints of the FAA inspectors faulted the cozy relationship between the FAA and the airline companies. Ultimately, the FAA grounded American and Southwest fleets of MD-80s for the mandated maintenance and repairs. American Airlines CEO Gerald Arpey said he believed that "the safety of our MD-80 fleet was never at issue."

Whistle-Blowing

Employee disclosure of illegal, immoral, or illegitimate practices on the employer's part is called **whistle-blowing**.[59] No organization can rely exclusively on codes of conduct and ethical structures to prevent all unethical behavior. Holding organizations accountable depends to some degree on individuals who are willing to blow the whistle if they detect illegal, dangerous, or unethical activities. Whistle-blowers often report wrongdoing to outsiders, such as regulatory agencies, senators, or newspaper reporters. Some firms have instituted innovative programs and confidential hotlines to encourage and support internal whistle-blowing. For this practice to be an effective ethical safeguard, however, companies must view whistle-blowing as a benefit to the company and make dedicated efforts to protect whistle-blowers.[60] Pricewaterhouse Coopers conducted a Global Economic Crime survey and reported that the two most effective investments in ethics programs are internal auditing and support of whistle-blowers.[61]

Without effective protective measures, whistle-blowers suffer. Whistle-blowing has become widespread, but it is still risky for employees, who can lose their jobs, be ostracized by coworkers, or be transferred to lower-level positions. Consider what happened when Linda Kimble reported that the car rental agency where she worked was pushing the sale of insurance to customers who already had coverage. Within a few weeks after making the complaint to top managers, Kimble was fired. The 2002 Sarbanes-Oxley Act provides some safety for whistle-blowers like Kimble. People fired for reporting wrongdoing can file a complaint under the law and are eligible for back pay, attorney's fees, and a chance to get their old job back, as Kimble did. The impact of the legislation is still unclear, but many whistle-blowers fear that they will suffer even more hostility if they return to the job after winning a case under Sarbanes-Oxley.[62]

Many managers still look on whistle-blowers as disgruntled employees who aren't good team players. Yet to maintain high ethical standards, organizations need people who are willing to point out wrongdoing. Managers can be trained to view whistle-blowing as a benefit rather than a threat, and systems can be set up to effectively protect employees who report illegal or unethical activities.

Strive to be an ethical leader by adhering to high standards in your personal and professional behavior. As a new manager, use tools such as codes of ethics, ethics training programs, and ethics offices to promote ethical behavior in your unit and help people resolve ethical dilemmas. Treasure whistle-blowers who have the courage to point out wrongdoing, and set up organizational systems to protect them.

TakeaMoment

The Business Case for Ethics and Social Responsibility

Most managers now realize that paying attention to ethics and social responsibility is as important a business issue as paying attention to costs, profits, and growth. In the United States, varied stakeholders are increasingly pushing new reporting initiatives connected to the sustainability movement that emphasize *the triple bottom line* of economic, social, and environmental performance.

Naturally, the relationship of a corporation's ethics and social responsibility to its financial performance concerns both managers and management scholars and has generated a lively debate.[63] One concern of managers is whether good citizenship will hurt performance—after all, ethics programs and social responsibility cost money. A number of studies, undertaken to determine whether heightened ethical and social responsiveness increases or decreases financial performance, provided varying results but generally found a positive relationship between social responsibility and financial performance.[64] For example, a study of the financial performance of large U.S. corporations considered "best corporate citizens" found that they enjoy both superior reputations and superior financial performance.[65] Similarly, Governance Metrics International, an independent corporate governance ratings agency in New York, reports that the stocks of companies run on more selfless principles perform better than those run in a self-serving manner.[66] Although results from these studies are not proof, they do provide an indication that use of resources for ethics and social responsibility does not hurt companies.[67] Moreover, one survey found that 70 percent of global CEOs believe corporate social responsibility is vital to their companies' profitability.[68]

Companies are also making an effort to measure the nonfinancial factors that create value. Researchers find, for example, that people prefer to work for companies that demonstrate a high level of ethics and social responsibility; thus, these organizations can attract and retain high-quality employees.[69] Customers pay attention too. A study by

Walker Research indicates that, price and quality being equal, two-thirds of customers say they would switch brands to do business with a company that is ethical and socially responsible.[70] Enlightened companies realize that integrity and trust are essential elements in sustaining successful and profitable business relationships with an increasingly connected web of employees, customers, suppliers, and partners. Although doing the right thing might not always be profitable in the short run, many managers believe it can provide a competitive advantage by developing a level of trust that money can't buy.

ch5   A MANAGER'S ESSENTIALS: WHAT HAVE WE LEARNED?

- Ethics is the code of moral principles that governs behavior with respect to what is right or wrong. An ethical issue is present in any situation when the actions of an individual or organization may harm or benefit others. Ethical decisions and behavior are typically guided by a value system. Four value-based approaches that serve as criteria for ethical decision making are utilitarian, individualism, moral-rights, and justice.

- For an individual manager, the ability to make ethical choices depends partly on whether the person is at a preconventional, conventional, or postconventional level of moral development.

- Corporate social responsibility concerns a company's values toward society. The model for evaluating social performance uses four criteria: economic, legal, ethical, and discretionary.

- The question of how an organization can be a good corporate citizen is complicated because organizations respond to many different stakeholders, including customers, employees, stockholders and suppliers. Some organizations are extending their field of stakeholders through bottom-of-the-pyramid business activities.

- One social issue of growing concern is responsibility to the natural environment. The philosophy of sustainability emphasizes economic development that meets the needs of today while preserving resources for the future.

- Managers can help organizations be ethical and socially responsible by practicing ethical leadership and using mechanisms such as codes of ethics, ethics committees, chief ethics officers, training programs, and procedures to protect whistleblowers. After years of scandal, many managers are recognizing that managing ethics and social responsibility is just as important as paying attention to costs, profits, and growth. Companies that are ethical and socially responsible perform as well as—and often better than—those that are not socially responsible.

ch5   DISCUSSION QUESTIONS

1. Dr. Martin Luther King, Jr., said, "As long as there is poverty in the world, I can never be rich. . . . As long as diseases are rampant, I can never be healthy. . . . I can never be what I ought to be until you are what you ought to be." Discuss this quote with respect to the material in this chapter. Would this idea be true for corporations, too?

2. Environmentalists are trying to pass laws for oil spills that would remove all liability limits for the oil companies. This change would punish corporations financially. Is this approach the best way to influence companies to be socially responsible?

3. Choose two of the dilemmas listed on page 167. First apply the utilitarian approach to ethical decision making in each situation, and then apply the moral-rights approach. Did you reach the same or different conclusions depending on the approach used? Which do you think is generally the better approach for managers to use?

4. Imagine yourself in a situation of being encouraged to inflate your expense account. Do you think your choice would be more affected by your individual moral development or by the cultural values of the company for which you worked? Explain.

5. Is it socially responsible for organizations to undertake political activity or join with others in a trade association to influence the government? Discuss.

6. Was it ethical during the 1990s for automobile manufacturers to attempt to accommodate an ever-increasing consumer appetite for SUVs with their low fuel efficiency? Was it good business?

7. A noted business executive said, "A company's first obligation is to be profitable. Unprofitable enterprises can't afford to be socially responsible." Do you agree? Discuss.

8. Do you believe it is ethical for companies to compile portfolios of personal information about their Web site visitors without informing them? What

about organizations monitoring their employees' use of the Web? Discuss.

9. Which do you think would be more effective for shaping long-term ethical behavior in an organization: a written code of ethics combined with ethics training or strong ethical leadership? Which would have more impact on you? Why?

10. Lincoln Electric considers customers and employees to be more important stakeholders than shareholders. Is it appropriate for management to define some stakeholders as more important than others? Should all stakeholders be considered equal?

11. Do you think a social entrepreneur can run a profitable business with a primary goal of improving society? Discuss.

ch5 MANAGEMENT IN PRACTICE: EXPERIENTIAL EXERCISE

Ethical Work Climates

Answer the following questions by circling the number that best describes an organization for which you have worked.

Disagree ① ② ③ ④ ⑤ Agree

1. What is the best for everyone in the company is the major consideration here.

   1 2 3 4 5

2. Our major concern is always what is best for the other person.

   1 2 3 4 5

3. People are expected to comply with the law and professional standards over and above other considerations.

   1 2 3 4 5

4. In this company, the first consideration is whether a decision violates any law.

   1 2 3 4 5

5. It is very important to follow the company's rules and procedures here.

   1 2 3 4 5

6. People in this company strictly obey the company policies.

   1 2 3 4 5

7. In this company, people are mostly out for themselves.

   1 2 3 4 5

8. People are expected to do anything to further the company's interests, regardless of the consequences.

   1 2 3 4 5

9. In this company, people are guided by their own personal ethics.

   1 2 3 4 5

10. Each person in this company decides for himself or herself what is right and wrong.

    1 2 3 4 5

Scoring and Interpretation

Subtract each of your scores for questions 7 and 8 from the number 6. Then, add up your score for all 10 questions: _____. These questions measure the dimensions of an organization's ethical climate. Questions 1 and 2 measure caring for people, questions 3 and 4 measure lawfulness, questions 5 and 6 measure rules adherence, questions 7 and 8 measure emphasis on financial and company performance, and questions 9 and 10 measure individual independence. A total score above 40 indicates a highly positive ethical climate. A score from 30 to 40 indicates above-average ethical climate. A score from 20 to 30 indicates a below-average ethical climate, and a score below 20 indicates a poor ethical climate.

Go back over the questions and think about changes that you could have made to improve the ethical climate in the organization. Discuss with other students what you could do as a manager to improve ethics in future companies you work for.

SOURCE: Based on Bart Victor and John B. Cullen, "The Organizational Bases of Ethical Work Climates," *Administrative Science Quarterly* 33 (1988), 101–125.

ch5 MANAGEMENT IN PRACTICE: ETHICAL DILEMMA

Should We Go Beyond the Law?

Nathan Rosillo stared out his office window at the lazy curves and lush, green, flower-lined banks of the Dutch Valley River. He'd grown up near here, and he envisioned the day his children would enjoy the river as he had as a child. But now his own company might make that a risky proposition.

Nathan is a key product developer at Chem-Tech Corporation, an industry leader. Despite its competitive position, Chem-Tech experienced several quarters of dismal financial performance. Nathan and his team developed a new lubricant product that the company sees as the turning point in its declining fortunes. Top executives are thrilled that they can produce the new product at a significant cost savings because of recent changes in environmental regulations. Regulatory agencies loosened requirements on reducing and recycling wastes, which means Chem-Tech can now release waste directly into the Dutch Valley River.

Nathan is as eager as anyone to see Chem-Tech survive this economic downturn, but he doesn't think this route is the way to do it. He expressed his opposition regarding the waste dumping to both the plant manager and his direct supervisor, Martin Feldman. Martin has always supported Nathan, but this time was different. The plant manager, too, turned a deaf ear. "We're meeting government standards," he'd said. "It's up to them to protect the water. It's up to us to make a profit and stay in business."

Frustrated and confused, Nathan turned away from the window, his prime office view mocking his inability to protect the river he loved. He knew the manufacturing vice president was visiting the plant next week. Maybe if he talked with her, she would agree that the decision to dump waste materials in the river was ethically and socially irresponsible. But if she didn't, he would be skating on thin ice. His supervisor had already accused him of not being a team player. Maybe he should just be a passive bystander—after all, the company isn't breaking any laws.

What Would You Do?

1. Talk to the manufacturing vice president and emphasize the responsibility Chem-Tech has as an industry leader to set an example. Present her with a recommendation that Chem-Tech participate in voluntary pollution reduction as a marketing tool, positioning itself as the environmentally friendly choice.

2. Mind your own business and just do your job. The company isn't breaking any laws, and if ChemTech's economic situation doesn't improve, a lot of people will be thrown out of work.

3. Call the local environmental advocacy group and get them to stage a protest of the company.

SOURCE: Adapted from Janet Q. Evans,"What Do You Do: What If Polluting Is Legal?" *Business Ethics* (Fall 2002): 20.

ch5 CASE FOR CRITICAL ANALYSIS

Empress Luxury Lines

From what computer technician Kevin Pfeiffer just told him, it looked to Antonio Melendez as if top management at Empress Luxury Lines finally found a way to fund the computer system upgrade he'd been requesting ever since he'd taken the job two years ago.

It all began innocently enough, Kevin said. When he reported to the luxury cruise line's corporate headquarters, his supervisor Phil Bailey informed him that the computer system had been hit by a power surge during the fierce thunderstorms that rolled through southern Florida the night before. "Check out the damage, and report directly back to me," Phil instructed.

When Kevin delivered what he thought would be good news—the damaged underground wires and computer circuits could be repaired to the tune of about $15,000—he couldn't understand why

Phil looked so deflated. "Go out to the reception area. I've got to call Roger," Phil snapped, referring to Empress's CFO—and Antonio's boss. In a few minutes, Phil called Kevin back into the office and instructed him to dig up nearly all the underground wire and cable and then haul it all off before the insurance adjustor appeared. If Kevin carried out Phil's orders, he knew the costs would balloon astronomically to about a half-million dollars, a tidy sum that would go a long way toward covering the costs of a computer system upgrade, as Phil pointed out.

Kevin took a deep breath and refused, even though as a new hire he was still on probation. When Antonio congratulated Kevin on his integrity, the technician shook his head. "Didn't really matter," he said. "On my way back to my cubicle, Matt passed me on his way to do the deed."

Antonio could guess at the motivation behind the scam. During the 1990s, Empress increased its fleet of ships in response to the healthy demand for its luxury cruises during the stock market bubble. But the bubble burst, the nation was traumatized by September 11, and some of the vacationers who did venture onto cruises were felled by an outbreak of the Norwalk virus. Bookings fell off precipitously. To top it all off, the 2005 hurricanes hit, forcing Empress to write piles of refund checks for their Caribbean and Gulf cruises while coping with steep increases in fuel costs. Seriously sagging earnings explained why Antonio's requests for that system upgrade went unheeded.

He could also guess at the likely consequences if he chose to do the right thing. Since taking the job, he'd heard rumors that Empress successfully defrauded insurance companies before he arrived. He dismissed them at the time, but now he wasn't so sure. No confidential mechanism was in place for employees to report wrong-doing internally, and no protections were available for whistle-blowers. Shaken, Antonio wasn't feeling at all confident that, even if he bypassed the CFO, he would find upper-level management all that eager to thwart the scheme. He had a hunch that the person most likely to be penalized was the whistle-blower.

"I debated about just calling the insurance company," Kevin said, "but I decided to come to you first." So what should Antonio do? Should he advise Kevin to go ahead and report Empress to the insurance company? Or should he treat Kevin's communication as confidential and deal with the situation himself, in effect putting only his own job in jeopardy? And really, considering the high degree of personal risk and the low probability that the problem would actually be addressed, should he just sweep the problem under the rug?

Questions

1. When determining what his obligations are to his subordinate, Kevin Pfeiffer, what decision would Antonio Melendez most likely reach if he applied the utilitarian approach to decision making? What conclusions would probably result if he employed the individualism approach?

2. Put yourself in Antonio's position and decide realistically what you would do. Is your response at a preconventional, conventional, or postconventional level of moral development? How do you feel about your response?

3. If Antonio or Kevin were fired because they reported Empress's fraud, would they be justified in removing all traces of their employment at the cruise line from their resumes so they don't have to explain to a prospective employer why they were fired? Why or why not?

SOURCES: Based on Don Soeken, "On Witnessing a Fraud," *Business Ethics* (Summer 2004): 14; Amy Tao, "Have Cruise Lines Weathered the Storm?" *BusinessWeek Online* (September 11, 2003), http://www.businessweek.com/bwdaily/dnflash/sep2003/nf20030911_6693_db014.htm; and Joan Dubinsky, "A Word to the Whistle-Blower," *Workforce* (July 2002): 28.

ch5 ON THE JOB VIDEO CASE

Organic Valley Plants the Seeds of Social Responsibility

Many organizations treat social responsibility as if it were a separate division—the department of good deeds. They support volunteerism among employees, use environmentally friendly packaging, and sponsor special programs in the community. All of these activities are to be commended. But very few commercial organizations can actually claim to be based on the principles of social responsibility. The Organic Valley Cooperative is an exception. Based in Wisconsin, Organic Valley is a cooperative of small farmers whose products are certified to be produced without pesticides, synthetic hormones, or antibiotics, including organic milk, cheese, butter, spreads, creams, eggs, vegetables, juice, and meat.

Nearly two decades ago, a few farmers who believed strongly in the value to society of practicing organic agriculture and saving family farms got together to form a cooperative. By acting together, these farmers could better control their fate. They could control supply, negotiate with larger customers, and reach more consumers who wanted their products. And they could set their own milk prices. Instead of being forced to accept prices subject to wild fluctuations in the open marketplace, these farmers began to set their own. This practice alone may be the single most important factor in the ability of family farms to survive. In one recent year, the milk price paid to Organic Valley farmers was 60 percent higher than the price paid to conventional dairy farmers. Organic Valley has actually received criticism for this practice, particularly from its creditors. But the cooperative holds firm. "Lowering the milk price would have been as easy as falling off a log," argues Organic Valley's CEO George Siemon. "But one of our objectives is to pay our farmers a good price. . . . We have a pay program the farmers expect us to deliver on. These relationships are the most important thing."

Today, Organic Valley is being called the most successful organic cooperative in the world. The cooperative has 630 members farming 100,000 acres in 16 states, with a waiting list. Sales are hitting upwards of $200 million per year and growing. Member farmers are the cooperative's major stakeholders. With assistance from Organic Valley employees, the farmers govern the cooperative by serving on the board and executive committees. Organic Valley's structure is designed so it will be able to sustain itself from one generation to the next, ensuring the survival of family farms and sustainable, organic agriculture.

Sweet Ridge Organic Dairy is one of the cooperative's farms, operated by Paul Deutsch in Westby, Wisconsin. Deutsch owns twenty-six cows that are milked twice a day and allowed to graze over pasture-land the rest of the time—unlike cows in many larger, conventional dairy farms, which are kept in stalls 24 hours a day and may be given hormones or antibiotics. It costs more to run an organic dairy farm, where in addition to grass the cows are fed organic corn, alfalfa, and other grains, and the cows need more grazing land. But Deutsch isn't spending money on chemicals or vet bills. He estimates that he makes about 30 percent profit each year because consumers are happy to pay more for products they know are more healthful for themselves and their families. "Many parents have read the *Consumer Reports* studies and the National Academy of Science reports and know that organic for their kids is like seatbelts in a car," notes Theresa Marquez, Organic Valley's director of sales and marketing. "The organic category has been growing steadily at 20 percent, and organic milk, with 27+ percent annual growth, is driving the growth of the category. The implementation of the National Organic Program in the U.S. . . . further established the organic market as one that is here to stay. Consumers want organic."

Organic Valley has helped the economies of several rural areas. When a large federal dam project in southwestern Wisconsin was cancelled after displacing more than 140 local farmers from their land, many lost their livelihoods. As Organic Valley became established, it created employment opportunities—both on the farms and in the cooperative offices—for hundreds of residents in the area. "Going organic saved our farm," says cooperative farmer Mike Gehl, whose family has operated a Wisconsin farm for 154 years and five generations. Now Gehl and others like him can look forward to the next generation of farming.

Questions

1. In addition to the farmers, who are Organic Valley's other stakeholders?

2. Describe at least one ethical challenge that Organic Valley may face during turbulent times.

SOURCES: Company Web site, *http://www.organicvalley.coop.com*, accessed August 2, 2004; Judy Ettenhofer, "Organic Valley a Big Success," *The Capital Times*, July 29, 2004, *http://www.madison.com*; "Organic Valley Posts Record Level Pay Price to Farmers," *OFARM*, December 30, 2003, *http://www.ofarm.org*; Organic Valley press kit.

---

ch5 BIZ FLIX VIDEO CASE

The Bourne Identity

Jason Bourne (Matt Damon) cannot remember who he is, but others believe he is an international assassin. Bourne tries to learn his identity with the help of his new friend and lover Marie (Franka Potente). Meanwhile, while CIA agents pursue him across Europe trying to kill him, Bourne slowly discovers that he is an extremely well-trained and lethal agent. The story, which is loosely based on Robert Ludlum's 1981 novel, was previously filmed in 1988 as a television miniseries starring Richard Chamberlain.

This scene is an edited version of the "Bourne's Game" sequence near the end of the film. Jason Bourne kills the hired assassin who tried to kill him the day after Jason and Marie arrived at the home of Eamon (Tim Dutton). Eamon is Marie's friend but is a stranger to Jason. Jason uses the dead man's cell phone after returning to his apartment in Paris, France. He presses the redial button, which connects him to Conklin (Chris Cooper), the CIA manager who is looking for him. Listen carefully to Jason's conversation with Conklin as he walks along the right bank of the Seine River in Paris.

What to Watch for and Ask Yourself

1. Does Jason Bourne describe a plan to Conklin? If he does, what are the plan's elements? What is Bourne's goal?

2. Does Bourne assess the plan's execution to determine if it conforms to his goal? If so, what does he do?

3. Was Bourne's plan successfully carried out? Why or why not? How does this scene relate to organizational strategic planning?

ch5 ENDNOTES

1. This example comes from Susan Pulliam, "Crossing the Line; At Center of Fraud, WorldCom Official Sees Life Unravel," *The Wall Street Journal*, March 24, 2005; and S. Pulliam, "Over the Line: A Staffer Ordered to Commit Fraud Balked, Then Caved," *The Wall Street Journal*, June 23, 2003.
2. Bethany McLean, "Why Enron Went Bust," *Fortune* (December 24, 2001): 58–68; survey results reported in Patricia Wallington, "Honestly?!" *CIO* (March 15, 2003): 41–42.
3. Mike Esterl, "Executive Derision: In Germany, Scandals Tarnish Business Elite," *The Wall Street Journal*, March 4, 2008.
4. Gordon F. Shea, *Practical Ethics* (New York: American Management Association, 1988); and Linda K. Treviño, "Ethical Decision Making in Organizations; A Person-Situation Interactionist Model," *Academy of Management Review* 11 (1986): 601–617.
5. Thomas M. Jones, "Ethical Decision Making by Individuals in Organizations: An Issue-Contingent Model," *Academy of Management Review* 16(1991): 366–395.
6. Shelby D. Hunt and Jared M. Hansen, "Understanding Ethical Diversity in Organizations," *Organizational Dynamics* 36, no 2 (2007): 202–216.
7. John R. Emshwiller and Alexei Barrionuevo, "U.S. Prosecutors File Indictment Against Skilling," *The Wall Street Journal*, February 20, 2004.
8. See Clinton W. McLemore, *Street-Smart Ethics: Succeeding in Business*

Without Selling Your Soul (Louisville, KY: Westminster John Knox Press, 2003), for a cogent discussion of some ethical and legal issues associated with Enron's collapse.
9. Rushworth M. Kidder, "The Three Great Domains of Human Action," *Christian Science Monitor*, January 30, 1990.
10. Linda K. Treviño and Katherine A. Nelson, *Managing Business Ethics: Straight Talk About How to Do It Right* (New York: John Wiley & Sons, Inc. 1995), p. 4.
11. Jones, "Ethical Decision Making by Individuals in Organizations."
12. Based on a question from a General Electric employee ethics guide, reported in Kathryn Kranhold, "U.S. Firms Raise Ethics Focus," *The Wall Street Journal*, November 28, 2005.
13. Based on information in Constance E. Bagley, "The Ethical Leader's Decision Tree," *Harvard Business Review* (February 2003): 18–19.
14. Based on information in Vadim Liberman, "Scoring on the Job," *Across the Board* (November–December 2003): 46–50.
15. From Jeffrey Kluger, "What Makes Us Moral? *Time* (December 3, 2007): 54–60.
16. "The Morality Quiz," at http://www.time.com/morality (accessed February 19, 2008).
17. This discussion is based on Gerald F. Cavanagh, Dennis J. Moberg, and Manuel Velasquez, "The Ethics of Organizational Politics," *Academy of Management Review* 6 (1981): 363–374; Justin G. Longenecker,

Joseph A. McKinney, and Carlos W. Moore, "Egoism and Independence: Entrepreneurial Ethics," *Organizational Dynamics* (Winter 1988): 64–72; Carolyn Wiley, "The ABCs of Business Ethics: Definitions, Philosophies, and Implementation," *IM* (February 1995): 22–27; and Mark Mallinger, "Decisive Decision Making: An Exercise Using Ethical Frameworks," *Journal of Management Education* (August 1997): 411–417.
18. Michael J. McCarthy, "Now the Boss Knows Where You're Clicking," and "Virtual Morality: A New Workplace Quandary," *The Wall Street Journal*, October 21, 1999; and Jeffrey L. Seglin, "Who's Snooping on You?" *Business 2.0* (August 8, 2000): 202–203.
19. John Kekes, "Self-Direction: The Core of Ethical Individualism," in *Organizations and Ethical Individualism*, ed. Konstanian Kolenda (New York: Praeger, 1988), pp. 1–18.
20. Tad Tulega, *Beyond the Bottom Line* (New York: Penguin Books, 1987).
21. L. Kohlberg, "Moral Stages and Moralization: The Cognitive-Developmental Approach," in *Moral Development and Behavior: Theory, Research, and Social Issues*, ed. T. Lickona (New York: Holt, Rinehart & Winston, 1976), pp. 31–83; L. Kohlberg, "Stage and Sequence: The Cognitive-Developmental Approach to Socialization," in *Handbook of Socialization Theory and Research*, ed. D. A. Goslin (Chicago: Rand McNally, 1969); Linda K. Treviño, Gary

R. Weaver, and Scott J. Reynolds, "Behavioral Ethics in Organizations: A Review, *Journal of Management* 32, no 6 (December 2006): 951–990; and Jill W. Graham, "Leadership, Moral Development, and Citizenship Behavior," *Business Ethics Quarterly* 5, no. 1 (January 1995): 43–54.

22. See Thomas Donaldson and Thomas W. Dunfee, "When Ethics Travel: The Promise and Peril of Global Business Ethics," *California Management Review* 41, No. 4 (Summer 1999): 45–63.

23. Transparency International, "The BPI 2006—The Ranking," www .transparency.org/policy_research/ surveys_indices/bpi/bpi_2006 (accessed February 18, 2007).

24. Eugene W. Szwajkowski, "The Myths and Realities of Research on Organizational Misconduct," in *Research in Corporate Social Performance and Policy*, ed. James E. Post (Greenwich, CT: JAI Press, 1986), 9:103–122; and Keith Davis, William C. Frederick, and Robert L. Blostrom, *Business and Society: Concepts and Policy Issues* (New York: McGraw-Hill, 1979).

25. Douglas S. Sherwin, "The Ethical Roots of the Business System," *Harvard Business Review* 61 (November–December 1983): 183–192.

26. Nancy C. Roberts and Paula J. King, "The Stakeholder Audit Goes Public," *Organizational Dynamics* (Winter 1989): 63–79; Thomas Donaldson and Lee E. Preston, "The Stakeholder Theory of the Corporation: Concepts, Evidence, and Implications," *Academy of Management Review* 20, no. 1 (1995): 65–91; and Jeffrey S. Harrison and Caron H. St. John, "Managing and Partnering with External Stakeholders," *Academy of Management Executive* 10, no. 2 (1996): 46–60.

27. Clay Chandler, "The Great Wal-Mart of China," *Fortune* (July 25, 2005): 104–116; and Charles Fishman, "The Wal-Mart You Don't Know—Why Low Prices Have a High Cost," *Fast Company* (December 2003): 68–80.

28. David Wheeler, Barry Colbert, and R. Edward Freeman, "Focusing on Value: Reconciling Corporate Social Responsibility, Sustainability, and a Stakeholder Approach in a Networked World," *Journal of General*

Management 28, no. 3 (Spring 2003): 1–28; James E. Post, Lee E. Preston, and Sybille Sachs, "Managing the Extended Enterprise: The New Stakeholder View," *California Management Review* 45, no. 1 (Fall 2002): 6–28; and Peter Fritsch and Timothy Mapes, "Seed Money; In Indonesia, A Tangle of Bribes Creates Trouble for Monsanto," *The Wall Street Journal*, April 5, 2005.

29. Max B. E. Clarkson, "A Stakeholder Framework for Analyzing and Evaluating Corporate Social Performance," *Academy of Management Review* 20, no. 1 (1995): 92–117.

30. C. K. Prahalad and S. L. Hart, "The Fortune at the Bottom of the Pyramid," *Strategy + Business* 26 (2006): 54–67.

31. Rob Walker, "Cleaning Up," *New York Times Magazine* (June 10, 2007): 20.

32. Ibid.

33. This definition is based on Marc J. Epstein and Marie-Josée Roy, "Improving Sustainability Performance: Specifying, Implementing and Measuring Key Principles," *Journal of General Management* 29, no. 1 (Autumn 2003): 15–31, World Commission on Economic Development, *Our Common Future* (Oxford: Oxford University Press, 1987): and Marc Gunther, "Tree Huggers, Soy Lovers, and Profits," *Fortune* (June 23, 2003): 98–104.

34. Cornelia Dean, "Executive on a Mission: Saving the Planet," *The New York Times*, May 22, 2007.

35. John Carey, "Hugging the Tree Huggers," *BusinessWeek* (March 12, 2007): 66–68.

36. Reported in Kate O'Sullivan, "Virtue Rewarded," *CFO* (October 2006): 47–52.

37. Carey, "Hugging the Tree Huggers."

38. Mark Borden, Jeff Chu, Charles Fishman, Michael A. Prospero, and Danielle Sacks, "50 Ways to Green Your Business," *Fast Company* (November, 2007).

39. Mark S. Schwartz and Archie B. Carroll, "Corporate Social Responsibility: A Three-Domain Approach," *Business Ethics Quarterly* 13, no. 4 (2003): 503–530; and Archie B. Carroll, "A Three-Dimensional Conceptual Model of Corporate Performance," *Academy of Management Review* 4 (1979): 497–505. For a discussion of various models for

evaluating corporate social performance, also see Diane L. Swanson, "Addressing a Theoretical Problem by Reorienting the Corporate Social Performance Model," *Academy of Management Review* 20, no. 1 (1995): 43–64.

40. Milton Friedman, *Capitalism and Freedom* (Chicago: University of Chicago Press, 1962), p. 133; and Milton Friedman and Rose Friedman, *Free to Choose* (New York: Harcourt Brace Jovanovich, 1979).

41. Eugene W. Szwajkowski, "Organizational Illegality: Theoretical Integration and Illustrative Application," *Academy of Management Review* 10 (1985): 558–567.

42. Reported in Ronald W. Clement, "Just How Unethical is American Business?" *Business Horizons* 49 (2006): 313–327.

43. David J. Fritzsche and Helmut Becker, "Linking Management Behavior to Ethical Philosophy—An Empirical Investigation," *Academy of Management Journal* 27 (1984): 165–175.

44. John Hechinger, "Financial-Aid Directors Received Payments from Preferred Lender; Student Loan Xpress Puts Three Managers on Leave Amid Multiple Inquiries," *The Wall Street Journal*, April 10, 2007; and Kathy Chu, "3 University Financial Aid Chiefs Suspended," *USA Today*, April 6, 2007, http://www .usatoday.com/money/industries/ banking/2007-04-06-loans-usat_N .htm (accessed April 6, 2007).

45. O'Sullivan, "Virtue Rewarded."

46. Katie Hafner and Claudi H. Deutsch, "When Good Will Is Also Good Business," *The New York Times*, September 14, 2005, www .nytimes.com.

47. Saul W. Gellerman, "Managing Ethics from the Top Down," *Sloan Management Review* (Winter 1989): 73–79.

48. Michael E. Brown and Linda K. Treviño, "Ethical Leadership: A Review and Future Directions," *The Leadership Quarterly* 17 (2006): 595–616; Gary R. Weaver, Linda Klebe Treviño, and Bradley Agle, "'Somebody I Look Up To': Ethical Role Models in Organizations," *Organizational Dynamics* 34, no. 4 (2005): 313–330; and L. K. Treviño, G. R. Weaver, David G. Gibson, and Barbara Ley Toffler, "Managing

Ethics and Legal Compliance: What Works and What Hurts?" *California Management Review* 41, no. 2 (Winter 1999): 131–151.

49. Ibid.

50. Treviño et al., "Managing Ethics and Legal Compliance."

51. Carolyn Wiley, "The ABC's of Business Ethics: Definitions, Philosophies, and Implementation," *IM* (January–February 1995): 22–27; Joseph L. Badaracco and Allen P. Webb, "Business Ethics: A View from the Trenches," *California Management Review* 37, no. 2 (Winter 1995): 8–28; and Ronald B. Morgan, "Self- and Co-Worker Perceptions of Ethics and Their Relationships to Leadership and Salary," *Academy of Management Journal* 36, no. 1 (February 1993): 200–214.

52. Journal Communications—Code of Ethics, from Codes of Ethics Online, The Center for the Study of Ethics in the Professions, Illinois Institute of Technology, www.iit.edu/departments/csep/PublicWWW/codes/index.html.

53. Cheryl Rosen, "A Measure of Success? Ethics after Enron," *Business Ethics* (Summer 2006): 22–26.

54. Alan Yuspeh, "Do the Right Thing," *CIO* (August 1, 2000): 56–58.

55. Reported in Rosen, "A Measure of Success? Ethics after Enron."

56. Beverly Geber, "The Right and Wrong of Ethics Offices," *Training* (October 1995): 102–118.

57. Kranhold, "U.S. Firms Raise Ethics Focus" and "Our Actions: GE 2005 Citizenship Report," General Electric Company, 2005.

58. Amy Zipkin, "Getting Religion on Corporate Ethics," *The New York Times*, October 18, 2000.

59. Marcia Parmarlee Miceli and Janet P. Near, "The Relationship among Beliefs, Organizational Positions, and Whistle-Blowing Status: A Discriminant Analysis," *Academy of Management Journal* 27 (1984): 687–705.

60. Eugene Garaventa, "*An Enemy of the People* by Henrik Ibsen: The Politics of Whistle-Blowing," *Journal of Management Inquiry* 3, no. 4 (December 1994): 369–374; Marcia P. Miceli and Janet P. Near, "Whistleblowing: Reaping the Benefits," *Academy of Management Executive* 8, no. 3 (1994): 65–74.

61. Reported in Rosen, "A Measure of Success? Ethics after Enron."

62. Jayne O'Donnell, "Blowing the Whistle Can Lead to Harsh Aftermath, Despite Law," *USA Today*, July 31, 2005, www.usatoday.com.

63. Homer H. Johnson, "Does It Pay to Be Good? Social Responsibility and Financial Performance," *Business Horizons* (November–December 2003): 34–40; Jennifer J. Griffin and John F. Mahon, "The Corporate Social Performance and Corporate Financial Performance Debate: Twenty-Five Years of Incomparable Research," *Business and Society* 36, no. 1 (March 1997): 5–31; Bernadette M. Ruf, Krishnamurty Muralidar, Robert M. Brown, Jay J. Janney, and Karen Paul, "An Empirical Investigation of the Relationship between Change in Corporate Social Performance and Financial Performance: A Stakeholder Theory Perspective," *Journal of Business Ethics* 32, no. 2 (July 2001): 143; Philip L. Cochran and Robert A. Wood, "Corporate Social Responsibility and Financial Performance," *Academy of Management Journal* 27 (1984): 42–56.

64. Paul C. Godfrey, "The Relationship Between Corporate Philanthropy and Shareholder Wealth: A Risk Management Perspective," *Academy of Management Review* 30, no. 4 (2005): 777–798; Oliver Falck and Stephan Heblich, "Corporate Social Responsibility: Doing Well by Doing Good," *Business Horizons* 50 (2007): 247–254; J. A. Pearce II and J. P. Doh, "The High Impact of Collaborative Social Initiatives"; Curtis C. Verschoor and Elizabeth A. Murphy, "The Financial Performance of Large U.S. Firms and Those with Global Prominence: How Do the Best Corporate Citizens Rate?" *Business and Society Review* 107, no. 3 (Fall 2002): 371–381; Johnson, "Does It Pay to Be Good?"; Dale Kurschner, "5 Ways Ethical Business Creates Fatter Profits," *Business Ethics* (March–April 1996): 20–23. Also see studies reported in Lori Ioannou, "Corporate America's Social Conscience," *Fortune* (May 26, 2003): S1–S10.

65. Verschoor and Murphy, "The Financial Performance of Large U.S. Firms."

66. Phred Dvorak, "Finding the Best Measure of 'Corporate Citizenship,'" *The Wall Street Journal*, July 2, 2007.

67. Jean B. McGuire, Alison Sundgren, and Thomas Schneeweis, "Corporate Social Responsibility and Firm Financial Performance," *Academy of Management Journal* 31 (1988): 854–872; and Falck and Heblich, Corporate Social Responsibility: Doing Well by Doing Good."

68. Vogel, "Is There a Market for Virtue?"

69. Daniel W. Greening and Daniel B. Turban, "Corporate Social Performance as a Competitive Advantage in Attracting a Quality Workforce," *Business and Society* 39, no. 3 (September 2000): 254; and O'Sullivan, "Virtue Rewarded."

70. "The Socially Correct Corporate Business," in Leslie Holstrom and Simon Brady, "The Changing Face of Global Business," *Fortune* (July 24, 2000): S1–S38.

2
Environment

General Motors
Part Two: The Environment of Management
The Volt: GM's Ultimate Green Machine

Imagine that you are one of millions of Americans whose commute to school or work is less than 40 miles round trip. Each morning, you hop in a sleek compact and drive off to your destination. At night, you park safely in the garage and plug your vehicle into a standard household electric socket for bedtime. After repeating this pattern for months, you never use a drop of gas or emit an ounce of emissions. Moreover, charging your vehicle costs you just 80 cents each day and consumes less energy annually than your own home refrigerator.

If you are one of the thousands of excited consumers lining up to purchase the 2010 Chevy Volt, this scenario is not fantasy—it's your future. In fact, it's the future that General Motors (GM) envisions for each one of America's more than 200 million licensed drivers.

In a move to reinvent the automobile for the needs of the twenty-first century, GM unveiled its first electric car during the company's historic 2008 centennial celebration. The Volt, with its emissions-free driving and 2010 delivery date, promises to become the ultimate green machine for eco-minded consumers everywhere.

While the cost of operating the aerodynamic electric compact is roughly equivalent to the price of a cup of coffee, the driving experience is priceless. The electric drive unit delivers 150 horsepower, 0-to-60 acceleration in nine seconds, and top speeds of 100 miles per hour. Drivers who make longer trips than the battery's 40-mile range get an automatic recharge from Volt's gas-powered generator. And although it runs on batteries, the Volt is no golf cart. The environmentally friendly four-door vehicle features a sporty-yet-sophisticated stance, aerodynamic design, closed front grille, and more. The futuristic cockpit takes cues from the latest in design trends—the metallic-white center control console could pass for a next-generation iPod.

How did GM go from being the world's largest manufacturer of gas-guzzling Hummers and Escalades to an electric-car company producing what one observer has called a "Viper for tree huggers"? The dramatic shift is related to multiple threats in the organization's external environment.

First, there's oil: Wildly fluctuating gas prices—such as the $5-per-gallon spike in 2008—have caused drivers to moderate driving habits and stay away from dealerships. Then, there's government regulation: The Democrat-controlled U.S. Congress overwhelmingly passed the Energy Independence and Security Act of 2007, which in addition to banning the use of ordinary incandescent light bulbs, raised corporate average fuel economy (CAFE) standards on automakers to a fleetwide average of 35 mpg. Next, there's the philosophy of sustainability: Many leaders in business and government see environmental "clean" technology as a way of striking a balance between today's economic development needs and those of future generations. Another pressure comes from lobbyists: Powerful voices sounding the alarm on impending global catastrophe have demanded that manufacturers put the brakes on industry to save the planet. Finally, there's the competition: "Green" is an important buzzword in business today, and vehicles like Toyota Prius and the Tesla Roadster that leave a small carbon footprint are putting pressure on GM to get out in front.

Whatever the economic, political, and social forces driving big changes at GM, leadership is determined to create a new culture of innovation and change. Whether it's the emissions-free promise of the Volt, the gravity-defying fuel efficiency of the Chevy Tahoe Hybrid, or the next-generation thinking of the hydrogen-powered Cadillac Provoq, the presence of exciting alternative-fuel vehicles sends a message to stakeholders that the future of the automobile is still in Detroit.

Questions

1. What management strategies might be most effective in helping GM adapt to uncertainty and change in its external environment?

2. What obstacles does GM face as it attempts to bring its corporate culture into alignment with the needs and challenges of the twenty-first century?

3. As GM continues its attempts to demonstrate good corporate citizenship, what complex issues and obstacles may frustrate its efforts?

SOURCES: Peter Fairley, "The New CAFE Standards—Fuel Standards Will Likely Be Achievable But Won't Encourage Innovation," *Technology Review*, January 15, 2008, http://www.technologyreview.com/energy/20067 (accessed October 11, 2008); Anita Lienert, "Aerodynamic Chevrolet Volt Electrifies GM's 100th-Anniversary Celebration," *Inside Line*, September 16, 2008, http://www.edmunds.com/

insideline (accessed October 11, 2008); Robert Snell, "GM Enters Its Second Century by Finally Taking Wraps off Volt," *The Detroit News*, September 17, 2008, http://www.detnews.com (accessed October 11, 2008); U.S. Department of Transportation, "Distribution of Licensed Drivers—2006," Federal Highway Administration, Highway Statistics 2006 Table DL-20, http://www.fhwa.dot.gov/policy/ohim/hs06/htm/ dl20.htm; David Welch, "GM Charges Up the Electric Chevy Volt—GM Introduces the Chevy Volt, a Sleek Electric Car Capable of 40 mpg on a Single Charge," *BusinessWeek*, September, 17, 2008, http://www .businessweek.com/lifestyle/content/sep2008/bw20080916_356100 .htm (accessed October 11, 2008).

2 Environment

© GETTY IMAGES/DIGITAL VISION

Learning Outcomes

After studying this chapter, you should be able to:

1. Define goals and plans and explain the relationship between them.

2. Explain the concept of organizational mission and how it influences goal setting and planning.

3. Describe the types of goals an organization should have and how managers use strategy maps to align goals.

4. Define the characteristics of effective goals.

5. Describe the four essential steps in the management by objectives (MBO) process.

6. Explain the difference between single-use plans and standing plans.

7. Describe and explain the importance of contingency planning, scenario building, and crisis planning in today's environment.

8. Summarize the guidelines for high-performance planning in a fast-changing environment.

Managerial Planning and Goal Setting

1 Introduction

2 Environment

3 Planning

4 Organizing

5 Controlling

6 Leading

Does Goal Setting Fit Your Management Style?

Are you a good planner? Do you set goals and identify ways to accomplish them? This questionnaire will help you understand how your work habits fit with making plans and setting goals. Answer the following questions as they apply to your work or study habits. Please indicate whether each item is Mostly True or Mostly False for you.

	Mostly True	Mostly False
1. I have clear, specific goals in several areas of my life.	_____	_____
2. I have a definite outcome in life I want to achieve.	_____	_____
3. I prefer general to specific goals.	_____	_____
4. I work better without specific deadlines.	_____	_____
5. I set aside time each day or week to plan my work.	_____	_____
6. I am clear about the measures that indicate when I have achieved a goal.	_____	_____
7. I work better when I set more challenging goals for myself.	_____	_____
8. I help other people clarify and define their goals.	_____	_____

SCORING AND INTERPRETATION: Give yourself one point for each item you marked as Mostly True except items 3 and 4. For items 3 and 4 give yourself one point for each one you marked Mostly False. A score of 5 or higher suggests a positive level of goal-setting behavior and good preparation for a new manager role in an organization. If you scored 4 or less you might want to evaluate and begin to change your goal-setting behavior. An important part of a new manager's job is setting goals, measuring results, and reviewing progress for the department and subordinates.

These questions indicate the extent to which you have already adopted the disciplined use of goals in your life and work. But if you scored low, don't despair. Goal setting can be learned. Most organizations have goal setting and review systems that new managers use. Not everyone thrives under a disciplined goal-setting system, but as a new manager, setting goals and assessing results are tools that will enhance your impact. Research indicates that setting clear, specific, and challenging goals in key areas will produce better performance.

One of the primary responsibilities of managers is to decide where the organization should go in the future and how to get it there. In some organizations, typically small ones, planning is informal. In others, managers follow a well-defined planning framework. The company establishes a basic mission and periodically develops formal goals and plans for carrying it out. Large organizations such as Royal Dutch/Shell, IBM, and United Way undertake a comprehensive planning exercise each year—reviewing their missions, goals, and plans to meet environmental changes or the expectations of important stakeholders such as the community, owners, or customers.

Of the four management functions—planning, organizing, leading, and controlling—described in Chapter 1, planning is considered the most fundamental. Everything else stems from planning. Yet planning also is the most controversial management function. How do managers plan for the future in a constantly changing environment? The economic, political, and social turmoil of recent years has sparked a renewed interest in organizational planning, particularly planning for unexpected problems and events. Yet planning cannot read an uncertain future. Planning cannot tame a turbulent environment. A statement by General Colin Powell, former U.S. Secretary of State, offers a warning for managers: "No battle plan survives contact with the enemy."[1] Does that mean it's useless to make plans? Of course not. No plan can be perfect, but without plans and goals, organizations and employees flounder. However, good managers understand that plans should grow and change to meet new conditions.

In this chapter, we explore the process of planning and consider how managers develop effective plans. Special attention is given to goal setting, for that is where planning starts. Then, we discuss the various types of plans that managers use to help the organization achieve those goals. We also take a look at planning approaches that help managers deal with uncertainty, such as contingency planning, scenario building, and crisis planning. Finally, we examine new approaches to planning that emphasize the involvement of employees, and sometimes other stakeholders, in strategic thinking and execution. Chapter 7 will look at strategic planning in depth and examine a number of strategic options managers can use in a competitive environment. In Chapter 8, we look at management decision making. Proper decision-making techniques are crucial to selecting the organization's goals, plans, and strategic options.

OVERVIEW OF GOALS AND PLANS

A **goal** is a desired future state that the organization attempts to realize.[2] Goals are important because organizations exist for a purpose, and goals define and state that purpose. A **plan** is a blueprint for goal achievement and specifies the necessary resource allocations, schedules, tasks, and other actions. Goals specify future ends; plans specify today's means. The concept of **planning** usually incorporates both ideas; it means determining the organization's goals and defining the means for achieving them.[3]

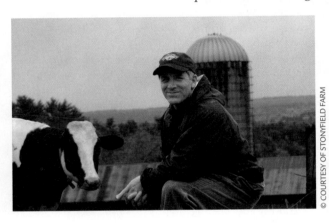

Concept Connection   From its beginning as a seven-cow farm in New England to a $300 million organic yogurt business, Stonyfield Farm has incorporated environmental responsibility into its **organizational planning.** Today, every operational plan encompasses Stonyfield's **goal** of carbon-neutral operations. CEO Gary Hirshberg believes that businesses can be more profitable and help save the planet at the same time.

Levels of Goals and Plans

Exhibit 6.1 illustrates the levels of goals and plans in an organization. The planning process starts with a formal mission that defines the basic purpose of the organization, especially for external audiences. The mission is the basis for the strategic (company) level of goals and plans, which in turn shapes the tactical (divisional) level and the operational (departmental) level.[4] Top managers are typically responsible for establishing *strategic* goals and plans that reflect a commitment to both organizational efficiency and effectiveness, as described in Chapter 1. *Tactical* goals and plans are the responsibility of middle managers, such as the heads of major divisions or functional units. A division manager will formulate tactical plans that focus on the major actions the division must take to fulfill its part in the strategic plan set by top management. *Operational* plans identify the specific procedures or processes needed at lower levels of the organization, such as individual departments and employees. Front-line managers and supervisors develop operational plans that focus on specific tasks and processes and that help meet tactical and strategic goals. Planning at each level supports the other levels.

Purposes of Goals and Plans

goal A desired future state that the organization attempts to realize.

plan A blueprint specifying the resource allocations, schedules, and other actions necessary for attaining goals.

planning The act of determining the organization's goals and the means for achieving them.

Uncertainty about the future and the complexity of today's environment overwhelm many managers and cause them to focus on operational issues and short-term results rather than long-term goals and plans. However, planning generally positively affects a company's performance.[5] In addition to improving financial and operational performance, explicit goals and plans at each level illustrated in Exhibit 6.1 benefit organizations because they send important messages to both external and internal audiences:[6]

■ *Legitimacy.* An organization's mission describes what the organization stands for and its reason for existence. It symbolizes legitimacy to external audiences such as investors, customers, suppliers, and the local community. The mission helps them look on the company in a favorable light. A strong mission also has an impact on

EXHIBIT | 6.1

Levels of Goals/Plans and
Their Importance

3 Planning

employees, enabling them to become committed to the organization because they identify with its overall purpose and reason for existence.

- *Source of motivation and commitment.* Goals and plans enhance employees' motivation and commitment by reducing uncertainty and clarifying what they should accomplish. Lack of a clear goal can hamper motivation because people don't understand what they're working toward. Whereas a goal provides the "why" of an organization or subunit's existence, a plan tells the "how." A plan lets employees know what actions to undertake to achieve the goal.

- *Resource allocation.* Goals help managers decide where they need to allocate resources, such as employees, money, and equipment. For example, DuPont has a goal of generating 25 percent of revenues from renewable resources by 2010. This goal lets managers know they need to use resources to develop renewable and biodegradable materials, acquire businesses that produce products with renewable resources, and buy equipment that reduces waste, emissions, and energy usage.[7]

- *Guides to action.* Goals and plans provide a sense of direction. They focus attention on specific targets and direct employee efforts toward important outcomes. To see how goals can guide action, consider Guitar Center, one of the fastest-growing retailers in the United States. Managers give specific goals to sales teams at every Guitar Center store each morning, and employees do whatever they need to, short of losing the company money, to meet the targets. The fast-growing retailer's unwritten mantra of "Take the deal" means that salespeople are trained to take any profitable deal, even at razor-thin margins, to meet daily sales targets.[8]

- *Rationale for decisions.* Through goal setting and planning, managers clarify what the organization is trying to accomplish. They can make decisions to ensure that internal policies, roles, performance, structure, products, and expenditures will be made in accordance with desired outcomes. Decisions throughout the organization will be in alignment with the plan.

- *Standard of performance.* Because goals define desired outcomes for the organization, they also serve as performance criteria. They provide a standard of assessment. If an organization wishes to grow by 15 percent, and actual growth is 17 percent, managers will have exceeded their prescribed standard.

EXHIBIT | 6.2

The Organizational
Planning Process

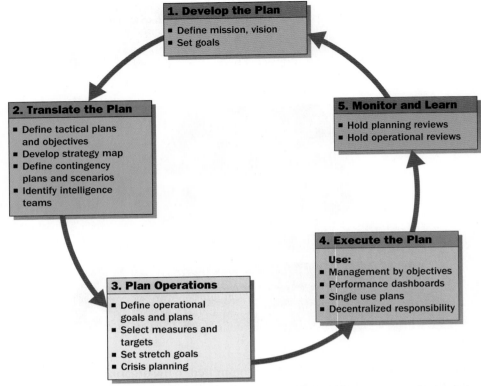

SOURCE: Based on Robert S. Kaplan and David P. Norton, "Mastering the Management System," *Harvard Business Review* (January 2008): 63–77.

The Organizational Planning Process

The overall planning process, illustrated in Exhibit 6.2, prevents managers from thinking merely in terms of day-to-day activities. The process begins when managers develop the overall plan for the organization by clearly defining mission and strategic (company-level) goals. Second, they translate the plan into action, which includes defining tactical plans and objectives, developing a strategic map to align goals, formulating contingency and scenario plans, and identifying intelligence teams to analyze major competitive issues. Third, managers lay out the operational factors needed to achieve goals. This involves devising operational goals and plans, selecting the measures and targets that will be used to determine if things are on track, and identifying stretch goals and crisis plans that might need to be put into action. Tools for executing the plan include management by objectives, performance dashboards, single-use plans, and decentralized responsibility. Finally, managers periodically review plans to learn from results and shift plans as needed, starting a new planning cycle.

TakeaMoment | As a new manager, what approach will you take to goal setting and planning? Complete the New Manager Self-Test on page 163 to get some insight into your planning approach from the way you study as a student.

GOALS IN ORGANIZATIONS

Setting goals starts with top managers. The overall planning process begins with a mission statement and goals for the organization as a whole.

New Manager Self-Test

Your Approach to Studying

Your approach to studying may be a predictor of your planning approach as a new manager. Answer the questions below as they apply to your study behavior. Please answer whether each item below is Mostly True or Mostly False for you.

	Mostly True	Mostly False
1. Before I tackle an assignment, I try to work out the reasoning behind it.	_____	_____
2. When I am reading I stop occasionally to reflect on what I am trying to get out of it.	_____	_____
3. When I finish my work, I check it through to see if it really meets the assignment.	_____	_____
4. Now and then, I stand back from my studying to think generally how successful it is going.	_____	_____
5. I frequently focus on the facts and details because I do not see the overall picture.	_____	_____
6. I write down as much as possible during lectures, because I often am not sure what is really important.	_____	_____
7. I try to relate ideas to other topics or courses whenever possible.	_____	_____
8. When I am working on a topic, I try to see in my own mind how all the ideas fit together.	_____	_____
9. It is important to me to see the bigger picture within which a new concept fits.	_____	_____

SCORING AND INTERPRETATION. Give yourself one point for each item you marked as Mostly True except items 5 and 6. For items 5 and 6 give yourself one point for each one you marked Mostly False. An important part of a new manager's job is to plan ahead, which involves grasping the bigger picture. The items above measure *metacognitive awareness*, which means to step back and see the bigger picture of one's own learning activities. This same approach enables a manager to step back and see the big picture required for effective planning, monitoring, and evaluating an organization. If you scored 3 or fewer points you may be caught up in the details of current activities. A score of 7 or above suggests that you see yourself in a bigger picture, which is an approach to studying that very well may reflect a successful planning aptitude.

SOURCE: Adapted from Kristin Backhaus and Joshua P. Liff, "Cognitive Styles and Approaches to Studying in Management Education," *Journal of Management Education* 31 (August 2007): 445–466; and A. Duff, "Learning Styles Measurement: The Revised Approaches to Studying Inventory," *Bristol Business School Teaching and Research Review* 3 (2000).

3 Planning

Organizational Mission

At the top of the goal hierarchy is the **mission**—the organization's reason for existence. The mission describes the organization's values, aspirations, and reason for being. A well-defined mission is the basis for development of all subsequent goals

mission The organization's reason for existence.

Concept Connection   A candle-scented office in a cozy yellow house that feels like a retreat from the stresses of life: Does that sound like a trip to the dentist? It's part of what sets the Washington, D.C., practice of Dr. Lynn Locklear apart. Her **mission,** she says, is "to provide a level of services and dental care that significantly enhances the quality of your life." Dr. Locklear takes a holistic approach, viewing dental health as linked to a person's overall physical and emotional well-being. That philosophy helped Locklear's business boom and earned her recognition as the 2006 *Black Enterprise* "Business Innovator of the Year."

and plans. Without a clear mission, goals and plans may be developed haphazardly and not take the organization in the direction it needs to go.

The formal **mission statement** is a broadly stated definition of purpose that distinguishes the organization from others of a similar type. A well-designed mission statement can enhance employee motivation and organizational performance.[9] The content of a mission statement often focuses on the market and customers and identifies desired fields of endeavor. Some mission statements describe company characteristics such as corporate values, product quality, location of facilities, and attitude toward employees. The mission statement of Volvo Group is shown in Exhibit 6.3. Such short, straightforward mission statements describe basic business activities and purposes as well as the values that guide the company. Another example of this type of mission statement is that of State Farm Insurance:

> State Farm's mission is to help people manage the risks of everyday life, recover from the unexpected, and realize their dreams.
>
> We are people who make it our business to be like a good neighbor; who built a premier company by selling and keeping promises through our marketing partnership; who bring diverse talents and experiences to our work of serving the State Farm customer.
>
> Our success is built on a foundation of shared values—quality service and relationships, mutual trust, integrity, and financial strength.[10]

Because of mission statements such as those of Volvo Group and State Farm, employees as well as customers, suppliers, and stockholders know the company's stated purpose and values.

mission statement A broadly stated definition of the organization's basic business scope and operations that distinguishes it from similar types of organizations.

strategic goals Broad statements of where the organization wants to be in the future; pertain to the organization as a whole rather than to specific divisions or departments.

strategic plans The action steps by which an organization intends to attain strategic goals.

Goals and Plans

Strategic goals, sometimes called *official goals*, are broad statements describing where the organization wants to be in the future. These goals pertain to the organization as a whole rather than to specific divisions or departments.

Strategic plans define the action steps by which the company intends to attain strategic goals. The strategic plan is the blueprint that defines the organizational activities and resource allocations—in the form of cash, personnel, space, and facilities—required for meeting these targets. Strategic planning tends to be long term and may define organizational action steps from two to five years in the future. The purpose of strategic plans is to turn organizational goals into realities within that time period. Consider the new strategic goals and plans at Borders, the number two book retailer in the United States.

Borders Group Inc.

Innovative Way

It's a tough environment for booksellers today. A sluggish book market, combined with competition from discounters, has put tremendous pressure on traditional book retailers to find the right approach to keep growing and thriving.

Borders Group revolutionized bookselling in the 1990s by building huge superstores, and managers stayed with the strategic goals of building more bricks-and-mortar stores even after the Internet changed the rules of the game. A partnership with Amazon was the extent of Borders' online selling. Now, managers are realizing the bricks-and-mortar approach no longer works. Online book sales are soaring, while sales at U.S. bookstores have sagged.

VOLVO GROUP MISSION STATEMENT

By creating value for our customers, we create value for our shareholders.

We use our exertise to create transport-related products and services of superior quality, safety and environmental care for demanding customers in selected segments.

We work with energy, passion and respect for the individual.

SOURCE: AB Volvo. Reprinted with permission.

Recently named CEO George Jones announced a new strategic goal of making Borders a force in online bookselling.

To achieve the goal, Borders is ending its alliance with Amazon and opening its own branded e-commerce site, giving Borders Rewards members the chance to earn benefits online, which they weren't able to do through Amazon. Managers are giving up on the idea of expanding the book superstore concept internationally and plan to sell off or franchise most of Borders' 73 overseas stores. The plan also calls for closing some of its U.S. stores, including nearly half of the smaller Waldenbooks outlets.[11]

The Borders CEO knows that achieving the goal "won't be a slam dunk," but he sees it as the best way to keep Borders relevant in the book retailing industry. The new strategic goals and plans, he believes, will revive the company by enabling Borders to provide greater benefits to customers and partner with a variety of companies for innovative projects.

After strategic goals are formulated, the next step is defining **tactical goals**, which are the results that major divisions and departments within the organization intend to achieve. These goals apply to middle management and describe what major subunits must do for the organization to achieve its overall goals.

Tactical plans are designed to help execute the major strategic plans and to accomplish a specific part of the company's strategy.[12] Tactical plans typically have a shorter time horizon than strategic plans—over the next year or so. The word *tactical* originally comes from the military. In a business or nonprofit organization, tactical plans define what major departments and organizational subunits will do to implement the organization's strategic plan. For example, the overall strategic plan of a large florist might involve becoming the number one telephone and Internet-based purveyor of flowers, which requires high-volume sales during peak seasons such as Valentine's Day and Mother's Day. Human resource managers will develop tactical plans to ensure that the company has the dedicated order takers and customer service representatives it needs during these critical periods. Tactical plans might include cross-training employees so they can switch to different jobs as departmental needs change, allowing order takers to transfer to jobs at headquarters during off-peak times to prevent burnout, and using regular order takers to train and supervise temporary workers during peak seasons.[13] These actions help top managers implement their overall strategic plan. Normally, it is the middle manager's job to take the broad strategic plan and identify specific tactical plans.

The results expected from departments, work groups, and individuals are the **operational goals**. They are precise and measurable. "Process 150 sales applications

tactical goals Goals that define the outcomes that major divisions and departments must achieve for the organization to reach its overall goals.

tactical plans Plans designed to help execute major strategic plans and to accomplish a specific part of the company's strategy.

operational goals Specific, measurable results expected from departments, work groups, and individuals within the organization.

© STUART RAMSON/ASSOCIATED PRESS

Concept Connection In 2001, California fashion house BCBG Max Azria Group was facing possible bankruptcy. Its **strategic goal** was clear: growth. But, its expansion had gone awry. Undeterred, CEO Max Azria hired Ben Malka as president. Together they formulated a new **strategic plan,** obtained $53 million in financing, and got to work. BCBG introduced new lines, concluded licensing agreements, and dramatically increased the number of retail outlets worldwide through acquisitions and by opening new stores. In 2006, BCBG expected to realize $1 billion in sales for the first time. Here Azria and his wife Lubov, who is a BCBG creative designer, acknowledge applause at a New York fashion show.

each week," "achieve 90 percent of deliveries on time," "reduce overtime by 10 percent next month," and "develop two new online courses in accounting" are examples of operational goals. Managers at the Internal Revenue Service (IRS) set an operational goal of providing accurate responses to 85 percent of taxpayer questions.[14]

Operational plans are developed at the lower levels of the organization to specify action steps toward achieving operational goals and to support tactical plans. The operational plan is the department manager's tool for daily and weekly operations. Goals are stated in quantitative terms, and the department plan describes how goals will be achieved. Operational planning specifies plans for department managers, supervisors, and individual employees. Schedules are an important component of operational planning. Schedules define precise time frames for the completion of each operational goal required for the organization's tactical and strategic goals. Operational planning also must be coordinated with the budget, because resources must be allocated for desired activities.

TakeaMoment | Go to the experiential exercise on page 179 that pertains to developing action plans for accomplishing strategic goals.

Aligning Goals with Strategy Maps

Effectively designed organizational goals are aligned; that is, they are consistent and mutually supportive so that the achievement of goals at low levels permits the attainment of high-level goals. Organizational performance is an outcome of how well these interdependent elements are aligned, so that individuals, teams, departments, and so forth are working in concert to attain specific goals that ultimately help the organization achieve high performance and fulfill its mission.[15]

An increasingly popular technique for achieving *goal alignment* is the strategy map. A **strategy map** is a visual representation of the key drivers of an organization's success and shows how specific goals and plans in each area are linked.[16] The strategy map provides a powerful way for managers to see the cause-and-effect relationships among goals and plans. The simplified strategy map in Exhibit 6.4 illustrates four key areas that contribute to a firm's long-term success—learning and growth, internal processes, customer service, and financial performance—and how the various goals and plans in each area link to the other areas. The idea is that learning and growth goals serve as a foundation to help achieve goals for excellent internal business processes. Meeting business process goals, in turn, enables the organization to meet goals for customer service and satisfaction, which helps the organization achieve its financial goals and optimize its value to all stakeholders.

In the strategy map shown in Exhibit 6.4, the organization has learning and growth goals that include developing employees, enabling continuous learning and knowledge sharing, and building a culture of innovation. Achieving these will help the organization build internal business processes that promote good relationships with suppliers and partners, improve the quality and flexibility of operations, and excel at developing

operational plans Plans developed at the organization's lower levels that specify action steps toward achieving operational goals and that support tactical planning activities.

strategy map A visual representation of the key drivers of an organization's success, showing the cause-and-effect relationships among goals and plans.

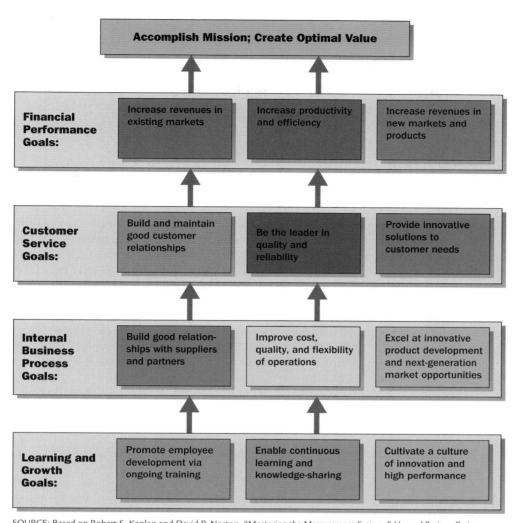

EXHIBIT | 6.4

A Strategy Map for Aligning Goals

Accomplish Mission; Create Optimal Value

Financial Performance Goals:
- Increase revenues in existing markets
- Increase productivity and efficiency
- Increase revenues in new markets and products

Customer Service Goals:
- Build and maintain good customer relationships
- Be the leader in quality and reliability
- Provide innovative solutions to customer needs

Internal Business Process Goals:
- Build good relationships with suppliers and partners
- Improve cost, quality, and flexibility of operations
- Excel at innovative product development and next-generation market opportunities

Learning and Growth Goals:
- Promote employee development via ongoing training
- Enable continuous learning and knowledge-sharing
- Cultivate a culture of innovation and high performance

SOURCE: Based on Robert S. Kaplan and David P. Norton, "Mastering the Management System," *Harvard Business Review* (January 2008): 63–77; and R. S. Kaplan and D. P. Norton, "Having Trouble with Your Strategy? Then Map It," *Harvard Business Review* (September–October 2000): 167–176.

innovative products and services. Accomplishing internal process goals, in turn, enables the organization to maintain strong relationships with customers, be a leader in quality and reliability, and provide innovation solutions to emerging customer needs. At the top of the strategy map, the accomplishment of these lower-level goals helps the organization increase revenues in existing markets, increase productivity and efficiency, and grow through selling new products and services and serving new markets segments.

In a real-life organization, the strategy map would typically be more complex and would state concrete, specific goals relevant to the particular business. However, the generic map in Exhibit 6.4 gives an idea of how managers can map goals and plans so that they are mutually supportive. The strategy map is also a good way to communicate goals, because everyone in the organization can see what part they play in helping the organization accomplish its mission.

OPERATIONAL PLANNING

Managers use operational goals to direct employees and resources toward achieving specific outcomes that enable the organization to perform efficiently and effectively. One consideration is how to establish effective goals. Then managers use a number of planning approaches, including management by objectives, single-use plans, and standing plans.

3 Planning

EXHIBIT | 6.5

Characteristics of Effective
Goal Setting

Goal Characteristics

- Specific and measurable
- Defined time period
- Cover key result areas
- Challenging but realistic
- Linked to rewards

Criteria for Effective Goals

Research has identified certain factors, listed in Exhibit 6.5, that characterize effective goals. First and foremost, goals need to be *specific and measurable*. When possible, operational goals should be expressed in quantitative terms, such as increasing profits by 2 percent, having zero incomplete sales order forms, or increasing average teacher effectiveness ratings from 3.5 to 3.7. Not all goals can be expressed in numerical terms, but vague goals have little motivating power for employees. By necessity, goals are qualitative as well as quantitative. The important point is that the goals be precisely defined and allow for measurable progress. Effective goals also have a *defined time period* that specifies the date on which goal attainment will be measured. School administrators might set a deadline for improving teacher effectiveness ratings, for instance, at the end of the 2009 school term. When a goal involves a two- to three-year time horizon, setting specific dates for achieving parts of it is a good way to keep people on track toward the goal.

Goals should *cover key result areas*. Goals cannot be set for every aspect of employee behavior or organizational performance; if they were, their sheer number would render them meaningless. Instead, managers establish goals based on the idea of *choice and clarity*. A few carefully chosen, clear, and direct goals can more powerfully focus organizational attention, energy, and resources.[17] Managers should set goals that are *challenging but realistic*. When goals are unrealistic, they set employees up for failure and lead to a decrease in employee morale. However, if goals are too easy, employees may not feel motivated. Goals should also be *linked to rewards.* The ultimate impact of goals depends on the extent to which salary increases, promotions, and awards are based on goal achievement. Employees pay attention to what gets noticed and rewarded in the organization.[18]

TakeaMoment | As a new manager, establish operational goals that are in alignment with the tactical and strategic goals set at higher levels in the organization. Make goals specific, measurable, and challenging, but realistic. Remember that a few carefully chosen goals are powerful for directing employee energy and motivation. Reward people when they meet goals.

Management by Objectives

Described by famed management scholar Peter Drucker in his 1954 book, *The Practice of Management*, management by objectives has remained a popular and compelling method for defining goals and monitoring progress toward achieving them. **Management by objectives (MBO)** is a system whereby managers and employees define goals for every department, project, and person and use them to monitor subsequent performance.[19] A model of the essential steps of the MBO system is presented in Exhibit 6.6. Four major activities make MBO successful:[20]

management by objectives (MBO) A method of management whereby managers and employees define goals for every department, project, and person and use them to monitor subsequent performance.

1. *Set goals.* Setting goals involves employees at all levels and looks beyond day-to-day activities to answer the question "What are we trying to accomplish?" Managers heed the criteria of effective goals described in the previous section and make sure to assign responsibility for goal accomplishment. However, goals

EXHIBIT | 6.6 Model of the MBO Process

Step 1: Set Goals
- Corporate Strategic Goals
- Departmental Goals
- Individual Goals

Step 2: Develop Action Plans

Action Plans

Review Progress

Step 3: Review Progress

Take Corrective Action

Appraise Performance

Step 4: Appraise Overall Performance

should be jointly derived. Mutual agreement between employee and supervisor creates the strongest commitment to achieving goals. In the case of teams, all team members may participate in setting goals.

2. **Develop action plans.** An *action plan* defines the course of action needed to achieve the stated goals. Action plans are made for both individuals and departments.

3. **Review progress.** A periodic progress review is important to ensure that action plans are working. These reviews can occur informally between managers and subordinates, where the organization may wish to conduct three-, six-, or nine-month reviews during the year. This periodic checkup allows managers and employees to see whether they are on target or whether corrective action is needed. Managers and employees should not be locked into predefined behavior and must be willing to take whatever steps are necessary to produce meaningful results. The point of MBO is to achieve goals. The action plan can be changed whenever goals are not being met.

4. **Appraise overall performance.** The final step in MBO is to carefully evaluate whether annual goals have been achieved for both individuals and departments. Success or failure to achieve goals can become part of the performance appraisal system and the designation of salary increases and other rewards. The appraisal of departmental and overall corporate performance shapes goals for the next year. The MBO cycle repeats itself on an annual basis.

The specific application of MBO must fit the needs of each company. For example, Siemens used MBO to improve its overall financial performance.

Siemens of Germany, which makes everything from mobile phones to gas-turbine generators to lightbulbs, has always had great engineers bent on producing products of the highest quality. But in recent years, managers have learned that competing with the likes of U.S.-based General Electric and Korea's Samsung takes more than quality—it also requires speed to market, relentless innovation, and ruthless attention to costs. Within two years, Siemens' profits sank by two-thirds and company shares fell even faster. CEO Heinrich von Pierer developed a plan for getting Siemens back on track, with a specific goal (MBO step 1) of strengthening the overall business to be in financial shape for listing on a U.S. stock exchange within three years.

Managers developed an action plan (MBO step 2) that included: (1) cutting the time it takes to develop and produce new products; (2) selling or closing poor-performing units and strengthening remaining businesses through acquisitions to achieve world leadership;

Innovative Way

Siemens

3
Planning

(3) setting tough profit targets for managers and tying pay to performance; and (4) converting accounting practices to report results according to U.S. accounting standards. Managers of the various business divisions then developed action plans for employees in their own units. Progress was reviewed (MBO step 3) at quarterly meetings where managers from the 14 business units reported on their advancements directly to von Pierer.

Managers were required to explain if benchmarks weren't met and how shortcomings would be corrected. At the end of each year of the turnaround plan, an overall performance appraisal was held for each business and the corporation as a whole (MBO step 4). Managers who met goals were rewarded; those who had consistently failed to meet them were let go, with the poorest performers going first. Since the plan was implemented, Siemens dramatically improved its speed and overall financial performance. The MBO system helped to energize manager and employee actions companywide toward goals deemed critical by top management.[21]

Many companies, including Intel, Tenneco, Black & Decker, and DuPont, have adopted MBO, and most managers think MBO is an effective management tool.[22] Managers believe they are better oriented toward goal achievement when MBO is used. In recent years, the U.S. Congress required that federal agencies use a type of MBO system to focus government employees on achieving specific outcomes.[23] Like any system, MBO achieves benefits when used properly but results in problems when used improperly. Benefits and problems are summarized in Exhibit 6.7.

The benefits of the MBO process can be many. Corporate goals are more likely to be achieved when they focus manager and employee efforts. Using a performance measurement system, such as MBO, helps employees see how their jobs and performance contribute to the business, giving them a sense of ownership and commitment.[24] Performance is improved when employees are committed to attaining the goal, are motivated because they help decide what is expected, and are free to be resourceful. Goals at lower levels are aligned with and enable the attainment of goals at top management levels.

Problems with MBO occur when the company faces rapid change. The environment and internal activities must have some stability for performance to be measured and compared against goals. Setting new goals every few months allows no time for action plans and appraisal to take effect. Also, poor employer-employee relations reduce effectiveness because of an element of distrust that may be present between managers and workers. Sometimes goal "displacement" occurs if employees focus exclusively on their operational goals to the detriment of other teams or departments. Overemphasis on operational goals can harm the attainment of overall goals. Another problem arises in mechanistic organizations characterized by rigidly defined tasks and rules that may not be compatible with MBO's emphasis on mutual determination of goals by employee and supervisor. In addition, when participation is discouraged, employees will lack the training and values to jointly set goals with employers. Finally, if MBO becomes a process of filling out annual paperwork rather than energizing employees to achieve goals, it becomes an empty exercise. Once the

EXHIBIT | 6.7

MBO Benefits and Problems

Benefits of MBO	Problems with MBO
1. Manager and employee efforts are focused on activities that will lead to goal attainment.	1. Constant change prevents MBO from taking hold.
2. Performance can be improved at all company levels.	2. An environment of poor employer-employee relations reduces MBO effectiveness.
3. Employees are motivated.	3. Strategic goals may be displaced by operational goals.
4. Departmental and individual goals are aligned with company goals.	4. Mechanistic organizations and values that discourage participation can harm the MBO process.
	5. Too much paperwork saps MBO energy.

paperwork is completed, employees forget about the goals, perhaps even resenting the paperwork in the first place.

Single-Use and Standing Plans

Single-use plans are developed to achieve a set of goals that are not likely to be repeated in the future. **Standing plans** are ongoing plans that provide guidance for tasks or situations that occur repeatedly within the organization. Exhibit 6.8 outlines the major types of single-use and standing plans. Single-use plans typically include both programs and projects. The primary standing plans are organizational policies, rules, and procedures. Standing plans generally pertain to such matters as employee illness, absences, smoking, discipline, hiring, and dismissal. Many companies are discovering a need to develop standing plans regarding the use of e-mail, as discussed in the Manager's Shoptalk box.

single-use plans Plans that are developed to achieve a set of goals that are unlikely to be repeated in the future.

standing plans Ongoing plans that are used to provide guidance for tasks performed repeatedly within the organization.

Manager's Shoptalk

Regulating E-Mail in the Workplace

Top executives around the globe are discovering that casual e-mail messages can come back to haunt them—in court. The American Management Association (AMA) surveyed 1,100 companies and found that 14 percent of them had been ordered to disclose e-mail messages. Eight brokerage firms were fined $8 million for not keeping and producing e-mail in accordance with SEC guidelines. Some companies have had to pay millions to settle sexual harassment lawsuits arising from inappropriate e-mail.

As with any powerful tool, e-mail has the potential to be hazardous, backfiring not only on the employee but on the organization as well. One study found that "potentially dangerous or nonproductive" messages account for fully 31 percent of all company e-mail. Experts say a formal written policy is the best way for companies to protect themselves, and they offer some tips for managers on developing effective policies governing the use of e-mail.

- *Make clear that all e-mail and its contents are the property of the company.* Many experts recommend warning employees that the company reserves the right to read any messages transmitted over its system. "Employees need to understand that a company can access employees' e-mail at any time without advance notice or consent," says lawyer Pam Reeves. This rule helps to discourage frivolous e-mails or those that might be considered crude and offensive.

- *Tie the policy to the company's sexual harassment policy or other policies governing employee behavior on the job.* Starwood Hotel and Resorts ousted its CEO after an investigation uncovered e-mails that seem to substantiate claims that he made sexual advances to female

employees. In almost all sexual harassment cases, judges have ruled that the use of e-mail is considered part of the workplace environment.

- *Establish clear guidelines on matters such as the use of e-mail for jokes and other nonwork-related communications, the sending of confidential messages, and how to handle junk e-mail.* At Prudential Insurance, for example, employees are prohibited from using company e-mail to share jokes, photographs, or any kind of nonbusiness information.

- *Establish guidelines for deleting or retaining messages.* Retention periods of 30 to 90 days for routine messages are typical. Most organizations also set up a centralized archive for retaining essential e-mail messages.

- *Consider having policies pop up on users' screens when they log on.* It is especially important to remind employees that e-mail belongs to the employer and may be monitored.

The field of computer forensics is booming, and even deleted e-mails can usually be tracked down. An effective policy is the best step companies can take to manage the potential risks of e-mail abuse.

SOURCES: "E-Mail: The DNA of Office Crimes," *Electric Perspectives* 28, no. 5 (September–October 2003): 4; Marcia Stepanek with Steve Hamm, "When the Devil Is in the E-Mails," *BusinessWeek* (June 8, 1998): 72–74; Joseph McCafferty, "The Phantom Menace," *CFO* (June 1999): 89–91; "Many Company Internet and E-Mail Policies Are Worth Revising," *The Kiplinger Letter* (February 21, 2003): 1; and Carol Hymowitz, "Personal Boundaries Shrink as Companies Punish Bad Behavior," *The Wall Street Journal*, June 18, 2007.

3 Planning

EXHIBIT | 6.8

Major Types of Single-Use
and Standing Plans

Single-Use Plans	Standing Plans

Program
 • Plans for attaining a one-time organizational goal
 • Major undertaking that may take several years to complete
 • Large in scope; may be associated with several projects
   Examples: Building a new headquarters
   Converting all paper files to digital
	Policy
	 • Broad in scope—general guide to action
	 • Based on organization's overall goals/strategic plan
	 • Defines boundaries within which to make decisions
	   Examples: Sexual harassment policies
	   Internet and e-mail usage policies

Project
 • Also a set of plans for attaining a one-time goal
 • Smaller in scope and complexity than a program; shorter in horizon
 • Often one part of a larger program
   Examples: Renovating the office
   Setting up a company intranet
	Rule
	 • Narrow in scope
	 • Describes how a specific action is to be performed
	 • May apply to specific setting
	   Examples: No eating rule in areas of company where employees are visible to the public
	
	 Procedure
	 • Sometimes called a standard operating procedure
	 • Defines a precise series of steps to attain certain goals
	   Examples: Procedures for issuing refunds
	   Procedures for handling employee grievances

contingency plans Plans
that define company responses
to specific situations, such
as emergencies, setbacks, or
unexpected conditions.

PLANNING FOR A TURBULENT ENVIRONMENT

As increasing turbulence and uncertainty shake the business world, managers have turned to innovative planning approaches that help brace the organization for unexpected—even unimaginable—events. Three critical planning methods are contingency planning, building scenarios, and crisis planning.

Contingency Planning

When organizations are operating in a highly uncertain environment or dealing with long time horizons, sometimes planning can seem like a waste of time. Indeed, inflexible plans may hinder rather than help an organization's performance in the face of rapid technological, social, economic, or other environmental change. In these cases, managers can develop multiple future alternatives to help them form more adaptive plans.

Contingency plans define company responses to be taken in the case of emergencies, setbacks, or unexpected conditions. To develop contingency plans, managers identify important factors in the environment, such as possible economic downturns, declining markets, increases in cost of supplies, new technological developments, or safety accidents. Managers then forecast a range of alternative responses to the most

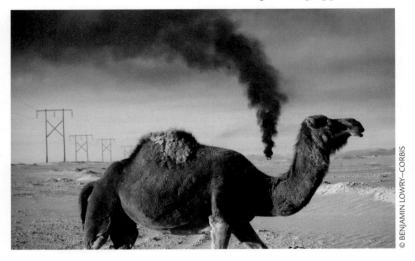

Concept Connection A desert flare marks the area where geologists discovered Libya's rich Zilten oilfield in the 1950s. At their peak in 1970, Libyan oil fields operated by Occidental Petroleum were producing 660,000 barrels a day, more than the company's total oil production in 2003. Today, with economic sanctions against Libya lifted by the U.S. government, big oil companies like Occidental, Chevron Texaco, and Exxon Mobil are again ready to do business with Libya's National Oil Corporation. Yet, the current environment of terrorist threats and general uncertainty means managers have to be prepared for whatever might happen. They are busy developing **contingency plans** to define how their companies will respond in case of unexpected setbacks associated with renewed Libyan operations. Companies are willing to take the risks because the potential rewards are huge.

likely high-impact contingencies, focusing on the worst case.[25] For example, if sales fall 20 percent and prices drop 8 percent, what will the company do? Managers can develop contingency plans that might include layoffs, emergency budgets, new sales efforts, or new markets. A real-life example comes from FedEx, which has to cope with some kind of unexpected disruption to its service somewhere in the world on a daily basis. In one recent year alone, managers activated contingency plans related to more than two dozen tropical storms, an air traffic controller strike in France, and a blackout in Los Angeles. The company also has contingency plans in place for events such as labor strikes, social upheavals in foreign countries, or incidents of terrorism.[26]

Building Scenarios

An extension of contingency planning is a forecasting technique known as scenario building.[27] **Scenario building** involves looking at current trends and discontinuities and visualizing future possibilities. Rather than looking only at history and thinking about what has been, managers think about what *could be*. The events that cause the most damage to companies are those that no one even conceived of, such as the collapse of the World Trade Center towers in New York due to terrorist attack. Managers can't predict the future, but they can rehearse a framework within which future events can be managed. With scenario building, a broad base of managers mentally rehearses different scenarios based on anticipating varied changes that could affect the organization. Scenarios are like stories that offer alternative vivid pictures of what the future will be like and how managers will respond. Typically, two to five scenarios are developed for each set of factors, ranging from the most optimistic to the most pessimistic view.[28] Scenario building forces managers to mentally rehearse what they would do if their best-laid plans collapse.

Royal Dutch/Shell has long used scenario building to help managers navigate the instability and uncertainty of the oil industry. A classic example is the scenario Shell managers rehearsed in 1970 that focused on an imagined accident in Saudi Arabia that severed an oil pipeline, which in turn decreased supply. The market reacted by increasing oil prices, which allowed OPEC nations to pump less oil and make more money. This story caused managers to reexamine the standard assumptions about oil price and supply and imagine what would happen and how they would respond if OPEC increased prices. Nothing in the exercise told Shell managers to expect an embargo, but by rehearsing this scenario, they were much more prepared than the competition when OPEC announced its first oil embargo in October 1973. The company's speedy response to a massive shift in the environment enabled Shell to move in two years' from being the world's eighth largest oil company to being number two.[29]

As a new manager, get in the mind-set of scenario planning. Go to http://www
.shell.com/scenarios, where Shell Oil publishes the outline of its annual scenario planning exercise. You might also want to do an Internet search and type in "national intelligence agency scenarios" to find links to reports of global trends and scenario planning done by various organizations.

TakeaMoment

Crisis Planning

Surveys of companies' use of management techniques reveal that the use of contingency and scenario planning surged after the September 11, 2001, terrorist attacks in the United States and has remained high ever since, reflecting a growing emphasis on managing uncertainty.[30] Some firms also engage in *crisis planning* to enable them to cope with unexpected events that are so sudden and devastating that they have the potential to destroy the organization if managers aren't prepared with a quick and appropriate response.

scenario building Looking at trends and discontinuities and imagining possible alternative futures to build a framework within which unexpected future events can be managed.

EXHIBIT | **6.9**

Essential Stages of Crisis Planning

Crisis Planning

Prevention
- Build relationships.
- Detect signals from environment.

Preparation
- Designate crisis management team and spokesperson.
- Create detailed crisis management plan.
- Set up effective communications system.

SOURCE: Based on information in W. Timothy Coombs, *Ongoing Crisis Communication: Planning, Managing, and Responding* (Thousand Oaks, CA: Sage Publications, 1999).

Crises have become integral features of organizations in today's world. Consider events such as the death of a 17-year-old girl due to a botched transplant at Duke University Hospital, deaths due to e-coli bacteria from Jack-in-the-Box hamburgers, the shooting rampage at Virginia Tech University, or the crash of the *Columbia* space shuttle. Although crises may vary, a carefully thought-out and coordinated plan can be used to respond to any disaster. In addition, crisis planning reduces the incidence of trouble, much like putting a good lock on a door reduces burglaries.[31] Exhibit 6.9 outlines two essential stages of crisis planning.[32]

- **Crisis Prevention.** The *crisis prevention* stage involves activities managers undertake to try to prevent crises from occurring and to detect warning signs of potential crises. A critical part of the prevention stage is building open, trusting relationships with key stakeholders such as employees, customers, suppliers, governments, unions, and the community. By developing favorable relationships, managers can often prevent crises from happening and respond more effectively to those that cannot be avoided. For example, organizations that have open, trusting relationships with employees and unions may avoid crippling labor strikes. Coca-Cola suffered a major crisis in Europe because it failed to respond quickly to reports of "foul-smelling" Coke in Belgium. A former CEO observed that every problem the company has faced in recent years "can be traced to a singular cause: We neglected our relationships."[33]

- **Crisis Preparation.** The *crisis preparation* stage includes all the detailed planning to handle a crisis when it occurs. Three steps in the preparation stage are: (1) designating a crisis management team and spokesperson, (2) creating a detailed crisis management plan, and (3) setting up an effective communications system. The crisis management team, for example, is a cross-functional group of people who are designated to swing into action if a crisis occurs. The organization should also designate a spokesperson who will be the voice of the company during the crisis.[34] The crisis management plan (CMP) is a detailed, written plan that specifies the steps to be taken,

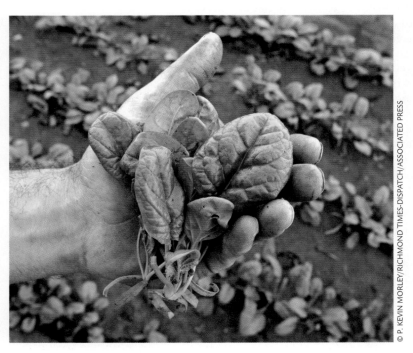

© P. KEVIN MORLEY/RICHMOND TIMES-DISPATCH/ASSOCIATED PRESS

Concept Connection Looks harmless, doesn't it? But three people died and nearly 200 became ill after E. coli-contaminated spinach grown in central California reached consumers throughout the United States. Government and the food industry activated **crisis management plans** to contain the public health menace. Producers voluntarily recalled spinach products, grocers swept shelves clear of bagged spinach, and the FDA worked tirelessly to determine the cause. Various groups also proposed future **prevention** measures. Some advocated more stringent government regulation, while others argued for producers doing more product testing and a better job of tracking produce from field to table.

and by whom, if a crisis occurs. The CMP should include the steps for dealing with various types of crises, such as natural disasters like fires or earthquakes, normal accidents like economic crises or industrial accidents, and abnormal events such as product tampering or acts of terrorism.[35] A key point is that a crisis management plan should be a living, changing document that is regularly reviewed, practiced, and updated as needed.

PLANNING FOR HIGH PERFORMANCE

The purpose of planning and goal setting is to help the organization achieve high performance. The process of planning is changing to be more in tune with today's environment and the shifting attitudes of employees. Traditionally, strategy and planning have been the domain of top managers. Today, however, managers involve people throughout the organization, which can spur higher performance because people understand the goals and plans and buy into them.

Traditional Approaches to Planning

Traditionally, corporate planning has been done entirely by top executives, by consulting firms, or, most commonly, by central planning departments. **Central planning departments** are groups of planning specialists who report directly to the CEO or president. This approach was popular during the 1970s. Planning specialists were hired to gather data and develop detailed strategic plans for the corporation as a whole. This planning approach was top down because goals and plans were assigned to major divisions and departments from the planning department after approval by the president.

This approach worked well in many applications and is still popular with some companies. However, formal planning increasingly is being criticized as inappropriate for today's fast-paced environment. Central planning departments may be out of touch with the constantly changing realities faced by front-line managers and employees, which may leave people struggling to follow a plan that no longer fits the environment and customer needs. In addition, formal plans dictated by top managers and central planning departments can inhibit employee innovation and learning.

Go to the ethical dilemma on pages 179–180 that pertains to potential problems with high performance planning.   TakeaMoment

High-Performance Approaches to Planning

A fresh approach to planning is to involve everyone in the organization, and sometimes outside stakeholders as well, in the planning process. The evolution to a new approach began with a shift to **decentralized planning**, which means that planning experts work with managers in major divisions or departments to develop their own goals and plans. Managers throughout the company come up with their own creative solutions to problems and become more committed to following through on the plans. As the environment became even more volatile, top executives saw the benefits of pushing decentralized planning even further, by having planning experts work directly with line managers and front-line employees to develop dynamic plans that meet fast-changing needs.

In a complex and competitive business environment, strategic thinking and execution become the expectation of every employee.[36] Planning comes alive when employees are involved in setting goals and determining the means to reach them. Here are some guidelines for planning in the new workplace.

central planning department
A group of planning specialists who develop plans for the organization as a whole and its major divisions and departments and typically report directly to the president or CEO.

decentralized planning
Managers work with planning experts to develop their own goals and plans.

© GARY VOLINSKY

Concept Connection Netflix is trying to meet a **stretch goal** of improving its Internet movie recommendation system ("people who liked this movie also rented...") by 10 percent. In October 2006, the company invited the biggest math brains in the world to compete for a $1 million prize to reach that goal. In the first year, more than 2,500 teams from a dozen countries submitted entries. At the one-year anniversary, a team of AT&T researchers (Chris Volinsky, Yehuda Koren, and Bob Bell) won a $50,000 progress award for improving the system by 8.43 percent. Some speculate that a 10 percent improvement is unobtainable. By May 2008, the team had reached a 9.15 percent improvement of the system.

Set Stretch Goals for Excellence **Stretch goals** are reasonable yet highly ambitious goals that are so clear, compelling, and imaginative that they fire up employees and engender excellence. Stretch goals are typically so far beyond the current levels that people have to be innovative to find ways to reach them. An extension of the stretch goal is the *big hairy audacious goal* or *BHAG*. The phrase was first proposed by James Collins and Jerry Porras in their 1996 article entitled "Building Your Company's Vision."[37] Since then, it has evolved to a term used to describe any goal that is so big, inspiring, and outside the prevailing paradigm that it hits people in the gut and shifts their thinking. At the same time, however, goals must be seen as achievable or employees will be discouraged and demotivated.[38]

Stretch goals and BHAGs have become extremely important because things move fast. A company that focuses on gradual, incremental improvements in products, processes, or systems will get left behind. Managers can use these goals to compel employees to think in new ways that can lead to bold, innovative breakthroughs. Motorola used stretch goals to achieve *Six Sigma* quality, which has now become the standard for numerous companies. Managers first set a goal of a tenfold increase in quality over a two-year period. After this goal was met, they set a new stretch goal of a hundredfold improvement over a four-year period.[39]

Use Performance Dashboards People need a way to see how plans are progressing and gauge their progress toward achieving goals. Companies began using *business performance dashboards* as a way for executives to keep track of key performance metrics, such as sales in relation to targets, number of products on back order, or percentage of customer service calls resolved within specified time periods. Today, dashboards are evolving into organization-wide systems that help align and track goals across the enterprise. Exhibit 6.10 shows a business performance dashboard from Celequest that can deliver real-time key performance metrics to any employee's desktop. The true power of dashboards comes from applying them throughout the company, even on the factory floor, so that all employees can track progress toward goals, see when things are falling short, and find innovative ways to get back on course toward reaching the specified targets. At Emergency Medical Associates, a physician-owned medical group that manages emergency rooms for hospitals in New York and New Jersey, dashboards enable the staff to see when performance thresholds related to patient wait times, for example, aren't being met at various hospitals.[40] Some dashboard systems also incorporate software that lets users perform what-if scenarios to evaluate the impact of various alternatives for meeting goals.

TakeaMoment | As a new manager, involve others in planning and goal setting to enhance commitment and performance. Set stretch goals to encourage innovation and excellence. Make use of business performance dashboards to help people track progress toward goals, and deploy intelligence teams to analyze major competitive issues.

stretch goal A reasonable yet highly ambitious, compelling goal that energizes people and inspires excellence.

Deploy Intelligence Teams Anticipating and managing uncertainty and turbulence in the environment is a crucial part of planning, which means managers need good intelligence to make informed choices about goals and plans. A growing

EXHIBIT | 6.10 A Performance Dashboard for Planning

SOURCE: © Celequest, PR Newswire Photo Service (Newscom).

number of leading companies are using intelligence teams to manage this challenge. An **intelligence team** is a cross-functional group of managers and employees, usually led by a competitive intelligence professional, who work together to gain a deep understanding of a specific business issue, with the aim of presenting insights, possibilities, and recommendations about goals and plans related to that issue.[41] Intelligence teams are useful when the organization confronts a major intelligence challenge. For example, consider a large financial services firm that learns that an even-larger rival is potentially moving to compete directly with one of its major profit-generating businesses. Top managers might form an intelligence team to identify when and how this might happen and how it might affect the organization. Intelligence teams can provide insights that enable managers to make more informed decisions about goals, as well as to devise contingency plans and scenarios related to major strategic issues.

intelligence team A cross-functional group of managers and employees who work together to gain a deep understanding of a specific competitive issue and offer insight and recommendations for planning.

ch6 A MANAGER'S ESSENTIALS: WHAT HAVE WE LEARNED?

- This chapter discussed organizational planning, which involves defining goals and developing plans with which to achieve them.

- An organization exists for a single, overriding purpose known as its *mission*—the basis for strategic goals and plans. Goals within the organization begin with strategic goals followed by tactical and operational goals. Plans are defined similarly, with strategic, tactical, and operational plans used to achieve the goals. Managers can use strategy maps to clearly align goals and communicate them throughout the organization.

- Managers formulate goals that are specific and measurable, cover key result areas, are challenging but realistic, have a defined time period, and are linked to rewards.

- The chapter described several types of operational plans, including management by objectives, single-use and standing plans, and contingency plans. Two extensions of contingency planning are scenario building and crisis planning. Scenarios are alternative vivid pictures of what the future might be like. They provide a framework for managers to cope with unexpected or unpredictable events. Crisis planning involves the stages of prevention and preparation.

- In the past, planning was almost always done entirely by top managers, consultants, or central planning departments. During turbulent times, planning is decentralized and people throughout the organization are involved in establishing dynamic plans that can meet rapidly changing needs in the environment.

- Some guidelines for high-performance planning in a turbulent environment include setting stretch goals for excellence, using performance dashboards, and organizing intelligence teams.

ch6 DISCUSSION QUESTIONS

1. Companies such as Wal-Mart and Valero Energy Corp. were days ahead of FEMA in responding to relief operations after Katrina and Rita devastated the Gulf Coast in the fall of 2005. Why do you think they were able to respond more quickly? What types of planning would help federal, state, and local governments prepare for unexpected events?

2. Write a brief mission statement for a local business with which you are familiar. How might having a clear, written mission statement benefit a small organization?

3. What strategic plans could the college or university at which you are taking this management course adopt to compete for students in the marketplace? Would these plans depend on the school's goals?

4. If you were a top manager of a medium-sized real estate sales agency, would you use MBO? If so, give examples of goals you might set for managers and sales agents.

5. A new business venture must develop a comprehensive business plan to borrow money to get started. Companies such as FedEx, Nike, and Rolm Corporation say they did not follow the original plan closely. Does that mean that developing the plan was a waste of time for these eventually successful companies?

6. When using MBO as a manager, how would you go about achieving mutual agreement between you and your employees to create strong commitment toward achieving the goals? What would you do if a fundamental disagreement between you and your employees arose about goal achievement?

7. How do you think planning in today's organizations compares to planning 25 years ago? Do you think planning becomes more important or less important in a world where everything is changing fast and crises are a regular part of organizational life? Why?

8. Assume Southern University decides to (1) raise its admission standards, and (2) initiate a business fair to which local townspeople will be invited. What types of plans might it use to carry out these two activities?

9. In what types of organizations do you think event-based planning would be most useful? What about scenario planning? Why?

10. Come up with a stretch goal for some aspect of your own life. How do you determine whether it makes sense to pursue a stretch goal?

ch6 MANAGEMENT IN PRACTICE: EXPERIENTIAL EXERCISE

Company Crime Wave

Senior managers in your organization are concerned about internal theft. Your department has been assigned the task of writing an ethics policy that defines employee theft and prescribes penalties. Stealing goods is easily classified as theft, but other activities are more ambiguous. Before writing the policy, go through the following list and decide which behaviors should be defined as stealing and whether penalties should apply. Discuss the items with your department members until agreement is reached. Classify each item as an example of (1) theft, (2) acceptable behavior, or (3) in between with respect to written policy. Is it theft when an employee

- Gets paid for overtime not worked?
- Takes a longer lunch or coffee break than authorized?
- Punches a time card for another?
- Comes in late or leaves early?

- Fakes injury to receive workers' compensation?
- Takes care of personal business on company time?
- Occasionally uses company copying machines or makes long-distance telephone calls for personal purposes?
- Takes a few stamps, pens, or other supplies for personal use?
- Takes money from the petty cash drawer?
- Uses company vehicles or tools for own purposes but returns them?
- Damages merchandise so a cohort can purchase it at a discount?
- Accepts a gift from a supplier?

Now consider those items rated "in between." Do these items represent ethical issues as defined in Chapter 5? How should these items be handled in the company's written policy?

ch6 MANAGEMENT IN PRACTICE: ETHICAL DILEMMA

Inspire Learning Corp.

When the idea first occurred to her, it seemed like such a win-win situation. Now she wasn't so sure.

Marge Brygay was a hard-working sales rep for Inspire Learning Corporation, a company intent on becoming the top educational software provider in five years. That newly adopted strategic goal translated into an ambitious million-dollar sales target for each of Inspire's sales reps. At the beginning of the fiscal year, her share of the sales department's operational goal seemed entirely reasonable to Marge. She believed in Inspire's products. The company had developed innovative, highly regarded math, language, science, and social studies programs for the K–12 market. What set the software apart was a foundation in truly cutting-edge research. Marge had seen for herself how Inspire programs could engage whole classrooms of normally unmotivated kids; the significant rise in test scores on those increasingly important standardized tests bore out her subjective impressions.

But now, just days before the end of the year, Marge's sales were $1,000 short of her million-dollar goal. The sale that would have put her comfortably over the top fell through due to last-minute cuts in one large school system's budget. At first, she was nearly overwhelmed with frustration, but then it occurred to her that if she contributed $1,000 to Central High, the inner-city high school in her territory probably most in need of what she had for sale, they could purchase the software and put her over the top.

Her scheme would certainly benefit Central High students. Achieving her sales goal would make Inspire happy, and it wouldn't do her any harm, either professionally or financially. Making the goal would earn her a $10,000 bonus check that would come in handy when the time came to write out that first tuition check for her oldest child, who had just been accepted to a well-known, private university.

Initially, it seemed like the perfect solution all the way around. The more she thought about it, though, the more it didn't quite sit well with her conscience. Time was running out. She needed to decide what to do.

What Would You Do?

1. Donate the $1,000 to Central High, and consider the $10,000 bonus a good return on your gift.

2. Accept the fact you didn't quite make your sales goal this year. Figure out ways to work smarter next year to increase the odds of achieving your target.

3. Don't make the donation, but investigate whether any other ways were available to help Central High raise the funds that would allow them to purchase the much-needed educational software.

SOURCE: Based on Shel Horowitz, "Should Mary Buy Her Own Bonus?" *Business Ethics* (Summer 2005): 34.

ch6 CASE FOR CRITICAL ANALYSIS

H.I.D.

Consultant Keith Houck strode into the conference room in Bill Collins's wake. Bill, the president of H.I.D., had hired Keith to help the hotel company's management team with their strategic planning. Wasting no time, Bill introduced Keith to human resources director Karen Setz, marketing head Tony Briggs, hotel operations chief Dave King, and accountant Art Johnson. Already written in large block letters on an easel in the front of the room was the company's 10-year-old mission statement: "H.I.D. strives to exceed the expectations of our guests by providing excellent value in well-run hotels located off the beaten track. In this way, we will meet our profit, quality, and growth goals."

Keith, of course, had digested all of the background materials the president had sent him, so he knew the company currently owned 21 properties: the original 10 Holiday Inns and 2 Quality Inns, all in Georgia, plus 8 hotels in Canada and a property in the Caribbean, acquired since Bill assumed the presidency five years ago. Keith was also well aware that even though H.I.D. was a reasonably profitable company, Bill wasn't satisfied.

The consultant started the ball rolling by asking each person in the room to describe his or her vision for domestic operations over the next 10 years. How many hotels should H.I.D. own? Where should they be located, and what should the target market be? As the managers shared their views, Keith summarized their answers on the flip chart.

The consultant wasn't at all surprised that Bill's goals were the most ambitious. He advocated for an intermediate goal of adding 27 properties in five years and a long-term goal of 50 in 10 years. The other managers didn't come close, calling for only 15 hotels to be added in five years and no more than 20 over a decade. The H.I.D. senior managers just sat and stared at the figures.

Keith asked for reactions. After an uncomfortable silence, Dave was the first to jump into the fray. "We can't build something like five hotels a year. We would outpace our income. And we couldn't run them, certainly not given our current staffing. I don't see how we could afford to hire the people we'd need." Art nodded in agreement.

"You know, we've always concentrated on medium-priced hotels in smaller towns where we don't have much competition," pointed out Tony.

Karen jumped in. "Well, do we need to think about moving to bigger towns now, like maybe Jacksonville? We've got one property in Atlanta already. Maybe we should look into building another one there."

"Why stick so close to home?" asked Bill. "You know, we're already looking at the possibility of going to Jacksonville. But why stop there? We've got an interesting opportunity out in California, and we might have another one in New Jersey."

Keith was beginning to fully appreciate the breadth and depth of the job he had on his hands. He looked at the mission statement, reviewed the list of current properties, and realized as he listened to the managers that nothing really matched up. So, now what should he do?

Questions

1. What are the causes of the confusion confronting Keith Houck? Is H.I.D. ready to formulate a strategic plan? Why or why not?

2. If you were Keith Houck, what questions would you ask the managers? What steps would you recommend in your effort to help H.I.D. successfully formulate strategic goals and plans?

3. If you were Bill Collins, what might you have done differently during your tenure as H.I.D. president?

SOURCE: Based on a case provided by James Higgins.

ch6   ON THE JOB VIDEO CASE

Organic Valley Grows Up

Every business starts small. Sometimes it begins in a garage or a basement. Sometimes it starts in a small storefront. Organic Valley Cooperative planted its seeds in the lands and barns of half a dozen family farmers in Wisconsin nearly 20 years ago. And despite the alarming trend in which more than 6 million U.S. family farms have closed during this time period, Organic Valley is growing. Starting a business like this, building it, and growing into a larger organization is a process filled with all kinds of challenges and setbacks. The conventional challenges include the search for financial resources, an uncertain market, potential competitors, changing regulations, and issues of supply and demand. But farming comes with its own set of potential setbacks—drought, flooding, tornadoes, and disease among animals, just to name a few. Organic Valley has managed to face these challenges and grow from a few dairy farms to more than 630 organic farms on 100,000 acres in 16 states across the United States. Here is how they did it.

Driven by their belief that food—meat, produce, and dairy products—should be free of pesticides, antibiotics, and synthetic hormones, the first group of Organic Valley farmers set up a cooperative with an office in tiny LaFarge, Wisconsin, whose population is still less than 800. Even as a small group, Organic Valley was able to provide a consistent, stable price to farmers for their products, particularly milk. This consistency allowed the farmers to pay off debts and grow their own businesses. The cooperative obtained financing from bank loans and private stock that was available to select investors (mostly the cooperative farmers themselves), with set returns on profits. As more and more farmers joined the cooperative—and as consumer demand for organic products increased—sales increased, organizational staff increased by 30 to 50 employees per year, and ultimately the cooperative itself needed more office space.

Committed to remaining in LaFarge, Organic Valley searched for ways to expand. LaFarge is so small that there isn't much land available to lease or buy, so the cooperative spread out among mobile office trailers, houses, the town community center, an unused feed mill, and several abandoned business offices around town. Since the cooperative didn't have a single room that could accommodate more than twelve people, it had to rent a room from the town for larger meetings. Workers were scattered around town, packed into tiny rooms, riding bicycles from office to office when they needed to meet with each other. But

this fragmented, frugal way of doing business bought Organic Valley time—and money—to build a real headquarters. And just when it seemed that the cooperative was about to burst at the seams, construction on One Organic Way in LaFarge was completed.

The new office looks like a barn. The 49,210-square-foot structure also has plenty of room for more growth. Constructed of many recycled materials, it contains a state-of-the-art energy recovery system that exchanges warm and cool air throughout the building, as well as systems for using natural light and solar power. As the staffers pour in and spread out, enjoying their new-found elbow room, Organic Valley plans to hire even more employees, helping to bolster the local economy. Employees now get to enjoy organic foods served in the cafeteria, a mile-long nature path around the property, and locker rooms with showers. They still ride bikes as their major on-site transportation—but now it is for fun.

There are some risks involved in Organic Valley's growth. For example, other businesses aren't stampeding LaFarge to join the cooperative's lead. So if the cooperative falters or fails, or if Organic Valley decides to leave town, the $5.9 million headquarters has little or no resale or rental value. And agriculture is always a risky business. But Organic Valley's founders, members, and investors already know this. Organic Valley's CEO George Siemon sums it up by saying that in business, entrepreneurs must be prepared for three things: what happens if they are wildy successful, what happens if they are moderately successful, and what happens if they fail. If they are ready for all three, they'll do all right.

Questions

1. Farmers are natural entrepreneurs. What personal traits would you say Organic Valley's farmers must have in order to succeed?

2. Two methods of financing were mentioned in the case. What other types of financing might Organic Valley and its farmers obtain?

3. At what stage of growth would you place Organic Valley, according to Exhibit 6.9 in the chapter? Why?

SOURCES: Company Web site, *http://www.organicvalley.coop*; accessed August 2, 2004; Judy Ettenhofer, "Organic Valley a Big Success," *The Capital Times*, July 29, 2004, *http://www.madison.com*; "Organic Valley to Hold Ribbon-Cutting Ceremony for New $5.9 Million Green Design Headquarters," press release, July 20, 2004, *http://www .organicvalley.coop*; "Organic Valley Posts Record Level Pay Price to Farmers," *OFARM*, December 30, 2003, *http://www.ofarm.org/news*.

ch6   BIZ FLIX VIDEO CASE

Blue Crush

Anne Marie Chadwick (Kate Bosworth) and her friends Eden (Michelle Rodriguez) and Lena (Sanoe Lake) work as hotel maids to support their commitment to surfing the magnificent waves of Hawaii's North Shore. They live in a simple beach shack where Anne Marie also cares for her sister Penny (Mika Boorem). Anne Marie trains daily to compete in the Pipe Masters surf competition. She also must fight off nagging fears from a nearly fatal surfing accident. Professional quarterback Matt Tollman (Matthew Davis) asks her to teach him to surf, and their romance soon presents another distraction for Anne Marie. *Blue Crush* is easy to watch and features some extraordinary surfing sequences including many with professional surfers.

This scene comes from the "No Fear" sequence near the end of the film. Anne Marie was thrown from her board during her first ride, almost re-creating her earlier accident. The judges gave her a score of 4.6, enough to move her into this second round. She now competes against top surfer Keala Kennelly (herself). Anne Marie has not yet had a scoring ride in this round. Kennelly has more points than Anne Marie but encourages and coaches her to catch a wave and have no fear. This section of the scene follows Kennelly's efforts to encourage Anne Marie to successfully ride "The Pipe."

What to Watch for and Ask Yourself

1. Describe the level of risk in Anne Marie's strategy.

2. What level of competitive advantage does Anne Marie have?

3. What parallels do you see between Anne Marie's involvement in the competition and a modern manager's experience in the competitive business environment? Perform a SWOT analysis for Anne Marie.

ch6   ENDNOTES

1. Quoted in Oren Harari, "Good/Bad News About Strategy," *Management Review* (July 1995): 29–31.

2. Amitai Etzioni, *Modern Organizations* (Englewood Cliffs, NJ: Prentice Hall, 1984), p. 6.

3. Ibid.

4. Max D. Richards, *Setting Strategic Goals and Objectives*, 2nd ed. (St. Paul, MN: West, 1986).

5. C. Chet Miller and Laura B. Cardinal, "Strategic Planning and Firm Performance: A Synthesis of More Than Two Decades of Research," *Academy of Management Journal* 37, no. 6 (1994): 1649–1685.

6. This discussion is based on Richard L. Daft and Richard M. Steers, *Organizations: A Micro/Macro Approach* (Glenview, IL: Scott, Foresman, 1986), pp. 319–321; Herbert A. Simon, "On the Concept of Organizational Goals," *Administrative Science Quarterly* 9 (1964): 1–22; and Charles B. Saunders and Francis D. Tuggel, "Corporate Goals," *Journal of General Management* 5 (1980): 3–13.

7. Marc Gunther, "Tree Huggers, Soy Lovers, and Profits," *Fortune* (June 23, 2003): 98–104.

8. Paul Sloan, "The Sales Force That Rocks," *Business 2.0* (July 2005): 102–107.

9. Mary Klemm, Stuart Sanderson, and George Luffman, "Mission Statements: Selling Corporate Values to Employees," *Long-Range Planning* 24, no. 3 (1991): 73–78; John A. Pearce II and Fred David, "Corporate Mission Statements: The Bottom Line," *Academy of Management Executive* (1987): 109–116; Jerome H. Want, "Corporate Mission: The Intangible Contributor to Performance," *Management Review* (August 1986): 46–50; and Forest R. David and Fred R. David, "It's Time to Redraft Your Mission Statement," *Journal of Business Strategy* (January–February 2003): 11–14.

10. "Tennessee News and Notes from State Farm," State Farm Mutual Automobile Insurance Company, 2004.

11. Jeffrey A. Trachtenberg, "Borders Business Plan Gets a Rewrite; It Will Reopen Web Site, Give Up Most Stores Abroad, Close Many Waldenbooks," *Wall Street Journal*, March 22, 2007, B1. Copyright 2007 by Dow Jones & Company, Inc. Reproduced with permission of Dow Jones & Company, Inc. in the format Textbook via Copyright Clearance Center.

12. Paul Meising and Joseph Wolfe, "The Art and Science of Planning at the Business Unit Level," *Management Science* 31 (1985): 773–781.

13. Based in part on information about 1-800-Flowers, in Jenny C. McCune, "On the Train Gang," *Management Review* (October 1994): 57–60.

14. "Study: IRS Employees Often Steer Taxpayers Wrong on Law Questions," *Johnson City Press*, September 4, 2003.

15. Geary A. Rummler and Kimberly Morrill, "The Results Chain," *TD* (February 2005): 27–35; and John C. Crotts, Duncan R. Dickson, and Robert C. Ford, "Aligning Organizational Processes with Mission: The Case of Service Excellence,"

Academy of Management Executive 19, no. 3 (August 2005): 54–68.

16. This discussion is based on Robert S. Kaplan and David P. Norton, "Mastering the Management System," *Harvard Business Review* (January 2008): 63–77; and Robert S. Kaplan and David P. Norton, "Having Trouble with Your Strategy? Then Map It," *Harvard Business Review* (September–October 2000): 167–176.

17. Sayan Chatterjee, "Core Objectives: Clarity in Designing Strategy," *California Management Review* 47, no. 2 (Winter 2005): 33–49.

18. Edwin A. Locke, Gary P. Latham, and Miriam Erez, "The Determinants of Goal Commitment," *Academy of Management Review* 13 (1988): 23–39.

19. Peter F. Drucker, *The Practice of Management* (New York: Harper & Row, 1954); George S. Odiorne, "MBO: A Backward Glance," *Business Horizons* 21 (October 1978): 14–24.

20. Jan P. Muczyk and Bernard C. Reimann, "MBO as a Complement to Effective Leadership," *The Academy of Management Executive* 3 (1989): 131–138; and W. Giegold, *Objective Setting and the MBO Process*, vol. 2 (New York: McGraw-Hill, 1978).

21. Jack Ewing, "Siemens Climbs Back," *BusinessWeek* (June 5, 2000): 79–82.

22. John Ivancevich, J. Timothy McMahon, J. William Streidl, and Andrew D. Szilagyi, "Goal Setting: The Tenneco Approach to Personnel Development and Management Effectiveness," *Organizational Dynamics* (Winter 1978): 48–80.

23. Brigitte W. Schay, Mary Ellen Beach, Jacqueline A. Caldwell, and Christelle LaPolice, "Using Standardized Outcome Measures in the Federal Government," *Human Resource Management* 41, no. 3 (Fall 2002): 355–368.

24. Eileen M. Van Aken and Garry D. Coleman, "Building Better Measurement," *Industrial Management* (July–August 2002): 28–33.

25. Curtis W. Roney, "Planning for Strategic Contingencies," *Business Horizons* (March–April 2003): 35–42; and "Corporate Planning: Drafting a Blueprint for Success," *Small Business Report* (August 1987): 40–44.

26. Ellen Florian Kratz, "For FedEx, It Was Time to Deliver," *Fortune* (October 3, 2005): 83–84.

27. This section is based on Steven Schnaars and Paschalina Ziamou, "The Essentials of Scenario Writing," *Business Horizons* (July–August 2001): 25–31; Audrey Schriefer and Michael Sales, "Creating Strategic Advantage with Dynamic Scenarios," *Strategy & Leadership* 34, no. 3 (2006): 31–42; Geoffrey Colvin, "An Executive Risk Handbook," *Fortune* (October 3, 2005): 69–70; and Syed H. Akhter, "Strategic Planning, Hypercompetition, and Knowledge Management," *Business Horizons* (January–February 2003): 19–24.

28. Peter Cornelius, Alexander Van de Putte, and Mattia Romani, "Three Decades of Scenario Planning in Shell," *California Management Review* 48, no. 1 (Fall 2005); and Schnaars and Ziamou, "The Essentials of Scenario Writing."

29. Colvin, "An Executive Risk Handbook"; and Ian Wylie, "There Is No Alternative To . . . ," *Fast Company* (July 2002): 106–110.

30. Bain & Company Management Tools and Trends Survey, reported in Darrell Rigby and Barbara Bilodeau, "A Narrowing Focus on Preparedness," *Harvard Business Review* (July–August 2007): 21–22.

31. Ian Mitroff with Gus Anagnos, *Managing Crises Before They Happen* (New York: AMACOM, 2001); Ian Mitroff and Murat C. Alpaslan, "Preparing for Evil," *Harvard Business Review* (April 2003): 109–115.

32. This discussion is based largely on W. Timothy Coombs, *Ongoing Crisis Communication: Planning, Managing, and Responding* (Thousand Oaks, CA: Sage Publications, 1999).

33. Ian I. Mitroff, "Crisis Leadership," *Executive Excellence* (August 2001): 19; Andy Bowen, "Crisis Procedures that Stand the Test of Time," *Public Relations Tactics* (August 2001): 16.

34. Christine Pearson, "A Blueprint for Crisis Management," *Ivey Business Journal* (January–February 2002): 69–73.

35. See Mitroff and Alpaslan, "Preparing for Evil," for a discussion of the "wheel of crises" outlining the many different kinds of crises organizations may face.

36. Harari, "Good News/Bad News about Strategy."

37. James C. Collins and Jerry I. Porras, "Building Your Company's Vision," *Harvard Business Review* (September–October 1996): 65–77.

38. Steven Kerr and Steffan Landauer, "Using Stretch Goals to Promote Organizational Effectiveness and Personal Growth: General Electric and Goldman Sachs," *Academy of Management Executive* 18, no. 4 (November 2004): 134–138.

39. See Kenneth R. Thompson, Wayne A. Hockwarter, and Nicholas J. Mathys, "Stretch Targets: What Makes Them Effective?" *Academy of Management Executive* 11, no. 3 (August 1997): 48.

40. Doug Bartholomew, "Gauging Success," *CFO-IT* (Summer 2005): 17–19.

41. This section is based on Liam Fahey and Jan Herring, "Intelligence Teams," *Strategy & Leadership* 35, no. 1 (2007): 13–20.

3
Planning

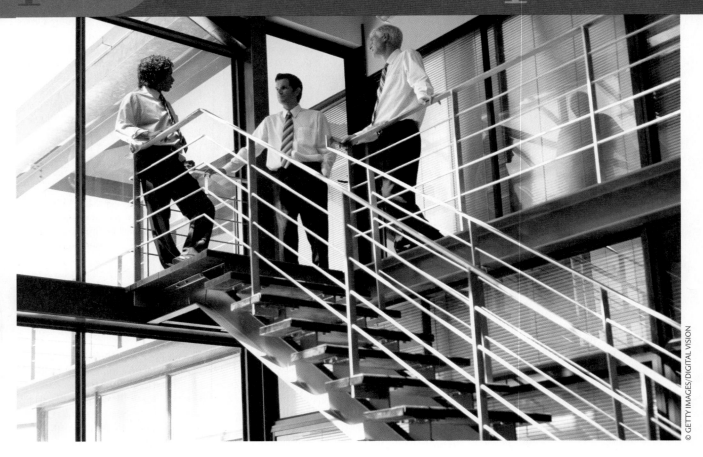

© GETTY IMAGES/DIGITAL VISION

Learning Outcomes

After studying this chapter, you should be able to:

1. Define the components of strategic management and discuss the levels of strategy.

2. Describe the strategic management process and SWOT analysis.

3. Define corporate-level strategies and explain the BCG matrix, portfolio, and diversification approaches.

4. Describe Porter's competitive forces and strategies.

5. Discuss new trends in strategy, including innovation from within and strategic partnerships.

6. Discuss the organizational dimensions used for strategy execution.

1 Introduction
2 Environment
3 Planning
4 Organizing
5 Controlling
6 Leading

Strategy Formulation and Implementation

WHAT IS YOUR STRATEGY STRENGTH?[1]

As a new manager, what are your strengths concerning strategy formulation and implementation? To find out, think about how *you handle challenges and issues* in your school or job. Then mark (a) or (b) for each of the following items, depending on which is more descriptive of your behavior. There are no right or wrong answers. Respond to each item as it best describes how you respond to work situations.

1. When keeping records, I tend to
   _____ **a.** Be careful about documentation.
   _____ **b.** Be haphazard about documentation.

2. If I run a group or a project, I
   _____ **a.** Have the general idea and let others figure out how to do the tasks.
   _____ **b.** Try to figure out specific goals, timelines, and expected outcomes.

3. My thinking style could be more accurately described as
   _____ **a.** Linear thinker, going from A to B to C.
   _____ **b.** Thinking like a grasshopper, hopping from one idea to another.

4. In my office or home things are
   _____ **a.** Here and there in various piles.
   _____ **b.** Laid out neatly or at least in reasonable order.

5. I take pride in developing
   _____ **a.** Ways to overcome a barrier to a solution.
   _____ **b.** New hypotheses about the underlying cause of a problem.

6. I can best help strategy by encouraging
   _____ **a.** Openness to a wide range of assumptions and ideas.
   _____ **b.** Thoroughness when implementing new ideas.

7. One of my strengths is
   _____ **a.** Commitment to making things work.
   _____ **b.** Commitment to a dream for the future.

8. I am most effective when I emphasize
   _____ **a.** Inventing original solutions.
   _____ **b.** Making practical improvements.

SCORING AND INTERPRETATION: Managers have differing strengths and capabilities when it comes to formulating and implementing strategy. Here's how to determine yours. For *Strategic Formulator* strength, score one point for each (a) answer marked for questions 2, 4, 6, and 8, and for each (b) answer marked for questions 1, 3, 5, and 7. For *Strategic Implementer* strength, score one point for each (b) answer marked for questions 2, 4, 6, and 8, and for each (a) answer marked for questions 1, 3, 5, and 7. Which of your two scores is higher and by how much? The higher score indicates your strategy strength.

Formulator and Implementer are two important ways new managers bring value to strategic management. New managers with implementer strengths tend to work within the situation and improve it by making it more efficient and reliable. Leaders with the formulator strength push toward out-of-the-box strategies and like to seek dramatic breakthroughs. Both styles are essential to strategic management. Strategic formulators often use their skills in creating whole new strategies, and strategic implementers often work with strategic improvements and implementation.

If the difference between your two scores is two or less, you have a balanced formulator/implementer style and work well in both arenas. If the difference is four or five points, you have a moderately strong style and probably work best in the area of your strength. And if the difference is seven or eight points, you have a distinctive strength and almost certainly would want to work in the area of your strength rather than in the opposite domain.

How important is strategic management? It largely determines which organizations succeed and which ones struggle. How did Best Buy overtake Circuit City as the player to beat in consumer electronics retailing, or Hewlett-Packard gain an impressive lead over Dell in personal computer sales? A big part of the reason is the strategies managers chose and how effectively they were executed.

Every company is concerned with strategy. Apple has succeeded in recent years with a strategy of fierce product innovation. In one year alone, three major new products—the iPhone, iPod Touch, and Leopard OS—led to triple-digit revenue growth for the once-struggling maker of computers.[2] McDonald's devised a new strategy of downsizing its menu items and adding healthier products in response to changes in the environment. Super-sized french fries and soft drinks were eliminated in favor of fresh salads and low-fat items to counter public accusations that McDonald's was responsible for Americans' growing waistlines. Now the fast-food icon is expanding to include specialty coffee drinks and smoothies to try to lure more teenagers and young adults.[3] Strategic blunders can hurt a company. For example, Kodak stumbled by failing to plan for the rapid rise of digital photography, assuming sales of film and paper would stay strong for years to come. Between 2001 and 2005, Kodak's earnings dropped about 60 percent as interest in film photography tanked.[4]

Managers at McDonald's, Kodak, and Apple are all involved in strategic management. They are finding ways to respond to competitors, cope with difficult environmental changes, meet changing customer needs, and effectively use available resources. Strategic management has taken on greater importance in today's environment because managers are responsible for positioning their organizations for success in a world that is constantly changing.

Chapter 6 provided an overview of the types of goals and plans that organizations use. In this chapter, we will explore strategic management, which is one specific type of planning. First, we define the components of strategic management and discuss the purposes and levels of strategy. Then, we examine several models of strategy formulation at the corporate and business levels. Finally, we discuss the tools managers use to execute their strategic plans.

THINKING STRATEGICALLY

What does it mean to think strategically? Strategic thinking means to take the long-term view and to see the big picture, including the organization and the competitive environment, and consider how they fit together. Strategic thinking is important for both businesses and nonprofit organizations. In for-profit firms, strategic planning typically pertains to competitive actions in the marketplace. In nonprofit organizations such as the Red Cross or The Salvation Army, strategic planning pertains to events in the external environment.

Research has shown that strategic thinking and planning positively affect a firm's performance and financial success.[5] Most managers are aware of the importance of strategic planning, as evidenced by a *McKinsey Quarterly* survey. Fifty-one percent of responding executives whose companies had no formal strategic planning process said they were dissatisfied with the company's development of strategy, compared to only 20 percent of those at companies that had a formal planning process.[6] CEOs at successful companies make strategic thinking and planning a top management priority. For an organization to succeed, the CEO must be actively involved in making the tough choices and trade-offs that define and support strategy.[7] However, senior executives at today's leading companies want middle- and low-level managers to think strategically as well. Understanding the strategy concept and the levels of strategy is an important start toward strategic thinking.

TakeaMoment | Complete the New Manager Self-Test on page 187 to get some idea about your strategic thinking ability. As a new manager, practice thinking strategically by studying your department's or your organization's environment, market, and competitors. Think about what the long-term future might hold and how you think the company can best be positioned to stay competitive.

New Manager Self-Test

Your Approach to Studying, Part 2

Your approach to studying may reveal whether you have the ability to think strategically. Answer the questions below as they apply to your study behavior. Please answer whether each item below is Mostly True or Mostly False for you.

	Mostly True	Mostly False
1. One way or another, I manage to obtain whatever books and materials I need for studying.	_____	_____
2. I make sure I find study conditions that let me do my work easily.	_____	_____
3. I put effort into making sure I have the most important details at my fingertips.	_____	_____
4. When I read an article or book, I try to work out for myself what is being said.	_____	_____
5. I know what I want to get out of this course, and I am determined to achieve it.	_____	_____
6. When I am working on a new topic, I try to see in my mind how the ideas fit together.	_____	_____
7. It is important to me to follow the argument and see the reasoning behind something.	_____	_____
8. I look at the evidence carefully and then try to reach my own conclusions about things I am studying.	_____	_____
9. When I am reading, I think how the ideas fit in with previous material.	_____	_____

SCORING AND INTERPRETATION: The items above represent a *strategic approach* to studying. Strategy means knowing your desired outcomes, how to acquire factual knowledge, thinking clearly about tactics and cause-effect relationships, and implementing behaviors that will achieve the desired outcomes. Give yourself one point for each item you marked as Mostly True. If you scored 3 or lower you probably are not using a strategic approach to studying. A score of 6 or above suggests a strategic approach to studying that will likely translate into strategic management ability as a new manager.

SOURCE: Adapted from Kristin Backhaus and Joshua P. Liff, "Cognitive Styles and Approaches to Studying in Management Education," *Journal of Management Education,* 31 (August 2007): 445–466, and A. Duff, "Learning Styles Measurement: The Revised Approaches to Studying Inventory," *Bristol Business School Teaching and Research Review,* 3 (2000).

3 Planning

WHAT IS STRATEGIC MANAGEMENT?

Strategic management refers to the set of decisions and actions used to formulate and execute strategies that will provide a competitively superior fit between the organization and its environment so as to achieve organizational goals.[8] Managers ask questions such as the following: What changes and trends are occurring in the competitive environment? Who are our competitors and what are their strengths and weaknesses? Who are our customers? What products or services should we offer, and how can we offer them most efficiently? What does the future hold for our industry, and how can we change the rules of the game? Answers to these questions help managers make choices about how to position their organizations in the environment with respect to rival companies.[9] Superior organizational performance is not a matter of luck. It is determined by the choices that managers make.

strategic management The set of decisions and actions used to formulate and implement strategies that will provide a competitively superior fit between the organization and its environment so as to achieve organizational goals.

strategy The plan of action that prescribes resource allocation and other activities for dealing with the environment, achieving a competitive advantage, and attaining organizational goals.

competitive advantage What sets the organization apart from others and provides it with a distinctive edge in the marketplace.

core competence A business activity that an organization does particularly well in comparison to competitors.

Purpose of Strategy

The first step in strategic management is to define an explicit **strategy**, which is the plan of action that describes resource allocation and activities for dealing with the environment, achieving a competitive advantage, and attaining the organization's goals. **Competitive advantage** refers to what sets the organization apart from others and provides it with a distinctive edge for meeting customer or client needs in the marketplace. The essence of formulating strategy is choosing how the organization will be different.[10] Managers make decisions about whether the company will perform different activities or will execute similar activities differently than its rivals do. Strategy necessarily changes over time to fit environmental conditions, but to remain competitive, companies develop strategies that focus on core competencies, develop synergy, and create value for customers.

Concept Connection When the U.S. Marines needed rugged motorcycles, they looked to manufacturers of on- and off-road bikes. But most motorcycles run on gasoline, which is the wrong fuel for military purposes. Hayes Diversified Technologies had the competitive advantage. After twenty years of building adapted motorcycles for the Marines and the Army Special Forces, Hayes had developed a **core competence** in technology that addresses the fuel limitations faced by the military. Most military machines run on JB8 fuel, a formulation of diesel and kerosene. Hayes Diversified's new HDT M1030M1 motorcycle is designed for diesel service, so Hayes readily won the contract.

COURTESY OF HAYES DIVERSIFIED TECHNOLOGIES

Exploit Core Competence A company's **core competence** is something the organization does especially well in comparison to its competitors. A core competence represents a competitive advantage because the company acquires expertise that competitors do not have. A core competence may be in the area of superior research and development, expert technological know-how, process efficiency, or exceptional customer service.[11] At VF, a large apparel company that owns Vanity Fair, Nautica, Wrangler, and The North Face, strategy focuses on the company's core competencies of operational efficiency and merchandising know-how. When VF bought The North Face, for example, its distribution systems were so poor that stores were getting ski apparel at the end of winter and camping gear at the end of summer. The company's operating profit margin was minus 35 percent. Managers at VF revamped The North Face's sourcing, distribution, and financial systems and within five years doubled sales to $500 million and improved profit margins to a healthy 13 percent.[12]

Gaylord Hotels, which has large hotel and conference centers in several states as well as the Opryland complex near Nashville, Tennessee, thrives based on a strategy of superior service for large group meetings.[13] Robinson Helicopter succeeds through superior technological know-how for building small, two-seater helicopters used for everything from police patrols in Los Angeles to herding cattle in Australia.[14] In each case, leaders identified what their company does especially well and built strategy around it.

Build Synergy When organizational parts interact to produce a joint effect that is greater than the sum of the parts acting alone, **synergy** occurs. The organization may attain a special advantage with respect to cost, market power, technology, or management skill. When properly managed, synergy can create additional value with existing resources, providing a big boost to the bottom line.[15] Synergy was the motivation for Pepsi to buy Frito-Lay for instance, and for News Corp. to buy MySpace.

Synergy can also be obtained by good relationships between organizations. For example, the Disney Channel invites magazines such as *J-14*, *Twist*, and *Popstar* to visit the set of shows like "Hannah Montana" and "High School Musical," gives reporters access for interviews and photo shoots, and provides brief videos for the magazines to post on their Web sites. The synergy keeps preteen interest booming for both the television shows and the magazines.[16]

Deliver Value Delivering value to the customer is at the heart of strategy. Value can be defined as the combination of benefits received and costs paid. Managers help their companies create value by devising strategies that exploit core competencies and attain synergy. To compete with the rising clout of satellite television, for example, cable companies such as Time-Warner Cable and Comcast are offering *value packages* that offer a combination of basic cable, digital premium channels, video on demand, high-speed Internet, and digital phone service for a reduced cost.

Consider how Save-A-Lot has grown into one of the most successful grocery chains in the United States with a strategy based on exploiting core competencies, building synergy, and providing value to customers.

© ASHLEY TWIGGS/THE CHRISTIAN SCIENCE MONITOR/GETTY IMAGES

3 Planning

Concept Connection Rather than trying to be all things to all pizza lovers, Upper Crust Pizza founder Jordan Tobins aims to grow by doing one thing better than anyone else. That one thing is his Neopolitan-style pizza, prepared here by Antonio Carlos Filho. The Boston-area pizza chain has succeeded with a **business-level strategy** of focusing on high quality in a limited product line. As Upper Crust fan and former General Electric CEO Jack Welch enthused, "You could faint just describing the flavor of the sauce, and the crust puts you over the edge."

synergy The condition that exists when the organization's parts interact to produce a joint effect that is greater than the sum of the parts acting alone.

Innovative Way

Save-A-Lot

When most supermarket executives look at the inner city, they see peeling paint, low-income customers, rampant crime, and low profits. Save-A-Lot looks at the inner city and sees opportunity. Save-A-Lot was started in the late 1970s, when Bill Moran noticed that low-income and rural areas were poorly served by large supermarkets. Moran began opening small stores in low-rent areas and stocking them with a limited number of low-priced staples. Moran hand-wrote price signs and built crude shelves out of particle board. He made his own labels from low-quality paper, which suppliers then slapped on generic products.

Save-A-Lot has thrived ever since by using its core competency of cost efficiency, which enables the stores to sell goods at prices 40 percent lower than major supermarkets. Unlike the typical supermarket, which is about 45,000 square feet, Save-A-Lot stores use a compact 16,000-square-foot no-frills format, targets areas with dirt-cheap rent, and courts households earning less than $35,000 a year. Save-A-Lot stores don't have bakeries, pharmacies, or grocery baggers. Labor costs are kept ultra low. For example, whereas most grocery managers want employees to keep displays well-stocked and tidy, Save-A-Lot managers tell people to let the displays sell down before restocking.

Save-A-Lot has obtained synergy by developing good relationships with a few core suppliers. Most supermarkets charge manufacturers slotting fees to put their products on shelves, but not Save-A-Lot. In addition, the company doesn't ask suppliers to take back damaged goods. It just sticks up a hand-written "Oops" sign and marks prices even lower. Customers love it. Now, even branded food makers want a slice of the Save-A-Lot pie. Procter & Gamble, for example, developed a low-priced version of Folgers, and the chain also sells low-priced brands of cheese from Kraft and cereal from General Mills.[17]

TakeaMoment | **As a new manager, can you identify the core competence of your team or department and identify ways that it can contribute to the overall organization's strategy? Who are your team's or department's customers, and how can you deliver value?**

Levels of Strategy

Another aspect of strategic management concerns the organizational level to which strategic issues apply. Strategic managers normally think in terms of three levels of strategy, as illustrated in Exhibit 7.1.[18]

■ *What Business Are We In?* This is the question managers address when they consider corporate-level strategy. **Corporate-level strategy** pertains to the organization as a whole and the combination of business units and product lines that make up the corporate entity. Strategic actions at this level usually relate to the acquisition of new businesses; additions or divestments of business units, plants, or product lines; and joint ventures with other corporations in new areas. An example of corporate-level strategy is Brunswick, which was once associated primarily with billiard tables and bowling gear. CEO George Buckley is transforming Brunswick into the "Toyota of boating" by selling off unprofitable businesses and buying companies such as Sea Pro, Hatteras, and Princecraft to give Brunswick a slice of every boating niche.[19]

■ *How Do We Compete?* **Business-level strategy** pertains to each business unit or product line. Strategic decisions at this level concern amount of advertising, direction and extent of research and development, product changes, new-product development, equipment and facilities, and expansion or contraction of product and service lines. Many companies have opened e-commerce units as a part of business-level strategy. For example, NutriSystem Inc. was bankrupt a decade ago, but managers reinvented the company as an Internet distributor, shipping customers a month's worth of shelf-stable diet food. People can track their progress online and get virtual counseling when they need a boost. The Internet strategy and a new approach to advertising pushed sales from just $27 million in 2002 to more than $775 million in 2007.[20]

corporate-level strategy The level of strategy concerned with the question "What business are we in?" Pertains to the organization as a whole and the combination of business units and product lines that make it up.

business-level strategy The level of strategy concerned with the question "How do we compete?" Pertains to each business unit or product line within the organization.

EXHIBIT | **7.1** Three Levels of Strategy in Organizations

Corporate-Level Strategy: What business are we in?

Corporation

Business-Level Strategy: How do we compete?

Consumer Products Unit | Biotechnology Unit | Media Unit

Functional-Level Strategy: How do we support the business-level strategy?

Finance | R&D | Manufacturing | Marketing

SOURCES: Milton Leontiades, *Strategies for Diversification and Change* (Boston: Little, Brown, 1980): 63; and Dan E. Schendel and Charles W. Hofer, eds., *Strategic Management: A New View of Business Policy and Planning* (Boston: Little, Brown, 1979): 11–14.

Go to the ethical dilemma on page 207 that pertains to corporate grand strategy. | TakeaMoment

- *How Do We Support the Business-Level Strategy?* **Functional-level strategy** pertains to the major functional departments within the business unit. Functional strategies involve all of the major functions, including finance, research and development, marketing, and manufacturing. The functional-level strategy for NutriSystem's marketing department, for example, is to feature real-life customers in direct-response print and television ads that steer dieters to the company's Web site.

THE STRATEGIC MANAGEMENT PROCESS

The overall strategic management process is illustrated in Exhibit 7.2. It begins when executives evaluate their current position with respect to mission, goals, and strategies. They then scan the organization's internal and external environments and identify strategic factors that might require change. Internal or external events might indicate a need to redefine the mission or goals or to formulate a new strategy at either the corporate, business, or functional level. The final stage in the strategic management process is implementation of the new strategy.

Strategy Formulation Versus Execution

Strategy formulation includes the planning and decision making that lead to the establishment of the firm's goals and the development of a specific strategic plan.[21] **Strategy formulation** may include assessing the external environment and internal problems and integrating the results into goals and strategy. This process is in contrast to **strategy execution**, which is the use of managerial and organizational tools to direct resources toward accomplishing strategic results.[22] Strategy execution is the administration and implementation of the strategic plan. Managers may use persuasion, new equipment, changes in organization structure, or a revised reward system to ensure that employees and resources are used to make formulated strategy a reality.

functional-level strategy
The level of strategy concerned with the question "How do we support the business-level strategy?" Pertains to all of the organization's major departments.

strategy formulation The stage of strategic management that involves the planning and decision making that lead to the establishment of the organization's goals and of a specific strategic plan.

strategy execution The stage of strategic management that involves the use of managerial and organizational tools to direct resources toward achieving strategic outcomes.

3 Planning

EXHIBIT | 7.2 The Strategic Management Process

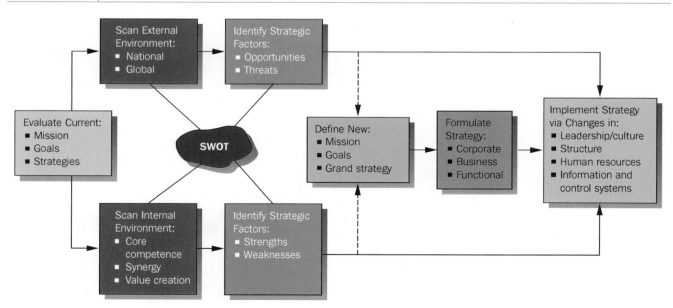

SWOT Analysis

Formulating strategy often begins with an assessment of the internal and external factors that will affect the organization's competitive situation. **SWOT analysis** includes a search for strengths, weaknesses, opportunities, and threats that affect organizational performance. External information about opportunities and threats may be obtained from a variety of sources, including customers, government reports, professional journals, suppliers, bankers, friends in other organizations, consultants, or association meetings. Many firms hire special scanning organizations to provide them with newspaper clippings, Internet research, and analyses of relevant domestic and global trends. In addition, many companies are hiring competitive intelligence professionals to scope out competitors, as we discussed in Chapter 3, and using intelligence teams, as described in Chapter 6.

Executives acquire information about internal strengths and weaknesses from a variety of reports, including budgets, financial ratios, profit and loss statements, and surveys of employee attitudes and satisfaction. Managers spend 80 percent of their time giving and receiving information. Through frequent face-to-face discussions and meetings with people at all levels of the hierarchy, executives build an understanding of the company's internal strengths and weaknesses.

TakeaMoment

> Go to the experiential exercise on page 206 that pertains to strategy formulation and strategy execution. Before reading further, you might also want to review your strategic strengths as determined by your responses to the questionnaire at the beginning of this chapter.

Internal Strengths and Weaknesses *Strengths* are positive internal characteristics that the organization can exploit to achieve its strategic performance goals. *Weaknesses* are internal characteristics that might inhibit or restrict the organization's performance. Some examples of what executives evaluate to interpret strengths and weaknesses are given in Exhibit 7.3. The information sought typically pertains to specific functions such as marketing, finance, production, and R&D. Internal analysis also examines overall organization structure, management competence and quality, and human resource characteristics. Based on their understanding of these areas, managers can determine their strengths or weaknesses compared with other companies.

SWOT analysis Analysis of the strengths, weaknesses, opportunities, and threats (SWOT) that affect organizational performance

EXHIBIT | 7.3

Checklist for Analyzing
Organizational Strengths
and Weaknesses

Management and Organization	Marketing	Human Resources
Management quality	Distribution channels	Employee experience, education
Staff quality	Market share	Union status
Degree of centralization	Advertising efficiency	Turnover, absenteeism
Organization charts	Customer satisfaction	Work satisfaction
Planning, information, control systems	Product quality	Grievances
	Service reputation	
	Sales force turnover	
Finance	**Production**	**Research and Development**
Profit margin	Plant location	Basic applied research
Debt-equity ratio	Machinery obsolescence	Laboratory capabilities
Inventory ratio	Purchasing system	Research programs
Return on investment	Quality control	New-product innovations
Credit rating	Productivity/efficiency	Technology innovations

External Opportunities and Threats *Threats* are characteristics of the external environment that may prevent the organization from achieving its strategic goals. *Opportunities* are characteristics of the external environment that have the potential to help the organization achieve or exceed its strategic goals. Executives evaluate the external environment with information about the ten sectors described in Chapter 3. The task environment sectors are the most relevant to strategic behavior and include the behavior of competitors, customers, suppliers, and the labor supply. The general environment contains those sectors that have an indirect influence on the organization but nevertheless must be understood and incorporated into strategic behavior. The general environment includes technological developments, the economy, legal-political and international events, natural resources, and sociocultural changes. Additional areas that might reveal opportunities or threats include pressure groups, interest groups, creditors, and potentially competitive industries.

Social networking company Facebook, which was at first a site for college students, provides an example of how managers can use SWOT analysis in formulating an appropriate strategy.

Concept Connection The effects of this oil fire in Iraq were felt thousands of miles away—in the executive suites at companies such as United Airlines, US Airways, and Delta in the United States. The major air carriers, already struggling, were devastated when the price of fuel spiked in the spring and summer of 2008. Uncertainty about oil costs and supplies is a significant **external threat** to the nation's airlines. Other threats include stiff competition from low-cost carriers and the lingering fear of terrorism.

Facebook Inc.

Innovative Way

MySpace is still in the lead in online social networking, but Facebook is getting all the attention. The startup grew rapidly in the first four years after 23-year-old Mark Zuckerberg founded it while still a student at Harvard University. To keep Facebook growing, the young CEO made some strategic decisions that can be understood by looking at the company's strengths, weaknesses, opportunities, and threats.

Facebook's *strengths* include technological know-how and an aggressive and innovative culture. In addition, Facebook has a major partnership with Microsoft, which has invested $240 million, brokers banner ads for the company, and is developing tools that make it easy to create links between Windows applications and Facebook's network. Since Facebook expanded beyond students, membership has boomed, and Facebook is preferred over MySpace by older users and the Silicon Valley tech set. Work networks on Facebook are exploding. The primary *weakness* is a lack of management expertise to help the company meet the challenges of growing up.

The biggest *threat* to the company is that Facebook is still spending more cash than it is bringing in. In addition, Zuckerberg is gaining a reputation in the industry as an arrogant and standoffish manager, which could hurt Facebook's chances of successful partnerships. *Opportunities* abound to expand the company's operations internationally and to take advantage of Facebook's popularity to introduce features that can command higher Web advertising rates and bring in more revenue.

What does SWOT analysis suggest for Facebook? Zuckerberg is trying to capitalize on Facebook's popularity by making it a place for companies to provide services to members. For example, Prosper.com developed a Facebook application for its service that allows members to lend one another money at negotiated interest rates. Non-Internet companies such as Red Bull have also developed Facebook applications to reach Facebook's vast customer base. Companies that put applications on the Facebook Web site can experience a sort of viral popularity as word spreads among millions of members.

To implement the strategy, Zuckerberg is bringing in executives with more strategy experience than himself, such as Chamath Palihapitiya, a former AOL manager, as vice president of product marketing, and Sheryl Sandberg, formerly of Google, as chief operating officer. These managers have the traditional skills Facebook needs to execute the new strategy both in the United States and internationally.[23]

It's too soon to tell if Facebook's strategy is working.[24] Zuckerberg is continuing his efforts to build a more seasoned executive team to keep growing and avoid damaging mistakes as Facebook pursues its strategy.

FORMULATING CORPORATE-LEVEL STRATEGY

Portfolio Strategy

Individual investors often wish to diversify in an investment portfolio with some high-risk stocks, some low-risk stocks, some growth stocks, and perhaps a few income bonds. In much the same way, corporations like to have a balanced mix of business divisions called **strategic business units (SBUs)**. An SBU has a unique business mission, product line, competitors, and markets relative to other SBUs in the corporation.[25] Executives in charge of the entire corporation generally define an overall strategy and then bring together a portfolio of strategic business units to carry it out. **Portfolio strategy** pertains to the mix of business units and product lines that fit together in a logical way to provide synergy and competitive advantage for the corporation. Managers don't like to become too dependent on one business. For example, at United Technologies Corporation (UTC), the aerospace-related business units have been struggling through one of the worst slumps in history. However, UTC's Otis Elevator division is keeping the corporation's sales and profits strong. Otis has a commanding share of the worldwide market for new elevators and escalators. In addition, the unit provides a steady revenue stream from elevator maintenance, repair, and upgrade. The elevators in the Waldorf-Astoria, for example, were installed in 1931 and have been steadily upgraded by Otis ever since.[26] One useful way to think about portfolio strategy is the BCG matrix.

The BCG Matrix

The BCG (for Boston Consulting Group) matrix is illustrated in Exhibit 7.4. The **BCG matrix** organizes businesses along two dimensions—business growth rate and market share.[27] *Business growth rate* pertains to how rapidly the entire industry is increasing. *Market share* defines whether a business unit has a larger or smaller share than competitors. The combinations of high and low market share and high and low business growth provide four categories for a corporate portfolio.

strategic business unit (SBU) A division of the organization that has a unique business mission, product line, competitors, and markets relative to other SBUs in the same corporation.

portfolio strategy The organization's mix of strategic business units and product lines that fit together in such a way as to provide the corporation with synergy and competitive advantage.

BCG matrix A concept developed by the Boston Consulting Group that evaluates strategic business units with respect to the dimensions of business growth rate and market share.

EXHIBIT 7.4

The BCG Matrix

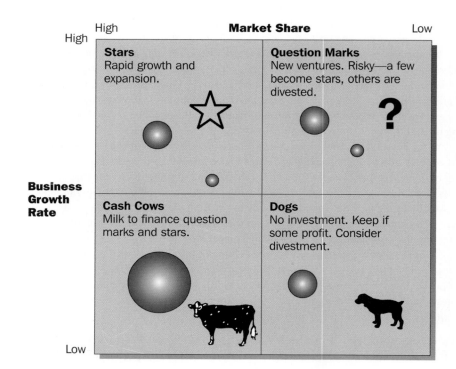

The *star* has a large market share in a rapidly growing industry. The star is important because it has additional growth potential, and profits should be plowed into this business as investment for future growth and profits. The star is visible and attractive and will generate profits and a positive cash flow even as the industry matures and market growth slows.

The *cash cow* exists in a mature, slow-growth industry but is a dominant business in the industry, with a large market share. Because heavy investments in advertising and plant expansion are no longer required, the corporation earns a positive cash flow. It can milk the cash cow to invest in other, riskier businesses.

The *question mark* exists in a new, rapidly growing industry, but has only a small market share. The question mark business is risky: It could become a star, or it could fail. The corporation can invest the cash earned from cash cows in question marks with the goal of nurturing them into future stars.

The *dog* is a poor performer. It has only a small share of a slow-growth market. The dog provides little profit for the corporation and may be targeted for divestment or liquidation if turnaround is not possible.

The circles in Exhibit 7.4 represent the business portfolio for a hypothetical corporation. Circle size represents the relative size of each business in the company's portfolio. Most large organizations, such as General Electric (GE), have businesses in more than one quadrant, thereby representing different market shares and growth rates.

General Electric

Since he took over as General Electric's CEO, Jeff Immelt has been reshuffling the corporation's mix of businesses in a way that he believes will better position GE for the long term. GE is investing heavily in its stars and question marks to ensure that its portfolio will continue to include cash cows in a future that might be very different from today's world.

The most famous cash cows in General Electric's portfolio are the appliance division and lighting, which hold a large share of a stable market and account for a big portion of sales and profits. The GE Security division has star status, and GE is pumping money into development of new products for hot areas such as fire safety, industrial security, and homeland security. GE Healthcare is also a star, and managers are investing research dollars to become a leader in the growing business of biosciences and personalized medicine. Some products under development might not hit the marketplace for a decade but hold the promise of huge returns.

GE's renewable energy business is still a question mark. The company moved into wind and solar power and biogas with acquisitions such as Enron Wind. Managers hope the division can become a star, but the potential demand for renewable energy is uncertain at this point.

GE's consumer finance division is also a question mark. Top executives are currently overhauling the brand image of consumer finance to see whether it will revive the division enough to keep it in the portfolio. If they decide the division is a dog, GE will sell it off as they did the less profitable and slow-growing insurance business.[28]

Diversification Strategy

The strategy of moving into new lines of business, as GE did by getting into healthcare, finance, and alternative forms of energy, is called **diversification**. Other examples of diversification include Apple's entry into the mobile phone business with the iPhone, the move by News Corporation into online social networking with the acquisition of MySpace, and Nestlé's entry into the pet food business with the purchase of Ralston.

The purpose of diversification is to expand the firm's business operations to produce new kinds of valuable products and services. When the new business is related to the company's existing business activities, the organization is implementing a strategy of **related diversification**. For example, GE's move into renewable energy and Nestlé's move into pet foods are linked to these firms' existing energy and nutrition businesses. **Unrelated diversification** occurs when an organization expands into a totally new line of

diversification A strategy of moving into new lines of business.

related diversification Moving into a new business that is related to the company's existing business activities.

unrelated diversification Expanding into a totally new line of business.

business, such as GE's entry into consumer finance or food company Sara Lee's move into the intimate apparel business. With unrelated diversification, the company's lines of business aren't logically associated with one another; therefore, it can be difficult to make the strategy successful. Most companies are giving up on unrelated diversification strategies, selling off unrelated businesses to focus on core areas.

A firm's managers may also pursue diversification opportunities to create value through a strategy of vertical integration. **Vertical integration** means the company expands into businesses that either produce the supplies needed to make products or that distribute and sell those products to customers. For example, E & J Gallo Winery started a new business to make its own wine bottles rather than buying them from a supplier.[29] Gallo could make bottles more cheaply than it could buy them, enabling managers to reduce costs. In addition, the new division enabled the company to distinguish its wines with unique bottle shapes. An example of diversifying to distribute products comes from Apple, which opened retail stores to increase visibility and sell its innovative products to customers. The strategy was a big success. Customers can try the products before they buy and get free help on how to use Macintosh computers, iPods and iPhones, Apple software, and accessories like digital cameras. [30]

FORMULATING BUSINESS-LEVEL STRATEGY

Now we turn to strategy formulation within the strategic business unit, in which the concern is how to compete. A popular and effective model for formulating strategy is Porter's competitive forces and strategies. Michael E. Porter studied a number of business organizations and proposed that business-level strategies are the result of five competitive forces in the company's environment.[31] More recently, Porter examined the impact of the Internet on business-level strategy.[32] New Web-based technology is influencing industries in both positive and negative ways, and understanding this impact is essential for managers to accurately analyze their competitive environments and design appropriate strategic actions.

Porter's Five Competitive Forces

Exhibit 7.5 illustrates the competitive forces that exist in a company's environment and indicates some ways Internet technology is affecting each area. These forces help determine a company's position vis-à-vis competitors in the industry environment.

1. *Potential new entrants.* Capital requirements and economies of scale are examples of two potential barriers to entry that can keep out new competitors. It is far more costly to enter the automobile industry, for instance, than to start a specialized mail-order business. In general, Internet technology has made it much easier for new companies to enter an industry by curtailing the need for such organizational elements as an established sales force, physical assets such as buildings and machinery, or access to existing supplier and sales channels.

2. *Bargaining power of buyers.* Informed customers become empowered customers. The Internet provides easy access to a wide array of information about products, services, and competitors, thereby greatly increasing the bargaining power of end consumers. For example, a customer shopping for a car can gather extensive information about various options, such as wholesale prices for new cars or average value for used vehicles, detailed specifications, repair records, and even whether a used car has ever been involved in an accident.

3. *Bargaining power of suppliers.* The concentration of suppliers and the availability of substitute suppliers are significant factors in determining supplier power. The sole supplier of engines to a manufacturer of small airplanes will have great power, for example. The impact of the Internet in this area can be both positive

vertical integration Expanding into businesses that either produce the supplies needed to make products or that distribute and sell those products.

EXHIBIT | **7.5** Porter's Five Forces Affecting Industry Competition

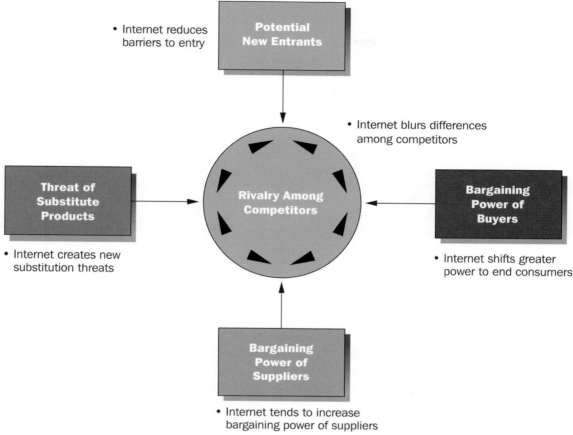

- Internet reduces barriers to entry

Potential New Entrants

- Internet blurs differences among competitors

Threat of Substitute Products

Rivalry Among Competitors

Bargaining Power of Buyers

- Internet creates new substitution threats

- Internet shifts greater power to end consumers

Bargaining Power of Suppliers

- Internet tends to increase bargaining power of suppliers

SOURCES: Based on Michael E. Porter, *Competitive Strategy: Techniques for Analyzing Industries and Competitors* (New York: Free Press, 1980); and Michael E. Porter, "Strategy and the Internet," *Harvard Business Review* (March 2001): 63–78.

and negative. That is, procurement over the Web tends to give a company greater power over suppliers, but the Web also gives suppliers access to a greater number of customers, as well as the ability to reach end users. Overall, the Internet tends to raise the bargaining power of suppliers.

4. ***Threat of substitute products.*** The power of alternatives and substitutes for a company's product may be affected by changes in cost or in trends such as increased health consciousness that will deflect buyer loyalty. Companies in the sugar industry suffered from the growth of sugar substitutes; manufacturers of aerosol spray cans lost business as environmentally conscious consumers chose other products. The Internet created a greater threat of new substitutes by enabling new approaches to meeting customer needs. For example, offers of low-cost airline tickets over the Internet hurt traditional travel agencies.

5. ***Rivalry among competitors.*** As illustrated in Exhibit 7.5, rivalry among competitors is influenced by the preceding four forces, as well as by cost and product differentiation. With the leveling force of the Internet and information technology, it has become more difficult for many companies to find ways to distinguish themselves from their competitors, which intensifies rivalry. Porter referred to the "advertising slugfest" when describing the scrambling and jockeying for position that occurs among fierce rivals within an industry. Nintendo and Sony are fighting for control of the video game console industry, Netflix and Blockbuster are competing for the mail order movie rental business, and Pepsi and Coke are still battling it out in the cola wars.

| As a new manager, examine the competitive forces that are affecting your organization. What can you do as a lower-level manager to help the firm find or keep its competitive edge through a differentiation, cost-leadership, or focus strategy?

Competitive Strategies

In finding its competitive edge within these five forces, Porter suggests that a company can adopt one of three strategies: differentiation, cost leadership, or focus. The organizational characteristics typically associated with each strategy are summarized in Exhibit 7.6.

- **Differentiation.** The **differentiation** strategy involves an attempt to distinguish the firm's products or services from others in the industry. The organization may use creative advertising, distinctive product features, exceptional service, or new technology to achieve a product perceived as unique. Examples of products that have benefited from a differentiation strategy include Harley-Davidson motorcycles, Snapper lawn equipment, and Gore-Tex fabrics, all of which are perceived as distinctive in their markets. Service companies such as Starbucks, Whole Foods Market, and IKEA also use a differentiation strategy.

    A differentiation strategy can reduce rivalry with competitors if buyers are loyal to a company's brand. Successful differentiation can also reduce the bargaining power of large buyers because other products are less attractive, which also helps the firm fight off threats of substitute products. In addition, differentiation erects entry barriers in the form of customer loyalty that a new entrant into the market would have difficulty overcoming.

- **Cost leadership.** With a **cost leadership** strategy, the organization aggressively seeks efficient facilities, pursues cost reductions, and uses tight cost controls to produce products more efficiently than competitors. A low-cost position means that the company can undercut competitors' prices and still offer comparable quality and earn a reasonable profit. For example, Comfort Inn and Motel 6 are low-priced alternatives to Four Seasons or Marriott.

differentiation A type of competitive strategy with which the organization seeks to distinguish its products or services from that of competitors.

cost leadership A type of competitive strategy with which the organization aggressively seeks efficient facilities, cuts costs, and employs tight cost controls to be more efficient than competitors.

EXHIBIT | 7.6

Organizational Characteristics of Porter's Competitive Strategies

Strategy	Organizational Characteristics
Differentiation	Acts in a flexible, loosely knit way, with strong coordination among departments
	Strong capability in basic rewards
	Creative flair, thinks "out of the box"
	Strong marketing abilities
	Rewards employee innovation
	Corporate reputation for quality or technological leadership
Cost Leadership	Strong central authority; tight cost controls
	Maintains standard operating procedures
	Easy-to-use manufacturing technologies
	Highly efficient procurement and distribution systems
	Close supervision, finite employee empowerment
Focus	Frequent, detailed control reports
	May use combination of above policies directed at particular strategic target
	Values and rewards flexibility and customer intimacy
	Measures cost of providing service and maintaining customer loyalty
	Pushes empowerment to employees with customer contact

SOURCES: Based on Michael E. Porter, *Competitive Strategy: Techniques for Analyzing Industries and Competitors* (New York: The Free Press: 1980); Michael Treacy and Fred Wiersema, "How Market Leaders Keep Their Edge," *Fortune* (February 6, 1995): 88–98; and Michael A. Hitt, R. Duane Ireland, and Robert E. Hoskisson, *Strategic Management* (St. Paul, MN: West, 1995), p. 100–113.

Being a low-cost producer provides a successful strategy to defend against the five competitive forces in Exhibit 7.5. The most efficient, low-cost company is in the best position to succeed in a price war while still making a profit. Likewise, the low-cost producer is protected from powerful customers and suppliers, because customers cannot find lower prices elsewhere, and other buyers would have less slack for price negotiation with suppliers. If substitute products or potential new entrants occur, the low-cost producer is better positioned than higher-cost rivals to prevent loss of market share. The low price acts as a barrier against new entrants and substitute products.[33]

■ **Focus.** With a **focus** strategy, the organization concentrates on a specific regional market or buyer group. The company will use either a differentiation or cost leadership approach, but only for a narrow target market. Save-A-Lot, described earlier, uses a focused cost leadership strategy, putting stores in low-income areas. Edward Jones Investments, a St. Louis-based brokerage house, uses a focused differentiation strategy, building its business in rural and small town America and providing clients with conservative, long-term investment advice. Management scholar and consultant Peter Drucker once said the safety-first orientation means Edward Jones delivers a product "that no Wall Street house has ever sold before: peace of mind."[34]

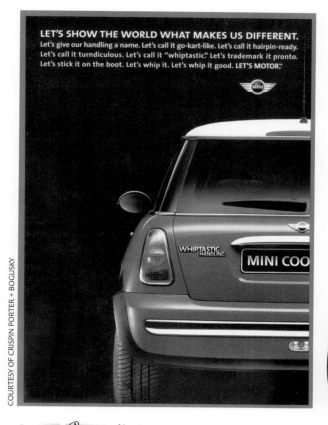

COURTESY OF CRISPIN PORTER + BOGUSKY

LET'S SHOW THE WORLD WHAT MAKES US DIFFERENT.
Let's give our handling a name. Let's call it go-kart-like. Let's call it hairpin-ready. Let's call it turndiculous. Let's call it "whiptastic." Let's trademark it pronto. Let's stick it on the boot. Let's whip it. Let's whip it good. **LET'S MOTOR.**

Concept Connection The MINI's trademarked term "Whiptastic Handling" is one of the ways the company distinguishes itself in the automobile industry. MINI, a division of BMW of North America, is thriving with its **differentiation strategy**. The company trademarked the Whiptastic name to emphasize that driving a MINI Cooper is unlike anything else. Customers seem to agree; sales are zooming.

Managers should think carefully about which strategy will provide their company with its competitive advantage. Gibson Guitar Corporation, famous in the music world for its innovative, high-quality products, found that switching to a low-cost strategy to compete against Japanese rivals such as Yamaha and Ibanez actually hurt the company. When managers realized people wanted Gibson products because of their reputation, not their price, they went back to a differentiation strategy and invested in new technology and marketing.[35] In his studies, Porter found that some businesses did not consciously adopt one of these three strategies and were stuck with no strategic advantage. Without a strategic advantage, businesses earned below-average profits compared with those that used differentiation, cost leadership, or focus strategies. Similarly, a five-year study of management practices in hundreds of businesses, referred to as the *Evergreen Project,* found that a clear strategic direction was a key factor that distinguished winners from losers.[36]

NEW TRENDS IN STRATEGY

Organizations have been in a merger and acquisition frenzy in recent years. J. P. Morgan Chase and Bank One merged, AT&T bought Cingular Wireless, and Disney merged with ABC. Some companies still seek to gain or keep a competitive edge by acquiring new capabilities via mergers and acquisitions. Yet today, a decided shift has occurred toward enhancing the organization's existing capabilities as the primary means of growing and innovating. Another current trend is using strategic partnerships as an alternative to mergers and acquisitions.

focus A type of competitive strategy that emphasizes concentration on a specific regional market or buyer group.

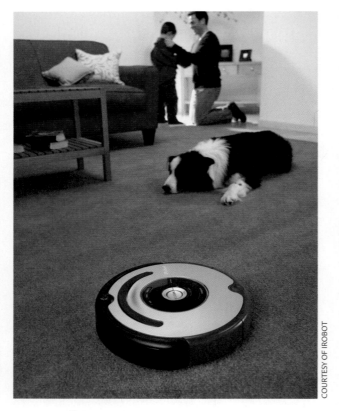

Concept Connection The technology company iRobot is
best known for the Roomba—a pet-like robotic vacuum, shown here
with a live flesh-and-blood pet. But iRobot also fulfils a more serious
purpose of providing military robots that perform dangerous jobs such
as clearing caves and sniffing out bombs. The company's **dynamic
capabilities** approach included sending an engineer to Afghanistan for
field testing and learning. For its consumer products, iRobot primarily
uses internal interdisciplinary teams to incubate ideas. But **partnerships**
feed iRobot's innovation machine, as well, such as when the company
partnered with an explosives-sensor company to develop its bomb-
sniffing bot.

Innovation from Within

The strategic approach referred to as **dynamic capabilities**
means that managers focus on leveraging and developing
more from the firm's existing assets, capabilities, and core
competencies in a way that will provide a sustained competitive advantage.[37] Learning, reallocation of existing
assets, and internal innovation are the route to addressing new challenges in the competitive environment and
meeting new customer needs. For example, General Electric, as described earlier, has acquired a number of other
companies to enter a variety of diverse businesses. Yet
today, the emphasis at GE is not on making deals but
rather on stimulating and supporting internal innovation. Instead of spending billions to buy new businesses,
CEO Jeff Immelt is investing in internal "Imagination
Breakthrough" projects that will take GE into internally
developed new lines of business, new geographic areas,
or a new customer base. The idea is that getting growth
out of existing businesses is cheaper and more effective
than trying to buy it from outside.[38]

Another example of dynamic capabilities is IBM,
which many analysts had written off as a has-been in the
early 1990s. Since then, new top managers have steered
the company through a remarkable transformation by
capitalizing on IBM's core competence of expert technology by learning new ways to apply it to meet changing
customer needs. By leveraging existing capabilities to
provide solutions to major customer problems rather than
just selling hardware, IBM has moved into businesses as
diverse as life sciences, banking, and automotive.[39]

Strategic Partnerships

Internal innovation doesn't mean companies always go
it alone, however. Collaboration with other organiza-
tions, sometimes even with competitors, is an important part of how today's successful companies enter new areas of business. Consider Procter & Gamble (P&G)
and Clorox. The companies are fierce rivals in cleaning products and water purifi-
cation, but both profited by collaborating on a new plastic wrap. P&G researchers
invented a wrap that seals tightly only where it is pressed, but P&G didn't have a
plastic wrap category. Managers negotiated a strategic partnership with Clorox to
market the wrap under the well-established Glad brand name, and Glad Press &
Seal became one of the company's most popular products.[40]

The Internet is both driving and supporting the move toward partnership thinking.
The ability to rapidly and smoothly conduct transactions, communicate information,
exchange ideas, and collaborate on complex projects via the Internet means that companies such as Citigroup, Dow Chemical, and Herman Miller have been able to enter entirely
new businesses by partnering in business areas that were previously unimaginable.[41]

dynamic capabilities
Leveraging and developing
more from the firm's existing
assets, capabilities, and core
competencies in a way that will
provide a sustained competitive
advantage.

GLOBAL STRATEGY

Many organizations operate globally and pursue a distinct strategy as the focus of
global business. Senior executives try to formulate coherent strategies to provide
synergy among worldwide operations for the purpose of fulfilling common goals.

Yet managers face a strategic dilemma between the need for global integration and national responsiveness.

The various global strategies are shown in Exhibit 7.7. Recall from Chapter 4 that the first step toward a greater international presence is when companies begin exporting domestically produced products to selected countries. The *export strategy* is shown in the lower left corner of the exhibit. Because the organization is domestically focused, with only a few exports, managers have little need to pay attention to issues of either local responsiveness or global integration. Organizations that pursue further international expansion must decide whether they want each global affiliate to act autonomously or whether activities should be standardized and centralized across countries. This choice leads managers to select a basic strategy alternative such as globalization versus multidomestic strategy. Some corporations may seek to achieve both global integration and national responsiveness by using a transnational strategy.

Concept Connection AT&T is the exclusive service provider for the iPhone. This **strategic partnership** with Apple provided AT&T with new, younger customers and a hipper image. AT&T CEO Randall Stephenson, here with his iPhone, struck the deal to provide growth in the wireless service market.

Globalization

When an organization chooses a strategy of **globalization**, it means that product design and advertising strategies are standardized throughout the world.[42] This approach is based on the assumption that a single global market exists for many consumer and industrial products. The theory is that people everywhere want to buy the same products and live the same way. People everywhere want to drink Coca-Cola and eat McDonald's hamburgers.[43] A globalization

globalization The standardization of product design and advertising strategies throughout the world.

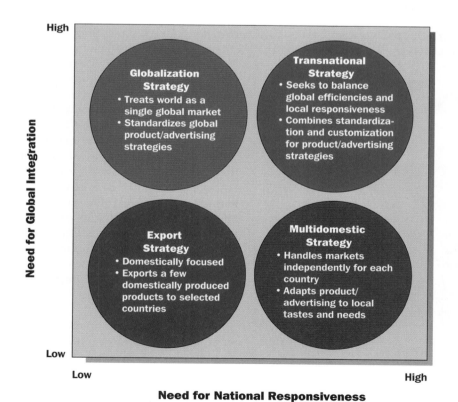

EXHIBIT | **7.7**

Global Corporate Strategies

High

Need for Global Integration

Globalization Strategy
• Treats world as a single global market
• Standardizes global product/advertising strategies

Transnational Strategy
• Seeks to balance global efficiencies and local responsiveness
• Combines standardization and customization for product/advertising strategies

Export Strategy
• Domestically focused
• Exports a few domestically produced products to selected countries

Multidomestic Strategy
• Handles markets independently for each country
• Adapts product/advertising to local tastes and needs

Low

Low   **High**

Need for National Responsiveness

SOURCES: Based on Michael A. Hitt, R. Duane Ireland, and Robert E. Hoskisson, *Strategic Management: Competitiveness and Globalization* (St. Paul, MN; West, 1995), p. 239; and Thomas M. Begley and David P. Boyd, "The Need for a Corporate Global Mindset," *MIT Sloan Management Review* (Winter 2003): 25–32.

strategy can help an organization reap efficiencies by standardizing product design and manufacturing, using common suppliers, introducing products around the world faster, coordinating prices, and eliminating overlapping facilities. For example, Gillette Company has large production facilities that use common suppliers and processes to manufacture products whose technical specifications are standardized around the world.[44]

Globalization enables marketing departments alone to save millions of dollars. One consumer products company reports that, for every country where the same commercial runs, the company saves $1 million to $2 million in production costs alone. More millions have been saved by standardizing the look and packaging of brands.[45]

Multidomestic Strategy

multidomestic strategy The modification of product design and advertising strategies to suit the specific needs of individual countries.

transnational strategy A strategy that combines global coordination to attain efficiency with flexibility to meet specific needs in various countries.

When an organization chooses a **multidomestic strategy**, it means that competition in each country is handled independently of industry competition in other countries. Thus, a multinational company is present in many countries, but it encourages marketing, advertising, and product design to be modified and adapted to the specific needs of each country.[46] Many companies reject the idea of a single global market. They have found that the French do not drink orange juice for breakfast, that laundry detergent is used to wash dishes in parts of Mexico, and that people in the Middle East prefer toothpaste that tastes spicy. Service companies also have to consider their global strategy carefully. The 7-Eleven convenience store chain uses a multidomestic strategy because the product mix, advertising approach, and payment methods need to be tailored to the preferences, values, and government regulations in different parts of the world. For example, in Japan, customers like to use convenience stores to pay utility and other bills. 7-Eleven Japan also set up a way for people to pick up and pay for purchases made over the Internet at their local 7-Eleven market.[47]

Transnational Strategy

A **transnational strategy** seeks to achieve both global integration and national responsiveness.[48] A true transnational strategy is difficult to achieve, because one goal requires close global coordination while the other goal requires local flexibility. However, many industries are finding that, although increased competition means they must achieve global efficiency, growing pressure to meet local needs demands national responsiveness.[49] One company that effectively uses a transnational strategy is Caterpillar, Inc., a heavy equipment manufacturer. Caterpillar achieves global efficiencies by designing its products to use many identical components and centralizing manufacturing of components in a few large-scale facilities. However, assembly plants located in each of Caterpillar's major markets add certain product features tailored to meet local needs.[50]

Although most multinational companies want to achieve some degree of global integration to hold costs down, even global products may require some customization to meet government regulations in various countries or some tailoring to fit consumer preferences. In addition, some products are better suited for standardization than others. Most large

Concept Connection Since first going international in 1971, Dallas-based Mary Kay Inc. has expanded to more than 30 markets on five continents. The company uses a **multidomestic strategy** that handles competition independently in each country. In China, for example, Mary Kay is working on lotions that incorporate traditional Chinese herbs, and it sells skin whiteners there, not bronzers. As Mary Kay China President Paul Mak (pictured here) explains, Chinese women prize smooth white skin. Managers' efforts in China have paid off. Estimates are that by 2015, more Mary Kay product will be sold in China than in the rest of the world combined.

multinational corporations with diverse products and services will attempt to use a partial multidomestic strategy for some product or service lines and global strategies for others. Coordinating global integration with a responsiveness to the heterogeneity of international markets is a difficult balancing act for managers, but it is increasingly important in today's global business world.

STRATEGY EXECUTION

The final step in the strategic management process is strategy execution—how strategy is implemented or put into action. Many people argue that execution is the most important, yet the most difficult, part of strategic management.[51] Indeed, many struggling companies may have file drawers full of winning strategies, but managers can't effectively execute them.[52]

No matter how brilliant the formulated strategy, the organization will not benefit if it is not skillfully executed. Strategy execution requires that all aspects of the organization be in congruence with the strategy and that every individual's efforts be coordinated toward accomplishing strategic goals.[53] Strategy execution involves using several tools—parts of the firm that can be adjusted to put strategy into action—as illustrated in Exhibit 7.8. Once a new strategy is selected, it is implemented through changes in leadership, structure, information and control systems, and human resources.[54] The Manager's Shoptalk box gives some further tips for strategy execution.

- **Leadership.** The primary key to successful strategy execution is leadership. *Leadership* is the ability to influence people to adopt the new behaviors needed for putting the strategy into action. Leaders use persuasion, motivation techniques, and cultural values to support the new strategy. They might make speeches to employees, build coalitions of people who support the new strategic direction, and persuade middle managers to go along with their vision for the company. At IBM, for example, CEO Sam Palmisano used leadership to get people aligned with the strategy of getting IBM intimately involved in revamping and even running

EXHIBIT | **7.8** Tools for Putting Strategy into Action

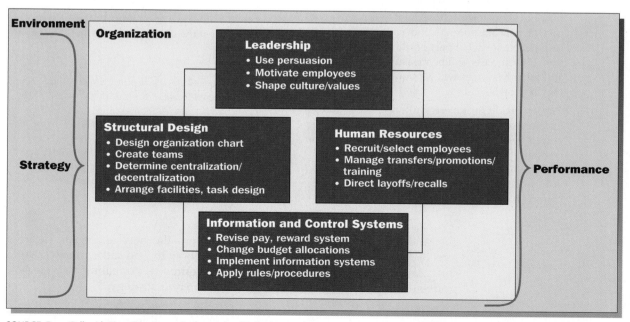

SOURCE: From Galbraith/Kazanjian. *Strategy Implementation*, 2E. © 1986 South-Western, Cengage Learning. Reproduced by permission. www.cengage.com/permissions.

Manager's Shoptalk

Tips for Effective Strategy Execution

One survey found that only 57 percent of responding firms reported that managers successfully executed the new strategies they had devised. Strategy gives a company a competitive edge only if it is skillfully executed through the decisions and actions of front-line managers and employees. Here are a few clues for creating an environment and process conducive to effective strategy execution.

1. *Build commitment to the strategy.* People throughout the organization have to buy into the new strategy. Managers make a deliberate and concentrated effort to bring front-line employees into the loop so they understand the new direction and have a chance to participate in decisions about how it will be executed. When Saab managers wanted to shift their strategy, they met with front-line employees and dealers to explain the new direction and ask for suggestions and recommendations on how to put it into action. Clear, measurable goals and rewards that are tied to implementation efforts are also important for gaining commitment.

2. *Devise a clear execution plan.* Too often, managers put forth great effort to formulate a strategy and next to none crafting a game plan for its execution. Without such a plan, managers and staff are likely to lose sight of the new strategy when they return to the everyday demands of their jobs. For successful execution, translate the strategy into a simple, streamlined plan that breaks the implementation process into a series of short-term actions, with a timetable for each step. Make sure the plan spells out who is responsible for what part of the strategy execution, how success will be measured and tracked, and what resources will be required and how they will be allocated.

3. *Pay attention to culture.* Culture drives strategy, and without the appropriate cultural values, employees' behavior will be out of sync with the company's desired positioning in the marketplaces. For example, Air Canada's CEO made a sincere commitment to making the airline the country's customer service leader. However,

employee behavior didn't change because the old culture values supported doing things the way they had always been done.

4. *Take advantage of employees' knowledge and skills.* Managers need to get to know their employees on a personal basis so they understand how people can contribute to strategy execution. Most people want to be recognized and want to be valuable members of the organization. People throughout the organization have unused talents and skills that might be crucial for the success of a new strategy. In addition, managers can be sure people get training so they are capable of furthering the organization's new direction.

5. *Communicate, communicate, communicate.* Top managers have to continually communicate, through words and actions, their firm commitment to the strategy. In addition, managers have to keep tabs on how things are going, identify problems, and keep people informed about the organization's progress. Managers should break down barriers to effective communication across functional and hierarchical boundaries, often bringing customers into the communication loop as well. Information systems should provide accurate and timely information to the people who need it for decision making.

Executing strategy is a complex job that requires everyone in the company to be aligned with the new direction and working to make it happen. These tips, combined with the information in the text, can help managers meet the challenge of putting strategy into action.

SOURCES: Brooke Dobni, "Creating a Strategy Implementation Environment," *Business Horizons* (March–April 2003): 43–46; Michael K. Allio, "A Short Practical Guide to Implementing Strategy," *Journal of Business Strategy* (August 2005): 12–21; "Strategy Execution: Achieving Operational Excellence," *Economist Intelligence Unit* (November 2004); and Thomas W. Porter and Stephen C. Harper, "Tactical Implementation: The Devil Is in the Details," *Business Horizons* (January–February 2003): 53–60.

customers' business operations. To implement the new approach, he invested tons of money to teach managers at all levels how to lead rather than control their staff. And he talked to people all over the company, appealing to their sense of pride and uniting them behind the new vision and strategy.[55]

■ *Structural Design. Structural design* pertains to managers' responsibilities, their degree of authority, and the consolidation of facilities, departments, and divisions. Structure also pertains to such matters as centralization versus decentralization and the design of job tasks. Trying to execute a strategy that conflicts with structural design, particularly in relation to managers' authority and responsibility, is a top obstacle to putting strategy into action effectively.[56] Many new strategies require making changes in organizational structure, such as adding or changing positions, reorganizing to teams, redesigning jobs, or shifting managers' responsibility and accountability. At IBM, Palmisano dismantled the executive committee that previously presided over strategic initiatives and replaced it with committees made up of people from all over the company. In addition, the entire firm was reorganized into teams that work directly with customers. As the company moves into a new business such as insurance claims processing or supply-chain optimization, IBM assigns SWAT teams to work with a handful of initial clients to learn what customers want and deliver it fast. Practically every job in the giant corporation was redefined to support the new strategy.[57]

■ *Information and Control Systems. Information and control systems* include reward systems, pay incentives, budgets for allocating resources, information technology systems, and the organization's rules, policies, and procedures. Changes in these systems represent major tools for putting strategy into action.[58] For example, Pizza Hut has made excellent use of sophisticated information technology to support a differentiation strategy of continually innovating with new products. Data from point-of-sale customer transactions goes into a massive data warehouse. Managers can mine the data for competitive intelligence that enables them to predict trends as well as better manage targeted advertising and direct-mail campaigns.[59] Information technology can also be used to support a low-cost strategy, such as Wal-Mart has done by accelerating checkout, managing inventory, and controlling distribution.[60]

■ *Human Resources.* The organization's *human resources* are its employees. The human resource function recruits, selects, trains, transfers, promotes, and lays off employees to achieve strategic goals. Longo Toyota of El Monte, California, recruits a highly diverse workforce to create a competitive advantage in selling cars and trucks. The staff speaks more than 30 languages and dialects, which gives Longo a lead because research shows that minorities prefer to buy a vehicle from someone who speaks their language and understands their culture.[61] Training employees is also important because it helps them understand the purpose and importance of a new strategy, overcome resistance, and develop the necessary skills and behaviors to implement the strategy. Southwest supports its low-cost strategy by cross-training employees to perform a variety of functions, minimizing turnover time of planes.[62]

ch7   A MANAGER'S ESSENTIALS: WHAT HAVE WE LEARNED?

■ This chapter described important concepts of strategic management. Strategic management begins with an evaluation of the organization's current mission, goals, and strategy. This evaluation is followed by situation analysis (called SWOT analysis), which examines opportunities and threats in the external environment as well as strengths and weaknesses within the organization. Situation analysis leads to the formulation of explicit strategies, which indicate how the company intends to achieve a competitive advantage. Managers formulate strategies that focus on core competencies, develop synergy, and create value.

■ Strategy formulation takes place at three levels: corporate, business, and functional. Frameworks for corporate strategy include portfolio strategy, the BCG matrix, and diversification strategy. An approach to business-level strategy is Porter's competitive forces and strategies. The Internet is having a profound impact on the competitive environment, and managers should consider its influence when analyzing the five competitive forces and formulating business strategies. Once business strategies have been formulated, functional strategies for supporting them can be developed.

■ New approaches to strategic thought emphasize innovation from within and strategic partnerships rather than acquiring skills and capabilities through mergers and acquisitions.

- Even the most creative strategies have no value if they cannot be translated into action. Execution is the most important and most difficult part of strategy. Managers put strategy into action by aligning all parts of the organization to be in congruence with the new strategy. Four areas that managers focus on for strategy execution are leadership, structural design, information and control systems, and human resources.

- Many organizations also pursue a separate global strategy. Managers can choose to use a globalization strategy, a multidomestic strategy, or a transnational strategy as the focus of global operations.

ch7 DISCUSSION QUESTIONS

1. In 2004, Kmart emerged from bankruptcy and acquired Sears. Based on your experience in the two stores, how would you define the core competencies of the two retailers? Do you think the store changes so far show evidence of the synergy the dealmakers hoped for?

2. How might a corporate management team go about determining whether it should formulate a growth strategy or a stability strategy? What factors should they take into consideration? What kinds of information should they collect?

3. You are a middle manager helping to implement a new corporate cost-cutting strategy, and you're meeting skepticism, resistance, and in some cases, outright hostility from your subordinates. In what ways might you or the company have been able to avoid this situation? Where do you go from here?

4. Perform a situation (SWOT) analysis for the school or university you attend. Do you think university administrators consider the same factors when devising their strategy?

5. Do you think the movement toward corporate collaborations, alliances, and partnership rather than competition is a passing phenomenon or here to stay? What skills would make a good manager in a strategic alliance with another company? What

skills would make a good manager operating in competition with another company?

6. Using Porter's competitive strategies, how would you describe the strategies of Wal-Mart, Bloomingdale's, and Target? Do any of these companies also use partnership strategies? Discuss.

7. Walt Disney Company has four major strategic business units: movies (including Miramax and Touchstone), theme parks, consumer products, and television (ABC and cable). Place each of these SBUs on the BCG matrix based on your knowledge of them.

8. As an administrator for a medium-sized hospital, you and the board of directors have decided to change to a drug dependency hospital from a short-term, acute-care facility. How would you go about implementing this strategy?

9. If you are the CEO of a global company, how might you determine whether a globalization, a transnational, or a multidomestic strategy would work best for your enterprise? What factors would influence your decision? How would your choice reflect the products or services your company is offering?

10. Describe how the Internet increases the bargaining power of consumers, one of Porter's five competitive forces. Have you felt increased power as a consumer because of the Internet? Explain.

ch7 MANAGEMENT IN PRACTICE: EXPERIENTIAL EXERCISE

Developing Strategy for a Small Business

Instructions: Your instructor may ask you to do this exercise individually or as part of a group. Select a local business with which you (or group members) are familiar. Complete the following activities.

Activity 1 Perform a SWOT analysis for the business.

    Strengths:

    Weaknesses:

    Opportunities:

    Threats:

Activity 2 Write a statement of the business's current strategy.

Activity 3 Decide on a goal you would like the business to achieve in two years, and write a statement of proposed strategy for achieving that goal.

Activity 4 Write a statement describing how the proposed strategy will be implemented.

Activity 5 What have you learned from this exercise?

ch7   MANAGEMENT IN PRACTICE: ETHICAL DILEMMA

The Spitzer Group

Irving Silberstein, marketing director for The Spitzer Group, a growing regional marketing and corporate communications firm, was hard at work on an exciting project. He was designing Spitzer's first word-of-mouth campaign for an important client, a manufacturer of beauty products.

In a matter of just a few years, word-of-mouth advertising campaigns morphed from a small fringe specialty to a mainstream marketing technique embraced by no less than consumer product giant Procter & Gamble (P&G). The basic idea was simple, really. You harnessed the power of existing social networks to sell your products and services. The place to start, Irving knew, was to take a close look at how P&G's in-house unit, Vocalpoint, conducted its highly successful campaigns, both for its own products and those of its clients.

Because women were key purchasers of P&G consumer products, Vocalpoint focused on recruiting mothers with extensive social networks, participants known internally by the somewhat awkward term, *connectors*. The Vocalpoint Web page took care to emphasize that participants were members of an "exclusive" community of moms who exerted significant influence on P&G and other major companies. Vocalpoint not only sent the women new product samples and solicited their opinions, but it also carefully tailored its pitch to the group's interests and preoccupations so the women would want to tell their friends about a product. For example, it described a new dishwashing foam that was so much fun to use, kids would actually volunteer to clean up the kitchen, music to any mother's ears. P&G then furnished the mothers with coupons to hand out if they wished. It's all voluntary, P&G pointed out. According to a company press release issued shortly before Vocal-point went national in early 2006, members "are never obligated to do or say anything."

One of the things Vocalpoint members weren't obligated to say, Irving knew, was that the women were essentially unpaid participants in a P&G-sponsored marketing program. When asked about the policy, Vocalpoint CEO Steve Reed replied, "We have a deeply held belief you don't tell the consumer what to say." However, skeptical observers speculated that what the company really feared was that the women's credibility might be adversely affected if their Vocalpoint affiliation were known. Nondisclosure really amounted to lying for financial gain, Vocalpoint's critics argued, and furthermore the whole campaign shamelessly exploited personal relationships for commercial purposes. Others thought the critics were making mountains out of molehills. P&G wasn't forbidding participants from disclosing their ties to Vocalpoint and P&G. And the fact that they weren't paid meant the women had no vested interest in endorsing the products.

So as Irving designs the word-of-mouth campaign for his agency's client, just how far should he emulate the company that even its detractors acknowledge as a master of the technique?

What Would You Do?

1. Don't require Spitzer "connectors" to reveal their affiliation with the corporate word-of-mouth marketing campaign. They don't have to recommend a product they don't believe in.

2. Require that Spitzer participants reveal their ties to the corporate marketing program right up front before they make a recommendation.

3. Instruct Spitzer participants to reveal their participation in the corporate marketing program only if directly asked by the person they are talking to about the client's products.

SOURCES: Robert Berner, "I Sold It Through the Grapevine," *BusinessWeek* (May 29, 2006): 32–34; "Savvy Moms Share Maternal Instincts; Vocalpoint Offers Online Moms the Opportunity to be a Valuable Resource to Their Communities," *Business Wire* (December 6, 2005); and "Word of Mouth Marketing: To Tell or Not To Tell," *AdRants .com* (May 2006), www.adrants.com/2006/05/word-of-mouth-marketing-to-tell-or-not-to.php.

ch7   CASE FOR CRITICAL ANALYSIS

Edmunds Corrugated Parts & Services

Larry Edmunds grimaces as he tossed his company's latest quarterly earnings onto his desk. When Virginia-based Edmunds Corrugated Parts & Service Co.'s sales surged past the $10 million mark awhile back, he was certain the company was well-positioned for steady growth. Today the company, which provided precision machine parts and service to the domestic corrugated box industry, still enjoys a dominant market share and is showing a profit, though not quite the profit seen in years past. However, it is no longer possible to ignore the fact that revenues were beginning to show clear signs of stagnation.

More than two decades ago, Larry's grandfather loaned him the money to start the business and then handed over the barn on what had been the family's Shenandoah Valley farm to serve as his first factory. Today, he operates from a 50,000 square-foot factory located near I-81 just a few miles from that old barn. The business allowed him to realize what had once seemed an almost impossible goal: He was making a good living without having to leave his close-knit extended family and rural roots. He also felt a sense of satisfaction at employing about 100 people, many of them neighbors. They were among the most hard-working, loyal workers you'd find anywhere. However, many of his original employees were now nearing retirement. Replacing those skilled workers was going to be difficult, he realized from experience. The area's brightest and best young people were much more likely to move away in search of employment than their parents had been. Those who remained behind just didn't seem to have the work ethic Larry had come to expect in his employees.

He didn't feel pressured by the emergence of any new direct competitors. After slipping slightly a couple years ago, Edmunds's formidable market share—based on its reputation for reliability and exceptional, personalized service—was holding steady at 75 percent. He did feel plagued, however, by higher raw material costs resulting from the steep increase in steel prices. But the main source of concern stemmed from changes in the box industry itself. The industry had never been particularly recession resistant, with demand fluctuating with manufacturing output. Now alternative shipping products were beginning to make their appearance, mostly flexible plastic films and reusable plastic containers. It remained to be seen how much of a dent they'd make in the demand for boxes.

More worrying, consolidation in the paper industry had wiped out hundreds of the U.S. plants that Edmunds once served, with many of the survivors either opening overseas facilities or entering into joint ventures abroad. The surviving manufacturers were investing in higher quality machines that broke down less frequently, thus requiring fewer of Edmunds's parts. Still, he had

to admit that although the highly fragmented U.S. corrugated box industry certainly qualified as a mature one, no one seriously expected U.S. manufacturers to be dislodged from their position as major producers for both the domestic and export markets.

Edmunds was clearly at a crossroads. If Larry wanted that steady growth he'd assumed he could count on not so long ago, he suspect that business as usual wasn't going to work. But if he wanted the company to grow, what was the best way to achieve that goal? Should he look into developing new products and services, possibly serving industries other than the box market? Should he investigate the possibility of going the mergers and acquisitions route or look for a partnership opportunity? He thought about the company's rudimentary Web page, one that did little beside give a basic description of the company, and wondered whether he could find ways of making better use of the Internet? Was it feasible for Edmunds to find new markets by exporting its parts globally?

All he knew for sure was that once he decided where to take the company from here, he would sleep better.

Questions

1. What would the SWOT analysis look like for this company?

2. What role do you expect the Internet to play in the corrugated box industry? What are some ways that Edmunds could better use the Internet to foster growth?

3. Which of Porter's competitive strategies would you recommend that Edmunds follow? Why? Which of the strategies do you think would be least likely to succeed?

SOURCES: Based on Ron Stodghill,"Boxed Out," *FSB* (April 2005): 69–72; "SIC 2653 Corrugated and Solid Fiber Boxes," *Encyclopedia of American Industries*, www.referenceforbusiness.com/industries/Paper-Allied/Corrugated-Solid-Fiber-Boxes.html; "Paper and Allied Products," *U.S. Trade and Industry Outlook 2000*, 10-12 to 10-15; and "Smurfit-Stone Container: Market Summary," *BusinessWeek Online* (May 4, 2006), research.businessweek.com/business_summary.asp? Symbol=SSCC.

ch7 ON THE JOB VIDEO CASE

Timbuk2: The Message Is in the Bag

Picture yourself on a bike, weaving in and out of city traffic, pedaling as fast as you can through a maze of streets, dodging taxicabs and pedestrians, carrying your cargo on your back. Now picture yourself making dozens of deliveries in a day, pedaling an

eight- or nine-hour shift in blazing sun, pouring rain, stinging sleet, or even blowing snow. This is the life of a bicycle messenger. Timbuk2, founded in San Francisco more than 15 years ago by former bicycle messenger Rob Honeycutt, manufactures what seems to be a specialized product: messenger bags for cyclists who make their living delivering documents door to door. Today, Timbuk2 still manufactures professional bags for bike messengers. But the firm has expanded its offerings to include fashion bags for other consumers—and its goals and plans are much broader than they were fifteen years ago.

"Our goal for the future is to remain faithful to our working-class urban roots, while expanding our unique qualities and design sensibilities to a broader range of products and a wider audience," states Timbuk2's Web site. Mark Dwight, CEO of the firm, echoes this sentiment. Dwight's job as CEO is to focus on the big picture—overall goals and how to achieve them. "The difference between strategy and goals is, goals are the endpoint and strategy is the way to get there. The actual steps you take would be the tactics," Dwight explains. Timbuk2's current goal is to move from a tiny, specialized market into a broader market. "Our roots are in the bicycle messenger market . . . a subculture that is very interesting. . . . However, it isn't really a market; there's no growth there. So what we're trying to do is build from that heritage, that authenticity that gives value to our brand as a lifestyle brand," says Dwight.

Formulating the strategies to achieve the goals requires careful planning. "We are building a lifestyle brand; we are [also] trying to build brand equity because that ultimately is the value of this company," notes Dwight. "Then, when we go to sell the company or take it public, there's value there." So every effort, from the development of new products to the marketing of existing ones, focuses on strengthening the Timbuk2 brand in consumers' minds. Dwight and his staff plan to "develop a product portfolio that asserts our position in existing markets, moves into new markets, and really creates a sense of lifestyle . . . so when you think of Timbuk2 . . . you think of an emotional concept, a brand, a lifestyle."

Timbuk2 is already moving rapidly toward its goals. Sit in on a Timbuk2 planning meeting, and you'll hear lots of ideas and opinions flying back and forth—how to design a new bag, how to market it, how to offer it over the Web. "I don't want to see any of this hardware," says Dwight, pointing to a sketch in one design meeting. "That's Coach. We're not Coach." When reminded that chrome hardware is popular

among today's consumers, he does not back down. He wants Timbuk2's bags to have a look that is distinctive. So far, they have managed to offer a variety of bags for a variety of needs—without chrome hardware. Consumers can pick up a water-resistant bag with quick-release buckles that allow yoga followers to snap out their practice mats with ease, weather-proof travel bags with destination stickers superimposed on the flaps, and colorful, messenger-style laptop computer bags for commuters who want to blend durability with style. The bags don't come cheap; with the addition of custom features, consumers can pay $100 or more for their Timbuk2 bags. But a good purse or travel bag from another maker can cost just as much or more.

Timbuk2 hasn't forgotten bicycle messengers, even with its new focus. The professionals can still visit the Timbuk2 Web site and "build" customized professional bags—selecting from four different sizes, several fabrics, and an array of colors. In addition, as part of a celebration of the firm's heritage, Timbuk2 has planned to collaborate with Joe Urich, San Francisco bike messenger and design student at the California College of Arts (CCA), to design two new, industrial-strength messenger bags for his colleagues. These new bags will be designed specifically to meet requirements of working messengers. "I hope it goes well," says Urich. The project should succeed—after all, who knows better how to design a messenger bag than the messenger himself?

Questions

1. Do Timbuk2's goals have the characteristics of effective goals? Why or why not?

2. Does Timbuk2 represents a high performance approach to planning? Why or why not?

3. Using what you know about Timbuk2, write a brief mission statement for the organization.

SOURCES: Company Web site, *http://www.tumbuk2. com*, accessed August 13, 2004; "Timbuk2's Groovy Bag," *Yoga Journal*, July/August 2004, *http://www.yogajournal com*; Larry Armstrong, "Green with Envy," *BusinessWeek*, [no pub info], *http://www.businessweek.com*; "In Style Every Mile," *Organic Style*, May 2004, *www.organicstyle.com*.

3
Planning

---

ch7   BIZ FLIX VIDEO CASE

Dr. Seuss' How the Grinch Stole Christmas

Readers and lovers of Dr. Seuss's original tale may be put off by Ron Howard's loose adaptation of the story.

Whoville, a magical, mythical land that exists inside a snowflake, features two types of life: the Whos who love Christmas and the Grinch (Jim Carrey) who hates it. Cindy Lou Who (Taylor Momsen) tries to bring the Grinch back to Yuletide celebrations, an effort that backfires on all involved. Sparkling special effects will dazzle most viewers and likely distract them from the film's departures from the original story.

This scene is an edited version of the "Second Thoughts" sequence early in the film. Just before this scene, fearless Cindy Lou entered the Grinch's lair to invite him to be the Holiday Cheermeister at the Whobilation One-thousand Celebration. In typical Grinch fashion, he pulls the trap door on Cindy Lou who unceremoniously slides out of his lair to land on a snowy Whoville street. The Grinch now must decide

whether to accept the invitation. The film continues with the Cheermeister award ceremony.

What to Watch for and Ask Yourself

1. What are the Grinch's decision alternatives or options?

2. What decision criteria does the Grinch use to choose from the alternatives?

3. Describe the steps in the Grinch's decision-making process.

ch7 ENDNOTES

1. This questionnaire is adapted from Dorothy Marcic and Joe Seltzer, *Organizational Behavior: Experiences and Cases* (Cincinnati, OH: South-Western, 1998), pp. 284–287, and William Miller, *Innovation Styles* (Global Creativity Corporation, 1997).

2. "The World's Most Innovative Companies," *Fast Company* (March 2008): 92–118.

3. Janet Adamy, "McDonald's Takes on a Weakened Starbucks; Food Giant to Install Specialty Coffee Bars," *The Wall Street Journal*, January 7, 2008.

4. Nanette Byrnes and Peter Burrows, "Where Dell Went Wrong," *BusinessWeek* (February 19, 2007): 62–63; William M. Bulkeley, "SofterView; Kodak Sharpens Digital Focus on Its Best Customers: Women," *The Wall Street Journal*, July 6, 2005.

5. Chet Miller and Laura B. Cardinal, "Strategic Planning and Firm Performance: A Synthesis of More than Two Decades of Research," *Academy of Management Journal* 37, no. 6 (1994): 1649–1665.

6. Renee Dye and Olivier Sibony, "How to Improve Strategic Planning," *McKinsey Quarterly*, no. 3 (2007).

7. Keith H. Hammonds, "Michael Porter's Big Ideas," *Fast Company* (March 2001): 150–156.

8. John E. Prescott, "Environments as Moderators of the Relationship between Strategy and Performance," *Academy of Management Journal* 29 (1986): 329–346; John A. Pearce II and Richard B. Robinson, Jr., *Strategic Management: Strategy, Formulation, and Implementation*, 2nd ed.

(Homewood, IL: Irwin, 1985); and David J. Teece, "Economic Analysis and Strategic Management," *California Management Review* 26 (Spring 1984): 87–110.

9. Jack Welch, "It's All in the Sauce," excerpt from his book, *Winning*, in *Fortune* (April 18, 2005): 138–144; and Constantinos Markides, "Strategic Innovation," *Sloan Management Review* (Spring 1997): 9–23.

10. Michael E. Porter, "What Is Strategy?" *Harvard Business Review* (November–December 1996): 61–78.

11. Arthur A. Thompson, Jr., and A. J. Strickland III, *Strategic Management: Concepts and Cases*, 6th ed. (Homewood, IL: Irwin, 1992); and Briance Mascarenhas, Alok Baveja, and Mamnoon Jamil, "Dynamics of Core Competencies in Leading Multinational Companies," *California Management Review* 40, no. 4 (Summer 1998): 117–132.

12. Michael V. Copeland, "Stitching Together an Apparel Power-house," *Business 2.0* (April 2005): 52–54.

13. "Gaylord Says Hotels Prosper by Becoming Destinations," *The Tennessean*, July 24, 2005, http://www.tennessean.com.

14. Chris Woodyard, "Big Dreams for Small Choppers Paid Off," *USA Today*, September 11, 2005, http://www.usatoday.com.

15. Michael Goold and Andrew Campbell, "Desperately Seeking Synergy," *Harvard Business Review* (September–October 1998): 131–143.

16. Elizabeth Olson, "OMG! Cute Boys, Kissing Tips and Lots of Pics, As Magazines Find a Niche," *The New York Times*, May 28, 2007.

17. Janet Adamy, "Bare Essentials; To Find Growth, No-Frills Grocer Goes Where Other Chains Won't," *Wall Street Journal* (August 30, 2005): A1, A8. Copyright 2005 by Dow Jones & Company, Inc.. Reproduced with permission of Dow Jones & Company, Inc. in the format Textbook via Copyright Clearance Center.

18. Milton Leontiades, *Strategies for Diversification and Change* (Boston: Little, Brown, 1980), p. 63; and Dan E. Schendel and Charles W. Hofer, eds., *Strategic Management: A New View of Business Policy and Planning* (Boston: Little, Brown, 1979), pp. 11–14.

19. Georgia Flight, "Powerboating's New Powerhouse," *Business 2.0* (November 2005): 62–67.

20. NutriSystem profile, "Hot Growth Special Report 2006, *BusinessWeek* (June 5, 2006), http://www.businessweek.com/hot_growth/2006/company/20.htm; Christopher Palmeri, "How NutriSystem Got Fat and Happy," *BusinessWeek* (September 19, 2005): 82–84; and "NutriSystem Announces Fourth Quarter and Year End 2007 Results," http://phx.corporate-ir.net/phoenix.zhtml?c=66836&p=irol-newsArticle&ID=1109858&highlight= (accessed March 3, 2008).

21. Milton Leontiades, "The Confusing Words of Business Policy," *Academy of Management Review* 7 (1982): 45–48.

22. Lawrence G. Hrebiniak and William F. Joyce, *Implementing Strategy* (New York: Macmillan, 1984).

23. David Kirkpatrick, "Facebook's Plan To Hook Up the World," *Fortune* (June 11, 2007): 127–130; Brad Stone, "Facebook Expands Into MySpace's Territory," *The New York Times*, May 25, 2007; and Vauhini Vara, "Facebook CEO Seeks Help as Site Suffers Growing Pains," *The Wall Street Journal*, March 5, 2008.

24. Vara, "Facebook CEO Seeks Help."

25. Frederick W. Gluck, "A Fresh Look at Strategic Management," *Journal of Business Strategy* 6 (Fall 1985): 4–19.

26. J. Lynn Lunsford, "Going Up; United Technologies' Formula: A Powerful Lift from Elevators," *The Wall Street Journal*, July 2, 2003.

27. Thompson and Strickland, *Strategic Management*; and William L. Shanklin and John K. Ryans, Jr., "Is the International Cash Cow Really a Prize Heifer?" *Business Horizons* 24 (1981): 10–16.

28. Diane Brady, "The Immelt Revolution," *BusinessWeek* (March 28, 2005): 64–73.

29. Example cited in Gareth R. Jones and Jennifer M. George, *Contemporary Management*, 4th ed. (Boston, MA: McGraw-Hill Irwin, 2006), p. 283.

30. Steve Lohr, "Apple, a Success at Stores, Bets Big on Fifth Avenue," *The New York Times*, May 19, 2006; and Brent Schlender, "How Big Can Apple Get?" *Fortune* (February 21, 2005): 66–76.

31. Michael E. Porter, "The Five Competitive Forces That Shape Strategy," *Harvard Business Review* (January 2008): 7993; Michael E. Porter, *Competitive Strategy* (New York: Free Press, 1980), pp. 36–46; Danny Miller, "Relating Porter's Business Strategies to Environment and Structure: Analysis and Performance Implementations," *Academy of Management Journal* 31 (1988): 280–308; and Michael E. Porter, "From Competitive Advantage to Corporate Strategy," *Harvard Business Review* (May–June 1987): 43–59.

32. Michael E. Porter, "Strategy and the Internet," *Harvard Business Review* (March 2001): 63–78.

33. Andrew Park and Peter Burrows, "Dell, the Conqueror," *BusinessWeek* (September 24, 2001): 92–102; and Thompson and Strickland, *Strategic Management*.

34. Richard Teitelbaum, "The Wal-Mart of Wall Street," *Fortune* (October 13, 1997): 128–130.

35. Joshua Rosenbaum, "Guitar Maker Looks for a New Key," *The Wall Street Journal*, February 11, 1998.

36. Nitin Nohria, William Joyce, and Bruce Roberson, "What Really Works," *Harvard Business Review* (July 2003): 43–52.

37. This discussion is based on J. Bruce Harreld, Charles A. O'Reilly III, and Michael L. Tushman, "Dynamic Capabilities at IBM: Driving Strategy into Action," *California Management Review* 49, no. 4 (2007).

38. Diane Brady, "The Immelt Revolution," *BusinessWeek* (March 28, 2005): 64–73.

39. Harreld et al., "Dynamic Capabilities at IBM."

40. Alice Dragoon, "A Travel Guide to Collaboration," *CIO* (November 15, 2004): 68–75.

41. Don Tapscott, "Rethinking Strategy in a Networked World," *Strategy & Business*, no. 24 (Third Quarter 2001): 34–41.

42. Kenichi Ohmae, "Managing in a Borderless World," *Harvard Business Review* (May–June 1990): 152–161.

43. Theodore Levitt, "The Globalization of Markets," *Harvard Business Review* (May–June 1983): 92–102.

44. Cesare Mainardi, Martin Salva, and Muir Sanderson, "Label of Origin: Made on Earth," *strategy + business*, no. 15 (Second Quarter, 1999).

45. Joanne Lipman, "Marketers Turn Sour on Global Sales Pitch Harvard Guru Makes," *The Wall Street Journal*, May 12, 1988.

46. Michael E. Porter, "Changing Patterns of International Competition," *California Management Review* 28 (Winter 1986): 40.

47. Mohanbir Sawhney and Sumant Mandal, "What Kind of Global Organization Should You Build?" *Business 2.0* (May 2000): 213.

48. Based on Michael A. Hitt, R. Duane Ireland, and Robert E. Hoskisson, *Strategic Management: Competitiveness and Globalization* (St. Paul, MN: West, 1995), p. 238.

49. Anil K. Gupta and Vijay Govindarajan, "Converting Global Presence into Global Competitive Advantage," *Academy of Management Executive* 15, no. 2 (2001): 45–56.

50. Thomas S. Bateman and Carl P. Zeithaml, *Management: Function and Strategy*, 2nd ed. (Homewood, IL: Irwin, 1993), p. 231.

51. Lawrence G. Hrebiniak, "Obstacles to Effective Strategy Implementa-

tion," *Organizational Dynamics* 35, no. 1 (2006): 12–31; Eric M. Olson, Stanley F. Slater, and G. Tomas M. Hult, "The Importance of Structure and Process to Strategy Implementation," *Business Horizons* 48 (2005): 47–54; L. J. Bourgeois III and David R. Brodwin, "Strategic Implementation: Five Approaches to an Elusive Phenomenon," *Strategic Management Journal* 5 (1984): 241–264; Anil K. Gupta and V. Govindarajan, "Business Unit Strategy, Managerial Characteristics, and Business Unit Effectiveness at Strategy Implementation," *Academy of Management Journal* (1984): 25–41; and Jeffrey G. Covin, Dennis P. Slevin, and Randall L. Schultz, "Implementing Strategic Missions: Effective Strategic, Structural, and Tactical Choices," *Journal of Management Studies* 31, no. 4 (1994): 481–505.

52. Based on a statement by Louis Gerstner, quoted in Harreld et al., "Dynamic Capabilities at IBM."

53. Olson, Slater, and Hult, "The Importance of Structure and Process to Strategy Implementation."

54. Jay R. Galbraith and Robert K. Kazanjian, *Strategy Implementation: Structure, Systems and Process*, 2nd ed. (St. Paul, MN: West, 1986); and Paul C. Nutt, "Selecting Tactics to Implement Strategic Plans," *Strategic Management Journal* 10 (1989): 145–161.

55. Spencer E. Ante, "The New Blue," *BusinessWeek* (March 17, 2003): 80–88.

56. Survey results reported in Hrebiniak, "Obstacles to Effective Strategy Implementation."

57. Steve Hamm, "Beyond Blue," *BusinessWeek* (April 18, 2005): 68–76.

58. Gupta and Govindarajan, "Business Unit Strategy"; and Bourgeois and Brodwin, "Strategic Implementation."

59. Obasi Akan, Richard S. Allen, Marilyn M. Helms, and Samuel A. Spralls III, "Critical Tactics for Implementing Porter's Generic Strategies," *Journal of Business Strategy* 27, no. 1 (2006): 43–53.

60. Nitin Nohria, William Joyce, and Bruce Roberson, "What Really Works," *Harvard Business Review* (July 2003): 43–52.

61. Akan et al., "Critical Tactics for Implementing Porter's Generic Strategies."

62. Ibid.

3
Planning

© GETTY IMAGES/DIGITAL VISION

Chapter Outline

Learning Outcomes

After studying this chapter, you should be able to:

1. Explain why decision making is an important component of good management.

2. Discuss the difference between programmed and nonprogrammed decisions and the decision characteristics of certainty and uncertainty.

3. Describe the ideal, rational model of decision making and the political model of decision making.

4. Explain the process by which managers actually make decisions in the real world.

5. Identify the six steps used in managerial decision making.

6. Describe four personal decision styles used by managers, and explain the biases that frequently cause managers to make bad decisions.

7. Identify and explain techniques for innovative group decision making.

Managerial Decision Making

1 Introduction
2 Environment
3 Planning
4 Organizing
5 Controlling
6 Leading

HOW DO YOU MAKE DECISIONS?

Most of us make decisions automatically and without realizing that people have diverse decision-making behaviors, which they bring to management positions. Think back to how you make decisions in your personal, student, or work life, especially where other people are involved. Please answer whether each of the following items is Mostly True or Mostly False for you.

	Mostly True	Mostly False
1. I like to decide quickly and move on to the next thing.	_____	_____
2. I would use my authority to make the decision if certain I was right.	_____	_____
3. I appreciate decisiveness.	_____	_____
4. There is usually one correct solution to a problem.	_____	_____
5. I identify everyone who needs to be involved in the decision.	_____	_____
6. I explicitly seek conflicting perspectives.	_____	_____
7. I use discussion strategies to reach a solution.	_____	_____
8. I look for different meanings when faced with a great deal of data.	_____	_____
9. I take time to reason things through and use systematic logic.	_____	_____

SCORING AND INTERPRETATION: All nine items in the list reflect appropriate decision-making behavior, but items 1–4 are more typical of new managers. Items 5–8 are typical of successful senior manager decision making. Item 9 is considered part of good decision making at all levels. If you checked Mostly True for three or four of items 1–4 and 9, consider yourself typical of a new manager. If you checked Mostly True for three or four of items 5–8 and 9, you are using behavior consistent with top managers. If you checked a similar number of both sets of items, your behavior is probably flexible and balanced.

New managers typically use a different decision behavior than seasoned executives. The decision behavior of a successful CEO may be almost the opposite of a first-level supervisor. The difference is due partly to the types of decisions and partly to learning what works at each level. New managers often start out with a more directive, decisive, command-oriented behavior and gradually move toward more openness, diversity of viewpoints, and interactions with others as they move up the hierarchy.[1]

Managers often are referred to as *decision makers*, and every organization grows, prospers, or fails as a result of decisions by its managers. Many manager decisions are strategic, such as whether to build a new factory, move into a new line of business, or sell off a division. Yet managers also make decisions about every other aspect of an organization, including structure, control systems, responses to the environment, and human resources. Managers scout for problems, make decisions for solving them, and monitor the consequences to see whether additional decisions are required. Good decision making is a vital part of good management because decisions determine how the organization solves its problems, allocates resources, and accomplishes its goals.

The business world is full of evidence of both good and bad decisions. Apple, which seemed all but dead in the mid-1990s, became the world's most admired company in 2008 based on decisions made by CEO Steve Jobs and other top managers. No longer just a maker of computers, Apple is now in the music player business, the cell phone business, and the retailing business, among others. iTunes is now the second-largest seller of music behind Wal-Mart.[2] Cadillac's sales made a comeback after managers ditched stuffy golf and yachting sponsorships and instead tied in with top Hollywood movies.[3] On the other hand, Maytag's decision to introduce the Neptune Drying Center was a complete flop. The new $1,200 product was hyped as a breakthrough in laundry, but the six-foot-tall Drying Center wouldn't fit into most people's existing laundry rooms. Or consider the decision of Timex managers to replace the classic tag line, "It takes a licking and keeps on ticking," with the bland "Life is ticking." The desire to modernize their company's image led Timex managers to ditch one of the most recognizable advertising slogans in the world in favor of a lame and rather depressing new one.[4] Decision making is not easy. It must be done amid ever-changing factors, unclear information, and conflicting points of view.

Chapters 6 and 7 described strategic planning. This chapter explores the decision process that underlies strategic planning. Plans and strategies are arrived at through decision making; the better the decision making, the better the strategic planning. First, we examine decision characteristics. Then we look at decision-making models and the steps executives should take when making important decisions. The chapter also explores some biases that can cause managers to make bad decisions. Finally, we examine some techniques for innovative group decision making.

TYPES OF DECISIONS AND PROBLEMS

A **decision** is a choice made from available alternatives. For example, an accounting manager's selection among Colin, Tasha, and Carlos for the position of junior auditor is a decision. Many people assume that making a choice is the major part of decision making, but it is only a part.

Decision making is the process of identifying problems and opportunities and then resolving them. Decision making involves effort both before and after the actual choice. Thus, the decision as to whether to select Colin, Tasha, or Carlos requires the accounting manager to ascertain whether a new junior auditor is needed, determine the availability of potential job candidates, interview candidates to acquire necessary information, select one candidate, and follow up with the socialization of the new employee into the organization to ensure the decision's success.

decision A choice made from available alternatives.

decision making The process of identifying problems and opportunities and then resolving them.

programmed decision A decision made in response to a situation that has occurred often enough to enable decision rules to be developed and applied in the future.

nonprogrammed decision A decision made in response to a situation that is unique, is poorly defined and largely unstructured, and has important consequences for the organization.

Programmed and Nonprogrammed Decisions

Management decisions typically fall into one of two categories: programmed and nonprogrammed. **Programmed decisions** involve situations that have occurred often enough to enable decision rules to be developed and applied in the future.[5] Programmed decisions are made in response to recurring organizational problems. The decision to reorder paper and other office supplies when inventories drop to a certain level is a programmed decision. Other programmed decisions concern the types of skills required to fill certain jobs, the reorder point for manufacturing inventory, exception reporting for expenditures ten percent or more over budget, and selection of freight routes for product deliveries. Once managers formulate decision rules, subordinates and others can make the decision, freeing managers for other tasks.

TakeaMoment | **Go to the ethical dilemma on pages 233–234 that pertains to making nonprogrammed decisions.**

Nonprogrammed decisions are made in response to situations that are unique, are poorly defined and largely unstructured, and have important consequences for the organization. Many nonprogrammed decisions involve strategic planning because uncertainty is great and decisions are complex. Decisions to build a new factory, develop a new product or service, enter a new geographical market, or relocate headquarters to another city are all nonprogrammed decisions. One good example of a nonprogrammed decision is ExxonMobil's decision to form a consortium to drill for oil in Siberia. One of the largest foreign investments in Russia, the consortium committed $4.5 billion before pumping the first barrel and expects a total capital cost of $12 billion-plus. The venture could produce 250,000 barrels a day, about 10 percent of ExxonMobil's global production. But if things go wrong, the oil giant will take a crippling hit.

Facing Certainty and Uncertainty

One primary difference between programmed and nonprogrammed decisions relates to the degree of certainty or uncertainty that managers deal with in making the decision. In a perfect world, managers would have all the information necessary for making decisions. In reality, however, some things are unknowable; thus, some decisions will fail to solve the problem or attain the desired outcome. Managers try to obtain information about decision alternatives that will reduce decision uncertainty. Every decision situation can be organized on a scale according to the availability of information and the possibility of failure. The four positions on the scale are certainty, risk, uncertainty, and ambiguity, as illustrated in Exhibit 8.1. Whereas programmed decisions can be made in situations involving certainty, many situations that managers deal with every day involve at least some degree of uncertainty and require nonprogrammed decision making.

Concept Connection When Martha Stewart, shown here leaving the courthouse, was found guilty of lying to federal investigators and sentenced to five months in prison, top managers at her company, Martha Stewart Living Omnimedia, also felt the sting. CEO Sharon Patrick was faced with unique challenges for which plans had not been made. Patrick made the **nonprogrammed decision** to downplay Martha Stewart's presence in the company, including downsizing the Stewart name on the flagship *Living* magazine cover.

EXHIBIT | 8.1

Conditions That Affect the Possibility of Decision Failure

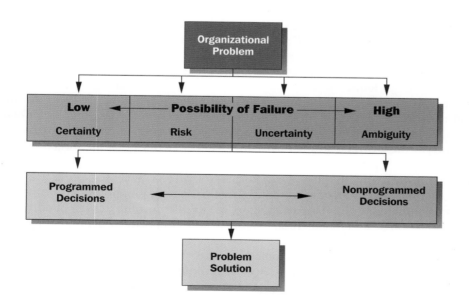

Certainty Certainty means that all the information the decision maker needs is fully available.[6] Managers have information on operating conditions, resource costs or constraints, and each course of action and possible outcome. For example, if a company considers a $10,000 investment in new equipment that it knows for certain will yield $4,000 in cost savings per year over the next five years, managers can calculate a before-tax rate of return of about 40 percent. If managers compare this investment with one that will yield only $3,000 per year in cost savings, they can confidently select the 40 percent return. However, few decisions are certain in the real world. Most contain risk or uncertainty.

Risk Risk means that a decision has clear-cut goals and that good information is available, but the future outcomes associated with each alternative are subject to chance. However, enough information is available to allow the probability of a successful outcome for each alternative to be estimated.[7] Statistical analysis might be used to calculate the probabilities of success or failure. The measure of risk captures the possibility that future events will render the alternative unsuccessful. For example, to make restaurant location decisions, McDonald's can analyze potential customer demographics, traffic patterns, supply logistics, and the local competition and come up with reasonably good forecasts of how successful a restaurant will be in each possible location.[8]

Uncertainty Uncertainty means that managers know which goals they wish to achieve, but information about alternatives and future events is incomplete. Factors that may affect a decision, such as price, production costs, volume, or future interest rates, are difficult to analyze and predict. Managers may have to make assumptions from which to forge the decision even though it will be wrong if the assumptions are incorrect. Former U.S. Treasury Secretary Robert Rubin defined uncertainty as a situation in which even a good decision might produce a bad outcome.[9] Managers face uncertainty every day. Many problems have no clear-cut solution, but managers rely on creativity, judgment, intuition, and experience to craft a response.

TakeaMoment	As a new manager, consider the degree of risk, uncertainty, or ambiguity in a specific decision you face. Develop decision rules for programmed decisions and let other people handle the decisions. Save your time and energy for coping with complex, nonprogrammed decisions.

certainty The situation in which all the information the decision maker needs is fully available.

risk A situation in which a decision has clear-cut goals and good information is available, but the future outcomes associated with each alternative are subject to chance.

uncertainty The situation that occurs when managers know which goals they wish to achieve, but information about alternatives and future events is incomplete.

ambiguity A condition in which the goals to be achieved or the problem to be solved is unclear, alternatives are difficult to define, and information about outcomes is unavailable.

Ambiguity and Conflict Ambiguity is by far the most difficult decision situation. Ambiguity means that the goals to be achieved or the problem to be solved is unclear, alternatives are difficult to define, and information about outcomes is unavailable.[10] Ambiguity is what students would feel if an instructor created student groups, told each group to complete a project, but gave the groups no topic, direction, or guidelines whatsoever. In some situations, managers involved in a decision create ambiguity because they see things differently and disagree about what they want. Managers in different departments often have different priorities and goals for the decision, which can lead to conflicts over decision alternatives. For example, at Rockford Health Services, the decision about implementing a new self-service benefits system wasn't clear-cut. Human resources (HR) managers wanted the system, which would allow employees to manage their own benefits and free up HR employees for more strategic activities, but the high cost of the software licenses conflicted with finance managers' goals of controlling costs. In addition, if HR got the new system, it meant managers in other departments might not get their projects approved.[11]

A highly ambiguous situation can create what is sometimes called a *wicked decision problem*. Wicked decisions are associated with conflicts over goals and decision alternatives, rapidly changing circumstances, fuzzy information, and unclear links among decision elements.[12] Sometimes managers will come up with a "solution" only to realize that they hadn't clearly defined the real problem to begin with.[13] Managers have a difficult time coming to grips with the issues and must conjure up reasonable scenarios in the absence of clear information.

DECISION-MAKING MODELS

The approach managers use to make decisions usually falls into one of three types—the classical model, the administrative model, or the political model. The choice of model depends on the manager's personal preference, whether the decision is programmed or nonprogrammed, and the degree of uncertainty associated with the decision.

Concept Connection   Former NBA Lakers player Magic Johnson is known as a sports star, but he's also a smart businessman. Johnson opened his first twelve-screen cinema in south central Los Angeles while he was still a Lakers player. Despite the **uncertainty** involved in opening businesses in long-ignored urban communities, Johnson established Magic Johnson Enterprises to bring entertainment options and jobs to these areas. Today, the company owns or operates numerous Starbucks, AMC Magic Johnson Theater complexes, Burger Kings, T.G.I. Fridays, 24 Hour Fitness Magic Sport centers, and SodexhoMagic in underserved communities.

The Ideal, Rational Model

The **classical model** of decision making is based on rational economic assumptions and manager beliefs about what ideal decision making should be. This model has arisen within the management literature because managers are expected to make decisions that are economically sensible and in the organization's best economic interests. The four assumptions underlying this model are as follows:

1. The decision maker operates to accomplish goals that are known and agreed on. Problems are precisely formulated and defined.

2. The decision maker strives for conditions of certainty, gathering complete information. All alternatives and the potential results of each are calculated.

3. Criteria for evaluating alternatives are known. The decision maker selects the alternative that will maximize the economic return to the organization.

4. The decision maker is rational and uses logic to assign values, order preferences, evaluate alternatives, and make the decision that will maximize the attainment of organizational goals.

The classical model of decision making is considered to be **normative**, which means it defines how a decision maker *should* make decisions. It does not describe how managers actually make decisions so much as it provides guidelines on how to reach an ideal outcome for the organization. The ideal, rational approach of the classical model is often unattainable by real people in real organizations, but the model has value because it helps decision makers be more rational and not rely entirely on personal preference in making decisions.

The classical model is most useful when applied to programmed decisions and to decisions characterized by certainty or risk because relevant information is available and probabilities can be calculated. For example, new analytical software programs automate many programmed decisions, such as freezing the account of a customer who has failed to make payments, determining the cell phone service plan that is most appropriate for a particular customer, or sorting insurance claims so that cases are handled most efficiently.[14] Airlines use automated systems to optimize seat pricing, flight scheduling, and crew assignment decisions. Retailers such as the Home Depot and Gap use software programs to analyze sales data and decide when, where, and how much to mark down prices. Many companies use systems that capture information about customers to help managers evaluate risks and make credit decisions.[15]

The growth of quantitative decision techniques that use computers has expanded the use of the classical approach. Quantitative techniques include such things as decision trees, payoff matrices, break-even analysis, linear programming, forecasting,

classical model A decision-making model based on the assumption that managers should make logical decisions that will be in the organization's best economic interests.

normative An approach that defines how a decision maker should make decisions and provides guidelines for reaching an ideal outcome for the organization.

and operations research models. Southwest Airlines uses quantitative models to help retain its position as the industry's low-cost leader.

Southwest's wacky, people-oriented culture has often been cited as a key factor in the company's success. But managers point out that keeping a hawk's eye on costs is just as much a part of the culture as silliness and fun.

One way managers keep a lid on costs is by applying technology to support decision making. Consider the use of a new breed of simulation software to help make decisions about the airline's freight operations. BiosGroup, a joint venture between Santa Fe Institute biologist Stuart Kauffman and the consulting firm Cap Gemini Ernst & Young, uses adaptive, agent-based computer modeling to help companies solve complex operations problems. For the Southwest project, the computer simulation model represented individual baggage handlers and other employees; the model was created to see how thousands of individual day-to-day decisions and interactions determined the behavior of the airline's overall freight operation.

A BiosGroup team spent many hours interviewing all the employees whose jobs related to freight handling. Then, they programmed the computer to simulate the people in the freight house who accepted a customer's package, those who figured out which flight the package should go on, those on the ramp who were loading the planes, and so forth. When the computer ran a simulation of a week's worth of freight operations, various aspects of operations were measured—such as how many times employees had to load and unload cargo or how often freight had to be stored overnight. The simulation indicated that, rather than unloading cargo from incoming flights and putting it on the next direct flight to its destination, Southwest would be better off to just let the freight take the long way around. Paradoxically, this approach turned out to usually get the freight to its destination faster and saved the time and cost of unloading and reloading.

Southwest managers lost no time in implementing the decision to change the freight handling system. By applying technology to find a more efficient way of doing things, Southwest is saving an estimated $10 million over five years.[16]

How Managers Actually Make Decisions

Another approach to decision making, called the **administrative model**, is considered to be **descriptive**, meaning that it describes how managers actually make decisions in complex situations rather than dictating how they *should* make decisions according to a theoretical ideal. The administrative model recognizes the human and environmental limitations that affect the degree to which managers can pursue a rational decision-making process. In difficult situations, such as those characterized by nonprogrammed decisions, uncertainty, and ambiguity, managers are typically unable to make economically rational decisions even if they want to.[17]

Bounded Rationality and Satisficing The administrative model of decision making is based on the work of Herbert A. Simon. Simon proposed two concepts that were instrumental in shaping the administrative model: bounded rationality and satisficing. **Bounded rationality** means that people have limits, or boundaries, on how rational they can be. The organization is incredibly complex, and managers have the time and ability to process only a limited amount of information with which to make decisions.[18] Because managers do not have the time or cognitive ability to process complete information about complex decisions, they must satisfice. **Satisficing** means that decision makers choose the first solution alternative that satisfies minimal decision criteria. Rather than pursuing all alternatives to identify the single solution that will maximize economic returns, managers will opt for the first solution that appears to solve the problem, even if better solutions are presumed to exist. The decision maker cannot justify the time and expense of obtaining complete information.[19]

administrative model A decision-making model that describes how managers actually make decisions in situations characterized by nonprogrammed decisions, uncertainty, and ambiguity.

descriptive An approach that describes how managers actually make decisions rather than how they should make decisions according to a theoretical ideal.

bounded rationality The concept that people have the time and cognitive ability to process only a limited amount of information on which to base decisions.

satisficing To choose the first solution alternative that satisfies minimal decision criteria, regardless of whether better solutions are presumed to exist.

As a new manager, choose the right decision approach. Use the classical model when problems are clear-cut, goals are agreed on, and clear information is available. For the classical model, use analytical procedures, including new software programs, to calculate the potential results of each alternative. When goals are vague or conflicting, decision time is limited, and information is unclear, use bounded rationality, satisficing, and intuition for decision making.

TakeaMoment

Managers sometimes generate alternatives for complex problems only until they find one they believe will work. For example, several years ago, then-CEO William Smithburg of Quaker attempted to thwart takeover attempts but had limited options. He satisficed with a quick decision to acquire Snapple, thinking he could use the debt acquired in the deal to discourage a takeover. The acquisition had the potential to solve the problem at hand; thus, Smithburg looked no further for possibly better alternatives.[20]

The administrative model relies on assumptions different from those of the classical model and focuses on organizational factors that influence individual decisions. According to the administrative model:

1. Decision goals often are vague, conflicting, and lack consensus among managers. Managers often are unaware of problems or opportunities that exist in the organization.

2. Rational procedures are not always used, and, when they are, they are confined to a simplistic view of the problem that does not capture the complexity of real organizational events.

3. Managers' searches for alternatives are limited because of human, information, and resource constraints.

4. Most managers settle for a satisficing rather than a maximizing solution, partly because they have limited information and partly because they have only vague criteria for what constitutes a maximizing solution.

intuition The immediate comprehension of a decision situation based on past experience but without conscious thought.

Intuition Another aspect of administrative decision making is intuition. **Intuition** represents a quick apprehension of a decision situation based on past experience but without conscious thought.[21] Intuitive decision making is not arbitrary or irrational because it is based on years of practice and hands-on experience that enable managers to quickly identify solutions without going through painstaking computations. In today's fast-paced business environment, intuition plays an increasingly important role in decision making. A survey of managers conducted by Christian and Timbers found that nearly half of executives say they rely more on intuition than on rational analysis to run their companies.[22]

Psychologists and neuroscientists have studied how people make good decisions using their intuition under extreme time pressure and uncertainty.[23] Good intuitive decision making is based on an ability to recognize patterns at lightning speed. When people have a depth of experience and knowledge in a particular area, the right decision often comes quickly and effortlessly as a recognition of information that has been largely forgotten by the

© STAN GODLEWSKI PHOTOGRAPHY

Concept Connection "Lots of people hear what I'm doing and think, 'That's a crazy idea!'" says Russell Simmons. The successful entrepreneur, who heads the New York-based media firm Rush Communications Inc., has relied on his **intuition** to build a half-billion dollar empire on one profitable "crazy idea" after another. It all began with his belief that he could go mainstream with the vibrant rap music he heard in African American neighborhoods. In 1983, he started the pioneering hip-hop Def Jam record label, launching the careers of Beastie Boys, LL Cool J, and Run-DMC, among others. He's since moved on to successful ventures in fashion, media, consumer products, and finance.

conscious mind. For example, firefighters make decisions by recognizing what is typical or abnormal about a fire, based on their experiences. Similarly, in the business world, managers continuously perceive and process information that they may not consciously be aware of, and their base of knowledge and experience helps them make decisions that may be characterized by uncertainty and ambiguity.

However, intuitive decisions don't always work out, and managers should take care to apply intuition under the right circumstances and in the right way rather than considering it a magical way to make important decisions.[24] Managers may walk a fine line between two extremes: on the one hand, making arbitrary decisions without careful study; and on the other, relying obsessively on rational analysis. One is not better than the other, and managers need to take a balanced approach by considering both rationality and intuition as important components of effective decision making.[25]

TakeaMoment | **Do you tend to analyze things or rely on gut feelings when it comes to making an important decision? Complete the New Manager Self-Test below to find out your predominant approach.**

New ManagerSelf-Test

Making Important Decisions

How do you make important personal decisions? To find out, think about a time when you made an important career decision or made a large purchase or investment. To what extent do each of the words below describe how you reached the final decision? Please check <u>five</u> words below that best describe how you made your final choice.

1. Logic _____

2. Inner knowing _____

3. Data _____

4. Felt sense _____

5. Facts _____

6. Instincts _____

7. Concepts _____

8. Hunch _____

9. Reason _____

10. Feelings _____

SCORING AND INTERPRETATION. The odd-numbered items pertain to a linear decision style and the even-numbered items pertain to a nonlinear decision approach. Linear means using logical *rationality* to make decisions; nonlinear means to use primarily *intuition* to make decisions. Of the five words you chose, how many represent rationality versus intuition? If all five words are either linear or nonlinear, then that is clearly your dominant decision approach. If four words are either linear or nonlinear, then that approach would be considered your preference. Rationality approach means a preference for the *rational model* of decision making as described in the text. Intuition approach suggests a preference for the *satisficing* and *intuition* models.

SOURCE: Charles M. Vance, Kevin S. Groves, Yongsun Paik, and Herb Kindler, "Understanding and Measuring Linear-Nonlinear Thinking Style for Enhanced Management Education and Professional Practice" *Academy of Management Learning & Education* 6, no. 2 (2007): 167–185.

Political Model

The third model of decision making is useful for making nonprogrammed decisions when conditions are uncertain, information is limited, and there are manager conflicts about what goals to pursue or what course of action to take. Most organizational decisions involve many managers who are pursuing different goals, and they have to talk with one another to share information and reach an agreement. Managers often engage in coalition building for making complex organizational decisions. A **coalition** is an informal alliance among managers who support a specific goal. *Coalition building* is the process of forming alliances among managers. In other words, a manager who supports a specific alternative, such as increasing the corporation's growth by acquiring another company, talks informally to other executives and tries to persuade them to support the decision. Without a coalition, a powerful individual or group could derail the decision-making process. Coalition building gives several managers an opportunity to contribute to decision making, enhancing their commitment to the alternative that is ultimately adopted.[26]

The political model closely resembles the real environment in which most managers and decision makers operate. For example, interviews with CEOs in high-tech industries found that they strived to use some type of rational process in making decisions, but the way they actually decided things was through a complex interaction with other managers, subordinates, environmental factors, and organizational events.[27] Decisions are complex and involve many people, information is often ambiguous, and disagreement and conflict over problems and solutions are normal. The political model begins with four basic assumptions:

1. Organizations are made up of groups with diverse interests, goals, and values. Managers disagree about problem priorities and may not understand or share the goals and interests of other managers.

2. Information is ambiguous and incomplete. The attempt to be rational is limited by the complexity of many problems as well as personal and organizational constraints.

3. Managers do not have the time, resources, or mental capacity to identify all dimensions of the problem and process all relevant information. Managers talk to each other and exchange viewpoints to gather information and reduce ambiguity.

4. Managers engage in the push and pull of debate to decide goals and discuss alternatives. Decisions are the result of bargaining and discussion among coalition members.

An example of the political model was when AOL chief executive Jonathan Miller built a coalition to support the development of a Yahoo-like free Web site. Opposition to offering AOL's rich content for free was strong, but Miller talked with other executives and formed a coalition that supported the move as the best way to rejuvenate the declining AOL in the shifting Internet service business. The decision proved to be a turning point, making AOL once more a relevant force on the Web and enticing tech titans such as Google and Microsoft as potential partners.[28]

The key dimensions of the classical, administrative, and political models are listed in Exhibit 8.2. Research into decision-making procedures found rational, classical

coalition An informal alliance among managers who support a specific goal.

EXHIBIT | **8.2**

Characteristics of Classical, Administrative, and Political Decision-Making Models

Classical Model	Administrative Model	Political Model
Clear-cut problem and goals	Vague problem and goals	Pluralistic; conflicting goals
Condition of certainty	Condition of uncertainty	Condition of uncertainty/ambiguity
Full information about alternatives and their outcomes	Limited information about alternatives and their outcomes	Inconsistent viewpoints; ambiguous information
Rational choice by individual for maximizing outcomes	Satisficing choice for resolving problem using intuition	Bargaining and discussion among coalition members

3 Planning

procedures to be associated with high performance for organizations in stable environments. However, administrative and political decision-making procedures and intuition have been associated with high performance in unstable environments in which decisions must be made rapidly and under more difficult conditions.[29]

TakeaMoment | As a new manager, use your political skills to reach a decision in the midst of disagreement about goals or problem solutions. Talk with other managers or employees and negotiate to gain support for the goal or solution you favor. Learn to compromise and to support others when appropriate.

© DON MURRAY/GETTY IMAGES

Concept Connection Jon Bon Jovi is a rock star and entrepreneur who co-owns the Philadelphia Soul, an expansion team of the Arena Football League (AFL). Bon Jovi and his partner, businessman Craig Spencer, spotted an **opportunity** to capitalize on Bon Jovi's personality and fame, as well as his savvy marketing skills, by acquiring the franchise. Bon Jovi personally made decisions such as naming the team the Soul (because "anybody can have soul," he says) and creating a mascot (the Soul Man), and he is actively involved in decisions regarding everything from advertising budgets to where to place the autograph tables after a game.

problem A situation in which organizational accomplishments have failed to meet established goals.

opportunity A situation in which managers see potential organizational accomplishments that exceed current goals.

diagnosis The step in the decision-making process in which managers analyze underlying causal factors associated with the decision situation.

DECISION-MAKING STEPS

Whether a decision is programmed or nonprogrammed and regardless of managers' choice of the classical, administrative, or political model of decision making, six steps typically are associated with effective decision processes. These steps are summarized in Exhibit 8.3.

Recognition of Decision Requirement

Managers confront a decision requirement in the form of either a problem or an opportunity. A **problem** occurs when organizational accomplishment is less than established goals. Some aspect of performance is unsatisfactory. An **opportunity** exists when managers see potential accomplishment that exceeds specified current goals. Managers see the possibility of enhancing performance beyond current levels.

Awareness of a problem or opportunity is the first step in the decision sequence and requires surveillance of the internal and external environment for issues that merit executive attention.[30] This process resembles the military concept of gathering intelligence. Managers scan the world around them to determine whether the organization is satisfactorily progressing toward its goals.

Some information comes from periodic financial reports, performance reports, and other sources that are designed to discover problems before they become too serious. Managers also take advantage of informal sources. They talk to other managers, gather opinions on how things are going, and seek advice on which problems should be tackled or which opportunities embraced.[31] Recognizing decision requirements is difficult because it often means integrating bits and pieces of information in novel ways. For example, the failure of U.S. intelligence leaders to recognize the imminent threat of Al Qaeda prior to September 11, 2001, terrorist attacks has been attributed partly to the lack of systems that could help leaders put together myriad snippets of information that pointed to the problem.[32]

Diagnosis and Analysis of Causes

Once a problem or opportunity comes to a manager's attention, the understanding of the situation should be refined. **Diagnosis** is the step in the decision-making process in which managers analyze underlying causal factors associated with the decision situation.

Kepner and Tregoe, who conducted extensive studies of manager decision making, recommend that managers ask a series of questions to specify underlying causes, including the following:

- What is the state of disequilibrium affecting us?

- When did it occur?

EXHIBIT | 8.3

Six Steps in the Managerial
Decision-Making Process

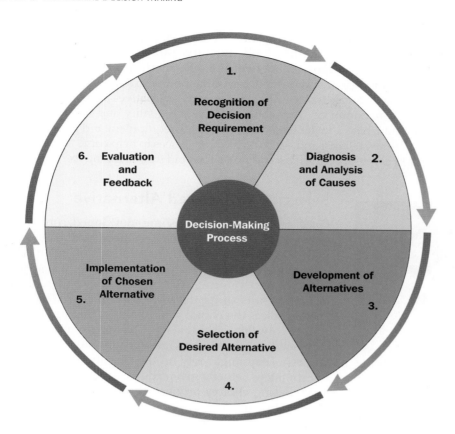

- Where did it occur?
- How did it occur?
- To whom did it occur?
- What is the urgency of the problem?
- What is the interconnectedness of events?
- What result came from which activity?[33]

Such questions help specify what actually happened and why. Managers at Avon are struggling to diagnose the underlying factors in the company's recent troubles. After six straight years of growing sales and earnings, revenues sagged, overhead spiked, and the stock price plummeted. CEO Andrea Jung and other top managers are examining the myriad problems facing Avon, tracing the pattern of the decline, and looking at the interconnectedness of issues such as changing consumer interests, tight government regulations in developing countries, decreases in incentives for direct sales representatives, an approach of handling manufacturing and marketing in each country independently, preventing the company from achieving economies of scale, and weak internal communications that allowed problems to go unnoticed.[34]

Development of Alternatives

The next stage is to generate possible alternative solutions that will respond to the needs of the situation and correct the underlying causes.

For a programmed decision, feasible alternatives are easy to identify and in fact usually are already available within the organization's rules and procedures. Non-programmed decisions, however, require developing new courses of action that will meet the company's needs. For decisions made under conditions of high uncertainty, managers may develop only one or two custom solutions that will satisfice for handling the problem. However, studies find that limiting the search for alternatives is a primary cause of decision failure in organizations.[35]

Decision alternatives can be thought of as tools for reducing the difference between the organization's current and desired performance. For example, to improve sales at fast-food giant McDonald's, executives considered alternatives such as using mystery shoppers and unannounced inspections to improve quality and service, motivating demoralized franchisees to get them to invest in new equipment and programs, taking R&D out of the test kitchen and encouraging franchisees to help come up with successful new menu items, and closing some stores to avoid cannibalizing its own sales.[36]

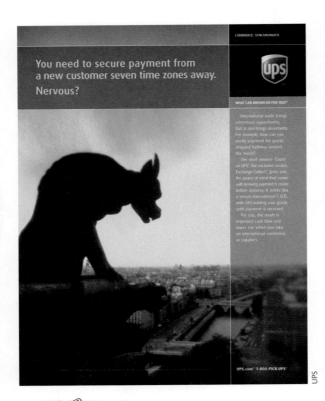

Concept Connection UPS knows many businesses have a low **risk propensity** when it comes to matters affecting their cash flow. The company's UPS Capital Insurance division reduces customers' risk of delayed payments through a variety of trade insurance policies. This advertisement for Exchange Collect promises peace of mind for companies dealing with international customers or suppliers. The service works like a secure international C.O.D., with UPS securing payment on behalf of the customer before delivering goods. For UPS customers, the results are improved cash flow and less risk.

Selection of Desired Alternative

Once feasible alternatives are developed, one must be selected. The decision choice is the selection of the most promising of several alternative courses of action. The best alternative is one in which the solution best fits the overall goals and values of the organization and achieves the desired results using the fewest resources.[37] The manager tries to select the choice with the least amount of risk and uncertainty. Because some risk is inherent for most nonprogrammed decisions, managers try to gauge prospects for success. They might rely on their intuition and experience to estimate whether a given course of action is likely to succeed. Basing choices on overall goals and values can also effectively guide managers' selection of alternatives. Recall from Chapter 3 Valero Energy's decision to keep everyone on the payroll after Hurricane Katrina hit the Gulf Coast, while other refineries shut down and laid off workers. For Valero managers, the choice was easy based on values of putting employees first. Valero's values-based decision making helped the company zoom from number 23 to number 3 on *Fortune* magazine's list of best companies to work for—and enabled Valero to get back to business weeks faster than competitors.[38]

Choosing among alternatives also depends on managers' personality factors and willingness to accept risk and uncertainty. **Risk propensity** is the willingness to undertake risk with the opportunity of gaining an increased payoff. The level of risk a manager is willing to accept will influence the analysis of cost and benefits to be derived from any decision. Consider the situations in Exhibit 8.4. In each situation, which alternative would you choose? A person with a low risk propensity would tend to take assured moderate returns by going for a tie score, building a domestic plant, or pursuing a career as a physician. A risk taker would go for the victory, build a plant in a foreign country, or embark on an acting career.

Implementation of Chosen Alternative

risk propensity The willingness to undertake risk with the opportunity of gaining an increased payoff.

implementation The step in the decision-making process that involves using managerial, administrative, and persuasive abilities to translate the chosen alternative into action.

The **implementation** stage involves the use of managerial, administrative, and persuasive abilities to ensure that the chosen alternative is carried out. This step is similar to the idea of strategy execution described in Chapter 7. The ultimate success of the chosen alternative depends on whether it can be translated into action.[39] Sometimes an alternative never becomes reality because managers lack the resources or energy needed to make things happen. Implementation may require discussion with people affected by the decision. Communication, motivation, and leadership skills must be used to see that the decision is carried out. When employees see that

For each of the following decisions, which alternative would you choose?

1. In the final seconds of a game with the college's traditional rival, the coach of a college football team may choose a play that has a 95 percent chance of producing a tie score or one with a 30 percent chance of leading to victory or to sure defeat if it fails.

2. The president of a Canadian company must decide whether to build a new plant within Canada that has a 90 percent chance of producing a modest return on investment or to build it in a foreign country with an unstable political history. The latter alternative has a 40 percent chance of failing, but the returns would be enormous if it succeeded.

3. A college senior with considerable acting talent must choose a career. She has the opportunity to go on to medical school and become a physician, a career in which she is 80 percent likely to succeed. She would rather be an actress but realizes that the opportunity for success is only 20 percent.

EXHIBIT | 8.4

Decision Alternatives with Different Levels of Risk

managers follow up on their decisions by tracking implementation success, they are more committed to positive action.[40]

Evaluation and Feedback

In the evaluation stage of the decision process, decision makers gather information that tells them how well the decision was implemented and whether it was effective in achieving its goals. Feedback is important because decision making is a continuous, never-ending process. Decision making is not completed when a manager or board of directors votes yes or no. Feedback provides decision makers with information that can precipitate a new decision cycle. The decision may fail, thus generating a new analysis of the problem, evaluation of alternatives, and selection of a new alternative. Many big problems are solved by trying several alternatives in sequence, each providing modest improvement. Feedback is the part of monitoring that assesses whether a new decision needs to be made.

To illustrate the overall decision-making process, including evaluation and feedback, consider the decision to introduce a new deodorant at Tom's of Maine.

Innovative Way

Tom's of Maine

Tom's of Maine, known for its all-natural personal hygiene products, saw an opportunity to expand its line with a new natural deodorant. However, the opportunity quickly became a problem when the deodorant worked only half of the time with half of the customers who used it, and its all-recyclable plastic dials were prone to breakage.

The problem of the failed deodorant led founder Tom Chappell and other managers to analyze and diagnose what went wrong. They finally determined that the company's product development process had run amok. The same group of merry product developers was responsible from conception to launch of the product. They were so attached to the product that they failed to test it properly or consider potential problems, becoming instead "a mutual admiration society." Managers considered several alternatives for solving the problem. The decision to publicly admit the problem and recall the deodorant was an easy one for Chappell, who runs his company on principles of fairness and honesty. Not only did the company apologize to its customers, but it also listened to their complaints and suggestions. Chappell himself helped answer calls and letters. Even though the recall cost the company $400,000 and led to a stream of negative publicity, it ultimately helped improve relationships with customers.

Evaluation and feedback also led Tom's of Maine to set up *acorn groups,* from which it hopes mighty oaks of successful products will grow. Acorn groups are cross-departmental teams that will shepherd new products from beginning to end. The cross-functional teams are a mechanism for catching problems—and new opportunities—that ordinarily would be missed. They pass on their ideas and findings to senior managers and the product-development team.

Tom's was able to turn a problem into an opportunity, thanks to evaluation and feedback. Not only did the disaster ultimately help the company solidify relationships with customers, but it also led to a formal mechanism for learning and sharing ideas—something the company did not have before.[41]

Tom's of Maine's decision illustrates all the decision steps, and the process ultimately ended in success. Strategic decisions always contain some risk, but feedback and follow-up decisions can help get companies back on track. By learning from their decision mistakes, managers can turn problems into opportunities.

PERSONAL DECISION FRAMEWORK

Imagine you were a manager at Tom's of Maine, the Boeing Company, a local movie theater, or the public library. How would you go about making important decisions that might shape the future of your department or company? So far we have discussed a number of factors that affect how managers make decisions. For example, decisions may be programmed or nonprogrammed, situations are characterized by various levels of uncertainty, and managers may use the classical, administrative, or political model of decision making. In addition, the decision-making process follows six recognized steps.

However, not all managers go about making decisions in the same way. In fact, significant differences distinguish the ways in which individual managers may approach problems and make decisions concerning them. These differences can be explained by the concept of personal **decision styles**. Exhibit 8.5 illustrates the role of personal style in the decision-making process. Personal decision style refers to distinctions among people with respect to how they evaluate problems, generate alternatives, and make choices. Research has identified four major decision styles: directive, analytical, conceptual, and behavioral.[42]

1. The *directive style* is used by people who prefer simple, clear-cut solutions to problems. Managers who use this style often make decisions quickly because they do not like to deal with a lot of information and may consider only one or two alternatives. People who prefer the directive style generally are efficient and rational and prefer to rely on existing rules or procedures for making decisions.

2. Managers with an *analytical style* like to consider complex solutions based on as much data as they can gather. These individuals carefully consider alternatives and often base their decisions on objective, rational data from management control systems and other sources. They search for the best possible decision based on the information available.

3. People who tend toward a *conceptual style* also like to consider a broad amount of information. However, they are more socially oriented than those with an analytical style and like to talk to others about the problem and possible alternatives for solving it. Managers using a conceptual style consider many broad alternatives, rely on information from both people and systems, and like to solve problems creatively.

4. The *behavioral style* is often the style adopted by managers having a deep concern for others as individuals. Managers using this style like to talk to people one-on-one and understand their feelings about the problem and the effect of a given

decision styles Differences among people with respect to how they perceive problems and make decisions.

EXHIBIT | 8.5   Personal Decision Framework

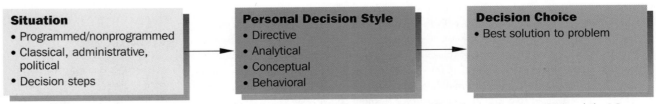

SOURCE: Based on A. J. Rowe, J. D. Boulgaides, and M. R. McGrath, **Managerial Decision Making** (Chicago: Science Research Associates, 1984); and Alan J. Rowe and Richard O. Mason, **Managing with Style: A Guide to Understanding, Assessing, and Improving Your Decision Making** (San Francisco: Jossey-Bass, 1987).

decision on them. People with a behavioral style usually are concerned with the personal development of others and may make decisions that help others achieve their goals.

To learn more about how you rate on these four styles, go to the experiential exercise on pages 232–233 that evaluates your personal decision style. | TakeaMoment

Many managers have a dominant decision style. One example is Jeff Zucker at NBC Entertainment. Zucker uses a primarily conceptual style, which makes him well suited to the television industry. He consults with dozens of programmers about possible new shows and likes to consider many broad alternatives before making decisions.[43] However, managers frequently use several different styles or a combination of styles in making the varied decisions they confront daily. A manager might use a directive style for deciding on which printing company to use for new business cards, yet shift to a more conceptual style when handling an interdepartmental conflict. The most effective managers are able to shift among styles as needed to meet the situation. Being aware of one's dominant decision style can help a manager avoid making critical mistakes when his or her usual style may be inappropriate to the problem at hand.

WHY DO MANAGERS MAKE BAD DECISIONS?

Managers are faced with a relentless demand for decisions, from solving minor problems to implementing major strategic changes. Even the best manager will make mistakes, but managers can increase their percentage of good decisions by understanding some of the factors that cause people to make bad ones. Most bad decisions are errors in judgment that originate in the human mind's limited capacity and in the natural biases managers display during decision making. Awareness of the following six biases can help managers make more enlightened choices:[44]

1. *Being influenced by initial impressions.* When considering decisions, the mind often gives disproportionate weight to the first information it receives. These initial impressions, statistics, or estimates act as an anchor to our subsequent thoughts and judgments. Anchors can be as simple as a random comment by a colleague or a statistic read in a newspaper. Past events and trends also act as anchors. For example, in business, managers frequently look at the previous year's sales when estimating sales for the coming year. Giving too much weight to the past can lead to poor forecasts and misguided decisions.

2. *Justifying past decisions.* Many managers fall into the trap of making choices that justify their past decisions, even if those decisions no longer seem valid. Consider managers who invest tremendous time and energy into improving the performance of a problem employee whom they now realize should never have been hired in the first place. Another example is when a manager continues to pour money into a failing project, hoping to turn things around. People don't like to make mistakes, so they continue to support a flawed decision in an effort to justify or correct the past.

3. *Seeing what you want to see.* People frequently look for information that supports their existing instinct or point of view and avoid information that contradicts it. This bias affects where managers look for information, as well as how they interpret the information they find. People tend to give too much weight to supporting information

© COPYRIGHT AP IMAGES

Concept Connection Facebook founder Mark Zuckerberg stepped into a hole when he decided to retrofit his site with a feature named Beacon. Beacon was designed to pass information about customer Web activity to participating vendors, providing a new source of revenue for Facebook. But when Beacon was implemented, Facebook was slammed with complaints about privacy intrusion and a lawsuit. What caused this poor decision? Based on the wild popularity of his social network site and his rapid rise in the business world, Zuckerbeg was probably **overly confident** about how users would receive Beacon. Facebook management quickly decided to make it easier for customers to opt-out of the service.

and too little to information that conflicts with their established viewpoints. It is important for managers to be honest with themselves about their motives and to examine all the evidence with equal rigor. Having a devil's advocate is also a good way to avoid seeing only what you want to see.

4. *Perpetuating the status quo.* Managers may base decisions on what has worked in the past and fail to explore new options, dig for additional information, or investigate new technologies. For example, DuPont clung to its cash cow, nylon, despite growing evidence in the scientific community that a new product, polyester, was superior for tire cords. Celanese, a relatively small competitor, blew DuPont out of the water by exploiting this new evidence, quickly capturing 75 percent of the tire market.

5. *Being influenced by problem framing.* The decision response of a manager can be influenced by the mere wording of a problem. For example, consider a manager faced with a decision about salvaging the cargo of three barges that sank off the coast of Alaska. If managers are given the option of approving plan A that has a 100 percent chance of saving the cargo of one of the three barges, worth $200,000, or plan B that has a one-third chance of saving the cargo of all three barges, worth $600,000 and a two-thirds chance of saving nothing, most managers choose option A. The same problem with a negative frame would give managers a choice of selecting plan C that has a 100 percent chance of losing two of the three cargoes, worth $400,000 or plan D that has a two-thirds chance of losing all three cargoes but a one-third chance of losing no cargo. With this framing, most managers choose option D. Because both problems are identical, the decision choice depends strictly on how the problem is framed.

6. *Overconfidence.* Most people overestimate their ability to predict uncertain outcomes. Before making a decision, managers have unrealistic expectations of their ability to understand the risk and make the right choice. Overconfidence is greatest when answering questions of moderate to extreme difficulty. For example, when people are asked to define quantities about which they have little direct knowledge ("What was Wal-Mart's 2007 revenue?" "What was the market value of Google as of March 14, 2008?"), they overestimate their accuracy. Evidence of overconfidence is illustrated in cases in which subjects were so certain of an answer that they assigned odds of 1,000 to 1 of being correct but in fact were correct only about 85 percent of the time. When uncertainty is high, managers may unrealistically expect that they can successfully predict outcomes and hence select the wrong alternative.

TakeaMoment

As a new manager, be aware of biases that can cloud your judgment and lead to bad decisions. The Manager's Shoptalk describes a new way of thinking about decision making that can help you avoid decision traps such as overconfidence, seeing only what you want to see, or justifying past decisions.

INNOVATIVE GROUP DECISION MAKING

The ability to make fast, widely supported, high-quality decisions on a frequent basis is a critical skill in today's fast-moving organizations.[45] In many industries, the rate of competitive and technological change is so extreme that opportunities are fleeting, clear and complete information is seldom available, and the cost of a slow decision means lost business or even company failure. Do these factors mean managers should make the majority of decisions on their own? No. The rapid pace of the business environment calls for just the opposite—that is, for people throughout the organization to be involved in decision making and have the information, skills, and freedom they need to respond immediately to problems and questions.

Manager's Shoptalk

Evidence-Based Management

At a time when decision making is so important, many managers do not know how to make a good choice among alternatives. Using evidence-based decision making can help. Evidence-based decision making simply means a commitment to make more informed and intelligent decisions based on the best available facts and evidence. It means being aware of our biases and seeking and examining evidence with rigor. Managers practice evidence-based decision making by being careful and thoughtful rather than carelessly relying on assumptions, past experience, rules of thumb, or intuition.

Here are some ideas for applying evidence-based decision making:

- *Demand Evidence.* Educate people throughout the organization to use data and facts to the extent possible to inform their decisions. Many manager problems are uncertain, and hard facts and data aren't available, but by always asking for evidence, managers can avoid relying on faulty assumptions. Managers at one computer company kept blaming the marketing staff for the trouble the company had selling their products in retail stores. Then, members of the senior team posed as mystery shoppers and tried to buy the company's computers. They kept encountering sales clerks that tried to dissuade them from purchasing the firm's products, citing the excessive price, clunky appearance, and poor customer service. Real-world observations told them something that was very different from what they assumed.

- *Practice the Five Whys.* One simple way to get people to think more broadly and deeply about problems rather than going with a superficial understanding and a first response is called the Five Whys. For every problem, managers ask "Why?" not just once, but five times. The first *why* generally produces a superficial explanation for the problem, and each subsequent *why* probes deeper into the causes of the problem and potential solutions.

- *Do a Post-Mortem.* A technique many companies have adopted from the U.S. Army to encourage examination of the evidence and continuous learning is the after-action review. After implementation of any significant decision, managers evaluate what worked, what didn't, and how to do things better. Many problems are solved by trial and error. For example, post-mortem reviews of decisions regarding attacks from roadside bombs in Iraq led soldiers to suggest implementation of an overall counterinsurgency strategy rather than relying so much on technology.

- *Balance Decisiveness and Humility.* The best decision makers have a healthy appreciation for what they don't know. They're always questioning and encouraging others to question their knowledge and assumptions. They foster a culture of inquiry, observation, and experimentation.

SOURCES: Based on Jeffrey Pfeffer and Robert I. Sutton, "Evidence-Based Management," *Harvard Business Review* (January 2006): 62–74; Rosemary Stewart, *Evidence-based Decision Making* (Abingdon, UK: Radcliffe Publishing, 2002); Joshua Klayman, Richard P. Larrick, and Chip Heath, "Organizational Repairs," *Across the Board* (February 2000): 26–31; and Peter Eisler, Blake Morrison, and Tom Vanden Brook, "Strategy That's Making Iraq Safer Was Snubbed for Years," *USA Today*, December 19, 2007.

3 Planning

Managers do make some decisions as individuals, but decision makers more often are part of a group. Indeed, major decisions in the business world rarely are made entirely by an individual.

Start with Brainstorming

Brainstorming uses a face-to-face interactive group to spontaneously suggest a wide range of alternatives for decision making. The keys to effective brainstorming are that people can build on one another's ideas; all ideas are acceptable, no matter how crazy they seem; and criticism and evaluation are not allowed. The goal is to generate as many ideas as possible. Brainstorming has been found to be highly effective for

brainstorming A technique that uses a face-to-face group to spontaneously suggest a broad range of alternatives for decision making.

quickly generating a wide range of alternate solutions to a problem, but it does have some drawbacks. For one thing, people in a group often want to conform to what others are saying, a problem sometimes referred to as *groupthink*. Others may be concerned about pleasing the boss or impressing colleagues. In addition, many creative people simply have social inhibitions that limit their participation in a group session or make it difficult to come up with ideas in a group setting. In fact, one study found that when four people are asked to "brainstorm" individually, they typically come up with twice as many ideas as a group of four brainstorming together.

One recent approach, electronic brainstorming, takes advantage of the group approach while overcoming some disadvantages. **Electronic brainstorming**, sometimes called *brainwriting*, brings people together in an interactive group over a computer network.[46] One member writes an idea, another reads it and adds other ideas, and so on. Studies show that electronic brainstorming generates about 40 percent more ideas than individuals brainstorming alone, and 25 to 200 percent more ideas than regular brainstorming groups, depending on group size.[47] Why? Because the process is anonymous, the sky's the limit in terms of what people feel free to say. People can write down their ideas immediately, avoiding the possibility that a good idea might slip away while the person is waiting for a chance to speak in a face-to-face group. Social inhibitions and concerns are avoided, which typically allows for a broader range of participation. Another advantage is that electronic brainstorming can potentially be done with groups made up of employees from around the world, further increasing the diversity of alternatives.

Engage in Rigorous Debate

An important key to better decision making is to encourage a rigorous debate of the issue at hand.[48] Good managers recognize that constructive conflict based on divergent points of view can bring a problem into focus, clarify people's ideas, stimulate creative thinking, create a broader understanding of issues and alternatives, and improve decision quality.[49] Chuck Knight, the former CEO of Emerson Electric, always sparked heated debates during strategic planning meetings. Knight believed rigorous debate gave people a clearer picture of the competitive landscape and forced managers to look at all sides of an issue, helping them reach better decisions.[50]

Stimulating rigorous debate can be done in several ways. One way is by ensuring that the group is diverse in terms of age and gender, functional area of expertise, hierarchical level, and experience with the business. Some groups assign a **devil's advocate**, who has the role of challenging the assumptions and assertions made by the group.[51] The devil's advocate may force the group to rethink its approach to the problem and avoid reaching premature conclusions. Jeffrey McKeever, CEO of MicroAge, often plays the devil's advocate, changing his position in the middle of a debate to ensure that other executives don't just go along with his opinions.[52]

Another approach is to have group members develop as many alternatives as they can as quickly as they can.[53] It allows the team to work with multiple alternatives and encourages people to advocate ideas they might not prefer simply to encourage debate. Still another way to encourage constructive conflict is to use a technique called **point-counterpoint**, which breaks a decision-making group into two subgroups and assigns them different, often competing responsibilities.[54] The groups then develop and exchange proposals and discuss and debate the various options until they arrive at a common set of understandings and recommendations.

Avoid Groupthink

It is important for managers to remember that some disagreement and conflict is much healthier than blind agreement. Pressures for conformity exist in almost any group, and particularly when people in a group like one another they tend to avoid anything that might create disharmony. **Groupthink** refers to the tendency of people in groups to suppress contrary opinions.[55] When people slip into groupthink, the desire for

electronic brainstorming
Bringing people together in an interactive group over a computer network to suggest alternatives; sometimes called *brainwriting*.

devil's advocate A decision-making technique in which an individual is assigned the role of challenging the assumptions and assertions made by the group to prevent premature consensus.

point-counterpoint A decision-making technique in which people are assigned to express competing points of view.

groupthink The tendency of people in groups to suppress contrary opinions.

harmony outweighs concerns over decision quality. Group members emphasize maintaining unity rather than realistically challenging problems and alternatives. People censor their personal opinions and are reluctant to criticize the opinions of others.

Author and scholar Jerry Harvey coined the related term *Abilene paradox* to illustrate the hidden pressures for conformity that can exist in groups.[56] Harvey tells the story of how members of his extended family sat sweltering on the porch in 104-degree heat in a small town about 50 miles from Abilene, Texas. When someone suggested driving to a café in Abilene, everyone went along with the idea, even though the car was not air conditioned. Everyone was miserable and returned home exhausted and irritable. Later, each person admitted that they hadn't wanted to make the trip and thought it was a ridiculous idea. They only went because they thought the others wanted to go.

Know When to Bail

In a fast-paced environment, good managers encourage risk taking and learning from mistakes, but they also aren't hesitant to pull the plug on something that isn't working. Research has found that managers and organizations often continue to invest time and money in a solution despite strong evidence that it is not appropriate. This tendency is referred to as **escalating commitment**. Managers might block or distort negative information because they don't want to be responsible for a bad decision, or they might simply refuse to accept that their solution is wrong. A recent study in Europe verified that even highly successful managers often miss or ignore warning signals because they become committed to a decision and believe if they persevere it will pay off.[57] As companies face increasing competition, complexity, and change, it is important that managers don't get so attached to their own ideas that they're unwilling to recognize when to move on. According to Stanford University professor Robert Sutton, the key to successful creative decision making is to "fail early, fail often, and pull the plug early."[58]

escalating commitment
Continuing to invest time and resources in a failing decision.

3 Planning

---

ch8   A MANAGER'S ESSENTIALS: WHAT HAVE WE LEARNED?

- This chapter made several important points about the process of organizational decision making. The study of decision making is important because it describes how managers make successful strategic and operational decisions. Managers confront many types of decisions, including programmed and nonprogrammed, and these decisions differ according to the amount of risk, uncertainty, and ambiguity in the environment.

- Three decision-making approaches were described: the classical model, which is an ideal, rational model of decision making; the administrative model, which is more descriptive of how managers actually make decisions; and the political model, which takes into consideration the discussion and coalition building that many decisions involve.

- Decision making should involve six basic steps: problem recognition, diagnosis of causes, development of alternatives, choice of an alternative, implementation of the alternative, and feedback and evaluation. Another factor affecting decision making is the manager's personal decision style. The four major decision styles are directive, analytical, conceptual, and behavioral.

- Being aware of common biases that cloud judgment can help managers avoid decision traps and make better choices. Biases to watch out for include being influenced by initial impressions, trying to correct or justify past flawed decisions, seeing only what you want to see, perpetuating the status quo, being influenced by problem framing, and being overconfident.

■ Many manager decisions are made as part of a group. In addition, involving lower level employees in decision making contributes to individual and organizational learning. Managers can use the following guidelines to support innovative group decision making: start with brainstorming; engage in rigorous debate; avoid groupthink; and know when to bail. These techniques can improve the quality and effectiveness of decision making in an uncertain or fast-changing environment.

ch8   DISCUSSION QUESTIONS

1. You are a busy partner in a legal firm, and an experienced secretary complains of continued headaches, drowsiness, dry throat, and occasional spells of fatigue and flu. She tells you she believes air quality in the building is bad and would like something to be done. How would you respond?

2. Why do you think decision making is considered a fundamental part of management effectiveness?

3. Explain the difference between risk and ambiguity. How might decision making differ for a risky versus ambiguous situation?

4. Analyze three decisions you made over the past six months. Which of these were programmed and which were nonprogrammed? Which model—the classical, administrative, or political—best describes the approach you took to make each decision?

5. What opportunities and potential problems are posed by the formation of more than one coalition within an organization, each one advocating a different direction or alternatives? What steps can you take as a manager to make sure that dueling coalitions result in construction discussion rather than dissension?

6. The Vroom-Jago model for group decision making has been criticized as being less than perfect.

What do you think are the major criticisms of the model?

7. As a new, entry-level manager, how important is it to find ways to compensate for your relative lack of experience when trying to determine which alternative before you is most likely to succeed? What are some ways you can meet this challenge?

8. List some possible advantages and disadvantages to using computer technology for managerial decision making.

9. Do you think intuition is a valid approach to making decisions in an organization? Why or why not? How might intuition be combined with a rational decision approach?

10. Do you see a conflict between today's emphasis on risk taking and learning and the six steps in Exhibit 8.3 that are associated with effective decision making? Discuss.

11. What do you think is your dominant decision style? Which style are you most comfortable using? Which style feels least comfortable? What are the implications for the type of job you might want to seek?

12. What do you see as the advantages and disadvantages of electronic brainstorming versus face-to-face brainstorming?

ch8   MANAGEMENT IN PRACTICE: EXPERIENTIAL EXERCISE

What's Your Personal Decision Style?

Read each of the following questions and circle the answer that best describes you. Think about how you typically act in a work or school situation and mark the answer that first comes to mind. There are no right or wrong answers.

1. In performing my job or class work, I look for:
   a. practical results
   b. the best solution
   c. creative approaches or ideas
   d. good working conditions

2. I enjoy jobs that:
   a. are technical and well-defined
   b. have a lot of variety
   c. allow me to be independent and creative
   d. involve working closely with others

3. The people I most enjoy working with are:
   a. energetic and ambitious
   b. capable and organized
   c. open to new ideas
   d. agreeable and trusting

4. When I have a problem, I usually:
   a. rely on what has worked in the past
   b. apply careful analysis
   c. consider a variety of creative approaches
   d. seek consensus with others

5. I am especially good at:
   a. remembering dates and facts
   b. solving complex problems
   c. seeing many possible solutions
   d. getting along with others

6. When I don't have much time, I:
   a. make decisions and act quickly
   b. follow established plans or priorities
   c. take my time and refuse to be pressured
   d. ask others for guidance and support

7. In social situations, I generally:
   a. talk to others
   b. think about what's being discussed
   c. observe
   d. listen to the conversation

8. Other people consider me:
   a. aggressive
   b. disciplined
   c. creative
   d. supportive

9. What I dislike most is:
   a. not being in control
   b. doing boring work
   c. following rules
   d. being rejected by others

10. The decisions I make are usually:
    a. direct and practical
    b. systematic or abstract
    c. broad and flexible
    d. sensitive to others' needs

Scoring and Interpretation

These questions rate your personal decision style, as described in the text and listed in Exhibit 9.5.

Count the number of *a* answers. They provide your *directive* score.

Count the number of *b* answers for your *analytical* score.

The number of *c* answers is your *conceptual* score.

The number of *d* answers is your *behavioral* score.

What is your dominant decision style? Are you surprised, or does this result reflect the style you thought you used most often?

SOURCE: Adapted from Alan J. Rowe and Richard O. Mason, *Managing with Style: A Guide to Understanding, Assessing, and Improving Decision Making* (San Francisco: Jossey-Bass, 1987): 40–41.

3
Planning

---

ch8   MANAGEMENT IN PRACTICE: ETHICAL DILEMMA

The No-Show Consultant

Jeffrey Moses was facing one of the toughest decisions of his short career as a manager with International Consulting. Andrew Carpenter, one of his best consultants, was clearly in trouble, and his problems were affecting his work. International Consulting designs, installs, and implements complex back-office software systems for companies all over the world. About half the consultants work out of the main office, while the rest, including Carpenter, work primarily from home.

This Monday morning, Moses had gotten an irate call from a major New York client saying Carpenter never showed up at the company's headquarters, where the client had been expecting his new computer system to go live for the first time. In calling around to other customers on the East Coast trying to locate the missing consultant, Moses heard other stories. Carpenter had also missed a few other appointments—all on Monday mornings—but no one had felt the need to report it because he had

called to reschedule. In addition, he practically came to blows with an employee who challenged him about the capabilities of the new system, and he inexplicably walked out of one customer's office in the middle of the day without a word to anyone. Another client reported that the last time he saw Carpenter he appeared to have a serious hangover. Most of the clients liked Carpenter, but they were concerned that his behavior was increasingly erratic. One client suggested that she would prefer to work with someone else. As for the major New York customer, he preferred that Andrew rather than a new consultant finish the project, but they were also demanding that International eat half the $250,000 consultant's fee.

After Moses finally located Carpenter by calling his next-door neighbor, Andrew confessed that he'd had a "lost weekend" and been too drunk to get on the plane. He then told Moses that his wife had left and taken their two-year-old son with her. He admitted that he had been drinking a little more than usual lately, but insisted that he was getting himself under control and promised no more problems. "I'm really not an alcoholic or anything," he said. "I've just been upset about Brenda leaving, and I let it get out of hand this weekend." Moses told Carpenter that if he would get to New York and complete the project, all would be forgiven.

Now, however, he wondered whether he should really just let things slide. Moses talked to Carpenter's team leader about the situation and was told that the leader was aware of his recent problems but thought everything would smooth itself over. "Consultants with his knowledge, level of skill, and willingness to travel are hard to find. He's well-liked among all the customers; he'll get his act together." However, when Moses discussed the problem with Carolyn Walter, vice president of operations, she argued that Carpenter should be dismissed. "You're under no obligation to keep him just because you said you would," she pointed out. "This was a major screw-up, and it's perfectly legal to fire someone for absenteeism. Your calls to customers should make it clear that this situation was not a one-time thing. Get rid of him now before things get worse. If you think eating half that $250,000 fee hurts now, just think what could happen if this behavior continues."

What Would You Do?

1. Give him a month's notice and terminate. He's known as a good consultant, so he probably won't have any trouble finding a new job, and you'll avoid any further problems associated with his emotional difficulties and his possible alcohol problem.

2. Let it slide. Missing the New York appointment is Carpenter's first big mistake. He says he is getting things under control and you believe he should be given a chance to get himself back on track.

3. Let Carpenter know that you care about what he's going through, but insist that he take a short paid leave and get counseling to deal with his emotional difficulties and evaluate the seriousness of his problems with alcohol. If the alcohol abuse continues, require him to attend a treatment program or find another job.

SOURCES: Based on information in Jeffrey L. Seglin, "The Savior Complex," *Inc.* (February 1999): 67–69; and Nora Johnson, "'He's Been Beating Me,' She Confided," *Business Ethics* (Summer 2001): 21.

---

ch8 CASE FOR CRITICAL ANALYSIS

Pinnacle Machine Tool Co.

Don Anglos had to decide whether to trust his gut or his head, and he had to make that decision by next week's board meeting. Either way, he knew he was bound to make at least a member or two of his senior management team unhappy.

The question at hand was whether Pinnacle Co., the small, publicly held Indiana-based machine tool company he led as CEO, should attempt to acquire Hoilman Inc. Hoilman was a company known for the cutting-edge sensor technology and communications software it had developed to monitor robotics equipment. Anglos had just heard a credible rumor that one of Pinnacle's chief competitors was planning a hostile takeover of the company. Coincidentally, Don Anglos knew Hoilman well because he had recently held exploratory talks about the possibility of a joint venture designed to develop similar technology capable of monitoring a broad range of manufacturing equipment. The joint venture did not work out. But now, by acquiring Hoilman, Pinnacle could develop software that transmitted real-time information on its customers' equipment, enabling it to set itself apart by providing top-notch service far more sophisticated than its current standard maintenance and service contracts.

Don, a hard-charging 48-year-old, firmly believed that bigger was better. It was a premise that had served his Greek immigrant father well as he built a multimillion-dollar business from nothing by acquiring one commercial laundry after another. The CEO had to admit, though, that getting bigger in the machine tool industry, currently a slow-growing sector facing increasing competition from low-priced foreign manufacturers, was going to be a challenge. Still, he had been convinced to sign on as Pinnacle's CEO four years ago not only because the company had relatively healthy earnings, but also because his sixth sense told him the company had growth potential. He hadn't been entirely sure where that potential lay, but he was a problem-solver with a proven track record of successfully spotting new market opportunities. In the past, he acted on hunches, which had paid off handsomely.

So far, Anglos had managed to modestly nudge Pinnacle's revenue growth and increase its market share through aggressive pricing that successfully kept customers from switching to several potential foreign rivals. But those moves inevitably chipped away at the company's healthy profit margins. In any case, he recognized he'd taken the company down that road as far as he could. It was time for a real change in strategy. Instead of concentrating on manufacturing, he wanted to transform Pinnacle into a high-tech service company. Such a drastic metamorphosis was going to require a new, service-oriented corporate culture, he admitted, but it was the only way he could see achieving the growth and profitability he envisioned. Acquiring Hoilman looked like a good place to start, but this option would be gone if Hoilman sold out to another firm.

Jennifer Banks, services division head, was enthusiastic about both the acquisition and the new strategy. "Acquiring Hoilman is the chance of a lifetime," she crowed. Not all the senior managers agreed. In particular, CFO Sam Lodge advanced arguments against the acquisition that were hard to dismiss. The timing was wrong, he insisted. Pinnacle's recent drop in profitability hadn't escaped Wall Street's attention, and the further negative impact on earnings that would result from the Hoilman acquisition wasn't likely to make already wary investors feel any better. But then Sam shocked Don by offering an even more fundamental critique. "Getting into the service business is a mistake, Don. It's what everybody's doing right now. Just look at the number of our competitors who've already taken steps to break into the services market. What makes you think we'll come out on top? And when I look at our customers, I just don't see any evidence that even if they wanted to, they could afford to buy any add-on services any time soon."

With such a big decision, Don's head had to agree with Lodge's position that was based on his usual CFO thoroughness with number-crunching. But his gut wasn't so sure. Sometimes, he thought, you just have to go with your instincts. And his instincts were champing at the bit to go after Hoilman.

Questions

1. What steps in the decision-making process have Don Anglos and Pinnacle taken? Which ones have they not completed?

2. Which decision-making style best describes Don's approach: directive, analytical, conceptual, or behavioral? Which style best describes Sam Lodge's approach?

3. What leadership style is Anglos employing? Is it the participation style you'd recommend based on a Vroom-Jago analysis of the situation? Why or why not?

4. Would you recommend that Pinnacle attempt to acquire Hoilman? If so, why? If not, what alternatives would you suggest?

SOURCE: Based on Paul Hemp, "Growing for Broke," Harvard Business Review (September 2002): 27–37.

---

ch8 ON THE JOB VIDEO CASE

Timbuk2: Make the Swirl as Famous as the Swoosh

"We want to make the *Swirl* as famous as the *Swoosh*," says Timbuk2's CEO Mark Dwight with a chuckle. While he may be joking by comparing his firm's logo to the Nike *Swoosh*, Dwight isn't kidding. When Dwight took over as head of Timbuk2 a few years ago, the company was on a downward slide, losing money because it had only one product to offer to a narrow market—a bag for bicycle messengers. Granted, the bag came in several sizes and colors—but Dwight realized that Timbuk2 couldn't survive, let alone grow, on the strength of one messenger bag. So Dwight and his managers developed corporate- and business-level strategies to achieve the goal of turning the company around and then achieving growth: increasing and broadening the product line to reach into new markets, developing the brand while remaining true to the company's heritage, finding new distribution channels, creating alliances with other firms, and outsourcing some production to maintain quality but reduce costs.

To achieve the sales goal of $25 million in five years, the Timbuk2 design, production, and marketing teams set about developing new products. Meanwhile, the sales staff renewed their efforts with Timbuk2's existing bags and customers. The expanded product line now includes yoga bags, CD cases, travel bags, duffels, graphic-arts totes, and laptop/commuter bags, among others. "We now have a [product] portfolio that you can shake the trees with," says Geoff Sacco. "It's not just about asking customers, 'Can you buy some more messenger bags?'" More products means more potential sales to more markets. For instance, a chic traveler might want to carry a Timbuk2 bag; a yoga student might choose a Timbuk2 bag for her yoga mat, water bottle, and other gear; a cyclist might choose the new Shortcut, a convertible waist pack that contains easy-access pockets and reflective patches for night riding.

However, Mark Dwight and his staff are determined to remain true to Timbuk2's original customers, the bicycle messengers. They are the firm's longstanding customers, and Dwight wants to be careful not to leave them behind. To that end, Timbuk2 is developing the new professional messenger bag called the Tag Junkie—referring to a term used by messengers—in collaboration with a California design student who also happens to be a bike messenger. Whenever new designs are reviewed in meetings, Dwight and his staff discuss the elements of a bag that make it stand out as a Timbuk2 brand—so that each bag is consistent with the image of the Timbuk2 brand.

Developing new distribution channels is an important strategy for Timbuk2. One is the Internet. The firm's Web site is already profitable, so building on that strength makes sense. A current popular feature of the site is "Build Your Own Bag," where customers can combine sizes, fabrics, colors, and features to create their own customized bags.

Developing products that can be used successfully with other firms' products is a creative strategy. Recently, Timbuk2 has begun manufacturing bags specifically to fit Apple laptops—much to the delight of Apple users. One reviewer who tried the Commute XL Laptop Messenger Bag for his Apple Macintosh 17" Powerbook was pleased with several features, including the strap, padded back, durable construction (a Timbuk2 hallmark), and waterproof interior (making it a good all-weather commuter bag).

Timbuk2's decision to outsource production of some of its bags to China—most are made in a factory near the company's offices in San Francisco—drew criticism from a few customers. However, the firm defended the move by explaining that doing so actually allowed the San Francisco factory to remain open and active. The laptop bags, explains their Web site, "are much more complex to build and require substantially more labor and a variety of very expensive machines we don't have here in our factory." So the bags are made in China to strict quality specifications—and can be sold in the United States at a more reasonable price.

To make certain that each of these strategies is being implemented effectively, Mark Dwight meets weekly with his management staff and daily with his operations staff. We "look at performance on an ongoing basis," says Dwight. "How do I know if we picked the right strategy? The results that we've seen so far indicate that we're on the right path. There are examples of other [firms] that have done the same thing and they created substantial, lasting enterprises on this strategy."

Questions

1. In which category would you place Timbuk2's grand strategy? Why?

2. How would you define Timbuk2's core competency?

3. Identify one strength, weakness, opportunity, and threat for Timbuk2.

SOURCES: Company Web site, *http://www.timbuk2.com*, accessed August 13, 2004; "Timbuk2—New Stuff," *Cross Country Skier*, January 2004, *http://www.findarticles.com*; product review, *mymac.com*, January 2004, *http://www.mymac.com*.

ch8 BIZ FLIX VIDEO CASE

The Paper

This engaging film shows the ethical dilemmas and stress of producing the *New York Sun*, a daily metropolitan newspaper. Metro Editor Henry Hackett (Michael Keaton) races against the clock to publish a story about a major police scandal that could send two young African American men to jail. He is in constant conflict with Managing Editor Alicia Clark (Glenn Close) who is more concerned about controlling the budget than about running accurate stories. Hackett is also under constant pressure from his wife Marty (Marisa Tomei), who is pregnant with their first child. While Hackett tries to get his story, Marty urges him to take a less demanding job at *The Sentinel*.

This scene is an edited version of the "The Managing Editor" sequence, which occurs early in *The Paper*. It shows a staff meeting that takes place the day after the *Sun* missed a story about a murder and other shootings with racial overtones. Instead, the *Sun* ran a front-page story about parking problems. At the meeting, Senior Editor Bernie White (Robert Duvall) discusses his preferences in front-page stories.

What to Watch for and Ask Yourself

1. Senior Editor Bernie White wants to reach a specific goal with the next edition of the *New York Sun*. What is this goal?

2. What method of departmentalization best describes the organizational structure at the *Sun*: functional, product, customer, geographic, or matrix? Explain your choice.

3. Is the organizational structure of the *Sun* appropriate for reaching White's goal? Why or why not?

ch8 ENDNOTES

1. See Kenneth R. Brousseau, Michael L. Driver, Gary Hourihan, and Rikard Larsson, "The Seasoned Executive's Decision Making Style," *Harvard Business Review* (February 2006): 110ff, for a discussion of how decision-making behavior evolves as managers progress in their careers.

2. Betsy Morris, "What Makes Apple Golden?" *Fortune* (March 17, 2008): 68–74.

3. Michael V. Copeland and Owen Thomas, "Hits (& Misses)," *Business 2.0* (January–February 2004): 126.

4. Michael V. Copeland, "Stuck in the Spin Cycle," *Business 2.0* (May 2005): 74–75; Adam Horowitz, Mark Athitakis, Mark Lasswell, and Owen Thomas, "101 Dumbest Moments in Business," *Business 2.0* (January–February 2004): 72–81.

5. Herbert A. Simon, *The New Science of Management Decision* (Englewood Cliffs, NJ: Prentice Hall, 1977), p. 47.

6. Samuel Eilon, "Structuring Unstructured Decisions," *Omega 13* (1985): 369–377; and Max H. Bazerman, *Judgment in Managerial Decision Making* (New York: Wiley, 1986).

7. James G. March and Zur Shapira, "Managerial Perspectives on Risk and Risk Taking," *Management Science* 33 (1987): 1404–1418; and Inga Skromme Baird and Howard Thomas, "Toward a Contingency Model of Strategic Risk Taking," *Academy of Management Review* 10 (1985): 230–243.

8. Hugh Courtney, "Decision-Driven Scenarios for Assessing Four Levels of Uncertainty," *Strategy & Leadership* 31, no. 1 (2003): 14–22.

9. Reported in David Leonhardt, "This Fed Chief May Yet Get a Honeymoon," *The New York Times*, August 23, 2006.

10. Michael Masuch and Perry LaPotin, "Beyond Garbage Cans: An AI Model of Organizational Choice," *Administrative Science Quarterly* 34 (1989): 38–67; and Richard L. Daft and Robert H. Lengel, "Organizational Information Requirements, Media Richness and Structural Design," *Management Science* 32 (1986): 554–571.

11. Ben Worthen, "Cost Cutting Versus Innovation: Reconcilable Difference," *CIO* (October 1, 2004): 89–94.

12. David M. Schweiger, William R. Sandberg, and James W. Ragan, "Group Approaches for Improving Strategic Decision Making: A Comparative Analysis of Dialectical Inquiry, Devil's Advocacy, and Consensus," *Academy of Management Journal* 29 (1986): 51–71; and Richard O. Mason and Ian I. Mitroff, *Challenging Strategic Planning Assumptions* (New York: Wiley Interscience, 1981).

13. Michael Pacanowsky, "Team Tools for Wicked Problems," *Organizational Dynamics* 23, no. 3 (Winter 1995): 36–51.

14. Thomas H. Davenport and Jeanne G. Harris, "Automated Decision Making Comes of Age," *MIT Sloan Management Review* (Summer 2005): 83–89; and Stacie McCullough, "On the Front Lines," *CIO* (October 15, 1999): 78–81.

15. Julie Schlosser, "Markdown Lowdown," *Fortune* (January 12, 2004): 40; Srinivas Bollapragada, Prasanthi Ganti, Mark Osborn, James Quaile, and Kannan Ramanathan, "GE's Energy Rentals Business Automates Its Credit Assessment Process," *Interfaces* 33, no. 5 (September–October 2003): 45–56.

16. Mitchell Waldrop, "Chaos, Inc.," *Red Herring* (January 2003): 38–40; Andy Serwer, "Southwest Airlines: The Hottest Thing in the Sky," *Fortune* (March 8, 2004): 86–106; Perry Flint, "The Darkest Hour," *Air Transport World* (December 2005): 52–53; *Southwest Airlines 2005 Annual Report*, www.southwest.com/ investor_relations/swaar05.pdf; and John Heimlich, "State of the Industry Q&A," Air Transport Association of America, Inc. (April 11, 2006), www .airlines.org/econ/d.aspx?nid=9630.

17. Herbert A. Simon, *The New Science of Management Decision* (New York: Harper & Row, 1960), pp. 5–6; and Amitai Etzioni, "Humble Decision Making," *Harvard Business Review* (July–August 1989): 122–126.

18. James G. March and Herbert A. Simon, *Organizations* (New York: Wiley, 1958).

19. Herbert A. Simon, *Models of Man* (New York: Wiley, 1957), pp. 196–205; and Herbert A. Simon, *Administrative Behavior*, 2nd ed. (New York: Free Press, 1957).

20. Paul C. Nutt, "Expanding the Search for Alternatives During Strategic Decision Making," *Academy of Management Executive* 18, no. 4 (2004): 13–28.

21. Weston H. Agor, "The Logic of Intuition: How Top Executives Make Important Decisions," *Organizational Dynamics* 14 (Winter 1986): 5–18; and Herbert A. Simon, "Making Management Decisions: The Role of Intuition and Emotion," *Academy of Management Executive* 1 (1987): 57–64. For a recent review of research, see Erik Dane and Michael G. Pratt, "Exploring Intuition and Its Role in Managerial Decision Making," *Academy of Management Review* 32, no. 1 (2007): 33–54.

22. Study reported in C. Chet Miller and R. Duane Ireland, "Intuition in Strategic Decision Making: Friend or Foe in the Fast-Paced 21st Century?" *Academy of Management Executive* 19, no. 1 (2005): 19–30.

23. See Gary Klein, *Intuition at Work: Why Developing Your Gut Instincts Will Make You Better at What You Do* (New York: Doubleday, 2002); Kurt Matzler, Franz Bailom, and Todd A. Mooradian, "Intuitive Decision Making," *MIT Sloan Management Review* 49, no. 1 (Fall 2007): 13–15; Malcolm Gladwell, *Blink: The Power of Thinking Without Thinking* (New York: Little Brown, 2005); and Sharon Begley, "Follow Your Intuition: The Unconscious You May Be the Wiser Half," *The Wall Street Journal*, August 30, 2002.

24. Miller and Ireland, "Intuition in Strategic Decision Making," and Eric Bonabeau, "Don't Trust Your Gut," *Harvard Business Review* (May 2003): 116ff.

25. Eugene Sadler-Smith and Erella Shefy, "The Intuitive Executive: Understanding and Applying 'Gut Feel' in Decision Making," *Academy of Management Executive* 18, no. 4 (2004): 76–91; Simon, "Making Management Decisions," and Ann

3 Planning

Langley, "Between 'Paralysis by Analysis' and 'Extinction by Instinct,'" *Sloan Management Review* (Spring 1995): 63–76.

26. William B. Stevenson, Jon L. Pierce, and Lyman W. Porter, "The Concept of 'Coalition' in Organization Theory and Research," *Academy of Management Review* 10 (1985): 256–268.

27. George T. Doran and Jack Gunn, "Decision Making in High-Tech Firms: Perspectives of Three Executives," *Business Horizons* (November–December 2002): 7–16.

28. Stephanie N. Mehta and Fred Vogelstein, "AOL: The Relaunch," *Fortune* (November 14, 2005): 78–84.

29. James W. Fredrickson, "Effects of Decision Motive and Organizational Performance Level on Strategic Decision Processes," *Academy of Management Journal* 28 (1985): 821–843; James W. Fredrickson, "The Comprehensiveness of Strategic Decision Processes: Extension, Observations, Future Directions," *Academy of Management Journal* 27 (1984): 445–466; James W. Dean, Jr., and Mark P. Sharfman, "Procedural Rationality in the Strategic Decision-Making Process," *Journal of Management Studies* 30, no. 4 (July 1993): 587–610; Nandini Rajagopalan, Abdul M. A. Rasheed, and Deepak K. Datta, "Strategic Decision Processes: Critical Review and Future Directions," *Journal of Management* 19, no. 2 (1993): 349–384; and Paul J. H. Schoemaker, "Strategic Decisions in Organizations: Rational and Behavioral Views," *Journal of Management Studies* 30, no. 1 (January 1993): 107–129.

30. Marjorie A. Lyles and Howard Thomas, "Strategic Problem Formulation: Biases and Assumptions Embedded in Alternative Decision-Making Models," *Journal of Management Studies* 25 (1988): 131–145; and Susan E. Jackson and Jane E. Dutton, "Discerning Threats and Opportunities," *Administrative Science Quarterly* 33 (1988): 370–387.

31. Richard L. Daft, Juhani Sormumen, and Don Parks, "Chief Executive Scanning, Environmental Characteristics, and Company Performance: An Empirical Study" (unpublished manuscript, Texas A&M University, 1988).

32. Jena McGregor, "Gospels of Failure," *Fast Company* (February 2005): 62–67.

33. C. Kepner and B. Tregoe, *The Rational Manager* (New York: McGraw-Hill, 1965).

34. Nanette Byrnes, "Avon: More Than Cosmetic Changes," *BusinessWeek* (March 12, 2007): 62–63.

35. Paul C. Nutt, "Expanding the Search for Alternatives During Strategic Decision Making," *Academy of Management Executive* 18, no. 4 (2004): 13–28; and P. C. Nutt, "Surprising But True: Half the Decisions in Organizations Fail," *Academy of Management Executive* 13, no. 4 (1999): 75–90.

36. Pallavi Gogoi and Michael Arndt, "Hamburger Hell," *BusinessWeek* (March 3, 2003): 104.

37. Peter Mayer, "A Surprisingly Simple Way to Make Better Decisions," *Executive Female* (March–April 1995): 13–14; and Ralph L. Keeney, "Creativity in Decision Making with Value-Focused Thinking," *Sloan Management Review* (Summer 1994): 33–41.

38. Janet Guyon, "The Soul of a Money-making Machine," *Fortune* (October 3, 2005): 113–120; Robert Levering and Milton Moskowitz, "And the Winners Are . . . (The 100 Best Companies to Work For)," *Fortune* (January 23, 2006): 89–108.

39. Mark McNeilly, "Gathering Information for Strategic Decisions, Routinely," *Strategy & Leadership* 30, no. 5 (2002): 29–34.

40. Ibid.

41. Jenny C. McCune, "Making Lemonade," *Management Review* (June 1997): 49–53; and Douglas S. Barasch, "God and Toothpaste," *New York Times,* December 22, 1996.

42. Based on A. J. Rowe, J. D. Boulgaides, and M. R. McGrath, *Managerial Decision Making* (Chicago: Science Research Associates, 1984); and Alan J. Rowe and Richard O. Mason, *Managing with Style: A Guide to Understanding, Assessing, and Improving Your Decision Making* (San Francisco: Jossey-Bass, 1987).

43. Mark Gunther, "Jeff Zucker Faces Life Without *Friends*," *Fortune,* May 12, 2003, http://money.cnn.com/magazines/fortune/fortune_archive/2003/05/12/342332/index.htm (accessed August 13, 2008).

44. This section is based on John S. Hammond, Ralph L. Keeney, and

Howard Raiffa, *Smart Choices: A Practical Guide to Making Better Decisions* (Boston: Harvard Business School Press, 1999); Max H. Bazerman and Dolly Chugh, "Decisions Without Blinders," *Harvard Business Review* (January 2006): 88–97; J. S. Hammond, R. L. Keeney, and H. Raiffa, "The Hidden Traps in Decision Making," *Harvard Business Review* (September–October 1998): 47–58; Oren Harari, "The Thomas Lawson Syndrome," *Management Review* (February 1994): 58–61; Dan Ariely, "Q&A: Why Good CIOs Make Bad Decisions," *CIO* (May 1, 2003): 83–87; Leigh Buchanan, "How to Take Risks in a Time of Anxiety," *Inc.* (May 2003): 76–81; and Max H. Bazerman, *Judgment in Managerial Decision Making,* 5th ed. (New York: John Wiley & Sons, 2002).

45. Kathleen M. Eisenhardt, "Strategy as Strategic Decision Making," *Sloan Management Review* (Spring 1999): 65–72.

46. R. B. Gallupe, W. H. Cooper, M. L. Grise, and L. M. Bastianutti, "Blocking Electronic Brainstorms," *Journal of Applied Psychology* 79 (1994): 77–86; R. B. Gallupe and W. H. Cooper, "Brainstorming Electronically," *Sloan Management Review* (Fall 1993): 27–36; and Alison Stein Wellner, "A Perfect Brainstorm," *Inc.* (October 2003): 31–35.

47. Wellner, "A Perfect Brainstorm"; Gallupe and Cooker, "Brainstorming Electronically."

48. Michael A. Roberto, "Making Difficult Decisions in Turbulent Times," *Ivey Business Journal* (May–June 2003): 1–7.

49. Eisenhardt, "Strategy as Strategic Decision Making"; and David A. Garvin and Michael A. Roberto, "What You Don't Know About Making Decisions," *Harvard Business Review* (September 2001): 108–116.

50. Roberto, "Making Difficult Decisions in Turbulent Times."

51. David M. Schweiger and William R. Sandberg, "The Utilization of Individual Capabilities in Group Approaches to Strategic Decision Making," *Strategic Management Journal* 10 (1989): 31–43; and "The Devil's Advocate," *Small Business Report* (December 1987): 38–41.

52. Doran and Gunn, "Decision Making in High-Tech Firms."

53. Eisenhardt, "Strategy as Strategic Decision Making."

54. Garvin and Roberto, "What You Don't Know About Making Decisions."

55. Irving L. Janis, *Groupthink: Psychological Studies of Policy Decisions and Fiascoes*, 2nd ed. (Boston: Houghton Mifflin, 1982).

56. Jerry B. Harvey, "The Abilene Paradox: The Management of Agreement," *Organizational Dynamics* (Summer 1988): 17–43.

57. Hans Wissema, "Driving Through Red Lights; How Warning Signals Are Missed or Ignored," *Long Range Planning* 35 (2002): 521–539.

58. Ibid.

General Motors
Part Three: Planning
The Moment of Decision: Can Management Fix GM's Financial Crisis?

In the months leading up to 2009, news leaked that General Motors (GM) was pitching a merger to other Big Three automakers. Although they are famous cross-town rivals, GM, Ford, and Chrysler are facing a brutal common enemy: global economic crisis. As the companies struggled to survive the worst sales slump in decades, an unexpected meltdown in the U.S. mortgage industry spawned an international credit crisis, freezing cash flows worldwide.

Unable to obtain money, and burning through $1 billion of its own reserves monthly, GM set out to find partners who might circle the wagons to stave off bankruptcy. Chairman Rick Wagoner and President Frederick Henderson met with Ford executives Alan Mulally and William Ford Jr. to propose merging their companies to survive the economic downturn. After numerous meetings, Mr. Mulally and Mr. Ford concluded that Ford Motor Company could reorganize better on its own. Not willing to give up on the idea, Wagoner took his pitch to Chrysler.

The past few years have been a moment of decision for GM. With the world's top automaker inching close to a financial precipice, senior executives have begun making tough choices and seeking out innovative solutions to rescue the organization.

Of the many possible options for saving GM, a merger strategy is perhaps the boldest. First, a merger could solidify GM's position as global sales leader over Japanese rival Toyota, which in recent years has challenged GM's status as the world's top automaker. Although its position as top automaker is not unimportant, the bigger problem is cash: GM doesn't have any. The company reported losses of $18.7 billion in the first half of 2008, and the ensuing plunge of shares to their lowest levels since 1950 left the company valued at just $3 billion. Against that backdrop, Chrysler's $11 billion cash horde looked especially inviting to Wagoner and his executive management teams.

Not surprisingly, analysts were divided about a merger option. Van Conway, a merger and acquisitions expert and partner at Conway & MacKenzie, cheered GM's survival instinct. "You want to be the last man standing here because the car market is going to come back." However, Erich Merkle, an analyst at the accounting firm Crowe Horwath, did not applaud the move. "If you put two auto companies together, both that are losing money, both that are losing market share, you've just got an auto company that's losing market share faster and losing more money."

Management has other options for performing what amounts to emergency bypass surgery on the 100-year-old company. For example, in July 2008, Wagoner announced a plan to cut $10 billion in costs while raising $5 billion through asset sales through the end of 2009. Within months, the iconic Hummer brand was up for sale. Next followed a steady drumbeat of plant closings throughout the Midwest—even the company's Detroit headquarters was rumored to be up for sale.

Among GM's most difficult decisions has been what to do about skyrocketing labor costs. The United Auto Workers Union, once a symbol of workforce stability and fairness, has become a financial albatross around GM's neck. GM spends as much as $1,635 on every vehicle sold to cover benefits for active and retired U.S. workers. In addition, with all compensation perks factored in, pay for GM workers adds up to $73 per hour. Toyota pays nothing for retirees and only $215 per vehicle to cover active-worker benefits. Management addressed the imbalance in 2006 by offering 126,000 employees as much as $140,000 to sever all ties with the company. The massive buyout was part of a four-point restructuring plan announced in 2005 to achieve $7 billion in cost reductions.

Yet of all the tricks GM has up its sleeve to manage its financial crisis, one option is reportedly off the table. In a written statement to the press, management acknowledged "unprecedented challenges" related to global financial markets. The statement firmly added, "But bankruptcy protection is not an option GM is considering. Bankruptcy would not be in the interests of our employees, stockholders, suppliers, or customers."

Questions

1. What planning approaches and methods might GM adopt to help manage its turbulent environment and respond effectively to global economic crisis?

2. In what way does a merger solution to GM's financial crisis represent strategic thinking and planning?

3. As GM's managers continue making decisions that affect the company's ultimate survival, what prevents them from making purely rational decisions, and what common decision-making errors must they guard against?

SOURCES: Jeff Green, "GM Is Said to Be in Preliminary Talks With Chrysler," *Bloomberg*, October 11, 2008, http://www.bloomberg.com (accessed October 12, 2008); Alex Taylor III, "Deepening Gloom at General Motors," *Fortune* (June 19, 2008), http://money.cnn .com/2008/06/19/news/companies/taylor_gm.fortune/index.htm (accessed October 13, 2008); "Toyota Zooms Past GM," *The Street .com*, April 24, 2007, http://www.thestreet.com (accessed October 12, 2008); Bill Vlasic, "G.M. Said to Seek Merger with Ford Before Chrysler," *The New York Times*, October 11, 2008, http://www.nytimes .com/2008/10/12/business/12auto.html (accessed October 15, 2008); "General Motors Could Sell Detroit Headquarters to Raise Cash," *Boston Herald*, October 7, 2008, http://www.bostonherald.com (accessed October 13, 2008); Alex Taylor III, "Behind Ford's Scary $12.7 Billion Loss—The Big Three Are Hemorrhaging Money, and Struggling to Stay Competitive with Foreign Rivals," *Fortune* (January 26, 2007), http://money.cnn.com/2007/01/26/news/companies/ pluggedin_taylor_ford.fortune/index.htm (accessed October 10, 2008); "Ford, GM Say They Won't File for Bankruptcy," *MSNBC.com*, October 10, 2008, http://www.msnbc.msn.com/id/27101859 (accessed October 12, 2008); David Kiley, "Can GM Make It?" *BusinessWeek Online*, October 9, 2008, http://www.businessweek.com/lifestyle/content/oct2008/ bw2008109_718575.htm (accessed October 12, 2008); Tom Krisher, "General Motors Putting Hummer Brand and French Factory Up for Sale," The Associated Press, September 24, 2008, http://www .canadaeast.com/article/article/425760 (accessed October 12, 2008); Sharon Silke Carty, "GM Offers Buyouts to 126,000," *USA Today*, March 27, 2006, http://www.usatoday.com (accessed October 10, 2008); Tom Krisher, "Analysts: GM Would Need Cash to Acquire Chrysler," *ABC News*, October 11, 2008, http://abcnews.go.com/ Business/wireStory?id=6009470 (accessed October 14, 2008); Rick Haglund, "Why GM and Chrysler? You May Not Like the Answer," *Mlive.com*, October 15, 2008, http://www.mlive.com (accessed October 15, 2008); Alex Taylor III, "Gentlemen, Start Your Turnaround," *Fortune* (January 8, 2008), http://money.cnn.com/2008/01/07/news/companies/ gm_turnaround.fortune/index.htm (accessed October 15, 2008); "Global Auto Market May 'Collapse' in 2009—J.D. Power Points to Growing Concerns Around Credit Availability," *MSNBC.com*, October 10, 2008, http://www.msnbc.msn.com/id/27114183 (accessed October 13, 2008).

© GETTY IMAGES / DIGITAL VISION

Learning Outcomes

After studying this chapter, you should be able to:

1. Discuss the fundamental characteristics of organizing, including such concepts as work specialization, chain of command, span of management, and centralization versus decentralization.

2. Describe functional and divisional approaches to structure.

3. Explain the matrix approach to structure and its application to both domestic and international organizations.

4. Describe the contemporary team and virtual network structures and why they are being adopted by organizations.

5. Explain why organizations need coordination across departments and hierarchical levels, and describe mechanisms for achieving coordination.

6. Identify how structure can be used to achieve an organization's strategic goals.

Designing Adaptive Organizations

WHAT ARE YOUR LEADERSHIP BELIEFS?[1]

The fit between a new manager and the organization is often based on personal beliefs about the role of leaders. Things work best when organization design matches a new manager's beliefs about his or her leadership role. To understand your leadership beliefs, please answer each item below as Mostly True or Mostly False for you.

Think about the extent to which each statement reflects your beliefs about a leader's role in an organization. Mark as Mostly True the four statements that are *most* true for you, and mark as Mostly False the four that are *least* true for you.

	Mostly True	Mostly False
1. A leader should take charge of the group or organization.	_____	_____
2. The major tasks of a leader are to make and communicate decisions.	_____	_____
3. Group and organization members should be loyal to designated leaders.	_____	_____
4. The responsibility for taking risks lies with the leaders.	_____	_____
5. Leaders should foster member discussions about the future.	_____	_____
6. Successful leaders make everyone's learning their highest priority.	_____	_____
7. An organization needs to be always changing the way it does things to adapt to a changing world.	_____	_____
8. Everyone in an organization should be responsible for accomplishing organizational goals.	_____	_____

SCORING AND INTERPRETATION: Each question pertains to one of two subscales of *leadership beliefs*. Questions 1–4 reflect *position-based* leadership beliefs. This is the belief that the most competent and loyal people are placed in positions of leadership where they assume responsibility and authority for the group or organization. Questions 5–8 reflect *nonhierarchical* leadership beliefs. This belief is that the group or organization faces a complex system of adaptive challenges, and leaders see their job as facilitating the flow of information among members and their full engagement to respond to those challenges. The subscale for which you checked more items Mostly True may reveal your personal beliefs about position-based versus nonhierarchical leadership. Position-based beliefs typically work for managers in a traditional vertical heirarchy or mechanistic organization. Nonhierarchical beliefs typically work for managers engaged with horizontal organizing or organic organizations, such as managing teams, projects, and reengineering.

A manager's work is influenced by how the company is organized. New managers are typically more comfortable and more effective working in an organization system that is compatible with their leadership beliefs. Yet all organizations wrestle with the question of structural design, and reorganization often is necessary to reflect a new strategy, changing market conditions, or innovative technology. Good managers understand and learn to work within a variety of structural configurations.

In recent years, many companies have realigned departmental groupings, chains of command, and horizontal coordination mechanisms to attain new strategic goals. Managers at Nissan created cross-functional teams to enhance horizontal collaboration. Microsoft reorganized into three divisions that each focus on a primary business line to increase flexibility in developing and delivering new products. Among CEO Robert Nardelli's plans for getting struggling automaker Chrysler back on track is a

1 Introduction
2 Environment
3 Planning
4 Organizing
5 Controlling
6 Leading

Concept Connection   Successful artist Shepard Fairey has proven himself to be an effective manager too. Fairey runs his own marketing design firm, Studio Number One, a studio to design unique graphics and logos used in untraditional advertising campaigns, and on labels for clothing, soft drinks, and other products. Fairey manages a creative team of seven full-time employees and a handful of part-timers and interns. Even in a small organization such as this, **organizing** is a critical part of good management. Fairey has to be sure people are assigned and coordinated to do all the various jobs necessary to satisfy clients such as Express, Levi's, and Dr. Pepper/Seven Up. The right **organization structure** enables Studio Number One to be "fast, deadline-sensitive, and responsive."

organizing The deployment of organizational resources to achieve strategic goals.

organization structure The framework in which the organization defines how tasks are divided, resources are deployed, and departments are coordinated.

organization chart The visual representation of an organization's structure.

work specialization The degree to which organizational tasks are subdivided into individual jobs; also called division of labor.

major reorganization that includes outsourcing some operations to developing countries.[2] Each of these organizations is using fundamental concepts of organizing.

Organizing is the deployment of organizational resources to achieve strategic goals. The deployment of resources is reflected in the organization's division of labor into specific departments and jobs, formal lines of authority, and mechanisms for coordinating diverse organization tasks.

Organizing is important because it follows from strategy—the topic of Part 3. Strategy defines *what* to do; organizing defines *how* to do it. Structure is a powerful tool for reaching strategic goals, and a strategy's success often is determined by its fit with organizational structure. Part 4 explains the variety of organizing principles and concepts used by managers. This chapter covers fundamental concepts that apply to all organizations and departments, including organizing the vertical structure and using mechanisms for horizontal coordination. Chapter 10 discusses how organizations can be structured to facilitate innovation and change. Chapters 11 and 12 consider how to use human resources to the best advantage within the organization's structure.

ORGANIZING THE VERTICAL STRUCTURE

The organizing process leads to the creation of organization structure, which defines how tasks are divided and resources deployed. **Organization structure** is defined as: (1) the set of formal tasks assigned to individuals and departments; (2) formal reporting relationships, including lines of authority, decision responsibility, number of hierarchical levels, and span of managers' control; and (3) the design of systems to ensure effective coordination of employees across departments.[3] Ensuring coordination across departments is just as critical as defining the departments to begin with. Without effective coordination systems, no structure is complete.

The set of formal tasks and formal reporting relationships provides a framework for vertical control of the organization. The characteristics of vertical structure are portrayed in the **organization chart**, which is the visual representation of an organization's structure.

A sample organization chart for a water bottling plant is illustrated in Exhibit 9.1. The plant has four major departments—accounting, human resources, production, and marketing. The organization chart delineates the chain of command, indicates departmental tasks and how they fit together, and provides order and logic for the organization. Every employee has an appointed task, line of authority, and decision responsibility. The following sections discuss several important features of vertical structure in more detail.

Work Specialization

Organizations perform a wide variety of tasks. A fundamental principle is that work can be performed more efficiently if employees are allowed to specialize.[4] **Work specialization**, sometimes called *division of labor*, is the degree to which organizational tasks are subdivided into separate jobs. Work specialization in Exhibit 9.1 is

EXHIBIT | **9.1** Organization Chart for a Water Bottling Plant

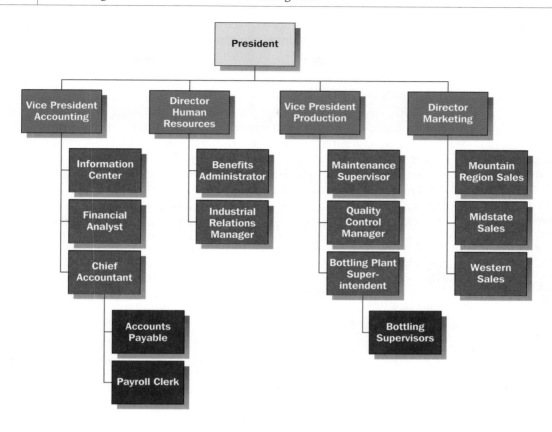

illustrated by the separation of production tasks into bottling, quality control, and maintenance. Employees within each department perform only the tasks relevant to their specialized function. When work specialization is extensive, employees specialize in a single task. Jobs tend to be small, but they can be performed efficiently. Work specialization is readily visible on an automobile assembly line where each employee performs the same task over and over again. It would not be efficient to have a single employee build the entire automobile, or even perform a large number of unrelated jobs.

Despite the apparent advantages of specialization, many organizations are moving away from this principle. With too much specialization, employees are isolated and do only a single, boring job. In addition, too much specialization creates separation and hinders the coordination that is essential for organizations to be effective. Many companies are implementing teams and other mechanisms that enhance coordination and provide greater challenge for employees.

Chain of Command

The **chain of command** is an unbroken line of authority that links all persons in an organization and shows who reports to whom. It is associated with two underlying principles. *Unity of command* means that each employee is held accountable to only one supervisor. The *scalar principle* refers to a clearly defined line of authority in the organization that includes all employees. Authority and responsibility for different tasks should be distinct. All persons in the organization should know to whom they report as well as the successive management levels all the way to the top. In Exhibit 9.1, the payroll clerk reports to the chief accountant, who in turn reports to the vice president, who in turn reports to the company president.

chain of command An unbroken line of authority that links all individuals in the organization and specifies who reports to whom.

4

Organizing

Authority, Responsibility, and Delegation The chain of command illustrates the authority structure of the organization. **Authority** is the formal and legitimate right of a manager to make decisions, issue orders, and allocate resources to achieve organizationally desired outcomes. Authority is distinguished by three characteristics:[5]

1. *Authority is vested in organizational positions, not people.* Managers have authority because of the positions they hold, and other people in the same positions would have the same authority.

2. *Authority is accepted by subordinates.* Although authority flows top-down through the organization's hierarchy, subordinates comply because they believe that managers have a legitimate right to issue orders. The *acceptance theory of authority* argues that a manager has authority only if subordinates choose to accept his or her commands. If subordinates refuse to obey because the order is outside their zone of acceptance, a manager's authority disappears.[6]

3. *Authority flows down the vertical hierarchy.* Positions at the top of the hierarchy are vested with more formal authority than are positions at the bottom.

Responsibility is the flip side of the authority coin. **Responsibility** is the duty to perform the task or activity as assigned. Typically, managers are assigned authority commensurate with responsibility. When managers have responsibility for task outcomes but little authority, the job is possible but difficult. They rely on persuasion and luck. When managers have authority exceeding responsibility, they may become tyrants, using authority toward frivolous outcomes.[7]

authority The formal and legitimate right of a manager to make decisions, issue orders, and allocate resources to achieve organizationally desired outcomes.

responsibility The duty to perform the task or activity an employee has been assigned.

accountability The fact that the people with authority and responsibility are subject to reporting and justifying task outcomes to those above them in the chain of command.

TakeaMoment

Go to the ethical dilemma on page 270 that pertains to issues of authority, responsibility, and delegation.

Accountability is the mechanism through which authority and responsibility are brought into alignment. **Accountability** means that the people with authority and responsibility are subject to reporting and justifying task outcomes to those above them in the chain of command.[8] For organizations to function well, everyone needs to know what they are accountable for and accept the responsibility and authority for performing it. Accountability can be built into the organization structure. For example, at Whirlpool, incentive programs tailored to different hierarchical levels provide strict accountability. Performance of all managers is monitored, and bonus payments are tied to successful outcomes. Another example comes from Caterpillar Inc., which got hammered by new competition in the mid-1980s and reorganized to build in accountability.

Caterpillar Inc.

Innovative Way

Caterpillar, which makes large construction equipment, engines, and power systems, had almost total control of its markets until the mid-1980s, when a combination of global recession and runaway inflation opened the door to a host of new competitors, including Japan's Komatsu. The company was losing $1 million a day seven days a week in the mid-1980s.

When George Schaefer took over as CEO, he and other top managers decided to undertake a major transformation to make sure Caterpillar wasn't caught flat-footed again. They started with structure. One major problem Schaefer saw was that the organization didn't have clear accountability. Schaefer pushed authority, responsibility, and accountability dramatically downward by reorganizing Caterpillar into several new business divisions that would be judged on divisional profitability. Business units could now design their own products, develop their own manufacturing processes, and set their own prices rather than getting permission or directives from headquarters. The division managers were strictly accountable for how they used their new decision-making authority. Each division was judged on profitability and return on assets (ROA), and any division that couldn't demonstrate 15 percent ROA was subject to elimination. The CEO held regular meetings with each division president and kept notes of what they said they would achieve. Then at the next meeting, he would review each manager's performance compared to his or her commitments. The compensation plan was also overhauled to base managers' bonuses on meeting divisional plan targets.

Previously, if things went wrong, division managers would blame headquarters. The clear accountability of the new structure forced people to find solutions to their problems rather than assigning blame.[9]

Some top managers at Caterpillar had trouble letting go of authority in the new structure because they were used to calling all the shots, but the new structure was an important part of returning the company to profitability. Another important concept related to authority is delegation.[10] **Delegation** is the process managers use to transfer authority and responsibility to positions below them in the hierarchy. Most organizations today encourage managers to delegate authority to the lowest possible level to provide maximum flexibility to meet customer needs and adapt to the environment. However, as at Caterpillar, many managers find delegation difficult. When managers can't delegate, they undermine the role of their subordinates and prevent people from doing their jobs effectively. Techniques for effective delegation are discussed in the Manager's Shoptalk box.

As a new manager, delegate authority and responsibility to employees so they can quickly respond to customer needs and other shifts in the environment. Don't hoard control and limit the effectiveness and creativity of others.

TakeaMoment

Line and Staff Authority An important distinction in many organizations is between line authority and staff authority, reflecting whether managers work in line or staff departments in the organization's structure. *Line departments* perform tasks that reflect the organization's primary goal and mission. In a software company, line departments make and sell the product. In an Internet-based company, line departments would be those that develop and manage online offerings and sales. *Staff departments* include all those that provide specialized skills in support of line departments. Staff departments have an advisory relationship with line departments and typically include marketing, labor relations, research, accounting, and human resources.

Line authority means that people in management positions have formal authority to direct and control immediate subordinates. **Staff authority** is narrower and includes the right to advise, recommend, and counsel in the staff specialists' area of expertise. Staff authority is a communication relationship; staff specialists advise managers in technical areas. For example, the finance department of a manufacturing firm would have staff authority to coordinate with line departments about which accounting forms to use to facilitate equipment purchases and standardize payroll services.

Span of Management

The **span of management** is the number of employees reporting to a supervisor. Sometimes called the *span of control*, this characteristic of structure determines how closely a supervisor can monitor subordinates. Traditional views of organization design recommended a span of management of about seven subordinates per manager. However, many lean organizations today have spans of management as high as 30, 40, and even higher. For example, at Consolidated Diesel's team-based engine assembly plant, the span of management is 100.[11] Research over the past 40 or so years shows that span of management varies widely and that several factors influence the span.[12] Generally, when supervisors must be closely involved with subordinates, the span should be small, and when supervisors need little involvement with subordinates, it can be large. The following section describes the factors that are associated with less supervisor involvement and thus larger spans of control.

delegation The process managers use to transfer authority and responsibility to positions below them in the hierarchy.

line authority A form of authority in which individuals in management positions have the formal power to direct and control immediate subordinates.

staff authority A form of authority granted to staff specialists in their area of expertise.

span of management The number of employees reporting to a supervisor; also called *span of control*.

Manager'sShoptalk

How to Delegate

The attempt by top management to decentralize decision making often gets bogged down because middle managers are unable to delegate. Managers may cling tightly to their decision making and task responsibilities. Failure to delegate occurs for a number of reasons: Managers are most comfortable making familiar decisions; they feel they will lose personal status by delegating tasks; they believe they can do a better job themselves; or they have an aversion to risk—they will not take a chance on delegating because performance responsibility ultimately rests with them.

Yet decentralization offers an organization many advantages. Decisions are made at the right level, lower-level employees are motivated, and employees have the opportunity to develop decision-making skills. Overcoming barriers to delegation in order to gain these advantages is a major challenge. The following approach can help each manager delegate more effectively:

1. *Delegate the whole task.* A manager should delegate an entire task to one person rather than dividing it among several people. This type of delegation gives the individual complete responsibility and increases his or her initiative while giving the manager some control over the results.

2. *Select the right person.* Not all employees have the same capabilities and degree of motivation. Managers must match talent to task if delegation is to be effective. They should identify subordinates who made independent decisions in the past and show a desire for more responsibility.

3. *Ensure that authority equals responsibility.* Merely assigning a task is not effective delegation. Managers often load subordinates with increased responsibility but do not extend their decision-making range. In addition to having responsibility for completing a task, the worker must be given the authority to make decisions about how best to do the job.

4. *Give thorough instruction.* Successful delegation includes information on what, when, why, where, who, and how. The subordinate must clearly understand the task and the expected results. It is a good idea to write down all provisions discussed, including required resources and when and how the results will be reported.

5. *Maintain feedback.* Feedback means keeping open lines of communication with the subordinate to answer questions and provide advice, but without exerting too much control. Open lines of communication make it easier to trust subordinates. Feedback keeps the subordinate on the right track.

6. *Evaluate and reward performance.* Once the task is completed, the manager should evaluate results, not methods. When results do not meet expectations, the manager must assess the consequences. When they do meet expectations, the manager should reward employees for a job well done with praise, financial rewards when appropriate, and delegation of future assignments.

Are You a Positive Delegator?

Positive delegation is the way an organization implements decentralization. Do you help or hinder the decentralization process? If you answer yes to more than three of the following questions, you may have a problem delegating:

- I tend to be a perfectionist.
- My boss expects me to know all the details of my job.
- I don't have the time to explain clearly and concisely how a task should be accomplished.
- I often end up doing tasks myself.
- My subordinates typically are not as committed as I am.
- I get upset when other people don't do the task right.
- I really enjoy doing the details of my job to the best of my ability.
- I like to be in control of task outcomes.

SOURCES: Thomas R. Horton "Delegation and Team Building: No Solo Acts Please," *Management Review* (September 1992): 58–61; Andrew E. Schwartz, "The Why, What, and to Whom of Delegation," *Management Solutions* (June 1987): 31–38; "Delegation," *Small Business Report* (June 1986): 38–43; and Russell Wild, "Clone Yourself," *Working Woman* (May 2000): 79–80.

1. Work performed by subordinates is stable and routine.

2. Subordinates perform similar work tasks.

3. Subordinates are concentrated in a single location.

4. Subordinates are highly trained and need little direction in performing tasks.

5. Rules and procedures defining task activities are available.

6. Support systems and personnel are available for the manager.

7. Little time is required in nonsupervisory activities such as coordination with other departments or planning.

8. Managers' personal preferences and styles favor a large span.

The average span of control used in an organization determines whether the structure is tall or flat. A **tall structure** has an overall narrow span and more hierarchical levels. A **flat structure** has a wide span, is horizontally dispersed, and has fewer hierarchical levels.

Having too many hierarchical levels and narrow spans of control is a common structural problem for organizations. The result may be routine decisions that are made too high in the organization, which pulls higher-level executives away from important long-range strategic issues, and it limits the creativity and innovativeness of lower-level managers in solving problems.[13] The trend in recent years has been toward wider spans of control as a way to facilitate delegation.[14] Exhibit 9.2 illustrates how an international metals company was reorganized. The multilevel set of managers shown in panel *a* was replaced with ten operating managers and nine staff specialists reporting directly to the CEO, as shown in panel *b*. The CEO welcomed this wide span of 19 management subordinates because it fit his style, his management

© UNITED STATES NAVY

Concept Connection Prior to the early 1990s, there were seven management layers at Electric Boat Corporation's Quonset Point facility in Rhode Island, which fabricates and assembles U.S. Navy nuclear submarines. This **tall structure** resulted in high costs and a lengthy chain of command that slowed decision making. After the General Dynamics Corporation subsidiary re-engineered itself into a **flat structure** with only three layers, overhead and indirect labor costs were cut by 50 percent, and communications, efficiency, and productivity all improved. The Best Manufacturing Practice (BPM) Center of Excellence ranks Electric Boat's practices as among the best. BPM is a partnership of the Office of Naval Research, the Commerce Department, and the University of Maryland.

tall structure A management structure characterized by an overall narrow span of management and a relatively large number of hierarchical levels.

flat structure A management structure characterized by an overall broad span of control and relatively few hierarchical levels.

4 Organizing

EXHIBIT | **9.2** Reorganization to Increase Span of Management for President of an International Metals Company

a. Old, Tall Structure

President

Executive Vice President
— Staff Specialists (6)

Executive Vice President
— Operating Managers (5)
— Staff Specialists (3)

Executive Vice President
— Operating Managers (4)
— Staff Specialists (5)

Vice President
— Operating Managers (10)
— Staff Specialists (5)

b. New, Flat Structure

President

Operating Managers (10)   Staff Specialists (9)

team was top quality and needed little supervision, and they were all located on the same floor of an office building.

Centralization and Decentralization

Centralization and decentralization pertain to the hierarchical level at which decisions are made. **Centralization** means that decision authority is located near the top of the organization. With **decentralization**, decision authority is pushed downward to lower organization levels. Organizations may have to experiment to find the correct hierarchical level at which to make decisions. For example, most large school systems are highly centralized. However, a study by William Ouchi found that three large urban school systems that shifted to a decentralized structure giving school principals and teachers more control over staffing, scheduling, and teaching methods and materials performed better and more efficiently than centralized systems of similar size.[15]

In the United States and Canada, the trend over the past 30 years has been toward greater decentralization of organizations. Decentralization is believed to relieve the burden on top managers, make greater use of employees' skills and abilities, ensure that decisions are made close to the action by well-informed people, and permit more rapid response to external changes. However, this trend does not mean that every organization should decentralize all decisions. Managers should diagnose the organizational situation and select the decision-making level that will best meet the organization's needs. Factors that typically influence centralization versus decentralization are as follows:

1. *Greater change and uncertainty in the environment are usually associated with decentralization.* A good example of how decentralization can help cope with rapid change and uncertainty occurred following Hurricane Katrina. Mississippi Power restored power in just 12 days thanks largely to a decentralized management system that empowered people at the electrical substations to make rapid on-the-spot decisions.[16]

2. *The amount of centralization or decentralization should fit the firm's strategy.* Top executives at New York City Transit are decentralizing the subway system to let managers of individual subway lines make almost every decision about what happens on the tracks, in the trains, and in the stations. Decentralization fits the strategy of responding faster and more directly to customer complaints or other problems. Previously, a request to fix a leak causing slippery conditions in a station could languish for years because the centralized system slowed decision making to a crawl.[17] Taking the opposite approach, Procter & Gamble recentralized some of its operations to take a more focused approach and leverage the giant company's capabilities across business units.[18]

3. *In times of crisis or risk of company failure, authority may be centralized at the top.* When Honda could not get agreement among divisions about new car models, President Nobuhiko Kawamoto made the decision himself.[19]

DEPARTMENTALIZATION

centralization The location of decision authority near top organizational levels.

decentralization The location of decision authority near lower organizational levels.

departmentalization The basis on which individuals are grouped into departments and departments into the total organization.

Another fundamental characteristic of organization structure is **departmentalization**, which is the basis for grouping positions into departments and departments into the total organization. Managers make choices about how to use the chain of command to group people together to perform their work. Five approaches to structural design reflect different uses of the chain of command in departmentalization, as illustrated in Exhibit 9.3. The functional, divisional, and matrix are traditional approaches that rely on the chain of command to define departmental groupings and reporting relationships along the hierarchy. Two innovative approaches are the use of teams and virtual networks, which have emerged to meet changing organizational needs in a turbulent global environment.

EXHIBIT | 9.3 Five Approaches to Structural Design

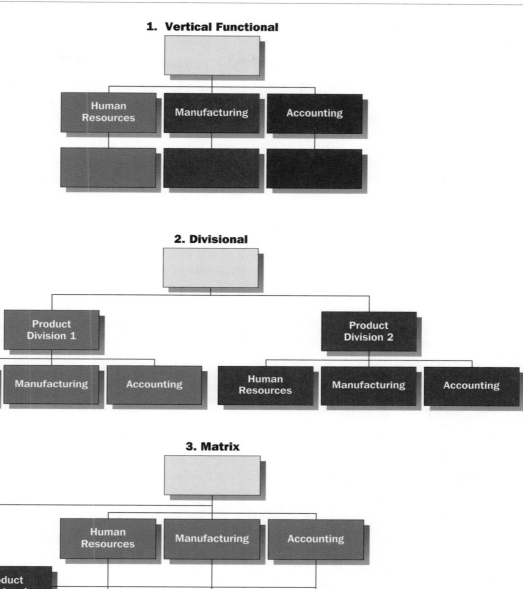

1. Vertical Functional

Human Resources | Manufacturing | Accounting

2. Divisional

Product Division 1 — Human Resources | Manufacturing | Accounting

Product Division 2 — Human Resources | Manufacturing | Accounting

3. Matrix

Human Resources | Manufacturing | Accounting

Product Division 1

Product Division 2

4. Team-Based

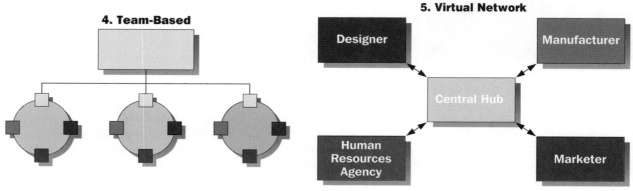

5. Virtual Network

Designer | Manufacturer

Central Hub

Human Resources Agency | Marketer

The basic difference among structures illustrated in Exhibit 9.3 is the way in which employees are departmentalized and to whom they report.[20] Each structural approach is described in detail in the following sections.

Vertical Functional Approach

What It Is **Functional structure** is the grouping of positions into departments based on similar skills, expertise, work activities, and resource use. A functional structure can be thought of as departmentalization by organizational resources, because each type of functional activity—accounting, human resources, engineering, and manufacturing—represents specific resources for performing the organization's task. People, facilities, and other resources representing a common function are grouped into a single department. One example is Blue Bell Creameries, which relies on in-depth expertise in its various functional departments to produce high-quality ice creams for a limited regional market. The quality control department, for example, tests all incoming ingredients and ensures that only the best go into Blue Bell's ice cream. Quality inspectors also test outgoing products and, because of their years of experience, can detect the slightest deviation from expected quality. Blue Bell also has functional departments such as sales, production, maintenance, distribution, research and development, and finance.[21]

functional structure The grouping of positions into departments based on similar skills, expertise, and resource use.

divisional structure An organization structure in which departments are grouped based on similar organizational outputs.

How It Works Refer back to Exhibit 9.1 on page 245 for an example of a functional structure. The major departments under the president are groupings of similar expertise and resources, such as accounting, human resources, production, and marketing. Each of the functional departments is concerned with the organization as a whole. The marketing department is responsible for all sales and marketing, for example, and the accounting department handles financial issues for the entire company.

The functional structure is a strong vertical design. Information flows up and down the vertical hierarchy, and the chain of command converges at the top of the organization. In a functional structure, people within a department communicate primarily with others in the same department to coordinate work and accomplish tasks or implement decisions that are passed down the hierarchy. Managers and employees are compatible because of similar training and expertise. Typically, rules and procedures govern the duties and responsibilities of each employee, and employees at lower hierarchical levels accept the right of those higher in the hierarchy to make decisions and issue orders.

Divisional Approach

What It Is In contrast to the functional approach, in which people are grouped by common skills and resources, the **divisional structure** occurs when departments are grouped together based on similar organizational outputs. The divisional structure is sometimes called a *product structure, program structure,* or *self-contained unit structure.* Each of these terms means essentially the same thing: Diverse departments are brought together to produce a single organizational output, whether it is a product, a program, or service to a single customer.

Most large corporations have separate divisions that perform different tasks, use different technologies, or serve different customers. When a huge organization produces products for different markets, the divisional structure works because each division is an autonomous business. For example, United Technologies Corporation (UTC), which is among the 50 largest U.S. industrial firms, has numerous divisions, including Carrier (air conditioners and heating), Otis (elevators and escalators), Pratt & Whitney (aircraft engines), and Sikorsky (helicopters).[22]

Concept Connection Mary Berner started her job as chief executive of Reader's Digest Association by realigning its business units. She broke up the book and magazine units and reorganized them along consumer interests. This new **divisional structure** created ad-friendly clusters of consumer interests such as the new Food and Entertaining unit, which includes magazines *Every Day with Rachael Ray* and *Taste of Home* along with Allrecipes.com.

How It Works Functional and divisional structures are illustrated in Exhibit 9.4. In the divisional structure, divisions are created as self-contained units with separate functional departments for each division. For example, in Exhibit 9.4, each functional department resource needed to produce the product is assigned to each division. Whereas in a functional structure, all R&D engineers are grouped together and work on all products, in a divisional structure separate R&D departments are created within each division. Each department is smaller and focuses on a single product line or customer segment. Departments are duplicated across product lines.

The primary difference between divisional and functional structures is that the chain of command from each function converges lower in the hierarchy. In a divisional structure, differences of opinion among research and development, marketing, manufacturing, and finance would be resolved at the divisional level rather than by the president. Thus, the divisional structure encourages decentralization. Decision making is pushed down at least one level in the hierarchy, freeing the president and other top managers for strategic planning.

Geographic- or Customer-Based Divisions An alternative for assigning divisional responsibility is to group company activities by geographic region or customer group. For example, the Internal Revenue Service shifted to a structure focused on four distinct taxpayer (customer) groups: individuals, small businesses, corporations, and nonprofit or government agencies.[23] Top executives at Citigroup are considering reorganizing to a geographic structure to give the giant global corporation a more unified face to local customers.[24] A global geographic structure is illustrated in Exhibit 9.5. In a geographic-based structure, all functions in a specific country or region report to the same division manager. The structure focuses company activities on local market conditions. Competitive advantage may come from the production or sale of a product or service adapted to a given country or region. Colgate-Palmolive Company is organized into regional divisions in North America, Europe, Latin America, the Far East, and the South Pacific.[25] The structure works for Colgate because personal care products often need to be tailored to cultural values and local customs.

Large nonprofit organizations such as the United Way, National Council of YMCAs, Habitat for Humanity International, and the Girl Scouts of the USA also frequently use a type of geographical structure, with a central headquarters and semiautonomous local units. The national organization provides brand recognition, coordinates

EXHIBIT | **9.4** Functional Versus Divisional Structures

EXHIBIT | **9.5** Geographic-Based Global Organization Structure

fund-raising services, and handles some shared administrative functions, while day-to-day control and decision making are decentralized to local or regional units.[26]

Matrix Approach

What It Is The **matrix approach** combines aspects of both functional and divisional structures simultaneously in the same part of the organization. The matrix structure evolved as a way to improve horizontal coordination and information sharing.[27] One unique feature of the matrix is that it has dual lines of authority. In Exhibit 9.6, the functional hierarchy of authority runs vertically, and the divisional hierarchy of authority runs horizontally. The vertical structure provides traditional control within functional departments, and the horizontal structure provides coordination across departments. The matrix structure therefore supports a formal chain of command for both functional (vertical) and divisional (horizontal) relationships. As a result of this dual structure, some employees actually report to two supervisors simultaneously.

matrix approach An organization structure that uses functional and divisional chains of command simultaneously in the same part of the organization.

EXHIBIT | **9.6** Dual-Authority Structure in a Matrix Organization

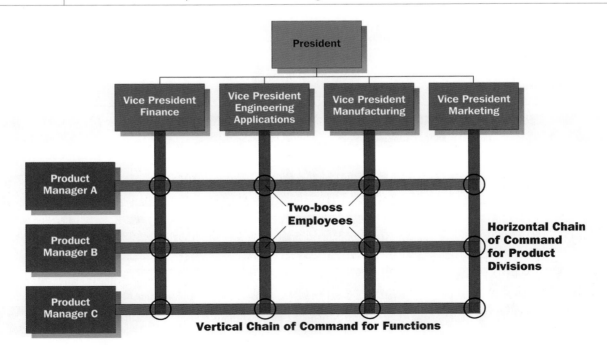

How It Works The dual lines of authority make the matrix unique. To see how the matrix works, consider the global matrix structure illustrated in Exhibit 9.7. The two lines of authority are geographic and product. The geographic boss in Germany coordinates all subsidiaries in Germany, and the plastics products boss coordinates the manufacturing and sale of plastics products around the world. Managers of local subsidiary companies in Germany would report to two superiors, both the country boss and the product boss. The dual authority structure violates the unity-of-command concept described earlier in this chapter but is necessary to give equal emphasis to both functional and divisional lines of authority. Dual lines of authority can be confusing, but after managers learn to use this structure, the matrix provides excellent coordination simultaneously for each geographic region and each product line.

The success of the matrix structure depends on the abilities of people in key matrix roles. **Two-boss employees**, those who report to two supervisors simultaneously, must resolve conflicting demands from the matrix bosses. They must work with senior managers to reach joint decisions. They need excellent human relations skills with which to confront managers and resolve conflicts. The **matrix boss** is the product or functional boss, who is responsible for one side of the matrix. The top leader is responsible for the entire matrix. The **top leader** oversees both the product and functional chains of command. His or her responsibility is to maintain a power balance between the two sides of the matrix. If disputes arise between them, the problem will be kicked upstairs to the top leader.[28]

Team Approach

What It Is Probably the most widespread trend in departmentalization in recent years has been the implementation of team concepts. The vertical chain of command is a powerful means of control, but passing all decisions up the hierarchy takes too long and keeps responsibility at the top. The team approach gives managers a way to delegate authority, push responsibility to lower levels, and be more flexible and responsive in the competitive global environment. Chapter 19 will discuss teams in detail.

How It Works One approach to using teams in organizations is through **cross-functional teams**, which consist of employees from various functional departments

> **two-boss employees**
> Employees who report to two supervisors simultaneously.
>
> **matrix boss** The product or functional boss, responsible for one side of the matrix.
>
> **top leader** The overseer of both the product and functional chains of command, responsible for the entire matrix.
>
> **cross-functional teams** A group of employees from various functional departments that meet as a team to resolve mutual problems.

Concept Connection Hospitals and other health care providers face a great need for **coordination** because medical care needs to be integrated. For instance, collaborative care, like this **cross-functional team** of a nurse, doctor, and dietitian, helps patients with chronic illnesses require fewer emergency department visits. Rush University Medical Center in Chicago started its Virtual Integrated Practice project to give physicians in private practice access to teams of physicians, dieticians, pharmacists, and social workers. VIP replicates the collaboration that can occur in a hospital setting by enabling members to share information via email, phone, and fax.

4 Organizing

EXHIBIT | 9.7 Global Matrix Structure

who are responsible to meet as a team and resolve mutual problems. Team members typically still report to their functional departments, but they also report to the team, one member of whom may be the leader. Cross-functional teams are used to provide needed horizontal coordination to complement an existing divisional or functional structure. A frequent use of cross-functional teams is for change projects, such as new product or service innovation.

The second approach is to use **permanent teams**, groups of employees who are organized in a way similar to a formal department. Each team brings together employees from all functional areas focused on a specific task or project, such as parts supply and logistics for an automobile plant. Emphasis is on horizontal communication and information sharing because representatives from all functions are coordinating their work and skills to complete a specific organizational task. Authority is pushed down to lower levels, and front-line employees are often given the freedom to make decisions and take action on their own. Team members may share or rotate team leadership. With a **team-based structure**, the entire organization is made up of horizontal teams that coordinate their work and work directly with customers to accomplish the organization's goals. At SEI, an investment services company, all work is distributed among 140 or so teams. Some are permanent, such as those that serve major customers or focus on specific markets, but many are designed to work on short-term projects or problems. Most desks are on wheels, and computer links called *pythons* drop from the ceiling in SEI's open office environment. As people change assignments, they unplug their pythons and move to a new locations to work on the next project.[29]

permanent teams A group of participants from several functions who are permanently assigned to solve ongoing problems of common interest.

team-based structure Structure in which the entire organization is made up of horizontal teams that coordinate their activities and work directly with customers to accomplish the organization's goals.

virtual network structure An organization structure that disaggregates major functions to separate companies that are brokered by a small headquarters organization.

The Virtual Network Approach

What It Is The most recent approach to departmentalization extends the idea of horizontal coordination and collaboration beyond the boundaries of the organization. In a variety of industries, vertically integrated, hierarchical organizations are giving way to loosely interconnected groups of companies with permeable boundaries.[30] *Outsourcing*, which means farming out certain activities, such as manufacturing or credit processing, has become a significant trend. In addition, partnerships, alliances, and other complex collaborative forms are now a leading approach to accomplishing strategic goals. In the music industry, firms such as Vivendi Universal and Sony have formed networks of alliances with Internet service providers, digital retailers, software firms, and other companies to bring music to customers in new ways.[31] Some organizations take this networking approach to the extreme to create an innovative structure. The **virtual network structure** means that the firm subcontracts most of its major functions to separate companies and coordinates their activities from a small headquarters organization.[32] Indian telecom company Bharti Tele-Ventures Ltd., for example, outsources everything except marketing and customer management.[33]

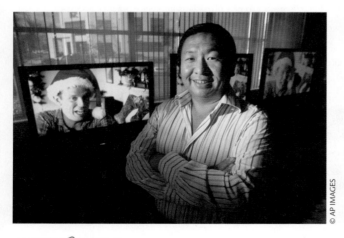

Concept Connection   William Wang, founder of Vizio, Inc., produces a competitively priced plasma television using the **virtual network approach**. Wang keeps costs down by running a lean operation, outsourcing manufacturing, research and development, and technical support. Vizio plasma televisions are priced about 50 percent lower than most brands. "I would never imagine four or five years ago that Sony would look at us a competitor," says Wang.

How It Works The organization may be viewed as a central hub surrounded by a network of outside specialists, as illustrated in Exhibit 9.8. Rather than being housed under one roof, services such as accounting, design, manufacturing, and distribution are outsourced to separate organizations that are connected electronically to the central office.[34] Networked computer systems, collaborative software, and the Internet enable organizations to exchange data and information so rapidly and smoothly that a loosely connected network

EXHIBIT 9.8 Network Approach to Departmentalization

of suppliers, manufacturers, assemblers, and distributors can look and act like one seamless company.

The idea behind networks is that a company can concentrate on what it does best and contract out other activities to companies with distinctive competence in those specific areas, which enables a company to do more with less.[35] Strida, a company based in Birmingham, England, provides an example of the virtual network approach.

Innovative Way

Strida

How do two people run an entire company that sells thousands of high-tech folding bicycles all over the world? Steedman Bass and Bill Bennet do it with a virtual network approach that outsources design, manufacturing, customer service, logistics, accounting, and just about everything else to other organizations.

Bass, an avid cyclist, got into the bicycle business when he and his partner Bennet bought the struggling British company Strida, which was having trouble making enough quality bicycles to meet even minimum orders. The partners soon realized why Strida was struggling. The design for the folding bicycle was a clever engineering idea, but it was a manufacturing nightmare. Bass and Bennet immediately turned over production engineering and new product development to an American bicycle designer, still with intentions of building the bikes at the Birmingham factory. However, a large order from Italy sent them looking for other options. Eventually, they transferred all manufacturing to Ming Cycle Company of Taiwan, which builds the bikes with parts sourced from parts manufacturers in Taiwan and mainland China.

Finally, the last piece of the puzzle was to contract with a company in Birmingham that would take over everything else—from marketing to distribution. Bass and Bennet concentrate their energies on managing the partnerships that make the network function smoothly.[36]

With a network structure such as that used at Strida, it is difficult to answer the question "where is the organization?" in traditional terms. The different organizational parts may be spread all over the world. They are drawn together contractually and coordinated electronically, creating a new form of organization. Much like building blocks, parts of the network can be added or taken away to meet changing needs.[37]

A similar approach to networking is called the **modular approach**, in which a manufacturing company uses outside suppliers to provide entire chunks of a product, which are then assembled into a final product by a handful of workers. The Canadian firm Bombardier's Continental business jet is made up of about a dozen huge modular components from all over the world: the engines from the United States, the nose and cockpit from Canada, the fuselage from Northern Ireland, the tail from Taiwan, the wings from Japan, and so forth.[38] Automobile manufacturers are leaders in using the modular approach. The modular approach hands off

modular approach The process by which a manufacturing company uses outside suppliers to provide large components of the product, which are then assembled into a final product by a few workers.

4
Organizing

responsibility for engineering and production of entire sections of an automobile, such as the chassis or interior, to outside suppliers. Suppliers design a module, making some of the parts themselves and subcontracting others. These modules are delivered right to the assembly line, where a handful of employees bolt them together into a finished vehicle.[39]

Advantages and Disadvantages of Each Structure

Each of these approaches to departmentalization—functional, divisional, matrix, team, and network—has strengths and weaknesses. The major advantages and disadvantages of each are listed in Exhibit 9.9.

Functional Approach Grouping employees by common task permits economies of scale and efficient resource use. For example, at American Airlines, all information technology (IT) people work in the same, large department. They have the expertise and skills to handle almost any IT problem for the organization. Large, functionally based departments enhance the development of in-depth skills because people work on a variety of related problems and are associated with other experts within their own department. Because the chain of command converges at the top, the functional structure also provides a way to centralize decision making and provide unified direction from top managers. The primary disadvantages reflect barriers that exist across departments. Because people are separated into distinct departments, communication and coordination across functions are often poor, causing a slow response to environmental changes. Innovation and change require involvement of several departments. Another problem is that decisions involving more than one department may pile up at the top of the organization and be delayed.

Divisional Approach By dividing employees and resources along divisional lines, the organization will be flexible and responsive to change because each unit is small and tuned in to its environment. By having employees working on a single product line, the concern for customers' needs is high. Coordination across functional departments is better because employees are grouped together in a single location and committed

EXHIBIT | 9.9 Structural Advantages and Disadvantages

Structural Approach	Advantages	Disadvantages
Functional	Efficient use of resources; economies of scale In-depth skill specialization and development Top manager direction and control	Poor communication across functional departments Slow response to external changes; lagging innovation Decisions concentrated at top of hierarchy, creating delay
Divisional	Fast response, flexibility in unstable environment Fosters concern for customer needs Excellent coordination across functional departments	Duplication of resources across divisions Less technical depth and specialization Poor coordination across divisions
Matrix	More efficient use of resources than single hierarchy Flexibility, adaptability to changing environment Interdisciplinary cooperation, expertise available to all divisions	Frustration and confusion from dual chain of command High conflict between two sides of the matrix Many meetings, more discussion than action
Team	Reduced barriers among departments, increased compromise Shorter response time, quicker decisions Better morale, enthusiasm from employee involvement	Dual loyalties and conflict Time and resources spent on meetings Unplanned decentralization
Virtual Network	Can draw on expertise worldwide Highly flexible and responsive Reduced overhead costs	Lack of control; weak boundaries Greater demands on managers Employee loyalty weakened

to one product line. Great coordination exists within divisions; however, coordination *across* divisions is often poor. Problems occurred at Hewlett-Packard, for example, when autonomous divisions went in opposite directions. The software produced in one division did not fit the hardware produced in another. Thus, the divisional structure was realigned to establish adequate coordination across divisions. Another major disadvantage is duplication of resources and the high cost of running separate divisions. Instead of a single research department in which all research people use a single facility, each division may have its own research facility. The organization loses efficiency and economies of scale. In addition, the small size of departments within each division may result in a lack of technical specialization, expertise, and training.

Matrix Approach The matrix structure is controversial because of the dual chain of command. However, the matrix can be highly effective in a complex, rapidly changing environment in which the organization needs to be flexible and adaptable.[40] The conflict and frequent meetings generated by the matrix allow new issues to be raised and resolved. The matrix structure makes efficient use of human resources because specialists can be transferred from one division to another. The major problem is the confusion and frustration caused by the dual chain of command. Matrix bosses and two-boss employees have difficulty with the dual reporting relationships. The matrix structure also can generate high conflict because it pits divisional against functional goals in a domestic structure, or product line versus country goals in a global structure. Rivalry between the two sides of the matrix can be exceedingly difficult for two-boss employees to manage. This problem leads to the third disadvantage: time lost to meetings and discussions devoted to resolving this conflict. Often the matrix structure leads to more discussion than action because different goals and points of view are being addressed. Managers may spend a great deal of time coordinating meetings and assignments, which takes time away from core work activities.[41]

As a new manager, understand the advantages and disadvantages of each approach to departmentalization. Recognize how each structure can provide benefits but might not be appropriate for every organization and situation.

TakeaMoment

4 Organizing

Team Approach The team concept breaks down barriers across departments and improves coordination and cooperation. Team members know one another's problems and compromise rather than blindly pursue their own goals. The team concept also enables the organization to more quickly adapt to customer requests and environmental changes and speeds decision making because decisions need not go to the top of the hierarchy for approval. Another big advantage is the morale boost. Employees are typically enthusiastic about their involvement in bigger projects rather than narrow departmental tasks. At video games company Ubisoft, for example, each studio is set up so that teams of employees and managers work collaboratively to develop new games. Employees don't make a lot of money, but they're motivated by the freedom they have to propose new ideas and put them into action.[42]

Yet the team approach has disadvantages as well. Employees may be enthusiastic about team participation, but they may also experience conflicts and dual loyalties. A cross-functional team may make different work demands on members than do their department managers, and members who participate in more than one team must resolve these conflicts. A large amount of time is devoted to meetings, thus increasing coordination time. Unless the organization truly needs teams to coordinate complex projects and adapt to the environment, it will lose production efficiency with them. Finally, the team approach may cause too much decentralization. Senior department managers who traditionally made decisions might feel left out when a team moves ahead on its own. Team members often do not see the big picture of the corporation and may make decisions that are good for their group but bad for the organization as a whole.

Virtual Network Approach The biggest advantages to a virtual network approach are flexibility and competitiveness on a global scale. The extreme flexibility of a network approach is illustrated by today's "war on terrorism." Most experts agree that the primary reason the insurgency is so difficult to fight is that it is a far-flung collection of groups that share a specific mission but are free to act on their own. "Attack any single part of it, and the rest carries on largely untouched," wrote one journalist after talking with U.S. and Iraqi officials. "It cannot be decapitated, because the insurgency, for the most part, has no head."[43] One response of the United States and its allies is to organize into networks to quickly change course, put new people in place as needed, and respond to situations and challenges as they emerge.[44]

Similarly, today's business organizations can benefit from a flexible network approach that lets them shift resources and respond quickly. A network organization can draw on resources and expertise worldwide to achieve the best quality and price and can sell its products and services worldwide. Flexibility comes from the ability to hire whatever services are needed, and to change a few months later without constraints from owning plant, equipment, and facilities. The organization can continually redefine itself to fit new product and market opportunities. This structure is perhaps the leanest of all organization forms because little supervision is required. Large teams of staff specialists and administrators are not needed. A network organization may have only two or three levels of hierarchy, compared with ten or more in traditional organizations.[45]

One of the major disadvantages is lack of hands-on control. Managers do not have all operations under one roof and must rely on contracts, coordination, negotiation, and electronic linkages to hold things together. Each partner in the network necessarily acts in its own self-interest. The weak and ambiguous boundaries create higher uncertainty and greater demands on managers for defining shared goals, coordinating activities, managing relationships, and keeping people focused and motivated.[46] Finally, in this type of organization, employee loyalty can weaken. Employees might feel they can be replaced by contract services. A cohesive corporate culture is less likely to develop, and turnover tends to be higher because emotional commitment between organization and employee is weak.[47]

ORGANIZING FOR HORIZONTAL COORDINATION

One reason for the growing use of teams and networks is that many companies are recognizing the limits of traditional vertical organization structures in a fast-shifting environment. In general, the trend is toward breaking down barriers between departments, and many companies are moving toward horizontal structures based on work processes rather than departmental functions.[48] However, regardless of the type of structure, every organization needs mechanisms for horizontal integration and coordination. The structure of an organization is not complete without designing the horizontal as well as the vertical dimensions of structure.[49]

The Need for Coordination

As organizations grow and evolve, two things happen. First, new positions and departments are added to deal with factors in the external environment or with new strategic needs. For example, in recent years, most colleges and universities established in-house legal departments to cope with increasing government regulations and a greater threat of lawsuits in today's society. Whereas small schools once relied on outside law firms, legal counsel is now considered crucial to the everyday operation of a college or university.[50] Many organizations establish information technology departments to manage the proliferation of new information systems. As companies add positions and departments to meet changing needs, they grow more complex, with hundreds of positions and departments performing incredibly diverse activities.

Second, senior managers have to find a way to tie all these departments together. The formal chain of command and the supervision it provides is effective, but it is not enough. The organization needs systems to process information and enable communication among people in different departments and at different levels. **Coordination** refers to the quality of collaboration across departments. Without coordination, a company's left hand will not act in concert with the right hand, causing problems and conflicts. Coordination is required regardless of whether the organization has a functional, divisional, or team structure. Employees identify with their immediate department or team, taking its interest to heart, and they may not want to compromise with other units for the good of the organization as a whole.

The dangers of poor coordination are reflected in what Lee Iacocca said about Chrysler Corporation in the 1980s:

> What I found at Chrysler were 35 vice presidents, each with his own turf. . . . I couldn't believe, for example, that the guy running engineering departments wasn't in constant touch with his counterpart in manufacturing. But that's how it was. Everybody worked independently. I took one look at that system and I almost threw up. That's when I knew I was in really deep trouble.
>
> I'd call in a guy from engineering, and he'd stand there dumbfounded when I'd explain to him that we had a design problem or some other hitch in the engineering-manufacturing relationship. He might have the ability to invent a brilliant piece of engineering that would save us a lot of money. He might come up with a terrific new design. There was only one problem: He didn't know that the manufacturing people couldn't build it. Why? Because he had never talked to them about it. Nobody at Chrysler seemed to understand that interaction among the different functions in a company is absolutely critical. People in engineering and manufacturing almost have to be sleeping together. These guys weren't even flirting![51]

If one thing changed at Chrysler (now DaimlerChrysler) in the years before Iacocca retired, it was improved coordination. Cooperation among engineering, marketing, and manufacturing enabled the rapid design and production of the popular PT Cruiser, for example.

The problem of coordination is amplified in the international arena, because organizational units are differentiated not only by goals and work activities but also by geographical distance, time differences, cultural values, and perhaps language. How can managers ensure that needed coordination will take place in their company, both domestically and globally? Coordination is the outcome of information and cooperation. Managers can design systems and structures to promote horizontal coordination. At Whirlpool, for example, managers decentralized operations to support a global strategy, giving more authority and responsibility to teams of designers and engineers in developing countries like Brazil, and established outsourcing relationships with manufacturers in China and India.[52] Exhibit 9.10 illustrates the evolution of organizational structures, with a growing emphasis on horizontal coordination. Although the vertical functional structure is effective in stable environments, it does

coordination The quality of collaboration across departments.

EXHIBIT | 9.10

Evolution of Organization Structures

Traditional Vertical Structure

Cross-Functional Teams and Project Managers

Reengineering to Horizontal Teams

not provide the horizontal coordination needed in times of rapid change. Innovations such as cross-functional teams, task forces, and project managers work within the vertical structure but provide a means to increase horizontal communication and cooperation. The next stage involves reengineering to structure the organization into teams working on horizontal processes. The vertical hierarchy is flattened, with perhaps only a few senior executives in traditional support functions such as finance and human resources.

Task Forces, Teams, and Project Management

A **task force** is a temporary team or committee designed to solve a short-term problem involving several departments.[53] Task force members represent their departments and share information that enables coordination. For example, the Shawmut National Corporation created a task force in human resources to consolidate all employment services into a single area. The task force looked at job banks, referral programs, employment procedures, and applicant tracking systems; found ways to perform these functions for all Shawmut's divisions in one human resource department; and then disbanded.[54] In addition to creating task forces, companies also set up *cross-functional teams,* as described earlier. A cross-functional team furthers horizontal coordination because participants from several departments meet regularly to solve ongoing problems of common interest.[55] This team is similar to a task force except that it works with continuing rather than temporary problems and might exist for several years. Team members think in terms of working together for the good of the whole rather than just for their own department.

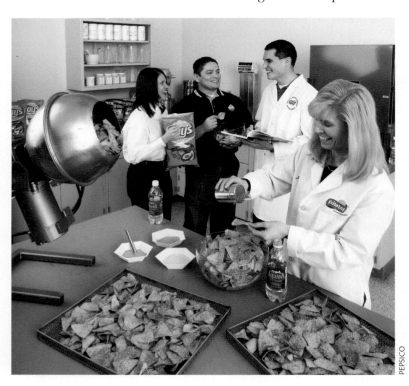

Companies also use project managers to increase coordination between functional departments. A **project manager** is a person who is responsible for coordinating the activities of several departments for the completion of a specific project.[56] Project managers are critical today because many organizations are continually reinventing themselves, creating flexible structures, and working on projects with an ever-changing assortment of people and organizations.[57] Project managers might work on several different projects at one time and might have to move in and out of new projects at a moment's notice.

Concept Connection   Frito-Lay, a subsidiary of PepsiCo Inc., thrives on the introduction of new products such as Lay's Cool Guacamole potato chips and Doritos Guacamole tortilla chips. A **task force** that included members of Adelante, the Frito-Lay network for Hispanic employees, helped develop both products. In the photo, Frito-Lay researchers and Adelante members check the quality of the new guacamole chips.

The distinctive feature of the project manager position is that the person is not a member of one of the departments being coordinated. Project managers are located outside of the departments and have responsibility for coordinating several departments to achieve desired project outcomes. General Mills, Procter & Gamble, and General Foods all use product managers to coordinate their product lines. A manager is assigned to each line, such as Cheerios, Bisquick, and Hamburger Helper. Product managers set budget goals, marketing targets, and strategies and obtain the cooperation from advertising, production, and sales personnel needed for implementing product strategy.

task force A temporary team or committee formed to solve a specific short-term problem involving several departments.

project manager A person responsible for coordinating the activities of several departments on a full-time basis for the completion of a specific project.

As a new manager, be a team or task force member who reaches out to facilitate horizontal coordination. Don't limit yourself to your own function. Share information across departmental boundaries to improve horizontal communication and understanding. Build your people skills to influence and persuade as an effective project manager.

TakeaMoment

In some organizations, project managers are included on the organization chart, as illustrated in Exhibit 9.11. The project manager is drawn to one side of the chart to indicate authority over the project but not over the people assigned to it. Dashed lines to the project manager indicate responsibility for coordination and communication with assigned team members, but department managers retain line authority over functional employees. Project managers might also have titles such as product manager, integrator, program manager, or process owner. Project managers need excellent people skills. They use expertise and persuasion to achieve coordination among various departments, and their jobs involve getting people together, listening, building trust, confronting problems, and resolving conflicts and disputes in the best interest of the project and the organization.

Many organizations move to a stronger horizontal approach such as the use of permanent teams, project managers, or process owners after going through a redesign procedure called reengineering.

Reengineering

Reengineering, sometimes called *business process reengineering,* is the radical redesign of business processes to achieve dramatic improvements in cost, quality, service, and speed.[58] Because the focus of reengineering is on process rather than function, reengineering generally leads to a shift away from a strong vertical structure to one emphasizing stronger horizontal coordination and greater flexibility in responding to changes in the environment.

Reengineering changes the way managers think about how work is done in their organizations. Rather than focusing on narrow jobs structured into distinct, functional departments, they emphasize core processes that cut horizontally across the company and involve teams of employees working to provide value directly to customers.[59] A **process** is an organized group of related tasks and activities that work together to transform inputs into outputs and create value. Common examples of processes include new product development, order fulfillment, and customer service.[60]

Reengineering frequently involves a shift to a horizontal team-based structure, as described earlier in this chapter. All the people who work on a particular process have easy access to one another so they can easily communicate and coordinate their efforts, share knowledge, and provide value to customers.[61] Consider how reengineering at Alcoa's Michigan Casting Center led to the formation of manufacturing teams that became the fundamental organizational unit.

reengineering The radical redesign of business processes to achieve dramatic improvements in cost, quality, service, and speed.

process An organized group of related tasks and activities that work together to transform inputs into outputs and create value.

4 Organizing

EXHIBIT 9.11 Example of Project Manager Relationships to Other Departments

Innovative Way

Michigan Casting Center (MCC) is now North America's largest supplier of aluminum steering knuckles for automotive suspension systems. However, in the mid-1990s, quality and delivery problems, combined with operational inefficiency and high turnover, almost put the company under.

At the time, MCC was organized by function, with the manufacturing function built around work processes that served all product lines, as illustrated in Part A of Exhibit 9.12. No one had accountability for moving a product efficiently through the entire manufacturing process to the end customer. Managers operated in isolated silos, focused solely on their own area of responsibility rather than the overall success of the manufacturing department.

A team of managers reengineered manufacturing to organize work around product flow paths, as illustrated in Part B of Exhibit 9.12. The new organization created focus and ownership at the product level by giving leaders responsibility and accountability across all work processes related to a specific product. Support staff members were assigned accountability for specific product lines, making them a part of the manufacturing teams as well. Cell leaders were empowered to solve problems and make decisions, leading to a deeper level of engagement, feeling of ownership, and sense of pride. Eventually, teams became capable of running the plant on their own, freeing managers to focus on strategic issues.

Operational efficiency, product quality, and delivery performance all improved dramatically under the reengineered system. For example, defective parts returned per million decreased from more than 6,000 to around 20 four years later. And by synchronizing internal activities, MCC was able to more effectively synchronize production with customers' requirements. Giving employees expanded jobs, clearer accountability, and more autonomy led to greater job satisfaction and commitment too. Voluntary turnover, which had been as high as 42 percent a year, decreased to around 4 percent.[62]

As illustrated by this example, reengineering can lead to stunning results, but, like all business ideas, it has its drawbacks. Organizations often have difficulty realigning power relationships and management processes to support work redesign, and thus may not reap the intended benefits of reengineering. According to some estimates, 70 percent of reengineering efforts fail to reach their intended goals.[63] Because reengineering is expensive, time consuming, and usually painful to implement, it seems best suited to companies that are facing serious competitive threats.

TakeaMoment | **As a potential new manager, check out your authority role models by completing the New Manager Self-Test on page 266.**

STRUCTURE FOLLOWS STRATEGY

Vertical hierarchies continue to thrive because they often provide important benefits for organizations, However, in today's environment, organizations with stronger horizontal designs typically perform better.[64] How do managers know whether to design a structure that emphasizes the formal, vertical hierarchy or one with an emphasis on horizontal communication and collaboration? The answer lies in the organization's strategic goals. The right structure is designed to fit the organization's strategy. A recent study demonstrated that business performance is strongly influenced by how well the company's structure is aligned with its strategic intent, so managers strive to pick strategies and structures that are congruent.[65]

TakeaMoment | **As a new manager, understand how structure fits the organization's strategic goals. Design the right mix of structural characteristics to enable the organization to effectively implement its strategy.**

EXHIBIT | 9.12 Reengineering Manufacturing at Michigan Casting Center

SOURCES: Dan Groszkiewicz and Brent Warren, "Alcoa's Michigan Casting Center Runs the Business from the Bottom Up," *Journal of Organizational Excellence* (Spring 2006): 13–23. (used with permission).

In Chapter 7, we discussed several strategies that business firms can adopt. Two strategies proposed by Porter are differentiation and cost leadership.[66] With a differentiation strategy, the organization attempts to develop innovative products unique to the market. With a cost leadership strategy, the organization strives for internal efficiency.

New Manager Self-Test

Authority Role Models

An organization's structure is based on authority. Expectations about authority for a new manager are often based on experiences in your first authority figures and role models—Mom and Dad. To understand your authority role models, please answer each of the following items as Mostly True or Mostly False for you. Think about each statement as it applies to the parent or parents who made primary decisions about raising you.

	Mostly True	Mostly False
1. My parent(s) believed that children should get their way in the family as often as the parents do.	_____	_____
2. When a family policy was established, my parent(s) discussed the reasoning behind it with the children.	_____	_____
3. My parent(s) believed it was for my own good if I was made to conform to what they thought was right.	_____	_____
4. My parent(s) felt the children should make up our own minds about what we wanted to do, even if they did not agree with us.	_____	_____
5. My parent(s) directed my activities through reasoning and discussion.	_____	_____
6. My parent(s) was clear about who was the boss in the family.	_____	_____
7. My parent(s) allowed me to decide most things for myself without a lot of direction.	_____	_____
8. My parent(s) took the children's opinions into consideration when making family decisions.	_____	_____
9. If I didn't meet parental rules and expectations, I could expect to be punished.	_____	_____

SCORING AND INTERPRETATION: Each question pertains to one of three subscales of **parental authority**. Questions 1, 4, and 7 reflect *permissive* parental authority, questions 2, 5, and 8 indicate *flexible* authority, and questions 3, 6, and 9 indicate *authoritarian* parental authority. The subscale for which you checked more items Mostly True may reveal personal expectations from your early role models that shape your comfort with authority as a new manager. *Authoritarian* expectations typically would fit in a traditional vertical structure with fixed rules and a clear hierarchy of authority (mechanistic organization characteristics). *Flexible* authority expectations typically would fit with horizontal organizing, such as managing teams, projects, and reengineering (organic organization characteristics). Because most organizations thrive on structure, *permissive* expectations may be insufficient to enforce accountability under any structure. How do you think your childhood role models affect your authority expectations? Remember, this questionnaire is just a guide because your current expectations about authority may not directly reflect your childhood experiences.

SOURCE: Adapted from John R. Buri, "Parental Authority Questionnaire," *Journal of Personality and Social Assessment* 57 (1991): 110–119.

Typically, strategic goals of cost efficiency occur in more stable environments while goals of innovation and flexibility occur in more uncertain environments. The terms *mechanistic* and *organic* can be used to explain structural responses to strategy and the environment.[67] Goals of efficiency and a stable environment are associated with a mechanistic system. This type of organization typically has a rigid, vertical, centralized structure, with most decisions made at the top. The organization is highly specialized and characterized by rules, procedures, and a clear hierarchy of authority. With goals of innovation and a rapidly changing environment, however, the organization tends to be much looser, free-flowing, and adaptive, using an organic system. The structure is more horizontal, and decision-making authority is decentralized. People at lower levels have more responsibility and authority for solving problems, enabling the organization to be more fluid and adaptable to changes.[68]

Go to the experiential exercise on pages 269–270 that pertains to organic versus mechanistic structure.   TakeaMoment

Exhibit 9.13 shows a simplified continuum that illustrates how different structural approaches are associated with strategy and the environment. The pure functional structure is appropriate for achieving internal efficiency goals in a stable environment. The vertical functional structure uses task specialization and a strict chain of command to gain efficient use of scarce resources, but it does not enable the organization to be flexible or innovative. In contrast, horizontal teams are appropriate when the primary goal is innovation and the organization needs flexibility to cope with an uncertain environment. Each team is small, is able to be responsive, and has the people and resources necessary for performing its task. The flexible horizontal structure enables organizations to differentiate themselves and respond quickly to the demands of a shifting environment but at the expense of efficient resource use.

Exhibit 9.13 also illustrates how other forms of structure represent intermediate steps on the organization's path to efficiency or innovation. The functional structure with cross-functional teams and project managers provides greater coordination and flexibility than the pure functional structure. The divisional structure promotes differentiation because each division can focus on specific products and customers, although divisions tend to be larger and less flexible than small teams. Exhibit 9.13 does not include all possible structures, but it illustrates how structures can be used to facilitate the organization's strategic goals.

EXHIBIT | 9.13 Relationship of Structural Approach to Strategy and the Environment

ch9   A MANAGER'S ESSENTIALS: WHAT HAVE WE LEARNED?

- Fundamental characteristics of organization structure include work specialization, chain of command, authority and responsibility, span of management, and centralization and decentralization. These dimensions represent the vertical hierarchy and define how authority and responsibility are distributed.

- Another major concept is departmentalization, which describes how organization employees are grouped. Three traditional approaches are functional, divisional, and matrix; contemporary approaches are team and virtual network structures. The functional approach groups employees by common skills and tasks. The opposite structure is divisional, which groups people by organizational output such that each division has a mix of functional skills and tasks. The matrix structure uses two chains of command simultaneously, and some employees have two bosses. The team approach uses permanent teams and cross-functional teams to achieve better coordination and employee commitment than is possible with a purely functional structure. The network approach means that a firm concentrates on what it does best and subcontracts other functions to separate organizations that are connected to the headquarters electronically.

- Each organization form has advantages and disadvantages and can be used by managers to meet the needs of the competitive situation. In addition, managers adjust elements of the vertical structure, such as the degree of centralization or decentralization, to meet changing needs.

- As organizations grow, they add new departments, functions, and hierarchical levels. A major problem for management is how to tie the whole organization together. Horizontal coordination mechanisms provide coordination across departments and include reengineering, task forces, project managers, and horizontal teams.

- The correct structural approach is influenced by the firm's strategic goals. When a firm's strategy is to differentiate its products or services, an organic flexible structure using teams, decentralization, and empowered employees is appropriate. A mechanistic structure is appropriate for a low-cost strategy, which typically occurs in a stable environment. The structure needs to be looser and more flexible when environmental uncertainty is high.

ch9   DISCUSSION QUESTIONS

1. Sandra Holt, manager of Electronics Assembly, asked Hector Cruz, her senior technician, to handle things in the department while Sandra worked on the budget. She needed peace and quiet for at least a week to complete her figures. After 10 days, Sandra discovered that Hector had hired a senior secretary, not realizing that Sandra had promised interviews to two other people. Evaluate Sandra's approach to delegation.

2. Many experts note that organizations have been making greater use of teams in recent years. What factors might account for this trend?

3. An organizational consultant was heard to say, "Some aspect of functional structure appears in every organization." Do you agree? Explain.

4. The divisional structure is often considered almost the opposite of a functional structure. Do you agree? Briefly explain the major differences in these two approaches to departmentalization.

5. Some people argue that the matrix structure should be adopted only as a last resort because the dual chains of command can create more problems than they solve. Discuss. Do you agree or disagree? Why?

6. What is the virtual network approach to structure? Is the use of authority and responsibility different compared with other forms of departmentalization? Explain.

7. The Hay Group published a report that some managers have personalities suited to horizontal relationships such as project management that

achieve results with little formal authority. Other managers are more suited to operating roles with much formal authority in a vertical structure. In what type of structure—functional, matrix, team, or virtual network—would you feel most comfortable managing? Which structure would be the most challenging for you? Give your reasons.

8. Experts say that organizations are becoming increasingly decentralized, with authority, decision-making responsibility, and accountability being pushed farther down into the organization. How will this trend affect what will be asked of you as a new manager? The chapter suggested that structure should be designed to fit strategy. Some theorists argue that strategy should be designed to fit the organization's structure. With which theory do you agree? Explain.

9. Carnival Cruise Lines provides pleasure cruises to the masses. Carnival has several ships and works on high volume/low price rather than offering luxury cruises. What would you predict about the organization structure of a Carnival Cruise ship compared with a company that had smaller ships for wealthy customers? Discuss why an organization in an uncertain environment requires more horizontal relationships than one in a certain environment.

10. What is the difference between manufacturing and service technology? How would you classify a university, a local discount store, a nursery school? How would you expect the structure of a service organization to differ from that of a manufacturing organization?

11. What impact does the growing use of digital technology have on organizational structure? Would you expect the structure of an Internet-based organization such as eBay, which operates almost entirely online, to be different from a bricks-and-mortar company such as General Electric that uses the Internet for business-to-business transactions with vendors? Why or why not?

ch9 MANAGEMENT IN PRACTICE: EXPERIENTIAL EXERCISE

Organic Versus Mechanistic Organization Structure

Interview an employee at your university, such as a department head or secretary. Have the employee answer the following 13 questions about his or her job and organizational conditions. Then, answer the same set of questions for a job you have held.

Disagree Strongly ① ② ③ ④ ⑤ Agree Strongly

1. Your work would be considered routine.

   1 2 3 4 5

2. A clearly known way is established to do the major tasks you encounter.

   1 2 3 4 5

3. Your work has high variety and frequent exceptions.

   1 2 3 4 5

4. Communications from above consist of information and advice rather than instructions and directions.

   1 2 3 4 5

5. You have the support of peers and your supervisor to do your job well.

   1 2 3 4 5

6. You seldom exchange ideas or information with people doing other kinds of jobs.

   1 2 3 4 5

7. Decisions relevant to your work are made above you and passed down.

   1 2 3 4 5

8. People at your level frequently have to figure out for themselves what their jobs are for the day.

   1 2 3 4 5

9. Lines of authority are clear and precisely defined.

   1 2 3 4 5

10. Leadership tends to be democratic rather than autocratic in style.

    1 2 3 4 5

11. Job descriptions are written and up-to-date for each job.

    1 2 3 4 5

12. People understand each other's jobs and often do different tasks.

    1 2 3 4 5

13. A manual of policies and procedures is available to use when a problem arises.

    1 2 3 4 5

Scoring and Interpretation

To obtain the total score, subtract the scores for questions 1, 2, 6, 7, 9, 11, and 13 from the number 6 and total the adjusted scores.

Total Score, Employee: _____

Total Score, You: _____

Compare the total score for a place you have worked to the score of the university employee you interviewed. A total score of 52 or above suggests that you or the other respondent is working in an organic organization. The score reflects a loose, flexible structure that is often associated with uncertain environments and small-batch or service technology. People working in this structure feel empowered. Many organizations today are moving in the direction of flexible structures and empowerment.

A score of 26 or below suggests a mechanistic structure. This structure utilizes traditional control and functional specialization, which often occurs in a certain environment, a stable organization, and routine or mass-production technology. People in this structure may feel controlled and constrained.

Discuss the pros and cons of organic versus mechanistic structure. Does the structure of the employee you interviewed fit the nature of the organization's environment, strategic goals, and technology? How about the structure for your own workplace? How might you redesign the structure to make the work organization more effective?

ch9   MANAGEMENT IN PRACTICE: ETHICAL DILEMMA

A Matter of Delegation

Tom Harrington loved his job as an assistant quality-control officer for Rockingham Toys. After six months of unemployment, he was anxious to make a good impression on his boss, Frank Golopolus. One of his new responsibilities was ensuring that new product lines met federal safety guidelines. Rockingham had made several manufacturing changes over the past year. Golopolus and the rest of the quality-control team had been working 60-hour weeks to trouble-shoot the new production process.

Harrington was aware of numerous changes in product safety guidelines that he knew would impact the new Rockingham toys. Golopolus was also aware of the guidelines, but he was taking no action to implement them. Harrington wasn't sure whether his boss expected him to implement the new procedures. The ultimate responsibility was his boss's, and Harrington was concerned about moving ahead on his own. To cover for his boss, he continued to avoid the questions he received from the factory floor, but he was beginning to wonder whether Rockingham would have time to make changes with the Christmas season rapidly approaching.

Harrington felt loyalty to Golopolus for giving him a job and didn't want to alienate him by interfering. However, he was beginning to worry what might happen if he didn't act. Rockingham had a fine product safety reputation and was rarely challenged on matters of quality. Should he question Golopolus about implementing the new safety guidelines?

What Would You Do?

1. Prepare a memo to Golopolus, summarizing the new safety guidelines that affect the Rockingham product line and requesting his authorization for implementation.

2. Mind your own business. Golopolus hasn't said anything about the new guidelines and you don't want to overstep your authority. You've been unemployed and need this job.

3. Send copies of the reports anonymously to the operations manager, who is Golopolus's boss.

SOURCE: Based on Doug Wallace, "The Man Who Knew Too Much," *Business Ethics*, 2 (March–April 1993): 7–8.

ch9   CASE FOR CRITICAL ANALYSIS

FMB&T

Marshall Pinkard, president and CEO of FMB&T, a growing California-based regional commercial and consumer retail bank, clicked on an e-mail from Ayishia Coles. Ayishia was the bright, hard-working, self-confident woman who'd recently come onboard as the bank's executive vice president and chief information officer. The fact that the person in Coles's position in the company's traditional vertical organization now reported directly to him and was a full-fledged member of the executive committee reflected FMB&T's recognition of just how important information technology was to all aspects of its increasingly competitive business. The successful, leading-edge banks were the ones using information technology not only to operate efficiently, but also to help them focus more effectively on customer needs. Marshall settled back to read what he expected would be a report on how she was settling in. He was sadly mistaken.

After a few months on the job, Ayishia Coles was frustrated. What she needed from him, she wrote, was a clear statement of her responsibilities and authority. The way Ayishia saw it, the relationship between information technology and the bank's other business units was muddled, often causing considerable confusion, friction, and inefficiency. Typically someone from retail banking or marketing, for example, came to her department with a poorly defined problem, such as how to link up checking account records with investment records, and they always expected a solution the same day. What made the situation even more vexing was that more often than not, the problem crossed organizational lines. She found that generally the more work units the problem affected, the less likely it was that any single unit took responsibility for defining exactly what they wanted IT to do. Who exactly was supposed to be getting all these units together and coordinating requests? When she tried to step into the breach and act as a facilitator, unit managers usually didn't welcome her efforts.

Despite the vagueness of their requests, the work units still expected IT to come up with a solution—and come up with it quickly. All of these expectations seemed almost calculated to drive the methodical IT folks mad. Before taking on a problem, they wanted to make sure they thoroughly understood all of its dimensions so that the solution would fit seamlessly into the existing systems. This coordination took time that other parts of the bank weren't willing to give IT.

In addition, Ayishia knew the IT staff was increasingly feeling underutilized. The staff wanted to identify opportunities for dazzling new IT developments to contribute to business strategies, but it found itself limited to applications work. Ayishia's greatest concern was the president of a large regional branch who was actively campaigning to locate decentralized IT departments in each large branch under branch authority so that work would be completed faster to meet branch needs. He said it would be better to let work-units coordinate their own IT departments rather than run everything though corporate IT. Under that scenario, Ayishia Coles' department could end up one-half its current size.

Marshall leaned back in his high-backed executive chair and sighed. At the very least, he needed to clarify Ayishia's authority and responsibilities as she had asked him to do. But he recognized that the new vice president was talking about a much larger can of worms. Was it time to rethink the bank's entire organizational structure?

Questions

1. What are the main organizational causes of the frustration that Ayishia Coles feels?

2. If you were Marshall Pinkard, how would you address both Ayishia's request for clarification about her authority and responsibilities and the underlying problems her e-mail brings to his attention? Can the problems be addressed with minor adjustments, or would you need to consider a drastic overhaul of the bank's organizational structure? What environmental and technological factors would influence your decision?

3. Sketch a general chart for the type of organization that you think would work best for IT at FMB&T.

SOURCES: Based on Perry Glasser, "In CIOs We Trust," *CIO Enterprise,* (June 15, 1999): 34–44; Stephanie Overby, "What Really Matters: Staying in the Game," *CIO Magazine* (October 1, 2004), www.cio.com/archive/100104/role.html; and Alenka Grealish, "Banking Trends in 2005 That Will Make A Difference," *Bank Systems & Technology* (December 14, 2004): www.banktech.com/news/showarticle.jhtml?articleid=55301770.

4

Organizing

ch9 ON THE JOB VIDEO CASE

Timbuk2: CEO Sets a Course

Making decisions is a big part of any manager's job. Making the decisions that determine the direction a company will take is the job of a CEO. Mark Dwight, CEO of Timbuk2, is comfortable with this role, even though it means sometimes making unpopular decisions—or even making mistakes. Timbuk2's 45 workers tend to be young, so Dwight sees himself as the senior manager in more ways than one. "I'm the experienced executive here, and it's my charter to manage the company," he

explains. "It's not a democracy. I ask the people that I think have a good perspective on [an] issue, who are affected by the issue, we discuss it, and I make a command decision based on those inputs. Hopefully, people think I make educated, informed decisions. That's my job."

Most of the decisions Dwight is referring to are nonprogrammed decisions—such as the design of a new product or the type of fabric to use. These decisions can affect sales, the brand image, and even the overall performance of the company. During one recent meeting on the new Tag Junkie bags (whose working name may be changed, requiring another decision), Dwight and his managerial staff discussed whether to invest in a costly, high-performance fabric for the bag. The cost of the fabric could potentially put the price of the bag out of reach for the average professional bike messenger. But in talking about it, the group speculated that the bag could successfully reach the motorcycle market. With night reflectors and highly durable, weatherproof fabric, the bag could be very appealing to motorcyclists—and could be offered at a higher price. Then the group discussed the working name of the product line—Tag Junkie, a term used by bike messengers and also the name of the original Timbuk2 messenger bag. Did they want to resurrect the name for the final product or try something new? The group tossed around the name Pro Series—and everyone liked the ring of it. "It sounds fast," observed marketing manager Macy Allatt. But the decision was not yet final, since the group wanted to weigh the consequences of a name change in the bike messenger market.

"Mark is the guy with the vision," says Allatt. "He will drive the decision making, but he's very open to taking input from other people. When decisions need to be made, everyone sits down and we hash it out, and when we come out of the room, we feel like we're going to make some progress."

Just about every decision facing Mark Dwight has some degree of uncertainty. He knows that he wants Timbuk2 to achieve $25 million in sales in five years; he knows he wants the firm to reach new markets such as motorcycle riders and yet rejuvenate the bike messenger market; he knows the firm needs to find new distribution channels. But there's no guarantee that a single decision is the right one. Still, Dwight believes he is ultimately responsible

for deciding which way to go. "We have to make a decision and move on," he remarks. "Sometimes we make mistakes, but it's better to move to a new place than sit around and talk about it." One recent decision involved moving the production of certain bags to China to cut production costs. Despite receiving criticism for the move, particularly because so many textile factories surrounding Timbuk2's hometown of San Francisco have been closed, Dwight hung tight to his decision, insisting that transferring some production overseas would actually help the San Francisco factory stay open. So far, Dwight has been able to maintain the San Francisco plant. Increased orders for the firm's artistic Graphic Messenger Bags have actually resulted in hiring more employees at the San Francisco facility.

As a leader, Dwight doesn't mind taking the heat. "I'm a strong personality. . . . It's my job to call the shots, and I can be very dictatorial about it." If he's right, future success for Timbuk2 is in the bag.

Questions

1. What part do you think intuition plays in Mark Dwight's decision making? Why?

2. How would you categorize Dwight's leadership participation style on the Vroom-Jago model? Why?

3. Which of the new "decision approaches for turbulent times" that are described in the chapter does Dwight use?

SOURCES: Company Web site, *http://www.timbuk2.com*, accessed August 13, 2004; Brad Stone, "Homegrown," *Newsweek*, April 19, 2004, *http://www.msnbc.com*.

---

ch9 BIZ FLIX VIDEO CASE

Apollo 13

This film dramatically portrays the Apollo 13 mission to the moon that almost ended in disaster. Only innovative problem solving and decision making amid massive ambiguity saved the crew. Almost any scene dramatically makes this point. Flight Director Gene Kranz wrote a book describing the mission and the actions that prevented disaster.

A zero gravity simulator, a KC-135 four-engine jet aircraft (NASA's "Vomit Comet"), helped create the film's realistic weightless scenes. These scenes required 600 parabolic loops over 10 days of filming.[1] See the later Biz Flix exercise for a discussion of another scene from *Apollo 13*.

This scene is a composite built from portions of the "Carbon Dioxide Problem" sequence, which occurs a little after the midway point of the film, and parts of the "With Every Breath . . ." sequence, which appears about seven minutes later. The scene's first part follows the nearly complete shutdown of the Apollo 13 module to save battery power. Mission Control has detected rising carbon dioxide levels in the module, which could kill the astronauts if NASA engineers on the ground cannot solve the problem. The film continues with the Apollo 13 crew building a carbon dioxide filter designed by the engineers.

What to Watch for and Ask Yourself

1. What is the problem in this scene?
2. What are the engineers' options for solving the problem?
3. Does this scene show innovation and innovative behavior? If so, in what form?

[1] J. Craddock, Ed. *VideoHound's Golden Movie Retriever*, (Farmington Hills, MI: The Gale Group, Inc.), 2000.

ch9 ENDNOTES

1. This questionnaire is based on Richard M. Wielkiewicz, "The Leadership Attitudes and Beliefs Scale: An Instrument for Evaluating College Students' Thinking About Leadership and Organizations," *Journal of College Student Development* 41 (May/June-2000): 335–346.
2. Carlos Ghosn, "Saving the Business Without Losing the Company," *Harvard Business Review* (January 2002): 37–45; Jay Greene, "Less Could Be More at Microsoft," *BusinessWeek* (October 3, 2005): 40; Josée Valcourt, "Chrysler Begins Overhaul in Engineering," *The Wall Street Journal*, February 19, 2008.
3. John Child, *Organization: A Guide to Problems and Practice*, 2nd ed. (London: Harper & Row, 1984).
4. Adam Smith, *The Wealth of Nations* (New York: Modern Library, 1937).
5. This discussion is based on Richard L. Daft, *Organization Theory and Design*, 4th ed. (St. Paul, MN: West, 1992), pp. 387–388.
6. C. I. Barnard, *The Functions of the Executive* (Cambridge, MA: Harvard University Press, 1938).
7. Thomas A. Stewart, "CEOs See Clout Shifting," *Fortune* (November 6, 1989): 66.
8. Michael G. O'Loughlin, "What Is Bureaucratic Accountability and How Can We Measure It?" *Administration & Society* 22, no. 3 (November 1990): 275–302; and Brian Dive, "When Is an Organization Too Flat?" *Across the Board* (July–August 2003): 20–23.
9. Gary L. Neilson and Bruce A. Pasternack, "The Cat That Came Back," *Strategy + Business*, no. 40 (August 17, 2005): 32–45.
10. Carrie R. Leana, "Predictors and Consequences of Delegation," *Academy of Management Journal* 29 (1986): 754–774.
11. Curtis Sittenfeld, "Powered by the People," *Fast Company* (July–August 1999): 178–189.
12. Barbara Davison, "Management Span of Control: How Wide Is Too Wide?" *Journal of Business Strategy* 24, no. 4 (2003): 22–29; Paul D. Collins and Frank Hull, "Technology and Span of Control: Woodward Revisited," *Journal of Management Studies* 23 (March 1986): 143–164; David D. Van Fleet and Arthur G. Bedeian, "A History of the Span of Management," *Academy of Management Review* 2 (1977): 356–372; and C. W. Barkdull, "Span of Control—A Method of Evaluation," *Michigan Business Review* 15 (May 1963): 25–32.
13. Gary Neilson, Bruce A. Pasternack, and Decio Mendes, "The Four Bases of Organizational DNA," *Strategy + Business*, no. 33 (December 10, 2003): 48–57.
14. Barbara Davison, "Management Span of Control"; Brian Dive, "When Is an Organization Too Flat?"; and Brian Dumaine, "What the Leaders of Tomorrow See," *Fortune* (July 3, 1989): 48–62; and Raghuram G. Rajan and Julie Wulf, "The Flattening Firm: Evidence from Panel Data on the Changing Nature of Corporate Hierarchies," working paper, reported in Caroline Ellis, "The Flattening Corporation," *MIT Sloan Management Review* (Summer 2003): 5.
15. William G. Ouchi, "Power to the Principals: Decentralization in Three Large School Districts," *Organization Science* 17, no. 2 (March-April 2006): 298–307.
16. Dennis Cauchon, "The Little Company That Could," *USA Today*, October 9, 2005, http://www.usatoday.com.
17. William Newman, "Management of Subways to Be Split," *The New York Times*, December 6, 2007.
18. Steffan M. Lauster and J. Neely, "The Core's Competence," *Strategy + Business*, issue 38 (April 15, 2005): 40–49.
19. Clay Chandler and Paul Ingrassia, "Just as U.S. Firms Try Japanese Management, Honda Is Centralizing," *The Wall Street Journal*, April 11, 1991.
20. The following discussion of structural alternatives draws from Jay R. Galbraith, *Designing Complex Organizations* (Reading, MA: Addison-Wesley, 1973); Jay R. Galbraith, *Organization Design* (Reading, MA: Addison-Wesley, 1977); Jay R. Galbraith, *Designing Dynamic Organizations* (New York: AMACOM, 2002); Robert Duncan, "What Is the Right Organization Structure?" *Organizational Dynamics* (Winter 1979): 59–80; N. Anand and Richard L. Daft, "What Is the Right Organization Design?" *Organizational Dynamics* 36, no. 4 (2007): 329–344; and J. McCann and Jay R. Galbraith, "Interdepartmental Relations," in *Handbook of Organizational Design*,

ed. P. Nystrom and W. Starbuck (New York: Oxford University Press, 1981), pp. 60–84.

21. Based on the story of Blue Bell Creameries in Richard L. Daft, *Organization Theory and Design*, 9th ed. (Mason, OH: South-Western, 2007), p. 103.

22. Anand and Daft, "What Is the Right Organization Design?"

23. Eliza Newlin Carney, "Calm in the Storm," *Government Executive* (October 2003): 57–63; and http:// www.irs.gov (accessed April 20, 2004).

24. David Enrich and Carrick Mollenkamp, "Citi's Focus: Out with Old, In with Profit Drivers," *The Wall Street Journal*, February 20, 2008.

25. Robert J. Kramer, *Organizing for Global Competitiveness: The Geographic Design* (New York: The Conference Board, 1993), pp. 29–31.

26. Maisie O'Flanagan and Lynn K. Taliento, "Nonprofits: Ensuring That Bigger Is Better," *McKinsey Quarterly*, no. 2 (2004): 112ff.

27. Lawton R. Burns, "Matrix Management in Hospitals: Testing Theories of Matrix Structure and Development," *Administrative Science Quarterly* 34 (1989): 349–368; Carol Hymowitz, "Managers Suddenly Have to Answer to a Crowd of Bosses," *The Wall Street Journal*, August 12, 2003.

28. Stanley M. Davis and Paul R. Lawrence, *Matrix* (Reading, MA: Addison-Wesley, 1977).

29. Alfred P. West, Jr., and Yoram (Jerry) Wind, "Putting the Organization on Wheels: Workplace Design at SEI," *California Management Review* 49, no. 2 (Winter 2007): 138–153.

30. Melissa A. Schilling and H. Kevin Steensma, "The Use of Modular Organizational Forms: An Industry-Level Analysis," *Academy of Management Journal*, 44, no. 6 (December 2001): 1149–1169.

31. Susan G. Cohen and Don Mankin, "Complex Collaborations for the New Global Economy," *Organizational Dynamics* 31, no. 2 (2002): 117–133; David Lei and John W. Slocum Jr., "Organizational Designs to Renew Competitive Advantage," *Organizational Dynamics* 31, no. 1 (2002): 1–18.

32. Raymond E. Miles and Charles C. Snow, "The New Network Firm: A Spherical Structure Built on a Human Investment Philosophy,"

Organizational Dynamics (Spring 1995): 5–18; and Raymond E. Miles, Charles C. Snow, John A. Matthews, Grant Miles, and Henry J. Coleman, Jr., "Organizing in the Knowledge Age: Anticipating the Cellular Form," *Academy of Management Executive* 11, no. 4 (1997): 7–24.

33. Jena McGregor, with Michael Arndt, Robert Berner, Ian Rowley, Kenji Hall, Gail Edmondson, Steve Hamm, Moon Ihlwan, and Andy Reinhardt, "The World's Most Innovative Companies," *BusinessWeek* (April 24, 2006), http://www .businessweek.com.

34. Raymond E. Miles and Charles C. Snow, "Organizations: New Concepts for New Forms," *California Management Review* 28 (Spring 1986): 62–73; and "Now, The Post-Industrial Corporation," *BusinessWeek* (March 3, 1986): 64–74.

35. N. Anand, "Modular, Virtual, and Hollow Forms of Organization Design," working paper, London Business School (2000); Don Tapscott, "Rethinking Strategy in a Networked World," *Strategy & Business*, issue 24 (Third Quarter 2001): 34–41.

36. Malcolm Wheatley, "Cycle Company with a Virtual Spin," *MT* (September 2003): 78–81.

37. Gregory G. Dess, Abdul M. A. Rasheed, Kevin J. McLaughlin, and Richard L. Priem, "The New Corporate Architecture," *Academy of Management Executive* 9, no. 3 (1995): 7–20.

38. Philip Siekman, "The Snap-Together Business Jet," *Fortune* (January 21, 2002): 104[A]–104[H].

39. Kathleen Kerwin, "GM: Modular Plants Won't Be a Snap," *BusinessWeek* (November 9, 1998): 168, 172.

40. Robert C. Ford and W. Alan Randolph, "Cross-Functional Structures: A Review and Integration of Matrix Organization and Project Management," *Journal of Management* 18, no. 2 (1992): 267–294; and Paula Dwyer with Pete Engardio, Zachary Schiller, and Stanley Reed, "Tearing Up Today's Organization Chart," *BusinessWeek/Twenty-First Century Capitalism*, 80–90.

41. These disadvantages are based on Michael Goold and Andrew Campbell, "Making Matrix Structures Work: Creating Clarity on Unit Roles and Responsibilities," *European Management Journal* 21, no. 3

(June 2003): 351–363; Hymowitz, "Managers Suddenly Have to Answer to a Crowd of Bosses"; and Dwyer et al., "Tearing Up Today's Organization Chart."

42. Geoff Keighley, "Massively Multinational Player," *Business 2.0* (September 2005): 64–66.

43. Dexter Filkins, "Profusion of Rebel Groups Helps Them Survive in Iraq," *The New York Times*, December 2, 2005, http://www. nytimes.com.

44. Scott Shane and Neil A. Lewis, "At Sept. 11 Trial, Tale of Missteps and Mismanagement," *The New York Times*, March 31, 2006, http://www .nytimes.com.

45. Raymond E. Miles, "Adapting to Technology and Competition: A New Industrial Relations System for the Twenty-First Century," *California Management Review* (Winter 1989): 9–28; and Miles and Snow, "The New Network Firm."

46. Dess et al., "The New Corporate Architecture"; Henry W. Chesbrough and David J. Teece, "Organizing for Innovation: When Is Virtual Virtuous?" *The Innovative Entrepreneur* (August 2002): 127–134; N. Anand, "Modular, Virtual, and Hollow Forms," and M. Lynne Markus, Brook Manville, and Carole E. Agres, "What Makes a Virtual Organization Work?" *Sloan Management Review* (Fall 2000): 13–26.

47. Anand and Daft, "What Is the Right Organization Design?"

48. Laurie P. O'Leary, "Curing the Monday Blues: A U.S. Navy Guide for Structuring Cross-Functional Teams," *National Productivity Review* (Spring 1996): 43–51; and Alan Hurwitz, "Organizational Structures for the 'New World Order,'" *Business Horizons* (May–June 1996): 5–14.

49. Jay Galbraith, Diane Downey, and Amy Kates, *Designing Dynamic Organizations*, chapter 4, "Processes and Lateral Capability" (New York: AMACOM, 2002).

50. Sara Lipka, "The Lawyer Is In," *The Chronicle of Higher Education* (July 1, 2005): A19, A21.

51. Lee Iacocca with William Novak, *Iacocca: An Autobiography* (New York: Phantom Books, 1984), pp. 152–153.

52. Miriam Jordan and Jonathan Karp, "Machines for the Masses," *The Wall Street Journal*, December 9, 2003.

53. William J. Altier, "Task Forces: An Effective Management Tool," *Management Review* (February 1987): 52–57.

54. "Task Forces Tackle Consolidation of Employment Services," *Shawmut News*, Shawmut National Corporation (May 3, 1989): 2.

55. Henry Mintzberg, *The Structure of Organizations* (Englewood Cliffs, NJ: Prentice Hall, 1979).

56. Paul R. Lawrence and Jay W. Lorsch, "New Managerial Job: The Integrator," *Harvard Business Review* (November–December 1967): 142–151.

57. Ronald N. Ashkenas and Suzanne C. Francis, "Integration Managers: Special Leaders for Special Times," *Harvard Business Review* (November–December 2000): 108–116.

58. This discussion is based on Michael Hammer and Steven Stanton, "How Process Enterprises *Really* Work," *Harvard Business Review* (November–December 1999): 108–118; Richard L. Daft, *Organization Theory and Design*, 5th ed. (Minneapolis, MN: West Publishing Company, 1995), p. 238; Raymond L. Manganelli and Mark M. Klein, "A Framework for Reengineering," *Management Review* (June 1994): 9–16; and Barbara Ettorre, "Reengineering Tales from the Front," *Management Review* (January 1995): 13–18.

59. Hammer and Stanton, "How Process Enterprises *Really* Work."

60. Michael Hammer, definition quoted in "The Process Starts Here," *CIO* (March 1, 2000): 144–156; and David A. Garvin, "The Processes of Organization and Management," *Sloan Management Review* (Summer 1998): 33–50.

61. Frank Ostroff, *The Horizontal Organization: What the Organization of the Future Looks Like and How It Delivers Value to Customers* (New York: Oxford University Press, 1999).

62. Dan Groszkiewicz and Brent Warren, "Alcoa's Michigan Casting Center Runs the Business from the Bottom Up," *Journal of Organizational Excellence* (Spring 2006): 13–23.

63. Erik Brynjolfsson, Amy Austin Renshaw, and Marshall Van Alstyne, "The Matrix of Change," *Sloan Management Review* (Winter 1997): 37–54.

64. Harold J. Leavitt, "Why Hierarchies Thrive," *Harvard Business Review* (March 2003): 96–102, provides a discussion of the benefits and problems of hierarchies. See Timothy Galpin, Rod Hilpirt, and Bruce Evans, "The Connected Enterprise: Beyond Division of Labor," *Journal of Business Strategy* 28, no. 2 (2007): 38–47, for a discussion of the advantages of horizontal over vertical designs.

65. Eric M. Olson, Stanley F. Slater, and G. Tomas M. Hult, "The Importance of Structure and Process to Strategy Implementation," *Business Horizons* 48 (2005): 47–54.

66. Michael E. Porter, *Competitive Strategy* (New York: Free Press, 1980), pp. 36–46.

67. Tom Burns and G. M. Stalker, *The Management of Innovation* (London: Tavistock, 1961).

68. John A. Coutright, Gail T. Fairhurst, and L. Edna Rogers, "Interaction Patterns in Organic and Mechanistic Systems," *Academy of Management Journal* 32 (1989): 773–802.

© STOCKBYTE

Learning Outcomes

After studying this chapter, you should be able to:

1. Define organizational change and explain the forces driving innovation
   and change in today's organizations.

2. Identify the three innovation strategies managers implement for changing
   products and technologies.

3. Explain the value of creativity, idea incubators, horizontal linkages, open
   innovation, idea champions, and new-venture teams for innovation.

4. Discuss why changes in people and culture are critical to any change
   process.

5. Define organization development (OD) and large group interventions.

6. Explain the OD stages of unfreezing, changing, and refreezing.

7. Identify sources of resistance to change.

8. Explain force-field analysis and other implementation tactics that can be
   used to overcome resistance.

Managing Change and Innovation

ARE YOU INNOVATIVE?[1]

Think about your current life. Indicate whether each item below is Mostly True or Mostly False for you.

	Mostly True	Mostly False
1. I am always seeking new ways to do things.	_____	_____
2. I consider myself creative and original in my thinking and behavior.	_____	_____
3. I rarely trust new gadgets until I see whether they work for people around me.	_____	_____
4. In a group or at work, I am often skeptical of new ideas.	_____	_____
5. I typically buy new foods, gear, and other innovations before other people.	_____	_____
6. I like to spend time trying out new things.	_____	_____
7. My behavior influences others to try new things.	_____	_____
8. Among my co-workers, I will be among the first to try out a new idea or method.	_____	_____

SCORING AND INTERPRETATION: *Personal Innovativeness* reflects the awareness of the need to innovate and a readiness to try new things. Innovativeness is also thought of as the degree to which a person adopts innovations earlier than other people in the peer group. Innovativeness is considered a positive thing for people in many companies where individuals and organizations are faced with a constant need to change.

To compute your score on the Personal Innovativeness scale, add the number of Mostly True answers to items 1, 2, 5, 6, 7, 8 above and the Mostly False answers to items 3 and 4 for your score. A score of six to eight indicates that you are very innovative and likely are one of the first people to adopt changes. A score of four to five would suggest that you are average or slightly above average in innovativeness compared to others. A score of zero to three means that you may prefer the tried and true and hence are not excited about new ideas or innovations. As a new manager, a high score suggests you will emphasize innovation and change. A low score suggests you may prefer stability and established methods.

Glance through recent back issues of just about any business magazine and you will see them: *Wired* magazine's "Wired 40" list of the most innovative companies. *Fast Company*'s "Fast 50 World's Most Innovative Companies." *Business Week*'s "Twenty Five Most Innovative Companies in the World." Everyone's talking about innovation and extolling the virtues of companies that do it right. Innovation is at the top of everyone's priority list today, but managing innovation and change has always been an important management capability. If organizations don't successfully change and innovate, they die. Consider that just 71 of the companies on *Fortune* magazine's first list of America's 500 largest corporations, compiled in 1955, survived the next half-century.[2]

Every organization sometimes faces the need to change swiftly and dramatically to cope with a changing environment. For example, Nokia is still the world's largest maker of cell phone handsets, but it lost its leading position in the United States by failing to match popular products like the Motorola Razr and Apple iPhone.[3] Samsung Electronics was becoming a brand associated with cheap, low-quality knockoffs until managers implemented new processes that transformed the company into a hotbed of innovation. "We cannot live without change," said Samsung Vice Chairman and CEO Jong-Yong Yun. "The race for survival in this world is not to the strongest, but to the most adaptive."[4]

In this chapter, we look at how organizations can be designed to respond to the environment through internal change and development. First we look at two key aspects

1 Introduction
2 Environment
3 Planning
4 Organizing
5 Controlling
6 Leading

of change in organizations: introducing new products and technologies, and changing people and culture. Then we examine how managers implement change, including overcoming resistance.

INNOVATION AND THE CHANGING WORKPLACE

In today's topsy-turvy world, managing change and innovation is taking center stage. Some observers of business trends suggest that the *knowledge economy* of the late 1900s and early 2000s is rapidly being transformed into the *creativity economy*. As more high-level knowledge work is outsourced to less-developed countries, companies in the United States, Europe, and Japan are evolving to the next level—generating economic value from creativity, imagination, and innovation.[5]

Sometimes, change and innovation are spurred by forces outside the organization, such as when a powerful retailer such as Wal-Mart demands annual price cuts or when a key supplier goes out of business. Many U.S. companies had to revise administrative procedures to comply with provisions of the Sarbanes-Oxley corporate governance reform law. In China, organizations feel pressure from the government to increase wages to help workers cope with rising food costs.[6] These outside forces compel managers to look for greater efficiencies in operations and other changes to keep their organizations profitable. Other times, managers within the company want to initiate major changes, such as forming employee-participation teams, introducing new products, or instituting new training systems, but they don't know how to make the changes successful. Organizations must embrace many types of change. Businesses must develop improved production technologies, create new products and services desired in the marketplace, implement new administrative systems, and upgrade employees' skills.

Today's successful companies are continually innovating. For example, Johnson & Johnson Pharmaceuticals uses biosimulation software from Entelos that compiles all known information about a disease such as diabetes or asthma and runs extensive virtual tests of new drug candidates. With a new-drug failure rate of 50 percent even at the last stage of clinical trials, the process helps scientists cut the time and expense of early testing and focus their efforts on the most promising prospects. Telephone companies are investing in technology to push deeper into the television and broadband markets. Automakers are perfecting fuel-cell power systems that could make today's internal combustion engine as obsolete as the steam locomotive.[7] Computer companies are developing computers that are smart enough to configure themselves, balance huge workloads, and know how to anticipate and fix problems before they happen.[8] Organizations that change successfully are both profitable and admired. Innovative companies such as Target and Procter & Gamble have seen median profit margin growth of 3.4 percent a year since 1995, compared to only 0.4 percent for the median among Standard & Poor's Global 1200 companies.[9]

organizational change The adoption of a new idea or behavior by an organization.

Organizational change is defined as the adoption of a new idea or behavior by an organization.[10] Many organizations struggle with changing successfully. In some cases, employees don't have the desire or motivation to come up with new ideas, or their ideas never get heard by managers who could put them into practice. In other cases, managers learn about good ideas but have trouble getting cooperation from employees for implementation. Successful change requires that organizations be capable of both creating and implementing ideas, which means the organization must learn to be *ambidextrous*.[11]

© AP IMAGES

Concept Connection   Swimmer Michael Phelps, who scored an historic eight gold medals at the Olympics in Beijing, wears the new Speedo LZR Racer one-piece suit. Olympic swimmers wearing the LZR Racer broke 25 world records. Speedo's "world's-fastest-swimsuit" **innovation** was developed with help from NASA scientists. The seams of the suit are ultrasonically sealed and wind-tunnel tested for surface drag. Each athlete gets a 3-D body scan to create a suit with core support in critical areas to make swimmers more streamlined. The $550 price was a good deal for Phelps. His sponsor Speedo gave him a $1 million bonus for his record-breaking eight-medal win.

An **ambidextrous approach** means incorporating structures and processes that are appropriate for both the creative impulse and for the systematic implementation of innovations. For example, a loose, flexible structure and greater employee freedom are excellent for the creation and initiation of ideas; however, these same conditions often make it difficult to implement a change because employees are less likely to comply. Or, as one scholar put it, companies "that are healthy enough to consider innovation are also hearty enough to resist change."[12] With an ambidextrous approach, managers encourage flexibility and freedom to innovate and propose new ideas with creative departments, venture teams, and other mechanisms we will discuss in this chapter, but they use a more rigid, centralized, and standardized approach for implementing innovations. In the following section, we discuss technology and product changes, which typically rely on new ideas that bubble up from lower levels of the organization.

CHANGING *THINGS:* NEW PRODUCTS AND TECHNOLOGIES

Introducing new products and technologies is a vital area for innovation. A **product change** is a change in the organization's product or service outputs. Product and service innovation is the primary way in which organizations adapt to changes in markets, technology, and competition.[13] Examples of new products include Apple's iPhone 3G, Glad Force Flex trash bags, and the hydrogen-powered BMW Hydrogen 7. The introduction of *e-file*, which allows online filing of tax returns, by the U.S. Internal Revenue Service (IRS) is an example of a new service innovation. Product changes are related to changes in the technology of the organization. A **technology change** is a change in the organization's production process—how the organization does its work. Technology changes are designed to make the production of a product or service more efficient. The adoption of automatic mail sorting machines by the U.S. Postal Service is one example of a technology change.

Three critical innovation strategies for changing products and technologies are illustrated in Exhibit 10.1.[14] The first strategy, *exploration*, involves designing the organization to encourage creativity and the initiation of new ideas. The strategy of *cooperation* refers to creating conditions and systems to facilitate internal and external coordination and knowledge sharing. Finally, *entrepreneurship* means that managers put in place processes and structures to ensure that new ideas are carried forward for acceptance and implementation.

Exploration

Exploration is the stage where ideas for new products and technologies are born. Managers design the organization for exploration by establishing conditions that encourage creativity and allow new ideas to spring forth. **Creativity**, which refers to the generation of novel ideas that might meet perceived needs or respond to opportunities for the organization, is the essential first step in innovation.[15] People noted

ambidextrous approach Incorporating structures and processes that are appropriate for both the creative impulse and for the systematic implementation of innovations.

product change A change in the organization's product or service outputs.

technology change A change that pertains to the organization's production process.

creativity The generation of novel ideas that might meet perceived needs or offer opportunities for the organization.

Exploration	Cooperation	Entrepreneurship
• Creativity • Experimentation • Idea incubators	• Horizontal coordination mechanisms • Customers, partners • Open innovation	• Idea champions • New venture teams • Skunkworks • New venture fund

EXHIBIT | 10.1

Three Innovative Strategies for New Products and Technologies

SOURCE: Based on Patrick Reinmoeller and Nicole van Baardwijk, "The Link Between Diversity and Resilience," *MIT Sloan Management Review* (Summer 2005): 61–65.

© ROBYN TWOMEY

Concept Connection   Innovative companies such as Intuit want everyone to continually be coming up with new ideas. Founder Scott Cook and CEO Steve Bennett, shown here, encourage **creativity** during the **exploration phase** by embracing failure as readily as they do success. "I've had my share of really bad ideas," Cook admits. Yet failure can have hidden possibilities. Sticky notes, such as those shown here on Intuit's board, were invented at 3M Corporation based on a failed product—a not-very-sticky adhesive that resulted from a chemist's attempts to create a superglue. Post-it Notes became one of the best-selling office products ever.

for their creativity include Edwin Land, who invented the Polaroid camera, and Swiss engineer George de Mestral, who created Velcro after noticing the tiny hooks on the burrs caught on his wool socks. These people saw unique and creative opportunities in a familiar situation. Stanford University's Technology Ventures program recently sponsored a contest challenging people to come up with creative uses for everyday objects, such as rubber bands. Ignacio Donoso Olive, a computer science student in Ecuador, connected bands to form an elastic hem around the mesh canopies that are hung over beds at night to combat malaria. The elastic band helps prevent the canopies, usually tucked under mattresses, from slipping loose and giving deadly entrance to mosquitoes.[16]

Characteristics of highly creative people are illustrated in the left-hand column of Exhibit 10.2. Creative people often are known for originality, open-mindedness, curiosity, a focused approach to problem solving, persistence, a relaxed and playful attitude, and receptivity to new ideas.[17] Creativity can also be designed into organizations. Companies or departments within companies can be organized to be creative and initiate ideas for change. Most companies want more highly creative employees and often seek to hire creative individuals. However, the individual is only part of the story, and each of us has some potential for creativity. Managers are responsible for creating a work environment that allows creativity to flourish.[18]

EXHIBIT | 10.2

Characteristics of Creative People and Organizations

The Creative Individual	The Creative Organization or Department
1. Conceptual fluency Open-mindedness	1. Open channels of communication Contact with outside sources Overlapping territories; cross-pollination of ideas across disciplines Suggestion systems, brainstorming, freewheeling discussions
2. Originality	2. Assigning nonspecialists to problems Eccentricity allowed Hiring outside your comfort zone
3. Less authority Independence Self-confidence	3. Decentralization, loosely defined positions, loose control Acceptance of mistakes; rewarding risk-taking People encouraged to challenge their bosses
4. Playfulness Undisciplined exploration Curiosity	4. Freedom to choose and pursue problems Not a tight ship, playful culture, doing the impractical Freedom to discuss ideas; long time horizon
5. Persistence Commitment Focused approach	5. Resources allocated to creative personnel and projects without immediate payoff Reward system encourages innovation Absolution of peripheral responsibilities

SOURCES: Based on Gary A. Steiner, ed., *The Creative Organization* (Chicago: University of Chicago Press, 1965): 16–18; Rosabeth Moss Kanter, "The Middle Manager as Innovator," *Harvard Business Review* (July–August 1982): 104–105; James Brian Quinn, "Managing Innovation: Controlled Chaos," *Harvard Business Review* (May–June 1985): 73–84; Robert I. Sutton, "The Weird Rules of Creativity," *Harvard Business Review* (September 2001): 94–103; and Bridget Finn, "Playbook: Brainstorming for Better Brainstorming," *Business 2.0* (April 2005), 109–114.

The characteristics of creative organizations correspond to those of individuals, as illustrated in the right-hand column of Exhibit 10.2. Creative organizations are loosely structured. People find themselves in a situation of ambiguity, assignments are vague, territories overlap, tasks are loosely defined, and much work is done through teams. Managers in creative companies embrace risk and experimentation. They involve employees in a varied range of projects, so that people are not stuck in the rhythm of routine jobs, and they drive out the fear of making mistakes that can inhibit creative thinking.[19] Creative organizations have an internal culture of playfulness, freedom, challenge, and grass-roots participation.[20] To keep creativity alive at Google, managers let people spend 20 percent of their time working on any project they choose. People who interview for a job at the company are often asked, "If you could change the world using Google's resources, what would you build?" Google's managers instill a sense of creative fearlessness, which is part of the reason Google shows up at the top of numerous lists of most innovative companies.[21] Exhibit 10.3 shows the top ten innovative companies from one recent list.

As a new manager, you can inspire people to be more creative by giving them opportunities to explore ideas outside their regular jobs and encouraging them to experiment and take risks. Be open-minded and willing to listen to "crazy ideas," and let people know it's okay to make mistakes.

TakeaMoment

Another popular way to encourage new ideas within the organization is the **idea incubator**. An idea incubator provides a safe harbor where ideas from employees throughout the company can be developed without interference from company bureaucracy or politics.[22] Yahoo started an offsite incubator to speed up development of ideas and be more competitive with Google. Dubbed "Brickhouse" and located in a hip section of San Francisco, the idea incubator gets about 200 ideas submitted each month and a panel sorts out the top 5 to 10. "The goal is to take the idea, develop it, and make sure it's seen by senior management quickly," says Salim Ismail, head of Brickhouse.[23]

idea incubator An in-house program that provides a safe harbor where ideas from employees throughout the organization can be developed without interference from company bureaucracy or politics.

Go to the experiential exercise on page 297 that pertains to creativity in organizations.

TakeaMoment

Cooperation

Another important aspect of innovation is providing mechanisms for both internal and external coordination. Ideas for product and technology innovations typically originate at lower levels of the organization and need to flow horizontally across

4 Organizing

EXHIBIT | 10.3

The World's Most Innovative Companies

Rank	Company	Headquarters In:	Most Known For:
1	Apple	United States	New Products
2	Google	United States	Customer Experience
3	Toyota Motor Co.	Japan	Work Processes
4	General Electric	United States	Work Processes
5	Microsoft	United States	New Products
6	Tata Group	India	New Products
7	Nintendo	Japan	New Products
8	Procter & Gamble	United States	Work Processes
9	Sony	Japan	New Products
10	Nokia	Finland	New Products

SOURCE: "The World's 50 Most Innovative Companies," *BusinessWeek* (April 28, 2008), http://bwnt.businessweek.com/interactive_reports/innovative_companies/ (accessed May 6, 2008).

departments. In addition, people and organizations outside the firm can be rich sources of innovative ideas. Lack of innovation is widely recognized as one of the biggest problems facing today's businesses. Consider that 72 percent of top executives surveyed by *BusinessWeek* and the Boston Consulting Group reported that innovation is a top priority, yet almost half said they are dissatisfied with their results in that area.[24] Thus, many companies are undergoing a transformation in the way they find and use new ideas, focusing on improving both internal and external coordination.

Internal Coordination Successful innovation requires expertise from several departments simultaneously, and failed innovation is often the result of failed cooperation.[25] Consider the partner at a large accounting firm who was leading a team of 50 experts to develop new services. After a year of effort, they'd come up with few ideas, and the ones they had produced weren't successful. What went wrong? The leader had divided the team into three separate groups, so that researchers would come up with ideas, then hand them off to technical specialists, who in turn passed them along to marketers. Because the groups were working in isolation, much time and energy was spent on ideas that didn't meet technical specialists' criteria or that the marketers knew wouldn't work commercially.[26]

Companies that successfully innovate usually have the following characteristics:

1. People in marketing have a good understanding of customer needs.
2. Technical specialists are aware of recent technological developments and make effective use of new technology.
3. Members from key departments—research, manufacturing, marketing—cooperate in the development of the new product or service.[27]

horizontal linkage model An approach to product change that emphasizes shared development of innovations among several departments.

One approach to successful innovation is called the **horizontal linkage model**, which is illustrated in the center circle of Exhibit 10.4.[28] The model shows that the research, manufacturing, and sales and marketing departments within an organization simultaneously contribute to new products and technologies. People from these departments meet frequently in teams and task forces to share ideas and solve problems. Research

EXHIBIT 10.4

Coordination Model for Innovation

people inform marketing of new technical developments to learn whether they will be useful to customers. Marketing people pass customer complaints to research to use in the design of new products and to manufacturing people to develop new ideas for improving production speed and quality. Manufacturing informs other departments whether a product idea can be manufactured within cost limits.

The horizontal linkage model is increasingly important in today's high-pressure business environment that requires rapidly developing and commercializing products and services. This kind of teamwork is similar to a rugby match wherein players run together, passing the ball back and forth as they move downfield.[29] Speed is emerging as a pivotal strategic weapon in the global marketplace for a wide variety of industries.[30] Some companies use fast-cycle teams to deliver products and services faster than competitors, giving them a significant strategic advantage. A **fast-cycle team** is a multifunctional, and sometimes multinational, team that works under stringent timelines and is provided with high levels of resources and empowerment to accomplish an accelerated product development project.[31]

Even as a new manager, you can make sure people are communicating and cooperating across organizational boundaries. Implement mechanisms to help your team or department members stay in touch with what's happening in other departments and in the marketplace.

External Coordination Exhibit 10.4 also illustrates that organizations look outside their boundaries to find and develop new ideas. Engineers and researchers stay aware of new technological developments. Marketing personnel pay attention to shifting market conditions and customer needs. Some organizations build formal strategic partnerships such as alliances and joint ventures to improve innovation success.

Today's most successful companies are including customers, strategic partners, suppliers, and other outsiders directly in the product and service development process. One of the hottest trends is *open innovation*.[32] In the past, most businesses generated their own ideas in house and then developed, manufactured, marketed, and distributed them, a closed innovation approach. Today, however, forward-looking companies are trying a different method. **Open innovation** means extending the search for and commercialization of new ideas beyond the boundaries of the organization and even beyond the boundaries of the industry. In a survey conducted by IBM and *Industry Week* magazine, 40 percent of respondents identified collaborating with customers and suppliers as having the most significant impact on product development time-to-market.[33] Procter & Gamble, not so long ago a stodgy consumer products company, has become one of the country's hottest innovators and a role model for the open innovation process.

© JB REED/BLOOMBERG NEWS /LANDOV

Take a Moment

fast-cycle team A multifunctional team that is provided with high levels of resources and empowerment to accomplish an accelerated product development project.

open innovation Extending the search for and commercialization of new ideas beyond the boundaries of the organization.

4 Organizing

Concept Connection
Google co-founders Larry Page (left) and Sergey Brin (right) take the stage during the September 2008 unveiling of the HTC G1 phone by T-Mobile, the first mobile phone to run on Google's Android software. Using an **open innovation** approach, Google issued a call for anyone to develop new software applications for its open-platform Android. The company's Developer Challenge will award a total of $10 million for the best new applications.

The SwifferVac. Crest Spin Brush. Mr. Clean Magic Eraser. Valentino Rock 'n Rose Eau de Parfum. Olay Regenerist. These are some of Procter & Gamble's best-selling products—and all of them were developed in whole or in part by someone outside of P&G. The technology for the Mr. Clean Magic Eraser was originally developed by Germany's BASF for sound-proofing and insulation in the construction and automotive industries. The Crest Spin Brush was invented by a small entrepreneurial firm in Cleveland.

Procter & Gamble CEO A. G. Lafley set a goal to get 50 percent of the company's innovation from outside the organization, up from about 35 percent in 2004 and only 10 percent in 2000. The company's top executives estimated that for every P&G researcher there were 200 scientists elsewhere who were just as good, so why not tap into that vast pool of creativity and talent? P&G developed a detailed, well-organized process for open innovation with its Connect and Develop strategy, which taps into networks of inventors, scientists, academics, partners, and suppliers to embrace the collective brains of the world. When P&G wanted to make snacks more fun by printing trivia questions, animal facts, jokes, and cartoon characters on its Pringles potato crisps, it drew up a technology brief defining the problem and circulated it throughout the global network. It turned out that a small bakery in Bologna, Italy, had an ink-jet method for printing edible images on cakes that P&G was able to adapt for use on the potato crisps. The innovation of Pringles Prints helped P&G's North America Pringles division achieve double-digit growth for the next two years.

But P&G doesn't just look for extensions of its current product categories. An important part of its open innovation process is networking with external scientists in totally new areas that could lead to totally new businesses. For instance, who would have thought that the company that brings us Tide and Pampers could rival beauty titan Chanel in premium fragrance sales?[34]

In line with the new way of thinking we discussed in Chapter 1, which sees partnership and collaboration as more important than independence and competition, the boundaries between an organization and its environment are becoming porous, as illustrated by the P&G examples. Through open innovation, ideas flow back and forth among different people and companies that engage in partnerships, joint ventures, licensing agreements, and other alliances.

Entrepreneurship

The third aspect of product and technology innovation is creating mechanisms to make sure new ideas are carried forward, accepted, and implemented. Managers can directly influence whether entrepreneurship flourishes in the organization by expressing support of entrepreneurial activities, giving employees a degree of autonomy, and rewarding learning and risk-taking.[35] One important matter is fostering idea champions. The formal definition of an **idea champion** is a person who sees the need for and champions productive change within the organization.

Remember: Change does not occur by itself. Personal energy and effort are required to successfully promote a new idea. When Texas Instruments studied 50 of its new-product introductions, a surprising fact emerged: Without exception, every new product that failed lacked a zealous champion. In contrast, most of the new products that succeeded had a champion. Managers made an immediate decision: No new product would be approved unless someone championed it. Research confirms that successful new ideas are generally those that are backed by someone who believes in the idea wholeheartedly and is determined to convince others of its value.[36]

Sometimes a new idea is rejected by management, but champions are passionately committed to a new product or idea despite rejection by others. For example, Robert Vincent was fired twice by two different division managers at a semiconductor company. Both times, he convinced the president and chairman of the board to reinstate him to continue working on his idea for an airbag sensor that measures acceleration and deceleration. He couldn't get approval for research funding, so Vincent pushed to finish another project in half the time and used the savings to support the new product development.[37]

idea champion A person who sees the need for and champions productive change within the organization.

Championing an idea successfully requires roles in organizations, as illustrated in Exhibit 10.5. Sometimes a single person may play two or more of these roles, but successful innovation in most companies involves an interplay of different people, each adopting one role. The *inventor* comes up with a new idea and understands its technical value but has neither the ability nor the interest to promote it for acceptance within the organization. The *champion* believes in the idea, confronts the organizational realities of costs and benefits, and gains the political and financial support needed to bring it to reality. The *sponsor* is a high-level manager who approves the idea, protects the idea, and removes major organizational barriers to acceptance. The *critic* counterbalances the zeal of the champion by challenging the concept and providing a reality test against hard-nosed criteria. The critic prevents people in the other roles from adopting a bad idea.[38]

As a new manager, have the courage to promote useful change. Are you an idea champion for changes or new ideas you believe in? To find out, complete the New Manager Self Test on page 286.

TakeaMoment

Another way to facilitate entrepreneurship is through a **new-venture team**. A new-venture team is a unit separate from the rest of the organization that is responsible for developing and initiating a major innovation.[39] Whenever BMW Group begins developing a new car, the project's team members—from engineering, design, production, marketing, purchasing, and finance—are relocated to a separate Research and Innovation Center, where they work collaboratively to speed the new product to market.[40] New-venture teams give free rein to members' creativity because their separate facilities and location unleash people from the restrictions imposed by organizational rules and procedures. These teams typically are small, loosely structured, and flexible, reflecting the characteristics of creative organizations described in Exhibit 10.2.

One variation of a new-venture team is called a **skunkworks**.[41] A skunkworks is a separate small, informal, highly autonomous, and often secretive group that focuses on breakthrough ideas for the business. The original skunkworks, which still exists, was created by Lockheed Martin more than 50 years ago. The essence of a skunkworks is that highly talented people are given the time and freedom to let creativity reign.[42] The laser printer was invented by a Xerox researcher who was transferred to a skunkworks, the Xerox Palo Alto Research Center (PARC), after his ideas about using lasers were stifled within the company for being "too impractical and expensive."[43] Companies such as Cargill and IBM are launching entirely new businesses by using entrepreneurship groups similar to a skunkworks.[44] Good ideas that don't fit existing businesses are transferred for development to a separate formal organization, called

new-venture team A unit separate from the mainstream of the organization that is responsible for developing and initiating innovations.

skunkworks A separate small, informal, highly autonomous, and often secretive group that focuses on breakthrough ideas for the business.

4 Organizing

EXHIBIT | **10.5** Four Roles in Organizational Change

Inventor	Champion	Sponsor	Critic
Develops and understands technical aspects of idea	Believes in idea	High-level manager who removes organizational barriers	Provides reality test
Does not know how to win support for the idea or make a business of it	Visualizes benefits	Approves and protects idea within organization	Looks for shortcomings
	Confronts organizational realities of cost, benefits		Defines hard-nosed criteria that idea must pass
	Obtains financial and political support		
	Overcomes obstacles		

SOURCES: Based on Harold L. Angle and Andrew H. Van de Ven, "Suggestions for Managing the Innovation Journey," in *Research in the Management of Innovation: The Minnesota Studies*, ed. A. H. Van de Ven, H. L. Angle, and Marshall Scott Poole (Cambridge, MA: Ballinger/Harper & Row, 1989); and Jay R. Galbraith, "Designing the Innovating Organization," *Organizational Dynamics* (Winter 1982): 5–25.

new-venture fund A fund providing resources from which individuals and groups can draw to develop new ideas, products, or businesses.

the Emerging Business Accelerator at Cargill and the Emerging Business Opportunities program at IBM. One idea from IBM's EBO program, a digital media business to help manage video, audio, and still images, grew into a $1.7 billion business in only three years.[45]

A related idea is the **new-venture fund**, which provides resources from which individuals and groups can draw to develop new ideas, products, or businesses. At

New Manager Self-Test

Taking Charge of Change

As a new manager, do you have what it takes to be an idea champion? Will you initiate change? Think of a job you held for a period of time. Answer the following questions according to your behaviors and perspective on that job. Please answer whether each item is Mostly True or Mostly False for you.

	Mostly True	Mostly False
1. I often tried to adopt improved procedures for doing my job.	_____	_____
2. I felt a personal sense of responsibility to bring about change in my workplace.	_____	_____
3. I often tried to institute new work methods that were more effective for the company.	_____	_____
4. I often tried to change organizational rules or policies that were nonproductive or counterproductive.	_____	_____
5. It was up to me to bring about improvement in my workplace.	_____	_____
6. I often made constructive suggestions for improving how things operated.	_____	_____
7. I often tried to implement new ideas for pressing organizational problems.	_____	_____
8. I often tried to introduce new structures, technologies, or approaches to improve efficiency.	_____	_____

SCORING AND INTERPRETATION: An important part of a new manager's job is to facilitate improvements through innovation and change. Will you be a champion for change? Your answers to the questions may indicate the extent to which you have a natural inclination toward taking charge of change. Not everyone thrives in a position of initiating change, but as a new manager, initiating change within the first six months will enhance your impact.

Give yourself one point for each item you marked as Mostly True. If you scored 4 or less you may not have been flexing your change muscles on the job. You may need to become more active at taking charge of change. Moreover, you may need to be in a more favorable change situation. Research indicates that jobs with open-minded management, where change is believed likely to succeed and be rewarded, increase a person's initiative. So the organization in which you are a new manager plus your own inclination will influence your initiation of change. A score of 5 or more suggests a positive level of previous change initiation behavior and solid preparation for a new manager role as an idea champion.

SOURCE: Based on Elizabeth W. Morrison and Corey C. Phelps, "Taking Charge at Work: Extrarole Efforts to Initiate Workplace Change," *Academy of Management Journal* 42 (1999): 403–419.

3M, scientists can apply for Genesis Grants to work on innovative project ideas. 3M awards from 12 to 20 of these grants each year, ranging from $50,000 to $100,000 each, for researchers to hire supplemental staff, acquire equipment, or whatever is needed to develop the new idea.[46] With these programs, the support and assistance of senior managers are often just as important as the funding.[47]

Go to the ethical dilemma on page 298 that pertains to structural change. | TakeaMoment

CHANGING PEOPLE AND CULTURE

All successful changes involve changes in people and culture as well. Changes in people and culture pertain to how employees think—changes in mind-set. **People change** concerns just a few employees, such as sending a handful of middle managers to a training course to improve their leadership skills. **Culture change** pertains to the organization as a whole, such as when the IRS shifted its basic mind-set from an organization focused on collection and compliance to one dedicated to informing, educating, and serving customers (taxpayers).[48] Large-scale culture change is not easy. Indeed, managers routinely report that changing people and culture is their most difficult job.[49] Two specific tools that can smooth the process are training and development programs and organization development (OD).

Training and Development

Training is one of the most frequently used approaches to changing people's mindsets. A company might offer training programs to large blocks of employees on subjects such as teamwork, diversity, emotional intelligence, quality circles, communication skills, or participative management.

Successful companies want to provide training and development opportunities for everyone, but they might particularly emphasize training and development for managers, with the idea that the behavior and attitudes of managers will influence people throughout the organization and lead to culture change. A number of Silicon Valley companies, including Intel, Advanced Micro Devices (AMD), and Sun Microsystems, regularly send managers to the Growth and Leadership Center (GLC), where they learn to use emotional intelligence to build better relationships. Nick Kepler, director of technology development at AMD, was surprised to learn how his emotionless approach to work was intimidating people and destroying the rapport needed to shift to a culture based on collaborative teamwork.[50]

Organization Development

Organization development (OD) is a planned, systematic process of change that uses behavioral science knowledge and techniques to improve an organization's health and effectiveness through its ability to adapt to the environment, improve internal relationships, and increase learning and problem-solving capabilities.[51] OD focuses on the human and social aspects of the organization and works to change attitudes and relationships among employees, helping to strengthen the organization's capacity for adaptation and renewal.[52]

OD can help managers address at least three types of current problems:[53]

1. *Mergers/acquisitions.* The disappointing financial results of many mergers and acquisitions are caused by the failure of executives to determine whether the administrative style and corporate culture of the two companies fit. Executives may concentrate on potential synergies in technology, products, marketing, and control systems but fail to recognize that two firms may have widely different

people change A change in the attitudes and behaviors of a few employees in the organization.

culture change A major shift in the norms, values, attitudes, and mind-set of the entire organization.

organization development (OD) The application of behavioral science techniques to improve an organization's health and effectiveness through its ability to cope with environmental changes, improve internal relationships, and increase learning and problem-solving capabilities.

values, beliefs, and practices. These differences create stress and anxiety for employees, and these negative emotions affect future performance. Cultural differences should be evaluated during the acquisition process, and OD experts can be used to smooth the integration of two firms.

2. *Organizational decline/revitalization.* Organizations undergoing a period of decline and revitalization experience a variety of problems, including a low level of trust, lack of innovation, high turnover, and high levels of conflict and stress. The period of transition requires opposite behaviors, including confronting stress, creating open communication, and fostering creative innovation to emerge with high levels of productivity. OD techniques can contribute greatly to cultural revitalization by managing conflicts, fostering commitment, and facilitating communication.

3. *Conflict management.* Conflict can occur at any time and place within a healthy organization. For example, a product team for the introduction of a new software package was formed at a computer company. Made up of strong-willed individuals, the team made little progress because members could not agree on project goals. At a manufacturing firm, salespeople promised delivery dates to customers that were in conflict with shop supervisor priorities for assembling customer orders. In a publishing company, two managers disliked each other intensely. They argued at meetings, lobbied politically against each other, and hurt the achievement of both departments. Organization development efforts can help resolve these kinds of conflicts, as well as conflicts that are related to growing diversity and the global nature of today's organizations.

team building A type of OD intervention that enhances the cohesiveness of departments by helping members learn to function as a team.

survey feedback A type of OD intervention in which questionnaires on organizational climate and other factors are distributed among employees and their results reported back to them by a change agent.

Organization development can be used to solve the types of problems just described and many others. However, to be truly valuable to companies and employees, organization development practitioners go beyond looking at ways to settle specific problems. Instead, they become involved in broader issues that contribute to improving organizational life, such as encouraging a sense of community, pushing for an organizational climate of openness and trust, and making sure the company provides employees with opportunities for personal growth and development.[54]

OD Activities OD consultants use a variety of specialized techniques to help meet OD goals. Three of the most popular and effective are the following:

© DANIEL LEVIN/GETTY IMAGES

Concept Connection **Organization development** specialists have long recognized that fun can be a powerful tool in the serious business of **team building**. Here, Target Corporation store employees engage in some group problem solving. While holding hands, each member must wriggle through two hula hoops without breaking the human chain. Such noncompetitive games not only break the ice but also give team members practice in working cooperatively to achieve a common goal.

1. *Team-building activities.* Team building enhances the cohesiveness and success of organizational groups and teams. For example, a series of OD exercises can be used with members of cross-departmental teams to help them learn to act and function as a team. An OD expert can work with team members to increase their communication skills, facilitate their ability to confront one another, and help them accept common goals.

2. *Survey-feedback activities.* Survey feedback begins with a questionnaire distributed to employees on values, climate, participation, leadership, and group cohesion within their organization. After the survey is completed, an OD consultant meets with groups of employees to provide feedback about their responses and the problems identified. Employees are engaged in problem solving based on the data.

3. *Large-group interventions.* In recent years, the need for bringing about fundamental organizational change in today's complex, fast-changing world prompted a growing interest in applications of OD techniques to large group settings.[55] The **large-group intervention** approach brings together participants from all parts of the organization—often including key stakeholders from outside the organization as well—to discuss problems or opportunities and plan for change. A large-group intervention might involve 50 to 500 people and last several days. The idea is to include everyone who has a stake in the change, gather perspectives from all parts of the system, and enable people to create a collective future through sustained, guided dialogue.

Large-group interventions reflect a significant shift in the approach to organizational change from earlier OD concepts and approaches. Exhibit 10.6 lists the primary differences between the traditional OD model and the large-scale intervention model of organizational change.[56] In the newer approach, the focus is on the entire system, which takes into account the organization's interaction with its environment. The source of information for discussion is expanded to include customers, suppliers, community members, even competitors, and this information is shared widely so that everyone has the same picture of the organization and its environment. The acceleration of change when the entire system is involved can be remarkable. In addition, learning occurs across all parts of the organization simultaneously, rather than in individuals, small groups, or business units. The result is that the large-group approach offers greater possibilities for fundamental, radical transformation of the entire culture, whereas the traditional approach creates incremental change in a few individuals or small groups at a time. General Electric's Work-Out Program provides an excellent example of the large-group intervention approach.

large-group intervention
An approach that brings together participants from all parts of the organization (and may include key outside stakeholders as well) to discuss problems or opportunities and plan for major change.

General Electric's Work-Out

Innovative Way

4 Organizing

GE's Work-Out began in large-scale off-site meetings facilitated by a combination of top leaders, outside consultants, and human resources specialists. In each business unit, the basic pattern was the same. Hourly and salaried workers came together from many different parts of the organization in an informal three-day meeting to discuss and solve problems. Gradually, the Work-Out events began to include external stakeholders such as suppliers and customers as well as employees. Today, Work-Out is not an event, but a process of how work is done and problems are solved at GE.

The format for Work-Out includes seven steps:

1. Choose a work process or problem for discussion.

2. Select an appropriate cross-functional team, to include external stakeholders.

3. Assign a "champion" to follow through on recommendations.

4. Meet for several days and come up with recommendations to improve processes or solve problems.

EXHIBIT 10.6

OD Approaches to Culture Change

	Traditional Organization Development Model	Large-Group Intervention Model
Focus for action:	Specific problem or group	Entire system
Information Source:	Organization	Organization and environment
Distribution:	Limited	Widely shared
Time frame:	Gradual	Fast
Learning:	Individual, small group	Whole organization
Change process:	Incremental change	Rapid transformation

SOURCE: Adapted from Barbara Benedict Bunker and Billie T. Alban, "Conclusion: What Makes Large Group Interventions Effective," *Journal of Applied Behavioral Science* 28, no. 4 (December 1992): 579–591.

5. Meet with leaders, who are asked to respond to recommendations on the spot.

6. Hold additional meetings as needed to implement the recommendations.

7. Start the process all over again with a new process or problem.

GE's Work-Out process forces a rapid analysis of ideas, the creation of solutions, and the development of a plan for implementation. Over time, this large-group process creates an organizational culture where ideas are rapidly translated into action and positive business results.[57]

Large-group interventions represent a significant shift in the way leaders think about change and reflect an increasing awareness of the importance of dealing with the entire system, including external stakeholders, in any significant change effort.

TakeaMoment

As a new manager, look for and implement training opportunities that can help people shift their attitudes, beliefs, and behaviors toward what is needed for team, department, and organization success. Use organization development consultants and techniques such as team building, survey feedback, and large-group intervention for widespread change.

OD Steps Organization development experts acknowledge that changes in corporate culture and human behavior are tough to accomplish and require major effort. The theory underlying OD proposes three distinct stages for achieving behavioral and attitudinal change: (1) unfreezing, (2) changing, and (3) refreezing.[58]

The first stage, **unfreezing**, means that people throughout the organization are made aware of problems and the need for change. This stage creates the motivation for people to change their attitudes and behaviors. Unfreezing may begin when managers present information that shows discrepancies between desired behaviors or performance and the current state of affairs. In addition, managers need to establish a sense of urgency to unfreeze people and create an openness and willingness to change. The unfreezing stage is often associated with *diagnosis*, which uses an outside expert called a *change agent*. The **change agent** is an OD specialist who performs a systematic diagnosis of the organization and identifies work-related problems. He or she gathers and analyzes data through personal interviews, questionnaires, and observations of meetings. The diagnosis helps determine the extent of organizational problems and helps unfreeze managers by making them aware of problems in their behavior.

The second stage, **changing**, occurs when individuals experiment with new behavior and learn new skills to be used in the workplace. This process is sometimes known as intervention, during which the change agent implements a specific plan for training managers and employees. The changing stage might involve a number of specific steps.[59] For example, managers put together a coalition of people with the will and power to guide the change, create a vision for change that everyone can believe in, and widely communicate the vision and plans for change throughout the company. In addition, successful change involves using emotion as well as logic to persuade people and empowering employees to act on the plan and accomplish the desired changes.

The third stage, **refreezing**, occurs when individuals acquire new attitudes or values and are rewarded for them by the organization. The impact of new behaviors is evaluated and reinforced. The change agent supplies new data that show positive changes in performance. Managers may provide updated data to employees that demonstrate positive changes in individual and organizational performance. Top executives celebrate successes and reward positive behavioral changes. At this stage, changes are institutionalized in the organizational culture, so that employees begin to view the changes as a normal, integral part of how the organization operates. Employees may also participate in refresher courses to maintain and reinforce the new behaviors.

unfreezing The stage of organization development in which participants are made aware of problems to increase their willingness to change their behavior.

change agent An OD specialist who contracts with an organization to facilitate change.

changing The intervention stage of organization development in which individuals experiment with new workplace behavior.

refreezing The reinforcement stage of organization development in which individuals acquire a desired new skill or attitude and are rewarded for it by the organization.

IMPLEMENTING CHANGE

The final step to be managed in the change process is *implementation*. A new, creative idea will not benefit the organization until it is in place and being fully used. Executives at companies around the world are investing heavily in change and innovation projects, but many of them say they aren't very happy with their results.[60] One frustration for managers is that employees often seem to resist change for no apparent reason. To effectively manage the implementation process, managers should be aware of the reasons people resist change and use techniques to enlist employee cooperation. Major, corporate-wide changes can be particularly challenging, as discussed in the Manager's Shoptalk box.

Need for Change

Many people are not willing to change unless they perceive a problem or a crisis. However, many problems are subtle, so managers have to recognize and then make others aware of the need for change.[61]

One way managers sense a need for change is through the appearance of a **performance gap**—a disparity between existing and desired performance levels. They then try to create a sense of urgency so that others in the organization will recognize and understand the need for change (similar to the OD concept of *unfreezing*). Recall from Chapter 7 the discussion of SWOT analysis. Managers are responsible for monitoring threats and opportunities in the external environment as well as strengths and weaknesses within the organization to determine whether a need for change exists. Big problems are easy to spot, but sensitive monitoring systems are needed to detect gradual changes that can fool managers into thinking their company is doing fine. An organization may be in greater danger when the environment changes slowly, because managers may fail to trigger an organizational response.

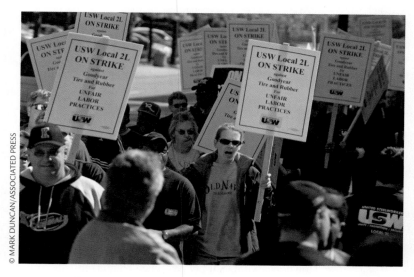

Concept Connection Fear of job loss is one of the biggest reasons for **resistance to change.** Managers at Goodyear Tire & Rubber Co. decided the company needed to outsource some of its private label business to compete with low-cost foreign producers. Unfortunately, the change would lead to plant closings in the U.S. After having made major concessions several years earlier to help the ailing tire manufacturer, United Steelworkers Union members were strongly opposed to further job losses. Despite months of talks, the two sides failed to reach an agreement and 15,000 USW members went on strike.

Resistance to Change

Getting others to understand the need for change is the first step in implementation. Yet most changes will encounter some degree of resistance. Idea champions often discover that other employees are unenthusiastic about their new ideas. Members of a new-venture group may be surprised when managers in the regular organization do not support or approve their innovations. Managers and employees not involved in an innovation often seem to prefer the status quo. People resist change for several reasons, and understanding them can help managers implement change more effectively.

Self-Interest People typically resist a change they believe conflicts with their self-interests. A proposed change in job design, structure, or technology may lead to an increase in employees' workload, for example, or a real or perceived loss of power, prestige, pay, or benefits. The fear of personal loss is perhaps the biggest obstacle to organizational

performance gap A disparity between existing and desired performance levels.

Concept *Connection*   Marathon Oil Corporation took a creative approach to **implementing change** by using this Discovery Map to engage all 2,400 or so employees in the switch to using a new enterprise resource planning system. The ERP software system from SAP would impact all employees and operations at the international oil and gas production company and was seen as critical to the company's future competitiveness. Paradigm Learning, Inc., a Florida-based consulting firm, created the Discovery Map that visually communicates Marathon's change initiatives: its current reality and challenges, its vision for the future, and how to get there from here—with the new ERP system shown as the bridge.

change.[62] At Fabcon, which makes huge precast concrete wall panels for commercial buildings, employees resisted a new experimental automation process because it added to their workload and reduced their productivity. "They were already working long days; they want to go home, and they didn't want to spend time doing R &D," says Fabcon's CEO Michael Le Jeune.[63] Managers began working with the foremen to show them how the process could eventually save time and effort, and the change was eventually a success.

Lack of Understanding and Trust   Employees often distrust the intentions behind a change or do not understand the intended purpose of a change. If previous working relationships with an idea champion have been negative, resistance may occur. One manager had a habit of initiating a change in the financial reporting system about every 12 months and then losing interest and not following through. After the third

Manager's Shoptalk

Making Change Stick

Employees are not always receptive to change. A combination of factors can lead to rejection of, or even outright rebellion against, management's "new and better ideas."

Consider what happened when managers at Lands' End Inc. of Dodgeville, Wisconsin, tried to implement a sweeping overhaul incorporating many of today's management trends—teams, 401(k) plans, peer reviews, and the elimination of guards and time clocks. Despite managers' best efforts, employees balked. They had liked the old family-like atmosphere and uncomplicated work environment, and they considered the new requirement for regular meetings a nuisance. "We spent so much time in meetings that we were getting away from the basic stuff of taking care of business," says one employee. Even a much-ballyhooed new mission statement seemed "pushy." One long-time employee complained, "We don't need anything hanging over our heads telling us to do something we're already doing."

Confusion and frustration reigned at Lands' End and was reflected in an earnings drop of 17 percent. Eventually, a new CEO initiated a return to the familiar "Lands' End Way" of doing things. Teams were disbanded, and many of the once-promising initiatives were shelved as workers embraced what was familiar.

The inability of people to adapt to change is not new. Neither is the failure of management to sufficiently lay the groundwork to prepare employees for change. Harvard professor John P. Kotter established an eight-step plan for implementing change that can provide a greater potential for successful transformation of a company:

1. Establish a sense of urgency through careful examination of the market and identification of opportunities and potential crises.

2. Form a powerful coalition of managers able to lead the change.

3. Create a vision to direct the change and the strategies for achieving that vision.

4. Communicate the vision throughout the organization.

5. Empower others to act on the vision by removing barriers, changing systems, and encouraging risk taking.

6. Plan for and celebrate visible, short-term performance improvements.

7. Consolidate improvements, reassess changes, and make necessary adjustments in the new programs.

8. Articulate the relationship between new behaviors and organizational success.

Major change efforts can be messy and full of surprises, but following these guidelines can break down resistance and mean the difference between success and failure.

SOURCES: Gregory A. Patterson, "Lands' End Kicks Out Modern New Managers, Rejecting a Makeover," *The Wall Street Journal*, April 3, 1995; and John P. Kotter, "Leading Changes: Why Transformation Efforts Fail," *Harvard Business Review* (March–April 1995): 59–67.

time, employees no longer went along with the change because they did not trust the manager's intention to follow through to their benefit.

Uncertainty *Uncertainty* is the lack of information about future events. It represents a fear of the unknown. Uncertainty is especially threatening for employees who have a low tolerance for change and fear anything out of the ordinary. They do not know how a change will affect them and worry about whether they will be able to meet the demands of a new procedure or technology.[64] For example, union leaders at an American auto manufacturer resisted the introduction of employee participation programs. They were uncertain about how the program would affect their status and thus initially opposed it.

Different Assessments and Goals Another reason for resistance to change is that people who will be affected by an innovation may assess the situation differently from an idea champion or new-venture group. Critics frequently voice legitimate disagreements over the proposed benefits of a change. Managers in each department pursue different goals, and an innovation may detract from performance and goal achievement for some departments. For example, if marketing gets the new product it wants for customers, the cost of manufacturing may increase, and the manufacturing superintendent thus will resist. Resistance may call attention to problems with the innovation. At a consumer products company in Racine, Wisconsin, middle managers resisted the introduction of a new employee program that turned out to be a bad idea. The managers truly believed that the program would do more harm than good.[65]

These reasons for resistance are legitimate in the eyes of employees affected by the change. The best procedure for managers is not to ignore resistance but to diagnose the reasons and design strategies to gain acceptance by users.[66] Strategies for overcoming resistance to change typically involve two approaches: the analysis of resistance through the force-field technique and the use of selective implementation tactics to overcome resistance.

Force-Field Analysis

Force-field analysis grew from the work of Kurt Lewin, who proposed that change was a result of the competition between *driving* and *restraining forces*.[67] Driving forces can be thought of as problems or opportunities that provide motivation for change within the organization. Restraining forces are the various barriers to change, such as a lack of resources, resistance from middle managers, or inadequate employee skills. When a change is introduced, management should analyze both the forces that drive change (problems and opportunities) as well as the forces that resist it (barriers to change). By selectively removing forces that restrain change, the driving forces will be strong enough to enable implementation, as illustrated by the move from A to B in Exhibit 10.7. As barriers are reduced or removed, behavior will shift to incorporate the desired changes.

force-field analysis The process of determining which forces drive and which resist a proposed change.

EXHIBIT | **10.7** Using Force-Field Analysis to Change from Traditional to Just-in-Time Inventory System

Just-in-time (JIT) inventory control systems schedule materials to arrive at a company just as they are needed on the production line. In an Ohio manufacturing company, management's analysis showed that the driving forces (opportunities) associated with the implementation of JIT were: (1) the large cost savings from reduced inventories, (2) savings from needing fewer workers to handle the inventory, and (3) a quicker, more competitive market response for the company. Restraining forces (barriers) discovered by managers were: (1) a freight system that was too slow to deliver inventory on time, (2) a facility layout that emphasized inventory maintenance over new deliveries, (3) worker skills inappropriate for handling rapid inventory deployment, and (4) union resistance to loss of jobs. The driving forces were not sufficient to overcome the restraining forces.

To shift the behavior to JIT, managers attacked the barriers. An analysis of the freight system showed that delivery by truck provided the flexibility and quickness needed to schedule inventory arrival at a specific time each day. The problem with facility layout was met by adding four new loading docks. Inappropriate worker skills were attacked with a training program to instruct workers in JIT methods and in assembling products with uninspected parts. Union resistance was overcome by agreeing to reassign workers no longer needed for maintaining inventory to jobs in another plant. With the restraining forces reduced, the driving forces were sufficient to allow the JIT system to be implemented.

TakeaMoment | **As a new manager, recognize that people often have legitimate and rational reasons for resisting change. Don't try to bulldoze a change through a wall of resistance. Use force-field analysis to evaluate the forces that are driving a change and those that are restraining it. Try communication and education, participation, and negotiation to melt resistance, and be sure to enlist the support of top-level managers. Use coercion to implement a change only when absolutely necessary.**

Implementation Tactics

The other approach to managing implementation is to adopt specific tactics to overcome resistance. Researchers have studied various methods for dealing with resistance to change. The following five tactics, summarized in Exhibit 10.8, have proven successful.[68]

EXHIBIT | **10.8**

Tactics for Overcoming
Resistance to Change

Approach	When to Use
Communication, education	• Change is technical. • Users need accurate information and analysis to understand change.
Participation	• Users need to feel involved. • Design requires information from others. • Users have power to resist.
Negotiation	• Group has power over implementation. • Group will lose out in the change.
Coercion	• A crisis exists. • Initiators clearly have power. • Other implementation techniques have failed.
Top management support	• Change involves multiple departments or reallocation of resources. • Users doubt legitimacy of change.

SOURCE: Based on J.P. Kotter and L.A. Schlesinger, "Choosing Strategies for Change," *Harvard Business Review* 57 (March–April 1979): 106–114.

Communication and Education *Communication* and *education* are used when solid information about the change is needed by users and others who may resist implementation. Education is especially important when the change involves new technical knowledge or users are unfamiliar with the idea. Canadian Airlines International spent a year and a half preparing and training employees before changing its entire reservations, airport, cargo, and financial systems as part of a new "Service Quality" strategy. Smooth implementation resulted from this intensive training and communications effort, which involved 50,000 tasks, 12,000 people, and 26 classrooms around the world.[69] Managers should also remember that implementing change requires speaking to people's hearts (touching their feelings) as well as to their minds (communicating facts). Emotion is a key component in persuading and influencing others. People are much more likely to change their behavior when they both understand the rational reasons for doing so and see a picture of change that influences their feelings.[70]

Participation *Participation* involves users and potential resisters in designing the change. This approach is time consuming, but it pays off because users understand and become committed to the change. At Learning Point Associates, which needed to change dramatically to meet new challenges, the change team drew up a comprehensive road map for transformation but had trouble getting the support of most managers. The managers argued that they hadn't been consulted about the plans and didn't feel compelled to participate in implementing them.[71] Research studies have shown that proactively engaging front-line employees in upfront planning and decision making about changes that affect their work results in much smoother implementation.[72] Participation also helps managers determine potential problems and understand the differences in perceptions of change among employees.

Negotiation Negotiation is a more formal means of achieving cooperation. *Negotiation* uses formal bargaining to win acceptance and approval of a desired change. For example, if the marketing department fears losing power if a new management structure is implemented, top managers may negotiate with marketing to reach a resolution. Companies that have strong unions frequently must formally negotiate change with the unions. The change may become part of the union contract reflecting the agreement of both parties.

Coercion *Coercion* means that managers use formal power to force employees to change. Resisters are told to accept the change or lose rewards or even their jobs. In most cases, this approach should not be used because employees feel like victims, are angry at change managers, and may even sabotage the changes. However, coercion may be necessary in crisis situations when a rapid response is urgent. For example, a number of top managers at Coca-Cola had to be reassigned or let go after they refused to go along with a new CEO's changes for revitalizing the sluggish corporation.[73]

Top Management Support The visible support of top management also helps overcome resistance to change. *Top management support* symbolizes to all employees that the change is important for the organization. One survey found that 80 percent of companies that are successful innovators have top executives who frequently reinforce the importance of innovation both verbally and symbolically.[74] Top management support is especially important when a change involves multiple departments or when resources are being reallocated among departments. Without top management support, changes can get bogged down in squabbling among departments. Moreover, when change agents fail to enlist the support of top executives, these leaders can inadvertently undercut the change project by issuing contradictory orders.

Managers can soften resistance and facilitate change and innovation by using smart techniques. At Remploy Ltd., needed changes were at first frightening and confusing to Remploy's workers, 90 percent of whom have some sort of disability. However, by communicating with employees, providing training, and closely involving them in the change process, managers were able to smoothly implement the new procedures and work methods. As machinist Helen Galloway put it, "Change is frightening, but because we all have a say, we feel more confident making those changes."[75]

ch10 A MANAGER'S ESSENTIALS: WHAT HAVE WE LEARNED?

- Change is inevitable in organizations, and successful innovation is vital to the health of companies in all industries. This chapter discussed the techniques available for managing the change process. Two key aspects of change in organizations are changing products and technologies and changing people and culture.

- Three essential innovation strategies for changing products and technologies are exploration, cooperation, and entrepreneurship. Exploration involves designing the organization to promote creativity, imagination, and idea generation. Cooperation requires mechanisms for internal coordination, such as horizontal linkages across departments, and mechanisms for connecting with external parties. One popular approach is open innovation, which extends the search for and commercialization of ideas beyond the boundaries of the organization. Entrepreneurship includes encouraging idea champions and establishing new-venture teams, skunkworks, and new-venture funds.

- People and culture changes pertain to the skills, behaviors, and attitudes of employees. Training and organization development are important approaches to changing people's mind-sets and corporate culture. The OD process entails three steps: unfreezing (diagnosis of the problem), the actual change (intervention), and refreezing (reinforcement of new attitudes and behaviors). Popular OD techniques include team building, survey feedback, and large-group interventions.

- Implementation of change first requires that people see a need for change. Managers should be prepared to encounter resistance. Some typical reasons for resistance include self-interest, lack of trust, uncertainty, and conflicting goals. Force-field analysis is one technique for diagnosing barriers, which often can be removed. Managers can also draw on the implementation tactics of communication, participation, negotiation, coercion, or top management support.

ch10 DISCUSSION QUESTIONS

1. Times of shared crisis, such as the September 11, 2001, terrorist attack on the World Trade Center or the Gulf Coast hurricanes in 2005, can induce many companies that have been bitter rivals to put their competitive spirit aside and focus on cooperation and courtesy. Do you believe this type of change will be a lasting one? Discuss.

2. A manager of an international chemical company said that few new products in her company were successful. What would you advise the manager to do to help increase the company's success rate?

3. What is meant by the terms *internal* and *external forces for change*? Which forces do you think are causes of change in a university? In a pharmaceuticals firm?

4. As a manager, how would you deal with resistance to change when you suspect employee fears of job loss are well-founded?

5. How might businesses use the Internet to identify untapped customer needs through open innovation? What do you see as the major advantages and disadvantages of the open innovation approach?

6. Why do organizations experience resistance to change? What techniques can managers use to overcome resistance?

7. Explain force-field analysis. Use examples from your own experience to analyze the driving and restraining forces for a change.

8. Which role or roles—the inventor, champion, sponsor, or critic—would you most like to play in the innovation process? Which roles would you be least comfortable playing? Why do you think idea champions are so essential to the initiation of change?

9. You are a manager, and you believe the expense reimbursement system for salespeople is far too slow, taking weeks instead of days. How would you go about convincing other managers that this problem needs to be addressed?

10. Do the underlying values of organization development differ from assumptions associated with other types of change? Discuss.

11. How do large-group interventions differ from OD techniques such as team building and survey feedback?

ch10 MANAGEMENT IN PRACTICE: EXPERIENTIAL EXERCISE

Is Your Company Creative?

An effective way to assess the creative climate of an organization for which you have worked is to fill out the following questionnaire. Answer each question based on your work experience in that firm. Discuss the results with members of your group, and talk about whether changing the firm along the dimensions in the questions would make it more creative.

Instructions: Answer each of the following questions using the five-point scale (*Note:* No rating of 4 is used):

⓪ We never do this.
① We rarely do this.
② We sometimes do this.
③ We frequently do this.
⑤ We always do this.

1. We are encouraged to seek help anywhere inside or outside the organization with new ideas for our work unit.

   0 1 2 3 5

2. Assistance is provided to develop ideas into proposals for management review.

   0 1 2 3 5

3. Our performance reviews encourage risky, creative efforts, ideas, and actions.

   0 1 2 3 5

4. We are encouraged to fill our minds with new information by attending professional meetings and trade fairs, visiting customers, and so on.

   0 1 2 3 5

5. Our meetings are designed to allow people to freewheel, brainstorm, and generate ideas.

   0 1 2 3 5

6. All members contribute ideas during meetings.

   0 1 2 3 5

7. Meetings often involve much spontaneity and humor.

   0 1 2 3 5

8. We discuss how company structure and our actions help or spoil creativity within our work unit.

   0 1 2 3 5

9. During meetings, the chair is rotated among members.

   0 1 2 3 5

10. Everyone in the work unit receives training in creativity techniques and maintaining a creative climate.

    0 1 2 3 5

Scoring and Interpretation

Add your total score for all 10 questions: _____

To measure how effectively your organization fosters creativity, use the following scale:

Highly effective: 35–50
Moderately effective: 20–34
Moderately ineffective: 10–19
Ineffective: 0–9

SOURCE: Adapted from Edward Glassman, *Creativity Handbook: Idea Triggers and Sparks That Work* (Chapel Hill, NC: LCS Press, 1990). Used by permission.

4
Organizing

ch10   MANAGEMENT IN PRACTICE: ETHICAL DILEMMA

Crowdsourcing

Last year, when Ai-Lan Nguyen told her friend, Greg Barnwell, that Asheville, North Carolina-based Off the Hook Tees, was going to experiment with crowdsourcing, he warned her she wouldn't like the results. Now, as she was about to walk into a meeting called to decide whether to adopt this new business model, she was afraid her friend had been right.

Crowdsourcing uses the Internet to invite anyone, professionals and amateurs alike, to perform tasks such as product design that employees usually perform. In exchange, contributors receive recognition—but little or no pay. Ai-Lan, as vice president of operations for Off the Hook, a company specializing in witty T-shirts aimed at young adults, upheld the values of founder Chris Woodhouse, who like Ai-Lan was a graphic artist. Before he sold the company, the founder always insisted that T-shirts be well-designed by top-notch graphic artists to make sure each screen print was a work of art. Those graphic artists reported to Ai-Lan.

During the past 18 months, Off the Hook's sales stagnated for the first time in its history. The crowdsourcing experiment was the latest in a series of attempts to jump-start sales growth. Last spring, Off the Hook issued its first open call for T-shirt designs and then posted the entries on the Web so people could vote for their favorites. The top five vote-getters were handed over to the in-house designers, who tweaked the submissions until they met the company's usual quality standards.

When CEO Rob Taylor first announced the company's foray into crowdsourcing, Ai-Lan found herself reassuring the designers that their positions were not in jeopardy. Now Ai-Lan was all but certain she would have to go back on her word. Not only had the crowdsourced tees sold well, but Rob had put a handful of winning designs directly into production, bypassing the design department altogether. Customers didn't notice the difference.

Ai-Lan concluded that Rob was ready to adopt some form of the Web-based crowdsourcing because it made T-shirt design more responsive to consumer desires. Practically speaking, it reduced the uncertainty that surrounded new designs, and it dramatically lowered costs. The people who won the competitions were delighted with the exposure it gave them.

However, when Ai-Lan looked at the crowdsourced shirts with her graphic artist's eye, she felt that the designs were competent, but none achieved the aesthetic standards attained by her in-house designers. Crowdsourcing essentially replaced training and expertise with public opinion. That made the artist in her uncomfortable.

More distressing, it was beginning to look as if Greg had been right when he'd told her that his working definition of crowdsourcing was "a billion amateurs want your job." It was easy to see that if Off the Hook adopted crowdsourcing, she would be handing out pink slips to most of her design people, long-time employees whose work she admired. "Sure, crowdsourcing costs the company less, but what about the human cost?" Greg asked.

What future course should Ai-Lan argue for at the meeting? And what personal decisions did she face if Off the Hook decided to put the crowd completely in charge when it came to T-shirt design?

What Would You Do?

1. Go to the meeting and argue for abandoning crowdsourcing for now in favor of maintaining the artistic integrity and values that Off the Hook has always stood for.

2. Accept the reality that because Off the Hook's CEO Rob Taylor strongly favors crowdsourcing, it's a fait accompli. Be a team player and help work out the details of the new design approach. Prepare to lay off graphic designers as needed.

3. Accept the fact that converting Off the Hook to a crowdsourcing business model is inevitable, but because it violates your own personal values, start looking for a new job elsewhere.

SOURCES: Based on Paul Boutin, "Crowdsourcing: Consumers as Creators," *BusinessWeek Online* (July 13, 2006), www.businessweek.com/innovate/content/jul2006/id20060713_55844.htm?campaign_id=search; Jeff Howe, "The Rise of Crowdsourcing," *Wired* (June 2006), www.wired.com/wired/archive/14.06/crowds.html; and Jeff Howe, Crowdsourcing Blog, www.crowdsourcing.com.

ch10 CASE FOR CRITICAL ANALYSIS

Southern Discomfort

Jim Malesckowski remembers the call of two weeks ago as if he just put down the telephone receiver. "I just read your analysis and I want you to get down to Mexico right away," Jack Ripon, his boss and chief executive officer, had blurted in his ear. "You know we can't make the plant in Oconomo work anymore—the costs are just too high. So go down there, check out what our operational costs would be if we move, and report back to me in a week."

At that moment, Jim felt as if a shiv had been stuck in his side, just below the rib cage. As president of the Wisconsin Specialty Products Division of Lamprey, Inc., he knew quite well the challenge of dealing with high-cost labor in a third-generation, unionized U.S. manufacturing plant. And although he had done the analysis that led to his boss's knee-jerk response, the call still stunned him. There were 520 people who made a living at Lamprey's Oconomo facility, and if it closed, most of them wouldn't have a journeyman's prayer of finding another job in the town of 9,000 people.

Instead of the $16-per-hour average wage paid at the Oconomo plant, the wages paid to the Mexican workers—who lived in a town without sanitation and with an unbelievably toxic effluent from industrial pollution—would amount to about $1.60 an hour on average. That's a savings of nearly $15 million a year for Lamprey, to be offset in part by increased costs for training, transportation, and other matters.

After two days of talking with Mexican government representatives and managers of other companies in the town, Jim had enough information to develop a set of comparative figures of production and shipping costs. On the way home, he started to outline the report, knowing full well that unless some miracle occurred, he would be ushering in a blizzard of pink slips for people he had come to appreciate.

The plant in Oconomo had been in operation since 1921, making special apparel for persons suffering injuries and other medical conditions. Jim had often talked with employees who would recount stories about their fathers or grandfathers working in the same Lamprey company plant—the last of the original manufacturing operations in town.

But friendship aside, competitors had already edged past Lamprey in terms of price and were dangerously close to overtaking it in product quality. Although both Jim and the plant manager had tried to convince the union to accept lower wages, union leaders resisted. In fact, on one occasion when Jim and the plant manager tried to discuss a cell manufacturing approach, which would cross-train employees to perform up to three different jobs, local union leaders could barely restrain their anger. Yet probing beyond the fray, Jim sensed the fear that lurked under the union reps' gruff exterior. He sensed their vulnerability, but could not break through the reactionary bark that protected it.

A week has passed and Jim just submitted his report to his boss. Although he didn't specifically bring up the point, it was apparent that Lamprey could put its investment dollars in a bank and receive a better return than what its Oconomo operation is currently producing.

Tomorrow, he'll discuss the report with the CEO. Jim doesn't want to be responsible for the plant's dismantling, an act he personally believes would be wrong as long as there's a chance its costs can be lowered. "But Ripon's right," he says to himself. "The costs are too high, the union's unwilling to cooperate, and the company needs to make a better return on its investment if it's to continue at all. It sounds right but feels wrong. What should I do?"

Questions

1. What forces for change are evident at the Oconomo plant?

2. What is the primary type of change needed—changing "things" or changing the "people and culture?" Can the Wisconsin plant be saved by changing things alone, by changing people and culture, or must both be changed? Explain your answer.

3. What do you think is the major underlying cause of the union leaders' resistance to change? If you were Jim Malesckowski, what implementation tactics would you use to try to convince union members to change in order to save the Wisconsin plant?

SOURCE: Doug Wallace, "What Would You Do?" *Business Ethics* (March/April 1996), 52–53. Reprinted with permission.

ch10   ON THE JOB VIDEO CASE

Lonely Planet: Structure That Makes Sense

When travelers Tony and Maureen Wheeler founded Lonely Planet in the early 1970s, they didn't intend to create a globe-spanning company. They didn't necessarily plan to start a publishing company. As newlyweds, they had just completed an overland trip from London through Asia, winding up in Australia. All they really wanted to do was finance their next trip—it never occurred to them to stop traveling around the world. So they wrote and published the first Lonely Planet guidebook, *Across Asia on the Cheap;* it was an instant best-seller among world wanderers.

With just two people, the Wheelers naturally didn't think about organization. They traveled, wrote, and published whatever they wanted. By the mid 1970s, they had completed *Nepal and Trekking in the Himalayas* and were working on a group of guides covering Australia, Europe, Africa, and New Zealand. In 1981, *Lonely Planet India* was published and became a travel best-seller. By then, Lonely Planet had a staff of ten. It was time to get organized.

Today, Lonely Planet publishes more than 650 guidebooks, including specialized activity guides, "shoestring" or budget guides, international food guides, and phrasebooks. The firm is still owned by the Wheelers, employing 400 workers in offices in Melbourne; London; Paris; and Oakland, California. In addition, there are about 150 authors traveling and writing around the world. Lonely Planet has people to create maps, take photos, design book covers, sell books, and create marketing campaigns. There are also finance people and people who work with and manage the freelancers who are roaming the world. Managing all of these activities in four countries on three continents requires communication and coordination.

For example, each office is responsible for all sales and marketing efforts for its own region in order to address cultural and other environmental differences. In addition, a regional warehouse distributes all of that office's book titles to booksellers within the geographical area. Because Lonely Planet publishes books about world travel, having a presence in several key countries enhances the firm's credibility among readers. This organization gives the individual offices more flexibility in directing marketing messages to specific audiences and ensures that workers in each office know their region thoroughly. In addition, one of Lonely Planet's greatest assets is its local writers, according to David Zingarelli, managing editor for Lonely Planet USA. Being able to

meet with them in person and cultivate a relationship is a great advantage. Despite their relative independence, the offices must communicate with each other. So, managers rely on the Internet for regular communication and to create consistency among marketing messages.

Although regional offices may commission books for their areas—Lonely Planet USA commissions all the books for North and South America, as well as Central America—the headquarters in Australia actually produces all of the books. This centralization streamlines the production process, reduces costs by keeping cartographers and designers under one roof, and ensures that the books are designed and produced in a consistent fashion. In addition, negotiations with the printers in Hong Kong are more efficient and effective if they are conducted from a single location.

People who work at Lonely Planet love to travel, and they like the way the company is organized. "It's got all the excitement of working for a multinational . . . but without any of the . . . complexity of bureaucracy," explains one employee. "Working with other offices— Melbourne, Paris, London—as a global company and still being independently owned" is a positive experience, notes another. "It's a large company, but it's really small," he continues. Tony and Maureen Wheeler are still very much a presence in the company, visiting its worldwide offices and maintaining contact with many employees. There are some drawbacks to this far-flung method of managing; sometimes staffers grumble about the challenges of dealing with time differences, but they concede that this is a minor inconvenience. After all, if you work at a travel publisher because you love to travel, think about the possibilities. Perhaps you'll work in Australia this year and Paris next year. Maybe you've got the urge to set up shop in London. At Lonely Planet, there's almost always an opportunity to hit the road—and get paid for it.

Questions

1. In what ways is Lonely Planet decentralized? In what ways is it centralized?

2. Does Lonely Planet have a tall structure or a flat structure? Explain briefly.

3. In what ways does Lonely Planet achieve horizontal coordination across departments or offices?

SOURCES: Company Web site, *http://www.lonelyplanet.com,* accessed July 30, 2004; Lonely Planet press kit.

ch10 BIZ FLIX VIDEO CASE

Bowfinger

This film, which brought Steve Martin and Eddie Murphy together for the first time, offers a funny look at Hollywood film-making. Bobby Bowfinger (Martin), perhaps the least successful director in films, wants to produce a low-budget film with top star Kit Ramsey (Murphy). Bowfinger's problem: how to recruit a crew and cast with almost no budget while tricking Kit into appearing in his film.

Bowfinger interviews several candidates for the Kit Ramsey lookalike role. He rejects everyone until Jifferson (Jiff) Ramsey (also played by Murphy) auditions. This scene is an edited version of "The Look-alike"

sequence early in the film. It includes Jiff's audition, interview, and a brief look at his first day at work.

What to Watch for and Ask Yourself

1. Does Bobby Bowfinger have a set of valid selection criteria for filling the role of a Kit Ramsey look-alike? Does Bowfinger apply the criteria uniformly to each applicant?

2. Is Jiff Ramsey a good person-job fit in the screen role of Kit Ramsey?

3. Do you predict that Jiff Ramsey will be successful as a Kit Ramsey substitute?

ch10 ENDNOTES

1. Based on H. Thomas Hurt, Katherine Joseph, and Chester D. Cook, "Scales for the Measurement of Innovativeness," *Human Communication Research* 4, no. 1 (1977): 58–65, and John E. Ettlie and Robert D. O'Keefe, "Innovative Attitudes, Values, and Intentions in Organizations," *Journal of Management Studies* 19, no. 2 (1982): 163–182.

2. Reported in "90 Years in Business," *The Conference Board Review* (September–October 2006): 30–39.

3. Mark Landler, "Nokia Pushes to Regain U.S. Sales in Spite of Apple and Google, *The New York Times*, December 10, 2007.

4. Martin Fackler, "Electronics Company Aims to Create Break-Out Products," *The New York Times*, April 25, 2006; and Peter Lewis, "A Perpetual Crisis Machine," *Fortune* (September 19, 2005): 58–76.

5. Bruce Nussbaum, with Robert Berner and Diane Brady, "Get Creative," *BusinessWeek* (August 1, 2005): 60–68; Jena McGregor, Michael Arndt, Robert Berner, Ian Rowley, Kenji Hall, Gail Edmondson, Steve Hamm, Moon Ihlwan, and Andy Reinhardt, "The World's Most Innovative Companies," *Business-Week* (April 24, 2006), http://www.businessweek.com.

6. Keith Bracsher, "Newest Export Out of China: Inflation Fears," *The New York Times*, April 16, 2004, http://www.nytimes.com.

7. Scott Kirsner, "5 Technologies That Will Change the World," *Fast Company* (September 2003): 93–98; Peter Grant and Amy Schatz, "Battle Lines; For Cable Giants, AT&T Deal Is One More Reason to Worry," *The Wall Street Journal*, March 7, 2006; Stuart F. Brown, "The Automaker's Big-Time Bet

on Fuel Cells," *Fortune* (March 30, 1998): 122(B)–122(D); Alex Taylor III, "Billion-Dollar Bets," *Fortune* (June 27, 2005): 138–154.

8. Kirsner, "5 Technologies That Will Change the World."

9. David Henry, "Creativity Pays. Here's How Much," *BusinessWeek* (April 24, 2006): 76.

10. Richard L. Daft, "Bureaucratic vs. Nonbureaucratic Structure in the Process of Innovation and Change," in *Perspectives in Organizational Sociology: Theory and Research*, ed. Samuel B. Bacharach (Greenwich, CT: JAI Press, 1982), pp. 129–166.

11. Charles A. O"Reilly III and Michael L. Tushman, "The Ambidextrous Organization," *Harvard Business Review* (April 2004): 74–81; M. L. Tushman and C. A. O'Reilly III, "Building an Ambidextrous Organization: Forming

4 Organizing

Your Own 'Skunk Works,'" *Health Forum Journal* 42, no. 2 (March–April 1999): 20–23.

12. C. Brooke Dobni, "The Innovation Blueprint," *Business Horizons* (2006): 329–339.

13. Glenn Rifkin, "Competing Through Innovation: The Case of Broderbund," *Strategy + Business* 11 (Second Quarter 1998): 48–58; and Deborah Dougherty and Cynthia Hardy, "Sustained Product Innovation in Large, Mature Organizations: Overcoming Innovation-to-Organization Problems," *Academy of Management Journal* 39, no. 5 (1996): 1120–1153.

14. Adapted from Patrick Reinmoeller and Nicole van Baardwijk, "The Link Between Diversity and Resilience," *MIT Sloan Management Review* (Summer 2005): 61–65.

15. Teresa M. Amabile, "Motivating Creativity in Organizations: On Doing What You Love and Loving What You Do," *California Management Review* 40, no. 1 (Fall 1997): 39–58; Brian Leavy, "Creativity: The New Imperative," *Journal of General Management* 28, no. 1 (Autumn 2002): 70–85; and Timothy A. Matherly and Ronald E. Goldsmith, "The Two Faces of Creativity," *Business Horizons* (September–October 1985): 8.

16. Lee Gomes, "Our Columnist Judges a Brainstorming Bee, and Meets a Genius," *The Wall Street Journal*, March 5, 2008.

17. Gordon Vessels, "The Creative Process: An Open-Systems Conceptualization," *Journal of Creative Behavior* 16 (1982): 185–196.

18. Robert J. Sternberg, Linda A. O'Hara, and Todd I. Lubart, "Creativity as Investment," *California Management Review* 40, no. 1 (Fall 1997): 8–21; Amabile, "Motivating Creativity in Organizations"; Leavy, "Creativity: The New Imperative"; and Ken Lizotte, "A Creative State of Mind," *Management Review* (May 1998): 15–17.

19. James Brian Quinn, "Managing Innovation: Controlled Chaos," *Harvard Business Review* 63 (May–June 1985): 73–84; Howard H. Stevenson and David E. Gumpert, "The Heart of Entrepreneurship," *Harvard Business Review* 63 (March–April 1985): 85–94; Marsha Sinetar,

"Entrepreneurs, Chaos, and Creativity—Can Creative People Really Survive Large Company Structure?" *Sloan Management Review* 6 (Winter 1985): 57–62; and Constantine Andriopoulos, "Six Paradoxes in Managing Creativity: An Embracing Act," *Long Range Planning* 36 (2003): 375–388.

20. Cynthia Browne, "Jest for Success," *Moonbeams* (August 1989): 3–5; and Rosabeth Moss Kanter, *The Change Masters* (New York: Simon and Schuster, 1983).

21. Chuck Salter, "Google: The Faces and Voices of the World's Most Innovative Company," *Fast Company* (March 2008): 74–91.

22. Sherry Eng, "Hatching Schemes," *The Industry Standard* (November 27–December 4, 2000): 174–175.

23. Reena Jana, "Brickhouse: Yahoo's Hot Little Incubator," *IN* (November 2007): 14.

24. McGregor et al., "The World's Most Innovative Companies."

25. Barry Jaruzelski, Kevin Dehoff, and Rakesh Bordia, "Money Isn't Everything," *Strategy + Business*, no. 41 (December 5, 2005): 54–67; William L. Shanklin and John K. Ryans, Jr., "Organizing for High-Tech Marketing," *Harvard Business Review* 62 (November–December 1984): 164–171; and Arnold O. Putnam, "A Redesign for Engineering," *Harvard Business Review* 63 (May–June 1985): 139–144.

26. Rob Cross, Andrew Hargadon, Salvatore Parise, and Robert J. Thomas, "Business Insight (A Special Report); Together We Innovate: How Can Companies Come Up with New Ideas? By Getting Employees Working with One Another," *The Wall Street Journal*, September 15, 2007.

27. Andrew H. Van de Ven, "Central Problems in the Management of Innovation," *Management Science* 32 (1986): 590–607; Daft, *Organization Theory*; and Science Policy Research Unit, University of Sussex, *Success and Failure in Industrial Innovation* (London: Centre for the Study of Industrial Innovation, 1972).

28. Daft, *Organization Theory*.

29. Brian Dumaine, "How Managers Can Succeed Through Speed," *Fortune* (February 13, 1989): 54–59; and George Stalk, Jr., "Time—The

Next Source of Competitive Advantage," *Harvard Business Review* (July–August 1988): 41–51.

30. Steve Hamm, with Ian Rowley, "Speed Demons," *BusinessWeek* (March 27, 2006): 68–76; and John A. Pearce II, "Speed Merchants," *Organizational Dynamics* 30, no. 3 (2002): 191–205.

31. V. K. Narayanan, Frank L. Douglas, Brock Guernsey, and John Charnes, "How Top Management Steers Fast Cycle Teams to Success," *Strategy & Leadership* 30, no. 3 (2002): 19–27.

32. The discussion of open innovation is based on Henry Chesbrough, "The Era of Open Innovation," *MIT Sloan Management Review* (Spring 2003): 35–41; Julian Birkinshaw and Susan A. Hill, "Corporate Venturing Units: Vehicles for Strategic Success in the New Europe," *Organizational Dynamics* 34, no. 3 (2005): 247–257; Amy Muller and Liisa Välikangas, "Extending the Boundary of Corporate Innovation," *Strategy & Leadership* 30, no. 3 (2002): 4–9; Navi Radjou, "Networked Innovation Drives Profits," *Industrial Management* (January–February 2005): 14–21; Darrell Rigby and Barbara Bilodeau, "The Bain 2005 Management Tool Survey," *Strategy & Leadership* 33, no. 4 (2005): 4–12; Ian Mount, "The Return of the Lone Inventor," *FSB (Fortune Small Business)* (March 2005): 18; McGregor et al., "The World's Most Innovative Companies;" and Henry Chesbrough, "The Logic of Open Innovation: Managing Intellectual Property," *California Management Review* 45, no. 3 (Spring 2003): 33–58.

33. Reported in Jill Jusko, "A Team Effort," *Industry Week* (January 2007): 42, 45.

34. Larry Huston and Nabil Sakkab, "Connect and Develop; Inside Procter & Gamble's New Model for Innovation," *Harvard Business Review* (March 2006): 58–66; G. Gil Cloyd, "P&G's Secret: Innovating Innovation," *Industry Week* (December 2004): 26–34; Bettina von Stamm, "Collaboration with Other Firms and Customers: Innovation's Secret Weapon," *Strategy & Leadership* 32, no. 3 (2004): 16–20; Robert Berner,

"Why P&G's Smile Is So Bright," *BusinessWeek* (August 12, 2002): 58–60; Robert D. Hof, "Building an Idea Factory," *BusinessWeek* (October 11, 2004): 194–200; Patricia Sellers, "P&G: Teaching an Old Dog New Tricks," *Fortune* (May 31, 2004): 167–180; and Ellen Byron, "Bottle Curve; P&G's Push Into Perfume Tests a Stodgy Marketer," *The Wall Street Journal,* November 12, 2007.

35. Daniel T. Holt, Matthew W. Rutherford, and Gretchen R. Clohessy, "Corporate Entrepreneurship: An Empirical Look at Individual Characteristics, Context, and Process," *Journal of Leadership and Organizational Studies* 13, no. 4 (2007): 40–54.

36. Robert I. Sutton, "The Weird Rules of Creativity," *Harvard Business Review* (September 2001): 94–103.

37. Jane M. Howell, "The Right Stuff: Identifying and Developing Effective Champions of Innovation," *Academy of Management Executive* 19, no. 2 (2005): 108–119.

38. Harold L. Angle and Andrew H. Van de Ven, "Suggestions for Managing the Innovation Journey," in *Research in the Management of Innovation: The Minnesota Studies*, ed. A. H. Van de Ven, H. L. Angle, and Marshall Scott Poole (Cambridge, MA: Ballinger/Harper & Row, 1989).

39. C. K. Bart, "New Venture Units: Use Them Wisely to Manage Innovation," *Sloan Management Review* (Summer 1988): 35–43; Michael Tushman and David Nadler," Organizing for Innovation," *California Management Review* 28 (Spring 1986): 74–92; Peter F. Drucker, *Innovation and Entrepreneurship* (New York: Harper & Row, 1985); and Henry W. Chesbrough, "Making Sense of Corporate Venture Capital, *Harvard Business Review* (March 2002), http://www.hbsp. harvard.edu.

40. McGregor et al., "The World's Most Innovative Companies."

41. Christopher Hoenig, "Skunk Works Secrets," *CIO* (July 1, 2000): 74–76; and Tom Peters and Nancy Austin, *A Passion for Excellence: The Leadership Difference* (New York: Random House, 1985).

42. Hoenig, "Skunk Works Secrets."

43. Sutton, "The Weird Rules of Creativity."

44. Robert C. Wolcott and Michael J. Lippitz, "The Four Models of Corporate Entrepreneurship," *MIT Sloan Management Review* (Fall 2007): 75–82.

45. Wolcott and Lippitz, "The Four Models of Corporate Entrepreneurship"; Alan Deutschman, "Building a Better Skunkworks," *Fast Company* (March 2005): 69–73.

46. McGregor et al., "The World's Most Innovative Companies."

47. Wolcott and Lippitz, "The Four Models of Corporate Entrepreneurship."

48. E. H. Schein, "Organizational Culture," *American Psychologist* 45 (February 1990): 109–119; Eliza Newlin Carey, "Calm in the Storm."

49. Rosabeth Moss Kanter, "Execution: The Un-Idea," sidebar in Art Kleiner, "Our 10 Most Enduring Ideas," *Strategy + Business* no. 41 (December 12, 2005): 36–41.

50. Michelle Conlin, "Tough Love for Techie Souls," *BusinessWeek* (November 29, 1999): 164–170.

51. M. Sashkin and W. W. Burke, "Organization Development in the 1980s," *General Management* 13 (1987): 393–417; and Richard Beckhard, "What Is Organization Development?" in *Organization Development and Transformation: Managing Effective Change*, ed. Wendell L. French, Cecil H. Bell, Jr., and Robert A. Zawacki (Burr Ridge, IL: Irwin McGraw-Hill, 2000), pp. 16–19.

52. Wendell L. French and Cecil H. Bell, Jr., "A History of Organization Development," in French, Bell, and Zawacki, *Organization Development and Transformation*, pp. 20–42; and Christopher G. Worley and Ann E. Feyerherm, "Reflections on the Future of Organization Development," *The Journal of Applied Behavioral Science* 39, no. 1 (March 2003): 97–115.

53. Paul F. Buller, "For Successful Strategic Change: Blend OD Practices with Strategic Management," *Organizational Dynamics* (Winter 1988): 42–55; Robert M. Fulmer and Roderick Gilkey, "Blending Corporate Families: Management and Organization Development in a Postmerger Environment," *The*

Academy of Management Executive 2 (1988): 275–283; and Worley and Feyerherm, "Reflections on the Future of Organization Development."

54. W. Warner Burke, "The New Agenda for Organization Development," *Organizational Dynamics* (Summer 1997): 7–19.

55. This discussion is based on Kathleen D. Dannemiller and Robert W. Jacobs, "Changing the Way Organizations Change: A Revolution of Common Sense," *The Journal of Applied Behavioral Science* 28, no. 4 (December 1992): 480–498; and Barbara Benedict Bunker and Billie T. Alban, "Conclusion: What Makes Large Group Interventions Effective?" *The Journal of Applied Behavioral Science* 28, no. 4 (December 1992): 570–591.

56. B. B. Bunker and B. T. Alban, "Conclusion: What Makes Large Group Interventions Effective?" *Journal of Applied Behavioral Science* 28, no. 4 (December 1992): 572–591.

57. Dave Ulrich, Steve Kerr, and Ron Ashkenas, with Debbie Burke and Patrice Murphy, *The GE Work-Out: How to Implement GE's Revolutionary Method for Busting Bureaucracy and Attacking Organizational Problems—Fast!* (New York: McGraw-Hill, 2002); J. Quinn, "What a Work-Out!" *Performance* (November 1994): 58–63; and Bunker and Alban, "Conclusion: What Makes Large Group Interventions Effective?"

58. Kurt Lewin, "Frontiers in Group Dynamics: Concepts, Method, and Reality in Social Science," *Human Relations* 1 (1947): 5–41; and E. F. Huse and T. G. Cummings, *Organization Development and Change*, 3rd ed. (St. Paul, MN: West, 1985).

59. Based on John Kotter's eight-step model of planned change, which is described in John Kotter, *Leading Change* (Boston: Harvard Business School Press, 1996), pp. 20–25, and "Leading Change: Why Transformation Efforts Fail," *Harvard Business Review* (March–April, 1995): 59–67.

60. Pierre Loewe and Jennifer Dominiquini, "Overcoming the Barriers to Effective Innovation, *Strategy & Leadership* 34, no. 1 (2006): 24–31; and Jennifer Robison, "Innovation the Right Way: A Case Study in

How a Manufacturing Company Got Innovation Right," *Gallup Management Journal* (May 10, 2007).

61. John P. Kotter, *Leading Change* (Boston: Harvard University Press, 1996), pp. 20–25; and "Leading Change: Why Transformation Efforts Fail," *Harvard Business Review* (March–April, 1995): 59–67.

62. J. P. Kotter and L. A. Schlesinger, "Choosing Strategies for Change," *Harvard Business Review* 57 (March–April 1979): 106–114.

63. Robison, "Innovation the Right Way."

64. G. Zaltman and Robert B. Duncan, *Strategies for Planned Change* (New York: Wiley Interscience, 1977).

65. Leonard M. Apcar, "Middle Managers and Supervisors Resist Moves to More Participatory Management," *The Wall Street Journal*, September 16, 1985.

66. Dorothy Leonard-Barton and Isabelle Deschamps, "Managerial Influence in the Implementation of New Technology," *Management Science* 34 (1988): 1252–1265.

67. Kurt Lewin, *Field Theory in Social Science: Selected Theoretical Papers* (New York: Harper & Brothers, 1951).

68. Paul C. Nutt, "Tactics of Implementation," *Academy of Management Journal* 29 (1986): 230–261; Kotter and Schlesinger, "Choosing Strategies"; R. L. Daft and S. Becker, *Innovation in Organizations: Innovation Adoption in School Organizations* (New York: Elsevier, 1978); and R. Beckhard, *Organization Development: Strategies and Models* (Reading, MA: Addison-Wesley, 1969).

69. Rob Muller, "Training for Change," *Canadian Business Review* (Spring 1995): 16–19.

70. Gerard H. Seijts and Grace O'Farrell, "Engage the Heart: Appealing to the Emotions Facilitates Change," *Ivey Business Journal* (January–February 2003): 1–5; John P. Kotter and Dan S. Cohen, *The Heart of Change: Real-Life Stories of How People Change Their Organizations* (Boston: Harvard Business School Press, 2002); and Shaul Fox and Yair Amichai Hamburger, "The Power of Emotional Appeals in Promoting Organizational Change Programs," *Academy of Management Executive* 15, no. 4 (2001): 84–95.

71. Gina Burkhardt and Diane Gerard, "People: The Lever for Changing the Business Model at Learning Point Associates," *Journal of Organizational Excellence* (Autumn 2006): 31–43.

72. Henry Hornstein, "Using a Change Management Approach to Implement IT Programs," *Ivey Business Journal* (January–February 2008); Philip H. Mirvis, Amy L. Sales, and Edward J. Hackett, "The Implementation and Adoption of New Technology in Organizations: The Impact on Work, People, and Culture," *Human Resource Management* 30 (Spring 1991): 113–139; Arthur E. Wallach, "System Changes Begin in the Training Department," *Personnel Journal* 58 (1979): 846–848, 872; and Paul R. Lawrence, "How to Deal with Resistance to Change," *Harvard Business Review* 47 (January–February 1969): 4–12, 166–176.

73. Dean Foust with Gerry Khermouch, "Repairing the Coke Machine," *BusinessWeek* (March 19, 2001): 86–88.

74. Strategos survey results, reported in Loewe and Dominiquini, "Overcoming the Barriers to Effective Innovation."

75. Joy Persaud, "Strongest Links," *People Management* (May 29, 2003): 40–41.

© GETTY IMAGES/DIGITAL VISION

Learning Outcomes

After studying this chapter, you should be able to:

1. Explain the strategic role of human resource management.

2. Describe federal legislation and societal trends that influence human resource management.

3. Explain what the changing social contract between organizations and employees means for workers and human resource managers.

4. Show how organizations determine their future staffing needs through human resource planning.

5. Describe the tools managers use to recruit and select employees.

6. Describe how organizations develop an effective workforce through training and performance appraisal.

7. Explain how organizations maintain a workforce through the administration of wages and salaries, benefits, and terminations.

Managing Human Resources

1 Introduction

2 Environment

3 Planning

4 Organizing

5 Controlling

6 Leading

GETTING THE RIGHT PEOPLE ON THE BUS[1]

As a new manager, how much emphasis will you give to getting the right people on your team? How much emphasis on people is needed? Find out by answering the following questions based on your expectations and beliefs for handling the people part of your management job. Please answer whether each item is Mostly True or Mostly False for you.

	Mostly True	Mostly False
1. I will readily fire someone who isn't working out for the interests of the organization.	____	____
2. Selecting the right people for a winning business team is as important to me as it is to a winning sports team.	____	____
3. I expect to spend 40 percent to 60 percent of my management time on issues such as recruiting, developing, and placing people.	____	____
4. I will paint a realistic picture of negative job aspects that will help scare off the wrong people for the job.	____	____
5. My priority as a manager is first to hire the right people, second to put people in the right positions, and third to then decide strategy and vision.	____	____
6. With the right people on my team, problems of motivation and supervision will largely go away.	____	____
7. I expect that hiring the right people is a lengthy and arduous process.	____	____
8. I view firing someone as helping them find the place where they belong to find fulfillment.	____	____

SCORING AND INTERPRETATION: Most new managers are shocked at the large amount of time, effort, and skill required to recruit, place, and retain the right people. In recent years, the importance of "getting the right people on the bus" has been described in popular business books such as *Good to Great* and *Execution*. The right people can make an organization great; the wrong people can be catastrophic.

Give yourself one point for each item you marked as Mostly True. If you scored four or less you may be in for a shock as a new manager. People issues will take up most of your time, and if you don't handle people correctly, your effectiveness will suffer. You should learn how to get the right people on the bus, and how to get the wrong people off the bus. The faster you learn these lessons, the better new manager you will be. A score of five or more suggests you have the right understanding and expectations for becoming a manager and dealing with people on the bus.

Hiring and keeping quality employees is one of the most urgent concerns for today's organizations.[2] Employees give a company its primary source of competitive advantage, so talent management is a top priority for smart managers. The term **human resource management (HRM)** refers to the design and application of formal systems in an organization to ensure the effective and efficient use of human talent to accomplish organizational goals.[3] This system includes activities undertaken to attract, develop, and maintain an effective workforce. Managers have to find the right people, place them in positions where they can be most effective, and develop them so they contribute to company success.

human resource management (HRM)
Activities undertaken to attract, develop, and maintain an effective workforce within an organization.

307

Over the past decade, human resource management has shed its old "personnel" image and gained recognition as a vital player in corporate strategy.[4] Increasingly, large corporations are outsourcing routine HR administrative activities, freeing HRM staff from time-consuming paperwork and enabling them to take on more strategic responsibilities. Human resources tops Gartner Inc.'s list of most commonly outsourced business activities.[5]

All managers need to be skilled in the basics of human resource management. Flatter organizations often require that managers throughout the organization play an active role in recruiting and selecting the right employees, developing effective training programs, or creating appropriate performance appraisal systems. HRM professionals act to guide and assist line managers in managing human resources to achieve the organization's strategic goals.

THE STRATEGIC ROLE OF HRM IS TO DRIVE ORGANIZATIONAL PERFORMANCE

How a company manages talent may be the single most important factor in sustained competitive success. Today's best human resources departments not only support strategic objectives but also actively pursue an ongoing, integrated plan for furthering the organization's performance.[6] Research has found that effective human resource management has a positive impact on strategic performance, including higher employee productivity and stronger financial results.[7]

The Strategic Approach

The strategic approach to human resource management recognizes three key elements. First, all managers are involved in human resource management. Second, employees are viewed as assets. Employees, not buildings and machinery, give a company its competitive edge. Third, human resource management is a matching process, integrating the organization's strategy and goals with the correct approach to managing human capital.[8] In companies that take a strategic approach, HR managers are key players on the executive team and play a pivotal role in driving performance. At retailer Target, for example, the formal mission of the human resources department is to "drive company performance by building a fast, fun, and friendly team committed to excellence." To fulfill the mission, HR managers are directly involved in building a culture that distinguishes Target from other retailers, finding the right people to fit the culture, then creating training programs, compensation, and other mechanisms to develop and retain quality employees.[9] Some current strategic issues of particular concern to managers include the following:

- Right people to become more competitive on a global basis
- Right people for improving quality, innovation, and customer service
- Right people to retain during mergers and acquisitions
- Right people to apply new information technology for e-business

All of these strategic decisions determine a company's need for skills and employees.

TakeaMoment | **Go to the experiential exercise on pages 332–333 that pertains to your potential for strategic human resource management.**

This chapter examines the three primary goals of HRM as illustrated in Exhibit 11.1. HRM activities and goals do not take place inside a vacuum but within

EXHIBIT | 11.1 Strategic Human Resource Management

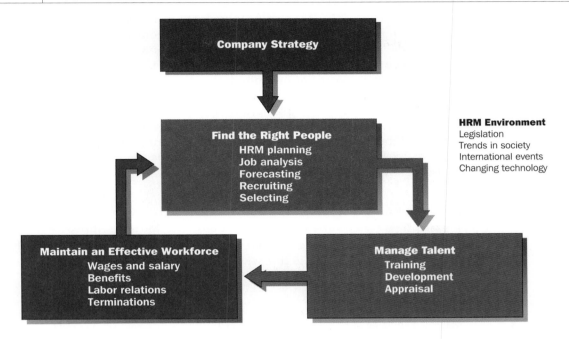

the context of issues and factors affecting the entire organization, such as globalization, changing technology, a growing need for rapid innovation, quick shifts in markets and the external environment, societal trends, government regulations, and changes in the organization's culture, structure, strategy, and goals.

The three broad HRM activities outlined in Exhibit 11.1 are to find the right people, manage talent so people achieve their potential, and maintain the workforce over the long term.[10] Achieving these goals requires skills in planning, recruiting, training, performance appraisal, wage and salary administration, benefit programs, and even termination.

human capital The economic value of the knowledge, experience, skills, and capabilities of employees.

4 Organizing

Building Human Capital to Drive Performance

Today, more than ever, strategic decisions are related to human resource considerations. In many companies, especially those that rely more on employee information, creativity, knowledge, and service rather than on production machinery, success depends on the ability to manage *human capital*.[11] **Human capital** refers to the economic value of the combined knowledge, experience, skills, and capabilities of employees.[12] To build human capital, HRM develops strategies for finding the best talent, enhancing their skills and knowledge with training programs and opportunities for personal and professional development, and providing compensation and benefits that support the sharing of knowledge and appropriately reward people for their contributions to the organization.

Concept Connection Lowe's 215,000 employees help customers with remodeling, building, and gardening ideas at its 1,575 stores. They cut lumber, blinds, pipe, and chains; thread pipes; assemble items; provide computer project design and landscape garden design; match paint colors; teach how-to clinics; and offer many other services. Managers know that providing superior customer service depends on **human capital**, so they invest in finding the best people and helping them develop and apply their combined knowledge, skills, experience, and talent.

The importance of human capital for business results is illustrated in Exhibit 11.2. The framework was developed by Accenture and used by software and services company SAP. SAP needed a way to evaluate and revise its human capital processes to shift to a new strategy requiring stronger customer focus and greater individual employee accountability. The idea is to show how investments in human capital contribute to stronger organizational performance and better financial results. The framework begins at the bottom (level 4) by assessing internal processes such as workforce planning, career development, learning management, and so forth. Managers use these activities to increase human capital capabilities (level 3), such as employee engagement or workforce adaptability. Enhanced capabilities, in turn, drive higher performance in key areas such as innovation or customer satisfaction (level 2). Finally, improvements in key performance areas lead to improved business results.[13]

TakeaMoment | As a new manager, recognize that human capital is the organization's most valuable asset. If you are involved in hiring decisions, look for the best people you can find, and then treat them like gold, with opportunities to learn, grow, and develop new skills and earn appropriate compensation and benefits.

EXHIBIT | 11.2 The Role and Value of Human Capital Investments

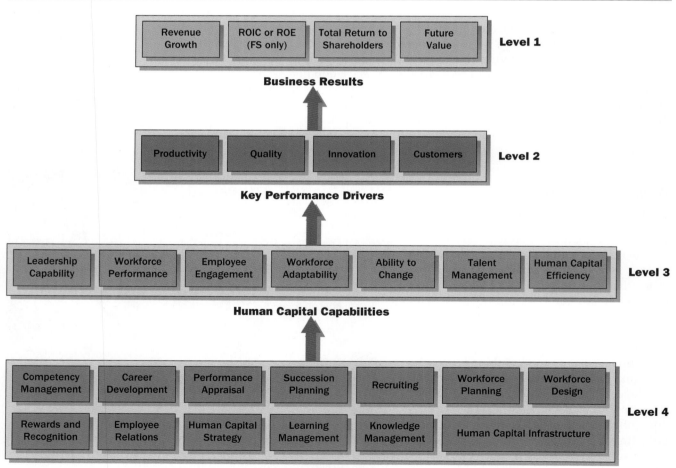

SOURCE: Susan Cantrell, James M. Benton, Terry Laudal, and Robert J. Thomas, "Measuring the Value of Human Capital Investments: The SAP Case," *Strategy & Leadership* 34, no. 2 (2006): 43–52. Copyright 2006 by Emerald Group Publishing Limited. Reproduced with permission of Emerald Group Publishing Limited in the format Textbook via Copyright Clearance Center.

Globalization

An issue of significant concern for today's organizations is competing on a global basis, and the success of a company's global business strategies is closely tied to the effectiveness of the organization's global HR strategies.[14] A subfield known as **international human resource management (IHRM)** specifically addresses the added complexity that results from coordinating and managing diverse people on a global scale.[15] Research in IHRM has revealed that, as the world becomes increasingly interconnected, some HR practices and trends are converging. However, IHRM managers need a high degree of cultural sensitivity and the ability to tailor and communicate policies and practices for different cultures.[16] What works in one country may not translate well to another. Exhibit 11.3 lists some interesting trends related to selection, compensation, performance appraisal, and training in different countries.

THE IMPACT OF FEDERAL LEGISLATION ON HRM

A number of federal laws have been passed to ensure equal employment opportunity (EEO). Some of the most significant legislation and executive orders are summarized in Exhibit 11.4. The point of the laws is to stop discriminatory practices that are unfair to specific groups and to define enforcement agencies for these laws. EEO legislation attempts to balance the pay given to men and women; provide employment opportunities without regard to race, religion, national origin, and gender; ensure fair treatment for employees of all ages; and avoid discrimination against disabled individuals.

The Equal Employment Opportunity Commission (EEOC) created by the Civil Rights Act of 1964 initiates investigations in response to complaints concerning discrimination. The EEOC is the major agency involved with employment discrimination. **Discrimination** occurs when some applicants are hired or promoted based on criteria that are not job relevant; for example, refusing to hire a black applicant for a job he is qualified to fill or paying a woman a lower wage than a man for the same work are discriminatory acts. When discrimination is found, remedies include providing back pay and taking affirmative action. **Affirmative action** requires that an employer take positive steps to guarantee equal employment opportunities for people within protected groups. An affirmative action plan is a formal document that can be reviewed by employees and enforcement agencies. The goal of organizational affirmative action is to reduce or eliminate internal inequities among affected employee groups.

international human resource management (IHRM) A subfield of human resource management that addresses the complexity that results from recruiting, selecting, developing, and maintaining a diverse workforce on a global scale.

discrimination The hiring or promoting of applicants based on criteria that are not job relevant.

affirmative action A policy requiring employers to take positive steps to guarantee equal employment opportunities for people within protected groups.

4
Organizing

EXHIBIT | 11.3   Some Trends in International Human Resource Management

Selection	• In Japan, HR managers focus on a job applicant's potential and his or her ability to get along with others. Less emphasis is placed on job-related skills and experience. • Employment tests are considered a crucial part of the selection process in Korea, whereas in Taiwan, the job interview is considered the most important criterion for selection.
Compensation	• Seniority-based pay is used to a greater extent in Asian and Latin countries. • China and Taiwan have surprisingly high use of pay incentives and are moving toward more incentives based on individual rather than group performance.
Performance Appraisal	• Across ten countries surveyed, managers consider recognizing subordinates' accomplishments, evaluating their goal achievement, planning their development, and improving their performance to be the most important reasons for performance appraisals.
Training	• In Mexico, managers consider training and development a reward to employees for good performance. • HR managers in Korea incorporate team-building into nearly all training and development practices.

SOURCE: Mary Ann Von Glinow, Ellen A. Drost, and Mary B. Teagarden, "Converging on IHRM Best Practices: Lessons Learned from a Globally Distributed Consortium on Theory and Practice," *Human Resource Management* 41, no. 1 (Spring 2002): 123–140.

EXHIBIT | **11.4** Major Federal Laws Related to Human Resource Management

Federal Law	Year	Provisions
Equal Opportunity/Discrimination Laws		
Civil Rights Act	1991	Provides for possible compensatory and punitive damages plus traditional back pay for cases of intentional discrimination brought under title VII of the 1964 Civil Rights Act. Shifts the burden of proof to the employer.
Americans with Disabilities Act	1990	Prohibits discrimination against qualified individuals by employers on the basis of disability and demands that "reasonable accommodations" be provided for the disabled to allow performance of duties.
Vocational Rehabilitation Act	1973	Prohibits discrimination based on physical or mental disability and requires that employees be informed about affirmative action plans.
Age Discrimination in Employment Act (ADEA)	1967 (amended 1978, 1986)	Prohibits age discrimination and restricts mandatory retirement.
Civil Rights Act, Title VII	1964	Prohibits discrimination in employment on the basis of race, religion, color, sex, or national origin.
Compensation/Benefits Laws Health Insurance Portability Accountability Act (HIPPA)	1996	Allows employees to switch health insurance plans when changing jobs and get the new coverage regardless of preexisting health conditions; prohibits group plans from dropping a sick employee.
Family and Medical Leave Act	1993	Requires employers to provide up to 12 weeks unpaid leave for childbirth, adoption, or family emergencies.
Equal Pay Act	1963	Prohibits sex differences in pay for substantially equal work.
Health/Safety Laws Consolidated Omnibus Budget Reconciliation Act (COBRA)	1985	Requires continued health insurance coverage (paid by employee) following termination.
Occupational Safety and Health Act (OSHA)	1970	Establishes mandatory safety and health standards in organizations.

Failure to comply with equal employment opportunity legislation can result in substantial fines and penalties for employers. Suits for discriminatory practices can cover a broad range of employee complaints. One issue of growing concern is *sexual harassment,* which is also a violation of Title VII of the Civil Rights Act. The EEOC guidelines specify that behavior such as unwelcome advances, requests for sexual favors, and other verbal and physical conduct of a sexual nature becomes sexual harassment when submission to the conduct is tied to continued employment or advancement or when the behavior creates an intimidating, hostile, or offensive work environment.[17] Sexual harassment will be discussed in more detail in Chapter 12.

Exhibit 11.4 also lists the major federal laws related to compensation and benefits and health and safety issues. The scope of human resource legislation is increasing at federal, state, and municipal levels. The working rights and conditions of women, minorities, older employees, and the disabled will likely receive increasing legislative attention in the future.

TakeaMoment | As a new manager, you may need to keep detailed records that document compliance with federal laws and regulations. Complete the New Manager Self-Test on page 313 to see if you have a natural orientation toward systematic record-keeping.

New Manager Self-Test

What Is Your HR Work Orientation?

As new manager, what is your orientation concerning day-to-day work issues? To find out, think about your preferences for the questions below. Circle *a* or *b* for each item depending on which one is accurate for you. There are no right or wrong answers.

1. The work elements I prefer are
   _____ a. Administrative
   _____ b. Conceptualizing

2. The work elements I prefer are
   _____ a. Creative
   _____ b. Organizing

3. My mode of living is
   _____ a. Conventional
   _____ b. Original

4. Which is more important to you?
   _____ a. How something looks (form)
   _____ b. How well it works (function)

5. I like to work with
   _____ a. A practical person
   _____ b. An idea person

6. I am more
   _____ a. Idealistic
   _____ b. Realistic

7. For weekend activities, I prefer to
   _____ a. Plan in advance
   _____ b. Be free to do what I want

8. A daily work routine for me is
   _____ a. Painful
   _____ b. Comfortable

SCORING AND INTERPRETATION: The HR department typically is responsible for monitoring compliance with federal laws, and it provides detailed and specific employee procedures and records for an organization. Every new manager is involved in HR activities for his or her direct reports, which involves systematic record keeping, awareness of applicable laws, and follow through. For your HR work orientation, score one point for each "a" answer circled for questions 1, 3, 5, 7 and one point for each "b" answer circled for questions 2, 4, 6, 8.

New managers with a high score (seven or eight) for HR work orientation tend to be practical, organized, good at record keeping, and meet commitments on time. New managers with a low score (one or two) on HR work orientation tend to be more free-spirited, creative, and conceptual. These managers tend to think out-of-the-box and may dislike the organization, routine, and legal record keeping required for efficient HR management. If your score is midrange (three to six), you may do well with HR work if you put your mind to it, but HR may not be your area of greatest strength.

4 Organizing

THE CHANGING NATURE OF CAREERS

Another current issue is the changing nature of careers and a shift in the relationship between employers and employees.

The Changing Social Contract

In the old social contract between organization and employee, the employee could contribute ability, education, loyalty, and commitment and expect in return that the company would provide wages and benefits, work, advancement, and training throughout the employee's working life. But volatile changes in the environment have disrupted this contract. Consider the following list found on a bulletin board at a company undergoing major restructuring:

- We can't promise you how long we'll be in business.
- We can't promise you that we won't be acquired.
- We can't promise that there'll be room for promotion.
- We can't promise that your job will exist when you reach retirement age.
- We can't promise that the money will be available for your pension.
- We can't expect your undying loyalty, and we aren't even sure we want it.[18]

Downsizing, outsourcing, rightsizing, and restructuring have led to the elimination of many positions in organizations. Employees who are left may feel little stability. The above list reflects a primarily negative view of the new employer-employee relationship, but there are positive aspects as well. Many people, particularly younger employees, like the expectation of responsibility and mobility embedded in the new social contract. Everyone is expected to be a self-motivated worker who is continuously acquiring new skills and demonstrating value to the organization.

Exhibit 11.5 lists some elements of the new social contract. The new contract is based on the concept of employability rather than lifetime employment. Individuals are responsible for developing their own skills and abilities, understanding their employer's business needs, and demonstrating their value to the organization. The employer, in turn, invests in creative training and development opportunities so that people will be more employable when the company no longer needs their services. This means offering challenging work assignments, opportunities to participate in decision making, and access to information and resources. In addition, an important challenge for HRM is revising performance evaluation, compensation, and reward practices to be compatible with the new social contract. Smart organizations contribute to employees' long-term success by offering extensive professional training and development opportunities, career information and assessment, and career coaching.[19]

EXHIBIT 11.5

The Changing Social Contract

	New Contract	Old Contract
Employee	• Employability; personal responsibility • Partner in business improvement • Learning; skill development	• Job security • A cog in the machine • Knowing
Employer	• Creative development opportunities • Lateral career moves; incentive compensation • Challenging assignments • Information and resources; decision-making authority	• Standard training programs • Traditional compensation package • Routine jobs • Limited information

SOURCES: Based on Louisa Wah, "The New Workplace Paradox," *Management Review* (January 1998): 7; and Douglas T. Hall and Jonathan E. Moss, "The New Protean Career Contract: Helping Organizations and Employees Adapt," *Organizational Dynamics* (Winter 1998): 22–37.

The new social contract can benefit both employees and organizations. However, some companies take the new approach as an excuse to treat people as economic factors to be used when needed and then let go. This attitude hurts morale, employee commitment, and organizational performance. Studies in both the United States and China, for example, have found lower employee and firm performance and decreased commitment in companies where the interaction between employer and employee is treated as a contractlike economic exchange rather than a genuine human and social relationship.[20]

As a new manager, appreciate the opportunities that are offered by the new social contract. Allow people to make genuine contributions of their talents to the organization, and provide them with challenging work and opportunities to learn new skills they can transfer to other jobs in the future.

TakeaMoment

Innovations in HRM

The rapid change and uncertainty in today's business environment bring significant new challenges for human resource management. Some important issues are becoming an employer of choice, addressing the needs of temporary employees and part-time workers, acknowledging growing employee demands for work/life balance, and humanely managing downsizing.

Becoming an Employer of Choice The old social contract may be broken for good, but today's best companies recognize the importance of treating people right and thinking for the long term rather than looking for quick fixes based on an economic exchange relationship with employees. An *employer of choice* is a company that is highly attractive to potential employees because of human resources practices that focus not just on tangible benefits such as pay and profit sharing, but also on intangibles (such as work/life balance, a trust-based work climate, and a healthy corporate culture), and that embraces a long-term view to solving immediate problems.[21] To engage people and spur high commitment and performance, an employer of choice chooses a carefully balanced set of HR strategies, policies, and practices that are tailored to the organization's own unique goals and needs.

contingent workers People who work for an organization, but not on a permanent or full-time basis, including temporary placements, contracted professionals, or leased employees.

4
Organizing

Using Temporary and Part-Time Employees Contingent workers are becoming a larger part of the workforce in both the United States and Europe. **Contingent workers** are people who work for an organization, but not on a permanent or full-time basis. These include temporary placements, contracted professionals, leased employees, or part-time workers.[22] The temporary staffing industry doubled between 2002 and 2007 and is projected to grow into a $200 billion industry by 2010.[23] People in temporary jobs do everything from data entry, to project management, to becoming the interim CEO. Although in the past, most temporary workers were in clerical and manufacturing positions, in recent years demand has grown for professionals, such as accountants and financial analysts, interim managers, information technology specialists, product managers, and even lawyers and health-care workers. A related trend is the use of *virtual teams*. Some are made up entirely of people who are hired on a project-by-project basis. Many companies depend on part-time or temporary employees to maintain flexibility.[24]

© ISAAC BREKKEN FOR THE NEW YORK TIMES/ REDUX IMAGES

Concept Connection The Federal Deposit Insurance Corporation is handling the increasing demand for its intervention in bank failures with **contingent professionals**, mostly retirees who bring the needed expertise. Gary Holloway, shown here, was recruited back after two years of retirement and now considers his office "on the road" as he travels to failing banks in his temporary job. An FDIC group swoops in like a SWAT team, sorts through a bank's troubled loans, sells assets, and reopens the bank under new ownership. Holloway brings to this task his experience with the FDIC during the 1980s savings and loan crisis, which resulted in 534 closings.

Promoting Work/Life Balance Initiatives that enable employees to lead a balanced life are a critical part of many organizations' retention strategies. One approach is to let people work part of the time from home or another remote location. **Telecommuting** means using computers and telecommunications equipment to do work without going to an office. The most recent report from the Bureau of Labor Statistics shows that 30.7 million people in the United States worked from home at least one day a week in 2004. This includes more than 100,000 employees of the federal government, according to the Office of Personnel Management.[25] Other forms of *flexible scheduling* are also important in today's workplace, and 55 percent of HRM professionals surveyed say they are willing to negotiate flexible work arrangements with interviewees and new employees.[26]

In addition, many companies have implemented broad work/life balance initiatives, partly in response to the shift in expectations among young employees.[27] Generation Y workers are a fast-growing segment of the workforce. Typically, Gen Y employees work smart and work hard on the job, but they refuse to let work be their whole life. Unlike their parents, who placed a high priority on career, Gen Y workers expect the job to accommodate their personal lives.[28]

Concept Connection When the Maytag operations closed in Newton, Iowa, Derek Winkel decided that was where he should locate his new company, Central Iowa Energy. Winkel knew he could **attract an effective workforce** for the biodiesel production company because there would be plenty of skilled and available labor in the area. Almost all of his employees are former Maytaggers.

© THOMAS STRAND

Rightsizing the Organization In some cases, organizations have more people than they need and have to let some employees go. **Rightsizing** refers to intentionally reducing the company's workforce to the point where the number of employees is deemed to be right for the company's current situation. Also called *downsizing*, planned reductions in the size of the workforce are a reality for many of today's companies. As the term *rightsizing* implies, the goal is to make the company stronger and more competitive by aligning the size of the workforce with the company's current needs. However, some researchers have found that massive cuts often fail to achieve the intended benefits and in some cases significantly harm the organization.[29] Unless HRM departments effectively and humanely manage the rightsizing process, layoffs can lead to decreased morale and performance. Managers can smooth the process by regularly communicating with employees and providing them with as much information as possible, providing assistance to workers who will lose their jobs, and using training and development to help address the emotional needs of remaining employees and enable them to cope with new or additional responsibilities.[30]

telecommuting Using computers and telecommunications equipment to perform work from home or another remote location.

rightsizing Intentionally reducing the company's workforce to the point where the number of employees is deemed to be right for the company's current situation.

matching model An employee selection approach in which the organization and the applicant attempt to match each other's needs, interests, and values.

FINDING THE RIGHT PEOPLE

Now let's turn to the three broad goals of HRM: finding, developing, and maintaining an effective workforce. The first step in finding the right people is human resource planning, in which managers or HRM professionals predict the need for new employees based on the types of vacancies that exist, as illustrated in Exhibit 11.6. The second step is to use recruiting procedures to communicate with potential applicants. The third step is to select from the applicants those persons believed to be the best potential contributors to the organization. Finally, the new employee is welcomed into the organization.

Underlying the organization's effort to attract employees is a matching model. With the **matching model**, the organization and the individual attempt to match

EXHIBIT | 11.6 Attracting an Effective Workforce

the needs, interests, and values that they offer each other.[31] For example, a small software developer might require long hours from creative, technically skilled employees. In return, it can offer freedom from bureaucracy, tolerance of idiosyncrasies, and potentially high pay. A large manufacturer can offer employment security and stability, but it might have more rules and regulations and require greater skills for "getting approval from the higher-ups." The individual who would thrive working for the software developer might feel stymied and unhappy working for a large manufacturer. Both the company and the employee are interested in finding a good match.

Human Resource Planning

Human resource planning is the forecasting of human resource needs and the projected matching of individuals with expected vacancies. Human resource planning begins with several questions:

- What new technologies are emerging, and how will these affect the work system?
- What is the volume of the business likely to be in the next five to ten years?
- What is the turnover rate, and how much, if any, is avoidable?

The responses to these questions are used to formulate specific questions pertaining to HR activities, such as the following:

- What types of engineers will we need, and how many?
- How many administrative personnel will we need to support the additional engineers?
- Can we use temporary, part-time, or virtual workers to handle some tasks?[32]

By anticipating future human resource needs, the organization can prepare itself to meet competitive challenges more effectively than organizations that react to problems only as they arise. One of the most successful applications of human resource planning occurred at the Tennessee Valley Authority.

human resource planning
The forecasting of human resource needs and the projected matching of individuals with expected job vacancies.

Tennessee Valley Authority (TVA)

Innovative Way

TVA created an eight-step plan that assesses future HR needs and formulates actions to meet those needs. The first step is laying the groundwork for later implementation of the program by creating planning and oversight teams within each business unit. Step two involves assessing processes and functions that can be benchmarked. Step three involves projecting the skills and employee numbers (demand data) that will be necessary to reach goals within each business unit. Once these numbers are in place, step four involves projecting the current employee numbers (supply data) over the planning horizon without new hires and taking into consideration the normal attrition of staff through death, retirement, resignation, and so forth. Comparison of the difference between supply and demand (step five) gives the future gap, or surplus situation. This knowledge enables HR to develop strategies and operational plans (step six). Step seven involves communicating the action plan to employees. The final step is to periodically evaluate and update the plan as the organization's needs change. When TVA faces a demand for additional employees, this process enables the company to recruit workers with the skills needed to help meet organizational goals.[33]

Recruiting

Recruiting is defined as "activities or practices that define the characteristics of applicants to whom selection procedures are ultimately applied."[34] Today, recruiting is sometimes referred to as *talent acquisition* to reflect the importance of the human factor in the organization's success.[35] Even when unemployment rates are high, companies often have trouble finding people with the skills the organization needs. A survey by Manpower Inc. of 33,000 employers in 23 countries found that 40 percent reported having difficulty finding and hiring the desired talent.[36]

Although we frequently think of campus recruiting as a typical recruiting activity, many organizations use *internal recruiting,* or *promote-from-within* policies, to fill their high-level positions.[37] Internal recruiting has two major advantages: It is less costly than an external search, and it generates higher employee commitment, development, and satisfaction because it offers opportunities for career advancement to employees rather than outsiders. Frequently, however, *external recruiting*—recruiting newcomers from outside the organization—is advantageous. Applicants are provided by a variety of outside sources including advertising, state employment services, online recruiting services, private employment agencies *(headhunters),* job fairs, and employee referrals.

recruiting The activities or practices that define the desired characteristics of applicants for specific jobs.

job analysis The systematic process of gathering and interpreting information about the essential duties, tasks, and responsibilities of a job.

job description A concise summary of the specific tasks and responsibilities of a particular job.

job specification An outline of the knowledge, skills, education, and physical abilities needed to adequately perform a job.

realistic job preview A recruiting approach that gives applicants all pertinent and realistic information about the job and the organization.

Assessing Organizational Needs Basic building blocks of human resource management include job analysis, job descriptions, and job specifications. **Job analysis** is a systematic process of gathering and interpreting information about the essential duties, tasks, and responsibilities of a job, as well as about the context within which the job is performed.[38] To perform job analysis, managers or specialists ask about work activities and work flow, the degree of supervision given and received in the job, knowledge and skills needed, performance standards, working conditions, and so forth. The manager then prepares a written **job description**, which is a clear and concise summary of the specific tasks, duties, and responsibilities, and **job specification**, which outlines the knowledge, skills, education, physical abilities, and other characteristics needed to adequately perform the job.

Job analysis helps organizations recruit the right kind of people and match them to appropriate jobs. For example, to enhance internal recruiting, Sara Lee Corporation identified six functional areas and 24 significant skills that it wants its finance executives to develop, as illustrated in Exhibit 11.7. Managers are tracked on their development and moved into other positions to help them acquire the needed skills.[39]

Realistic Job Previews Job analysis also enhances recruiting effectiveness by enabling the creation of **realistic job previews**. A realistic job preview (RJP) gives applicants all pertinent and realistic information—positive and negative—about the

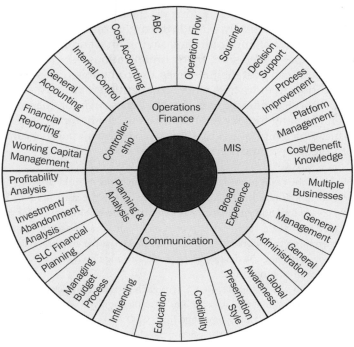

EXHIBIT | 11.7

Sara Lee's Required Skills for Finance Executives

SOURCE: Victoria Griffith, "When Only Internal Expertise Will Do," *CFO* (October 1998): 95–96, 102.

job and the organization.[40] RJPs contribute to greater employee satisfaction and lower turnover because they facilitate matching individuals, jobs, and organizations. Individuals have a better basis on which to determine their suitability to the organization and "self-select" into or out of positions based on full information.

Legal Considerations Organizations must ensure that their recruiting practices conform to the law. As discussed earlier in this chapter, equal employment opportunity (EEO) laws stipulate that recruiting and hiring decisions cannot discriminate on the basis of race, national origin, religion, or gender. The Americans with Disabilities Act underscored the need for well-written job descriptions and specifications that accurately reflect the mental and physical dimensions of jobs, so that people with disabilities will not be discriminated against. *Affirmative action* refers to the use of goals, timetables, or other methods in recruiting to promote the hiring, development, and retention of protected groups. Most large companies try to comply with affirmative action and EEO guidelines. Prudential Insurance Company's policy is presented in Exhibit 11.8. Prudential actively recruits employees and takes affirmative action steps to recruit individuals from all walks of life.

An Equal Opportunity Employer

EXHIBIT | 11.8

Prudential's Corporate Recruiting Policy

Prudential recruits, hires, trains, promotes, and compensates individuals without regard to race, color, religion or creed, age, sex, marital status, national origin, ancestry, liability for service in the armed forces of the United States, status as a special disabled veteran or veteran of the Vietnam era, or physical or mental handicap.

This is official company policy because: • we believe it is right
            • it makes good business sense
            • it is the law

We are also committed to an ongoing program of affirmative action in which members of underrepresented groups are actively sought out and employed for opportunities in all parts and at all levels of the company. In employing people from all walks of life, Prudential gains access to the full experience of our diverse society.

E-cruiting Today, much recruiting is done via the Internet.[41] *E-cruiting*, or recruiting job applicants online, dramatically extends the organization's recruiting reach, offering access to a wider pool of applicants and saving time and money. Besides posting job openings on company Web sites, many organizations use commercial recruiting sites where job seekers can post their résumés and companies can search for qualified applicants. In addition, in industries where competition for highly skilled employees is stiff, new online services emerge to help managers search for "passive candidates," people who aren't looking for jobs but might be the best fit for a company's opening. Red 5 Studios Inc. took a highly creative approach to recruit passive candidates in the hot market for videogame producers.

Red 5 Studios Inc.

Innovative Way

Several members of the team behind the popular online game "World of Warcraft" decided to start their own company, and Red 5 Studios was born. But the start-up quickly ran into a problem—how to attract good employees in an industry where competition for talent is stiff. The team decided to make a list of their "dream hires" and then set about recruiting them. They learned everything they could about each dream developer to personalize the pitch— searching on Google, playing the developer's games, tracking down the prospects' blogs and posts in industry forums, and so forth.

When the research was complete, Red 5 sent each prospect a package of boxes, nested like a Russian doll. In the final box was an iPod Shuffle engraved with the prospect's name and containing a recorded recruiting message from CEO Mark Kern. The recruiting strategy worked. Four months later, three of the passive candidates had joined Red 5 Studios, with another considering making the move.[42]

Concept Connection This ad from *Black Enterprise* magazine enhances **external recruiting** by giving potential applicants a **realistic job preview**. The applicant must possess critical skills such as speaking a foreign language, have a four-year college degree plus three years of professional work experience, be willing to live anywhere on assignment, be between the ages of 23 and 36, and be able to pass "a rigorous physical fitness test." If you possess these requirements, you can even apply online at http://www .fbijobs.com.

Innovations in Recruiting As the previous example shows, managers sometimes have to find innovative approaches to recruit the right people. Organizations look for ways to enhance their recruiting success. One highly effective method is getting referrals from current employees. Many organizations offer cash awards to employees who submits names of people who subsequently accept employment because referral by current employees is one of the cheapest and most reliable methods of external recruiting.[43] Companies also are increasingly searching among the membership of relevant trade groups, such as at trade shows, meetings, and on the associations' Web sites. "All the good candidates seem to belong to a particular association and the ones who aren't as skilled usually don't," explains one recruiter.[44]

Some organizations also turn to nontraditional sources to find dedicated employees, particularly in a tight labor market. For example, when Walker Harris couldn't find workers for his ice company on the west side of Chicago, Harris Ice, he began hiring former prison inmates, many of whom have turned out to be reliable, loyal employees.[45] In Louisville, Kentucky, where the traditional labor force is shrinking, companies such as UPS, Allied Van Lines, and General Electric are finding a source of hard-working employees among Asian, African, and Eastern European immigrants fleeing persecution.[46] Since 1998, Bank of America has hired and trained more than 3,000 former welfare recipients in positions that offer the potential for promotions and long-term careers. Numerous companies recruit older workers, who typically have lower turnover rates, especially for part-time jobs. The Home Depot offers "snowbird specials"—winter work in Florida and summers in Maine. Border's Bookstores entices retired teachers with book discounts and reading and discussion groups.[47] Recruiting on a global basis is on the rise as well. Public schools are recruiting teachers from overseas. High-tech companies are looking for qualified workers in foreign countries because they cannot find people with the right skills in the United States.[48]

Refer back to the opening questionnaire to test your own preparation as a new manager for recruiting and selecting the right people for your team. Do you have what it takes?

TakeaMoment

Selecting

The next step for managers is to select desired employees from the pool of recruited applicants. In the **selection** process, employers assess applicants' characteristics in an attempt to determine the "fit" between the job and applicant characteristics. Several selection devices are used for assessing applicant qualifications. The most frequently used are the application form, interview, employment test, and assessment center. Studies indicate that the greater the skill requirements and work demands of an open position, the greater the number and variety of selection tools the organization will use.[49] Human resource professionals may use a combination of devices to get an idea of a candidate's potential performance.

Application Form The **application form** is used to collect information about the applicant's education, previous job experience, and other background characteristics. Research in the life insurance industry shows that biographical information inventories can validly predict future job success.[50]

One pitfall to be avoided is the inclusion of questions that are irrelevant to job success. In line with affirmative action, the application form should not ask questions that will create an adverse impact on protected groups unless the questions are clearly related to the job.[51] For example, employers should not ask whether the applicant rents or owns his or her own home because (1) an applicant's response might adversely affect his or her chances at the job, (2) minorities and women may be less likely to own a home, and (3) home ownership is probably unrelated to job performance. By contrast, the CPA exam is relevant to job performance in a CPA firm; thus, it is appropriate to ask whether an applicant for employment has passed the CPA exam, even if only one-half of all female or minority applicants have done so versus nine-tenths of male applicants.

Interview The *interview* serves as a two-way communication channel that allows both the organization and the applicant to collect information that otherwise might be difficult to obtain. This selection technique is used in almost every job category in nearly every organization. It is another area where the organization can get into legal trouble if the interviewer asks questions that violate EEO guidelines. Exhibit 11.9 lists some examples of appropriate and inappropriate interview questions.

However, the interview is not generally a good predictor of job performance. One estimate is that conventional interviews have a .2 correlation with predicting a successful hire.[52] People can improve their chances of having a successful interview by understanding some common pet peeves that trigger a negative response from interviewers, as outlined in the Manager's Shoptalk on page 323.

Today's managers are trying different approaches to overcome the limitations of the interview. Some put candidates through a series of interviews, each one conducted by a different person and each one probing a different aspect of the candidate. Others use *panel interviews*, in which the candidate meets with several interviewers who take turns asking questions.[53] Some organizations also supplement traditional interviewing information with *computer-based interviews*. This type of interview typically requires a candidate to answer a series of multiple-choice questions tailored to the specific job.

4
Organizing

selection The process of determining the skills, abilities, and other attributes a person needs to perform a particular job.

application form A device for collecting information about an applicant's education, previous job experience, and other background characteristics.

EXHIBIT | 11.9   Employment Applications and Interviews: What Can You Ask?

Category	Okay to Ask	Inappropriate or Illegal to Ask
National origin	• The applicant's name • If applicant has ever worked under a different name	• The origin of applicant's name • Applicant's ancestry/ethnicity
Race	• Nothing	• Race or color of skin
Disabilities	• Whether applicant has any disabilities that might inhibit performance of job	• If applicant has any physical or mental defects • If applicant has ever filed workers' compensation claim
Age	• If applicant is over 18	• Applicant's age • When applicant graduated from high school
Religion	• Nothing	• Applicant's religious affiliation • What religious holidays applicant observes
Criminal record	• If applicant has ever been convicted of a crime	• If applicant has ever been arrested
Marital/family status	• Nothing	• Marital status, number of children or planned children • Childcare arrangements
Education and experience	• Where applicant went to school • Prior work experience	• When applicant graduated • Hobbies
Citizenship	• If applicant has a legal right to work in the United States	• If applicant is a citizen of another country

SOURCES: Based on "Appropriate and Inappropriate Interview Questions," in George Bohlander, Scott Snell, and Arthur Sherman, *Managing Human Resources*, 12th ed. (Cincinnati, OH: South-Western, 2001): 207; and "Guidelines to Lawful and Unlawful Preemployment Inquiries," Appendix E, in Robert L. Mathis and John H. Jackson, *Human Resource Management*, 2nd ed. (Cincinnati, OH: South-Western, 2002), 189–190.

The answers are compared to an ideal profile or to a profile developed on the basis of other candidates. Companies such as Pinkerton Security, Coopers & Lybrand, and Pic n' Pay Shoe Stores have found computer-based interviews to be valuable for searching out information regarding the applicant's honesty, work attitude, drug history, candor, dependability, and self-motivation.[54]

TakeaMoment | As a new manager, get the right people in the right jobs by assessing your team's or department's needs, offering realistic job previews, using a variety of recruiting and selecting methods, and striving to match the needs and interests of the individual to those of the organization.

Employment Test **Employment tests** may include intelligence tests, aptitude and ability tests, and personality inventories. Many companies today are particularly interested in personality inventories that measure such characteristics as openness to learning, initiative, responsibility, creativity, and emotional stability. Companies that put a premium on innovativeness and problem solving are also challenging applicants with *brain teasers*, having them ponder questions such as how many golf balls will fit inside a school bus. The answers aren't as important as how the applicant goes about solving the problem. See how you do answering the brain teasers in Exhibit 11.10 on page 324.

Assessment Center First developed by psychologists at AT&T, assessment centers are used to select individuals with high potential for managerial careers by such organizations as IBM, General Electric, and JCPenney.[55] **Assessment centers**

employment test A written or computer-based test designed to measure a particular attribute such as intelligence or aptitude.

assessment center A technique for selecting individuals with high managerial potential based on their performance on a series of simulated managerial tasks.

Manager's Shoptalk

What Makes a Good Interview Go Bad?

Have you ever had a job interview where everything seems to be going well but then takes a drastic turn for the worse? Understanding common blunders that tick off interviewers can make you more successful as both a job candidate and an interviewer. Here's one expert's list of the top seven:

1. *Not communicating enough.* People who won't talk drive interviewers crazy. These folks offer short answers to open-ended questions and don't follow up when the interviewer prods for more information.

2. *Not making eye contact.* Candidates who look around everywhere except at the interviewer provoke distrust. One expert advises extremely shy people to look at the interviewer's "third eye," just above and between the person's two eyes, to avoid this blunder.

3. *Talking too much.* Answering questions fully is important, but a candidate who babbles on and on puts most interviewers off.

4. *Using street slang or unprofessional language.* Street-speak doesn't fit most corporate domains. In addition, saying *like, uh,* or *um* every other word quickly loses an interviewer's attention.

5. *Stretching the truth.* People want to present themselves in the best light, but many candidates go too far, embellishing their skills, hiding past job failures, or outright lying about educational qualifications. Interviewers can often sense this, which destroys trust.

6. *Making a fashion statement.* In most cases, people should wear traditional professional dress for an interview.

7. *Failing to effectively close.* Interviewers like a candidate who closes the interview by stating their interest or asking about the next step in the process, rather than just letting the interview fade away.

There are even more outlandish blunders that occasionally occur. Here are some of the unusual things that have happened during job interviews, based on surveys of vice presidents and human resource directors at major U.S. corporations:

- The applicant announced she hadn't had lunch and proceeded to eat a hamburger and french fries in the interviewer's office.

- When asked if he had any questions about the job, the candidate answered, "Can I get an advance on my paycheck?"

- The applicant chewed bubble gum and constantly blew bubbles.

- The job candidate said the main thing he was looking for in a job was a quiet place where no one would bother him.

- The job applicant challenged the interviewer to arm wrestle.

SOURCES: Indira Dharchaudhuri, "Interviewers Pet Peeves," *Hindustan Times*, February 24, 2004; and Martha H. Peak, "What Color Is Your Bumbershoot?" *Management Review* (October 1989): 63.

4 Organizing

present a series of managerial situations to groups of applicants over a two- or three-day period, for example. One technique is the *in-basket simulation,* which requires the applicant to play the role of a manager who must decide how to respond to ten memos in his or her in-basket within a two-hour period. Panels of two or three trained judges observe the applicant's decisions and assess the extent to which they reflect interpersonal, communication, and problem-solving skills. At a Michigan auto parts plant that makes a joint-venture engine from Daimler-Chrysler, Mitsubishi, and Hyundai, applicants for plant manager go through four-hour "day-in-the-life" simulations in which they have to juggle memos, phone calls, and employee or job problems.[56]

Some organizations now use this technique for hiring front-line workers as well. Mercury Communications in England uses an assessment center to select customer assistants. Applicants participate in simulated exercises with customers and in various other exercises designed to assess their listening skills, customer sensitivity, and ability to cope under pressure.[57]

EXHIBIT | 11.10

Try Your Hand at Some Interview Brain Teasers

How would you answer the following questions in a job interview?

1. How would you weigh a jet plane without using scales?
2. Why are manhole covers round?
3. How many golf balls can fit inside a standard school bus?
4. How much should you charge to wash all the windows in Seattle?
5. You're shrunk and trapped in a blender that will turn on in 60 seconds. What do you do?

Answers: There might be many solutions to these questions. Here are some that interviewers consider good answers:

1. Fly it onto an aircraft carrier or other ship big enough to hold it. Paint a mark on the hull of the ship showing the water level. Then remove the jet. The ship will rise in the water. Now load the ship with items of known weight (100 lb. bales of cotton, for instance) until it sinks to exactly the line you painted on the hull. The total weight of the items will equal the weight of the jet.
2. A square cover might fall into its hole. If you hold a square manhole cover vertically and turn it a little, it will fall easily into the hole. In contrast, a round cover with a slight recess in the center can never fall in, no matter how it is held.
3. About 500,000, assuming the bus is 50 balls high, 50 balls wide, and 200 balls long.
4. Assuming 10,000 city blocks, 600 windows per block, five minutes per window, and a rate of $20 per hour, about $10 million.
5. Use the measurement marks on the side of the container to climb out.

SOURCES: These questions are used at companies such as Microsoft, Google, and eBay. Reported in Michael Kaplan, "Job Interview Brainteasers," *Business 2.0* (September 2007): 35–37; and William Poundstone, "Impossible Questions," *Across the Board* (September–October 2003): 44–48.

© AP IMAGES

Concept Connection **Employment tests** range from personality profiles to proficiency testing in specific skills required for a position. For a 911 operator position, an applicant should expect to take tests like data entry for speed and accuracy, 911 address checking, 911 grid map reading and direction accuracy, 911 memorization, customer service assessment, and a personal characteristics profile. Here, Rick Bias, 911 Communications Director for Morgan County, Missouri, oversees operations in the Public Service Answer Point Area.

Online Checks One of the newest ways of gauging whether a candidate is right for the company is by seeing what the person has to say about him or herself on social networking sites such as Facebook and MySpace. Recent college graduates looking for jobs have found doors closed to them because of risqué or teasing photos or vivid comments about drinking, drug use, or sexual exploits. Recruiters from more than two dozen companies told career counselors at New York University, for example, that if an applicant's online presentation raises red flags, the person isn't likely to even get an interview.[58] Companies today are not only interested in a candidate's educational and work qualifications, but also in personal characteristics and values that fit with the organization's culture. One recruiter said the open admission of excessive drinking and so forth makes managers question the applicant's maturity and judgment.

MANAGING TALENT

Following selection, the next goal of HRM is to develop employees into an effective workforce. Key development activities include training and performance appraisal.

Training and Development

Training and development represent a planned effort by an organization to facilitate employees' learning of job-related skills and behaviors.[59] Organizations spent some $58.5 billion on training in 2007, with more than $16 billion of that spent on outside learning products and services. Exhibit 11.11 shows some frequently used types and methods of training in today's organizations. One of the fastest growing methods is the use of podcasting, which jumped from 5 percent in 2006 to 15 percent in 2007.[60]

EXHIBIT | 11.11 Methods and Goals of Training

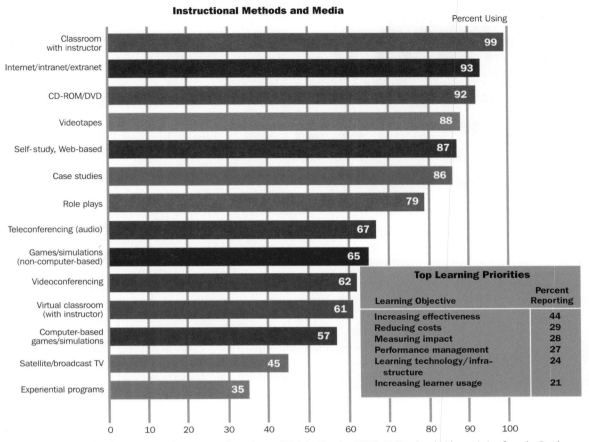

Instructional Methods and Media

Percent Using

Method	Percent
Classroom with instructor	99
Internet/intranet/extranet	93
CD-ROM/DVD	92
Videotapes	88
Self-study, Web-based	87
Case studies	86
Role plays	79
Teleconferencing (audio)	67
Games/simulations (non-computer-based)	65
Videoconferencing	62
Virtual classroom (with instructor)	61
Computer-based games/simulations	57
Satellite/broadcast TV	45
Experiential programs	35

Top Learning Priorities

Learning Objective	Percent Reporting
Increasing effectiveness	44
Reducing costs	29
Measuring impact	28
Performance management	27
Learning technology/infra-structure	24
Increasing learner usage	21

SOURCES: Methods data from Tammy Galvin, "2003 Industry Report," *Training* (October 2003): 21 (Reprinted with permission from the October 2003 issue of *Training* magazine, Copyright 2003, Bill Communications, Minneapolis, Minn. All rights reserved. Not for resale.); and "2007 Industry Report," *Training* (November–December 2007): 18.

On-the-Job Training The most common method of training is on-the-job training. In **on-the-job training (OJT)**, an experienced employee is asked to take a new employee "under his or her wing" and show the newcomer how to perform job duties. OJT has many advantages, such as few out-of-pocket costs for training facilities, materials, or instructor fees and easy transfer of learning back to the job. When implemented well, OJT is considered the fastest and most effective means of facilitating learning in the workplace.[61] One type of on-the-job training involves moving people to various types of jobs within the organization, where they work with experienced employees to learn different tasks. This *cross-training* may place an employee in a new position for as short a time as a few hours or for as long as a year, enabling the employee to develop new skills and giving the organization greater flexibility.

Corporate Universities Another popular approach to training and development is the corporate university. A **corporate university** is an in-house training and education facility that offers broad-based learning opportunities for employees—and frequently for customers, suppliers, and strategic partners as well—throughout their careers.[62] One well-known corporate university is Hamburger University, McDonald's worldwide training center, which has been in existence for more than 40 years. Numerous other companies, including IBM, FedEx, General Electric, Intel, Harley-Davidson, and Capital One, pump millions of dollars into corporate universities to continually build human capital.[63] Employees at Caterpillar attend courses at Caterpillar

on-the-job training (OJT) A type of training in which an experienced employee "adopts" a new employee to teach him or her how to perform job duties.

corporate university An in-house training and education facility that offers broad-based learning opportunities for employees.

4
Organizing

Concept Connection   "We don't do training," says Equifax senior vice president and chief learning officer Lynn Slavenski. "We do change." Slavenski oversaw the establishment of Equifax University for the consumer credit reporting company. What distinguishes **corporate universities** from most old-style training programs is that the courses—from classes teaching a specific technical skill to corporate-run MBA programs—are intentionally designed to foster the changes needed to achieve the organization's strategy.

University, which combines e-training, classroom sessions, and hands-on training activities. The U.S. Department of Defense runs Defense Acquisition University to provide ongoing training to 129,000 military and civilian workers in acquisitions, technology, and logistics.[64]

Promotion from Within Another way to further employee development is through promotion from within, which helps companies retain and develop valuable people. Promotions provide more challenging assignments, prescribe new responsibilities, and help employees grow by expanding and developing their abilities. The Peebles Hydro Hotel in Scotland is passionate about promoting from within as a way to retain good people and give them opportunities for growth. A maid has been promoted to head housekeeper, a wine waitress to restaurant head, and a student worker to deputy manager. The hotel also provides constant training in all areas. These techniques, combined with a commitment to job flexibility, have helped the hotel retain high-quality workers at a time when others in the tourism and hospitality industry are suffering from a shortage of skilled labor. Staff members with 10, 15, or even 20 years of service aren't uncommon at Hydro.[65]

Mentoring and Coaching For many management and professional jobs, traditional on-the-job training is supplemented or replaced by mentoring and coaching. With **mentoring**, an experienced employee guides and supports a newcomer or less-experienced employee. Mentors typically offer counsel regarding how to network and advance in the company in addition to guiding the employee in developing his or her skills and abilities. **Coaching** is a method of directing, instructing, and training a person with the goal to develop specific management skills. Coaching usually applies to higher-level managers who want to develop their personal competencies. For instance, a coach might observe a senior executive in action and provide feedback about how the executive can improve her interaction skills. Managers can also discuss difficult situations as they arise, with the coach helping them work through various alternative scenarios for dealing with the situation.[66]

Performance Appraisal

mentoring When an experienced employee guides and supports a less-experienced employee.

coaching A method of directing, instructing and training a person with the goal to develop specific management skills.

performance appraisal The process of observing and evaluating an employee's performance, recording the assessment, and providing feedback to the employee.

Performance appraisal comprises the steps of observing and assessing employee performance, recording the assessment, and providing feedback to the employee. During performance appraisal, skillful managers give feedback and praise concerning the acceptable elements of the employee's performance. They also describe performance areas that need improvement. Employees can use this information to change their job performance. Unfortunately, only three in ten employees in a recent survey believe their companies' performance review system actually helps to improve performance, indicating a need for improved methods of appraisal and feedback.[67]

Generally, HRM professionals concentrate on two things to make performance appraisal a positive force in their organizations: (1) the accurate assessment of performance through the development and application of assessment systems such as rating scales, and (2) training managers to effectively use the performance appraisal interview, so managers can provide feedback that will reinforce good performance and motivate employee development. Current thinking is that performance appraisal should be ongoing, not something that is done once a year as part of a consideration of raises.

Assessing Performance Accurately To obtain an accurate performance rating, managers acknowledge that jobs are multidimensional and performance thus may be multidimensional as well. For example, a sports broadcaster might perform well on the job-knowledge dimension; that is, she or he might be able to report facts and figures about the players and describe which rule applies when there is a questionable play on the field. But the same broadcaster might not perform as well on another dimension, such as communication. The person might be unable to express the information in a colorful way that interests the audience or might interrupt the other broadcasters. For performance to be rated accurately, the appraisal system should require the rater to assess each relevant performance dimension. A multidimensional form increases the usefulness of the performance appraisal and facilitates employee growth and development.

A recent trend in performance appraisal is called **360-degree feedback**, a process that uses multiple raters, including self-rating, as a way to increase awareness of strengths and weaknesses and guide employee development. Members of the appraisal group may include supervisors, coworkers, and customers, as well as the individual, thus providing appraisal of the employee from a variety of perspectives.[68] One study found that 26 percent of companies used some type of multirater performance appraisal.[69]

Another alternative performance-evaluation method is the *performance review ranking system.*[70] This method is increasingly coming under fire because it essentially evaluates employees by pitting them against one another. As most commonly used, a manager evaluates his or her direct reports relative to one another and categorizes each on a scale, such as A = outstanding performance (20 percent), B = high-middle performance (70 percent), or C = in need of improvement (10 percent). Some companies routinely fire those managers falling in the bottom 10 percent of the ranking. Proponents say the technique provides an effective way to assess performance and offer guidance for employee development. But critics of these systems, sometimes called *rank and yank,* argue that they are based on subjective judgments, produce skewed results, and discriminate against employees who are "different" from the mainstream. One study found that forced rankings that include firing the bottom 5 or 10 percent can lead to a dramatic improvement in organizational performance in the short term, but the benefits dissipate over several years as people become focused on competing with one another rather than improving the business.[71] Many companies are building more flexibility into the performance review ranking system, and some are abandoning it altogether.[72]

Despite these concerns, the appropriate use of performance ranking has been useful for many companies, especially as a short-term way to improve performance. Consider how a variation of the system helps U.S. restaurant chain Applebee's retain quality workers in the high-turnover restaurant business.

360-degree feedback A process that uses multiple raters, including self-rating, to appraise employee performance and guide development.

Innovative Way

Applebee's International Inc.

> Most people working in fast-food and casual dining restaurants don't stay long. Turnover of hourly employees is a perpetual problem, averaging more than 200 percent a year in the casual dining sector for the past 30 years. Applebee's managers wanted to reduce their turnover rate, but they also wanted to focus their retention efforts on the best people.
>
> A key aspect of the new retention strategy is the Applebee's Performance Management system. Twice a year, each hourly employee is rated on characteristics such as reliability, guest service, attitude, and teamwork. Managers then look at how each employee ranks with respect to all others in the restaurant, separating employees into the top 20 percent, the middle 60 percent, and the bottom 20 percent. Store managers are rewarded for retaining the top and middle performers.

The system is not the basis for firing low-ranking employees, but they usually leave soon enough anyway. Its value lies in helping managers focus their retention efforts on the more valuable employees. It's paying off. The turnover rate has dropped 50 percent since Applebee's began using the ranking system.[73]

Performance Evaluation Errors Although we would like to believe that every manager assesses employees' performance in a careful and bias-free manner, researchers have identified several rating problems.[74] One of the most dangerous is **stereotyping**, which occurs when a rater places an employee into a class or category based on one or a few traits or characteristics—for example, stereotyping an older worker as slower and more difficult to train. Another rating error is the **halo effect**, in which a manager gives an employee the same rating on all dimensions even if his or her performance is good on some dimensions and poor on others.

One approach to overcome performance evaluation errors is to use a behavior-based rating technique, such as the behaviorally anchored rating scale. The **behaviorally anchored rating scale (BARS)** is developed from critical incidents pertaining to job performance. Each job performance scale is anchored with specific behavioral statements that describe varying degrees of performance. By relating employee performance to specific incidents, raters can more accurately evaluate an employee's performance.[75]

Exhibit 11.12 illustrates the BARS method for evaluating a production line supervisor. The production supervisor's job can be broken down into several dimensions, such as equipment maintenance, employee training, or work scheduling. A behaviorally anchored rating scale should be developed for each dimension. The dimension in Exhibit 11.12 is work scheduling. Good performance is represented by a 4 or 5 on the scale and unacceptable performance as a 1 or 2. If a production supervisor's job has eight dimensions, the total performance evaluation will be the sum of the scores for each of eight scales.

stereotyping Placing an employee into a class or category based on one or a few traits or characteristics.

halo effect A type of rating error that occurs when an employee receives the same rating on all dimensions regardless of his or her performance on individual ones.

behaviorally anchored rating scale (BARS) A rating technique that relates an employee's performance to specific job-related incidents.

TakeaMoment

As a new manager evaluating subordinates, remember that jobs are multidimensional and people need to be evaluated separately on each relevant dimension so they can be rewarded appropriately and improve their performance where needed. Be aware of your own prejudices so you can avoid stereotyping people during evaluations.

EXHIBIT | 11.12   Example of a Behaviorally Anchored Rating Scale

Job: Production Line Supervisor
Work Dimension: Work Scheduling

Have no plan or schedule of work and no concept of realistic due dates. — **1**

Have a sound plan but neglect to keep track of target dates or to report schedule slippages or other problems as they occur. — **2**

Make a list of due dates and revise them but get frequently surprised by unforeseen events. — **3**

Usually satisfy time constraints, with time and cost overruns coming up infrequently. — **4**

Develop a comprehensive schedule, observe target dates, and update the status of operations relative to plans, making schedule modifications as quickly as necessary. — **5**

SOURCES: Based on J. P. Campbell, M. D. Dunnette, R. D. Arvey, and L. V. Hellervik, "The Development and Evaluation of Behaviorally Based Rating Scales," *Journal of Applied Psychology* 57 (1973): 15–22; and Francine Alexander, "Performance Appraisals," *Small Business Reports* (March 1989): 20–29.

MAINTAINING AN EFFECTIVE WORKFORCE

Now we turn to the topic of how managers and HRM professionals maintain a workforce that has been recruited and developed. Maintenance of the current workforce involves compensation, wage and salary systems, benefits, and occasional terminations.

Compensation

The term **compensation** refers to: (1) all monetary payments and (2) all goods or commodities used in lieu of money to reward employees.[76] An organization's compensation structure includes wages and/or salaries and benefits such as health insurance, paid vacations, or employee fitness centers. Developing an effective compensation system is an important part of human resource management because it helps to attract and retain talented workers. In addition, a company's compensation system has an impact on strategic performance.[77] Human resource managers design the pay and benefits systems to fit company strategy and to provide compensation equity.

Wage and Salary Systems Ideally, management's strategy for the organization should be a critical determinant of the features and operations of the pay system.[78] For example, managers may have the goal of maintaining or improving profitability or market share by stimulating employee performance. Thus, they should design and use a merit pay system rather than a system based on other criteria such as seniority.

The most common approach to employee compensation is *job-based pay,* which means linking compensation to the specific tasks an employee performs. However, these systems present several problems. For one thing, job-based pay may fail to reward the type of learning behavior needed for the organization to adapt and survive in today's environment. In addition, these systems reinforce an emphasis on organizational hierarchy and centralized decision making and control, which are inconsistent with the growing emphasis on employee participation and increased responsibility.[79]

Skill-based pay systems are becoming increasingly popular in both large and small companies, including Sherwin-Williams, Au Bon Pain, and Quaker Oats. Employees with higher skill levels receive higher pay than those with lower skill levels. At Quaker Oats pet food plant in Topeka, Kansas, for example, employees might start at something like $8.75 per hour but reach a top hourly rate of $14.50 when they master a series of skills.[80] Also called *competency-based pay,* skill-based pay systems encourage employees to develop their skills and competencies, thus making them more valuable to the organization as well as more employable if they leave their current jobs.

Compensation Equity Whether the organization uses job-based pay or skill-based pay, good managers strive to maintain a sense of fairness and equity within the pay structure and thereby fortify employee morale. **Job evaluation** refers to the process of determining the value or worth of jobs within an organization through an examination of job content. Job evaluation techniques enable managers to compare similar and dissimilar jobs and to determine internally equitable pay rates—that is, pay rates that employees believe are fair compared with those for other jobs in the organization.

Organizations also want to make sure their pay rates are fair compared to other companies. HRM managers may obtain **wage and salary surveys** that show what other organizations pay incumbents in jobs that match a sample of "key" jobs selected by the organization. These surveys are available from a number of sources, including the U.S. Bureau of Labor Statistics National Compensation Survey.

4
Organizing

compensation Monetary payments (wages, salaries) and nonmonetary goods/commodities (benefits, vacations) used to reward employees.

job evaluation The process of determining the value of jobs within an organization through an examination of job content.

wage and salary surveys Surveys that show what other organizations pay incumbents in jobs that match a sample of "key" jobs selected by the organization.

Pay-for-Performance Many of today's organizations develop compensation plans based on a *pay-for-performance standard* to raise productivity and cut labor costs in a competitive global environment. **Pay-for-performance**, also called *incentive pay*, means tying at least part of compensation to employee effort and performance, whether it be through merit-based pay, bonuses, team incentives, or various gain-sharing or profit-sharing plans. Data show that, while growth in base wages is slowing in many industries, the use of pay-for-performance has steadily increased since the early 1990s, with approximately 70 percent of companies now offering some form of incentive pay.[81] With pay-for-performance, incentives are aligned with the behaviors needed to help the organization achieve its strategic goals. Employees have an incentive to make the company more efficient and profitable because if goals are not met, no bonuses are paid.

Benefits

The best human resource managers know that a compensation package requires more than money. Although wage/salary is an important component, it is only a part. Equally important are the benefits offered by the organization. Benefits make up more than 40 percent of labor costs in the United States.[82]

Some benefits are required by law, such as Social Security, unemployment compensation, and workers' compensation. Other types of benefits, such as health insurance, vacations, and such things as on-site daycare or fitness centers are not required by law but are provided by organizations to maintain an effective workforce.

One reason benefits make up such a large portion of the compensation package is that health-care costs continue to increase. Many organizations are requiring that employees absorb a greater share of the cost of medical benefits, such as through higher co-payments and deductibles.

Computerization cuts the time and expense of administering benefits programs tremendously. At many companies, employees access their benefits package through an intranet, creating a "self-service" benefits administration.[83] This access also enables employees to change their benefits selections easily. Today's organizations realize that the "one-size-fits-all" benefits package is no longer appropriate, so they frequently offer *cafeteria-plan benefits packages* that allow employees to select the benefits of greatest value to them.[84] Other companies use surveys to determine which combination of fixed benefits is most desirable. The benefits packages provided by large companies attempt to meet the needs of all employees.

Termination

Despite the best efforts of line managers and HRM professionals, the organization will lose employees. Some will retire, others will depart voluntarily for other jobs, and still others will be forced out through mergers and cutbacks or for poor performance.

TakeaMoment | **Even as a new manager, play a role in how people are compensated. Consider skill-based pay systems and incentive pay to encourage high performers. Don't be dismayed if some people have to be let go. If people have to be laid off or fired, do it humanely. Go to the ethical dilemma on pages 333–334 that pertains to termination of employees for poor performance.**

pay-for-performance Incentive pay that ties at least part of compensation to employee effort and performance.

The value of termination for maintaining an effective workforce is two-fold. First, employees who are poor performers can be dismissed. Productive employees often resent disruptive, low-performing employees who are allowed to stay with the company and receive pay and benefits comparable to theirs. Second, employers can use exit interviews as a valuable HR tool, regardless of whether the employee leaves voluntarily or is forced out. An **exit interview** is an interview conducted with departing employees to determine why they are leaving. Sixty-eight percent of companies surveyed by the Society for Human Resource Management say they either routinely or occasionally conduct formal exit interviews.[85] The value of the exit interview is to provide an inexpensive way to learn about pockets of dissatisfaction within the organization and hence find ways to reduce future turnover.[86] The oil services giant Schlumberger includes an exit interview as part of a full-scale investigation of every departure, with the results posted online so managers all around the company can get insight into problems.[87] However, in many cases, employees who leave voluntarily are reluctant to air uncomfortable complaints or discuss their real reasons for leaving. Companies such as T-Mobile, Campbell Soup, and Conair found that having people complete an online exit questionnaire yields more open and honest information. When people have negative things to say about managers or the company, the online format is a chance to speak their mind without having to do it in a face-to-face meeting.[88]

For companies experiencing downsizing through mergers or because of global competition or a shifting economy, often a large number of managers and workers are terminated at the same time. In these cases, enlightened companies try to find a smooth transition for departing employees. By showing genuine concern in helping laid-off employees, a company communicates the value of human resources and helps maintain a positive corporate culture.

exit interview An interview conducted with departing employees to determine the reasons for their termination.

ch11 A MANAGER'S ESSENTIALS: WHAT HAVE WE LEARNED?

- This chapter described several important points about human resource management in organizations. All managers are responsible for human resources, and most organizations have a human resource department that works with line managers to ensure a productive workforce.

- Human resource management plays a key strategic role in driving organizational performance, through building human capital and enabling the company to be more competitive on a global basis.

- The HR department must also implement procedures to reflect federal and state legislation and respond to changes in working relationships and career directions. The old social contract of the employee being loyal to the company and the company taking care of the employee until retirement no longer holds. Employees are responsible for managing their own careers.

- Current issues of concern to HRM are becoming an employer of choice, addressing the needs of temporary and part-time employees, implementing work/life balance initiatives, and humanely managing downsizing.

- The first goal of HRM is to attract an effective workforce through human resource planning, recruiting, and employee selection. The second is to develop an effective workforce. Newcomers are introduced to the organization and to their jobs through orientation and training programs. Moreover, employees are evaluated through performance appraisal programs. The third goal is to maintain an effective workforce through wage and salary systems, benefits packages, and termination procedures. In many organizations, information technology is being used to more effectively meet all three of these important HR goals.

ch11 DISCUSSION QUESTIONS

1. It is the year 2018. In your company, central planning has given way to frontline decision making, and bureaucracy has given way to teamwork. Shop floor workers use handheld computers and robots. A labor shortage currently affects many job openings, and the few applicants you do attract lack skills to work in teams, make their own production decisions, or use sophisticated technology. As vice president of human resource management since 2006, what should you have done to prepare for this situation?

2. If you were asked to advise a private company about its equal employment opportunity responsibilities, what two points would you emphasize as most important?

3. How might the human resource activities of recruiting, performance appraisal, and compensation be related to corporate strategy?

4. Think back to your own job experience. What human resource management activities described in this chapter were performed for the job you filled? Which ones were absent?

5. How "valid" do you think the information obtained from a personal interview versus an employment test versus an assessment center would be for predicting effective job performance for a college professor? For an assembly-line worker in a manufacturing plant? Discuss.

6. How do you think the growing use of telecommuters, contingent workers, and virtual teams affect human resource management? How can managers improve recruiting and retention of these new kinds of employees?

7. If you are in charge of training and development, which training option or options—such as on-the-job training, cross-training, classroom, self-directed, or computer-based—would you be likely to choose for your company's production line manager? A customer service representative? An entry-level accountant?

8. If you were to draw up a telecommuting contract with an employee, what would it look like? Include considerations such as job description, compensation and benefits, performance measures, training, and grounds for dismissal.

9. How would you go about deciding whether to use a job-based, skills-based, or pay-for-performance compensation plan for employees in a textile manufacturing plant? For wait staff in a restaurant? For salespeople in an insurance company?

10. What purpose do exit interviews serve for human resource management?

ch11 MANAGEMENT IN PRACTICE: EXPERIENTIAL EXERCISE

Do You Want to Be an HR Manager?

The following questions are based on a Human Resources Capability Model developed by the Australian Public Service (APS) for HR managers who work in government agencies. People who work with HR managers complete a 72-item questionnaire assessing a range of expectations for the HR manager. The results are given to the manager, who then works to improve low scores. The following questions give a glimpse of the expectations for APS HR managers. Please think about how other people would rate you as a potential HR manager and then respond to each statement by rating yourself on how well you think you would fulfill each expectation.

① = not well at all; ② = not very well; ③ = moderately well; ④ = very well; ⑤ = extremely well

Bringing HR to the Business

1. Has a detailed knowledge of current HR approaches, tools, and technology.

   1 2 3 4 5

2. Understands the human behavior triggers that affect or improve organizational performance.

   1 2 3 4 5

Connecting HR with the Business

3. Maintains knowledge of the business through frequent interaction with people in the workplace.

   1 2 3 4 5

4. Presents strong business cases for HR initiatives.

   1 2 3 4 5

Partnering with the Business

5. Establishes and maintains good relationships across the organization.

   1 2 3 4 5

6. Guides the top executive and line managers in actively managing people issues.

   1 2 3 4 5

Achieving High-Quality Business Results

7. Applies business acumen to HR decisions.

   1 2 3 4 5

8. Continuously monitors HR initiatives to maintain consistency with business outcomes.

   1 2 3 4 5

Bringing Ideas to the Business

9. Continually looks for ways to enhance or create new HR methods to achieve business outcomes.

   1 2 3 4 5

10. Critically evaluates and explores alternatives to the way things are done.

    1 2 3 4 5

Scoring and Interpretation

Correct answers are not the point of the preceding questions. The subscales (Bringing HR to the Business, Partnering with Business, etc.), represent elements of the HR Capability Model that APS HR managers are expected to master. Any questions for which you receive a 4 or 5 would be strong areas for you. If you aspire to become an HR manager it would be good to study the entire model at the following Web site: *http://www.apsc.gov.au/publications01/hrmodel.htm.*

SOURCE: Based on "Human Resources Capability Model," Australian Public Service Commission, Australian Government, as reported at *http://www.apsc.gov.au/publications01/hrmodel.htm.*

4 Organizing

ch11 MANAGEMENT IN PRACTICE: ETHICAL DILEMMA

A Conflict of Responsibilities

As director of human resources, Tess Danville was asked to negotiate a severance deal with Terry Winston, the Midwest regional sales manager for Cyn-Com Systems. Winston's problems with drugs and alcohol had become severe enough to precipitate his dismissal. His customers were devoted to him, but top management was reluctant to continue gambling on his reliability. Lives depended on his work as the salesperson and installer of Cyn-Com's respiratory diagnostic technology. Winston had been warned twice to clean up his act, but had never succeeded. Only his unique blend of technical knowledge and high-powered sales ability had saved him before.

Now the vice president of sales asked Danville to offer Winston the option of resigning rather than being fired if he would sign a noncompete agreement and agree to go into rehabilitation. Cyn-Com would also extend a guarantee of confidentiality on the abuse issue and a good work reference as thanks for the millions of dollars of business that Winston had brought to Cyn-Com. Winston agreed to take the deal. After his departure, a series of near disasters was uncovered as a result of Winston's mismanagement. Some of his maneuvers to cover up his mistakes bordered on fraud.

Today, Danville received a message to call the human resource director at a cardiopulmonary technology company to give a personal reference on Terry

Winston. From the area code, Danville could see that he was not in violation of the noncompete agreement. She had also heard that Winston had completed a 30-day treatment program as promised. Danville knew she was expected to honor the confidentiality agreement, but she also knew that if his shady dealings had been discovered before his departure, he would have been fired without any agreement. Now she was being asked to give Winston a reference for another medical sales position.

What Would You Do?

1. Honor the agreement, trusting Winston's rehabilitation is complete on all levels and that he is now ready for a responsible position. Give a good recommendation.

2. Contact the vice president of sales and ask him to release you from the agreement or to give the reference himself. After all, he made the agreement. You don't want to lie.

3. Without mentioning specifics, give Winston such an unenthusiastic reference that you hope the other human resources director can read between the lines and believe that Winston will be a poor choice.

---

ch11   CASE FOR CRITICAL ANALYSIS

Waterway Industries

Lee Carter and her husband, Jack Schiffer, became two of Waterway Industries most valuable managers almost by accident. But now, if the snatch of conversation CEO Cyrus Maher just overheard on his way to get coffee meant what he thought it did, he was in danger of losing the very people who'd contributed most to Waterway's recent growth surge.

Cyrus had met Lee and Jack, both paddling enthusiasts, when he was advisor to a university outing club. Lee had been majoring in marketing at the time, while Jack was studying engineering. He took a liking to the young couple and offered them part-time work at Waterways, then a small manufacturer of high-quality canoes in upstate New York. After graduation, the newlyweds decided to stay on full-time and take a breather before launching their demanding professional careers. That was 10 years ago.

When Lee and Jack joined Waterway, they found a laid-back atmosphere. Even as Waterway had grown steadily over the years, it continued to attract shop-floor employees who loved water sports and enjoyed making quality products they themselves used in their off-hours. Workers spent time good-naturedly horsing around with each other, but they got their work done on time. In fact, on nice days, they often completed their tasks early so they could leave by midafternoon and get some canoeing in before dark.

In late 2003, Lee took a hard look at the slowing demand for canoes and the rapidly growing kayak market. "Cyrus," she asked, "have you ever thought about making kayaks?" Intrigued, Cyrus gave Lee and Jack the go-ahead to see what they could do. Jack responded by designing a compact, inexpensive, lightweight kayak that immediately found favor among baby boomers looking for a way to have some fun. Lee established a formal marketing department to drive sales. That's when things really took off. Many Waterway canoe customers placed sizable kayak orders, and a number of private labels asked Cyrus to make kayaks for their companies.

Energized by their success, Cyrus, Lee, Jack (who'd recently been named design department head), and other Waterway managers developed a long-range strategic plan that called for aggressive growth, new product designs, and nationwide marketing and distribution by 2008. These ambitious plans resulted in an increased workload and a faster-paced work environment. Waterway managers provided employees across-the-board pay raises.

In Cyrus's opinion, the pay increases were more than reasonable, but lately he has heard complaints, both from the shop floor and from managers. He is dealing with compensation issues the way he always has—on a case-by-case basis. When a plant manager suggested top hourly performers receive additional wage increases, Cyrus turned it down, contending that Waterway's wages were in line with other manufacturers in rural New York. Shortly afterwards, a new automotive parts plant offering a slightly higher wage lured away three of Waterway's best workers.

When the company's CFO threatened to leave unless his compensation package included profit-sharing, Cyrus appeased him with a pay increase and extra vacation. But Lee and Jack have been more insistent. What they feel they deserve, in view of their contribution to the company's growth, is a share in the profits. He turned them down, and now, if he heard correctly, they are considering a lucrative job offer from a competing company.

What should the CEO do? He sees Lee and Jack's point of view, but would the other managers understand if he granted the couple the part ownership in the company he'd denied the others? And how would the hourly workers react?

Questions

1. Does Waterway's current compensation system seem to fit the company's strategy of aggressive growth and product innovation? How might it be changed to achieve a better fit?

2. Specifically, how would you gather the data and design a competitive compensation system for Waterway? Would your approach be different for hourly workers versus managers? Would you treat all managers equally?

3. How might nonfinancial incentives play a role in helping Waterway retain hourly shop workers? How can they help keep aggressive and ambitious professionals such as Lee and Jack?

SOURCES: Based on Robert D. Nicoson, "Growing Pains," *Harvard Business Review* (July–August 1996): 20–36.

---

ch11 ON THE JOB VIDEO CASE

Original Penguin Spreads Its Wings

Change is hard for companies—especially for large companies, which have large numbers of people and systems to manage. But in many cases, change can be positive, especially when it is in response to an opportunity for growth. Chris Kolbe is a master of change. Now vice president of Original Penguin, Chris essentially runs the division for its parent company, Perry Ellis International. He got there by finding himself in the unique position of rediscovering a languishing bird—and bringing it back to life.

Original Penguin was a 1950s icon—the penguin logo appeared on Munsingwear Penguin knit sport shirts for men, mostly golfers. Eventually, its popularity faded, and Perry Ellis International later acquired the brand. Chris Kolbe was working in merchandising at retailer Urban Outfitters when he conceived the idea of rejuvenating the penguin—but with a new twist and for a new market. Starting with a few new shirts, which sold out almost immediately, the "new" Original Penguin began to grow, and Perry Ellis tapped Kolbe to complete the transformation as head of a new venture team.

Despite the fact that the Original Penguin flagship store in New York boasts an oversized vintage photo of Kolbe's family, including his father wearing one of the "original" Munsingwear Penguin golf shirts, Kolbe recognizes that the fashion industry is a hotbed of change—and any clothing company that wants to survive must embrace innovation. "The fashion business is a young business," observes Kolbe. "It's about having fresh ideas. . . . What can happen is, if you stop having those brands in your pipeline, things start to dry up. . . . We realized Penguin could be one of those brands." So Kolbe and his team have focused on designs and clothing items that appeal to a younger market, both men and women, between the ages of 17 and 30.

While Kolbe could certainly be called the idea champion for this project, he does not work alone. He has a team of highly creative fashion-industry professionals, including David Bedwell, Creative Director. "We changed the brand a bit to really reach out to a different market today than maybe the market it was reaching in the past . . . yet keeping a classic twist on it," says Bedwell.

Consumers who wander into the new Original Penguin store will find an entire line of trendy, yet classic clothing and accessories. "We try to create an environment that our clothes will live in," explains Bedwell. Store displays show quirky, unconventional clothing combinations—such as a striped top with plaid pants. And visitors may wander through the "garden" or the "bedroom" to look at different outfits. Yes, shoppers can still buy knit sport shirts—in new colors and designs—but they can also pick up belts, shoes, and even bikinis.

If it sounds as though Kolbe and his team have free rein from Perry Ellis, they don't. Instead, they have a loose rein. They have a great deal of freedom to take risks, be creative, and make decisions. But Perry Ellis is taking the ultimate risk, and Kolbe knows that. The company does require regular updates on key financial and sales numbers. "The best

4
Organizing

thing about being young is you don't know the odds you're up against. . . . The risk for Perry Ellis was equally significant because they finance everything," says Kolbe.

Kolbe envisions the current fashion lines as the beginning of more innovation for Original Penguin and Perry Ellis. He also understands that change takes time and patience. "It takes a couple of years to see results, so it takes a certain amount of perseverance," he acknowledges. But he is excited about the future. "We've been able to bring a lot of influence and fresh ideas to a company that was searching. You can start to be a catalyst for a larger business."

Questions

1. In what ways might creativity be designed into the Original Penguin division of Perry Ellis International?

2. Why has it been important for Perry Ellis to give freedom to a new venture team in order to relaunch Original Penguin?

3. In what respects does Original Penguin represent a cultural change for Perry Ellis?

SOURCE: Company Web site, *http://www.originalpenguin.com*, accessed July 30, 2004.

ch11   BIZ FLIX VIDEO CASE

The Breakfast Club

John Hughes's careful look at teenage culture in a suburban high school outside Chicago focuses on a group of teenagers from the school's subcultures. They start their Saturday detention with nothing in common. Over the day they learn each others' most inner secrets. The highly memorable characters—the Jock, the Princess, the Criminal, the Kook, and the Brain—leave lasting impressions. (If you have seen the film, try to recall which actor or actress played each character.)

This scene shows the detainees at lunchtime. It is an edited version of the "Lunch Time" sequence

that appears in the first third of the film. Carefully study each character's behavior to answer the questions below.

What to Watch for and Ask Yourself

1. Which Big Five personality dimensions describe each character in this scene?

2. Which characters show positive affectivity? Which show negative affectivity?

3. Are any of these characters Type A personalities or Type B personalities? If so, which ones?

ch11   ENDNOTES

1. Based on ideas presented in Jim Collins, *Good to Great: Why Some Companies Make the Leap . . . and Others Don't* (New York: Harper Business, 2001).

2. Results of a McKinsey Consulting survey, reported in Leigh Branham, "Planning to Become an Employer of Choice," *Journal of Organizational Excellence* (Summer 2005): 57–68.

3. Robert L. Mathis and John H. Jackson, *Human Resource Management: Essential Perspectives*, 2nd ed. (Cincinnati, OH: South-Western Publishing, 2002), p. 1.

4. See James C. Wimbush, "Spotlight on Human Resource Management," *Business Horizons* 48 (2005): 463–467; Jonathan Tompkins, "Strategic Human Resources Management in Government: Unresolved Issues," *Public Personnel Management* (Spring 2002): 95–110; Noel M. Tichy, Charles J. Fombrun, and Mary Anne Devanna, "Strategic Human Resource Management," *Sloan Management Review* 23 (Winter 1982): 47–61; Cynthia A. Lengnick-Hall and Mark L. Lengnick-Hall, "Strategic Human Resources Management: A Review of the Literature and a Proposed Typology," *Academy of Management Review* 13 (July 1988): 454–470; Eugene B. McGregor, *Strategic Management of Human Knowledge, Skills, and Abilities*, (San Francisco: Jossey-Bass, 1991).

5. Edward E. Lawler III, "HR on Top," *Strategy + Business*, no. 35 (Second Quarter 2004): 21–25.

6. P. Wright, G. McMahan, and A. McWilliams, "Human Resources and Sustained Competitive Advantage: A Resource-Based Perspective," *International Journal of Human Resource* Management 5 (1994): 301–326; Tompkins, "Strategic Human Resource Management in Government: Unresolved Issues"; and Wimbush, "Spotlight on Human Resource Management."

7. B. Becker and M. Huselid, "High Performance Work Systems and Firm Performance: A Synthesis of Research and Managerial Implications," *Research in Personnel and Human Resources Management* 16 (1998): 53–101; S. Ramlall, "Measuring Human Resource Management's Effectiveness in Improving Performance," *Human Resource Planning* 26 (2003): 51; Mark A. Huselid, Susan E. Jackson, and Randall S. Schuler, "Technical and Strategic Human Resource Management Effectiveness as Determinants of Firm Performance," *Academy of Management Journal* 40, no. 1 (1997): 171–188; and John T. Delaney and Mark A. Huselid, "The Impact of Human Resource Management Practices on Perceptions of Organizational Performance," *Academy of Management Journal* 39, no. 4 (1996): 949–969.

8. James N. Baron and David M. Kreps, "Consistent Human Resource Practices," *California Management Review* 41, no. 3 (Spring 1999): 29–53.

9. Sunil J. Ramlall, "Strategic HR Management Creates Value at Target," *Journal of Organizational Excellence* (Spring 2006): 57–62.

10. Cynthia D. Fisher, "Current and Recurrent Challenges in HRM," *Journal of Management* 15 (1989): 157–180.

11. Floyd Kemske, "HR 2008: A Forecast Based on Our Exclusive Study," *Workforce* (January 1998): 46–60.

12. This definition and discussion is based on George Bollander, Scott Snell, and Arthur Sherman, *Managing Human Resources*, 12th ed. (Cincinnati, OH: South-Western, 2001), pp. 13–15; and Harry Scarbrough, "Recipe for Success," *People Management* (January 23, 2003): 22–25.

13. Susan Cantrell, James M. Benton, Terry Laudal, and Robert J. Thomas, "Measuring the Value of Human Capital Investments: The SAP Case," *Strategy & Leadership* 34, no. 2 (2006): 43–52.

14. Rich Wellins and Sheila Rioux, "The Growing Pains of Globalizing HR," *Training and Development* (May 2000): 79–85.

15. Helen DeCieri, Julie Wolfram Cox, and Marilyn S. Fenwick, "Think Global, Act Local: From Naive Comparison to Critical Participation in the Teaching of Strategic International Human Resource Management," *Tamara: Journal of Critical Postmodern Organization Science* 1, no. 1 (2001): 68ff; S. Taylor, S. Beecher, and N. Napier, "Towards an Integrative Model of Strategic Human Resource Management," *Academy of Management Review* 21 (1996): 959–985; Mary Ann Von Glinow, Ellen A. Drost, and Mary B. Teagarden, "Converging on IHRM Best Practices: Lessons Learned from a Globally Distributed Consortium on Theory and Practice," *Human Resource Management* 41, no. 1 (Spring 2002): 123–140.

16. Von Glinow, Drost, and Teagarden, "Converging on IHRM Best Practices"; and Jennifer J. Laabs, "Must-Have Global HR Competencies," *Workforce* 4, no. 2 (1999): 30–32.

17. Section 1604.1 of the EEOC Guidelines based on the Civil Rights Act of 1964, Title VII.

18. Reported in D. T. Hall and P. H. Mirvis, "The New Protean Career: Psychological Success and the Path with a Heart," in D. T. Hall & Associates, *The Career is Dead—Long Live the Career: A Relational Approach to Careers* (San Francisco: Jossey-Bass, 1995), pp. 15–45.

19. Based on Douglas T. Hall and Jonathan E. Moss, "The New Protean Career Contract: Helping Organizations and Employees Adapt," *Organizational Dynamics* (Winter 1998): 22–37; and M. V. Roehling, M. A. Cavanaugh, L. M. Moynihan, and W. R. Boswell, "The Nature of the New Employment Relationship: A Content Analysis of the Practitioner and Academic Literatures," *Human Resource Management* 39, no. 4 (2000): 305–320.

20. A. S. Tsui, J. L. Pearce, L. W. Porter, and A. M. Tripoli, "Alternative Approaches to the Employee-Organization Relationship: Does Investment in Employees Pay Off?" *Academy of Management Journal* 40 (1997): 1089–1121; D. Wang, A. S. Tsui, Y. Zhang, and L. Ma, "Employment Relationships and Firm Performance: Evidence from an Emerging Economy," *Journal of Organizational Behavior* 24 (2003): 511–535.

21. Based on Branham, "Planning to Become an Employer of Choice."

22. This discussion is based on Jaclyn Fierman, "The Contingency Workforce," *Fortune* (January 24, 1994): 30–31; Kris Maher, "More People Pushed Into Part-Time Work Force," *The Wall Street Journal*, March 8, 2008; Marshall Goldsmith, "The Contingent Workforce," *BusinessWeek* (May 23, 2007), http://www.businessweek.com/careers/content/may2007/ca20070523_580432.htm (accessed April 8, 2008); and John Tagliabue, "Europe No Longer Shuns Part-Time and Temporary Jobs," *The New York Times*, May 11, 2006.

23. Goldsmith, "The Contingent Workforce."

24. Thomas Frank, "TSA Struggles to Reduce Persistent Turnover," *USA Today*, February 25, 2008.

25. Ellen Gragg, "Are Telecommuting and Flextime Dead?" *Office Solutions* (January/February 2006): 28ff; Stephen Barr, "Working from Home a Work in Progress," *The Washington Post*, June 19, 2007.

26. Gragg, "Are Telecommuting and Flextime Dead?"

27. John Challenger, "There Is No Future for the Workplace," *Public Management* (February 1999): 20–23; Susan Caminiti, "Work-Life," *Fortune* (September 19, 2005): S1–S17.

28. Stephanie Armour, "Generation Y: They've Arrived at Work With a New Attitude," *USA Today*, November 6, 2005, http://www.usatoday.com; Ellyn Spragins, "The Talent Pool," *FSB* (October 2005): 92–101; and Caminiti, "Work-Life."

29. James R. Morris, Wayne F. Cascio, and Clifford Young, "Downsizing

4 Organizing

After All These Years: Questions and Answers About Who Did It, How Many Did It, and Who Benefited From It," *Organizational Dynamics* (Winter 1999): 78–86; William McKinley, Carol M. Sanchez, and Allen G. Schick, "Organizational Downsizing: Constraining, Cloning, Learning," *Academy of Management Executive* 9, no. 3 (1995): 32–42; and Brett C. Luthans and Steven M. Sommer, "The Impact of Downsizing on Workplace Attitudes," *Group and Organization Management* 2, no. 1 (1999): 46–70.

30. Effective downsizing techniques are discussed in detail in Bob Nelson, "The Care of the Un-Downsized," *Training and Development* (April 1997): 40–43; Shari Caudron, "Teaching Downsizing Survivors How to Thrive," *Personnel Journal* (January 1996): 38; Joel Brockner, "Managing the Effects of Layoffs on Survivors," *California Management Review* (Winter 1992): 9–28; and Kim S. Cameron, "Strategies for Successful Organizational Downsizing," *Human Resource Management* 33, no. 2 (Summer 1994): 189–211.

31. James G. March and Herbert A. Simon, *Organizations* (New York: Wiley, 1958).

32. Dennis J. Kravetz, *The Human Resources Revolution* (San Francisco: Jossey-Bass, 1989).

33. David E. Ripley, "How to Determine Future Workforce Needs," *Personnel Journal* (January 1995): 83–89.

34. J. W. Boudreau and S. L. Rynes, "Role of Recruitment in Staffing Utility Analysis," *Journal of Applied Psychology* 70 (1985): 354–366.

35. Megan Santosus, "The Human Capital Factor," *CFO-IT* (Fall 2005): 26–27.

36. Reported in Robert E. Ployhart, "Staffing in the 21st Century: New Challenges and Strategic Opportunities," *Journal of Management* 32, no. 6 (December 2006): 868–897.

37. Brian Dumaine, "The New Art of Hiring Smart," *Fortune* (August 17, 1987): 78–81.

38. This discussion is based on Mathis and Jackson, *Human Resource Management*, chapter 4, pp. 49–60.

39. Victoria Griffith, "When Only Internal Expertise Will Do," *CFO* (October 1998): 95–96, 102.

40. J. P. Wanous, *Organizational Entry* (Reading, MA: Addison-Wesley, 1980).

41. Samuel Greengard, "Technology Finally Advances HR," *Workforce* (January 2000): 38–41; and Scott Hays, "Hiring on the Web," *Workforce* (August 1999): 77–84.

42. Simona Covel, "Start-Up Lures Talent with Creative Pitch," *The Wall Street Journal*, June 4, 2007.

43. Kathryn Tyler, "Employees Can Help Recruit New Talent," *HR Magazine* (September 1996): 57–60.

44. Sarah E. Needleman, "If You Want to Stand Out, Join the Crowd," *The Wall Street Journal*, August 14, 2007.

45. Ron Stodghill, "Soul on Ice," *FSB* (October 2005): 129–134.

46. Miriam Jordan, "Bourbon, Baseball Bats, and Not the Bantu," *The Wall Street Journal*, September 18, 2007.

47. Milt Freudenheim, "More Help Wanted: Older Workers Please Apply," *The New York Times*, March 23, 2005, http://www.nytimes.com.

48. "Bank of America to Hire 850 Ex-Welfare Recipients," *Johnson City Press*, January 14, 2001; E. Blacharczyk, "Recruiters Challenged by Economy, Shortages, Unskilled," *HR News* (February 1990): B1; Victoria Rivkin, "Visa Relief," *Working Woman* (January 2001): 15.

49. Wimbush, "Spotlight on Human Resource Management."

50. P. W. Thayer, "Somethings Old, Somethings New," *Personnel Psychology* 30 (1977): 513–524.

51. J. Ledvinka, *Federal Regulation of Personnel and Human Resource Management* (Boston: Kent, 1982); and *Civil Rights Act*, Title VII, Section 2000e *et seq.*, *U. S. Code* 42 (1964).

52. Reported in Stephanie Clifford, "The New Science of Hiring," *Inc. Magazine* (August 2006): 90–98.

53. George Bohlander, Scott Snell, and Arthur Sherman, *Managing Human Resources*, 12th ed. (Cincinnati, OH: South-Western, 2001). p. 202.

54. Ibid.

55. "Assessment Centers: Identifying Leadership through Testing," *Small Business Report* (June 1987): 22–24; and W. C. Byham, "Assessment Centers for Spotting Future Managers," *Harvard Business Review* (July–August 1970): 150–167.

56. Erin White, "Walking a Mile in Another's Shoes—Employers Champion Tests of Job Candidates to Gauge Skills at 'Real World' Tasks" (Theory and Practice column), *The Wall Street Journal*, January 16, 2006.

57. Mike Thatcher, "'Front-line' Staff Selected by Assessment Center," *Personnel Management* (November 1993): 83.

58. Alan Finder, "For Some, Online Persona Undermines a Resumé," *The New York Times*, June 11, 2006.

59. Bernard Keys and Joseph Wolfe, "Management Education and Development: Current Issues and Emerging Trends," *Journal of Management* 14 (1988): 205–229.

60. "2007 Industry Report," *Training* (November-December 2007): 8–24.

61. William J. Rothwell and H. C. Kazanas, *Improving On-the-Job Training: How to Establish and Operate a Comprehensive OJT Program* (San Francisco: Jossey-Bass, 1994).

62. Jeanne C. Meister, "The Brave New World of Corporate Education," *The Chronicle of Higher Education* (February 9, 2001): B10; and Meryl Davids Landau, "Corporate Universities Crack Open Their Doors," *The Journal of Business Strategy* (May–June 2000): 18–23.

63. Meister, "The Brave New World of Corporate Education"; Edward E. Gordon, "Bridging the Gap," *Training* (September 2003): 30; and John Byrne, "The Search for the Young and Gifted," *BusinessWeek* (October 4, 1999): 108–116.

64. Doug Bartholomew, "Taking the E-Train," *Industry Week* (June 2005): 34–37; Joel Schettler, "Defense Acquisition University: Weapons of Mass Instruction," *Training* (February 2003): 20–27.

65. Jim Dow, "Spa Attraction," *People Management* (May 29, 2003): 34–35.

66. See C. H. Deutsch, "A New Kind of Whistle-Blower: Company Refines Principles of Coaching and Teamwork," *The New York Times*, May 7, 1999; and B. Filipczak, "The Executive Coach: Helper or Healer?" *Training* (March 1998): 30–36.

67. Survey by HR consulting firm Watson Wyatt, reported in Kelley Holland, "Performance Reviews: Many Need Improvement," *The New York Times*, September 10, 2006.

68. Walter W. Tornow, "Editor's Note: Introduction to Special Issue on 360-Degree Feedback," *Human Resource Management* 32, no. 2–3 (Summer–Fall 1993): 211–219; and Brian O'Reilly, "360 Feedback Can Change Your Life," *Fortune* (October 17, 1994): 93–100.

69. Kris Frieswick, "Truth & Consequences," *CFO* (June 2001): 56–63.

70. This discussion is based on Dick Grote, "Forced Ranking: Behind the Scenes," *Across the Board* (November–December 2002): 40–45; Matthew Boyle, "Performance Reviews: Perilous Curves Ahead," *Fortune* (May 28, 2001): 187–188; Carol Hymowitz, "Ranking Systems Gain Popularity But Have Many Staffers Riled," *The Wall Street Journal*, May 15, 2001; and Frieswick, "Truth & Consequences."

71. Reported in McGregor, "The Struggle to Measure Performance."

72. Ibid.

73. Erin White, "How to Reduce Turnover—Restaurant Chain Retains Workers Using Rankings and Rewards," *The Wall Street Journal*, November 21, 2005; and Lou Kaucic, "Finding Your Stars," *Microsoft Executive Circle* (Summer 2003): 14.

74. V. R. Buzzotta, "Improve Your Performance Appraisals," *Management Review* (August 1988): 40–43; and H. J. Bernardin and R. W. Beatty, *Performance Appraisal: Assessing Human Behavior at Work* (Boston: Kent, 1984).

75. Bernardin and Beatty, *Performance Appraisal*.

76. Richard I. Henderson, *Compensation Management: Rewarding Performance*, 4th ed. (Reston, VA: Reston, 1985).

77. L. R. Gomez-Mejia, "Structure and Process Diversification, Compensation Strategy, and Firm Performance," *Strategic Management Journal* 13 (1992): 381–397; and E. Montemayor, "Congruence Between Pay Policy and Competitive Strategy in High-Performing Firms," *Journal of Management* 22, no. 6 (1996): 889–908.

78. Renée F. Broderick and George T. Milkovich, "Pay Planning, Organization Strategy, Structure and 'Fit': A Prescriptive Model of Pay," paper presented at the 45th Annual Meeting of the Academy of Management, San Diego, August 1985.

79. E. F. Lawler, III, *Strategic Pay: Aligning Organizational Strategies and Pay Systems* (San Francisco: Jossey-Bass, 1990); and R. J. Greene, "Person-Focused Pay: Should It Replace Job-Based Pay?" *Compensation and Benefits Management* 9, no. 4 (1993): 46–55.

80. L. Wiener, "No New Skills? No Raise," *U.S. News and World Report* (October 26, 1992): 78.

81. Data from Hewitt Associates, Bureau of Labor Statistics, reported in Michelle Conlin and Peter Coy, with Ann Therese Palmer, and Gabrielle Saveri, "The Wild New Workforce," *BusinessWeek* (December 6, 1999): 39–44.

82. *2005 Employee Benefits Study*, (Washington, DC: U. S. Chamber of Commerce, 2005), http://www .uschamber.com/press/releases/ 2006/april/06-72.htm, (accessed April 11, 2008).

83. Frank E. Kuzmits, "Communicating Benefits: A Double-Click Away," *Compensation and Benefits Review* 30, no. 5 (September–October 1998): 60–64; and Lynn Asinof, "Click and Shift: Workers Control Their Benefits Online," *The Wall Street Journal*, November 27, 1997.

84. Robert S. Catapano-Friedman, "Cafeteria Plans: New Menu for the '90s," *Management Review* (November 1991): 25–29.

85. Society for Human Resource Management 2006 Talent Management Survey Report, reported in "Formal Findings," *The Wall Street Journal*, June 4, 2007.

86. Scott Westcott, "Goodbye and Good Luck," *Inc. Magazine* (April 2006): 40–42.

87. Nanette Byrnes, "Star Search," *BusinessWeek* (October 10, 2005): 68–78.

88. Mike Brewster, "No Exit," *Fast Company* (April 2005): 93.

4
Organizing

© GETTY IMAGES/DIGITAL VISION

Learning Outcomes

After studying this chapter, you should be able to:

1. Understand the pervasive demographic changes occurring in the domestic and global marketplace and how corporations are responding.

2. Understand how the definition of diversity has grown to recognize a broad spectrum of differences among employees, and appreciate the dividends of a diverse workforce.

3. Recognize the complex attitudes, opinions, and issues that employees bring to the workplace, including prejudice, discrimination, stereotypes, and ethnocentrism.

4. Recognize the factors that affect women's opportunities, including the glass ceiling, the opt-out trend, and the female advantage.

5. Explain the five steps in developing cultural competence in the workplace.

6. Describe how diversity initiatives and training programs help create a climate that values diversity.

7. Understand how multicultural teams and employee network groups help organizations respond to the rapidly changing and complex workplace.

Managing Diversity

DO YOU KNOW YOUR BIASES?[1]

As a new manager, your day-to-day behavior will send signals about your biases and values. Some personal biases are active and well known to yourself and others. Other biases are more subtle, and the following questions may provide some hints about where you are biased and don't know it. Please answer whether each item is Mostly True or Mostly False for you.

	Mostly True	Mostly False
1. I prefer to be in work teams with people who think like me.	_____	_____
2. I have avoided talking about culture differences with people I met from different cultures because I didn't want to say the wrong thing.	_____	_____
3. My mind has jumped to a conclusion without first hearing all sides of a story.	_____	_____
4. The first thing I notice about people is the physical characteristics that make them different from the norm.	_____	_____
5. Before I hire someone, I have a picture in mind of what they should look like.	_____	_____
6. I typically ignore movies, magazines, and TV programs that are targeted toward groups and values that are different from mine.	_____	_____
7. When someone makes a bigoted remark or joke, I don't confront them about it.	_____	_____
8. I prefer to not discuss sensitive topics such as race, age, gender, sexuality, or religion at work.	_____	_____
9. There are people I like but would feel uncomfortable inviting to be with my family or close friends.	_____	_____

SCORING AND INTERPRETATION: Give yourself one point for each item you marked as Mostly True. The ideal score is zero, but few people reach the ideal. Each question reflects an element of "passive bias," which can cause people different from you to feel ignored or disrespected by you. Passive bias may be more insidious than active discrimination because it excludes people from opportunities for expression and interaction. If you scored 5 or more, you should take a careful look at how you think and act toward people different from yourself. The sooner you learn to actively include diverse views and people, the better new manager you will be.

Sweeping demographic changes in the U.S. population have transformed today's society, creating a cultural mosaic of diverse people. The nation's minority population, for example, is now 100.7 million, making about one in three U.S. residents a minority. Roughly 32 million people speak Spanish at home, and nearly half of these people say they don't speak English very well, according to Census Bureau figures.[2] These demographic shifts, among others, are prompting companies in the United States and abroad to take notice because these trends open up new markets. To capitalize on those opportunities, organizations have recognized that their workplaces need to reflect the diversity in the marketplace. "Our country's consumer base is so varied," says Shelley Willingham-Hinton, president of the National Organization for

1 Introduction
2 Environment
3 Planning
4 Organizing
5 Controlling
6 Leading

Diversity in Sales and Marketing. "I can't think of how a company can succeed without having that kind of diversity with their employees."[3]

Forward-thinking organizations agree and are taking steps to attract and retain a workforce that reflects the cultural diversity of the population. They take seriously the fact that there is a link between the diversity of the workforce and financial success in the marketplace. To be successful, these organizations are hiring workers who share the same cultural background as the customers they are trying to reach. Avon, for example, turned around its inner-city markets by putting African-American and Hispanic managers in charge of marketing to these populations.[4]

Today's organizations recognize that diversity is no longer just the right thing to do; it is a business imperative and perhaps the single most important factor of the twenty-first century for organization performance.[5] Companies that ignore diversity will have a hard time competing in a multicultural global environment. As Ted Childs, director of diversity at IBM, put it, "Diversity is the bridge between the workplace and the marketplace."[6] The global corporations listed in Exhibit 12.1 have been recognized as leaders in corporate diversity. They have made diversity a top priority and have taken steps toward creating a corporate culture that values equality and reflects today's multicultural consumer base.

In this chapter, we explore why demographic changes in the U.S. and global marketplace have prompted corporations to place high value on creating a diverse workforce. The chapter considers the advantages of a diverse workforce and the challenges in managing one. We look at the myriad complex issues that face managers and employees in a diverse workplace, including prejudice, stereotypes, discrimination, and ethnocentrism. Factors that specifically affect women—the glass ceiling, the opt-out trend, and the female advantage—are also considered. After a review of the steps toward cultural competence, the chapter concludes by presenting an overview of initiatives taken by corporations to create an environment that welcomes and values a broad spectrum of diversity among its employees.

THE CHANGING WORKPLACE

When Brenda Thomson, the director of diversity and leadership education at the Las Vegas MGM Mirage, steps into one of the company's hotel lobbies, she closes her eyes and listens. "It's amazing all the different languages I can hear just standing in the lobbies of any of our hotels," she says. "Our guests come from all over the world, and it really makes us realize the importance of reflecting that diversity in our workplace."[7] The diversity Thomson sees in the lobbies of the MGM Mirage hotels is a small reflection of the cultural diversity seen in the larger domestic and global workplaces.

EXHIBIT | 12.1

Leaders in Corporate Diversity

Allstate	Marriott International
American Express	Merrill Lynch
Bank of America	Pepsi Bottling Group
Bausch & Lomb	Pricewaterhouse Coopers
Citigroup	Procter & Gamble
Consolidated Edison Company of New York	Starwood Resorts
Daimler Chrysler	The Coca-Cola Company
Deloitte & Touche USA	UPS
Eastman Kodak	Verizon
Ernst & Young	Wachovia
FedEx	Wells Fargo
IBM	Xerox
JP Morgan Chase	

SOURCE: Susan Caminiti, "The Diversity Factor," *Fortune* (October 29, 2007): 95–105.

Diversity in the United States

Today's U.S. corporations reflect the country's image as a melting pot, but with a difference. In the past, the United States was a place where people of different national origins, ethnicities, races, and religions came together and blended to resemble one another. Opportunities for advancement were limited to those workers who easily fit into the mainstream of the larger culture. Some immigrants chose desperate measures to fit in, such as abandoning their native languages, changing their last names, and sacrificing their own unique cultures. In essence, everyone in workplace organizations was encouraged to share similar beliefs, values, and lifestyles despite differences in gender, race, and ethnicity.[8]

Now organizations recognize that everyone is not the same and that the differences people bring to the workplace are valuable.[9] Rather than expecting all employees to adopt similar attitudes and values, managers are learning that these differences enable their companies to compete globally and to tap into rich sources of new talent. Although diversity in North America has been a reality for some time, genuine efforts to accept and *manage* diverse people began only in recent years. Exhibit 12.2 lists some interesting milestones in the history of corporate diversity.

Diversity in corporate America has become a key topic, in part because of the vast changes occurring in today's workplace and consumer base. The average worker is older now, and many more women, people of color, and immigrants are seeking job and advancement opportunities. The following statistics illustrate some of the changes reshaping the workplace.

- *Aging workforce.* Baby boomers continue to affect the workplace as this massive group of workers progresses through its life stages. A baby boomer turns 60 every seven seconds, continuously bumping up the average age of the workforce.[10] In 1986, the median age of the U.S. labor force was 35.4 years. It increased to 40.8 years in 2006 and will increase to 42.1 years in 2016.[11]

- *Growth in Hispanic and Asian workers.* The greatest increase in employment will occur with Asians and Hispanics. In fact, the number of Hispanics in the workforce will increase by 6 million between 2006 and 2016, with 27 million Hispanics in the workforce by 2016.[12] Exhibit 12.3 on page 345 shows the growth in employment among different racial and ethnic groups in the United States.

- *Minority purchasing power.* Hispanics, African Americans, and Asian Americans together represent $1.5 trillion in annual purchasing power.[13]

- *Growth in foreign-born population.* During the 1990s, the foreign-born population of the United States nearly doubled, and immigrants now number more than 37.5 million, meaning that almost one in eight people living in the United States was born in another country, the highest percentage since the 1920s.[14]

So far, the ability of organizations to manage diversity has not kept pace with these demographic trends, thus creating a number of significant challenges for minority workers and women. Progress for women and minorities in both pay and leadership roles has stalled or regressed at many U.S. corporations, as reflected in these statistics: 75 percent of 357 global senior executives report their companies have one or no minorities among their top executives, and 56 percent say they have one or no women among their top executives.[15] This inequality shapes perceptions about who can assume leadership roles. And the pay gap between white men and every other group still exists.[16] Corporations that truly value diversity will recognize pay inequality and discrimination in the workplace and make progress toward eliminating them.

As a new manager, you will be challenged to create a workplace that is inclusive and bias-free. You may have the courage to take an active stand against prejudice and inappropriate, disrespectful behavior. But will you inadvertently exclude people who are different from the mainstream? Refer back to your score on the opening questionnaire concerning passive bias.

TakeaMoment

4
Organizing

EXHIBIT | 12.2

Some Milestones in the
History of Corporate
Diversity

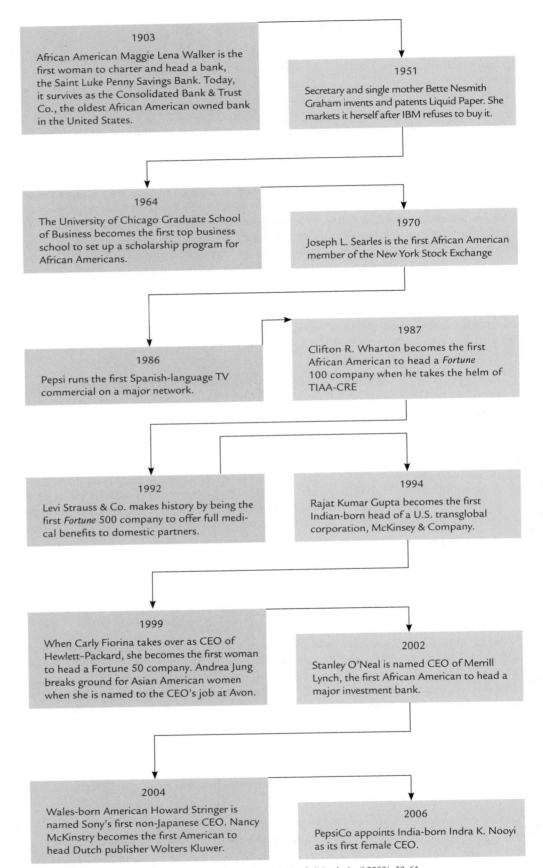

1903
African American Maggie Lena Walker is the first woman to charter and head a bank, the Saint Luke Penny Savings Bank. Today, it survives as the Consolidated Bank & Trust Co., the oldest African American owned bank in the United States.

1951
Secretary and single mother Bette Nesmith Graham invents and patents Liquid Paper. She markets it herself after IBM refuses to buy it.

1964
The University of Chicago Graduate School of Business becomes the first top business school to set up a scholarship program for African Americans.

1970
Joseph L. Searles is the first African American member of the New York Stock Exchange

1986
Pepsi runs the first Spanish-language TV commercial on a major network.

1987
Clifton R. Wharton becomes the first African American to head a *Fortune* 100 company when he takes the helm of TIAA-CRE

1992
Levi Strauss & Co. makes history by being the first *Fortune* 500 company to offer full medical benefits to domestic partners.

1994
Rajat Kumar Gupta becomes the first Indian-born head of a U.S. transglobal corporation, McKinsey & Company.

1999
When Carly Fiorina takes over as CEO of Hewlett-Packard, she becomes the first woman to head a Fortune 50 company. Andrea Jung breaks ground for Asian American women when she is named to the CEO's job at Avon.

2002
Stanley O'Neal is named CEO of Merrill Lynch, the first African American to head a major investment bank.

2004
Wales-born American Howard Stringer is named Sony's first non-Japanese CEO. Nancy McKinstry becomes the first American to head Dutch publisher Wolters Kluwer.

2006
PepsiCo appoints India-born Indra K. Nooyi as its first female CEO.

SOURCE: "Spotlight on Diversity," special advertising section, *MBA Jungle* (March–April 2003): 58–61.

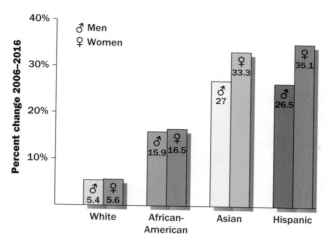

EXHIBIT | 12.3

Growth in Employment from 2006 to 2016 by Group

SOURCE: Bureau of Labor Statistics.

Diversity on a Global Scale

Implications of an increasingly diverse workforce are not limited to the United States. For example, the aging of the population is a global phenomenon. In addition, for organizations operating globally, social and cultural differences may create more difficulties and conflicts than any other sources. For instance, U.S. managers trying to transfer their diversity policies and practices to European divisions haven't considered the complex and social cultural systems in Europe. Even the meaning of diversity presents problems. In many European languages, the closest word implies separation rather than the inclusion sought by U.S. diversity programs.[17]

Foreign firms doing business in the United States face similar challenges understanding and dealing with diversity issues. For example, Japanese leaders at Toyota Motor Company seriously bungled the handling of a sexual harassment complaint in the company's North American division, leading to a lawsuit. When Sayaka Kobayashi sent a letter to Dennis Cuneo, senior vice president of Toyota North America, saying she had endured months of romantic and sexual advances from her boss, Cuneo told her he would discuss the issue with the boss, Hideaki Otaka. However, Cuneo allegedly said that he didn't want to offend the man (a cultural norm), so he planned to say it was Kobayashi's boyfriend who was upset about the overtures. This chapter's Manager's Shoptalk lists some interesting tips for foreign managers working in the United States to help them understand and relate to Americans. Do you agree that these statements provide a good introduction to American culture for a non-native?

National cultures are intangible, pervasive, and difficult to comprehend. However, it is imperative that managers in organizations learn to understand local cultures and deal with them effectively.[18] Many companies have taken this challenge seriously and have experienced growth in the global marketplace. For example, Honeywell has a growing role in the global marketplace with 118,000 employees operating in more than 100 countries. Today, 54 percent of its employees work outside the United States. Honeywell made the global connection and incorporated diversity as part of its global strategies and believes that diversity provides the energy to fuel its high-performance culture and achieve sustainable competitive advantage.[19] The director of diversity at Kraft General Foods concurs. "Being global means that our customers are diverse. Our stockholders are diverse. The population which is available to us, our productivity, creativity, innovation, and people who supply us are diverse. There is no way we can run a business effectively without a deep understanding and accommodating all of these elements."[20]

Manager'sShoptalk

A GUIDE FOR EXPATRIATE MANAGERS IN AMERICA

Although each person is different, individuals from a specific country typically share certain values and attitudes. Managers planning to move to a foreign country can learn about these broad value patterns to help them adjust to working and living abroad. The following characteristics are often used to help foreign managers understand what Americans are like.

1. *Americans are informal.* They tend to treat everyone alike, even when individuals differ significantly in age or social status.

2. *Americans are direct and decisive.* To some foreigners, this behavior may seem abrupt or even rude. Typically, Americans don't "beat around the bush," which means they don't talk around things but get right to the point. They quickly define a problem and decide on the course of action they believe is most likely to get the desired results.

3. *Americans love facts.* They value statistics, data, and information in any form.

4. *Americans are competitive.* They like to keep score, whether at work or play. Americans like to win, and they don't tolerate failure well. Some foreigners might think Americans are aggressive or overbearing. For example, Americans are not at all shy about selling themselves. In fact, it's expected.

5. *Americans believe in work.* For many, commitment to work and career comes first. In general, Americans rarely take time off, even if a family member is ill. They don't believe in long vacations—even corporation presidents often take only two weeks, if that.

6. *Americans are independent and individualistic.* They place a high value on freedom and believe that people can control their own destinies.

7. *Americans are questioners.* They ask a lot of questions, even of someone they have just met. Some of these questions may seem pointless (How ya' doin'?) or personal (What kind of work do you do?).

8. *Americans dislike silence.* They would rather talk about the weather than deal with silence in a conversation.

9. *Americans value punctuality.* They keep appointment calendars and live according to schedules and clocks.

10. *Americans pay close attention to appearances.* They take note of designer clothing and good grooming. They may in fact seem obsessed with bathing, eliminating body odors, and wearing clean clothes.

How many of these statements do you agree with? Discuss them with your friends and classmates, including people from different countries and members of different subcultural groups from the United States.

SOURCES: Winston Fletcher, "The American Way of Work," *Management Today* (August 1, 2005): 46; "What Are Americans Like?" Exhibit 4-6 in Stephen P. Robbins and Mary Coulter, *Management*, 8th ed. (Upper Saddle River, NJ: Pearson Prentice Hall, 2005), as adapted from M. Ernest, ed., *Predeparture Orientation Handbook: For Foreign Students and Scholars Planning to Study in the United States* (Washington, DC: U.S. Information Agency, Bureau of Cultural Affairs, 1984), p. 103–105; Amanda Bennett, "American Culture Is Often a Puzzle for Foreign Managers in the U.S.," *The Wall Street Journal*, February 12, 1986; "Don't Think Our Way's the Only Way," *The Pryor Report* (February 1988): 9; and B. Wattenberg, "The Attitudes Behind American Exceptionalism," *U.S. News and World Report* (August 7, 1989): 25.

MANAGING DIVERSITY

Whether operating on a national or global scale, organizations recognize that their consumer base is changing, and they cannot prosper and succeed without a diverse workforce. Let's first explore the expanding definition of *diversity* and consider the dividends of cultivating a diverse workforce.

What Is Diversity?

diversity All the ways in which employees differ.

Diversity is defined as all the ways in which people differ.[21] Diversity wasn't always defined this broadly. Decades ago, many companies defined diversity in terms of race, gender, age, lifestyle, and disability. That focus helped create awareness, change mind-sets, and create new opportunities for many. Today, companies are embracing a more inclusive definition of diversity that recognizes a spectrum of differences that influence how employees approach work, interact with each other, derive satisfaction from their work, and define who they are as people in the workplace.[22]

Exhibit 12.4 illustrates the difference between the traditional model and the inclusive model of diversity. The dimensions of diversity shown in the traditional model include inborn differences that are immediately observable and include race, gender, age, and physical ability. However, the inclusive model of diversity includes *all* of the ways in which employees differ, including aspects of diversity that can be acquired or changed throughout one's lifetime. These dimensions may have less impact than those included only in the traditional model but nevertheless affect a person's self-definition and worldview and the way the person is viewed by others. For example, the inclusive model of diversity recognizes people with different spiritual beliefs. As part of its diversity program, Target addresses issues of faith in its Minneapolis store. Muslim cashiers who object to ringing up pork products due to religious beliefs are allowed to wear gloves, shift to other positions, or transfer to other stores.[23]

Concept Connection Successful organizations seek a **diverse and inclusive workforce.** Indra Nooyi was named CEO of PepsiCo in 2006 after twelve years with the food and beverage giant, spending most of those years leading its global strategy. Both *Fortune* and *Forbes* magazines named the Indian-born executive one of the most powerful women in America. "I am not your normal, nondiverse CEO. I am everything that this company took forth in diversity and inclusion, and it has all come together with me," says Nooyi.

© AP IMAGES

Go to the ethical dilemma on pages 366–367 that pertains to accommodating religious practices in the workplace.

TakeaMoment

EXHIBIT 12.4 Traditional vs. Inclusive Models of Diversity

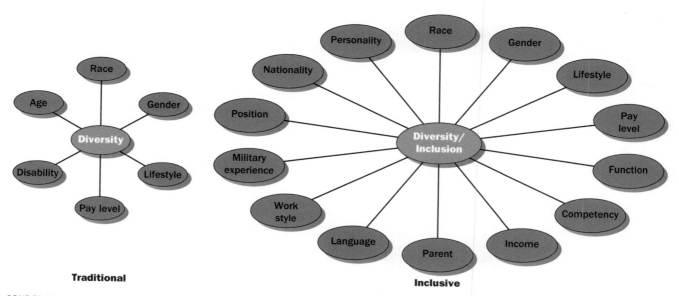

SOURCE: Reproduced by permission. Anthony Oshiotse and Richard O'Leary, "Corning Creates an Inclusive Culture to Drive Technology Innovation and Performance," *Wiley InterScience, Global Business and Organizational Excellence,* 26 no. 3 (March/April 2007): 12.

Concept Connection Many people are opting to stay in the workforce long past retirement age, giving managers opportunities to enhance **workforce diversity** by incorporating older employees. When CPI Aerostructures in Edgewood, New York, earned new contracts to provide spare parts to the U.S. government, CEO Edward J. Fred needed skilled mechanics ready to work. He was flooded with inquiries from retired mechanics, many well past the age of 65. Fred hired two seniors as part-time workers, and two as full-time employees. The decision gave CPI flexibility in scheduling, experienced workers to serve as teachers to younger colleagues, and a workplace culture that increased pride in the work for employees of all ages.

With 35 percent of its domestic workforce made up of African-Americans, Hispanics, Asian Americans, and other minorities, UPS is widely recognized for its commitment to diversity. For the past seven consecutive years, a *Fortune* magazine survey has ranked UPS as one of the "50 Best Companies for Minorities." In addition, minorities hold 85 senior management positions, with African Americans filling 52 of those posts, and five of the company's board of directors are African American.[24] Positive statistics like this help UPS attract and retain a diverse workforce. UPS believes that the diversity reflected in its workforce is the key to its effectiveness.

Yet, a diverse workforce poses unique challenges for managers at UPS and elsewhere. Employees with different backgrounds bring different opinions and ideas. Conflict, anxiety, and misunderstandings may increase. Embracing these differences and using them to improve company performance can be challenging. **Managing diversity**, a key management skill in today's global economy, means creating a climate in which the potential advantages of diversity for organizational or group performance are maximized while the potential disadvantages are minimized.[25]

Dividends of Workplace Diversity

Corporations that build strong, diverse organizations reap numerous dividends as described below and shown in Exhibit 12.5[26]. The dividends of diversity include the following:

- *Better use of employee talent.* Companies with the best talent are the ones with the best competitive advantage. But attracting a diverse workforce is not enough; companies must also provide career opportunities and advancement for its minority and women employees to retain them.

- *Increased understanding of the marketplace.* The consumer market is becoming increasingly diverse. A diverse workforce is better able to anticipate and respond to changing consumer needs. Ford Motor Company realized it could reach its business objectives only if it created a workforce that reflected the multicultural face of the country. So it assembled a workforce made up of 25 percent minorities

managing diversity
Creating a climate in which the potential advantages of diversity for organizational or group performance are maximized while the potential disadvantages are minimized.

EXHIBIT | **12.5**

Dividends of Workplace Diversity

- Better use of employee talent
- Increased understanding of the marketplace
- Enhanced breadth of understanding in leadership positions
- Increased quality of team problem solving
- Reduced costs associated with high turnover, absenteeism, and lawsuits

SOURCE: Gail Robinson and Kathleen Dechant, "Building a Business Case for Diversity," *Academy of Management Executive* 11, no. 3 (1997): 22.

(18.4 percent are African American) to foster a culture of inclusion, winning it a spot on *Black Enterprise's* "40 Best Companies for Diversity."[27]

- **Enhanced breadth of understanding in leadership positions.** Homogeneous top management teams tend to be myopic in their perspectives. According to Niall FitzGerald of Unilever, "It is important for any business operating in an increasingly complex and rapidly changing environment to deploy a broad range of talents. That provides a breadth of understanding of the world and environment and a fusion of the very best values and different perspectives which make up that world."[28]

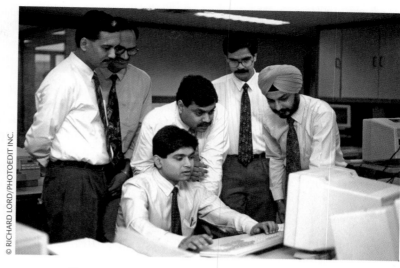

Concept Connection With roughly half of its 66,000 employees working outside the United States, it's not surprising that American Express is an acknowledged leader in managing **global diversity.** These East Indian staff members are shown in the company's Delhi offices. American Express developed a training module, "Valuing Diversity and Practicing Inclusion," for managers throughout the world, but executives let local facilitators customize the tool to fit their cultures. "We always allow them a period of time to be able to adapt, modify, and customize . . . so that it resonates well with employees," explains Henry Hernandez, vice president and chief diversity officer.

- **Increased quality of team problem solving.** Teams with diverse backgrounds bring different perspectives to a discussion that result in more creative ideas and solutions.[29] Although 85 percent of Ernst & Young's senior leadership is still male, the company is taking steps to create a more diverse leadership team because it's better for business. "We know you get better solutions when you put a diverse team at the table. People come from different backgrounds and they have different frames of reference. When you put these people together, you get the best solution for our clients," says Billie Williamson, director of flexibility and gender equity strategy at Ernst & Young.[30]

- **Reduced costs associated with high turnover, absenteeism, and lawsuits.** Companies that foster a diverse workforce reduce turnover, absenteeism, and the risk of lawsuits. Because family responsibilities contribute to turnover and absenteeism, many companies now offer child-care and elder-care benefits, flexible work arrangements, telecommuting, and part-time employment to accommodate employee responsibilities at home. Discrimination lawsuits are also a costly side effect of a discriminatory work environment. A racial harassment suit against Lockheed Martin Corporation cost the company $2.5 million, the largest individual racial-discrimination payment obtained by the Equal Employment Opportunity Commission.[31]

These benefits of diversity are important for all organizations, but they are critical for agencies like the Federal Bureau of Investigation that are striving to keep communities safe in today's complex multicultural world. Not so long ago, if you were a woman or member of a minority group, you didn't stand a chance of becoming an FBI agent. Today, however, the agency's goal is to reflect the diversity of U.S. society.

How does the FBI gain credibility and obtain the information it needs to investigate and solve crimes? One way is by looking and thinking like the people in the communities where it seeks information. Each of the FBI's 56 field offices gets a report card on how well they've done in terms of making their offices reflective of the community. Each office is responsible for bringing minorities and women on board and providing them with advancement opportunities.

In addition, the FBI's national recruitment office was launched specifically to develop programs for recruiting women and minorities. One innovative initiative was the EdVenture Partners Collegiate Marketing Program, which worked with two historically African-American universities. The program gave students college credit and funding to devise and implement a local marketing plan for the FBI. As a result of the program, the agency received 360 minority applications. "In many cases, the students' perceptions about the FBI were totally

Federal Bureau of Investigation (FBI)

Innovative Way

4 Organizing

changed," says Gwen Hubbard, acting chief of the national recruitment office. "Initially, we were not viewed as an employer of choice by the diverse student populations." The EdVenture Partners program is being expanded to eight colleges and universities. Another initiative is a minority summer intern program, which started with 21 full-time student interns and is being expanded to at least 40.

These programs on the national level, along with emphasis in the field offices on reflecting the local communities, ensure that the Federal Bureau of Investigation recruits diverse candidates. Today, the FBI has thousands of female and minority agents. Top leaders are also focusing on ways to make sure those people have full opportunity to move up the ranks so that there is diversity at leadership levels as well.[32]

FACTORS SHAPING PERSONAL BIAS

To reap the benefits of diversity described above, organizations are seeking managers who will serve as catalysts in the workplace to reduce barriers and eliminate obstacles for disadvantaged people. *Managing diversity*, therefore, has become a sought after management skill. To successfully manage a diverse workgroup and create a positive, productive environment for all employees, managers need to start with an understanding of the complex attitudes, opinions, and issues that already exist in the workplace or that employees bring into the workplace. These include several factors that shape personal bias: prejudice, discrimination, stereotypes, and ethnocentrism.

Prejudice, Discrimination, and Stereotypes

Prejudice is the tendency to view people who are different as being deficient. If someone acts out their prejudicial attitudes toward people who are the targets of their prejudice, **discrimination** has occurred.[33] Paying a woman less than a man for the same work is gender discrimination. Mistreating people because they have a different ethnicity is ethnic discrimination. Although blatant discrimination is not as widespread as in the past, bias in the workplace often shows up in subtle ways: a lack of choice assignments, the disregard by a subordinate of a minority manager's directions, or the ignoring of comments made by women and minorities at meetings. A survey by Korn Ferry International found that 59 percent of minority managers surveyed had observed a racially motivated double standard in the delegation of assignments.[34] Their perceptions are supported by a study that showed minority managers spend more time in the "bullpen" waiting for their chance and then have to prove themselves over and over again with each new assignment. Minority employees typically feel that they have to put in longer hours and extra effort to achieve the same status as their white colleagues. "It's not enough to be as good as the next person," says Bruce Gordon, president of Bell Atlantic's enterprise group. "We have to be better."[35]

A number of federal and state laws outlaw different types of discrimination, as discussed in Chapter 11. These include the following:

- Title VII of the Civil Rights Act of 1964, which prohibits discrimination on the basis of race, color, religion, national origin, and sex.

- The Equal Pay Act of 1963, which prohibits employers from paying different wages to men and women who perform essentially the same work under similar working conditions.

- The Americans with Disabilities Act, which prohibits discrimination against persons with disabilities.

- The Age Discrimination in Employment Act, which prohibits discrimination against individuals who are age 40 or above.[36]

A major component of prejudice is **stereotyping**, a rigid, exaggerated, irrational belief associated with a particular group of people.[37] To be successful managing

prejudice The tendency to view people who are different as being deficient.

discrimination When someone acts out their prejudicial attitudes toward people who are the targets of their prejudice.

stereotype A rigid, exaggerated, irrational belief associated with a particular group of people.

diversity, managers need to eliminate harmful stereotypes from their thinking, shedding any biases that negatively affect the workplace. Managers can learn to *value differences*, which means they recognize cultural differences and see the differences with an appreciative attitude. To facilitate this attitude, managers can learn about cultural patterns and typical beliefs of groups to help understand why people act the way they do. It helps to understand the difference between these two ways of thinking, most notably that stereotyping is a barrier to diversity but valuing cultural differences facilitates diversity. These two different ways of thinking are described below and illustrated in Exhibit 12.6.[38]

- *Stereotypes are often based on folklore, media portrayals, and other unreliable sources of information.* In contrast, legitimate cultural differences are backed up by systematic research of real differences.

- *Stereotypes contain negative connotations.* On the other hand, managers who value diversity view differences as potentially positive or neutral. For example, the observation that Asian males are typically less aggressive does not imply they are inferior or superior to white males—it simply means that there is a difference.

- *Stereotypes assume that all members of a group have the same characteristics.* Managers who value diversity recognize that individuals within a group of people may or may not share the same characteristics of the group.[39]

What judgmental beliefs or attitudes do you have that influence your feelings about people who belong to certain groups? To successfully manage diversity, you will need to shed stereotypes while still appreciating the differences among people.

TakeaMoment

Not only should managers rid themselves of stereotypical thinking, they should also recognize the stereotype threat that may jeopardize the performance of at-risk employees. **Stereotype threat** describes the psychological experience of a person who, usually engaged in a task, is aware of a stereotype about his or her identity group suggesting that he or she will not perform well on that task.[40] Suppose you are a member of a minority group presenting complicated market research results to your management team and are anxious about making a good impression. Assume that some members of your audience have a negative stereotype about your identity group. As you ponder this, your anxiety skyrockets and your confidence is shaken. Understandably, your presentation suffers because you are distracted by worries and self-doubt as you invest energy in overcoming the stereotype. The feelings you are experiencing are called *stereotype threat.*

People most affected by stereotype threat are those we consider as disadvantaged in the workplace due to negative stereotypes—racial and ethnic minorities, members of lower socioeconomic classes, women, older people, gay and bisexual men, and people with disabilities. Although anxiety about performing a task may be normal,

stereotype threat A psychological experience of a person who, usually engaged in a task, is aware of a stereotype about his or her identify group suggesting that he or she will not perform well on that task.

EXHIBIT | **12.6** Difference Between Stereotyping and Valuing Cultural Differences

Stereotyping	Valuing Cultural Differences
Is based on false assumptions, anecdotal evidence, or impressions without any direct experience with a group	Views based on cultural differences verified by scientific research methods
Assigns negative traits to members of a group	Views cultural differences as positive or neutral
Assumes that all members of a group have the same characteristics	Does not assume that all individuals within a group have the same characteristics
Example: Suzuko Akoi is an Asian; therefore, she is not aggressive by white, male standards.	Example: As a group, Asians tend to be less aggressive than white, male Americans.

SOURCE: Adapted from Taylor Cox, Jr., and Ruby L. Beale, *Developing Competency to Manage Diversity: Readings, Cases, and Activities* (San Francisco: Berrett-Koehler Publishers, Inc.).

4 Organizing

people with stereotype threat feel an extra scrutiny and worry that their failure will reflect not only on themselves as individuals but on the larger group to which they belong. As Beyoncé Knowles said, "It's like you have something to prove, and you don't want to mess it up and be a negative reflection on black women."[41]

Ethnocentrism

Valuing diversity by recognizing, welcoming, and cultivating differences among people so they can develop their unique talents and be effective organizational members is difficult to achieve. Ethnocentrism can be a roadblock to this type of thinking. **Ethnocentrism** is the belief that one's own group and subculture are inherently superior to other groups and cultures. Ethnocentrism makes it difficult to value diversity. Viewing one's own culture as the best culture is a natural tendency among most people. Moreover, the business world still tends to reflect the values, behaviors, and assumptions based on the experiences of a rather homogeneous, white, middle-class, male workforce. Indeed, most theories of management presume that workers share similar values, beliefs, motivations, and attitudes about work and life in general. These theories presume one set of behaviors best helps an organization to be productive and effective and therefore should be adopted by all employees.[42]

Ethnocentric viewpoints and a standard set of cultural practices produce a **monoculture**, a culture that accepts only one way of doing things and one set of values and beliefs, which can cause problems for minority employees. People of color, women, gay people, the disabled, the elderly, and other diverse employees may feel undue pressure to conform, may be victims of stereotyping attitudes, and may be presumed deficient because they are different. White, heterosexual men, many of whom do not fit the notion of the "ideal" employee, may also feel uncomfortable with the monoculture and resent stereotypes that label white males as racists and sexists. Valuing diversity means ensuring that *all* people are given equal opportunities in the workplace.[43]

The goal for organizations seeking cultural diversity is pluralism rather than a monoculture and ethnorelativism rather than ethnocentrism. **Ethnorelativism** is the belief that groups and subcultures are inherently equal. **Pluralism** means that an organization accommodates several subcultures. Movement toward pluralism seeks to fully integrate into the organization the employees who otherwise would feel isolated and ignored. To promote pluralism in its Mountain View corporate headquarters, chefs at Google's corporate cafeteria ensure that its menu accommodates the different tastes of its ethnically diverse workforce.

ethnocentrism The belief that one's own group or subculture is inherently superior to other groups or cultures.

monoculture A culture that accepts only one way of doing things and one set of values and beliefs.

ethnorelativism The belief that groups and subcultures are inherently equal.

pluralism An environment in which the organization accommodates several subcultures, including employees who would otherwise feel isolated and ignored.

Google

Innovative Way

Employees in Google's corporate headquarters come from all corners of the world, but they feel a little closer to home when they see familiar foods from their homeland on the cafeteria menu. With a goal of satisfying a diverse, ethnically varied palate, Google's first food guru and chef Charlie Ayers designed menus that reflected his eclectic tastes yet also met the needs of an increasingly diverse workforce. He created his own dishes, searched all types of restaurants for new recipes, and often got some of his best ideas from foreign-born employees. For example, a Filipino accountant offered a recipe for chicken *adobo*, a popular dish from her native country. Scattered around the Googleplex are cafes specializing in Southwestern, Italian, California-Mediterranean, and vegetarian cuisines. And because more and more Googlers originally hail from Asia, employees can find sushi at the Japanese-themed Pacific Café or Thai red curry beef at the East Meets West Café.

Google believes food can be a tool for supporting an inclusive workplace. The array of menu options gives people a chance to try new things and learn more about their coworkers. And Google knows that when people need a little comfort and familiarity, nothing takes the edge off of working in a foreign country like eating food that reminds you of home.[44]

Many of today's organizations, like Google, are making conscious efforts to shift from a monoculture perspective to one of pluralism. Others, however, are still hindered by stereotypical thinking. Consider a recent report from the National Bureau of Economic Research, entitled "Are Greg and Emily More Employable than Lakisha and Jamal?" which shows that employers often unconsciously discriminate against job applicants based solely on the Afrocentric names on their résumé. In interviews prior to the research, most human resource managers surveyed said they expected only a small gap and some expected to find a pattern of reverse discrimination. The results showed instead that white-sounding names got 50 percent more callbacks than black-sounding names, even when skills and experience were equal.[45] Discrimination's reach extends beyond U.S. borders. One study conducted in France revealed that a job candidate with a North African-sounding name had three times less chance than one with a French-sounding name to get an interview.[46]

Factors Affecting Women's Careers

Despite years of progress by women in the workforce, many find their career goals are still unattainable or difficult to achieve. In addition, men as a group still have the benefit of higher wages and faster promotions. In the United States in 2005, for example, women employed full-time earned 81 cents for every dollar that men earned.[47] Both the glass ceiling and the decision to "opt out" of a high-pressure career have an impact on women's advancement opportunities and pay. Yet women are sometimes favored in leadership roles for demonstrating behaviors and attitudes that help them succeed in the workplace, a factor called "the female advantage."

Glass Ceiling

The **glass ceiling** is an invisible barrier that separates women from top management positions. They can look up through the ceiling and see top management, but prevailing attitudes and stereotypes are invisible obstacles to their own advancement. This barrier also impedes the career progress of minorities.

In addition, women and minorities are often excluded from informal manager networks and often don't get access to the type of general and line management experience that is required for moving to the top.[48] Research suggests the existence of *glass walls* that serve as invisible barriers to important lateral movement within the organization. Glass walls, like exclusion from manager networks, bar experience in areas such as line supervision that would enable women and minorities to advance vertically.[49]

Evidence that the glass ceiling persists is the distribution of women and minorities, who are clustered at the bottom levels of the corporate hierarchy. Among minority groups, women have made the biggest strides in recent years, but they still represent only 15.7 percent of corporate officers in America's 500 largest companies, up from 12.5 percent in 2000 and 8.7 percent in 1995.[50] In 2007, just seven companies, or 1 percent, among the *Fortune* 500 companies had female CEOs.[51] And both male and female African Americans and Hispanics continue to hold only a small percentage of all management positions in the United States.[52]

Women and minorities also make less money. As shown in Exhibit 12.7, African-American men earn about 22 percent less, white women 24 percent less, and Hispanic men 37 percent less than white males. Minority women fare even worse, with African-American women earning 35 percent less and Hispanic women 46 percent less than white males.[53]

Another sensitive issue related to the glass ceiling is homosexuals in the workplace. Many gay men and lesbians believe they will not be accepted as they are and risk losing their jobs or their chances for advancement. Gay employees of color are particularly hesitant to disclose their sexual orientation at work because by doing so they risk a double dose of discrimination.[54] Although some examples of openly gay corporate leaders can be found, such as David Geffen, co-founder of DreamWorks SKG, and Ford Vice Chairman Allan D. Gilmour, most managers still believe staying in the closet is the only way they can succeed at work. Thus, gays and lesbians often

glass ceiling Invisible barrier that separates women and minorities from top management positions.

EXHIBIT | 12.7

The Wage Gap

SOURCE: "2006 Median Annual Earnings by Race and Sex," U.S. Census Bureau, Current Population Survey, 2007 Annual Social and Economic Supplement, http://www.infoplease.com/us/census/median-earnings-by-race-2006.html.

fabricate heterosexual identities to keep their jobs or avoid running into the glass ceiling they see other employees encounter.

Opt-Out Trend

Many women are never hitting the glass ceiling because they choose to get off the fast track long before it comes into view. In recent years, an ongoing discussion concerns something referred to as the *opt-out trend*. In a recent survey of nearly 2,500 women and 653 men, 37 percent of highly qualified women report that they voluntarily left the workforce at some point in their careers, compared to only 24 percent of similarly qualified men.[55]

Quite a debate rages over the reasons for the larger number of women who drop out of mainstream careers. Opt-out proponents say women are deciding that corporate success isn't worth the price in terms of reduced family and personal time, greater stress, and negative health effects.[56] For example, Marge Magner left her job as CEO of Citigroup's Consumer Group after suffering both the death of her mother and a personal life-changing accident in the same year. In evaluating her reasons, Magner said she realized that "life is about everything, not just the work."

One school of thought says women don't want corporate power and status in the same way that men do, and clawing one's way up the corporate ladder has become less appealing. Yet critics argue that this view is just another way to blame women themselves for the dearth of female managers at higher levels.[57] Vanessa Castagna, for example, left JCPenney after decades with the company not because she wanted more family or personal time but because she kept getting passed over for top jobs.[58] Although some women are voluntarily leaving the fast track, many more genuinely want to move up the corporate ladder but find their paths blocked. Fifty-five percent of executive women surveyed by Catalyst said they aspire to senior leadership levels.[59] In addition, a survey of 103 women voluntarily leaving executive jobs in *Fortune* 1000 companies found that corporate culture was cited as the number one reason for leaving.[60] The greatest disadvantages of women leaders stem largely from prejudicial attitudes and a heavily male-oriented corporate culture.[61] Some years ago, when Procter & Gamble asked the female executives it considered "regretted losses" (that is, high performers the company wanted to retain) why they left their jobs, the most common answer was that they didn't feel valued by the company.[62]

New Manager's Self-Test

Are You Tuned Into Gender Differences?

How much do you know about gender differences in behavior? Please answer whether each item below is True or False. Answer all questions before looking at the answers at the bottom of the page.

	True	False
1. Men control the content of conversations, and they work harder to keep conversations going.	_____	_____
2. Women use less personal space than men.	_____	_____
3. A male speaker is listened to more carefully than a female speaker even when they make an identical presentation.	_____	_____
4. In the classroom, male students receive more reprimands and criticism.	_____	_____
5. Men are more likely to interrupt women than to interrupt other men.	_____	_____
6. Female managers communicate with more emotional openness and drama than male managers.	_____	_____
7. Women are more likely to answer questions not addressed to them.	_____	_____
8. In general, men smile more than women do.	_____	_____
9. Both male and female direct reports see female managers as better communicators than male managers.	_____	_____
10. In a classroom, teachers are more likely to give verbal praise to female students.	_____	_____

SCORING AND INTERPRETATION: Check your answers below. If you scored seven or more correctly, consider yourself perceptive and observant about gender behavior. If you scored three or fewer, you may want to tune in to the gender dynamics you are missing.

SOURCE: Myra Sadker and Joyce Kaser, *The Communications Gender Gap* (Washington, DC: Mid-Atlantic Center for Sex Equity, 1984).

Answers 1: False (men control content, women work harder); 2: True; 3: True; 4: True; 5: True; 6: False (managers of both sexes communicate about the same way); 7: False; 8: False (women smile more); 9: True; 10: False.

4 Organizing

The Female Advantage

Some people think women might actually be better managers, partly because of a more collaborative, less hierarchical, relationship-oriented approach that is in tune with today's global and multicultural environment.[63] As attitudes and values change with changing generations, the qualities women seem to naturally possess may lead to a gradual role reversal in organizations. For example, a stunning gender reversal is taking place in U.S. education, with girls taking over almost every leadership role from kindergarten to graduate school. In addition, women of all races and ethnic groups are outpacing men in earning bachelor's and master's degrees. In most higher education institutions, women make up 58 percent of enrolled students.[64] By 2010, the Department of Education expects the girl-boy ratio to be 60 to 40.[65] Among 25- to 29-year-olds, 32 percent of women have college degrees, compared to 27 percent of men. Women are rapidly closing the M.D. and Ph.D. gap, and they make up about half of all U.S. law students, half of all undergraduate business majors, and about 30 percent of MBA candidates. Overall, women's participation in both the labor force and civic affairs steadily increased since the mid-1950s, while men's participation has slowly but steadily declined.[66]

According to James Gabarino, an author and professor of human development at Cornell University, women are "better able to deliver in terms of what modern society requires of people—paying attention, abiding by rules, being verbally competent, and dealing with interpersonal relationships in offices."[67] His observation is supported by the fact that female managers are typically rated higher by subordinates on interpersonal skills as well as on factors such as task behavior, communication, ability to motivate others, and goal accomplishment.[68] Recent research found a correlation between balanced gender composition in companies (that is, roughly equal male and female representation) and higher organizational performance. Moreover, a study by Catalyst indicates that organizations with the highest percentage of women in top management financially outperform, by about 35 percent, those with the lowest percentage of women in higher-level jobs.[69]

TakeaMoment | Complete the New Manager Self-Test on page 355 to generate more awareness of gender differences in behavior.

CULTURAL COMPETENCE

A corporate culture, as discussed in Chapter 3, is defined by the values, beliefs, understandings, and norms shared by members of the organization. Although some corporate cultures foster diversity, many managers struggle to create a culture that values and nurtures its diverse employees. Managers who have made strategic decisions to foster diversity need a plan that moves a corporate culture toward one that reduces obstacles for disadvantaged employees. A successful diversity plan leads to a workforce that demonstrates *cultural competence* in the long run. **Cultural competence** is the ability to interact effectively with people of different cultures.[70]

Exhibit 12.8 illustrates the five-step process for implementing a diversity plan.[71] These steps create cultural competence among employees by helping them better understand, communicate with, and successfully interact with diverse coworkers.

Step 1: Uncover diversity problems in the organization. Most doctors can't make a medical diagnosis without first examining the patient. Similarly, organizations cannot assess their progress toward cultural competence without first investigating where the culture is right now. A *cultural audit* is a tool that identifies problems or areas needing improvement in a corporation's culture. The cultural audit is completed by employees who answer the following types of questions: How do promotion rates compare? Is there pay disparity between managers in the same pay grade? Does a glass ceiling limit the advancement of women and minorities? Answers to

cultural competence The ability to interact effectively with people of different cultures.

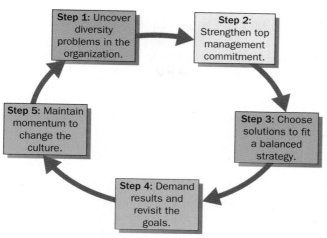

EXHIBIT 12.8

Five Steps to Develop Diversity

SOURCE: Based on Ann M. Morrison, *The New Leaders: Guidelines on Leadership Diversity in America* (San Francisco: Jossey-Bass Publishers, 1992), p. 160.

these questions help managers assess the cultural competence of the organization and focus their diversity efforts on specific problems.

Step 2: Strengthen top management commitment. The most important component of a successful diversity strategy is management commitment, leadership, and support.[72] Some of the ways that top managers demonstrate their support of diversity efforts are by allocating time and money to diversity activities, supporting the recommendations of problem-solving task forces, and communicating the commitment to diversity through speeches and vision and mission statements. Committed top managers also make diversity a priority by setting an example for others to follow.

Step 3: Choose solutions to fit a balanced strategy. The best solutions to diversity problems are those that address the organization's most pressing problems uncovered during Step 1. To be most effective, solutions should be presented in a balanced strategy and address three factors: education, enforcement, and exposure. *Education* may include new training programs that improve awareness and diversity skills. *Enforcement* means providing incentives for employees who demonstrate new behaviors and disciplinary action for those who violate diversity standards. A good example is Denny's restaurants. After facing discrimination lawsuits in the early 1990s, Denny's rebounded with a multifaceted diversity program that included 25 percent discretionary bonuses to all senior managers who significantly improved their record of hiring and promoting minority workers.[73] *Exposure* involves exposing traditional managers to nontraditional peers to help break down stereotypical beliefs. For example, a company might team a white male manager with a female African-American manager.

Step 4: Demand results and revisit the goals. The simple rule "what doesn't get measured doesn't get done" applies to diversity efforts. Diversity performance should be measured by numerical goals to ensure solutions are being implemented successfully. Numerical goals demonstrate that diversity is tied to business objectives. Examples of numerical goals might include tracking the salaries, rates of promotion, and managerial positions for women and minorities. But these personnel statistics don't completely measure an organization's progress toward cultural competence. Other measures might include productivity and profitability tied to diversity efforts, employee opinions about their coworkers, and an assessment of the corporation's ability to provide a satisfying work environment for all employees.[74]

Step 5: Maintain momentum to change the culture. Success with any of the previous four steps is a powerful motivator for continuing diversity efforts. Corporations should use these successes as fuel to move forward and leverage for more progress.

4 Organizing

DIVERSITY INITIATIVES AND PROGRAMS

Today's managers choose from a variety of solutions that create cultural competence. As described in Step 3 of Exhibit 12.8, organizations may develop initiatives and programs that address their unique diversity problems. These initiatives may include: (1) changing structures and policies, (2) focusing on diversity recruiting, (3) establishing mentor relationships, (4) accommodating special needs; and (5) offering training and education.

Changing Structures and Policies

Many policies within organizations originally were designed to fit the stereotypical male employee. Now leading companies are changing structures and policies to facilitate and support diversity. A survey of *Fortune* 1,000 companies conducted by the Center for Creative Leadership found that 85 percent of companies surveyed have formal policies against racism and gender discrimination, and 76 percent have structured grievance procedures and complaint review processes.[75] Companies are also developing policies to support the recruitment and career advancement of diverse employees. At least half of *Fortune* 1,000 companies have staff dedicated exclusively to encouraging diversity. Increasingly, organizations such as Procter & Gamble, Ernst & Young, and Allstate Insurance are tying managers' bonuses and promotions to how well they diversify the workforce. Exhibit 12.9 illustrates some of the most common diversity initiatives.

mentor A higher-ranking, senior organizational member who is committed to providing upward mobility and support to a protégé's professional career.

Expanding Recruitment Efforts

For many organizations, a new approach to recruitment means making better use of formal recruiting strategies, offering internship programs to give people opportunities, and developing creative ways to draw on previously unused labor markets. Nationwide's Scholars Program brings in Hispanic and African-American college students for a three-year program that includes summer internships and yearlong mentoring.[76] Marathon Ashland Petroleum created a six-point recruiting strategy to increase diversity, including: (1) recruiting corporate-wide and cross-functionally, (2) building relationships with first- and second-tiered schools to recruit minority students, (3) offering internships for racial and ethnic minorities, (4) offering minority scholarships, (5) establishing informal mentoring programs, and (6) forming affiliations with minority organizations.[77]

Establishing Mentor Relationships

The successful advancement of diverse group members means that organizations must find ways to eliminate the glass ceiling. One of the most successful structures to accomplish this goal is the mentoring relationship. A **mentor** is a higher-ranking organizational member who is committed to providing upward mobility and support to a protégé's professional career.[78] Mentoring provides minorities and women with direct training and inside information on the norms and expectations of the organization. A mentor also acts as a friend or counselor,

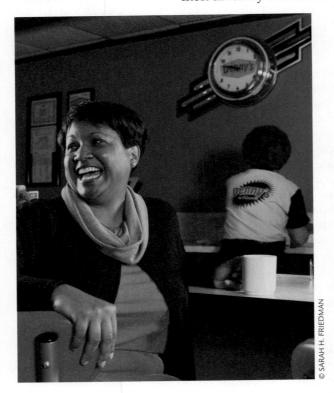

© SARAH H. FRIEDMAN

Concept Connection   Denny's Restaurants, which was hit with a series of discrimination lawsuits in the early 1990s, has been **changing structures and policies** to promote and support diversity. The company responded to the discrimination charges with aggressive minority hiring and supplier-diversity efforts. In July 2006, *Black Enterprise* magazine ranked Denny's at the top of its list of "Best 40 Companies for Diversity." Around 51 percent of Denny's employees, 43 percent of franchisees, and 36 percent of managers are members of minority groups.

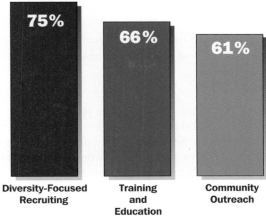

75%

66%

61%

**Diversity-Focused
Recruiting**

**Training
and
Education**

**Community
Outreach**

SOURCE: Adapted from data in "Impact of Diversity Initiatives on
the Bottom Line: A SHRM Survey of the *Fortune* 1000,"pp; S12-S14, in
Fortune, special advertising section, "Keeping Your Edge: Managing a
Diverse Corporate Culture," produced in association with the Society
for Human Resource Management, http://www.fortune.com/sections.

enabling the employee to feel more confident and capable. Joseph Cleveland has
made a point of helping young African
Americans navigate the corporate maze
in his career at General Electric and Lockheed Martin. For Pamela Blow-Mitchell,
Cleveland's mentoring changed the course
of her career and enabled her to seize
opportunities she might otherwise have
missed. "He kind of dunked down deep in
the organization to initiate a conversation
with someone that he saw potential in,"
said Mitchell. "At the time, I could not see
the range of opportunities, but I trusted
his advice."[79]

One researcher who studied the career
progress of high-potential minorities found
that those who advance the furthest all
share one characteristic—a strong mentor or network of mentors who nurtured
their professional development.[80] However,
research also indicates that minorities, as
well as women, are much less likely than
men to develop mentoring relationships.[81]
Women and minorities might not seek mentors because they feel that job competency
should be enough to succeed, or they might feel uncomfortable seeking out a mentor
when most of the senior executives are white males. Women might fear that initiating a
mentoring relationship could be misunderstood as a romantic overture, whereas male
mentors may think of women as mothers, wives, or sisters rather than as executive
material. Cross-race mentoring relationships sometimes leave both parties uncomfortable, but the mentoring of minority employees must often be across race because of
the low number of minorities in upper-level positions. The few minorities and women
who have reached the upper ranks often are overwhelmed with mentoring requests
from people like themselves, and they may feel uncomfortable in highly visible minor-
ity-minority or female-female mentoring relationships, which isolate them from the
white male status quo.

© STEVEN RUBIN/THE IMAGE WORKS

Concept Connection Fannie Mae, a major provider of home mortgage
funds, was in the news for all the wrong reasons after the U.S. government seized
control of it and Freddie Mac to avoid a collapse of the giant firms due to losses from
mortgage defaults. Fannie Mae's CEO was ousted and the firm is being restructured,
but the company's commitment to workforce diversity remains solid. Fannie Mae
offers a structured **mentoring program** to enhance individual capabilities and career
development. Here the director of legal operations is mentoring two Fannie Mae
employees. A partnership with a more experienced employee provides valuable insights
and contacts for minorities and women wanting to advance their skills and careers.

4 Organizing

Even as a new manager, you may have an opportunity to act as a mentor to a younger or less-experienced minority employee. Use your interpersonal skills to build the person's confidence and help him or her develop valuable contacts. Assist the employee in navigating the office politics and learning the unwritten rules about how things are done in the organization.

The solution is for organizations to overcome some of the barriers to mentor relationships between white males and minorities. When organizations can institutionalize the value of white males actively seeking women and minority protégés, the benefits will mean that women and minorities will be steered into pivotal jobs and positions critical to advancement. Mentoring programs also are consistent with the Civil Rights Act of 1991 that requires the diversification of middle and upper management.

Accommodating Special Needs

Many people have special needs of which top managers may be unaware. For example, if numerous people entering the organization at the lower level are single parents, the company can reassess job scheduling and opportunities for child care. If a substantial labor pool is non-English–speaking, training materials and information packets can be provided in another language, or the organization can provide English language classes.

In many families today, both parents work, which means that the company can provide structures to deal with child care, maternity or paternity leave, flexible work schedules, telecommuting or home-based employment, and perhaps part-time employment or seasonal hours that reflect the school year. The key to attracting and keeping elderly or disabled workers may include long-term-care insurance and special health or life insurance benefits. Alternative work scheduling also may be important for these groups of workers. Organizations struggling with generational diversity must find ways to meet the needs of workers at different ages and places in the life cycle.[82] Pitney Bowes created the Life Balance Resources program to help employees in different generations cope with life cycle issues, such as helping Generation Y workers find their first apartments or cars, assisting Generation X employees in locating child care or getting home loans, helping baby boomers plan for retirement, and aiding older workers in researching insurance and long-term care options.[83]

Another issue for U.S. companies is that racial/ethnic minorities and immigrants often had fewer educational opportunities than other groups. Some companies work with high schools to provide fundamental skills in literacy and math, or they provide these programs within the company to upgrade employees to appropriate educational levels. The movement toward providing educational services for employees can be expected to increase for immigrants and the economically disadvantaged in the years to come.

Providing Diversity Skills Training

Most of today's organizations provide special training, called **diversity training**, to help people identify their own cultural boundaries, prejudices, and stereotypes and develop the skills for managing and working in a diverse workplace. By some estimates, about $80 billion has been invested in corporate diversity programs over the past ten years, much of it spent on training.[84] Working or living within a multicultural context requires a person to use interaction skills that transcend the skills typically effective when dealing with others from one's own in-group.[85]

The first step is typically *diversity awareness training* to make employees aware of the assumptions they make and to increase people's sensitivity and openness to those who are different from them. A basic aim of awareness training is to help people recognize that hidden and overt biases direct their thinking about specific individuals and groups. If people can come away from a training session recognizing that they prejudge people and that this tendency needs to be consciously addressed in

diversity training Special training designed to educate employees about the importance of diversity, make people aware of their own biases, and teach them skills for communicating and working in a diverse workplace.

communications with and treatment of others, an important goal of diversity awareness training has been reached.

The next step is *diversity skills training* to help people learn how to communicate and work effectively in a diverse environment. Rather than just attempting to increase employees' understanding and sensitivity, this training gives people concrete skills they can use in everyday situations, such as how to handle conflict in a constructive manner or how to modify nonverbal communication such as body language and facial expression.[86] Verizon Communications uses an online training tool where managers can tap into various diversity scenarios that might occur in the workplace and see how they can manage them in an appropriate way.[87] In addition to online training, companies may also use classroom sessions, experiential exercises, videotapes or DVDs, and outside consulting firms that help organizations with diversity management issues.

Concept Connection A counselor for Camba, a social services group in New York City, directs a role-playing session during a course to help immigrants apply for jobs at Whole Foods Market. The grocer helped Camba develop the course to support its **diversity recruiting** goals. The classes include instruction on organic foods, customer service training, and tours of a Whole Foods Market.

Increasing Awareness of Sexual Harassment

Sexual harassment creates an unhealthy and unproductive work environment. To eliminate it, companies may offer sexual harassment awareness programs that create awareness of what defines sexual harassment and the legal ramifications of violations. Although psychological closeness between men and women in the workplace may be a positive experience, sexual harassment is not. Sexual harassment is illegal. As a form of sexual discrimination, sexual harassment in the workplace is a violation of Title VII of the 1964 Civil Rights Act. Sexual harassment in the classroom is a violation of Title VIII of the Education Amendment of 1972. The following list categorizes various forms of sexual harassment as defined by one university:

- *Generalized.* This form involves sexual remarks and actions that are not intended to lead to sexual activity but that are directed toward a coworker based solely on gender and reflect on the entire group.

- *Inappropriate/offensive.* Though not sexually threatening, it causes discomfort in a coworker, whose reaction in avoiding the harasser may limit his or her freedom and ability to function in the workplace.

- *Solicitation with promise of reward.* This action treads a fine line as an attempt to "purchase" sex, with the potential for criminal prosecution.

- *Coercion with threat of punishment.* The harasser coerces a coworker into sexual activity by using the threat of power (through recommendations, grades, promotions, and so on) to jeopardize the victim's career.

- *Sexual crimes and misdemeanors.* The highest level of sexual harassment, these acts would, if reported to the police, be considered felony crimes and misdemeanors.[88]

Statistics in Canada indicate that between 40 and 70 percent of women and about 5 percent of men have been sexually harassed at work.[89] The situation in the United States is just as dire. Over a ten-year period, the Equal Employment Opportunity Commission shows a 150 percent increase in the number of sexual harassment cases filed annually.[90] About 10 percent of those were filed by males. The Supreme Court held that same-sex harassment as well as harassment of men by female coworkers is just as illegal as the harassment of women by men. In the suit that prompted the court's decision, a male oil-rig worker claimed he was singled out by other members of the all-male crew for crude sex play, unwanted touching, and threats of rape.[91] A growing number of men are urging recognition that sexual harassment is not just a woman's problem.[92]

TakeaMoment

> As a new manager, be careful about a romantic relationship in the workplace. In particular, steer clear of such relationships with superiors or subordinates, which is a slippery ethical area. Know what sexual harassment means, and make sure everyone in your team or department understands that sexual harassment is disrespectful and against the law.

NEW DIVERSITY INITIATIVES

Ninety-one percent of companies responding to a survey by the Society for Human Resource Management believe that diversity initiatives help maintain a competitive advantage. Some specific benefits they cited include improving employee morale, decreasing interpersonal conflict, facilitating progress in new markets, and increasing the organization's creativity.[93] In addition to the ideas already discussed, two new approaches to diversity management—multicultural teams and employee networks—have arisen in response to the rapid change and complexity of the twenty-first–century organization.

Multicultural Teams

Companies have long known that putting together teams made up of members from different functional areas results in better problem solving and decision making. Now, they are recognizing that **multicultural teams**—teams made up of members from diverse national, racial, ethnic, and cultural backgrounds—provide even greater potential for enhanced creativity, innovation, and value in today's global marketplace.[94] Research indicates that diverse teams generate more and better alternatives to problems and produce more creative solutions than homogeneous teams.[95] A team made up of people with different perspectives, backgrounds, and cultural values creates a healthy mix of ideas and leads to greater creativity and better decisions.

Some organizations, such as RhonePoulenc Rorer (RPR), based in Collegeville, Pennsylvania, are committed to mixing people from diverse countries and cultures, from the top to the bottom of the organization. Fifteen nationalities are represented in RPR's top management teams, including a French CEO, an Austrian head of operations, an American general counsel, an Egyptian head of human resources, and an Italian director of corporate communications.[96]

Despite their many advantages,[97] multicultural teams are more difficult to manage because of the increased potential for miscommunication and misunderstanding. Multicultural teams typically have more difficulty learning to communicate and work together smoothly, but with effective cross-cultural training and good management, teams can learn to work well together.[98] One management team videotaped its meetings so members could see how their body language reflects cultural differences. An American manager remarked, "I couldn't believe how even my physical movements dominated the table, while Ron [a Filipino American] . . . actually worked his way off-camera within the first five minutes."[99]

Employee Network Groups

Employee network groups are based on social identity, such as gender or race, and are organized by employees to focus on concerns of employees from that group.[100]

multicultural teams Teams made up of members from diverse national, racial, ethnic, and cultural backgrounds.

employee network groups Groups based on social identity, such as gender or race, and organized by employees to focus on concerns of employees from that group.

Network groups pursue a variety of activities, such as meetings to educate top managers, mentoring programs, networking events, training sessions and skills seminars, minority intern programs, and community volunteer activities. These activities give people a chance to meet, interact with, and develop social and professional ties to others throughout the organization, which may include key decision makers. Network groups are a powerful way to reduce social isolation for women and minorities, help these employees be more effective, and enable members to achieve greater career advancement. A recent study confirms that network groups can be important tools for helping organizations retain managerial-level minority employees.[101] For example, Best Buy's Julie Gilbert launched a women's leadership forum, known as WOLF, to get more women involved in solving core business problems and to pull frontline employees into the top ranks. Gilbert's WOLF teams choose a project, create a solution, and then implement the ideas in stores within three months. The end result is that recruitment of women regional sales managers at Best Buy is up 100 percent over the previous year, and turnover among women managers has dropped almost 10 percentage points.[102]

An important characteristic of network groups is that they are created informally by employees, not the organization, and membership is voluntary. Employee networks for minorities who have faced barriers to advancement in organizations, including African Americans, Hispanics, American Indians, Asian Americans, women, gays and lesbians, and disabled employees, show tremendous growth. Even managers who once thought of minority networks as "gripe groups" are now seeing them as essential to organizational success because they help to retain minority employees, enhance diversity efforts, and spark new ideas that can benefit the organization.[103] At Kraft Foods, networks are considered critical to the success of multicultural teams because they build awareness and acceptance of cultural differences and help people feel more comfortable working together.[104] In general, female and minority employees who participate in a network group feel more pride about their work and are more optimistic about their careers than those who do not have the support of a network.[105]

ch12 A MANAGER'S ESSENTIALS: WHAT HAVE WE LEARNED?

- The domestic and global marketplace is experiencing dramatic demographic changes, including an aging population and growing immigrant and minority populations. Savvy managers recognize that their workforces should reflect this cultural diversity.

- Diversity is defined as all the ways in which employees differ. This definition has been broadened in recent years to be more inclusive and recognize a broad spectrum of characteristics including age, religion, physical ability, race, ethnicity, sexual preference, and more. Because of the complexities of managing a diverse workforce, *managing diversity* is a key management skill today.

- The dividends of diversity are numerous and include better use of employee talent, increased understanding of customers in the marketplace, enhanced breadth of understanding in leadership positions, increased quality of team problem-solving, and reduced costs associated with high turnover, absenteeism, and lawsuits.

- All employees bring to the workplace opinions and attitudes that affect their ability to treat people equally. Some of these issues include prejudice, discrimination, and stereotyping. The performance of minorities and other disadvantaged workers may be affected by a *stereotype threat*, a psychological reaction by employees that is triggered by worry and concern that others may doubt their abilities due to unfair stereotypes. Managers should be aware of the challenges minority employees face and be prepared to handle them, including issues related to ethnocentrism, the glass ceiling, the opt-out trend, and the female advantage.

■ When a corporate culture embraces diversity and fosters an environment where all people thrive equally, they have achieved cultural competence. The five steps toward cultural competence involve identifying diversity issues, strengthening top management commitment, choosing solutions, demanding results, and maintaining momentum.

■ Two strategies frequently used by corporations to enhance advancement opportunities for diverse group members include establishing mentoring relationships and accommodating the unique needs of employees. Mentoring relationships can provide upward mobility and support to a protégé's professional career. By accommodating the special needs of employees, organizations demonstrate their care and concern for employees.

■ Training programs give people the tools and information they need to treat coworkers fairly and without bias. Training programs may include diversity skills training and sexual harassment training. Two recent approaches to supporting and leveraging the power of diversity in organizations are multicultural teams and employee network groups.

ch12 DISCUSSION QUESTIONS

1. If you were a senior manager at a company such as Mitsubishi, Allstate Insurance, or Wal-Mart, how would you address the challenges faced by minority employees?

2. Some people argue that social class is a major source of cultural differences, yet social class is not listed as a primary or secondary dimension in Exhibit 12.4. Discuss reasons it is not there.

3. Evaluate your own experiences so far with people from other backgrounds. How well do you think those experiences prepared you to understand the unique needs and dilemmas of a diverse workforce?

4. What is the glass ceiling, and why do you think it has proven to be such a barrier to women and minorities?

5. How might employee network groups contribute to the advancement of women and minorities to higher-level positions in an organization?

6. In preparing an organization to accept diversity, do you think it is more important to change the corporate culture or to change structures and policies? Explain.

7. If a North American corporation could choose either high-context or low-context communications, which do you think would be best for the company's long-term health? Discuss.

8. Why do you think a large number of women are opting out of corporate management? Discuss whether this trend is likely to continue over the next 10 years.

9. As a manager, how would you accommodate the special needs of different groups (e.g., single parents, older workers, or employees with poor English language skills or religious restrictions) without appearing to show favoritism or offending other groups?

10. How can organizations strike a balance between respecting and meeting the needs of a diverse workforce and shaping a high-performance corporate culture where shared values contribute to the accomplishment of strategic goals?

11. You are a manager at an organization that has decided it needs a more diverse workforce. What steps or techniques will you use to accomplish this goal? What steps will you take to retain diverse employees once you have successfully recruited them?

ch12 MANAGEMENT IN PRACTICE: EXPERIENTIAL EXERCISE

How Tolerant Are You?

For each of the following questions, circle the answer that best describes you.

1. Most of your friends
   a. are very similar to you
   b. are very different from you and from each other
   c. are like you in some respects but different in others

2. When someone does something you disapprove of, you
   a. break off the relationship
   b. tell how you feel but keep in touch
   c. tell yourself it matters little and behave as you always have

3. Which virtue is most important to you?
   a. kindness
   b. objectivity
   c. obedience

4. When it comes to beliefs, you
   a. do all you can to make others see things the same way you do
   b. actively advance your point of view but stop short of argument
   c. keep your feelings to yourself

5. Would you hire a person who has had emotional problems?
   a. no
   b. yes, provided the person shows evidence of complete recovery
   c. yes, if the person is suitable for the job

6. Do you voluntarily read material that supports views different from your own?
   a. never
   b. sometimes
   c. often

7. You react to old people with
   a. patience
   b. annoyance
   c. sometimes a, sometimes b

8. Do you agree with the statement, "What is right and wrong depends upon the time, place, and circumstance"?
   a. strongly agree
   b. agree to a point
   c. strongly disagree

9. Would you marry someone from a different race?
   a. yes
   b. no
   c. probably not

10. If someone in your family were homosexual, you would
    a. view this as a problem and try to change the person to a heterosexual orientation
    b. accept the person as a homosexual with no change in feelings or treatment
    c. avoid or reject the person

11. You react to little children with
    a. patience
    b. annoyance
    c. sometimes a, sometimes b

12. Other people's personal habits annoy you
    a. often
    b. not at all
    c. only if extreme

13. If you stay in a household run differently from yours (cleanliness, manners, meals, and other customs), you
    a. adapt readily
    b. quickly become uncomfortable and irritated
    c. adjust for a while, but not for long

14. Which statement do you agree with most?
    a. We should avoid judging others because no one can fully understand the motives of another person.
    b. People are responsible for their actions and have to accept the consequences.
    c. Both motives and actions are important when considering questions of right and wrong.

Scoring and Interpretation

Circle your score for each of the answers and total the scores:

1. a = 4; b = 0; c = 2
2. a = 4; b = 2; c = 0
3. a = 0; b = 2; c = 4
4. a = 4; b = 2; c = 0
5. a = 4; b = 2; c = 0
6. a = 4; b = 2; c = 0
7. a = 0; b = 4; c = 2
8. a = 0; b = 2; c = 4
9. a = 0; b = 4; c = 2

4 Organizing

10. a = 2; b = 0; c = 4

11. a = 0; b = 4; c = 2

12. a = 4; b = 0; c = 2

13. a = 0; b = 4; c = 2

14. a = 0; b = 4; c = 2

Total Score

0–14: If you score 14 or below, you are a very tolerant person and dealing with diversity comes easily to you.

15–28: You are basically a tolerant person and others think of you as tolerant. In general, diversity presents few problems for you; you may be broad-minded in some areas and have less tolerant ideas in other areas of life, such as attitudes toward older people or male-female social roles.

29–42: You are less tolerant than most people and should work on developing greater tolerance of people different from you. Your low tolerance level could affect your business or personal relationships.

43–56: You have a very low tolerance for diversity. The only people you are likely to respect are those with beliefs similar to your own. You reflect a level of intolerance that could cause difficulties in today's multicultural business environment.

SOURCE: Adapted from the Tolerance Scale by Maria Heiselman, Naomi Miller, and Bob Schlorman, Northern Kentucky University, 1982. In George Manning, Kent Curtis, and Steve McMillen, *Building Community: The Human Side of Work*, (Cincinnati, OH: Thomson Executive Press, 1996): 272–277.

ch12 MANAGEMENT IN PRACTICE: ETHICAL DILEMMA

Sunset Prayers

Frank Piechowski, plant manager for a Minnesota North Woods Appliance Corp. refrigerator plant, just received his instructions from the vice president for manufacturing. He was to hire 40 more temporary workers through Twin Cities Staffing, the local labor agency North Woods used. Frank already knew from past experience that most, if not all, of the new hires available to work the assembly line would be Muslim Somali refugees, people who had immigrated to Minnesota from their war-torn native country en masse over the past 15 years.

North Woods, like all appliance manufacturers, was trying to survive in a highly competitive, mature industry. Appliance companies were competing mainly on price. The entrance of large chains such as Best Buy and Home Depot only intensified the price wars, not to mention that consumers could easily do comparison shopping before leaving home by logging onto the Internet. The pressure to keep production costs low was considerable.

That's where the Somali workers came in. In an effort to keep labor costs low, North Woods was relying more and more on temporary workers rather than increasing the ranks of permanent employees. Frank was quite pleased with the Somalis already at work on the assembly line. Although few in number, they were responsible, hard-working, and willing to work for the wages he could afford to pay.

It was the first time this son of Polish immigrants had ever come into contact with Muslims, but so far, it had gone well. Frank had established a good working relationship with the Somalis' spokesperson, Halima Adan, who explained that unlike most Western faiths, Islamic religious practices were inextricably woven into everyday life. So together, they worked out ways to accommodate Muslim customs. Frank authorized changes in the plant's cafeteria menu so the Somali workers had more options that conformed to their dietary restrictions, and he allowed women to wear traditional clothing as long as they weren't violating safety standards.

After learning that the Somalis would need to perform at least some of the ceremonial washing and prayers they were required to do five times a day during work hours, the plant manager set aside a quiet, clean room where they could observe their 15-minute rituals during their breaks and at sunset. The Maghrib sunset prayers second shift workers had to perform were disruptive to a smooth workflow. Compared to their midday and afternoon rituals, the Muslim faithful had considerably less leeway as to when they said the sunset prayers, and of course, the sun set at a slightly different time each day. But so far, they'd all coped.

But what was he going to do about the sunset prayers with an influx of 40 Somali workers that would dramatically increase the number of people who would need to leave the line to pray? Was it time to modify his policy? He knew that Title VII of the Civil Right Act required that he make "reasonable" accommodations to his employees' religious practices unless doing so would impose an "undue hardship" on the employer. Had he reached the point where the accommodations Halima Adan would probably request crossed the line from reasonable to unreasonable? But if he changed his policy, did he risk alienating his workforce?

What Would You Do?

1. Continue the current policy that leaves it up to the Muslim workers as to when they leave the assembly line to perform their sunset rituals.

2. Try to hire the fewest possible Muslim workers so the work line will be efficient on second shift.

3. Ask the Muslim workers to delay their sunset prayers until a regularly scheduled break occurs, pointing out that North Woods is primarily a place of business, not a house of worship.

SOURCES: Based on Rob Johnson, "30 Muslim Workers Fired for Praying on Job at Dell," *The Tennessean,* (March 10, 2005): http://tennessean.com/local/archives/05/03/66733769.shtml?Element_ID=66733769; Anayat Durrani, "Religious Accommodation for Muslim Employees," *Workforce.com,* www.workforce.com/archive/feature/22/26/98/index.php?ht=muslim%20muslim; U.S. Equal Employment Opportunity Commission, "Questions and Answers about Employer Responsibilities Concerning the Employment of Muslims, Arabs, South Asians, and Sikhs," www.eeoc.gov/facts/backlash-employer.html; and U.S. Department of Commerce, Office of Health and Consumer Goods, "2005 Appliance Industry Outlook," *Trade.gov,* www.ita.doc.gov/td/ocg/outlook05_appliances.pdf.

ch12 CASE FOR CRITICAL ANALYSIS

Draper Manufacturing

"You see what I'm up against?" asked Ralph Draper wearily as he escorted Ted Hanrahan, a diversity consultant, into his modest office on a rainy October day. Ralph was the new CEO of Draper Manufacturing, a small mattress manufacturer. He'd recently moved back to Portland, Oregon, his hometown, to take over the reins of the family-owned company from his ailing father. Ralph and Ted had just come from a contentious meeting of Draper's top managers that vividly illustrated the festering racial tensions Ralph wanted Ted to help alleviate.

It hadn't taken long for sales manager Brent Myers to confront shipping and receiving department head Adam Fox, an African American and the only non-white manager. "Why can't your boys get orders shipped out on time?" Brent demanded. "Isn't there some way you can get them to pay a little less attention to their bling and a little more to their responsibilities?" Adam Fox shot back angrily, "If you tightwads actually hired enough people to get the job done, there wouldn't be any problem." The other managers sat by silently, looking acutely uncomfortable, until the quality control head worked in a joke about his wife. Most laughed loudly, and Ralph took the opportunity to steer the conversation to other agenda topics.

The main challenge Draper faces is the price of oil, which had passed $60 per barrel mark that summer. In addition to powering its operations and shipping, petroleum is an essential raw material for many mattress components, from polyester and thread to foam. Then the Gulf hurricanes caused severe shortages of TDI, the chemical used to make polyurethane foam, a key component. So far, the company had passed its cost increases on to the consumer, but with increased competition from low-priced Asian imports, no one knew how long that strategy would work. To survive in mattress manufacturing, Draper needs to find ways to lower costs and increase productivity. Ralph completely understands why Brent is pressuring Adam to ship orders out more quickly.

The current workforce reflects Draper's determination to keep labor costs low. It employs 90 people full-time, the majority of whom are Asian and Hispanic immigrants and African Americans. Although women make up 75 percent of the workforce, nearly all of the shipping department employees are young African American men. Instead of adding to its permanent workforce, the company hires part-time workers from time to time, mostly Hispanic females. It tends to engage Asians as mechanics and machine operators because human resources head Teresa Burns believes they have superior technical skills. The result is a diverse but polarized workforce. "This is a time everyone needs to pull together," said Ralph. "But what's happening is that each minority group sticks to itself. The blacks and Asians rarely mix, and most of the Mexicans stay to themselves and speak only in Spanish."

When two of the older white shipping employees retired last year, Ralph didn't replace them, hoping to improve efficiency by cutting salary costs. "It seems to me that some of our workers are just downright lazy sometimes." said Ralph. "I myself have talked to Adam about pushing his kids to develop a work ethic. But he insists on blaming the company for the department's problems. You can see why we want your help."

Questions

1. Based on the information in the case, at what stage of diversity awareness do managers at Draper Manufacturing seem to be? Discuss.

2. If you were the shipping and receiving or human resources manager, how do you think you would feel about working at Draper? What are some of the challenges you might face at this company?

3. If you were Ted Hanrahan, what suggestions would you make to Draper's managers to help them move toward successfully managing diversity issues?

SOURCES: Based on "Northern Industries," a case prepared by Rae Andre of Northeastern University; "Interesting Times Indeed. Let's Review, Shall We?" *BedTimes* (December 2005): www.sleepproducts .org/Content/ContentGroups/BEDtimes1/20052/December6/ Interesting_times_indeed.htm; and Jacqueline A. Gilbert, Norma Carr-Rufino, John M. Ivancevich and Millicent Lownes-Jackson, "An Empirical Examination of Inter-Ethnic Stereotypes: Comparing Asian American and African American Employees," *Public Personnel Management* (Summer 2003): 251–266.

---

ch12 ON THE JOB VIDEO CASE

PepsiCo Puts People First

Whether a company employs five or five thousand people, its greatest resource is those workers. Many of today's companies view their workforces as part of their overall competitive strategy—the best people producing the best products. Human resource managers at large firms such as PepsiCo may be viewed as strategic business partners. No longer do they simply sign paychecks, approve vacations, and process health benefit claims. At PepsiCo, HR managers play an integral role in the day-to-day success of the business.

Headquartered in Purchase, New York, PepsiCo is a global organization, with more than 143,000 employees worldwide. The company produces and markets such brands as PepsiCo beverages, Frito-Lay snacks, Gatorade and Tropicana drinks, and Quaker Foods. PepsiCo brand products are available in nearly 200 countries and territories. But recruiting, selecting, training, and managing more than 100,000 workers requires planning to meet the career needs of so many people. To foster long-term career growth, PepsiCo offers a variety of programs and has created its own PepsiCo Career Growth Model, which offers job opportunities to promote employees' knowledge and skills, and abilities in leadership capability, functional excellence, knowing the business, and critical experiences.

PepsiCo's HR managers follow their own Human Resources Competency Model, which defines four key roles played by the HR department:

- As a *strategic partner,* the HR department is charged with aligning the human resource strategy with the business strategy of PepsiCo.

- As a *change agent,* the department focuses on facilitating and leading organization transformation and change initiatives.

- As a *technical functional expert,* the HR department emphasizes mastering and driving efficiency and effectiveness in the core information and administrative processes.

- As an *employee champion,* the department drives employee satisfaction, commitment, and engagement.

Both of these models indicate a high degree of structure within PepsiCo, and the structure helps ensure that everyone's career, benefits, and other needs are met. Employees have a choice of flexible benefits. At Quaker Oats, workers may select time off for adoption, apply for a student loan, or take a leave of absence under the QuakerFlex benefits program. At many locations, they may even enjoy free oatmeal in the morning!

Regardless of job level or brand, PepsiCo looks for the best workers to contribute to the overall performance of the company. "Excellent performance . . . does not happen on its own," writes chairman and CEO Steve Reinemund on the company's Web site. "Our people make it happen. In order to sustain this level of success, we need to ensure that we continue to attract, retain, and develop great people in all of our businesses." At PepsiCo's online Career Center, potential job candidates will find information on what the company looks for in its employees. In turn, PepsiCo offers its workers opportunities such as "exciting career challenges," "world-class training and development," and "excellent compensation." This, in essence, is PepsiCo's social contract with its employees.

Keeping all of this in mind, consider the job of Darryl Claiborne, HR manager for regional sales at PepsiCo's Frito-Lay division. Claiborne works with Frito-Lay's route sales reps, who sell and deliver their products directly to retailers. Claiborne and his reps understand that their success correlates directly with Frito-Lay's profitability. So, as an HR strategic partner, Claiborne looks for ways to help his reps manage and grow their business. Claiborne communicates regularly with his reps, on how well they are doing and where they need help. He continually reengineers their routes to make sure they can steadily increase sales. Claiborne embraces the company's "Know the Business" principles, the set of guidelines created to help managers understand the company, its mission, and the way its employees achieve success. "PepsiCo—Taste the Success!" invites the company Web site. Claiborne, his route sales reps, and more than 140,000 other employees intend to do just that.

Questions

1. In what ways could Darryl Claiborne be considered an employee champion?

2. Why is this important to PepsiCo's efforts to build human capital?

3. In essence, Darryl Claiborne engages in on-the-job training as he communicates with and accompanies his reps on their sales rounds. How is this an important part of their effectiveness as a workforce?

SOURCES: Company Web sites, *http://www.pepsico.com* and *http://www.pepsicojobs.com*, accessed August 19, 2004; PepsiCo career and HR materials, "Knowing the Business: Resources Guide" and "Career Framework: Functional Competency Model."

4 Organizing

ch12 BIZ FLIX VIDEO CASE

U-571

This action-packed thriller deals with a U.S. submarine crew's efforts to retrieve an Enigma encryption device from a disabled German submarine during World War II. After the crew gets the device, the U.S. submarine sinks, and they must use the German submarine to escape from enemy destroyers. The film's almost nonstop action and extraordinary special effects will look and sound best with a home theater system.

This scene is an edited composite of the "To Be a Captain" sequence early in the film. The S33, an older U.S. submarine, is embarking on a secret mission. Before departure, the S33's officers receive a briefing on their mission from Office of Naval Intelligence representatives on board. Executive officer Lt. Andrew Tyler (Matthew McConaughey) reports on the submarine's status to Lt. Commander Mike Dahlgren (Bill Paxton). The film continues with the S33 finding the disabled German submarine.

What to Watch for and Ask Yourself

1. What aspects of leadership does Dahlgren say are important for a submarine commander?

2. Which leadership behaviors or traits does he emphasize?

3. Are these traits or behaviors right for this situation? Why or why not?

ch12 ENDNOTES

1. Lawrence Otis Graham, *Proversity: Getting Past Face Values and Finding the Soul of People* (New York: John Wiley & Sons, 1997).

2. Russ Wiles, "Businesses Encourage Employees to Learn Spanish," *USA Today,* December 7, 2007 http://www.usatoday.com/money/workplace/2007-12-08-spanish_n.htm?loc=interstitialskip (accessed March 17, 2008).

3. Susan Caminiti, "The Diversity Factor," *Fortune* (October 19, 2007): 95–105.

4. Gail Robinson and Kathleen Dechant, *Academy of Management Executive* 11, no. 3 (1997): 26.

5. Michael L. Wheeler, "Diversity: The Performance Factor," *Harvard Business Review* (March 2005): S1–S7.

6. Ibid.

7. Caminiti, "The Diversity Factor."

8. M. Fine, F. Johnson, and M. S. Ryan, "Cultural Diversity in the Workforce," *Public Personnel Management* 19 (1990): 305–319.

9. Taylor H. Cox, "Managing Cultural Diversity: Implications for Organizational Competitiveness," *Academy of Management Executive* 5, no. 3 (1991): 45–56; and Faye Rice, "How to Make Diversity Pay," *Fortune* (August 8, 1994): 78–86.

10. U.S. Department of Labor, Report of the Taskforce on the Aging of the American Workforce, February, 2008, http://www.bls.gov (accessed March 13, 2008).

11. The Bureau of Labor Statistics.

12. Ibid.

13. Kimberly L. Allers with Nadira A. Hira, "The Diversity List," *Fortune* (August 22, 2005); Elizabeth Wasserman, "A Race for Profits," *MBA Jungle* (March–April 2003): 40–41; Amy Aronson, "Getting Results: Corporate Diversity, Integration, and Market Penetration," special advertising section, *BusinessWeek* (October 20, 2003).

14. Immigrant statistics from the U.S. Census Bureau reported in "Census Numbers Show Education Divide Among Immigrant Groups," *USA Today* (September 27, 2007), http://www.cnn.com/2007/US/09/26/census.immigrants.ap/index.html?loc=interstitialskip (accessed August 25, 2008).

15. Joseph Daniel McCool, "Diversity Pledges Ring Hollow," *BusinessWeek,* February 28, 2008, http://search.businessweek.com/Search?searchTerm=diversity+pledges+ring+hollow&resultsPerPage=20 (accessed March 11, 2008).

16. "On Diversity, America Isn't Putting Its Money Where Its Mouth Is," *The Wall Street Journal*, February 25, 2008.

17. Helen Bloom, "Can the U.S. Export Diversity?" *Across the Board* (March/April 2002): 47–51.

18. Richard L. Daft, *The Leadership Experience,* (Cincinnati, OH: Cengage Learning, 2008), p. 340.

19. Honeywell Web site, http://www.honeywell.com (accessed March 4, 2008).

20. Michael L. Wheeler, "Diversity: Business Rationale and Strategies," The Conference Board, Report No. 1130-95-RR, 1995, p. 14.

21. Ibid.

22. Anthony Oshiotse and Richard O'Leary, "Corning Creates an Inclusive Culture to Drive Technology Innovation and Performance," *Wiley InterScience*, Global Business and Organizational Excellence, 26 no. 3 (March/April 2007): 10.

23. Elizabeth D. Macgillivray, H. Juanita M. Beecher, and Deirdre Golden, "Legal Developments—Religion at Work," *Wiley InterScience* (November/December 2007): 67.

24. UPS Web site, http://www.ups.com/pressroom/us/awards/citizenship (accessed March 6, 2008).

25. Taylor Cox, Jr., and Ruby L. Beale, *Developing Competency to Manage Diversity* (San Francisco: Berrett-Koehler Publishers, Inc., 1997), p. 2.

26. Gail Robinson and Kathleen Dechant, "Building a Business Case for Diversity," *Academy of Management Executive* 11, no. 3 (1997): 22.

27. Sonie Alleyne and Nicole Marie Richardson, "The 40 Best Companies for Diversity," *Black Enterprise* 36, no. 12 (July 2006): 15.

28. Robinson and Dechant, "Building a Business Case for Diversity," 27.

29. Ibid., 22.

30. Carol Hymowitz, "Coaching Men on Mentoring Women Is Ernst & Young Partner's Mission," *The Wall Street Journal Online,* June 14, 2007, www.wsj.com (accessed July 9, 2007).

31. Kris Maher, "Lockheed Settles Racial-Discrimination Suits," *The Wall Street Journal Online,* January 3, 2008, http://online.wsj.com/article_print/SB119932555019663957.html (accessed March 11, 2008).

32. "Diversity in the Federal Government," report of a roundtable discussion on "Addressing Diversity Issues in the Government," July 10, 2003, moderated by Omar Wasow, executive director of BlackPlanet.com, reported in *The New York Times Magazine* (September 14, 2003): 95–99.

33. Norma Carr-Ruffino, *Managing Diversity: People Skills for a Multicultural Workplace* (Tucson, AZ: Thomson Executive Press, 1996), p. 92.

34. Roy Harris, "The Illusion of Inclusion," *CFO* (May 2001): 42–50.

35. Stephanie N. Mehta, "What Minority Employees Really Want," *Fortune* (June 10, 2000): 181–186.

36. Vivek Wadhwa, "The True Cost of Discrimination," *BusinessWeek,* June 6, 2006 http://www.businessweek.com/smallbiz/content/jun2006 (accessed March 7, 2008).

37. Carr-Ruffino, *Managing Diversity: People Skills for a Multicultural Workplace,* pp. 98–99.

38. Cox and Beale, "Developing Competency to Manage Diversity," p. 79.

39. Ibid, pp. 80–81.

40. Loriann Roberson and Carol T. Kulik, "Stereotype Threat at Work," *Academy of Management Perspectives* 21, no. 2 (May 2007): 25–27.

41. Ibid., 26.

42. Robert Doktor, Rosalie Tung, and Mary Ann von Glinow, "Future Directions for Management Theory Development," *Academy of Management Review* 16 (1991): 362–365; and Mary Munter, "Cross-Cultural Communication for Managers," *Business Horizons* (May–June 1993): 69–78.

43. Renee Blank and Sandra Slipp, "The White Male: An Endangered Species?" *Management Review* (September 1994): 27–32; Michael S. Kimmel, "What Do Men Want?" *Harvard Business Review* (November–December 1993): 50–63; and Sharon Nelton, "Nurturing Diversity," *Nation's Business* (June 1995): 25–27.

44. Jim Carlton, "Dig In," *The Wall Street Journal* (November 14, 2005); Tony DiRomualdo, "Is Google's Cafeteria a Competitive Weapon?" *Wisconsin Technology Network* (August 30, 2005), http://wistechnology.com/article.php?id=2190; Marc Ramirez, "Tray Chic: At Work, Cool Cafeterias, Imaginative Menus," *The Seattle Times*, November 21, 2005, http://seattletimes.nwsource.com/html/living/2002634266_cafes21.html?pageid=display-in-the-news.module&pageregion=itn-body.

45. Marianne Bertrand and Sendhil Mullainathan, "Are Emily and Greg More Employable than Lakisha and Jamal?" National Bureau of Economic Research report, as reported in L. A. Johnson, "What's in a Name: When Emily Gets the Job Over Lakisha," *The Tennessean*, January 4, 2004.

46. Marie Valla, "France Seeks Path to Workplace Diversity," *The Wall Street Journal*, January 3, 2007.

47. Alice H. Eagly and Linda L. Carli, "Leadership," *Harvard Business Review* (September, 2007): 64.

48. Sheila Wellington, Marcia Brumit Kropf, and Paulette R. Gerkovich, "What's Holding Women Back?" *Harvard Business Review* (June 2003): 18–19.

49. Julie Amparano Lopez, "Study Says Women Face Glass Walls as Well as Ceilings," *The Wall Street Journal*, March 3, 1992; Ida L. Castro, "Q: Should Women Be Worried About the Glass Ceiling in the Workplace?" *Insight* (February 10, 1997): 24–27; Debra E. Meyerson and Joyce K. Fletcher, "A Modest Manifesto for Shattering the Glass Ceiling," *Harvard Business Review* (January–February 2000): 127–136; and Wellington, Brumit Kropf, and Gerkovich, "What's Holding Women Back?"; Annie Finnigan, "Different Strokes," *Working Woman* (April 2001): 42–48.

50. Catalyst survey results reported in Jason Forsythe, "Winning with Diversity," *The New York Times Magazine* (March 28, 2004): 65–72.

51. Eagly and Carli, "Leadership," 64.

52. Jory Des Jardins, "I Am Woman (I Think)," *Fast Company* (May 2005): 25–26; Lisa Belkin, "The Opt-Out Revolution," *The New York Times Magazine* (October 26, 2003): 43–47, 58; Finnigan, "Different Strokes," 42–48; and Meyerson and Fletcher, "A Modest Manifesto for Shattering the Glass Ceiling."

53. Statistics from the U.S. Census Bureau, Current Population Survey, 2004 Annual Social and Economic Supplement, as reported in "2003 Median Annual Earnings by Race and Sex," http://www.infoplease.com/ipa/A0197814.html; and "The Economics of Gender and Race: Examining the Wage Gap in the United States," The Feminist Majority Foundation Choices Campus Campaign, http://www.feministcampus.org.

54. Cliff Edwards, "Coming Out in Corporate America," *BusinessWeek* (December 15, 2003): 64–72; Belle Rose Ragins, John M. Cornwell, and Janice S. Miller, "Heterosexism in the Workplace: Do Race and Gender Matter?" *Group & Organization Management* 28, no. 1 (March 2003): 45–74.

55. Sylvia Ann Hewlett and Carolyn Buck Luce, "Off-Ramps and On-Ramps; Keeping Talented Women on the Road to Success," *Harvard Business Review* (March 2005): 43–54.

56. Belkin, "The Opt-Out Revolution."

57. C. J. Prince, "Media Myths: The Truth About the Opt-Out Hype," *NAFE Magazine* (Second Quarter 2004): 14–18; Patricia Sellers, "Power: Do Women Really Want It?" *Fortune* (October 13, 2003): 80–100.

58. Jia Lynn Yang, "Goodbye to All That," *Fortune* (November 14, 2005): 169–170.

59. Sheila Wellington, Marcia Brumit Kropf, and Paulette R. Gerkovich, "What's Holding Women Back?" *Harvard Business Review* (June 2003): 18–19.

60. The Leader's Edge/Executive Women Research 2002 survey, reported in "Why Women Leave," *Executive Female* (Summer 2003): 4.

61. Barbara Reinhold, "Smashing Glass Ceilings: Why Women Still Find It Tough to Advance to the Executive Suite," *Journal of Organizational Excellence* (Summer 2005): 43–55; Des Jardins, "I Am Woman (I Think)"; and Alice H. Eagly and Linda L. Carli, "The Female Leadership Advantage: An Evaluation of the Evidence," *The Leadership Quarterly* 14 (2003): 807–834.

62. Claudia H. Deutsch, "Behind the Exodus of Executive Women: Boredom," *USA Today*, May 2, 2005.

63. Eagly and Carli, "The Female Leadership Advantage"; Reinhold, "Smashing Glass Ceilings"; Sally Helgesen, *The Female Advantage: Women's Ways of Leadership* (New York: Doubleday Currency, 1990); Rochelle Sharpe, "As Leaders, Women Rule: New Studies Find that Female Managers Outshine Their Male Counterparts in Almost Every Measure," *BusinessWeek* (November 20, 2000): 5ff; and Del Jones, "2003: Year of the Woman Among the Fortune 500?" (December 30, 2003): 1B.

64. Tamar Lewin, "At Colleges, Women Are Leaving Men in the Dust," *The New York Times Online*, July 9, 2006, http://www.nytimes.com/2006/07/09/education/09college.html?_r=1&scp=1&sq=at%20colleges,%20women%20are%20leaving%20men%20in%20the%20dust&st=cse&oref=slogin (accessed March 13, 2008).

65. Alex Kingsbury, "Admittedly Unequal," *U.S. News & World Report* (June 25, 2007): 50.

4
Organizing

66. Michelle Conlin, "The New Gender Gap," and Michelle Conlin, "A Better Education Equals Higher Pay," *BusinessWeek* (May 26, 2003): 74–82.

67. Quoted in Conlin, "The New Gender Gap."

68. Kathryn M. Bartol, David C. Martin, and Julie A. Kromkowski, "Leadership and the Glass Ceiling: Gender and Ethnic Group Influences on Leader Behaviors at Middle and Executive Managerial Levels," *The Journal of Leadership and Organizational Studies* 9, no. 3 (2003): 8–19; Bernard M. Bass and Bruce J. Avolio, "Shatter the Glass Ceiling: Women May Make Better Managers," *Human Resource Management* 33, no. 4 (Winter 1994): 549–560; and Rochelle Sharpe, "As Leaders, Women Rule," 75–84.

69. Dwight D. Frink, Robert K. Robinson, Brian Reithel, Michelle M. Arthur, Anthony P. Ammeter, Gerald R. Ferris, David M. Kaplan, and Hubert S. Morrisette, "Gender Demography and Organization Performance: A Two-Study Investigation with Convergence," *Group & Organization Management* 28, no. 1 (March 2003): 127–147; Catalyst research project cited in Reinhold, "Smashing Glass Ceilings."

70. Mercedes Martin and Billy Vaughn (2007), *Strategic Diversity & Inclusion Management*, pp. 31–36.

71. Ann M. Morrison, *The New Leaders: Guidelines on Leadership Diversity in America* (San Francisco: Jossey-Bass Publishers, 1992), p. 235.

72. Michael L. Wheeler, "Diversity: Business Rationale and Strategies," The Conference Board, Report No. 1130-95-RR, 1995, p. 25.

73. Alleyne and Richardson, "The 40 Best Companies for Diversity," 100.

74. Morrison, "*The New Leaders.*"

75. Reported in "Strength Through Diversity for Bottom-Line Success," *Working Woman* (March 1999).

76. Finnigan, "Different Strokes."

77. "Diversity in an Affiliated Company," cited in Vanessa J. Weaver, "Winning with Diversity," *BusinessWeek* (September 10, 2001).

78. Melanie Trottman, "A Helping Hand," *The Wall Street Journal*, November 14, 2005; B. Ragins, "Barriers to Mentoring: The Female Manager's Dilemma," *Human Relations* 42, no. 1 (1989): 1–22; and Belle Rose Ragins, Bickley Townsend, and Mary Mattis, "Gender Gap in the Executive Suite: CEOs and Female Executives Report on Breaking the Glass Ceiling," *Academy of Management Executive* 12, no. 1 (1998): 28–42.

79. Trottman, "A Helping Hand."

80. David A. Thomas, "The Truth About Mentoring Minorities—Race Matters," *Harvard Business Review* (April 2001): 99–107.

81. Mary Zey, "A Mentor for All," *Personnel Journal* (January 1988): 46–51.

82. Joanne Sujansky, "Lead a Multi-Generational Workforce," *The Business Journal of Tri-Cities, Tennessee–Virginia* (February 2004): 21–23.

83. "Keeping Your Edge: Managing a Diverse Corporate Culture," *Fortune* (June 3, 2001).

84. Kimberly L. Allers, "Won't It Be Grand When We Don't Need Diversity Lists?" *Fortune* (August 22, 2005): 101.

85. J. Black and M. Mendenhall, "Cross-Cultural Training Effectiveness: A Review and a Theoretical Framework for Future Research," *Academy of Management Review* 15 (1990): 113–136.

86. Laura Egodigwe, "Back to Class," *The Wall Street Journal*, November 14, 2005.

87. Lee Smith, "Closing the Gap," *Fortune* (November 14, 2005): 211–218.

88. "Sexual Harassment: Vanderbilt University Policy" (Nashville, TN: Vanderbilt University, 1993).

89. Rachel Thompson, "Sexual Harassment: It Doesn't Go with the Territory," *Horizons* 15, no. 3 (Winter 2002): 22–26.

90. Statistics reported in Jim Mulligan and Norman Foy, "Not in My Company: Preventing Sexual Harassment," *Industrial Management* (September/October 2003): 26–29; also see *EEOC Charge Complaints*, http://www.eeoc.gov.

91. Jack Corcoran, "Of Nice and Men," *Success* (June 1998): 65–67.

92. Barbara Carton, "At Jenny Craig, Men Are Ones Who Claim Sex Discrimination," *The Wall Street Journal*, November 29, 1994.

93. "Impact of Diversity Initiatives on the Bottom Line: A SHRM Survey of the Fortune 1000" (pp. S12–S14), in *Fortune*, "Keeping Your Edge: Managing a Diverse Corporate Culture," produced in association with the Society for Human Resource Management (June 3, 2001), http://www.fortune.com/sections.

94. Joseph J. Distefano and Martha L. Maznevski, "Creating Value with Diverse Teams in Global Management," *Organizational Dynamics* 29, no. 1 (Summer 2000): 45–63; and Finnigan, "Different Strokes."

95. W. E. Watson, K. Kumar, and L. K. Michaelsen, "Cultural Diversity's Impact on Interaction Process and Performance: Comparing Homogeneous and Diverse Task Groups," *Academy of Management Journal* 36 (1993): 590–602; G. Robinson and K. Dechant, "Building a Business Case for Diversity," *Academy of Management Executive* 11, no. 3 (1997): 21–31; and D. A. Thomas and R. J. Ely, "Making Differences Matter: A New Paradigm for Managing Diversity," *Harvard Business Review* (September–October 1996): 79–90.

96. Marc Hequet, Chris Lee, Michele Picard, and David Stamps, "Teams Get Global," *Training* (December 1996): 16–17.

97. See Distefano and Maznevski, "Creating Value with Diverse Teams" for a discussion of the advantages of multicultural teams.

98. Watson, Kumar, and Michaelsen, "Cultural Diversity's Impact on Interaction Process and Performance."

99. Distefano and Maznevski, "Creating Value with Diverse Teams."

100. This definition and discussion is based on Raymond A. Friedman, "Employee Network Groups: Self-Help Strategy for Women and Minorities," *Performance Improvement Quarterly* 12, no. 1 (1999): 148–163.

101. Raymond A. Friedman and Brooks Holtom, "The Effects of Network Groups on Minority Employee Turnover Intentions," *Human Resource Management* 41, no. 4 (Winter 2002): 405–421.

102. Diane Brady and Jena McGregar, "What Works in Women's Networks," *BusinessWeek* (June 18, 2007): 58.

103. Wasserman, "A Race for Profits."

104. Finnigan, "Different Strokes."

105. Raymond A. Friedman, Melinda Kane, and Daniel B. Cornfield, "Social Support and Career Optimism: Examining the Effectiveness of Network Groups Among Black Managers," *Human Relations* 51, no. 9 (1998): 1155–1177; "Diversity in the New Millennium," *Working Woman* (March 2000).

General Motors
Part Four: Organizing
Diversity Equals Opportunity at General Motors

William "Billy" Durant and Henry Ford are celebrated founders of the two greatest automobile companies in America's history: General Motors (GM) and Ford Motor Company. Ford was the famous inventor who introduced the Model T, the world's first affordable automobile. Durant was an entrepreneur whose Flint, Michigan, carriage business manufactured a variety of luxury models and farm wagons for diverse customers.

Although both were pioneers of the auto industry, their approaches could not have been more different. Whereas Ford remained focused on one brand and one vehicle, Durant dreamed of a whole family of car companies, each producing different models for different kinds of consumers and needs. Not satisfied owning only GM Buick in 1908, Durant proceeded to acquire Oldsmobile, Cadillac, and Oakland Motor Car Company. (Pontiac), among others, bringing them under one roof alongside Chevrolet, which he co-founded on the side.

The story of William Durant is a powerful metaphor for the spirit of diversity that infuses the work and culture of GM today. In the global marketplace, managers interact with people of different cultures, languages, beliefs, and values. Recognizing diversity, and the unique way people with different backgrounds interact and communicate, is key to success in the international arena.

As GM celebrates 100 years of auto manufacturing greatness, its workforce is increasingly made up of people of all ethnicities and walks of life. The company is home to a variety of employee-resource groups, including the African Ancestry Network, the Hispanic Initiative Team, the Native American Cultural Network, the People with Disabilities Group, and the Veteran's Affinity Group. Employees who join these special support groups discover a wealth of resources for career and personal development.

By promoting a workforce that is as diverse as its customer base, GM brings a broad range of ideas and voices to bear on tough business challenges. "By valuing and respecting differences and similarities in the workplace, we will be in a better position to win in the marketplace," said Rod Gillum, vice president of corporate responsibility and diversity at GM. "It is our goal to recruit and retain diverse talent that reflects our global customers and to create an environment where everyone can fully contribute in creating great GM products and services."

The top automaker has made great strides toward Gillum's goal. *DiversityInc* magazine ranks GM among its Top 50 Companies for Diversity. The magazine writes that GM shows "unbiased retention" in hiring people of all races, ethnicities, and gender—and at all levels of the organization. To appear in the magazine's rankings, companies must demonstrate a commitment to diversity in four areas: CEO commitment, human capital, organizational communications, and supplier diversity.

Cultivating a broad multinational workforce means eliminating glass ceilings that discourage groups from participating fully in the company. Edward T. Welburn is GM's vice president of global design, heading up a multinational division with 11 design centers around the world. Appointed in 2005, Welburn is the sixth person to hold this position, and the first African-American. Under his leadership, GM unified its design efforts worldwide by establishing coordinated collaboration between 1,900 designers in eight countries. The results speak for themselves. Whether it's the sleek luxury of the Cadillac CTS or the retrospective cool of the 2010 Chevy Camaro, GM's most exciting new concepts are developing rapidly under Welburn's watchful eye. Hired by GM in 1972, Welburn appears to have been born for the job. "All I ever wanted to do was design cars," the design chief says.

Yet for any diversity initiative to thrive in an organization, it must have support all the way to the top. CEO Rick Wagoner understands the challenges of the new millennium as well as diversity's role in meeting those challenges. "At General Motors, we know that to succeed in today's global marketplace, we need a diverse workforce, one that brings together a wide range of talents, ideas, experiences, and perspectives."

Questions

1. What do you think are the most compelling advantages of diversity presented here?

2. What challenges do managers face in creating a diverse workplace, and how might they respond to these challenges?

3. Do you think that GM's encouragement of employee networks always leads to a culture of diversity and cooperation? Explain.

SOURCES: Bryce G. Hoffman, "Legendary Execs: 7 Notable Presidents Who Helped Shape GM," *The Detroit News*, August 30, 2008, http://

www.detnews.com (accessed October 13 2008); David Phillips, "Legacy of Innovation," *The Detroit News*, September 16, 2008, http://www .detnews.com (accessed October 15, 2008); General Motors, "African Americans Take the Driver's Seat in GM Product Development," *The Inside Scoop*, vol. 1, no. 2 (February 2007), http://www.gmdynamic .com/newsletter/diversity/feb_07/feb-stry1.html (accessed October 14, 2008); Katie Merx, "GM Turns 100 with Focus on Future," *USA Today*, January 1, 2008, http://www.usatoday.com/money/autos/2008-01-01-gm-birthday_N.htm (accessed October 13, 2008); "2008 DiversityInc Top 50 Companies for Diversity: General Motors" *DiversityInc* (June 2, 2008), http://www.diversityinc.com/public/3335.cfm (accessed October 13, 2008); General Motors, "Leadership from a Design Perspective— GM Design Chief Addresses Entrepreneurs' Conference," *The Inside Scoop*, vol. 2, no. 6 (June 2008), http://www.gmdynamic.com/newsletter/diversity/june_08/story2.html (accessed October 14, 2008); General Motors Web site, "Senior Leadership Group: Edward T. Welburn Jr., GM Vice President, Global Design," http://www.gm.com/corporate/investor_information/corp_gov/bios/welburn.jsp (accessed October 14, 2008).

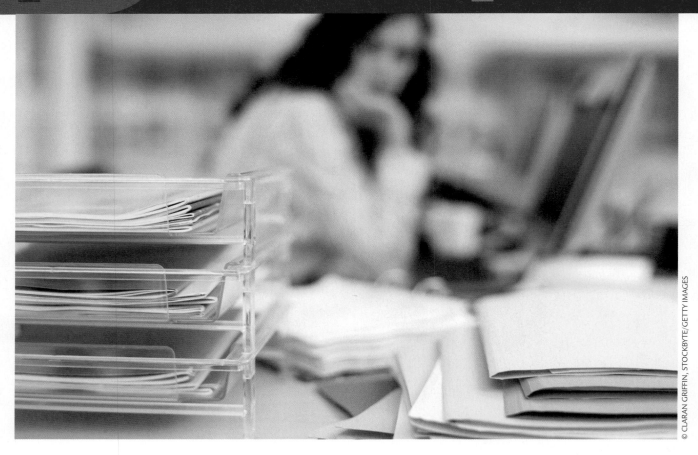

© CLARAN GRIFFIN, STOCKBYTE/GETTY IMAGES

pt5 **chapter13**

Chapter Outline

Learning Outcomes

After studying this chapter, you should be able to:

1. Define organizational control and explain why it is a key management function.

2. Explain the benefits of using the balanced scorecard to track performance and control of the organization.

3. Explain the four steps in the control process.

4. Discuss the use of financial statements, financial analysis, and budgeting as management controls.

5. Contrast the hierarchical and decentralized methods of control.

6. Identify the benefits of open-book management.

7. Describe the concept of total quality management and major TQM techniques, such as quality circles, benchmarking, Six Sigma principles, reduced cycle time, and continuous improvement.

8. Identify current trends in quality and financial control, including ISO 9000, economic value-added and market value-added systems, activity-based costing, and corporate governance, and discuss their impact on organizations.

1 Introduction

2 Environment

3 Planning

4 Organizing

5 Controlling

6 Leading

Managing Quality and Performance

WHAT IS YOUR ATTITUDE TOWARD ORGANIZATIONAL REGULATION AND CONTROL?[1]

Managers have to control people for organizations to survive, yet control should be the right amount and type. Companies are often less democratic than the society of which they are a part. Think honestly about your beliefs toward the regulation of other people and answer each item that follows as Mostly True or Mostly False.

	Mostly True	Mostly False
1. I believe people should be guided more by feelings and less by rules.	_____	_____
2. I think employees should be on time to work and to meetings.	_____	_____
3. I believe efficiency and speed are not as important as letting everyone have their say when making a decision.	_____	_____
4. I think employees should conform to company policies.	_____	_____
5. I let my significant other make the decision and have his or her way most of the time.	_____	_____
6. I like to tell other people what to do.	_____	_____
7. I am more patient with the least capable people.	_____	_____
8. I like to have things running "just so."	_____	_____

SCORING AND INTERPRETATION: Give yourself one point for each Mostly True answer to the odd-numbered questions and one point for each Mostly False answer to the even-numbered questions. A score of six or above suggests you prefer decentralized control for other people in organizations. A score of three or less suggests a preference for more control and bureaucracy in a company. Enthusiastic new managers may exercise too much of their new control and get a negative backlash. However, too little control may mean less accountability and productivity. The challenge for new managers is to strike the right balance for the job and people involved.

Control is an important issue facing every manager in every organization, but new managers sometimes have a hard time finding the correct degree of control that will keep people productive without squelching their motivation and creativity. Managers face many control issues, including controlling work processes, regulating employee behavior, setting up basic systems for allocating financial resources, developing human resources, analyzing financial performance, and evaluating overall profitability. Another important aspect is quality control.

Consider the quality control challenge facing U.S. Army managers. Every week, dozens of war-battered Humvees from Iraq are shipped to a 36,000-acre army depot in Texarkana, Texas. Called the Red River Army Depot, it is one of the army's oldest and most important maintenance and storage bases. Faced with a shrinking defense budget, military experts had to find ways to repair the Humvees faster and with fewer personnel. They studied quality control processes used in the private sector and spearheaded the most ambitious business effort in the 231-year history of the U.S. Army: an attempt to adopt a quality control theory, Lean Six Sigma, across the entire service. "We need to free up resources so we can apply them to the operating side of the army. We need to equip our soldiers better and faster," says Mike Kirby, deputy under secretary of the army for business transformation. The new quality control process includes a highly efficient assembly line where horns blare every 23 minutes to indicate station changes. The results are impressive: the facility now turns out 32 mission-ready Humvees a day, compared with three a week in 2004. And the new process has lowered the cost of repair for one vehicle from $89,000 to $48,000. Optimistic projections claim the army could be saving billions of dollars each year in a decade.[2]

This chapter introduces basic mechanisms for controlling the organization. We begin by summarizing the objectives of the control process and the use of the balanced scorecard to measure performance. Then we discuss the four steps in the control process and methods for controlling financial performance, including the use of budgets and financial statements. The next sections examine the changing philosophy of control, today's approach to total quality management, and recent trends such as ISO certification, economic value-added and market value-added systems, activity-based costing, and corporate governance.

THE MEANING OF CONTROL

organizational control The systematic process through which managers regulate organizational activities to make them consistent with expectations established in plans, targets, and standards of performance.

It seemed like a perfect fit. In the chaotic aftermath of 2005's Hurricane Katrina, the American Red Cross needed private-sector help to respond to the hundreds of thousands of people seeking emergency aid. Staffing company Spherion Corporation had the expertise to hire and train temporary workers fast, and the company had a good track record working with the Red Cross. Yet Red Cross officials soon noticed something odd: An unusually large number of Katrina victim money orders, authorized by employees at the Spherion-staffed call center, were being cashed near the call center itself—in Bakersfield, California, far from the hurricane-ravaged area. A federal investigation found that some call-center employees were issuing money orders to fake hurricane victims and cashing the orders for themselves. Fortunately, the fraud was discovered quickly, but the weak control systems that allowed the scam to occur got both the Red Cross and Spherion into a public relations and political mess.[3]

A lack of control can have repercussions that damage an organization's health, hurt its reputation, and threaten its future. One area in which many managers are implementing stronger controls is employee use of the Internet and e-mail, as described in the Manager's Shoptalk.

Organizational control refers to the systematic process of regulating organizational activities to make them consistent with the expectations established in plans, targets, and standards of performance. In a classic article on the control function, Douglas S. Sherwin summarizes the concept as follows: "The essence of control is action which adjusts operations to predetermined standards, and its basis is information in the hands of managers."[4] Thus, effectively controlling an organization requires information about performance standards and actual performance, as well as actions taken to correct any deviations from the standards. To effectively control an organization, managers need to decide what information is essential, how they will obtain that information, and how they can and should respond to it. Having the correct data is essential. Managers decide which standards, measurements, and metrics are needed to effectively monitor and control the organization and set up systems for obtaining that information. For example, an important metric for a pro football or basketball team

COURTESY OF HONEYWELL, INC.

Concept Connection A new philosophy about **organizational control** involves lower-level workers in management and control decisions. At the Honeywell Industrial Automation and Control facility in Phoenix, employees' quality-control decisions cut defect rates by 70 percent, inventory by 46 percent, and customer lead times by an average of 75 percent.

Manager'sShoptalk

Cyberslackers Beware: The Boss Is Watching

When employees have access to the Internet's vast resources, and the ability to communicate quickly via e-mail and instant messaging with anyone in the world, that's got to be good for productivity, right?

Not necessarily, as many organizations are discovering. Many companies are experiencing a growing problem with "cyberslackers," people who spend part of their workday sending personal e-mails, shopping, or downloading music and videos that hog available bandwidth and sometimes introduce viruses. In addition, it takes just a few bad apples engaging in harmful and possibly illegal activities, such as harassing other employees over the Web, to cause serious problems for their employers. So it's not surprising that the use of sophisticated software to both block employees' access to certain sites and monitor their Internet and e-mail use has grown exponentially.

A certain degree of vigilance is clearly warranted. However, enlightened managers strive for a balanced approach that protects the organization's interests while at the same time maintaining a positive, respectful work environment. Surveillance overkill can sometimes cost more than it saves, and it can also have a distinctly negative impact on employee morale. At the very least, employees may feel as though they're not being treated as trustworthy, responsible adults.

Here are some guidelines for creating an effective but fair "acceptable use policy" for workplace Internet use.

- *Make sure employees understand that they have no legal right to privacy in the workplace.* The courts so far have upheld an organization's right to monitor any and all employee activities on computers purchased by an employer for work purposes.

- *Create a written Internet policy.* Make sure you clearly state what qualifies as a policy violation by giving clear, concrete guidelines for acceptable use of e-mail, the Internet, and any other employer-provided hardware or software. For

example, spell out the types of Web sites that are never to be visited while at work and what constitutes acceptable e-mail content. Are employees ever permitted to use the Web for personal use? If so, specify what they can do, for how long, and whether they need to confine their personal use to lunchtime or breaks. List the devices you'll be checking and tell them the filtering and monitoring procedures you have in place. Get employees to sign a statement saying they've read and understand the policy.

- *Describe the disciplinary process.* Give people a clear understanding of the consequences of violating the organization's Internet and electronic use policy. Make sure they know the organization will cooperate if a criminal investigation arises.

- *Review the policy at regular intervals.* You'll need to modify your guidelines as new technologies and devices appear.

Managers should remember that monitoring e-mail and Internet use doesn't have to be an all-or-nothing process. Some organizations use continuous surveillance; others only screen when they believe a problem exists, or they disseminate a policy and leave enforcement to the honor system. Look carefully at your workforce and the work they're doing, and assess your potential liability and security needs. Then come up with a policy and monitoring plan that makes sense for your organization.

SOURCES: Lorraine Cosgrove Ware, "People Watching," *CIO* (August 15, 2005): 24; Art Lambert, "Technology in the Workplace: A Recipe for Legal Trouble," *Workforce.com* (February 14, 2005): www.workforce.com Technical Resource Group, "Employee E-mail and Internet Usage Monitoring: Issues and Concerns," www.picktrg.com; Pui-Wing Tam, Erin White, Nick Wingfield, and Kris Maher, "Snooping E-Mail by Software Is Now a Workplace Norm," *The Wall Street Journal*, March 9, 2005; and Ann Sherman, "Firms Address Worries over Workplace Web Surfing," *Broward Daily Business Review* (May 17, 2006): 11.

5 Controlling

might be the number of season tickets, which reduces the organization's dependence on more labor-intensive box-office sales.[5]

Choosing Standards and Measures

Most organizations focus on measuring and controlling financial performance, such as sales, revenue, and profit. Yet managers increasingly recognize the need to measure other intangible aspects of performance to manage the value-creating activities of the contemporary organization.[6] British Airways, for example, measures its performance in key areas of customer service because its strategy is to compete on superior service in an industry dominated by companies that compete on price. Underpinning this strategy is a belief that delivery of excellent service will result in higher levels of customer retention and profitability. Thus, British Airways measures and controls areas of customer service that have the greatest impact on a customer's service experience, including in-flight service, meal rating, baggage claim, and executive club membership.[7] Instead of relying only on financial measures to judge the company's performance, British Airways uses a number of different operational measures to track performance and control the organization.

The Balanced Scorecard

Like British Airways, many firms are now taking a more balanced perspective of company performance, integrating various dimensions of control that focus on markets and customers as well as employees and financials.[8] Organizations recognize that relying exclusively on financial measures can result in short-term, dysfunctional behavior. Nonfinancial measures provide a healthy supplement to the traditional financial measures, and companies are investing significant sums in developing more balanced measurement systems as a result.[9] The **balanced scorecard** is a comprehensive management control system that balances traditional financial measures with operational measures relating to a company's critical success factors.[10]

A balanced scorecard contains four major perspectives, as illustrated in Exhibit 13.1: financial performance, customer service, internal business processes, and the organization's capacity for learning and growth.[11] Within these four areas, managers identify key performance metrics the organization will track. The *financial performance* perspective reflects a concern that the organization's activities contribute to improving short- and long-term financial performance. It includes traditional measures such as net income and return on investment. *Customer service* indicators measure such things as how customers view the organization, as well as customer retention and satisfaction. *Business process* indicators focus on production and operating statistics, such as order fulfillment or cost per order. A good example of business process indicators comes from Facebook, one of the fastest-rising dot-coms in history. One of the internal activities it measures is the number of minutes visitors spend at its site. In March 2008, Facebook visitors spent a whopping 20 billion minutes at the site, compared to 6.4 billion minutes a year earlier. By measuring "minutes per visitor," Facebook is able to track its performance and adjust its strategy in response.[12]

The final component of the balanced scorecard looks at the organization's *potential for learning and growth*, focusing on how well resources and human capital are being managed for the company's future. Metrics may include such things as employee retention and the introduction of new products. The components of the scorecard are designed in an integrative manner, as illustrated in Exhibit 13.1.

Managers record, analyze, and discuss these various metrics to determine how well the organization is achieving its strategic goals. The balanced scorecard is an effective tool for managing and improving performance only if it is clearly linked to a well-defined organizational strategy and goals.[13] At its best, use of the scorecard cascades down from the top levels of the organization so that everyone becomes involved in thinking about and discussing strategy.[14] The scorecard has become the core management control system for many organizations, including well-known organizations such as Bell Emergis (a division of Bell Canada), ExxonMobil, Cigna Insurance, Hilton Hotels Corporation, and even some units of the U.S. federal government.[15] As with all management systems, the balanced scorecard is not right for every organization in every situation. The simplicity of the system causes some managers to underestimate the time and commitment that is needed for the approach to become a truly useful management control system. If managers implement the balanced scorecard using a *performance measurement* orientation rather than a *performance*

balanced scorecard A comprehensive management control system that balances traditional financial measures with measures of customer service, internal business processes, and the organization's capacity for learning and growth.

EXHIBIT | 13.1 The Balanced Scorecard

Financial

Customers

Internal Business Processes

Learning and Growth

SOURCES: Based on Robert S. Kaplan and David P. Norton, "Using the Balanced Scorecard as a Strategic Management System," *Harvard Business Review* (January–February 1996): 75–85; and Chee W. Chow, Kamal M. Haddad, and James E. Williamson, "Applying the Balanced Scorecard to Small Companies," *Management Accounting* 79, no. 2 (August 1997): 21–27.

management approach that links targets and measurements to corporate strategy, use of the scorecard can actually hinder or even decrease organizational performance.[16]

FEEDBACK CONTROL MODEL

All well-designed control systems involve the use of feedback to determine whether performance meets established standards. Managers need feedback, for example, in each of the four categories of the balanced scorecard. British Airways ties its use of the balanced scorecard to a feedback control model. Scorecards are used as the agenda for monthly management meetings. Managers focus on the various elements of the scorecard to set targets, evaluate performance, and guide discussion about what further actions need to be taken.[17] In this section, we examine the key steps in the feedback control model and then look at how the model applies to organizational budgeting.

Steps of Feedback Control

Managers set up control systems that consist of the four key steps illustrated in Exhibit 13.2: Establish standards, measure performance, compare performance to standards, and make corrections as necessary.

EXHIBIT | 13.2   Feedback Control Model

Establish Standards of Performance Within the organization's overall strategic plan, managers define goals for organizational departments in specific, operational terms that include a *standard of performance* against which to compare organizational activities. A standard of performance could include "reducing the reject rate from 15 to 3 percent," "increasing the corporation's return on investment to 7 percent," or "reducing the number of accidents to one per each 100,000 hours of labor." Managers should carefully assess what they will measure and how they will define it. In the auto industry, crash test ratings provide a standard of performance established by the National Highway Traffic Safety Administration. When crash test ratings are below standard, managers rethink design and manufacturing processes to improve crash test results. Although Daimler's ultra-tiny Smart ForTwo car won a Five Star rating for driver protection, it won just a Three Star rating for passenger protection, indicating the need for improved passenger safety features.[18]

Tracking such measures as customer service, employee involvement, or, for auto manufacturers, crash test results, is an important supplement to traditional financial and operational performance measurement, but many companies have a hard time identifying and defining nonfinancial measurements.[19] To effectively evaluate and reward employees for the achievement of standards, managers need clear standards that reflect activities that contribute to the organization's overall strategy in a significant way. Standards should be defined clearly and precisely so employees know what they need to do and can determine whether their activities are on target.[20]

Measure Actual Performance Most organizations prepare formal reports of quantitative performance measurements that managers review daily, weekly, or monthly. These measurements should be related to the standards set in the first step of the control process. For example, if sales growth is a target, the organization should have a means of gathering and reporting sales data. If the organization has identified appropriate measurements, regular review of these reports helps managers stay aware of whether the organization is doing what it should. Technology is aiding many organizations in measuring performance. For example, GPS tracking devices installed on government-issued vehicles are helping many communities reduce waste and abuse, in part by catching employees shopping, working out at the gym, or otherwise loafing while on the clock. Although some claim this technology is intrusive, city officials claim that tracking the whereabouts of government employees has deterred abuses and saved taxpayers money. In Denver, 76 vehicles equipped with GPS units were driven 5,000 fewer miles than the unequipped fleet during the same period the year before, indicating the value of this type of quantitative measure.[21]

In most companies, managers do not rely exclusively on quantitative measures. They get out into the organization to see how things are going, especially for such goals as increasing employee participation or improving customer satisfaction. Managers have to observe for themselves whether employees are participating in decision making and have opportunities to add to and share their knowledge. Interaction with customers is necessary for managers to really understand whether activities are meeting customer needs.

Compare Performance to Standards The third step in the control process is comparing actual activities to performance standards. When managers read computer reports or walk through the plant, they identify whether actual performance meets, exceeds, or falls short of standards. Typically, performance reports simplify such comparisons by placing the performance standards for the reporting period alongside the actual performance for the same period and by computing the variance—that is, the difference between each actual amount and the associated standard. To correct the problems that most require attention, managers focus on variances.

When performance deviates from a standard, managers must interpret the deviation. They are expected to dig beneath the surface and find the cause of the problem. If the sales goal is to increase the number of sales calls by 10 percent and a salesperson achieved an increase of 8 percent, where did she fail to achieve her goal? Perhaps several businesses on her route closed, additional salespeople were assigned to her area by competitors, or she needs training in making cold sales calls more effectively. Managers should take an inquiring approach to deviations to gain a broad understanding of factors that influence performance. Effective management control involves subjective judgment and employee discussions, as well as objective analysis of performance data.

EVAN KAFKA

Concept Connection Is it possible to make scientific discovery efficient? Managers at pharmaceuticals company Wyeth think so. They devised a streamlined research and development system driven by ambitious, quantifiable **standards of performance**. Managers routinely **compare performance to standards** and issue automated scorecards for each individual. Wyeth ties compensation to accomplishment of these all-or-nothing targets. "If the goal was to discover 12 drugs, 11 drugs are worth no points," says Wyeth Research President Robert Ruffolo Jr., who oversaw the reengineering effort. So far, the approach has yielded impressive results. With no additional investment, Wyeth has seen the number of new drugs that emerge from the early discovery phase increase fourfold.

As a new manager, apply the feedback control model to determine whether your team is functioning well or if changes are needed. Define clear standards of performance, measure outcomes regularly, and work with team members to take corrective actions when necessary.

TakeaMoment

Take Corrective Action Managers also determine what changes, if any, are needed. In a traditional top-down approach to control, managers exercise their formal authority to make necessary changes. They may encourage employees to work harder, redesign the production process, or fire employees. In contrast, managers using a participative control approach collaborate with employees to determine the corrective action necessary. As an example, Toyota's commitment to continuous improvement is reflected in its philosophy of "Problems First." In staff meetings, factory managers are asked to present their "problems first," triggering problem-solving sessions with managers that generate solutions. This approach reflects the company's commitment to seeking out better ways to manufacture cars. "Even with projects that had been a general success, we would ask, 'What didn't go well so we can make it better?'" says James Wiseman, vice president of corporate affairs for Toyota manufacturing in North America.[22]

Managers may wish to provide positive reinforcement when performance meets or exceeds standards. For example, they may reward a department that has exceeded its planned goals or congratulate employees for a job well done. Managers should

5
Controlling

not ignore high-performing departments at the expense of taking corrective actions elsewhere. The online auction company eBay provides a good illustration of the feedback control model.

eBay

As CEO of eBay, one of Meg Whitman's guiding rules was "If you can't measure it, you can't control it." Whitman has moved on to other pursuits, but eBay is still a company obsessed with performance measurement. Top managers personally monitor a slew of performance metrics, including standard measurements such as site visitors, new users, and time spent on the site, as well as the ratio of eBay's revenues to the value of goods traded.

Managers and employees throughout the company also monitor performance almost obsessively. Category managers, for example, have clear standards of performance for their auction categories (such as sports memorabilia, jewelry and watches, health and beauty, and fashion). They are constantly measuring, tweaking, and promoting their categories to meet or outperform the targets.

Top managers believe getting a firm grip on performance measurement is essential for a company to know where to spend money, where to assign more personnel, and which projects to promote or abandon. But performance measurement isn't just about numbers. At eBay, "it's all about the customer," and gauging customer (user) satisfaction requires a mix of methods, such as surveys, monitoring eBay's discussion boards, and personal contact. Managers get their chance to really connect with users at the annual eBay Live conference. There, they wander the convention hall floor talking with anyone and everyone about their eBay experiences. [23]

By defining standards, using a combination of measurement approaches, and comparing performance to standards, eBay managers are able to identify trouble spots and move quickly to take corrective action when and where it's needed.

Application to Budgeting

Budgetary control, one of the most commonly used methods of managerial control, is the process of setting targets for an organization's expenditures, monitoring results and comparing them to the budget, and making changes as needed. As a control device, budgets are reports that list planned and actual expenditures for cash, assets, raw materials, salaries, and other resources. In addition, budget reports usually list the variance between the budgeted and actual amounts for each item.

TakeaMoment | Go to the experiential exercise on page 401 that pertains to budgetary control.

A budget is created for every division or department within an organization, no matter how small, as long as it performs a distinct project, program, or function. The fundamental unit of analysis for a budget control system is called a responsibility center. A **responsibility center** is defined as any organizational department or unit under the supervision of a single person who is responsible for its activity. [24] A three-person appliance sales office in Watertown, New York, is a responsibility center, as is a quality control department, a marketing department, and an entire refrigerator manufacturing plant. The manager of each unit has budget responsibility. Top managers use budgets for the company as a whole, and middle managers traditionally focus on the budget performance of their department or division. Budgets that managers typically use include expense budgets, revenue budgets, cash budgets, and capital budgets.

responsibility center An organizational unit under the supervision of a single person who is responsible for its activity.

expense budget A budget that outlines the anticipated and actual expenses for a responsibility center.

Expense Budget An **expense budget** includes anticipated and actual expenses for each responsibility center and for the total organization. An expense budget may show all types of expenses or may focus on a particular category, such as materials or research and development expenses. When actual expenses exceed budgeted amounts, the difference signals the need for managers to identify whether a problem exists and take corrective action if needed. The difference may arise from inefficiency, or expenses may be higher because the organization's sales are growing faster than anticipated. Conversely, expenses below budget may signal exceptional efficiency or possibly the failure to meet some other standards, such as a desired level of sales or quality of service. Either way, expense budgets help identify the need for further investigation but do not substitute for it.

Revenue Budget A **revenue budget** lists forecasted and actual revenues of the organization. In general, revenues below the budgeted amount signal a need to investigate the problem to see whether the organization can improve revenues. In contrast, revenues above budget would require determining whether the organization can obtain the necessary resources to meet the higher-than-expected demand for its products or services. Managers then formulate action plans to correct the budget variance.

Cash Budget The **cash budget** estimates receipts and expenditures of money on a daily or weekly basis to ensure that an organization has sufficient cash to meet its obligations. The cash budget shows the level of funds flowing through the organization and the nature of cash disbursements. If the cash budget shows that the firm has more cash than necessary to meet short-term needs, the company can arrange to invest the excess to earn interest income. In contrast, if the cash budget shows a payroll expenditure of $20,000 coming at the end of the week but only $10,000 in the bank, the organization must borrow cash to meet the payroll.

Capital Budget The **capital budget** lists planned investments in major assets such as buildings, heavy machinery, or complex information technology systems, often involving expenditures over more than a year. Capital expenditures not only have a large impact on future expenses, they also are investments designed to enhance profits. Therefore, a capital budget is necessary to plan the impact of these expenditures on cash flow and profitability. Controlling involves not only monitoring the amount of capital expenditures but also evaluating whether the assumptions made about the return on the investments are holding true. Managers can evaluate whether continuing investment in particular projects is advisable, as well as whether their procedures for making capital expenditure decisions are adequate. Some companies, including Boeing, Merck, Shell, United Technologies, and Whirlpool, evaluate capital projects at several stages to determine whether they are still in line with the company's strategy.[25]

Budgeting is an important part of organizational planning and control. Many traditional companies use **top-down budgeting**, which means that the budgeted amounts for the coming year are literally imposed on middle- and lower-level managers.[26] These managers set departmental budget targets in accordance with overall company revenues and expenditures specified by top executives. Although the top-down process provides some advantages, the movement toward employee empowerment, participation, and learning means that many organizations are adopting **bottom-up budgeting**, a process in which lower-level managers anticipate their departments' resource needs and pass them up to top management for approval.[27] Companies of all kinds are increasingly involving line managers in the budgeting process. At the San Diego Zoo, scientists, animal keepers, and other line managers use software and templates to plan their department's budget needs because, as CFO Paula Brock says, "Nobody knows that side of the business better than they do."[28] Each of the 145 zoo departments also does a monthly budget close and reforecast so that resources can be redirected as needed to achieve goals within budget constraints. Thanks to the bottom-up process, for example, the zoo was able to quickly redirect resources to protect its valuable exotic bird collection from an outbreak of a highly infectious bird disease without significantly damaging the rest of the organization's budget.[29]

revenue budget A budget that identifies the forecasted and actual revenues of the organization.

cash budget A budget that estimates and reports cash flows on a daily or weekly basis to ensure that the company has sufficient cash to meet its obligations.

capital budget A budget that plans and reports investments in major assets to be depreciated over several years.

top-down budgeting A budgeting process in which middle- and lower-level managers set departmental budget targets in accordance with overall company revenues and expenditures specified by top management.

bottom-up budgeting A budgeting process in which lower-level managers budget their departments' resource needs and pass them up to top management for approval.

5 Controlling

FINANCIAL CONTROL

In every organization, managers need to watch how well the organization is performing financially. Not only do financial controls tell whether the organization is on sound financial footing, but they can be useful indicators of other kinds of performance problems. For example, a sales decline may signal problems with products, customer service, or sales force effectiveness.

Financial Statements

Financial statements provide the basic information used for financial control of an organization. Two major financial statements—the balance sheet and the income statement—are the starting points for financial control.

The **balance sheet** shows the firm's financial position with respect to assets and liabilities at a specific point in time. An example of a balance sheet is presented in Exhibit 13.3. The balance sheet provides three types of information: assets, liabilities, and owners' equity. *Assets* are what the company owns, and they include *current assets* (those that can be converted into cash in a short time period) and *fixed assets* (such as buildings and equipment that are long term in nature). *Liabilities* are the firm's debts, including both *current debt* (obligations that will be paid by the company in the near future) and *long-term debt* (obligations payable over a long period). *Owners' equity* is the difference between assets and liabilities and is the company's net worth in stock and retained earnings.

The **income statement**, sometimes called a profit-and-loss statement or P&L for short, summarizes the firm's financial performance for a given time interval, usually one year. A sample income statement is shown in Exhibit 13.4. Some organizations calculate the income statement at three-month intervals during the year to see whether they are on target for sales and profits. The income statement shows revenues coming into the organization from all sources and subtracts all expenses, including cost of goods sold, interest, taxes, and depreciation. The *bottom line* indicates the net income—profit or loss—for the given time period.

The owner of Aahs!, a specialty retailing chain in California, used the income statement to detect that sales and profits were dropping significantly during the summer months.[30] He immediately evaluated company activities and closed two money-losing

balance sheet A financial statement that shows the firm's financial position with respect to assets and liabilities at a specific point in time.

income statement A financial statement that summarizes the firm's financial performance for a given time interval; sometimes called a profit-and-loss statement.

EXHIBIT | 13.3 Balance Sheet

**New Creations Landscaping
Consolidated Balance Sheet
December 31, 2009**

Assets			Liabilities and Owners' Equity		
Current assets:			Current liabilities:		
Cash	$ 25,000		Accounts payable	$200,000	
Accounts receivable	75,000		Accrued expenses	20,000	
Inventory	500,000		Income taxes payable	30,000	
Total current assets		$ 600,000	Total current liabilities		$ 250,000
Fixed assets:			Long-term liabilities:		
Land	250,000		Mortgages payable	350,000	
Buildings and fixtures	1,000,000		Bonds outstanding	250,000	
Less depreciation	200,000		Total long-term liabilities		$ 600,000
Total fixed assets		1,050,000	Owners' equity:		
			Common stock	540,000	
			Retained earnings	260,000	
			Total owners' equity		800,000
Total assets		$1,650,000	Total liabilities and net worth		$1,650,000

EXHIBIT 13.4

Income Statement

New Creations Landscaping
Income Statement
For the Year Ended December 31, 2009

Gross sales	$3,100,000	
Less sales returns	200,000	
Net sales		$2,900,000
Less expenses and cost of goods sold:		
Cost of goods sold	2,110,000	
Depreciation	60,000	
Sales expenses	200,000	
Administrative expenses	90,000	2,460,000
Operating profit		440,000
Other income		20,000
Gross income		460,000
Less interest expense	80,000	
Income before taxes		380,000
Less taxes	165,000	
Net income		$ 215,000

stores. He also began a training program to teach employees how to increase sales and cut costs to improve net income. This use of the income statement follows the control model described in the previous section, beginning with setting targets, measuring actual performance, and then taking corrective action to improve performance to meet targets.

Financial Analysis: Interpreting the Numbers

A manager needs to be able to evaluate financial reports that compare the organization's performance with earlier data or industry norms. These comparisons enable the manager to see whether the organization is improving and whether it is competitive with others in the industry. The most common financial analysis focuses on ratios, statistics that express the relationships between performance indicators such as profits and assets, sales, and inventory. Ratios are stated as a fraction or proportion; Exhibit 13.5 summarizes some financial ratios, which are measures of an organization's liquidity, activity, profitability, and leverage. These ratios are among the most common, but many measures are used. Managers decide which ratios reveal the most important relationships for their business.

Liquidity Ratios A **liquidity ratio** indicates an organization's ability to meet its current debt obligations. For example, the *current ratio* (current assets divided by current liabilities) tells whether the company has sufficient assets to convert into cash to pay off its debts, if needed. If a hypothetical company, Oceanographics, Inc., has current assets of $600,000 and current liabilities of $250,000, the current ratio is 2.4, meaning it has sufficient funds to pay off immediate debts 2.4 times. This level for the current ratio is normally considered a satisfactory margin of safety.

liquidity ratio A financial ratio that indicates the organization's ability to meet its current debt obligations.

EXHIBIT 13.5

Common Financial Ratios

Liquidity Ratios	
Current ratio	Current assets/Current liabilities
Activity Ratios	
Inventory turnover	Total sales/Average inventory
Conversion ratio	Purchase orders/Customer inquiries
Profitability Ratios	
Profit margin on sales	Net income/Sales
Gross margin	Gross income/Sales
Return on assets (ROA)	Net income/Total assets
Leverage Ratios	
Debt ratio	Total debt/Total assets

Activity Ratios An **activity ratio** measures internal performance with respect to key activities defined by management. For example, *inventory turnover* is calculated by dividing total sales by average inventory. This ratio tells how many times the inventory is used up to meet the total sales figure. If inventory sits too long, money is wasted. Dell Inc. achieved a strategic advantage by minimizing its inventory costs. Dividing Dell's annual sales by its small inventory generates an inventory turnover rate of 35.7.[31] Another type of activity ratio, the *conversion ratio*, is purchase orders divided by customer inquiries. This ratio is an indicator of a company's effectiveness in converting inquiries into sales. For example, if Cisco Systems moves from 26.5 to 28.2 percent conversion ratio, more of its inquiries are turned into sales, indicating better sales activity.

Profitability Ratios Managers analyze a company's profits by studying **profitability ratios**, which state profits relative to a source of profits, such as sales or assets. One important profitability ratio is the *profit margin on sales*, which is calculated as net income divided by sales. Similarly, *gross margin* is the gross (before-tax) profit divided by total sales. Managers at Tesco.com, the online grocery service of Britain's top supermarket chain, pay close attention to the profit margin. Tesco.com managers implemented strict financial controls from the beginning. The online division was immediately profitable, earning about $6 on the average online sale, whereas U.S.-based Webvan, which eventually failed, lost about $100 per sale because of its huge start-up costs and high operating expenses.[32]

    Another profitability measure is *return on total assets (ROA)*, which is a percentage representing what a company earned from its assets, computed as net income divided by total assets. ROA is a valuable yardstick for comparing a company's ability to generate earnings with other investment opportunities. In basic terms, the company should be able to earn more by using its assets to operate the business than it could by putting the same investment in the bank. Caterpillar Inc., which produces construction and mining equipment, uses return on assets as its main measure of performance. It sets ROA standards for each area of the business and uses variances from the standards to identify whether the company is fully using its assets and improving operational efficiency. Since it began using ROA standards, Caterpillar has enjoyed double-digit returns.[33]

Leverage Ratios *Leverage* refers to funding activities with borrowed money. A company can use leverage to make its assets produce more than they could on their own. However, too much borrowing can put the organization at risk such that it will be unable to keep up with repayment of its debt. Managers therefore track their *debt ratio*, or total debt divided by total assets, to make sure it does not exceed a level they consider acceptable. Lenders may consider a company with a debt ratio above 1.0 to be a poor credit risk.

THE CHANGING PHILOSOPHY OF CONTROL

Managers' approach to control is changing in many of today's organizations. In connection with the shift to employee participation and empowerment, many companies are adopting a *decentralized* rather than a *hierarchical* control process. Hierarchical control and decentralized control represent different philosophies of corporate culture, which was discussed in Chapter 3. Most organizations display some aspects of both hierarchical and decentralized control, but managers generally emphasize one or the other, depending on the organizational culture and their own beliefs about control.

Hierarchical versus Decentralized Approaches

Hierarchical control involves monitoring and influencing employee behavior through extensive use of rules, policies, hierarchy of authority, written documentation, reward systems, and other formal mechanisms.[34] In contrast, decentralized

---

activity ratio A financial ratio that measures the organization's internal performance with respect to key activities defined by management.

profitability ratio A financial ratio that describes the firm's profits in terms of a source of profits (for example, sales or total assets).

hierarchical control The use of rules, policies, hierarchy of authority, reward systems, and other formal devices to influence employee behavior and assess performance.

control relies on cultural values, traditions, shared beliefs, and trust to foster compliance with organizational goals. Managers operate on the assumption that employees are trustworthy and willing to perform effectively without extensive rules and close supervision.

Exhibit 13.6 contrasts the use of hierarchical and decentralized methods of control. Hierarchical methods define explicit rules, policies, and procedures for employee behavior. Control relies on centralized authority, the formal hierarchy, and close personal supervision. Responsibility for quality control rests with quality control inspectors and supervisors rather than with employees. Job descriptions generally are specific and task related, and managers define minimal standards for acceptable employee performance. In exchange for meeting the standards, individual employees are given extrinsic rewards such as wages, benefits, and possibly promotions up the hierarchy. Employees rarely participate in the control process, with any participation being formalized through mechanisms such as grievance procedures. With hierarchical control, the organizational culture is somewhat rigid, and managers do not consider culture a useful means of controlling employees and the organization. Technology often is used to control the flow and pace of work or to monitor employees, such as by measuring the number of minutes employees spend on phone calls or how many keystrokes they make at the computer.

Hierarchical control techniques can enhance organizational efficiency and effectiveness. Many employees appreciate a system that clarifies what is expected of them, and they may be motivated by challenging, but achievable goals.[35] However, although many managers effectively use hierarchical control, too much control can backfire. Employees resent being watched too closely, and they may try to sabotage the control system. One veteran truck driver expressed his unhappiness with electronic monitoring to a *Wall Street Journal* reporter investigating the use of devices that monitor truck locations. According to the driver, "It's getting worse and worse all the time. Pretty soon they'll want to put a chip in the drivers' ears and make them robots." He added that he occasionally escapes the relentless monitoring by parking under an overpass to take a needed nap out of the range of the surveillance satellites.[36]

EXHIBIT | **13.6** Hierarchical and Decentralized Methods of Control

	Hierarchical Control	**Decentralized Control**
Basic Assumptions	People are incapable of self-discipline and cannot be trusted. They need to be monitored and controlled closely.	People work best when they are fully committed to the organization.
Actions	Uses detailed rules and procedures; formal control systems.	Features limited use of rules; relies on values, group and self-control, selection, and socialization.
	Uses top-down authority, formal hierarchy, position power, quality control inspectors.	Relies on flexible authority, flat structure, expert power; everyone monitors quality.
	Relies on task-related job descriptions.	Relies on results-based job descriptions; emphasizes goals to be achieved.
	Emphasizes extrinsic rewards (pay, benefits, status).	Emphasizes extrinsic and intrinsic rewards (meaningful work, opportunities for growth).
	Features rigid organizational culture; distrust of cultural norms as means of control.	Features adaptive culture; culture recognized as means for uniting individual, team, and organizational goals for overall control.
Consequences	Employees follow instructions and do *just* what they are told.	Employees take initiative and seek responsibility.
	Employees feel a sense of indifference toward work.	Employees are actively engaged and committed to their work.
	Employee absenteeism and turnover is high.	Employee turnover is low.

SOURCES: Based on Naresh Khatri, Alok Bavega, Suzanne A. Boren, and Abate Mammo, "Medical Errors and Quality of Care: From Control to Commitment," *California Management Review* 48, no. 3 (Spring, 2006): 118; Richard E. Walton, "From Control to Commitment in the Workplace," *Harvard Business Review* (March–April 1985): 76–84; and Don Hellriegel, Susan E. Jackson, and John W. Slocum, Jr., *Management*, 8th ed. (Cincinnati, Ohio: South-Western, 1999), p. 663.

5
Controlling

Decentralized control is based on values and assumptions that are almost opposite to those of hierarchical control. Rules and procedures are used only when necessary. Managers rely instead on shared goals and values to control employee behavior. The organization places great emphasis on the selection and socialization of employees to ensure that workers have the appropriate values needed to influence behavior toward meeting company goals. No organization can control employees 100 percent of the time, and self-discipline and self-control are what keep workers performing their jobs up to standard. Empowerment of employees, effective socialization, and training all can contribute to internal standards that provide self-control.

With decentralized control, power is more dispersed and is based on knowledge and experience as much as position. The organizational structure is flat and horizontal, as discussed in Chapter 9, with flexible authority and teams of workers solving problems and making improvements. Everyone is involved in quality control on an ongoing basis. Job descriptions generally are results-based, with an emphasis more on the outcomes to be achieved than on the specific tasks to be performed. Managers use not only extrinsic rewards such as pay, but the intrinsic rewards of meaningful work and the opportunity to learn and grow. Technology is used to empower employees by giving them the information they need to make effective decisions, work together, and solve problems. People are rewarded for team and organizational success as well as their individual performance, and the emphasis is on equity among employees. Employees participate in a wide range of areas, including setting goals, determining standards of performance, governing quality, and designing control systems.

With decentralized control, the culture is adaptive, and managers recognize the importance of organizational culture for uniting individual, team, and organizational goals for greater overall control. Ideally, with decentralized control, employees will pool their areas of expertise to arrive at procedures that are better than managers could come up with working alone.

decentralized control The use of organizational culture, group norms, and a focus on goals, rather than rules and procedures, to foster compliance with organizational goals.

open-book management Sharing financial information and results with all employees in the organization.

TakeaMoment | What is your philosophy of control? As a new manager, will you tend to watch things closely or give others freedom to perform? Complete the New Manager Self-Test on page 391 to get some feedback on your own approach to control.

Concept Connection Honest Tea co-founder and CEO Seth Goldman (left) practices **open book management**—sharing with employees information on sales, profit and loss, growth rate, expenses, salaries as a lump sum, stock price, and capitalization. Here, Goldman tours Castle's Co-Packer, which produces and bottles organic brewed teas for his company, with *Beverage World* magazine editor Sarah Theodore (center) and Brian Dworkin of Castle's. When Coca-Cola bought 40 percent of Honest Tea, Goldman says, "we insisted on an arrangement that allowed all of our employees to invest alongside Coke in the transaction—there's no question that this structure has contributed to the passion and entrepreneurial spirit of our team."

Open-Book Management

One important aspect of decentralized control in many organizations is open-book management. An organization that promotes information sharing and teamwork admits employees throughout the organization into the loop of financial control and responsibility to encourage active participation and commitment to goals. **Open-book management** allows employees to see for themselves—through charts, computer printouts, meetings, and so forth—the financial condition of the company. Second, open-book management shows the individual employee how his or her job fits into the big picture and affects the financial future of the organization. Finally, open-book management ties employee rewards to the company's overall success. With training in interpreting the financial data, employees can see the interdependence and importance of each function. If they are rewarded according to performance, they become motivated to take responsibility for their entire team or function, rather than merely their individual jobs.[37] Cross-functional communication and cooperation are also enhanced.

New Manager Self-Test

What Is Your Control Approach?

As a new manager, how will you control your work unit? What is your natural control approach? Please answer whether each item below is Mostly True or Mostly False for you.

	Mostly True	Mostly False
1. I find myself losing sight of long-term goals when there is a short-term crisis.		
2. I prefer complex to simple problems and projects.		
3. I am good at mapping out steps needed to complete a project.		
4. I make most decisions without needing to know an overall plan.		
5. I keep my personal books and papers in good order.		
6. I prefer tasks that challenge my thinking ability.		
7. I think about how my behavior relates to outcomes I desire.		
8. I like to be part of a situation where results are measured and count for something.		

SCORING AND INTERPRETATION: Control systems are designed and managed via a manager's "systems" thinking. Systems thinking considers how component parts of system interact to achieve desired goals. Systems thinking means seeing the world in an organized way and thinking about underlying cause-effect relationships. Give yourself one point for each Mostly True answer to items 2, 3, 5 to 8 and one point for each Mostly False answer to items 1 and 4. A score of six or above means that you appear to have a natural orientation toward systems thinking and control. You see the world in an organized way and focus on cause-effect relationships that produce outcomes. If you scored three or less, you probably are not very focused on control issues and relationships. You may not be interested or have the time to understand complex relationships. As a new manager, you may have to put extra effort into understanding control relationships to produce the outcomes you and the organization desire.

5 Controlling

The goal of open-book management is to get every employee thinking and acting like a business owner. To get employees to think like owners, management provides them with the same information owners have: what money is coming in and where it is going. Open-book management helps employees appreciate why efficiency is important to the organization's success as well as their own. Open-book management turns traditional control on its head. Development Counsellors International, a New York City public relations firm, found an innovative way to involve employees in the financial aspects of the organization.

When Andrew Levine took over as president of Development Counsellors International (DCI), the public relations firm founded by his father in 1960, he was eager to try open-book management. His first step was to add a financial segment to the monthly staff meeting, but employees just seemed bored. Most of them had no interest or skills in finance, statistics, and ratios.

Rather than providing standard training, Levine had an idea: Why not appoint a different staffer each month to be CFO for the day. That person would be required to figure out the financials and then present the financial reports at the monthly staff meeting. His first appointment was the receptionist, Sergio Barrios, who met with Levine and the company's chief financial officer to go over the figures, look at any unusual increases or decreases in revenue or expenses, and talk about ideas to spark discussion. Levine was astounded by the reaction of staffers at the monthly meeting. Unlike Levine or another manager, Barrios was new to accounting and consequently explained things in a way that any layperson could understand. In addition, employees wanted to support Barrios as "one of their own," so they paid more attention and asked more questions.

At each monthly meeting, the CFO of the day goes through a breakdown of the company's sales and expenses, points out irregularities and trends in the numbers, takes questions from other staff members, and sparks discussion of current financial issues. At the end of the report, the person reveals the bottom line, indicating whether the company met its profit goal for the month. Each time DCI's accumulated profit hits another $100,000 increment during the course of the year, 30 percent is distributed to employees.[38]

DCI has been profitable ever since Levine began the CFO-of-the-day program. In addition, employees are happier with their jobs, so turnover has decreased. Clients tend to stick around longer too, because employees put more effort into building relationships. "Nobody wants to see a zero next to their client in the income column," Levine says.[39]

Managers in some countries have more trouble running an open-book company because prevailing attitudes and standards encourage confidentiality and even secrecy concerning financial results. Many businesspeople in countries such as China, Russia, and India, for example, are not accustomed to publicly disclosing financial details, which can present problems for multinational companies operating there.[40] Exhibit 13.7 lists a portion of a recent *Opacity Index*, which offers some indication of the degree to which various countries are open regarding economic matters. The higher the rating, the more opaque, or hidden, the economy of that country. In the partial index in Exhibit 13.7, Nigeria has the highest opacity rating at 57, and Finland the lowest at 9. The United States has an opacity rating of 23, a slight increase since the previous ratings. In countries with higher ratings, financial figures are typically closely guarded and managers may be discouraged from sharing information with employees and the public. Globalization is beginning to have an impact on economic opacity in various countries by encouraging a convergence toward global accounting standards that support more accurate collection, recording, and reporting of financial information. Thus, most countries have improved their ratings over the past few years. Indonesia, Singapore, and Ireland all show significant decreases in opacity since the 2005-2006 ratings, for example.

TOTAL QUALITY MANAGEMENT

Another popular approach based on a decentralized control philosophy is **total quality management (TQM)**, an organization-wide effort to infuse quality into every activity in a company through continuous improvement. Managing quality is a concern for every organization. The Yugo was the lowest-priced car on the market when it was introduced in the United States in 1985, yet four years later, the division went bankrupt, largely as a result of quality problems in both products and services.[41] In contrast, Toyota has steadily gained market share over the past several decades and has taken over General Motors as the world's top-selling auto maker. The difference

total quality management (TQM) An organization-wide commitment to infusing quality into every activity through continuous improvement.

EXHIBIT | 13.7

International Opacity Index:
Which Countries Have the
Most Secretive Economies?

Country	2007–2008 Opacity Score	2005–2006 Score
Nigeria	57	60
Venezuela	48	50
Saudi Arabia	47	52
China	45	48
India	44	44
Indonesia	41	56
Russia	41	45
Mexico	37	43
Taiwan	34	33
South Korea	31	35
South Africa	26	32
Japan	25	26
United States	23	21
Canada	22	24
Germany	17	27
Ireland	16	25
Singapore	14	28
Hong Kong	12	19
Finland	9	17

The higher the opacity score, the more secretive the national economy, meaning that prevailing attitudes and standards discourage openness regarding financial results and other data.

SOURCE: Joel Kurtzman and Glenn Yago, "Opacity Index, 2007–2008: Measuring Global Business Risks," published by Milken Institute (April 2008), http://www.milkeninstitute.org/pdf/2008OpacityIndex.pdf (accessed June 16, 2008).

comes down to quality. Toyota is a model of what happens when a company makes a strong commitment to total quality management.

TQM became attractive to U.S. managers in the 1980s because it had been successfully implemented by Japanese companies, such as Toyota, Canon, and Honda, which were gaining market share and an international reputation for high quality. The Japanese system was based on the work of such U.S. researchers and consultants as Deming, Juran, and Feigenbaum, whose ideas attracted U.S. executives after the methods were tested overseas.[42] The TQM philosophy focuses on team-work, increasing customer satisfaction, and lowering costs. Organizations implement TQM by encouraging managers and employees to collaborate across functions and departments, as well as with customers and suppliers, to identify areas for improvement, no matter how small. Each quality improvement is a step toward perfection and meeting a goal of zero defects. Quality control becomes part of the day-to-day business of every employee, rather than being assigned to specialized departments.

TQM Techniques

The implementation of total quality management involves the use of many techniques, including quality circles, benchmarking, Six Sigma principles, reduced cycle time, and continuous improvement.

Quality Circles One technique for implementing the decentralized approach of TQM is to use quality circles. A **quality circle** is a group of 6 to 12 volunteer employees who meet regularly to discuss and solve problems affecting the quality of their work.[43] At a set time during the workweek, the members of the quality circle meet, identify problems, and try to find solutions. Circle members are free to collect data and take surveys. Many companies train people in team building, problem solving,

quality circle A group of 6 to 12 volunteer employees who meet regularly to discuss and solve problems affecting the quality of their work.

and statistical quality control. The reason for using quality circles is to push decision making to an organization level at which recommendations can be made by the people who do the job and know it better than anyone else.

Benchmarking Introduced by Xerox in 1979, benchmarking is now a major TQM component. **Benchmarking** is defined as "the continuous process of measuring products, services, and practices against the toughest competitors or those companies recognized as industry leaders to identify areas for improvement."[44] The key to successful benchmarking lies in analysis. Starting with its own mission statement, a company should honestly analyze its current procedures and determine areas for improvement. As a second step, a company carefully selects competitors worthy of copying. For example, Xerox studied the order fulfillment techniques of L. L. Bean, the Freeport, Maine, mail-order firm, and learned ways to reduce warehouse costs by 10 percent. Companies can emulate internal processes and procedures of competitors, but must take care to select companies whose methods are compatible. Once a strong, compatible program is found and analyzed, the benchmarking company can then devise a strategy for implementing a new program.

COURTESY OF STARWOOD HOTELS & RESORTS WORLD-WIDE; PHOTO PROVIDED BY BUSINESSWEEK

Concept Connection The idea for "Unwind" events, such as this performance of traditional dance in the lobby of the Westin Kuala Lumpur in Malaysia, came from the staff of the Westin Chicago River North as a way to improve profitability and guest service. Unwind events are aimed at business travelers and designed to encourage guest interaction. **Six Sigma** specialists at each unit of Starwood Hotels & Resorts Worldwide facilitate the development of projects from the ideas of local staff. After rolling out a prototype, performance metrics are used to gauge the success or failure of the new projects. The Unwind program alone produced 120 new events, one for each Westin hotel.

Six Sigma Six Sigma quality principles were first introduced by Motorola in the 1980s and were later popularized by General Electric, where former CEO Jack Welch praised Six Sigma for quality and efficiency gains that saved the company billions of dollars. Based on the Greek letter *sigma*, which statisticians use to measure how far something deviates from perfection, **Six Sigma** is a highly ambitious quality standard that specifies a goal of no more than 3.4 defects per million parts. That essentially means being defect-free 99.9997 percent of the time.[45] However, Six Sigma has deviated from its precise definition to become a generic term for a quality-control approach that takes nothing for granted and emphasizes a disciplined and relentless pursuit of higher quality and lower costs. The discipline is based on a five-step methodology referred to as *DMAIC* (Define, Measure, Analyze, Improve, and Control, pronounced "de-May-ick" for short), which provides a structured way for organizations to approach and solve problems.[46]

Effectively implementing Six Sigma requires a major commitment from top management, because Six Sigma involves widespread change throughout the organization. Hundreds of organizations have adopted some form of Six Sigma program in recent years. Highly committed companies, including ITT Industries, Motorola, General Electric, Allied Signal, ABB Ltd., and the DuPont Company, send managers to weeks of training to become qualified as Six Sigma "black belts." These black belts lead projects aimed at improving targeted areas of the business.[47] Although originally applied to manufacturing, Six Sigma has evolved to a process used in all industries and affecting every aspect of company operations, from human resources to customer service. Textron, whose products include Cessna jets and E-Z-Go golf carts, has trained nearly 10,000 in-house experts in Six Sigma and uses it in both its manufacturing and service sectors. Textron CEO Lewis Campbell offers proof that it's working. "Even though Cessna has been producing planes for 89 years and jets since 1972, they recently reduced by 17 percent the labor hours required to make their single-piston aircraft. That's a big number. They've taken the inspection time from 10 days to five. Textron financial used to take 320 hours each month collecting interest from customers. They've got that down to 56 hours."[48] Exhibit 13.8 lists some statistics that illustrate why Six Sigma is important for both manufacturing and service organizations.

benchmarking The continuous process of measuring products, services, and practices against major competitors or industry leaders.

Six Sigma A quality control approach that emphasizes a relentless pursuit of higher quality and lower costs.

99 Percent Amounts to:	Six Sigma Amounts to:
117,000 pieces of lost first-class mail per hour	1 piece of lost first-class mail every two hours
800,000 mishandled personal checks each day	3 mishandled checks each day
23,087 defective computers shipped each month	8 defective computers shipped each month
7.2 hours per month without electricity	9 seconds per month without electricity

SOURCE: Based on data from *Statistical Abstract of the United States*, U.S. Postal Service, as reported in Tracy Mayor, "Six Sigma Comes to IT: Targeting Perfection," *CIO* (December 1, 2003): 62–70.

EXHIBIT | 13.8

The Importance of Quality Improvement Programs

Reduced Cycle Time Cycle time has become a critical quality issue in today's fast-paced world. **Cycle time** refers to the steps taken to complete a company process, such as making an airline reservation, processing an online order, or opening a retirement fund. The simplification of work cycles, including dropping barriers between work steps and among departments and removing worthless steps in the process, enables a TQM program to succeed. Even if an organization decides not to use quality circles or other techniques, substantial improvement is possible by focusing on improved responsiveness and acceleration of activities into a shorter time. Reduction in cycle time improves overall company performance as well as quality.[49]

L. L. Bean is a recognized leader in cycle time control. Workers used flowcharts to track their movements, pinpoint wasted motions, and completely redesign the order-fulfillment process. Today, a computerized system breaks down an order based on the geographic area of the warehouse in which items are stored. Items are placed on conveyor belts, where electronic sensors re-sort the items for individual orders. After orders are packed, they are sent to a FedEx facility on site. Improvements such as these have enabled L. L. Bean to process most orders within two hours after the order is received.[50]

cycle time The steps taken to complete a company process.

continuous improvement The implementation of a large number of small, incremental improvements in all areas of the organization on an ongoing basis.

Continuous Improvement In North America, crash programs and designs have traditionally been the preferred method of innovation. Managers measure the expected benefits of a change and favor the ideas with the biggest payoffs. In contrast, Japanese companies have realized extraordinary success from making a series of mostly small improvements. This approach, called **continuous improvement**, or *kaizen*, is the implementation of a large number of small, incremental improvements in all areas of the organization on an ongoing basis. In a successful TQM program, all employees learn that they are expected to contribute by initiating changes in their own job activities. The basic philosophy is that improving things a little bit at a time, all the time, has the highest probability of success. Innovations can start simple, and employees can build on their success in this unending process. Here's how one auto parts plant benefits from a TQM and continuous improvement philosophy.

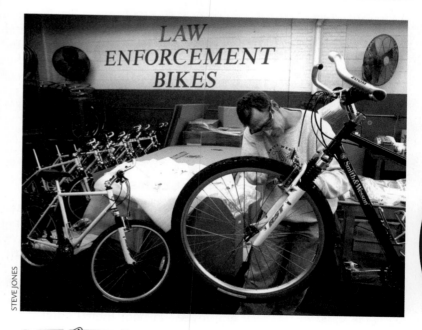

STEVE JONES

Concept Connection University of Miami public safety officers used to take a hit-or-miss approach to auto theft. The result: cars continued to disappear. To upgrade their tactics, a **continuous improvement** team collected data, analyzed it, and pinpointed exactly where and when thieves were most likely to strike. Now a marked patrol car and security guards on bicycles, similar to the ones being assembled by Smith & Wesson employees here, patrol known campus "hot spots." Car thefts dropped by approximately 75 percent. The continuous improvement effort continues because "ten auto thefts may seem like a small number, but it is ten more than we want."

5 Controlling

The Dana Corporation's Perfect Circle Products Franklin Steel Products Plant in Franklin, Kentucky, manufactures as many as 3,500 different part numbers, primarily for automakers Ford, General Motors, and DaimlerChrysler, as well as thousands of after-market products. In one recent year, the company churned out about 60 million oil-ring expanders, for example.

Despite the high-volume, high-mix environment, Dana Franklin has maintained a 99 percent on-time delivery rate to customers since 2001. For the first six months of 2004, customer complaints were zero per million products sold, and the customer reject rate was zero parts per million. The plant has been named one of *Industry Week* magazine's 10 Best North American Manufacturing Facilities a record-setting six times. These results are amazing accomplishments for the plant's small workforce (just 44 production and management personnel), especially considering that some of the equipment they use is more than 50 years old. Yet the philosophy here is that with each unit produced, with each hour, with each day and each week, the plant gets just a little bit better. As plant manager Tim Parys says, "We've sort of adopted the Japanese philosophy in that the worst that the equipment ever runs is the day that you put it on the floor."

In addition to continuous improvement on the plant floor, typically two or three active Six Sigma initiatives are underway at any time in the plant. Almost everyone in the plant is a Six Sigma green belt or black belt. Dana Franklin holds regular four-day *kaizen* events, in which team members selected from the entire workforce focus on eliminating wasteful materials, activities, and processes. Production technician Ronnie Steenbergen is convinced that *kaizen* works and can enable the factory to squeeze out even more improvements from its "old machines."[51]

Unfortunately, despite the effectiveness of the Franklin plant and the quality of its parts and service, production cutbacks by U.S. automakers, along with pressure from the automakers for ever-lower prices even as the cost of raw materials was skyrocketing, pushed parent company Dana into bankruptcy. The company is now struggling to restructure and survive in an increasingly tough industry.[52] Yet Dana remains committed to a strong continuous improvement program. "As we pursue improved financial performance, we are taking aggressive actions to enhance our operational excellence. Chief among these are the establishment of shared, targeted metrics across all of our businesses; the implementation of the Dana Operating System, a coordinated approach to drive continuous improvement throughout our operations; and the review of our global manufacturing footprint to ensure that we are producing the right products in the right places to best serve the needs of our customers," said CEO Gary Convis.[53]

TQM Success Factors

Despite its promise, total quality management does not always work. A few firms have had disappointing results. In particular, Six Sigma principles might not be appropriate for all organizational problems, and some companies have expended tremendous energy and resources for little payoff.[54] Many contingency factors (listed in Exhibit 13.9) can influence the success of a TQM program. For example, quality circles are most beneficial when employees have challenging jobs; participation in a quality circle can contribute to productivity because it enables employees to pool their knowledge and solve interesting problems. TQM also tends to be most successful when it enriches jobs and improves employee motivation. In addition, when participating in the quality program improves workers' problem-solving skills, productivity is likely to increase. Finally, a quality program has the greatest chance of success in a corporate culture that values quality and stresses continuous improvement as a way of life, as at the Dana Franklin plant just described.

Positive Factors	Negative Factors
• Tasks make high skill demands on employees.	• Management expectations are unrealistically high.
• TQM serves to enrich jobs and motivate employees.	• Middle managers are dissatisfied about loss of authority.
• Problem-solving skills are improved for all employees.	• Workers are dissatisfied with other aspects of organizational life.
• Participation and teamwork are used to tackle significant problems.	• Union leaders are left out of QC discussions.
• Continuous improvement is a way of life.	• Managers wait for big, dramatic innovations.

EXHIBIT 13.9

Quality Program Success Factors

TRENDS IN QUALITY AND FINANCIAL CONTROL

Many companies are responding to changing economic realities and global competition by reassessing organizational management and processes—including control mechanisms. Some of the major trends in quality and financial control include international quality standards, economic value-added and market value-added systems, activity-based costing, and increased corporate governance.

International Quality Standards

One impetus for total quality management in the United States is the increasing significance of the global economy. Many countries have adopted a universal benchmark for quality management practices, **ISO 9000 standards**, which represent an international consensus of what constitutes effective quality management as outlined by the International Organization for Standardization.[55] Hundreds of thousands of organizations in 157 countries, including the United States, have been certified against ISO 9000 standards to demonstrate their commitment to quality. Europe continues to lead in the total number of certifications, but the greatest number of new certifications in recent years has been in the United States. One of the more interesting organizations to recently become ISO certified was the Phoenix, Arizona, Police Department's Records and Information Bureau. In today's environment, where the credibility of law enforcement agencies has been called into question, the bureau wanted to make a clear statement about its commitment to quality and accuracy of information provided to law enforcement personnel and the public.[56] ISO certification has become the recognized standard for evaluating and comparing companies on a global basis, and more U.S. companies are feeling the pressure to participate to remain competitive in international markets. In addition, many countries and companies require ISO certification before they will do business with an organization.

As a new manager, be aware of current trends in financial and quality control. Learn quality principles, new financial control systems, and open-book management and apply what works for your situation.

TakeaMoment

ISO 9000 standards A set of standards that represent an international consensus of what constitutes effective quality management, as outlined by the International Organization for Standardization.

New Financial Control Systems

In addition to traditional financial tools, managers are using systems such as economic value-added, market value-added, activity-based costing, and corporate governance to provide effective financial control.

5
Controlling

Economic Value-Added (EVA) Hundreds of companies, including AT&T, Quaker Oats, the Coca-Cola Company, and Philips Petroleum Company, have set up **economic value-added (EVA)** measurement systems as a new way to gauge financial performance. EVA can be defined as a company's net (after-tax) operating profit minus the cost of capital invested in the company's tangible assets.[57] Measuring performance in terms of EVA is intended to capture all the things a company can do to add value from its activities, such as run the business more efficiently, satisfy customers, and reward shareholders. Each job, department, process, or project in the organization is measured by the value added. EVA can also help managers make more cost-effective decisions. At Boise Cascade, the vice president of IT used EVA to measure the cost of replacing the company's existing storage devices against keeping the existing storage assets that had higher maintenance costs. Using EVA demonstrated that buying new storage devices would lower annual maintenance costs significantly and easily make up for the capital expenditure.[58]

Market Value-Added (MVA) **Market value-added (MVA)** adds another dimension because it measures the stock market's estimate of the value of a company's past and projected capital investment projects. For example, when a company's market value (the value of all outstanding stock plus the company's debt) is greater than all the capital invested in it from shareholders, bondholders, and retained earnings, the company has a positive MVA, an indication that it has increased the value of capital entrusted to it and thus created shareholder wealth. A positive MVA usually, although not always, goes hand-in-hand with a high overall EVA measurement.[59] For example, in one study, General Electric had both the highest MVA and the highest EVA in its category (companies were categorized by size). Microsoft was ranked second in MVA but had a lower EVA rating than GE and many other companies. This comparison indicates that the stock market believes Microsoft has greater opportunities for further growth, which will, in turn, increase its EVA.[60]

Activity-Based Costing (ABC) Managers measure the cost of producing goods and services so they can be sure they are selling those products for more than the cost to produce them. Traditional methods of costing assign costs to various departments or functions, such as purchasing, manufacturing, human resources, and so on. With a shift to more horizontal, flexible organizations has come a new approach called **activity-based costing (ABC)**, which allocates costs across business processes. ABC attempts to identify all the various activities needed to provide a product or service and allocate costs accordingly. For example, an activity-based costing system might list the costs associated with processing orders for a particular product, scheduling production for that product, producing it, shipping it, and resolving problems with it. Because ABC allocates costs across business processes, it provides a more accurate picture of the cost of various products and services.[61] In addition, it enables managers to evaluate whether more costs go to activities that add value (meeting customer deadlines, achieving high quality) or to activities that do not add value (such as processing internal paperwork). They can then focus on reducing costs associated with nonvalue-added activities.

Corporate Governance Today, many organizations are moving toward increased control from the top in terms of **corporate governance**, which refers to the system of governing an organization so that the interests of corporate shareholders are protected. The matter of corporate governance has come to the forefront in light of the failure of top executives and corporate directors to provide adequate oversight and control at failed companies such as Enron, HealthSouth, Adelphia, and WorldCom. In some cases, financial reporting systems were manipulated to produce false results and hide internal failures. The financial reporting systems and the roles of boards of directors are being scrutinized in organizations around the world to ensure that top leaders are keeping a close eye on the activities of lower-level managers and employees.

economic value-added (EVA) A control system that measures performance in terms of after-tax profits minus the cost of capital invested in tangible assets.

market value-added (MVA) A control system that measures the stock market's estimate of the value of a company's past and expected capital investment projects.

activity-based costing (ABC) A control system that identifies the various activities needed to provide a product and allocates costs accordingly.

corporate governance The system of governing an organization so the interests of corporate owners are protected.

Some of the corporate failures could be attributed to *undercontrol* because top managers did not keep personal tabs on everything in a large, global organization. Many of the CEOs who have been indicted in connection with financial misdeeds have claimed that they were unaware that misconduct was going on. In some cases, these claims might be true, but they reflect a significant breakdown in control. In response, the U.S. government enacted the Sarbanes-Oxley Act of 2002, often referred to as SOX, which requires several types of reforms, including better internal monitoring to reduce the risk of fraud, certification of financial reports by top leaders, improved measures for external auditing, and enhanced public financial disclosure. SOX has been unpopular with many business leaders, largely because of the expense of complying with the act. In addition, some critics argue that SOX is creating a culture of *overcontrol* that is stifling innovation and growth. Even among those who agree that government regulation is needed, calls for a more balanced regulatory scheme that requires transparency and objectivity without restraining innovation are growing.[62]

As a new manager, keep in mind that overcontrol can be just as detrimental to your team's performance as undercontrol. Find a balance between oversight and control on the one hand and mutual trust and respect on the other. Go to the ethical dilemma on page 401 that pertains to new workplace control issues.

TakeaMoment

Overcontrol of employees can be damaging to an organization as well. Managers might feel justified in monitoring e-mail and Internet use, as described in the Shoptalk earlier in this chapter, for example, yet employees often resent and feel demeaned by close monitoring that limits their personal freedom and makes them feel as if they are constantly being watched. Excessive control of employees can lead to demotivation, low morale, lack of trust, and even hostility among workers. Managers have to find an appropriate balance, as well as develop and communicate clear policies regarding workplace monitoring. Although oversight and control are important, good organizations also depend on mutual trust and respect among managers and employees.

ch13 A MANAGER'S ESSENTIALS: WHAT HAVE WE LEARNED?

- Organizational control is the systematic process through which managers regulate organizational activities to meet planned goals and standards of performance. Most organizations measure and control performance using financial measures. Increasingly, more organizations are measuring less tangible aspects of performance.

- The balanced scorecard is a comprehensive management control system that balances traditional measures with operational measures relating to a company's critical success factors. The four major perspectives of the balanced scorecard are financial performance, customer service, internal business processes, and the organization's capacity for learning and growth.

- The feedback control model involves using feedback to determine whether performance meets established standards. Well-designed control systems include four key steps: establish standards, measure performance, compare performance to standards, and make corrections as necessary.

- Budgetary control is one of the most commonly used forms of managerial control. Managers might use expense budgets, revenue budgets, cash budgets, and capital budgets. Other financial controls include use of the balance sheet, income statement, and financial analysis of these documents.

5
Controlling

- The philosophy of controlling has shifted to reflect changes in leadership methods. Traditional hierarchical controls emphasize establishing rules and procedures, then monitoring employee behavior to make sure the rules and procedures are followed. With decentralized control, employees assume responsibility for monitoring their own performance.

- Open-book management is used in decentralized organizations to share with all employees the financial condition of a company. Open-book management encourages active participation in achieving organizational goals, helps the employee understand how his or her job affects the financial success of the organization, and allows employees to see the interdependence and importance of each business function.

- Total quality management is an organization-wide effort to infuse quality into every activity in a company through continuous improvement. Although based on work of U.S. researchers and consultants, TQM was initially adopted and made popular by Japanese firms. TQM techniques include quality circles, benchmarking, Six Sigma, reduced cycle time, and continuous improvement.

- Recent trends in control include the use of international quality standards, economic value-added (EVA) and market value-added (MVA) systems, activity-based costing (ABC), and corporate governance.

ch13 DISCUSSION QUESTIONS

1. You're a manager who employs a participative control approach. You've concluded that corrective action is necessary to improve customer satisfaction, but first you need to convince your employees that the problem exists. What kind of evidence do you think employees will find more compelling: quantitative measurements or anecdotes from your interactions with customers? Explain your answer.

2. How might a public school system use feedforward control to identify the best candidates for its teaching positions?

3. What are some examples of feedback control that might be used in a family-style restaurant? In a large hospital?

4. Think of a class you've taken in the past. What standards of performance did your professor establish? How was your actual performance measured? How was your performance compared to the standards? Do you think the standards and methods of measurement were fair? Were they appropriate to your assigned work? Why or why not?

5. Some critics argue that Six Sigma is a collection of superficial changes that often result in doing a superb job of building the wrong product or offering the wrong service. Do you agree or disagree? Explain.

6. In what ways could a university benefit from bureaucratic control? In what ways might it benefit from decentralized control? Overall, which approach do you think would be best at your college or university? Why?

7. What types of analysis can managers perform to help them diagnose a company's financial condition? How might a review of financial statements help managers diagnose other kinds of performance problems as well?

8. Why is benchmarking an important component of total quality management (TQM) programs? Do you believe a company could have a successful TQM program without using benchmarking?

9. How might activity-based costing provide better financial control tools for managers of a company such as Kellogg that produces numerous food products?

10. Why do you think today's managers would want to use the balanced scorecard to measure and control organizational performance? Think of two different kinds of organizations. Do you think the balanced scorecard approach is equally suitable for them both? Why or why not?

ch13 MANAGEMENT IN PRACTICE: EXPERIENTIAL EXERCISE

Is Your Budget in Control?

By the time you are in college, you are in charge of at least some of your own finances. How well you manage your personal budget may indicate how well you will manage your company's budget on the job. Respond to the following statements to evaluate your own budgeting habits. If the statement doesn't apply directly to you, respond the way you think you would behave in a similar situation.

1. I spend all my money as soon as I get it.　Yes　No

2. At the beginning of each week (or month, or term), I write down all my fixed expenses.　Yes　No

3. I never seem to have any money left over at the end of the week (or month).　Yes　No

4. I pay all my expenses, but I never seem to have any money left over for fun.　Yes　No

5. I am not putting any money away in savings right now; I'll wait until after I graduate from college.　Yes　No

6. I can't pay all my bills.　Yes　No

7. I have a credit card, but I pay the balance in full each month.　Yes　No

8. I take cash advances on my credit card.　Yes　No

9. I know how much I can spend on eating out, movies, and other entertainment each week.　Yes　No

10. I pay cash for everything.　Yes　No

11. When I buy something, I look for value and determine the best buy.　Yes　No

12. I lend money to friends whenever they ask, even if it leaves me short of cash.　Yes　No

13. I never borrow money from friends.　Yes　No

14. I am putting aside money each month to save for something that I really need.　Yes　No

Scoring and Interpretation

Yes responses to statements 2, 9, 10, 13, and 14 point to the most disciplined budgeting habits; *yes* responses to 4, 5, 7, and 11 reveal adequate budgeting habits; yes responses to 1, 3, 6, 8, and 12 indicate the poorest budgeting habits. If you have answered honestly, chances are you'll have a combination of all three. Look to see where you can improve your budgeting.

ch13 MANAGEMENT IN PRACTICE: ETHICAL DILEMMA

The Wages of Sin?

Chris Dykstra, responsible for loss prevention at West-wind Electronics, took a deep breath before he launched into making his case for the changes he was proposing in the company's shoplifting policy. He knew convincing Ross Chenoweth was going to be a hard sell. Ross, the president and CEO, was the son of the founder of the local, still family-owned consumer electronics chain based in Phoenix, Arizona. He'd inherited not only the company but also his father's strict moral code.

"I think it's time to follow the lead of other stores," Chris began. He pointed out that most other retailers didn't bother calling the police and pressing charges unless the thief had shoplifted merchandise worth more than $50 to $100. In contrast, Westwind currently had the zero-tolerance policy toward theft that

Ross's father had put in place when he started the business. Chris wanted to replace that policy with one that only prosecuted individuals between 18 and 65, had stolen more than $20 worth of goods, and had no previous history of theft at Westwind. In the case of first-time culprits under 18 or over 65, he argued for letting them off with a strict warning regardless of the value of their ill-gotten goods. Repeat offenders would be arrested.

"Frankly, the local police are getting pretty tired of having to come to our stores every time a teenager sticks a CD in his jacket pocket," Chris pointed out. "And besides, we just can't afford the costs associated with prosecuting everyone." Every time he pressed charges against a shoplifter who'd made off with a $10 item, Westwind lost money. The company had to engage a lawyer and pay employees overtime for

5

Controlling

their court appearances. In addition, Chris was looking at hiring more security guards to keep up with the workload. Westwind was already in a battle it was losing at the moment with the mass retailers who were competing all too successfully on price, so passing on the costs of its zero-tolerance policy to customers wasn't really an option. "Let's concentrate on catching dishonest employees and those organized theft rings. They're the ones who are really hurting us," Chris concluded.

There was a long pause after Chris finished his carefully prepared speech. Ross thought about his recently deceased father, both an astute businessman and a person for whom honesty was a key guiding principle. If he were sitting here today, he'd no doubt say that theft was theft, that setting a minimum was tantamount to saying that stealing was acceptable just as long as you don't steal too much. He looked at Chris. "You know, we've both got teenagers. Is this really a message you want to send out, especially to kids? You know as well as I do that there's nothing they like better than testing limits. It's almost an invitation to see if you can beat the system." But then Ross faltered as he found himself glancing at the latest financial figures on his desk—another in a string of quarterly losses. If Westwind went under, a lot of

employees would be looking for another way to make a living. In his heart, he believed in his father's high moral standards, but he had to ask himself: Just how moral could Westwind afford to be?

What Would You Do?

1. Continue Westwind's zero-tolerance policy toward shoplifting. It's the right thing to do—and it will pay off in the end in higher profitability because the chain's reputation for being tough on crime will reduce overall losses from theft.

2. Adopt Chris Dykstra's proposed changes and show more leniency to first-time offenders. It is a more cost-effective approach to the problem than the current policy, plus it stays close to your father's original intent.

3. Adopt Chris Dykstra's proposed changes with an even higher limit of $50 or $100, which is still less than the cost of prosecution. In addition, make sure the policy isn't publicized. That way you'll reduce costs even more and still benefit from your reputation for prosecuting all shoplifters.

SOURCE: Based on Michael Barbaro,"Some Leeway for the Small Shoplifter," *The New York Times* (July 13, 2006): section C, 1.

---

ch13 CASE FOR CRITICAL ANALYSIS

Lincoln Electric

Imagine having a management system that is so successful people refer to it with capital letters—the Lincoln Management System—and other businesses benchmark their own systems by it. That is the situation of Ohio-based Lincoln Electric. For a number of years, other companies have tried to figure out Lincoln Electric's secret—how management coaxes maximum productivity and quality from its workers, even during difficult financial times. Lately, however, Lincoln Electric has been trying to solve a mystery of its own: Why is the company having such difficulty exporting a management system abroad that has worked so well at home?

Lincoln Electric is a leading manufacturer of welding products, welding equipment, and electric motors, with more than $1 billion in sales and 6,000 workers worldwide. The company's products are used for cutting, manufacturing, and repairing other metal products. Although it is now a publicly traded company,

members of the Lincoln family still own more than 60 percent of the stock.

Lincoln uses a diverse control approach. Tasks are precisely defined, and individual employees must exceed strict performance goals in order to achieve top pay. The incentive and control system is powerful. Production workers are paid on a piece-rate basis, plus merit pay based on performance. Employees also are eligible for annual bonuses, which fluctuate according to the company's profits, and they participate in stock purchase plans. A worker's bonus is based on four factors: work productivity, work quality, dependability, and cooperation with others. Some factory workers at Lincoln have earned more than $100,000 a year.

However, the Lincoln system succeeds largely because of an organizational culture based on openness and trust, shared control, and an egalitarian spirit. To begin with, the company has earned employee trust with its no layoff policy. In fact, the last time it laid off anyone was in 1951. Although the line between managers and workers at Lincoln is firmly drawn, managers respect the expertise of production workers and value their contributions to many aspects of the business. The company has an open-door policy for all top executives, middle managers, and production workers, and regular face-to-face communication is encouraged. Workers are expected to challenge management if they believe practices or compensation rates are unfair. Most workers are hired right out of high school, then trained and cross-trained to perform different jobs. Some eventually are promoted to executive positions, because Lincoln believes in promoting from within. Many Lincoln workers stay with the company for life.

One of Lincoln's founders felt that organizations should be based on certain values, including honesty, trustworthiness, openness, self-management, loyalty, accountability, and cooperativeness. These values continue to form the core of Lincoln's culture, and management regularly rewards employees who manifest them. Because Lincoln so effectively socializes employees, they exercise a great degree of self-control on the job. Each supervisor oversees 100 workers, and less tangible rewards complement the piece-rate incentive system. Pride of workmanship and feelings of involvement, contribution, and esprit de corps are intrinsic rewards that flourish at Lincoln Electric. Cross-functional teams, empowered to make decisions, take responsibility for product planning, development, and marketing. Information about the company's operations and financial performance is openly shared with workers throughout the company.

Lincoln emphasizes anticipating and solving customer problems. Sales representatives are given the technical training they need to understand customer needs, help customers understand and use Lincoln's products, and solve problems. This customer focus is backed by attention to the production process through the use of strict accountability standards and formal measurements for productivity, quality, and innovation for all employees. In addition, a software program called Rhythm helps streamline the flow of goods and materials in the production process.

Lincoln's system worked so well in the United States that senior executives decided to extend it overseas. Lincoln built or purchased eleven plants in Japan, South America, and Europe, with plans to run the plants from the United States using Lincoln's expertise with management control systems.

Managers saw the opportunity to beat local competition by applying manufacturing control incentive systems to reduce costs and raise production in plants around the world. The results were abysmal and nearly sunk the company. Managers at international plants failed to meet their production and financial goals every year—they exaggerated the goals sent to Lincoln's managers in order to receive more resources, especially during the recession in Europe and South America. Many overseas managers had no innate desire to increase sales, and workers were found sleeping on benches because not enough work was available. The European labor culture was hostile to the piecework and bonus control system. The huge losses in the international plants, which couldn't seem to adopt Lincoln's vaunted control systems, meant the company would have to borrow money to pay U.S. workers' bonuses, or forgo bonuses for the first time in Lincoln's history. Top managers began to wonder. Had they simply done a poor job of applying the Lincoln Management System to other cultures, or was it possible that it simply wasn't going to work abroad?

Questions

1. What types of control described in the chapter—feedforward, concurrent, or feedback—are illustrated in this case? Would you characterize Lincoln's control approach as primarily bureaucratic or decentralized? Explain your answers.

2. Based on what you've just read, what do you think makes the Lincoln System so successful in the United States?

3. What is the problem with transporting Lincoln's control systems to other national cultures? What suggestions would you make to Lincoln's managers to make future international manufacturing plants more successful?

4. Should Lincoln borrow money and pay bonuses to avoid breaking trust with its U.S. workers? Why or why not?

SOURCES: Based on Herb Greenberg, "Why Investors May Do Well with Firms That Avoid Layoffs," *The Wall Street Journal* (September 9, 2006): B4; Mark Gottlieb, "Feeding the Dragon," *Industry Week* 251, no. 1 (February 2002): 54–55; Donald Hastings, "Lincoln Electric's Harsh Lessons from International Expansion," *Harvard Business Review* (May–June, 1999): 3–11; and Joseph Maciariello, "A Pattern of Success: Can This Company Be Duplicated?" *Drucker Management* 1, no. 1 (Spring 1997): 7–11.

5 Controlling

ch13 ON THE JOB VIDEO CASE

The NEADS Team: People and Dogs

All the teams you have encountered in this chapter have been teams of people. NEADS, the National Education for Assistance Dog Services, functions with teams of people as well. But another type of teamwork is central to the mission of NEADS: the team of human and dog. NEADS acquires, raises, trains, and matches service dogs to meet the needs of people with limited physical mobility or deafness. A typical service dog may be trained to respond to a blaring smoke alarm or ringing telephone, nudge a light switch on or off with its nose, or retrieve items for an owner. Since this partnership is intended to last a lifetime, it is important for the match to be perfect.

It takes about two years to train a service dog—and that requires a lot of teamwork. Since NEADS is a nonprofit organization, it must be creative in the way it recruits and uses volunteers. These volunteers include high school students, families, and prisoners. High school students may help NEADS puppy trainers begin to expose the youngest dogs to experiences they will encounter in their lives as service dogs, such as sitting by a wheelchair or walking next to a cane. Families become part of the team when, at four months of age, the puppies are placed in foster care for the next part of their education. Volunteer families agree to feed, love, and raise the puppies so they become accustomed to the distractions and energy of the real world. Professional dog trainers from NEADS visit regularly to work with the families and dogs to ensure that the dogs receive the proper training in preparation for their later work. Since 1998, prison inmates in Massachusetts and Connecticut have participated in a foster care program as well. While a puppy lives at the prison, a small team from NEADS visits regularly to monitor the puppy's development. Another set of volunteers participate in a program called Pups on Parole, during which they take the puppies outside the prison for field trips to shopping malls, supermarkets, business districts, parks, and the like. In addition, a professional trainer works with the prisoners and puppies. The partnership with prisons has required another level of teamwork, with state agencies. NEADS

executive director Sheila O'Brien says this relationship has been highly successful. "The commissioner felt very strongly that inmates should give back to the society that they violated, in a safe way." Working with the dogs has proved to be a safe and effective program for inmates. In fact, the dogs who live with prisoners return to NEADS more advanced in their readiness for formal training than those who live with families.

The puppies live in their foster homes until they are about a year and a half old—then they return to the NEADS farm to continue their education. Here, they receive advanced training from professional dog trainers. When a dog's training is complete, its new owner arrives on campus for a two-week stay, during which the person and dog become a team. The dog and person have been matched through an extensive process that involves a team of people interviewers and dog trainers. During this intensive get-acquainted and training period, "they learn to love each other, respect each other, and work together," explains O'Brien.

O'Brien emphasizes that, "Even though the concentration at this point is on the team, meaning two— the dog and the person—there are still many team members working behind the stage to facilitate this coming together." She refers to volunteers who raise funds to cover the cost of receiving a dog, as well as those who greet new clients and help them become familiar and comfortable with the NEADS campus. "What makes these teams work so cohesively is that everyone knows what the outcome should be," says O'Brien. "Everyone is working toward getting a dog and person together and making sure this dog provides the independence that this disabled or deaf person needs. Everyone has that in sight. Everyone just works toward that end."

Questions

1. Describe the characteristics of a typical NEADS team, using the criteria discussed in the chapter.

2. What factors determine the cohesiveness of NEADS teams?

3. Describe a situation in which conflict might arise in a NEADS team.

SOURCE: Organization Web site, *http://www.neads.org.*

ch13 BIZ FLIX VIDEO CASE

Casino

Martin Scorsese's lengthy, complex, and beautifully filmed *Casino* offers a close look at the gambling casinos of Las Vegas and their organized crime connections in the 1970s. It completes his trilogy that began with *Mean Streets* (1973) and continued with *Goodfellas* (1990). In *Casino*, ambition, greed, drugs, and sex ultimately destroy the mob's gambling empire. The film includes strong performances by Robert De Niro, Joe Pesci, and Sharon Stone. The violence and expletive-filled dialogue give *Casino* an R rating.

This scene, which comes from the beginning of "The Truth about Las Vegas" sequence, opens the film and establishes important background about casino operations. Listen carefully to Sam Rothstein's (De Niro) voice-over. He quickly describes the casino's operation and explains how it tries to reach its goals.

What to Watch for and Ask Yourself

1. What type of operations management does this scene show—manufacturing operations management or service operations management?

2. Are the customers directly involved in this operation? If they are, in what way? What likely effects does their involvement have on the casino's operation and its management?

3. Does the casino have independent or interdependent operations processes?

SOURCE: J. Craddock, Ed. *VideoHound's Golden Movie Retriever*, (Farmington Hills, MI: The Gale Group, Inc.), 2000.

ch13 ENDNOTES

1. Adapted from J. J. Ray, "Do Authoritarians Hold Authoritarian Attitudes?" *Human Relations* 29 (1976): 307–325.

2. Sally B. Connelly, "Lean and Mean," Inside Business, *Time* (August, 2006): A4.

3. Yochi J. Dreazen, "More Katrina Woes: Incidents of Fraud at Red Cross Centers," *The Wall Street Journal*, October 19, 2005.

4. Douglas S. Sherwin, "The Meaning of Control," *Dunn's Business Review* (January, 1956).

5. Russ Banham, "Nothin' But Net Gain," *eCFO* (Fall 2001): 32–33.

6. "On Balance," a *CFO* Interview with Robert Kaplan and David Norton, *CFO* (February 2001): 73–78; and Bill Birchard, "Intangible Assets + Hard Numbers = Soft Finance," *Fast Company* (October 1999): 316–336.

7. Andy Neely and Mohammed Al Najjar, "Management Learning Not Management Control: The True Role of Performance Measurement," *California Management Review* 48, no. 3 (Spring 2006): 105.

8. This discussion is based on a review of the balanced scorecard in Richard L. Daft, *Organization Theory and Design*, 7th ed. (Cincinnati, OH: South-Western, 2001), pp. 300–301.

9. Neely and Al Najjar, pp. 105 and 112.

10. Robert Kaplan and David Norton, "The Balanced Scorecard: Measures That Drive Performance," *Harvard Business Review* (January–February 1992): 71–79; and Chee W. Chow, Kamal M. Haddad, and James E. Williamson, "Applying the Balanced Scorecard to Small Companies," *Management Accounting* 79, no. 2 (August 1997): 21–27.

11. Based on Kaplan and Norton, "The Balanced Scorecard"; Chow, Haddad, and Williamson, "Applying the Balanced Scorecard"; and Cathy Lazere, "All Together Now," *CFO* (February 1998): 28–36.

12. Jessi Hempil, "Finding Cracks in Facebook," *Fortune* (May 13,

5 Controlling

2008), http://money.cnn
.com/2008/05/12/technology/
cracks_facebook_hempel.fortune/
index.htm?postversion=2008051308
(accessed May 14, 2008).

13. Geert J. M. Braam and Edwin J.
Nijssen, "Performance Effects of Us-
ing the Balanced Scorecard: A Note
on the Dutch Experience," *Long
Range Planning* 37 (2004): 335–349;
Kaplan and Norton, "The Balanced
Scorecard"; and Cam Scholey,
"Strategy Maps: A Step-by-Step
Guide to Measuring, Managing, and
Communicating the Plan," *Journal
of Business Strategy* 26, no. 3 (2005):
12–19.

14. Nils-Göran Olve, Carl-Johan Petri,
Jan Roy, and Sofie Roy, "Twelve Years
Later: Understanding and Realizing
the Value of Balanced Scorecards,"
Ivey Business Journal (May–June
2004); Eric M. Olson and Stanley
F. Slater, "The Balanced Score-
card, Competitive Strategy, and
Performance," *Business Horizons*
(May–June 2002): 11–16; and Eric
Berkman, "How to Use the Balanced
Scorecard," *CIO* (May 15, 2002):
93–100.

15. Ibid.; and Brigitte W. Schay, Mary
Ellen Beach, Jacqueline A. Caldwell,
and Christelle LaPolice, "Using
Standardized Outcome Measures in
the Federal Government," *Human
Resource Management* 41, no. 3 (Fall
2002): 355–368.

16. Braam and Nijssen, "Performance
Effects of Using the Balanced
Scorecard."

17. Olve et al., "Twelve Years Later: Understanding and Realizing the Value
of Balanced Scorecards."

18. Peter Valdes-Dapena, "Tiny Smart
Car Gets Crash Test Kudos," *Fortune*
(May 14, 2008), http://money.cnn
.com/2008/05/14/autos/smart_
fortwo_iihs_crash_test/index.htm
(accessed May 14, 2008).

19. Richard E. Crandall, "Keys to
Better Performance Measurement,"
Industrial Management (January–
February 2002): 19–24; Christopher
D. Ittner and David F. Larcker,
"Coming Up Short on Nonfinancial
Performance Measurement,"
Harvard Business Review (Novem-
ber 2003): 88–95.

20. Crandall, "Keys to Better Performance Measurement."

21. Frank Eltman, "Tracking Systems
Help Cities Monitor Employees,

Save," *The Tennessean*, November
16, 2007.

22. Charles Fishman, "No Satisfaction,"
Fast Company (December 2006/
January 2007): 88.

23. Adam Lashinsky, "Meg and the
Machine," *Fortune* (September 1,
2003): 68–78.

24. Sumantra Ghoshal, *Strategic Control*
(St. Paul, MN: West, 1986), Chap-
ter 4; and Robert N. Anthony, John
Dearden, and Norton M. Bedford,
Management Control Systems, 5th
ed. (Homewood, IL: Irwin, 1984).

25. John A. Boquist, Todd T. Milbourn,
and Anjan V. Thakor, "How Do You
Win the Capital Allocation Game?"
Sloan Management Review (Winter
1998): 59–71.

26. Anthony, Dearden, and Bedford,
Management Control Systems.

27. Participation in budget setting is
described in a number of stud-
ies, including Neil C. Churchill,
"Budget Choice: Planning versus
Control," *Harvard Business Review*
(July–August 1984): 150–164; Peter
Brownell, "Leadership Style, Bud-
getary Participation, and Managerial
Behavior," *Accounting Organizations
and Society* 8 (1983): 307–321; and
Paul J. Carruth and Thurrell O.
McClandon, "How Supervisors
React to 'Meeting the Budget' Pres-
sure," *Management Accounting* 66
(November 1984): 50–54.

28. Tim Reason, "Budgeting in the Real
World," *CFO* (July 2005): 43–48.

29. Ibid.

30. Bruce G. Posner, "How to Stop Worrying and Love the Next Recession,"
Inc. (April 1986): 89–95.

31. Lawrence M. Fisher, "Inside Dell
Computer Corporation," *Strategy
and Business* 10, (First Quarter
1998): 68–75; and Randy Myers,
"Cash Crop: The 2000 Working
Capital Survey," *CFO* (August 2000):
59–69.

32. Andy Reinhardt, "Tesco Bets Small—
And Wins Big," *BusinessWeek e.biz*
(October 1, 2001): EB26–EB32.

33. Robin Goldwyn Blumenthal, "'Tis
the Gift to Be Simple," *CFO* (January
1998): 61–63.

34. William G. Ouchi, "Markets,
Bureaucracies, and Clans," *Administrative Science Quarterly* 25
(1980): 129–141; and B. R. Baligia
and Alfred M. Jaeger, "Multinational
Corporations: Control Systems
and Delegation Issues," *Journal of

International Business Studies* (Fall
1984): 25–40.

35. Sherwin, "The Meaning of Control."

36. Anna Wilde Mathews, "New Gadgets Track Truckers' Every Move," *The
Wall Street Journal*, July 14, 1997.

37. Perry Pascarella, "Open the Books to
Unleash Your People," *Management
Review* (May 1998): 58–60.

38. Nadine Heintz, "Everyone's a CFO,"
Inc. (September 2005): 42, 45.

39. Ibid.

40. Mel Mandell, "Accounting Challenges
Overseas," *World Trade* (December
1, 2001).

41. John A. Parnell, C. W. Von Bergen,
and Barlow Soper, "Profiting from
Past Triumphs and Failures: Har-
nessing History for Future Success,"
SAM Advanced Management Journal
(Spring 2005): 36–59.

42. A. V. Feigenbaum, *Total Quality Con-
trol: Engineering and Management*
(New York: McGraw-Hill, 1961);
John Lorinc, "Dr. Deming's Traveling
Quality Show," *Canadian Business*
(September 1990): 38–42; Mary
Walton, *The Deming Management
Method* (New York: Dodd-Meade
& Co., 1986); and J. M. Juran and
Frank M. Gryna, eds., *Juran's Qual-
ity Control Handbook*, 4th ed. (New
York: McGraw-Hill, 1988).

43. Edward E. Lawler III and Susan A.
Mohrman, "Quality Circles after
the Fad," *Harvard Business Review*
(January–February 1985): 65–71; and
Philip C. Thompson, *Quality Circles:
How to Make Them Work in America*
(New York: AMACOM, 1982).

44. D. J. Ford, "Benchmarking HRD,"
Training and Development (July
1993): 37–41.

45. Tracy Mayor, "Six Sigma Comes to
IT: Targeting Perfection," *CIO* (De-
cember 1, 2003): 62–70; Hal Plotkin,
"Six Sigma: What It Is and How to
Use It," *Harvard Management Up-
date* (June 1999): 3–4; Tom Rancour
and Mike McCracken, "Applying 6
Sigma Methods for Breakthrough
Safety Performance," *Professional
Safety* 45, no. 10 (October 2000):
29–32; G. Hasek, "Merger Mar-
ries Quality Efforts," *Industry Week*
(August 21, 2000): 89–92; and Lee
Clifford, "Why You Can Safely Ignore
Six Sigma," *Fortune* (January 22,
2001): 140.

46. Dick Smith and Jerry Blakeslee "The
New Strategic Six Sigma," *Training
& Development* (September 2002):

45–52; Michael Hammer and Jeff Goding, "Putting Six Sigma in Perspective," *Quality* (October 2001): 58–62; and Mayor, "Six Sigma Comes to IT."

47. Plotkin, "Six Sigma: What It Is"; Timothy Aeppel, "Nicknamed 'Nag,' She's Just Doing Her Job," *The Wall Street Journal*, May 14, 2002; John S. McClenahen, "ITT's Value Champion," *IndustryWeek* (May 2002): 44–49.

48. "CEO Expects Good Things as Textron Does Six Sigma Right," *USA Today*, January 21, 2008.

49. Philip R. Thomas, Larry J. Gallace, and Kenneth R. Martin, *Quality Alone Is Not Enough* (New York: American Management Association, 1992).

50. Kate Kane, "L. L. Bean Delivers the Goods," *Fast Company* (August–September 1997): 104–113.

51. George Taninecz, "Change for the Better," *Industry Week* (October 2004): 49–50; and "Dana Corporation Earns Record Sixth Industry Week 10 Best Plants Award," *PR Newswire* (September 27, 2004): 1.

52. Sholnn Freeman, "Auto Parts Maker Files Chapter 11; Rising Costs, Cuts in Detroit Prompt Move by Dana Corp.," *The Washington Post*, March 4, 2006; and Doron Levin, "Dana's Bankruptcy Is Payback to Ford, Other Automakers," *Pittsburgh Post-Gazette*, March 9, 2006.

53. "Dana Holding Corporation Reports First-Quarter 2008 Results," www.http://dana.mediaroom.com/index.php/press_releases/2144 (accessed May 15, 2008).

54. Clifford, "Why You Can Safely Ignore Six Sigma"; and Hammer and Goding, "Putting Six Sigma in Perspective."

55. Syed Hasan Jaffrey, "ISO 9001 Made Easy," *Quality Progress* 37, no. 5 (May 2004): 104; Frank C. Barnes, "ISO 9000 Myth and Reality: A Reasonable Approach to ISO 9000," *SAM Advanced Management Journal* (Spring 1998): 23–30; and Thomas H. Stevenson and Frank C. Barnes, "Fourteen Years of ISO 9000: Impact, Criticisms, Costs, and Benefits," *Business Horizons* (May–June 2001): 45–51.

56. David Amari, Don James, and Cathy Marley, "ISO 9001 Takes On a New Role—Crime Fighter," *Quality Progress* 37, no. 5 (May 2004): 57ff.

57. Don L. Bohl, Fred Luthans, John W. Slocum Jr., and Richard M. Hodgetts, "Ideas That Will Shape the Future of Management Practice," *Organizational Dynamics* (Summer 1996): 7–14.

58. John Berry, "How to Apply EVA to I.T.," *CIO* (January 15, 2003): 94–98.

59. Stephen Taub, "MVPs of MVA," *CFO* (July 2003): 59–66; and K. Lehn and A. K. Makhija, "EVA and MVA as Performance Measures and Signals for Strategic Change," *Strategy & Leadership* (May–June 1996): 34–38.

60. Taub, "MVPs of MVA."

61. Sidney J. Baxendale, "Activity-Based Costing for the Small Business: A Primer," *Business Horizons* (January–February 2001): 61–68; Terence C. Pare, "A New Tool for Managing Costs," *Fortune* (June 14, 1993): 124–129; and Don L. Bohl, Fred Luthans, John W. Slocum Jr., and Richard M. Hodgetts, "Ideas That Will Shape the Future of Management Practice," *Organizational Dynamics* (Summer 1996): 7–14.

62. "Business: The Trial of Sarbanes-Oxley; Regulating Business," *The Economist* (April 22, 2006): 69; and Maurice R. Greenberg, "Regulation, Yes; Strangulation, No," *The Wall Street Journal*, August 21, 2006.

5 Controlling

pt5

chapter14

© GETTY IMAGES/DIGITAL VISION

Learning Outcomes

After studying this chapter, you should be able to:

1. Define *operations management* and describe its application within manufacturing and service organizations.

2. Explain today's partnership approach to supply chain management.

3. Summarize considerations in designing facilities layout.

4. Discuss new technologies used for manufacturing and service operations, and explain what is meant by lean manufacturing.

5. Explain why small inventories are preferred by most organizations and describe just-in-time inventory management.

6. Identify ways in which information technology has transformed the manager's job.

7. Describe different types of IT systems used in today's organizations and how they support daily operations and decision making.

8. Summarize the key components of e-business and explain common e-business strategies.

Managing the Value Chain, Information Technology, and E-Business

1 Introduction
2 Environment
3 Planning
4 Organizing
5 Controlling
6 Leading

WHICH SIDE OF YOUR BRAIN DO YOU USE?[1]

The following questions ask you to describe your behavior. For each question, check the answer that best describes you.

1. I am usually running late for class or other appointments:
   _____ **a.** Yes
   _____ **b.** No

2. When taking a test I prefer:
   _____ **a.** Subjective questions (discussion or essay)
   _____ **b.** Objective questions (multiple choice)

3. When making decisions, I typically:
   _____ **a.** Go with my gut—what feels right
   _____ **b.** Carefully weigh each option

4. When solving a problem, I would more likely:
   _____ **a.** Take a walk, mull things over, then discuss
   _____ **b.** Write down alternatives, prioritize them, then pick the best

5. I consider time spent daydreaming as:
   _____ **a.** A viable tool for planning my future
   _____ **b.** A waste of time

6. To remember directions, I typically:
   _____ **a.** Visualize the information
   _____ **b.** Make notes

7. My work style is mostly:
   _____ **a.** To juggle several things at once
   _____ **b.** To concentrate on one task at a time until complete

8. My desk, work area, or laundry area are typically:
   _____ **a.** Cluttered
   _____ **b.** Neat and organized

SCORING AND INTERPRETATION: People have two thinking processes—one visual and intuitive, which is often referred to as *right-brained thinking*, and the other verbal and analytical, referred to as *left-brained thinking*. The thinking process you prefer predisposes you to certain types of knowledge and information—visual charts and operations dashboards vs. written reports, intuitive suggestions vs. quantitative data—as effective input to your thinking and decision making.

Count the number of checked "a" items and "b" items. Each "a" represents right-brain processing, and each "b" represents left-brain processing. If you scored six or higher on either, you have a distinct processing style. If you checked less than six for either, you probably have a balanced style. New managers typically need left-brain processing to handle data and to justify decisions. At middle and upper management levels, right-brain processing enables visionary thinking and strategic insights.

Managers are inundated with data and information, particularly in today's world of computers and the Internet. As suggested by the opening questionnaire, some people prefer written reports with lots of explicit data, while others like a visual presentation and a broad overview. Both styles are useful, and as managers grow in their abilities, they typically learn to use and appreciate a balanced approach.

This chapter describes techniques for the planning and control of manufacturing and service operations and the use of information technology in today's organizations. Whereas the previous chapter described overall control concepts, this chapter will focus on the control of production operations and the use of information systems for management and control. First, we define operations management and supply chain management, consider specific operational design issues, such as facilities layout and the use of technology in the production system, and take a close look at inventory management. The second part of the chapter explores the application of information technology, including management information and enterprise resource planning systems, use of the Internet, and strategies for e-business.

THE ORGANIZATION AS A VALUE CHAIN

In Chapter 1, the organization was described as a system used for transforming inputs into outputs. At the center of this transformation process is the **technical core**, which is the heart of the organization's production of its product or service.[2] In an automobile company, the technical core includes the plants that manufacture automobiles. In a university, the technical core includes the academic activities of teaching and research.

As illustrated in Exhibit 14.1, the organization can be thought of as a *value chain* that receives inputs from the environment, such as raw materials and other resources, and adds value by transforming them into products and services for customers. Inputs into the technical core typically include materials and equipment, human resources, land and buildings, and information. Outputs from the technical core are the goods and services produced by the organization and sold or provided to customers and clients. Operations strategy and control feedback shape the quality of outputs and the efficiency of operations within the technical core.

The topic of operations management pertains to the day-to-day management of the technical core, as illustrated in Exhibit 14.1, including acquiring inputs, transforming them, and distributing outputs. **Operations management** is formally defined as the field of management that specializes in the production of goods and services and uses special tools and techniques for solving production problems. In essence, operations managers are concerned with all the activities involved in converting inputs into outputs, including decisions about matters such as how and where to obtain raw materials, where to locate facilities and what equipment to install in them, and how to get products or services to customers. For example, PepsiCo has gotten into the farming business to get the raw materials it needs to build its snack foods business in emerging markets. Sales of Western-style snack foods are growing fast in China and other developing countries, and Pepsi wants to be the global leader. However, getting the tens of millions of potatoes needed to

technical core The heart of the organization's production of its product or service.

operations management The field of management that focuses on the physical production of goods or services and uses specialized techniques for solving manufacturing problems.

EXHIBIT | **14.1**　The Organization As a Value Chain

serve the Chinese market alone turned out to be a major problem. Today, Pepsi is the largest private potato grower in China and also has potato programs in Russia, South Africa, and Poland.[3] Pepsi's operations managers also have to consider the best location to manufacture snack foods for global markets, how to get raw materials to manufacturing facilities, and how to efficiently produce products and get them onto store shelves.

manufacturing organization An organization that produces physical goods.

service organization An organization that produces nonphysical outputs that require customer involvement and cannot be stored in inventory.

Manufacturing and Service Operations

Although terms such as *production* and *operations* seem to imply manufacturing, operations management applies to service organizations as well. The service sector has increased three times as fast as the manufacturing sector in the North American economy. More than half of all businesses in the United States are service organizations and two-thirds of the U.S. workforce is employed in services, such as hospitals, hotels and resorts, retail, financial services, information services, or telecommunications firms. Exhibit 14.2 shows differences between manufacturing and service organizations.

Manufacturing organizations are those that produce physical goods, such as cars, video games, television sets, or golf balls. In contrast, **service organizations** produce nonphysical outputs, such as medical, educational, communication, or transportation services for customers. Doctors, consultants, online auction companies, and the local barber all provide services. Services also include the sale of merchandise. Although merchandise is a physical good, the service company does not manufacture it but merely sells it as a service to the customer.

Services differ from manufactured products in two ways. First, the service customer is involved in the actual production process.[4] The patient actually visits the doctor to receive the service, and it's difficult to imagine a hairstylist providing services without direct customer contact. The same is true for airlines, restaurants, and banks. Second, manufactured goods can be placed in inventory, whereas service outputs, being intangible, cannot be stored. Manufactured products such as clothes, food, cars, or iPods all can be put in warehouses and sold at a later date. However, a hairstylist cannot wash, cut, and style hair in advance and leave it on the shelf for the customer's arrival, nor can a doctor place examinations in inventory. The service must be created and provided for the customer exactly when he or she wants it.

Despite the differences between manufacturing and service firms, they face similar operational problems. First, each kind of organization is concerned with scheduling. A medical clinic must schedule appointments

© BECKFORD ENTERPRISES/PRNEWSFOTO (NEWSCOM)

Concept Connection   A doctor's office is a classic example of a **service operation**, but Dr. Rita Beckford doesn't limit her practice of medicine to the clinic. Her mission is to empower people everywhere to take control of their own health. Beckford didn't need anyone to tell her that her post-pregnancy weight of 210 pounds put her at risk for the diabetes that killed her grandmother. So she shed more than 80 pounds, became a certified fitness instructor, and offered her services to medical clinics, community centers, and churches. Beckford's popular exercise routines became the core of a DVD, *Home with Dr. B.*, and she also offers her services as a motivational speaker.

EXHIBIT | **14.2**

Differences Between Manufacturing and Service Organizations

Manufacturing Organizations	Service Organizations
Produce physical goods	Produce nonphysical outputs
Goods inventoried for later consumption	Simultaneous production and consumption
Quality measured directly	Quality perceived and difficult to measure
Standardized output	Customized output
Production process removed from consumer	Consumer participates in production process
Facilities site moderately important to business success	Facilities site crucial to success of firm
Capital intensive	Labor intensive
Examples:	*Examples:*
Automobile manufacturers	Airlines
Steel companies	Hotels
Soft-drink companies	Law firms

SOURCES: Based on Richard L. Daft, *Organization Theory and Design* (Cincinnati, OH: South-Western, 2005), p. 256; and Byron J. Finch and Richard L. Luebbe, *Operations Management* (Fort Worth, TX: Dryden Press, 1995), p. 50.

5 Controlling

so that doctors' and patients' time will be used efficiently. Second, both manufacturing and service organizations must obtain materials and supplies. Third, both types of organizations are concerned with quality and productivity. Because many operational problems are similar, operations management tools and techniques can and should be applied to service organizations as readily as they are to manufacturing operations.

TakeaMoment | As a new manager, think about your team as part of a value chain that receives inputs, adds value, and provides outputs to customers or clients. Help your team implement operations techniques to achieve superior customer responsiveness, innovation, quality, and efficiency.

Supply Chain Management

To operate efficiently, innovate, and produce high-quality items that meet customers' needs, the organization must have reliable deliveries of high-quality, reasonably priced supplies and materials. It also requires an efficient and reliable system for distributing finished products, making them readily accessible to customers. Operations managers therefore recognize that they need to manage the entire supply chain. **Supply chain management** is the term for managing the sequence of suppliers and purchasers covering all stages of processing from obtaining raw materials to distributing finished goods to final consumers.[5]

supply chain management
Managing the sequence of suppliers and purchasers, covering all stages of processing from obtaining raw materials to distributing finished goods to final consumers.

The most recent advances in supply chain management involve using Internet technologies to achieve the right balance of low inventory levels and customer responsiveness. An e-supply chain creates a seamless, integrated link that stretches from customers to suppliers by establishing electronic linkages between the organization and these external partners for the sharing and exchange of data.[6] Dell's integrated supply chain, illustrated in Exhibit 14.3 provides an excellent example.

EXHIBIT | 14.3   Dell Computer's Integrated Supply Chain

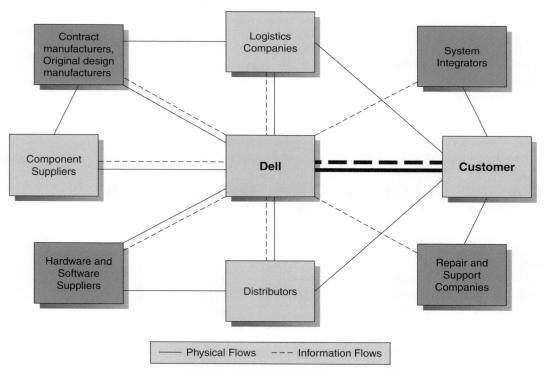

SOURCE: Jason Dedrick and Kenneth L. Kraemer, "The Impacts of IT on Firm and Industry Structure: The Personal Computer Industry," *California Management Review* 47, no. 3 (Spring 2005): 132. Used with permission.

Dell has struggled in recent years due to poor strategic decisions, but it thrived for decades because managers found the most efficient way to make, sell, and deliver personal computers.

Dell is electronically connected to suppliers, contract manufacturers, and distributors, as shown in Exhibit 14.3, so that everyone along the supply chain has almost completely transparent information about sales, orders, shipments, and other data. That means, for instance, that suppliers have data about orders and production levels and know what parts Dell's factories are going to need and when they'll need them. Distributors know when computers will be ready for shipment and where they'll be going. At the end of the supply chain, Dell develops close connections to customers through a range of channels, including online sales and services, call centers, and a direct sales force and technical personnel serving larger customers. Dell's role in the supply chain is to manage the electronic information flows and physical connections among suppliers, partners, and customers.[7]

Innovative Way

Dell Inc.

Despite Dell's recent problems, AMR Research still ranks it as the third best-performing supply chain in the world, with Apple ranked at number 1, Nokia at number 2, Wal-Mart at number 6, and the British supermarket chain Tesco at number 12.[8]

Enterprise integration through the use of electronic linkages is creating a level of cooperation not previously imaginable for many organizations. Supplier relationships used to be based on an *arm's-length* approach, in which an organization spreads purchases among many suppliers and encourages them to compete with one another. With integration, more companies are opting for a *partnership* approach, which involves cultivating intimate relationships with a few carefully selected suppliers and collaborating closely to coordinate tasks that benefit both parties.

Integrating every company along the supply chain also means a quicker response to end consumers by reducing the time it takes to move critical data through the information pipeline. Manufacturers have immediate access to sales data and can deliver new products, even custom orders, as needed. An integrated supply chain enables managers at fashion chain Zara stores to order hot selling items and have them in stock two days later.[9] Ford Motor Company has been undergoing a supply-chain makeover intended to enable the company to manufacture cars on a reasonable build-to-order basis, so that customers no longer have to wait months for delivery of the car of their dreams.[10]

Managing a supply chain means asserting influence and gaining cooperation without having formal authority over suppliers, which requires interpersonal and political skills. Take the New Manager Self-Test on page 414 to learn about your political skills.

TakeaMoment

FACILITIES LAYOUT

Another important consideration for operations management is planning the facilities layout for producing goods or services. The four most common types of layout are process, product, cellular, and fixed-position, shown in Exhibit 14.4.

Process Layout

As illustrated in Exhibit 14.4(a), a **process layout** in a manufacturing firm is one in which all machines that perform a similar function or task are grouped together. In a machine shop, the lathes perform a similar function and are located together in one section. The grinders are in another section of the shop. Service organizations also use process layouts. In a bank, the loan officers are in one area, the tellers in another, and the managers in a third.

The advantage of the process layout is that it has the potential for economies of scale and reduced costs. For example, having all painting done in one spray-painting area means that fewer machines and people are required to paint all products for

process layout A facilities layout in which machines that perform the same function are grouped together in one location.

5
Controlling

New Manager Self-Test

Political Skills

How good are you at influencing people horizontally across an organization? To learn something about your skills, answer the questions that follow. Please answer whether each item that follows is Mostly True or Mostly False for you.

	Mostly True	Mostly False
1. I am able to communicate easily and effectively with others.	_____	_____
2. I spend a lot of time at work developing connections with people outside my area.	_____	_____
3. I instinctively know the right thing to say or do to influence others.	_____	_____
4. I am good at using my connections outside my area to get things done at work.	_____	_____
5. When communicating with others, I am absolutely genuine in what I say and do.	_____	_____
6. It is easy for me to reach out to new people.	_____	_____
7. I make strangers feel comfortable and at ease around me.	_____	_____
8. I am good at sensing the motivations and hidden agendas of others.	_____	_____

SCORING AND INTERPRETATION: Give yourself one point for each item marked as Mostly True. A score of six or higher suggests active political skills and a good start for your career as a new manager. If you scored three or less, you may want to focus more on building horizontal relationships as you progress in your career.

Political skills help a new manager build personal and organizational relationships that enhance the team's outcomes. New managers often learn task and people skills first. Political skills tend to be subtle and are typically mastered after gaining management experience.

SOURCE: Adapted from Gerald R. Ferris, Darren C. Treadway, Robert W. Kolodinsky, Wayne A. Hochwarter, Charles J. Kacmer, Ceasar Douglas, and Dwight D. Frink, "Development and Validation of the Political Skill Inventory, *Journal of Management* 31 (February 2005): 126–152.

the organization. In a bank, having all tellers located in one controlled area provides increased security. Placing all operating rooms together in a hospital makes it possible to control the environment for all rooms simultaneously.

The drawback to the process layout, as illustrated in Exhibit 14.4(a), is that the actual path a product or service takes can be long and complicated. A product may need several different processes performed on it and thus must travel through many different areas before production is complete.

Product Layout

product layout A facilities layout in which machines and tasks are arranged according to the sequence of steps in the production of a single product.

Exhibit 14.4(b) illustrates a **product layout**—one in which machines and tasks are arranged according to the progressive steps in producing a single product. The automobile assembly line is a classic example, because it produces a single product starting from the raw materials to the finished output. Many fast-food restaurants use the

EXHIBIT 14.4

Basic Production Layouts

(a) Process Layout

(b) Product Layout

(c) Cellular Layout

(d) Fixed-Position Layout

SOURCES: Based on J. T. Black, "Cellular Manufacturing Systems Reduce Setup Time, Make Small Lot Production Economical," *Industrial Engineering* (November 1983): 36–48; and Richard J. Schonberger, "Plant Layout Becomes Product-Oriented with Cellular, Just-in-Time Production Concepts," *Industrial Engineering* (November 1983): 66–77.

product layout, with activities arranged in sequence to produce hamburgers or fried chicken, depending on the products available.

The product layout is efficient when the organization produces or provides huge volumes of identical products or services. Note in Exhibit 14.4(b) that two lines have paint areas. This duplication of functions can be economical only if the volume is high enough to keep each paint area busy working on specialized products.

Cellular Layout

Illustrated in Exhibit 14.4(c) is an innovative layout, called **cellular layout**, based on group-technology principles. In a manufacturing plant, all machines dedicated to sequences of operations are grouped into cells, as shown in the exhibit. In a service organization, all the people who work on a process, such as insurance claims processing, are organized into cells where they can see and easily communicate with one another. Work flows from one station to another, similar to materials movement in the manufacturing plant.[11] Grouping technology into cells provides some of the efficiencies of both process and product layouts. Even more important, the U-shaped cells in Exhibit 14.4(c) provide efficiencies in material and tool handling and inventory movement. Employees work in clusters that facilitate teamwork and joint problem solving. Staffing flexibility is enhanced because people are cross-trained so that each worker can perform all the tasks, assisting coworkers as needed.

Fixed-Position Layout

As shown in Exhibit 14.4(d), the **fixed-position layout** is one in which the product remains in one location, and employees and equipment are brought to it. The fixed-position layout is used to create a product or service that is either large or one of a kind. Product examples include aircraft, ships, and buildings. The product cannot be moved from function to function or along an assembly line; rather, the people, materials, and machines all come to the fixed-position site for assembly and processing. London-based Imagination Ltd., Europe's largest independent design and communications agency, provides an interesting service example.

Imagination Ltd.

Innovative Way

Imagination Ltd. has made a name for itself by producing highly theatrical and award-winning events and programs. Consider the event staged for the launch of the *Harry Potter and the Prisoner of Azkaban* DVD and video. Eight hundred guests were invited to Middle Temple, an historic London building where Imagination employees had recreated four movie sets, among them the Great Hall at the Hogwarts School of Witchcraft and Wizardry.

Getting the décor right was a top priority, but Imagination's employees faced a challenge because Middle Temple is a working dining room during the week. They had to work outside regular dining hours and keep everything top-secret, not so easy to do when you're suspending 200 battery-powered candles from the ceiling and making arrangements to transport Harry Potter himself to the party. The event, designed to attract international media for client Warner Home Video, was a resounding success and generated more than $9.5 million worth of free advertising.[12] example.

The fixed-position layout is not good for high volume, but it is often necessary for large, bulky products, special events, and custom orders like the one-of-a-kind launch of the *Harry Potter and the Prisoner of Azkaban* DVD. Many manufacturers are adapting the fixed-position layout to speed up production. Boeing now builds many of its planes on a type of moving assembly line, which cut in half the time it takes to assemble a single-aisle 737. Airbus uses assembly stations, moving the plane only from one major workstation to the next, with the idea that a glitch in one plane won't slow a whole production line.[13]

cellular layout A facilities layout in which machines dedicated to sequences of production are grouped into cells in accordance with group-technology principles.

fixed-position layout A facilities layout in which the product remains in one location and the required tasks and equipment are brought to it.

TECHNOLOGY AUTOMATION

A goal for many of today's operations managers is to find the right combination of technology and management to most efficiently produce goods and services. Let's look at three advances in manufacturing and service operations.

Radio-Frequency Identification (RFID)

flexible manufacturing system A small or medium sized automated production line that can be adapted to produce more than one product line.

Radio-frequency identification (RFID) uses electronic tags that can identify and track individual items such as books, jugs of laundry detergent, automobiles, or even people. One of the best-known uses of RFID is OnStar, which is a satellite-based RFID system used in automobiles. RFID tags emit radio signals that can be read remotely by electronic readers and provide precise, real-time information about the location of specific items, whether it be a Cadillac with a dead battery, a misplaced book in a bookstore, or a pallet of merchandise in a warehouse.[14] Although RFID is also used by manufacturing firms, the technology has revolutionized services. The biggest names in retail, including Wal-Mart, Home Depot, Carrefour, and Tesco, are taking advantage of the new technology. Dutch bookseller Selexyz tags every book on its shelves with RFID, which increases profits and cuts costs since there's no more taking inventory by hand, fewer lost books, and fewer returns to publishers.[15] The potential of RFID for streamlining inventory management and cutting costs for retailers is enormous, which has prompted many companies to require that suppliers use the new technology.

© AP PHOTO/JOHN FROSCHAUER

Concept Connection Because its manufactured goods are too large and cumbersome to move along a traditional assembly line, Boeing Corporation typically uses a **fixed-position layout**. Products, such as this 787 Dreamliner, remain in one location, and employees, components, and equipment are brought to them for assembly. To increase speed and flexibility, Boeing has begun implementing a hybrid system for some of its products. After the wings and landing gear have been attached, a plane such as the 737 is dragged toward the door at two inches a minute, with workers moving along it on a float-like apparatus. Boeing's goal is to push a 737 out the door in only five days.

Other service firms use RFID as well. New York's E-Z Pass and California's FasTrak both use RFID to speed cars through toll booths, for example.[16] The U.S. Department of Defense requires suppliers to use RFID on shipping pallets and cases, enabling the military to easily track shipments of combat-support goods and other items.[17] Amusement parks put RFID wrist bands on children so they can be quickly located if they get separated from their parents.[18] The technology might even ameliorate the age-old problem of lost luggage, which is maddening for passengers and costly for airlines. An RFID baggage-tagging system in use at the Las Vegas McCarran International Airport reduced lost luggage by about 20 percent, and bags that do go astray are located more quickly.[19]

Flexible Manufacturing Systems

Advanced technology has also revolutionized manufacturing. The use of automated production lines that can be quickly adapted to produce more than one kind of product is called a **flexible manufacturing system**.[20] The machinery uses sophisticated computer technology to coordinate and integrate the machines. Automated functions include loading, unloading, storing parts, changing tools, and machining. The computer can instruct the machines to change parts, machining, and tools when a new product must be produced. Human operators make adjustments to the computer, not the production machinery itself, dramatically cutting the time and expense of making changes. This approach is a breakthrough compared with the traditional assembly line in which a single line is restricted to a single product. With a flexible

© FABRIZIO COSTANTINI FOR THE NEW YORK TIMES

Concept Connection   At its East Liberty, Ohio, facility, Honda can shift within minutes from making a Ridgeline truck to making the subcompact Civic. A **flexible manufacturing system** enables this quick-changeover and lets Honda build the Civic Sedan, Civic GX (natural gas powered), Element, Honda CR-V, and Ridgeline truck on the same assembly line with little disruption. As part of the system, the factory has 200-plus robots for welding, which can be quickly reprogrammed by an operator as they shift from one model to another. This flexibility helps Honda respond faster than competitors to changing consumer interests as gas prices fluctuate.

manufacturing system, a single production line can be readily adapted to small batches of different products based on computer instructions.

At the Nissan factory in Canton, Mississippi, for example, minivans, pickup trucks, and sport utility vehicles can all be sent down the same assembly line. Robotic arms on machines are programmed to weld in the spots needed for different vehicles. Highly automated painting machines are programmed to paint all kinds of vehicles one after another, with no down time for reconfiguration.[21] Many of Matsushita Electric's Factories did away with assembly lines altogether in favor of clusters of robots controlled by software that can quickly shift gears to make the hottest electronic gadgets and ease up on slow sellers.[22]

Lean Manufacturing

Lean manufacturing, sometimes called *lean production*, combines advanced technology with innovative management methods, using highly trained employees who take a painstaking approach to problem solving at every stage of the production process to cut waste and improve quality and productivity. Lean manufacturing was pioneered by Toyota, and the concept has spread around the world to both manufacturing and service organizations.

Technology plays a key role in lean manufacturing. Companies make full use of flexible manufacturing systems, and equipment is often designed to stop automatically so that a defect can be fixed. However, the heart of the process is not machines or technology, but people.[23] For example, Toyota's operations are admired worldwide as a model of quality and efficiency, but this success is not merely a result of using the right machines or setting the right standards. Toyota's system combines techniques, systems, and management philosophy, such as commitment to employee empowerment and a creative culture. Besides installing the methodology for running an efficient assembly line, such as *just-in-time* shipments of supplies, managers must instill the necessary attitudes, such as concern for quality and a desire to innovate.[24]

lean manufacturing Manufacturing process using highly trained employees at every stage of the production process to cut waste and improve quality.

inventory The goods that the organization keeps on hand for use in the production process up to the point of selling the final products to customers.

finished-goods inventory Inventory consisting of items that have passed through the complete production process but have yet to be sold.

work-in-process inventory Inventory composed of the materials that still are moving through the stages of the production process.

raw materials inventory Inventory consisting of the basic inputs to the organization's production process.

INVENTORY MANAGEMENT

Inventory is the goods the organization keeps on hand for use in the production process. Most organizations have three types of inventory: finished goods prior to shipment, work in process, and raw materials.

Finished-goods inventory includes items that have passed through the entire production process but have not been sold. This inventory is highly visible. The new cars parked in the storage lot of an automobile factory are finished-goods inventory, as are the hamburgers and french fries stacked under the heat lamps at a McDonald's restaurant. Finished-goods inventory is expensive, because the organization has invested labor and other costs to make the finished product.

Work-in-process inventory includes the materials moving through the stages of the production process that are not completed products. Work-in-process inventory in an automobile plant includes engines, wheel and tire assemblies, and dashboards waiting to be installed. In a fast-food restaurant, the french fries in the fryer and hamburgers on the grill are work-in-process inventory.

Raw materials inventory includes the basic inputs to the organization's production process. This inventory is cheapest, because the organization has not yet invested labor in it. Steel, wire, glass, and paint are raw materials inventory for an auto plant. Meat patties, buns, and raw potatoes are the raw materials inventory in a fast-food restaurant.

The Importance of Inventory

Inventory management is vitally important to organizations, because inventory sitting idly on the shop floor or in the warehouse costs money. Many years ago, a firm's wealth was measured by its inventory. Today inventory is recognized as an unproductive asset in cost-conscious firms. Dollars not tied up in inventory can be used in other productive ventures. Keeping inventory low is especially important for high-tech firms, because so many of their products lose value quickly as they are replaced by more innovative and lower-cost models. For example, the value of a completed personal computer falls rapidly; even if shelf space for PCs were free, a company would lose money on its PC inventory.[25] Service firms are concerned with inventory too, which is a big part of the reason for the growth of RFID, as described earlier.

The Japanese analogy of rocks and water describes the current thinking about the importance of inventory.[26] As illustrated in Exhibit 14.5, the water is the inventory in the organization. The higher the water, the less managers have to worry about the rocks, which represent problems. In operations management, these problems apply to scheduling, facilities layout, or quality. When the water level goes down, managers see the rocks and must deal with them. When inventories are reduced, the problems of a poorly designed and managed operations process also are revealed. The problems then must be solved. When inventory can be kept at an absolute minimum, operations management is considered excellent.

As a new manager, recognize the importance of inventory management. Consider a just-in-time inventory system to enhance productivity and efficiency.

TakeaMoment

Just-in-Time Inventory

Just-in-time (JIT) inventory systems are designed to reduce the level of an organization's inventory and its associated costs, aiming to push to zero the amount of time that raw materials and finished products are sitting in the factory, being inspected, or in transit.[27] Sometimes these systems are referred to as *stockless systems, zero inventory systems*, or *kanban systems*. Each system centers on the concept that suppliers deliver materials only at the exact moment needed, thereby reducing raw material inventories to zero. Moreover, work-in-process inventories are kept to a minimum because goods are produced only as needed to service the next stage of production. Finished-goods inventories are minimized by matching them exactly to sales demand. Just-in-time systems have tremendous advantages. Reduced inventory level frees productive capital for other company uses. In addition, JIT plays a crucial role in enhancing flexibility. A study of manufacturing firms in seven countries found that those that were performing better in terms of flexibility ranked just-in-time as one of their top two improvement initiatives, along with total quality management, as defined in the previous chapter.[28]

just-in-time (JIT) inventory system An inventory control system that schedules materials to arrive precisely when they are needed on a production line.

5 Controlling

EXHIBIT | **14.5**   Large Inventories Hide Operations Management Problems

SOURCE: Based on R. J. Schonberger, *Japanese Manufacturing Techniques: Nine Hidden Lessons in Simplicity* (New York: Free Press, 1982).

Recall the analogy of the rocks and the water. To reduce inventory levels to zero means that all management and coordination problems will surface and must be resolved. Scheduling must be scrupulously precise and logistics tightly coordinated. For example, follow the movement of a shipment of odometers and speedometers from a supplier in Winchester, Virginia, to the Nissan plant in Canton, Mississippi.

Thursday, 9 a.m.:   A truck arrives at the supplier. As workers load the parts, drivers check on-board computers for destination, route, and estimated time of arrival (ETA) data.

Friday, 3 a.m.:   The truck arrives at Canton, Mississippi, and approaches a switching yard two miles from the Nissan plant, parking in a computer-assigned spot. The driver downloads a key-shaped floppy disk from the on-board computer into the trucking company's main-frame, which relays the performance report directly to Nissan.

Friday, 12:50 p.m.: The trailer leaves the switching yard at a designated time and arrives at a predetermined receiving dock at the Nissan plant, where workers unload the parts and send them to the production line just in time.[29]

The coordination required by JIT demands that information be shared among everyone in the supply chain. Communication between only adjoining links in the supply chain is too slow. Rather, coordination requires a kind of information web in which members of the supply chain share information simultaneously with all other participants, often using Internet technologies and perhaps RFID.[30]

INFORMATION TECHNOLOGY HAS TRANSFORMED MANAGEMENT

Advanced information technology makes just-in-time inventory management work seamlessly, but it has also transformed management in many other ways. An organization's **information technology (IT)** consists of the hardware, software, telecommunications, database management, and other technologies it uses to store data and make them available in the form of information for organizational decision making. In general, information technology has positive implications for the practice of management.

Boundaries Dissolve; Collaboration Reigns

Walk into the video conference room at Infosys Technologies, a leader in India's out-sourcing and software industry, and the first thing you'll see is a wall-size flat-screen television. On that screen, Infosys can hold virtual meetings of the key players from its entire global supply chain for any project at any time of the day or night.[31]

Time, distance, and other boundaries between individuals, departments, and organizations are irrelevant in today's business world. Collaboration is what it's all about. Information technology can connect people around the world for the sharing and exchange of information and ideas. As historian Thomas L. Friedman puts it, "Wherever you look today . . . hierarchies are being flattened and value is being created less and less within vertical silos and more and more through horizontal collaboration within companies, between companies, and among individuals."[32]

Knowledge Management

Information technology plays a key role in managers' efforts to support and leverage organizational knowledge. **Knowledge management** refers to the efforts to systematically gather knowledge, organize it, make it widely available throughout the organization, and foster a culture of continuous learning and knowledge sharing.[33]

information technology (IT)
The hardware, software, telecommunications, database management, and other technologies used to store, process, and distribute information.

knowledge management
The process of systematically gathering knowledge, making it widely available throughout the organization, and fostering a culture of learning.

Knowledge is not the same thing as data or information, although it uses both. **Data** are simple, absolute facts and figures that, in and of themselves, may be of little use. A company might have data that show 30 percent of a particular product is sold to customers in Florida. To be useful to the organization, the data are processed into finished *information* by connecting them with other data—for example, nine out of ten of the products sold in Florida are bought by people over the age of sixty. **Information** is data that have been linked with other data and converted into a useful context for specific use. **Knowledge** goes a step further; it is a conclusion drawn from the information after it is linked to other information and compared to what is already known. Knowledge, as opposed to information and data, always has a human factor. Books can contain information, but the information becomes knowledge only when a person absorbs it and puts it to use.[34]

IT systems facilitate knowledge management by enabling organizations to collect and store tremendous amounts of data, analyze that data so it can be transformed into information and knowledge, and share knowledge all across the enterprise. The most common organizational approach to knowledge management is sharing knowledge via information technology.[35] A variety of new software tools support collaboration and knowledge sharing through services such as Web conferencing, knowledge portals, content management, and the use of *wikis*. A **knowledge management portal** is a single, personalized point of access for employees to multiple sources of information on the corporate intranet. A **wiki** uses software to create a Web site that allows anyone with access to create, share, and edit content through a simple brower-based user interface. Organizations typically use a variety of IT systems to facilitate the collection, analysis, and sharing of information and knowledge.

Another IT application for knowledge management is the use of **business intelligence software** that analyzes data and extracts useful insights, patterns, and relationships that might be significant.[36] The application of business intelligence software at Cendant Hotel Group lets managers know immediately when a huge surge of interest in triple rooms in San Diego or Phoenix happens, enabling the company to add inventory or adjust offerings on its Web site. Similarly, managers in other firms can identify sets of products that particular market segments purchase, patterns of transactions that signal possible fraud, or patterns of product performance that may indicate defects.

Management Information Systems

A **management information system (MIS)** is a computer-based system that provides information and support for effective managerial decision making. The central elements of a management information system are illustrated in Exhibit 14.6.

data Raw, unsummarized, and unanalyzed facts and figures.

information Data that have been converted into a meaningful and useful context for the receiver.

knowledge A conclusion drawn from information after it is linked to other information and compared to what is already known.

knowledge management portal A single point of access for employees to multiple sources of information that provides personalized access on the corporate intranet.

wiki Web site that allows anyone with access, inside or outside the organization, to create, share, and edit content through a simple, browser-based user interface.

business intelligence software software that analyzes data from multiple sources and extracts useful insights, patterns, and relationships that might be significant.

management information system (MIS) A computer-based system that provides information and support for effective managerial decision making.

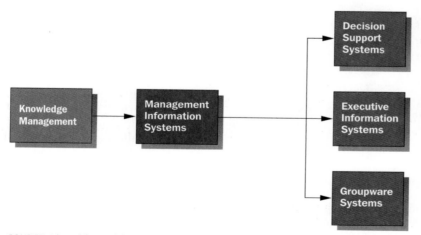

EXHIBIT | 14.6

Basic Elements of Management Information Systems

5
Controlling

SOURCE: Adapted from Ralph M. Stair and George W. Reynolds, *Principles of Information Systems: A Managerial Approach*, 4th ed. (Cambridge, MA: Course Technology, 1999), p. 391.

decision support system (DSS) An interactive, computer-based system that uses decision models and specialized databases to support organization decision makers.

executive information system (EIS) A management information system designed to facilitate strategic decision making at the highest levels of management by providing executives with easy access to timely and relevant information.

business performance dashboard A system that pulls data from a variety of organizational systems and databases; gauges the data against key performance metrics; pulls out the right nuggets of information; and delivers information to managers in a graphical, easy-to-interpret format.

groupware Software that works on a computer network or the Internet to facilitate information sharing, collaborative work, and group decision making.

enterprise resource planning (ERP) system A networked information system that collects, processes, and provides information about an organization's entire enterprise, from identification of customer needs and receipt of orders to distribution of products and receipt of payments.

MISs typically support strategic decision-making needs of mid-level and top management. However, as technology becomes more widely accessible, more employees are wired into networks, and organizations push decision making downward in the hierarchy, these kinds of systems are seeing use at all levels of the organization. For example, when a production supervisor needs to make a decision about production scheduling, he or she may need data on the anticipated number of orders in the coming month, inventory levels, and availability of computers and personnel. The MIS can provide these data. At Veterans Administration (VA) hospitals around the country, a sophisticated MIS called Vista enables people all across the organization to access complete patient information and provide better care. The VA, once considered subpar, has been transformed by technology into one of the highest-quality, most cost-effective medical providers in the United States.[37]

Management information systems typically include decision support systems, executive information systems, and groupware.

Decision support systems (DSSs) are interactive, computer-based information systems that rely on decision models and specialized databases to support decision makers. With electronic spreadsheets and other decision support software, users can pose a series of what-if questions to test alternatives they are considering. Based on the assumptions used in the software or specified by the user, managers can explore various alternatives and receive tentative information to help them choose the alternative with the best outcome. Big retailers such as Home Depot, Bloomingdale's, and Gap use decision support systems to help them gauge when to mark down prices and what items to discount, for example.[38]

Executive information systems (EISs) are management information systems to facilitate strategic decision making at the highest level of management. These systems are typically based on software that provides easy access to large amounts of complex data and can analyze and present information in a timely fashion. EISs provide top management with quick access to relevant internal and external information and, if designed properly, can help them diagnose problems as well as develop solutions. Many companies use executive information systems that enable top managers to view a *dashboard* of key performance indicators on their PCs or laptops. A **business performance dashboard** uses software to present key business information (e.g., sales data, fill rates for orders, or profits per product line) in graphical, easy-to-interpret form and can alert managers to any deviations or unusual patterns in the data. Dashboards pull data from a variety of organizational systems and databases, gauge the data against key performance metrics, and pull out the right nuggets of information to deliver to top managers for analysis and action.[39] The effective use of business performance dashboards is further discussed in this chapter's Manager's Shoptalk.

Modern information technology systems also recognize that many organizational and managerial activities involve groups of people working together to solve problems and meet customer needs. **Groupware** is software that works on a computer network or via the Internet to link people or workgroups across a room or around the globe. The software enables managers or team members to communicate, share information, and work simultaneously on the same document, chart, or diagram and see changes and comments as they are made by others. Sometimes called *collaborative work systems*, groupware systems allow people to interact with one another in an electronic meeting space and at the same time take advantage of computer-based support data.

Concept Connection Alliance Steel Services increased revenues by 500 percent in three years after CEO Michael Zweigbaum invested in a computer inventory management system. This family-run scrap metal business went from pen and paper management to a computerized system that captures each scrap delivery with a photo, weight, and grade. Zweigbaum uses a **business performance dashboard** to monitor how often and how efficiently the inventory moves. He credits the management system's precision for enabling Alliance to sell more brass, copper, and titanium to developing countries, which increased profits.

© THOMAS STRAND

Enterprise Resource Planning Systems

Another key IT component for many companies is an approach to information management called enterprise resource planning. **Enterprise resource planning (ERP) systems** integrate

Manager's Shoptalk

Putting Performance Dashboards to Work

It's first thing in the morning. You sit down at your computer, coffee cup in hand, and click on an icon. Attractively arrayed on the screen is current information organized under various headings—for example, "Calendar," "Tasks," "Key Performance Indicators," "Sales by Manager," and those always eye-catching "Alerts." Critical information about your business is presented in colorful tables, pie charts, graphs, and other visual displays. With just a glance, you're up-to-date on everything you need to know before you start your day. If you're puzzled by a particular figure or alarmed by an alert, you just click on the item and start "drilling down" into the data until you get a detailed picture of exactly what is going on. Welcome to the world of business performance dashboards.

As impressive as the technology is, it's the way organizations design and use dashboards that determines whether they turn out to be a boon or a distracting bane. Here are some tips.

- **Don't contribute to information overload.** Because dashboards collate information from many databases and programs, it's all too easy to construct a Web page that delivers too much information. To make dashboards useful, carefully choose what data will be tracked and what information will be displayed. Make sure it's what employees need to know to do their jobs better.

- **Let line managers and employees drive the development.** Always remember that designing a dashboard is primarily a strategic project,

not a technical one. The IT department can help implement the dashboard, but it is the responsibility of managers to determine its content. One way to make sure people get the right information is to solicit input from end users during the design process.

- **Carefully assess who needs a dashboard.** At General Electric, business unit chiefs use dashboards, but CEO Jeffrey Immelt rarely does. Immelt doesn't want to get so mired in the details that he loses sight of the big picture. On the other hand, using dashboards to push information farther down into the organization can help employees at all levels see from day to day in concrete terms exactly how their actions contribute to an organization's success or failure in achieving its goals.

- **Don't forget the human touch.** Having all the latest facts and figures at your fingertips is certainly valuable, but it's only part of what managers need to know to run an effective organization. Getting out and talking to employees and customers is still just as important.

SOURCES: Spencer E. Ante, "Giving the Boss the Big Picture," *BusinessWeek* (February 13, 2006): 48–51; Tad Leahy, "Warming Up to Performance Dashboards," *Business-FinanceMag.com* (June 1, 2006), http://businessfinancemag.com/article/warming-performance-dashboards-0601; and Doug Bartholomew, "Gauging Success," *CFO-IT* (Summer 2005): 17–19.

SOURCE: Dundas Data Visualization, www.dundas.com.

EXHIBIT | 14.7 Example of ERP Applications

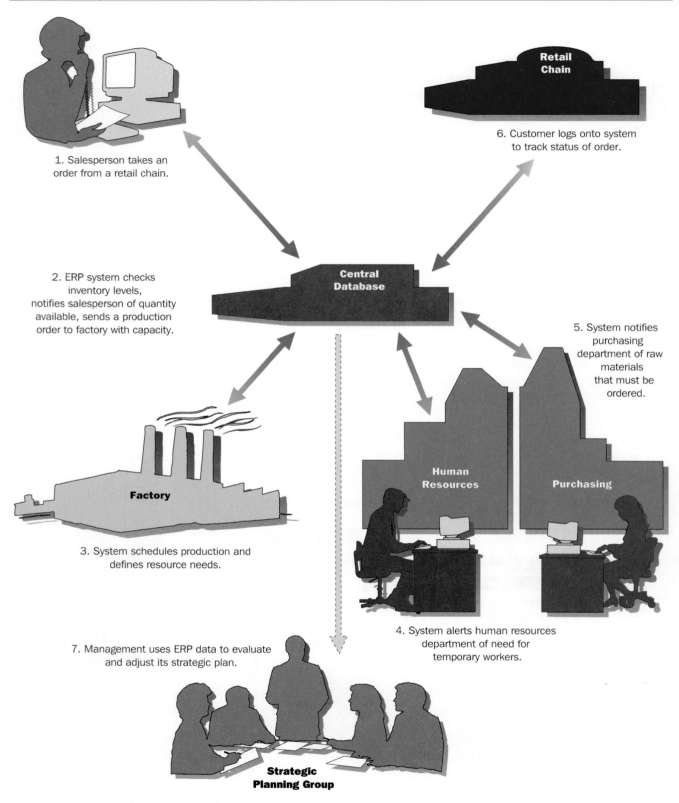

1. Salesperson takes an order from a retail chain.

2. ERP system checks inventory levels, notifies salesperson of quantity available, sends a production order to factory with capacity.

Central Database

Retail Chain

6. Customer logs onto system to track status of order.

5. System notifies purchasing department of raw materials that must be ordered.

Factory

3. System schedules production and defines resource needs.

Human Resources

Purchasing

4. System alerts human resources department of need for temporary workers.

7. Management uses ERP data to evaluate and adjust its strategic plan.

Strategic Planning Group

SOURCE: Adapted from Gail Edmondson, "Silicon Valley on the Rhine," *BusinessWeek* (November 2, 1997): 162–166.

and optimize all the various business processes across the entire firm.[40] A recent study by AMR Research indicates that the use of ERP continues to grow, with nearly half of the companies surveyed planning to spend more than $10 million on ERP activities. The study also showed an increase in the percentage of employees who are using ERP systems in organizations.[41]

An enterprise resource planning system can become the backbone of an organization's operations. It collects, processes, and provides information about an organization's entire enterprise, including orders, product design, production, purchasing, inventory, distribution, human resources, receipt of payments, and forecasting of future demand. Such a system links these areas of activity into a network, as illustrated in Exhibit 14.7.

When a salesperson takes an order, the ERP system checks to see how the order affects inventory levels, scheduling, human resources, purchasing, and distribution. The system replicates organizational processes in software, guides employees through the processes step by step, and automates as many of them as possible. For example, the software can automatically cut an accounts payable check as soon as a clerk confirms that goods have been received in inventory, send an online purchase order immediately after a manager has authorized a purchase, or schedule production at the most appropriate plant after an order is received.[42] In addition, because the system integrates data about all aspects of operations, managers and employees at all levels can see how decisions and actions in one part of the organization affect other parts, using this information to make better decisions. Customers and suppliers are typically linked into the information exchange as well. When carefully implemented, ERP can cut costs, shorten cycle time, enhance productivity, and improve relationships with customers and suppliers.

A NEW GENERATION OF INFORMATION TECHNOLOGY

The force that is fueling growth on the Internet today isn't a bunch of dot-com start-ups, or even long-established companies making waves in the online world. Instead, power has shifted to the individual, with blogs, wikis, and social networking becoming the most explosive outbreaks in the world of information technology since the emergence of the World Wide Web.[43] A **blog** is a running Web log that allows an individual to post opinions and ideas about anything from the weather and dating relationships to a company's products, management, or business practices. An entire industry has sprung up to help managers navigate the world of blogs, such as monitoring what is being said about the company, implementing damage control strategies, and tracking what the majority of the world is thinking, minute by minute, to help the organization respond to emerging trends and opportunities.[44] In addition, managers at companies such as McDonald's, Marriott International, and even the once-secretive Boeing are posting blogs of their own to communicate with employees and customers and present the company's side of the story to the public.[45]

Companies are also tapping into the power of new IT applications as powerful collaboration tools within organizations, using group blogs, wikis, social networking, and peer-to-peer file sharing. The simplicity and informality of blogs make them an easy and comfortable medium for people to communicate and share ideas, both with colleagues and outsiders. As described earlier, a *wiki* is similar to a blog and uses software to create a Web site that allows people to

blog Web log that allows individuals to post opinions and ideas.

© BEN BAKER/REDUX

5 Controlling

Concept Connection Jeffrey Kalmikoff (left) and Jake Nichell (right), owners of Threadless, built a $30 million business through a **social network** where users are both customers and part of the supply chain. Their online T-shirt business uses Facebook, Twitter, Flickr, MySpace, and the company website to interact with the Threadless community. Designers submit designs for T-shirts, and online participants vote for the best designs. Winners receive a cash prize of $2,500 and reprint fees for designs that are printed on T-shirts. Threadless has been connecting online with designers since 2000 and opened its first retail location in Chicago in 2007.

create, share, and edit content through a browser-based interface. Rather than simply sharing opinions and ideas as with a blog, wikis are free-form, allowing people to edit what they find on the site and add content.[46] The best-known example of a wiki is the online encyclopedia Wikipedia, where thousands of volunteer contributors have written, edited, and policed more than 9 million entries in more than a hundred languages.[47] Boeing and BMW both use wiki software to open much of their design work to partner organizations.

Social networking, also referred to as *social media* or *user-generated content*, is an extension of blogs and wikis.[48] Sites such as MySpace, Facebook, and Friendster provide an unprecedented peer-to-peer communication channel, where people interact in an online community, sharing personal data and photos, producing and sharing all sorts of information and opinions, or unifying activists and raising funds. Smart companies are finding ways to benefit from the phenomenon. Work networks on Facebook and MySpace are exploding, and some companies, including Dow Chemical, JPMorgan Chase, and Lockheed Martin, are starting their own in-house social networks as a way to facilitate information sharing.[49]

TakeaMoment | As a new manager, incorporate new IT tools to extend the power of your organization's management information systems. Recognize that people need different tools, depending on their work as well as how they like to process and use information. Go to the experiential exercise on page 431 that pertains to how you use information for decision making.

Peer-to-peer file sharing, such as that pioneered by Napster for sharing music online, enables PCs to communicate directly with one another over the Internet, bypassing central databases, servers, control points, and Web pages.[50] Peer-to-peer software lets any individual's computer "talk" directly to another PC without an intermediary, enhancing the opportunities for information sharing and collaboration. Peer-to-peer technology improves efficiency by eliminating the need for setting up and managing huge central storage systems. GlaxoSmithKline uses P2P technology to let its employees and researchers outside the company share their drug test data digitally and work collaboratively on new projects. Law firm Baker & McKenzie uses it to allow major clients to tap directly into its attorneys' files stored on computers worldwide.[51]

THE INTERNET AND E-BUSINESS

In recent years, most organizations have incorporated the Internet as part of their information technology strategy.[52] Both business and nonprofit organizations quickly realized the potential of the Internet for expanding their operations globally, improving business processes, reaching new customers, and making the most of their resources. Exhibit 14.8 shows the popular iPod nano, one of the many products that Apple sells over the Internet and in retail stores.

Numerous organizations today are involved in some type of e-business. **E-business** can be defined as any business that takes place by digital processes over a computer network rather than in physical space. Most commonly today, it refers to electronic linkages over the Internet with customers, partners, suppliers, employees, or other key constituents. **E-commerce** is a more limited term that refers specifically to business exchanges or transactions that occur electronically.

Some organizations, such as eBay, Amazon.com, Expedia, and Yahoo! would not exist without the Internet. However, most traditional, established organizations, including General Electric; the City of Madison, Wisconsin; Macy's; and the U.S. Postal Service, also make extensive use of the Internet, and we will focus on these types of organizations in the remainder of this section.

social networking Online interaction in a community format where people share personal information and photos, produce and share all sorts of information and opinions, or unify activists and raise funds.

peer-to-peer file sharing File sharing that allows PCs to communicate directly with one another over the Internet, bypassing central databases, servers, control points, and Web pages.

e-business Any business that takes place by digital processes over a computer network rather than in physical space.

e-commerce Business exchanges or transactions that occur electronically.

EXHIBIT | 14.8

Apple Sells Products in Retail Stores and via the Internet

Exhibit 14.9 illustrates the key components of e-business for two organizations, a manufacturing company and a retail chain. First, each organization operates an **intranet**, an internal communications system that uses the technology and standards of the Internet but is accessible only to people within the company. The next component is a system that allows the separate companies to share data and information. An **extranet** is an external communications system that uses the Internet and is shared by two or more organizations. With an extranet, each organization moves certain data outside of its private intranet, but makes the data available only to the other companies sharing the extranet. The final piece of the overall system is the Internet, which is accessible to the general public. Organizations make some information available to the public through their Web sites, which may include products or services offered for sale.

intranet An internal communications system that uses the technology and standards of the Internet but is accessible only to people within the organization.

extranet An external communications system that uses the Internet and is shared by two or more organizations.

EXHIBIT | 14.9

The Key Components of E-Business for Two Traditional Organizations

5 Controlling

SOURCE: Based on Jim Turcotte, Bob Silveri, and Tom Jobson, "Are You Ready for the E-Supply Chain?" *APICS—The Performance Advantage* (August 1998): 56–59.

Concept Connection   Blair Corporation is a multichannel direct marketer of apparel and home merchandise for value-conscious customers. In 2003, Blair launched an Internet division aimed at **market expansion**. Using a variety of tools and techniques, including virtual catalogs, Blair.com added 170,000 new-to-file customers in its first year, with an average age nearly 15 years younger than their traditional core customers: "proof of the power of this new channel."

The first step toward a successful e-business for an established firm is for managers to determine why they need such a business to begin with.[53] Failure to align the e-business initiative with corporate strategy can lead to e-business failure. Two basic strategic approaches for traditional organizations setting up an Internet operation are illustrated in Exhibit 14.10. Some companies embrace e-business primarily to expand into new markets and reach new customers. Others use e-business as a route to increased productivity and cost efficiency.

E-Business Strategy: Market Expansion

An Internet division allows a company to establish direct links to customers and expand into new markets. The organization can provide access around the clock to a worldwide market. ESPN.com, for example, is the biggest Internet draw for sports, attracting a devoted audience of 18- to 34-year-old men, an audience that is less and less interested in traditional television. The site's ESPN360, a customizable high-speed service, offers super-sharp video clips of everything from *SportsCenter* to poker tournaments, as well as behind-the-scenes coverage. To reach young viewers, other television networks, including Comedy Central, E. W. Scripps Networks, which owns HGTV and the Food Network, CBS Broadcasting, and NBC Universal, have also launched high-speed broadband channels to deliver short videos, pilots of new shows, or abbreviated and behind-the-scenes looks.[54] Retailers have also been big winners with a market expansion strategy. JCPenney was one of the first traditional retailers to launch a Web site.

JCPenney   *Innovative Way*

Not so long ago, the century-old JCPenney department store chain had so many troubles that some analysts predicted it wouldn't survive. Today, however, the retailer is thriving, thanks in part to managers' mastery of e-business.

Penney was one of the first traditional retailers to launch a Web site in 1994. Though that initial site sold only one product—Power Rangers—it gave the company invaluable experience for expansion once the Internet really took off. Today, Penney has one of the most productive online stores among mainstream retailers. The Web site has enabled the company to attract a younger customer base than those who typically shop at Penney and find ways to lure them into bricks-and-mortar stores. Penney embraced the Internet wholeheartedly, encouraging cooperation between its Web site and stores from the beginning. It was the one of the first

EXHIBIT | 14.10

Strategies for Engaging Clicks with Bricks

to allow customers to pick up and return items bought online at their local store, and it was the first to give online shoppers a way to check which clothes are in stock at local stores. It's no wonder Penney's ranks among the top five Web sites in terms of the number of paying customers it attracts.[55]

Like JCPenney, most retailers selling products online also now use their Web sites to drive more traffic into stores. Bloomingdale's tapped into the social networking phenomenon by sponsoring a three-day event that allowed people to try on outfits in front of an interactive mirror that connected them to their friends via the Internet. Most other big retailers also now let online shoppers pick up purchases at the local store. Circuit City promises that online purchases will be ready for pickup in 24 minutes—if they're not, the customer gets a $24 gift card. Getting people to the store gives staff a chance to push accessory items and increase sales.[56]

Go to the ethical dilemma on page 432 that pertains to using the Internet for market expansion.   TakeaMoment

E-Business Strategy: Increasing Efficiency

With this approach, the e-business initiative is seen primarily as a way to improve the bottom line by increasing productivity and cutting costs. Automakers such as Toyota, General Motors, and Ford, for example, use e-business to reduce the cost of ordering and tracking parts and supplies and to implement just-in-time manufacturing. At Nibco, a manufacturer of piping products, 12 plants and distribution centers automatically share data on inventory and orders via the Internet, resulting in about 70 percent of orders being automated. The technology has helped Nibco trim its inventory by 13 percent, as well as respond more quickly to changes in orders from customers.[57]

Several studies attest to real and significant gains in productivity from e-business.[58] Even the smallest companies can realize gains. Rather than purchasing parts from a local supplier at premium rates, a small firm can access a worldwide market and find the best price, or negotiate better terms with the local supplier.[59] Service firms and government agencies can benefit too. New York City became the first city to use the Internet to settle personal injury claims more efficiently. Using NYC Comptroller's Cybersettle Service, lawyers submit blind offers until a match is hit. If an agreement can't be reached, the parties go back to face-to-face negotiations. The city saved $17 million in less than two years by settling 1,137 out of 7,000 claims online and reduced settlement times from four years to nine months.[60]

ch14   A MANAGER'S ESSENTIALS: WHAT HAVE WE LEARNED?

5 Controlling

- This chapter described several points about operations management and the use of information for management and control. Operations management pertains to the tools and techniques used to manage the organization's core production process. These techniques apply to both manufacturing and service organizations.

- Supply chain management is a crucial area for operations, and today's managers use Internet and computer-based technology to manage the sequence of suppliers and purchasers covering all stages of processing from obtaining raw materials to distributing finished goods to consumers. Other important considerations for operations management include facilities layout and technology automation, including RFID, flexible manufacturing systems, and lean manufacturing. The chapter also discussed inventory management. Three types of inventory are raw materials, work in process, and finished goods. Just-in-time inventory is an effective technique for minimizing inventory levels.

- Managers rely on information technology for the efficient management and control of operations. Information technology and e-business has transformed management and contributes to enhanced collaboration and knowledge sharing. Sophisticated information technology systems can gather huge amounts of data and transform them into useful information for decision makers. Management information systems that support operations and decision making include decision support systems, executive information systems, and collaborative work systems. An important IT solution for improving business operations is enterprise resource planning (ERP). Knowledge management is also an important application for new technology. Key technologies for knowledge management are business intelligence software and knowledge management portals on the corporate intranet.

- Collaborative work systems allow groups of managers or employees to share information, collaborate electronically, and have access to computer-based support data for group decision making and problem solving. New IT tools, including blogs, wikis, social networking, and peer-to-peer file sharing, extend the power of the organization's collaborative systems.

- Most organizations have incorporated the Internet and e-business as part of their information technology strategy. Traditional organizations use an online division primarily for market expansion or to increase productivity and reduce costs.

ch14   DISCUSSION QUESTIONS

1. Business writer Nicholas Carr argued that because computers and software have become so available and affordable, it's getting harder to achieve a competitive edge by being a technology leader. Do you agree or disagree? Explain your answer.

2. What types of information technology do you as a student use on a regular basis? How might your life be different if this technology were not available to you?

3. Has the growth of increasingly sophisticated management information systems (MIS) changed the importance of personal experience and intuition in decision making? In other words, does MIS make decision making more of a science than an art?

4. How might the organizers of an upcoming Olympics use an extranet to get all the elements of the event up and running on schedule?

5. You are a manager assigned the task of deciding how to blend your organization's traditional operations with a new Internet initiative for both purchasing and sales. What are the main factors you would consider? What information would you collect?

6. If you were a manager in charge of new product marketing, what are some ways you might harness the power of blogs and social networking sites to help market your latest products?

7. The openness of wikis is both their strength and their weakness. As a business owner, how would you take advantage of this new technology but guard against its potential problems, such as their vulnerability to mistakes, pranks, inaccurate and self-serving posts, and cybervandalism?

8. Define the difference between explicit knowledge and tacit knowledge and give an example of each from your own experience. How can knowledge management systems be designed to promote the sharing of both explicit and tacit knowledge?

9. Do you believe information overload is a problem for today's students? For managers or employees in an organization where you have worked? How might people deal with information overload?

10. How is e-business affecting the way organizations are structured and the way jobs are designed?

11. Have you ever used peer-to-peer file-sharing technology? Discuss your experiences—positive and negative—with P2P.

ch14 MANAGEMENT IN PRACTICE: EXPERIENTIAL EXERCISE

What Is Your MIS Style?

For each of the following 14 statements, circle the number that indicates how much you agree that each statement is characteristic of you. The questions refer to how you use information and make decisions.

Disagree Strongly ① ② ③ ④ ⑤ Strongly Agree

1. I like to wait until all relevant information is examined before deciding something.

   1 2 3 4 5

2. I prefer information that can be interpreted in several ways and leads to different but acceptable solutions.

   1 2 3 4 5

3. I like to keep gathering data until an excellent solution emerges.

   1 2 3 4 5

4. To make decisions, I often use information that means different things to different people.

   1 2 3 4 5

5. I want just enough data to make a decision quickly.

   1 2 3 4 5

6. I act on logical analysis of the situation rather than on my "gut feelings" about the best alternative.

   1 2 3 4 5

7. I seek information sources or people that will provide me with many ideas and details.

   1 2 3 4 5

8. I try to generate more than one satisfactory solution for the problem faced.

   1 2 3 4 5

9. When reading something, I confine my thoughts to what is written rather than search for additional understanding.

   1 2 3 4 5

10. When working on a project, I try to narrow, not broaden, the scope so it is clearly defined.

    1 2 3 4 5

11. I typically acquire all possible information before making a final decision.

    1 2 3 4 5

12. I like to work on something I've done before rather than take on a complicated problem.

    1 2 3 4 5

13. I prefer clear, precise data.

    1 2 3 4 5

14. When working on a project, I like to explore various options rather than maintain a narrow focus.

    1 2 3 4 5

Scoring and Interpretation

Your information-processing style determines the extent to which you will benefit from computer-based information systems. First, subtract each of your scores for questions 5, 6, 9, 10, 12, and 13 from the number 6 and indicate the adjusted score next to each question. Use the adjusted scores to calculate your totals as follows:

The odd-numbered questions pertain to the "amount of information" you like to use. Your total score for odd-numbered questions: _____. A score of 28 or more suggests you prefer a large amount of information. A score of 14 or less indicates you like a small amount.

The even-numbered questions pertain to the "focus of information" you prefer. Your total score for even-numbered questions: _____. A score of 28 or more suggests you are comfortable with ambiguous, multifocused information, while a score of 14 or less suggests you like clear, unifocused data.

If you are a person who likes a large amount of information and clear, focused data, you will tend to make effective use of management information systems. You could be expected to benefit greatly from an EIS or MIS in your company. If you are a person who prefers a small amount of information and data that are multifocused, you would probably not get the information you need to make decisions through formal information systems. You probably won't utilize EIS or MIS to a great extent, preferring instead to get decision data from other convenient sources, including face-to-face discussions.

SOURCES: This questionnaire is adapted from Richard L. Daft and Norman B. Macintosh, "A Tentative Exploration into the Amount and Equivocality of Information Processing in Organizational Work Units," *Administrative Science Quarterly* 26 (1981): 207–224; and Dorothy Marcic, *Organizational Behavior: Experiences and Cases,* 4th ed. (St. Paul, MN: West, 1995).

5 Controlling

ch14   MANAGEMENT IN PRACTICE: ETHICAL DILEMMA

Manipulative or Not?

As head of the marketing department for Butter Crisp Snack Foods, 55-year-old Frank Bellows has been forced to learn a lot about the Internet in recent years. Although he initially resisted the new technology, Frank has gradually come to appreciate the potential of the Internet for serving existing customers and reaching potential new ones. In fact, he has been one of the biggest supporters of the company's increasing use of the Internet to stay in touch with customers.

However, something about this new plan just doesn't feel right. At this morning's meeting, Keith Deakins, Butter Crisp's CEO, announced that the company would soon be launching a Web site geared specifically to children. Although Deakins has the authority to approve the site on his own, he has asked all department heads to review the site and give their approval for its launch. He then turned the meeting over to the Information Technology team that developed the new site, which will offer games and interactive educational activities. The team pointed out that although it will be clear that Butter Crisp is the sponsor of the site, the site will not include advertising of Butter Crisp products. So far, so good, Frank thinks. However, he knows that two of the young hot-shot employees in his department have been helping to develop the site and that they provided a list of questions that children will be asked to answer online. Just to enter the Web site, for example, a user must provide name, address, gender, e-mail address, and favorite TV show. In return, users receive "Crisp Cash," a form of virtual money that they can turn in for toys, games, Butter Crisp samples, and other prizes. After they enter the site, children can earn more Crisp Cash by providing other information about themselves and their families.

Frank watched the demonstration and agreed that the Web site does indeed have solid educational content. However, he is concerned about the tactics for gathering information from children when that information will almost certainly be used for marketing purposes. So far, it seems that the other department heads are solidly in favor of launching the Web site. Frank is wondering whether he can sign his approval with a clear conscience. He also knows that several groups, including the national PTA and the Center for Media Education, are calling for stricter governmental controls regarding collecting information from children via the Internet.

What Would You Do?

1. Stop worrying about it. There's nothing illegal about what Butter Crisp is proposing to do, and any personal information gathered will be closely guarded by the company. Children can't be harmed in any way by using the new Web site.

2. Begin talking with other managers and try to build a coalition in support of some stricter controls, such as requiring parental permission to enter areas of the site that offer Crisp Cash in exchange for personal information.

3. Contact the Center for Media Education and tell them you suspect Butter Crisp intends to use the Web site to conduct marketing research. The Center might be able to apply pressure that would make it uncomfortable enough for Deakins to pull the plug on the new kid's Web site.

SOURCE: Based on Denise Gellene, "Internet Marketing to Kids Is Seen as a Web of Deceit," *Los Angeles Times* (March 29, 1996): A1, A20.

ch14   CASE FOR CRITICAL ANALYSIS

Tri-Angle Equipment and Leasing

Joe Jett, president of Tri-Angle Equipment and Leasing, which owns several agricultural equipment dealerships in the midwestern United States, tried computers 15 years ago. He didn't like them, and he didn't think he needed information technology to run his business.

But as the company grew, Jett realized he had taken on more debt than he was comfortable with, so he hired a chief financial officer named Dan Fraley. Jett also got back into the information technology

game, investing $150,000 in a proprietary inventory and accounting system. When Jett and Fraley approached Citigroup's Global Equipment Finance Division seeking better financing for the company, Jett was surprised that Citigroup seemed to be more interested in Tri-Angle's information technology capacity than it was in how many million-dollar machines the company had sold. As a Citigroup representative explained, "The theory goes that if you can trust the computer systems, you can trust the company's numbers."

Tri-Angle wanted to borrow a significant amount of money, so Citigroup sent information technology consultants to evaluate the company's systems and make sure they were capable of generating the sort of accurate monthly financial reports required by the firm for such a sizable loan. Tri-Angle was already on the right track with the new inventory and accounting system, so the necessary data were in the database. However, the consultants soon learned that it was difficult to translate the data into quality information. For instance, if someone wanted a list of accounts receivable that were past due, the database would spit out 500 pages of indecipherable codes and numbers. "None of the answers just popped out of the computer," recalls Fraley.

Fraley began using a software program called Monarch (ironically, already installed on the computer) to turn the data into useful information printed on neat, readable spreadsheets. In the process, Tri-Angle not only qualified for a $5 million loan, but also discovered some of its own poor business practices. For example, Jett and Fraley found more than $100,000 worth of outdated, unused parts that could be returned to manufacturers. As Tri-Angle's ability to turn data into quality information has increased, the leaders are able to see at a moment's notice how the company is performing. They can see immediately which pieces of equipment are being sold or leased and which are not—and on which sales lots. In addition, salespeople, who now carry laptops, can enter sales figures directly into a customer's file using contract management software. When a salesperson gives a customer a quote, it is automatically e-mailed to Jett. As soon as Jett opens the e-mail, the quote is deposited in the central database for later reference.

With the success of Monarch and other management information systems, Jett is now thinking about moving into the world of e-business. He has read about extranets, Web pages, customer relationship management software, and the like, and he wonders how these new technologies might help his business.

Questions

1. With its newfound reliance on information technology, do you think Tri-Angle might fall into a trap of poor information quality or information overload? Why or why not?

2. How does information technology contribute to Tri-Angle's knowledge management? What other strategic advantages does MIS provide?

3. What would you recommend to Tri-Angle as a first step into e-business? Why?

SOURCES: Based on Joshua Macht, "The Accidental Automator," *Inc. Tech*, no. 2 (1997): 66–71.

---

ch14 ON THE JOB VIDEO CASE

Numi Organic Tea: Managing the Value Chain, Information Technology, and E-Business

When Brian Durkee shows up at Numi Organic Tea every day to work as the director of operations, he's on a mission to make Numi a worldwide leader in sustainable supply chain management—and he gets right to work. Setting up and maintaining an efficient enterprise resource planning (ERP) system turned out to be much easier than converting Chinese suppliers to profoundly different farming methods and ways of doing business.

Numi was initially run on Excel spreadsheets and QuickBooks, which was hard to imagine after walking through Numi's box-filled distribution center in Oakland, California. Durkee pointed out that those are tools used by most start-up companies. Numi had just begun to implement an ERP system with integrated inventory management and accounting when Durkee joined the company. He's still in awe of what the system can do. "We're managing our inventories in multiple countries through the same software program. All we do now is simply go into the system and push a button to say we want to make a particular product, and the system pulls all the lots and materials for us and allocates the inventory." It's that simple!

Durkee can calculate the inventory's value and cost of goods at any time, too. "The enhancements we've made in our technology have helped us in tremendous ways. It has helped reduce costs, improve customer service, and most importantly, it has helped

5 Controlling

us manage our business more efficiently." With clients like Costco, Target, and Safeway, quality and efficiency are essential. The system also keeps everyone working on the same page, because it provides a clear, real-time picture of what's happening.

Although just-in-time (JIT) inventory sounds great, it's not possible for Numi. Because its teas are grown by carefully chosen suppliers who adhere to Numi's standards for organics and fair trade, Durkee can't simply pick up the phone to order more tea or ask his suppliers to grow it instantaneously. The concept of a raw materials inventory doesn't really apply to Numi either, because tea, its raw material, always requires a labor investment. To effectively manage his inventory, Durkee uses sales forecasts to make plans for tea production. JIT doesn't work for its specialty bamboo packaging either because the boxes are handmade. Big changes in forecasts are difficult to address given these constraints. Luckily, tea leaves aren't perishable once dried and packaged, so Numi can confidently build up its finished goods inventory, knowing the products will sell sooner rather than later.

The people who grow and package Numi tea are a vital part of the supply chain and the operation's technical core. Durkee said the best part of his job is working with supply partners to improve working conditions. And although Numi tea is grown all over the world, its partners in China have the most trouble comprehending Numi's fair-trade and organic practices. No matter how many times Durkee asked the owner of the packaging plant in China to install air conditioning for the workers, the owner couldn't

understand Durkee's assertion that 120 degree temperatures constitute inhumane conditions. Ultimately, Durkee lied and said the hot temperatures affected the quality of the tea. Within two days, the factory was fully air-conditioned. Durkee has also been working with tea suppliers to change the conditions for workers who have historically lived on-site in dorm-size rooms with 10 or 12 people. Numi will not partner with anyone who does not comply with the company's standards.

Numi is redefining and expanding the ways companies bring value and quality to the value chain. Although Numi doesn't practice lean manufacturing per se, ongoing efforts to make its supply chain more sustainable reduce waste on many levels—energy, natural resources, and packaging materials. In the eyes of Numi customers, organic and fair-trade products possess more value. They also view organically grown products as safer, healthier, and of higher quality than non-organics. Anyone finding it difficult to quantify value Numi-style, should eavesdrop on Numi customers as they chat enthusiastically on Numi's blog.

Discussion Questions

1. What challenges are inherent in an agricultural production process?
2. How does depending on a big finished-goods inventory make Numi vulnerable?
3. Beyond the impact on workers, how might fair-trade practices affect product quality and costs?

---

ch14   BIZ FLIX VIDEO CASE

The Good Shepherd

Edward Wilson (Matt Damon) graduates from Yale University and joins the Office of Strategic Services, the intelligence unit that preceded the Central Intelligence Agency (CIA). His career unfolds during World War II and into the 1960s. Wilson's strong work focus and shallow family focus develop many issues for him that he does not easily resolve. The film's centerpiece is Wilson's task of finding why the Bay of

Pigs invasion of Cuba has failed. Many strong performances and unusual intercutting of scenes from various periods make an engaging cinematic experience.

Information Technology

These scenes appear in two parts with a title screen separating Part I from Part II. You can view the scenes continuously or pause after Part I to consider the questions below.

Part I: Beginning the Information Development. This scene is part of DVD Chapter 7, "Uses of Information." It begins with the Photography Technical Officer (Christopher Evan Welch) saying to Edward Wilson, "The photograph is particularly dark." The scene ends after the Sound Technical Officer (Tuc Watkins) says, "We are going to keep playing with it." The film holds a shot on Wilson and then cuts to a 1941 London air raid.

Part II: Continuing the Information Development. This scene begins with a shot of Wilson and two lines of titling that read, "C.I.A. Technical Services April 23, 1961." A woman's voice-over says her lover is safe with her. This scene ends after Wilson's question about their schedule and the answer of going as fast as possible. The film cuts to an aerial shot of the Soviet sector of Berlin with a German voice-over.

What to Watch for and Ask Yourself

- Which parts of these scenes show data? Which parts show information?

- These film scenes show the information technology used during the 1960s at the CIA. Compare it to this chapter's discussion of modern information technology. What are the similarities and differences?

- The chapter described knowledge management as efforts to systematically gather and organize knowledge for an organization. Identify the activities in this scene that show knowledge management activities.

ch14 ENDNOTES

1. Adapted from Carolyn Hopper, *Practicing Management Skills* (New York: Houghton Mifflin, 2003); and Jacquelyn Wonder and Priscilla Donovan, "Mind Openers," *Self* (March 1984).
2. James D. Thompson, *Organizations in Action* (New York: McGraw-Hill, 1967).
3. Chad Terhune, "Growing Pains; To Bag China's Snack Market, Pepsi Takes Up Potato Farming," *The Wall Street Journal*, December 19, 2005.
4. Gregory B. Northcraft and Richard B. Chase, "Managing Service Demand at the Point of Delivery," *Academy of Management Review* 10 (1985): 66–75; and Richard B. Chase and David A. Tanski, "The Customer Contact Model for Organization Design," *Management Science* 29 (1983): 1037–1050.
5. Definition based on Steven A. Melnyk and David R. Denzler, *Operations Management: A Value-Driven Approach* (Burr Ridge, IL: Richard D. Irwin, 1996), p. 613.
6. Based on Jim Turcotte, Bob Silveri, and Tom Jobson, "Are You Ready for the E-Supply Chain?" *APICS–The Performance Advantage* (August 1998): 56–59.
7. Jason Dedrick and Kenneth L. Kraemer, "The Impacts of IT on Firm and Industry Structure: The Personal Computer Industry," *California Management Review* 47, no. 3 (Spring 2005): 122–142; Kathryn Jones, "The Dell Way," *Business 2.0* (February 2003): 61–66; and Stewart Deck, "Fine Line," *CIO* (February 1, 2000): 88–92.
8. "The AMR Research Supply Chain Top 25 for 2008," http://www.amrresearch.com/supplychain-top25/# (accessed May 30, 2008).
9. Cecilie Rohwedder and Keith Johnson, "Pace-Setting Zara Seeks More Speed To Fight Its Rising Cheap-Chic Rivals," *The Wall Street Journal*, February 20, 2008.
10. Russ Banham, "Caught in the Middle," *CFO* (May 2001): 69–74.
11. Nancy Lea Hyer and Karen A. Brown, "Work Cells with Staying Power: Lessons for Process–Complete Operations," *California Management Review* 46, no. 1 (Fall 2003): 27–52.
12. Kelly Wardle, "One Enchanted Evening," *Special Events*, http://www.specialevents.com/corporate/events_one_enchanted_evening_20060203/index.html (accessed May 27, 2008).
13. Daniel Michaels and J. Lynn Lunsford, "Streamlined Plane Making," *The Wall Street Journal*, April 1, 2005.
14. Dean Elmuti and Michael Abebe, "RFID Reshapes the Global Supply Chain," *Industrial Management* (March–April 2005): 27–31; John Teresko, "Plant Strategies: Winning with Wireless," *Industry Week* (June 2003): 60–66; and Meridith Levinson, "The RFID Imperative," *CIO* (December 1, 2003): 78–91; and "ZDNet Definition for: RFID," from *Computer Desktop Encyclopedia*, http://dictionary.zdnet.com/definition/RFID.html (accessed May 27, 2008).
15. Erick Schonfeld, "Tagged for Growth," *Business 2.0* (December 2006): 58–61.
16. Maryanne Murray Buechner, "Cracking the Code," *FSB: Fortune Small Business* (March 2004): 72–73.
17. Barnaby J. Feder, "Military to Urge Suppliers to Adopt Radio ID Tags," *The New York Times*, November 12, 2005.
18. "ZDNet Definition for: RFID."
19. Scott McCartney, "The Middle Seat: A New Way to Prevent Lost

5 Controlling

Luggage," *The Wall Street Journal*, February 27, 2007.

20. Sumer C. Aggarwal, "MRP, JIT, OPT, FMS?" *Harvard Business Review* 63 (September–October 1985): 8–16; and Paul Ranky, *The Design and Operation of Flexible Manufacturing Systems* (New York: Elsevier, 1983).

21. David Welch, "How Nissan Laps Detroit," *BusinessWeek* (December 22, 2003): 58–60.

22. Kenji Hall, "No One Does Lean Like the Japanese," *BusinessWeek* (July 10, 2006): 40–41.

23. Peter Strozniak, "Toyota Alters Face of Production," *Industry Week* (August 13, 2001): 46–48; and Jeffrey K. Liker and James M. Morgan, "The Toyota Way in Services: The Case of Lean Product Development," *Academy of Management Perspectives* (May 2006): 5–20.

24. Art Kleiner, "Leaning Toward Utopia," *Strategy + Business*, no. 39 (Second Quarter 2005): 76–87; Fara Warner, "Think Lean," *Fast Company* (February 2002): 40, 42; Norihiko Shirouzu, "Gadget Inspector: Why Toyota Wins Such High Marks on Quality Surveys," *The Wall Street Journal*, March 15, 2001; and James P. Womack and Daniel T. Jones, *The Machine That Changed the World: The Story of Lean Production* (New York: HarperCollins, 1991).

25. Evan Ramstad, "Compaq Stumbles Amid New Pressures on PCs," *The Wall Street Journal*, March 9, 1998.

26. R. J. Schonberger, *Japanese Manufacturing Techniques: Nine Hidden Lessons in Simplicity* (New York: Free Press, 1982).

27. Luciana Beard and Stephen A. Butler, "Introducing JIT Manufacturing: It's Easier Than You Think," *Business Horizons* (September–October 2000): 61–64.

28. Robert J. Vokurka, Rhonda R. Lummus, and Dennis Krumwiede, "Improving Manufacturing Flexibility: The Enduring Value of JIT and TQM," *SAM Advanced Management Journal* (Winter 2007): 14–21.

29. Based on Ronald Henkoff, "Delivering the Goods," *Fortune* (November 28, 1994): 64–78.

30. Noel P. Greis and John D. Kasarda, "Enterprise Logistics in the Information Era," *California Management Review* 39, no. 4 (Summer 1997):

55–78; "Kanban: The Just-in-Time Japanese Inventory System," *Small Business Report* (February 1984): 69–71; and Richard C. Walleigh, "What's Your Excuse for Not Using JIT?" *Harvard Business Review* 64 (March–April 1986): 38–54.

31. Thomas L. Friedman, "It's a Flat World, After All," *The New York Times Magazine* (April 3, 2005): 32–37.

32. Ibid.

33. Based on Andrew Mayo, "Memory Bankers," *People Management* (January 22, 1998): 34–38; William Miller, "Building the Ultimate Resource," *Management Review* (January 1999), 42–45; and Todd Datz, "How to Speak Geek," *CIO Enterprise*, Section 2 (April 15, 1999), 46–52.

34. Richard McDermott, "Why Information Technology Inspired But Cannot Deliver Knowledge Management," *California Management Review* 41, no. 4 (Summer 1999), 103–117.

35. Thomas H. Davenport, Laurence Prusak, and Bruce Strong, "Business Insight (A Special Report): Organization; Putting Ideas to Work: Knowledge Management Can Make a Difference—But It Needs to Be More Pragmatic," *The Wall Street Journal*, March 10, 2008.

36. Meridith Levinson, "Business Intelligence: Not Just for Bosses Anymore," *CIO* (January 15, 2006): 82–88; and Alice Dragoon, "Business Intelligence Gets Smart," *CIO* (September 15, 2003): 84–91.

37. David Stires, "How the VA Healed Itself," *Fortune* (May 15, 2006): 130–136.

38. Julie Schlosser, "Markdown Lowdown," *Fortune* (January 12, 2004): 40.

39. Spencer E. Ante, "Giving the Boss the Big Picture," *BusinessWeek* (February 13, 2006): 48–51; Doug Bartholomew, "Gauging Success," *CFO-IT* (Summer 2005): 17–19; Russ Banham, "Seeing the Big Picture: New Data Tools Are Enabling CEOs to Get a Better Handle on Performance Across Their Organizations," *Chief Executive* (November 2003): 46.

40. This discussion is based on Judy Sweeney and Simon Jacobson, "ERP Breaks," *Industry Week* (January 2007): 11a–13a; and Vincent A. Mabert, Ashok Soni, and M. A.

Venkataramanan, "Enterprise Resource Planning: Common Myths Versus Evolving Reality," *Business Horizons* (May–June 2001): 69–76.

41. Sweeney and Jacobson, "ERP Breaks."

42. Derek Slater, "What Is ERP?" *CIO Enterprise* (May 15, 1999): 86.

43. Anya Kamenetz, "The Network Unbound," *Fast Company* (June 2006): 68ff; and Stephen Baker and Heather Green, "Blogs Will Change Your Business," *BusinessWeek* (May 2, 2005): 56–67.

44. Baker and Green, "Blogs Will Change Your Business."

45. Stanley Holmes, "Into the Wild Blog Yonder," *BusinessWeek* (May 22, 2006): 8486; and Erin White, Joann S. Lublin, and David Kesmodel, "Executives Get the Blogging Bug," *The Wall Street Journal*, July 13, 2007.

46. Cindy Waxer, "Workers of the World—Collaborate," *FSB* (April 2005): 57–58.

47. Evelyn Nussenbaum, "Technology to Boost Teamwork," *Forbes Small Business* (February 2008): 51–54; and Russ Juskalian, "Wikinomics Could Change Everything As Concept of Sharing Spreads," *USA Today*, January 2, 2007, http://www.usatoday.com (accessed January 2, 2007).

48. This discussion of social networks is based on Kamenetz, "The Network Unbound."

49. Brad Stone, "Facebook Expands Into MySpace's Territory," *The New York Times*, May 25, 2007; and Heather Green, "The Water Cooler is Now on the Web," *BusinessWeek* (October 1, 2007).

50. Spencer E. Ante with Amy Borrus and Robert D. Hof, "In Search of the Net's Next Big Thing," *BusinessWeek* (March 26, 2001): 140–141; Amy Cortese, "Peer to Peer: P2P Taps the Power of Distant Computers in a Way That Could Transform Whole Industries," *BusinessWeek* 50, Supplement to *BusinessWeek* (Spring 2001): 194–196.

51. Mark Roberti, "Peer-to-Peer Isn't Dead," *The Industry Standard* (April 23, 2001): 58–59.

52. Jim Turcotte, Bob Silveri, and Tom Jobson, "Are You Ready for the E-Supply Chain?" *APICS–The Performance Advantage* (August 1998): 56–59.

53. This discussion is based on Long W. Lam and L. Jean Harrison-Walker, "Toward an Objective-Based Typology of E-Business Models," *Business Horizons* (November–December 2003): 17–26; and Detmar Straub and Richard Klein, "E-Competitive Transformations," *Business Horizons* (May–June 2001): 3–12.

54. Tom Lowry, "In the Zone," *Business-Week* (October 17, 2005): 66–78; Tom Lowry, "TV's New Parallel Universe," *BusinessWeek* (November 14, 2005): 72–74.

55. Robert Berner, "J. C. Penney Gets the Net," *BusinessWeek* (May 7, 2007): 70; and "Jcpenney.Com Celebrates 10th Anniversary Of Online Shopping," *Business Wire* (November 8, 2004).

56. Nanette Byrnes, "More Clicks at the Bricks," *BusinessWeek* (December 17, 2007): 50–52.

57. "The Web Smart 50," *BusinessWeek* (November 21, 2005): 82–112.

58. Jonathan L. Willis, "What Impact Will E-Commerce Have on the U.S. Economy?" *Economic Review— Federal Reserve Bank of Kansas City* 89, no. 2 (Second Quarter 2004): 53ff; Timothy J. Mullaney with Heather Green, Michael Arndt, Robert D. Hof, and Linda Himelstein, "The E-Biz Surprise," *Business Week* (May 12, 2003): 60–68.

59. Straub and Klein, "E-Competitive Transformations."

60. "The Web Smart 50."

General Motors
Part Six: Controlling
General Motors Gives Design Teams the Green Light

With all the bad news about layoffs, outsourcing, and plant closings at General Motors (GM), it's not hard to guess what keeps many GM employees up at night. However, with the company's renewed mission to reinvent the automobile, and with a new $25 billion bailout from the federal government for automakers who invest in green technology, at least one group at GM is sleeping a little easier.

E-Flex Systems, the hybrid-vehicle task force behind the 2010 Chevy Volt, recently received the green light from senior management to design cleaner more energy-efficient vehicles. And now with a $25 billion credit line from the feds, GM's group of more than 600 engineers and designers is hard at work developing high-quality low-emissions vehicles for the future.

In videotaped comments posted on the company's FastLane blog, Bob Lutz, GM's vice chairman of global product development, explained the automaker's perspective on quality. "If you ask me, 'Are we satisfied where we are in quality?' the answer has to be 'No.' Because until you're absolutely perfect, which no company will ever be, this is really an area where you strive."

Although quality may be a never-ending pursuit, getting it right may be more important than ever before in GM's history. In recent years, the company has overhauled design processes to make way for alternative-fuel vehicles like the Chevy Tahoe hybrid, the hydrogen-powered Equinox SUV, and the battery-powered Volt. Such uncharted waters could prove treacherous if controls are not in place to measure performance and provide swift corrective action when problems arise.

In the case of the Chevy Volt, E-Flex teams are keeping a close eye on the car's plug-in electric drive unit—especially the mission-critical lithium-ion batteries that deliver Volt's 40 miles of gas-free driving. As anyone with a laptop computer knows, battery technology is improving slowly. Drawbacks of batteries include limited storage capacity, cost of production, performance deterioration, and life cycle—and they're heavy, too. "It's the biggest challenge we have with this car," says Andrew Farah, chief engineer of the E-Flex Systems group. To ensure quality in Volt's state-of-the-art battery technology, engineers are testing batteries from Massachusetts-based supplier A123 Systems as well as packs from Compact Power, a subsidiary of LG Chem.

While not on par with the V-8 engines GM pioneered in the past, Volt's electric drive train produces plenty of pep. The unit delivers 150 horsepower, 273 pound-feet of torque, speeds of 100 miles per hour, and 0-to-60 in nine seconds. "That doesn't sound like a golf cart to me," quipped Tony Posawatz, vehicle line director for the Volt. "It'll be fun to drive."

But Volt's game-changing fuel efficiency also comes from its unique design. The Volt seats only four people, allowing integration of a six-foot T-shaped battery that sits economically under the center spine and rear seats. As Global Design Vice President Ed Welburn notes, "The battery is so integrated into the design that it's like, 'where is it?'" Precisely the point, according to chief engineer Farah. "The whole idea is to integrate it. You don't want to have a battery with some wheels."

GM product-development teams have more ordinary concerns as well. Although the Volt's electric motor is pivotal, Lutz notes that consumers are more likely to notice things like precise body fits and the radiance of the paint job. "These are things that people associate with quality," says the vice chairman. "They like to have an object that looks like it was put together with great care and by somebody that had a lot of respect for the ultimate customer." As Lutz sees it, the customer is always at the center of GM's commitment to quality. "We shoot not only for absence of problems, but we especially shoot for a joyous owner experience."

Questions

1. How might GM use organizational control to ensure that the Chevy Volt meets the expectations set for it during the vehicle's early planning stages?

2. Which total quality management (TQM) techniques may not be applicable to GM as it pioneers next-generation alternative-fuel vehicles?

3. Would the partnership approach to supply chain management improve GM's procurement of materials for new energy-efficient vehicles? Why or why not?

SOURCES: Michael Kanellos, "Does GM Now Mean 'Green Motors'?" *CNET News*, December 14, 2007, http://news.cnet.com/Does-GM-now-mean-green-motors/2100-11389_3-6222853.html (accessed October 13, 2008); Robert Snell, "GM Enters Its Second Century by Finally Taking Wraps Off Volt," *The Detroit News*, September 17, 2008, http://www.detnews.com (accessed October 11, 2008); "GM Starts Its Next 100 Years with New Approach," *The Bay City Times*, September 28, 2008, http://blog.mlive.com/bcopinion/2008/09/gm_starts_its_

next_100_years_w.html (accessed October 11, 2008); James Quinn, "GM Steers Towards Green Funding," *Telegraph*, October 13, 2008, http://www.telegraph.co.uk (accessed October 14, 2008); Chuck Squatriglia, "GM Dedicates Design Studio to Electric Vehicles," *Wired*, December 11, 2007, http://www.wired.com/cars/futuretransport/news/2007/12/eflex (accessed October 13, 2008); General Motors,

"The Case for GM: Has GM Closed the Quality Gap?," videotaped interview with Bob Lutz, GM FastLane Blog, October 6, 2008, http://fastlane.gmblogs.com (accessed October 13, 2008); David Welch, "GM Charges Up the Electric Chevy Volt," *BusinessWeek Online*, September 17, 2008, http://www.businessweek.com/lifestyle/content/sep2008/bw20080916_356100.htm (accessed October 13, 2008).

5
Controlling

© GETTY IMAGES/DIGITAL VISION

Learning Outcomes

After studying this chapter, you should be able to:

1. Define attitudes and explain their relationship to personality, perception, and behavior.

2. Discuss the importance of work-related attitudes.

3. Identify major personality traits and describe how personality can influence workplace attitudes and behaviors.

4. Define the four components of emotional intelligence and explain why they are important for today's managers.

5. Explain how people learn in general and in terms of individual learning styles.

6. Discuss the effects of stress and identify ways individuals and organizations can manage stress to improve employee health, satisfaction, and productivity.

Dynamics of Behavior in Organizations

1 Introduction
2 Environment
3 Planning
4 Organizing
5 Controlling
6 Leading

ARE YOU SELF-CONFIDENT?

Self-confidence is the foundation for many important behaviors of a new manager. To learn something about your level of self-confidence, answer the following questions. Please answer whether each item is Mostly True or Mostly False for you.

	Mostly True	Mostly False
1. I have lots of confidence in my decisions.	_____	_____
2. I would like to change some things about myself.	_____	_____
3. I am satisfied with my appearance and personality.	_____	_____
4. I would be nervous about meeting important people.	_____	_____
5. I come across as a positive person.	_____	_____
6. I sometimes think of myself as a failure.	_____	_____
7. I am able to do things as well as most people.	_____	_____
8. I find it difficult to believe nice things someone says about me.	_____	_____

SCORING AND INTERPRETATION: Many good things come from self-confidence. How self-confident are you? Give yourself one point for each *odd-numbered* item above marked as Mostly True and one point for each *even-numbered* item marked Mostly False. If you scored three or less, your self-confidence may not be very high. You might want to practice new behavior in problematic areas to develop greater confidence. A score of 6 or above suggests a high level of self-confidence and a solid foundation on which to begin your career as a new manager.

If a new manager lacks self-confidence, he or she is more likely to avoid difficult decisions and confrontations and may tend to overcontrol subordinates, which is called micromanaging. A lack of self-confidence also leads to less sharing of information and less time hiring and developing capable people. Self-confident managers, by contrast, can more easily delegate responsibility, take risks, give credit to others, confront problems, and assert themselves for the good of their team.

Managers' attitudes, personality characteristics, values, and personal qualities such as self-confidence affect their behavior, including how they handle work situations and relate to others. These characteristics can profoundly affect the workplace and influence employee motivation, morale, and job performance. Equally important is managers' ability to understand others. Insight into why people behave the way they do is a part of good management.

People are an organization's most valuable resource—and the source of some of managers' most difficult problems. Individuals differ in many ways. Some are quiet and shy while others are gregarious; some are perpetual optimists while others tend to look at the negative side of things. People bring their individual differences to work each day, and these differences in attitudes, personality, and so forth influence how they interpret assignments, whether they like to be told what to do, how they handle challenges, and how they interact with others.

Three basic leadership skills are at the core of identifying and solving people problems: (1) diagnosing, or gaining insight into the situation a manager is trying to influence, (2) adapting individual behavior and resources to meet the needs of the situation, and (3) communicating in a way that others can understand and accept. Thus, managers need a grounding in the principles of organizational behavior—that is, the ways individuals and groups tend to act in organizations. By increasing their knowledge of individual differences in the areas of attitudes, personality, perception, learning, and stress management, managers can understand and lead employees and colleagues through many workplace challenges. This chapter introduces basic principles of organizational behavior in each of these areas.

ORGANIZATIONAL BEHAVIOR

Organizational behavior, commonly called OB, is an interdisciplinary field dedicated to the study of human attitudes, behavior, and performance in organizations. OB draws concepts from many disciplines, including psychology, sociology, cultural anthropology, industrial engineering, economics, ethics, and vocational counseling, as well as the discipline of management. The concepts and principles of organizational behavior are important to managers because in every organization human beings ultimately make the decisions that control how the organization acquires and uses resources. Those people may cooperate with, compete with, support, or undermine one another. Their beliefs and feelings about themselves, their coworkers, and the organization shape what they do and how well they do it. People can distract the organization from its strategy by engaging in conflict and misunderstandings, or they can pool their diverse talents and perspectives to accomplish much more as a group than they could ever do as individuals.

Organizational citizenship refers to the tendency of people to help one another and put in extra effort that goes beyond job requirements to contribute to the organization's success. An employee demonstrates organizational citizenship by being helpful to coworkers and customers, doing extra work when necessary, and looking for ways to improve products and procedures. These behaviors enhance the organization's performance and contribute to positive relationships both within the organization and with customers. Managers can encourage organizational citizenship by applying their knowledge of human behavior, such as selecting people with positive attitudes, managing different personalities, putting people in jobs where they can thrive, and enabling employees to cope with and learn from workplace challenges.[1]

organizational behavior An interdisciplinary field dedicated to the study of how individuals and groups tend to act in organizations.

organizational citizenship Work behavior that goes beyond job requirements and contributes as needed to the organization's success.

attitude A cognitive and affective evaluation that predisposes a person to act in a certain way.

ATTITUDES

Most students have probably heard the expression that someone "has an attitude problem," which means some consistent quality about the person affects his or her behavior in a negative way. An employee with an attitude problem might be hard to get along with, might constantly gripe and cause problems, and might persistently resist new ideas. We all seem to know intuitively what an attitude is, but we do not consciously think about how strongly attitudes affect our behavior. Defined formally, an **attitude** is an evaluation—either positive or negative—that predisposes a person to act in a certain way. Understanding employee attitudes is important to managers because attitudes determine how people perceive the work environment, interact with others, and behave on the job. Emerging research is revealing the importance of positive attitudes to both individual and organizational success. For example, studies have found that the characteristic most common to top executives is an optimistic attitude. People rise to the top because they have the ability to see opportunities where others see problems and can instill in others a sense of hope and possibility for the future.[2]

Managers strive to develop and reinforce positive attitudes among all employees, because happy, positive people are healthier, more effective, and more productive.[3] Some companies, such as David's Bridal, the nation's largest bridal store chain, are applying scientific research to improve employee attitudes—and sales performance.

Concept Connection JetBlue founder David Neeleman illustrates the **positive attitude** and **optimism** that are common traits of successful leaders. Neeleman was shocked when the board of directors of JetBlue removed him as CEO after the highly reported stranding of 131,000 passengers during the 2007 Valentine's Day ice storm. At the time, Neeleman said he would never found another airline, but now he is launching a new low-cost carrier, Azul (Portuguese for *blue*) in Brazil. "Every time a door closes, another one opens up," Neeleman says. "And so I'm excited to be off to the country of my birth to start something new."

Planning a wedding can be one of the most joyful experiences in a woman's life—and one of the most nerve-wracking. The salespeople at David's Bridal, a 267-store chain owned by Federated Department Stores, bear the brunt of these intense emotions. For many, dealing with those emotions can be overwhelming and exhausting, translating into negative attitudes and impatience with already-stressed customers.

Managers turned to new research on happiness to help employees cope and develop more positive attitudes. In a pilot training program based on the work of psychologist Martin Seligman, salespeople were taught how to feel more cheerful with techniques such as "emotion regulation," "impulse control," and "learned optimism." These techniques enable salespeople to be more calm and centered with harried, indecisive brides-to-be, which helps customers stay calm and centered as well. The constructive behavior translates into better sales, meaning employees make better commissions, which in turn contributes to more positive attitudes toward the job.[4]

David's Bridal

Innovative Way

As this example shows, sometimes negative attitudes can result from characteristics of the job, such as a high stress level, but managers can find ways to help people have better attitudes. Managers should pay attention to negative attitudes because they can be both the result of underlying problems in the workplace as well as a contributor to forthcoming problems.[5]

Components of Attitudes

One important step for managers is recognizing and understanding the *components* of attitudes, which is particularly important when attempting to change attitudes.

Behavioral scientists consider attitudes to have three components: cognitions (thoughts), affect (feelings), and behavior.[6] The cognitive component of an attitude includes the beliefs, opinions, and information the person has about the object of the attitude, such as knowledge of what a job entails and opinions about personal abilities. The affective component is the person's emotions or feelings about the object of the attitude, such as enjoying or hating a job. The behavioral component of an attitude is the person's intention to behave toward the object of the attitude in a certain way. Exhibit 15.1 illustrates the three components of a positive attitude toward one's job. The cognitive element is the conscious thought that "my job is interesting and challenging." The affective element is the feeling that "I love this job." These elements, in turn, are related to the behavioral component—an employee might arrive at work early because he or she is happy with the job.

The emotional (affective) component is often the stronger factor in affecting behavior, so managers should be aware of situations that involve strong feelings. However, as a general rule, changing just one component—cognitions, affect, or behavior—can contribute to an overall change in attitude. Suppose a manager concludes that some employees have the attitude that the manager should make all the decisions affecting the department, but the manager prefers that employees assume more decision-making responsibility. To change the underlying attitude, the manager would consider whether to educate employees about the areas in which they can make good decisions (changing the cognitive component), build enthusiasm with pep talks about the satisfaction of employee empowerment (changing the affective component), or simply insist that employees make their own decisions (behavioral component) with the expectation that, once they experience the advantages of decision-making authority, they will begin to like it.

As a new manager, be mindful of your own attitude and how it affects people who work for you. A positive attitude can go a long way toward helping others feel good about themselves and their work responsibilities. If you want to change employees' attitudes, don't underestimate the strength of the emotions.

TakeaMoment

6 Leading

EXHIBIT | 15.1

Components of an Attitude

Cognitive...thoughts...

"My job is interesting."

Affective...feelings...
"I love my job."

Behavioral...intention to act...
"I'm going to get to work early with a smile on my face."

Attitude: Job Satisfaction

High-Performance Work Attitudes

The attitudes of most interest to managers are those related to work, especially attitudes that influence how well employees perform. Two attitudes that might relate to high performance are satisfaction with one's job and commitment to the organization.

Job Satisfaction A positive attitude toward one's job is called **job satisfaction**. In general, people experience this attitude when their work matches their needs and interests, when working conditions and rewards (such as pay) are satisfactory, when they like their coworkers, and when they have positive relationships with supervisors. You can take the quiz in Exhibit 15.2 to better understand some of the factors that contribute to job satisfaction.

Many managers believe job satisfaction is important because they think satisfied employees will do better work. In fact, research shows that the link between satisfaction and performance is generally small and is influenced by other factors.[7] For example, the importance of satisfaction varies according to the amount of control the employee has; an employee doing routine tasks may produce about the same output no matter how he or she feels about the job. Managers of today's knowledge workers, however, often rely on job satisfaction to keep motivation and enthusiasm high. They can't afford to lose talented, highly skilled workers. Regrettably, a survey by International Survey Research found that Gen X employees, those who are carrying the weight of much of today's knowledge work, are the least satisfied of all demographic groups.[8]

Managers create the environment that determines whether employees have positive or negative attitudes toward their jobs.[9] A related attitude is organizational commitment.

job satisfaction A positive attitude toward one's job.

EXHIBIT | 15.2   Rate Your Job Satisfaction

Think of a job—either a current or previous job—that was important to you, and then answer the following questions with respect to how satisfied you were with that job. Please answer the six questions with a number 1–5 that reflects the extent of your satisfaction.

| 1 = Very dissatisfied | 3 = Neutral | 5 = Very satisfied |
| 2 = Dissatisfied | 4 = Satisfied | |

	1	2	3	4	5
1. Overall, how satisfied are you with your job?	1	2	3	4	5
2. How satisfied are you with the opportunities to learn new things?	1	2	3	4	5
3. How satisfied are you with your boss?	1	2	3	4	5
4. How satisfied are you with the people in your work group?	1	2	3	4	5
5. How satisfied are you with the amount of pay you receive?	1	2	3	4	5
6. How satisfied are you with the advancement you are making in the organization?	1	2	3	4	5

Scoring and Interpretation: Add up your responses to the six questions to obtain your total score: _____. The questions represent various aspects of satisfaction that an employee may experience on a job. If your score is 24 or above, you probably feel satisfied with the job. If your score is 12 or below, you probably do not feel satisfied. What is your level of performance in your job, and is your performance related to your level of satisfaction?

SOURCES: These questions were adapted from Daniel R. Denison, *Corporate Culture and Organizational Effectiveness* (New York: John Wiley, 1990); and John D. Cook, Susan J. Hepworth, Toby D. Wall, and Peter B. Warr, *The Experience of Work: A Compendium and Review of 249 Measures and their Use* (San Diego, CA: Academic Press, 1981).

Organizational Commitment Organizational commitment refers to an employee's loyalty to and engagement with the organization. An employee with a high degree of organizational commitment is likely to say *we* when talking about the company. Such a person likes being a part of the organization and tries to contribute to its success. This attitude is illustrated by an incident at the A. W. Chesterton company, a manufacturer of mechanical seals and pumps. When two Chesterton pumps that supply water on Navy ship *USS John F. Kennedy* failed on a Saturday night just before the ship's scheduled departure, the team that produces the seals swung into action. Two members worked through the night to make new seals and deliver them to be installed before the ship left port.[10]

organizational commitment
Loyalty to and heavy involvement in one's organization.

Most managers want to enjoy the benefits of loyal, committed employees, including low turnover and employee willingness to do more than the job's basic requirements. Results of a Towers Perrin-ISR survey of more than 360,000 employees from 41 companies around the world indicate that companies with highly committed employees perform better.[11] Alarmingly, another recent survey suggests that commitment levels around the world are relatively low. Only one-fifth of the respondents were categorized as fully engaged, that is, reflecting a high level of commitment. In the United States, the percentage classified as fully engaged was 29 percent, compared to 54 percent in Mexico, 37 in percent in Brazil, and 36 percent in India, Countries where employees reflect similar or lower levels of commitment than the U. S. include Canada at 23 percent, Spain at 19 percent, Germany at 17 percent, China at 16 percent, the United Kingdom at 14 percent, France at 12 percent, and Japan at only 3 percent.[12]

MARCIO JOSE SANCHEZ/ASSOCIATED PRESS

Concept Connection   "To shake the hand of someone who was nearly dead—there's no feeling like that in the world." That's how one physician assistant (PA) explained why he finds the profession so fulfilling. **Job satisfaction** is extraordinarily high for PAs, such as Jim Johnson, shown here helping patients in a makeshift medical tent after Hurricane Katrina hit Gulfport, Mississippi. A recent survey reported that 90 percent would make the same career choice all over again. In addition to good pay and flexible working conditions, PAs relish the autonomy of the job, a chance to help others, the challenge of diagnosing and treating a variety of ailments, and working as part of a team.

6 Leading

Trust in management decisions and integrity is one important component of organizational commitment.[13] Unfortunately, in recent years, many employees in the U.S. have lost that trust. Just 28 percent of people surveyed by *Fast Company* magazine said they think the CEO of their company has integrity. Another survey by Ajilon Professional Staffing found that only 29 percent of employees reported believing their boss cared about them and looked out for their interests.[14] Managers can promote stronger organizational commitment by being honest and trustworthy in their business dealings, keeping employees informed, giving them a say in decisions, providing the necessary training and other resources that enable them to succeed, treating them fairly, and offering rewards they value.

Conflicts Among Attitudes

Sometimes a person may discover that his or her attitudes conflict with one another or are not reflected in behavior. For example, a person's high level of organizational commitment might conflict with a commitment to family members. If employees routinely work evenings and weekends, their long hours and dedication to the job might conflict with their belief that family ties are important. This conflict can create a state of **cognitive dissonance**, a psychological discomfort that occurs when individuals recognize inconsistencies in their own attitudes and behaviors.[15] The theory of cognitive dissonance, developed by social psychologist Leon Festinger in the 1950s, says that people want to behave in accordance with their attitudes and usually will take corrective action to alleviate the dissonance and achieve balance.

In the case of working overtime, people who can control their hours might restructure responsibilities so that they have time for both work and family. In contrast, those who are unable to restructure workloads might develop an unfavorable attitude toward the employer, reducing their organizational commitment. They might resolve their dissonance by saying they would like to spend more time with their kids but their unreasonable employer demands that they work too many hours.

PERCEPTION

Another critical aspect of understanding behavior is perception. **Perception** is the cognitive process people use to make sense out of the environment by selecting, organizing, and interpreting information from the environment. Because of individual differences in attitudes, personality, values, interests, and so forth, people often "see" the same thing in different ways. A class that is boring to one student might be fascinating to another. One student might perceive an assignment to be challenging and stimulating, whereas another might find it a silly waste of time.

We can think of perception as a step-by-step process, as shown in Exhibit 15.3. First, we observe information (sensory data) from the environment through our senses: taste, smell, hearing, sight, and touch. Next, our mind screens the data and will select only the items we will process further. Third, we organize the selected data

cognitive dissonance A condition in which two attitudes or a behavior and an attitude conflict.

perception The cognitive process people use to make sense out of the environment by selecting, organizing, and interpreting information.

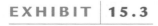

EXHIBIT | 15.3

The Perception Process

Observing information via the senses → Screening the information and selecting what to process → Organizing the selected data into patterns for interpretation and response into meaningful patterns for interpretation and response. Most differences in perception among people at work are related to how they select and organize sensory data. You can experience differences in perceptual organization by looking at the visuals in Exhibit 15.4. What do you see in part *a* of Exhibit 15.4? Most people see this as a dog, but others see only a series of unrelated ink blots. Some people will see the figure in part *b* as a beautiful young woman while others will see an old one. Now look at part *c*. How many blocks do you see—six or seven? Some people have to turn the figure upside down before they can see seven blocks. These visuals illustrate how complex perception is.

Perceptual Selectivity

We are bombarded by so much sensory data that it is impossible to process it all. Thus, we tune in to some things and tune out others. **Perceptual selectivity** is the process by which individuals subconsciously screen and select the various objects and stimuli that vie for their attention.

People typically focus on stimuli that satisfy their needs and that are consistent with their attitudes, values, and personality. For example, employees who need positive feedback to feel good about themselves might pick up on positive statements made by a supervisor but tune out most negative comments. A supervisor could use this understanding to tailor feedback in a positive way to help the employee improve work performance. The influence of needs on perception has been studied in laboratory experiments and found to have a strong impact on what people perceive.[16]

Characteristics of the stimuli themselves also affect perceptual selectivity. People tend to notice stimuli that stand out against other stimuli or that are more intense than surrounding stimuli. Examples would be a loud noise in a quiet room or a bright red dress at a party where most women are wearing basic black. People also tend to notice things that are familiar to them, such as a familiar voice in a crowd, as well as things that are new or different from their previous experiences. In addition, *primacy* and *recency* are important to perceptual selectivity. People pay relatively greater attention to sensory data that occur toward the beginning of an event or toward the end. Primacy supports the old truism that first impressions really do count, whether it be on a job interview, meeting a date's parents, or participating in a new social group. Recency reflects the reality that the last impression might be a lasting impression. For example, Malaysian Airlines discovered its value in building customer loyalty. A woman traveling with a nine-month-old might find the flight itself an exhausting blur, but one such traveler enthusiastically told people for years how Malaysian Airlines flight attendants helped her with baggage collection and ground transportation.[17]

perceptual selectivity The process by which individuals screen and select the various stimuli that vie for their attention.

EXHIBIT | **15.4** Perception—What Do You See?

a. Do you see the dog?

b. Old woman or young woman?

c. How many blocks?

Perceptual Distortions

Once people select the sensory data to be perceived, they begin grouping the data into recognizable patterns (perceptual organization). Of particular concern in the work environment are **perceptual distortions**, errors in perceptual judgment that arise from inaccuracies in any part of the perceptual process.

One common perceptual error is **stereotyping**, the tendency to assign an individual to a group or broad category (e.g., female, black, elderly; or male, white, disabled) and then to attribute widely held generalizations about the group to the individual. Thus, someone meets a new colleague, sees he is in a wheelchair, assigns him to the category "physically disabled," and attributes to this colleague generalizations she believes about people with disabilities, which may include a belief that he is less able than other coworkers. However, the person's inability to walk should not be seen as indicative of lesser abilities in other areas. Stereotyping prevents people from truly knowing those they classify in this way. In addition, negative stereotypes prevent talented people from advancing in an organization and fully contributing their talents to the organization's success.

The **halo effect** occurs when the perceiver develops an overall impression of a person or situation based on one characteristic, either favorable or unfavorable. In other words, a halo blinds the perceiver to other characteristics that should be used in generating a more complete assessment. The halo effect can play a significant role in performance appraisal, as we discussed in Chapter 11. For example, a person with an outstanding attendance record may be assessed as responsible, industrious, and highly productive; another person with less-than-average attendance may be assessed as a poor performer. Either assessment may be true, but it is the manager's job to be sure the assessment is based on complete information about all job-related characteristics and not just his or her preferences for good attendance.

Projection is the tendency of perceivers to see their own personal traits in other people; that is, they project their own needs, feelings, values, and attitudes into their judgment of others. A manager who is achievement oriented might assume that subordinates are as well. This assumption might cause the manager to restructure jobs to be less routine and more challenging, without regard for employees' actual satisfaction.

Perceptual defense is the tendency of perceivers to protect themselves against ideas, objects, or people that are threatening. People perceive things that are satisfying and pleasant but tend to disregard things that are disturbing and unpleasant. In essence, people develop blind spots in the perceptual process so that negative sensory data do not hurt them.

Attributions

Among the judgments people make as part of the perceptual process are attributions. **Attributions** are judgments about what caused a person's behavior—something about the person or something about the situation. An *internal attribution* says characteristics of the person led to the behavior. ("Susan missed the deadline because she's careless and lazy.") An *external attribution* says something about the situation caused the person's behavior. ("Susan missed the deadline because she couldn't get the information she needed in a timely manner.") Attributions are important because they help people decide how to handle a situation. In the case of the missed deadline, a manager who blames it on the employee's personality will view Susan as the problem and might give her unfavorable performance reviews and less attention and support. In contrast, a manager who blames the behavior on the situation might try to prevent such situations in the future, such as by improving horizontal communication mechanisms so people get the information they need in a timely way.

Social scientists have studied the attributions people make and identified three factors that influence whether an attribution will be external or internal.[18] These three factors are illustrated in Exhibit 15.5.

perceptual distortions Errors in perceptual judgment that arise from inaccuracies in any part of the perceptual process.

stereotyping The tendency to assign an individual to a group or broad category and then attribute generalizations about the group to the individual.

halo effect An overall impression of a person or situation based on one characteristic, either favorable or unfavorable.

projection The tendency to see one's own personal traits in other people.

perceptual defense The tendency of perceivers to protect themselves by disregarding ideas, objects, or people that are threatening to them.

attributions Judgments about what caused a person's behavior—either characteristics of the person or of the situation.

Observed Behavior

EXHIBIT | 15.5

Factors Influencing Whether Attributions Are Internal or External

Does the person behave in this way in other situations?

Yes Low distinctiveness ⟹ Internal attribution

No High distinctiveness ⟹ External attribution

Does the person have a history of behaving this way at other times?

Yes High consistency ⟹ Internal attribution

No Low consistency ⟹ External attribution

Do other people behave in this way in similar situations?

Yes High consensus ⟹ External attribution

No Low consensus ⟹ Internal attribution

1. *Distinctiveness.* Whether the behavior is unusual for that person (in contrast to a person displaying the same kind of behavior in many situations). If the behavior is distinctive, the perceiver probably will make an *external* attribution.

2. *Consistency.* Whether the person being observed has a history of behaving in the same way. People generally make *internal* attributions about consistent behavior.

3. *Consensus.* Whether other people tend to respond to similar situations in the same way. A person who has observed others handle similar situations in the same way will likely make an *external* attribution; that is, it will seem that the situation produces the type of behavior observed.

In addition to these general rules, people tend to have biases that they apply when making attributions. When evaluating others, we tend to underestimate the influence of external factors and overestimate the influence of internal factors. This tendency is called the **fundamental attribution error**. Consider the case of someone being promoted to CEO. Employees, outsiders, and the media generally focus on the characteristics of the person that allowed him or her to achieve the promotion. In reality, however, the selection of that person might have been heavily influenced by external factors, such as business conditions creating a need for someone with a strong financial or marketing background at that particular time.

Another bias that distorts attributions involves attributions we make about our own behavior. People tend to overestimate the contribution of internal factors to their successes and overestimate the contribution of external factors to their failures. This tendency, called the **self-serving bias**, means people give themselves too much credit for what they do well and give external forces too much blame when they fail. Thus, if your manager says you don't communicate well enough, and you think your manager doesn't listen well enough, the truth may actually lie somewhere in between.

PERSONALITY AND BEHAVIOR

In recent years, many employers showed heightened interest in matching people's personalities to the needs of the job and the organization. An individual's **personality** is the set of characteristics that underlie a relatively stable pattern of behavior in

fundamental attribution error The tendency to underestimate the influence of external factors on another's behavior and to overestimate the influence of internal factors.

self-serving bias The tendency to overestimate the contribution of internal factors to one's successes and the contribution of external factors to one's failures.

personality The set of characteristics that underlie a relatively stable pattern of behavior in response to ideas, objects, or people in the environment.

response to ideas, objects, or people in the environment. Managers who appreciate the ways their employees' personalities differ have insight into what kinds of leadership behavior will be most influential.

Personality Traits

In common use, people think of personality in terms of traits, the fairly consistent characteristics a person exhibits. Researchers investigated whether any traits stand up to scientific scrutiny. Although investigators examined thousands of traits over the years, their findings fit into five general dimensions that describe personality. These dimensions, often called the "Big Five" personality factors, are illustrated in Exhibit 15.6.[19] Each factor may contain a wide range of specific traits. The **Big Five personality factors** describe an individual's extroversion, agreeableness, conscientiousness, emotional stability, and openness to experience:

1. *Extroversion.* The degree to which a person is outgoing, sociable, assertive, and comfortable with interpersonal relationships.

2. *Agreeableness.* The degree to which a person is able to get along with others by being good-natured, likable, cooperative, forgiving, understanding, and trusting.

3. *Conscientiousness.* The degree to which a person is focused on a few goals, thus behaving in ways that are responsible, dependable, persistent, and achievement oriented.

Big Five personality factors Dimensions that describe an individual's extroversion, agreeableness, conscientiousness, emotional stability, and openness to experience.

4. *Emotional stability.* The degree to which a person is calm, enthusiastic, and self-confident, rather than tense, depressed, moody, or insecure.

5. *Openness to experience.* The degree to which a person has a broad range of interests and is imaginative, creative, artistically sensitive, and willing to consider new ideas.

EXHIBIT | **15.6** The Big Five Personality Traits

Each individual's collection of personality traits is different; it is what makes us unique. But, although each *collection* of traits varies, we all share many common traits. The following phrases describe various traits and behaviors. Rate how accurately each statement describes you, based on a scale of 1 to 5, with 1 being very inaccurate and 5 very accurate. Describe yourself as you are now, not as you wish to be. There are no right or wrong answers.

1 2 3 4 5
Very Inaccurate   Very Accurate

Extroversion						Neuroticism (Low Emotional Stability)					
I am usually the life of the party.	1	2	3	4	5	I often feel critical of myself.	1	2	3	4	5
I feel comfortable around people.	1	2	3	4	5	I often envy others.	1	2	3	4	5
I am talkative.	1	2	3	4	5	I am temperamental.	1	2	3	4	5

Agreeableness						Openness to New Experiences					
I am kind and sympathetic.	1	2	3	4	5	I am imaginative.	1	2	3	4	5
I have a good word for everyone.	1	2	3	4	5	I prefer to vote for liberal political candidates.	1	2	3	4	5
I never insult people.	1	2	3	4	5	I really like art.	1	2	3	4	5

Conscientiousness					
I am systematic and efficient.	1	2	3	4	5
I pay attention to details.	1	2	3	4	5
I am always prepared for class.	1	2	3	4	5

Which are your most prominent traits? For fun and discussion, compare your responses with those of classmates.

As illustrated in the exhibit, these factors represent a continuum. That is, a person may have a low, moderate, or high degree of each quality. Answer the questions in Exhibit 15.6 to see where you fall on the Big Five scale for each of the factors. Having a moderate-to-high degree of each of the Big Five personality factors is considered desirable for a wide range of employees, but this isn't always a key to success. For example, having an outgoing, sociable personality (extraversion) is considered desirable for managers, but many successful top leaders, including Bill Gates, Charles Schwab, and Steven Spielberg, are introverts, people who become drained by social encounters and need time alone to reflect and recharge their batteries. One study found that four in ten top executives test out to be introverts.[20] Thus, the quality of extraversion is not as significant as is often presumed. Traits of agreeableness, on the other hand, seem to be particularly important in today's collaborative organizations. The days are over when a hard-driving manager can run roughshod over others to earn a promotion. Companies want managers who work smoothly with others and get help from lots of people inside and outside the organization. Executive search firm Korn/Ferry International examined data from millions of manager profiles since the early 2000s and found that the most successful executives today are team-oriented leaders who gather information and work collaboratively with many different people.[21]

Concept Connection Marriott carefully screens candidates for critical customer service positions, such as the hotel concierge shown here. One important way managers determine whether people have the "right stuff" is through **personality testing**. During the application process, candidates answer a series of questions about their beliefs, attitudes, work habits, and how they might handle situations, enabling Marriott to identify people with interests and motivations that are compatible with company values. As managers re-evaluate Marriott's mission and goals, the test also evolves. Some fear personality tests have too much influence, determining not just who gets hired, but who even gets an interview.

One recent book argues that the secret to success in work and in life is *likability*. We all know we're more willing to do something for someone we like than for someone we don't, whether it is a teammate, a neighbor, a professor, or a supervisor. Managers can increase their likability by developing traits of agreeableness, including being friendly and cooperative, understanding other people in a genuine way, and striving to make people feel positive about themselves.[22]

Many companies, including JCPenney, DuPont, Toys "R" Us, and the Union Pacific Railroad, use personality testing to hire, evaluate, or promote employees. Surveys show that at least 30 percent of organizations use some kind of personality testing for hiring.[23] Entrepreneurial companies such as eHarmony are using sophisticated personality testing to match singles through online dating services.

Innovative Way

eHarmony

Online dating has grown into a half-billion dollar industry in just over ten years. Personality tests are central to some of these organizations' strategies, and eHarmony is one of the most comprehensive at pursuing so-called serious daters, people who are searching for a lasting relationship.

The eHarmony Compatibility Matching System employs an exhaustive 436-question personality survey that is based on founder Neil Clark Warren's past professional experience and his company's research into long-lived marriages. Warren, who holds both divinity and clinical psychology degrees, believes the unions most likely to succeed are those between people who share at least 10 of the 29 personality traits eHarmony measures.

Does the approach work? So far, the only company to track relationships it has helped create is eHarmony. Claiming to have helped bring about 16,000 marriages in 2005 alone, the company conducted an in-house study it says showed eHarmony couples enjoyed higher levels of marital satisfaction than those who had met through other channels.[24]

Despite growing use of personality tests, there is so far little hard evidence showing them to be valid predictors of job—or relationship—success.

Emotional Intelligence

In recent years, new insights into personality are emerging through research in the area of *emotional intelligence*. Emotional intelligence (EQ) includes four basic components:[25]

1. *Self-awareness.* The basis for all the other components; being aware of what you are feeling. People who are in touch with their feelings are better able to guide their own lives and actions. A high degree of self-awareness means you can accurately assess your own strengths and limitations and have a healthy sense of self-confidence.

2. *Self-management.* The ability to control disruptive or harmful emotions and balance one's moods so that worry, anxiety, fear, or anger do not cloud thinking and get in the way of what needs to be done. People who are skilled at self-management remain optimistic and hopeful despite setbacks and obstacles. This ability is crucial for pursuing long-term goals. MetLife found that applicants who failed the regular sales aptitude test but scored high on optimism made 21 percent more sales in their first year and 57 percent more in their second year than those who passed the sales test but scored high on pessimism.[26]

3. *Social awareness.* The ability to understand others and practice *empathy*, which means being able to put yourself in someone else's shoes, to recognize what others are feeling without them needing to tell you. People with social awareness are capable of understanding divergent points of view and interacting effectively with many different types of people.

4. *Relationship management.* The ability to connect to others, build positive relationships, respond to the emotions of others, and influence others. People with relationship management skills know how to listen and communicate clearly, and they treat others with compassion and respect.

Studies show a positive relationship between job performance and high levels of emotional intelligence in a variety of jobs. Numerous organizations, including the U.S. Air Force and Canada Life, use EQ tests to measure such things as self-awareness, ability to empathize, and capacity to build positive relationships.[27] Altera Corporation uses "empathy coaches" to help its salespeople develop greater social awareness and see things from their customers' point of view.[28] EQ seems to be particularly important for jobs such as sales that require a high degree of social interaction. It's also critical for managers, who are responsible for influencing others and building positive attitudes and relationships in the organization. Managers with low emotional intelligence can undermine employee morale and harm the organization.

TakeaMoment | **Complete the New Manager Self-Test on page 453 to assess your own level of emotional intelligence. You might also want to refer back to the questionnaire related to self-confidence at the beginning of this chapter. Self-confidence strongly influences a new manager's EQ.**

Attitudes and Behaviors Influenced by Personality

An individual's personality influences his or her work-related attitudes and behaviors. As a new manager, you will have to manage people with a wide variety of personality characteristics. This chapter's Shoptalk discusses how managers can cope with the challenge of bridging personality differences. Four areas related to personality that are of particular interest to managers are locus of control, authoritarianism, Machiavellianism, and problem-solving styles.

New Manager Self-Test

What's Your EQ?

Understanding yourself and others is a major part of new manager's job. To learn about your insights into self and others, answer each item below as Mostly True or Mostly False for you.

	Mostly True	Mostly False
1. **I am aware of sensations and emotions within my body.**	_____	_____
2. **I am slow to react to others' slights or negative actions toward me.**	_____	_____
3. **I can tell my friends' moods from their behavior.**	_____	_____
4. **I am good at building consensus among others.**	_____	_____
5. **I have a good sense of why I have certain feelings.**	_____	_____
6. **I calm down right away if upset and am quick to forgive.**	_____	_____
7. **I often sense the impact of my words or behavior on others.**	_____	_____
8. **Other people are happier when I am around.**	_____	_____

SCORING AND INTERPRETATION: The categories of emotional intelligence are below. Give yourself one point for each item marked Mostly True.

Self-Awareness: Items 1, 5
Self-Management: Items 2, 6,
Social Awareness: Items 3, 7
Relationship Management: Items 4, 8

These are the four dimensions of EQ described in the text. If you scored 2 on a dimension, you probably do well on it. If you scored 0 on a dimension, you may want to work on that aspect of your EQ before becoming a manager. The important thing as a manager is to know and guide yourself, to understand the emotional state of others, and to guide your relationships in a positive direction.

Locus of Control People differ in terms of what they tend to accredit as the cause of their success or failure. Their **locus of control** defines whether they place the primary responsibility within themselves or on outside forces.[29] Some people believe that their own actions strongly influence what happens to them. They feel in control of their own fate. These individuals have a high *internal* locus of control. Other people believe that events in their lives occur because of chance, luck, or outside people and events. They feel more like pawns of their fate. These individuals have a high *external* locus of control.

Research on locus of control shows real differences in behavior across a wide range of settings. People with an internal locus of control are easier to motivate because they believe the rewards are the result of their behavior.

locus of control The tendency to place the primary responsibility for one's success or failure either within oneself (internally) or on outside forces (externally).

6 Leading

Manager's Shoptalk

Bridging the Personality Gap

Personality differences among employees make the life of a new manager interesting—and sometimes exasperating. Consultant Deborah Hildebrand took a lighthearted look at this issue by comparing the manager to a ringmaster at the circus. Here are a few of the "performers" managers encounter:

- **The Lion Tamer.** These people are fiercely independent and like to be in control. They are willing to tackle the biggest, toughest projects but aren't typically good team players. The manager can give lion tamers some freedom, but make sure they understand who is ultimately in charge. Lion tamers crave recognition. Praising them for their accomplishments is a sure way to keep them motivated and prevent them from acting out to draw attention to themselves.

- **The Clown.** Everybody loves him (or her), but the clown tends to goof off a little too much, as well as disrupt the work of others. Keeping this person focused is the key to keeping him or her productive. A little micromanaging can be a good thing with a clown. It's also good to put clowns in jobs where socializing is a key to productivity and success.

- **Sideshow Performers.** These are the knife throwers, fire eaters, and sword swallowers. They have unique strengths and skills but tend to get overwhelmed with broad projects. These folks are expert team members because they like to combine their talents with others to make up a whole. Don't ask a sideshow performer to do a lion tamer's job.

This list is intended to be humorous, but in the real world of management, working with different personalities isn't always a laughing matter. Differences at work can create an innovative environment but also lead to stress, conflict, and bad feelings. Managers can learn to work more effectively with different personality types by following some simple tips.

1. **Understand your own personality and how you react to others.** Try to avoid judging people based on limited knowledge. Realize that everyone has many facets to their personality.

2. **Treat everyone with respect.** People like to be accepted and appreciated for who they are. Even if you find someone's personality grating, remain professional and keep your frustration and irritation to yourself.

3. **When leading a team or group, make sure everyone has an equal chance to participate.** Don't let the outgoing members dominate the scene.

4. **Remember that everyone wants to fit in.** No matter their personalities, people typically take on behavior patterns that are the norm for their environment. Managers can create norms that keep everyone focused on positive interactions and high performance.

SOURCES: Based on Deborah S. Hildebrand, "Managing Different Personalities," Suite101.com (June 25, 2007), http://businessmanagement.suite101.com/article.cfm/managing_different_personalities; Jamie Walters and Sarah Fenson, "Building Rapport with Different Personalities," *Inc.com* (March 2000), http://www.inc.com/articles/2000/03/17713.html; Tim Millett, "Learning to Work with Different Personality Types," http://ezinearticles.com/?Learning-To-Work-With-Different-Personality-Types&id=725606; and Carol Ritberter, "Understanding Personality: The Secret to Managing People," http://www.dreammanifesto.com/understanding-personality-the-secret-of-managing-people.html (accessed April 17, 2008).

They are better able to handle complex information and problem solving, are more achievement oriented, but are also more independent and therefore more difficult to manage. By contrast, people with an external locus of control are harder to motivate, less involved in their jobs, more likely to blame others when faced with a poor performance evaluation, but more compliant and conforming and, therefore, easier to manage.[30]

Do you believe luck plays an important role in your life, or do you feel that you control your own fate? To find out more about your locus of control, read the instructions and complete the questionnaire in Exhibit 15.7.

authoritarianism The belief that power and status differences should exist within the organization.

Authoritarianism Authoritarianism is the belief that power and status differences should exist within the organization.[31] Individuals high in authoritarianism tend to be concerned with power and toughness, obey recognized authority above them,

EXHIBIT | 15.7 Measuring Locus of Control

Your Locus of Control

This questionnaire is designed to measure locus-of-control beliefs. Researchers using this questionnaire in a study of college students found a mean of 51.8 for men and 52.2 for women, with a standard deviation of 6 for each. The higher your score on this question-naire, the more you tend to believe that you are generally responsible for what happens to you; in other words, higher scores are as-sociated with internal locus of control. Low scores are associated with external locus of control. Scoring low indicates that you tend to believe that forces beyond your control, such as powerful other people, fate, or chance, are responsible for what happens to you.

For each of these 10 questions, indicate the extent to which you agree or disagree using the following scale:

1 = strongly disagree   4 = neither disagree nor agree   7 = strongly agree
2 = disagree   5 = slightly agree
3 = slightly disagree   6 = agree

	1	2	3	4	5	6	7
1. When I get what I want, it is usually because I worked hard for it.	1	2	3	4	5	6	7
2. When I make plans, I am almost certain to make them work.	1	2	3	4	5	6	7
3. I prefer games involving some luck over games requiring pure skill.	1	2	3	4	5	6	7
4. I can learn almost anything if I set my mind to it.	1	2	3	4	5	6	7
5. My major accomplishments are entirely due to my hard work and ability.	1	2	3	4	5	6	7
6. I usually don't set goals because I have a hard time following through on them.	1	2	3	4	5	6	7
7. Competition discourages excellence.	1	2	3	4	5	6	7
8. Often people get ahead just by being lucky.	1	2	3	4	5	6	7
9. On any sort of exam or competition, I like to know how well I do relative to everyone else.	1	2	3	4	5	6	7
10. It's pointless to keep working on something that's too difficult for me.	1	2	3	4	5	6	7

Scoring and Interpretation

To determine your score, reverse the values you selected for questions 3, 6, 7, 8, and 10 (1 = 7, 2 = 6, 3 = 5, 4 = 4, 5 = 3, 6 = 2, 7 = 1). For example, if you strongly disagree with the statement in question 3, you would have given it a value of 1. Change this value to a 7. Reverse the scores in a similar manner for questions 6, 7, 8, and 10. Now add the point values for all 10 questions together. Your score _____

SOURCES: Adapted from J. M. Burger, *Personality: Theory and Research* (Belmont, CA: Wadsworth, 1986): 400–401, cited in D. Hellriegel, J.W. Slocum, Jr., and R.W.Woodman, *Organizational Behavior*, 6th ed. (St. Paul, MN: West, 1992): 97–100. Original source: D. L. Paulhus, "Sphere-Specific Measures of Perceived Control," *Journal of Personality and Social Psychology*, 44, 1253–1265.

stick to conventional values, critically judge others, and oppose the use of subjective feelings. The degree to which managers possess authoritarianism will influence how they wield and share power. The degree to which employees possess authoritarianism will influence how they react to their managers. If a manager and employees differ in their degree of authoritarianism, the manager may have difficulty leading effectively. The trend toward empowerment and shifts in expectations among younger employ-ees for more equitable relationships contribute to a decline in strict authoritarianism in many organizations.

Machiavellianism Another personality dimension that is helpful in understand-ing work behavior is **Machiavellianism**, which is characterized by the acquisition of power and the manipulation of other people for purely personal gain. Machiavel-lianism is named after Niccolo Machiavelli, a sixteenth-century author who wrote *The Prince*, a book for noblemen of the day on how to acquire and use power.[32] Psy-chologists developed instruments to measure a person's Machiavellianism (Mach) orientation.[33] Research shows that high Machs are predisposed to being pragmatic, capable of lying to achieve personal goals, more likely to win in win-lose situations, and more likely to persuade than be persuaded.[34]

Different situations may require people who demonstrate one or the other type of behavior. In loosely structured situations, high Machs actively take control, while low Machs accept the direction given by others. Low Machs thrive in highly structured situations, while high Machs perform in a detached, disinterested way. High Machs are particularly good in jobs that require bargaining skills or that involve substantial rewards for winning.[35]

Machiavellianism The ten-dency to direct much of one's behavior toward the acquisition of power and the manipulation of other people for personal gain.

Problem-Solving Styles and the Myers–Briggs Type Indicator Managers also need to realize that individuals solve problems and make decisions in different ways. One approach to understanding problem-solving styles grew out of the work of psychologist Carl Jung. Jung believed differences resulted from our preferences in how we go about gathering and evaluating information.[36] According to Jung, gathering information and evaluating information are separate activities. People gather information either by *sensation* or *intuition*, but not by both simultaneously. Sensation-type people would rather work with known facts and hard data and prefer routine and order in gathering information. Intuitive-type people would rather look for possibilities than work with facts and prefer solving new problems and using abstract concepts.

Evaluating information involves making judgments about the information a person has gathered. People evaluate information by *thinking* or *feeling*. These represent the extremes in orientation. Thinking-type individuals base their judgments on impersonal analysis, using reason and logic rather than personal values or emotional aspects of the situation. Feeling-type individuals base their judgments more on personal feelings such as harmony and tend to make decisions that result in approval from others.

According to Jung, only one of the four functions—sensation, intuition, thinking, or feeling—is dominant in an individual. However, the dominant function usually is backed up by one of the functions from the other set of paired opposites. Exhibit 15.8 shows the four problem-solving styles that result from these matchups, as well as occupations that people with each style tend to prefer.

Two additional sets of paired opposites not directly related to problem solving are *introversion–extroversion* and *judging–perceiving*. Introverts gain energy by focusing on personal thoughts and feelings, whereas extroverts gain energy from being around others and interacting with others. On the judging versus perceiving dimension, people with a judging preference like certainty and closure and tend to make decisions quickly based on available data. Perceiving people, on the other hand, enjoy ambiguity, dislike deadlines, and may change their minds several times as they gather large amounts of data and information to make decisions.

EXHIBIT 15.8 Four Problem-Solving Styles

Personal Style	Action Tendencies	Likely Occupations
Sensation-Thinking	• Emphasizes details, facts, certainty • Is a decisive, applied thinker • Focuses on short-term, realistic goals • Develops rules and regulations for judging performance	• Accounting • Production • Computer programming • Market research • Engineering
Intuitive-Thinking	• Prefers dealing with theoretical or technical problems • Is a creative, progressive, perceptive thinker • Focuses on possibilities using impersonal analysis • Is able to consider a number of options and problems simultaneously	• Systems design • Systems analysis • Law • Middle/top management • Teaching business, economics
Sensation-Feeling	• Shows concern for current, real-life human problems • Is pragmatic, analytical, methodical, and conscientious • Emphasizes detailed facts about people rather than tasks • Focuses on structuring organizations for the benefit of people	• Directing supervisor • Counseling • Negotiating • Selling • Interviewing
Intuitive-Feeling	• Avoids specifics • Is charismatic, participative, people oriented, and helpful • Focuses on general views, broad themes, and feelings • Decentralizes decision making, develops few rules and regulations	• Public relations • Advertising • Human Resources • Politics • Customer service

A widely used personality test that measures how people differ on all four of Jung's sets of paired opposites is the **Myers–Briggs Type Indicator (MBTI)**. The MBTI measures a person's preferences for introversion versus extroversion, sensation versus intuition, thinking versus feeling, and judging versus perceiving. The various combinations of these four preferences result in 16 unique personality types.

Go to the experiential exercise on pages 465–466 that pertains to evaluating your Myers–Briggs personality type.

TakeaMoment

Each of the 16 different personality types can have positive and negative consequences for behavior. Based on the limited research that has been done, the two preferences that seem to be most strongly associated with effective management in a variety of organizations and industries are thinking and judging.[37] However, people with other preferences can also be good managers. One advantage of understanding your natural preferences is to maximize your innate strengths and abilities. Dow Chemical manager Kurt Swogger believes the MBTI can help put people in the right jobs—where they will be happiest and make the strongest contribution to the organization.

Innovative Way

Dow Chemical

When Kurt Swogger arrived at Dow Chemical's plastics business in 1991, it took anywhere from 6 to 15 years to launch a new product—and the unit hadn't launched a single one for 3 years. Ten years later, a new product launch took just 2 to 4 years, and Swogger's R&D team was launching hit after hit.

What changed? "The biggest obstacle to launching great new products was not having the right people in the right jobs," says Swogger. He began reassigning people based on his intuition and experience, distinguishing pure inventors from those who could add value later in the game and still others who were best at marketing the new products. Swogger says he was right-on about 60 percent of the time. If someone didn't work out after six months, he'd put him or her in another assignment.

Seeking a better way to determine people's strengths, Swogger began using the Myers–Briggs Type Indicator (MBTI), predicting which types would be best suited to each stage of the product development and launch cycles. After administering the test to current and former Dow plastics employees, he found some startling results. In 1991, when Swogger came on board, the match between the right personality type and the right role was only 29 percent. By 2001, the rate had jumped to 93 percent. Swogger's next step was to administer the MBTI to new hires, so he could immediately assign people to jobs that matched their natural thinking and problem-solving styles, leading to happier employees and higher organizational performance.[38]

Other organizations also use the MBTI, with 89 of the *Fortune* 100 companies recently reporting that they use the test in hiring and promotion decisions.[39] Putting the right people in the right jobs is a vital skill for managers, whether they do it based on intuition and experience or by using personality tests such as the MBTI.

Person–Job Fit

An important responsibility of managers is to try to match employee and job characteristics so that work is done by people who are well suited to do it. The extent to which a person's ability and personality match the requirements of a job is called **person–job fit**. When managers achieve person–job fit, employees are more likely to contribute and have higher levels of job satisfaction and commitment.[40] The importance of person–job fit became apparent during the dot-com heyday of the late 1990s. People who rushed to Internet companies in hopes of finding a new challenge—or making a quick buck—found themselves floundering in jobs for which they were

Myers–Briggs Type Indicator (MBTI) Personality test that measures a person's preference for introversion vs. extroversion, sensation vs. intuition, thinking vs. feeling, and judging vs. perceiving.

person–job fit The extent to which a person's ability and personality match the requirements of a job.

6 Leading

Concept Connection   Andrew Field, who owns a $25 million printing services company, PrintingForLess.com, uses dogs to help him create the **person-environment fit** when hiring new employees. The dog-friendly policy started at the company's inception when Field began bringing his Border collie and black Labrador mix Jessie (far left) to work on a daily basis. The idea caught on and now as many as fifteen dogs frequent the office with their owners. With rules such as owner accountability, a dog review board, and a dog-approval process, employees find the dogs are a great release for stress. Fields says that the dog policy helps him make good hires; candidates who respond favorably to the canine rule are likely to fit in with the office culture.

unsuited. One manager recruited by a leading executive search firm lasted less than two hours at his new job. The search firm, a division of Russell Reynolds Associates, later developed a "Web Factor" diagnostic to help determine whether people have the right personality for dot-com jobs, including such things as a tolerance for risk and uncertainty, an obsession with learning, and a willingness to do whatever needs doing, regardless of job title.[41]

A related concern is *person–environment fit*, which looks not only at whether the person and job are suited to one another but also at how well the individual will fit in the overall organizational environment. An employee who is by nature strongly authoritarian, for example, would have a hard time in an organization such as W. L. Gore and Associates, which has few rules, no hierarchy, no fixed or assigned authority, and no bosses. Many of today's organizations pay attention to person–environment fit from the beginning of the recruitment process. Texas Instruments' Web page includes an area called Fit Check that evaluates personality types anonymously and gives a prospective job candidate the chance to evaluate whether he or she would be a good match with the company.[42]

LEARNING

learning A change in behavior or performance that occurs as the result of experience.

Years of schooling condition many of us to think that learning is something students do in response to teachers in a classroom. With this view, in the managerial world of time deadlines and concrete action, learning seems remote—even irrelevant. However, successful managers need specific knowledge and skills as well as the ability to adapt to changes in the world around them. Managers have to learn. **Learning** is a change in behavior or performance that occurs as the result of experience. Two individuals who undergo similar experiences— for example, a business transfer to a foreign country—probably will differ in how they adapt their behaviors to (that is, learn from) the experience. In other words, each person learns in a different way.

The Learning Process

One model of the learning process, shown in Exhibit 15.9, depicts learning as a four-stage cycle.[43] First, a person encounters a concrete experience. This event is followed by thinking and reflective observation, which lead to abstract conceptualization and, in turn, to active experimentation. The results of the experimentation generate new experiences, and the cycle repeats. The

Concept Connection   Jenny Craig, the pioneering weight-loss company, believes in **continuous learning** for both employees and clients. Its program combines Web-based tools with more traditional methods, including videos and sessions led by instructors, such as trainer Jeri Dawn Martel, shown here. Employees undergo an extensive orientation, as well as several days of training each time they assume new responsibilities. In addition, headquarters provides over 600 centers with product and services updates for their semimonthly staff meetings and in-depth training materials for quarterly continuing education courses.

EXHIBIT | 15.9

The Experiential Learning Cycle

arrows in the model indicate that this process is a recurring cycle. People continually test their conceptualizations and adapt them as a result of their personal reflections and observations about their experiences.

Learning Styles

Individuals develop personal learning styles that vary in terms of how much they emphasize each stage of the learning cycle. These differences occur because the learning process is directed by individual needs and goals. For example, an engineer might place greater emphasis on abstract concepts, while a salesperson might emphasize concrete experiences. Because of these preferences, personal learning styles typically have strong and weak points.

Questionnaires can assess a person's strong and weak points as a learner by measuring the relative emphasis the person places on each of the four learning stages shown in Exhibit 15.9: concrete experience, reflective observation, abstract conceptualization, and active experimentation. Some people have a tendency to overemphasize one stage of the learning process or to avoid some aspects of learning. Not many people have totally balanced profiles, but the key to effective learning is competence in each of the four stages when it is needed.

Researchers have identified four fundamental learning styles, outlined in Exhibit 15.10, labeled Diverger, Assimilator, Converger, and Accommodator. Each style combines elements of the four stages of the learning cycle.[44] The exhibit lists some questions that can help you understand your dominant learning abilities and identifies some occupations you might enjoy based on your dominant style. For example, people whose dominant style is Accommodator are often drawn to sales and marketing. Those with a primarily Diverger style might enjoy human resource management.

As a new manager, determine your natural learning style to understand how you approach problems, use your learning strengths, and better relate to people who have different styles. As you grow in your management responsibilities, strive for a balance among the four learning stages shown in Exhibit 15.9.

TakeaMoment

6 Leading

EXHIBIT | 15.10 What's Your Learning Style?

Learning Style Type	Dominant Learning Abilities	Is This Your Style?	You Might Be Good At:
Diverger	• Concrete experience • Reflective observation	• Are you good at generating ideas, seeing a situation from multiple perspectives, and being aware of meaning and value? • Are you interested in people, culture, and the arts?	• Human resource management • Counseling • Organization development specialist
Assimilator	• Abstract conceptualization • Reflective observation	• Are you good at inductive reasoning, creating theoretical models, and combining disparate observations into an integrated explanation? • Do you tend to be less concerned with people than ideas and abstract concepts?	• Research • Strategic planning
Converger	• Abstract conceptualization • Active experimentation	• Are you good at making decisions, the practical application of ideas, and hypothetical deductive reasoning? • Do you prefer dealing with technical tasks rather than interpersonal issues?	• Engineering
Accommodator	• Concrete experience • Active experimentation	• Are you good at implementing decisions, carrying out plans, and getting involved in new experiences? • Do you tend to be at ease with people but are sometimes seen as impatient or pushy?	• Marketing • Sales

STRESS AND STRESS MANAGEMENT

Now let's turn our attention to a problem almost every manager will encounter at some time in his or her career: workplace stress. Formally defined, **stress** is an individual's physiological and emotional response to external stimuli that place physical or psychological demands on the individual and create uncertainty and lack of personal control when important outcomes are at stake.[45] These stimuli, called *stressors*, produce some combination of frustration (the inability to achieve a goal, such as the inability to meet a deadline because of inadequate resources) and anxiety (such as the fear of being disciplined for not meeting deadlines).

TakeaMoment | **Go to the ethical dilemma on page 467 that pertains to organizational sources of stress.**

People's responses to stressors vary according to their personalities, the resources available to help them cope, and the context in which the stress occurs. When the level of stress is low relative to a person's coping resources, stress can be a positive force, stimulating desirable change and achievement. However, too much stress is associated with many negative consequences, including sleep disturbances, drug and alcohol abuse, headaches, ulcers, high blood pressure, and heart disease. People who are experiencing the ill effects of too much stress may become irritable or withdraw from interactions with their coworkers, take excess time off, and have more health problems. In the United States, an estimated one million people each day don't show up for work because of stress.[46] Similarly, a survey in the United Kingdom found that 68 percent of nonmanual workers and 42 percent of manual workers reported missing work because of stress-related illness.[47] Just as big a problem for organizations as absenteeism is *presenteeism*, which refers to people who go to work but are too stressed and distracted to be productive.[48] Clearly, too much stress is harmful to employees as well as to companies.

stress A physiological and emotional response to stimuli that place physical or psychological demands on an individual.

Type A and Type B Behavior

Researchers observed that some people seem to be more vulnerable than others to the ill effects of stress. From studies of stress-related heart disease, they categorized people as having behavior patterns called Type A and Type B.[49] The **Type A behavior** pattern includes extreme competitiveness, impatience, aggressiveness, and devotion to work. In contrast, people with a **Type B behavior** pattern exhibit less of these behaviors. They consequently experience less conflict with other people and a more balanced, relaxed lifestyle. Type A people tend to experience more stress-related illness than Type B people.

Most Type A individuals are high-energy people and may seek positions of power and responsibility. By pacing themselves and learning control and intelligent use of their natural high-energy tendencies, Type A individuals can be powerful forces for innovation and leadership within their organizations. However, many Type A personalities cause stress-related problems for themselves, and sometimes for those around them. Type B individuals typically live with less stress unless they are in high-stress situations. A number of factors can cause stress in the workplace, even for people who are not naturally prone to high stress.

Causes of Work Stress

Workplace stress is skyrocketing worldwide. The World Congress on Health and Safety at Work presented studies suggesting that job-related stress may be as big a danger to the world's people as chemical and biological hazards.[50] The number of people in the United States who say they are overworked grew from 28 percent in 2001 to 44 percent in 2005, and one-third of Americans between the ages of 25 and 39 say they feel burned out by their jobs. Surveys in Canada consistently peg work as the top source of stress for people in that country. In India, growing numbers of young software professionals and call-center workers are falling prey to depression, anxiety, and other mental illnesses because of increasing workplace stress.[51] And in France, companies did some serious soul searching after the notes of three engineers who committed suicide within five months implied that workplace stress was a major factor in their decision to end their lives.[52]

Most people have a general idea of what a stressful job is like: difficult, uncomfortable, exhausting, even frightening. Managers can better cope with their own stress and establish ways for the organization to help employees cope if they define the conditions that tend to produce work stress. One way to identify work stressors is to think about stress caused by the demands of job tasks and stress caused by interpersonal pressures and conflicts.

- *Task demands* are stressors arising from the tasks required of a person holding a particular job. Some kinds of decisions are inherently stressful: those made under time pressure, those that have serious consequences, and those that must be made with incomplete information. For example, emergency room doctors are under tremendous stress as a result of the task demands of their jobs. They regularly have to make quick decisions based on limited information that may determine whether a patient lives or dies. Almost all jobs, especially those of managers, have some level of stress associated with task demands. Task demands also sometimes cause stress because of **role ambiguity**, which means that people are unclear about what task behaviors are expected of them.

- *Interpersonal demands* are stressors associated with relationships in the organization. Although in some cases interpersonal relationships can alleviate stress, they also can be a source of stress when the group puts pressure on an individual or when conflicts arise between individuals. Managers can resolve many conflicts using techniques that will be discussed in Chapter 19. **Role conflict** occurs when an individual perceives incompatible demands from others. Managers often feel role conflict because the demands of their superiors conflict with those of the

Type A behavior Behavior pattern characterized by extreme competitiveness, impatience, aggressiveness, and devotion to work.

Type B behavior Behavior pattern that lacks Type A characteristics and includes a more balanced, relaxed lifestyle.

role ambiguity Uncertainty about what behaviors are expected of a person in a particular role.

Role conflict Incompatible demands of different roles.

employees in their department. They may be expected to support employees and provide them with opportunities to experiment and be creative, while at the same time top executives are demanding a consistent level of output that leaves little time for creativity and experimentation.

TakeaMoment | **As a new manager, learn to recognize the conditions that cause stress in the workplace and then change what you can to alleviate unnecessary or excessive stress for employees. Remember that not all stress is negative, but try to help people manage stress in a healthy way.**

Innovative Responses to Stress Management

Organizations that want to challenge their employees and stay competitive will never be stress-free, but healthy workplaces promote the physical and emotional well-being of their employees. Managers have direct control over many of the things that cause people stress, including their own behavior. Exhibit 15.11 lists some of the top things managers do to cause excessive and unnecessary stress.

Concept Connection **Many companies help employees manage stress** by offering discounts to local gyms. At SALO, LLC, a financial staffing firm in Minneapolis, employees can exercise as they work. Here, co-owners Amy Langer and John Folkstead walk as they meet. Langer and Folkstead experimented with a few treadmill desks to help get their employees and themselves moving more. The desks were such a hit with the staff that they installed twelve more stations. Employees report they have more energy and have lost weight since the treadmill desks were installed.

© PETE CROUSER/SALO LLC

A variety of techniques can help individuals manage stress. Among the most basic strategies are those that help people stay healthy: exercising regularly, getting plenty of rest, and eating a healthful diet. Although individuals can pursue stress management strategies on their own, today's enlightened companies support healthy habits to help people manage stress and be more productive. Stress costs businesses billions of dollars a year in absenteeism, lower productivity, staff turnover, accidents, and higher health insurance and workers' compensation costs.[53] Taking care of employees has become a business as well as an ethical priority. In Britain, employers are required to meet certain minimal conditions to manage workplace stress, such as ensuring that employees are not exposed to a poor physical work environment, have the necessary skills and training to meet their job requirements, and are given a chance to offer input into the way their work is done.[54]

Helping employees manage stress can be as simple as encouraging people to take regular breaks and vacations. Consider that more than a third of U.S. employees surveyed by the Families and Work Institute currently don't take their full allotment of vacation time.[55] Here are

EXHIBIT | 15.11

How Managers Create Stress for Employees

Working for a bad boss is a major cause of workplace stress. Here are some things bad bosses do to create stress for their subordinates:

1. Impose unreasonable demands and overwhelming workloads.
2. Don't let people have a say in how they do their work.
3. Create perpetual doubt about how well employees are performing.
4. Refuse to get involved in conflicts between employees; let them work it out.
5. Fail to give people credit for their contributions and achievements.
6. Keep people guessing about what is expected of them.
7. Bully and harass people to keep them on their toes.
8. Don't allow people to form a community; tell them work isn't a social club.

SOURCES: Based on "Getting the Least From Your Staff," sidebar in Don Mills, "Running on High Octane or Burning Out Big Time?" *National Post*, April 8, 2006; Donna Callea, "Workers Feeling the Burn; Employee Burnout a New Challenge to Productive, Morale, Experts Say," *News Journal*, March 27, 2006; and Joe Humphreys, "Stress Will Be Main Cause of Workplace Illness by 2020," *Irish Times*, July 27, 2005.

some proactive approaches managers are taking to combat the growing stress level in today's workplace:

- Some companies, including BellSouth, First Union, and Tribble Creative Group, have designated *quiet rooms* or meditation centers where employees can take short, calming breaks at any time they feel the need.[56] The time off is a valuable investment when it allows employees to approach their work with renewed energy and a fresh perspective.

- Wellness programs provide access to nutrition counseling and exercise facilities. A worldwide study of wellness programs conducted by the Canadian government found that for each dollar spent, the company gets from $1.95 to $3.75 return payback from benefits.[57]

- Training programs and conferences can help people identify stress and teach them coping mechanisms. Training managers to recognize warning signs is critical.

- Manager intervention is a growing trend in enlightened companies. At Boston Consulting Group, for instance, the boss steps in if he or she sees someone working too hard or displaying signs of excessive stress. Mark Ostermann says, "It was a great feeling [to have the boss provide support]. I didn't have to complain to anyone. They were proactive in contacting me."[58]

- Broad work–life balance initiatives that may include flexible work options such as telecommuting and flexible hours, as well as benefits such as onsite daycare or eldercare, fitness centers, and personal services such as pickup and delivery of dry cleaning. *Daily flextime* is considered by many employees to be the most effective work–life practice, which means giving employees the freedom to vary their hours as needed, such as leaving early to take an elderly parent shopping or taking time off to attend a child's school play.[59]

The study of organizational behavior reminds managers that employees are *human* resources with human needs. By acknowledging the personal aspects of employees' lives, these various initiatives communicate that managers and the organization care about employees. In addition, managers' attitudes make a tremendous difference in whether employees are stressed out and unhappy or relaxed, energetic, and productive.

ch15 A MANAGER'S ESSENTIALS: WHAT HAVE WE LEARNED?

- The principles of organizational behavior describe how people as individuals and groups behave and affect the performance of the organization as a whole. Desirable work-related attitudes include job satisfaction and organizational commitment. Employees' and managers' attitudes can strongly influence employee motivation, performance, and productivity. Three components of attitudes are cognitions, emotions, and behavior.

- Attitudes affect people's perceptions, and vice versa. Individuals often "see" things in different ways. The perceptual process includes perceptual selectivity and perceptual organization. Perceptual distortions, such as stereotyping, the halo effect, projection, and perceptual defense, are errors in judgment that can arise from inaccuracies in the perception process. Attributions are judgments that individuals make about whether a person's behavior was caused by internal or external factors.

- Another area of interest is personality, the set of characteristics that underlie a relatively stable pattern of behavior. One way to think about personality is the

Big Five personality traits of extroversion, agreeableness, conscientiousness, emotional stability, and openness to experience. Some important work-related attitudes and behaviors influenced by personality are locus of control, authoritarianism, Machiavellianism, and problem-solving styles. A widely used personality test is the Myers–Briggs Type Indicator. Managers want to find a good person–job fit by ensuring that a person's personality, attitudes, skills, abilities, and problem-solving styles match the requirements of the job and the organizational environment. New insight into personality has been gained through research in the area of emotional intelligence (EQ). Emotional intelligence includes the components of self-awareness, self-management, social awareness, and relationship management.

■ Even though people's personalities may be relatively stable, individuals can learn new behaviors. Learning refers to a change in behavior or performance that occurs as a result of experience. The learning process goes through a four-stage cycle, and individual learning styles differ. Four learning styles are Diverger, Assimilator, Converger, and Accommodator. Rapid changes in today's marketplace create a need for ongoing learning. They may also create greater stress for many of today's workers. The causes of work stress include task demands and interpersonal demands. Individuals and organizations can alleviate the negative effects of stress by engaging in a variety of techniques for stress management.

ch15   DISCUSSION QUESTIONS

1. If you were trying to change a subordinate's attitude, which approach do you think would be more effective: changing cognition, affect, or behavior? Why? Why is it important for managers to have an understanding of organizational behavior? Do you think a knowledge of OB might be more important at some managerial levels than at others? Discuss.

2. In what ways might the cognitive and affective components of attitude influence the behavior of employees who are faced with learning an entirely new set of computer-related skills in order to retain their jobs at a manufacturing facility?

3. Suggest a way that a manager might be able to use his or her understanding of perceptual selectivity and organization to communicate more effectively with subordinates. What steps might managers at a company that is about to merge with another company take to promote organizational commitment among employees?

4. In the Big Five personality factors, extroversion is considered a "good" quality to have. Why might introversion be an equally positive quality?

5. Why do you think surveys show that Generation X employees (those born between 1961 and 1981) experience the least job satisfaction of all demographic groups? Do you expect this finding to be true throughout their careers?

6. What is meant by perceptual selectivity? Explain some characteristics of the perceiver and of the stimuli that might affect perception?

7. Which of the four components of emotional intelligence do you consider most important to an effective manager in today's world? Why?

8. How might understanding whether an employee has an internal or an external locus of control help a manager better communicate with, motivate, and lead the employee?

9. You are a manager, and you realize that one of your employees repeatedly teases coworkers born in India that they come from a backward country with pagan beliefs. How would you decide whether it's necessary to respond to the situation? If you decide to intervene, what would your response be? Why is it important for managers to achieve person-job fit when they are hiring employees?

10. Review Exhibit 15.10. Which learning style best characterizes you? How can you use this understanding to improve your learning ability? To improve your management skills?

11. Describe a time when you experienced role ambiguity or role conflict. What stress management techniques did you use to cope with the stress this situation created?

12. Why do you think workplace stress seems to be skyrocketing? Do you think it is a trend that will continue? Explain the reasons for your answer. Do you think it is the responsibility of managers and organizations to help employees manage stress? Why or why not?

ch15 MANAGEMENT IN PRACTICE: EXPERIENTIAL EXERCISE

Personality Assessment: Jung's Typology and the Myers-Briggs Type Indicator

For each of the following items, circle either a or b. In some cases, both a and b may apply to you. You should decide which is more like you, even if it is only slightly more true.

1. I would rather
   a. Solve a new and complicated problem
   b. Work on something that I have done before

2. I like to
   a. Work alone in a quiet place
   b. Be where "the action" is

3. I want a boss who
   a. Establishes and applies criteria in decisions
   b. Considers individual needs and makes exceptions

4. When I work on a project, I
   a. Like to finish it and get some closure
   b. Often leave it open for possible change

5. When making a decision, the most important considerations are
   a. Rational thoughts, ideas, and data
   b. People's feelings and values

6. On a project, I tend to
   a. Think it over and over before deciding how to proceed
   b. Start working on it right away, thinking about it as I go along

7. When working on a project, I prefer to
   a. Maintain as much control as possible
   b. Explore various options

8. In my work, I prefer to
   a. Work on several projects at a time, and learn as much as possible about each one
   b. Have one project that is challenging and keeps me busy

9. I often
   a. Make lists and plans whenever I start something and may hate to seriously alter my plans
   b. Avoid plans and just let things progress as I work on them

10. When discussing a problem with colleagues, it is easy for me
    a. To see "the big picture"
    b. To grasp the specifics of the situation

11. When the phone rings in my office or at home, I usually
    a. Consider it an interruption
    b. Don't mind answering it

12. The word that describes me better is
    a. Analytical
    b. Empathetic

13. When I am working on an assignment, I tend to
    a. Work steadily and consistently
    b. Work in bursts of energy with "downtime" in between

14. When I listen to someone talk on a subject, I usually try to
    a. Relate it to my own experience and see whether it fits
    b. Assess and analyze the message

15. When I come up with new ideas, I generally
    a. "Go for it"
    b. Like to contemplate the ideas some more

16. When working on a project, I prefer to
    a. Narrow the scope so it is clearly defined
    b. Broaden the scope to include related aspects

17. When I read something, I usually
    a. Confine my thoughts to what is written there
    b. Read between the lines and relate the words to other ideas

18. When I have to make a decision in a hurry, I often
    a. Feel uncomfortable and wish I had more information
    b. Am able to do so with available data

19. In a meeting, I tend to
    a. Continue formulating my ideas as I talk about them
    b. Speak out only after I have carefully thought the issue through

20. In work, I prefer spending a great deal of time on issues of
    a. Ideas
    b. People

21. In meetings, I am most often annoyed with people who
    a. Come up with many sketchy ideas
    b. Lengthen the meeting with many practical details

22. I tend to be
    a. A morning person
    b. A night owl

23. My style in preparing for a meeting is
    a. To be willing to go in and be responsive
    b. To be fully prepared and sketch an outline of the meeting

24. In meetings, I would prefer for people to
    a. Display a fuller range of emotions
    b. Be more task-oriented

6
Leading

25. I would rather work for an organization where
    a. My job was intellectually stimulating
    b. I was committed to its goals and mission
26. On weekends, I tend to
    a. Plan what I will do
    b. Just see what happens and decide as I go along
27. I am more
    a. Outgoing
    b. Contemplative

28. I would rather work for a boss who is
    a. Full of new ideas
    b. Practical

In the following, choose the word in each pair that appeals to you more:

29. a. Social   b. Theoretical
30. a. Ingenuity   b. Practicality
31. a. Organized   b. Adaptable
32. a. Active   b. Concentration

Scoring and Interpretation

Count one point for each of the following items that you circled in the inventory.

Score for I (Introversion)	Score for E (Extroversion)	Score for S (Sensing)	Score for N (Intuition)
2a	2b	1b	1a
6a	6b	10b	10a
11a	11b	13a	13b
15b	15a	16a	16b
19b	19a	17a	17b
22a	22b	21a	21b
27b	27a	28b	28a
32b	32a	30b	30a
Totals _____	_____	_____	_____

Circle the one with more points:
I or E
(If tied on I/E, don't count #11)

Circle the one with more points:
S or N
(If tied on S/N, don't count #16)

Score for T (Thinking)	Score for F (Feeling)	Score for J (Judging)	Score for P (Perceiving)
3a	3b	4a	4b
5a	5b	7a	7b
12a	12b	8b	8a
14b	14a	9a	9b
20a	20b	18b	18a
24b	24a	23b	23a
25a	25b	26a	26b
29b	29a	31a	31b
Totals _____	_____	_____	_____

Circle the one with more points:
T or F
(If tied on T/F, don't count #24)

Circle the one with more points:
J or P
(If tied on J/P, don't count #23)

Your Score Is: I or E _____ S or N _____ T or F _____ J or P _____

Your MBTI type is _____ (example: INTJ; ESFP; etc.)

The Myers-Briggs Type Indicator (MBTI), based on the work of psychologist Carl Jung, is the most widely used personality assessment instrument in the world. The MBTI, which was described in the chapter text, identifies 16 different "types," shown with their dominant characteristics in the chart on page 600. Remember that no one is a pure type; however, each individual has preferences for introversion versus extroversion, sensing versus intuition, thinking versus feeling, and judging versus perceiving. Read the description of your type as determined by your scores in the survey. Do you believe the description fits your personality?

SOURCE: From *Organizational Behavior: Experience and Cases*, 4th ed. by Dorothy Marcic. © 1995. Reprinted with permission of South-Western, a division of Thomson Learning: http://www. thomsonrights.com.

ch15 MANAGEMENT IN PRACTICE: ETHICAL DILEMMA

Should I Fudge the Numbers?

Sara MacIntosh recently joined MicroPhone, a large telecommunications company, to take over the implementation of a massive customer service training project. The program was created by Kristin Cole, head of human resources and Sara's new boss. According to the grapevine, Kristin was hoping this project alone would give her the "star quality" she needed to earn a coveted promotion. Industry competition was heating up, and MicroPhone's strategy called for being the best at customer service, which meant having the most highly trained people in the industry, especially those who worked directly with customers. Kristin's new training program called for an average of one full week of intense customer service training for each of 3,000 people and had a price tag of about $40 million.

Kristin put together a team of overworked staffers to develop the training program, but now she needed someone well qualified and dedicated to manage and implement the project. Sara, with eight years of experience, a long list of accomplishments, and advanced degrees in finance and organizational behavior, seemed perfect for the job. However, during a thorough review of the proposal, Sara discovered some assumptions built into the formulas that raised red flags. She approached Dan Sotal, the team's coordinator, about her concerns, but the more Dan tried to explain how the financial projections were derived, the more Sara realized that Kristin's proposal was seriously flawed. No matter how she tried to work them out, the most that could be squeezed out of the $40 million budget was 20 hours of training per person, not the 40 hours everyone expected for such a high price tag.

Sara knew that, although the proposal had been largely developed before she came on board, it would bear her signature. As she carefully described the problems with the proposal to Kristin and outlined the potentially devastating consequences, Kristin impatiently tapped her pencil. Finally, she stood up, leaned forward, and interrupted Sara, quietly saying, "Sara, make the numbers work so that it adds up to 40 hours and stays within the $40 million budget." Sara glanced up and replied, "I don't think it can be done unless we either change the number of employees who are to be trained or the cost figure. . . ." Kristin's smile froze on her face and her eyes began to snap as she again interrupted. "I don't think you understand what I'm saying. We have too much at stake here. *Make the previous numbers work.*" Stunned, Sara belatedly began to realize that Kristin was ordering her to fudge the numbers. She felt an anxiety attack coming on as she wondered what she should do.

What Would You Do?

1. Make the previous numbers work. Kristin and the entire team have put massive amounts of time into the project and they all expect you to be a team player. You don't want to let them down. Besides, this project is a great opportunity for you in a highly visible position.

2. Stick to your principles and refuse to fudge the numbers. Tell Kristin you will work overtime to help develop an alternate proposal that stays within the budget by providing more training to employees who work directly with customers and fewer training hours for those who don't have direct customer contact.

3. Go to the team and tell them what you've been asked to do. If they refuse to support you, threaten to reveal the true numbers to the CEO and board members.

SOURCE: Adapted from Doug Wallace, "Fudge the Numbers or Leave," *Business Ethics* (May–June 1996): 58–59. Adapted with permission.

ch15 CASE FOR CRITICAL ANALYSIS

Reflex Systems

As the plane took off from the L.A. airport for Chicago and home, Henry Rankin tried to unwind, something that didn't come naturally to the Reflex Systems software engineer. He needed time to think, and the flight from Los Angeles was a welcome relief. He went to L.A. to help two members of his project team solve technical glitches in software.

Rankin had been pushing himself and his team hard for three months now, and he didn't know when they would get a break. Rankin was responsible for the technical implementation of the new customer relationship management software being installed for western and eastern sales offices in L.A. and Chicago. The software was badly needed to improve follow-up sales for his company, Reflex Systems.

Reflex sold exercise equipment to high schools and colleges through a national force of 310 salespeople. Reflex also sold products to small and medium-sized businesses for recreation centers.

Rankin knew CEO Mike Frazer saw the new CRM software as the answer to one of the exercise equipment manufacturer's most persistent problems. Even though Reflex's low prices generated healthy sales, follow-up service was spotty. Consequently, getting repeat business from customers—high schools, colleges, and corporate recreation centers—was an uphill battle. Excited by the prospect of finally removing this major roadblock, Frazer ordered the CRM software installed in just 10 weeks, a goal Rankin privately thought was unrealistic. He also felt the project budget wasn't adequate. Rankin thought about meeting the next day with his three Chicago team members, and about the status update he would give his boss, Nicole Dyer, the senior vice president for Information Technology. Rankin remembered that Dyer had scheduled 10 weeks for the CRM project. He had always been a top performer by driving himself hard, and had been in his management position three years now. He was good with technology, but was frustrated when members of his five-person team didn't seem as committed. Dyer told him last week that she didn't feel a sense of urgency from his team. How could she think that? Rankin requested that team members work evenings and weekends because the budget was too tight to fill a vacant position. They agreed to put in the hours, although they didn't seem enthusiastic.

Still, Frazer was the boss, so if he wanted the job done in 10 weeks, Rankin would do everything in his power to deliver, even if it meant the entire team worked nights and weekends. He wasn't asking any more of his subordinates than he was asking of himself, as he frequently reminded them when they came to him with bloodshot eyes and complained about the hours. Rankin thought back to a flight one month ago when he returned to Chicago from L.A. Sally Phillips sat next to him. Phillips was on one of five members on Rankin's team and told him she had an offer from a well-known competitor. The money was less, but she was interested in the quality of life aspect of the company. Phillips asked for feedback on how she was doing and about her career prospects at Reflex. Rankin said he didn't want her to leave, but what more could he say? She got along well with people but she wasn't as technically gifted as some on the team. Rankin needed her help to finish the project and he told her so. Two weeks later she turned in her letter

of resignation, and now the team was shorthanded. Rankin was also aware that his own possible promotion in two years, when Nicole Dyer was eligible for retirement, depended on his success with this project. He would just take up the slack himself. He loved studying, analyzing, and solving technical problems when he could get time alone.

Henry Rankin knew that Nicole Dyer had noticed a lack of commitment on the part of the team members. He wondered whether she had discussed the team's performance with Frazer as well. Rankin hadn't noticed any other problems, but he recalled his partner on the project, Sam Matheny, saying that two Chicago team members, Bob Finley and Lynne Johnston, were avoiding each other. How did Sam know that? Matheny was in charge of nontechnical sales implementation of the CRM project, which meant training salespeople, redesigning sales procedures, updating customer records, and so forth. Rankin called Finley and Johnston to his office and said he expected them to get along for the good of the project. Finley said he had overreacted to Johnston from lack of sleep, and wondered when the project would be over. Rankin wasn't certain because of all the problems with both software and hardware, but he said the project shouldn't last more than another month.

As the plane taxied to the gate, an exhausted Rankin couldn't quell his growing fears that as the deadline fast approached, the project team was crumbling. How could he meet that deadline? As the plane taxied to the gate at Chicago, Rankin wondered about the project's success. Was there more to managing this team than working hard and pushing others hard? Even he was tired. Maybe he would ask his wife when he got home. He hadn't seen her or the kids for a week, but they had not complained.

Questions

1. What personality and behavior characteristics does Henry Rankin exhibit? Do you think these traits contribute to a good person-job fit for him? If you were an executive coach hired to help Rankin be a better manager, what would you say to him? Why?

2. Does Rankin display type A or type B behavior? What are the causes of stress for his team?

3. If you were Rankin, how would you have handled your team members (Sally Phillips, Bob Finley, and Lynne Johnston)? Be specific. What insights or behaviors would make Rankin a better manager?

Diversity at PepsiCo

Imagine trying to manage and accommodate the needs of more than 140,000 people at once. Imagine a variety of voices, languages, cultures, ethnic backgrounds, families, lifestyles, ages, and geographies all vying for attention, all bearing the name PepsiCo. That's the challenge of managers throughout PepsiCo. From the top down, PepsiCo embraces diversity and inclusion in its worldwide workforce. Top executives, including CEO Steve Reinemund, believe that nurturing diversity in the organization is not only a matter of responsible ethics but also good business. Because PepsiCo offers products to such a diverse array of customers, it makes sense for the PepsiCo workforce to mirror the market. In addition, a facility's workforce will likely reflect the local population. However, embracing a philosophy of diversity is entirely different from implementing it. Here is how PepsiCo takes on this global task.

Although some of the divisions may use different program models, the Frito-Lay North American Diversity/Inclusion Model is a good example of how PepsiCo builds a measurable framework for diversity. The model was developed so that managers could implement and track diversity programs under their jurisdictions. It addresses five key areas, ranging from "evolving the culture" to "leveraging our people systems." By following a structure, the human resource department and other managers can develop and implement specific programs to meet the needs of their employees.

One such program is the development of employee networks throughout divisions. PepsiCo's employee networks are usually grassroots groups created on the basis of a common characteristic, such as gender or ethnic background. These networks provide opportunities for support and mentoring as employees develop their careers at PepsiCo. But the networks also help PepsiCo reach its diverse customer base. Ideas for new products, marketing efforts, and other projects grow out of the employee networks. For example, a new guacamole chip came from the Hispanic employee network, Adelante. In one recent year, Frito-Lay sold $100 million Lay's guacamole chips.

Regardless of the characteristics of a particular network, all PepsiCo employee networks have similar missions and goals:

- to become business partners that are focused on key organizational issues
- to offer resources to PepsiCo based on their unique perspectives and experiences

- to pave the way for employees to grow in their careers
- to provide opportunities for group members to network with each other and business leaders
- to become ambassadors for PepsiCo, creating opportunities for community involvement

Each division sponsors its own networks, depending on its population of workers. For example, Frito-Lay has the Black Employees Association (BEA), Adelante (Hispanic employee network), Asians in Motion (AIM), EQUAL (gay, lesbian, bisexual, and transgender employee network), and Women's Initiative Network (WIN).

In addition to the formation of employee networks, PepsiCo has established a formal, three-level inclusion training program. At level 1, division presidents and their teams participate in a course that covers issues of cultural differences and similarities; components of culture such as values and communication styles; models for individual and organizational change; and exercises. Level 2 training aimed at all business managers throughout the United States businesses, is designed to provide managers with the skills to lead teams of diverse workers. It focuses on enhancing self-awareness, conducting difficult conversations, recognizing people's strengths, and managing conflict. Level 3 training is intended to reinforce the previous two levels of training for ongoing efforts to promote diversity and inclusion throughout the company.

PepsiCo believes that diversity can be harnessed as a powerful tool for growth, even during turbulent times. It's more than coming up with an idea for a new chip; it brings together groups of people who can work to meet the needs of consumers.

Questions

1. Would you describe PepsiCo as being ethnocentric, ethnorelativistic, or somewhere in between? Why?

2. Why is it important for upper-level managers at PepsiCo to receive diversity and inclusion training?

3. Do you think that PepsiCo's encouragement of employee networks actually works against diversity and the formation of multicultural teams? Why or why not?

SOURCE: Company Web site, http://www.pepsico.com, accessed August 16, 2004.

ch15 BIZ FLIX VIDEO CASE

For Love of the Game

Billy Chapel (Kevin Costner), a 20-year veteran pitcher with the Detroit Tigers, learns just before the season's last game that the team's new owners want to trade him. He also learns that his partner Jane Aubrey (Kelly Preston) intends to leave him. Faced with these daunting blows, Chapel wants to pitch a perfect final game. Director Sam Raimi's love of baseball shines through in some striking visual effects.

This scene is a slightly edited version of the "Just Throw" sequence, which begins the film's exciting closing scenes in which Chapel pitches his last game. In this scene, the Tigers' catcher Gus Sinski (John C. Reilly) comes out to the pitching mound to talk to Billy.

What to Watch for and Ask Yourself

1. What is Billy Chapel's level of esteem needs at this point in the game?

2. Do you expect Gus Sinski's talk to have any effect on Chapel? If it will, what will be the effect?

3. What rewards potentially exist for Billy Chapel? Remember, this is the last baseball game of his career.

ch15 ENDNOTES

1. See Michael West, "Hope Springs," *People Management* (October 2005): 38ff ; and Mark C. Bolino, William H. Turnley, and James M. Bloodgood, "Citizenship Behaviors and the Creation of Social Capital in Organizations," *Academy of Management Review* 27, no. 4 (2002): 505–522.

2. Reported in Del Jones, "Optimism Puts Rose-Colored Tint in Glasses of Top Execs," *USA Today*, December 15, 2005, http://www.usatoday.com.

3. Jerry Krueger and Emily Killham, "At Work, Feeling Good Matters," *Gallup Management Journal* (December 8, 2005).

4. Jeffrey Zaslow, "Pursuits: Happiness, Inc.," *The Wall Street Journal*, March 18, 2006.

5. John W. Newstrom and Keith Davis, *Organizational Behavior: Human Behavior at Work*, 11th ed. (Burr Ridge, IL: McGraw-Hill Irwin, 2002): chapter 9.

6. S. J. Breckler, "Empirical Validation of Affect, Behavior, and Cognition as Distinct Components of Attitude," *Journal of Personality and Social Psychology* (May 1984): 1191–1205; and J. M. Olson and M. P. Zanna, "Attitudes and Attitude Change," *Annual Review of Psychology* 44 (1993): 117–154.

7. M. T. Iaffaldano and P. M. Muchinsky, "Job Satisfaction and Job Performance: A Meta-Analysis," *Psychological Bulletin* (March 1985): 251–273; C. Ostroff, "The Relationship Between Satisfaction, Attitudes, and Performance: An Organizational Level Analysis," *Journal of Applied Psychology* (December 1992): 963–974; and M. M. Petty, G. W. McGee, and J. W. Cavender, "A Meta-Analysis of the Relationship Between Individual Job Satisfaction and Individual Performance," *Academy of Management Review* (October 1984): 712–721.

8. "Worried at Work: Generation Gap in Workplace Woes," International Survey Research, http://www.isrsurveys.com (accessed May 19, 2004).

9. Tony Schwartz, "The Greatest Sources of Satisfaction in the Workplace Are Internal and Emotional," *Fast Company* (November 2000): 398–402.

10. William C. Symonds, "Where Paternalism Equals Good Business," *BusinessWeek* (July 20, 1998), 16E4, 16E6.

11. "Engaged Employees Drive the Bottom Line," Towers Perrin-International Survey Research, http://www.isrinsight.com/pdf/solutions/EngagementBrochureFinalUS.pdf (accessed November 14, 2008).

12. "Closing the Engagement Gap: A Road Map for Driving Superior Business Performance," (Towers Perrin Global Workforce Study, 2007–2008), http://links.mkt304.com/ctt?kn=1&m=1506453&r=MTUwMTY1NjAy NDkS1&b=2&j=NjE1NjYwMzQS1&mt=2&rj=NjE1MzQwMzcS1 (accessed on November 18, 2008).

13. W. Chan Kin and Renée Mauborgne, "Fair Process: Managing in the Knowledge Economy," *Harvard Business Review* (January 2003), 127–136.

14. Survey results reported in Del Jones, "Optimism Puts Rose-Colored Tint in Glasses of Top Execs," *USA Today* (December 15, 2005).

15. For a discussion of cognitive dissonance theory, see Leon A. Festinger, *Theory of Cognitive Dissonance* (Stanford, CA: Stanford University Press, 1957).

16. J. A. Deutsch, W. G. Young, and T. J. Kalogeris, "The Stomach Signals Satiety," *Science* (April 1978): 22–33.

17. Richard B. Chase and Sriram Dasu, "Want to Perfect Your Company's Service? Use Behavioral Science," *Harvard Business Review* (June 2001): 79–84.

18. H. H. Kelley, "Attribution in Social Interaction," in E. Jones et al., eds., *Attribution: Perceiving the Causes of Behavior* (Morristown, NJ: General Learning Press, 1972).

19. See J. M. Digman, "Personality Structure: Emergence of the Five-Factor Model," *Annual Review of Psychology* 41 (1990): 417–440; M. R. Barrick and M. K. Mount, "Autonomy as a Moderator of the Relationships Between the Big Five Personality Dimensions and

Job Performance," *Journal of Applied Psychology* (February 1993): 111–118; and J. S. Wiggins and A. L. Pincus, "Personality: Structure and Assessment," *Annual Review of Psychology* 43 (1992): 473–504.

20. Del Jones, "Not All Successful CEOs Are Extroverts," *USA Today*, June 6, 2006, http://www.usatoday.com/money/companies/management/2006-06-06-shy-ceo-usat_x.htm.

21. Reported in Christopher Palmeri, "Putting Managers to the Test," *BusinessWeek* (November 20, 2006): 82.

22. Tim Sanders, *The Likeability Factor: How to Boost Your L-Factor and Achieve the Life of Your Dreams* (New York: Crown, 2005).

23. Lisa Takeuchi Cullen, "SATs for J-O-B-S," *Time* (April 3, 2006): 89.

24. Lori Gottlieb, "How Do I Love Thee?" *The Atlantic Monthly* (March 2006): 58–70; Rachel Lehmann-Haupt, "Is the Right Chemistry a Click Nearer?" *The New York Times*, February 12, 2006; Christopher Palmeri, "Dr. Warren's Lonely Hearts Club," *BusinessWeek Online* (February 20, 2006): http://www.business-week.com/magazine/content/06_08/b3972111.htm

25. Daniel Goleman, "Leadership That Gets Results," *Harvard Business Review* (March–April 2000): 79–90; Richard E. Boyatzis and Daniel Goleman, *The Emotional Competence Inventory–University Edition*, The Hay Group, 2001; and Daniel Goleman, *Emotional Intelligence: Why It Can Matter More than IQ* (New York: Bantam Books, 1995).

26. Alan Farnham, "Are You Smart Enough to Keep Your Job?" *Fortune* (January 15, 1996): 34–47.

27. Hendrie Weisinger, *Emotional Intelligence at Work* (San Francisco: Jossey–Bass, 2000); D. C. McClelland, "Identifying Competencies with Behavioral-Event Interviews," *Psychological Science* (Spring 1999): 331–339; Daniel Goleman, "Leadership That Gets Results," *Harvard Business Review* (March–April 2000): 78–90; D. Goleman, *Working with Emotional Intelligence* (New York: Bantam Books, 1999); and Lorie Parch, "Testing ... 1,2,3," *Working Woman* (October 1997): 74–78.

28. Cliff Edwards, "Death of a Pushy Salesman," *BusinessWeek* (July 3, 2006): 108–109.

29. J. B. Rotter, "Generalized Expectancies for Internal versus External Control of Reinforcement," *Psychological Monographs* 80, no. 609 (1966).

30. See P. E. Spector, "Behavior in Organizations as a Function of Employee's Locus of Control," *Psychological Bulletin* (May 1982): 482–497.

31. T. W. Adorno, E. Frenkel-Brunswick, D. J. Levinson, and R. N. Sanford, *The Authoritarian Personality* (New York: Harper & Row, 1950).

32. Niccolo Machiavelli, *The Prince*, trans. George Bull (Middlesex: Penguin, 1961).

33. Richard Christie and Florence Geis, *Studies in Machiavellianism* (New York: Academic Press, 1970).

34. R. G. Vleeming, "Machiavellianism: A Preliminary Review," *Psychological Reports* (February 1979): 295–310.

35. Christie and Geis, *Studies in Machiavellianism*.

36. Carl Jung, *Psychological Types* (London: Routledge and Kegan Paul, 1923).

37. Mary H. McCaulley, "Research on the MBTI and Leadership: Taking the Critical First Step," keynote address, The Myers–Briggs Type Indicator and Leadership: An International Research Conference, January 12–14, 1994.

38. Alison Overhold, "Are You a Polyolefin Optimizer? Take This Quiz!" *Fast Company* (April 2004): 37.

39. Reported in Cullen, "SATs for J-O-B-S."

40. Charles A. O'Reilly III, Jennifer Chatman, and David F. Caldwell, "People and Organizational Culture: A Profile Comparison Approach to Assessing Person-Organization Fit," *Academy of Management Journal* 34, no. 3 (1991): 487–516.

41. Anna Muoio, "Should I Go .Com?" *Fast Company* (July 2000): 164–172.

42. Michelle Leder, "Is That Your Final Answer?" *Working Woman* (December–January 2001): 18.

43. David A. Kolb, "Management and the Learning Process," *California Management Review* 18, no. 3 (Spring 1976): 21–31.

44. See David. A. Kolb, I. M. Rubin, and J. M. McIntyre, *Organizational Psychology: An Experimental Approach*, 3rd ed. (Englewood Cliffs, NJ: Prentice Hall, 1984): 27–54.

45. T. A. Beehr and R. S. Bhagat, *Human Stress and Cognition in Organizations: An Integrated Perspective*

(New York: Wiley, 1985); and Bruce Cryer, Rollin McCraty, and Doc Childre, "Pull the Plug on Stress," *Harvard Business Review* (July 2003): 102–107.

46. Reported in Brian Nadel, "The Price of Pressure," special advertising feature, *Fortune* (December 11, 2006): 143–146.

47. Health and Safety Authority survey, reported in Joe Humphreys, "Stress Will Be Main Cause of Workplace Illness by 2020," *Irish Times*, July 27, 2005.

48. Don Mills, "Running on High Octane or Burning Out Big Time? Stress Flunkies," *National Post*, April 8, 2006.

49. M. Friedman and R. Rosenman, *Type A Behavior and Your Heart* (New York: Knopf, 1974).

50. Reported in "Work Stress Is Costly," *Morning Call*, October 18, 2005.

51. Families and Work Institute survey, reported in "Reworking Work," *Time* (July 25, 2005): 50–55; Spherion survey, reported in Donna Callea, "Workers Feeling the Burn: Employee Burnout a New Challenge to Productivity, Morale, Experts Say," *News Journal*, March 27, 2006); Mills, Running on High Octane or Burning Out Big Time?; Vani Doraisamy, "Young Techies Swell the Ranks of the Depressed," *The Hindu*, October 11, 2005.

52. Jenna Goudreau, "Dispatches from the War on Stress," *BusinessWeek* (August 6, 2007): 74–75.

53. Claire Sykes, "Say Yes to Less Stress," *Office Solutions* (July–August 2003): 26; and Andrea Higbie, "Quick Lessons in the Fine Old Art of Unwinding," *The New York Times*, February 25, 2001.

54. Donalee Moulton, "Buckling Under the Pressure," *OH & S Canada* 19, no. 8 (December 2003): 36.

55. Rosabeth Moss Kanter, "Balancing Work and Life," Knight-Ridder Tribune News Service, April 8, 2005.

56. Leslie Gross Klass, "Quiet Time at Work Helps Employee Stress," *Johnson City Press*, January 28, 2001.

57. Moulton, "Buckling Under the Pressure."

58. Goudreau, "Dispatches from the War on Stress."

59. David T. Gordon, "Balancing Act," *CIO* (October 15, 2001): 58–62.

© GETTY IMAGES/DIGITAL VISION

Learning Outcomes

After studying this chapter, you should be able to:

1. Define leadership and explain its importance for organizations.

2. Describe how leadership is changing in today's organizations.

3. Identify personal characteristics associated with effective leaders.

4. Define task-oriented behavior and people-oriented behavior and explain how these categories are used to evaluate and adapt leadership style.

5. Describe Hersey and Blanchard's situational theory and its application to subordinate participation.

6. Discuss how leadership fits the organizational situation and how organizational characteristics can substitute for leadership behaviors.

7. Describe transformational leadership and when it should be used.

8. Explain how followership is related to effective leadership.

9. Identify sources of leader power and the tactics leaders use to influence others.

10. Explain servant leadership and moral leadership and their importance in contemporary organizations.

Leadership

1 Introduction

2 Environment

3 Planning

4 Organizing

5 Controlling

6 Leading

WHAT'S YOUR PERSONAL STYLE?

Ideas about effective leadership change over time. To understand your approach to leadership, think about your personal style toward others or toward a student group to which you belong, and then answer each item below as Mostly True or Mostly False for you.

	Mostly True	Mostly False
1. I am a modest, unassuming person.	___	___
2. When a part of a group, I am more concerned about how the group does than how I do.	___	___
3. I prefer to lead with quiet modesty rather than personal assertiveness.	___	___
4. I feel personally responsible if the team does poorly.	___	___
5. I act with quiet determination.	___	___
6. I resolve to do whatever needs doing to produce the best result for the group.	___	___
7. I am proactive to help the group succeed.	___	___
8. I facilitate high standards for my group's performance.	___	___

SCORING AND INTERPRETATION: A recent view of leadership called Level Five Leadership says that the most successful leaders have two prominent qualities: humility and will. Give yourself one point for each item marked Mostly True.

> Humility: Items 1, 2, 3, 4
> Will: Items 5, 6, 7, 8

Humility means a quiet, modest, self-effacing manner. A humble person puts group or organizational success ahead of one's personal success. "Will" means a quiet but fierce resolve to stay the course to achieve the group's desired outcome and to help the group succeed. The traits of humility and will are opposite the traditional idea of leadership as loud and self-centered. If you scored 3 or 4 on either humility or will, you are on track to level 5 leadership, which says that ordinary people often make excellent leaders.

In the previous chapter, we explored differences in attitudes and personality that affect behavior. Some of the most important attitudes for the organization's success are those of its leaders, because leader attitudes and behaviors play a critical role in shaping employee attitudes, such as their job satisfaction and organizational commitment. Yet there are as many variations among leaders as there are among other individuals, and many different styles of leadership can be effective.

Different leaders behave in different ways depending on their individual differences as well as their followers' needs and the organizational situation. Consider the differing styles of Pat McGovern, founder and chair of IDG, a technology publishing and research firm that owns magazines such as *CIO*, *PC World*, and *Computerworld*, and Tom Siebel, CEO of software company Siebel Systems. McGovern treats each employee to lunch at the Ritz on his or her tenth anniversary with IDG to tell them how important they are to the success of the company. He personally thanks almost every person in every business unit once a year, which takes about a month of his time. Managers provide him with a list of accomplishments for all their direct reports, which McGovern memorizes the night before his visit so he can congratulate people on specific accomplishments. In addition to appreciating and caring about employees, McGovern also shows that he believes in them by decentralizing decision making so that people have the autonomy to make their own decisions about how best to accomplish organizational goals. Tom Siebel, in contrast, is known as a disciplined and dispassionate manager who remains somewhat aloof from his employees and likes to maintain strict control over every aspect of the business. He enforces a dress code, sets tough goals and standards, and holds people strictly accountable. "We go to work to realize our professional ambitions, not to have a good time," Siebel says.[1] Both Siebel and McGovern have been successful as leaders, although their styles are quite different.

This chapter explores one of the most widely discussed and researched topics in management—leadership. Here we define leadership and explore how managers develop leadership qualities. We look at some important leadership approaches for contemporary organizations, as well as examine trait, behavioral, and contingency theories of leadership effectiveness, discuss charismatic and transformational leadership, explore the role of followership, and consider how leaders use power and influence to get things done. The final section of the chapter discusses servant leadership and moral leadership, two enduring approaches that have received renewed emphasis in recent years. Chapters 17 through 19 will look in detail at many of the functions of leadership, including employee motivation, communication, and encouraging teamwork.

THE NATURE OF LEADERSHIP

Perhaps no topic is more important to organizational success than leadership. In most situations, a team, military unit, or volunteer organization is only as good as its leader. Consider the situation in Iraq, as U.S. military advisors strive to build Iraqi forces that can take over security duties without support from coalition troops. Many

trainers say they encounter excellent individual soldiers and junior leaders but that many of the senior commanders are stuck in old authoritarian patterns that undermine their units. Whether an Iraqi unit succeeds or fails often comes down to one person—its commander—so advisors are putting emphasis on finding and strengthening good leaders.[2] Top leaders make a difference in business organizations as well. Baron Partners Fund picks stocks based largely on an evaluation of companies' senior executives, because it believes top leaders who are smart, honorable, and treat their employees right typically lead their companies to greater financial success and greater shareholder returns.[3] The approach has proved successful, helping Baron's diversified stock fund consistently perform well.

Among all the ideas and writings about leadership, three aspects stand out—people, influence, and goals. Leadership occurs among people, involves the use of influence, and is used to attain goals.[4] *Influence* means that the relationship among people is not passive. Moreover, influence is designed to achieve some end or goal. Thus, **leadership** as defined here is the ability to influence people toward the attainment of goals. This definition captures the idea that leaders are involved with other people in the achievement of goals. Leadership is reciprocal, occurring *among* people.[5] Leadership is a "people" activity, distinct from administrative paper shuffling or problem-solving activities.

Concept Connection CEO Matt Rubel moved Payless Shoes from bargain shopping to the frontlines of fashion. Under his **leadership,** Kansas-based Payless opened a design studio in Manhattan and partnered with young designers to offer exclusive designer shoes and handbags. He took the helm in 2005, and in 2006 Payless nearly doubled its earnings. Thanks to Rubel's makeover, Payless is luring fashion-conscious consumers who wouldn't have considered shopping there before. In 2007, *Footwear News* named Rubel its "Person of the Year."

CONTEMPORARY LEADERSHIP

leadership The ability to influence people toward the attainment of organizational goals.

The concept of leadership evolves as the needs of organizations change. That is, the environmental context in which leadership is practiced influences which approach might be most effective, as well as what kinds of leaders are most admired by society.

The technology, economic conditions, labor conditions, and social and cultural mores of the times all play a role. A significant influence on leadership styles in recent years is the turbulence and uncertainty of the environment. Ethical and economic difficulties, corporate governance concerns, globalization, changes in technology, new ways of working, shifting employee expectations, and significant social transitions have contributed to a shift in how we think about and practice leadership.

Of particular interest for leadership in contemporary times is a *postheroic approach* that focuses on the subtle, unseen, and often unrewarded acts that good leaders perform every day, rather than on the grand accomplishments of celebrated business heroes.[6] During the 1980s and 1990s, leadership became equated with larger-than-life personalities, strong egos, and personal ambitions. In contrast, the postheroic leader's major characteristic is humility.[7] **Humility** means being unpretentious and modest rather than arrogant and prideful. Humble leaders don't have to be in the center of things. They quietly build strong, enduring companies by developing and supporting others rather than touting their own abilities and accomplishments. The idea of the leader as a lone hero is deeply embedded in our culture, but the challenges of recent years have spurred leaders to take a more collaborative, integrated approach. A study by the Center for Creative Leadership found that more than 84 percent of business leaders surveyed agree that the definition of effective leadership has changed since the turn of the century, with many of them citing interdependence as a key to success.[8] Two approaches that are in tune with postheroic leadership for today's times are Level 5 leadership and interactive leadership.

TakeaMoment

What did your score on the "Personal Style" questions at the beginning of this chapter say about your humility? Go to the ethical dilemma on pages 497–498 that pertains to postheroic leadership for turbulent times.

Level 5 Leadership

A study conducted by Jim Collins and his research associates identified the critical importance of what Collins calls *Level 5 leadership* in transforming companies from merely good to truly great organizations.[9] As described in his book *Good to Great: Why Some Companies Make the Leap . . . and Others Don't*, Level 5 leadership refers to the highest level in a hierarchy of manager capabilities, as illustrated in Exhibit 16.1.

A key characteristic of Level 5 leaders is an almost complete lack of ego, coupled with a fierce resolve to do what is best for the organization. In contrast to the view of great leaders as larger-than-life personalities with strong egos and big ambitions, Level 5 leaders often seem shy and unpretentious. Although they accept full responsibility for mistakes, poor results, or failures, Level 5 leaders give credit for successes to other people. For example, Joseph F. Cullman III, former CEO of Philip Morris, staunchly refused to accept credit for the company's long-term success, citing his great colleagues, successors, and predecessors as the reason for the accomplishments. Another example is Darwin E. Smith. When he was promoted to CEO of Kimberly-Clark, Smith questioned whether the board really wanted to appoint him because he didn't believe he had the qualifications a CEO needed.

humility Being unpretentious and modest rather than arrogant and prideful.

Kimberly-Clark

Few people have ever heard of Darwin Smith, who led Kimberly-Clark from 1971 to 1991—and that's probably just the way he wanted it. Smith was somewhat shy and awkward in social situations, and he was never featured in splashy articles in *Fortune* magazine or *The Wall Street Journal*. Yet anyone who interpreted his appearance and demeanor as a sign of ineptness soon learned differently. Smith demonstrated an aggressive determination to revive Kimberly-Clark, which at the time was a stodgy old paper company that had seen years of falling stock prices. When he took over, the company's core business was in coated paper. Convinced that this approach doomed the company to mediocrity, Smith took the controversial step of selling the company's paper mills and investing all its resources in consumer products such as Kleenex and Huggies diapers.

Innovative Way

6
Leading

EXHIBIT | 16.1 Level 5 Hierarchy

Level 5: Level 5 Executive
Builds enduring greatness through a paradoxical
blend of personal humility and professional will.

Level 4: Effective Leader
Catalyzes commitment to and vigorous
pursuit of a clear and compelling vision,
stimulating higher performance standards.

Level 3: Competent Manager
Organizes people and resources toward the
effective and efficient pursuit of predetermined
objectives.

Level 2: Contributing Team Member
Contributes individual capabilities to the
achievement of group objectives and works
effectively with others in a group setting.

Level 1: Highly Capable Individual
Makes productive contributions through talent,
knowledge, skills, and good work habits.

SOURCE: Jim Collins, *Good to Great: Why Some Companies Make the Leap . . . and Others Don't* (New York: HarperCollins, 2001), 20. Copyright © 2001 by Jim Collins. Reprinted with permission from Jim Collins.

Over his 20 years as CEO, Smith turned Kimberly-Clark into the leading consumer paper products company in the world, beating rivals Scott Paper and Procter & Gamble. The company generated cumulative stock returns that were 4.1 times greater than those of the general market. When asked about his exceptional performance after his retirement, Smith said simply, "I never stopped trying to become qualified for the job."[10]

As the example of Darwin Smith illustrates, despite their personal humility, Level 5 leaders have a strong will to do whatever it takes to produce great and lasting results for their organizations. They are extremely ambitious for their companies rather than for themselves. This goal becomes highly evident in the area of succession planning. Level 5 leaders develop a solid corps of leaders throughout the organization, so that when they leave the company can continue to thrive and grow even stronger. Egocentric leaders, by contrast, often set their successors up for failure because it will be a testament to their own greatness if the company doesn't perform well without them. Rather than building an organization around "a genius with a thousand helpers," Level 5 leaders want everyone to develop to their fullest potential.

Interactive Leadership

The focus on minimizing personal ambition and developing others is also a hallmark of interactive leadership. **Interactive leadership** means that the leader favors a consensual and collaborative process, and influence derives from relationships rather than position power and formal authority.[11] For example, Nancy Hawthorne, former chief financial officer at Continental Cablevision Inc., felt that her role as a leader was to delegate tasks and authority to others and to help them be more effective. "I was being traffic cop and coach and facilitator," Hawthorne says. "I was always into building a department that hummed."[12]

Interest in interactive leadership grew partly from observations about the differences in how women and men lead. Research indicates that women's style of leadership is typically different from most men's and is particularly suited to today's organizations.[13] Using data from actual performance evaluations, one study found that when rated by peers, subordinates, and bosses, female managers score significantly

interactive leadership A leadership style characterized by values such as inclusion, collaboration, relationship building, and caring.

higher than men on abilities such as motivating others, fostering communication, and listening.[14] Another study of leaders and their followers in organizations including businesses, universities, and government agencies found that women typically score higher on social and emotional skills, which are crucial for interactive leadership.[15] However, men can be interactive leaders as well, as illustrated by the example of Pat McGovern of IDG earlier in the chapter. For McGovern, having personal contact with employees and letting them know they're appreciated is a primary responsibility of leaders. The characteristics associated with interactive leadership are emerging as valuable qualities for both male and female leaders in today's workplace. Values associated with interactive leadership include personal humility, inclusion, relationship building, and caring.

As a new manager, will your interpersonal style fit the contemporary leadership approaches described in the text? To find out, complete the New Manager Self-Test below.

TakeaMoment

New Manager Self-Test

Interpersonal Patterns

The majority of a new manager's work is accomplished through interpersonal relationships. To understand your relationship pattern, consider the following verbs. These 20 verbs describe some of the ways people feel and act from time to time. Think about your behavior in groups. How do you feel and act in groups? Check the five verbs that best describe your behavior in groups as you see it.

_____ acquiesce	_____ coordinate	_____ lead
_____ advise	_____ criticize	_____ oblige
_____ agree	_____ direct	_____ relinquish
_____ analyze	_____ disapprove	_____ resist
_____ assist	_____ evade	_____ retreat
_____ concede	_____ initiate	_____ withdraw
_____ concur	_____ judge	

SCORING AND INTERPRETATION: Two underlying patterns of interpersonal behavior are represented in the preceding list: *dominance* (authority or control) and *sociability* (intimacy or friendliness). Most individuals tend either to like to control things (high dominance) or to let others control things (low dominance). Similarly, most persons tend to be either warm and personal (high sociability) or somewhat distant and impersonal (low sociability). In the following diagram, circle the five verbs in the list that you used to describe yourself. The set of ten verbs in either horizontal row (sociability dimension) or vertical column (dominance dimension) in which three or more are circled represents your tendency in interpersonal behavior.

	High Dominance	Low Dominance
High Sociability	advises coordinates directs initiates leads	acquiesces agrees assists concurs obliges
Low Sociability	analyzes criticizes disapproves judges resists	concedes evades relinquishes retreats withdraws

Your behavior pattern suggested in the diagram is a clue to your interpersonal style as a new manager. Which of the quadrants provides the best description of you? Is that the type of leader you aspire to become? Generally speaking, the high sociability and high dominance pattern reflects the type of leader to which many new managers aspire. How does your pattern correspond to the Level 5 and interactive leadership patterns described in the text?

SOURCE: David W. Johnson and Frank P. Johnson, *Joining Together: Group Theory and Group Skills*, 8th ed. (New York: Allyn and Bacon, 2003), pp. 189–190. Used with permission.

FROM MANAGEMENT TO LEADERSHIP

Hundreds of books and articles have been written in recent years about the differences between management and leadership. Good management is essential in organizations, yet good managers have to be leaders too, because distinctive qualities are associated with management and leadership that provide different strengths for the organization. As shown in Exhibit 16.2, management and leadership reflect two different sets of qualities and skills that frequently overlap within a single individual. A person might have more of one set of qualities than the other, but ideally a manager develops a balance of both manager and leader qualities.[16]

A primary distinction between management and leadership is that management promotes stability, order, and problem solving within the existing organizational structure and systems. This ensures that suppliers are paid, customers invoiced, products and services produced on time, and so forth. Leadership, on the other hand, promotes vision, creativity, and change. Leadership means questioning the status quo so that outdated, unproductive, or socially irresponsible norms can be replaced to meet new challenges. Consider the challenge Susan Decker faces as she runs the day-to-day business as the new president of Yahoo. Decker will need excellent management skills to improve financial results, oversee operational details, make tough decisions, and work with managers to execute Yahoo's strategy. She will also need consummate leadership abilities to create and inspire people with a vision that can help Yahoo emerge from under the shadow of search leader Google to find the key to recruiting and retaining top-notch talent and to rebuild the sagging morale inside the company.[17]

Leadership cannot replace management; it should be in addition to management. Good management is needed to help the organization meet current commitments, while good leadership is needed to move the organization into the future. Leadership's power comes from being built on the foundation of a well-managed organization.

EXHIBIT | 16.2

Leader and Manager
Qualities

MANAGER QUALITIES

MIND
Rational
Consulting
Persistent
Problem solving
Tough-minded
Analytical
Structured
Deliberate
Authoritative
Stabilizing
Position power

LEADER QUALITIES

SOUL
Visionary
Passionate
Creative
Flexible
Inspiring
Innovative
Courageous
Imaginative
Experimental
Initiates change
Personal power

SOURCE: Based on Genevieve Capowski, "Anatomy of a Leader: Where Are the Leaders of Tomorrow?" *Management Review* (March 1994): 12.

LEADERSHIP TRAITS

Early efforts to understand leadership success focused on the leader's traits. **Traits** are the distinguishing personal characteristics of a leader, such as intelligence, honesty, self-confidence, and even appearance. The early research looked at leaders who had achieved a level of greatness, and hence was referred to as the *Great Man* approach. The idea was relatively simple: Find out what made these people great, and select future leaders who already exhibited the same traits or could be trained to develop them. Generally, early research found only a weak relationship between personal traits and leader success.[18]

In recent years, interest in examining leadership traits has reemerged. In addition to personality traits, physical, social, and work-related characteristics of leaders have been studied.[19] Exhibit 16.3 summarizes the physical, social, and personal leadership characteristics that have received the greatest research support. However, these characteristics do not stand alone. The appropriateness of a trait or set of traits depends on the leadership situation. The same traits do not apply to every organization or situation. Further studies expand the understanding of leadership beyond the personal traits of the individual to focus on the dynamics of the relationship between leaders and followers.

BEHAVIORAL APPROACHES

The inability to define effective leadership based solely on traits led to an interest in looking at the behavior of leaders and how it might contribute to leadership success or failure. Two basic leadership behaviors identified as important for leadership are *task-oriented behavior* and *people-oriented behavior*. These two *metacategories*, or broadly defined behavior categories, were found to be applicable to effective leadership in a variety of situations and time periods.[20] Although they are not the only important leadership behaviors, concern for tasks and concern for people must be shown at some reasonable level. Thus, many approaches to understanding leadership use these metacategories as a basis for study and comparison. Important research programs on leadership behavior were conducted at Ohio State University, University of Michigan, and University of Texas.

Concept Connection Linda St. Clair (right) has been both an artistic-director of theater productions and a personnel manager for a technology firm. Her **interactive leadership style** worked equally well in both settings. As a theater director, she articulated a clear overarching vision, supported individual artists, encouraged collaborative relationships—and then let the creative process take its course. The job of a manager isn't very different. "When I was at my best in the corporation," she recalls, "I helped people get what they needed to be effectively creative." Good leaders, St. Clair believes, know how to build relationships and act not as a commander but rather as a coach, guide, and mentor.

traits Distinguishing personal characteristics, such as intelligence, values, and appearance.

EXHIBIT | **16.3** Personal Characteristics of Leaders

Physical Characteristics	**Personality**	**Work-Related Characteristics**
Energy	Self-confidence	Achievement drive, desire to excel
Physical stamina	Honesty and integrity	Conscientiousness in pursuit of goals
	Enthusiasm	Persistence against obstacles, tenacity
	Desire to lead	
	Independence	
Intelligence and Ability	**Social Characteristics**	
Intelligence, cognitive ability	Sociability, interpersonal skills	**Social Background**
Knowledge	Cooperativeness	Education
Judgment, decisiveness	Ability to enlist cooperation	Mobility
	Tact, diplomacy	

SOURCES: Based on Bernard M. Bass, *Bass & Stogdill's Handbook of Leadership: Theory, Research, and Managerial Applications*, 3rd ed. (New York: The Free Press, 1990), pp. 80–81; and S. A. Kirkpatrick and E. A. Locke, "Leadership: Do Traits Matter?" *Academy of Management Executive* 5, no. 2 (1991): 48–60.

6 Leading

Ohio State Studies

Researchers at The Ohio State University surveyed leaders to study hundreds of dimensions of leader behavior.[21] They identified two major behaviors: consideration and initiating structure.

Consideration falls in the category of people-oriented behavior and is the extent to which the leader is mindful of subordinates, respects their ideas and feelings, and establishes mutual trust. Considerate leaders are friendly, provide open communication, develop teamwork, and are oriented toward their subordinates' welfare.

Initiating structure is the degree of task behavior, that is, the extent to which the leader is task oriented and directs subordinate work activities toward goal attainment. Leaders with this style typically give instructions, spend time planning, emphasize deadlines, and provide explicit schedules of work activities.

Consideration and initiating structure are independent of each other, which means that a leader with a high degree of consideration may be either high or low on initiating structure. A leader may have any of four styles: high initiating structure–low consideration, high initiating structure–high consideration, low initiating structure–low consideration, or low initiating structure–high consideration. The Ohio State research found that the high consideration–high initiating structure style achieved better performance and greater satisfaction than the other leader styles. The value of the high-high style is illustrated by Bob LaDouceur, the coach of an extraordinary high school football team.

The De La Salle Spartans

Innovative Way

The De La Salle Spartans football team pulled off a 151-game winning streak that lasted for a decade—despite the fact that many of the players had previously been derided as "undersized" and "untalented." Year after year, competing against bigger schools and tougher players, the De La Salle Spartans just kept on winning.

Years ago, coach Bob LaDouceur sized up his team of demoralized players and made a decision. He was going to teach these guys what it takes to win, and then make it a day-to-day process. LaDouceur directs close attention to the tasks needed to accomplish the goal of winning. He keeps his players on a year-round strength and conditioning program. Each practice is methodical, and LaDouceur tells his players to leave every practice just a little bit better than they were when it started.

However, the coach hasn't just institutionalized the process of drills, workouts, and practices. He has also institutionalized a process of building bonds and intimacy among his players. "If a team has no soul," LaDouceur says, "you're just wasting your time." Tasks are important, but for LaDouceur, people always come first. "It's not about how we're getting better physically, it's about how we're getting better as people," he says. During the off season, players go camping and rafting together and volunteer for community service. When the season starts, the team attends chapel together for readings and songs. After every practice, a dinner is held at a player's home. As tensions build during the season, players are encouraged to speak their hearts, to confess their fears and shortcomings, and to talk about their commitments and expectations of themselves for the next game.[22]

The high–high leadership style of coach Bob LaDouceur has accomplished remarkable results. Yet research indicates that the high–high style is not always necessarily the best. Studies suggest that effective leaders may be high on consideration and low on initiating structure or low on consideration and high on initiating structure, depending on the situation.[23]

Michigan Studies

Studies at the University of Michigan at about the same time took a different approach by comparing the behavior of effective and ineffective supervisors.[24] The most effective supervisors were those who focused on the subordinates' human needs to "build effective work groups with high performance goals." The Michigan researchers used the term *employee-centered leaders* for leaders who established high performance goals

consideration A type of behavior that describes the extent to which the leader is sensitive to subordinates, respects their ideas and feelings, and establishes mutual trust.

initiating structure A type of leader behavior that describes the extent to which the leader is task oriented and directs subordinate work activities toward goal attainment.

and displayed supportive behavior toward subordinates. The less-effective leaders were called *job-centered leaders*; these leaders tended to be less concerned with goal achievement and human needs in favor of meeting schedules, keeping costs low, and achieving production efficiency.

The Leadership Grid

Building on the work of the Ohio State and Michigan studies, Blake and Mouton of the University of Texas proposed a two-dimensional theory called the managerial grid, which was later restated by Blake and McCanse as the **leadership grid**.[25] The model and five of its seven major management styles are depicted in Exhibit 16.4. Each axis on the grid is a nine-point scale, with 1 meaning low concern and 9 meaning high concern.

Team management (9, 9) often is considered the most effective style and is recommended for leaders because organization members work together to accomplish tasks. *Country club management* (1, 9) occurs when primary emphasis is given to people rather than to work outputs. *Authority-compliance management* (9, 1) occurs when efficiency in operations is the dominant orientation. *Middle-of-the-road management* (5, 5) reflects a moderate amount of concern for both people and production. *Impoverished management* (1, 1) means the absence of a management philosophy; managers exert little effort toward interpersonal relationships or work accomplishment.

leadership grid A two-dimensional leadership theory that measures the leader's concern for people and for production.

> **TakeaMoment**
>
> As a new manager, realize that both task-oriented behavior and people-oriented behavior are important, although some situations call for a greater degree of one over the other. Go to the experiential exercise on pages 496–497 to measure your degree of task orientation and people orientation.

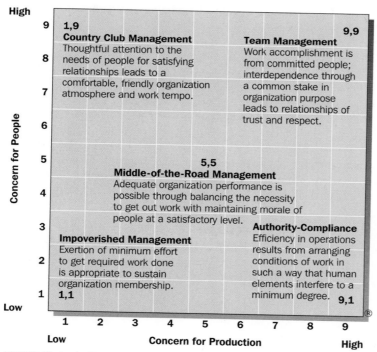

EXHIBIT 16.4

The Leadership Grid Figure

SOURCE: The Leadership Grid figure, Paternalism figure, and Opportunism figure from Robert R. Blake and Anne Adams McCanse, *Leadership Dilemmas-Grid Solutions* (formerly the Managerial Grid by Robert R. Blake and Jane S. Mouton) (Houston: Gulf Publishing Company, 1991). Grid figure, p. 29; Paternalism figure, p. 30; Opportunism figure, p. 31. Copyright © 1991 by Blake and Mouton, and Scientific Methods, Inc. Reproduced by permission of the owners.

6
Leading

CONTINGENCY APPROACHES

How can two people with widely different styles both be effective leaders? The next group of theories builds on the leader-follower relationship of behavioral approaches to explore how the organizational situation influences leader effectiveness. These theories are termed **contingency approaches** and include the situational theory of Hersey and Blanchard, the leadership model developed by Fiedler and his associates, and the substitutes-for-leadership concept.

Hersey and Blanchard's Situational Theory

The **situational theory** of leadership is an interesting extension of the behavioral theories summarized in the leadership grid (see Exhibit 16.4). Hersey and Blanchard's approach focuses a great deal of attention on the characteristics of followers in determining appropriate leadership behavior. The point of Hersey and Blanchard is that subordinates vary in readiness level. People low in task readiness—because of little ability or training or insecurity—need a different leadership style than those who are high in readiness and have good ability, skills, confidence, and willingness to work.[26] According to the situational theory, a leader can adopt one of four leadership styles, based on a combination of relationship (concern for people) and task (concern for production) behavior. The appropriate style depends on the readiness level of followers.

Exhibit 16.5 summarizes the relationship between leader style and follower readiness. The *telling style* reflects a high concern for tasks and a low concern for people

contingency approach A model of leadership that describes the relationship between leadership styles and specific organizational situations.

situational theory A contingency approach to leadership that links the leader's behavioral style with the task readiness of subordinates.

EXHIBIT | 16.5

Hersey and Blanchard's Situational Theory of Leadership

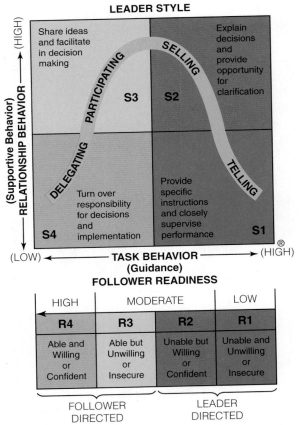

and relationships. This highly directive style involves giving explicit directions about how tasks should be accomplished. The *selling style* is based on a high concern for both people and tasks. With this approach, the leader explains decisions and gives subordinates a chance to ask questions and gain clarity and understanding about work tasks. The next leader behavior style, the *participating style,* is based on a combination of high concern for people and relationships and low concern for production tasks. The leader shares ideas with subordinates, gives them a chance to participate, and facilitates decision making. The fourth style, the *delegating style,* reflects a low concern for both relationships and tasks. This leader style provides little direction and little support because the leader turns over responsibility for decisions and their implementation to subordinates.

The bell-shaped curve in Exhibit 16.5 is called a prescriptive curve because it indicates when each leader style should be used. The readiness level of followers is indicated in the lower part of the exhibit. R1 is low readiness and R4 represents high readiness. The telling style is for low readiness followers because people are unable or unwilling—because of poor ability and skills, little experience, or insecurity—to take responsibility for their own task behavior. The leader is specific, telling people exactly what to do, how to do it, and when. The selling and participating styles work for followers at moderate readiness levels. For example, followers might lack some education and experience for the job but have high confidence, interest, and willingness to learn. As shown in the exhibit, the selling style is effective in this situation because it involves giving direction but also includes seeking input from others and clarifying tasks rather than simply instructing that they be performed. When followers have the necessary skills and experience but are somewhat insecure in their abilities or lack high willingness, the participating style enables the leader to guide followers' development and act as a resource for advice and assistance. When followers demonstrate high readiness, that is, they have high levels of education, experience, and readiness to accept responsibility for their own task behavior, the delegating style can effectively be used. Because of the high readiness level of followers, the leader can delegate responsibility for decisions and their implementation to subordinates who have the skills, abilities, and positive attitudes to follow through. The leader provides a general goal and sufficient authority to do the task as followers see fit.

To apply the Hersey and Blanchard model, the leader diagnoses the readiness level of followers and adopts the appropriate style—telling, selling, participating, or delegating. Using the incorrect style can hurt morale and performance. Consider what happened when Lawrence Summers, former president of Harvard University, tried to use a primarily telling style with followers who were at high readiness levels. Summers employed an assertive top-down style with followers who think of themselves not as employees but as partners in an academic enterprise. Faculty members at most universities have long been accustomed to decentralized, democratic decision making and having a say in matters such as department mergers or new programs of study. Summers made many decisions on his own that followers thought should be put to a faculty vote. Summers' leadership approach led to serious conflicts with some faculty members and demands for his ouster. Eventually, a vote of no confidence from faculty convinced Summers to resign with many of his goals and plans for the university unrealized.[27]

Fiedler's Contingency Theory

Whereas Hersey and Blanchard focused on the characteristics of followers, Fiedler and his associates looked at some other elements of the organizational situation to assess when one leadership style is more effective than another.[28] The starting point for Fiedler's theory is the extent to which the leader's style is task oriented or relationship (people) oriented. Fiedler considered a person's leadership style to be relatively fixed and difficult to change; therefore, the basic idea is to match the leader's style with the situation most favorable for his or her effectiveness. By diagnosing leadership style and the organizational situation, the correct fit can be arranged.

Concept Connection At Earnest Partners, an asset management firm in Atlanta, Georgia, the quality of **leader-member relationships** is high. CEO Paul Viera has gained the respect and trust of colleagues and followers because he has proven that he has the integrity, skills, and commitment to keep the company thriving. Viera can be characterized as a **task-oriented leader** because he is focused, prepared, and competitive, and he expects others to be as well. According to Fielder's contingency theory, Viera's style succeeds at Earnest because of positive leader-member relations, strong leader position power, and jobs that contain some degree of task structure.

Situation: Favorable or Unfavorable? The suitability of a person's leadership style is determined by whether the situation is favorable or unfavorable to the leader. The favorability of a leadership situation can be analyzed in terms of three elements: the quality of relationships between leader and followers, the degree of task structure, and the extent to which the leader has formal authority over followers.[29]

A situation would be considered *highly favorable* to the leader when leader-member relationships are positive, tasks are highly structured, and the leader has formal authority over followers. In this situation, followers trust, respect, and have confidence in the leader. The group's tasks are clearly defined, involve specific procedures, and have clear, explicit goals. In addition, the leader has formal authority to direct and evaluate followers, along with the power to reward or punish. A situation would be considered *highly unfavorable* to the leader when leader-member relationships are poor, tasks are highly unstructured, and the leader has little formal authority. In a highly unfavorable situation, followers have little respect for or confidence and trust in the leader. Tasks are vague and ill-defined and lacking in clear-cut procedures and guidelines. The leader has little formal authority to direct subordinates and does not have the power to issue rewards or punishments.

Matching Leader Style to the Situation

Combining the three situational characteristics yields a variety of leadership situations, ranging from highly favorable to highly unfavorable. When Fiedler examined the relationships among leadership style and situational favorability, he found the pattern shown in Exhibit 16.6. Task-oriented leaders are more effective when the situation is either highly favorable or highly unfavorable. Relationship-oriented leaders are more effective in situations of moderate favorability.

The task-oriented leader excels in the favorable situation because everyone gets along, the task is clear, and the leader has power; all that is needed is for someone to lead the charge and provide direction. Similarly, if the situation is highly unfavorable to the leader, a great deal of structure and task direction is needed. A strong leader will define task structure and establish authority over subordinates.

EXHIBIT | 16.6   How Leader Style Fits the Situation

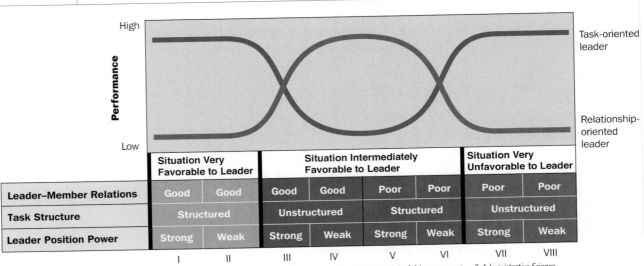

	Situation Very Favorable to Leader		Situation Intermediately Favorable to Leader				Situation Very Unfavorable to Leader	
Leader–Member Relations	Good	Good	Good	Good	Poor	Poor	Poor	Poor
Task Structure	Structured		Unstructured		Structured		Unstructured	
Leader Position Power	Strong	Weak	Strong	Weak	Strong	Weak	Strong	Weak
	I	II	III	IV	V	VI	VII	VIII

SOURCE: Based on Fred E. Fiedler, "The Effects of Leadership Training and Experience: A Contingency Model Interpretation," *Administrative Science Quarterly* 17 (1972): 455.

Because leader-member relations are poor anyway, a strong task orientation will make no difference in the leader's popularity. For example, researchers at the University of Chicago looked at CEOs of companies in turnaround situations—where companies typically have high debt loads and a need to improve results in a hurry—and found that tough-minded, task-focused characteristics such as analytical skills, a focus on efficiency, and setting high standards were more valuable leader qualities that were relationships skills such as good communication, listening, and teamwork.[30]

The relationship-oriented leader performs better in situations of intermediate favorability because human relations skills are important in achieving high group performance. In these situations, the leader may be moderately well liked, have some power, and supervise jobs that contain some ambiguity. A leader with good interpersonal skills can create a positive group atmosphere that will improve relationships, clarify task structure, and establish position power.

A leader, then, needs to know two things to use Fiedler's contingency theory. First, the leader should know whether he or she has a relationship- or task-oriented style. Second, the leader should diagnose the situation and determine whether leader-member relations, task structure, and position power are favorable or unfavorable.

Fiedler believed fitting leader style to the situation can yield big dividends in profits and efficiency.[31] On the other hand, the model has also been criticized.[32] For one thing, some researchers have challenged the idea that leaders cannot adjust their styles as situational characteristics change. Despite criticisms, Fiedler's model has continued to influence leadership studies. Fiedler's research called attention to the importance of finding the correct fit between leadership style and the situation.

TakeaMoment

As a new manager, remember that different situations and different followers may require different approaches to leadership. Pay attention to the situation and the followers to determine how much structure and direction you need to provide.

Substitutes for Leadership

The contingency leadership approaches considered so far focus on the leaders' style, the subordinates' nature, and the situation's characteristics. The final contingency approach suggests that situational variables can be so powerful that they actually substitute for or neutralize the need for leadership.[33] This approach outlines those organizational settings in which a leadership style is unimportant or unnecessary.

Exhibit 16.7 shows the situational variables that tend to substitute for or neutralize leadership characteristics. A **substitute** for leadership makes the leadership style unnecessary or redundant. For example, highly professional subordinates who know how to do their tasks do not need a leader who initiates structure for them and tells them what to do. A **neutralizer** counteracts the leadership style and prevents the

substitute A situational variable that makes a leadership style unnecessary or redundant.

neutralizer A situational variable that counteracts a leadership style and prevents the leader from displaying certain behaviors.

EXHIBIT | 16.7

Substitutes and Neutralizers for Leadership

Variable		Task-Oriented Leadership	People-Oriented Leadership
Organizational variables	Group cohesiveness	Substitutes for	Substitutes for
	Formalization	Substitutes for	No effect on
	Inflexibility	Neutralizes	No effect on
	Low position power	Neutralizes	Neutralizes
	Physical separation	Neutralizes	Neutralizes
Task characteristics	Highly structured task	Substitutes for	No effect on
	Automatic feedback	Substitutes for	No effect on
	Intrinsic satisfaction	No effect on	Substitutes for
Group characteristics	Professionalism	Substitutes for	Substitutes for
	Training/experience	Substitutes for	No effect on

leader from displaying certain behaviors. For example, if a leader has absolutely no position power or is physically removed from subordinates, the leader's ability to give directions to subordinates is greatly reduced.

Situational variables in Exhibit 16.7 include characteristics of the group, the task, and the organization itself. When followers are highly professional and experienced, both leadership styles are less important. People do not need much direction or consideration. With respect to task characteristics, highly structured tasks substitute for a task-oriented style, and a satisfying task substitutes for a people-oriented style. With respect to the organization itself, group cohesiveness substitutes for both leader styles. Formalized rules and procedures substitute for leader task orientation. Physical separation of leader and subordinate neutralizes both leadership styles.

The value of the situations described in Exhibit 16.7 is that they help leaders avoid leadership overkill. Leaders should adopt a style with which to complement the organizational situation. Consider the work situation for bank tellers. A bank teller performs highly structured tasks, follows clear written rules and procedures, and has little flexibility in terms of how to do the work. The head teller should not adopt a task-oriented style, because the organization already provides structure and direction. The head teller should concentrate on a people-oriented style to provide a more pleasant work environment. In other organizations, if group cohesiveness or intrinsic satisfaction meets employees' social needs, the leader is free to concentrate on task-oriented behaviors. The leader can adopt a style complementary to the organizational situation to ensure that both task needs and people needs of the work group will be met.

charismatic leader A leader who has the ability to motivate subordinates to transcend their expected performance.

TakeaMoment | As a new manager, avoid leadership overkill. Don't use a task-oriented style if the job already provides clear structure and direction. Concentrate instead on people and relationships. Remember that professional employees typically need less leadership.

Concept Connection Leon Gorman stepped up to save the family business when his grandfather L.L. Bean died in 1967. Demonstrating **visionary leadership**, Gorman preserved the identity of the Maine-based outdoorsman clothing and supplies business while turning it into a successful multichannel billion-dollar enterprise. He improved employee morale and customer service by introducing stakeholder values that link success to customers, employees, stockholders, communities, and the environment. Employees are encouraged to provide feedback on products after testing them on tax-deductible field trips. The U.S. Department of Labor recognized L.L. Bean in its *Trendsetter Report* for avoiding overseas manufacturers that use "sweatshop" labor.

CHARISMATIC AND TRANSFORMATIONAL LEADERSHIP

Research has also looked at how leadership can inspire and motivate people beyond their normal levels of performance. Some leadership approaches are more effective than others for bringing about high levels of commitment and enthusiasm. Two types with a substantial impact are charismatic and transformational.

Charismatic and Visionary Leadership

Charisma has been referred to as "a fire that ignites followers' energy and commitment, producing results above and beyond the call of duty."[34] The **charismatic leader** has the ability to inspire and motivate people to do more than they would normally do, despite obstacles and personal sacrifice. Followers are willing to put aside their own interests for the sake of the team, department, or organization. The impact of charismatic leaders is normally from: (1) stating a lofty vision of an imagined future that employees identify with; (2) displaying an ability to understand and empathize with followers; and (3) empowering and trusting subordinates to accomplish results.[35] Charismatic leaders tend to be less predictable because they create an atmosphere of change, and they may be obsessed by visionary ideas that excite, stimulate, and drive other people to work hard.

Charismatic leaders include Mother Theresa, Sam Walton, Alexander the Great, Steve Jobs, David Koresh, Oprah Winfrey, Martin Luther King Jr., and Osama bin Laden. Charisma can be used for positive outcomes that benefit the group, but it can also be used for self-serving purposes that lead to deception, manipulation, and exploitation of others. When charismatic leaders respond to organizational problems in terms of the needs of the entire group rather than their own emotional needs, they can have a powerful, positive influence on organizational performance.[36]

Charismatic leaders are skilled in the art of *visionary leadership*. A **vision** is an attractive, ideal future that is credible yet not readily attainable. Vision is an important component of both charismatic and transformational leadership. Visionary leaders speak to the hearts of employees, letting them be part of something bigger than themselves. Where others see obstacles or failures, they see possibility and hope.

Charismatic leaders typically have a strong vision for the future, almost an obsession, and they can motivate others to help realize it.[37] These leaders have an emotional impact on subordinates because they strongly believe in the vision and can communicate it to others in a way that makes the vision real, personal, and meaningful. This chapter's Manager's Shoptalk provides a short quiz to help you determine whether you have the potential to be a charismatic leader.

vision An attractive, ideal future that is credible yet not readily attainable.

Manager's Shoptalk

Are You a Charismatic Leader?

If you were the head of a major department in a corporation, how important would each of the following activities be to you? Answer yes or no to indicate whether you would strive to perform each activity.

1. Help subordinates clarify goals and how to reach them.
2. Give people a sense of mission and overall purpose.
3. Help get jobs out on time.
4. Look for the new product or service opportunities.
5. Use policies and procedures as guides for problem solving.
6. Promote unconventional beliefs and values.
7. Give monetary rewards in exchange for high performance from subordinates.
8. Command respect from everyone in the department.
9. Work alone to accomplish important tasks.
10. Suggest new and unique ways of doing things.
11. Give credit to people who do their jobs well.
12. Inspire loyalty to yourself and to the organization.
13. Establish procedures to help the department operate smoothly.
14. Use ideas to motivate others.
15. Set reasonable limits on new approaches.
16. Demonstrate social nonconformity.

The even-numbered items represent behaviors and activities of charismatic leaders. Charismatic leaders are personally involved in shaping ideas, goals, and direction of change. They use an intuitive approach to develop fresh ideas for old problems and seek new directions for the department or organization. The odd-numbered items are considered more traditional management activities, or what would be called *transactional leadership*. Managers respond to organizational problems in an impersonal way, make rational decisions, and coordinate and facilitate the work of others. If you answered yes to more even-numbered than odd-numbered items, you may be a potential charismatic leader.

SOURCES: Based on "Have You Got It?" a quiz that appeared in Patricia Sellers, "What Exactly Is Charisma?" *Fortune* (January 15, 1996): 68–75; Bernard M. Bass, *Leadership and Performance Beyond Expectations* (New York: Free Press, 1985); and Lawton R. Burns and Selwyn W. Becker, "Leadership and Managership," in S. Shortell and A. Kaluzny, eds., *Health Care Management* (New York: Wiley, 1986).

6
Leading

Transformational Versus Transactional Leadership

Transformational leaders are similar to charismatic leaders, but they are distinguished by their special ability to bring about innovation and change by recognizing followers' needs and concerns, helping them look at old problems in new ways, and encouraging them to question the status quo. Transformational leaders inspire followers not just to believe in the leader personally, but to believe in their own potential to imagine and create a better future for the organization. Transformational leaders create significant change in both followers and the organization.[38]

Transformational leadership can be better understood in comparison to *transactional leadership*.[39] **Transactional leaders** clarify the role and task requirements of subordinates, initiate structure, provide appropriate rewards, and try to be considerate to and meet the social needs of subordinates. The transactional leader's ability to satisfy subordinates may improve productivity. Transactional leaders excel at management functions. They are hardworking, tolerant, and fair minded. They take pride in keeping things running smoothly and efficiently. Transactional leaders often stress the impersonal aspects of performance, such as plans, schedules, and budgets. They have a sense of commitment to the organization and conform to organizational norms and values. Transactional leadership is important to all organizations, but leading change requires a different approach.

Transformational leaders have the ability to lead changes in the organization's mission, strategy, structure, and culture, as well as to promote innovation in products and technologies. Transformational leaders do not rely solely on tangible rules and incentives to control specific transactions with followers. They focus on intangible qualities such as vision, shared values, and ideas to build relationships, give larger meaning to diverse activities, and find common ground to enlist followers in the change process.[40]

A recent study confirmed that transformational leadership has a positive impact on follower development and follower performance. Moreover, transformational leadership skills can be learned and are not ingrained personality characteristics.[41] However, some personality traits may make it easier for a leader to display transformational leadership behaviors. For example, studies of transformational leadership have found that the trait of agreeableness, as discussed in the previous chapter, is positively associated with transformational leaders.[42] In addition, transformational leaders are typically emotionally stable and positively engaged with the world around them, and they have a strong ability to recognize and understand others' emotions.[43] These characteristics are not surprising considering that these leaders accomplish change by building networks of positive relationships.

FOLLOWERSHIP

transformational leader A leader distinguished by a special ability to bring about innovation and change.

transactional leader A leader who clarifies subordinates' role and task requirements, initiates structure, provides rewards, and displays consideration for subordinates.

critical thinking Thinking independently and being mindful of the effect of one's behavior on achieving goals.

uncritical thinking Failing to consider the possibilities beyond what one is told; accepting others' ideas without thinking.

No discussion of leadership is complete without a consideration of followership. Leadership matters, but without effective followers no organization can survive. Leaders can develop an understanding of their followers and how to help them be most effective.[44] Many of the qualities that define a good leader are the same qualities as those possessed by a good follower. Understanding differences in followers can improve one's effectiveness as both a follower and a leader. One model of followership is illustrated in Exhibit 16.8. Robert E. Kelley conducted extensive interviews with managers and their subordinates and came up with five *follower styles*, which are categorized according to two dimensions, as shown in the exhibit.[45]

The first dimension is the quality of independent, **critical thinking** versus dependent, **uncritical thinking**. Independent critical thinkers are mindful of the effects of their own and others' behavior on achieving organizational goals. They can weigh the impact of their boss's and their own decisions and offer constructive criticism, creativity, and innovation. Conversely, a dependent, uncritical thinker does not consider possibilities beyond what he or she is told, does not contribute to the cultivation of the organization, and accepts the supervisor's ideas without thinking.

Independent, critical thinking

Alienated | Effective

Pragmatic Survivor

Passive | Conformist

Dependent, uncritical thinking

Passive / Active

SOURCE: From THE POWER OF FOLLOWERSHIP by Robert E. Kelley, p. 97, copyright © 1992 by Consultants to Executives and Organizations, Ltd. Used by permission of Doubleday, a division of Random House, Inc.

EXHIBIT | 16.8

Styles of Followership

The second dimension of follower style is active versus passive behavior. An active follower participates fully in the organization, engages in behavior that is beyond the limits of the job, demonstrates a sense of ownership, and initiates problem solving and decision making. A passive follower, by contrast, is characterized by a need for constant supervision and prodding by superiors. Passivity is often regarded as laziness; a passive person does nothing that is not required and avoids added responsibility.

The extent to which an individual is active or passive and is a critical, independent thinker or a dependent, uncritical thinker determines whether the person will be an alienated follower, a passive follower, a conformist, a pragmatic survivor, or an effective follower, as illustrated in Exhibit 16.8:

1. The **alienated follower** is a passive, yet independent, critical thinker. Alienated employees are often effective followers who have experienced setbacks and obstacles, perhaps promises broken by their superiors. Thus, they are capable, but they focus exclusively on the shortcomings of their boss. Often cynical, alienated followers are able to think independently, but they do not participate in developing solutions to the problems or deficiencies they see. These people waste valuable time complaining about their boss without offering constructive feedback.

2. The **conformist** participates actively in a relationship with the boss but doesn't use critical thinking skills. In other words, a conformist typically carries out any and all orders regardless of the nature of the request. The conformist participates willingly, but without considering the consequences of what he or she is being asked to do—even at the risk of contributing to a harmful endeavor. A conformist is concerned only with avoiding conflict. This follower style might reflect an individual's overdependent attitude toward authority, yet it can also result from rigid rules and authoritarian environments that create a culture of conformity.

3. The **pragmatic survivor** has qualities of all four extremes—depending on which style fits with the prevalent situation. This type of person uses whatever style best benefits his or her own position and minimizes risk. Pragmatic survivors often emerge when an organization is going through desperate times, and managers find themselves doing whatever is needed to get themselves through the difficulty. Within any given company, some 25 to 35 percent of people tend to be pragmatic survivors, avoiding risks and fostering the status quo.[46]

alienated follower A person who is an independent, critical thinker but is passive in the organization.

conformist A follower who participates actively in the organization but does not use critical thinking skills.

pragmatic survivor A follower who has qualities of all four follower styles, depending on which fits the prevalent situation.

4. The **passive follower** exhibits neither critical, independent thinking nor active participation. Being passive and uncritical, these people show neither initiative nor a sense of responsibility. Their activity is limited to what they are told to do, and they accomplish things only with a great deal of supervision. Passive followers leave the thinking to the boss. Often, this style is the result of a micromanaging boss who encourages passive behavior. People learn that to show initiative, accept responsibility, or think creatively is not rewarded, and may even be punished by the boss, so they grow increasingly passive.

5. The **effective follower** is both a critical, independent thinker and active in the organization. Effective followers behave the same toward everyone, regardless of their position in the organization. They develop an equitable relationship with their leaders and do not try to avoid risk or conflict. These people are capable of self-management, they discern strengths and weaknesses in themselves and their bosses, they are committed to something bigger than themselves, and they work toward competency, solutions, and positive impact. Effective followers recognize that they have power in their relationships with superiors; thus, they have the courage to manage upward, to initiate change, and to put themselves at risk or in conflict with the boss if they believe it serves the best interest of the team or organization.

POWER AND INFLUENCE

Both followers and leaders use power and influence to get things done in organizations.

Power is the potential ability to influence the behavior of others.[47] Sometimes the terms *power* and *influence* are used synonymously, but there are distinctions between the two. Basically, **influence** is the effect a person's actions have on the attitudes, values, beliefs, or behavior of others. Whereas power is the capacity to cause a change in a person, influence may be thought of as the degree of actual change.

Power results from an interaction of leader and followers. Some power comes from an individual's position in the organization. Power may also come from personal sources, such as an individual's personal interests, goals, and values, as well as from sources such as access to information or important relationships. Followers as well as leaders can tap into a variety of power sources.

Position Power

The traditional manager's power comes from the organization. The manager's position gives him or her the power to reward or punish subordinates to influence their behavior. Legitimate power, reward power, and coercive power are all forms of position power used by managers to change employee behavior.

Legitimate Power Power coming from a formal management position in an organization and the authority granted to it is called **legitimate power**. Once a person has been selected as a supervisor, most employees understand that they are obligated to follow his or her direction with respect to work activities. Subordinates accept this source of power as legitimate, which is why they comply.

Reward Power Another kind of power, **reward power**, stems from the authority to bestow rewards on other people. Managers may have access to formal rewards, such as pay increases or promotions. They also have at their disposal such rewards as praise, attention, and recognition. Managers can use rewards to influence subordinates' behavior.

passive follower A person who exhibits neither critical independent thinking nor active participation.

effective follower A critical, independent thinker who actively participates in the organization.

power The potential ability to influence others' behavior.

influence The effect a person's actions have on the attitudes, values, beliefs, or behavior of others.

legitimate power Power that stems from a formal management position in an organization and the authority granted to it.

reward power Power that results from the authority to bestow rewards on other people.

Coercive Power The opposite of reward power is **coercive power**. It refers to the authority to punish or recommend punishment. Managers have coercive power when they have the right to fire or demote employees, criticize, or withdraw pay increases. If an employee does not perform as expected, the manager has the coercive power to reprimand him, put a negative letter in his file, deny him a raise, and hurt his chances for a promotion.

Personal Power

In contrast to the external sources of position power, personal power most often comes from internal sources, such as an individual's special knowledge or personal characteristics. Personal power is the primary tool of the leader, and it is becoming increasingly important as more businesses are run by teams of workers who are less tolerant of authoritarian management.[48] Two types of personal power are expert power and referent power.

Expert Power Power resulting from a person's special knowledge or skill regarding the tasks being performed is referred to as **expert power**. When someone is a true expert, others go along with recommendations because of his or her superior knowledge. Followers as well as leaders can possess expert power. For example, some managers lead teams in which members have expertise that the leader lacks. Some leaders at top management levels may lack expert power because subordinates know more about technical details than they do.

© TIM DILLON/USA TODAY

Concept Connection UPS employees joke that when Mike Eskew became CEO, he'd only worked for the company for 30 years. This bit of office humor reflects UPS's long-standing promote-from-within approach to management development. UPS managers gain **expert power** by working their way up from the bottom. For example, when Eskew arrived as a young industrial engineer, his first assignment was to redraw a parking lot so it could accommodate more trucks. Today, he's using his thorough understanding of the business to help move the $43 billion company from package delivery into global supply chain management. Eskew retired in 2008, having completed the five-year tenure that's become customary for UPS CEOs.

Referent Power **Referent power** comes from an individual's personal characteristics that command others' identification, respect, and admiration so they wish to emulate that individual. Referent power does not depend on a formal title or position. When employees admire a supervisor because of the way she deals with them, the influence is based on referent power. Referent power is most visible in the area of charismatic leadership. In social and religious movements, we often see charismatic leaders who emerge and gain a tremendous following based solely on their personal power.

Other Sources of Power

There are additional sources of power that are not linked to a particular person or position but rather to the role an individual plays in the overall functioning of the organization. These important sources include personal effort, relationships with others, and information.

Personal Effort People who show initiative, work beyond what is expected of them, take on undesirable but important projects, and show interest in learning about the organization and industry often gain power as a result. Managers come to depend on particular subordinates, for instance, whom they know they can count on to take on a disagreeable job or put forth extra effort when it's necessary. However, these people aren't pushovers. Related to personal effort is the individual's willingness to be assertive in asking for what she wants and needs from superiors.

coercive power Power that stems from the authority to punish or recommend punishment.

expert power Power that stems from special knowledge of or skill in the tasks performed by subordinates.

referent power Power that results from characteristics that command subordinates' identification with, respect and admiration for, and desire to emulate the leader.

6 Leading

Network of Relationships People who are enmeshed in a network of relationships have greater power. A leader or employee with many relationships knows what's going on in the organization and industry, whereas one who has few interpersonal connections is often in the dark about important activities or changes. Developing positive associations with superiors or other powerful people is a good way to gain power, but people with the greatest power are those who cultivate relationships with individuals at all levels, both inside and outside the organization.

Information Information is a primary business resource, and people who have access to information and control over how and to whom it is distributed are typically powerful. To some extent, access to information is determined by a person's position in the organization. Top managers typically have access to more information than middle managers, who in turn have access to more information than lower-level supervisors or front-line employees.

TakeaMoment | As a new manager, you may not have a lot of position power. Build your power by strengthening your knowledge and skills, putting forth personal effort, and developing positive relationships. Interpersonal influence tactics will serve you well throughout your career, even as your position power increases.

Interpersonal Influence Tactics

The next question is how leaders use their power to implement decisions and facilitate change. Leaders often use a combination of influence strategies, and people who are perceived as having greater power and influence typically are those who use a wider variety of tactics. One survey of a few hundred leaders identified more than 4,000 different techniques these people used to influence others.[49]

However, these tactics fall into basic categories that rely on understanding the principles that cause people to change their behavior and attitudes. Exhibit 16.9 lists seven principles for asserting influence. Notice that most of these involve the use of personal power rather than relying solely on position power or the use of rewards and punishments.[50]

1. *Use rational persuasion.* The most frequently used influence strategy is to use facts, data, and logical argument to persuade others that a proposed idea, request, or decision is appropriate. Using rational persuasion can often be highly effective, because most people have faith in facts and analysis.[51] Rational persuasion is most successful when a leader has technical knowledge and expertise related to the issue at hand (expert power), although referent power is also used. That is, in addition to facts and figures, people also have to believe in the leader's credibility.

2. *Make people like you.* Recall our discussion of *likability* from the previous chapter. People would rather say yes to someone they like than to someone they don't. Effective leaders strive to create goodwill and favorable impressions.

EXHIBIT | 16.9

Seven Interpersonal Influence Tactics for Leaders

1. Use rational persuasion.
2. Make people like you.
3. Rely on the rule of reciprocity.
4. Develop allies.
5. Be assertive—ask for what you want.
6. Make use of higher authority.
7. Reward the behaviors you want.

When a leader shows consideration and respect, treats people fairly, and demonstrates trust in others, people are more likely to want to help and support the leader by doing what he or she asks. In addition, most people like a leader who makes them feel good about themselves, so leaders should never underestimate the power of praise.

3. *Rely on the rule of reciprocity.* Leaders can influence others through the exchange of benefits and favors. Leaders share what they have—whether it is time, resources, services, or emotional support. The feeling among people is nearly universal that others should be paid back for what they do, in one form or another. This unwritten "rule of reciprocity" means that leaders who do favors for others can expect that others will do favors for them in return.[52]

4. *Develop allies.* Effective leaders develop networks of allies, people who can help the leader accomplish his or her goals. Leaders talk with followers and others outside of formal meetings to understand their needs and concerns as well as to explain problems and describe the leader's point of view. They strive to reach a meeting of minds with others about the best approach to a problem or decision.[53]

5. *Ask for what you want.* Another way to influence others is to make a direct and personal request. Leaders have to be explicit about what they want, or they aren't likely to get it. An explicit proposal is sometimes accepted simply because others have no better alternative. Also, a clear proposal or alternative will often receive support if other options are less well-defined.

6. *Make use of higher authority.* Sometimes to get things done leaders have to use their formal authority, as well as gain the support of people at higher levels to back them up. However, research has found that the key to successful use of formal authority is to be knowledgeable, credible, and trustworthy—that is, to demonstrate expert and referent power as well as legitimate power. Managers who become known for their expertise, who are honest and straightforward with others, and who inspire trust can exert greater influence than those who simply issue orders.[54]

7. *Reward the behaviors you want.* Leaders can also use organizational rewards and punishments to influence others' behavior. The use of punishment in organizations is controversial, but negative consequences almost always occur for inappropriate or undesirable behavior. Leaders should not rely solely on reward and punishment as a means for influencing others, but combined with other tactics that involve the use of personal power, rewards can be highly effective.

Research indicates that people rate leaders as "more effective" when they are perceived to use a variety of influence tactics. But not all managers use influence in the same way. Studies have found that leaders in human resources, for example, tend to use softer, more subtle approaches such as building goodwill, using favors, and developing allies, whereas those in finance are inclined to use harder, more direct tactics such as formal authority and assertiveness.[55]

LEADERSHIP AS SERVICE

To close this chapter, let's look at two timeless leadership approaches that are gaining renewed attention in today's environment of ethical scandals and weakened employee trust. Characteristics of servant leadership and moral leadership can be successfully used by leaders in all situations to make a positive difference.

Servant Leadership

Some leaders operate from the assumption that work exists for the development of the worker as much as the worker exists to do the work.[56] The concept of servant leadership, first described by Robert Greenleaf in 1970, has gained renewed interest in recent years as companies recover from ethical scandals and compete to attract and retain the best human talent.[57]

Servant leaders transcend self-interest to serve others and the organization.[58] They operate on two levels: for the fulfillment of their subordinates' goals and needs and for the realization of the larger purpose or mission of their organization. Servant leaders give things away—power, ideas, information, recognition, credit for accomplishments, even money. Harry Stine, founder of Stine Seed Company in Adel, Iowa, casually announced to his employees at the company's annual postharvest luncheon that they would each receive $1,000 for each year they had worked at the company. For some loyal workers, that amounted to a $20,000 bonus.[59] Servant leaders truly value other people. They are trustworthy and they trust others. They encourage participation, share power, enhance others' self-worth, and unleash people's creativity, full commitment, and natural impulse to learn and contribute. Servant leaders can bring their followers' higher motives to the work and connect their hearts to the organizational mission and goals.

Servant leaders often work in the nonprofit world because it offers a natural way to apply their leadership drive and skills to serve others. But servant leaders also succeed in business. Ari Weinzweig and Paul Saginaw, co-founders of Zingerman's Community of Businesses, built a $30 million food, restaurant, and training company using servant leadership principles. The leaders are continually asking employees, *What can I do for you?* "People give me assignments all the time," Weinzweig says. "Sometimes I'm the note-taker. . . . Sometimes I'm on my hands and knees wiping up what people spilled. We have to learn to be good followers."[60]

servant leader A leader who works to fulfill subordinates' needs and goals as well as to achieve the organization's larger mission.

moral leadership Distinguishing right from wrong and choosing to do right in the practice of leadership.

Moral Leadership

Because leadership can be used for good or evil, to help or to harm others, all leadership has a moral component. Leaders carry a tremendous responsibility to use their power wisely and ethically. Sadly, in recent years, too many have chosen to act from self-interest and greed rather than behaving in ways that serve and uplift others. The disheartening ethical climate in American business has led to a renewed interest in moral leadership. **Moral leadership** is about distinguishing right from wrong and choosing to do right. It means seeking the just, the honest, the good, and the decent behavior in the practice of leadership.[61] Moral leaders remember that business is about values, not just economic performance.

Distinguishing the right thing to do is not always easy, and doing it is sometimes even harder. Leaders are often faced with right-versus-right decisions, in which several responsibilities conflict with one another.[62] Commitments to superiors, for example, may mean a leader feels the need to hide unpleasant news about pending layoffs from followers. Moral leaders strive to find the moral answer or compromise, rather than taking the easy way out. Consider Katherine Graham, the long-time leader of *The Washington Post*, when she was confronted with a decision in 1971 about what to do with the Pentagon Papers, a leaked Defense Department study that showed Nixon administration deceptions about the Vietnam War. Graham admitted she was terrified—she knew she was risking the whole company on the decision, possibly inviting prosecution under the Espionage Act, and jeopardizing thousands of employees' jobs. She decided to go ahead with the story, and reporters Bob Woodward and Carl Bernstein made Watergate—and *The Washington Post*—a household name.[63]

© HERMAN MILLER

Concept Connection Fifty years ago, D. J. De Pree created environmental sustainability programs at Herman Miller, which designs and manufactures office furnishings. De Pree displayed **moral leadership** by acting on his belief that businesses should be careful stewards of natural resources. His innovative directives—such as that all employees should be able to look out a window from no more than 75 feet and that 50 percent of company-developed land should be green space—are still followed. Today, the company benefits from lower energy expenses by harvesting natural daylight. The Design Yard, located in Holland, Michigan, received Gold LEED (Leadership in Energy and Environmental Design) recognition.

Clearly, moral leadership requires **courage**, the ability to step forward through fear and act on one's values and conscience. As we discussed in Chapter 5, leaders often behave unethically simply because they lack courage. Most people want to be liked, and it is easy to do the wrong thing in order to fit in or impress others. One example might be a leader who holds his tongue in order to "fit in with the guys" when colleagues are telling sexually or racially offensive jokes. Moral leaders summon the fortitude to do the right thing even if it is unpopular. Standing up for what is right is the primary way in which leaders create an environment of honesty, trust, and integrity in the organization.

courage The ability to step forward through fear and act on one's values and conscience.

ch16 A MANAGER'S ESSENTIALS: WHAT HAVE WE LEARNED?

- This chapter covered several important ideas about leadership. The concept of leadership continues to evolve and change with the changing times. Of particular interest in today's turbulent environment is a postheroic leadership approach. Two significant concepts in line with the postheroic approach are Level 5 leadership and interactive leadership, which is common among women leaders. Level 5 leaders are characterized by personal humility combined with a strong determination to build a great organization that will thrive beyond the leader's direct influence. Interactive leadership emphasizes relationships and helping others develop to their highest potential and may be particularly well-suited to today's workplace.

- The early research on leadership focused on personal traits such as intelligence, energy, and appearance. Later, research attention shifted to leadership behaviors that are appropriate to the organizational situation. Behavioral approaches dominated the early work in this area; task-oriented behavior and people-oriented behavior were suggested as essential behaviors that lead work groups toward high performance. The Ohio State and Michigan approaches and the managerial grid are in this category. Contingency approaches include Hersey and Blanchard's situational theory, Fiedler's theory, and the substitutes-for-leadership concept.

- Leadership concepts have evolved from the transactional approach to charismatic and transformational leadership behaviors. Charismatic leadership is the ability to articulate a vision and motivate followers to make it a reality. Transformational leadership extends charismatic qualities to guide and foster dramatic organizational change.

- Being a good follower is an important component of being a good leader, as effective leaders and effective followers share similar characteristics. An effective follower is both independent and active in the organization. Being an effective follower depends on not becoming alienated, conforming, or passive.

- Leadership involves the use of power to influence others. Sources of power are both position-based (legitimate, reward, and coercive) and person-based (expert and referent). Other important sources of power in organizations are personal effort, a network of relationships, and access to information. Leaders rely more on personal power than position power, and they use a variety of interpersonal influence tactics to implement decisions and accomplish goals.

- Two enduring approaches that reflect the idea of leadership as service are servant leadership and moral leadership. Servant leaders facilitate the growth, goals, and development of others to liberate their best qualities in pursuing the organization's mission. Moral leadership means seeking to do the honest and decent thing in the practice of leadership. Leaders can make a positive difference by applying characteristics of servant and moral leadership.

6 Leading

ch16 DISCUSSION QUESTIONS

1. Do you think leadership style is fixed and unchangeable for a leader or flexible and adaptable? Discuss.

2. Suggest some personal traits that you believe would be useful to a business leader today. Are these traits more valuable in some situations than in others?

3. What is the difference between trait theories and behavioral theories of leadership?

4. Suggest the sources of power that would be available to a leader of a student government organization. What sources of power may not be available? To be effective, should student leaders keep power to themselves or delegate power to other students?

5. What skills and abilities does a manager need to lead effectively in a virtual environment? Do you believe a leader with a consideration style or an initiating-structure style would be more successful as a virtual leader? Explain your answer.

6. What is transformational leadership? Give examples of organizational situations that would call for transformational, transactional, or charismatic leadership.

7. How does Level 5 leadership differ from the concept of servant leadership? Do you believe anyone has the potential to become a Level 5 leader? Discuss.

8. Do you think leadership is more important or less important in today's flatter, team-based organizations? Are some leadership styles better suited to such organizations as opposed to traditional hierarchical organizations? Explain.

9. Consider the leadership position of a senior partner in a law firm. What task, subordinate, and organizational factors might serve as substitutes for leadership in this situation?

10. Do you see yourself as having leader qualities or manager qualities? Do you think you will become a better leader/manager by developing the characteristics you already have or by trying to develop the characteristics you don't have? Discuss.

ch16 MANAGEMENT IN PRACTICE: EXPERIENTIAL EXERCISE

T–P Leadership Questionnaire: An Assessment of Style

Some leaders deal with general directions, leaving details to subordinates. Other leaders focus on specific details with the expectation that subordinates will carry out orders. Depending on the situation, both approaches may be effective. The important issue is the ability to identify relevant dimensions of the situation and behave accordingly. Through this questionnaire, you can identify your relative emphasis on two dimensions of leadership: task orientation (T) and people orientation (P). These approaches are not opposites; and an individual can rate high or low on either or both.

Directions: The following items describe aspects of leadership behavior. Respond to each item according to the way you would most likely act if you were the leader of a work group. Circle whether you would most likely behave in the described way: always (A), frequently (F), occasionally (O), seldom (S), or never (N).

1. I would most likely act as the spokesperson of the group.

   A   F   O   S   N

2. I would encourage overtime work.

   A   F   O   S   N

3. I would allow members complete freedom in their work.

   A   F   O   S   N

4. I would encourage the use of uniform procedures.

   A   F   O   S   N

5. I would permit members to use their own judgment in solving problems.

   A   F   O   S   N

6. I would stress being ahead of competing groups.

   A   F   O   S   N

7. I would speak as a representative of the group.

   A   F   O   S   N

8. I would needle members for greater effort.

   A   F   O   S   N

9. I would try out my ideas in the group.

   A   F   O   S   N

10. I would let members do their work the way they think best.

    A   F   O   S   N

11. I would be working hard for a promotion.

    A   F   O   S   N

12. I would tolerate postponement and uncertainty.

    A   F   O   S   N

13. I would speak for the group if visitors were present.

A   F   O   S   N

14. I would keep the work moving at a rapid pace.

A   F   O   S   N

15. I would turn the members loose on a job and let them go to it.

A   F   O   S   N

16. I would settle conflicts when they occur in the group.

A   F   O   S   N

17. I would get swamped by details.

A   F   O   S   N

18. I would represent the group at outside meetings.

A   F   O   S   N

19. I would be reluctant to allow the members any freedom of action.

A   F   O   S   N

20. I would decide what should be done and how it should be done.

A   F   O   S   N

21. I would push for increased production.

A   F   O   S   N

22. I would let some members have authority that I could keep.

A   F   O   S   N

23. Things would usually turn out as I had predicted.

A   F   O   S   N

24. I would allow the group a high degree of initiative.

A   F   O   S   N

25. I would assign group members to particular tasks.

A   F   O   S   N

26. I would be willing to make changes.

A   F   O   S   N

27. I would ask the members to work harder.

A   F   O   S   N

28. I would trust the group members to exercise good judgment.

A   F   O   S   N

29. I would schedule the work to be done.

A   F   O   S   N

30. I would refuse to explain my actions.

A   F   O   S   N

31. I would persuade others that my ideas are to their advantage.

A   F   O   S   N

32. I would permit the group to set its own pace.

A   F   O   S   N

33. I would urge the group to beat its previous record.

A   F   O   S   N

34. I would act without consulting the group.

A   F   O   S   N

35. I would ask that group members follow standard rules and regulations.

A   F   O   S   N

T_____   P_____

Scoring and Interpretation

The T–P Leadership Questionnaire is scored as follows:

a. Circle the statements numbered 8, 12, 17, 18, 19, 30, 34, and 35.

b. Write the number 1 in front of the circled number if you responded S (seldom) or N (never) to that statement.

c. Also write a number 1 in front of the statement numbers not circled if you responded A (always) or F (frequently).

d. Circle the number 1s that you have written in front of the following statements: 3, 5, 8, 10, 15, 18, 19, 22, 24, 26, 28, 30, 32, 34, and 35.

e. Count the circled number 1s. This total is your score for concern for people. Record the score in the blank following the letter P at the end of the questionnaire.

f. Count uncircled number 1s. This total is your score for concern for task. Record this number in the blank following the letter T.

SOURCE: The T–P Leadership Questionnaire was adapted by J. B. Ritchie and P. Thompson in *Organization and People* (New York: West, 1984). Copyright 1969 by the American Educational Research Association. Adapted by permission of the publisher.

ch16 MANAGEMENT IN PRACTICE: ETHICAL DILEMMA

Too Much of a Good Thing?

Not long ago, Jessica Armstrong, vice president of administration for Delaware Valley Chemical Inc., a New Jersey-based multinational company, made a point of stopping by department head Darius Harris's office and lavishly praising him for his volunteer work with an after-school program for disadvantaged children in a nearby urban neighborhood. Now she was about to summon him to her office so she could take him to task for dedication to the same volunteer work.

It was Carolyn Clark, Harris's secretary, who'd alerted her to the problem. "Darius told the community center he'd take responsibility for a fundraising mass mailing. And then he asked me to edit the letter he'd drafted, make all the copies, stuff the envelopes, and get it into the mail—most of this on my own time," she reported, still obviously indignant. "When I told him, 'I'm sorry, but that's not my job,' he looked me straight in the eye and asked when I'd like to schedule my upcoming performance appraisal."

Several of Harris's subordinates also volunteered with the program. After chatting with them, Armstrong concluded most were volunteering out of a desire to stay on the boss's good side. It was time to talk to Harris.

"Oh, come on," responded Harris impatiently when Armstrong confronted him. "Yes, I asked for her help as a personal favor to me. But I only brought up the appraisal because I was going out of town, and we needed to set some time aside to do the evaluation." Harris went on to talk about how important working for the after-school program was to him personally. "I grew up in that neighborhood, and if it hadn't been for the people at the center, I wouldn't be here today," he said. Besides, even if he had pressured employees to help out—and he wasn't saying he had—didn't all the emphasis the company was putting on employee volunteerism make it okay to use employees' time and company resources?

After Harris left, Armstrong thought about the conversation. There was no question Delaware Valley actively encouraged employee volunteerism—and not just because it was the right thing to do. It was a chemical company with a couple of unfortunate accidental spills in its recent past that caused environmental damage and community anger.

Volunteering had the potential to help employees acquire new skills, create a sense of camaraderie, and play a role in recruiting and retaining talented people. But most of all, it gave a badly needed boost to the company's public image. Recently, Delaware Valley took every opportunity to publicize its employees' extracurricular community work on its Web site and in company publications. And the company created the annual Delaware Prize, which granted cash awards ranging from $1,000 to $5,000 to outstanding volunteers.

So now that Armstrong had talked with everyone concerned, just what was she going to do about the dispute between Darius Harris and Carolyn Clark?

What Would You Do?

1. Tell Carolyn Clark that employee volunteerism is important to the company and that while her performance evaluation will not be affected by her decision, she should consider helping Harris because it is an opportunity to help a worthy community project.

2. Tell Darius Harris that the employee volunteer program is just that: a volunteer program. Even though the company sees volunteerism as an important piece of its campaign to repair its tarnished image, employees must be free to choose whether to volunteer. He should not ask for the help of his direct reports with the after-school program.

3. Discipline Darius Harris for coercing his subordinates to spend their own time on his volunteer work at the community after-school program. This action will send a signal that coercing employees is a clear violation of leadership authority.

---

ch16   CASE FOR CRITICAL ANALYSIS

Mountain West Health Plans Inc.

"Be careful what you wish for," thought Martin Quinn, senior vice president for service and operations for the Denver-based health insurance company, Mountain West Health Plans, Inc. When there was an opening for a new director of customer service last year due to Evelyn Gustafson's retirement, he'd seen it as the perfect opportunity to bring someone in to control the ever-increasing costs of the labor-intensive department. He'd been certain he had found just the person in Erik Rasmussen, a young man in his late twenties with a shiny new bachelor's degree in business administration.

A tall, unflappable woman, Evelyn Gustafson consistently showed warmth and concern toward her mostly female, non-unionized employees as they sat in their noisy cubicles, fielding call after call about Mountain West's products, benefits, eligibility, and

claims. Because she had worked her way up from a customer service representative position herself, she could look her subordinates right in the eye after they'd fielded a string of stressful calls and tell them she knew exactly how they felt. She did her best to offset the low pay by accommodating the women's needs with flexible scheduling, giving them frequent breaks, and offering plenty of training opportunities that kept them up-to-date in the health company's changing products and in the latest problem-solving and customer service techniques.

Her motto was: "Always put yourself in the subscriber's shoes." She urged representatives to take the time necessary to thoroughly understand the subscriber's problem and do their best to see that it was completely resolved by the call's completion. Their job was important, she told them. Subscribers counted on them to help them negotiate the often Byzantine complexities of their coverage. Evelyn's subordinates adored her, as demonstrated by the 10 percent turnover rate, compared to the typical 25 to 45 percent rate for customer service representatives. Mountain West subscribers were generally satisfied, although Quinn did hear some occasional grumbling about the length of time customers spent on hold.

However, whatever her virtues, Gustafson firmly resisted all attempts to increase efficiency and lower costs in a department where salaries accounted for close to 70 percent of the budget. That's where Erik Rasmussen came in. Upper-level management charged him with the task of bringing costs under control. Eager to do well in his first management position, the hard-working, no-nonsense young man made increasing the number of calls per hour each representative handled a priority. For the first time ever, the company measured the representatives' performance against statistical standards that emphasized speed, recorded the customer service calls, and used software that generated automated work schedules based on historical information and projected need. Efficient, not flexible, scheduling was the goal. In addition, the company cut back on training.

The results, Martin Quinn had to admit, were mixed. With more efficient scheduling and clear performance standards in place, calls per hour increased dramatically, and subscribers spent far less time on hold. The department's costs were finally heading downwards, but department morale was spiraling downwards as well, with the turnover rate currently at 30 percent and climbing. And Quinn was beginning to hear more complaints from subscribers who'd received inaccurate information from inexperienced or representatives who sounded rushed.

It was time for Rasmussen's first performance review. Quinn knew the young manager was about to walk into his office ready to proudly recite the facts and figures that documented the department's increased efficiency. What kind of an evaluation was he going to give Rasmussen? Should he recommend some mid-course corrections?

Questions

1. How would you describe Evelyn Gustafson's leadership style? What were its strengths and weaknesses? What were the sources of her influence?

2. How would you describe Erik Rasmussen's leadership style as he tried to effect change? What are its strengths and weaknesses? What are the sources of his influence?

3. If you were Martin Quinn, would you recommend modifications in Erik Rasmussen's leadership style that you would like him to adopt? Do you think it will be possible for Rasmussen to make the necessary changes? If not, why not? If you do think change is possible, how would you recommend the desired changes be facilitated?

SOURCES: Based on Gary Yukl, *Leadership in Organizations*, 4th ed. (Englewood Cliffs, NJ: Prentice Hall, 1998): 66–67; and "Telephone Call Centers: The Factory Floors of the 21st Century," *Knowledge @ Wharton* (April 10, 2002): http://knowledge.wharton.upenn.edu/index .cfm?fa=viewArticle&ID=540.

ch16 ON THE JOB VIDEO CASE

P.F. Chang Serves Its Workers Well

Have you ever sat down in a restaurant and immediately thought, "This place is great?" You can tell by the atmosphere that diners are happy and staff members enjoy their jobs. Your server seems genuinely glad to see you. On the flip side, you've probably been to at least one restaurant where the staff was rushed or surly, the service slow—and you don't even recall the food because the service was so poor. You're likely to return to the first restaurant and recommend it to others. However, you're unlikely to give the second restaurant another chance. Restaurant managers face the challenge every day of putting the right person in the right job, creating a team that works well together, fostering positive work attitudes, and helping employees manage stress. Managers at P.F. Chang's, which owns and operates 97 full-service, casual dining Asian bistros and 33 contemporary Chinese diners across the country, greet these challenges with gusto.

Founded in 1993, P.F. Chang's prides itself in being able to offer "fresh, contemporary, and consistently outstanding" fare at every one of its restaurants. Selections of rice, noodles, grains, dumplings, vegetables, meat, poultry, and seafood are served at each restaurant, with mixtures of traditional Chinese foods and innovative dishes from Southeast Asia. P.F. Chang's strives to create an exceptional dining experience for every customer—and that includes a friendly, knowledgeable staff. Whether guests choose the full-service casual dining experience at P.F. Chang's bistros or the quick-service, limited-menu option of the Pei Wei Asian diners, they receive the same high quality of food and service.

How does an organization this large—and spread out—foster positive attitudes and high performance among its workers? Roxanne Pronk, Regional Vice President of Operations, explains P.F. Chang's approach. First, she notes, restaurant workers are typically young, working for hourly wages (and tips), and struggling to establish themselves in their lives and careers. So, when they arrive at work, they are not necessarily thinking about the needs of customers but are thinking about themselves. According to Pronk, most restaurants deal with these problems through the use of discipline and negative reinforcement— which results in unhappy employees and a high degree of turnover. But P.F. Chang's takes a different approach. If a worker begins to exhibit a pattern of poor behavior, such as arriving late to work, his or her manager sits down with the employee, asks whether everything is all right and how the manager might be able to help turn things around. Pronk notes that this caring and respectful treatment has a profound effect on workers' attitudes about their jobs.

By treating employees with respect, restaurant managers find that they can expect more from their staffs—and get it. Unlike many hourly restaurant employees, those at P.F. Chang's have the authority to make decisions that benefit customers. For example, if a customer is dissatisfied with a meal, the server has the authority to offer a replacement or a free meal. If a customer requests butter—which is not an ingredient found in Asian cuisine—the server can ask a busboy to run to the nearest market to buy butter for the customer's meal. Giving employees the freedom to make decisions has had a huge impact on their attitude and performance, says Pronk. Of course, workers are also held accountable for their behavior and their performance, but they welcome the responsibility.

Managers at P.F. Chang's restaurant receive extensive training in how to create and nurture a positive attitude among their employees, and all workers receive an employee handbook, which clearly spells out exactly what is expected of them. In addition, every work shift at P.F. Chang's begins with a staff meeting which acts as a sort of pep rally to motivate workers to head into their shifts with an upbeat outlook. The Chang's culture is made up of trust, respect, accountability, commitment, and passion. "We believe that every employee and member of our management team must embody our messages as well as our values," explains the Web site. That's a recipe for some delicious dining.

Questions

1. Managers at P.F. Chang's address the affective component of workers' attitudes. Why is this an important step for them to take?

2. In what ways does P.F. Chang's create organizational commitment among its workers?

3. How might a manager at P.F. Chang's use the Big Five personality factors to assess whether a candidate for a position on the wait staff would be suitable?

SOURCES: Company Web site, *http://www.pfchangs.com*, accessed August 26, 2004; "Work Force Still Top Concern for CEOs," *The Phoenix Business Journal*, May 24, 2004, *http://phoenix.bizjournals.com*.

---

ch16 BIZ FLIX VIDEO CASE

Patch Adams

Hunter "Patch" Adams (Robin Williams), a maverick medical student, believes that laughter is the best medicine. The rest of the medical community believes that medicine is the best medicine. Unlike traditional doctors who remain aloof, Patch Adams wants to be close to his patients. Williams's wackiness comes through clearly in this film, which is based on a true story.

This scene comes from the film's early sequence "The Experiment," which takes place after the students' medical school orientation. Patch Adams and fellow medical student Truman Schiff (Daniel London) leave the University Diner. They begin Patch's experiment for changing the programmed responses of people they meet on the street. Along the way, they stumble upon a meat packers' convention where this scene occurs.

What to Watch for and Ask Yourself

1. What parts of the communication process appear in this scene? Note each part of the process that you see in the scene.

2. What type of communication does this scene show: Small group, large audience, or persuasive?

3. Do you think Patch Adams is an effective communicator? Why or why not?

ch16 ENDNOTES

1. Leigh Buchanan, "Pat McGovern . . . For Knowing the Power of Respect," segment in "25 Entrepreneurs We Love," *Inc Magazine* (April 2004): 110–147; Melanie Warner, "Confessions of a Control Freak," *Fortune* (September 4, 2000): 130–140.

2. Greg Jaffe, "Change of Command; A Marine Captain Trains Iraqi Colonel to Take Over Fight," *The Wall Street Journal*, February 24, 2005; and Jackie Spinner, "Training a New Army from the Top Down; U.S. Military Struggles to ëBuild Leaders,'" *Washington Post*, November 1, 2005.

3. Kevin Kelleher, "How To . . . Spot Great Chief Executives," *Business 2.0* (April 2005): 42.

4. Gary Yukl, "Managerial Leadership: A Review of Theory and Research," *Journal of Management* 15 (1989): 251–289.

5. James M. Kouzes and Barry Z. Posner, "The Credibility Factor: What Followers Expect from Their Leaders," *Management Review* (January 1990): 29–33.

6. Joseph L. Badaracco, Jr. "A Lesson for the Times: Learning From Quiet Leaders," *Ivey Business Journal* (January–February 2003): 1–6; and Matthew Gwyther, "Back to the Wall," *Management Today* (February 2003): 58–61.

7. See J. Andrew Morris, Céleste M. Brotheridge, and John C. Urbanski, "Bringing Humility to Leadership: Antecedents and Consequences of Leader Humility," *Human Relations* 58, no. 10 (2005): 1323–1350; Linda Tischler, "The CEO's New Clothes," *Fast Company* (September 2005): 27–28; James C. Collins, *From Good to Great: Why Some Companies Make the Leap . . . And Others Don't* (New York: HarperCollins 2001); Charles A. O'Reilly III and Jeffrey Pfeffer, *Hidden Value: How Great Companies Achieve Extraordinary Results with Ordinary People* (Boston, MA: Harvard Business School Press, 2000); Rakesh Khurana, "The Curse of the Superstar CEO," *Harvard Business Review* (September 2002): 60–66, excerpted from his book, *Searching for a Corporate Savior: The Irrational Quest for Charismatic CEOs* (Princeton, NJ: Princeton University Press, 2002); and Joseph Badaracco, *Leading Quietly* (Boston, MA: Harvard Business School Press, 2002).

8. Center for Creative Leadership study, reported in Andre Martin, "What Is Effective Leadership Today?" *Chief Executive* (July–August 2006): 24; and "The Demise of the Heroic Leader," *Leader to Leader* (Fall 2006): 55–56.

9. Jim Collins, "Level 5 Leadership: The Triumph of Humility and Fierce Resolve," *Harvard Business Review* (January 2001): 67–76; Jim Collins, "Good to Great," *Fast Company* (October 2001): 90–104; A. J. Vogl, "Onward and Upward" (an interview with Jim Collins), *Across the Board* (September–October 2001): 29–34; and Jerry Useem, "Conquering Vertical Limits," *Fortune* (February 19, 2001): 84–96.

10. Collins, "Level 5 Leadership."

11. Judy B. Rosener, *America's Competitive Secret: Utilizing Women as a Management Strategy* (New York: Oxford University Press, 1995), pp. 129–135.

12. Rochelle Sharpe, "As Leaders, Women Rule," *BusinessWeek* (November 20, 2000): 75–84.

13. Alice H. Eagly and Linda L. Carli, "The Female Leadership Advantage: An Evaluation of the Evidence," *The Leadership Quarterly* 14 (2003): 807–834; Rosener, *America's Competitive Secret*; Judy B. Rosener, "Ways Women Lead," *Harvard Business Review* (November–December 1990): 119–125; Sally Helgesen, *The Female Advantage: Women's Ways of Leadership* (New York: Currency/Doubleday, 1990); and Bernard M. Bass and Bruce J. Avolio, "Shatter the Glass Ceiling: Women May Make Better Managers," *Human Resource Management* 33, no. 4 (Winter 1994): 549–560.

14. Sharpe, "As Leaders, Women Rule," 75–84.

15. Kevin S. Groves, "Gender Differences in Social and Emotional Skills and Charismatic Leadership," *Journal of Leadership and Organizational Studies* 11, no. 3 (2005): 30ff.

16. Gary Yukl and Richard Lepsinger, "Why Integrating the Leading and Managing Roles Is Essential for Organizational Effectiveness," *Organizational Dynamics* 34, no. 4 (2005): 361–375.

17. Miguel Helft, "Can She Turn Yahoo Into, Well, Google?" *The New York Times*, July 1, 2007; and Miguel Helft, "Industry Insiders Praise Yahoo Choice for Key Post," *The New York Times*, December 7, 2006.

18. G. A. Yukl, *Leadership in Organizations* (Englewood Cliffs, NJ: Prentice Hall, 1981); and S. C. Kohs and K. W. Irle, "Prophesying Army Promotion," *Journal of Applied Psychology* 4 (1920): 73–87.

19. R. Albanese and D. D. Van Fleet, *Organizational Behavior: A Managerial Viewpoint* (Hinsdale, IL: The Dryden Press, 1983).

20. Gary Yukl, Angela Gordon, and Tom Taber, "A Hierarchical Taxonomy of Leadership Behavior: Integrating a Half Century of Behavior Research," *Journal of Leadership and Organizational Studies* 9, no. 1 (2002): 13–32.

21. C. A. Schriesheim and B. J. Bird, "Contributions of the Ohio State Studies to the Field of Leadership," *Journal of Management* 5 (1979): 135–145; and C. L. Shartle, "Early Years of the Ohio State University Leadership Studies," *Journal of Management* 5 (1979): 126–134.

22. Don Wallace, "The Soul of a Sports Machine," *Fast Company* (October 2003): 100–102; and Neil Hayes, *When the Game Stands Tall. The Story of the De La Salle Spartans and Football's Longest Winning Streak* (Berkeley, CA: Frog, Ltd./North Atlantic Books, 2005).

23. P. C. Nystrom, "Managers and the High-High Leader Myth," *Academy of Management Journal* 21 (1978): 325–331; and L. L. Larson, J. G. Hunt, and Richard N. Osborn, "The Great High-High Leader Behavior Myth: A Lesson from Occam's Razor," *Academy of Management Journal* 19 (1976): 628–641.

24. R. Likert, "From Production- and Employee-Centeredness to Systems 1–4," *Journal of Management* 5 (1979): 147–156.

25. Robert R. Blake and Jane S. Mouton, *The Managerial Grid III* (Houston, TX: Gulf, 1985).

26. Paul Hersey and Kenneth H. Blanchard, *Management of Organizational Behavior: Utilizing Human Resources*, 4th ed. (Englewood Cliffs, NJ: Prentice Hall, 1982).

27. Robert Tomsho and John Hechinger, "Crimson Blues; Harvard Clash Pits Brusque Leader Against Faculty," *The Wall Street Journal*, February 18, 2005; and Ruth R. Wisse, "Cross Country; Coup d' Ecole," *The Wall Street Journal*, February 23, 2006.

28. Fred E. Fiedler, "Assumed Similarity Measures as Predictors of Team Effectiveness," *Journal of Abnormal and Social Psychology* 49 (1954): 381–388; F. E. Fiedler, *Leader Attitudes and Group Effectiveness* (Urbana, IL: University of Illinois Press, 1958); and F. E. Fiedler, *A Theory of Leadership Effectiveness* (New York: McGraw-Hill, 1967).

29. Fred E. Fiedler and M. M. Chemers, *Leadership and Effective Management* (Glenview, IL: Scott, Foresman, 1974).

30. Reported in George Anders, "Theory & Practice: Tough CEOs Often Most Successful, a Study Finds," *The Wall Street Journal*, November 19, 2007.

31. Fred E. Fiedler, "Engineer the Job to Fit the Manager," *Harvard Business Review* 43 (1965): 115–122; and F. E. Fiedler, M. M. Chemers, and L. Mahar, *Improving Leadership Effectiveness: The Leader Match Concept* (New York: Wiley, 1976).

32. R. Singh, "Leadership Style and Reward Allocation: Does Least Preferred Coworker Scale Measure Tasks and Relation Orientation?" *Organizational Behavior and Human Performance* 27 (1983): 178–197; and D. Hosking, "A Critical Evaluation of Fiedler's Contingency Hypotheses," *Progress in Applied Psychology* 1 (1981): 103–154.

33. S. Kerr and J. M. Jermier, "Substitutes for Leadership: Their Meaning and Measurement," *Organizational Behavior and Human Performance* 22 (1978): 375–403; and Jon P. Howell and Peter W. Dorfman, "Leadership and Substitutes for Leadership among Professional and Nonprofessional Workers," *Journal of Applied Behavioral Science* 22 (1986): 29–46.

34. Katherine J. Klein and Robert J. House, "On Fire: Charismatic Leadership and Levels of Analysis," *Leadership Quarterly* 6, no. 2 (1995): 183–198.

35. Jay A. Conger and Rabindra N. Kanungo, "Toward a Behavioral Theory of Charismatic Leadership in Organizational Settings," *Academy of Management Review* 12 (1987): 637–647; Jaepil Choi, "A Motivational Theory of Charismatic Leadership: Envisioning, Empathy, and Empowerment," *Journal of Leadership and Organizational Studies* 13, no. 1 (2006): 24ff; and William L. Gardner and Bruce J. Avolio, "The Charismatic Relationship: A Dramaturgical Perspective," *Academy of Management Review* 23, no. 1 (1998): 32–58.

36. Robert J. House and Jane M. Howell, "Personality and Charismatic Leadership," *Leadership Quarterly* 3, no. 2 (1992): 81–108; and Jennifer O'Connor, Michael D. Mumford, Timothy C. Clifton, Theodore L. Gessner, and Mary Shane Connelly, "Charismatic Leaders and Destructiveness: A Historiometric Study," *Leadership Quarterly* 6, no. 4 (1995): 529–555.

37. Robert J. House, "Research Contrasting the Behavior and Effects of Reputed Charismatic vs. Reputed Non-Charismatic Leaders," paper presented as part of a symposium, "Charismatic Leadership: Theory and Evidence," Academy of Management, San Diego, 1985.

38. Bernard M. Bass, "Theory of Transformational Leadership Redux," *Leadership Quarterly* 6, no. 4 (1995): 463–478; Noel M. Tichy and Mary Anne Devanna, *The Transformational Leader* (New York: John Wiley & Sons, 1986); and Badrinarayan Shankar Pawar and Kenneth K. Eastman, "The Nature and Implications of Contextual Influences on Transformational Leadership: A Conceptual Examination," *Academy of Management Review* 22, no. 1 (1997) 80–109.

39. The terms *transactional* and *transformational* come from James M. Burns, *Leadership* (New York: Harper & Row, 1978); and Bernard M. Bass, "Leadership: Good, Better, Best," *Organizational Dynamics* 13 (Winter 1985): 26–40.

40. Richard L. Daft and Robert H. Lengel, *Fusion Leadership: Unlocking the Subtle Forces that Change People and Organizations* (San Francisco: Berrett-Koehler, 1998).

41. Taly Dvir, Dov Eden, Bruce J. Avolio, and Boas Shamir, "Impact of Transformational Leadership on Follower Development and Performance: A Field Experiment," *Academy of Management Journal* 45, no. 4 (2002): 735–744.

42. Robert S. Rubin, David C. Munz, and William H. Bommer, "Leading From Within: The Effects of Emotion Recognition and Personality on Transformational Leadership Behavior," *Academy of Management Journal* 48, no. 5 (2005): 845–858; and Timothy A. Judge and Joyce E. Bono, "Five-Factor Model of Personality and Transformational Leadership," *Journal of Applied Psychology* 85, no. 5 (October 2000): 751ff.

43. Rubin et al., "Leading from Within."

44. Barbara Kellerman, "What Every Leader Needs to Know About Followers," *Harvard Business Review* (December 2007): 84–91.

45. Robert E. Kelley, *The Power of Followership* (New York: Doubleday, 1992).

46. Ibid., 117–118.

47. Henry Mintzberg, *Power In and Around Organizations* (Englewood Cliffs, NJ: Prentice Hall, 1983); and Jeffrey Pfeffer, *Power in Organizations* (Marshfield, MA: Pitman, 1981).

48. Jay A. Conger, "The Necessary Art of Persuasion," *Harvard Business Review* (May–June 1998): 84–95.

49. D. Kipnis, S. M. Schmidt, C. Swaffin-Smith, and I. Wilkinson, "Patterns of Managerial Influence: Shotgun Managers, Tacticians, and Politicians," *Organizational Dynamics* (Winter 1984): 58–67.

50. These tactics are based on Kipnis et al., "Patterns of Managerial Influence"; and Robert B. Cialdini, "Harnessing the Science of Persuasion," *Harvard Business Review* (October 2001): 72–79.

51. Kipnis et al., "Patterns of Managerial Influence"; and Jeffrey Pfeffer, *Managing with Power: Politics and Influence in Organizations* (Boston: Harvard Business School Press, 1992), chapter 15.

52. Ibid.

53. V. Dallas Merrell, *Huddling: The Informal Way to Management Success* (New York: AMACOM, 1979).

54. Robert B. Cialdini, *Influence: Science and Practice*, 4th ed. (Boston: Pearson Allyn & Bacon, 2000).

55. Harvey G. Enns and Dean B. McFarlin, "When Executives Influence Peers, Does Function Matter?" *Human Resource Management* 4, no. 2 (Summer 2003): 125–142.

56. Daft and Lengel, *Fusion Leadership*.

57. Leigh Buchanan, "In Praise of Selflessness: Why the Best Leaders Are Servants," *Inc. Magazine* (May 2007): 33–35.

58. Robert K. Greenleaf, *Servant Leadership: A Journey into the Nature of Legitimate Power and Greatness* (Mahwah, NJ: Paulist Press, 1977).

59. Anne Fitzgerald, "Christmas Bonus Stuns Employees," *The Des Moines Register*, December 20, 2003, http://www.desmoinesregister.com.

60. Buchanan, "In Praise of Selflessness."

61. Richard L. Daft, *The Leadership Experience*, 3rd ed. (Cincinnati, OH: South-Western, 2005), chapter 6.

62. Badaracco, "A Lesson for the Times: Learning From Quiet Leaders."

63. Jim Collins, "The 10 Greatest CEOs of All Time," *Fortune* (July 21, 2003): 54–68.

© GETTY IMAGES/DIGITAL VISION

Learning Outcomes

After studying this chapter, you should be able to:

1. Define *motivation* and explain the difference between intrinsic and extrinsic rewards.

2. Identify and describe content theories of motivation based on employee needs.

3. Identify and explain process theories of motivation.

4. Describe the reinforcement perspective and how it can be used to motivate employees.

5. Discuss major approaches to job design and how job design influences motivation.

6. Explain how empowerment heightens employee motivation.

7. Describe ways that managers can create a sense of meaning and importance through employee engagement.

Motivating Employees

ARE YOU ENGAGED OR DISENGAGED?[1]

The term *employee engagement* is becoming popular in the corporate world. To learn what engagement means, answer the following questions twice—(1) once for a course you both enjoyed and performed well and (2) a second time for a course you did not enjoy and performed poorly. Please mark a "1" to indicate whether each item is Mostly True or Mostly False for the course you enjoyed and performed well. Please mark a "2" to indicate whether each item is Mostly True or Mostly False for the course you did not enjoy and performed poorly.

	Mostly True	Mostly False
1. I made sure to study on a regular basis.	_____	_____
2. I put forth effort.	_____	_____
3. I found ways to make the course material relevant to my life.	_____	_____
4. I found ways to make the course interesting to me.	_____	_____
5. I raised my hand in class.	_____	_____
6. I had fun in class.	_____	_____
7. I participated actively in small group discussions.	_____	_____
8. I helped fellow students.	_____	_____

SCORING AND INTERPRETATION: Engagement means that people involve and express themselves in their work, going beyond the minimum effort required. Engagement typically has a positive relationship with both personal satisfaction and performance. If this relationship was true for your classes, the number of "1s" in the Mostly True column will be higher than the number of "2s." You might expect a score of 6 or higher for a course in which you were engaged, and possibly 3 or lower if you were disengaged.

The challenge for a new manager is to learn to engage subordinates in the same way your instructors in your favorite classes were able to engage you. Teaching is similar to managing. What techniques did your instructors use to engage students? Which techniques can you use to engage people when you become a new manager?

Most people begin a new job with energy and enthusiasm, but employees can lose their drive if managers fail in their role as motivators. It can be a problem for even the most successful of organizations and the most admired of managers, when experienced, valuable employees lose the motivation and commitment they once felt, causing a decline in their performance. One secret for success in organizations is motivated and engaged employees.

Motivation is a challenge for managers because motivation arises from within employees and typically differs for each person. For example, Janice Rennie makes $350,000 a year selling residential real estate in Toronto; she attributes her success to the fact that she likes to listen carefully to clients and then find houses to meet their needs. Greg Storey is a skilled machinist who is challenged by writing programs for numerically controlled machines. After dropping out of college, he swept floors in a machine shop and was motivated to learn to run the machines. Frances Blais sells educational books and software. She is a top salesperson, but she doesn't care about the $50,000-plus commissions: "I'm not even thinking money when I'm selling. I'm really on a crusade to help children read well." In stark contrast, Rob Michaels gets sick to his stomach before he goes to work. Rob is a telephone salesperson who spends all day trying to get people to buy products they do not need, and the rejections are painful. His motivation is money; he earned $120,000 in the past year and cannot make nearly that much doing anything else.[2]

1 Introduction

2 Environment

3 Planning

4 Organizing

5 Controlling

6 Leading

Rob is motivated by money, Janice by her love of listening and problem solving, Frances by the desire to help children read, and Greg by the challenge of mastering numerically controlled machinery. Each person is motivated to perform, yet each has different reasons for performing. With such diverse motivations among individuals, how do managers find the right way to motivate employees toward common organizational goals?

This chapter reviews several approaches to employee motivation. First, we define motivation and the types of rewards managers use. Then, we examine several models that describe the employee needs and processes associated with motivation. We also look at the use of reinforcement for motivation, as well as examine how job design—changing the structure of the work itself—can affect employee satisfaction and productivity. Finally, we discuss the trend of empowerment and look at how managers imbue work with a sense of meaning by fostering employee engagement.

THE CONCEPT OF MOTIVATION

motivation The arousal, direction, and persistence of behavior.

intrinsic reward The satisfaction received in the process of performing an action.

extrinsic reward A reward given by another person.

Most of us get up in the morning, go to school or work, and behave in ways that are predictably our own. We respond to our environment and the people in it with little thought as to why we work hard, enjoy certain classes, or find some recreational activities so much fun. Yet all these behaviors are motivated by something. **Motivation** refers to the forces either within or external to a person that arouse enthusiasm and persistence to pursue a certain course of action. Employee motivation affects productivity, and part of a manager's job is to channel motivation toward the accomplishment of organizational goals.[3] The study of motivation helps managers understand what prompts people to initiate action, what influences their choice of action, and why they persist in that action over time.

A simple model of human motivation is illustrated in Exhibit 17.1. People have *needs*—such as for recognition, achievement, or monetary gain—that translate into an internal tension that motivates specific behaviors with which to fulfill the need.

To the extent that the behavior is successful, the person is rewarded in the sense that the need is satisfied. The reward also informs the person that the behavior was appropriate and can be used again in the future.

Rewards are of two types: intrinsic and extrinsic. **Intrinsic rewards** are the satisfactions a person receives in the process of performing a particular action. The completion of a complex task may bestow a pleasant feeling of accomplishment, or solving a problem that benefits others may fulfill a personal mission. Frances Blais sells educational materials for the intrinsic reward of helping children read well. **Extrinsic rewards** are given by another person, typically a manager, and include promotions, pay increases, and bonuses. They originate externally, as a result of pleasing others. Rob Michaels, who hates his sales job, nevertheless is motivated by the extrinsic reward of high pay. Although extrinsic rewards are important, good managers strive to help people achieve intrinsic rewards as well. The most talented and innovative employees are rarely motivated exclusively by rewards

PHOTO COURTESY OF THE CONTAINER STORE

Concept Connection The Container Store has the motto that one great person equals three good people. Here, an employee and Elfa storage system designer works with a couple to design a custom storage plan. Getting hired is quite competitive at the retailer that has been on *Fortune* magazine's list of 100 Best Companies to Work for in America year after year since 2000. Employees get **intrinsic rewards** from knowing they were selected to work for this winning company. The Container Store also puts its money where its motto is—providing the **extrinsic rewards** of entry level pay that is 50 to 100 percent higher than average retail pay, a 40 percent merchandise discount, and health insurance for part-time as well as full-time employees.

EXHIBIT | 17.1 A Simple Model of Motivation

NEED Creates desire to fulfill needs (food, friendship, recognition, achievement) → **BEHAVIOR** Results in actions to fulfill needs → **REWARDS** Satisfy needs; intrinsic or extrinsic rewards

FEEDBACK Reward informs person whether behavior was appropriate and should be used again.

such as money and benefits, or even praise and recognition. Instead, they seek satisfaction from the work itself.[4] For example, at Google, people are motivated by an idealistic goal of providing "automated universal transference," which basically means unifying data and information around the world and totally obliterating language barriers via the Internet. People are energized by the psychic rewards they get from working on intellectually stimulating and challenging technical problems, as well as by the potentially beneficial global impact of their work.[5]

As a new manager, remember that people will be more engaged when they do things they really like. To reinforce this understanding, refer back to your answers on the questionnaire at the beginning of this chapter.

TakeaMoment

The importance of motivation as illustrated in Exhibit 17.1 is that it can lead to behaviors that reflect high performance within organizations. Studies have found that high employee motivation goes hand-in-hand with high organizational performance and profits.[6] It is the responsibility of managers to find the right combination of motivational techniques and rewards to satisfy employees' needs and simultaneously encourage high work performance.

Some ideas about motivation, referred to as *content theories*, stress the analysis of underlying human needs and how needs can be satisfied in the workplace. *Process theories* concern the thought processes that influence behavior. They focus on how people seek rewards in work circumstances. *Reinforcement theories* focus on employee learning of desired work behaviors. In Exhibit 17.1, content theories focus on the concepts in the first box, process theories on those in the second, and reinforcement theories on those in the third.

CONTENT PERSPECTIVES ON MOTIVATION

Content theories emphasize the needs that motivate people. At any point in time, people have a variety of needs. These needs translate into an internal drive that motivates specific behaviors in an attempt to fulfill the needs. In other words, our needs are like a hidden catalog of the things we want and will work to get. To the extent that managers understand employees' needs, they can design reward systems to meet them and direct employees' energies and priorities toward attaining organizational goals.

content theories A group of theories that emphasize the needs that motivate people.

hierarchy of needs theory A content theory that proposes that people are motivated by five categories of needs—physiological, safety, belongingness, esteem, and self-actualization—that exist in a hierarchical order.

The Hierarchy of Needs

Probably the most famous content theory was developed by Abraham Maslow.[7] Maslow's **hierarchy of needs theory** proposes that people are motivated by multiple

6 Leading

needs and that these needs exist in a hierarchical order, as illustrated in Exhibit 17.2. Maslow identified five general types of motivating needs in order of ascendance:

1. *Physiological needs.* These most basic human physical needs include food, water, and oxygen. In the organizational setting, they are reflected in the needs for adequate heat, air, and base salary to ensure survival.

2. *Safety needs.* These needs include a safe and secure physical and emotional environment and freedom from threats—that is, for freedom from violence and for an orderly society. In an organizational workplace, safety needs reflect the needs for safe jobs, fringe benefits, and job security.

3. *Belongingness needs.* These needs reflect the desire to be accepted by one's peers, have friendships, be part of a group, and be loved. In the organization, these needs influence the desire for good relationships with coworkers, participation in a work group, and a positive relationship with supervisors.

4. *Esteem needs.* These needs relate to the desire for a positive self-image and to receive attention, recognition, and appreciation from others. Within organizations, esteem needs reflect a motivation for recognition, an increase in responsibility, high status, and credit for contributions to the organization.

5. *Self-actualization needs.* These needs include the need for self-fulfillment, which is the highest need category. They concern developing one's full potential, increasing one's competence, and becoming a better person. Self-actualization needs can be met in the organization by providing people with opportunities to grow, be creative, and acquire training for challenging assignments and advancement.

According to Maslow's theory, low-order needs take priority—they must be satisfied before higher-order needs are activated. The needs are satisfied in sequence: Physiological needs come before safety needs, safety needs before social needs, and so on. A person desiring physical safety will devote his or her efforts to securing a safer environment and will not be concerned with esteem needs or self-actualization needs. Once a need is satisfied, it declines in importance and the next higher need is activated.

A study of employees in the manufacturing department of a major health-care company in the United Kingdom provides some support for Maslow's theory. Most line workers emphasized that they worked at the company primarily because of the good pay, benefits, and job security. Thus, employees' lower-level physiological and safety needs were being met. When questioned about their motivation, employees indicated the importance of positive social relationships with both peers and supervisors (belongingness needs) and a desire for greater respect and recognition from management (esteem needs).[8]

EXHIBIT | 17.2   Maslow's Hierarchy of Needs

Fulfillment off the Job	Need Hierarchy	Fulfillment on the Job
Education, religion, hobbies, personal growth	Self-Actualization Needs	Opportunities for training, advancement, growth, and creativity
Approval of family, friends, community	Esteem Needs	Recognition, high status, increased responsibilities
Family, friends, community groups	Belongingness Needs	Work groups, clients, coworkers, supervisors
Freedom from war, pollution, violence	Safety Needs	Safe work, fringe benefits, job security
Food, water, oxygen	Physiological Needs	Heat, air, base salary

As a new manager, recognize that some people are motivated primarily to satisfy lower-level physiological and safety needs, while others want to satisfy higher-level needs. Learn which lower- and higher-level needs motivate you by completing the experiential exercise on pages 527–528.

TakeaMoment

ERG Theory

Clayton Alderfer proposed a modification of Maslow's theory in an effort to simplify it and respond to criticisms of its lack of empirical verification.[9] His **ERG theory** identified three categories of needs:

1. *Existence needs.* The needs for physical well-being.
2. *Relatedness needs.* The needs for satisfactory relationships with others.
3. *Growth needs.* The needs that focus on the development of human potential and the desire for personal growth and increased competence.

The ERG model and Maslow's need hierarchy are similar because both are in hierarchical form and presume that individuals move up the hierarchy one step at a time. However, Alderfer reduced the number of need categories to three and proposed that movement up the hierarchy is more complex, reflecting a **frustration-regression principle**, namely, that failure to meet a high-order need may trigger a regression to an already fulfilled lower-order need. Thus, a worker who cannot fulfill a need for personal growth may revert to a lower-order need and redirect his or her efforts toward making a lot of money. The ERG model therefore is less rigid than Maslow's need hierarchy, suggesting that individuals may move down as well as up the hierarchy, depending on their ability to satisfy needs.

Need hierarchy theory helps explain why organizations find ways to recognize employees, encourage their participation in decision making, and give them opportunities to make significant contributions to the organization and society. At Sterling Bank, with headquarters in Houston, Texas, there are no *bank tellers*. These positions are now front-line managers who have the opportunity to make decisions and contribute ideas for improving the business.[10] USAA, which offers insurance, mutual funds, and banking services to five million members of the military and their families, provides another example.

ERG theory A modification of the needs hierarchy theory that proposes three categories of needs: existence, relatedness, and growth.

frustration-regression principle The idea that failure to meet a high-order need may cause a regression to an already satisfied lower-order need.

USAA

USAA's customer service agents are on the front lines in helping families challenged by war and overseas deployment manage their financial responsibilities. Managers recognize that the most important factor in the company's success is the relationship between USAA members and these front-line employees.

To make sure that relationship is a good one, USAA treats customer service reps, often considered the lowest rung on the corporate ladder, like valued professionals. People have a real sense that they're making life just a little easier for military members and their families, which gives them a feeling of pride and importance. Employees are organized into small, tightly knit "expert teams" and are encouraged to suggest changes that will benefit customers. Service reps don't have scripts to follow, and calls aren't timed. Employees know they can take whatever time they need to give the customer the best possible service.

Giving people the opportunity to make genuine contributions has paid off. In a study by Forrester Research, 81 percent of USAA customers said they believe the company does what's best for them, rather than what's best for the bottom line. Compare that to about 20 percent of customers for other financial services firms.[11]

Innovative Way

A recent survey found that employees who contribute ideas at work, such as customer service reps at USAA, are more likely to feel valued, committed, and motivated. In addition, when employees' ideas are implemented and recognized, a motivational effect often ripples throughout the workforce.[12]

Many companies are finding that creating a humane work environment that allows people to achieve a balance between work and personal life is also a great high-level motivator. Flexibility in the workplace, including options such as telecommuting, flexible hours, and job sharing, is highly valued by today's employees because it enables them to manage their work and personal responsibilities. Flexibility is good for organizations too. Employees who have control over their work schedules are significantly less likely to suffer job burnout and are more highly committed to their employers, as shown in Exhibit 17.3. This idea was supported by a survey conducted at Deloitte, which found that client service professionals cited workplace flexibility as a strong reason for wanting to stay with the firm. Another study at Prudential Insurance found that work-life satisfaction and work flexibility directly correlated to job satisfaction, organizational commitment, and employee retention.[13]

A Two-Factor Approach to Motivation

Frederick Herzberg developed another popular theory of motivation called the *two-factor theory*.[14] Herzberg interviewed hundreds of workers about times when they were highly motivated to work and other times when they were dissatisfied and unmotivated. His findings suggested that the work characteristics associated with dissatisfaction were quite different from those pertaining to satisfaction, which prompted the notion that two factors influence work motivation.

The two-factor theory is illustrated in Exhibit 17.4. The center of the scale is neutral, meaning that workers are neither satisfied nor dissatisfied. Herzberg believed that two entirely separate dimensions contribute to an employee's behavior at work. The first, called **hygiene factors**, involves the presence or absence of job dissatisfiers, such as working conditions, pay, company policies, and interpersonal relationships. When hygiene factors are poor, work is dissatisfying. However, good hygiene factors simply remove the dissatisfaction; they do not in themselves cause people to become highly satisfied and motivated in their work.

The second set of factors does influence job satisfaction. **Motivators** focus on high-level needs and include achievement, recognition, responsibility, and opportunity for growth. Herzberg believed that when motivators are absent, workers are neutral toward work, but when motivators are present, workers are highly motivated and satisfied. Thus, hygiene factors and motivators represent two distinct factors that influence motivation. Hygiene factors work only in the area of dissatisfaction. Unsafe working conditions or a noisy work environment will cause people to be dissatisfied, but their correction will not lead to a high level of motivation and satisfaction. Motivators such as challenge, responsibility, and recognition must be in place before employees will be highly motivated to excel at their work.

hygiene factors Factors that involve the presence or absence of job dissatisfiers, including working conditions, pay, company policies, and interpersonal relationships.

motivators Factors that influence job satisfaction based on fulfillment of high-level needs such as achievement, recognition, responsibility, and opportunity for growth.

EXHIBIT | 17.3

The Motivational Benefits of Job Flexibility

SOURCE: WFD Consulting data, as reported in Karol Rose, "Work-Life Effectiveness," *Fortune* (September 29, 2003): S1–S17.

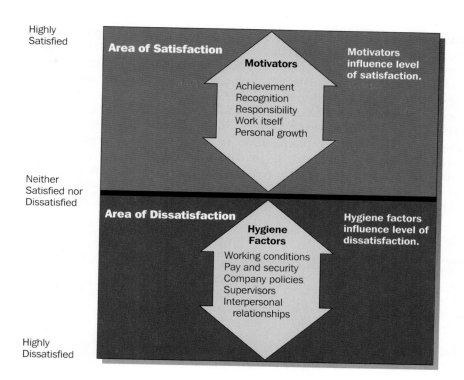

EXHIBIT | 17.4

Herzberg's Two-Factor Theory

The implication of the two-factor theory for managers is clear. On one hand, providing hygiene factors will eliminate employee dissatisfaction but will not motivate workers to high achievement levels. On the other hand, recognition, challenge, and opportunities for personal growth are powerful motivators and will promote high satisfaction and performance. The manager's role is to remove dissatisfiers—that is, to provide hygiene factors sufficient to meet basic needs—and then to use motivators to meet higher-level needs and propel employees toward greater achievement and satisfaction.

Acquired Needs

The *acquired needs theory*, developed by David McClelland, proposes that certain types of needs are acquired during the individual's lifetime. In other words, people are not born with these needs but may learn them through their life experiences.[15] The three needs most frequently studied are these:

1. *Need for achievement.* The desire to accomplish something difficult, attain a high standard of success, master complex tasks, and surpass others.
2. *Need for affiliation.* The desire to form close personal relationships, avoid conflict, and establish warm friendships.
3. *Need for power.* The desire to influence or control others, be responsible for others, and have authority over others.

Early life experiences typically determine whether people acquire these needs. If children are encouraged to do things for themselves and receive reinforcement, they will acquire a need to achieve. If they are reinforced for forming warm human relationships, they will develop a need for affiliation. If they get satisfaction from controlling others, they will acquire a need for power.

For more than 20 years, McClelland studied human needs and their implications for management. People with a high need for achievement are frequently entrepreneurs. People who have a high need for *affiliation* are successful integrators, whose job is to coordinate the work of several departments in an organization.[16] Integrators include brand managers and project managers who must have excellent people skills. A high need for *power* often is associated with successful attainment of top levels in the organizational hierarchy. For example, McClelland studied managers at AT&T for 16 years and found that those with a high need for power were more likely to follow a path of continued promotion over time. More than half of the employees at the top levels had a high need for power. In contrast, managers with a high need for achievement but a low need for power tended to peak earlier in their careers and at a lower level. The reason is that achievement needs can be met through the task itself, but power needs can be met only by ascending to a level at which a person has power over others.

In summary, content theories focus on people's underlying needs and label those particular needs that motivate behavior. The hierarchy of needs theory, the ERG theory, the two-factor theory, and the acquired needs theory all help managers understand what motivates people. In this way, managers can design work to meet needs and hence elicit appropriate and successful work behaviors.

process theories A group of theories that explain how employees select behaviors with which to meet their needs and determine whether their choices were successful.

goal-setting theory A motivation theory in which specific, challenging goals increase motivation and performance when the goals are accepted by subordinates and these subordinates receive feedback to indicate their progress toward goal achievement.

PROCESS PERSPECTIVES ON MOTIVATION

Process theories explain how people select behavioral actions to meet their needs and determine whether their choices were successful. Important perspectives in this area include goal-setting, equity theory, and expectancy theory.

Goal-Setting

Recall from Chapter 6 our discussion of the importance and purposes of goals. Numerous studies have shown that specific, challenging targets significantly enhance people's motivation and performance levels.[17] You have probably noticed in your own life that you are more motivated when you have a specific goal, such as making an A on a final exam, losing 10 pounds before spring break, or earning enough money during the summer to buy a used car.

Goal-setting theory, described by Edwin Locke and Gary Latham, proposes that managers can increase motivation and enhance performance by setting specific, challenging goals, then helping people track their progress toward goal achievement by providing timely feedback. Key components of goal-setting theory include the following:[18]

- *Goal specificity* refers to the degree to which goals are concrete and unambiguous. Specific goals such as "visit one new customer each day," or "sell $1,000 worth of merchandise a week" are more motivating than vague goals such as "keep in touch with new customers" or "increase merchandise sales." For example, a lack of clear, specific goals is cited as a major cause of the failure of pay-for-performance incentive plans in many organizations.[19] Vague goals can be frustrating for employees.

- In terms of *goal difficulty*, hard goals are more motivating than easy ones. Easy goals provide little challenge for employees and don't require them to increase their output. Highly ambitious but achievable goals ask people to stretch their abilities and provide a basis for greater feelings of accomplishment and personal effectiveness. A study in Germany found that, over a three-year period, only employees who perceived their goals as difficult reported increases in positive emotions and feelings of job satisfaction and success.[20]

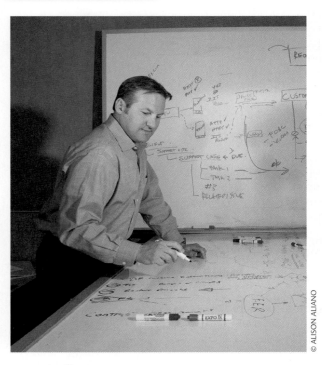

© ALISON ALIANO

Concept Connection At Computerized Facility Integration, **clear, specific goals** enhance employee motivation and commitment. CFI's turnover is 4 percent, dramatically lower than the industry average of 30 percent. Every employee—from clerical help to senior management—receives a monthly bonus for meeting established targets. "It varies by role, of course, but we clearly state what everyone should be achieving, and we reward people accordingly," says founder and CEO Robert Verdun. "One of the big advantages of this bonus system is that it obliges us to keep communicating." The Southfield, Michigan, company installs and services technology systems in office buildings and factories.

- *Goal acceptance* means that employees have to "buy into" the goals and be committed to them. Having people participate in setting goals is a good way to increase acceptance and commitment. At Aluminio del Caroni, a state-owned aluminum company in southeastern Venezuela, plant workers felt a renewed sense of commitment when top leaders implemented a *co-management* initiative that has managers and lower-level employees working together to set budgets, determine goals, and make decisions. "The managers and the workers are running this business together," said one employee who spends his days shoveling molten aluminum down a channel from an industrial oven to a cast. "It gives us the motivation to work hard."[21]

- Finally, the component of *feedback* means that people get information about how well they are doing in progressing toward goal achievement. It is important for managers to provide performance feedback on a regular, ongoing basis. However, self-feedback, where people are able to monitor their own progress toward a goal, has been found to be an even stronger motivator than external feedback.[22]

Why does goal setting increase motivation? For one thing, it enables people to focus their energies in the right direction. People know what to work toward, so they can direct their efforts toward the most important activities to accomplish the goals. Goals also energize behavior because people feel compelled to develop plans and strategies that keep them focused on achieving the target. Specific, difficult goals provide a challenge and encourage people to put forth high levels of effort. In addition, when goals are achieved, pride and satisfaction increase, contributing to higher motivation and morale.[23]

As a new manager, use specific, challenging goals to keep people focused and motivated. Have team members participate in setting goals and determining how to achieve them. Give regular feedback on how people are doing.

TakeaMoment

Equity Theory

Equity theory focuses on individuals' perceptions of how fairly they are treated compared with others. Developed by J. Stacy Adams, equity theory proposes that people are motivated to seek social equity in the rewards they expect for performance.[24]

According to equity theory, if people perceive their compensation as equal to what others receive for similar contributions, they will believe that their treatment is fair and equitable. People evaluate equity by a ratio of inputs to outcomes. Inputs to a job include education, experience, effort, and ability. Outcomes from a job include pay, recognition, benefits, and promotions. The input-to-outcome ratio may be compared to another person in the work group or to a perceived group average. A state of **equity** exists whenever the ratio of one person's outcomes to inputs equals the ratio of another's outcomes to inputs.

Inequity occurs when the input-to-outcome ratios are out of balance, such as when a new, inexperienced employee receives the same salary as a person with a high level of education or experience. Interestingly, perceived inequity also occurs in the other direction. Thus, if an employee discovers she is making more money than other people who contribute the same inputs to the company, she may feel the need to correct the inequity by working harder, getting more education, or considering lower pay. Studies of the brain have shown that people get less satisfaction from money they receive without having to earn it than they do from money they work to receive.[25] Perceived inequity creates tensions within individuals that motivate them to bring equity into balance.[26]

The most common methods for reducing a perceived inequity are these:

- ***Change work effort.*** A person may choose to increase or decrease his or her inputs to the organization. Individuals who believe they are underpaid may reduce their level of effort or increase their absenteeism. Overpaid people may increase effort on the job.

equity theory A process theory that focuses on individuals' perceptions of how fairly they are treated relative to others.

equity A situation that exists when the ratio of one person's outcomes to inputs equals that of another's.

6
Leading

- *Change outcomes.* A person may change his or her outcomes. An underpaid person may request a salary increase or a bigger office. A union may try to improve wages and working conditions to be consistent with a comparable union whose members make more money.

- *Change perceptions.* Research suggests that people may change perceptions of equity if they are unable to change inputs or outcomes. They may artificially increase the status attached to their jobs or distort others' perceived rewards to bring equity into balance.

- *Leave the job.* People who feel inequitably treated may decide to leave their jobs rather than suffer the inequity of being under- or overpaid. In their new jobs, they expect to find a more favorable balance of rewards.

expectancy theory A process theory that proposes that motivation depends on individuals' expectations about their ability to perform tasks and receive desired rewards.

E → P expectancy Expectancy that putting effort into a given task will lead to high performance.

The implication of equity theory for managers is that employees indeed evaluate the perceived equity of their rewards compared to others'. Inequitable pay puts pressure on employees that is sometimes almost too great to bear. They attempt to change their work habits, try to change the system, or leave the job.[27] Consider Deb Allen, who went into the office on a weekend to catch up on work and found a document accidentally left on the copy machine. When she saw that some new hires were earning $200,000 more than their counterparts with more experience, and that "a noted screw-up" was making more than highly competent people, Allen began questioning why she was working on weekends for less pay than many others were receiving. Allen became so demoralized by the inequity that she quit her job three months later.[28]

TakeaMoment | As a new manager, be alert to feelings of inequity among your team members. Don't play favorites, such as regularly praising some while overlooking others making similar contributions. Keep equity in mind when you make decisions about compensation and other rewards.

Expectancy Theory

Concept Connection Circuit City managers are using **expectancy theory** principles to help meet employees' needs while attaining organizational goals. By creating an incentive program that is a commission-based plan designed to provide the highest compensation to sales counselors who are committed to serving every customer, Circuit City achieves its volume and profitability objectives. The incentive program is also used in other areas such as distribution, where employees are recognized for accomplishment in safety, productivity, and attendance.

Expectancy theory suggests that motivation depends on individuals' expectations about their ability to perform tasks and receive desired rewards. Expectancy theory is associated with the work of Victor Vroom, although a number of scholars have made contributions in this area.[29] Expectancy theory is concerned not with identifying types of needs but with the thinking process that individuals use to achieve rewards. Consider Amy Huang, a university student with a strong desire for a B in her accounting course. Amy has a C+ average and one more exam to take. Amy's motivation to study for that last exam will be influenced by: (1) the expectation that hard study will lead to an A on the exam and (2) the expectation that an A on the exam will result in a B for the course. If Amy believes she cannot get an A on the exam or that receiving an A will not lead to a B for the course, she will not be motivated to study exceptionally hard.

Expectancy theory is based on the relationship among the individual's *effort*, the individual's *performance*, and the desirability of *outcomes* associated with high performance. These elements and the relationships among them are illustrated in Exhibit 17.5. The keys to expectancy theory are the expectancies for the relationships among effort, performance, and the value of the outcomes to the individual.

E → P expectancy involves determining whether putting effort into a task will lead to high performance. For this expectancy to be high, the individual must have the ability, previous experience, and necessary equipment, tools, and opportunity to perform. Let's consider a simple sales example. If Carlos, a salesperson at the Diamond Gift Shop, believes that increased selling effort will lead to higher personal sales,

EXHIBIT | **17.5** Major Elements of Expectancy Theory

we can say that he has a high E → P expectancy. However, if Carlos believes he has neither the ability nor the opportunity to achieve high performance, the expectancy will be low, and so will be his motivation.

P → O expectancy involves determining whether successful performance will lead to the desired outcome or reward. If the P → O expectancy is high, the individual will be more highly motivated. If the expectancy is that high performance will not produce the desired outcome, motivation will be lower. If Carlos believes that higher personal sales will lead to a pay increase, we can say that he has a high P → O expectancy. He might be aware that raises are coming up for consideration and talk with his supervisor or other employees to see if increased sales will help him earn a better raise. If not, he will be less motivated to work hard.

Valence is the value of outcomes, or attraction to outcomes, for the individual. If the outcomes that are available from high effort and good performance are not valued by employees, motivation will be low. Likewise, if outcomes have a high value, motivation will be higher. If Carlos places a high value on the pay raise, valence is high and he will have a high motivational force. On the other hand, if the money has low valence for Carlos, the overall motivational force will be low. For an employee to be highly motivated, all three factors in the expectancy model must be high.[30]

Expectancy theory attempts not to define specific types of needs or rewards but only to establish that they exist and may be different for every individual. One employee might want to be promoted to a position of increased responsibility, and another might have high valence for good relationships with peers. Consequently, the first person will be motivated to work hard for a promotion and the second for the opportunity of a team position that will keep him or her associated with a group. Recent studies substantiate the idea that rewards need to be individualized to be motivating. A recent finding from the U.S. Department of Labor shows that the number 1 reason people leave their jobs is because they "don't feel appreciated." Yet Gallup's analysis of 10,000 workgroups in 30 industries found that making people feel appreciated depends on finding the right kind of reward for each individual. Some people prefer tangible rewards or gifts, while others place high value on words of recognition. In addition, some want public recognition while others prefer to be quietly praised by someone they admire and respect.[31]

P → O expectancy Expectancy that successful performance of a task will lead to the desired outcome.

valence The value or attraction an individual has for an outcome.

As a new manager, how would you manage expectations and use rewards to motivate subordinates to perform well? Complete the New Manager Self-Test on page 516 to learn more about your approach to motivating others.

TakeaMoment

New Manager Self-Test

Your Approach to Motivating Others

Think about situations in which you were in a student group or organization. Think about your informal approach as a leader and answer the questions below. Indicate whether each item below is Mostly False or Mostly True for you.

1. I ask the other person what rewards they value for high performance.

2. I only reward people if their performance is up to standard.

3. I find out if the person has the ability to do what needs to be done.

4. I use a variety of rewards (treats, recognition) to reinforce exceptional performance.

5. I explain exactly what needs to be done for the person I'm trying to motivate.

6. I generously and publicly praise people who perform well.

7. Before giving somebody a reward, I find out what would appeal to that person.

8. I promptly commend others when they do a better-than-average job.

SCORING AND INTERPRETATION: The questions above represent two related aspects of motivation theory. For the aspect of *expectancy theory*, sum the points for Mostly True to the odd-numbered questions. For the aspect of *reinforcement theory*, sum the points for Mostly True for the even-numbered questions. The scores for my approach to motivation are:

My use of expectancy theory _____

My use of reinforcement theory _____

These two scores represent how you apply the motivational concepts of expectancy and reinforcement in your role as an informal leader. Three or more points on *expectancy theory* means you motivate people by managing expectations. You understand how a person's effort leads to performance and make sure that high performance leads to valued rewards. Three or more points for *reinforcement theory* means that you attempt to modify people's behavior in a positive direction with frequent and prompt positive reinforcement. New managers often learn to use reinforcements first, and as they gain more experience are able to apply expectancy theory.

SOURCES: These questions are based on D. Whetten and K. Cameron, *Developing Management Skills*, 5th ed. (Upper Saddle River, NJ: Prentice-Hall, 2002), pp. 302–303; and P. M. Podsakoff, S. B. Mackenzie, R. H. Moorman, and R. Fetter, "Transformational Leader Behaviors and Their Effects on Followers' Trust in Leader, Satisfaction, and Organizational Citizenship Behaviors," *Leadership Quarterly* 1, no. 2 (1990): 107–142.

---

reinforcement theory A motivation theory based on the relationship between a given behavior and its consequences.

behavior modification The set of techniques by which reinforcement theory is used to modify human behavior.

law of effect The assumption that positively reinforced behavior tends to be repeated, and unreinforced or negatively reinforced behavior tends to be inhibited.

reinforcement Anything that causes a given behavior to be repeated or inhibited.

positive reinforcement The administration of a pleasant and rewarding consequence following a desired behavior.

REINFORCEMENT PERSPECTIVE ON MOTIVATION

The reinforcement approach to employee motivation sidesteps the issues of employee needs and thinking processes described in the content and process theories. **Reinforcement theory** simply looks at the relationship between behavior and its consequences. It focuses on changing or modifying employees' on-the-job behavior through the appropriate use of immediate rewards and punishments.

Behavior modification is the name given to the set of techniques by which reinforcement theory is used to modify human behavior.[32] The basic assumption underlying behavior modification is the **law of effect**, which states that behavior that is positively reinforced tends to be repeated, and behavior that is not reinforced tends not to be repeated. **Reinforcement** is defined as anything that causes a certain behavior to be repeated or inhibited. The four reinforcement tools are positive reinforcement, avoidance learning, punishment, and extinction, as summarized in Exhibit 17.6.

- **Positive reinforcement** is the administration of a pleasant and rewarding consequence following a desired behavior, such as praise for an employee who

EXHIBIT | 17.6 Changing Behavior with Reinforcement

Positive Reinforcement
Increases likelihood that behavior will be repeated

Avoidance Learning
Increases likelihood that behavior will be repeated

Punishment
Reduces likelihood that behavior will be repeated

Extinction
Reduces likelihood that behavior will be repeated

SOURCE: Based on Richard L. Daft and Richard M. Steers, *Organizations: A Micro/Macro Approach* (Glenview, IL: Scott, Foresman, 1986), p. 109.

arrives on time or does a little extra work. Research shows that positive reinforcement does help to improve performance. Moreover, nonfinancial reinforcements such as positive feedback, social recognition, and attention are just as effective as financial incentives.[33] One study of employees at fast-food drive-thru windows, for example, found that performance feedback and supervisor recognition had a significant effect on increasing the incidence of "up-selling," or asking customers to increase their order.[34] Indeed, many people value factors other than money. Nelson Motivation Inc. conducted a survey of 750 employees across various industries to assess the value they placed on various rewards. Cash and other monetary awards came in dead last. The most valued rewards involved praise and manager support and involvement.[35]

- **Avoidance learning** is the removal of an unpleasant consequence following a desired behavior. Avoidance learning is sometimes called *negative reinforcement*. Employees learn to do the right thing by avoiding unpleasant situations. Avoidance learning occurs when a supervisor stops criticizing or reprimanding an employee once the incorrect behavior has stopped.

- **Punishment** is the imposition of unpleasant outcomes on an employee. Punishment typically occurs following undesirable behavior. For example, a supervisor may berate an employee for performing a task incorrectly. The supervisor expects that the negative outcome will serve as a punishment and reduce the likelihood

© CLAY PETERSON/THE CALIFORNIAN/ASSOCIATED PRESS

Concept Connection Farm managers apply **positive reinforcement** by basing a fruit or vegetable picker's pay on the amount he or she harvests. A variation on this individual piece-rate system is a relative incentive plan that bases each worker's pay on the ratio of the individual's productivity to average productivity among all co-workers. A study of Eastern and Central European pickers in the United Kingdom found that workers' productivity declined under the relative plan. Researchers theorized that fast workers didn't want to hurt their slower colleagues, so they reduced their efforts. The study authors suggested a team-based scheme—where everyone's pay increased if the team did well—would be more effective.

avoidance learning The removal of an unpleasant consequence when an undesirable behavior is corrected.

punishment The imposition of an unpleasant outcome following undesirable behavior.

of the behavior recurring. The use of punishment in organizations is controversial and often criticized because it fails to indicate the correct behavior. However, almost all managers report that they find it necessary to occasionally impose forms of punishment ranging from verbal reprimands to employee suspensions or firings.[36]

- **Extinction** is the withdrawal of a positive reward. Whereas with punishment, the supervisor imposes an unpleasant outcome such as a reprimand, extinction involves withholding pay raises, bonuses, praise, or other positive outcomes. The idea is that behavior that is not positively reinforced will be less likely to occur in the future. A good example of the use of extinction comes from Cheektowaga (New York) Central Middle School, where students with poor grades or bad attitudes are excluded from extracurricular activities such as athletic contests, dances, crafts, or ice-cream socials.[37]

Reward and punishment motivational practices dominate organizations. According to the Society for Human Resource Management, 84 percent of all companies in the United States offer some type of monetary or nonmonetary reward system, and 69 percent offer incentive pay, such as bonuses, based on an employee's performance.[38] However, in other studies, more than 80 percent of employers with incentive programs have reported that their programs are only somewhat successful or not working at all.[39] Despite the testimonies of organizations that enjoy successful incentive programs, criticism of these "carrot-and-stick" methods is growing, as discussed in the Manager's Shoptalk.

TakeaMoment | **As a new manager, remember that reward and punishment practices are limited motivational tools because they focus only on extrinsic rewards and lower-level needs. Using intrinsic rewards to meet higher level needs is important too.**

JOB DESIGN FOR MOTIVATION

A *job* in an organization is a unit of work that a single employee is responsible for performing. A job could include writing tickets for parking violators in New York City, performing MRIs at Salt Lake Regional Medical Center, reading meters for Pacific Gas and Electric, or doing long-range planning for the WB Television Network. Jobs are an important consideration for motivation because performing their components may provide rewards that meet employees' needs. Managers need to know what aspects of a job provide motivation as well as how to compensate for routine tasks that have little inherent satisfaction. **Job design** is the application of motivational theories to the structure of work for improving productivity and satisfaction. Approaches to job design are generally classified as job simplification, job rotation, job enlargement, and job enrichment.

Job Simplification

Job simplification pursues task efficiency by reducing the number of tasks one person must do. Job simplification is based on principles drawn from scientific management and industrial engineering. Tasks are designed to be simple, repetitive, and standardized. As complexity is stripped from a job, the worker has more time to concentrate on doing more of the same routine task. Workers with low skill levels can perform the job, and the organization achieves a high level of efficiency. Indeed, workers are interchangeable because they need little training or skill and exercise little judgment. As a motivational technique, however, job simplification has failed. People dislike routine and boring jobs and react in a number of negative ways, including sabotage,

extinction The withdrawal of a positive reward.

job design The application of motivational theories to the structure of work for improving productivity and satisfaction.

job simplification A job design whose purpose is to improve task efficiency by reducing the number of tasks a single person must do.

Manager'sShoptalk

The Carrot-and-Stick Controversy

Everybody thought Rob Rodin was crazy when he decided to wipe out all individual incentives for his sales force at Marshall Industries, a large distributor of electronic components based in El Monte, California. He did away with all bonuses, commissions, vacations, and other awards and rewards. All salespeople would receive a base salary plus the opportunity for profit sharing, which would be the same percent of salary for everyone, based on the entire company's performance. Six years later, Rodin says productivity per person has tripled at the company, but still he gets questions and criticism about his decision.

Rodin is standing right in the middle of a big controversy in modern management. Do financial and other rewards really motivate the kind of behavior organizations want and need? A growing number of critics say no, arguing that carrot-and-stick approaches are a holdover from the Industrial Age and are inappropriate and ineffective in today's economy. Today's workplace demands innovation and creativity from everyone—behaviors that rarely are inspired by money or other financial incentives. Reasons for criticism of carrot-and-stick approaches include the following:

1. *Extrinsic rewards diminish intrinsic rewards.* When people are motivated to seek an extrinsic reward, whether it is a bonus, an award, or the approval of a supervisor, generally they focus on the reward rather than on the work they do to achieve it. Thus, the intrinsic satisfaction people receive from performing their jobs actually declines. When people lack intrinsic rewards in their work, their performance stays just adequate to achieve the reward offered. In the worst case, employees may cover up mistakes or cheat to achieve the reward. One study found that teachers who were rewarded for increasing test scores frequently used various forms of cheating, for example.

2. *Extrinsic rewards are temporary.* Offering outside incentives may ensure short-term success, but not long-term high performance. When

employees are focused only on the reward, they lose interest in their work. Without personal interest, the potential for exploration, creativity, and innovation disappears. Although the current deadline or goal may be met, better ways of working and serving customers will not be discovered and the company's long-term success will be affected.

3. *Extrinsic rewards assume people are driven by lower-level needs.* Rewards such as bonuses, pay increases, and even praise presume that the primary reason people initiate and persist in behavior is to satisfy lower-level needs. However, behavior also is based on yearnings for self-expression and on feelings of self-esteem and self-worth. Typical individual incentive programs don't reflect and encourage the myriad behaviors that are motivated by people's need to express themselves and realize their higher needs for growth and fulfillment.

Today's organizations need employees who are motivated to think, experiment, and continuously search for ways to solve new problems. Alfie Kohn, one of the most vocal critics of carrot-and-stick approaches, offers the following advice to managers regarding how to pay employees: "Pay well, pay fairly, and then do everything you can to get money off people's minds." Indeed some evidence indicates that money is not primarily what people work for. Managers should understand the limits of extrinsic motivators and work to satisfy employees' higher, as well as lower, needs. To be motivated, employees need jobs that offer self-satisfaction in addition to a yearly pay raise.

SOURCES: Alfie Kohn, "Incentives Can Be Bad for Business," *Inc.* (January 1998): 93–94; A. J. Vogl, "Carrots, Sticks, and Self-Deception" (an interview with Alfie Kohn), *Across the Board* (January 1994): 39–44; Geoffrey Colvin, "What Money Makes You Do," *Fortune* (August 17, 1998): 213–214; and Jeffrey Pfeffer, "Sins of Commission," *Business 2.0* (May 2004): 56.

---

absenteeism, and unionization. Job simplification is compared with job rotation and job enlargement in Exhibit 17.7.

Job Rotation

Job rotation systematically moves employees from one job to another, thereby increasing the number of different tasks an employee performs without increasing the complexity of any one job. For example, an autoworker might install windshields

job rotation A job design that systematically moves employees from one job to another to provide them with variety and stimulation.

EXHIBIT | 17.7 Types of Job Design

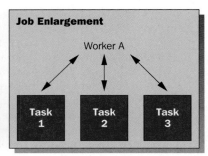

one week and front bumpers the next. Job rotation still takes advantage of engineering efficiencies, but it provides variety and stimulation for employees. Although employees might find the new job interesting at first, the novelty soon wears off as the repetitive work is mastered.

Companies such as Home Depot, Motorola, 1-800-Flowers, and Dayton Hudson have built on the notion of job rotation to train a flexible workforce. As companies break away from ossified job categories, workers can perform several jobs, thereby reducing labor costs and giving people opportunities to develop new skills. At Home Depot, for example, workers scattered throughout the company's vast chain of stores can get a taste of the corporate climate by working at in-store support centers, while associate managers can dirty their hands out on the sales floor.[40] Job rotation also gives companies greater flexibility. One production worker might shift among the jobs of drill operator, punch operator, and assembler, depending on the company's need at the moment. Some unions have resisted the idea, but many now go along, realizing that it helps the company be more competitive.[41]

Job Enlargement

Job enlargement combines a series of tasks into one new, broader job. This type of design is a response to the dissatisfaction of employees with oversimplified jobs. Instead of only one job, an employee may be responsible for three or four and will have more time to do them. Job enlargement provides job variety and a greater challenge for employees. At Maytag, jobs were enlarged when work was redesigned so that workers assembled an entire water pump rather than doing each part as it reached them on the assembly line. Similarly, rather than just changing the oil at a Precision Tune location, a mechanic changes the oil, greases the car, airs the tires, checks fluid levels, battery, air filter, and so forth. Then, the same employee is responsible for consulting with the customer about routine maintenance or any problems he or she sees with the vehicle.

Job Enrichment

Recall the discussion of Maslow's need hierarchy and Herzberg's two-factor theory. Rather than just changing the number and frequency of tasks a worker performs, **job enrichment** incorporates high-level motivators into the work, including job responsibility, recognition, and opportunities for growth, learning, and achievement. In an enriched job, employees have control over the resources necessary for performing it, make decisions on how to do the work, experience personal growth, and set their own work pace. Research shows that when jobs are designed to be controlled more by employees than by managers, people typically feel a greater sense of involvement, commitment, and motivation, which in turn contributes to higher morale, lower turnover, and stronger organizational performance.[42]

Many companies have undertaken job enrichment programs to increase employees' involvement, motivation, and job satisfaction. At Ralcorp's cereal manufacturing

job enlargement A job design that combines a series of tasks into one new, broader job to give employees variety and challenge.

job enrichment A job design that incorporates achievement, recognition, and other high-level motivators into the work.

plant in Sparks, Nevada, for example, assembly-line employees screen, interview, and train all new hires. They are responsible for managing the production flow to and from their upstream and downstream partners, making daily decisions that affect their work, managing quality, and contributing to continuous improvement. Enriched jobs have improved employee motivation and satisfaction, and the company has benefited from higher long-term productivity, reduced costs, and happier, more motivated employees.[43]

Job Characteristics Model

One significant approach to job design is the job characteristics model developed by Richard Hackman and Greg Oldham.[44] Hackman and Oldham's research concerned **work redesign**, which is defined as altering jobs to increase both the quality of employees' work experience and their productivity. Hackman and Oldham's research into the design of hundreds of jobs yielded the **job characteristics model**, which is illustrated in Exhibit 17.8. The model consists of three major parts: core job dimensions, critical psychological states, and employee growth-need strength.

Core Job Dimensions Hackman and Oldham identified five dimensions that determine a job's motivational potential:

1. *Skill variety.* The number of diverse activities that compose a job and the number of skills used to perform it. A routine, repetitive assembly-line job is low in variety, whereas an applied research position that entails working on new problems every day is high in variety.

2. *Task identity.* The degree to which an employee performs a total job with a recognizable beginning and ending. A chef who prepares an entire meal has more task identity than a worker on a cafeteria line who ladles mashed potatoes.

3. *Task significance.* The degree to which the job is perceived as important and having impact on the company or consumers. People who distribute penicillin and other medical supplies during times of emergencies would feel they have significant jobs.

4. *Autonomy.* The degree to which the worker has freedom, discretion, and self-determination in planning and carrying out tasks. A house painter can determine how to paint the house; a paint sprayer on an assembly line has little autonomy.

work redesign The altering of jobs to increase both the quality of employees' work experience and their productivity.

job characteristics model A model of job design that comprises core job dimensions, critical psychological states, and employee growth-need strength.

EXHIBIT | **17.8** The Job Characteristics Model

SOURCE: Adapted from J. Richard Hackman and G. R. Oldham, "Motivation through the Design of Work: Test of a Theory," *Organizational Behavior and Human Performance* 16 (1976): 256.

6 Leading

5. *Feedback.* The extent to which doing the job provides information back to the employee about his or her performance. Jobs vary in their ability to let workers see the outcomes of their efforts. A football coach knows whether the team won or lost, but a basic research scientist may have to wait years to learn whether a research project was successful.

The job characteristics model says that the more these five core characteristics can be designed into the job, the more the employees will be motivated and the higher will be performance, quality, and satisfaction.

Critical Psychological States The model posits that core job dimensions are more rewarding when individuals experience three psychological states in response to job design. In Exhibit 17.8, skill variety, task identity, and task significance tend to influence the employee's psychological state of *experienced meaningfulness of work.* The work itself is satisfying and provides intrinsic rewards for the worker. The job characteristic of autonomy influences the worker's *experienced responsibility.* The job characteristic of feedback provides the worker with *knowledge of actual results.* The employee thus knows how he or she is doing and can change work performance to increase desired outcomes.

Personal and Work Outcomes The impact of the five job characteristics on the psychological states of experienced meaningfulness, responsibility, and knowledge of actual results leads to the personal and work outcomes of high work motivation, high work performance, high satisfaction, and low absenteeism and turnover.

Employee Growth-Need Strength The final component of the job characteristics model is called *employee growth-need strength*, which means that people have different needs for growth and development. If a person wants to satisfy low-level needs, such as safety and belongingness, the job characteristics model has less effect. When a person has a high need for growth and development, including the desire for personal challenge, achievement, and challenging work, the model is especially effective. People with a high need to grow and expand their abilities respond favorably to the application of the model and to improvements in core job dimensions.

One interesting finding concerns the cross-cultural differences in the impact of job characteristics. Intrinsic factors such as autonomy, challenge, achievement, and recognition can be highly motivating in countries such as the United States. However, they may contribute little to motivation and satisfaction in a country such as Nigeria and might even lead to *demotivation.* A recent study indicates that the link between intrinsic characteristics and job motivation and satisfaction is weaker in economically disadvantaged countries with poor governmental social welfare systems, and in high power distance countries, as defined in Chapter 4.[45] Thus, the job characteristics model would be expected to be less effective in these countries.

INNOVATIVE IDEAS FOR MOTIVATING

Despite the controversy over carrot-and-stick motivational practices discussed in the Shoptalk box earlier in this chapter, organizations are increasingly using various types of incentive compensation as a way to motivate employees to higher levels of performance. Exhibit 17.9 summarizes several popular methods of incentive pay.

TakeaMoment | **Go to the ethical dilemma on pages 528–529 that pertains to the use of incentive compensation as a motivational tool.**

Program	Purpose
Pay for performance	Rewards individual employees in proportion to their performance contributions. Also called *merit pay.*
Gain sharing	Rewards all employees and managers within a business unit when predetermined performance targets are met. Encourages teamwork.
Employee stock ownership plan (ESOP)	Gives employees part ownership of the organization, enabling them to share in improved profit performance.
Lump-sum bonuses	Rewards employees with a one-time cash payment based on performance.
Pay for knowledge	Links employee salary with the number of task skills acquired. Workers are motivated to learn the skills for many jobs, thus increasing company flexibility and efficiency.
Flexible work schedule	*Flextime* allows workers to set their own hours. *Job sharing* allows two or more part-time workers to jointly cover one job. *Telecommuting,* sometimes called *flex-place,* allows employees to work from home or an alternative workplace.
Team-based compensation	Rewards employees for behavior and activities that benefit the team, such as cooperation, listening, and empowering others.
Lifestyle awards	Rewards employees for meeting ambitious goals with luxury items, such as high-definition televisions, tickets to big-name sporting events, and exotic travel.

EXHIBIT | 17.9

New Motivational Compensation Programs

Variable compensation and forms of "at risk" pay are key motivational tools that are becoming more common than fixed salaries at many companies. These programs can be effective if they are used appropriately and combined with motivational ideas that also provide employees with intrinsic rewards and meet higher-level needs. Effective managers don't use incentive plans as the sole basis of motivation. The most effective motivational programs typically involve much more than money or other external rewards. Two recent motivational trends are empowering employees and framing work to have greater meaning.

Empowering People to Meet Higher Needs

One significant way managers can meet higher motivational needs is to shift power down from the top of the organization and share it with employees to enable them to achieve goals. **Empowerment** is power sharing, the delegation of power or authority to subordinates in an organization.[46] Increasing employee power heightens motivation for task accomplishment because people improve their own effectiveness, choosing how to do a task and using their creativity.[47] Research indicates that most people have a need for *self-efficacy,* which is the capacity to produce results or outcomes, to feel that they are effective.[48]

Empowering employees involves giving them four elements that enable them to act more freely to accomplish their jobs: information, knowledge, power, and rewards.[49]

1. *Employees receive information about company performance.* In companies where employees are fully empowered, all employees have access to all financial and operational information.

2. *Employees have knowledge and skills to contribute to company goals.* Companies use training programs and other development tools to help employees acquire the knowledge and skills they need to contribute to organizational performance.

3. *Employees have the power to make substantive decisions.* Empowered employees have the authority to directly influence work procedures and organizational performance, such as through quality circles or self-directed work teams.

empowerment The delegation of power and authority to subordinates.

6 Leading

4. *Employees are rewarded based on company performance.* Organizations that empower workers often reward them based on the results shown in the company's bottom line. Organizations may also use other motivational compensation programs described in Exhibit 17.9 to tie employee efforts to company performance.

Many of today's organizations are implementing empowerment programs, but they are empowering workers to varying degrees. At some companies, empowerment means encouraging workers' ideas while managers retain final authority for decisions; at others it means giving employees almost complete freedom and power to make decisions and exercise initiative and imagination.[50] Current methods of empowerment fall along a continuum, as illustrated in Exhibit 17.10. The continuum runs from a situation in which front-line workers have almost no discretion, such as on a traditional assembly line, to full empowerment, where workers even participate in formulating organizational strategy.

Giving Meaning to Work Through Engagement

Another way to meet higher-level motivational needs and help people get intrinsic rewards from their work is to instill a sense of importance and meaningfulness. In recent years, managers have focused on employee engagement, which puts less

EXHIBIT | 17.10

A Continuum of Empowerment

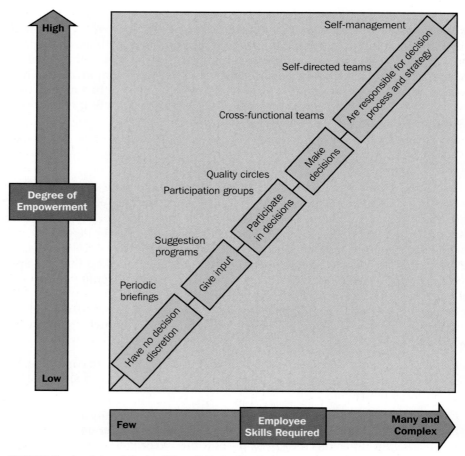

SOURCES: Based on Robert C. Ford and Myron D. Fottler, "Empowerment: A Matter of Degree," *Academy of Management Executive* 9, no. 3 (1995): 21–31; Lawrence Holpp, "Applied Empowerment," *Training* (February 1994): 39–44; and David P. McCaffrey, Sue R. Faerman, and David W. Hart, "The Appeal and Difficulties of Participative Systems," *Organization Science* 6, no. 6 (November–December 1995): 603–627.

emphasis on extrinsic rewards such as pay and more emphasis on fostering an environment in which people feel valued and effective. Employee **engagement** means that people enjoy their jobs and are satisfied with their work conditions, contribute enthusiastically to meeting team and organizational goals, and feel a sense of belonging and commitment to the organization. Fully engaged employees care deeply about the organization and actively seek out ways to serve the mission.[51]

How do managers develop engaged employees? Not by controlling and ordering them around, but by organizing the workplace in such a way that each person can learn, contribute, and grow. Good managers channel employee motivation toward the accomplishment of organizational goals by tapping into each individual's unique set of talents, skills, interests, attitudes, and needs. By treating each employee as an individual, good managers can put people in the right jobs and provide intrinsic rewards to every employee every day. Then, managers make sure people have what they need to perform, clearly define the desired outcomes, and get out of the way. At the Hotel Carlton in San Francisco, something as simple as buying new vacuum cleaners enhances employee engagement.

PHOTO COURTESY TURN HERE, PHOTO BY NAAMAH USSEY

Concept Connection Brad Inman (center), chairman and founder of TurnHere, Inc. of Emeryville, California, gathers his staff every day at 3 p.m. to kick around ideas, see works in progress, talk about the financial status of the company, and discuss how to meet revenue goals. "At first people thought I was crazy when I said we should all get together every day," says Inman, founder of the company that is a leading platform for online video production and provides studio-quality Internet video advertising for clients. But Inman believes involving and listening to employees is critical to **employee engagement**. "The key to retention is for people to feel they are contributing to building something, not just showing up," says Inman.

Innovative Way

Keeping low-skilled service employees engaged can be particularly challenging, but managers at Joie de Vivre Hospitality Inc. are continually searching for ways to do it. At the Hotel Carlton in San Francisco, which Joie de Vivre took over in 2003, one way was to buy a new vacuum for each of the 15 housekeepers and to replace it each year. Previous management had refused to replace the aging vacuums, despite numerous complaints from staff. Buying new vacuums made a big difference in employees' performance and motivation. "It just seems that [they] care more about us," one housekeeper said.

Caring about employees and helping them see their jobs as valuable and fun are top priorities for Joie de Vivre CEO Chip Conley. The company sponsors employee parties and awards, arranges annual employee retreats, and offers free classes on a variety of topics, including English as a second language. Most importantly, it pushes managers to seek and act on feedback from employees, to make the workplace feel like a community of caring, and to find ways to help people see how their jobs make a difference. It is essential, Conley says to "focus on the impact they're making rather than just on the task of cleaning the toilet."[52]

Hotel Carlton, Joie de Vivre Hospitality Inc.

One way to evaluate how a manager or a company is doing in engaging employees is a metric developed by Gallup Organization researchers called the Q12. This list of 12 questions provides a way to assess how managers are doing in creating an environment that helps employees thrive in the workplace. The Q12 includes questions such as whether employees know what is expected of them, have the resources they need to perform well, feel appreciated and recognized for doing good work, believe managers value their opinions, and have opportunities to learn and grow. The full list of 12 questions can be found in the book, *First Break All the Rules*, by researchers Marcus Cunningham and Curt Coffman.[53] When a majority of employees can answer

engagement A situation in which employees enjoy their work, contribute enthusiastically to meeting goals, and feel a sense of belonging and commitment to the organization.

6 Leading

the Q12 questions positively, the organization enjoys a highly motivated, engaged, and productive workforce.

Results of the Gallup study show that organizations where employees give high marks on the Q12 have less turnover, are more productive and profitable, and enjoy greater employee and customer loyalty.[54] Many companies have used the Q12 to pinpoint problems with motivation in the organization and find ways to solve them.

There also is a growing recognition that it is the behavior of managers that makes the biggest difference in whether people feel engaged at work.[55] Gallup Organization research conducted over 25 years indicates that the single most important variable in whether employees feel good about their work is the relationship they have with their direct supervisor.[56] Managers are responsible for keeping employees engaged and motivated so that they—and their organizations—thrive.

ch17   A MANAGER'S ESSENTIALS: WHAT HAVE WE LEARNED?

- This chapter introduced a number of important ideas about the motivation of people in organizations. Rewards are of two types: intrinsic rewards that result from the satisfactions a person receives in the process of performing a job, and extrinsic rewards such as promotions that are given by another person. Managers work to help employees receive both intrinsic and extrinsic rewards from their jobs.

- The content theories of motivation focus on the nature of underlying employee needs. Maslow's hierarchy of needs, Alderfer's ERG theory, Herzberg's two-factor theory, and McClelland's acquired needs theory all suggest that people are motivated to meet a range of needs.

- Process theories examine how people go about selecting rewards with which to meet needs. Goal-setting theory indicates that employees are more motivated if they have clear, specific goals and receive regular feedback concerning their progress toward meeting goals. Equity theory says that people compare their contributions and outcomes with others' and are motivated to maintain a feeling of equity. Expectancy theory suggests that people calculate the probability of achieving certain outcomes. Still another motivational approach is reinforcement theory, which says that employees learn to behave in certain ways based on the use of reinforcements.

- The application of motivational ideas is illustrated in job design and other motivational programs. Job design approaches include job simplification, job rotation, job enlargement, job enrichment, and the job characteristics model. Managers can change the structure of work to meet employees' high-level needs. The recent trend toward empowerment motivates by giving employees more information and authority to make decisions in their work while connecting compensation to the results.

- Employee engagement has become one of the hottest topics in management. By engaging employees, managers can instill employees with a sense of importance and meaningfulness, helping them reap intrinsic rewards and meet higher level needs. One way to measure the factors that determine whether people have high levels of engagement and motivation is the Q12, a list of 12 questions about the day-to-day realities of a person's job and workplace relationships.

ch17 DISCUSSION QUESTIONS

1. In response to security threats in today's world, the U.S. government federalized airport security workers. Many argued that simply making screeners federal workers would not solve the root problem: bored, low-paid, and poorly trained security workers have little motivation to be vigilant. How might these employees be motivated to provide the security that travel conditions now demand?

2. One small company recognizes an employee of the month, who is given a parking spot next to the president's space near the front door. What theories would explain the positive motivation associated with this policy?

3. Campbell Soup Company reduces accidents with a lottery. Each worker who works 30 days or more without losing a day for a job-related accident is eligible to win prizes in a raffle drawing. Why has this program been successful?

4. If an experienced secretary discovered that she made less money than a newly hired janitor, how would she react? What inputs and outcomes might she evaluate to make this comparison?

5. What intrinsic rewards do you experience in your role as a student? Extrinsic rewards? Are intrinsic or extrinsic rewards generally more important motivators for you?

6. Would you rather work for a supervisor high in need for achievement, need for affiliation, or need for power? Why? What are the advantages and disadvantages of each?

7. A survey of teachers found that two of the most important rewards were the belief that their work was important and a feeling of accomplishment. Is this consistent with Hackman and Oldham's job characteristics model? Explain.

8. The teachers in question 7 also reported that pay and benefits were poor, yet they continue to teach. Use Herzberg's two-factor theory to explain this finding.

9. What theories explain why employees who score high on the Q12 questionnaire are typically highly motivated and productive?

10. How can empowerment lead to higher motivation? Could a manager's empowerment efforts sometimes contribute to demotivation as well? Discuss.

11. Why might intrinsic factors such as achievement and recognition be less motivating in a poor country such as Nigeria than they are in the United States?

ch17 MANAGEMENT IN PRACTICE: EXPERIENTIAL EXERCISE

What Motivates You?

Indicate how important each characteristic is to you. Answer according to your feelings about the most recent job you had or about the job you currently hold. Circle the number on the scale that represents your feeling—1 (very unimportant) to 7 (very important).

1. The feeling of self-esteem a person gets from being in that job

   1 2 3 4 5 6 7

2. The opportunity for personal growth and development in that job

   1 2 3 4 5 6 7

3. The prestige of the job inside the company (i.e., regard received from others in the company)

   1 2 3 4 5 6 7

4. The opportunity for independent thought and action in that job

   1 2 3 4 5 6 7

5. The feeling of security in that job

   1 2 3 4 5 6 7

6. The feeling of self-fulfillment a person gets from being in that position (i.e., the feeling of being able to use one's own unique capabilities, realizing one's potential)

   1 2 3 4 5 6 7

7. The prestige of the job outside the company (i.e., the regard received from others not in the company)

   1 2 3 4 5 6 7

8. The feeling of worthwhile accomplishment in that job

   1 2 3 4 5 6 7

9. The opportunity in that job to give help to other people

   1 2 3 4 5 6 7

10. The opportunity in that job for participation in the setting of goals

    1 2 3 4 5 6 7

6 Leading

11. The opportunity in that job for participation in the determination of methods and procedures

1 2 3 4 5 6 7

12. The authority connected with the job

1 2 3 4 5 6 7

13. The opportunity to develop close friendships in the job

1 2 3 4 5 6 7

Scoring and Interpretation

Score the exercise as follows to determine what motivates you:

Rating for question 5 = _____.
Divide by 1 = _____ security.

Rating for questions 9 and 13 = _____.
Divide by 2 = _____ social.

Rating for questions 1, 3, and 7 = _____.
Divide by 3 = _____ esteem.

Rating for questions 4, 10, 11, and 12 = _____.
Divide by 4 = _____ autonomy.

Rating for questions 2, 6, and 8 = _____.
Divide by 3 = _____ self-actualization.

Your instructor has national norm scores for presidents, vice presidents, and upper middle-level, lower middle-level, and lower-level managers with which you can compare your mean importance scores. How do your scores compare with the scores of managers working in organizations?

SOURCE: Lyman W. Porter, *Organizational Patterns of Managerial Job Attitudes* (New York: American Foundation for Management Research, 1964): 17, 19. Used with permission.

---

ch17 MANAGEMENT IN PRACTICE: ETHICAL DILEMMA

To Renege or Not to Renege?

Federico Garcia, vice president of sales for Tacoma, Washington-based Puget Sound Building Materials, wasn't all that surprised by what company president Michael Otto and CFO James Wilson had to say during their meeting that morning.

Last year, launching a major expansion made sense to everyone at Puget, a well-established company that provided building materials as well as manufacturing and installation services to residential builders in the Washington and Oregon markets. Puget looked at the record new housing starts and decided it was time to move into the California and Arizona markets, especially concentrating on San Diego and Phoenix, two of the hottest housing markets in the country. Federico carefully hired promising new sales representatives and offered them hefty bonuses if they reached the goals set for the new territory over the next 12 months. All of the representatives had performed well, and three of them had exceeded Puget's goal—and then some. The incentive system he'd put in place had worked well. The sales reps were expecting handsome bonuses for their hard work.

Early on, however, it became all too clear that Puget had seriously underestimated the time it took to build new business relationships and the costs associated with the expansion, a mistake that was already eating into profit margins. Even more distressing were the most recent figures for new housing starts, which were heading in the wrong direction. As Michael said, "Granted, it's too early to tell if this is just a pause or the start of a real long-term downturn. But I'm worried. If things get worse, Puget could be in real trouble."

James looked at Federico and said, "Our lawyers built enough contingency clauses into the sales reps' contracts that we're not really obligated to pay those bonuses you promised. What would you think about not paying them?" Federico turned to the president, who said, "Why don't you think about it, and get back to us with a recommendation?"

Federico felt torn. On the one hand, he knew the CFO was correct. Puget wasn't, strictly speaking, under any legal obligation to pay out the bonuses, and the eroding profit margins were a genuine cause for concern. The president clearly wanted to not pay the bonuses. But Federico had created a first-rate sales force that had done exactly what he'd asked them to do. He prided himself on being a man of his word, someone others could trust. Could he go back on his promises?

What Would You Do?

1. Recommend to the president that a meeting be arranged with the sales representatives entitled to a bonus and tell them that their checks were going to be delayed until the Puget's financial picture clarified. The sales reps would be told that the company had a legal right to delay payment and that it may not be able to pay the bonuses if its financial situation continues to deteriorate.

2. Recommend a meeting with the sales representatives entitled to a bonus and tell them the company's deteriorating financial situation triggers one of the contingency clauses in their contract so that the company won't be issuing their bonus checks. Puget will just have to deal with the negative impact on sales rep motivation.

3. Recommend strongly to the president that Puget pay the bonuses as promised. The legal contracts and financial situation don't matter. Be prepared to resign if the bonuses are not paid as you promised. Your word and a motivated sales team mean everything to you.

SOURCE: Based on Doug Wallace, "The Company Simply Refused to Pay," *Business Ethics* (March–April 2000): 18; and Adam Shell, "Overheated Housing Market Is Cooling," *USA Today* (November 2, 2005): www.usatoday.com/money/economy/housing/2005-11-01-real-estate-usat_x.htm.

ch17 CASE FOR CRITICAL ANALYSIS

Kimbel's Department Store

Frances Patterson, Kimbel's CEO, looked at the latest "Sales by Manager" figures on her daily Web-based sales report. What did these up-to-the-minute numbers tell her about the results of Kimbel's trial of straight commission pay for its salespeople?

A regional chain of upscale department stores based in St. Louis, Kimbel's faces the challenge shared by most department stores these days: how to stop losing share of overall retail sales to discount store chains. A key component of the strategy the company formulated to counter this long-term trend is the revival of great customer service on the floor, once a hallmark of upscale stores. Frances knows Kimbel's has its work cut out for it. When she dropped in on several stores incognito a few years ago, she was dismayed to discover that finding a salesperson actively engaged with a customer was rare. In fact, finding a salesperson when a customer wanted to pay for an item was often difficult.

About a year and a half ago, the CEO read about a quiet revolution sweeping department store retailing. At stores such as Bloomingdale's and Bergdorf Goodman, managers put all salespeople on straight commission. Frances decided to give the system a year long try in two area stores.

Such a plan, she reasoned, would be good for Kimbel's if it lived up to its promise of attracting better salespeople, improving their motivation, and making them more customer-oriented. It could also potentially be good for employees. Salespeople in departments such as electronics, appliances, and jewelry, where expertise and highly personalized services paid off, had long worked solely on commission. But the majority of employees earn an hourly wage plus a meager 0.5 percent commission on total sales. Under the new scheme, all employees earn a 7 percent commission on sales. When she compared the two systems, she saw that a new salesclerk in women's wear would earn $35,000 on $500,000 in sales, as opposed to only $18,000 under the old scheme.

Now, with the trial period about to end, Frances notes that while overall sales in the two stores have increased modestly, so also has employee turnover. When the CEO examined the sales-by-manager figures, it was obvious that some associates had thrived and others had not. Most fell somewhere in the middle.

For example, Juan Santore is enthusiastic about the change—and for good reason. He works in women's designer shoes and handbags, where a single item can cost upwards of $1,000. Motivated largely by the desire to make lots of money, he's a personable, outgoing individual with an entrepreneurial streak. Ever since the straight commission plan took effect, he has put even more time and effort into cultivating relationships with wealthy customers, and it shows. His pay has increased an average of $150 per week.

It's a different story in the lingerie department, where even luxury items have more modest price tags. The lingerie department head, Gladys Weinholtz, said salespeople in her department are demoralized. Several valued employees had quit, and most miss the security of a salary. No matter how hard they work, they cannot match their previous earnings. "Yes, they're paying more attention to customers," conceded Gladys, "but they're so anxious about making ends meet, they tend to pounce on the poor women who wander into the department." Furthermore, lingerie sales associates are giving short shrift to duties such as handling complaints or returns that don't immediately translate into sales. "And boy, do they ever resent the sales superstars in the other departments," said Gladys.

The year is nearly up. It's time to decide. Should Frances declare the straight commission experiment a success on the whole and roll it out across the chain over the next six months?

Questions

1. What theories about motivation underlie the switch from salary to commission pay?

2. What needs are met under the commission system? Are they the same needs in the shoes and handbag department as they are in lingerie? Explain.

3. If you were Frances Patterson, would you go back to the previous compensation system, implement the straight commission plan in all Kimbel's stores, or devise and test some other compensation method? If you decided to test another system, what would it look like?

SOURCES: Based on Cynthia Kyle, "Commissions question—to pay . . . or not to pay?" *Michigan Retailer* (March 2003): www.retailers.com/news/retailers/03mar/mr0303commissions.html; "Opinion: Effective Retail Sales Compensation," *Furniture World Magazine* (March 7, 2006): www.furninfo.com/absolutenm/templates/NewsFeed.asp?articleid=6017; Terry Pristin, "Retailing's Elite Keep the Armani Moving Off the Racks," *The New York Times* (December 22, 2001): D1; Francine Schwadel, "Chain Finds Incentives a Hard Sell," *The Wall Street Journal* (July 5, 1990): B4; and Amy Dunkin, "Now Salespeople Really Must Sell for Their Supper," *BusinessWeek* (July 31, 1989): 50–52.

ch17   ON THE JOB VIDEO CASE

Leadership at P.F. Chang's

How do you manage 97 bistros and 33 diners at once? This isn't a riddle, it is actually the daily challenge of Rick Federico, chairman and CEO of P.F. Chang's, which owns and operates a chain of Asian restaurants across the country. During the time he has been head of the company, Federico has taken on the huge tasks of taking the company public and launching Pei Wei, the firm's chain of diners. In addition, he has developed management teams and laid out clear expectations for his employees. He has earned the respect of his managers, his workers, his customers, and even his competitors. He has won accolades and leadership awards. "Rick has done a great job of building a strong team culture and has built an organization that is based upon quality of execution," notes one colleague. "He has built P.F. Chang's into a concept that is craved and loved by its customers and team members." These characteristics are the attributes of a leader.

Rick Federico knows the restaurant industry. He began his career as a dishwasher for a steak house and worked his way up the management chain. So he understands everyone's job, from busboy to chef to manager. Perhaps that is why he feels comfortable fostering a team atmosphere at P.F. Chang's, giving employees the authority to make decisions to please customers and ultimately benefit the restaurant. And because he has so many contacts throughout the industry, he is able to attract the best staff, from hourly employees to restaurant managers. At the same time, he maintains a clear vision for the company as a whole. He believes that restaurants based on an Asian menu will continue to grow in popularity—and that developing a recognizable Asian brand is a huge opportunity. Everything at P.F. Chang's two types of restaurants—bistros and diners—is designed with this vision of growth in mind. From tableside cooking to replicas of 12th-century Chinese murals, the entire P.F. Chang's dining expe-rience is intended to leave a strong impression on customers, which is exactly what Federico wants.

While the restaurant industry in general has suffered during the past few years, P.F. Chang's has managed to grow. Federico is both philosophical and practical about the obstacles that every restaurant faces during uncertain times. "While so many of the challenges that face our industry are out of our control, our greatest challenge is also our greatest opportunity: our people," he says. "We are in the hospitality service industry, and our business is to provide our customers with an outstanding dining experience each and every time they walk through our doors." One way he accomplishes this goal is by empowering employees to make decisions, such as fulfilling special requests from customers. And because of its success, P.F. Chang's has been able to create hundreds of jobs across the country while other restaurant chains are laying off workers.

Federico expects results from every team, manager, and worker. But he expects no less from himself. "I'm a reflection of our employees," he muses. "I surround myself with people better than I am in certain areas." He believes his greatest tasks as a leader involve remaining focused on his customers, his workers, and the food they serve. As P.F. Chang's grows, he wants to be sure that the quality of service, atmosphere, and food are always at their highest. He's not afraid to look in the mirror for the solution to a problem. "I suppose the day I'm not an effective leader, I'll be out of here," he admits. For now, he'll be busy coming up with ways to make P.F. Chang's bigger, better, and eventually, a household name.

Questions

1. Describe some of Rick Federico's personal leadership traits.

2. Would you characterize Rick Federico as a charismatic or transformational leader? Why?

3. Which of the five sources of power does Rick Federico use most?

SOURCES: Company Web site, *http://www.pfchangs.com*, accessed August 26, 2004, Charles Bernstein, "Chief Execution Officer," *Chain Leader*, September 2004, 62–68; "Work Force Still Top Concern for CEOs," *The Phoenix Business Journal*, May 24, 2004, *http://phoenix .bizjournals.com*.

ch17 BIZ FLIX VIDEO CASE

Apollo 13

This film re-creates the heroic efforts of astronaut Jim Lovell (Tom Hanks), his crew, NASA, and Mission Control to return the damaged Apollo spacecraft to earth. Examples of both problem solving and decision making occur in almost every scene. See the earlier Biz Flix exercise for more information about this film and a discussion of another scene.

This scene takes place during day five of the mission about two-thirds of the way through the film. Early in Apollo 13's mission Jack Swigert (Kevin Bacon) stirred the oxygen tanks at the request of Mission Control. After this procedure, an explosion occurred, causing unknown damage to the command module. Before the scene takes place, the damage has forced the crew to move into the LEM (Lunar Exploration Module), which becomes their lifeboat for return to earth.

What to Watch for and Ask Yourself

1. What triggers the conflict in this scene?

2. Is this intergroup conflict or intragroup conflict? What effects can such conflict have on the group dynamics on board Apollo 13?

3. Does mission commander Jim Lovell successfully manage the group dynamics to return the group to a normal state?

6 Leading

ch17 ENDNOTES

1. Questions based on Mitchell M. Handelsman, William L. Briggs, Nora Sullivan, and Annette Towler, "A Measure of College Student Course Engagement," *Journal of Educational Research* 98 (January/February 2005): 184–191.

2. David Silburt, "Secrets of the Super Sellers," *Canadian Business* (January 1987): 54–59; "Meet the Savvy Supersalesmen," *Fortune* (February 4, 1985): 56–62; Michael Brody, "Meet Today's Young American Worker," *Fortune* (November 11, 1985): 90–98; and Tom Richman, "Meet the Masters. They Could Sell You Anything," *Inc.* (March 1985): 79–86.

3. Richard M. Steers and Lyman W. Porter, eds., *Motivation and Work Behavior*, 3rd ed. (New York: McGraw-Hill, 1983); Don Hellriegel, John W. Slocum, Jr., and Richard W. Woodman, *Organizational Behavior*, 7th ed. (St. Paul, MN: West, 1995), p. 170; and Jerry L. Gray and Frederick A. Starke, *Organizational Behavior: Concepts and Applications*, 4th ed. (New York: Macmillan, 1988), pp.104–105.

4. Carol Hymowitz, "Readers Tell Tales of Success and Failure Using Rating Systems," *The Wall Street Journal*, May 29, 2001.

5. Alan Deutschman, "Can Google Stay Google?" *Fast Company* (August 2005): 62–68.

6. See Linda Grant, "Happy Workers, High Returns," *Fortune* (January 12, 1998): 81; Elizabeth J. Hawk and Garrett J. Sheridan, "The Right Stuff," *Management Review* (June 1999): 43–48; Michael West and Malcolm Patterson, "Profitable Personnel," *People Management* (January 8, 1998): 28–31; Anne Fisher, "Why Passion Pays," *FSB* (September 2002): 58; and Curt Coffman and Gabriel Gonzalez-Molina, *Follow This Path: How the World's Great Organizations Drive Growth By Unleashing Human Potential* (New York: Warner Books, 2002).

7. Abraham F. Maslow, "A Theory of Human Motivation," *Psychological Review* 50 (1943): 370–396.

8. Sarah Pass, "On the Line," *People Management* (September 15, 2005): 38.

9. Clayton Alderfer, *Existence, Relatedness, and Growth* (New York: Free Press, 1972).

10. Robert Levering and Milton Moskowitz, "2004 Special Report: The 100 Best Companies To Work For," *Fortune* (January 12, 2004): 56–78.

11. Jena McGregor, "Employee Innovator; Winner: USAA," *Fast Company* (October 2005): 57.

12. Jeff Barbian, "C'mon, Get Happy," *Training* (January 2001): 92–96.

13. Karol Rose, "Work-Life Effectiveness," *Fortune* (September 29, 2003): S1–S17.

14. Frederick Herzberg, "One More Time: How Do You Motivate Employees?" *Harvard Business Review* (January 2003): 87–96.

15. David C. McClelland, *Human Motivation* (Glenview, IL: Scott, Foresman, 1985).

16. David C. McClelland, "The Two Faces of Power," in *Organizational Psychology*, ed. D. A. Colb, I. M. Rubin, and J. M. McIntyre (Englewood Cliffs, NJ: Prentice Hall, 1971), pp. 73–86.

17. See Gary P. Latham and Edwin A. Locke, "Enhancing the Benefits and Overcoming the Pitfalls of Goal Setting," *Organizational Dynamics* 35, no. 4 (2006): 332–338; Edwin A. Locke and Gary P. Latham, "Building a Practically Useful Theory of Goal Setting and Task Motivation: A 35-Year Odyssey," *The American Psychologist* 57, no. 9 (September 2002): 705ff; Gary P. Latham and Edwin A. Locke, "Self-Regulation through Goal Setting," *Organizational Behavior and Human Decision Processes* 50, no. 2 (December, 1991): 212–247; G. P. Latham and G. H. Seijts, "The Effects of Proximal and Distal Goals on Performance of a Moderately Complex Task," *Journal of Organizational Behavior* 20, no. 4 (1999): 421–428; P. C. Early, T. Connolly, and G. Ekegren, "Goals, Strategy Development, and Task Performance: Some Limits on the Efficacy of Goal Setting," *Journal of Applied Psychology* 74 (1989): 24–33; E. A. Locke, "Toward a Theory of Task Motivation and Incentives," *Organizational Behavior and Human Performance* 3 (1968): 157–189; Gerard H. Seijts, Ree M. Meertens, and Gerjo Kok, "The Effects of Task Importance and Publicness on the Relation Between Goal Difficulty and Performance," *Canadian Journal of Behavioural Science* 29, no. 1 (1997): 54ff.

18. Locke and Latham, "Building a Practically Useful Theory of Goal Setting and Task Motivation."

19. Edwin A. Locke, "Linking Goals to Monetary Incentives," *Academy of Management Executive* 18, no. 4 (2005): 130–133.

20. Latham and Locke, "Enhancing the Benefits and Overcoming the Pitfalls of Goal Setting."

21. Brian Ellsworth, "Making a Place for Blue Collars in the Boardroom," *The New York Times*, August 3, 2005.

22. J. M. Ivanecevich and J. T. McMahon, "The Effects of Goal Setting, External Feedback, and Self-Generated Feedback on Outcome Variables: A Field Experiment," *Academy of Management Journal* 25, no. 2 (June 1982): 359–372; G. P. Latham and E. A. Locke, "Self-Regulation Through Goal Setting," *Organizational Behavior and Human Decision Processes* 50, no. 2 (1991): 212–247.

23. Gary P. Latham, "The Motivational Benefits of Goal-Setting," *Academy of Management Executive* 18, no. 4 (2004): 126–129.

24. J. Stacy Adams, "Injustice in Social Exchange," in *Advances in Experimental Social Psychology*, 2nd ed., ed. L. Berkowitz (New York: Academic Press, 1965); and J. Stacy Adams, "Toward an Understanding of Inequity," *Journal of Abnormal and Social Psychology* (November 1963): 422–436.

25. "Study: The Brain Prefers Working Over Getting Money for Nothing," *TheJournalNews.com*, May 14, 2004, www.thejournalnews.com/apps/pbcs.dll/frontpage.

26. Ray V. Montagno, "The Effects of Comparison to Others and Primary Experience on Responses to Task Design," *Academy of Management Journal* 28 (1985): 491–498; and Robert P. Vecchio, "Predicting Worker Performance in Inequitable

Settings," *Academy of Management Review* 7 (1982): 103–110.

27. James E. Martin and Melanie M. Peterson, "Two-Tier Wage Structures: Implications for Equity Theory," *Academy of Management Journal* 30 (1987): 297–315.

28. Jared Sandberg, "Why You May Regret Looking at Papers Left on the Office Copier," *The Wall Street Journal*, June 20, 2006.

29. Victor H. Vroom, *Work and Motivation* (New York: Wiley, 1964); B. S. Gorgopoulos, G. M. Mahoney, and N. Jones, "A Path-Goal Approach to Productivity," *Journal of Applied Psychology* 41 (1957): 345–353; and E. E. Lawler III, *Pay and Organizational Effectiveness: A Psychological View* (New York: McGraw-Hill, 1981).

30. Richard L. Daft and Richard M. Steers, *Organizations: A Micro/Macro Approach* (Glenview, IL: Scott, Foresman, 1986).

31. Studies reported in Tom Rath, "The Best Way to Recognize Employees," *Gallup Management Journal* (December 9, 2004): 1–5; and Erin White, "Theory & Practice: Praise from Peers Goes a Long Way— Recognition Programs Help Companies Retain Workers as Pay Raises Get Smaller," *The Wall Street Journal*, December 19, 2005.

32. Alexander D. Stajkovic and Fred Luthans, "A Meta-Analysis of the Effects of Organizational Behavior Modification on Task Performance, 1975–95," *Academy of Management Journal* (October 1997): 1122–1149; H. Richlin, *Modern Behaviorism* (San Francisco: Freeman, 1970); and B. F. Skinner, *Science and Human Behavior* (New York: Macmillan, 1953).

33. Stajkovic and Luthans, "Effects of Organizational Behavior Modification on Task Performance," and Fred Luthans and Alexander D. Stajkovic, "Reinforce for Performance: The Need to Go Beyond Pay and Even Rewards," *Academy of Management Executive* 13, no. 2 (1999): 49–57.

34. Daryl W. Wiesman, "The Effects of Performance Feedback and Social Reinforcement on Up-Selling at Fast-Food Restaurants," *Journal of Organizational Behavior Management* 26, no. 4 (2006): 1–18.

35. Reported in Charlotte Garvey, "Meaningful Tokens of Appreciation," *HR Magazine* (August 2004): 101–105.

36. Kenneth D. Butterfield and Linda Klebe Treviño, "Punishment from the Manager's Perspective: A Grounded Investigation and Inductive Model," *Academy of Management Journal* 39, no. 6 (December 1996): 1479–1512; and Andrea Casey, "Voices from the Firing Line: Managers Discuss Punishment in the Workplace," *Academy of Management Executive* 11, no. 3 (1997): 93–94.

37. Winnie Hu, "School's New Rule for Pupils in Trouble: No Fun," *The New York Times*, April 4, 2008.

38. Amy Joyce, "The Bonus Question; Some Managers Still Strive to Reward Merit," *The Washington Post*, November 13, 2005.

39. Survey results from World at Work and Hewitt Associates, reported in Karen Kroll, "Benefits: Paying for Performance," *Inc.* (November 2004): 46; and Kathy Chu, "Firms Report Lackluster Results from Pay-for-Performance Plans," *The Wall Street Journal*, June 15, 2004.

40. Barbian, "C'mon, Get Happy."

41. Norm Alster, "What Flexible Workers Can Do," *Fortune* (February 13, 1989): 62–66.

42. Christine M. Riordan, Robert J. Vandenberg, and Hettie A. Richardson, "Employee Involvement Climate and Organizational Effectiveness," *Human Resource Management* 44, no. 4 (Winter 2005): 471–488.

43. Glenn L. Dalton, "The Collective Stretch," *Management Review* (December 1998): 54–59.

44. J. Richard Hackman and Greg R. Oldham, *Work Redesign* (Reading, MA: Addison-Wesley, 1980); and J. Richard Hackman and Greg Oldham, "Motivation through the Design of Work: Test of a Theory," *Organizational Behavior and Human Performance* 16 (1976): 250–279.

45. Xu Huang and Evert Van de Vliert, "Where Intrinsic Job Satisfaction Fails to Work: National Moderators of Intrinsic Motivation," *Journal of Organizational Behavior* 24 (2003): 157–179.

46. Edwin P. Hollander and Lynn R. Offermann, "Power and Leadership in Organizations," *American Psychologist* 45 (February 1990): 179–189.

47. Jay A. Conger and Rabindra N. Kanungo, "The Empowerment Process: Integrating Theory and Practice," *Academy of Management Review* 13 (1988): 471–482.

48. Ibid.

49. David E. Bowen and Edward E. Lawler III, "The Empowerment of Service Workers: What, Why, How, and When," *Sloan Management Review* (Spring 1992): 31–39; and Ray W. Coye and James A. Belohav, "An Exploratory Analysis of Employee Participation," *Group and Organization Management* 20, no. 1, (March 1995): 4–17.

50. This discussion is based on Robert C. Ford and Myron D. Fottler, "Empowerment: A Matter of Degree," *Academy of Management Executive* 9, no. 3 (1995): 21–31.

51. This definition is based on Mercer Human Resource Consulting's Employee Engagement Model, as described in Paul Sanchez and Dan McCauley, "Measuring and Managing Engagement in a Cross-Cultural Workforce: New Insights for Global Companies," *Global Business and Organizational Excellence* (November–December 2006): 41–50.

52. Phred Dvorak, "Hotelier Finds Happiness Keeps Staff Checked In" (Theory & Practice column), *The Wall Street Journal*, December 17, 2007.

53. Marcus Buckingham and Curt Coffman, *First, Break All the Rules: What the World's Gretest Managers Do Differently* (New York: Simon & Schuster, 1999).

54. Curt Coffman and Gabriel Gonzalez-Molina, *Follow This Path: How the World's Greatest Organizations Drive Growth by Unleashing Human Potential* (New York: Warner Books, 2002), as reported in Anne Fisher, "Why Passion Pays," *FSB* (September 2002): 58.

55. Theresa M. Welbourne, "Employee Engagement: Beyond the Fad and Into the Executive Suite," *Leader to Leader* (Spring 2007): 45–51.

56. This discussion is based on Tony Schwartz, "The Greatest Sources of Satisfaction in the Workplace are Internal and Emotional," *Fast Company* (November 2000): 398–402; Marcus Buckingham and Curt Coffman, *First, Break All the Rules: What the World's Greatest Managers Do Differently* (New York: Simon and Schuster, 1999); and Krueger and Killham, "At Work, Feeling Good Matters."

6 Leading

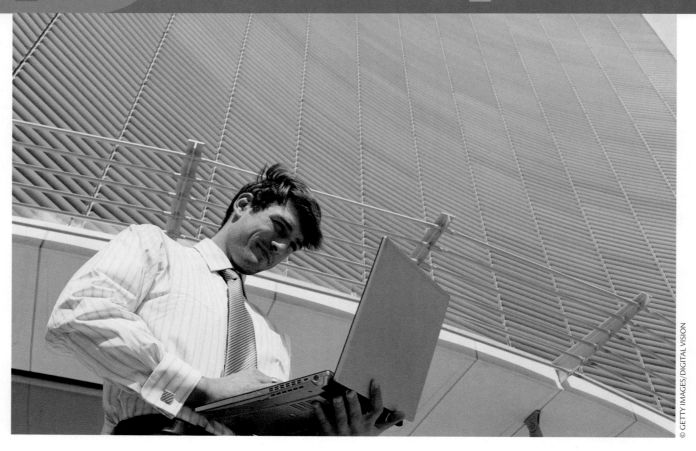

© GETTY IMAGES/DIGITAL VISION

Learning Outcomes

After studying this chapter, you should be able to:

1. Explain why communication is essential for effective management, and describe the communication process.

2. Describe the concept of channel richness, and explain how communication channels influence the quality of communication.

3. Understand how gender differences, nonverbal communication, and listening affect the effectiveness of communication.

4. Explain the difference between formal and informal organizational communications and the importance of each for organization management.

5. Identify how structure influences team communication outcomes.

6. Appreciate the role of personal communication channels in enhancing organizational communication.

7. Recognize the manager's role in creating dialogue, managing crisis communication, offering feedback, and creating a climate of trust.

Managing Communication

ARE YOU BUILDING A PERSONAL NETWORK?

How much effort do you put into developing connections with other people? Personal networks may help a new manager in the workplace. To learn something about your networking skills, answer the questions below. Please indicate whether each item is Mostly True or Mostly False for you in school or at work.

	Mostly True	Mostly False
1. I learn early on about changes going on in the organization and how they might affect me or my position.		
2. I network as much to help other people solve problems as to help myself.		
3. I am fascinated by other people and what they do.		
4. I frequently use lunches to meet and network with new people.		
5. I regularly participate in charitable causes.		
6. I maintain a list of friends and colleagues to whom I send holiday greeting cards.		
7. I maintain contact with people from previous organizations and school groups.		
8. I actively give information to subordinates, peers, and my boss.		

SCORING AND INTERPRETATION: Give yourself one point for each item marked as Mostly True. A score of six or higher suggests active networking and a solid foundation on which to begin your career as a new manager. When you create a personal network, you become well connected to get things done through a variety of relationships. Having sources of information and support helps a new manager gain career traction. If you scored three or less, you may want to focus more on building relationships if you are serious about a career as a manager. People with active networks tend to be more effective managers and have broader impact on the organization.

Personal networking is an important skill for managers because it enables them to get things done more smoothly and rapidly than they could do in isolation. Networking builds social, work, and career relationships that facilitate mutual benefit. How do managers build a personal network that includes a broad range of professional and social relationships? One key is knowing how to communicate effectively. In fact, communication is a vital factor in every aspect of the manager's job.

Organizations in today's complex business environment depend on effective communication to ensure business success. This is especially true in the competitive world of retailing. Target, ranked 33rd on the *Fortune* 500, banks on a steady stream of bold new product ideas to stay competitive against Wal-Mart and its low-price strategy. Yet Target managers know employee enthusiasm and knowledge is just as important as the products. Target educates employees with frequent communication about the company's vision, values, and strategic goals. Before trendsetting new products are launched in stores, for example, top managers thoroughly educate more than 150 marketing managers, PR representatives, and even the training staff on the marketing strategy behind each product. "We take the time to communicate to our broad organization what they do, why they're doing it, and how it fits the whole," explains CEO Gregg Steinhafel.[1]

Target's managers know that effective organizational communication leads to business success and impressive financial gains. A study by Watson Wyatt Worldwide found that companies with the most effective communication programs had a 47 percent higher total return to shareholders from 2002 to 2006 when compared with companies that had less effective communication.[2]

Not only does effective communication lead to better bottom-line results, but much of a manager's time is spent communicating. Managers spend at least 80 percent of every working day in direct communication with others. In other words, 48 minutes of every hour is spent in meetings, on the telephone, communicating online, or talking informally while walking around. The other 20 percent of a typical manager's time is spent doing desk work, most of which is also communication in the form of reading and writing.[3]

This chapter explains why managers should make effective communication a priority. First, we examine communication as a crucial part of the manager's job and describe a model of the communication process. Next, we consider the interpersonal aspects of communication, including communication channels, persuasion, gender differences, listening skills, and nonverbal communication that affect managers' ability to communicate. Then, we look at the organization as a whole and consider formal upward, downward, and horizontal communications as well as personal networks and informal communications. Finally, we describe the manager's role in creating dialogue, managing crisis communication, using feedback and learning to improve employee performance, and creating a climate of trust and openness.

strategic conversation Dialogue across boundaries and hierarchical levels about the team or organization's vision, critical strategic themes, and the values that help achieve important goals.

COMMUNICATION IS THE MANAGER'S JOB

Exhibit 18.1 illustrates the crucial role of managers as communication champions. Managers gather important information from both inside and outside the organization and then distribute appropriate information to others who need it. Managers' communication is *purpose-directed* in that it directs everyone's attention toward the vision, values, and desired goals of the team or organization and influences people to act in a way to achieve the goals. Managers facilitate *strategic conversations* by using open communication, actively listening to others, applying the practice of dialogue, and using feedback for learning and change. **Strategic conversation** refers to people talking across boundaries and hierarchical levels about the team or organization's vision, critical strategic themes, and the values that help achieve important goals.[4] For example, at Royal Philips Electronics, president Gerald Kleisterlee defined four strategic technology themes that he believes should define Philips's future in the industry: display, storage, connectivity, and digital video processing. These themes intentionally cross technology boundaries, which require that people communicate and collaborate across departments and divisions to accomplish goals.[5]

© BILL GREENBLATT/UPI/LANDOV

Concept Connection As **communication champion** for Marriott International, CEO Bill Marriott gathers information and communicates the vision, values, and goals of the company. Here he stops to congratulate employees on the opening of a new Renaissance Grand Hotel in downtown St. Louis. In his blog, Marriott on the Move at *www.blogs.marriott.com*, the CEO opens communication with Marriott customers and employees and shares his views on current events and how they affect the company's mission.

EXHIBIT | 18.1

The Manager as Communication Champion

External Information

Internal Information

Manager as Communication Champion

Purpose-Directed
- Direct attention to vision, values, desired outcomes
- Influence employee behavior

Strategic Conversations
- Open communication
- Listening
- Dialogue
- Feedback

Methods
- Rich channels
- Upward, downward, and horizontal channels
- Nonverbal communication
- Personal networks

SOURCES: Adapted from Henry Mintzberg, *The Nature of Managerial Work* (New York: Harper and Row, 1973); and Richard L. Daft, *The Leadership Experience*, 3rd ed. (Cincinnati, OH: South-Western, 2005), p. 346.

Communication permeates every management function described in Chapter 1.[6] For example, when managers perform the planning function, they gather information; write letters, memos, and reports; and meet with other managers to formulate the plan. When managers lead, they communicate to share a vision of what the organization can be and motivate employees to help achieve it. When managers organize, they gather information about the state of the organization and communicate a new structure to others. Communication skills are a fundamental part of every managerial activity.

What Is Communication?

A professor at Harvard once asked a class to define communication by drawing pictures. Most students drew a manager speaking or typing on a computer keyboard. Some placed "speech balloons" next to their characters; others showed pages flying from a printer. "No," the professor told the class, "none of you has captured the essence of communication." He went on to explain that communication means "to share," not "to speak" or "to write."

Communication is the process by which information is exchanged and understood by two or more people, usually with the intent to motivate or influence behavior. Communication is not just sending information. Honoring this distinction between *sharing* and *proclaiming* is crucial for successful management. A manager who does not listen is like a used-car salesperson who claims, "I sold a car—they just did not buy it." Management communication is a two-way street that includes listening and other forms of feedback. Effective communication, in the words of one expert, occurs as follows:

> When two people interact, they put themselves into each other's shoes, try to perceive the world as the other person perceives it, try to predict how the other will respond. Interaction involves reciprocal role-taking, the mutual employment of empathetic skills. The goal of interaction is

communication The process by which information is exchanged and understood by two or more people, usually with the intent to motivate or influence behavior.

6 Leading

the merger of self and other, a complete ability to anticipate, predict, and behave in accordance with the joint needs of self and other.[7]

It is the desire to share understanding that motivates executives to visit employees on the shop floor, hold small informal meetings, or eat with employees in the company cafeteria. The information that managers gather from direct communication with employees shapes their understanding of the organization.

The Communication Process

Many people think communication is simple. After all, we communicate every day without even thinking about it. However, communication usually is complex, and the opportunities for sending or receiving the wrong messages are innumerable. No doubt, you have heard someone say, "But that's not what I meant!" Have you ever received directions you thought were clear and yet still got lost? How often have you wasted time on misunderstood instructions?

To better understand the complexity of the communication process, note the key elements outlined in Exhibit 18.2. Two essential elements in every communication situation are the sender and the receiver. The *sender* is anyone who wishes to convey an idea or concept to others, to seek information, or to express a thought or emotion. The *receiver* is the person to whom the message is sent. The sender **encodes** the idea by selecting symbols with which to compose a message. The **message** is the tangible formulation of the idea that is sent to the receiver. The message is sent through a **channel**, which is the communication carrier. The channel can be a formal report, a telephone call, an e-mail message, or a face-to-face meeting. The receiver **decodes** the symbols to interpret the meaning of the message. Encoding and decoding are potential sources for communication errors, because knowledge, attitudes, and background act as filters and create *noise* when translating from symbols to meaning. Finally, **feedback** occurs when the receiver responds to the sender's communication with a return message. Without feedback, the communication is *one-way*; with feedback, it is *two-way*. Feedback is a powerful aid to communication effectiveness, because it enables the sender to determine whether the receiver correctly interpreted the message.

encode To select symbols with which to compose a message.

message The tangible formulation of an idea to be sent to a receiver.

channel The carrier of a communication.

decode To translate the symbols used in a message for the purpose of interpreting its meaning.

feedback A response by the receiver to the sender's communication.

TakeaMoment | As a new manager, become a communication champion by communicating across boundaries, actively listening to others, and using feedback to make improvements. Remember that effective communication requires sharing and achieving mutual understanding.

EXHIBIT | **18.2**

A Model of the Communication Process

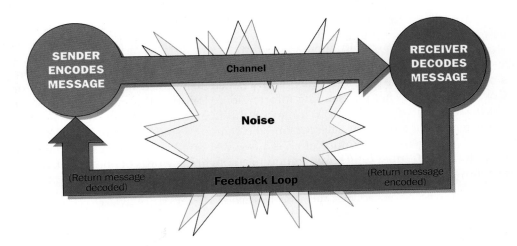

COMMUNICATING AMONG PEOPLE

The communication model in Exhibit 18.2 illustrates the components of effective communication. Communications can break down if sender and receiver do not encode or decode language in the same way.[8] We all know how difficult it is to communicate with someone who does not speak our language, and today's managers are often trying to communicate with people who speak many different native languages. The Manager's Shoptalk offers suggestions for communicating effectively with people who speak a different language.

Manager'sShoptalk

Breaking Down Language Barriers

In today's global business environment, odds are good you'll find yourself conversing with an employee, colleague, or customer who has limited skills in your native language. Here are some guidelines that will help you speak—and listen—more effectively.

1. *Keep your message simple.* Be clear about what you want to communicate, and keep to the point. Avoid slang. Using too many culturally narrow expressions, idioms, colloquialisms, and too much humor can cause your message to be totally lost in translation.

2. *Select your words with care.* Don't try to dazzle with your vocabulary. Choose simple words, and look for opportunities to use cognates—that is, words that resemble words in your listener's language. For example, *banco* in Spanish means "bank" in English. Assemble those simple words into equally simple phrases and short sentences. And be sure to avoid idioms, slang, jargon, and vague terminology such as *soon, often,* or *several.*

3. *Pay close attention to nonverbal messages.* Don't cover your mouth with your hand. Being able to see your lips helps your listener decipher what you are saying.

4. *Speak slowly and carefully.* In particular, avoid running words together. "Howyadoin?" won't make any sense to someone still struggling with the English language, for example.

5. *Allow for pauses.* If you're an American, your culture has taught you to avoid silence whenever possible. However, pauses give your listener time to take in what you have said, ask a question, or formulate a response.

6. *Fight the urge to shout.* Speaking louder doesn't make it any easier for someone to understand you. It also tends to be intimidating and could give the impression that you are angry.

7. *Pay attention to facial expressions and body language, but keep in mind that the meaning of such cues can vary significantly from culture to culture.* For example, Americans may view eye contact as a sign you're giving someone your full attention, but the Japanese consider prolonged eye contact rude.

8. *Check for comprehension frequently, and invite feedback.* Stop from time to time and make sure you're being understood, especially if the other person laughs inappropriately, never asks a question, or continually nods and smiles politely. Ask the listener to repeat what you've said in his or her own words. If you find the other person hasn't understood you, restate the information in a different way instead of simply repeating yourself. Similarly, listen carefully when the non-native speaks, and offer feedback so the person can check your understanding of his or her message.

Effective multicultural communication isn't easy, but a small investment in clear communication will result in trust and improved productivity.

SOURCES: Marshall Goldsmith, "Crossing the Cultural Chasm," *BusinessWeek.com*, May 30, 2007, http://www .businessweek.com/careers/content/may2007/ca20070530_ 521679.htm?chan=search (accessed April 8, 2008); "How to Communicate with a Non Native English Speaker," wikiHow, www.wikihow.com/ Communicate-With-a-Non-Native- English-Speaker; Sondra Thiederman, "Language Barriers: Bridging the Gap," www.thiederman.com/articles_detail .php?id=39; and "Communicating with Non-native Speakers," Magellan Health Services, www.magellanassist.com/mem/ library/default.asp?TopicId=95&CategoryId=0&ArticleId=5.

Many factors can lead to a breakdown in communications. For example, the selection of communication channel can determine whether the message is distorted by noise and interference. The listening skills of both parties and attention to nonverbal behavior can determine whether a message is truly shared. Thus, for managers to be effective communicators, they must understand how factors such as communication channels, the ability to persuade, gender differences, nonverbal behavior, and listening all work to enhance or detract from communication.

Communication Channels

Managers have a choice of many channels through which to communicate to other managers or employees. A manager may discuss a problem face-to-face, make a telephone call, use instant messaging, send an e-mail, write a memo or letter, or post an entry to a company blog, depending on the nature of the message. Research has attempted to explain how managers select communication channels to enhance communication effectiveness.[9] The research has found that channels differ in their capacity to convey information. Just as a pipeline's physical characteristics limit the kind and amount of liquid that can be pumped through it, a communication channel's physical characteristics limit the kind and amount of information that can be conveyed through it. The channels available to managers can be classified into a hierarchy based on information richness.

© POLYCOM, INC./PR NEWSWIRE PHOTO SERVICE

Concept Connection Videoconferencing systems, such as the Polycom high-definition system shown here, use increasingly sophisticated hardware and software to transmit both visual and verbal cues and provide feedback. On large screens in the front of the room, managers not only see and hear colleagues thousands of miles away, but they can also scrutinize displays of relevant information. These new systems provide **channel richness** once characteristic of only face-to-face meetings. Analysts expect that terrorism threats, possible pandemics, and expensive business travel will fuel at least a 20 percent annual increase in spending on videoconferencing systems in the foreseeable future.

The Hierarchy of Channel Richness Channel richness is the amount of information that can be transmitted during a communication episode. The hierarchy of channel richness is illustrated in Exhibit 18.3. The capacity of an information channel is influenced by three characteristics: (1) the ability to handle multiple cues simultaneously; (2) the ability to facilitate rapid, two-way feedback; and (3) the ability to establish a personal focus for the communication. Face-to-face discussion is the richest medium, because it permits direct experience, multiple information cues, immediate feedback, and personal focus. Face-to-face discussions facilitate the assimilation of broad cues and deep, emotional understanding of the situation. Telephone conversations are next in the richness hierarchy. Although eye contact, posture, and other body language cues are missing, the human voice can still carry a tremendous amount of emotional information.

Electronic messaging, such as e-mail and instant messaging, is increasingly being used for messages that were once handled via the telephone. However, in a survey by researchers at The Ohio State University, most respondents said they preferred the telephone or face-to-face conversation for communicating difficult news, giving advice, or expressing affection.[10] Because e-mail messages lack both visual and verbal cues and don't allow for interaction and feedback, messages can sometimes be misunderstood. Using e-mail to discuss disputes, for example, can lead to an escalation rather than a resolution of conflict.[11] Studies have found that e-mail messages tend to be much more blunt than other forms of communication, even other written communications. This bluntness can cause real problems when communicating cross-culturally, because some cultures consider directness rude or insulting.[12] Instant messaging

channel richness The amount of information that can be transmitted during a communication episode.

EXHIBIT | **18.3** A Continuum of Channel Richness

Advantages
Personal
Two-way
Fast feedback

Face-to-face
Communication

High
Channel Richness

Telephone

Electronic Messages
(email, IM, blogs)

Disadvantages
No permanent record
Spontaneous
Difficult to
disseminate

Advantages
Permanent record
Premeditated
Easy to
disseminate

Letters and Memos

Reports/Bulletins

Low
Channel Richness

Disadvantages
Impersonal
One-way
Slow feedback

alleviates the problem of miscommunication to some extent by allowing for immediate feedback. **Instant messaging (IM)** allows users to see who is connected to a network and share short-hand messages or documents with them instantly. A growing number of managers are using IM, indicating that it helps people get responses faster and collaborate more smoothly.[13] Overreliance on e-mail and IM can damage company communications because people stop talking to one another in a rich way that builds solid interpersonal relationships. However, some research indicates that electronic messaging can enable reasonably rich communication if the technology is used appropriately.[14] Organizations are also using videoconferencing that offers video capabilities to provide visual cues and greater channel richness.

Still lower on the hierarchy of channel richness are written letters and memos. Written communication can be personally focused, but it conveys only the cues written on paper and is slower to provide feedback. Impersonal written media, including fliers, bulletins, and standard computer reports, are the lowest in richness. These channels are not focused on a single receiver, use limited information cues, and do not permit feedback.

Selecting the Appropriate Channel It is important for managers to understand that each communication channel has advantages and disadvantages and that each can be an effective means of communication in the appropriate circumstances.[15] Channel selection depends on whether the message is routine or nonroutine. *Nonroutine messages* typically are ambiguous, concern novel events, and involve great potential for misunderstanding. They often are characterized by time pressure and surprise. Managers can communicate nonroutine messages effectively by selecting rich channels. *Routine* messages are simple and straightforward. They convey data or statistics or simply put into words what managers already agree on and understand. Routine messages can be efficiently communicated through a channel lower in richness, such as e-mail. Written communications should also be used when the communication is official and a permanent record is required.[16]

As a new manager, take care in choosing how to send a message. Don't use e-mail for difficult or emotional conversations that should be dealt with face-to-face or by telephone. E-mail is preferable for routine communications.

TakeaMoment

Consider the alert to consumers issued by the FDA following a widespread *E.coli* outbreak in September 2006. Tainted bagged spinach sickened 199 people in at least 26 states and resulted in one death. Grocers immediately pulled the product from shelves, and widespread news coverage warned the public not to consume any bagged spinach until the cause of the contamination could be identified. An

instant messaging (IM)
Electronic communication that allows users to see who is connected to a network and share information instantly.

immediate response was critical. This type of nonroutine communication forces a rich information exchange. The group facing such a communication challenge will meet face-to-face, brainstorm ideas, and provide rapid feedback to resolve the situation and convey the correct information. If, in contrast, an agency director is preparing a press release about a routine matter such as a policy change or new department members, less information capacity is needed. The director and public relations people might begin developing the press release with an exchange of memos, telephone calls, and e-mail messages.

The key is to select a channel to fit the message. During a major acquisition, one firm decided to send top executives to all major work sites of the acquired company, where most of the workers met the managers in person, heard about their plans for the company, and had a chance to ask questions. The results were well worth the time and expense of the personal face-to-face meetings because the acquired workforce saw their new managers as understanding, open, and willing to listen.[17] Communicating their nonroutine message about the acquisition in person prevented damaging rumors and misunderstandings. The choice of a communication channel can also convey a symbolic meaning to the receiver; in a sense, the medium becomes the message. The firm's decision to communicate face-to-face with the acquired workforce signaled to employees that managers cared about them as individuals.

Communicating to Persuade and Influence Others

Communication is not just for conveying information, but also to persuade and influence people. Although communication skills have always been important to managers, the ability to persuade and influence others is even more critical today. Businesses are run largely by cross-functional teams that are actively involved in making decisions. Issuing directives is no longer an appropriate or effective way to get things done.[18]

To persuade and influence, managers have to communicate frequently and easily with others. Yet some people find interpersonal communication experiences unrewarding or difficult and thus tend to avoid situations where communication is required. The term **communication apprehension** describes this avoidance behavior and is defined as "an individual's level of fear or anxiety associated with either real or anticipated communication." With training and practice, managers can overcome their communication apprehension and become more effective communicators.

TakeaMoment | **Go to the experiential exercise on pages 558–559 that pertains to your level of communication apprehension.**

communication apprehension An individual's level of fear or anxiety associated with interpersonal communications.

Effective persuasion doesn't mean telling people what you want them to do; instead, it involves listening, learning about others' interests and needs, and leading people to a shared solution.[19] Managers who forget that communication means *sharing*, as described earlier, aren't likely to be as effective at influencing or persuading others, as the founder and president of the executive coaching firm Valuedance learned the hard way.

Valuedance

Innovative Way

When Susan Cramm was asked by a client to help persuade the client's boss to support an initiative she wanted to launch, Cramm readily agreed. They scheduled a meeting with the boss, then held a series of planning sessions where the two discussed the current situation at the client's firm, weighed the options, and decided on the best approach for launching the initiative. Filled with enthusiasm and armed with a PowerPoint presentation, Cramm was sure the client's boss would see things their way.

An agonizing 15 minutes later, she was out the door, PowerPoint deck and all, having just had a lesson about the art of persuasion. What went wrong? Cramm had focused on the hard, rational matters and ignored the soft skills of relationship building, listening, and negotiating that are so crucial to persuading others. "Never did we consider the boss's views," Cramm said later about the planning sessions she and her client held to prepare for the meeting. "Like founding members of the 'it's all about me' club, we fell upon our swords, believing that our impeccable logic, persistence, and enthusiasm would carry the day."

With that approach, the meeting was over before it even began. The formal presentation shut down communications because it implied that Cramm had all the answers and the boss was just there to listen and agree.[20]

As this example shows, people stop listening to someone when that individual isn't listening to them. By failing to show interest in and respect for the boss's point of view, Cramm and her client lost the boss's interest from the beginning, no matter how suitable the ideas they were presenting. To effectively influence and persuade others, managers have to show they care about how the other person feels. Persuasion requires tapping into people's emotions, which can only be done on a personal, rather than a rational, impersonal level.

Gender Differences in Communication

As a new manager, you will undoubtedly encounter a variety of different communication styles in the workplace. Class, race, ethnicity, and gender are all factors that influence how people communicate. Managers should work hard to shed any innate or rigid opinions about a person's communication style so these beliefs don't hinder understanding or adversely affect personnel decisions, such as hiring or promoting. It is much more productive to recognize and appreciate differences in communication styles, thereby reducing some of the problems that naturally occur when a sender and receiver do not encode or decode language in the same way.

One difference managers encounter frequently relates to gender. How does gender affect communication style? For most women, although certainly not all, talking means *conversation* and is primarily a language of rapport, a way to establish connections and negotiate relationships. Women use their unique conversational style to show involvement, connection, and participation, such as by seeking similarities and matching experiences with others. They tend to interrupt less than men do and work hard to keep a conversation going. For most men, on the other hand, talk is primarily a means to preserve independence and negotiate and maintain status in a hierarchy. Men tend to use verbal language to exhibit knowledge and skill, such as by telling stories, joking, or passing on information.[21] Another notable difference related to communication in the workplace is how women and men claim credit for work accomplished. Because women typically seek to build rapport, they are inclined to downplay their expertise and accomplishments rather than display them. Men, on the other hand, tend to value their position at center stage, enjoy demonstrating their knowledge, and more easily take credit for their accomplishments.[22] When managers understand this gender difference, they can make an extra effort to encourage women to take credit when it is deserved.

Women and men also display differences in body language. Women tend to use more submissive gestures when communicating with men: using less body space, pulling in their body, tilting their heads while talking or listening, putting their hands in their laps more often, and lowering their eyes. Men tend to stare more, point more, take up more space, keep their heads straight, sit in a more outstretched position, and use larger, more sweeping gestures.[23] Grasping the different communication styles of men and women may help managers maximize every employee's talents and encourage both men and women to contribute more fully to the organization.

Concept Connection Rosa and Jorrick Battles, a successful entrepreneurial couple, manage **gender differences in communication** to plan their schedules and run their business. Women tend to build rapport and relationships in their communications by sharing information. Men tend to negotiate hierarchy and gather information to make decisions. Researchers show that women typically read more nonverbal cues to enrich their understanding. They also use questions that solicit participation. These differences can enhance or hinder communications in the workplace and in personal experiences. Communication problems send couples into therapy more than any other relationship issue.

TakeaMoment | As a new manager, use communication to tap into people's imagination and emotions. When influencing or persuading, first listen and strive to understand the other person's point of view. And pay attention to nonverbal communication.

Concept **Connection** Communication is conveyed not only by what is said, but also how it is said and the facial expressions and body language of the people involved. **Face-to-face communication** is the richest channel of communication because it facilitates these **nonverbal cues** and allows for immediate feedback. Important issues should be discussed face-to-face, such as in this meeting between two businesswomen.

© ARTIGA PHOTO/CORBIS

Nonverbal Communication

Body language is one aspect of nonverbal communication. **Nonverbal communication** refers to messages sent through human actions and behaviors rather than through words.[24] Managers are watched, and their behavior, appearance, actions, and attitudes are symbolic of what they value and expect of others.

Most of us have heard the saying that "actions speak louder than words." Indeed, we communicate without words all the time, whether we realize it or not. Most managers are astonished to learn that words themselves carry little meaning. A significant portion of the shared understanding from communication comes from the nonverbal messages of facial expression, voice, mannerisms, posture, and dress. Without these cues, miscommunication may occur.

Nonverbal communication occurs mostly face to face. One researcher found three sources of communication cues during face-to-face communication: the *verbal*, which are the actual spoken words; the *vocal*, which include the pitch, tone, and timbre of a person's voice; and *facial expressions*. According to this study, the relative weights of these three factors in message interpretation are as follows: verbal impact, 7 percent; vocal impact, 38 percent; and facial impact, 55 percent.[25] To some extent, we are all natural *face readers*, but facial expressions can be misinterpreted, suggesting that managers need to ask questions to make sure they're getting the right message. Managers can hone their skills at reading facial expressions and improve their ability to connect with and influence followers. Studies indicate that managers who seem responsive to the unspoken emotions of employees are more effective and successful in the workplace.[26]

Tuning in to the nonverbal messages of customers also has its benefits. In an effort to better serve customers during busy store hours, Ace Hardware turned employees into "customer quarterbacks" whose job was to read nonverbal messages of customers as they entered the store. Each customer was classified, based on nonverbal cues, as a browser, a mission shopper with no time to talk, or someone starting a new project. Customer quarterbacks would then interpret their nonverbal cues to determine how best to serve them.[27]

Listening

One of the most important tools of manager communication is listening, both to employees and customers. Most managers now recognize that important information flows from the bottom up, not the top down, and managers had better be tuned in.[28] Some organizations use innovative techniques for finding out what's on employees' and customers' minds. When Intuit's president and chief executive officer Stephen M. Bennett took over, the company instituted an annual employee survey that gives managers an opportunity to listen to employees' feelings on a range of company practices. Then, during the year, managers are encouraged to meet with subordinates to gather more feedback. Since instituting these listening strategies, turnover at Intuit has dropped from 24 percent to 12 percent. "Employees know that we are serious about asking for their feedback, and we listen and do something about it," Bennett says.[29]

nonverbal communication A communication transmitted through actions and behaviors rather than through words.

Managers are also tapping into the interactive nature of blogs to stay in touch with employees and customers. Blogs, running Web logs that allow people to post opinions, ideas, and information, provide a low-cost, always-fresh real-time link between organizations and customers, employees, the media, and investors.[30] One estimate is that 11 percent of *Fortune* 500 companies use blogs to keep in touch with stakeholders.[31] One of the most active and successful bloggers is Jonathan Schwartz, CEO of Sun Microsystems.

Innovative Way

Sun Microsystems

"One of the wonderful things about blogs is that I don't have to walk through campus to figure out what's on people's minds. I just go to blogs.sun.com, and I read what they're thinking," says Jonathan Schwartz, CEO of Sun Microsystems. Schwartz has his own blog that allows him to communicate efficiently to a large number and variety of stakeholders. "My No. 1 priority is ensuring my communications are broadly received. Blogging to me has become the most efficient form of communication. When I blog, I'm talking to the world," says Schwartz.

Not only do blogs give organizations a human voice, they also enable companies to influence opinion, tap into the expertise and ideas of core constituents, and treat employees and customers like friends rather than foes. Schwartz's blog is written in an informational, conversational style that keeps people coming back for more. Topics include updates on the company's mission, new product announcements, personal insights about his job as CEO, and responses to employee questions and concerns.

Although the number of top executives using blogs is relatively small today, Schwartz says, "In ten years, most of us will communicate directly with customers, employees, and the broader business community through blogs. For executives, having a blog is not going to be a matter of choice, any more than e-mail is today."[32]

Through his blog, Schwartz has gained access to volumes of feedback from customers and employees. He recognizes the value of listening to this feedback and responding with appropriate actions and information. Done correctly, listening is a vital link in the communication process, shown in Exhibit 18.2.

Listening involves the skill of grasping both facts and feelings to interpret a message's genuine meaning. Only then can the manager provide the appropriate response. Listening requires attention, energy, and skill. Although about 75 percent of effective communication is listening, most people spend only 30 to 40 percent of their time listening, which leads to many communication errors.[33] One of the secrets of highly successful salespeople is that they spend 60 to 70 percent of a sales call letting the customer talk.[34] However, listening involves much more than just not talking. Many people do not know how to listen effectively. They concentrate on formulating what they are going to say next rather than on what is being said to them. Our listening efficiency, as measured by the amount of material understood and remembered by subjects 48 hours after listening to a 10-minute message, is, on average, no better than 25 percent.[35]

What constitutes good listening? Exhibit 18.4 gives ten keys to effective listening and illustrates a number of ways to distinguish a bad listener from a good listener. A good listener finds areas of interest, is flexible, works hard at listening, and uses thought speed to mentally summarize, weigh, and anticipate what the speaker says. Good listening means shifting from thinking about self to empathizing with the other person and thus requires a high degree of emotional intelligence, as described in Chapter 15.

listening The skill of receiving messages to accurately grasp facts and feelings to interpret the genuine meaning.

As a new manager, your social disposition gives others glimpses into your managerial style. Are you friendly and approachable? A good listener? Goal-oriented? Take the New Manager Self-Test to learn more about your social disposition.

TakeaMoment

6
Leading

EXHIBIT | 18.4 Ten Keys to Effective Listening

Keys to Effective Listening	Poor Listener	Good Listener
1. Listen actively.	Is passive, laid back	Asks questions, paraphrases what is said
2. Find areas of interest.	Tunes out dry subjects	Looks for new learning
3. Resist distractions.	Is easily distracted; answers phone or sends text messages	Gives full attention, fights distractions, maintains concentration
4. Capitalize on the fact that thought is faster.	Tends to daydream	Mentally summarizes; weighs the evidence
5. Be responsive.	Avoids eye contact; is minimally involved	Nods and shows interest
6. Judge content, not delivery.	Tunes out if delivery is poor	Judges content; skips over delivery errors
7. Avoid premature judgment.	Has preconceptions	Does not judge until comprehension is complete
8. Listen for ideas.	Listens for facts	Listens to central themes
9. Work at listening.	Shows no energy; forgets what the speaker says	Works hard; exhibits active body state and eye contact
10. Exercise one's mind.	Resists difficult material in favor of light, recreational material	Uses heavier material as exercise for the mind

SOURCES: Adapted from Diann Daniel, "Seven Deadly Sins of (Not) Listening," http://www.cio.com/article/print/134801 (accessed April 8, 2008); Sherman K. Okum, "How to Be a Better Listener," *Nation's Business* (August 1975): 62; and Philip Morgan and Kent Baker, "Building a Professional Image: Improving Listening Behavior," *Supervisory Management* (November 1985): 34–38.

New Manager Self-Test

What Is Your Social Disposition?

How do you come across to others? What is your social disposition? To find out, please mark whether each item below is Mostly True or Mostly False for you.

	Mostly True	Mostly False
1. I want to climb the corporate ladder as high as I can.	_____	_____
2. I confront people when I sense a conflict.	_____	_____
3. People consider me cooperative and easy to work with.	_____	_____
4. I like to get right to the point.	_____	_____
5. I make quick decisions usually without consulting others.	_____	_____
6. I make a real effort to understand other peoples' point of view.	_____	_____
7. I enjoy competing and winning.	_____	_____
8. I like to get to the bottom line.	_____	_____
9. I take a personal interest in people.	_____	_____

SCORING AND INTERPRETATION: Give yourself one point for items 1, 2, 4, 5, 7, and 8 that you marked Mostly True and one point for items 3, 6, and 9 that you marked Mostly False. The questions pertain to whether your social disposition is one of being focused and driven toward personal success or whether you tend to come across as affable and friendly. If you scored seven or higher, you are probably ambitious and goal oriented. A score of three or less would mean that you probably are empathic, ask questions, and enjoy collaborating with others.

A person with a driven disposition may be promoted to manager, but may not be a good listener, fail to pick up on body language, or take time to engage in dialogue. A manager has to get things done through other people, and it helps to slow down, listen, build relationships, and take the time to communicate. Too much focus on your personal achievement may come across as uncaring. A new manager with a friendly disposition is often a good listener, makes inquiries, and experiences fewer communication mistakes.

SOURCE: Based on "Social Styles," in Paula J. Caproni, *Management Skills for Everyday Life: The Practical Coach,* 2nd ed. (Upper Saddle River, NJ: Prentice-Hall, 2005), pp. 200–203.

ORGANIZATIONAL COMMUNICATION

Another aspect of management communication concerns the organization as a whole. Organization-wide communications typically flow in three directions—downward, upward, and horizontally. Managers are responsible for establishing and maintaining formal channels of communication in these three directions. Managers also use informal channels, which means they get out of their offices and mingle with employees.

Formal Communication Channels

Formal communication channels are those that flow within the chain of command or task responsibility defined by the organization. The three formal channels and the types of information conveyed in each are illustrated in Exhibit 18.5.[36] Downward and upward communications are the primary forms of communication used in most traditional, vertically organized companies. However, many of today's organizations emphasize horizontal communication, with people continuously sharing information across departments and levels.

Electronic communication such as e-mail and instant messaging have made it easier than ever for information to flow in all directions. For example, the U.S. Army is using technology to rapidly transmit communications about weather conditions and the latest intelligence on the insurgency to lieutenants in the field in Iraq. Similarly, the U.S. Navy uses instant messaging to communicate within ships, across navy divisions, and even back to the Pentagon in Washington. "Instant messaging has allowed us to keep our crew members on the same page at the same time," says Lt. Cmdr. Mike Houston, who oversees the navy's communications program. "Lives are at stake in real time, and we're seeing a new level of communication and readiness."[37]

Downward Communication The most familiar and obvious flow of formal communication, **downward communication**, refers to the messages and information sent from top management to subordinates in a downward direction.

Managers can communicate downward to employees in many ways. Some of the most common are through speeches, messages in company newsletters, e-mail, information leaflets tucked into pay envelopes, material on bulletin boards, and policy

formal communication channel A communication channel that flows within the chain of command or task responsibility defined by the organization.

downward communication Messages sent from top management down to subordinates.

EXHIBIT | **18.5**

Downward, Upward, and Horizontal Communication in Organizations

6
Leading

and procedures manuals. Managers sometimes use creative approaches to downward communication to make sure employees get the message.

Managers also have to decide what to communicate about. It is impossible for managers to communicate with employees about everything that goes on in the organization, so they have to make choices about the important information to communicate.[38] Unfortunately, many U.S. managers could do a better job of effective downward communication. The results of one survey found that employees want open and honest communication about both the good and the bad aspects of the organization's performance. But when asked to rate their company's communication effectiveness on a scale of 0 to 100, the survey respondents' score averaged 69. In addition, a study of 1,500 managers, mostly at first and second management levels, found that 84 percent of these leaders perceive communication as one of their most important tasks, yet only 38 percent believe they have adequate communications skills.[39]

Managers can do a better job of downward communication by focusing on specific areas that require regular communication. Recall our discussion of purpose-directed communication from early in this chapter. Downward communication usually encompasses these five topics:

1. *Implementation of goals and strategies.* Communicating new strategies and goals provides information about specific targets and expected behaviors. It gives direction for lower levels of the organization. *Example:* "The new quality campaign is for real. We must improve product quality if we are to survive."

2. *Job instructions and rationale.* These directives indicate how to do a specific task and how the job relates to other organizational activities. *Example:* "Purchasing should order the bricks now so the work crew can begin construction of the building in two weeks."

3. *Procedures and practices.* These messages define the organization's policies, rules, regulations, benefits, and structural arrangements. *Example:* "After your first 90 days of employment, you are eligible to enroll in our company-sponsored savings plan."

4. *Performance feedback.* These messages appraise how well individuals and departments are doing their jobs. *Example:* "Joe, your work on the computer network has greatly improved the efficiency of our ordering process."

5. *Indoctrination.* These messages are designed to motivate employees to adopt the company's mission and cultural values and to participate in special ceremonies, such as picnics and United Way campaigns. *Example:* "The company thinks of its employees as family and would like to invite everyone to attend the annual picnic and fair on March 3."

A major problem with downward communication is *drop off*, the distortion or loss of message content. Although formal communications are a powerful way to reach all employees, much information gets lost—25 percent or so each time a message is passed from one person to the next. In addition, the message can be distorted if it travels a great distance from its originating source to the ultimate receiver. A tragic example is the following historical example.

> A reporter was present at a hamlet burned down by the U.S. Army 1st Air Cavalry Division in 1967. Investigations showed that the order from the division headquarters to the brigade was: "On no occasion must hamlets be burned down."
>
> The brigade radioed the battalion: "Do not burn down any hamlets unless you are absolutely convinced that the Viet Cong are in them."
>
> The battalion radioed the infantry company at the scene: "If you think there are any Viet Cong in the hamlet, burn it down."
>
> The company commander ordered his troops: "Burn down that hamlet."[40]

Information drop off cannot be completely avoided, but the techniques described in the previous sections can reduce it substantially. Using the right communication channel, consistency between verbal and nonverbal messages, and active listening can maintain communication accuracy as it moves down the organization.

Upward Communication Formal **upward communication** includes messages that flow from the lower to the higher levels in the organization's hierarchy. Most organizations take pains to build in healthy channels for upward communication. Employees need to air grievances, report progress, and provide feedback on management initiatives. Coupling a healthy flow of upward and downward communication ensures that the communication circuit between managers and employees is complete.[41] Five types of information communicated upward are the following:

1. *Problems and exceptions.* These messages describe serious problems with and exceptions to routine performance to make senior managers aware of difficulties. *Example:* "The printer has been out of operation for two days, and it will be at least a week before a new one arrives."

2. *Suggestions for improvement.* These messages are ideas for improving task-related procedures to increase quality or efficiency. *Example:* "I think we should eliminate step 2 in the audit procedure because it takes a lot of time and produces no results."

3. *Performance reports.* These messages include periodic reports that inform management how individuals and departments are performing. *Example:* "We completed the audit report for Smith & Smith on schedule but are one week behind on the Jackson report."

4. *Grievances and disputes.* These messages are employee complaints and conflicts that travel up the hierarchy for a hearing and possible resolution. *Example:* "The manager of operations research cannot get the cooperation of the Lincoln plant for the study of machine utilization."

5. *Financial and accounting information.* These messages pertain to costs, accounts receivable, sales volume, anticipated profits, return on investment, and other matters of interest to senior managers. *Example:* "Costs are 2 percent over budget, but sales are 10 percent ahead of target, so the profit picture for the third quarter is excellent."

Many organizations make a great effort to facilitate upward communication. Mechanisms include suggestion boxes, employee surveys, open-door policies, management information system reports, and face-to-face conversations between workers and executives.

Horizontal Communication **Horizontal communication** is the lateral or diagonal exchange of messages among peers or coworkers. It may occur within or across departments. The purpose of horizontal communication is not only to inform but also to request support and coordinate activities. Horizontal communication falls into one of three categories:

1. *Intradepartmental problem solving.* These messages take place among members of the same department and concern task accomplishment. *Example:* "Kelly, can you help us figure out how to complete this medical expense report form?"

2. *Interdepartmental coordination.* Interdepartmental messages facilitate the accomplishment of joint projects or tasks. *Example:* "Bob, please contact marketing and production and arrange a meeting to discuss the specifications for the new subassembly. It looks like we might not be able to meet their requirements."

3. *Change initiatives and improvements.* These messages are designed to share information among teams and departments

upward communication Messages transmitted from the lower to the higher levels in the organization's hierarchy.

horizontal communication The lateral or diagonal exchange of messages among peers or coworkers.

© ALAN DIAZ/ASSOCIATED PRESS

Concept Connection The National Oceanic and Atmospheric Administration (NOAA)—a decentralized, geographically dispersed agency with a mission to observe and describe changes in the entire earth's ecosystem—serves other coastal resource management groups with information, technology, and training. NOAA recently established the Office of Program Planning and Integration to improve **horizontal communication** and create a more coherent organization. For example, the new office solicits input during the strategic planning process from partners, stakeholders, and employees, such as oceanographers Michelle Zetwd and Chris Walters, shown here.

6
Leading

that can help the organization change, grow, and improve. *Example:* "We are streamlining the company travel procedures and would like to discuss them with your department."

Recall from Chapter 9 that many organizations build in horizontal communications in the form of task forces, committees, or even a matrix or horizontal structure to encourage coordination. At Chicago's Northwestern Memorial Hospital, two doctors created a horizontal task force to reduce the incidence of hospital-borne infections. The infection epidemic that kills nearly 100,000 people a year is growing worse worldwide, but Northwestern reversed the trend by breaking down communication barriers. Infectious-disease specialists Lance Peterson and Gary Noskin launched a regular Monday morning meeting involving doctors and nurses, lab technicians, pharmacists, computer technicians, admissions representatives, and even the maintenance staff. The enhanced communication paid off. Over a three-year period, Northwestern's rate of hospital-borne infections plunged 22 percent and was roughly half the national average.[42]

Team Communication Channels

A special type of horizontal communication is communicating in teams. At W. L. Gore, the chemical company best known for Gore-Tex, the core operating units are small, self-managing teams.[43] Its team members work together to accomplish tasks, and the team's communication structure influences both team performance and employee satisfaction.

Research into team communication has focused on two characteristics: the extent to which team communications are centralized and the nature of the team's task.[44] The relationship between these characteristics is illustrated in Exhibit 18.6. In a **centralized network**, team members must communicate through one individual to solve problems or make decisions. In a **decentralized network**, individuals can communicate freely with other team members. Members process information equally among themselves until all agree on a decision.[45]

In laboratory experiments, centralized communication networks achieved faster solutions for simple problems. Members could simply pass relevant information to a central person for a decision. Decentralized communications were slower for simple problems because information was passed among individuals until someone finally put the pieces together and solved the problem. However, for more complex problems, the decentralized communication network was faster. Because all necessary information was not restricted to one person, a pooling of information through widespread communications provided greater input into the decision. Similarly, the accuracy of problem solving was related to problem complexity. The centralized

centralized network A team communication structure in which team members communicate through a single individual to solve problems or make decisions.

decentralized network A team communication structure in which team members freely communicate with one another and arrive at decisions together.

EXHIBIT | 18.6

Effectiveness of Team Communication Networks

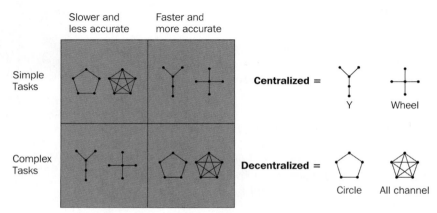

SOURCES: Adapted from A. Bavelas and D. Barrett, "An Experimental Approach to Organization Communication," *Personnel* 27 (1951): 366–371; M. E. Shaw, *Group Dynamics: The Psychology of Small Group Behavior* (New York: McGraw–Hill, 1976); and E. M. Rogers and R. A. Rogers, *Communication in Organizations* (New York: Free Press, 1976).

networks made fewer errors on simple problems but more errors on complex ones. Decentralized networks were less accurate for simple problems but more accurate for complex ones.[46]

The implication for organizations is as follows: In a highly competitive global environment, organizations typically use teams to deal with complex problems. When team activities are complex and difficult, all members should share information in a decentralized structure to solve problems. Teams need a free flow of communication in all directions.[47] Teams that perform routine tasks spend less time processing information, and thus communications can be centralized. Data can be channeled to a supervisor for decisions, freeing workers to spend a greater percentage of time on task activities.

Personal Communication Channels

Personal communication channels exist outside the formally authorized channels. These informal communications coexist with formal channels but may skip hierarchical levels, cutting across vertical chains of command to connect virtually anyone in the organization. In most organizations, these informal channels are the primary way information spreads and work gets accomplished. Three important types of personal communication channels are *personal networks*, the *grapevine, and written communication*.

Developing Personal Communication Networks
Personal networking refers to the acquisition and cultivation of personal relationships that cross departmental, hierarchical, and even organizational boundaries.[48] Smart managers consciously develop personal communication networks and encourage others to do so. In a communication network, people share information across boundaries and reach out to anyone who can further the goals of the team and organization. Exhibit 18.7 illustrates a communication network. Some people are central to the network while others play only a peripheral role. The key is that relationships are built across functional and hierarchical boundaries.

The value of personal networks for managers is that people who have more contacts have greater influence in the organization and get more accomplished. For example, in Exhibit 18.7, Sharon has a well-developed personal communication network, sharing information and assistance with many people across the marketing, manufacturing, and engineering departments. Contrast Sharon's contacts with those of Mike or Jasmine. Who do you think is likely to have greater access to resources and

personal communication channels Communication channels that exist outside the formally authorized channels and do not adhere to the organization's hierarchy of authority.

personal networking The acquisition and cultivation of personal relationships that cross departmental, hierarchical, and even organizational boundaries.

EXHIBIT | 18.7

An Organizational Communication Network

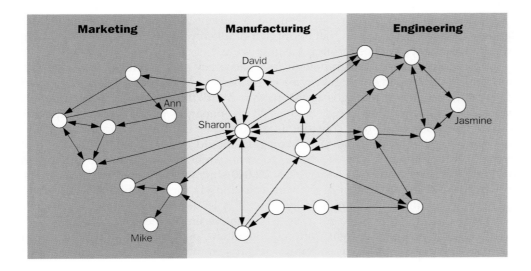

more influence in the organization? Here are a few tips from one expert networker for building a personal communication network:[49]

1. ***Build it before you need it.*** Smart managers don't wait until they need something to start building a network of personal relationships—by then, it's too late. Instead, they show genuine interest in others and develop honest connections.

2. ***Never eat lunch alone.*** People who excel at networking make an effort to be visible and connect with as many people as possible. Master networkers keep their social as well as business conference and event calendars full.

3. ***Make it win-win.*** Successful networking isn't just about getting what *you* want; it's also about making sure other people in the network get what *they* want.

4. ***Focus on diversity.*** The broader your base of contacts, the broader your range of influence. Build connections with people from as many different areas of interest as possible (both within and outside the organization).

Most of us know from personal experience that "who you know" sometimes counts for more than what you know. By cultivating a broad network of contacts, managers can significantly extend their influence and accomplish greater results.

TakeaMoment

As a new manager, it is essential to build and nurture a personal communication network. Refer back to the questionnaire at the beginning of the chapter to determine the effectiveness of your networking skills. Networking plugs you into the grapevine and supplements formal communication channels.

The Grapevine Although the word *gossip* has a negative connotation, it may actually be good for a company, especially during times of change, such as layoffs or downsizing. In fact, gossip can be an invaluable tool for managers who may be able to keep a better pulse on what's happening in the workplace by relying on information from employees who are known for spreading and knowing office gossip.[50] Gossip typically travels along the **grapevine**, an informal, person-to-person communication network that is not officially sanctioned by the organization.[51] The grapevine links employees in all directions, ranging from the CEO through middle management, support staff, and line employees. The grapevine will always exist in an organization, but it can become a dominant force when formal channels are closed. In such cases, the grapevine is actually a service because the information it provides helps makes sense of an unclear or uncertain situation. Employees use grapevine rumors to fill in information gaps and clarify management decisions. One estimate is that as much as 70 percent of all communication in a firm is carried out through its grapevine.[52] The grapevine tends to be more active during periods of change, excitement, anxiety, and sagging economic conditions. For example, a survey by professional employment services firm Randstad found that about half of all employees reported first hearing of major company changes through the grapevine.[53]

Surprising aspects of the grapevine are its accuracy and its relevance to the organization. About 80 percent of grapevine communications pertain to business-related topics rather than personal gossip. Moreover, from 70 to 90 percent of the details passed through a grapevine are accurate.[54] Many managers would like the grapevine to be destroyed because they consider its rumors to be untrue, malicious, and harmful, which typically is not the case. Managers should be aware that almost five of every six important messages are carried to some extent by the grapevine rather than through official channels. In a survey of 22,000 shift workers in varied industries, 55 percent said they get most of their information via the grapevine.[55] Smart managers understand the company's grapevine. "If a leader has his ear to the ground, gossip can be a way for him to get a sense of what his employees are thinking or feeling," says Mitch Kusy, an organizational consultant, psychologist, and professor at Antioch University.[56] In all cases, but particularly in times of crisis, executives need

grapevine An informal, person-to-person communication network of employees that is not officially sanctioned by the organization.

to manage communications effectively so that the grapevine is not the only source of information.[57]

Written Communication Written communication skills are becoming increasingly important in today's collaborative workplace. "With the fast pace of today's electronic communications, one might think that the value of fundamental writing skills has diminished in the workplace," said Joseph M. Tucci, president and CEO of EMC Corporation. "Actually, the need to write clearly and quickly has never been more important than in today's highly competitive, technology-driven global economy."[58]

Managers who are unable to communicate in writing will limit their opportunities for advancement. "Writing is both a 'marker' of high-skill, high-wage, professional work and a 'gatekeeper' with clear equity implications," says Bob Kerrey, president of New School University in New York and chair of the National Commission on Writing. Managers can improve their writing skills by following these guidelines:[59]

- *Respect the reader.* The reader's time is valuable; don't waste it with a rambling, confusing memo or e-mail that has to be read several times to try to make sense of it. Pay attention to your grammar and spelling. Sloppy writing indicates that you think your time is more important than that of your readers. You'll lose their interest—and their respect.

- *Know your point and get to it.* What is the key piece of information that you want the reader to remember? Many people just sit and write, without clarifying in their own mind what it is they're trying to say. To write effectively, know what your central point is and write to support it.

- *Write clearly rather than impressively.* Don't use pretentious or inflated language, and avoid jargon. The goal of good writing for business is to be understood the first time through. State your message as simply and as clearly as possible.

- *Get a second opinion.* When the communication is highly important, such as a formal memo to the department or organization, ask someone you consider to be a good writer to read it before you send it. Don't be too proud to take their advice. In all cases, read and revise the memo or e-mail a second and third time before you hit the send button.

A former manager of communication services at consulting firm Arthur D. Little Inc. has estimated that around 30 percent of all business memos and e-mails are written simply to get clarification about an earlier written communication that didn't make sense to the reader.[60] By following these guidelines, you can get your message across the first time.

INNOVATIONS IN ORGANIZATIONAL COMMUNICATION

Organizations with a high level of communication effectiveness develop strategies to encourage dialogue, manage crisis communication, use feedback to develop employees, and create a climate of trust and openness.

Dialogue

Dialogue is a group communication process in which people together create a stream of meaning that enables them to understand each other and share a view of the world.[61] People may start out at polar opposites, but by talking openly, they discover common ground, common issues, and common goals on which they can build a better future. Dialogue is never superficial; it is always a shared inquiry where the participants seek a greater understanding of each other. To build and maintain strong relationships, managers need to develop the ability to engage in dialogue. When Whole Foods CEO John Mackey was heckled by an animal rights activist at an

dialogue A group communication process aimed at creating a culture based on collaboration, fluidity, trust, and commitment to shared goals.

6
Leading

annual meeting, he agreed to a personal dialogue with the activist. Through careful listening and willingness to learn, he discovered some weaknesses in his company's policies on animal products and became a firm proponent of many of the activist's positions. Because of his ability to create a successful dialogue, he also converted the opponent into a vocal advocate for Whole Foods.[62]

A useful way to describe dialogue is to contrast it with discussion. The differences between dialogue and discussion are shown in Exhibit 18.8. The intent of discussion, generally, is to deliver one's point of view and persuade others to adopt it. A discussion is often resolved by logic or "beating down" opponents. Dialogue, by contrast, asks that participants suspend their attachments to a particular viewpoint so that a deeper level of listening, synthesis, and meaning can evolve from the group. A dialogue's focus is to reveal feelings and build common ground. Both forms of communication—dialogue and discussion—can result in change. However, the result of discussion is limited to the topic being deliberated, whereas the result of dialogue is characterized by group unity, shared meaning, and transformed mind-sets. As new and deeper solutions are developed, a trusting relationship is built among team members.[63]

Crisis Communication

Over the past few years, the sheer number and scope of crises have made communication a more demanding job for managers. Organizations face small crises every day, such as charges of racial discrimination, a factory fire, or a flu epidemic. Moreover, acts of intentional evil, such as bombings or kidnappings, continue to increase, causing serious repercussions for people and organizations.[64] Crises are like fires, and effective communications are the best way to douse them. The slower the response, the faster the crisis grows, fueled by misinformation, rumors, and fears. Prompt and thoughtful communications can counter confusion and replace it with confidence in the organization's leaders.[65] Managers can develop four primary skills for communicating in a crisis.[66]

EXHIBIT | 18.8

Dialogue and Discussion:
The Differences

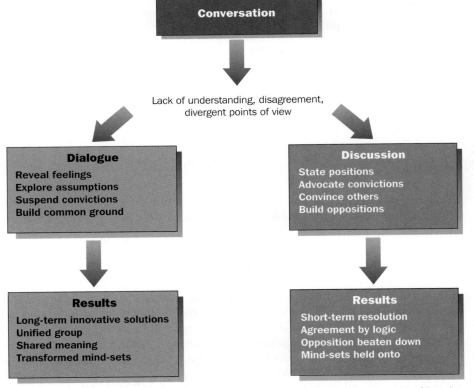

SOURCE: Adapted from Edgar Schein, "On Dialogue, Culture, and Organizational Learning," *Organizational Dynamics* (Autumn 1993): 46.

- *Maintain your focus.* Good crisis communicators don't allow themselves to be overwhelmed by the situation. Calmness and listening become more important than ever. Managers also learn to tailor their communications to reflect hope and optimism at the same time they acknowledge the current difficulties.

- *Be visible.* Many managers underestimate just how important their presence is during a crisis.[67] A manager's job is to step out immediately, both to reassure employees and respond to public concerns. Face-to-face communication with employees is crucial for letting people know that managers care about them and what they're going through.

- *Get the awful truth out.*[68] Effective managers gather as much information as they can, do their best to determine the facts, and tell the truth to employees and the public as soon as possible. Getting the truth out quickly prevents rumors and misunderstandings.

- *Communicate a vision for the future.* People need to feel that they have something to work for and look forward to. Moments of crisis present opportunities for managers to communicate a vision of a better future and unite people toward common goals.

Feedback and Learning

Feedback occurs when managers use evaluation and communication to help individuals and the organization learn and improve. It enables managers to determine whether they have been successful in communicating with others. Recall from Exhibit 18.2 that feedback is an important part of the communication process. However, despite its importance, feedback is often neglected. Giving and receiving feedback is typically difficult for both managers and employees. Yet, by avoiding feedback, people miss a valuable opportunity to help one another learn, develop, and improve.[69]

Successful managers focus their feedback to help develop the capabilities of subordinates, and they encourage critical feedback from employees. When managers enlist the whole organization in reviewing the outcomes of activities, they can quickly learn what works and what doesn't and use that information to improve the organization. Consider how the U.S. Army's feedback system promotes whole-system learning.

© RICK RYCRAFT/ASSOCIATED PRESS

Concept Connection   When an extortionist claimed to have placed seven pesticide-contaminated candy bars in Sydney area stores, manufacturer MasterFoods Australia-New Zealand's response was a textbook example of effective **crisis communication**. President Andy Weston-Webb announced, "It's not safe to eat Mars or Snickers bars" and immediately activated recall plans. MasterFoods launched a public relations campaign, which included interviews with Weston-Webb, full-page newspaper ads, a company hotline, and media access to the burial of 3 million candy bars in a deep pit. The two-month absence of the popular snacks cost the company more than $10 million. But MasterFoods emerged with its reputation intact. During the first week of the products' return, sales surged 300 percent.

Innovative Way   **U.S. Army**

At the National Training Center just south of Death Valley, U.S. Army troops engage in a simulated battle. The "enemy" has sent unmanned aerial vehicles (UAVs) to gather targeting data. When the troops fire on the UAVs, they reveal their location to attack helicopters hovering just behind a nearby ridge. After the exercise, unit members and their superiors hold an *after-action review* to review battle plans, discuss what worked and what didn't, and talk about how to do things better. Gen. William Hertzog suggests that inexpensive decoy UAVs might be just the thing to make a distracted enemy reveal its location. The observation became a "lesson learned" for the entire army, and UAVs became an important part of battle operations in Iraq.

Many researchers attribute the transformation of the army from a demoralized, dysfunctional organization following the Vietnam War into an elite force capable of effectively accomplishing Operation Iraqi Freedom to this unique feedback and learning system. In the U.S. Army, after-action reviews take just 15 minutes, and they occur after every identifiable event—large or small, simulated or real. The review involves asking four simple questions: What was supposed to happen? What actually happened? What accounts for any difference? What can we learn? It is a process of identifying mistakes, of innovating, and of continually learning from experience.

The lessons are based not only on simulated battles, but also on real-life experiences of soldiers in the field. The Center for Army Lessons Learned (CALL) sends experts into the field to observe after-action reviews, interview soldiers, and compile intelligence reports. Leaders in all army divisions are currently engaged in a detailed analysis of lessons learned during Operation Iraqi Freedom and Operation Enduring Freedom. The lessons will be used to train soldiers and develop action plans for resolving problems in future conflicts. For example, many of the problems and issues from a similar process following Operation Desert Storm had been resolved by the time of Operation Iraqi Freedom. A primary focus for current leaders is to improve training regarding the difficult shift from offensive operations to humanitarian and relief efforts.[70]

In this example, the organization is learning by communicating feedback about the consequences of field operations and simulated battles. Compiling what is learned and using communication feedback create an improved organization.

Climate of Trust and Openness

Perhaps the most important thing managers can do to enhance organizational communication is to create a *climate of trust and openness*. Open communication and dialogue can encourage people to communicate honestly with one another. Subordinates will feel free to transmit negative as well as positive messages without fear of retribution. Efforts to develop interpersonal skills among employees can also foster openness, honesty, and trust.

Second, managers should develop and use *formal communication channels* in all directions. Scandinavian Design uses two newsletters to reach employees. Dana Corporation has developed innovative programs such as the "Here's a Thought" board—called a HAT rack—to get ideas and feedback from workers. Other techniques include direct mail, bulletin boards, blogs, and employee surveys.

Third, managers should encourage the use of *multiple channels*, including both formal and informal communications. Multiple communication channels include written directives, face-to-face discussions, and the grapevine. For example, managers at GM's Packard Electric plant use multimedia, including a monthly newspaper, frequent meetings of employee teams, and an electronic news display in the cafeteria. Sending messages through multiple channels increases the likelihood that they will be properly received.

Fourth, the structure should *fit communication needs*. An organization can be designed to use teams, task forces, project managers, or a matrix structure as needed to facilitate the horizontal flow of information for coordination and problem solving. Structure should also reflect information needs. When team or department tasks are difficult, a decentralized structure should be implemented to encourage discussion and participation.

---

ch18   A MANAGER'S ESSENTIALS: WHAT HAVE WE LEARNED?

- A manager's communication is purpose-directed in that it unites people around a shared vision and goals and directs attention to the values and behaviors that achieve goals. Managers facilitate strategic conversations by using open communication, actively listening to others, applying the practice of dialogue, and using feedback for learning and change.

- Communication is the process in which information is exchanged and understood by two or more people. Two essential elements in every communication situation are the sender and the receiver. The sender encodes the idea by selecting symbols with which to compose a message and selecting a communication channel. The receiver decodes the symbols to interpret the meaning of the message. Feedback occurs when the receiver responds to the sender's communication with a return message.

- Communication among people can be affected by communication channels, gender differences, nonverbal communication, and listening skills. An important aspect of management communication is persuasion. The ability to persuade others to behave in ways that help accomplish the vision and goals is crucial to good management.

- Organization-wide communication typically flows in three directions: downward, upward, and horizontally. Managers are responsible for maintaining formal channels of communication in all three directions. Teams with complex tasks need to communicate successfully in all directions through a decentralized communication network.

- Personal communication channels exist outside formally authorized channels and include personal networks, the grapevine, and written communication. Managers with more contacts in their personal network have greater influence in the organization. The grapevine carries workplace gossip, a dominant force in organization communication when formal channels are closed. The ability to write clearly and quickly is increasingly important in today's collaborative work environment.

- To enhance organizational communication, managers should understand how to engage in dialogue, manage crisis communication, use feedback and learning to improve employee performance, and create a climate of trust and openness,

ch18 DISCUSSION QUESTIONS

1. Lee's Garage is an internal Wal-Mart Web site that CEO H. Lee Scott uses to communicate with the company's 1.5 million U.S. employees. A public relations associate screens employee questions, and Scott dictates his responses to an aide, who then posts them on the Web. What would you predict are the advantages and potential problems to this method of upper-level management's connecting with employees?

2. Describe the elements of the communication process. Give an example of each part of the model as it exists in the classroom during communication between teacher and students.

3. Why do you think stories are more effective than hard facts and figures in persuading others?

4. Try to recall an incident at school or work when information was passed primarily through the grapevine. How accurate were the rumors, and how did people react to them? How can managers control information that is processed through the grapevine?

5. What is the difference between a discussion and a dialogue? What steps might managers take to transform a discussion into a constructive dialogue?

6. What do you think are the major barriers to upward communication in organizations? Discuss.

7. What is the relationship between group member communication and group task? For example, how should communications differ in a strategic planning group and a group of employees who stock shelves in a grocery store?

8. Some senior managers believe they should rely on written information and computer reports because these yield more accurate data than do face-to-face communications. Do you agree? Why or why not?

9. Why is management by wandering around considered effective communication? How might managers encourage open and honest communication, as opposed to polite conversation and best behavior, when engaging in MBWA?

10. Assume that you have been asked to design a training program to help managers become better communicators. What would you include in the program?

6 Leading

ch18   MANAGEMENT IN PRACTICE: EXPERIENTIAL EXERCISE

Personal Assessment of Communication Apprehension

The following questions are about your feelings toward communication with other people. Indicate the degree to which each statement applies to you by marking (5) Strongly agree, (4) Agree, (3) Undecided, (2) Disagree, or (1) Strongly disagree. There are no right or wrong answers. Many of the statements are similar to other statements. Do not be concerned about their similarities. Work quickly, and just record your first impressions.

Disagree Strongly ① ② ③ ④ ⑤ **Agree Strongly**

1. When talking in a small group of acquaintances, I am tense and nervous.

   1   2   3   4   5

2. When presenting a talk to a group of strangers, I am tense and nervous.

   1   2   3   4   5

3. When conversing with a friend or colleague, I am calm and relaxed.

   1   2   3   4   5

4. When talking in a large meeting of acquaintances, I am calm and relaxed.

   1   2   3   4   5

5. When presenting a talk to a group of friends or colleagues, I am tense and nervous.

   1   2   3   4   5

6. When conversing with an acquaintance or colleague, I am calm and relaxed.

   1   2   3   4   5

7. When talking in a large meeting of strangers, I am tense and nervous.

   1   2   3   4   5

8. When talking in a small group of strangers, I am tense and nervous.

   1   2   3   4   5

9. When talking in a small group of strangers, I am tense and nervous.

   1   2   3   4   5

10. When presenting a talk to a group of acquaintances, I am calm and relaxed.

    1   2   3   4   5

11. When I am conversing with a stranger, I am calm and relaxed.

    1   2   3   4   5

12. When talking in a large meeting of friends, I am tense and nervous.

    1   2   3   4   5

13. When presenting a talk to a group of strangers, I am calm and relaxed.

    1   2   3   4   5

14. When conversing with a friend or colleague, I am tense and nervous.

    1   2   3   4   5

15. When talking in a large meeting of acquaintances, I am tense and nervous.

    1   2   3   4   5

16. When talking in a small group of acquaintances, I am calm and relaxed.

    1   2   3   4   5

17. When talking in a small group of strangers, I am calm and relaxed.

    1   2   3   4   5

18. When presenting a talk to a group of friends, I am calm and relaxed.

    1   2   3   4   5

19. When conversing with an acquaintance or colleague, I am tense and nervous.

    1   2   3   4   5

20. When talking in a large meeting of strangers, I am calm and relaxed.

    1   2   3   4   5

21. When presenting a talk to a group of acquaintances, I am tense and nervous.

    1   2   3   4   5

22. When conversing with a stranger, I am tense and nervous.

    1   2   3   4   5

23. When talking in a large meeting of friends or colleagues, I am calm and relaxed.

    1   2   3   4   5

24. When talking in a small group of friends or colleagues, I am tense and nervous.

    1   2   3   4   5

Scoring and Interpretation

This questionnaire permits computation of four subscores and one total score. Subscores relate to communication apprehension in four common situations—public speaking, meetings, group discussions, and interpersonal conversations. To compute your scores, add or subtract your scores for each item as indicated next.

Subscore/Scoring Formula

For each subscore, start with 18 points. Then add the scores for the plus (+) items and subtract the scores for the minus (−) items.

Public Speaking

18 + scores for items 2, 5, and 21; − scores for items 10, 13, and 18. Score = _____

Meetings

18 + scores for items 7, 12, and 15; − scores for items 4, 20, and 23. Score = _____

Group Discussions

18 + scores for items 1, 8, and 24; − scores for items 9, 16, and 17. Score = _____

Interpersonal Conversations

18 + scores for items 14, 19, and 22; − scores for items 3, 6, and 11. Score = _____

Total Score

Sum the four subscores for Total Score = _____

This personal assessment provides an indication of how much apprehension (fear or anxiety) you feel in a variety of communication settings. Total scores may range from 24 to 120. Scores above 72 indicate that you are more apprehensive about communication than the average person. Scores above 85 indicate a high level of communication apprehension. Scores below 59 indicate a low level of apprehension. These extreme scores (below 59 and above 85) are generally outside the norm. They suggest that the degree of apprehension you may experience in any given situation may not be associated with a realistic response to that communication situation.

Scores on the subscales can range from a low of 6 to a high of 30. Any score above 18 indicates some degree of apprehension. For example, if you score above 18 for the public speaking context, you are like the overwhelming majority of people.

To be an effective communication champion, you should work to overcome communication anxiety. The interpersonal conversations create the least apprehension for most people, followed by group discussions, larger meetings, and then public speaking. Compare your scores with another student. What aspect of communication creates the most apprehension for you? How do you plan to improve it?

SOURCES: J. C. McCroskey, "Measures of Communication-Bound Anxiety," *Speech Monographs* 37 (1970): 269–277; J. C. McCroskey and V. P. Richmond, "Validity of the PRCA as an Index of Oral Communication Apprehension," *Communication Monographs* 45 (1978): 192–203; J. C. McCroskey and V. P. Richmond, "The Impact of Communication Apprehension on Individuals in Organizations," *Communication Quarterly* 27 (1979): 55–61; J. C. McCroskey, *An Introduction to Rhetorical Communication* (Englewood Cliffs, NJ: Prentice Hall, 1982).

ch18 MANAGEMENT IN PRACTICE: ETHICAL DILEMMA

On Trial

When Werner and Thompson, a Los Angeles business and financial management firm, offered Iranian-born Firoz Bahmani a position as an accountant assistant one spring day in 2002, Bahmani felt a sense of genuine relief, but his relief was short-lived.

With his degree in accounting from a top-notch American university, he knew he was more than a little overqualified for the job. But time after time, he'd been rejected for suitable positions. His language difficulties were the reason most often given for his unsuccessful candidacy. Although the young man had grown up speaking both Farsi and French in his native land, he'd only begun to pick up English shortly before his arrival in the United States a few years ago. Impressed by his educational credentials and his quiet, courtly manner, managing partner Beatrice Werner overlooked his heavy accent and actively recruited him for the position, the only one available at the time. During his interview, she assured him he would advance in time.

It was clear to Beatrice that Firoz was committed to succeeding at all costs. But it soon also became apparent that Firoz and his immediate supervisor, Cathy Putnam, were at odds. Cathy was a seasoned account manager who had just transferred to Los Angeles from the New York office. Saddled with an enormous workload, she let Firoz know right from the start, speaking in her rapid-fire Brooklyn accent, that he'd need to get up to speed as quickly as possible.

Shortly before Cathy was to give Firoz his three-month probationary review, she came to Beatrice, expressed her frustration with Firoz's performance, and suggested that he be let go. "His bank reconciliations and financial report preparations are first-rate," Cathy admitted, "but his communication skills leave a lot to be desired. In the first place, I simply don't have the time to keep repeating the same directions over and over again when I'm trying to teach him his responsibilities. Then there's the fact that public contact is part of his written job description. Typically, he puts off making phone calls to dispute credit card charges or ask a client's staff for the information he needs. When he does finally pick up the phone . . . well, let's just say I've had more than one client mention how hard it is to understand what he's trying to say. Some of them are getting pretty exasperated."

"You know, some firms feel it's their corporate responsibility to help foreign-born employees learn English," Beatrice began. "Maybe we should help him find an English-as-a-second-language course and pay for it."

"With all due respect, I don't think that's our job," Cathy replied, with barely concealed irritation. "If you come to the United States, you should learn our language. That's what my mom's parents did when they came over from Italy. They certainly didn't expect anyone to hold their hands. Besides," she added, almost inaudibly, "Firoz's lucky we let him into this country."

Beatrice had mixed feelings. On one hand, she recognized that Werner and Thompson had every right to require someone in Firoz's position be capable of carrying out his public contract duties. Perhaps she had made a mistake in hiring him. But as the daughter of German immigrants herself, she knew firsthand both how daunting language and cultural barriers could be and that they could be overcome in time. Perhaps in part because of her family background, she had a passionate commitment to the firm's stated

goals of creating a diverse workforce and a caring, supportive culture. Besides she felt a personal sense of obligation to help a hard-working, promising employee realize his potential. What will she advise Cathy to do now that Firoz's probationary period is drawing to a close?

What Would You Do?

1. Agree with Cathy Putnam. Despite your personal feelings, accept that Firoz Bahmani is not capable of carrying out the accountant assistant's responsibilities. Make the break now, and give him his notice on the grounds that he cannot carry out one of the key stated job requirements. Advise him that a position that primarily involves paperwork would be a better fit for him.

2. Place Firoz with a more sympathetic account manager who is open to finding ways to help him improve his English and has the time to help him develop his assertiveness and telephone skills. Send Cathy Putnam to diversity awareness training.

3. Create a new position at the firm that will allow Firoz to do the reports and reconciliations for several account managers, freeing the account assistants to concentrate on public contact work. Make it clear that he will have little chance of future promotion unless his English improves markedly.

SOURCES: Mary Gillis, "Iranian Americans," *Multicultural America:* www.everyculture.com/multi/Ha-La/Iranian-Americans.html (accessed September 19, 2006); and Charlene Marmer Solomon, "Managing Today's Immigrants," *Personnel Journal* 72, no. 3 (February 1993): 56–65.

---

ch18   CASE FOR CRITICAL ANALYSIS

Hunter-Worth

Christmas was fast approaching. Just a short while ago, Chuck Moore, national sales manager for Hunter-Worth, a New York–based multinational toy manufacturer, was confident the coming holiday was going to be one of the company's best in years. At a recent toy expo, Hunter-Worth unveiled a new interactive plush toy that was cuddly, high-tech, and tied into a major holiday motion picture expected to be a smash hit. Chuck had thought the toy would do well, but frankly, the level of interest took him by surprise. The buyers at the toy fair raved, and the subsequent pre-order volume was extremely encouraging. It had all looked so promising, but now he couldn't shake a sense of impending doom.

The problem in a nutshell was that the Mexican subsidiary that manufactured the toy couldn't seem to

meet a deadline. Not only were all the shipments late so far, but they fell well short of the quantities ordered. Chuck decided to e-mail Vicente Ruiz, the plant manager, about the situation before he found himself in the middle of the Christmas season with parents clamoring for a toy he couldn't lay his hands on.

In a thoroughly professional e-mail that started with a friendly "Dear Vicente," Chuck inquired about the status of the latest order, asked for a production schedule for pending orders, and requested a specific explanation as to why the Mexican plant seemed to be having such difficulty shipping orders out on time. The reply appeared within the hour, but to his utter astonishment, it was a short message from Vicente's secretary. She acknowledged the receipt of his e-mail and assured him the Mexican plant would be shipping the order, already a week late, in the next ten days.

"That's it," Chuck fumed. "Time to take this to Sato." He prefaced his original e-mail and the secretary's reply with a terse note expressing his growing concern over the availability of what could well be this season's must-have toy. "Just what do I have to do to light a fire under Vicente?" he wrote. He then forwarded it all to his supervisor and friend, Michael Sato, the executive vice president for sales and marketing.

Next thing he knew, he was on the phone with Vicente—and the plant manager was furious. "Signor Moore, how dare you go over my head and say such things about me to my boss?" he sputtered, sounding both angry and slightly panicked. It seemed that Michael had forwarded Chuck's e-mail to Hunter-Worth's vice president of operations, who had sent it on to the Mexican subsidiary's president.

That turn of events was unfortunate, but Chuck wasn't feeling all that apologetic. "You could have prevented all this if you'd just answered the questions I e-mailed you last week," he pointed out. "I deserved more than a form letter—and from your secretary, no less."

"My secretary always answers my e-mails," replied Vicente. "She figures that if the problem is really urgent, you would pick up the phone and talk to me directly. Contrary to what you guys north of the border might think, we do take deadlines seriously here. There's only so much we can do with the supply problems we're having, but I doubt you're interested in hearing about those." And Vicente hung up the phone without waiting for a response.

Chuck was confused and disheartened. Things were only getting worse. How could he turn the situation around?

Questions

1. Based on Vicente Ruiz's actions and his conversation with Chuck Moore, what differences do you detect in cultural attitudes toward communications in Mexico as compared with the United States? Is understanding these differences important? Explain.

2. What was the main purpose of Chuck's communication to Vicente? To Michael Sato? What factors should he have considered when choosing a channel for his communication to Vicente? Are they the same factors he should have considered when communicating with Michael Sato?

3. If you were Chuck, what would you have done differently? What steps would you take at this point to make sure the supply of the popular new toy is sufficient to meet the anticipated demand?

SOURCES: Based on Harry W. Lane, *Charles Foster Sends an E-mail*, (London, Ontario: Ivey Publishing, 2005); Frank Unger and Roger Frankel, *Doing Business in Mexico: A Practical Guide on How to Break into the Market* (Council on Australia Latin America Relations and the Department of Foreign Affairs and Trade, 2002): 24–27; and Ignacio Hernandez, "Doing Business in Mexico—Business Etiquette—Understanding U.S.–Mexico Cultural Differences," *MexGrocer.com*: www.mexgrocer.com/business-in-mexico.html (accessed September 18, 2006).

ch18 ON THE JOB VIDEO CASE

P.F. Chang's Employees Taste the Fruits of Motivation

What motivates you? Do you run every morning to get fit, lose weight, or slide into that special pair of jeans? Do you study because you love what you are learning, or because you want good grades? Do you work every weekend for money to pay for college or for money to eat out with your friends? All of these motives are real and legitimate—they are what drive you to do the things you do. The same is true for workers everywhere, including P.F. Chang's bistros. It's easy to see what motivates managers and executives at P.F. Chang's: they want customers to love the food and atmosphere, they want their business to succeed and grow, and they want to earn a good living in return for their investment and hard work. "We

are truly glad you are here," says P.F. Chang's motto, "and we will do everything possible to make you want to come back again." This is the biggest motivation of all—to have customers come back.

But what motivates employees at P.F. Chang's— the wait staff, bartenders, hosts, chefs and kitchen crew, bus boys, and dishwashers? Historically, the restaurant industry has relied on a rigid hierarchy, with managers meting out punishments and rewards to hourly workers. The result has been a low degree of job satisfaction and a high degree of turnover. There might be some use of job rotation or job enlargement, but it is not an industry that is generally known for its embrace of a new workplace. P.F. Chang's, however, is different—and some may argue that the way its workers are treated is a major factor in the company's success.

Throughout the firm, Chairman and CEO Rick Federico introduced the concept of partnerships, rather than layers of management. Because they are empowered to hire their own team of workers, from the kitchen to the dining room, operating partners have a major stake in their restaurant's success. "Managers have a passion for the business," explains operating partner Jennifer Olson Hicks, "and we instill that in our employees." Hicks also notes that it is important for managers to be wherever they are needed in the restaurant—whether it is hosting, taking orders, or washing dishes. Setting this kind of example of commitment to the success of the organization can be a powerful motivator to employees.

All of P.F. Chang's restaurant workers are trained to understand more than just their jobs. They know the food and the way it is prepared; they know the wine list; they know what their guests want and how to provide it for them; and they know how P.F. Chang's operates as a company. In addition, the workers themselves are empowered to do just about whatever it takes to satisfy their customers. For example, wait staff are trained to guide new visitors through the Asian menu—termed the "limo ride" in company lingo—so they can select the food they will enjoy. Waiters don't just take orders, they provide a service through their knowledge of the menu, the food, and its preparation. In the kitchen, although workers may have specific jobs, ranging from line cook to sous chef, all employees understand the total picture. "Everyone knows what's going on in the kitchen," explains Paul Muller, corporate executive chef. He likens the performance of the kitchen staff to "a great baseball team."

P.F. Chang's also motivates by providing opportunity for advancement. Its continued growth "enables us to promote from within and offer members of our team the opportunity to enter management and further develop their business skills," notes CEO Federico. Finally, the firm offers a generous array of benefits, ranging from meal discounts to bonus plans to various retirement savings plans. P.F. Chang's sounds like a great place to eat—and an even better place to work.

Questions

1. P.F. Chang's offers a menu of extrinsic rewards to its workers. What are some of the intrinsic rewards?

2. In what ways might managers at P.F. Chang's use positive reinforcement for their kitchen crew or wait staff?

3. In what ways can P.F. Chang's employees use the four elements of empowerment to achieve the highest level of performance in their jobs?

SOURCES: Company training materials and company Web site, *http://www.pfchangs.com*, accessed September 8, 2004; Charles Bernstein, "Chief Execution Officer," *Chain Leader*, September 2004, pp. 62–68; "Work Force Still Top Concern for CEOs," *The Phoenix Business Journal*, May 24, 2004, *http://phoenix.bizjournals.com*.

---

ch18   BIZ FLIX VIDEO CASE

Scent of a Woman

Young Charlie Simms (Chris O'Donnell) wants to earn extra money over Thanksgiving weekend so that he can afford the airfare to go home during Christmas break. He becomes a guide and caretaker for ill-tempered, retired Lt. Col. Frank Slade (Al Pacino) who is blind. Charlie, from Gresham, Oregon, is quiet and reserved and has had little experience with the opposite sex. He attends the exclusive Baird Preparatory School on a scholarship. His wild New York City weekend with Frank Slade bonds them forever. This film is a remake of *Profumo di Donna*, a 1974 Italian film.

This scene follows Slade's morose moments in their hotel suite after the first day and night in Manhattan. Slade wants to sleep in and perhaps even die. Charlie convinces him to venture out on this beautiful day and go for a ride. They go to a Ferrari dealership where Slade convinces salesman Freddie Bisco (Leonard Gaines) to allow a 17-year-old driver and a blind man to take the Ferrari Cabriolet T for a test drive. This scene appears in the last third of the film and defines the continued bonding of Frank Slade and Charlie Simms.

What to Watch for and Ask Yourself

1. What pattern of control do these scenes show?

2. What are the control system's elements?

3. Do these scenes show a periodic or a continuous type of performance measurement?

ch18 ENDNOTES

1. Jennifer Reingold, "Target's Inner Circle," *Fortune* (March 31, 2008): 76–86.

2. "Effective Communication Strategy Impacts Bottom Line," *Executive's Tax & Management Report* (January 2008): 15.

3. Henry Mintzberg, *The Nature of Managerial Work* (New York: Harper & Row, 1973).

4. Phillip G. Clampitt, Laurey Berk, and M. Lee Williams, "Leaders as Strategic Communicators," *Ivey Business Journal* (May–June 2002): 51–55.

5. Ian Wylie, "Can Philips Learn to Walk the Talk?" *Fast Company* (January 2003): 44–45.

6. Fred Luthans and Janet K. Larsen, "How Managers Really Communicate," *Human Relations* 39 (1986): 161–178; and Larry E. Penley and Brian Hawkins, "Studying Interpersonal Communication in Organizations: A Leadership Application," *Academy of Management Journal* 28 (1985): 309–326.

7. D. K. Berlo, *The Process of Communication* (New York: Holt, Rinehart and Winston, 1960), p. 24.

8. Bruce K. Blaylock, "Cognitive Style and the Usefulness of Information," *Decision Sciences* 15 (Winter 1984): 74–91.

9. Robert H. Lengel and Richard L. Daft, "The Selection of Communication Media as an Executive Skill," *Academy of Management Executive* 2 (August 1988): 225–232; Richard L. Daft and Robert H. Lengel, "Organizational Information Requirements, Media Richness and Structural Design," *Managerial Science* 32 (May 1986): 554–572; and Jane Webster and Linda Klebe Treviño, "Rational and Social Theories as Complementary Explanations of Communication Media Choices: Two Policy-Capturing Studies," *Academy of Management Journal* 38, no. 6 (1995): 1544–1572.

10. Research reported in "E-mail Can't Mimic Phone Calls," *Johnson City Press*, September 17, 2000.

11. Raymond E. Friedman and Steven C. Currall, "E-Mail Escalation: Dispute Exacerbating Elements of Electronic Communication, http:// www.mba.vanderbilt.edu/ ray.friedman/pdf/emailescalation .pdf; Lauren Keller Johnson, "Does E-Mail Escalate Conflict?" *MIT Sloan Management Review* (Fall 2002): 14–15; and Alison Stein Wellner, "Lost in Translation," *Inc. Magazine* (September 2005): 37–38.

12. Wellner, "Lost in Translation"; Nick Easen, "Don't Send the Wrong Message; When E-Mail Crosses Borders, a Faux Pas Could Be Just a Click Away," *Business 2.0* (August 2005): 102.

13. Scott Kirsner, "IM Is Here. RU Prepared?" *Darwin Magazine* (February 2002): 22–24.

14. John R. Carlson and Robert W. Smud, "Channel Expansion Theory and the Experiential Nature of Media Richness Perceptions," *Academy of Management Journal* 42, no. 2 (1999): 153–170; R. Rice and G. Love, "Electronic Emotion," *Communication Research* 14 (1987): 85–108.

15. Ronald E. Rice, "Task Analyzability, Use of New Media, and Effectiveness: A Multi-Site Exploration of Media Richness," *Organizational Science* 3, no. 4 (November 1992): 475–500; and M. Lynne Markus, "Electronic Mail as the Medium of Managerial Choice," *Organizational Science* 5, no. 4 (November 1994): 502–527.

16. Richard L. Daft, Robert H. Lengel, and Linda Klebe Treviño, "Message Equivocality, Media Selection and Manager Performance: Implication for Information Systems," *MIS Quarterly* 11 (1987): 355–368.

17. Mary Young and James E. Post, "Managing to Communicate, Communicating to Manage: How Leading Companies Communicate with Employees," *Organizational Dynamics* (Summer 1993): 31–43.

18. Jay A. Conger, "The Necessary Art of Persuasion," *Harvard Business Review* (May–June 1998): 84–95.

19. Ibid.

20. Susan Cramm, "The Heart of Persuasion," *CIO* (July 1, 2005): 28–30.

21. Deborah Tannen, *You Just Don't Understand: Women and Men in Conversation* (New York: Ballantine Books, 1991), p. 77.

22. Ibid, p. 125.

23. Rosalind Barnett and Caryl Rivers, *Same Difference: How Gender Myths Are Hurting Our Relationships, Our Children, and Our Jobs* (New York: Perseus Books Group, 2004), p. 133.

24. I. Thomas Sheppard, "Silent Signals," *Supervisory Management* (March 1986): 31–33.

25. Albert Mehrabian, *Silent Messages* (Belmont, CA: Wadsworth, 1971); and Albert Mehrabian, "Communicating without Words," *Psychology Today* (September 1968): 53–55.

26. Meridith Levinson, "How to Be a Mind Reader," *CIO* (December 1, 2004): 72–76; Mac Fulfer, "Non-verbal Communication: How to Read What's Plain as the Nose . . . ," *Journal of Organizational Excellence* (Spring 2001): 19–27; Paul Ekman, *Emotions Revealed: Recognizing Faces and Feelings to Improve Communication and Emotional Life* (New York: Time Books, 2003).

27. Aili McConnon, "Ace Hardware: Calling the Right Play for Each Customer," *BusinessWeek* (February 21, 2008), http://www.businessweek .com/magazine/content/08_09/ b4073050445440.htm (accessed March 28, 2008).

28. C. Glenn Pearce, "Doing Something about Your Listening Ability," *Supervisory Management* (March 1989): 29–34; and Tom Peters, "Learning to Listen," *Hyatt Magazine* (Spring 1988): 16–21.

29. Kelley Holland, "Under New Management; The Silent May Have Something to Say," *The New York Times*, November 5, 2006, www .nytimes.com (accessed December 4, 2006).

30. Debbie Weil, *The Corporate Blogging Book* (New York: Penguin Group, 2006), p. 3.

31. Fortune 500 Business Blogging Wiki, http://www.socialtext.net/bizblogs/ index.cgi (accessed April 9, 2008).

32. Interview by Oliver Ryan, "Blogger in Chief," *Fortune* (November 13, 2006): 51.

33. M. P. Nichols, *The Lost Art of Listening* (New York: Guilford Publishing, 1995).

34. "Benchmarking the Sales Function," a report based on a study of 100 salespeople from small, medium,

6

Leading

and large businesses, conducted by Ron Volper Group Inc. Sales Consulting and Training, White Plains, New York (1996), as reported in "Nine Habits of Highly Successful Salespeople," *Inc. Small Business Success.*

35. Gerald M. Goldhaber, *Organizational Communication*, 4th ed. (Dubuque, IA: Brown, 1980), p. 189.

36. Richard L. Daft and Richard M. Steers, *Organizations: A Micro/Macro Approach* (New York: Harper Collins, 1986); and Daniel Katz and Robert Kahn, *The Social Psychology of Organizations*, 2nd ed. (New York: Wiley, 1978).

37. Greg Jaffe, "Tug of War: In the New Military, Technology May Alter Chain of Command," *The Wall Street Journal*, March 30, 2001; and Aaron Pressman, "Business Gets the Message," *The Industry Standard* (February 26, 2001): 58–59.

38. Phillip G. Clampitt, Robert J. DeKoch, and Thomas Cashman, "A Strategy for Communicating about Uncertainty," *Academy of Management Executive* 14, no. 4 (2000): 41–57.

39. Reported in Louise van der Does and Stephen J. Caldeira, "Effective Leaders Champion Communication Skills," *Nation's Restaurant News* (March 27, 2006): 20.

40. J. G. Miller, "Living Systems: The Organization," *Behavioral Science* 17 (1972): 69.

41. Michael J. Glauser, "Upward Information Flow in Organizations: Review and Conceptual Analysis," *Human Relations* 37 (1984): 613–643; and "Upward/ Downward Communication: Critical Information Channels," *Small Business Report* (October 1985): 85–88.

42. Thomas Petzinger, "A Hospital Applies Teamwork to Thwart An Insidious Enemy," *The Wall Street Journal*, May 8, 1998.

43. Gary Hamel, What Google, Whole Foods Do Best, *Fortune* (October 1, 2007): 124.

44. E. M. Rogers and R. A. Rogers, *Communication in Organizations* (New York: Free Press, 1976); and A. Bavelas and D. Barrett, "An Experimental Approach to Organization Communication," *Personnel* 27 (1951): 366–371.

45. This discussion is based on Daft and Steers, *Organizations.*

46. Bavelas and Barrett, "An Experimental Approach"; and M. E. Shaw, *Group Dynamics: The Psychology of Small Group Behavior* (New York: McGraw-Hill, 1976).

47. Richard L. Daft and Norman B. Macintosh, "A Tentative Exploration into the Amount and Equivocality of Information Processing in Organizational Work Units," *Administrative Science Quarterly* 26 (1981): 207–224.

48. This discussion of informal networks is based on Rob Cross, Nitin Nohria, and Andrew Parker, "Six Myths About Informal Networks," *MIT Sloan Management Review* (Spring 2002): 67–75; and Rob Cross and Laurence Prusak, "The People Who Make Organizations Go—or Stop," *Harvard Business Review* (June 2002): 105–112.

49. Tahl Raz, "The 10 Secrets of a Master Networker," *Inc.* (January 2003).

50. Stephanie Armour, "Office Gossip Has Never Traveled Faster, Thanks to Tech," *USA Today*, November 1, 2007, http://www.usatoday.com/tech/webguide/internetlife/2007-09-09-office-gossip-technology_n.htm (accessed March 28, 2008).

51. Keith Davis and John W. Newstrom, *Human Behavior at Work: Organizational Behavior*, 7th ed. (New York: McGraw-Hill, 1985).

52. Suzanne M. Crampton, John W. Hodge, and Jitendra M. Mishra, "The Informal Communication Network: Factors Influencing Grapevine Activity," *Public Personnel Management* 27, no. 4 (Winter 1998): 569–584.

53. Survey results reported in Jared Sandberg, "Ruthless Rumors and the Managers Who Enable Them," *The Wall Street Journal*, October 29, 2003.

54. Donald B. Simmons, "The Nature of the Organizational Grapevine," *Supervisory Management* (November 1985): 39–42; and Davis and Newstrom, *Human Behavior.*

55. Barbara Ettorre, "Hellooo. Anybody Listening?" *Management Review* (November 1997): 9.

56. Eilene Zimmerman, "Gossip Is Information by Another Name," *The New York Times*, February 3, 2008, http://www.nytimes.com/2008/02/03/jobs/03career.html?_r=1&scp=1&sq=Gossip%20Is%20Information%20by%20Another%20Name&st=cse&oref=slogin (accessed February 3, 2008).

57. Lisa A. Burke and Jessica Morris Wise, "The Effective Care, Handling, and Pruning of the Office Grapevine," *Business Horizons* (May–June 2003): 71–74; "They Hear It Through the Grapevine," cited in Michael Warshaw, "The Good Guy's Guide to Office Politics," *Fast Company* (April–May 1998): 157–178; and Carol Hildebrand, "Mapping the Invisible Workplace," *CIO Enterprise*, section 2 (July 15, 1998): 18–20.

58. The National Commission on Writing, "Writing Skills Necessary for Employment, Says Big Business," September 14, 2004, http://www.writingcommission.org/pr/writing_for_employ.html (accessed April 8, 2008).

59. Based on Michael Fitzgerald, "How to Write a Memorable Memo," *CIO* (October 15, 2005): 85–87; and Jonathan Hershberg, "It's Not Just What You Say," *Training* (May 2005): 50.

60. Mary Anne Donovan, "E-Mail Exposes the Literacy Gap," *Workforce* (November 2002): 15.

61. David Bohm, *On Dialogue* (Ojai, CA: David Bohm Seminars, 1989).

62. George Kohlrieser, "The Power of Authentic Dialogue," *Leader to Leader* (Fall 2006): 37.

63. This discussion is based on Glenna Gerard and Linda Teurfs, "Dialogue and Organizational Transformation," in *Community Building: Renewing Spirit and Learning in Business*, ed. Kazinierz Gozdz (New Leaders, 1995), pp. 142–153; and Edgar H. Schein, "On Dialogue, Culture, and Organizational Learning," *Organizational Dynamics* (Autumn 1993): 40–51.

64. Ian I. Mitroff and Murat C. Alpaslan, "Preparing for Evil," *Harvard Business Review* (April 2003): 109–115.

65. Brad Ritter and Janet Ritter, "Crisis Communication: Taking Center Stage With Confidence," *Government Finance Review* 23, no. 6 (December, 2007): 51.

66. This section is based on Leslie Wayne and Leslie Kaufman, "Leadership, Put to a New Test," *The New York Times*, September 16, 2001; Ian I. Mitroff, "Crisis Leadership," *Executive Excellence* (August 2001): 19; Jerry Useem, "What It Takes," *Fortune* (November 12, 2001): 126–132;

Andy Bowen, "Crisis Procedures That Stand the Test of Time," *Public Relations Tactics* (August 2001): 16; and Matthew Boyle, "Nothing Really Matters," *Fortune* (October 15, 2001): 261–264.

67. Stephen Bernhut, "Leadership, with Michael Useem," *Ivey Business Journal* (January–February 2002): 42–43.

68. Mitroff, "Crisis Leadership."

69. Jay M. Jackman and Myra H. Strober, "Fear of Feedback," *Harvard Business Review* (April 2003): 101–108;

and Dennis Tourish, "Critical Upward Communication: Ten Commandments for Improving Strategy and Decision Making," *Long Range Planning* 38 (2005): 485–503.

70. Thomas E. Ricks, "Army Devises System to Decide What Does, and Does Not, Work," *The Wall Street Journal*, May 23, 1997; Stephanie Watts Sussman, "CALL: A Model for Effective Organizational Learning," *Strategy* (Summer 1999): 14–15; John O'Shea, "Army: The

Leader as Learner-in-Chief," *The Officer* (June 2003): 31; Michael D. Maples, "Fires First in Combat—Train the Way We Fight," *Field Artillery* (July–August 2003): 1; Thomas E. Ricks, "Intelligence Problems in Iraq Are Detailed," *The Washington Post*, October 25, 2003; and Richard W. Koenig, "Forging Our Future: Using Operation Iraqi Freedom Phase IV Lessons Learned," *Engineer* (January–March 2004): 21–22.

pt6   chapter19

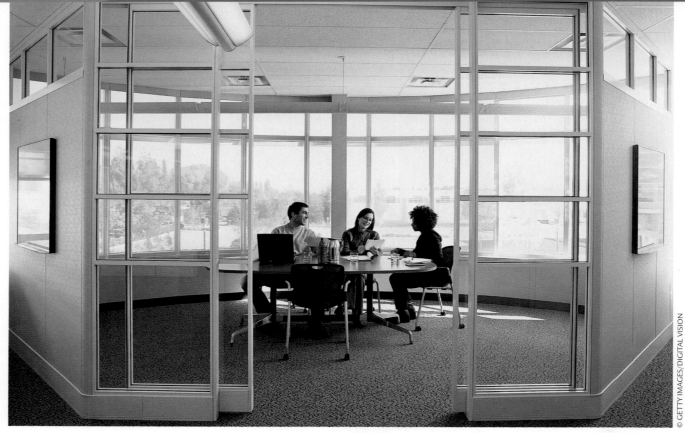

© GETTY IMAGES/DIGITAL VISION

Learning Outcomes

After studying this chapter, you should be able to:

1. Identify the types of teams in organizations.

2. Discuss some of the problems and challenges of teamwork.

3. Identify roles within teams and the type of role you could play to help a team be effective.

4. Explain the general stages of team development.

5. Identify ways in which team size and diversity of membership affects team performance.

6. Explain the concepts of team cohesiveness and team norms and their relationship to team performance.

7. Understand the causes of conflict within and among teams and how to reduce conflict.

8. Define the outcomes of effective teams and how managers can enhance team effectiveness.

Leading Teams

HOW DO YOU LIKE TO WORK?[1]

Your approach to your job or schoolwork may indicate whether you thrive on a team. Answer the questions below about your work preferences. Please answer whether each item below is Mostly True or Mostly False for you.

	Mostly True	Mostly False
1. I prefer to work on a team rather than do individual tasks.	_____	_____
2. Given a choice, I try to work by myself rather than face hassles of group work.	_____	_____
3. I enjoy the personal interaction when working with others.	_____	_____
4. I prefer to do my own work and let others do theirs.	_____	_____
5. I get more satisfaction from a group victory than an individual victory.	_____	_____
6. Teamwork is not worthwhile when people do not do their share.	_____	_____
7. I feel good when I work with others even when we disagree.	_____	_____
8. I prefer to rely on myself rather than others to do an assignment.	_____	_____

SCORING AND INTERPRETATION: Give yourself one point for each odd-numbered item you marked as Mostly True and one point for each even-numbered item you marked Mostly False. An important part of a new manager's job is to be both part of a team and to work alone. These items measure your preference for group work. Teamwork can be both frustrating and motivating. If you scored two or fewer points, you definitely prefer individual work. A score of seven or above suggests that you prefer working in teams. A score of three to six indicates comfort working alone and in a team. A new manager needs to do both.

Many people get their first management experience in a team setting, and you will probably sometimes have to work in a team as a new manager. Teams have become the primary way in which many companies accomplish their work, from the assembly line to the executive suite. Teams have real advantages, but it can sometimes be tough to work in a team. You may have already experienced the challenges of teamwork as a student, where you've had to give up some of your independence and rely on the team to perform well in order to earn a good grade.

Good teams can be highly productive, but teams aren't always successful. In a survey of manufacturing organizations, about 80 percent of respondents said they used some kind of teams, but only 14 percent of those companies rated their teaming efforts as highly effective. Just over half of the respondents said their efforts were only "somewhat effective," and 15 percent considered their efforts not effective at all.[2]

This chapter focuses on teams and their applications within organizations. We first look at why organizations use teams, discuss the dilemma of teamwork, and provide an overview of what makes an effective team. We define various types of teams, explore the stages of team development, and examine how characteristics such as size, cohesiveness, diversity, and norms influence team effectiveness. We also discuss how individuals can make contributions to teams, look at techniques for managing team conflict, and describe how negotiation can facilitate cooperation and teamwork. The final section of the chapter focuses on the outcomes of effective work teams within organizations. Teams are a central aspect of organizational life, and the ability to manage them is a vital component of manager and organization success.

WHY TEAMS AT WORK?

Why aren't organizations just collections of individuals going their own way and doing their own thing? Clearly, teamwork provides benefits or companies wouldn't continue to use this structural mechanism. Organizations are by their very nature made up of various individuals and groups that have to work together and coordinate their activities to accomplish objectives. Much work in organizations is *interdependent*, which means that individuals and departments rely on other individuals and departments for information or resources to accomplish their work. When tasks are highly interdependent, a team can be the best approach to ensuring the level of coordination, information sharing, and exchange of materials necessary for successful task accomplishment.

Concept Connection The power of effective **teamwork** is illustrated by Lance Armstrong's record-breaking accomplishment in winning the Tour de France seven consecutive years from 1999 to 2005. Armstrong, shown here in the yellow jersey with teammates during the 92nd Tour de France, succeeded not just as an individual but as part of a team. Members of the Discovery Channel Team (previously the U.S. Postal Service Cycling Team) united around a **shared purpose** of helping Armstrong win the 21-day competition, pacing his ride and protecting him from other cyclists and spectators.

What Is a Team?

A **team** is a unit of two or more people who interact and coordinate their work to accomplish a specific goal.[3] At Cirque du Soleil, the CEO, chief operating officer, chief financial officer, and vice president of creation function as a top management team to develop, coordinate, and oversee acrobatic troupes that travel to approximately 100 cities on four continents a year. Google assembles teams of three or four employees to assess new ideas and recommend whether they should be implemented. And at the Ralston Foods plant in Sparks, Nevada, teams of production workers handle all team hiring, scheduling, quality, budgeting, and disciplinary issues.[4]

The definition of a team has three components. First, two or more people are required. Second, people in a team have regular interaction. People who do not interact, such as when standing in line at a lunch counter or riding in an elevator, do not compose a team. Third, people in a team share a performance goal, whether to design a new handheld computing device, build an engine, or complete a class project.

Although a team is a group of people, the two terms are not interchangeable. An employer, a teacher, or a coach can put together a *group* of people and never build a *team*. The team concept implies a sense of shared mission and collective responsibility. Exhibit 19.1 lists the primary differences between groups and teams. One example of a true team comes from the military, where U.S. Navy surgeons, nurses, anesthesiologists, and technicians make up eight-person forward surgical teams that operated

team A unit of two or more people who interact and coordinate their work to accomplish a specific goal.

EXHIBIT | 19.1

Differences Between Groups and Teams

Group	Team
• Has a designated strong leader	• Shares or rotates leadership roles
• Holds individuals accountable	• Holds team accountable to each other
• Sets identical purpose for group and organization	• Sets specific team vision or purpose
• Has individual work products	• Has collective work products
• Runs efficient meetings	• Runs meetings that encourage open-ended discussion and problem solving
• Measures effectiveness indirectly by influence on business (such as financial performance)	• Measures effectiveness directly by assessing collective work
• Discusses, decides, delegates work to individuals	• Discusses, decides, shares work

SOURCE: Adapted from Jon R. Katzenbach and Douglas K. Smith, "The Discipline of Teams," *Harvard Business Review* (March–April 1995): 111–120.

for the first time ever in combat during Operation Iraqi Freedom. These teams were scattered over Iraq and were able to move to new locations and be set up within an hour. With a goal of saving the 15 to 20 percent of wounded soldiers and civilians who will die unless they receive critical care within 24 hours, members of these teams smoothly coordinated their activities to accomplish a critical shared mission.[5]

The Dilemma of Teams

If you've been in a class where the instructor announced that part of the grade would be based on a team project, you probably heard a few groans. The same thing happens in organizations. Some people love the idea of teamwork, others hate it, and many people have both positive and negative emotions about working as part of a team. There are three primary reasons teams present a dilemma for most people:

- *We have to give up our independence.* When people become part of a team, their success depends on the team's success; therefore, they are dependent on how well other people perform, not just on their own individual initiative and actions. Most people are comfortable with the idea of making sacrifices to achieve their own individual success, yet teamwork demands that they make sacrifices for *group* success.[6] The idea is that each person should put the team first, even if at times it hurts the individual. Many employees, particularly in individualistic cultures such as the United States, have a hard time appreciating and accepting that concept. Some cultures, such as Japan, have had greater success with teams because traditional Japanese culture values the group over the individual.

- *We have to put up with free riders.* Teams are sometimes made up of people who have different work ethics. The term **free rider** refers to a team member who attains benefits from team membership but does not actively participate in and contribute to the team's work. You might have experienced this frustration in a student project team, where one member put little effort into the group project but benefitted from the hard work of others when grades were handed out. Free riding is sometimes called *social loafing* because some members do not exert equal effort.[7]

- *Teams are sometimes dysfunctional.* Some companies have had great success with teams, but there are also numerous examples of how teams in organizations fail spectacularly.[8] A great deal of research and team experience over the past few decades has produced significant insights into what causes teams to succeed or fail. The evidence shows that how teams are managed plays the most critical role in determining how well they function.[9] Exhibit 19.2 lists five dysfunctions that are common in teams and describes the contrasting desirable characteristics that effective team leaders develop.

free rider A person who benefits from team membership but does not make a proportionate contribution to the team's work.

EXHIBIT | 19.2   Five Common Dysfunctions of Teams

Dysfunction	Effective Team Characteristics
Lack of Trust—People don't feel safe to reveal mistakes, share concerns, or express ideas.	**Trust**—Members trust one another on a deep emotional level; feel comfortable being vulnerable with one another.
Fear of Conflict—People go along with others for the sake of harmony; don't express conflicting opinions.	**Healthy Conflict**—Members feel comfortable disagreeing and challenging one another in the interest of finding the best solution.
Lack of Commitment—If people are afraid to express their true opinions, it's difficult to gain their true commitment to decisions.	**Commitment**—Because all ideas are put on the table, people can eventually achieve genuine buy-in around important goals and decisions.
Avoidance of Accountability—People don't accept responsibility for outcomes; engage in finger-pointing when things go wrong.	**Accountability**—Members hold one another accountable rather than relying on managers as the source of accountability.
Inattention to Results—Members put personal ambition or the needs of their individual departments ahead of collective results.	**Results Orientation**—Individual members set aside personal agendas; focus on what's best for the team. Collective results define success.

SOURCE: Based on Patrick Lencioni, *The Five Dysfunctions of a Team* (New York: John Wiley & Sons, 2002).

6 Leading

TakeaMoment | As a new manager, be aware of the dilemma teamwork creates. Some people will be energized and excited by the idea of working as part of a team, while others will be apprehensive, cynical, or annoyed. As a team leader, be alert to the possibility of free riding, and make sure work activities are distributed equitably.

HOW TO MAKE TEAMS EFFECTIVE

Smoothly functioning teams don't just happen. Stanford sociologist Elizabeth Cohen studied group work among young school children and found that only when teachers took the time to define roles, establish norms, and set goals did the groups function effectively as a team.[10] In organizations, effective teams are built by managers who take specific actions to help people come together and perform well as a team.

Some of the factors associated with team effectiveness are illustrated in Exhibit 19.3. Work team effectiveness is based on three outcomes—productive output, personal satisfaction, and the capacity to adapt and learn.[11] *Satisfaction* pertains to the team's ability to meet the personal needs of its members and hence maintain their membership and commitment. *Productive output* pertains to the quality and quantity of task outputs as defined by team goals. *Capacity to adapt and learn* refers to the ability of teams to bring greater knowledge and skills to job tasks and enhance the potential of the organization to respond to new threats or opportunities in the environment.

Model of Team Effectiveness

The model of team effectiveness in Exhibit 19.3 provides a structure for the remainder of this chapter. The factors that influence team effectiveness begin with the organizational context.[12] The organizational context in which the team operates is described in other chapters and includes such matters as structure, strategy, environment, culture, and reward systems. Within that context, managers define teams. Important team characteristics are the type of team, the team structure, and team composition. Managers must decide when to create permanent teams within the formal structure and when to use a temporary task team. The diversity of the team in terms of task-related knowledge and skills can have a tremendous impact on team processes and effectiveness. In addition, diversity in terms of gender and race affect a team's performance.[13] Team size and roles also are important.

These team characteristics influence processes internal to the team, which, in turn, affect output, satisfaction, and the team's contribution to organizational adaptability.

EXHIBIT | 19.3 Work Team Effectiveness Model

Good team leaders understand and manage stages of team development, cohesiveness, norms, and conflict to build an effective team. These processes are influenced by team and organizational characteristics and by the ability of members and leaders to direct these processes in a positive manner.

Effective Team Leadership

Team leaders play an important role in shaping team effectiveness. In addition to managing internal processes, there are three specific ways in which leaders contribute to team success:[14]

- *Rally people around a compelling purpose.* It is the leader's responsibility to articulate a clear, compelling purpose and direction, one of the key elements of effective teams. This ensures that everyone is moving in the same direction rather than floundering around wondering why the team was created and where it's supposed to be going.

- *Share power.* Good team leaders embrace the concept of teamwork in deeds as well as words. This means sharing power, information, and responsibility. It means letting team members who do the work have a say in how to do it. It requires that the leader have faith that team members will make good decisions, even if those decisions might not be the ones the leader would make.

- *Admit ignorance.* Often, people appointed to lead teams find that they don't know nearly as much as their teammates know. Good team leaders aren't afraid to admit their ignorance and ask for help. This serves as a *fallibility model* that lets people know that lack of knowledge, problems, concerns, and mistakes can be discussed openly without fear of appearing incompetent. Although it's hard for many managers to believe, admitting ignorance and being willing to learn from others can earn the respect of team members faster than almost any other behavior.

Go to the experiential exercise on page 590 that pertains to effective versus ineffective teams. | TakeaMoment

TYPES OF TEAMS

Organizations use many types of teams. Some are created as part of the organization's formal structure and others are designed to increase employee participation.

Formal Teams

Formal teams are created by the organization as part of the formal organization structure. Two common types of formal teams are vertical and horizontal, which typically represent vertical and horizontal structural relationships, as described in Chapter 9. These two types of teams are illustrated in Exhibit 19.4.

Vertical Team A **vertical team** is composed of a manager and his or her subordinates in the formal chain of command. Sometimes called a *functional team* or a *command team*, the vertical team may in some cases include three or four levels of hierarchy within a functional department. Typically, the vertical team includes a single department in an organization. The third-shift nursing team on the second floor of St. Luke's Hospital is a vertical team that includes nurses and a supervisor. A financial analysis department, a quality control department, an accounting department, and a human resource department are all vertical or command teams. Each is created by the organization to attain specific goals through members' joint activities and interactions.

formal team A team created by the organization as part of the formal organization structure.

vertical team A formal team composed of a manager and his or her subordinates in the organization's formal chain of command.

6 Leading

EXHIBIT | 19.4 Horizontal and Vertical Teams in an Organization

- – – – – Horizontal team for
          L21 modification project
────── Vertical engineering team

Horizontal Team A **horizontal team** is composed of employees from about the same hierarchical level but from different areas of expertise.[15] A horizontal team is drawn from several departments, is given a specific task, and may be disbanded after the task is completed. Horizontal teams include cross-functional teams, committees, and special purpose teams.

As described in Chapter 9, a *cross-functional team* is a group of employees from different departments formed to deal with a specific activity and existing only until the task is completed. Sometimes called a *task force*, the team might be used to create a new product in a manufacturing organization or a new history curriculum in a university. When several departments are involved, and many views have to be considered, tasks are best served with a horizontal, cross-functional team.

A **committee** generally is long-lived and may be a permanent part of the organization's structure. Membership is often decided by a person's title or position rather than by personal expertise. A committee needs official representation, compared with selection for a cross-functional team, which is based on personal qualifications for solving a problem. Committees typically are formed to deal with tasks that recur regularly. For example, a grievance committee handles employee grievances; an advisory committee makes recommendations in the areas of employee compensation and work practices; a worker-management committee may be concerned with work rules, job design changes, and suggestions for work improvement.[16]

Special-purpose teams, sometimes called *project teams*, are created outside the formal organization structure to undertake a project of special importance or creativity.[17] Examples include the team that developed the first IBM ThinkPad and the project team for the Motorola RAZR cell phone. A special-purpose team still is part of the formal organization and has its own reporting structure, but members perceive themselves as a separate entity.[18]

horizontal team A formal team composed of employees from about the same hierarchical level but from different areas of expertise.

committee A long-lasting, sometimes permanent team in the organization structure created to deal with tasks that recur regularly.

special-purpose team A team created outside the formal organization to undertake a project of special importance or creativity.

Self-Directed Teams

Some teams are designed to increase the participation of workers in decision making and the conduct of their jobs, with the goal of improving performance. Employee involvement started out simply with techniques such as information sharing with employees or asking employees for suggestions about improving the work. Gradually, companies moved toward greater autonomy for employees, which led first to problem-solving teams and then to self-directed teams.[19]

Problem-solving teams typically consist of 5 to 12 hourly employees from the same department who voluntarily meet to discuss ways of improving quality, efficiency, and the work environment. Recommendations are proposed to management for approval. The most widely known application is *quality circles*, first used by Japanese companies, in which employees focus on ways to improve quality in the production process. International Paper Company's Texarkana mill instituted a work systems team to focus on solving and preventing snafus in the logistically complex process of producing 1,800 to 1,900 tons of bleached board a day for packaging, milk cartons, drink cups, and folding cartons. This problem-solving team has played a significant role in helping the mill thrive amid brutal market conditions and stiff competition.[20]

Concept Connection At Lucasfilm Ltd., teams form around projects. To facilitate these **self-directed teams**, the company responsible for the *Star Wars* and *Indiana Jones* franchises moved its formerly separate divisions to a campus in the Presidio of San Francisco. An easily reconfigurable work environment encourages the sharing of ideas and technology between the visual effects division Industrial Light & Magic and LucasArts, the video game company. Project teams also work on visual effects for other films, like the visual effects for *Transformers* and the *Pirates of the Caribbean* franchise. In this photo, producer Julio Torres reviews work on LucasArts' video game *Star Wars: The Force Unleashed*.

As a company matures, problem-solving teams can gradually evolve into self-directed teams, which represent a fundamental change in how work is organized. **Self-directed teams** typically consist of 5 to 20 multiskilled workers who rotate jobs to produce an entire product or service or at least one complete aspect or portion of a product or service (e.g., engine assembly, insurance claim processing). The central idea is that the teams themselves, rather than managers or supervisors, take responsibility for their work, make decisions, monitor their own performance, and alter their work behavior as needed to solve problems, meet goals, and adapt to changing conditions.[21]

Self-directed teams are permanent teams that typically include the following elements:

- The team includes employees with several skills and functions, and the combined skills are sufficient to perform a major organizational task. A team may include members from the foundry, machining, grinding, fabrication, and sales departments, with members cross-trained to perform one another's jobs. The team eliminates barriers among departments, enabling excellent coordination to produce a product or service.

- The team is given access to resources such as information, equipment, machinery, and supplies needed to perform the complete task.

- The team is empowered with decision-making authority, which means that members have the freedom to select new members, solve problems, spend money, monitor results, and plan for the future.[22] Self-directed teams can enable employees to feel challenged, find their work meaningful, and develop a stronger sense of identity with the organization.

INNOVATIVE USES OF TEAMS

Some exciting new approaches to teamwork have resulted from advances in information technology, shifting employee expectations, and the globalization of business. Two types of teams that are increasingly being used are virtual teams and global teams.

Virtual Teams

A **virtual team** is made up of geographically or organizationally dispersed members who are linked primarily through advanced information and telecommunications technologies.[23] Although some virtual teams are made up of only organizational members, virtual teams often include contingent workers, members of partner organizations,

problem-solving team Typically 5 to 12 hourly employees from the same department who meet to discuss ways of improving quality, efficiency, and the work environment.

self-directed team A team consisting of 5 to 20 multiskilled workers who rotate jobs to produce an entire product or service, often supervised by an elected member.

virtual team A team made up of members who are geographically or organizationally dispersed, rarely meet face to face, and do their work using advanced information technologies.

customers, suppliers, consultants, or other outsiders. Team members use e-mail, instant messaging, telephone and text messaging, wikis and blogs, videoconferencing, and other technology tools to collaborate and perform their work, although they might also sometimes meet face to face. Many virtual teams are cross-functional teams that emphasize solving customer problems or completing specific projects. Others are permanent self-directed teams.

With virtual teams, team membership may change fairly quickly, depending on the tasks to be performed.[24] One of the primary advantages of virtual teams is the ability to rapidly assemble the most appropriate group of people to complete a complex project, solve a particular problem, or exploit a specific strategic opportunity. Virtual teams present unique challenges. Exhibit 19.5 lists some critical areas managers should address when leading virtual teams. Each of these areas is discussed in more detail below:[25]

- *Using technology to build relationships* is crucial for effective virtual teamwork. Leaders first select people who have the right mix of technical, interpersonal, and communication skills to work in a virtual environment, and then make sure they have opportunities to know one another and establish trusting relationships. Encouraging online social networking, where people can share photos and personal biographies, is one key to virtual team success. Leaders also build trust by making everyone's roles, responsibilities, and authority clear from the beginning, by shaping norms of full disclosure and respectful interaction, and by providing a way for everyone to stay up-to-date. In a study of which technologies make virtual teams successful, researchers found that round-the-clock virtual work spaces, where team members can access the latest versions of files, keep track of deadlines and timelines, monitor one another's progress, and carry on discussions between formal meetings, got top marks.[26] Today, many virtual teams use wikis to facilitate this kind of regular collaboration and open information sharing.

- *Shaping culture through technology* involves creating a virtual environment in which people feel safe to express concerns, admit mistakes, share ideas, acknowledge fears, or ask for help. Leaders reinforce a norm of sharing all forms of knowledge, and they encourage people to express "off-the-wall" ideas and ask for help when it's needed. Team leaders set the example by their own behavior. Leaders also make sure they bring diversity issues into the open and educate members early on regarding possible cultural differences that could cause communication problems or misunderstandings in a virtual environment.

- *Monitoring progress and rewarding members* means that leaders stay on top of the project's development and make sure everyone knows how the team is progressing toward meeting goals. Posting targets, measurements, and milestones in

EXHIBIT | 19.5

What Effective Virtual Team Leaders Do

Practice	How It's Done
Use Technology to Build Relationships	• Bring attention to and appreciate diverse skills and opinions • Use technology to enhance communication and trust • Ensure timely responses online • Manage online socialization
Shape Culture Through Technology	• Create a psychologically safe virtual culture • Share members' special experience/strengths • Engage members from cultures where they may be hesitant to share ideas
Monitor Progress and Rewards	• Scrutinize electronic communication patterns • Post targets and scorecards in virtual work space • Reward people through online ceremonies, recognition

SOURCE: Based on Table 1, Practices of Effective Virtual Team Leaders, in Arvind Malhotra, Ann Majchrzak, and Benson Rosen, "Leading Virtual Teams," *Academy of Management Perspectives* 21, no. 1 (February 2007): 60–69; and Table 2, "Best Practices" Solutions for Overcoming Barriers to Knowledge Sharing in Virtual Teams, in Benson Rosen, Stacie Furst, and Richard Blackburn, "Overcoming Barriers to Knowledge Sharing in Virtual Teams," *Organizational Dynamics* 36, no. 3 (2007): 259–273.

the virtual workspace can make progress explicit. Leaders also provide regular feedback, and they reward both individual and team accomplishments through such avenues as virtual award ceremonies and recognition at virtual meetings. They are liberal with praise and congratulations, but criticism or reprimands are handled individually rather than in the virtual presence of the team.

As the use of virtual teams grows, there is growing understanding of what makes them successful. Some experts suggest that managers solicit volunteers as much as possible for virtual teams, and interviews with virtual team members and leaders support the idea that members who truly want to work as a virtual team are more effective.[27] At Nokia, a significant portion of its virtual teams are made up of people who volunteered for the task.

In a study of 52 virtual teams in 15 leading multinational companies, London Business School researchers found that Nokia's teams were among the most effective, even though they were made up of people working in several different countries, across time zones and cultures. What makes Nokia's teams so successful?

Nokia managers are careful to select people who have a collaborative mind-set, and they form many teams with volunteers who are highly committed to the task or project. The company also tries to make sure some members of a team have worked together before, providing a base for trusting relationships. Making the best use of technology is critical. In addition to a virtual work space that team members can access 24 hours a day, Nokia provides an online resource where virtual workers are encouraged to post photos and share personal information. With the inability of members to get to know each another one of the biggest barriers to effective virtual teamwork, encouraging and supporting social networking has paid off for Nokia.[28]

Innovative Way

Nokia

Global Teams

As the example of Nokia shows, virtual teams are also sometimes global teams. **Global teams** are cross-border work teams made up of members of different nationalities whose activities span multiple countries.[29] Some global teams are made up of members who come from different countries or cultures and meet face-to-face, but many are virtual global teams whose members remain in separate locations around the world and conduct their work electronically.[30] For example, global teams of software developers at Tandem Services Corporation coordinate their work electronically so that the team is productive around the clock. Team members in London code a project and transmit the code each evening to members in the United States for testing. U.S. team members then forward the code they've tested to Tokyo for debugging. The next morning, the London team members pick up with the code debugged by their Tokyo colleagues, and another cycle begins.[31]

Global teams present enormous challenges for team leaders, who have to bridge gaps of time, distance, and culture.[32] In some cases, members speak different languages, use different technologies, and have different beliefs about authority, communication, decision making, and time orientation. For example, in some cultures, such as the United States, communication is explicit and direct, whereas in many other cultures meaning is embedded in the way the message is presented. U.S.-based team members are also typically highly focused on "clock time" and tend to follow rigid schedules, whereas many other cultures have a more relaxed, cyclical concept of time. These different cultural attitudes can affect work pacing, team communications, decision making, the perception of deadlines, and other issues, and provide rich soil for misunderstandings. No wonder when the executive council of *CIO* magazine asked global chief information officers to rank their greatest challenges, managing virtual global teams ranked as the most pressing issue.[33]

© MARK LEONG/REDUX

Concept Connection To update Lotus Symphony, a package of PC software applications, IBM assigned the project to teams in Beijing, China; Austin, Texas; Raleigh, North Carolina; and Boeblingen, Germany. Leading the project, the Beijing group—shown here with Michael Karasick (center), who runs the Beijing lab, and lead developer Yue Ma (right)—navigated the **global team** through the programming challenges. To help bridge the distance gap, IBM uses Beehive, a corporate social network similar to Facebook, where employees create profiles, list their interests, and post photos.

global team A work team made up of members of different nationalities whose activities span multiple countries; may operate as a virtual team or meet face-to-face.

6 Leading

Organizations using global teams invest the time and resources to adequately educate employees, such as Accenture, which trains all consultants and most of its services workers in how to effectively collaborate with international colleagues.[34] Managers working with global teams make sure all team members appreciate and understand cultural differences, are focused on clear goals, and understand their roles and responsibilities. For a global team to be effective, all team members must be willing to deviate somewhat from their own values and norms and establish new norms for the team.[35] As with virtual teams, carefully selecting team members, building trust, and sharing information are critical to success.

TEAM CHARACTERISTICS

After deciding the type of team to use, the next issue of concern to managers is designing the team for greatest effectiveness. Team characteristics of particular concern are size, diversity, and member roles.

Size

More than 30 years ago, psychologist Ivan Steiner examined what happened each time the size of a team increased, and he proposed that team performance and productivity peaked at about five—a quite small number. He found that adding additional members beyond five caused a decrease in motivation, an increase in coordination problems, and a general decline in performance.[36] Since then, numerous studies have found that smaller teams perform better, although most researchers say it's impossible to specify an optimal team size. One recent investigation of team size based on data from 58 software development teams found that the five best-performing teams ranged in size from three to six members.[37] Results of a recent Gallup poll in the United States show that 82 percent of employees agree that small teams are more productive.[38]

Teams need to be large enough to incorporate the diverse skills needed to complete a task, enable members to express good and bad feelings, and aggressively solve problems. However, they should also be small enough to permit members to feel an intimate part of the team and to communicate effectively and efficiently. In general, as a team increases in size, it becomes harder for each member to interact with and influence the others. Subgroups often form in larger teams and conflicts among them can occur. Turnover and absenteeism are higher because members feel less like an important part of the team.[39] Large projects can be split into components and assigned to several smaller teams to keep the benefits of small size. At Amazon .com, CEO Jeff Bezos established a "two-pizza rule." If a team gets so large that members can't be fed with two pizzas, it should be split into smaller teams.[40]

Concept Connection "As demographic shifts sweep our nation and our community, diversity in public relations is not just a good thing to do, but a necessary business reality," declares Judy Iannaccone, Rancho Santiago Community College District communications director. Her professional organization agrees. The Public Relations Society of America (PRSA) promotes inclusion among work teams with a diversity tool kit, career Web site, and speakers list. Each year, the Society recognizes individual chapters for outstanding diversity promotion efforts. The Orange County, California, PRSA diversity committee was one of the 2005 recipients. Iannaccone, a committee member, is second from the right.

Diversity

Because teams require a variety of skills, knowledge, and experience, it seems likely that heterogeneous teams would be more effective than homogeneous ones. In general, research supports this idea, showing that diverse teams produce more innovative solutions to problems.[41] Diversity in terms of functional area and skills, thinking styles, and personal characteristics is often a source of creativity. In addition, diversity may contribute to a healthy level of disagreement that leads to better decision making.

Research studies have confirmed that both functional diversity and gender diversity can have a positive impact on work team performance.[42] Racial, national, and ethnic diversity can also be good for teams, but in the short term these differences might hinder team interaction and performance. Teams made up of racially and culturally diverse members tend to have more difficulty learning to work well together, but, with effective leadership, the problems fade over time.[43]

As a new manager, remember that team effectiveness depends on selecting the right type of team for the task, balancing the team's size and diversity, and ensuring that both task and social needs are met.

TakeaMoment

Member Roles

For a team to be successful over the long run, it must be structured so as to both maintain its members' social well-being and accomplish its task. In successful teams, the requirements for task performance and social satisfaction are met by the emergence of two types of roles: task specialist and socioemotional.[44]

People who play the **task specialist role** spend time and energy helping the team reach its goal. They often display the following behaviors:

- *Initiate ideas.* Propose new solutions to team problems.
- *Give opinions.* Offer opinions on task solutions; give candid feedback on others' suggestions.
- *Seek information.* Ask for task-relevant facts.
- *Summarize.* Relate various ideas to the problem at hand; pull ideas together into a summary perspective.
- *Energize.* Stimulate the team into action when interest drops.[45]

People who adopt a **socioemotional role** support team members' emotional needs and help strengthen the social entity. They display the following behaviors:

- *Encourage.* Are warm and receptive to others' ideas; praise and encourage others to draw forth their contributions.
- *Harmonize.* Reconcile group conflicts; help disagreeing parties reach agreement.
- *Reduce tension.* Tell jokes or in other ways draw off emotions when group atmosphere is tense.
- *Follow.* Go along with the team; agree to other team members' ideas.
- *Compromise.* Will shift own opinions to maintain team harmony.[46]

Teams with mostly socioemotional roles can be satisfying, but they also can be unproductive. At the other extreme, a team made up primarily of task specialists will tend to have a singular concern for task accomplishment. This team will be effective for a short period of time but will not be satisfying for members over the long run. Effective teams have people in both task specialist and socioemotional roles. A well-balanced team will do best over the long term because it will be personally satisfying for team members as well as permit the accomplishment of team tasks.

TEAM PROCESSES

Now we turn our attention to internal team processes. Team processes pertain to those dynamics that change over time and can be influenced by team leaders. In this section, we discuss stages of development, cohesiveness, and norms. The fourth type of team process, conflict, will be covered in the next section.

task specialist role A role in which the individual devotes personal time and energy to helping the team accomplish its task.

socioemotional role A role in which the individual provides support for team members' emotional needs and social unity.

6 Leading

Stages of Team Development

After a team has been created, it develops through distinct stages.[47] New teams are different from mature teams. Recall a time when you were a member of a new team, such as a fraternity or sorority pledge class, a committee, or a small team formed to do a class assignment. Over time the team changed. In the beginning, team members had to get to know one another, establish roles and norms, divide the labor, and clarify the team's task. In this way, each member became part of a smoothly operating team. The challenge for leaders is to understand the stages of development and take action that will lead to smooth functioning.

Research findings suggest that team development is not random but evolves over definitive stages. One useful model for describing these stages is shown in Exhibit 19.6. Each stage confronts team leaders and members with unique problems and challenges.[48]

Forming The **forming** stage of development is a period of orientation and getting acquainted. Members break the ice and test one another for friendship possibilities and task orientation. Uncertainty is high during this stage, and members usually accept whatever power or authority is offered by either formal or informal leaders. During this initial stage, members are concerned about such things

forming The stage of team development characterized by orientation and acquaintance.

EXHIBIT | 19.6

Five Stages of Team Development

Forming:
Orientation, break the ice
Leader:
Facilitates social interchanges

Storming:
Conflict, disagreement
Leader:
Encourages participation, surfaces differences

Norming:
Establishment of order and cohesion
Leader:
Helps clarify team roles, norms, values

Performing:
Cooperation, problem solving
Leader:
Facilitates task accomplishment

Adjourning:
Task completion
Leader:
Brings closure, signifies completion

as "What is expected of me?" "What behavior is acceptable?" "Will I fit in?" During the forming stage, the team leader should provide time for members to get acquainted with one another and encourage them to engage in informal social discussions.

Storming

During the **storming** stage, individual personalities emerge. People become more assertive in clarifying their roles and what is expected of them. This stage is marked by conflict and disagreement. People may disagree over their perceptions of the team's goals or how to achieve them. Members may jockey for position, and coalitions or subgroups based on common interests may form. Unless teams can successfully move beyond this stage, they may get bogged down and never achieve high performance. During the storming stage, the team leader should encourage participation by each team member. Members should propose ideas, disagree with one another, and work through the uncertainties and conflicting perceptions about team tasks and goals.

Norming

During the **norming** stage, conflict is resolved, and team harmony and unity emerge. Consensus develops on who has the power, who are the leaders, and members' roles. Members come to accept and understand one another. Differences are resolved, and members develop a sense of team cohesion. During the norming stage, the team leader should emphasize unity within the team and help to clarify team norms and values.

Performing

During the **performing** stage, the major emphasis is on problem solving and accomplishing the assigned task. Members are committed to the team's mission. They are coordinated with one another and handle disagreements in a mature way. They confront and resolve problems in the interest of task accomplishment. They interact frequently and direct their discussions and influence toward achieving team goals. During this stage, the leader should concentrate on managing high task performance. Both socioemotional and task specialists contribute to the team's functioning.

storming The stage of team development in which individual personalities and roles emerge along with resulting conflicts.

norming The stage of team development in which conflicts developed during the storming stage are resolved and team harmony and unity emerge.

performing The stage of team development in which members focus on problem solving and accomplishing the team's assigned task.

adjourning The stage of team development in which members prepare for the team's disbandment.

Adjourning

The **adjourning** stage occurs in committees and teams that have a limited task to perform and are disbanded afterward. During this stage, the emphasis is on wrapping up and gearing down. Task performance is no longer a top priority. Members may feel heightened emotionality, strong cohesiveness, and depression or regret over the team's disbandment. At this point, the leader may wish to signify the team's disbanding with a ritual or ceremony, perhaps giving out plaques and awards to signify closure and completeness.

These five stages typically occur in sequence, but in teams that are under time pressure, they may occur quite rapidly. The stages may also be accelerated for virtual teams. For example, at McDevitt Street Bovis, a large construction management firm, bringing people together for a couple of days of team building helps teams move rapidly through the forming and storming stages.

MERCURY PHOENIX WNBA TEAM PHOTO

Concept Connection   To accomplish their goals—whether in the business world or on the basketball court—teams have to successfully advance to the **performing stage of team development**. The WNBA's Phoenix Mercury teammates shown here blend their talents and energies so effortlessly that they play the game not like separate people but like a coordinated piece of a whole. Phoenix recently began using psychological testing as part of the appraisal of new coaches and potential draft picks. Managers think testing gives them another tool for building a high-performance team. As part-owner Anne Mariucci puts it, "If a person isn't dotting the I's and crossing the T's, we know why, and we can surround that person with people who complement that. . . ."

McDevitt Street Bovis

Rather than the typical construction project characterized by conflicts, frantic scheduling, and poor communications, McDevitt Street Bovis wants its collection of contractors, designers, suppliers, and other partners to function like a true team—putting the success of the project ahead of their own individual interests.

The team-building process at Bovis is designed to take teams to the performing stage as quickly as possible by giving everyone an opportunity to get to know one another; explore the ground rules; and clarify roles, responsibilities, and expectations. The team is first divided into separate groups that may have competing objectives—such as the clients in one group, suppliers in another, engineers and architects in a third, and so forth—and asked to come up with a list of their goals for the project. Although interests sometimes vary widely in purely accounting terms, common themes almost always emerge. By talking about conflicting goals and interests, as well as what all the groups share, facilitators help the team gradually come together around a common purpose and begin to develop shared values that will guide the project. After jointly writing a mission statement for the team, each party says what it expects from the others, so that roles and responsibilities can be clarified. The intensive team-building session helps take members quickly through the forming and storming stages of development. "We prevent conflicts from happening," says facilitator Monica Bennett. Leaders at McDevitt Street Bovis believe building better teams builds better buildings.[49]

Team Cohesiveness

Another important aspect of the team process is cohesiveness. **Team cohesiveness** is defined as the extent to which members are attracted to the team and motivated to remain in it.[50] Members of highly cohesive teams are committed to team activities, attend meetings, and are happy when the team succeeds. Members of less cohesive teams are less concerned about the team's welfare. High cohesiveness is normally considered an attractive feature of teams.

Determinants of Team Cohesiveness Several characteristics of team structure and context influence cohesiveness. First is *team interaction*. When team members have frequent contact, they get to know one another, consider themselves a unit, and become more committed to the team.[51] Second is the concept of *shared goals*. If team members agree on purpose and direction, they will be more cohesive. Third is *personal attraction to the team*, meaning that members have similar attitudes and values and enjoy being together.

Two factors in the team's context also influence group cohesiveness. The first is the *presence of competition*. When a team is in moderate competition with other teams, its cohesiveness increases as it strives to win. Finally, *team success* and the favorable evaluation of the team by outsiders add to cohesiveness. When a team succeeds in its task and others in the organization recognize the success, members feel good, and their commitment to the team will be high.

Consequences of Team Cohesiveness The outcome of team cohesiveness can fall into two categories—morale and productivity. As a general rule, morale is higher in cohesive teams because of increased communication among members, a friendly team climate, maintenance of membership because of commitment to the team, loyalty, and member participation in team decisions and activities. High cohesiveness has almost uniformly good effects on the satisfaction and morale of team members.[52]

With respect to the productivity of the team as a whole, research findings suggest that cohesive teams have the potential to be productive, but the degree of productivity depends on the relationship between management and the working team. One study surveyed more than 200 work teams and correlated job performance with their cohesiveness.[53] Highly cohesive teams were more productive when team members felt management support and less productive when they sensed management hostility and negativism.

team cohesiveness The extent to which team members are attracted to the team and motivated to remain in it.

Team Norms

A **team norm** is an informal standard of conduct that is shared by team members and guides their behavior.[54] Norms are valuable because they provide a frame of reference for what is expected and acceptable.

Norms begin to develop in the first interactions among members of a new team.[55] Exhibit 19.7 illustrates four common ways in which norms develop. Sometimes, the first behaviors that occur in a team set a precedent. For example, at one company, a team leader began his first meeting by raising an issue and then "leading" team members until he got the solution he wanted. The pattern became ingrained so quickly into an unproductive team norm that members dubbed meetings the "Guess What I Think" game.[56] Other influences on team norms include critical events in the team's history, as well as behaviors, attitudes, and norms that members bring with them from outside the team.

Team leaders play an important role in shaping norms that will help the team be effective. For example, research shows that when leaders have high expectations for collaborative problem-solving, teams develop strong collaborative norms.[57] Making explicit statements about the desired team behaviors is a powerful way leaders influence norms. Explicit statements symbolize what counts and thus have considerable impact. Ameritech CEO Bill Weiss established a norm of cooperation and mutual support among his top leadership team by telling them bluntly that if he caught anyone trying to undermine the others, the guilty party would be fired.[58]

MANAGING TEAM CONFLICT

The final characteristic of team process is conflict. Conflict can arise among members within a team or between one team and another. **Conflict** refers to antagonistic interaction in which one party attempts to block the intentions or goals of another.[59] Competition, which is rivalry among individuals or teams, can have a healthy impact because it energizes people toward higher performance.[60]

team norm A standard of conduct that is shared by team members and guides their behavior.

conflict Antagonistic interaction in which one party attempts to thwart the intentions or goals of another.

EXHIBIT | 19.7

Four Ways Team Norms Develop

- Critical events in team's history
- Primacy: first-behavior precedents
- Explicit statements from leader or members
- Carryover from other experiences

Team Norms

Whenever people work together in teams, some conflict is inevitable. Bringing conflicts out into the open and effectively resolving them is one of the team leader's most challenging, yet most important, jobs. For example, studies of virtual teams indicate that how they handle internal conflicts is critical to their success, yet conflict within virtual teams tends to occur more frequently and take longer to resolve because people are separated by space, time, and cultural differences. Moreover, people in virtual teams tend to engage in more inconsiderate behaviors such as name-calling or insults than do people who work face-to-face.[61]

Balancing Conflict and Cooperation

Mild conflict can actually be beneficial to teams.[62] A healthy level of conflict helps to prevent **groupthink**, in which people are so committed to a cohesive team that they are reluctant to express contrary opinions. Author and scholar Jerry Harvey tells a story of how members of his extended family in Texas decided to drive 40 miles to Abilene on a hot day when the car's air conditioning didn't work. Everyone was miserable. Later, each person admitted they hadn't wanted to go but went along to please the others. Harvey used the term *Abilene paradox* to describe this tendency to go along with others for the sake of avoiding conflict.[63] Similarly, when people in work teams go along simply for the sake of harmony, problems typically result. Thus, a degree of conflict leads to better decision making because multiple viewpoints are expressed. Among top management teams, for example, low levels of conflict have been found to be associated with poor decision making.[64]

However, conflict that is too strong, that is focused on personal rather than work issues, or that is not managed appropriately can be damaging to the team's morale and productivity. Too much conflict can be destructive, tear relationships apart, and interfere with the healthy exchange of ideas and information.[65] Team leaders have to find the right balance between conflict and cooperation, as illustrated in Exhibit 19.8. Too little conflict can decrease team performance because the team doesn't benefit from a mix of opinions and ideas—even disagreements—that might lead to better solutions or prevent the team from making mistakes. At the other end of the spectrum, too much conflict outweighs the team's cooperative efforts and leads to a decrease in employee satisfaction and commitment, hurting team performance. A moderate amount of conflict that is managed appropriately typically results in the highest levels of team performance.

groupthink The tendency for people to be so committed to a cohesive team that they are reluctant to express contrary opinions.

TakeaMoment | Go to the ethical dilemma on page 591 that pertains to team cohesiveness and conflict.

EXHIBIT | **19.8**

Balancing Conflict and Cooperation

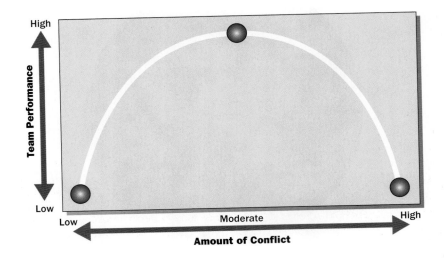

Causes of Conflict

Several factors can lead to conflict:[66] One of the primary causes of conflict is competition over resources, such as money, information, or supplies. When individuals or teams must compete for scarce or declining resources, conflict is almost inevitable. In addition, conflict often occurs simply because people are pursuing differing goals. Goal differences are natural in organizations. Individual salespeople's targets may put them in conflict with one another or with the sales manager. Moreover, the sales department's goals might conflict with those of manufacturing, and so forth.

Conflict may also arise from communication breakdowns. Poor communication can occur in any team, but virtual and global teams are particularly prone to communication breakdowns. For one thing, the lack of nonverbal cues in virtual interactions leads to more misunderstandings. In addition, trust issues can be a major source of conflict in virtual teams if members feel that they are being left out of important communication interactions.[67]

Styles to Handle Conflict

Teams as well as individuals develop specific styles for dealing with conflict, based on the desire to satisfy their own concern versus the other party's concern. A model that describes five styles of handling conflict is in Exhibit 19.9. The two major dimensions are the extent to which an individual is assertive versus cooperative in his or her approach to conflict.[68]

1. The *competing style* reflects assertiveness to get one's own way and should be used when quick, decisive action is vital on important issues or unpopular actions, such as during emergencies or urgent cost cutting.

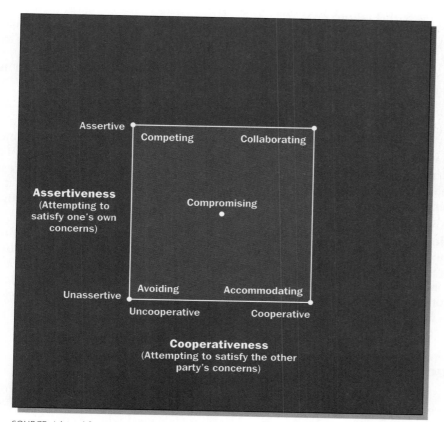

EXHIBIT | 19.9

A Model of Styles to Handle Conflict

SOURCE: Adapted from Kenneth Thomas, "Conflict and Conflict Management," in *Handbook of Industrial and Organizational Behavior*, ed. M. D. Dunnette (New York: John Wiley, 1976), p. 900.

2. The *avoiding style* reflects neither assertiveness nor cooperativeness. It is appropriate when an issue is trivial, when there is no chance of winning, when a delay to gather more information is needed, or when a disruption would be costly.

3. The *compromising style* reflects a moderate amount of both assertiveness and cooperativeness. It is appropriate when the goals on both sides are equally important, when opponents have equal power and both sides want to split the difference, or when people need to arrive at temporary or expedient solutions under time pressure.

4. The *accommodating style* reflects a high degree of cooperativeness, which works best when people realize that they are wrong, when an issue is more important to others than to oneself, when building social credits for use in later discussions, and when maintaining harmony is especially important.

5. The *collaborating style* reflects both a high degree of assertiveness and cooperativeness. The collaborating style enables both parties to win, although it may require substantial bargaining and negotiation. The collaborating style is important when both sets of concerns are too important to be compromised, when insights from different people need to be merged into an overall solution, and when the commitment of both sides is needed for a consensus.

TakeaMoment | As a new manager, appreciate that some conflict can be healthy, but don't let conflict reduce the team's effectiveness and well-being. Take the New Manager Self-Test on page 586 to learn about your personal style for handling conflict.

Effective team members vary their style to fit the specific situation. Each of the five styles is appropriate in certain cases. These styles of handling conflict are especially useful when an individual disagrees with others. But what does a manager or team leader do when a conflict erupts among others within a team or among teams for which the manager is responsible?

Research suggests the use of superordinate goals, mediation, and negotiation for resolving conflicts among people or departments:

- *Superordinate goals.* The larger objective that cannot be attained by a single party is identified as a **superordinate goal**.[69] It is similar to the concept of vision. A powerful vision often compels people to overcome conflicts and cooperate for the greater good. Similarly, a superordinate goal requires the cooperation of conflicting team members for achievement. People must pull together. To the extent that employees can be focused on team or organization goals, the conflict will decrease because they see the big picture and realize they must work together to achieve it.

- *Mediation.* Using a third party to settle a dispute is referred to as **mediation**. A mediator could be a supervisor, a higher-level manager, an outside consultant, or someone from the human resource department. The mediator can discuss the conflict with each party and work toward a solution. If a solution satisfactory to both sides cannot be reached, the parties might be willing to turn the conflict over to the mediator and abide by his or her solution.

superordinate goal A goal that cannot be reached by a single party.

mediation The process of using a third party to settle a dispute.

negotiation A conflict management strategy whereby people engage in give-and-take discussions and consider various alternatives to reach a joint decision that is acceptable to both parties.

Negotiation

One distinctive type of conflict management is **negotiation**, whereby people engage in give-and-take discussions and consider various alternatives to reach a joint decision that is acceptable to both parties. Negotiation is used when a conflict is formalized, such as between a union and management.

Types of Negotiation Conflicting parties may embark on negotiation from different perspectives and with different intentions, reflecting either an *integrative* approach or a *distributive* approach.

Integrative negotiation is based on a win-win assumption, in that all parties want to come up with a creative solution that can benefit both sides. Rather than viewing the conflict as a win-lose situation, people look at the issues from multiple angles, consider trade-offs, and try to "expand the pie" rather than divide it. With integrative negotiation, conflicts are managed through cooperation and compromise, which fosters trust and positive long-term relationships. **Distributive negotiation**, on the other hand, assumes the "size of the pie" is fixed and each party attempts to get as much of it as they can. One side wants to win, which means the other side must lose. With this win-lose approach, distributive negotiation is competitive and adversarial rather than collaborative, and does not typically lead to positive long-term relationships.[70]

Most experts emphasize the value of integrative negotiation for today's collaborative business environment. That is, the key to effectiveness is to see negotiation not as a zero-sum game but as a process for reaching a creative solution that benefits everyone.[71]

Concept Connection The closing of the pulp mill in Port Alice on Canada's Vancouver Island put 350 people out of work in a community of only 700. "There was no one in the village who didn't suffer," said employee Stu Roper. In late 2005, foreign investors bought the plant after British Columbia absolved the new owners of responsibility for past environmental damage, the community approved a five-year reduction in property taxes, and union members and Neucel management, pictured here, reached an agreement after contentious **distributive negotiation**. The newly christened Neucel mill produces high-purity cellulose used in a variety of industries.

Rules for Reaching a Win-Win Solution Achieving a win-win solution through integrative negotiation is based on four key strategies:[72]

1. *Separate the people from the problem.* For successful integrative negotiation, people stay focused on the problem and the source of conflict rather than attacking or attempting to discredit each other.

2. *Focus on interests, not current demands.* Demands are what each person wants from the negotiation, whereas interests are why they want them. Consider two sisters arguing over the last orange in the fruit bowl. Each insisted she should get the orange and refused to give up (demands). Then, the girls' aunt walks in and asks each of them *why* they want the orange (interests). As it turned out, one wanted to eat it and the other wanted the peel to use for a class project. By focusing on the interests, the sisters arrived at a solution that got each person what she wanted.[73] *Demands* create yes-or-no obstacles to effective negotiation, whereas *interests* present problems that can be solved creatively.

3. *Generate many alternatives for mutual gain.* Both parties in an integrative negotiation come up with a variety of options for solving the problem and engage in give-and-take discussions about which alternatives can get each side what it wants.

4. *Insist that results be based on objective standards.* Each party in a negotiation has its own interests and would naturally like to maximize its outcomes. Successful negotiation requires focusing on objective criteria and maintaining standards of fairness rather than using subjective judgments about the best solution.

integrative negotiation A collaborative approach to negotiation that is based on a win-win assumption, whereby the parties want to come up with a creative solution that benefits both sides of the conflict.

distributive negotiation A competitive and adversarial negotiation approach in which each party strives to get as much as it can, usually at the expense of the other party.

New Manager Self-Test

Managing Conflict

Conflicting opinions and perspectives occur in every team. The ability to handle conflict and disagreement is one mark of a successful new manager. To understand your approach to managing conflict, think about disagreements you have had with people on student teams or in other situations, then answer each of the following items as Mostly True or Mostly False for you.

	Mostly True	Mostly False
1. I typically assert my opinion to win a disagreement.	____	____
2. I often suggest solutions that combine others' points of view.	____	____
3. I prefer to not argue with team members.	____	____
4. I raise my voice to get other people to accept my position.	____	____
5. I am quick to agree when someone makes a good point.	____	____
6. I tend to keep quiet rather than argue with other people.	____	____
7. I stand firm in expressing my viewpoints during a disagreement.	____	____
8. I try to include other people's ideas to create a solution they will accept.	____	____
9. I like to smooth over disagreements so people get along.	____	____

SCORING AND INTERPRETATION: Three categories of conflict-handling strategies are measured in this instrument: competing, accommodating, and collaborating. By comparing your scores you can see your preferred conflict-handling strategy.

Give yourself one point for each item marked Mostly True.

Competing: Items 1, 4, 7

Accommodating: Items 2, 5, 8

Collaborating: Items 3, 6, 9

For which conflict-handling strategy do you score highest? New managers may initially be accommodating to get along with people until they size up the situation. A too-strong competing style may prevent subordinates from having a say in important matters. The collaborating style tries for a win-win solution and has the long-run potential to build a constructive team. How would your strategy differ if the other people involved in a disagreement were family members, friends, subordinates, or bosses?

WORK TEAM EFFECTIVENESS

Teams are the building blocks of today's organizations, but teams do not always live up to their potential or to the dreams managers have for them. In this section, we look at the positive outcomes of effective teams. By assessing teams in terms of productive output, personal satisfaction, and the capacity to adapt and learn, managers can better identify actions that will enhance work team effectiveness.[74]

Productive Output

One aspect of effectiveness relates to whether the team's output (such as decisions, products, or services) meets the requirements of customers or clients in terms of quality, quantity, and timeliness. An IBM team made up of members in the United States, Germany, and the United Kingdom, for example, used collaboration software as a virtual meeting room to solve a client's technical problem resulting from Hurricane Katrina within the space of just a few days.[75] Whether online or in physical space, effective meetings are essential to effective teamwork. The Manager's Shoptalk gives some tips for running a great meeting.

Effective teams can unleash enormous energy and creativity from employees. **Social facilitation** refers to the tendency for the presence of others to enhance one's motivation and performance. Simply being in the presence of other people has an energizing effect.[76] This benefit of teams is often lost in virtual and global teams because people are working in isolation from their teammates. Good virtual team leaders build in communication mechanisms that keep people interacting.

Satisfaction of Members

Another important question is whether the team experience contributes to the well-being, personal satisfaction, and development of its members. Effective teams provide multiple opportunities for people to satisfy their individual needs and to develop both personally and professionally.[77] As described in Chapter 17, employees have needs for belongingness and affiliation, and working in teams can help meet these needs. Participative teams can also reduce boredom, increase individuals' feeling of dignity and self-worth, and contribute to skill development because the whole person is employed. At Radius, a Boston restaurant, for example, two-person kitchen teams have full responsibility for their part of a meal, which gives them a greater sense of accomplishment and importance and enables them to expand their culinary and organizational skills.[78] People who have a satisfying team environment cope better with stress, enjoy their jobs, and have a higher level of organizational commitment.

Capacity to Adapt and Learn

A professor of management at Santa Clara University analyzed 14 years of National Basketball Association results and found that teams that had played together longer won more games. By playing together over a period of time, members learned to anticipate their teammates' moves and adapt their own behavior to defeat the competition.[79] The same thing happens in effective work teams, where members can anticipate one another's actions and respond appropriately. A good example is the emergency room trauma team at Massachusetts General Hospital, which functions so smoothly that the team switches leaders seamlessly depending on the crisis at hand. With each new emergency, direction may come from a doctor, nurse, intern, or technician—whoever is particularly experienced with the problem.[80] Over time, effective teams learn from experience and use that learning to revitalize and regenerate themselves, smoothly adapting to shifting organizational and competitive demands.[81]

social facilitation The tendency for the presence of others to influence an individual's motivation and performance.

6 Leading

Manager'sShoptalk

How to Run a Great Meeting

A recent survey in the United States and Britain found that people spend an average of 5.6 hours a week in meetings, yet 69 percent of respondents considered most of that time wasted. Meetings can be excellent avenues to solving problems, sharing information, and achieving shared goals, but good meetings don't just happen. Here are some tips on how to make meetings worthwhile and productive:

Prepare in Advance

Advance preparation is the single most important tool for running an efficient, productive meeting.

- *Define the purpose.* Is the meeting's purpose to share information, draw on participants' expertise and skills, elicit their commitment to a project, or coordinate the efforts required to accomplish a specific task? The leader needs to be clear about what the purpose is. If a meeting isn't essential, don't have it.

- *Invite the right people.* Meetings fail when too many, too few, or the wrong people are involved. Don't let the meeting get too big, but make sure everyone with a contribution to make or a stake in the topic is represented.

- *Prepare an agenda and identify the expected outcome.* Distributing a simple list of the topics to be discussed lets people know what to expect. If the meeting is for exploration only, say so. A lack of decision making can be frustrating if participants expect action to be taken.

Bring Out the Best During the Meeting

During the meeting, certain techniques will bring out the best in people and ensure a productive session:

- *Start on time, state the purpose, and review the agenda.* Starting on time has symbolic value, because it tells people that the topic is important and that the leader values their time. Begin by stating the meeting's explicit purpose and clarifying what should be accomplished by its conclusion.

- *Establish ground rules.* Outlawing cell phones, PDAs, and laptops can make sure people aren't distracted. Other rules concern how people should interact, such as emphasizing equal participation and respectful listening.

- *Create involvement.* Good leaders draw out the silent and control the talkative so that the meeting isn't dominated by one or two assertive people. In addition, they encourage a free flow

of ideas, provoke discussion with open-ended questions, and make sure everyone feels heard.

- *Keep it moving.* Allowing participants to waste time by getting into discussions of issues not on the agenda is a primary reason people hate meetings. Move the meeting along as needed to meet time constraints.

Attend to the End as Much as the Beginning

Review and follow-up is important to summarize and implement agreed-upon points.

- *End with a call to action.* Summarize the discussion, review any decisions made, and make sure everyone understands his or her assignments.

- *Follow up swiftly.* Send a short memo to summarize the meeting's key accomplishments, outline agreed-upon activities, and suggest schedules for implementation.

SOURCES: Based on Suzanne Bates, "Learning to Lead: Five Steps to Pain Free, Productive Meetings," *Supervision* (August 2006): 18–19; Beth Bratkovic, "Running an Effective Meeting," *Government Finance Review* (April 2007): 58–60; Phred Dvorak, "Corporate Meetings Go Through a Makeover," *The Wall Street Journal,* March 6, 2006; Antoney Jay, "How to Run a Meeting," *Harvard Business Review* (March–April 1976): 120–134; and Richard Axelrod, Emily M. Axelrod, Julie Beedon, and Robert Jacobs, "Creating Dynamic, Energy-Producing Meetings," *Leader to Leader* (Spring 2005): 53–58.

ch19 A MANAGER'S ESSENTIALS: WHAT HAVE WE LEARNED?

- Several important concepts about teams were described in this chapter. Teams can be effective in providing the coordination and information sharing needed to accomplish interdependent tasks. However, teams present a dilemma for many people. Individuals have to give up their independence and sometimes make sacrifices for the good of the team. Other potential problems are free riders and dysfunctional teams.

- Some teams are part of the formal structure, while others are designed to increase employee involvement and participation. Formal teams include vertical teams along the chain of command and horizontal teams such as cross-functional teams, committees, and special-purpose teams. Employee involvement via teams brings lower-level employees into decision processes to improve quality, efficiency, and job satisfaction. Companies typically start with problem-solving teams, which may evolve into self-directed teams that take on responsibility for management activities. Innovative approaches to teamwork include virtual teams and global teams, which place new demands on team leaders.

- Most teams go through systematic stages of development: forming, storming, norming, performing, and adjourning. Team characteristics that influence organizational effectiveness are size, diversity, cohesiveness, norms, and members' roles.

- All teams experience some conflict because of scarce resources, ambiguous responsibilities, communication breakdown, or goal conflicts. Some conflict is beneficial, but too much can hurt the team and the organization. Techniques for managing and resolving conflicts include superordinate goals, mediation, and negotiation.

- To identify ways to improve work team effectiveness, managers can assess teams in terms of productive output, personal satisfaction, and the capacity to adapt and learn.

ch19 DISCUSSION QUESTIONS

1. Volvo went to self-directed teams to assemble cars because of the need to attract and keep workers in Sweden, where pay raises are not a motivator (high taxes) and many other jobs are available. Are these factors good reasons for using a team approach? Discuss.

2. Trust is an important characteristic of a successful team. If you were a team leader, how would you go about building a culture of trust?

3. What factors in today's environment are contributing to an increasing use of virtual teams and global teams? Would you like to be part of a virtual team? Why or why not?

4. Suppose you are the leader of a team that has just been created to develop a new registration process at your college or university. How can you use an understanding of the stages of team development to improve your team's effectiveness?

5. Imagine yourself as a potential member of a team responsible for designing a new package for breakfast cereal. Do you think interpersonal skills would be equally important if the team is organized face-to-face versus a virtual team? Why or why not? Might different types of interpersonal skills be required for the two types of teams? Be specific.

6. If you were the leader of a special-purpose team developing a new computer game, and conflicts arose related to power and status differences among team members, what would you do? How might you use the various conflict-resolution techniques described in the chapter?

7. When you are a member of a team, do you adopt a task specialist or socioemotional role? Which role is more important for a team's effectiveness? Discuss.

8. Some people argue that the presence of an outside threat correlates with a high degree of team cohesion. Would you agree or disagree? Explain your answer. What is the relationship between team cohesiveness and team performance?

9. Describe the advantages and disadvantages of teams. In what situations might the disadvantages outweigh the advantages?

10. One company had 40 percent of its workers and 20 percent of its managers resign during the first year after reorganizing into teams. What might account for this dramatic turnover? How might managers ensure a smooth transition to teams?

ch19 MANAGEMENT IN PRACTICE: EXPERIENTIAL EXERCISE

Is Your Group a Cohesive Team?

Think about a student group with which you have worked. Answer the following questions as they pertain to the functioning of that group.

Disagree Strongly ① ② ③ ④ ⑤ **Agree Strongly**

1. Group meetings were held regularly and everyone attended.

   1 2 3 4 5

2. We talked about and shared the same goals for group work and grade.

   1 2 3 4 5

3. We spent most of our meeting time talking business, but discussions were open-ended and active.

   1 2 3 4 5

4. We talked through any conflicts and disagreements until they were resolved.

   1 2 3 4 5

5. Group members listened carefully to one another.

   1 2 3 4 5

6. We really trusted each other, speaking personally about what we really felt.

   1 2 3 4 5

7. Leadership roles were rotated and shared, with people taking initiative at appropriate times for the good of the group.

   1 2 3 4 5

8. Each member found a way to contribute to the final work product.

   1 2 3 4 5

9. I was really satisfied being a member of the group.

   1 2 3 4 5

10. We freely gave each other credit for jobs well done.

    1 2 3 4 5

11. Group members gave and received feedback to help the group do even better.

    1 2 3 4 5

12. We held each other accountable; each member was accountable to the group.

    1 2 3 4 5

13. Group members really liked and respected each other.

    1 2 3 4 5

Scoring and Interpretation

The questions here are about team cohesion. Add your scores for all 13 questions to obtain your total score: _____. If you scored 52 or greater, your group experienced authentic teamwork. Congratulations. If you scored between 39 and 51, you reached a positive group identity that might have been developed even further. If you scored between 26 and 38, group identity was weak and probably not all that satisfying. If you scored below 26, it was hardly a group at all, resembling a loose collection of individuals.

Remember, teamwork does not happen by itself. Individuals like you have to understand what a team is and then work to make it happen. What can you do to make a student group more like a team? Do you have the courage to take the initiative?

ch19 MANAGEMENT IN PRACTICE: ETHICAL DILEMMA

One for All and All for One?

Melinda Asbel watched as three of her classmates filed out of the conference room. Then she turned back to the large wooden table and faced her fellow members (a student and three faculty members) of the university's judiciary committee.

The three students—Joe Eastridge, Brad Hamil, and Lisa Baghetti—had just concluded their appeal against a plagiarism conviction stemming from a group project for an international marketing course. Melinda, who happened to be in the class with the students on trial, remembered the day the professor, Hank Zierden, had asked Joe, Brad, and Lisa, along with the group's leader, Paul Colgan, to stay after class. She happened to walk by the classroom a half hour later to see four glum students emerge. Even though Paul had a chagrined expression on his face, Joe was the one who looked completely shattered. It didn't take long for word to spread along the ever-active grapevine that Paul had admitted to plagiarizing his part of the group paper.

At the hearing, the students recounted how they'd quickly and unanimously settled on Paul to lead the group. He was by far the most able student among them, someone who managed to maintain a stellar GPA even while taking a full course load and holding down a part-time job. After the group worked together for weeks analyzing the problem and devising a marketing plan, Paul assigned a section of the final paper to each member. With the pressure of all those end-of-the-semester deadlines bearing down on them, everyone was delighted when Paul volunteered to write the company and industry background, the section that typically took the most time to produce. Paul gathered in everyone's contributions, assembled them into a paper, and handed out the final draft to the other members. They each gave it a quick read. They liked what they saw and thought they had a good chance for an A.

Unfortunately, as Paul readily admitted when Professor Zierden confronted them, he had pulled the section he'd contributed directly off the Internet. Pointing out the written policy he had distributed at the beginning of the semester stating that each group member was equally responsible for the final product, the professor gave all four students a zero for the project. The group project and presentation counted for 30 percent of the course grade.

Joe, Brad, and Lisa maintained they were completely unaware that Paul had cheated. "It just never occurred to us Paul would ever need to cheat," Brad said. They were innocent bystanders, the students argued. Why should they be penalized? Besides, the consequences weren't going to fall on each of them equally. Although Paul was suffering the embarrassment of public exposure, the failing group project grade would only put a dent in his solid GPA. Joe, on the other hand, was already on academic probation. A zero probably meant he wouldn't make the 2.5 GPA he needed to stay in the business program.

At least one of the faculty members of the judiciary committee supported Professor Zierden'a actions. "We're assigning more and more group projects because increasingly that's the way these students are going to find themselves working when they get real jobs in the real world," he said. "And the fact of the matter is that if someone obtains information illegally while on the job, it's going to put the whole corporation at risk for being sued, or worse."

Even though she could see merit to both sides, Melinda was going to have to choose. If you were Melinda, how would you vote?

What Would You Do?

1. Vote to exonerate the three group project members who didn't cheat. You're convinced they had no reason to suspect Paul Colgan of dishonesty. Exonerating them is the right thing to do.

2. Vote in support of Hank Zierden's decision to hold each individual member accountable for the entire project. The professor clearly stated his policy at the beginning of the semester, and the students should have been more vigilant. The committee should not undercut a professor's explicit policy.

3. Vote to reduce each of the three students' penalties. Instead of a zero, each student will receive only half of the possible total points for the project, which would be an F. You're still holding students responsible for the group project, but not imposing catastrophic punishment. This compromise both undercuts the professor's policy and punishes "innocent" team members to some extent, but not as severely.

SOURCE: Based on Ellen R. Stapleton, "College to Expand Policy on Plagiarism," The Ithancan Online (April 12, 2001): www.ithaca.edu/ithacan/articles/0104/12/news/0college_to_e.htm.

ch19 CASE FOR CRITICAL ANALYSIS

Acme Minerals Extraction Company

Several years ago, Acme Minerals Extraction Company introduced teams in an effort to solve morale and productivity problems at its Wichita plant. Acme used highly sophisticated technology, employing geologists, geophysicists, and engineers on what was referred to as the "brains" side of the business, as well as skilled and semiskilled labor on the "brawn" side to run the company's underground extracting operations. The two sides regularly clashed, and when some engineers locked several operations workers out of the office in 100-degree heat, the local press had a field day. The company hired Suzanne Howard to develop a program that would improve productivity and morale at the Wichita plant. The idea was that it would then be implemented at other Acme sites.

In Wichita, Howard had a stroke of luck in the form of Donald Peterson, a long-time Acme employee who was highly respected at the Wichita plant and was looking for one final challenging project before he retired. Peterson had served in just about every possible line and staff position at Acme over his 39-year career, and he understood the problems workers faced on both the brains and the brawn sides of the business. Howard was pleased when Peterson agreed to serve as leader for the Wichita pilot project.

Three functional groups at the Wichita plant included operations, made up primarily of hourly workers who operated and maintained the extracting equipment; the "below ground" group, consisting of engineers, geologists, and geophysicists who determined where and how to drill; and the "above ground" group of engineers in charge of cursory refinement and transportation of the minerals. Howard and Peterson decided the first step was to get these different groups talking to one another and sharing ideas. They instituted a monthly "problem chat," an optional meeting to which all employees were invited to discuss unresolved problems. At the first meeting, Howard and Peterson were the only two people who showed up. However, people gradually began to attend the meetings, and after about six months, they became lively problem-solving discussions that led to many improvements. For example, a maintenance worker complained that a standard piece of equipment failed repeatedly due to high levels of heat and sand contamination. Peterson listened carefully and then drew a facilities engineer into the discussion. The engineer came up with a new configuration better suited to the conditions, and downtime virtually disappeared.

Next, Howard and Peterson introduced teams to "select a problem and implement a tailored solution," or SPITS. These ad hoc groups were made up of members from each of the three functional areas. They were formed to work on a specific problem identified in a chat meeting and were then disbanded when the problem was solved. Acme gave SPITS the authority to address problems without seeking management approval. Some rocky moments occurred when engineers resented working with operations personnel, and vice versa. However, over time, and with Peterson's strong leadership, the groups eventually began to come together and focus on the issues rather than spending most of their time arguing.

Eventually, workers in Wichita were organized into permanent cross-functional teams that were empowered to make their own decisions and elect their own leaders. After a year and a half, things were really humming. The different groups weren't just working together; they had also started socializing together. At one of the problem chats, an operations worker jokingly suggested that the brains and the brawn should duke it out once a week to get rid of the tensions so they could focus all their energy on the job to be done. Several others joined in the joking, and eventually, the group decided to square off in a weekly softball game. Peterson had T-shirts printed up that said BRAINS and BRAWN. The softball games were well attended, and both sides usually ended up having a few beers together at a local bar afterward. Productivity and morale soared at the Wichita plant, and costs continued to decline.

The company identified the Lubbock plant as the next facility where Suzanne Howard and her team needed to introduce the cross-functional teams that had proven so successful in Kansas. Howard's team felt immense pressure from top management to get the team-based productivity project up and running smoothly and quickly at Lubbock. Top executives believed the lessons learned at Wichita would make implementing the program at other sites less costly and time-consuming. However, when Howard and her team attempted to implement the program at the Lubbock plant, things didn't go well. Because people weren't showing up for the problem chat meetings, the team made attendance mandatory. However, the meetings still produced few valuable ideas or suggestions. Although a few of the SPITS teams solved important problems, none of them showed the kind of commitment and enthusiasm Howard had seen in Wichita. In addition, the Lubbock workers refused to participate in the softball games and other team-building exercises that the team developed for them. Howard finally convinced some workers to join in the softball games by bribing them with free food and beer.

"If I just had a Donald Peterson in Lubbock, things would go a lot more smoothly," Howard thought. "These workers don't trust us the way workers in Wichita trusted him." It seemed that no matter how hard Howard and her team tried to make the project work in Lubbock, morale continued to decline and conflicts between the different groups of workers actually seemed to increase.

Questions

1. Suzanne Howard and Donald Peterson phased in permanent cross-functional teams in Wichita. What types of teams are the "problem chats" and SPITS groups? What stage or stages of team development did these groups evolve through?

2. What role did Donald Peterson play in the success of the Wichita team-based productivity project? What style did he employ to help reduce conflict between labor and the professionals? Do you agree with Suzanne Howard that if she just had a Donald Peterson in Lubbock, the project would succeed? Explain your answer.

3. What advice would you give Suzanne Howard and her team for improving the employee involvement climate, containing costs, and meeting production goals at the Lubbock plant?

SOURCES: Based on Michael C. Beers, "The Strategy That Wouldn't Travel," *Harvard Business Review* (November–December 1996): 18–31.

ch19 ON THE JOB VIDEO CASE

NEADS Creates Partnerships between People and Dogs

Suppose you woke up one day and couldn't see. Or perhaps you couldn't hear, couldn't speak, or couldn't walk. How would you communicate and interact with the world around you? Today's technology provides solutions to some of these challenges, but there is a live solution as well: assistance dogs. The National Education for Assistance Dog Services (NEADS) acquires, trains, and matches dogs with people who need assistance. Founded in 1976 as a nonprofit organization, NEADS is based in the rural community of Princeton, Massachusetts, where it adopts and trains dogs to serve their new owners.

Communication is central to success at NEADS. Communication between trainer and dog; between interviewer and client; between trainer and interviewer; and among the trio of client, trainer, and dog is a well-established process. Executive director Sheila O'Brien describes the importance of the process this way. "The match of client and dog is the most important thing that we do, because if we make a bad match, we can't salvage it in any way, shape, or form." Thus, while a trainer begins to work with a dog, developing the skills it will need in its new role—such as responding to a doorbell, ringing telephone, or activated smoke alarm—an interviewer reviews a client's application and conducts an in-person interview to learn as much about the client as possible. If the person has a hearing loss, the interviewer will ask how the loss occurred, how severe it is, and what the prognosis might be. Clients answer questions about lifestyle: Do they live in the city or the country? Do they work outside the home? How many people live in the home? Do they travel a lot? and so forth. They also have a chance to describe their expectations and preferences—whether they want a large or small dog, an energetic or quiet dog, a male or female dog. "The interviewer does have to listen on many levels," notes Shelia O'Brien. "[The interviewer must] ask questions and listen to the answers." Once the interview is complete, the interviewer and trainers meet to try to match dogs with clients.

The match meeting is lively. By now, the trainers know the characteristics of the dogs, and the interviewers know the personalities of their clients. "Match meetings have a lot of give and take," says O'Brien. "The lines of communication have got to be open." Sometimes, a match may seem close—but needs some tweaking. So a trainer will work further with the dog, and ultimately the client-dog pair, to create a smooth relationship.

Because NEADS staffers deal with different types of individuals, ranging from hearing-impaired clients to dogs in need of training, they are open to all kinds of communication. They don't view communication barriers as an obstacle. "I think my staff is of the opinion that the sky is the limit when it comes to communication," says O'Brien. If hearing or speaking is an issue, she explains, "We don't necessarily rely on voice . . . we rely on body language." Hand signals are often the best means of communication between a dog and a hearing-impaired client, so both are trained for their new language. Clients who will be receiving dogs live at the NEADS facility for two weeks while they learn how to communicate with

their new partners. "We have to be open to a wide variety of communication skills," says O'Brien. "We'll do what works. We'll use any kind of communication we can."

In its three decades of existence, NEADS has trained more than 650 client-dog teams. Because the program has been so successful, there is currently a two-year waiting period for clients who have been accepted into NEADS to receive their dogs. But when the match is made, it lasts a lifetime.

Questions

1. How would you describe the capacity and richness of the NEADS match meeting as a communication channel?

2. According to one study, the impact of facial expressions on message interpretation is 55 percent. How might this finding be used at NEADS?

3. Why are listening skills so important at NEADS?

SOURCE: Organization Web site, *http://www.neads.org*, accessed September 2, 2004.

ch19 BIZ FLIX VIDEO CASE

Lorenzo's Oil

This film tells the true story of young Lorenzo Odone who suffers from adrenoleukodystrophy (ALD), an incurable degenerative brain disorder. (Six actors and actresses play Lorenzo throughout the film.) Physicians and medical scientists offer little help to Lorenzo's desperate parents, Michaela (Susan Sarandon) and Augusto (Nick Nolte). They use their resources to learn about ALD to try to save their son. Director George Miller co-wrote the script, which benefited from his medical training as a physician.

Six months after Lorenzo's ALD diagnosis, his condition fails to improve with a restricted diet. Michaela and Augusto continue their research at the National Institutes of Health library in Bethesda, Maryland. Michaela finds a report of a critical Polish

experiment that showed positive effects of fatty acid manipulation in rats. Convinced that a panel of experts could systematically focus on their problem, they help organize the First International ALD Symposium. This scene is an edited version of the symposium sequence that appears about midway through the film. The film continues with the Odones' efforts to save their son.

What to Watch for and Ask Yourself

1. Do the scientists present data or information during the symposium?

2. If it is information, who transformed the data into information? Speculate about how such data became information.

3. What do you predict will be the next course of action for the Odones?

ch19 ENDNOTES

1. Based on Eric M. Stark, Jason D. Shaw, and Michelle K. Duffy, "Preference for Group Work, Winning Orientation, and Social Loafing Behavior in Groups," *Group & Organization Management* 32, no. 6 (December 2007): 699–723.

2. Industry Week/Manufacturing Performance Institute's Census of Manufacturers for 2004, reported in Traci Purdum, "Teaming, Take 2," *Industry Week* (May 2005): 41–43.

3. Carl E. Larson and Frank M. J. LaFasto, *TeamWork* (Newbury Park, CA: Sage, 1989).

4. Telis Demos, "Cirque du Balancing Act," *Fortune* (June 12, 2006): 114; Erin White, "How a Company Made Everyone a Team Player," *The Wall Street Journal*, August 13, 2007; David Kirkpatrick, "Inside Sam's $100 Billion Growth Machine," *Fortune* (June 14, 2004): 80–98; Daniel R. Kibbe and Jill Casner-Lotto, "Ralston Foods: From Greenfield to Maturity in a Team-Based Plant, *Journal of Organizational Excellence* (Summer 2002): 57–67.

5. "'Golden Hour' Crucial Time for Surgeons on Front Line," *Johnson City Press*, April 1, 2003.

6. Study by G. Clotaire Rapaille, reported in Karen Bernowski, "What Makes American Teams Tick?" *Quality Progress* 28, no. 1 (January 1995): 39–42.

7. Robert Albanese and David D. Van Fleet, "Rational Behavior in Groups: The Free-Riding Tendency," *Academy of Management Review* 10 (1985): 244–255.

8. David H. Freedman, "The Idiocy of Crowds" (What's Next column), *Inc. Magazine* (September 2006): 61–62.

9. "Why Some Teams Succeed (and So Many Don't)," *Harvard Management Update* (October 2006): 3–4.

10. Reported in Jerry Useem, "What's That Spell? Teamwork!" *Fortune* (June 12, 2006): 65–66.

11. Eric Sundstrom, Kenneth P. De-Meuse, and David Futrell, "Work Teams," *American Psychologist* 45 (February 1990): 120–133.

12. Deborah L. Gladstein, "Groups in Context: A Model of Task Group Effectiveness," *Administrative Science Quarterly* 29 (1984): 499–517.

13. Sujin K. Horwitz and Irwin B. Horwitz, "The Effects of Team Diversity on Team Outcomes: A Meta-Analytic Review of Team Demography," *Journal of Management* 33, no. 6 (December 2007): 987–1015; Dora C. Lau and J. Keith Murnighan, "Demographic Diversity and Faultlines: The Compositional Dynamics of Organizational Groups," *Academy of Management Review* 23, no. 2 (1998): 325–340.

14. Based on J. Richard Hackman, *Leading Teams: Setting the Stage for Great Performances* (Boston, MA: Harvard Business School Press, 2002), p. 62. Susan Caminiti, "What Team Leaders Need to Know," *Fortune* (February 20, 1995): 93–100; J. Thomas Buck, "The Rocky Road to Team-Based Management," *Training & Development* (April 1995): 35–38; and Lee G. Bolman and Terrence E. Deal, "What Makes a Team Work?" *Organizational Dynamics* (August, 1992): 34–44; Amy Edmondson, Richard Bohmer, and Gary Pisano, "Speeding Up Team Learning," *Harvard Business Review* (October 2001): 125–132; and Jeanne M. Wilson, Jill George, and Richard S. Wellings, with William C. Byham, *Leadership Trapeze: Strategies for Leadership in Team-Based Organizations* (San Francisco: Jossey-Bass, 1994), p. 14.

15. Thomas Owens, "Business Teams," *Small Business Report* (January 1989): 50–58.

16. "Participation Teams," *Small Business Report* (September 1987): 38–41.

17. Susanne G. Scott and Walter O. Einstein, "Strategic Performance Appraisal in Team-Based Organizations: One Size Does Not Fit All," *Academy of Management Executive* 15, no. 2 (2001): 107–116.

18. Larson and LaFasto, *TeamWork*.

19. James H. Shonk, *Team-Based Organizations* (Homewood, IL: Business One Irwin, 1992); and John Hoerr, "The Payoff from Teamwork," *BusinessWeek* (July 10, 1989): 56–62.

20. Jennifer Robison, "An International Paper Mill Saves Itself," *Gallup Management Journal* (December 14, 2006), http://gmj.gallup.com (accessed May 20, 2008).

21. Ruth Wageman, "Critical Success Factors for Creating Superb Self-Managing Teams," *Organizational Dynamics* (Summer 1997): 49–61.

22. Thomas Owens, "The Self-Managing Work Team," *Small Business Report* (February 1991): 53–65.

23. The discussion of virtual teams is based on Wayne F. Cascio and Stan Shurygailo, "E-Leadership and Virtual Teams," *Organizational Dynamics* 31, no. 4 (2002): 362–376; Anthony M. Townsend, Samuel M. DeMarie, and Anthony R. Hendrickson, "Virtual Teams: Technology and the Workplace of the Future," *Academy of Management Executive* 12, no. 3 (August 1998): 17–29; and Deborah L. Duarte and Nancy Tennant Snyder, *Mastering Virtual Teams* (San Francisco: Jossey-Bass, 1999).

24. Jessica Lipnack and Jeffrey Stamps, "Virtual Teams: The New Way to Work," *Strategy & Leadership* (January–February 1999): 14–19.

25. This discussion is based on Arvind Malhotra, Ann Majchrzak, and Benson Rosen, "Leading Virtual Teams," *Academy of Management Perspectives* 21, no. 1 (February 2007): 60–69; Benson Rosen, Stacie Furst, and Richard Blackburn, "Overcoming Barriers to Knowledge Sharing in Virtual Teams," *Organizational Dynamics* 36, no. 3 (2007): 259–273; Marshall Goldsmith, "Crossing the Cultural Chasm; Keeping Communication Clear and Consistent with Team Members from Other Countries Isn't Easy, Says Author Maya Hu-Chan," *BusinessWeek Online* (May 31, 2007), http://www.businessweek.com/careers/content/may2007/ca20070530_521679.htm (accessed August 24, 2007); and Bradley L. Kirkman, Benson Rosen, Cristina B. Gibson, Paul E. Tesluk, and Simon O. McPherson, "Five Challenges to Virtual Team Success: Lessons from Sabre, Inc.,"

Academy of Management Executive 16, no. 3 (2002): 67–79.

26. Ann Majchrzak, Arvind Malhotra, Jeffrey Stamps, and Jessica Lipnack, "Can Absence Make a Team Grow Stronger?" *Harvard Business Review* 82, no. 5 (May 2004): 131.

27. Lynda Gratton, "Working Together . . . When Apart," *The Wall Street Journal*, June 18, 2007; Kirkman et al., "Five Challenges to Virtual Team Success."

28. Pete Engardio, "A Guide for Multinationals: One of the Greatest Challenges for a Multinational Is Learning How to Build a Productive Global Team," *BusinessWeek* (August 20, 2007): 48–51; and Lynda Gratton, "Working Together . . . When Apart."

29. Vijay Govindarajan and Anil K. Gupta, "Building an Effective Global Business Team," *MIT Sloan Management Review* 42, no. 4 (Summer 2001): 63–71.

30. Charlene Marmer Solomon, "Building Teams Across Borders," *Global Workforce* (November 1998): 12–17.

31. Carol Saunders, Craig Van Slyke, and Douglas R. Vogel, "My Time or Yours? Managing Time Visions in Global Virtual Teams," *Academy of Management Executive* 18, no. 1 (2004): 19–31.

32. This discussion is based on Jeanne Brett, Kristin Behfar, and Mary C. Kern, "Managing Multicultural Teams," *Harvard Business Review* (November 2006): 84-91; and Saunders et al., "My Time or Yours?"

33. Richard Pastore, "Global Team Management: It's a Small World After All," *CIO* (January 23, 2008), http://www.cio.com/article/174750/ Global_Team_Management_It_s_a_ Small_World_After_All (accessed May 20, 2008).

34. Engardio, "A Guide for Multinationals."

35. Sylvia Odenwald, "Global Work Teams," *Training and Development* (February 1996): 54–57; and Debby Young, "Team Heat," *CIO* (September 1, 1998): 43–51.

36. Reported in Jia Lynn Yang, "The Power of Number 4.6," part of a special series, "Secrets of Greatness: Teamwork," *Fortune* (June 12, 2006): 122.

37. Martin Hoegl, "Smaller Teams—Better Teamwork: How to Keep Project Teams Small," *Business Horizons* 48 (2005): 209–214.

38. Reported in "Vive La Difference," box in Julie Connelly, "All Together Now," *Gallup Management Journal* (Spring 2002): 13–18.

39. For research findings on group size, see M. E. Shaw, *Group Dynamics*, 3rd ed. (New York: McGraw-Hill, 1981); G. Manners, "Another Look at Group Size, Group Problem-Solving and Member Consensus," *Academy of Management Journal* 18 (1975): 715–724; and Martin Hoegl, "Smaller Teams—Better Teamwork: How to Keep Project Teams Small," *Business Horizons* 48 (2005): 209–214.

40. Yang, "The Power of Number 4.6."

41. Warren E. Watson, Kamalesh Kumar, and Larry K. Michaelsen, "Cultural Diversity's Impact on Interaction Process and Performance: Comparing Homogeneous and Diverse Task Groups," *Academy of Management Journal* 36 (1993): 590–602; Gail Robinson and Kathleen Dechant, "Building a Business Case for Diversity," *Academy of Management Executive* 11, no. 3 (1997): 21–31; and David A. Thomas and Robin J. Ely, "Making Differences Matter: A New Paradigm for Managing Diversity," *Harvard Business Review* (September–October 1996): 79–90.

42. J. Stuart Bunderson and Kathleen M. Sutcliffe, "Comparing Alternative Conceptualizations of Functional Diversity in Management Teams: Process and Performance Effects," *Academy of Management Journal* 45, no. 5 (2002): 875–893; and Marc Orlitzky and John D. Benjamin, "The Effects of Sex Composition on Small Group Performance in a Business School Case Competition," *Academy of Management Learning and Education* 2, no. 2 (2003): 128–138.

43. Watson et al. "Cultural Diversity's Impact on Interaction Process and Performance."

44. George Prince, "Recognizing Genuine Teamwork," *Supervisory Management* (April 1989): 25–36; K. D. Benne and P. Sheats, "Functional Roles of Group Members," *Journal of Social Issues* 4 (1948): 41–49; and R. F. Bales, *SYMOLOG* Case Study Kit (New York: Free Press, 1980).

45. Robert A. Baron, *Behavior in Organizations*, 2nd ed. (Boston: Allyn & Bacon, 1986).

46. Ibid.

47. Kenneth G. Koehler, "Effective Team Management," *Small Business Report* (July 19, 1989): 14–16; and Connie J. G. Gersick, "Time and Transition in Work Teams: Toward a New Model of Group Development," *Academy of Management Journal* 31 (1988): 9–41.

48. Bruce W. Tuckman and Mary Ann C. Jensen, "Stages of Small-Group Development Revisited," *Group and Organizational Studies* 2 (1977): 419–427; and Bruce W. Tuckman, "Developmental Sequences in Small Groups," *Psychological Bulletin* 63 (1965): 384–399. See also Linda N. Jewell and H. Joseph Reitz, *Group Effectiveness in Organizations* (Glenview, IL: Scott, Foresman, 1981).

49. Thomas Petzinger Jr., "Bovis Team Helps Builders Construct a Solid Foundation" *The Wall Street Journal*, March 21, 1997.

50. Shaw, *Group Dynamics*.

51. Daniel C. Feldman and Hugh J. Arnold, *Managing Individual and Group Behavior in Organizations* (New York: McGraw-Hill, 1983).

52. Dorwin Cartwright and Alvin Zander, *Group Dynamics: Research and Theory*, 3rd ed. (New York: Harper & Row, 1968); and Elliot Aronson, *The Social Animal* (San Francisco: W. H. Freeman, 1976).

53. Stanley E. Seashore, *Group Cohesiveness in the Industrial Work Group* (Ann Arbor, MI: Institute for Social Research, 1954).

54. J. Richard Hackman, "Group Influences on Individuals," in *Handbook of Industrial and Organizational Psychology*, ed. M. Dunnette (Chicago: Rand McNally, 1976).

55. The following discussion is based on Daniel C. Feldman, "The Development and Enforcement of Group Norms," *Academy of Management Review* 9 (1984): 47–53.

56. Wilson et al., *Leadership Trapeze*, p. 12.

57. Simon Taggar and Robert Ellis, "The Role of Leaders in Shaping Formal Team Norms," *The Leadership Quarterly* 18 (2007): 105–120.

58. Geoffrey Colvin, "Why Dream Teams Fail," *Fortune* (June 12, 2006): 87–92.

59. Stephen P. Robbins, *Managing Organizational Conflict: A Nontraditional Approach* (Englewood Cliffs, NJ: Prentice Hall, 1974).

60. Daniel Robey, Dana L. Farrow, and Charles R. Franz, "Group Process and Conflict in System Development," *Management Science* 35 (1989): 1172–1191.

61. Yuhyung Shin, "Conflict Resolution in Virtual Teams," *Organizational Dynamics* 34, no. 4 (2005): 331–345.

62. Dean Tjosvold, Chun Hui, Daniel Z. Ding, and Junchen Hu, "Conflict Values and Team Relationships: Conflict's Contribution to Team Effectiveness and Citizenship in China," *Journal of Organizational Behavior* 24 (2003): 69–88; C. De Dreu and E. Van de Vliert, *Using Conflict in Organizations* (Beverly Hills, CA: Sage, 1997); and Kathleen M. Eisenhardt, Jean L. Kahwajy, and L. J. Bourgeois III, "Conflict and Strategic Choice: How Top Management Teams Disagree," *California Management Review* 39, no. 2 (Winter 1997): 42–62.

63. Jerry B. Harvey, "The Abilene Paradox: The Management of Agreement," *Organizational Dynamics* (Summer 1988): 17–43.

64. Eisenhardt et al., "Conflict and Strategic Choice."

65. Koehler, "Effective Team Management"; and Dean Tjosvold, "Making Conflict Productive," *Personnel Administrator* 29 (June 1984): 121.

66. This discussion is based in part on Richard L. Daft, *Organization Theory and Design* (St. Paul, MN: West, 1992), Chapter 15; and Paul M. Terry, "Conflict Management," *The Journal of Leadership Studies* 3, no. 2 (1996): 3–21.

67. Shin, "Conflict Resolution in Virtual Teams."

68. This discussion is based on K. W. Thomas, "Towards Multidimensional Values in Teaching: The Example of Conflict Behaviors," *Academy of Management Review* 2 (1977): 487.

69. Robbins, *Managing Organizational Conflict*.

70. "The Negotiation Process: The Difference Between Integrative and Distributive Negotiation," La Piana Associates Inc., http://www.lapiana .org/resources/tips/negotiations.

71. Rob Walker, "Take It or Leave It: The Only Guide to Negotiating You Will Ever Need," *Inc.* (August 2003): 75–82.

72. Based on Roger Fisher and William Ury, *Getting to Yes: Negotiating Agreement Without Giving In* (New York: Penguin, 1983).

73. This familiar story was reported in "The Difference Between Integrative and Distributive Negotiation."

74. Based in part on "A Note for Analyzing Work Groups," prepared by Linda A. Hill, Harvard Business School Publishing, http://www .hbsp.harvard.edu.

75. "Big and No Longer Blue," *The Economist* (January 21–27, 2006), http://www.economist.com.

76. R. B. Zajonc, "Social Facilitation," *Science* 149 (1965): 269–274; and Miriam Erez and Anit Somech, "Is Group Productivity Loss the Rule or the Exception? Effects of Culture and Group-Based Motivation," *Academy of Management Journal* 39, no. 6 (1996): 1513–1537.

77. Claire M. Mason and Mark A. Griffin, "Group Task Satisfaction; The Group's Shared Attitude to Its Task and Work Environment," *Group and Organizational Management* 30, no. 6 (2005): 625–652.

78. Gina Imperato, "Their Specialty? Teamwork," *Fast Company* (January–February 2000): 54–56.

79. Reported in Scott Thurm, "Theory & Practice: Teamwork Raises Everyone's Game—Having Employees Bond Benefits Companies More Than Promoting 'Stars,'" *The Wall Street Journal*, November 7, 2005.

80. Kenneth Labich, "Elite Teams Get the Job Done," *Fortune* (February 19, 1996): 90–99.

81. "A Note for Analyzing Effective Work Groups."

General Motors
Part Five: Leading
Blogs Take GM's Corporate Communication into Fast Lane

Whether it's the no-nonsense directness of legendary CEO Jack Welch, the point-by-point simplicity of financial guru Suze Orman, or the change-the-world idealism of Apple's Steve Jobs, effective communicators exhibit powerful mastery over their messages.

Yet in the age of new media and the Internet, getting one's point across requires mastery of both the message and medium. Thanks to blogs, texting, instant messaging, and social networking Web sites, leaders have more options than ever before for reaching large audiences.

Who exactly are the grand communicators of the digital age? The pimple-faced founders of Facebook? The 30-something search-engine geniuses at Google? Try Bob Lutz, the 77-year-old vice chairman of global product development at General Motors (GM). Lutz stunned the business community in 2005 when he ventured out into the blogosphere, exchanging his podium for podcasts and memoranda for message boards. Launched as the social media initiative of GM's Global Communications Group, Lutz's FastLane blog marked the first time an executive of a nontechnology Fortune 100 firm began blogging as a means of corporate communication.

Like other blogs, FastLane features commentary, product news, podcasts, video clips, photo galleries, user feedback, and twittering. Visitors to the blog—mostly car enthusiasts, members of the press, and GM employees—find information about auto shows, new vehicles, manufacturing breakthroughs, and more. With trademark informality, FastLane defines itself as "your source for the latest, greatest musings of GM leaders on topics relevant to the company, the industry and the global economy, and—most of all—to our customers."

Although the blogosphere is generally upbeat, blogs can become caldrons of conflict between adversarial groups. As a consequence of the blogosphere's reach and informal style, inartful comments may be published instantly on blogs and disseminated worldwide in seconds, creating severe headaches for public relations teams.

One such headache occurred in 2008 when off-the-cuff comments made during a closed-door session with journalists spread like wildfire across the blogosphere. Vice Chairman Lutz stated that hybrids didn't make "economic sense," adding that global warming was "a total crock." Critics seized on the moment to advance their crusade against the automaker. Lutz likewise took to his FastLane blog to respond.

"An offhand comment I made recently about the concept of global warming seems to have a lot of people heated, and it's spreading through the Internet like ragweed," wrote Lutz in his February 21, 2008, FastLane entry. "My opinions on the subject—like anyone's—are immaterial. General Motors is dedicated to the removal of cars and trucks from the environmental equation, period."

The vice chairman urged the public to ignore his personal musings and to focus instead on the company's push for clean transportation. "We're going to keep working on it—via E85, hybrids, hydrogen and fuel cells, and the electrification of the automobile." Lutz took the opportunity to praise GM's new electric car. "The Chevrolet Volt program is occurring under my personal watch, because I—and others in senior management—believe in it. I fully expect that it will revolutionize the automotive industry."

GM's ongoing support for FastLane shows that executives at the top automaker see blogging as a legitimate form of corporate communication. And no surprise: FastLane is an information center, marketing tool, crisis management instrument, and customer-feedback system wrapped up in one. If Lutz is any indication, the corporate blog is here to stay. Where else could an outspoken vice chairman find so versatile a megaphone.

Questions

1. Visit FastLane online to identify the blog's various communication channels and their channel richness.

2. Is the information posted at FastLane appropriate for a blog? Why or why not?

3. What unique communication benefits do blogs offer to GM executives?

SOURCES: Glenn Hunter, "GM's Lutz On Hybrids, Global Warming and Cars As Art," *D magazine* (January 30, 2008), http://frontburner.dmagazine.com/2008/01/30/gms-lutz-on-hybrids-global-warming-and-cars-as-art (accessed October 17, 2008); Rob Kelley, "Tahoe Hybrid SUV named 'Green Car of Year,'" *CNNMoney*, November 18, 2007, http://money.cnn.com/2007/11/15/autos/green_car/index.htm (accessed October 17, 2008); Bob Lutz, "Talk About a Crock," *FastLane Blog*, February 21, 2008, http://fastlane.gmblogs.com/archives/2008/02/talk_about_a_cr.html (accessed October 17, 2008); "Welcome to Fastlane," *FastLane Blog*, January 5, 2005, http://fastlane.gmblogs.com/archives/2005/01/welcome_to_fast_1.html (accessed October 17,

2008);"Half of GM Plants to Be Landfill-Free By Late 2010," *GreenBiz*, September 8, 2008, http://www.greenbiz.com/news/2008/09/08/half-gm-plants-be-landfill-free-by-late-2010 (accessed October 17, 2008); Kevin Krolicki,"GM Exec Stands by Calling Global Warming a 'Crock,'" *Reuters*, February 22, 2008, http://www.reuters.com (accessed October 17, 2008).

Characteristics Frequently Associated with Each Myers-Briggs Type

Sensing Types   **Intuitive Types**

ISTJ

Quiet, serious, earn success by thoroughness and dependability. Practical, matter-of-fact, realistic, and responsible. Decide logically what should be done and work toward it steadily, regardless of distractions. Take pleasure in making everything orderly and organized—their work, their home, their life. Value traditions and loyalty.

ISFJ

Quiet, friendly, responsible, and conscientious. Committed and steady in meeting their obligations. Thorough, painstaking, and accurate. Loyal, considerate, notice and remember specifics about people who are important to them, concerned with how others feel. Strive to create an orderly and harmonious environment at work and at home.

INFJ

Seek meaning and connection in ideas, relationships, and material possessions. Want to understand what motivates people and are insightful about others. Conscientious and committed to their firm values. Develop a clear vision about how best to serve the common good. Organized and decisive in implementing their vision.

INTJ

Have original minds and great drive for implementing their ideas and achieving their goals. Quickly see patterns in external events and develop long-range explanatory perspectives. When committed, organize a job and carry it through. Skeptical and independent, have high standards of competence and performance—for themselves and others.

ISTP

Tolerant and flexible, quiet observers until a problem appears, then act quickly to find workable solutions. Analyze what makes things work and readily get through large amounts of data to isolate the core of practical problems. Interested in cause and effect, organize facts using logical principles, value efficiency.

ISFP

Quiet, friendly, sensitive, and kind. Enjoy the present moment, what's going on around them. Like to have their own space and to work within their own time frame. Loyal and committed to their values and to people who are important to them. Dislike disagreements and conflicts, do not force their opinions or values on others.

INFP

Idealistic, loyal to their values and to people who are important to them. Want an external life that is congruent with their values. Curious, quick to see possibilities, can be catalysts for implementing ideas. Seek to understand people and to help them fulfill their potential. Adaptable, flexible, and accepting unless a value is threatened.

INTP

Seek to develop logical explanations for everything that interests them. Theoretical and abstract, interested more in ideas than in social interaction. Quiet, contained, flexible, and adaptable. Have unusual ability to focus in depth to solve problems in their area of interest. Skeptical, sometimes critical, always analytical.

ESTP

Flexible and tolerant, they take a pragmatic approach focused on immediate results. Theories and conceptual explanations bore them—they want to act energetically to solve the problem. Focus on the here-and-now, spontaneous, enjoy each moment that they can be active with others. Enjoy material comforts and style. Learn best through doing.

ESFP

Outgoing, friendly, and accepting. Exuberant lovers of life, people, and material comforts. Enjoy working with others to make things happen. Bring common sense and a realistic approach to their work, and make work fun. Flexible and spontaneous, adapt readily to new people and environments. Learn best by trying a new skill with other people.

ENFP

Warmly enthusiastic and imaginative. See life as full of possibilities. Make connections between events and information very quickly, and confidently proceed based on the patterns they see. Want a lot of affirmation from others, and readily give appreciation and support. Spontaneous and flexible, often rely on their ability to improvise and their verbal fluency.

ENTP

Quick, ingenious, stimulating, alert, and outspoken. Resourceful in solving new and challenging problems. Adept at generating conceptual possibilities and then analyzing them strategically. Good at reading other people. Bored by routine, will seldom do the same thing the same way, apt to turn to one new interest after another.

ESTJ

Practical, realistic, matter-of-fact. Decisive, quickly move to implement decisions. Organize projects and people to get things done, focus on getting results in the most efficient way possible. Take care of routine details. Have a clear set of logical standards, systematically follow them and want others to also. Forceful in implementing their plans.

ESFJ

Warmhearted, conscientious, and cooperative. Want harmony in their environment, work with determination to establish it. Like to work with others to complete tasks accurately and on time. Loyal, follow through even in small matters. Notice what others need in their day-by-day lives and try to provide it. Want to be appreciated for who they are and for what they contribute.

ENFJ

Warm, empathetic, responsive, and responsible. Highly attuned to the emotions, needs, and motivations of others. Find potential in everyone, want to help others fulfill their potential. May act as catalysts for individual and group growth. Loyal, responsive to praise and criticism. Sociable, facilitate others in a group, and provide inspiring leadership.

ENTJ

Frank, decisive, assume leadership readily. Quickly see illogical and inefficient procedures and policies, develop and implement comprehensive systems to solve organizational problems. Enjoy long-term planning and goal setting. Usually well informed, well read, enjoy expanding their knowledge and passing it on to others. Forceful in presenting their ideas.

Introverts (ISTJ, ISFJ, INFJ, INTJ, ISTP, ISFP, INFP, INTP)

Extraverts (ESTP, ESFP, ENFP, ENTP, ESTJ, ESFJ, ENFJ, ENTJ)

Managing Small Business Start-Ups

Do You Think Like an Entrepreneur?[1]

An entrepreneur faces many demands. Do you have the proclivity to start and build your own business? To find out, consider the extent to which each of the following statements characterizes your behavior. Please answer each of the following items as Mostly True or Mostly False for you.

	Mostly True	Mostly False
1. Give me a little information and I can come up with a lot of ideas.	_____	_____
2. I like pressure in order to focus.	_____	_____
3. I don't easily get frustrated when things don't go my way.	_____	_____
4. I identify how resources can be recombined to produce novel outcomes.	_____	_____
5. I enjoy competing against the clock to meet deadlines.	_____	_____
6. People in my life have to accept that nothing is more important than the achievement of my school, my sport, or my career goals.	_____	_____
7. I serve as a role model for creativity.	_____	_____
8. I think "on my feet" when carrying out tasks.	_____	_____
9. I am determined and action-oriented.	_____	_____

SCORING AND INTERPRETATION: Each question pertains to some aspect of improvisation, which is a correlate of entrepreneurial intentions. Entrepreneurial improvisation consists of three elements. Questions 1, 4, and 7 pertain to creativity/ingenuity, the ability to produce novel solutions under constrained conditions. Questions 2, 5, and 8 pertain to working under pressure/stress, the ability to excel under pressure-filled circumstances. Questions 3, 6, and 9 pertain to action/persistence, the determination to achieve goals and solve problems in the moment. If you answered "Mostly True" to at least two of three questions for each subscale or six of nine for all the questions, then consider yourself an entrepreneur in the making, with the potential to manage your own business. If you scored one or fewer "Mostly True" on each subscale or three or fewer for all nine questions, you might want to consider becoming a manager by working for someone else.

Many people dream of starting their own business. Some decide to start a business because they're inspired by a great idea or want the flexibility that comes from being self-employed. Others decide to go into business for themselves after they get laid off or find their opportunities limited in big companies. Interest in entrepreneurship and small business is at an all-time high. At college campuses across the United States, ambitious courses, programs, and centers teach the fundamentals of starting a small business. Entrepreneurs have access to business incubators, support networks, and online training courses. The enormous growth of franchising gives beginners an escorted route into a new business. In addition, the Internet opens new avenues for small business formation.

Today, the fastest growing segment of small business in both the United States and Canada is in one-owner operations, or *sole proprietorships*.[2] Sole proprietorships in the United States reached an all-time high of 19.5 million in 2004, the most recent year with statistics available.[3] After the crash of the dot-com boom, many of these entrepreneurs are finding opportunities in low-tech businesses such as landscaping, child care, and janitorial services. Overall, since the 1970s, the number of businesses in the United States economy has been growing faster than the labor force.[4]

However, running a small business is difficult and risky. The Small Business Administration reports that about 30 percent of small businesses fail within two years of opening and 56 percent fold after four years.[5] For high-tech businesses, the failure rate is even higher. Research indicates that the chances are only 6 in 1 million that an idea for a high-tech business eventually turns into a successful public company.[6] Yet despite the risks, people are entering the world of entrepreneurship at an unprecedented rate. In 2006, an estimated 649,700 new businesses were established in the United States, while an estimated 564,700 closed their doors for good.[7] Small business formation is the primary process by which an economy recreates and reinvents itself,[8] and the turbulence in the small business environment is evidence of a shifting but thriving U.S. economy.

WHAT IS ENTREPRENEURSHIP?

Entrepreneurship is the process of initiating a business venture, organizing the necessary resources, and assuming the associated risks and rewards.[9] An **entrepreneur** is someone who engages in entrepreneurship. An entrepreneur recognizes a viable idea for a business product or service and carries it out by finding and assembling the necessary resources—money, people, machinery, location—to undertake the business venture. Entrepreneurs also assume the risks and reap the rewards of the business. They assume the financial and legal risks of ownership and receive the business's profits.

A good example of entrepreneurship is Jeff Fluhr, who dropped out of Stanford during his first year of graduate school to launch StubHub, a leading Internet player in the burgeoning market of ticket reselling, an industry which by some estimates is doing $10 billion a year in volume. Hardworking and persistent, Fluhr struggled to raise money during the early days of the business, a time when many investors had been stung by the dot-com crash. His tenacity paid off as he convinced executives from Viacom Inc., Home Box Office, and Madison Square Garden to invest in his plan to reinvent the online ticket resale industry. StubHub gives consumers access to high-demand concert, theater, and sporting events that are usually unavailable, because promoters now reserve large blocks of tickets for fan club members, season ticket holders, and sponsors. StubHub allows sellers to list tickets at StubHub—free of charge—and sell them either by auction or at a fixed price. The company's two call centers receive approximately 2,500 calls a day and sell more than $200 million worth of tickets annually.[10] Fluhr, who comes from a family of entrepreneurs, was willing to take the risks and is now reaping the rewards of entrepreneurship.

Successful entrepreneurs have many different motivations, and they measure rewards in different ways. One study classified small business owners in five different categories, as illustrated in Exhibit A.1. Some people are *idealists*, who like the idea of working on something that is new, creative, or personally meaningful. *Optimizers* are rewarded by the personal satisfaction of being business owners. Entrepreneurs in the *sustainer* category like the chance to balance work and personal life and often don't want the business to grow too large, while *hard workers* enjoy putting in the long hours and dedication to build a larger, more profitable business. The *juggler* category includes entrepreneurs who like the chance a small business gives them to handle everything themselves. These high-energy people thrive on the pressure of paying bills, meeting deadlines, and making payroll.[11]

Compare the motivation of Paula Turpin to that of Greg Littlefield. Turpin borrowed a few thousand dollars to start a hair salon, Truly Blessed Styles, in Shirley, New York.

entrepreneurship The process of initiating a business venture, organizing the necessary resources, and assuming the associated risks and rewards.

entrepreneur Someone who recognizes a viable idea for a business product or service and carries it out.

Rewarded by chance to work on something new and creative

Thrive on the challenge of building a larger, more profitable business

Enjoy chance to balance work and personal life

| Idealists | Optimizers | Hard Workers | Jugglers | Sustainers |

Get personal satisfaction from being business owners

High-energy people who enjoy handling every detail of their own businesses

SOURCE: Based on a study conducted by Yankelovich Partners for Pitney Bowes in Mark Henricks, "Type-Cast," *Entrepreneur* (March 2000): 14–16.

She does all the cutting, styling, and coloring herself, while her mother helps schedule appointments and keeps the books. Turpin likes the flexibility and freedom of working for herself. Although she hopes to expand by adding beauty supplies, she doesn't want the headaches of managing a large business. Greg Littlefield quit his management job and started a cleaning service because he reasoned that it would never lack customers. From the beginning, when he was working two part-time jobs and cleaning buildings by himself at night, Littlefield had plans for expansion. Within a decade, Littlefield's firm, Professional Facilities Management, grew into a 900-employee company providing a range of services including housekeeping, landscaping, minor maintenance, and security services.[12] Greg Littlefield reflects the motivation of a *hard worker*, whereas Paula Turpin's motivation is more that of a *sustainer*.

Sometimes people start new businesses when they lose their jobs due to corporate downsizing. The major layoffs in the early 2000s provided just the push some latent entrepreneurs needed to strike out on their own. Some experts think an economic downturn is actually the best time to start a business. For one thing, a downturn opens up lots of opportunities because people are looking for lower costs and better ways of doing things. The economic climate also enables the new business to hire good people, forces the entrepreneur to keep costs in line, and provides the time needed to build something of lasting value rather than struggling to keep pace with rapid growth.[13]

ENTREPRENEURSHIP TODAY

Not so long ago, scholars and policy makers worried about the potential of small business to survive. The turbulence in the technology sector and the demise of many dot-com start-ups heightened concerns about whether small companies can compete with big business. However, entrepreneurship and small business, including high-tech start-ups, are vital, dynamic, and increasingly important parts of the U.S. economy. Small businesses represent 99.7 percent of all firms and employ about half of all private sector employees. In addition, small businesses have generated 60 to 80 percent of new jobs annually over the last decade.[14]

Entrepreneurship in other countries is also booming. The list of entrepreneurial countries around the world, shown in Exhibit A.2, is intriguing. A project monitoring entrepreneurial activity around the world reports that an estimated 47.4 percent of adults age 18 to 64 in Thailand are either starting up or managing new enterprises. The percentage in Peru is 39 percent; in Colombia, 33.6 percent. China and Argentina also show higher rates of entrepreneurial activity than the U.S. rate of 14.1 percent. China's boost in entrepreneurial activity continues to increase due to the rapid expansion of the Chinese economy, especially in the big cities.[15]

Country	Percentage of Individuals Age 18 to 64 Active in Starting or Managing a New Business, 2007
Thailand	47.4
Peru	39.0
Colombia	33.6
Venezuela	24.9
China	24.6
Argentina	24.1
Dominican Republic	23.2
Brazil	22.4
Chile	21.4
Iceland	19.8
Greece	18.7
Uruguay	18.5
Ireland	16.8
Portugal	15.4
Hong Kong	15.0

SOURCE: Table 1: Prevalence Rates of Entrepreneurial Activity Across Countries, 2007, in Niels Bosma, Kent Jones, Erkko Autio and Jonathan Levie, *Global Entrepreneurship Monitor 2007 Executive Report*, Babson College and the London Business School, March 14, 2008. Permission to reproduce this table has been kindly granted by the copyright holders. The GEM is an international consortium comprising of 42 countries in 2007. Our thanks go to the authors, researchers, funding bodies and other contributors who have made this possible.

Definition of Small Business

The U.S. Small Business Administration (SBA) defines a small business as "one that is independently owned and operated and which is not dominant in its field of operation."[16] Exhibit A.3 gives a few examples of how the SBA defines small business for a sample of industries.

However, the definition of small business is currently under revision in response to concerns from small business owners. After nationwide public hearings, the SBA determined that standards should be changed in light of shifting economic and industry conditions. Redefining small business size standards is a daunting task, but SBA leaders agree that the standards need to be more flexible in today's world. The SBA's definition has been revised a number of times over the years to reflect changing economic conditions.[17]

Exhibit A.3 also illustrates general categories of businesses most entrepreneurs start: manufacturing, retail, and Internet services. Additional categories of small businesses are construction, hospitality, communications, finance, and real estate.

Manufacturing	
Soft-drink manufacturing	Number of employees does not exceed 500
Electronic computer manufacturing	Number of employees does not exceed 1,000
Prerecorded CD, tape, and record producing	Number of employees does not exceed 750

Retail (Store and Nonstore)	
Sporting goods stores	Average annual receipts do not exceed $6.5 million
Electronic auctions	Average annual receipts do not exceed $23.0 million
Convenience stores	Average annual receipts do not exceed $6.5 million

Miscellaneous Internet Services	
Internet service providers	Average annual receipts do not exceed $23.0 million
Web search portals	Average annual receipts do not exceed $6.5 million
Internet publishing and broadcasting	Number of employees does not exceed 500

SOURCE: U.S. Small Business Administration, Table of Small Business Size Standards Matched to North American Industry Classification System Codes, http://www.sba.gov/idc/groups/public/documents/sba_homepage/serv_sstd_tablepdf.pdf (accessed June 23, 2008).

Impact of Entrepreneurial Companies

The impact of entrepreneurial companies on the U.S. economy is astonishing. According to the Small Business Administration, businesses with fewer than 500 employees represent 99.7 percent of all firms with employees in the United States, employ more than 50 percent of the nation's nonfarm private sector workers, and generate more than 50 percent of the nation's nonfarm gross domestic product (GDP). In addition, small businesses represent 97 percent of America's exporters and produce 28.6 percent of all export value.[18] In 2000, the status of the SBA administrator was elevated to a cabinet-level position in recognition of the importance of small business in the U.S. economy.[19]

Inspired by the growth of companies such as eBay, Google, and Amazon.com, entrepreneurs are still flocking to the Internet to start new businesses. In addition, demographic and lifestyle trends create new opportunities in areas such as environmental services, lawn care, computer maintenance, children's markets, fitness, and home health care. Entrepreneurship and small business in the United States is an engine for job creation and innovation.

- **Job Creation.** Researchers disagree over what percentage of new jobs is created by small business. Research indicates that the *age* of a company, more than its size, determines the number of jobs it creates. That is, virtually *all* new jobs in recent years have come from new companies, which include not only small companies but also new branches of huge, multinational organizations.[20] However, small companies still are thought to create a large percentage of new jobs in the United States. The SBA reports that small businesses create 65 percent or more of America's new jobs. Jobs created by small businesses give the United States an economic vitality no other country can claim. However, as reflected in Exhibit A.2 earlier in the chapter, entrepreneurial economic activity is dramatically expanding in other countries as well.

- **Innovation.** According to Cognetics, Inc., a research firm run by David Birch that traces the employment and sales records of some 9 million companies, new and smaller firms have been responsible for 55 percent of the innovations in 362 different industries and 95 percent of all radical innovations. In addition, fast-growing businesses, which Birch calls *gazelles*, produce twice as many product innovations per employee as do larger firms. Small firms that file for patents typically produce 13 to 14 times more patents per employee than large patenting firms.[21] Among the notable products for which small businesses can be credited are WD-40, the jet engine, and the shopping cart.

WHO ARE ENTREPRENEURS?

The heroes of American business—Henry Ford, Steve Jobs, Sam Walton, Bill Gates, Oprah Winfrey, Larry Page, Sergey Brin—are almost always entrepreneurs. Entrepreneurs start with a vision. Often they are unhappy with their current jobs and see an opportunity to bring together the resources needed for a new venture. However, the image of entrepreneurs as bold pioneers probably is overly romantic. A survey of the CEOs of the nation's fastest-growing small firms found that these entrepreneurs could be best characterized as hardworking and practical, with great familiarity with their market and industry.[22] For example, Jason Goldberg, T-Mobile USA's former strategic planning director, grew frustrated with the flood of unqualified candidates he received from popular job boards so he created Jobster as a new approach to online recruiting. Jobster takes advantage of the referring power of a social network, meaning that every job candidate is recommended by a trusted reference. Job recruiters reduce their risk of hiring an unknown candidate when they hire someone who comes with a referral. Striking a nerve with the hiring community, Jobster has signed 475 corporate clients since its launch in 2005, and its roster of clients is growing 30 percent every year.[23]

Diversity of Entrepreneurs

Entrepreneurs often have backgrounds and demographic characteristics that distinguish them from other people. Entrepreneurs are more likely to be the first-born within their families, and their parents are more likely to have been entrepreneurs. In addition, immigrants are more likely to start small businesses than native-born Americans.[24] Consider former veterinarian Salvador Guzman, who moved from Mexico to become a busboy in a friend's Mexican restaurant in Nashville, Tennessee. Energized by the opportunities to succeed in the United States as an entrepreneur, Guzman started his own restaurant with three partners and a savings of $18,000, joining more than 2.4 million self-employed immigrants in the United States. Now he owns 14 restaurants and the first Spanish-language radio station in Tennessee.[25]

Entrepreneurship offers opportunities for individuals who may feel blocked in established corporations. Women-owned and minority-owned businesses may be the emerging growth companies of the next decade. In 2005, women owned 6.5 million U.S. businesses that generated $950.6 billion in revenues and employed more than 7 million workers. In Canada as well, women entrepreneurs are thriving. Since 1989, the rate of small businesses started by women in Canada grew 60 percent faster than the growth in the number of small businesses started by men.[26] Statistics for minorities in the United States are also impressive, with minorities owning 4.1 million firms that generated $694 billion in revenues and employed 4.8 million people.[27] The number of new firms launched by minorities is growing about 17 percent a year, with African American businesses growing at a rate of about 26 percent a year. African American males between the ages of 25 and 35 start more businesses than any other group in the country. Moreover, the face of entrepreneurship for the future will be increasingly diverse. When Junior Achievement (an organization that educates young people about business) conducted a poll of teenagers ages 13 to 18, it found a much greater interest among minorities than whites in starting a business, as shown in Exhibit A.4.[28]

The types of businesses launched by minority entrepreneurs are also increasingly sophisticated. The traditional minority-owned mom-and-pop retail store or restaurant is being replaced by firms in industries such as financial services, insurance, and media. For example, Pat Winans, an African American who grew up in a Chicago ghetto, started Magna Securities, a successful institutional brokerage firm in New York City, with just $5,000. Ed Chin, a third-generation Chinese American, founded AIS Corporation to offer small and midsized companies the kind of sophisticated

EXHIBIT | A.4

A Glimpse of Tomorrow's Entrepreneurs

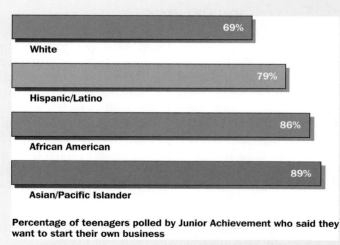

White 69%

Hispanic/Latino 79%

African American 86%

Asian/Pacific Islander 89%

Percentage of teenagers polled by Junior Achievement who said they want to start their own business

SOURCE: Junior Achievement Survey results reported in Cora Daniels, "Minority Rule," *FSB* (December 2003–January 2004): 65–66.

insurance packages usually available only to large companies. Chin originally found a niche by catering to the Asian marketplace, but word-of-mouth has helped his company expand beyond that market.[29]

Personality Traits

A number of studies have investigated the personality characteristics of entrepreneurs and how they differ from successful managers in established organizations. Some suggest that entrepreneurs in general want something different from life than do traditional managers. Entrepreneurs seem to place high importance on being free to achieve and maximize their potential. Some 40 traits are identified as being associated with entrepreneurship, but 6 have special importance.[30] These characteristics are illustrated in Exhibit A.5.

Internal Locus of Control The task of starting and running a new business requires the belief that you can make things come out the way you want. The entrepreneur not only has a vision but also must be able to plan to achieve that vision and believe it will happen. An **internal locus of control** is the belief by individuals that their future is within their control and that external forces have little influence. For entrepreneurs, reaching the future is seen as being in the hands of the individual. Many people, however, feel that the world is highly uncertain and that they are unable to make things come out the way they want. An **external locus of control** is the belief by individuals that their future is not within their control but rather is influenced by external forces. Entrepreneurs are individuals who are convinced they can make the difference between success and failure; hence, they are motivated to take the steps needed to achieve the goal of setting up and running a new business.

High Energy Level A business start-up requires great effort. Most entrepreneurs report struggle and hardship. They persist and work incredibly hard despite traumas and obstacles. A survey of business owners reported that half worked 60 hours or more per week. Another reported that entrepreneurs worked long hours, but that beyond 70 hours little benefit was gained. New business owners work long hours, with only 23 percent working fewer than 50 hours, which is close to a normal work-week for managers in established businesses.

Need to Achieve Another human quality closely linked to entrepreneurship is the **need to achieve**, which means that people are motivated to excel and pick situations in which success is likely.[31] People who have high achievement needs like to set their own goals, which are moderately difficult. Easy goals present no challenge; unrealistically difficult goals cannot be achieved. Intermediate goals are challenging and provide great satisfaction when achieved. High achievers also like to pursue goals for which they can obtain feedback about their success.

Self-Confidence People who start and run a business must act decisively. They need confidence about their ability to master the day-to-day tasks of the business. They must feel sure about their ability to win customers, handle the technical details, and keep the business moving. Entrepreneurs also have a general feeling of confidence that they can deal with anything in the future; complex, unanticipated problems can be handled as they arise.

Awareness of Passing Time Entrepreneurs tend to be impatient; they feel a sense of urgency. They want things to progress as if there is no tomorrow. They want things moving immediately and seldom procrastinate. Entrepreneurs seize the moment.

internal locus of control
The belief by individuals that their future is within their control and that external forces have little influence.

external locus of control
The belief by individuals that their future is not within their control but rather is influenced by external forces.

need to achieve A human quality linked to entrepreneurship in which people are motivated to excel and pick situations in which success is likely.

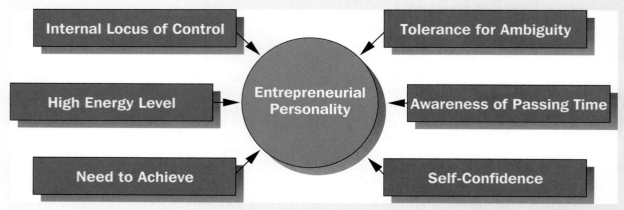

SOURCE: Adapted from Charles R. Kuehl and Peggy A. Lambing, *Small Business: Planning and Management* (Ft. Worth, TX: The Dryden Press, 1994): 45.

Tolerance for Ambiguity Many people need work situations characterized by clear structure, specific instructions, and complete information. **Tolerance for ambiguity** is the psychological characteristic that allows a person to be untroubled by disorder and uncertainty. This trait is important, because few situations present more uncertainty than starting a new business. Decisions are made without clear understanding of options or certainty about which option will succeed.

These personality traits and the demographic characteristics discussed earlier offer an insightful but imprecise picture of the entrepreneur. Successful entrepreneurs come in all ages, from all backgrounds, and may have a combination of personality traits. No one should be discouraged from starting a business because he or she doesn't fit a specific profile. One review of small business suggests that the three most important traits of successful entrepreneurs, particularly in a turbulent environment, are realism, flexibility, and passion. Even the most realistic entrepreneurs tend to underestimate the difficulties of building a business, so they need flexibility and a passion for their idea to survive the hurdles.[32]

SOCIAL ENTREPRENEURSHIP: AN INNOVATIVE APPROACH TO SMALL BUSINESS

In today's shifting business and social environment, a new breed of entrepreneur has emerged—the **social entrepreneur**. Social entrepreneurs are leaders who are committed to both good business and positive social change. They create new business models that meet critical human needs and solve important problems that remain unsolved by current economic and social institutions.[33] Consider Earl Martin Phalen, who founded BELL (Building Educated Leaders for Life) out of his Boston living room in 1992 to provide after-school and summer support services to low-income students in grades K–6. As an African American growing up in the state's foster care system, Bell understood firsthand how the right kind of support can change lives and communities. "To know that [somebody] supported me, and all of a sudden, it took my life from going to jail to going to Yale," he says of his motivation to start BELL. All 20 of the students in BELL's first class went on to college.[34]

Social entrepreneurship combines the creativity, business smarts, passion, and hard work of the traditional entrepreneur with a mission to change the world for the better. One writer referred to this new breed as a cross between Richard Branson, the high-powered CEO of Virgin Airlines, and Mother Teresa, a Catholic nun who dedicated her life to serving the poor.[35] Social entrepreneurs have a primary goal of improving

tolerance for ambiguity The psychological characteristic that allows a person to be untroubled by disorder and uncertainty.

social entrepreneur Entrepreneurial leaders who are committed to both good business and changing the world for the better.

society rather than maximizing profits, but they also emphasize solid business results, high performance standards, and accountability for results. The organizations created by social entrepreneurs may or may not make a profit, but the bottom line for these companies is always social betterment rather than economic return. For entrepreneur Peter Thum, founder of Ethos Water, the purpose of his business was to sell expensive bottled water in the West in stores like Starbucks and donate part of the profits to clean-water initiatives in developing countries such as Honduras and Kenya. By 2010, Ethos will give more than $10 million a year to nonprofits that fund safe-water projects.[36]

Social entrepreneurship is not new, but the phenomenon blossomed over the past 20 or so years. Exact figures for the number of social entrepreneurs are difficult to verify, but estimates number in the tens of thousands working around the world. The innovative organizations created by social entrepreneurs are defying the traditional boundaries between business and welfare.[37] One good illustration is Homeboy Industries, a company that started 12 years ago in a converted warehouse in Los Angeles. With 18 employees, Homeboy emphasizes rehabilitation of former gang members over revenue. The silk-screening part of the business generated $1.1 million last year, and the bakery produced another $3 million in revenue. Jesuit priest and founder Reverend Gregory Boyle explains that the "cash-producing part of the business brings in enough to pay for the free services." These services include therapy for former gang members, housing assistance, job development, counseling, and tattoo removal treatments. Boyle's goal is to hire and train the neighborhood's young men to break the cycle of gangs, crime, and imprisonment.[38]

LAUNCHING AN ENTREPRENEURIAL START-UP

Whether one starts a socially oriented company or a traditional for-profit small business, the first step in pursuing an entrepreneurial dream is to come up with a viable idea and then plan like crazy. Once someone has a new idea in mind, a business plan must be drawn and decisions must be made about legal structure, financing, and basic tactics, such as whether to start the business from scratch and whether to pursue international opportunities from the start.

Starting with the Idea

To some people, the idea for a new business is the easy part. They do not even consider entrepreneurship until they are inspired by an exciting idea. Other people decide they want to run their own business and set about looking for an idea or opportunity. Exhibit A.6 shows the most important reasons that people start a new business and

EXHIBIT | **A.6**   Sources of Entrepreneurial Motivation and New Business Ideas

Reasons for Starting a Business

41%	Joined Family Business
36%	To Control My Future
27%	To Be My Own Boss
25%	To Fulfill a Dream
5%	Downsized/Laid Off

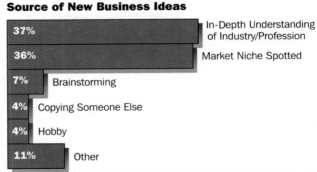

Source of New Business Ideas

37%	In-Depth Understanding of Industry/Profession
36%	Market Niche Spotted
7%	Brainstorming
4%	Copying Someone Else
4%	Hobby
11%	Other

SOURCES: John Case, "The Rewards," *Inc.* (May 15, 2001): 50–51; and Leslie Brokaw, "How to Start an Inc. 500 Company," *Inc.* (October 15, 1994): 51–65. Copyright 1994 and 2001 by Mansueto Ventures LLC. Reproduced with permission of Mansueto Ventures LLC in the format Textbook via Copyright Clearance Center.

the source of new business ideas. Note that 37 percent of business founders got their idea from an in-depth understanding of the industry, primarily because of past job experience. Interestingly, almost as many—36 percent—spotted a market niche that wasn't being filled.[39] After Camille Young decided to develop a healthier lifestyle and diet, she became frustrated trying to find organic food in Jersey City. Young explains, "I had to go to Manhattan to find organic food. It was annoying that Jersey City didn't even have a juice bar. Then I started thinking, Why don't I open one?" To fill this market niche, she opened two BaGua Juice stores that sell a variety of nutritious smoothies to health-conscious consumers.[40]

The trick for entrepreneurs is to blend their own skills and experience with a need in the marketplace. Acting strictly on one's own skills may produce something no one wants to buy. On the other hand, finding a market niche that one does not have the ability to fill doesn't work either. Both personal skill and market need typically must be present.

Writing the Business Plan

Once an entrepreneur is inspired by a new business idea, careful planning is crucial. A **business plan** is a document specifying the business details prepared by an entrepreneur prior to opening a new business. Planning forces the entrepreneur to carefully think through the issues and problems associated with starting and developing the business. Most entrepreneurs have to borrow money, and a business plan is absolutely critical for persuading lenders and investors to participate in the business. Studies show that small businesses with a carefully thought-out, written business plan are much more likely to succeed than those without one.[41] To attract the interest of venture capitalists or other potential investors, the entrepreneur should keep the plan crisp and compelling.

The details of a business plan may vary, but successful business plans generally share several characteristics:[42]

- Demonstrate a clear, compelling vision that creates an air of excitement.
- Provide clear and realistic financial projections.
- Profile potential customers and the target market.
- Include detailed information about the industry and competitors.
- Provide evidence of an effective entrepreneurial management team.
- Pay attention to good formatting and clear writing.
- Keep the plan short—no more than 50 pages.
- Highlight critical risks that may threaten business success.
- Spell out the sources and uses of start-up funds and operating funds.
- Capture the reader's interest with a killer summary.

Choosing a Legal Structure

Before entrepreneurs begin a business, and perhaps again as it expands, they must choose an appropriate legal structure for the company. The three basic choices are proprietorship, partnership, or corporation.

Sole Proprietorship A **sole proprietorship** is defined as an unincorporated business owned by an individual for profit. Proprietorships make up the majority of businesses in the United States. This form is popular because it is easy to start and has few legal requirements. A proprietor has total ownership and control of the company and can make all decisions without consulting anyone. However, this type of organization also has drawbacks. The owner has unlimited liability for the business, meaning that if someone sues, the owner's personal as well as business assets are at risk. Also, financing can be harder to obtain because business success rests on one person's shoulders.

business plan A document specifying the business details prepared by an entrepreneur prior to opening a new business.

sole proprietorship An unincorporated business owned by an individual for profit.

Partnership A **partnership** is an unincorporated business owned by two or more people. Partnerships, like proprietorships, are relatively easy to start. Two friends may reach an agreement to start a graphic arts company. To avoid misunderstandings and to make sure the business is well planned, it is wise to draw up and sign a formal partnership agreement with the help of an attorney. The agreement specifies how partners are to share responsibility and resources and how they will contribute their expertise. The disadvantages of partnerships are the unlimited liability of the partners and the disagreements that almost always occur among strong-minded people. A poll by *Inc.* magazine illustrated the volatility of partnerships. Fifty-nine percent of respondents considered partnerships a bad business move, citing reasons such as partner problems and conflicts. Partnerships often dissolve within five years. Respondents who liked partnerships pointed to the equality of partners (sharing of workload and emotional and financial burdens) as the key to a successful partnership.[43]

Corporation A **corporation** is an artificial entity created by the state and existing apart from its owners. As a separate legal entity, the corporation is liable for its actions and must pay taxes on its income. Unlike other forms of ownership, the corporation has a legal life of its own; it continues to exist regardless of whether the owners live or die. And the corporation, not the owners, is sued in the case of liability. Thus, continuity and limits on owners' liability are two principal advantages of forming a corporation. For example, a physician can form a corporation so that liability for malpractice will not affect his or her personal assets. The major disadvantage of the corporation is that it is expensive and complex to do the paperwork required to incorporate the business and to keep the records required by law. When proprietorships and partnerships are successful and grow large, they often incorporate to limit liability and to raise funds through the sale of stock to investors.

Arranging Financing

Most entrepreneurs are particularly concerned with financing the business. A few types of businesses can still be started with a few thousand dollars, but starting a business usually requires coming up with a significant amount of initial funding. An investment is required to acquire labor and raw materials and perhaps a building and equipment. High-tech businesses, for example, typically need from $50,000 to $500,000 just to get through the first six months, even with the founder drawing no salary.[44]

Many entrepreneurs rely on their own resources for initial funding, but they often have to mortgage their homes, depend on credit cards, borrow money from a bank, or give part of the business to a venture capitalist.[45] Exhibit A.7 summarizes the most common sources of start-up capital for entrepreneurs. The financing decision initially involves two options—whether to obtain loans that must be repaid (debt financing) or whether to share ownership (equity financing).

Debt Financing Borrowing money that has to be repaid at a later date to start a business is referred to as **debt financing**. One common source of debt financing for a start-up is to borrow from family and friends. Increasingly, entrepreneurs are using their personal credit cards as a form of debt financing. Another common source is a bank loan. Banks provide some 25 percent of all financing for small business. Sometimes entrepreneurs can obtain money from a finance company, wealthy individuals, or potential customers. A typical source of funds for businesses with high potential is through **angel financing**. Angels are wealthy individuals, typically with business experience and contacts, who believe in the idea for the start-up and are willing to invest their personal funds to help the business get started. Significantly, angels also provide advice and assistance as the entrepreneur is developing the company. The entrepreneur wants angels who can make business contacts, help find talented employees, and serve as all-around advisors.

partnership An unincorporated business owned by two or more people.

corporation An artificial entity created by the state and existing apart from its owners.

debt financing Borrowing money that has to be repaid at a later date in order to start a business.

angel financing Financing provided by a wealthy individual who believes in the idea for a start-up and provides personal funds and advice to help the business get started.

Appendix

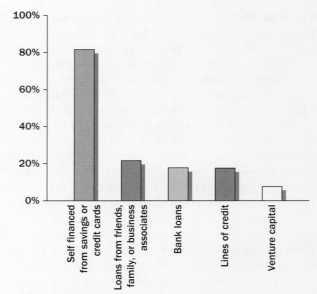

SOURCE: Jim Melloan, "The Inc. 5000," *Inc.* (September 1, 2006): 187.
Copyright 2006 by Mansueto Ventures LLC. Reproduced with permission of
Mansueto Ventures LLC in the format Textbook via Copyright Clearance Center.

Another form of loan financing is provided by the Small Business Administration (SBA). Staples, which started with one office supply store in Brighton, Massachusetts, in 1986, got its start toward rapid growth with the assistance of SBA financing. Today, Staples is North America's largest operator of office superstores, with 1,738 retail outlets in the United States and Canada, a thriving international presence in 27 countries, and $27 billion in sales.[46] SBA financing is especially helpful for people without substantial assets, providing an opportunity for single parents, minority group members, and others with a good idea but who might be considered high-risk by a traditional bank. The percentage of SBA loans to women, Hispanics, African Americans, and Asian Americans has increased significantly in recent years.[47]

Equity Financing Any money invested by owners or by those who purchase stock in a corporation is considered equity funds. **Equity financing** consists of funds that are invested in exchange for ownership in the company.

A **venture capital firm** is a group of companies or individuals that invests money in new or expanding businesses for ownership and potential profits. This form of capital is a potential for businesses with high earning and growth possibilities. Venture capitalists are particularly interested in high-tech businesses such as biotechnology, innovative online ventures, or telecommunications because they have the potential for high rates of return on investment.[48] The venture capital firm Lighthouse Capital Partners, for example, provided some of the early funding for Netflix, the online DVD rental service.[49] Venture capitalists also usually provide assistance, advice, and information to help the entrepreneur prosper. A growing number of minority-owned venture capital firms, such as Provender Capital, founded by African American entrepreneur Fred Terrell, are ensuring that minorities have a fair shot at acquiring equity financing.[50]

Tactics for Becoming a Business Owner

Aspiring entrepreneurs can become business owners in several different ways. They can start a new business from scratch, buy an existing business, or start a franchise. Another popular entrepreneurial tactic is to participate in a business incubator.

equity financing Financing that consists of funds that are invested in exchange for ownership in the company.

venture capital firm A group of companies or individuals that invests money in new or expanding businesses for ownership and potential profits.

Start a New Business One of the most common ways to become an entrepreneur is to start a new business from scratch. This approach is exciting because the entrepreneur sees a need for a product or service that has not been filled before and then sees the idea or dream become a reality. Ray Petro invested his $50,000 life savings and took out a $25,000 loan to launch Ray's Mountain Bike Indoor Park after learning from other mountain biking enthusiasts of their frustration with not being able to ride during the winter months. Taryn Rose started her shoe company, Taryn Rose International, after searching for stylish shoes that wouldn't destroy her feet while working long hours as an orthopedic surgeon.[51] The advantage of starting a business is the ability to develop and design the business in the entrepreneur's own way. The entrepreneur is solely responsible for its success. A potential disadvantage is the long time it can take to get the business off the ground and make it profitable. The uphill battle is caused by the lack of established clientele and the many mistakes made by someone new to the business. Moreover, no matter how much planning is done, a start-up is risky, with no guarantee that the new idea will work. Some entrepreneurs, especially in high-risk industries, develop partnerships with established companies that can help the new company get established and grow. Others use the technique of outsourcing—having some activities handled by outside contractors—to minimize the costs and risks of doing everything in-house.[52] For example, Philip Chigos and Mary Domenico are building their children's pajama business from the basement of their two-bedroom apartment, using manufacturers in China and Mexico to produce the goods and partnering with a local firm to receive shipments, handle quality control, and distribute finished products.[53]

Buy an Existing Business Because of the long start-up time and the inevitable mistakes, some entrepreneurs prefer to reduce risk by purchasing an existing business. This direction offers the advantage of a shorter time to get started and an existing track record. The entrepreneur may get a bargain price if the owner wishes to retire or has other family considerations. Moreover, a new business may overwhelm an entrepreneur with the amount of work to be done and procedures to be determined. An established business already has filing systems, a payroll tax system, and other operating procedures. Potential disadvantages are the need to pay for goodwill that the owner believes exists and the possible existence of ill will toward the business. In addition, the company may have bad habits and procedures or outdated technology, which may be why the business is for sale.

Buy a Franchise Franchising is perhaps the most rapidly growing path to entrepreneurship. The International Franchise Association reports that the country's 909,253 franchise outlets account for about $2.3 trillion in annual sales and are the source of 21 million jobs, 15.3 percent of all U.S. private-sector jobs.[54] **Franchising** is an arrangement by which the owner of a product or service allows others to purchase the right to distribute the product or service with help from the owner. The franchisee invests his or her money and owns the business but does not have to develop a new product, create a new company, or test the market. Franchises exist for weight-loss clinics, pet-sitting services, sports photography, bakeries, janitorial services, auto repair shops, real estate offices, and numerous other types of businesses, in addition to the traditional fast-food outlets. Exhibit A.8 lists the top ten fastest-growing franchises, including the type of business, the number of outlets, and the initial franchise costs. Initial franchise fees don't include the other start-up costs the entrepreneur will have to cover.

The powerful advantage of a franchise is that management help is provided by the owner. For example, Subway does not want a franchisee to fail. Subway has regional development agents who do the research to find good locations for Subway's sandwich outlets. The Subway franchisor also provides two weeks of training at company headquarters and ongoing operational and marketing support.[55] Franchisors provide an established name and national advertising to stimulate demand for the product or service. Potential disadvantages are the lack of control that occurs

franchising An arrangement by which the owner of a product or service allows others to purchase the right to distribute the product or service with help from the owner.

Top 10 Fastest-Growing
Franchises for 2008

Franchise	Type of Business	Number of Outlets	Franchise Costs
7–11	Convenience store	5,580	Varies
Subway	Submarine sandwich restaurant	21,344	$15,000
Dunkin' Donuts	Doughnut shop	5,451	$40,000—80,000
Pizza Hut	Pizza restaurant	4,757	$25,000
McDonald's	Hamburger restaurant	11,772	$45,000
Sonic Drive-in Restaurant	Drive-in hamburger restaurant	2,655	$45,000
KFC Corp.	Fast food chicken restaurant	4,287	$25,000
Intercontinental Hotels	Middle market lodging	2,541	Varies
Dominos Pizza	Pizza delivery	4,571	$25,000
RE/MAX Int'l	Real estate agency	4,315	$12,500—25,000

SOURCE: International Franchise Association, http://www.entrepreneur.com/franzone/fastestgrowing/index.html (accessed June 23, 2008).

when franchisors want every business managed in exactly the same way. In some cases, franchisors require that franchise owners use certain contractors or suppliers that might cost more than others would. In addition, franchises can be expensive, and the high start-up costs are followed with monthly payments to the franchisor that can run from 2 percent to 15 percent of gross sales.[56]

Entrepreneurs who are considering buying a franchise should investigate the company thoroughly. The prospective franchisee is legally entitled to a copy of franchisor disclosure statements, which include information on 20 topics, including litigation and bankruptcy history, identities of the directors and executive officers, financial information, identification of any products the franchisee is required to buy, and from whom those purchases must be made. The entrepreneur also should talk with as many franchise owners as possible, because they are among the best sources of information about how the company really operates.[57] Exhibit A.9 lists some specific questions entrepreneurs should ask about themselves and the company when considering buying a franchise. Answering such questions can improve the chances for a successful career as a franchisee.

business incubator An innovation that provides shared office space, management support services, and management advice to entrepreneurs.

Participate in a Business Incubator An attractive option for entrepreneurs who want to start a business from scratch is to join a business incubator. A **business incubator** typically provides shared office space, management support services, and

Sample Questions for Choosing a Franchise

Questions about the Entrepreneur	Questions about the Franchisor	Before Signing the Dotted Line
1. Will I enjoy the day-to-day work of the business?	1. What assistance does the company provide in terms of selection of location, setup costs, and securing credit; day-to-day technical assistance; marketing; and ongoing training and development?	1. Do I understand the risks associated with this business, and am I willing to assume them?
2. Do my background, experience, and goals make this opportunity a good choice for me?	2. How long does it take the typical franchise owner to start making a profit?	2. Have I had an advisor review the disclosure documents and franchise agreement?
3. Am I willing to work within the rules and guidelines established by the franchisor?	3. How many franchises changed ownership within the past year, and why?	3. Do I understand the contract?

SOURCES: Based on Thomas Love, "The Perfect Franchisee," *Nation's Business* (April 1998): 59–65; and Roberta Maynard, "Choosing a Franchise," *Nation's Business* (October 1996): 56–63.

management and legal advice to entrepreneurs. Incubators also give entrepreneurs a chance to share information with one another about local business, financial aid, and market opportunities. A recent innovation is the *virtual incubator*, which does not require that people set up on-site. These virtual organizations connect entrepreneurs with a wide range of experts and mentors and offer lower overhead and cost savings for cash-strapped small business owners. Christie Stone, co-founder of Ticobeans, a coffee distributor in New Orleans, likes the virtual approach because it gives her access to top-notch advice while allowing her to keep her office near her inventory.[58]

The concept of business incubators arose about two decades ago to nurture start-up companies. Business incubators have become a significant segment of the small business economy, with approximately 1,400 in operation in North America and an estimated 5,000 worldwide.[59] The incubators that are thriving are primarily not-for-profits and those that cater to niches or focus on helping women or minority entrepreneurs. These incubators include those run by government agencies and universities to boost the viability of small business and spur job creation. The great value of an incubator is the expertise of a mentor, who serves as advisor, role model, and cheerleader, and ready access to a team of lawyers, accountants, and other advisors. Incubators also give budding entrepreneurs a chance to network and learn from one another.[60] "The really cool thing about a business incubator is that when you get entrepreneurial people in one place, there's a synergistic effect," said Tracy Kitts, vice president and chief operating officer of the national Business Incubation Association. "Not only do they learn from staff, they learn tons from each other, and this really contributes to their successes."[61]

Starting an Online Business

Many entrepreneurs are turning to the Internet to expand their small businesses or launch a new venture. In fact, 12.1 percent of sole proprietors are engaging in e-commerce, up from 9.4 percent in 2005, according to a survey of 1,235 businesses.[62] Anyone with an idea, a personal computer, access to the Internet, and the tools to create a Web site can start an online business. These factors certainly fueled Ashley Qualls's desire to create a Web site that has become a destination for million of teenage girls. Starting at age 15, Ashley launched Whateverlife.com with a clever Web site, an $8 domain name, and a vision to provide free designs (hearts, flowers, celebrities) for MySpace pages. Her hobby exploded into a successful business with advertising revenue of more than $1 million so far. Ashley's motivation to start Whateverlife.com was fueled by an opportunity to turn a rewarding hobby into a thriving online business.[63]

Additional incentives for starting an online business include low overhead and the ability to work from home or any location. These are some of the incentives that motivated Landy Ung to launch 8coupons.com, a business that sends discount coupons directly to users' mobile phones via text messages. She and her boyfriend Wan His Yuan run the business from their 500-square-foot studio apartment, meaning headquarters is, effectively, their couch. Ung and Yuan have put $30,000 into the business, and operating costs remain low. The business demands many hours of hard work and diligence, however, frequently keeping both up until 3 a.m.[64]

Entrepreneurs who aspire to start online businesses follow the usual steps required to start a traditional business: identify a profitable market niche, develop an inspiring business plan, choose a legal structure, and determine financial backing. Beyond that, they need to be unusually nimble, persistent in marketing, savvy with technology, and skillful at building online relationships. Several steps required to start an online business are highlighted here.

- **Find a market niche.** To succeed in the competitive online market, aspiring entrepreneurs need to identify a market niche that isn't being served by other companies. Online businesses experience success when they sell unique, customized, or narrowly focused products or services to a well-defined target audience.

- **Create a professional Web site.** Online shoppers have short attention spans, so a Web site should entice them to linger. To improve customers' online experience, Web sites should be easy to navigate, intuitive, and offer menus that are easy to read and understand. Even "small-time" sites need "big-time" designs and should avoid common mistakes such as typos, excessively large files that are slow to load, too much information, and sensory overload.[65] FragranceNet.com competes with "big-time" competitors with a Web site that clearly communicates its value proposition (designer brands at discount prices), easy navigation, and superior customer service.[66]

- **Choose a domain name.** A domain name gives a company an address on the Web and a unique identity. Domain names should be chosen carefully and be easy to remember, pronounce, and spell. How is a domain name selected? The options for creating a domain name are many and include (1) using the company name (dell.com); (2) creating a domain name that describes your product or service (1-800-Flowers.com); or (3) choosing a domain name that doesn't have a specific meaning and provides options for expanding (Google.com).[67]

- **Build online relationships.** In a storefront business, business owners develop loyal customer relationships through personal attention and friendly service. In the virtual business world, however, business owners connect with customers primarily through an online experience. Creating a positive, online relationship with customers requires time and resources, as Marla Cilley, owner of FlyLady.net, discovered. Cilley cultivated a cultlike following to her Internet business by sharing personal encouragement and housecleaning advice to middle-aged homemakers who call themselves FlyLadies. Her adoring customers send her nearly 5,000 grateful messages each day. She hired a team of six offsite readers to respond to each one. Through positive customer experiences and shared testimonials, Cilley continues to grow her self-help empire.[68] This demanding process of responding to thousands of e-mails helps FlyLady.com develop a loyal following and strong customer relationships.

MANAGING A GROWING BUSINESS

Once an entrepreneurial business is up and running, how does the owner manage it? Often the traits of self-confidence, creativity, and internal locus of control lead to financial and personal grief as the enterprise grows. A hands-on entrepreneur who gave birth to the organization loves perfecting every detail. But after the start-up, continued growth requires a shift in management style. Those who fail to adjust to a growing business can be the cause of the problems rather than the solution.[69] In this section, we look at the stages through which entrepreneurial companies move and then consider how managers should carry out their planning, organizing, leading, and controlling.

Stages of Growth

Entrepreneurial businesses go through distinct stages of growth, with each stage requiring different management skills. The five stages are illustrated in Exhibit A.10.

1. *Start-up.* In this stage, the main problems are producing the product or service and obtaining customers. Several key issues facing managers are: Can we get enough customers? Will we survive? Do we have enough money? Burt's Bees was in the start-up stage when Roxanne Quimby was hand-making candles and personal care products from the beeswax of Burt Shavitz's bees and selling them at craft fairs in Maine.

2. *Survival.* At this stage, the business demonstrates that it is a workable business entity. It produces a product or service and has sufficient customers. Concerns here involve finances—generating sufficient cash flow to run the business and

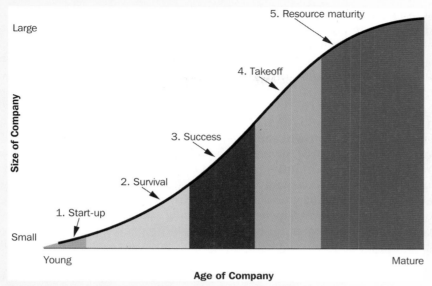

SOURCE: Based on Neil C. Churchill and Virginia L. Lewis, "The Five Stages of Small Business Growth," *Harvard Business Review* (May–June 1993): 30–50.

EXHIBIT | A.10

Five Stages of Growth for an Entrepreneurial Company

making sure revenues exceed expenses. The organization will grow in size and profitability during this period. Burt's Bees reached $3 million in sales by 1993, and Quimby moved the business from Maine to North Carolina to take advantage of state policies that helped her keep costs in line.

3. *Success.* At this point, the company is solidly based and profitable. Systems and procedures are in place to allow the owner to slow down if desired. The owner can stay involved or consider turning the business over to professional managers. Quimby chose to stay closely involved with Burt's Bees, admitting that she's a bit of a control freak about the business.

4. *Takeoff.* Here the key problem is how to grow rapidly and finance that growth. The owner must learn to delegate, and the company must find sufficient capital to invest in major growth. This period is pivotal in an entrepreneurial company's life. Properly managed, the company can become a big business. However, another problem for companies at this stage is how to maintain the advantages of "smallness" as the company grows. In 2003, Quimby sold 80 percent of Burt's Bees to AEA Investors, a private equity firm, for more than $175 million. She continued as CEO and focuses on continuing to grow the business.

5. *Resource maturity.* At this stage, the company's substantial financial gains may come at the cost of losing its advantages of small size, including flexibility and the entrepreneurial spirit. A company in this stage has the staff and financial resources to begin acting like a mature company with detailed planning and control systems.

Planning

In the early start-up stage, formal planning tends to be nonexistent except for the business plan described earlier in this chapter. The primary goal is simply to remain alive. As the organization grows, formal planning usually is not instituted until the success stage. Recall from Chapter 1 that planning means defining goals and deciding on the tasks and use of resources needed to attain them. Chapters 6, 7, and 8 describe how entrepreneurs can define goals and implement strategies and plans to meet them. It is important that entrepreneurs view their original business plan as a living document that evolves as the company grows or the market changes.

One planning concern for today's small businesses is the need to be Web-savvy. For many small companies today, their Web operations are just as critical as traditional warehouse management or customer service operations. The growing importance of e-business means entrepreneurs have to plan and allocate resources for Internet operations from the beginning and grow those plans as the company grows. Of the small companies that have Web sites, more than half say the site has broken even or paid for itself in greater efficiency, improved customer relationships, or increased business.[70]

Organizing

In the first two stages of growth, the organization's structure is typically informal, with all employees reporting to the owner. At about stage 3—success—functional managers often are hired to take over duties performed by the owner. A functional organization structure will begin to evolve with managers in charge of finance, manufacturing, and marketing. Another organizational approach is to use outsourcing, as described earlier. Method, a company launched by two 20-something entrepreneurs to develop a line of nontoxic cleaning products in fresh scents and stylish packaging, contracted with an industrial designer for the unique dish soap bottle and uses contract manufacturers in every region of the country to rapidly make products and get them to stores.[71]

During the latter stages of entrepreneurial growth, managers must learn to delegate and decentralize authority. If the business has multiple product lines, the owner may consider creating teams or divisions responsible for each line. The organization must hire competent managers and have sufficient management talent to handle fast growth and eliminate problems caused by increasing size. As an organization grows, it might also be characterized by greater use of rules, procedures, and written job descriptions. For example, Tara Cronbaugh started a small coffeehouse in a college town, but its success quickly led to the opening of three additional houses. With the rapid growth, Cronbaugh found that she needed a way to ensure consistency across operations. She put together an operations manual with detailed rules, procedures, and job descriptions so managers and employees at each coffeehouse would be following the same pattern.[72] Chapters 9 through 12 discuss organizing in detail.

Controlling

Financial control is important in each stage of the entrepreneurial firm's growth. In the initial stages, control is exercised by simple accounting records and by personal supervision. By stage 3—success—operational budgets are in place, and the owner should start implementing more structured control systems. During the takeoff stage, the company will need to make greater use of budgets and standard cost systems and use computer systems to provide statistical reports. These control techniques will become more sophisticated during the resource maturity stage.

As Amazon.com grew and expanded internationally, for example, entrepreneur and CEO Jeff Bezos needed increasingly sophisticated control mechanisms. Bezos hired a computer systems expert to develop a system to track and control all of the company's operations.[74] Control is discussed in Chapters 13 and 14.

Leading

The driving force in the early stages of development is the leader's vision. This vision, combined with the leader's personality, shapes corporate culture. The leader can signal cultural values of service, efficiency, quality, or ethics. Often entrepreneurs do not have good people skills but do have excellent task skills in either manufacturing or marketing. By the success stage of growth, the owner must either learn to motivate employees or bring in managers who can. Rapid takeoff is not likely to happen without employee cooperation. The president of Foreign Candy Company of Hull, Iowa, saw his company grow rapidly when he concentrated more on employee needs and less on financial results. He made an effort to communicate with employees, conducted surveys to learn how they were feeling about the company, and found ways to involve them in decision making. His shift in leadership style allowed the company to enter the takeoff stage with the right corporate culture and employee attitudes to sustain rapid growth.

Leadership also is important because many small firms have a hard time hiring qualified employees. Labor shortages often hurt small firms that grow rapidly. A healthy corporate culture can help attract and retain good people.[73] Chapters 15 through 19 present the dynamics of leadership.

A MANAGER'S ESSENTIALS: WHAT DID WE LEARN?

- *Entrepreneurship* is the process of initiating a business, organizing the necessary resources, and assuming the associated risks and rewards. Entrepreneurship plays an important role in the economy by stimulating job creation, innovation, and opportunities for minorities and women. An entrepreneur recognizes a viable idea for a business product or service and combines the necessary resources to carry it out. Entrepreneurs may be classified as *idealists, optimizers, sustainers, hard workers*, or *jugglers*.

- The Small Business Administration defines a *small business* as "one that is independently owned and operated and which is not dominant in its field of operation." The U.S. economy is ripe for entrepreneurial ventures, but entrepreneurial activity is also booming in other countries, with some of the highest rates in developing nations.

- Entrepreneurs place high importance on being free to achieve and maximize their potential. An entrepreneurial personality includes the traits of internal locus of control, high energy level, need to achieve, tolerance for ambiguity, awareness of passing time, and self-confidence.

- A new breed of entrepreneur, the *social entrepreneur*, is committed to both good business and positive social change. Social entrepreneurs sometime blur the line between business and social activism because they combine the creativity, business smarts, passion, and hard work of the traditional entrepreneur with a mission to improve the world.

- A business plan is a document specifying the business details prepared by an entrepreneur prior to opening a new business. Businesses with carefully written business plans are more likely to succeed than those without one. Small businesses may be organized as sole proprietorships, partnerships, or corporations. Initial funding for a small business may come from debt financing, borrowing money that has to be repaid, or equity financing, funds that are invested in exchange for ownership.

- Small businesses generally proceed through five stages of growth: start-up, survival, success, takeoff, and resource maturity. The management functions of planning, organizing, leading, and controlling should be tailored to each stage of growth.

DISCUSSION QUESTIONS

1. You are interested in being your own boss and have the chance to buy a franchise office supply store that is for sale in your city. You will need outside investors to help pay the franchise fees and other start up costs. How will you determine if this is a good entrepreneurial opportunity and make your decision about buying the store?

2. Over the past 20 years, entrepreneurship has been the fastest-growing course of study on campuses throughout the country. However, debate continues about whether you can teach someone to be an entrepreneur. Do you think entrepreneurship can be taught? Why or why not?

3. Why would small business ownership have great appeal to immigrants, women, and minorities?

4. Consider the six personality characteristics of entrepreneurs. Which two traits do you think are most like those of managers in large companies? Which two are least like those of managers in large companies?

5. How would you go about deciding whether you wanted to start a business from scratch, buy an existing business, or buy into a franchise? What information would you collect and analyze?

6. Many entrepreneurs say they did little planning, perhaps scratching notes on a legal pad. How is it possible for them to succeed?

7. What personal skills do you need to keep your financial backers feeling confident in your new business? Which skills are most useful when you're dealing with more informal sources such as family and friends versus receiving funds from stockhold-ers, a bank, or a venture capital firm? Would these considerations affect your financing strategy?

8. Many people who are successful at the start-up stage of a business are not the right people to carry the venture forward. How do you decide whether you're better suited to be a serial entrepreneur (start the business and then move on to start another) or whether you can guide the venture as it grows and matures?

9. How does starting an online business differ from starting a small business such as a local auto repair shop or delicatessen? Is it really possible for businesses that operate totally in cyberspace to build close customer relationships? Discuss.

10. Do you think entrepreneurs who launched a new business after deciding to leave a job on their own versus those who have been forced to leave a job as a result of downsizing are likely to have different traits? Which group is more likely to succeed? Why?

MANAGEMENT IN PRACTICE: EXPERIENTIAL EXERCISE

What's Your Entrepreneurial IQ?

Rate yourself on the following 15 behaviors and characteristics, according to the following scale.

① = Strongly disagree
② = Disagree
③ = Agree
④ = Strongly agree

1. I am able to translate ideas into concrete tasks and outcomes.

   1 2 3 4

2. When I am interested in a project, I tend to need less sleep.

   1 2 3 4

3. I am willing to make sacrifices to gain long-term rewards.

   1 2 3 4

4. Growing up, I was more of a risk-taker than a cautious child.

   1 2 3 4

5. I often see trends, connections, and patterns that are not obvious to others.

   1 2 3 4

6. I have always enjoyed spending much of my time alone.

   1 2 3 4

7. I have a reputation for being stubborn.

   1 2 3 4

8. I prefer working with a difficult but highly competent person to working with someone who is congenial but less competent.

   1 2 3 4

9. As a child, I had a paper route, lemonade stand, or other small enterprise.

   1 2 3 4

10. I usually keep New Year's resolutions.

    1 2 3 4

11. I'm not easily discouraged, and I persist when faced with major obstacles.

    1 2 3 4

12. I recover quickly from emotional setbacks.

    1 2 3 4

13. I would be willing to dip deeply into my "nest egg"—and possibly lose all I had saved—to go it alone.

    1 2 3 4

14. I get tired of the same routine day in and day out.

    1 2 3 4

15. When I want something, I keep the goal clearly in mind.

    1 2 3 4

Scoring and Interpretation

Total your score for the 15 items. If you tallied 50–60 points, you have a strong entrepreneurial IQ. A score of 30–50 indicates good entrepreneurial possibilities. Your chances of starting a successful entrepreneurial business are good if you have the desire and motivation. If you scored below 30, you probably do not have much entrepreneurial potential.

Go back over each question, thinking about changes you might make to become more or less entrepreneurial, depending on your career interests.

MANAGEMENT IN PRACTICE: ETHICAL DILEMMA

Closing the Deal

As the new, heavily recruited CEO of a high-technology start-up backed by several of Silicon Valley's leading venture capitalists, Chuck Campbell is flying high—great job, good salary, stock options, and a chance to be in on the ground floor and build one of the truly great twenty-first–century organizations. Just a few days into the job, Chuck participated in a presentation to a new group of potential investors for funding that could help the company expand marketing, improve its services, and invest in growth. By the end of the meeting, the investors had verbally committed $16 million in funding.

But things turned sour pretty fast. As Chuck was leaving about 9 p.m., the corporate controller, Betty Mars, who just returned from an extended leave, cornered him. He was surprised to find her working so late, but before he could even open his mouth, Betty blurted out her problem: The numbers Chuck had presented to the venture capitalists were flawed. "The assumptions behind the revenue growth plan are absolutely untenable," she said. "Not a chance of ever happening." Chuck was stunned. He told Betty to get on home and he'd stay and take a look at the figures.

At 11 p.m., Chuck was still sitting in his office wondering what to do. His research showed that the numbers were indeed grossly exaggerated, but most of them were at least statistically possible (however remote that possibility was!). However, what really troubled him was that the renewal income figure was just flat-out false—and it was clear that one member of the management team who participated in the presentation knew it was incorrect all along. To make matters worse, it was the renewal income figure that ultimately made the investment so attractive to the venture capital firm. Chuck knew what was at stake—no less than the life or death of the company itself. If he told the truth about the deceptive numbers, the company's valuation would almost certainly be slashed and the $16 million possibly canceled.

What Would You Do?

1. Say nothing about the false numbers. Of course, the company will miss the projections and have to come up with a good explanation, but, after all, isn't that par for the course among fledgling high-tech companies? Chances are the whole thing will blow over without a problem.

2. Go ahead and close the deal, but come clean later. Explain that the controller had been on an extended leave of absence and, because you had been on the job only a few days, you had not had time to personally do an analysis of the numbers.

3. Take swift action to notify the venture capitalists of the truth of the situation—and start cleaning house to get rid of people who would knowingly lie to close a deal.

SOURCE: Adapted from Kent Weber, "The Truth Could Cost You $16 Million," *Business Ethics* (March–April 2001): 18.

CASE FOR CRITICAL ANALYSIS

Emma's Parlor

Emma Lathbury's shoulders sagged as she flipped the cardboard sign hanging in the window of her tearoom's front door from "Open" to "Closed." The normally indefatigable 52-year-old owner of Emma's Parlor was bone-tired. Any doubts she'd harbored about the wisdom of seriously considering some major changes in her business were fast disappearing.

She hadn't felt this weary since she'd left nursing in the early 1990s. After years of working as an intensive care nurse—with its grueling hours, emotionally draining work, and lack of both respect and autonomy—she'd developed a bad case of burnout. At the time, she was convinced she could walk away from a secure, if difficult, profession and figure out a way of making a living that suited her high-energy, outgoing personality. Then one day, she noticed an 1870s-vintage Gothic Revival cottage for sale in the small Illinois farming community near where she'd grown up, and the answer to her dilemma came to her with a startling clarity. She'd get the financing, buy the house, and open up a cozy Victorian tearoom. Emma was certain she could make it work.

And she had. Her success was due in part to her unintentionally perfect timing. Specialty teas had taken off during the 1990s, with no end in sight to its current double-digit annual growth rate. But of course the solid performance of Emma's Parlor owed a good deal to its owner's hard work and all those 60- and 70-hour weeks she'd put in, which was more fun when she worked for herself. She'd personally chosen the precise shades of purple and plum for the cottage's exterior, hung the lace curtains, selected the fresh flowers that graced the small circular tables, hired the staff, and tracked down and tested recipes for the finger sandwiches, scones, jams, and Battenburg cake that earned her glowing reviews in numerous guidebooks and a national reputation. Quickly realizing that special events were key to attracting customers, she organized and publicized fanciful gatherings that drew everyone from children toting their favorite stuffed animals to an Alice-in-Wonderland affair to women dressed in their best outfits, complete with big floppy hats, to a Midwest version of a royal garden party. The tearoom, which now employed about 20 people, was nearly always completely booked.

Most of all, the former nurse developed a real expertise when it came to teas, becoming particularly fascinated by the medicinal benefits of herbal teas. She started by conducting evening workshops on the efficacy of organic teas in treating everything from a simple upset stomach to menopausal distress.

Eventually, she began blending her own Emma's Parlor Organic Teas and selling them to retail stores, restaurants, and individuals over the Web. As more and more publicity pointed to the benefits of tea, her Web-based business flourished, generating slightly less revenue than she was realizing from the tearoom. The profit margins were higher.

Despite the fulfillment she found in running her own business, it was getting too big for her to handle. Emma was beginning to experience the all-too-familiar symptoms of burnout. After she locked the front door, she made herself a soothing cup of rose-bud tea, kicked off her sensible shoes, and sat down to review her options. Maybe she could drop the tearoom and focus on the Internet business, or vice versa. She could try to master the fine art of delegation and turn Emma's Parlor over to an experienced restaurant manager, or she could take herself out of the picture by selling the tearoom outright. Then again, she could simply close the restaurant or the Internet business.

Questions

1. At what business stage is Emma's Parlor? At what stage is her Web-based organic tea business? What synergies exist between the two businesses? How critical do you think those synergies are to the success of each business?

2. How does Emma Lathbury fit the profile of the typical entrepreneur? Which of those traits are likely to continue to serve her well, and which might be counterproductive at this stage of her business?

3. After listing the pros and cons for each of Emma's options and considering her personality, which course of action would you recommend?

SOURCES: Based on Alison Stein Wellner, "Business Was Booming But the Richardsons Were Seriously Burned Out," *Inc. Magazine* (April 2006): 52–54; Mark Blumenthal, "Total Tea Sales in U.S. Forecast for $10 Billion in 2010," *HerbalGram* (2004): 61–62; and TeaMap Tearoom Directory, http://www.teamap.com.

ENDNOTES

1. Based on Keith M. Hmieleski and Andrew C. Corbett, "Proclivity for Improvisation as a Predictor of Entrepreneurial Intentions," *Journal of Small Business Management* 44, no. 1 (January 2006): 45–63; and "Do You Have an Entrepreneurial Mind?" *Inc.com* (October 19, 2005).

2. Elizabeth Olson, "They May Be Mundane, But Low-Tech Businesses Are Booming," *The New York Times*, April 28, 2005, http://www.nytimes.com/2005/04/28/business/28sbiz.html?_r=1&scp=1&sq=They%20May%20Be%20Mundane,%20But%20Low-Tech%20Businesses%20Are%20Booming&st=cse&oref=slogin; and "CIBC Report Predicts Canada Will Be Home to One Million Women Entrepreneurs By 2010," *Canada NewsWire* (June 28, 2005): 1.

3. U.S. Small Business Administration, http://www.sba.gov.

4. John Case, "Where We Are Now," *Inc.* (May 29, 2001): 18–19.

5. Amy E. Knaup, "Survival and Longevity in the Business Employment Dynamics Database," *Monthly Labor Review*, vol. 128, no. 5 (May 2005): 50–56; Brian Headd, "Redefining Business Success: Distinguishing Between Closure and Failure," *Small Business Economics*, vol. 21, no. 1 (August 2003): 51–61.

6. Reported in "Did You Know?" in J. Neil Weintraut, "Told Any Good Stories Lately?" *Business 2.0* (March 2000): 139–140.

7. U.S. Small Business Administration, www.sba.gov.

8. John Case, "Who's Looking at Start-Ups?" *Inc.* (May 29, 2001): 60.

9. Donald F. Kuratko and Richard M. Hodgetts, *Entrepreneurship: A Contemporary Approach*, 4th ed. (Fort Worth, TX: The Dryden Press, 1998), p. 30.

10. Steve Stecklow, "StubHub's Ticket to Ride," *The Wall Street Journal*, January, 17, 2006.

11. Study conducted by Yankelovich Partners, reported in Mark Henricks, "Type-Cast," *Entrepreneur* (March 2000): 14–16.

12. Olson, "Low-Tech Businesses Are Booming."

13. Norm Brodsky, "Street Smarts: Opportunity Knocks," *Inc.* (February 2002): 44–46; and Hilary Stout, "Start Low," *The Wall Street Journal*, May 14, 2001.

14. U.S. Small Business Administration, http://www.sba.gov.

15. Global Entrepreneurship Monitor, "Table 2: Prevalence Rates of Entrepreneurial Activity Across Countries, 2007," *2007 GEM Tables and Figures*, Babson College and the London Business School, March 14, 2008, http://www.gemconsortium.org/about.aspx?page=pub_gem_global_reports.

16. U.S. Small Business Administration, www. sba.gov.

17. Thuy-Doan Le Bee, "How Small Is Small? SBA Holds Hearings to Decide," *The Sacramento Bee*, June 29, 2005.

18. U.S. Small Business Administration, http://www.sba.gov.

19. Barbara Benham, "Big Government, Small Business," *Working Woman* (February 2001): 24.

20. Research and statistics reported in "The Job Factory," *Inc.* (May 29, 2001): 40–43.

21. Ian Mount, "The Return of the Lone Inventor," *FSB* (March 2005): 18; Office of Advocacy, U.S. Small Business Administration, www.sba.gov/advo.

22. John Case, "The Origins of Entrepreneurship," *Inc.* (June 1989): 51–53.

23. Jeanette Borzo, "Taking on the Recruiting Monster," *Business 2.0* (January/February 2007): 44.

24. Kauffman Foundation, http://www.kauffman.org.

25. "Small Business Ambassador," *FSB* (February 2007): 28.

26. U.S. Small Business Administration, www.sba.gov; "CIBC Report Predicts Canada Will Be Home to One Million Women Entrepreneurs by 2010," *Canada NewsWire* (June 28, 2005): 1.

27. U.S. Small Business Administration, www.sba.gov.

28. Statistics reported in Cora Daniels, "Minority Rule," *FSB* (December 2003–January 2004): 65–66; Elizabeth Olson, "New Help for the Black Entrepreneur," *The New York Times*, December 23, 2004; and David J. Dent, "The Next Black Power Movement," *FSB* (May 2003): 10–13.

29. Ellyn Spragins, "Pat Winans" profile, and Cora Daniels, "Ed Chin" profile, in "The New Color of Money," *FSB* (December 2003–January 2004): 74–87.

30. This discussion is based on Charles R. Kuehl and Peggy A. Lambing, *Small Business: Planning and Management*, 3rd ed. (Ft. Worth, TX: The Dryden Press, 1994).

31. David C. McClelland, *The Achieving Society* (New York: Van Nostrand, 1961).

32. Paulette Thomas, "Entrepreneurs' Biggest Problems—and How They Solve Them," *The Wall Street Journal* (March 17, 2003).

33. Definition based on Albert R. Hunt, "Social Entrepreneurs: Compassionate and Tough-Minded," *The Wall Street Journal* (July 13, 2000); David Puttnam, "Hearts Before Pockets," *The New Statesman* (February 9, 2004): 26; and Christian Seelos and Johanna Mair, "Social Entrepreneurship: Creating New Business Models to Serve the Poor," *Business Horizons* 48 (2005): 241–246.

34. Cheryl Dahle, "Filling the Void: The 2006 Social Capitalist Award Winners," *Fast Company* (January–February 2006): 50–61.

35. Putnam, "Hearts Before Pockets."

36. Jessica Harris, "Ethics in a Bottle," *FSB* (November 2007): 44.

37. Cheryl Dahle, "The Change Masters," *Fast Company* (January 2005): 47–58; David Bornstein, *How to Change the World: Social Entrepreneurs and the Power of New Ideas* (Oxford: Oxford University Press, 2004).

38. James Flanigan, "Small Businesses Offer Alternatives to Gang Life," *The New York Times*, March 20, 2008, http://www.nytimes.com/2008/03/20/business/smallbusiness/20edge.html (accessed June 23, 2008).

39. Leslie Brokaw, "How to Start an *Inc.* 500 Company," *Inc.* 500 (1994): 51–65.

40. Interview with Phaedra Hise, "A Chance to Prove My Worth," *FSB* (February 2007): 26.

41. Paul Reynolds, "The Truth about Start-Ups," *Inc.* (February 1995): 23; Brian O'Reilly, "The New Face of Small Businesses," *Fortune* (May 2, 1994): 82–88.

42. Based on Ellyn E. Spragins, "How to Write a Business Plan That Will Get You in the Door," *Small Business Success* (November 1990); Linda Elkins, "Tips for Preparing a Business Plan," *Nation's Business* (June 1996): 60R–61R; Carolyn M. Brown, "The Do's and Don'ts of Writing a Winning Business Plan," *Black Enterprise* (April 1996): 114–116; and Kuratko and Hodgetts, *Entrepreneurship*, 295–397. For a clear, thorough, step-by-step guide to writing an effective business plan, see Linda Pinson and Jerry Jinnett, *Anatomy of a Business Plan*, 5th ed. (Virginia Beach, VA: Dearborn, 2001).

43. The INC. FAXPOLL, *Inc.* (February 1992): 24.

44. Duncan MacVicar, "Ten Steps to a High-Tech Start-Up," *The Industrial Physicist* (October 1999): 27–31.

45. "Venture Capitalists' Criteria" *Management Review* (November 1985): 7–8.

46. "Staples Makes Big Business from Helping Small Businesses," *SBA Success Stories*, www.sba.gov/successstories.html (accessed on March 12, 2004);

http://www.staples.com/sbd/content/about/media/overview.html (accessed July 16, 2008).

47. Elizabeth Olson, "From One Business to 23 Million," *The New York Times*, March 7, 2004, http://query.nytimes.com/gst/fullpage.html?res=9C03E6D6113FF934A35750C0A9629C8B63 (accessed July 16, 2008).

48. "Where the Venture Money Is Going," *Business 2.0* (January–February 2004): 98.

49. Gary Rivlin, "Does the Kid Stay in the Picture?" *The New York Times*, February 22, 2005.

50. Dent, "The Next Black Power Movement."

51. Kristen Hampshire, "Roll With It," *FSB* (November 2005): 108–112; Jennifer Maxwell profile in Betsy Wiesendanger, "Labors of Love," *Working Woman* (May 1999): 43–56; Jena McGregor, Taryn Rose profile in "25 Top Women Business Builders," *Fast Company* (May 2005): 67–75.

52. Wendy Lea, "Dancing with a Partner," *Fast Company* (March 2000): 159–161.

53. Matt Richtel, "Outsourced All the Way," *The New York Times*, June 21, 2005, www.nytimes.com.

54. International Franchise Association, http://www.franchise.org/ (accessed June 23, 2008).

55. Quinne Bryant, "Who Owns 20+ Subway Franchises?" *The Business Journal of Tri-Cities Tennessee/Virginia* (August 2003): 42–43.

56. For a current discussion of the risks and disadvantages of owning a franchise, see Anne Fisher, "Risk

Reward," *FSB* (December 2005–January 2006): 44.

57. Anne Field, "Your Ticket to a New Career? Franchising Can Put Your Skills to Work in Your Own Business," in *Business Week Investor: Small Business* section, *Business-Week* (May 12, 2003): 100+; and Roberta Maynard, "Choosing a Franchise," *Nation's Business* (October 1996): 56–63.

58. Darren Dahl, "Getting Started: Percolating Profits." *Inc.* (February 2005): 38.

59. 2006 figures from the National Business Incubation Association http://www.nbia.org/resource_center/bus_inc_facts/index.php/ (accessed July 16, 2008).

60. Oringel, "Sowing Success."

61. Laura Novak, "For Women, a Recipe to Create a Successful Business," *The New York Times*, June 23, 2007, http://www.nytimes.com/2007/06/23/business/smallbusiness/23cocina.html?_r=1&sq=Laura%20Novak,%20â€œFor%20Women,%20a%20Recipe%20to%20Create%20a%20Successful%20Business&st=cse&adxnnl=1&oref=slogin&scp=1&adxnnlx=1225894278-APkyZ4kswGDrm3QtejIg6A (accessed June 23, 2008).

62. Sue Shellenbarger, "The Job That Follows You Wherever You May Roam," *The Wall Street Journal Online*, http://online.wsj.com/public/us (accessed July 10, 2008).

63. Chuck Salter, "Girl Power," *Fast Company* (September, 2007): 104.

64. Ellen Simon, "Starting Simple," *The Miami Herald*, November 13, 2007.

65. Jason R. Rich, *Unofficial Guide to Starting a Business Online*, 2nd ed. (New York: Wiley Publishing, 2006), p. 116.

66. Ellen Reid Smith, "e-loyalty: How to Keep Customers Coming Back to Your Website," HarperBusiness, p. 19.

67. Ibid, p. 127.

68. Susan G. Hauser, "Nagging for Dollars," *FSB* (September 2007): 76.

69. Carrie Dolan, "Entrepreneurs Often Fail as Managers," *The Wall Street Journal*, May 15, 1989.

70. George Mannes, "Don't Give Up on the Web," *Fortune* (March 5, 2001): 184[B]–184[L].

71. Bridgett Finn, "Selling Cool in a Bottle," *Business 2.0* (December 1, 2003), http://money.cnn.com/magazines/business2/business2_archive/2003/12/01/354202/index.htm (accessed November 5, 2008).

72. Amanda Walmac, "Full of Beans," *Working Woman* (February 1999): 38–40.

73. Udayan Gupta and Jeffery A. Tannenbaum, "Labor Shortages Force Changes at Small Firms," *The Wall Street Journal*, May 22, 1989; "Harnessing Employee Productivity," *Small Business Report* (November 1987): 46–49; and Molly Kilmas, "How to Recruit a Smart Team," *Nation's Business* (May 1995): 26–27.

74. Saul Hansell, "Listen Up! It's Time for a Profit: A Front Row Seat as Amazon Gets Serious," *The New York Times*, May 20, 2001.

Glossary

360-Degree Feedback A process that uses multiple raters, including self-rating, to appraise employee performance and guide development.

A

Accountability The fact that the people with authority and responsibility are subject to reporting and justifying task outcomes to those above them in the chain of command.

Achievement Culture A results-oriented culture that values competitiveness, personal initiative, and achievement.

Activity-Based Costing (ABC) A control system that identifies the various activities needed to provide a product and allocates costs accordingly.

Activity Ratio A financial ratio that measures the organization's internal performance with respect to key activities defined by management.

Adaptability Culture A culture characterized by values that support the company's ability to interpret and translate signals from the environment into new behavior responses.

Adjourning The stage of team development in which members prepare for the team's disbandment.

Administrative Model A decision-making model that describes how managers actually make decisions in situations characterized by nonprogrammed decisions, uncertainty, and ambiguity.

Administrative Principles A subfield of the classical management perspective that focuses on the total organization rather than the individual worker, delineating the management functions of planning, organizing, commanding, coordinating, and controlling.

Affirmative Action A policy requiring employers to take positive steps to guarantee equal employment opportunities for people within protected groups.

Alienated Follower A person who is an independent, critical thinker but is passive in the organization.

Ambidextrous Change Incorporating structures and processes that are appropriate for both the creative impulse and for the systematic implementation of innovations.

Ambiguity A condition in which the goals to be achieved or the problem to be solved is unclear, alternatives are difficult to define, and information about outcomes is unavailable.

Application Form A device for collecting information about an applicant's education, previous job experience, and other background characteristics.

Assessment Center A technique for selecting individuals with high managerial potential based on their performance on a series of simulated managerial tasks.

Attitude A cognitive and affective evaluation that predisposes a person to act in a certain way.

Attributions Judgments about what caused a person's behavior—either characteristics of the person or of the situation.

Authoritarianism The belief that power and status differences should exist within the organization.

Authority The formal and legitimate right of a manager to make decisions, issue orders, and allocate resources to achieve organizationally desired outcomes.

Avoidance Learning The removal of an unpleasant consequence when an undesirable behavior is corrected.

B

Balanced Scorecard A comprehensive management control system that balances traditional financial measures with measures of customer service, internal business processes, and the organization's capacity for learning and growth.

Balance Sheet A financial statement that shows the firm's financial position with respect to assets and liabilities at a specific point in time.

BCG Matrix A concept developed by the Boston Consulting Group that evaluates strategic business units with respect to the dimensions of business growth rate and market share.

Behaviorally Anchored Rating Scale (BARS) A rating technique that relates an employee's performance to specific job-related incidents.

Behavioral Sciences Approach A subfield of the humanistic management perspective that applies social science in an organizational context, drawing from economics, psychology, sociology, and other disciplines.

Behavior Modification The set of techniques by which reinforcement theory is used to modify human behavior.

Benchmarking The continuous process of measuring products, services, and practices against major competitors or industry leaders.

Big Five Personality Factors Dimensions that describe an individual's extroversion, agreeableness, conscientiousness, emotional stability, and openness to experience.

Blog Web log that allows individuals to post opinions and ideas.

Bottom of the Pyramid Concept The idea that large corporations can both alleviate social problems and make a profit by selling goods and services to the world's poorest people.

Bottom-Up Budgeting A budgeting process in which lower-level managers budget their departments' resource needs and pass them up to top management for approval.

Boundary-Spanning Roles Roles assumed by people and/or departments that link and coordinate the organization with key elements in the external environment.

Bounded Rationality The concept that people have the time and cognitive ability to process only a limited amount of information on which to base decisions.

Brainstorming A technique that uses a face-to-face group to spontaneously suggest a broad range of alternatives for decision making.

Bureaucratic Organizations A subfield of the classical management perspective that emphasized management on an impersonal, rational basis through such elements as clearly defined authority and responsibility, formal record-keeping, and separation of management and ownership.

Business Intelligence Software Software that analyzes data from multiple sources and extracts useful insights, patterns, and relationships that might be significant.

Business-Level Strategy The level of strategy concerned with the question "How do we compete?" Pertains to each business unit or product line within the organization.

Business Performance Dashboard A system that pulls data from a variety of organizational systems and databases; gauges the data against key performance metrics; pulls out the right nuggets of information; and delivers information to managers in a graphical, easy-to-interpret format.

C

Capital Budget A budget that plans and reports investments in major assets to be depreciated over several years.

Cash Budget A budget that estimates and reports cash flows on a daily or weekly basis to ensure that the company has sufficient cash to meet its obligations.

Cellular Layout A facilities layout in which machines dedicated to sequences of production are grouped into cells in accordance with group-technology principles.

Centralization The location of decision authority near top organizational levels.

Centralized Network A team communication structure in which team members communicate through a single individual to solve problems or make decisions.

Central Planning Department A group of planning specialists who develop plans for the organization as a whole and its major divisions and departments and typically report directly to the president or CEO.

Ceremony A planned activity at a special event that is conducted for the benefit of an audience.

Certainty The situation in which all the information the decision maker needs is fully available.

Chain of Command An unbroken line of authority that links all individuals in the organization and specifies who reports to whom.

Change Agent An OD specialist who contracts with an organization to facilitate change.

Changing The intervention stage of organization development in which individuals experiment with new workplace behavior.

Channel The carrier of a communication.

Channel Richness The amount of information that can be transmitted during a communication episode.

Charismatic Leader A leader who has the ability to motivate subordinates to transcend their expected performance.

Chief Ethics Officer A company executive who oversees ethics and legal compliance.

Classical Model A decision-making model based on the assumption that managers should make logical decisions that will be in the organization's best economic interests.

Classical Perspective A management perspective that emerged during the nineteenth and early twentieth centuries that emphasized a rational, scientific approach to the study of management and sought to make organizations efficient operating machines.

Closed System A system that does not interact with the external environment.

Coaching A method of directing, instructing and training a person with the goal to develop specific management skills.

Coalition An informal alliance among managers who support a specific goal.

Code of Ethics A formal statement of the organization's values regarding ethics and social issues.

Coercive Power Power that stems from the authority to punish or recommend punishment.

Cognitive Dissonance A condition in which two attitudes or a behavior and an attitude conflict.

Collectivism A preference for a tightly knit social framework in which individuals look after one another and organizations protect their members' interests.

Committee A long-lasting, sometimes permanent team in the organization structure created to deal with tasks that recur regularly.

Communication The process by which information is exchanged and understood by two or more people, usually with the intent to motivate or influence behavior.

Communication Apprehension An individual's level of fear or anxiety associated with interpersonal communications.

Compensation Monetary payments (wages, salaries) and nonmonetary goods/commodities (benefits, vacations) used to reward employees.

Compensatory Justice The concept that individuals should be compensated for the cost of their injuries by the party responsible and also that individuals should not be held responsible for matters over which they have no control.

Competitive Advantage What sets the organization apart from others and provides it with a distinctive edge in the marketplace.

Competitors Other organizations in the same industry or type of business that provide goods or services to the same set of customers.

Conceptual Skill The cognitive ability to see the organization as a whole and the relationships among its parts.

Conflict Antagonistic interaction in which one party attempts to thwart the intentions or goals of another.

Conformist A follower who participates actively in the organization but does not use critical thinking skills.

Consideration A type of behavior that describes the extent to which the leader is sensitive to subordinates, respects their ideas and feelings, and establishes mutual trust.

Consistency Culture A culture that values and rewards a methodical, rational, orderly way of doing things.

Content Theories A group of theories that emphasize the needs that motivate people.

Contingency Approach A model of leadership that describes the relationship between leadership styles and specific organizational situations.

Contingency Plans Plans that define company responses to specific situations, such as emergencies, setbacks, or unexpected conditions.

Contingency View An extension of the humanistic perspective in which the successful resolution of organizational problems is thought to depend on managers' identification of key variations in the situation at hand.

Contingent Workers People who work for an organization, but not on a permanent or full-time basis, including temporary placements, contracted professionals, or leased employees.

Continuous Improvement The implementation of a large number of small, incremental improvements in all areas of the organization on an ongoing basis.

Controlling The management function concerned with monitoring employees' activities, keeping the organization on track toward its goals, and making corrections as needed.

Coordination The quality of collaboration across departments.

Core Competence A business activity that an organization does particularly well in comparison to competitors.

Corporate Governance The system of governing an organization so the interests of corporate owners are protected.

Corporate-Level Strategy The level of strategy concerned with the question "What business are we in?" Pertains to the organization as a whole and the combination of business units and product lines that make it up.

Corporate Social Responsibility The obligation of organization management to make decisions and take actions that will enhance the welfare and interests of society as well as the organization.

Corporate University An in-house training and education facility that offers broad-based learning opportunities for employees.

Cost Leadership A type of competitive strategy with which the organization aggressively seeks efficient facilities, cuts costs, and employs tight cost controls to be more efficient than competitors.

Countertrade The barter of products for other products rather than their sale for currency.

Courage The ability to step forward through fear and act on one's values and conscience.

Creativity The generation of novel ideas that might meet perceived needs or offer opportunities for the organization.

Critical Thinking Thinking independently and being mindful of the effect of one's behavior on achieving goals.

Cross-Functional Teams A group of employees from various functional departments that meet as a team to resolve mutual problems.

Cultural Competence The ability to interact effectively with people of different cultures.

Cultural Intelligence (CQ) A person's ability to use reasoning and observation skills to interpret unfamiliar gestures and situations and devise appropriate behavioral responses.

Cultural Leader A manager who uses signals and symbols to influence corporate culture.

Culture The set of key values, beliefs, understandings, and norms that members of an organization share.

Culture Change A major shift in the norms, values, attitudes, and mind-set of the entire organization.

Culture Shock Feelings of confusion, disorientation, and anxiety that result from being immersed in a foreign culture.

Customer Relationship Management (CRM) Systems that help companies keep in close touch with customers, collect and manage customer data, and collaborate with customers to provide the most valuable products and services.

Customers People and organizations in the environment that acquire goods or services from the organization.

Cycle Time The steps taken to complete a company process.

D

Data Raw, unsummarized, and unanalyzed facts and figures.

Decentralization The location of decision authority near lower organizational levels.

Decentralized Control The use of organizational culture, group norms, and a focus on goals, rather than rules and procedures, to foster compliance with organizational goals.

Decentralized Network A team communication structure in which team members freely communicate with one another and arrive at decisions together.

Decentralized Planning Managers work with planning experts to develop their own goals and plans.

Decision A choice made from available alternatives.

Decision Making The process of identifying problems and opportunities and then resolving them.

Decision Styles Differences among people with respect to how they perceive problems and make decisions.

Decision Support System (DSS) An interactive, computer-based system that uses decision models and specialized databases to support organization decision makers.

Decode To translate the symbols used in a message for the purpose of interpreting its meaning.

Delegation The process managers use to transfer authority and responsibility to positions below them in the hierarchy.

Departmentalization The basis on which individuals are grouped into departments and departments into the total organization.

Descriptive An approach that describes how managers actually make decisions rather than how they should make decisions according to a theoretical ideal.

Devil's Advocate A decision-making technique in which an individual is assigned the role of challenging the assumptions and assertions made by the group to prevent premature consensus.

Diagnosis The step in the decision-making process in which managers analyze underlying causal factors associated with the decision situation.

Dialogue A group communication process aimed at creating a culture based on collaboration, fluidity, trust, and commitment to shared goals.

Differentiation A type of competitive strategy with which the organization seeks to distinguish its products or services from that of competitors.

Direct Investing An entry strategy in which the organization is involved in managing its production facilities in a foreign country.

Discretionary Responsibility Organizational responsibility that is voluntary and guided by the organization's desire to make social contributions not mandated by economics, law, or ethics.

Discrimination When someone acts out their prejudicial attitudes toward people who are the targets of their prejudice.

Distributive Justice The concept that different treatment of people should not be based on arbitrary characteristics. In the case of substantive differences, people should be treated differently in proportion to the differences among them.

Distributive Negotiation A competitive and adversarial negotiation approach in which each party strives to get as much as it can, usually at the expense of the other party.

Diversification A strategy of moving into new lines of business.

Diversity All the ways in which employees differ.

Diversity training Special training designed to educate employees about the importance of diversity, make people aware of their own biases, and teach them skills for communicating and working in a diverse workplace.

Divisional Structure An organization structure in which departments are grouped based on similar organizational outputs.

Downward Communication Messages sent from top management down to subordinates.

Dynamic Capabilities Leveraging and developing more from the firm's existing assets, capabilities, and core competencies in a way that will provide a sustained competitive advantage.

E

e-Business Any business that takes place by digital processes over a computer network rather than in physical space.

e-Commerce Business exchanges or transactions that occur electronically.

Economic Dimension The dimension of the general environment representing the overall economic health of the country or region in which the organization operates.

Economic Forces Forces that affect the availability, production, and distribution of a society's resources among competing users.

Economic Value-Added (EVA) A control system that measures performance in terms of after-tax profits minus the cost of capital invested in tangible assets.

Effective Follower A critical, independent thinker who actively participates in the organization.

Effectiveness The degree to which the organization achieves a stated goal.

Efficiency The use of minimal resources—raw materials, money, and people—to produce a desired volume of output.

Electronic Brainstorming Bringing people together in an interactive group over a computer network to suggest alternatives; sometimes called *brainwriting*.

Employee Network Groups Groups based on social identity, such as gender or race, and organized by employees to focus on concerns of employees from that group.

Employment Test A written or computer-based test designed to measure a particular attribute such as intelligence or aptitude.

Empowerment The delegation of power and authority to subordinates.

Encode To select symbols with which to compose a message.

Engagement A situation in which employees enjoy their work, contribute enthusiastically to meeting goals, and feel a sense of belonging and commitment to the organization.

Enterprise Resource Planning (ERP) System A networked information system that collects, processes, and provides information about an organization's entire enterprise, from identification of customer needs and receipt of orders to distribution of products and receipt of payments.

E → P Expectancy Expectancy that putting effort into a given task will lead to high performance.

Equity A situation that exists when the ratio of one person's outcomes to inputs equals that of another's.

Equity Theory A process theory that focuses on individuals' perceptions of how fairly they are treated relative to others.

ERG Theory A modification of the needs hierarchy theory that proposes three categories of needs: existence, relatedness, and growth.

Escalating Commitment Continuing to invest time and resources in a failing decision.

Ethical Dilemma A situation that arises when all alternative choices or behaviors are deemed undesirable because of potentially negative consequences, making it difficult to distinguish right from wrong.

Ethics The code of moral principles and values that governs the behaviors of a person or group with respect to what is right or wrong.

Ethics Committee A group of executives assigned to oversee the organization's ethics by ruling on questionable issues and disciplining violators.

Ethics Training Training programs to help employees deal with ethical questions and values.

Ethnocentrism The belief that one's own group or subculture is inherently superior to other groups or cultures.

Ethnorelativism The belief that groups and subcultures are inherently equal.

Euro A single European currency that replaced the currencies of 12 European nations.

Executive Information System (EIS) A management information system designed to facilitate strategic decision making at the highest levels of management by providing executives with easy access to timely and relevant information.

Exit Interview An interview conducted with departing employees to determine the reasons for their termination.

Expatriates Employees who live and work in a country other than their own.

Expectancy Theory A process theory that proposes that motivation depends on individuals' expectations about their ability to perform tasks and receive desired rewards.

Expense Budget A budget that outlines the anticipated and actual expenses for a responsibility center.

Expert Power Power that stems from special knowledge of or skill in the tasks performed by subordinates.

Exporting An entry strategy in which the organization maintains its production facilities within its home country and transfers its products for sale in foreign countries.

Extinction The withdrawal of a positive reward.

Extranet An external communications system that uses the Internet and is shared by two or more organizations.

Extrinsic Reward A reward given by another person.

F

Fast-Cycle Team A multifunctional team that is provided with high levels of resources and empowerment to accomplish an accelerated product development project.

Feedback A response by the receiver to the sender's communication.

Femininity A cultural preference for relationships, cooperation, group decision making, and quality of life.

Finished-Goods Inventory Inventory consisting of items that have passed through the complete production process but have yet to be sold.

First-Line Manager A manager who is at the first or second management level and is directly responsible for the production of goods and services.

Fixed-Position Layout A facilities layout in which the product remains in one location and the required tasks and equipment are brought to it.

Flat Structure A management structure characterized by an overall broad span of control and relatively few hierarchical levels.

Flexible Manufacturing System A small or medium sized automated production line that can be adapted to produce more than one product line.

Focus A type of competitive strategy that emphasizes concentration on a specific regional market or buyer group.

Force-Field Analysis The process of determining which forces drive and which resist a proposed change.

Formal Communication Channel A communication channel that flows within the chain of command or task responsibility defined by the organization.

Formal Team A team created by the organization as part of the formal organization structure.

Forming The stage of team development characterized by orientation and acquaintance.

Franchising A form of licensing in which an organization provides its foreign franchisees with a complete package of materials and services.

Free Rider A person who benefits from team membership but does not make a proportionate contribution to the team's work.

Frustration-Regression Principle The idea that failure to meet a high-order need may cause a regression to an already satisfied lower-order need.

Functional-Level Strategy The level of strategy concerned with the question "How do we support the business-level strategy?" Pertains to all of the organization's major departments.

Functional Manager A manager who is responsible for a department that performs a single functional task and has employees with similar training and skills.

Functional Structure The grouping of positions into departments based on similar skills, expertise, and resource use.

Fundamental Attribution Error The tendency to underestimate the influence of external factors on another's behavior and to overestimate the influence of internal factors.

G

General Environment The layer of the external environment that affects the organization indirectly.

General Manager A manager who is responsible for several departments that perform different functions.

Glass Ceiling Invisible barrier that separates women and minorities from top management positions.

Globalization The standardization of product design and advertising strategies throughout the world.

Global Outsourcing Engaging in the international division of labor so as to obtain the cheapest sources of labor and supplies regardless of country; also called *global sourcing*.

Global Team A work team made up of members of different nationalities whose activities span multiple countries; may operate as a virtual team or meet face-to-face.

Goal A desired future state that the organization attempts to realize.

Goal-Setting Theory A motivation theory in which specific, challenging goals increase motivation and performance when the goals are accepted by subordinates and these subordinates receive feedback to indicate their progress toward goal achievement.

Grapevine An informal, person-to-person communication network of employees that is not officially sanctioned by the organization.

Greenfield Venture The most risky type of direct investment, whereby a company builds a subsidiary from scratch in a foreign country.

Groupthink The tendency for people to be so committed to a cohesive team that they are reluctant to express contrary opinions.

Groupware Software that works on a computer network or the Internet to facilitate information sharing, collaborative work, and group decision making.

H

Halo Effect An overall impression of a person or situation based on one characteristic, either favorable or unfavorable; a type of rating error that occurs when an employee receives the same rating on all dimensions regardless of his or her performance on individual ones.

Hawthorne Studies A series of experiments on worker productivity begun in 1924 at the Hawthorne plant of Western Electric Company in Illinois; attributed employees' increased output to managers' better treatment of them during the study.

Hero A figure who exemplifies the deeds, character, and attributes of a strong corporate culture.

Hierarchical Control The use of rules, policies, hierarchy of authority, reward systems, and other formal devices to influence employee behavior and assess performance.

Hierarchy of Needs Theory A content theory that proposes that people are motivated by five categories of needs—physiological, safety, belongingness, esteem, and self-actualization—that exist in a hierarchical order.

High-Context Culture A culture in which communication is used to enhance personal relationships.

High-Performance Culture A culture based on a solid organizational mission or purpose that uses shared adaptive values to guide decisions and business practices and to encourage individual employee ownership of both bottom-line results and the organization's cultural backbone.

Horizontal Communication The lateral or diagonal exchange of messages among peers or coworkers.

Horizontal Linkage Model An approach to product change that emphasizes shared development of innovations among several departments.

Horizontal Team A formal team composed of employees from about the same hierarchical level but from different areas of expertise.

Human Capital The economic value of the knowledge, experience, skills, and capabilities of employees.

Humanistic Perspective A management perspective that emerged near the late nineteenth century and emphasized understanding human behavior, needs, and attitudes in the workplace.

Human Relations Movement A movement in management thinking and practice that emphasizes satisfaction of employees' basic needs as the key to increased worker productivity.

Human Resource Management (HRM) Activities undertaken to attract, develop, and maintain an effective workforce within an organization.

Human Resource Planning The forecasting of human resource needs and the projected matching of individuals with expected job vacancies.

Human Resources Perspective A management perspective that suggests jobs should be designed to meet higher-level needs by allowing workers to use their full potential.

Human Skill The ability to work with and through other people and to work effectively as a group member.

Humility Being unpretentious and modest rather than arrogant and prideful.

Hygiene Factors Factors that involve the presence or absence of job dissatisfiers, including working conditions, pay, company policies, and interpersonal relationships.

I

Idea Champion A person who sees the need for and champions productive change within the organization.

Idea Incubator An in-house program that provides a safe harbor where ideas from employees throughout the organization can be developed without interference from company bureaucracy or politics.

Implementation The step in the decision-making process that involves using managerial, administrative, and persuasive abilities to translate the chosen alternative into action.

Income Statement A financial statement that summarizes the firm's financial performance for a given time interval; sometimes called a profit-and-loss statement.

Individualism A preference for a loosely knit social framework in which individuals are expected to take care of themselves.

Individualism Approach The ethical concept that acts are moral when they promote the individual's best long-term interests, which ultimately leads to the greater good.

Influence The effect a person's actions have on the attitudes, values, beliefs, or behavior of others.

Information Data that have been converted into a meaningful and useful context for the receiver.

Information Technology (IT) The hardware, software, telecommunications, database management, and other technologies used to store, process, and distribute information.

Infrastructure A country's physical facilities that support economic activities.

Initiating Structure A type of leader behavior that describes the extent to which the leader is task oriented and directs subordinate work activities toward goal attainment.

Instant Messaging (IM) Electronic communication that allows users to see who is connected to a network and share information instantly.

Integrative Negotiation A collaborative approach to negotiation that is based on a win-win assumption, whereby the parties want to come up with a creative solution that benefits both sides of the conflict.

Intelligence Team A cross-functional group of managers and employees who work together to gain a deep understanding of a specific competitive issue and offer insight and recommendations for planning.

Interactive Leadership A leadership style characterized by values such as inclusion, collaboration, relationship building, and caring.

Internal Environment The environment that includes the elements within the organization's boundaries.

International Dimension Portion of the external environment that represents events originating in foreign countries as well as opportunities for U.S. companies in other countries.

International Human Resource Management (IHRM) A subfield of human resource management that addresses the complexity that results from recruiting, selecting, developing, and maintaining a diverse workforce on a global scale.

International Management The management of business operations conducted in more than one country.

Intranet An internal communications system that uses the technology and standards of the Internet but is accessible only to people within the organization.

Intrinsic Reward The satisfaction received in the process of performing an action.

Intuition The immediate comprehension of a decision situation based on past experience but without conscious thought.

Inventory The goods that the organization keeps on hand for use in the production process up to the point of selling the final products to customers.

Involvement Culture A culture that places high value on meeting the needs of employees and values cooperation and equality.

ISO Certification Certification based on a set of international standards for quality management, setting uniform guidelines for processes to ensure that products conform to customer requirements.

J

Job Analysis The systematic process of gathering and interpreting information about the essential duties, tasks, and responsibilities of a job.

Job Characteristics Model A model of job design that comprises core job dimensions, critical psychological states, and employee growth-need strength.

Job Description A concise summary of the specific tasks and responsibilities of a particular job.

Job Design The application of motivational theories to the structure of work for improving productivity and satisfaction.

Job Enlargement A job design that combines a series of tasks into one new, broader job to give employees variety and challenge.

Job Enrichment A job design that incorporates achievement, recognition, and other high-level motivators into the work.

Job Evaluation The process of determining the value of jobs within an organization through an examination of job content.

Job Rotation A job design that systematically moves employees from one job to another to provide them with variety and stimulation.

Job Satisfaction A positive attitude toward one's job.

Job Simplification A job design whose purpose is to improve task efficiency by reducing the number of tasks a single person must do.

Job Specification An outline of the knowledge, skills, education, and physical abilities needed to adequately perform a job.

Joint Venture A variation of direct investment in which an organization shares costs and risks with another firm to build a manufacturing facility, develop new products, or set up a sales and distribution network; a strategic alliance or program by two or more organizations.

Justice Approach The ethical concept that moral decisions must be based on standards of equity, fairness, and impartiality.

Just-In-Time (JIT) Inventory System An inventory control system that schedules materials to arrive precisely when they are needed on a production line.

K

Knowledge A conclusion drawn from information after it is linked to other information and compared to what is already known.

Knowledge Management The process of systematically gathering knowledge, making it widely available throughout the organization, and fostering a culture of learning.

Knowledge Management Portal A single point of access for employees to multiple sources of information that provides personalized access on the corporate intranet.

L

Labor Market The people available for hire by the organization.

Large-Group Intervention An approach that brings together participants from all parts of the organization (and may include key outside stakeholders as well) to discuss problems or opportunities and plan for major change.

Law of Effect The assumption that positively reinforced behavior tends to be repeated, and unreinforced or negatively reinforced behavior tends to be inhibited.

Leadership The ability to influence people toward the attainment of organizational goals.

Leadership Grid A two-dimensional leadership theory that measures the leader's concern for people and for production.

Leading The management function that involves the use of influence to motivate employees to achieve the organization's goals.

Lean Manufacturing Manufacturing process using highly trained employees at every stage of the production process to cut waste and improve quality.

Learning A change in behavior or performance that occurs as the result of experience.

Learning Organization An organization in which everyone is engaged in identifying and solving problems, enabling the organization to continuously experiment, improve, and increase its capability.

Legal-Political Dimension The dimension of the general environment that includes federal, state, and local government regulations and political activities designed to influence company behavior.

Legitimate Power Power that stems from a formal management position in an organization and the authority granted to it.

Licensing An entry strategy in which an organization in one country makes certain resources available to companies in another to participate in the production and sale of its products abroad.

Line Authority A form of authority in which individuals in management positions have the formal power to direct and control immediate subordinates.

Liquidity Ratio A financial ratio that indicates the organization's ability to meet its current debt obligations.

Listening The skill of receiving messages to accurately grasp facts and feelings to interpret the genuine meaning.

Locus of Control The tendency to place the primary responsibility for one's success or failure either within oneself (internally) or on outside forces (externally).

Long-Term Orientation A greater concern for the future and high value on thrift and perseverance.

Low-Context Culture A culture in which communication is used to exchange facts and information.

M

Machiavellianism The tendency to direct much of one's behavior toward the acquisition of power and the manipulation of other people for personal gain.

Management The attainment of organizational goals in an effective and efficient manner through planning, organizing, leading, and controlling organizational resources.

Management by Objectives (MBO) A method of management whereby managers and employees define goals for every department, project, and person and use them to monitor subsequent performance.

Management Information System (MIS) A computer-based system that provides information and support for effective managerial decision making.

Management Science Perspective A management perspective that emerged after World War II and applied mathematics, statistics, and other quantitative techniques to managerial problems.

Managing Diversity Creating a climate in which the potential advantages of diversity for organizational or group performance are maximized while the potential disadvantages are minimized.

Manufacturing Organization An organization that produces physical goods.

Market Entry Strategy An organizational strategy for entering a foreign market.

Market Value-Added (MVA) A control system that measures the stock market's estimate of the value of a company's past and expected capital investment projects.

Masculinity A cultural preference for achievement, heroism, assertiveness, work centrality, and material success.

Matching Model An employee selection approach in which the organization and the applicant attempt to match each other's needs, interests, and values.

Matrix Approach An organization structure that uses functional and divisional chains of command simultaneously in the same part of the organization.

Matrix Boss The product or functional boss, responsible for one side of the matrix.

Mediation The process of using a third party to settle a dispute.

Mentor A higher-ranking, senior organizational member who is committed to providing upward mobility and support to a protégé's professional career.

Mentoring When an experienced employee guides and supports a less-experienced employee.

Merger The combining of two or more organizations into one.

Message The tangible formulation of an idea to be sent to a receiver.

Middle Manager A manager who works at the middle levels of the organization and is responsible for major departments.

Mission The organization's reason for existence.

Mission Statement A broadly stated definition of the organization's basic business scope and operations that distinguishes it from similar types of organizations.

Modular Approach The process by which a manufacturing company uses outside suppliers to provide large components of the product, which are then assembled into a final product by a few workers.

Monoculture A culture that accepts only one way of doing things and one set of values and beliefs.

Moral Leadership Distinguishing right from wrong and choosing to do right in the practice of leadership.

Moral-Rights Approach The ethical concept that moral decisions are those that best maintain the rights of those people affected by them.

Motivation The arousal, direction, and persistence of behavior.

Motivators Factors that influence job satisfaction based on fulfillment of high-level needs such as achievement, recognition, responsibility, and opportunity for growth.

Multicultural Teams Teams made up of members from diverse national, racial, ethnic, and cultural backgrounds.

Multidomestic Strategy The modification of product design and advertising strategies to suit the specific needs of individual countries.

Multinational Corporation (MNC) An organization that receives more than 25 percent of its total sales revenues from operations outside the parent company's home country; also called *global corporation* or *transnational corporation.*

Myers–Briggs Type Indicator (MBTI) Personality test that measures a person's preference for introversion vs. extroversion, sensation vs. intuition, thinking vs. feeling, and judging vs. perceiving.

N

Natural Dimension The dimension of the general environment that includes all elements that occur naturally on earth, including plants, animals, rocks, and natural resources such as air, water, and climate.

Negotiation A conflict management strategy whereby people engage in give-and-take discussions and consider various alternatives to reach a joint decision that is acceptable to both parties.

Neutralizer A situational variable that counteracts a leadership style and prevents the leader from displaying certain behaviors.

New-Venture Fund A fund providing resources from which individuals and groups can draw to develop new ideas, products, or businesses.

New-Venture Team A unit separate from the mainstream of the organization that is responsible for developing and initiating innovations.

Nonprogrammed Decision A decision made in response to a situation that is unique, is poorly defined and largely unstructured, and has important consequences for the organization.

Nonverbal Communication A communication transmitted through actions and behaviors rather than through words.

Normative An approach that defines how a decision maker should make decisions and provides guidelines for reaching an ideal outcome for the organization.

Norming The stage of team development in which conflicts developed during the storming stage are resolved and team harmony and unity emerge.

O

On-the-Job Training (OJT) A type of training in which an experienced employee "adopts" a new employee to teach him or her how to perform job duties.

Open-Book Management Sharing financial information and results with all employees in the organization.

Open Innovation Extending the search for and commercialization of new ideas beyond the boundaries of the organization.

Open System A system that interacts with the external environment.

Operational Goals Specific, measurable results expected from departments, work groups, and individuals within the organization.

Operational Plans Plans developed at the organization's lower levels that specify action steps toward achieving operational goals and that support tactical planning activities.

Operations Management The field of management that focuses on the physical production of goods or services and uses specialized techniques for solving manufacturing problems.

Opportunity A situation in which managers see potential organizational accomplishments that exceed current goals.

Organization A social entity that is goal directed and deliberately structured.

Organizational Behavior An interdisciplinary field dedicated to the study of how individuals and groups tend to act in organizations.

Organizational Change The adoption of a new idea or behavior by an organization.

Organizational Citizenship Work behavior that goes beyond job requirements and contributes as needed to the organization's success.

Organizational Commitment Loyalty to and heavy involvement in one's organization.

Organizational Control The systematic process through which managers regulate organizational activities to make them consistent with expectations established in plans, targets, and standards of performance.

Organizational Environment All elements existing outside the organization's boundaries that have the potential to affect the organization.

Organization Chart The visual representation of an organization's structure.

Organization Development (OD) The application of behavioral science

techniques to improve an organization's health and effectiveness through its ability to cope with environmental changes, improve internal relationships, and increase learning and problem-solving capabilities.

Organization Structure The framework in which the organization defines how tasks are divided, resources are deployed, and departments are coordinated.

Organizing The management function concerned with assigning tasks, grouping tasks into departments, and allocating resources to departments; the deployment of organizational resources to achieve strategic goals.

Outsourcing Contracting out selected functions or activities of an organization to other organizations that can do the work more cost efficiently.

P

Passive Follower A person who exhibits neither critical independent thinking nor active participation.

Pay-for-Performance Incentive pay that ties at least part of compensation to employee effort and performance.

Peer-to-Peer File Sharing File sharing that allows PCs to communicate directly with one another over the Internet, bypassing central databases, servers, control points, and Web pages.

People Change A change in the attitudes and behaviors of a few employees in the organization.

Perception The cognitive process people use to make sense out of the environment by selecting, organizing, and interpreting information.

Perceptual Defense The tendency of perceivers to protect themselves by disregarding ideas, objects, or people that are threatening to them.

Perceptual Distortions Errors in perceptual judgment that arise from inaccuracies in any part of the perceptual process.

Perceptual Selectivity The process by which individuals screen and select the various stimuli that vie for their attention.

Performance The organization's ability to attain its goals by using resources in an efficient and effective manner.

Performance Appraisal The process of observing and evaluating an employee's performance, recording the assessment, and providing feedback to the employee.

Performance Gap A disparity between existing and desired performance levels.

Performing The stage of team development in which members focus on problem solving and accomplishing the team's assigned task.

Permanent Teams A group of participants from several functions who are permanently assigned to solve ongoing problems of common interest.

Personal Communication Channels Communication channels that exist outside the formally authorized channels and do not adhere to the organization's hierarchy of authority.

Personality The set of characteristics that underlie a relatively stable pattern of behavior in response to ideas, objects, or people in the environment.

Personal Networking The acquisition and cultivation of personal relationships that cross departmental, hierarchical, and even organizational boundaries.

Person–Job Fit The extent to which a person's ability and personality match the requirements of a job.

Plan A blueprint specifying the resource allocations, schedules, and other actions necessary for attaining goals.

Planning The management function concerned with defining goals for future organizational performance and deciding on the tasks and resources needed to attain them; the act of determining the organization's goals and the means for achieving them.

Pluralism An environment in which the organization accommodates several subcultures, including employees who would otherwise feel isolated and ignored.

P → O Expectancy Expectancy that successful performance of a task will lead to the desired outcome.

Point-Counterpoint A decision-making technique in which people are assigned to express competing points of view.

Political Forces The influence of political and legal institutions on people and organizations.

Political Instability Events such as riots, revolutions, or government upheavals that affect the operations of an international company.

Political Risk A company's risk of loss of assets, earning power, or managerial control due to politically based events or actions by host governments.

Portfolio Strategy The organization's mix of strategic business units and product lines that fit together in such a way as to provide the corporation with synergy and competitive advantage.

Positive Reinforcement The administration of a pleasant and rewarding consequence following a desired behavior.

Power The potential ability to influence others' behavior.

Power Distance The degree to which people accept inequality in power among institutions, organizations, and people.

Pragmatic Survivor A follower who has qualities of all four follower styles, depending on which fits the prevalent situation.

Prejudice The tendency to view people who are different as being deficient.

Pressure Group An interest group that works within the legal-political framework to influence companies to behave in socially responsible ways.

Problem A situation in which organizational accomplishments have failed to meet established goals.

Problem-Solving Team Typically 5 to 12 hourly employees from the same department who meet to discuss ways of improving quality, efficiency, and the work environment.

Procedural Justice The concept that rules should be clearly stated and consistently and impartially enforced.

Process An organized group of related tasks and activities that work together to transform inputs into outputs and create value.

Process Layout A facilities layout in which machines that perform the same function are grouped together in one location.

Process Theories A group of theories that explain how employees select behaviors with which to meet their needs and determine whether their choices were successful.

Product Change A change in the organization's product or service outputs.

Product Layout A facilities layout in which machines and tasks are arranged according to the sequence of steps in the production of a single product.

Profitability Ratio A financial ratio that describes the firm's profits in terms of a source of profits (for example, sales or total assets).

Programmed Decision A decision made in response to a situation that has occurred often enough to enable decision rules to be developed and applied in the future.

Projection The tendency to see one's own personal traits in other people.

Project Manager A person responsible for coordinating the activities of several departments on a full-time basis for the completion of a specific project; a manager responsible for a temporary work project that involves the participation of other people from various functions and levels of the organization.

Punishment The imposition of an unpleasant outcome following undesirable behavior.

Q

Quality Circle A group of 6 to 12 volunteer employees who meet regularly to discuss and solve problems affecting the quality of their work.

R

Raw Materials Inventory Inventory consisting of the basic inputs to the organization's production process.

Realistic Job Preview A recruiting approach that gives applicants all pertinent and realistic information about the job and the organization.

Recruiting The activities or practices that define the desired characteristics of applicants for specific jobs.

Reengineering The radical redesign of business processes to achieve dramatic improvements in cost, quality, service, and speed.

Referent Power Power that results from characteristics that command subordinates' identification with, respect and admiration for, and desire to emulate the leader.

Refreezing The reinforcement stage of organization development in which individuals acquire a desired new skill or attitude and are rewarded for it by the organization.

Reinforcement Anything that causes a given behavior to be repeated or inhibited.

Reinforcement Theory A motivation theory based on the relationship between a given behavior and its consequences.

Related Diversification Moving into a new business that is related to the company's existing business activities.

Responsibility The duty to perform the task or activity an employee has been assigned.

Responsibility Center An organizational unit under the supervision of a single person who is responsible for its activity.

Revenue Budget A budget that identifies the forecasted and actual revenues of the organization.

Reward Power Power that results from the authority to bestow rewards on other people.

Rightsizing Intentionally reducing the company's workforce to the point where the number of employees is deemed to be right for the company's current situation.

Risk A situation in which a decision has clear-cut goals and good information is available, but the future outcomes associated with each alternative are subject to chance.

Risk Propensity The willingness to undertake risk with the opportunity of gaining an increased payoff.

Role A set of expectations for one's behavior.

Role Ambiguity Uncertainty about what behaviors are expected of a person in a particular role.

Role Conflict Incompatible demands of different roles.

S

Satisficing To choose the first solution alternative that satisfies minimal decision criteria, regardless of whether better solutions are presumed to exist.

Scenario Building Looking at trends and discontinuities and imagining possible alternative futures to build a framework within which unexpected future events can be managed.

Scientific Management A subfield of the classical management perspective that emphasized scientifically determined changes in management practices as the solution to improving labor productivity.

Selection The process of determining the skills, abilities, and other attributes a person needs to perform a particular job.

Self-Directed Team A team consisting of 5 to 20 multiskilled workers who rotate jobs to produce an entire product or service, often supervised by an elected member.

Self-Serving Bias The tendency to overestimate the contribution of internal factors to one's successes and the contribution of external factors to one's failures.

Servant Leader A leader who works to fulfill subordinates' needs and goals as well as to achieve the organization's larger mission.

Service Organization An organization that produces nonphysical outputs that require customer involvement and cannot be stored in inventory.

Short-Term Orientation A concern with the past and present and a high value on meeting social obligations.

Single-Use Plans Plans that are developed to achieve a set of goals that are unlikely to be repeated in the future.

Situational Theory A contingency approach to leadership that links the leader's behavioral style with the task readiness of subordinates.

Six Sigma A quality control approach that emphasizes a relentless pursuit of higher quality and lower costs.

Skunkworks A separate small, informal, highly autonomous, and often secretive group that focuses on breakthrough ideas for the business.

Slogan A phrase or sentence that succinctly expresses a key corporate value.

Social Facilitation The tendency for the presence of others to influence an individual's motivation and performance.

Social Forces The aspects of a culture that guide and influence relationships among people—their values, needs, and standards of behavior.

Social Networking Online interaction in a community format where people share personal information and photos, produce and share all sorts of information and opinions, or unify activists and raise funds.

Sociocultural Dimension The dimension of the general environment representing the demographic characteristics, norms, customs, and values of the population within which the organization operates.

Socioemotional Role A role in which the individual provides support for team members' emotional needs and social unity.

Span of Management The number of employees reporting to a supervisor; also called *span of control.*

Special-Purpose Team A team created outside the formal organization to undertake a project of special importance or creativity.

Staff Authority A form of authority granted to staff specialists in their area of expertise.

Stakeholder Any group within or outside the organization that has a stake in the organization's performance.

Standing Plans Ongoing plans that are used to provide guidance for tasks performed repeatedly within the organization.

Stereotype A rigid, exaggerated, irrational belief associated with a particular group of people.

Stereotype Threat A psychological experience of a person who, usually engaged in a task, is aware of a stereotype about his or her identify group suggesting that he or she will not perform well on that task.

Stereotyping Placing an employee into a class or category based on one or a few traits or characteristics; the tendency to assign an individual to a group or broad category and then attribute generalizations about the group to the individual.

Storming The stage of team development in which individual personalities and roles emerge along with resulting conflicts.

Story A narrative based on true events and repeated frequently and shared among organizational employees.

Strategic Business Unit (SBU) A division of the organization that has a unique business mission, product line, competitors, and markets relative to other SBUs in the same corporation.

Strategic Conversation Dialogue across boundaries and hierarchical levels about the team or organization's vision, critical strategic themes, and the values that help achieve important goals.

Strategic Goals Broad statements of where the organization wants to be in the future; pertain to the organization as a whole rather than to specific divisions or departments.

Strategic Management The set of decisions and actions used to formulate and implement strategies that will provide a competitively superior fit between the organization and its environment so as to achieve organizational goals.

Strategic Plans The action steps by which an organization intends to attain strategic goals.

Strategy The plan of action that prescribes resource allocation and other activities for dealing with the environment, achieving a competitive advantage, and attaining organizational goals.

Strategy Execution The stage of strategic management that involves the use of managerial and organizational tools to direct resources toward achieving strategic outcomes.

Strategy Formulation The stage of strategic management that involves the planning and decision making that lead to the establishment of the organization's goals and of a specific strategic plan.

Strategy Map A visual representation of the key drivers of an organization's success, showing the cause-and-effect relationships among goals and plans.

Stress A physiological and emotional response to stimuli that place physical or psychological demands on an individual.

Stretch Goal A reasonable yet highly ambitious, compelling goal that energizes people and inspires excellence.

Substitute A situational variable that makes a leadership style unnecessary or redundant.

Subsystems Parts of a system that depend on one another for their functioning.

Superordinate Goal A goal that cannot be reached by a single party.

Suppliers People and organizations that provide the raw materials the organization uses to produce its output.

Supply Chain Management Managing the sequence of suppliers and purchasers, covering all stages of processing from obtaining raw materials to distributing finished goods to final customers.

Survey Feedback A type of OD intervention in which questionnaires on organizational climate and other factors are distributed among employees and their results reported back to them by a change agent.

Sustainability Economic development that meets the needs of the current population while preserving the environment for the needs of future generations.

SWOT Analysis Analysis of the strengths, weaknesses, opportunities, and threats (SWOT) that affect organizational performance

Symbol An object, act, or event that conveys meaning to others.

Synergy The condition that exists when the organization's parts interact to produce a joint effect that is greater than the sum of the parts acting alone; the concept that the whole is greater than the sum of its parts.

System A set of interrelated parts that function as a whole to achieve a common purpose.

Systemic Thinking Seeing both the distinct elements of a situation and the complex and changing interaction among those elements.

Systems Theory An extension of the humanistic perspective that describes organizations as open systems characterized by entropy, synergy, and subsystem interdependence.

T

Tactical Goals Goals that define the outcomes that major divisions and departments must achieve for the organization to reach its overall goals.

Tactical Plans Plans designed to help execute major strategic plans and to accomplish a specific part of the company's strategy.

Tall Structure A management structure characterized by an overall narrow span of management and a relatively large number of hierarchical levels.

Task Environment The layer of the external environment that directly influences the organization's operations and performance.

Task Force A temporary team or committee formed to solve a specific short-term problem involving several departments.

Task Specialist Role A role in which the individual devotes personal time and energy to helping the team accomplish its task.

Team A unit of two or more people who interact and coordinate their work to accomplish a specific goal.

Team-Based Structure Structure in which the entire organization is made up of horizontal teams that coordinate their activities and work directly with customers to accomplish the organization's goals.

Team Building A type of OD intervention that enhances the cohesiveness of departments by helping members learn to function as a team.

Team Cohesiveness The extent to which team members are attracted to the team and motivated to remain in it.

Team Norm A standard of conduct that is shared by team members and guides their behavior.

Technical Core The heart of the organization's production of its product or service.

Technical Skill The understanding of and proficiency in the performance of specific tasks.

Technological Dimension The dimension of the general environment that includes scientific and technological advancements in the industry and society at large.

Technology Change A change that pertains to the organization's production process.

Telecommuting Using computers and telecommunications equipment to perform work from home or another remote location.

Top-Down Budgeting A budgeting process in which middle- and lower-level managers set departmental budget targets in accordance with overall company revenues and expenditures specified by top management.

Top Leader The overseer of both the product and functional chains of command, responsible for the entire matrix.

Top Manager A manager who is at the top of the organizational hierarchy and is responsible for the entire organization.

Total Quality Management (TQM) A concept that focuses on managing the total organization to deliver quality to customers. Four significant elements of TQM are employee involvement, focus on the customer, benchmarking, and continuous improvement; an organization-wide commitment to infusing quality into every activity through continuous improvement.

Traits Distinguishing personal characteristics, such as intelligence, values, and appearance.

Transactional Leader A leader who clarifies subordinates' role and task requirements, initiates structure, provides rewards, and displays consideration for subordinates.

Transformational Leader A leader distinguished by a special ability to bring about innovation and change.

Transnational Strategy A strategy that combines global coordination to attain efficiency with flexibility to meet specific needs in various countries.

Two-Boss Employees Employees who report to two supervisors simultaneously.

Type A Behavior Behavior pattern characterized by extreme competitiveness, impatience, aggressiveness, and devotion to work.

Type B Behavior Behavior pattern that lacks Type A characteristics and includes a more balanced, relaxed lifestyle.

U

Uncertainty The situation that occurs when managers know which goals they wish to achieve, but information about alternatives and future events is incomplete.

Uncertainty Avoidance A value characterized by people's intolerance for uncertainty and ambiguity and resulting support for beliefs that promise certainty and conformity.

Uncritical Thinking Failing to consider the possibilities beyond what one is told; accepting others' ideas without thinking.

Unfreezing The stage of organization development in which participants are made aware of problems to increase their willingness to change their behavior.

Unrelated Diversification Expanding into a totally new line of business.

Upward Communication Messages transmitted from the lower to the higher levels in the organization's hierarchy.

Utilitarian Approach The ethical concept that moral behaviors produce the greatest good for the greatest number.

V

Valence The value or attraction an individual has for an outcome.

Vertical Integration Expanding into businesses that either produce the supplies needed to make products or that distribute and sell those products.

Vertical Team A formal team composed of a manager and his or her subordinates in the organization's formal chain of command.

Virtual Network Structure An organization structure that disaggregates major functions to separate companies that are brokered by a small headquarters organization.

Virtual Team A team made up of members who are geographically or organizationally dispersed, rarely meet face to face, and do their work using advanced information technologies.

Vision An attractive, ideal future that is credible yet not readily attainable.

W

Wage and Salary Surveys Surveys that show what other organizations pay incumbents in jobs that match a sample of "key" jobs selected by the organization.

Whistle-Blowing The disclosure by an employee of illegal, immoral, or illegitimate practices by the organization.

Wholly Owned Foreign Affiliate A foreign subsidiary over which an organization has complete control.

Wiki Web site that allows anyone with access, inside or outside the organization, to create, share, and edit content through a simple, browser-based user interface.

Work-in-Process Inventory Inventory composed of the materials that still are moving through the stages of the production process.

Work Redesign The altering of jobs to increase both the quality of employees' work experience and their productivity.

Work Specialization The degree to which organizational tasks are subdivided into individual jobs; also called division of labor.

Name Index

Company Index

Subject Index